MW01114985

# THE CONSTITUTIONAL
# LAW OF THE EUROPEAN
# UNION
## Third Edition

# LEXISNEXIS LAW SCHOOL ADVISORY BOARD

**William Araiza**
*Professor of Law*
Brooklyn Law School

**Ruth Colker**
*Distinguished University Professor &*
*Heck-Faust Memorial Chair in Constitutional Law*
Ohio State University Moritz College of Law

**Olympia Duhart**
*Associate Professor of Law*
Nova Southeastern University Shepard Broad Law School

**Samuel Estreicher**
*Dwight D. Opperman Professor of Law*
*Director, Center for Labor and Employment Law*
NYU School of Law

**David Gamage**
*Assistant Professor of Law*
UC Berkeley School of Law

**Joan Heminway**
*College of Law Distinguished Professor of Law*
University of Tennessee College of Law

**Edward Imwinkelried**
*Edward L. Barrett, Jr. Professor of Law*
UC Davis School of Law

**Paul Marcus**
*Haynes Professor of Law*
William and Mary Law School

**Melissa Weresh**
*Director of Legal Writing and Professor of Law*
Drake University Law School

# THE CONSTITUTIONAL LAW OF THE EUROPEAN UNION

## THIRD EDITION

**James D. Dinnage**
*MA (Cantab.) and Licence Spéciale en Droit Européen (Brussels)*
*Solicitor (England)*
*Attorney at Law (New York)*
*Special Legal Consultant (District of Columbia)*

**Jean-Luc Laffineur**
*Laffineur Law Firm*
*Avocat au Barreau de Bruxelles (Belgium)*
*LL.M. in International and European Business Law, University of London (England)*
*Maîtrise de Droit, Université de Paris II (France)*

ISBN: 978-0-7698-4600-2

**Library of Congress Cataloging-in-Publication Data**

Dinnage, James.
The constitutional law of the European Union / James D. Dinnage, Jean-Luc Laffineur. – 3rd ed.
p. cm.
Includes bibliographical references and index.
ISBN 978-0-7698-4600-2 (hardbound : alk. paper)
1. Constitutional law--European Union countries. I. Laffineur, Jean-Luc. II. Title.
    KJE4445.D56 2012
    342.24–dc23

2012006544

This publication is designed to provide authoritative information in regard to the subject matter covered. It is sold with the understanding that the publisher is not engaged in rendering legal, accounting, or other professional services. If legal advice or other expert assistance is required, the services of a competent professional should be sought.

LexisNexis and the Knowledge Burst logo are registered trademarks of Reed Elsevier Properties Inc., used under license. Matthew Bender and the Matthew Bender Flame Design are registered trademarks of Matthew Bender Properties Inc.

Copyright © 2012 Matthew Bender & Company, Inc., a member of LexisNexis. All Rights Reserved.

No copyright is claimed by LexisNexis or Matthew Bender & Company, Inc., in the text of statutes, regulations, and excerpts from court opinions quoted within this work. Permission to copy material may be licensed for a fee from the Copyright Clearance Center, 222 Rosewood Drive, Danvers, Mass. 01923, telephone (978) 750-8400.

NOTE TO USERS
To ensure that you are using the latest materials available in this area, please be sure to periodically check the LexisNexis Law School web site for downloadable updates and supplements at www.lexisnexis.com/lawschool.

Editorial Offices
121 Chanlon Rd., New Providence, NJ 07974 (908) 464-6800
201 Mission St., San Francisco, CA 94105-1831 (415) 908-3200
www.lexisnexis.com

MATTHEW◆BENDER

# DEDICATION

---

*To Eleftheria, Orlando and Hector*
Jean-Luc Laffineur, Brussels, September 2011

*To Karen and Russell, and all of my family.*
James Dinnage, Wilmington, DE, September 2011

# FOREWORD TO THE THIRD EDITION

Casebooks are not designed for judges. They know the law — that, at any event, is the fiction embraced by most European systems, including the Court of Justice of the EU. Nevertheless, this particular judge would have benefited significantly had he had this case book on his shelves when he was appointed and when he started drafting judgments. Similarly, I have no doubt that legal advisers — be they office-bound or advocates in court — would equally benefit. A danger to which all lawyers, whether judges or advisers, are subject is that of taking quotations out of context and applying them blindly. This book should prevent this by helping them to consider what has deliberately been unsaid in the judgments, what is said elsewhere, and the possible implication of applying words literally.

It starts by distilling much of EU law into a code (which it modestly describes as a Template) and follows this by 20 chapters that take an article of the Template and then set out the relevant law more fully. Each of these chapters starts with a brief elaboration of the proposition of the Template under examination and then continues with citations from the case law, legislative or administrative instruments from which the brief summary was drawn. Each of these citations is followed by an astute questionnaire on issues raised and not necessarily answered by the judgment or instrument under review.

One occasionally comes across advocates who embody the minimum amount of thought in the maximum amount of words. This book does the opposite. Adding my congratulations to those expressed by former Judge Bellamy in the previous forewords I commend it heartily.

**Konrad Schiemann**
**Luxembourg**
**6th October, 2011**

# FOREWORD TO THE SECOND EDITION

It is over 50 years since the Treaty establishing the European *Economic* Community (emphasis added) was signed in Rome on 25 March 1957, and longer still since the signature of its predecessor, the European Coal and Steel Treaty, on 18 April 1951. Since those now distant days, two trends have been particularly important. First, there has been a relatively constant process of adhesion of new Member States, from the original Six in the 1950s to 27 Member States today. The major accessions of 2004 and 2007, which brought a total of 12 Member States into what has now become the European Union, have been particularly significant. Secondly, the activities of the European Union have been progressively extended well beyond the economic aims of the original Treaties into fields never envisaged by the founding fathers — including a common foreign policy, justice and home affairs, asylum and immigration, citizenship, the protection of the environment, a single currency, at least among many Member States, and even, embryonically, defence. These changes are of course reflected in the adoption, in the 1993 Treaty of Maastricht, of the concept of the "European Union" as an umbrella term wider than, but including, the "European Community," from the title of which the word "Economic" was also dropped. If and when the Reform Treaty of 2007 is ratified, the "European Community" will itself pass into history and the whole complex structure will be subsumed under the single description "European Union."

These developments, among others, have created enormous pressures in the sphere with which this work is concerned, namely the Constitutional Law of the European Union. The Treaty of Rome is a cohesive and relatively simple document drafted in terms of general principles. In the clarity of its vision it is arguably one of the greatest documents produced in the second half of the twentieth century. However, the constitutional structure of the Union has become ever more complex. Among many changes we have had the Single European Act (1987), the Treaties of Maastricht (1993), Amsterdam (1997), and Nice (2003), numerous Treaties of Accession, the EEA Agreement of 1994, and a bewildering number of other Acts, Pacts, Charters, Decisions, Agreements and Conventions, accompanied by an array of pillars, opt-outs, protocols and procedures, re-enforced by an astonishing number of regulations and directives. An attempt to bring some kind of order into this diverse framework failed when the ill-fated and provocatively named Treaty Establishing a Constitution for Europe, signed in 2004, was rejected by the electorates of France and The Netherlands. The Reform Treaty of 2007, which revives some of the important elements of the failed 2004 Treaty, awaits ratification at the time of writing.

Against this background, a new edition of this work, first published in 1996, is warmly to be welcomed. With 27 Member States to be accommodated, three EEA States, and further candidates for accession waiting in the wings (including currently Croatia, Serbia, and Turkey), it is more important than ever to explain, as clearly as possible, the underlying principles of the constitution and governance of this unique phenomenon, the European Union. That is what this work achieves through the tried and tested case book method. Whether it is the autonomous nature of the EU legal system, including the

# FOREWORD TO THE SECOND EDITION

relationship between the Union and the Member States, the legislative competence of the EU, the complex process of EU Governance, or the relationship between the EU and the individual, including fundamental rights, this work covers every aspect of the subject.

In describing, through case law and materials, the constitutional structure of the Union, this book also charts much of the remarkable, in many ways inspiring, and certainly unique, story of the dynamic, and still continuing, process of European integration over the past 50 years. The Treaties and other instruments now provide, in effect, a supra-national constitutional framework for a territory stretching from the North of Finland to the Mediterranean, and from the Atlantic to the Black Sea, unparalled in history. We are all greatly indebted to the authors for this new edition of this comprehensive and authoritative work.

**Christopher Bellamy**
**London**
**April 2008**

# FOREWORD TO THE FIRST EDITION

The title itself reflects the innovative character of this magnificent new work. Not everyone would agree that the European Union, as such, was even a legal entity, let alone the proud possessor of "a constitution." But, as the authors point out, the absence of a single written document does not imply the absence of "constitutional" law. On the contrary, as this book demonstrates, the law of the European Union, and of the three Communities on which it is based, is a remarkable example of the dynamic development of constitutional principles for the governance of a unique form of political organization whose founding texts are often telegraphic to the point of obscurity.

However, because there is no one "constitutional" document, and because the legal system of the Union and its constituent parts has to be developed, as it goes along, drawing when necessary on the principles common to the member states, which themselves exhibit a rich legal, cultural and political diversity, it is also true that the constitutional law of the European Union is sometimes hard to find. It is the great merit of this work that the authors have assembled within a single corner and from a vast mosaic of different sources, a structured, articulate and comprehensive collection of the cases and materials needed for studying the constitutional aspects of the European Union unencumbered, so far as possible, by the details of the substantive law.

As the reader will also divine, it is not clear how "the process of creating an ever closer union among the peoples of Europe" (note: not among the "States" of Europe) will develop, constitutionally speaking, in the future, or how the Union will adapt itself to new challenges, notably to the East. Many constitutional issues concerning, for example, such basic matters as the respective powers of the executive and the legislature, and the relations between the Union, its constituent member states, and the citizens, are still being worked out on an almost daily basis (see for example the judgments of March 5, 1996 in joined cases C-46/and C-48/93 Brasserie du Pêcheur and Factortame, concerning State liability for legislative breach of Community Law). The Maastricht II Intergovernmental Conference, which opened in Turin on March 29, may mark a new phase in this development.

In these circumstances the present work is extremely opportune. Even if we cannot yet emulate Walter Bagehot who, writing in *The English Constitution* (1867), was able to distinguish between the *dignified* parts of the constitution "which excite and preserve the reverence of the population" and the *efficient* parts "by which it, in fact, works and rules" it is nonetheless vitally important that the constitutional aspects of the *acquis communautaire* should be readily accessible and comprehensible.

This book addresses that need. In my view the authors are to be congratulated.

**Christopher Bellamy**
**Luxembourg**
**1 April 1996**

# ACKNOWLEDGMENTS

We extend our thanks to the Publications Office of the European Union for its open policy in permitting reproduction of its publications, including case reports, legislation and other materials, which make up the bulk of the text in this book. Only European Union legislation printed in the paper edition of the *Official Journal of the European Union* is deemed authentic.

We wish also to thank the Incorporated Council of Law Reporting for kind permission to reproduce extracts from a number of English cases, specifically *Factortame v. Secretary of State for Transport, Thoburn et al. v. Sunderland City Council et al.* and *Maclaine Watson & Co. Ltd v. Department of Trade and Industry and Related Appeals.* Similarly, we thank Sweet & Maxwell for permission to reproduce extracts from the Common Market Law Reports translations of the following national court cases: *Administration des Douanes v. Société Cafés Jacques Vabre & J. Weigel et Cie Sàrl, Internationale Handelsgesellschaft mbH v. Einfuhr- und Vorratsstelle für Getreide und Futtermittel (Solange I); Brunner v. European Union Treaty; Blackburn v. Attorney General; Boisdet; Mccarthy's Ltd v. Smith; and Acciaierie San Michele SpA (in liquidation) v. High Authority of the ECSC.*

Our acknowledgment of the efforts of others with respect to the prior edition of this work should be repeated here, particularly as much of their work has supported this edition also. We are extremely grateful to Karen Dinnage, Arlene Steigler, and Suzanna Pierrepont for their invaluable assistance and patience, to Julian Joshua of the Steptoe and Johnson law firm in Brussels for his most helpful comments and to Maud Grunchard, Clémentine Leroy, Aurélie Perrichet, and Claire Martin of Cabinet d'avocats Laffineur. Our heartfelt thanks go to the library staff of Villanova University Law School, particularly Amy Spare, Matthew McGovern, and Robert Hegadorn for responding so promptly to our research requests, and to Maureen Carver, Assistant Dean for Student Records and Registrar, for assisting us in determining the extent of interest in U.S. law schools in EU Law. We would be remiss not to mention also the Villanova EU Law classes of 2007 through 2010 for bearing with us as we worked our way through the materials and navigated the various iterations of what became the Treaty of Lisbon. Their contributions were invaluable in helping us figure out what worked and what didn't, and the book is again much improved as a result.

Shortly after his retirement as President of the European Court of Justice in 1988, Lord Mackenzie Stuart (now sadly departed this life) visited the United States as a Woodrow Wilson Fellow. John Murphy and I were honored to have the opportunity to host him on a visit to the various historic sites in Philadelphia, followed by a dinner and seminar at Villanova University Law School. He had become extremely interested in the parallels between the judicial decisions from the early days of the United States and those of the European Communities and was clearly intrigued by what he saw and heard in Philadelphia. At the seminar in the evening he was full of fascinating insights and also provided highly entertaining and colorful accounts of some of his judgments. He was a leading inspiration for our original project.

Two other European Court judges have honored us by contributing Forewords to the various editions of this work. Sir Christopher Bellamy, who served on the General Court from 1992 to 1999, contributed the Foreword to the first and second editions. Sir Konrad

## ACKNOWLEDGMENTS

Schiemann, currently serving as a Judge at the Court of Justice, graciously agreed to provide the Foreword for this edition. We are indeed most grateful for their kind expressions of support and enthusiasm for our project.

# PREFACE

At the date of the first edition of this book, the European Union was "settling down", centered around a three-pillar structure: the European Community; the Common & Foreign Security policy and Justice Affairs and Home Affairs. The first pillar was based on the integration process among the Member States; the other two on cooperation between them. Integration and cooperation reflect the two ways the EU has always moved forward: the former being the area in which the Member States have abandoned most of their sovereignty, the latter being the area where they are the most reluctant to abandon it. There was general despondency that the new European Union had chosen the path of intergovernmental cooperation rather than integration.

How far we have come since then!

The Treaty of Amsterdam started the process of shifting TEU subject matter into the Community structure. After the subsequent rather disappointing Nice Treaty, the Member States took the more dramatic step of convening a process to rewrite the Treaties as a formalized Constitution, combining the Union and the Communities into one integrated structure, and indeed, a Constitution Treaty was signed. Although 18 Member States ratified it, the peoples of two of the six founding Member States rejected it in referenda. Was this, then, a rejection of the ideals of the Communities and the Union? Or was the Treaty a victim of other forces and worries that found a focal point for discontent? Would this turn of events set back the process of ever closer union for many years?

Whatever the reasons for rejection, the response of the Member States was relatively unequivocal. The process had to go to the next step if the Union were to be an effective force in dealing with the challenges of the twenty-first century and a membership that now stood at 27 states. Thus, in 2007, under the dedicated leadership of Germany as Chairman of the European Council, the practical and reforming elements of the Constitution Treaty were revived, shorn of the latter's more formal and controversial constitutional themes.

This effort resulted in the Treaty of Lisbon, which was eventually ratified by all Member States and came into effect on December 1, 2009. The creation of a single European Union based on the integrationist structure of the Community Treaties was achieved. With that came a remarkable degree of constitutional clarity, and this enabled us to create the constitutional template found in Chapter 1. The revisions to the organization of the book in this third edition reflect the structure of that template and at last enable an orderly, logical, and Treaty-based approach to the study of the Union's constitutional law.

Ironically, ever since the three-pillar structure was abandoned with the entry into force of the Lisbon Treaty, the EU's edifice has been shaking; threatened by the European sovereign debt crisis and the danger it is currently posing to the very existence of the Euro.

On September 28, 2011, the President of the European Commission, Mr. Barroso, said that the European governments could not be relied upon to lead deeper economic integration among Eurozone members and that *"For all this to work, we need more than ever the independent authority of the Commission."* By this statement, Mr. Barroso not only attempted to reestablish his authority and that of the European Commission; he also expressed the wish of many Europeans for more integration in order to solve the economic and financial problems currently faced by the EU. There is no doubt that the development of the EU will continue to revolve around these two concepts of integration and cooperation. The question remains whether the balance will lean towards one more than to the other in the coming years. The likelihood seems to be that a "permanent" and enlarged European Financial Stability Facility will continue to be constituted outside the Union's structure, thus preserving the Member States' sovereignty over economic and fiscal policy. Were it to be otherwise, Europeans would finally have to confront the possibility of a fiscal union. Politically this is probably not feasible today. Yet, with the TEU history as a model, is it not likely that this instrument will eventually move into the Union structure and become a Union competence? This would be such a radical step that the citizens of Europe ought surely to be given their say: they would be asked, finally, whether they wish to be part of a "United States of Europe", and an entirely new chapter in European history would begin.

This is a fascinating, though tense, moment of history to live through. There is always the possibility that events will overpower the unity of the Euro, that it will unravel and along with it the Union as a whole. Yet the Communities and the Union have survived crises in the past only to emerge stronger. It is our belief that the internal momentum for unification and the external pressures compelling it will once again prevail.

# THE EUROPEAN UNION FROM THE PERSPECTIVE OF THE UNITED STATES: A MESSAGE TO AMERICAN READERS

Dear Readers,

Now more than ever the importance of a deep understanding of EU Constitutional Law to American legal students and practioners is critical. Having experienced over many years firsthand the vibrant business and economic relationship between the U.S. and Europe, I can resoundingly attest to the EU's predominant role as America's premier trade and investment partner.

Unparalleled in its depth and breadth, this bilateral partnership easily is described by superlatives: the largest, the most complex, the most profitable, the wealthiest, and the longest in duration. In fact, the transatlantic economic partnership is the key driver of global prosperity and does indeed represent the biggest, most integrated, and most enduring relationship in the world.

America and the European Union account for a solid 50 percent of the world's economy, generating $5 trillion in total commercial sales each year and employing nearly 15 million workers on both sides of the Atlantic. With 54 percent of the world's GDP in terms of value and 40 percent in terms of purchasing power, it is no exaggeration to reaffirm that the transatlantic business bonds are second to none.

Equally impressive, the U.S. and Europe are each other's primary source and destination for foreign direct investment and notwithstanding fiscal and financial challenges, rates of growth are showing solid increases: in the last 10 years, American companies placed about $1.3 trillion into European FDI locations, a figure that represents more than 60 percent of total U.S. FDI for that same period. In tandem, Europe's share of total U.S. FDI in 2010 was roughly 52 percent and that proportion is expected to continue with more than half of the top foreign investors by country into the U.S. coming from Europe. By contrast, value of EU investment assets in the U.S. is three times the amount of the combined value in the so-called BRIC countries (Brazil, Russia, India, and China).

In terms of trade, the U.S. takes the number one position for EU exports of goods (well over 20 percent) and also is in the number one position of imports of EU services with about double that value, i.e., about 40 percent. Overall, America and the EU are each other's most important commercial partners when it comes to services trade and investment. The U.S. and European services economies have never been as interwoven as now in financial series, telecoms, utilities, insurance, advertising, computer services, and other related activities.

Moreover, even with recent past and current financial tribulations, American and EU financial markets continue to account for well over two-thirds of global banking assets, three-quarters of global financial services, 77 percent of all private and public debt securities, and almost 80 percent of all interest-rate derivatives.

These preeminent commercial, investment, financial, and trade connections require preeminent legal counsel and support to maintain their vibrancy. Europe is now and is expected for the next few years to remain the most profitable region to do business in the world for American firms. U.S. foreign affiliate income earned in Europe rose to an estimated $196 billion for the latest reporting period available — a record high.

Using this casebook as a reference, study of EU constitutional and other legal provisions, case

# A MESSAGE TO AMERICAN READERS

law, precedents, and relevant regulations will add immeasurably to your effectiveness as an attorney. With globalization's ever-strengthening reach, there is high probability that your clients will overwhelmingly want to do business with European companies. They, therefore, need American attorneys with knowledge of the European legal framework to ensure their success.

The Continent is frequently viewed as emblematic of centuries-old established borders, traditions, and precepts. However, the U.S. as a nation is much older than many of the modern nation-states we think of as iconic European: Italy, Ireland, the Czech Republic, Slovakia, and Belgium, just to name a few. The European Union in its present form has only been in existence for about 20 years (as of the time of this writing) and the euro as the single monetary unit was introduced as a functioning currency in daily use just a scant decade ago. Scanning today's headlines, we can safely say the "Union" is sometimes still more observed in its exception. Member states continue to exert tremendous autonomy and the resulting influence and effect, not only within Europe, but including in the U.S. and even worldwide, is unprecedented.

However, it is the shared affirmation and belief in common and deeply held values that will continue to infuse the transatlantic relationship with longevity and prosperity. These intersections of values complement the deeply interdependent transatlantic economy and the trust and confidence that have been created through the many collaborative years of trade and investment. Both partners are committed to the rule of law, the democratic process, and a free and fair market economy — all of which require attorneys with relevant competencies and expertise.

There is no doubt that the business and economic ties between the U.S. and Europe are second to none, and we share a common historical context, social traditions, and philosophical orientation that are reflected in some similar legal concepts as framework. However, despite these many commonalities, expectations and manner of doing business in each location are surprisingly different. Unlike their American counterparts, European business people are for the most part risk-averse, extremely loyal to local preference and are not as mobile as the average American worker. From a legal perspective, an interesting anomaly, one among many, is the American priority of security versus the European preference to favor privacy relating to sharing of, for example airline passenger and financial data and the tensions that are created when combating terrorism.

Thus, there is ample legal work to be accomplished in the transatlantic arena. Attorney services to protect and expand research and development, intellectual property rights, mergers and acquisitions, joint ventures, and strategic commercial alignments, and standardization in all manner of manufacturing and regulatory frameworks are just a few of the practice areas where clients will seek your counsel as they pursue access to lucrative European markets.

In conclusion, I cannot overemphasize the value of this text to those seeking to best advise clients seeking to engage in the competitive world of international business. I commend James Dinnage and Jean-Luc Laffineur for this impressive work. Today's world is truly a seamless universe. Therefore, even for those who believe they will focus their careers on areas only related to more local matters, familiarity with the issues presented here will serve them well.

Camille E. Sailer, Esq.

President

Board of Trustees

European American Chamber of Commerce — New Jersey/

Former Regional Commercial Counselor

Embassy of the United States of America in Brussels

# TABLE OF CONTENTS

# TABLE OF CONTENTS

# TABLE OF CONTENTS

# TABLE OF CONTENTS

# TABLE OF CONTENTS

# TABLE OF CONTENTS

# TABLE OF CONTENTS

# TABLE OF CONTENTS

# TABLE OF CONTENTS

# TABLE OF CONTENTS

# TABLE OF CONTENTS

# TABLE OF CONTENTS

# TABLE OF CONTENTS

# TABLE OF CONTENTS

# TABLE OF CONTENTS

# TABLE OF CONTENTS

# TABLE OF CONTENTS

# TABLE OF CONTENTS

# TABLE OF CONTENTS

# TABLE OF CONTENTS

# TABLE OF CONTENTS

# TABLE OF CONTENTS

# TABLE OF CONTENTS

# TABLE OF CONTENTS

# TABLE OF CONTENTS

# TABLE OF CONTENTS

# Part I

# THE EUROPEAN UNION AS AN INTERNATIONAL FEDERATION

# Chapter 1

# THE CONSTITUTIONAL FRAMEWORK

## § 1.01  INTRODUCTION

The European Union in its current form has existed only since December 1, 2009. It represents the current state of an ongoing process to create an ever closer union among the peoples of Europe that began with the European Coal and Steel Community 60 years earlier. The people who founded that Community saw it as a modest first step covering two basic industries. This was then followed by the establishment of the much broader European Economic Community (EEC), based on the same model, in 1957. After many amendments that filled out the original economic goals, a European Union was established in 1992 that provided a framework for broader political cohesion both in internal matters and foreign policy alongside the EEC (renamed simply the European Community or EC). Further treaties followed, so that by 2002, the Member States found themselves able to sponsor a convention for the drawing up of a Constitution for the Union, based on a revised composite Treaty. Although this document was signed by all Member States, it failed to garner popular support in The Netherlands and France, which both held referenda. Despite this failure, the momentum continued, culminating in the 2007 Treaty of Lisbon, which left the basic Treaties intact but amended them to round out a constitutional structure that can be legitimately described as an international federation.

The cases and materials in this book have been chosen to provide a relatively deep study of the constitutional aspects of the Union. Unfortunately, the treaties themselves are difficult to navigate and do not inherently lend themselves to a conceptual approach based on how we think of constitutions — government, competences, separation of powers, human rights. For this reason, we have devised a constitutional "template" that rearranges key treaty provisions in a more familiar order, filters out excessive detail and imports notions developed in the case law that are critical to the constitutional structure.

It is always a matter of debate as to what should or should not be in a Constitution. The U.S. Constitution at its inception was remarkably simple, while, by contrast, the German Basic Law is a much more lengthy document, sometimes going to a level of detail that might seem excessive. For the purposes of this Casebook, the primary motivation has been to find a means of conveying the essentials in as simple and familiar a manner as possible. In the case of the EU, it is suggested that such a document should lay out a description of:

- what the EU is, in terms of its membership, objectives, institutions and autonomous status (equates to the Preamble to the U.S. Constitution and the supremacy clause);

- the components of EU law (constitutional sources and legal acts of the Union),

- the Union legislature

- executive powers

- judicial powers
  (in each of the above three cases describing the structure, procedures and powers of each of the relevant institutions);

- the Union's competences,

- the limitations on the powers of the Member states to ensure the functioning of the internal market (where the case law is summarized, a necessary inclusion given that the actual treaty provisions on their own scarcely convey the true extent of the TFEU's reach in this regard);

- the position of the individual in relation to Union law (including fundamental rights and incorporation by reference of the Charter of Fundamental Rights); and

- relations between the Member States.

The template has no legal force whatsoever. Its purpose is simply to serve as an aid in promoting an understanding of the scope and functions of the European Union following the entry into force of the Treaty of Lisbon on December 1, 2009. There is no official document that claims to be the "Constitution of the European Union".

Key provisions and concepts of the Treaties have been selected and reorganized to bring out the essential constitutional structure of the Union in the post-Lisbon Treaty era. It is not intended to be a complete restatement of the Treaties.

The references in square brackets indicate the source of all of the provisions following the last preceding reference. "New TEU" refers to the Treaty on European Union post-Lisbon, "old TEU" to the pre-Lisbon text. "TFEU" refers to the Treaty on the Functioning of the European Union (formerly the Treaty establishing the European Community, referred to as "EC"). Articles or relevant elements of articles not previously appearing in the Treaties are designated as "(new)." Note that the EC references do not necessarily imply that the text of the TFEU provision has remained identical to that of the EC. In all cases it is the TFEU text that appears here. Some items are the result of case law, indicated by "*ECJ*". "Summary" indicates the authors' summary of more lengthy or disparate provisions.

## § 1.02  THE CONSTITUTIONAL TEMPLATE

### ARTICLE 1
### FOUNDATIONS OF THE EUROPEAN UNION

### Section 1.1 Purpose of the European Union

The sovereign states of Europe have established among themselves a European Union (the Union), on which they have conferred competences to attain objectives they have in common. The Union, which has existed since December 1, 2009 in its present form, is an organization established as the instrument for creating an ever closer union among the peoples of Europe, in which decisions are taken as openly as possible and as closely as possible to the citizen. The Union is intended to build on, and expand and improve the achievements of the prior organization of the same name and of the European Community, both of which it replaces and succeeds. [Summary and old TEU 1/new TEU 1]

### Section 1.2 Founding Principles

**1.2.1** The Union is founded on the values of respect for human dignity, freedom, democracy, equality, the rule of law and respect for human rights, including the rights of persons belonging to minorities. These values are common to the Member States in a society in which pluralism, non-discrimination, tolerance, justice, solidarity and equality between women and men prevail. [TEU 2 (new)]

**1.2.2** The functioning of the Union shall be founded on representative democracy.

Citizens are directly represented at Union level in the European Parliament.

Member States are represented in the European Council by their Heads of State or Government and in the Council by their governments, themselves democratically accountable either to their national Parliaments, or to their citizens.

Every citizen shall have the right to participate in the democratic life of the Union. Decisions shall be taken as openly and as closely as possible to the citizen.

Political parties at European level contribute to forming European political awareness and to expressing the will of citizens of the Union. [TEU 10]

### Section 1.3 Membership of the Union

**1.3.1** The countries that are Member States of the Union are listed in subsection 3.2.6. [Summary] The official languages of the Union are Bulgarian, Czech, Danish, Dutch, English, Estonian, Finnish, French, German, Greek, Hungarian, Irish, Italian, Latvian, Lithuanian, Maltese, Polish, Portuguese, Romanian, Slovak, Slovenian, Spanish and Swedish. [old TEU 53/new TEU 55]

**1.3.2** Any European State which respects the values referred to in Section 1.2 and is committed to promoting them may apply to become a member of the Union. After negotiation of the terms of accession by the Union and the applicant State, such accession shall be submitted for ratification by all the existing Member States in accordance with their respective constitutional requirements. [old TEU 49/new TEU 49]

**1.3.3** Any Member State may decide to withdraw from the Union in accordance with its own constitutional requirements. The Union shall negotiate and conclude an agreement with that State, setting out the arrangements for its withdrawal, taking account of the framework for its future relationship with the Union. [TEU 50 (new)]

**1.3.4** In case of a clear risk of serious breach, or actual persistent and serious breach by a Member State of the Union's values as described in Section 1.2 above, the Union may, subject to compliance with certain procedures, respectively take action to remove the risk or suspend the voting rights of that Member State in the Council [TEU 7/Summary and TFEU 354]

## 1.4 The Union's Institutions

**1.4.1** The Union acts through its institutions, which are:

- the European Parliament,
- the European Council,
- the Council,
- the European Commission,
- the Court of Justice of the European Union,
- the European Central Bank,
- the Court of Auditors. [old TEU 9/new TEU 13]

Additionally the Treaties or Union law provide for:

- the Economic and Social Committee; [EC 258/TFEU 301]
- the Committee of the Regions; [EC 265/TFEU 305]]
- the European Investment Bank [EC 266/TFEU 308]
- the European Police Office (Europol) [old TEU 30/TFEU 88]
- Eurojust [old TEU 31/TFEU 85]
- various specialized agencies. [TEU 42 (new) and legislation]

The European Parliament shall have its seat in Strasbourg where the 12 periods of monthly plenary sessions, including the budget session, shall be held. The periods of additional plenary sessions shall be held in Brussels. The committees of the European Parliament shall meet in Brussels. The General Secretariat of the European Parliament and its departments shall remain in Luxembourg.

The Council shall have its seat in Brussels. During the months of April, June and October, the Council shall hold its meetings in Luxembourg.

The Commission shall have its seat in Brussels. Certain departments shall be established in Luxembourg.

The Court of Justice of the European Union shall have its seat in Luxembourg.

The Court of Auditors shall have its seat in Luxembourg.

The Economic and Social Committee shall have its seat in Brussels.

The Committee of the Regions shall have its seat in Brussels.

The European Investment Bank shall have its seat in Luxembourg.

The European Central Bank shall have its seat in Frankfurt.

The European Police Office (Europol) shall have its seat in The Hague. [Protocol 6]

The President of the European Council shall be based in Brussels. The European Council may meet at any location chosen by the President. [Summary]

**1.4.2** In carrying out their missions, the institutions, bodies, offices and agencies of the Union shall have the support of an open, efficient and independent European administration. [TFEU 298 (new)]

## Section 1.5 Objectives of the Union

**1.5.1** The Union's aim is to promote peace, its values and the well-being of its peoples.

**1.5.2** The Union shall offer its citizens an area of freedom, security and justice without internal frontiers, in which the free movement of persons is ensured in conjunction with appropriate measures with respect to external border controls, asylum, immigration and the prevention and combating of crime. [old TEU 2/new TEU 3 and EC 61 and old TEU 29/TFEU 67]

**1.5.3** The Union shall adopt measures with the aim of establishing or ensuring the functioning of the internal market [old TEU 2/new TEU 3, EC 14/TFEU 26, EC 95 & 94/TFEU 114 & 115, EC 40/TFEU 46, EC 47/TFEU 53, EC 52/TFEU 59]. It shall work for the sustainable development of Europe based on balanced economic growth and price stability, a highly competitive social market economy, aiming at full employment and social progress, and a high level of protection and improvement of the quality of the environment. It shall promote scientific and technological advance.

It shall combat social exclusion and discrimination, and shall promote social justice and protection, equality between women and men, solidarity between generations and protection of the rights of the child.

It shall promote economic, social and territorial cohesion, and solidarity among Member States.

It shall respect its rich cultural and linguistic diversity, and shall ensure that Europe's cultural heritage is safeguarded and enhanced. [old TEU 2/new TEU 3]

**1.5.4** The Union shall establish an economic and monetary union whose currency is the euro. [old TEU 2/new TEU 3]

Certain Member States are permitted a derogation from the use of the euro and related obligations. [EC some provisions from 111- 124/TFEU 136-144 (partly new) and Protocol 15]

**1.5.5** The Union's competence in matters of common foreign and security policy shall cover all areas of foreign policy and all questions relating to the Union's security, including the progressive framing of a common defence policy that might lead to a common defence.

Within the framework of the principles and objectives of its external action, the Union shall conduct, define and implement a common foreign and security policy, based on the development of mutual political solidarity among Member States, the identification of questions of general interest and the achievement of an ever-increasing degree of convergence of Member States' actions. [old TEU 11/new TEU 24]

The Union's action on the international scene shall be guided by the principles which have inspired its own creation, development and enlargement, and which it seeks to advance in the wider world: democracy, the rule of law, the universality and indivisibility of human rights and fundamental freedoms, respect for human dignity, the principles of equality and solidarity, and respect for the principles of the United Nations Charter and international law.

The Union shall seek to develop relations and build partnerships with third countries, and international, regional or global organisations which share the principles referred to in the first subparagraph. It shall promote multilateral solutions to common problems, in particular in the framework of the United Nations.

The Union shall define and pursue common policies and actions, and shall work for a high degree of cooperation in all fields of international relations, in order to:

(a)    safeguard its values, fundamental interests, security, independence and integrity;

(b)    consolidate and support democracy, the rule of law, human rights and the principles of international law;

(c)    preserve peace, prevent conflicts and strengthen international security, in accordance with the purposes and principles of the United Nations Charter, with the principles of the Helsinki Final Act and with the aims of the Charter of Paris, including those relating to external borders;

(d)    foster the sustainable economic, social and environmental development of developing countries, with the primary aim of eradicating poverty;

(e)    encourage the integration of all countries into the world economy, including through the progressive abolition of restrictions on international trade;

(f)    help develop international measures to preserve and improve the quality of the environment and the sustainable management of global natural resources, in order to ensure sustainable development;

(g)    assist populations, countries and regions confronting natural or man-made disasters; and

(h)    promote an international system based on stronger multilateral cooperation and good global governance. [TEU 21(new)]

**1.5.6** The Union shall pursue its objectives by appropriate means commensurate with the competences which are conferred upon it in the Treaties. [old TEU 2/new TEU 3]

### Section 1.6 Legal Autonomy of the Union

**1.6.1** To enable the Union to pursue its objectives, the Member States have constituted the Union as a separate legal person [TEU 47 (new)].

**1.6.2** The Member States have limited their sovereign rights for the benefit of the Union and have transferred powers to it. [*ECJ*]

**1.6.3** Union law exists as an autonomous body of law within the legal systems of each Member State and, to the extent of any conflict with national laws, including the Constitution of each Member State, takes precedence over them. [*ECJ*/ Declaration 17]

### Section 1.7 Duties of the Member States

The Member States shall facilitate the achievement of the Union's tasks and refrain from any measure which could jeopardise the attainment of the Union's objectives. [EC 10/TEU 4]

**ARTICLE 2**
**THE COMPONENTS OF UNION LAW**

### Section 2.1 The Treaties

**2.1.1** The Union shall be founded on the Treaty on European Union and on the Treaty on the Functioning of the European Union, including the protocols, declarations and annexes thereto (the "Treaties"). Those two Treaties shall have the same legal value. [old TEU 1/new TEU 1]

**2.1.2** The Government of any Member State, the European Parliament or the Commission may submit to the Council proposals for the amendment of the Treaties. These proposals may, *inter alia*, serve either to increase or to reduce the competences conferred on the Union in the Treaties. If the proposals are approved by the European Council, the President of the European Council shall convene a Convention composed of representatives of the national Parliaments, of the Heads of State or Government of the Member States, of the European Parliament and of the Commission. The European Central Bank shall also be consulted in the case of institutional changes in the monetary area. The Convention shall examine the proposals for amendments and shall adopt by consensus a recommendation to a conference of representatives of the governments of the Member States.

The European Council may decide by a simple majority, after obtaining the consent of the European Parliament, not to convene a Convention should this not be justified by the extent of the proposed amendments. In the latter case, the European Council shall define the terms of reference for a conference of representatives of the governments of the Member States.

If consensus is reached, the amendments shall enter into force after being ratified by all the Member States in accordance with their respective constitutional requirements.

**2.1.3** The European Council may adopt a decision amending all or part of the provisions of the Treaty on the Functioning of the European Union relating to the internal market, the area of freedom, security and justice and Union policies. That decision shall not enter into force until it is approved by the Member States in accordance with their respective constitutional requirements. The decision shall not increase the competences conferred on the Union in the Treaties.

**2.1.4** Where the Treaty on the Functioning of the European Union or the provisions concerning the common foreign and security policy provides for the Council to act by unanimity in a given area or case, the European Council may adopt a decision authorising the Council to act by a qualified majority in that area or in that case. This subparagraph shall not apply to decisions with military implications or those in the area of defence.

Where the Treaty on the Functioning of the European Union provides for legislative acts to be adopted by the Council in accordance with a special legislative procedure, the European Council may adopt a decision allowing for the adoption of such acts in accordance with the ordinary legislative procedure.

Any initiative taken by the European Council on the basis of this subsection shall be notified to the national Parliaments. If a national Parliament makes known its opposition within six months of the date of such notification, the decision referred to in the first or the second subparagraph shall not be adopted. In the absence of opposition, the European Council may adopt the decision. [old TEU 48/new TEU 48]

**2.1.5** The Council may adopt provisions to confer jurisdiction on the Court of Justice of the European Union in disputes relating to the application of acts adopted on the basis of the Treaties which create European intellectual property rights. These provisions shall enter into force after their approval by the Member States in accordance with their respective constitutional requirements. [EC 229A/TFEU 262]

**2.1.6** In general, the Treaties are binding on the Member States and the Union's institutions. [Summary] However, precise and unconditional obligations imposed by the Treaty on the Functioning of the European Union on the Member States have direct effect within the legal systems of the Member States. [*ECJ*] The provisions of that Treaty described in Article 7 and Section 8.1 are directly effective, while the provisions concerning anticompetitive practices [EC 81 and 82/TFEU 101 and 102], non-discrimination on grounds of nationality [EC 39/TFEU 45] and gender discrimination in pay [EC 141/TFEU 157] are directly applicable in the legal systems of the Member States. [*ECJ*]

**2.1.7** The Treaties shall in no way prejudice the rules in Member States governing the system of property ownership. [EC 295/TFEU 345]

### Section 2.2 Fundamental Rights

**2.2.1** The Union recognizes the rights, freedoms and principles set forth in the Charter of Fundamental Rights of the European Union of 7 December 2000, as adopted at Strasbourg, on 12 December 2007. The Charter has legally binding force. It confirms the fundamental rights guaranteed by the European Convention for the Protection of Human Rights and Fundamental Freedoms and as they result from the constitutional traditions common to the Member States. Such rights, freedoms and principles shall have the same legal value as the Treaties and shall apply to the institutions of the Union, Union acts and any situation involving the implementation of Union law.

The provisions of the Charter shall not extend in any way the competences of the Union as defined in the Treaties. [old TEU 6/new TEU 6/Declaration 1]

**2.2.2** The Union shall accede to the to the Europoean Convention for the Protection of Human Rights and Fundamental Freedoms [TEU 6 (new)].

### Section 2.3 General Principles of law common to the Member States

Fundamental rights, as guaranteed by the European Convention for the Protection of Human Rights and Fundamental Freedoms and as they result from the constitutional traditions common to the Member States, shall constitute general principles of the Union's law. [old TEU 6/new TEU 6]

### Section 2.4 Union laws and executive acts

**2.4.1** To exercise the Union's competences, the institutions shall adopt regulations, directives, decisions, recommendations and opinions.

A regulation shall have general application. It shall be binding in its entirety and directly applicable in all Member States. [EC 249/TFEU 288]

A directive shall be binding, as to the result to be achieved, upon each Member State to which it is addressed, but shall leave to the national authorities the choice of form and methods. [EC 249/TFEU 288]. However, any provision of a directive that is precise and unconditional has direct effect in the legal systems of the Member States. [*ECJ*]

A decision shall be binding in its entirety. A decision which specifies those to whom it is addressed shall be binding only on them.

Recommendations and opinions shall have no binding force. [EC 249/TFEU 288]

**2.4.2** Agreements concluded by the Union are binding upon the institutions of the Union and on its Member States. [TFEU 216 (new)]

**2.4.3** Legal acts shall state the reasons on which they are based and shall refer to any proposals, initiatives, recommendations, requests or opinions required by the Treaties. [EC 253/TFEU 296] Every legal act derives its authority from a specific article (or in some cases, more than one article) in one of the Treaties. Each such article may specify the procedure and type of majority required to adopt it. [Summary]

**2.4.4** Legal acts of the Union must comply with the Treaties, the Charter of Fundamental Rights and the general principles of law common to the Member States. [Summary] The Union must respect international law in the exercise of its powers. [*ECJ*]

### Section 2.5 Selective applicability of Union Law in certain cases

**2.5.1** In specific instances described in the Treaties, some provisions of the Treaties and Union laws, including provisions relating to the use of the euro and the removal of immigration controls between Member States, do not apply or apply in a modified way to designated Member States. [Summary, and EC 105 – 120/TFEU 127-144, Protocols 4, 14 – 22, 30, 32, 34 and 36]

**2.5.2** Member States which wish to establish enhanced cooperation between themselves within the framework of the Union's non-exclusive competences may make use of its institutions and exercise those competences by applying the relevant provisions of the Treaties, subject to the limits and in accordance with the detailed arrangements laid down in the Treaties

Enhanced cooperation shall aim to further the objectives of the Union, protect its interests and reinforce its integration process. Such cooperation shall be open at any time to all Member States.

Acts adopted in the framework of enhanced cooperation shall bind only participating Member States. They shall not be regarded as part of the *acquis* which has to be accepted by candidate States for accession to the Union. [Old TEU 43-45/new TEU 20 and TFEU 82-87 and 326-334]

**2.5.3** The application of the Charter on Fundamental Rights in the United Kingdom and Poland is subject to certain restrictions. [Protocol 30/Declarations 61, 62]

**2.5.4** Acts adopted under the old TEU are subject to transitional provisions with some variation in legal effects among the Member States [Protocol 36]

### Section 2.6 Effects of Union law on individuals

Any Treaty provision or Union act that is directly applicable or directly effective has legal effects for individuals within the legal systems of the Member States to the extent and in the manner described in Article 8. [Summary]

**ARTICLE 3**
**THE LEGISLATURE**

### Section 3.1 The European Parliament

**3.1.1** The European Parliament shall be composed of representatives of the Union's citizens. They shall not exceed seven hundred and fifty in number, plus the President and shall be elected for a term of five years by direct universal suffrage in a free and secret ballot. [TEU 14 (new)]

The European Parliament shall draw up a proposal to lay down the provisions necessary for the election of its Members by direct universal suffrage in accordance with a uniform procedure in all Member States or in accordance with principles common to all Member States. Such measure shall be adopted in accordance with the special procedure laid down in the Treaties. [EC 190 (4) & (5)/TFEU 223]

**3.1.2** Representation of citizens shall be degressively proportional, that is to say, the number of citizens represented by each member increases with population size, with a minimum threshold of six members per Member State. No Member State shall be allocated more than ninety-six seats. At the initiative, and subject to the consent, of the European Parliament, the European Council shall decide on the composition of the European Parliament

**3.1.3** The European Parliament shall elect its President and its officers from among its members. [TEU 14 (new)]

**3.1.4** The European Parliament shall adopt legislation laying down the regulations and general conditions governing the performance of the duties of its Members. [EC 190(4) & (5)/TFEU 223] Members shall be entitled to compensation in accordance with the Statute for Members of the European Parliament and to the privileges and immunities laid down by the Treaties. [Summary]

**3.1.5** The European Parliament and the Council shall adopt legislation laying down the regulations governing political parties in the European Parliament and in particular the rules regarding their funding. [EC 191 2d subpara/TFEU 224]

**3.1.6** The European Parliament shall hold an annual session. It shall meet, without requiring to be convened, on the second Tuesday in March. It may meet in extraordinary part-session at the request of a majority of its component Members or at the request of the Council or of the Commission. [EC 196/TFEU 229]

**3.1.7** The European Parliament shall adopt its Rules of Procedure, acting by a majority of its Members. The proceedings of the European Parliament shall be published in the manner laid down in the Treaties and in its Rules of Procedure. [EC 199/TFEU 232]

**3.1.8** Save as otherwise provided in the Treaties, the European Parliament shall act by a majority of the votes cast. The Rules of Procedure shall determine the quorum. [EC 198/TFEU 231]

**3.1.9** The European Parliament shall, jointly with the Council, exercise legislative and budgetary functions. It shall exercise functions of political control and consultation [TEU 14] including:

- consent to certain international agreements [EC 300/TFEU 218]

- consent to the accession of a new Member State [old TEU 49/TEU 49]

- election of the President of the Commission [TEU 14 & 17 (new)]

- approval of the Commission composition proposed by the Council [TEU 17 (new)]

- censure of the Commission; [TEU 17 (new)]

- discharge of the implementation of the Union budget [EC 276/TFEU 319]

- consultation or consent with respect to other matters specified in the Treaties; [Summary]

■ regulation of the conduct of the Ombudsman [TFEU 228]

**3.1.10** In the course of its duties, the European Parliament may, at the request of a quarter of its component Members, set up a temporary Committee of Inquiry to investigate, without prejudice to the powers conferred by the Treaties on other institutions or bodies, alleged contraventions or maladministration in the implementation of Union law, except where the alleged facts are being examined before a court and while the case is still subject to legal proceedings. [EC 193/TFEU 226]

### Section 3.2 The Council

**3.2.1** The Council shall consist of a representative of each Member State at ministerial level, who may commit the government of the Member State in question and cast its vote. The Council shall meet in different configurations, the list of which shall be adopted by the European Council [TEU 16 (new)] The Council has both legislative and executive responsibilities. [Summary]

**3.2.2** A Committee of Permanent Representatives of the Governments of the Member States shall be responsible for preparing the work of the Council.

**3.2.3** The Council shall meet in public when it deliberates and votes on a draft legislative act.

**3.2.4** The Presidency of Council configurations, other than that of Foreign Affairs, shall be held by Member State representatives in the Council on the basis of equal rotation of six months each. [TEU 16 (new)]

**3.2.5** The Council shall meet when convened by its President on his own initiative or at the request of one of its Members or of the Commission. [EC 204/TFEU 237]

**3.2.6** The Council shall act by a qualified majority except where the Treaties provide otherwise. Until October 31 2014, where the Council is required to act by a qualified majority, the votes of its Members shall be weighted as follows:

| | |
|---|---|
| Belgium | 12 |
| Bulgaria | 12 |
| Czech Republic | 12 |
| Denmark | 7 |
| Germany | 29 |
| Estonia | 4 |
| Greece | 12 |
| Spain | 27 |
| France | 29 |
| Ireland | 7 |
| Italy | 29 |
| Cyprus | 4 |
| Latvia | 4 |
| Lithuania | 7 |
| Luxembourg | 4 |
| Hungary | 12 |
| Malta | 3 |

| | |
|---|---|
| Netherlands | 13 |
| Austria | 10 |
| Poland | 27 |
| Portugal | 12 |
| Romania | 15 |
| Slovenia | 4 |
| Slovakia | 7 |
| Finland | 7 |
| Sweden | 10 |
| United Kingdom | 29 |
| Total number of votes: | 341 |

Acts of the Council shall require for their adoption at least 255 votes in favour cast by a majority of the members where the Treaty on the Functioning of the European Union requires them to be adopted on a proposal from the Commission.

In other cases, for their adoption acts of the Council shall require at least 255 votes in favour, cast by at least two thirds of the members.

As from 1 November 2014, a qualified majority shall be defined as at least 55% of the members of the Council, comprising at least fifteen of them and representing Member States comprising at least 65% of the population of the Union.

A blocking minority must include at least four Council members, failing which the qualified majority shall be deemed attained.

Where the Council does not act on a proposal from the Commission or from the High Representative of the Union for Foreign Affairs and Security Policy, the qualified majority shall be defined as at least 72% of the members of the Council, representing Member States comprising at least 65% of the population of the Union.

Certain modifications to the above rules apply where not all Member States are permitted to participate due to derogations or exemptions from the obligations of the Treaties and also during a transitional period ending in 2017. [TEU 16 (new) & EC 205(1) & (2)/TFEU 238 and Protocol 36]

**3.2.7** Where it is required to act by a simple majority, the Council shall act by a majority of its component members.

**3.2.8** Abstentions by Members present in person or represented shall not prevent the adoption by the Council of acts which require unanimity. [EC 205 (1) & (2)/TFEU 238]

**3.2.9** Where a vote is taken, any Member of the Council may also act on behalf of not more than one other member. [EC 206/TFEU 239]

**3.2.10** The Council shall act by a simple majority regarding procedural matters and for the adoption of its Rules of Procedure. [EC 207/TFEU 240]

## Section 3.3 The Commission

**3.3.1** Union legislative acts may only be adopted on the basis of a Commission proposal, except where the Treaties provide otherwise. [TEU 17]

**3.3.2** The European Parliament may, acting by a majority of its component Members, request the Commission to submit any appropriate proposal on matters on which it considers that a Union act is required for the purpose of implementing the Treaties. If the Commission does not submit a proposal, it shall inform the European Parliament of the reasons. [EC 192/TFEU 225]

**3.3.3** Not less than one million citizens who are nationals of a significant number of Member States may take the initiative of inviting the European Commission, within the framework of its powers, to submit any appropriate proposal on matters where citizens consider that a legal act of the Union is required for the purpose of implementing the Treaties.

## Section 3.4 Legislative Procedures

**3.4.1** Any act adopted by the European Parliament and the Council, or by either institution with the participation of the other where a special legislative procedure is specified, shall be a legislative act. [TFEU 289 (new)]

Draft legislative acts shall be prepared by the Commission and shall be shared with the legislatures of the Member States. [Protocol 2] National Parliaments may send to the President of the Commission a reasoned opinion stating why they consider that a draft legislative act does not comply with the principle of subsidiarity. Where a reasoned opinion represents at least one third (a quarter for drafts in the area of freedom, security and justice) of all the votes allocated to the national parliaments, the draft must be reviewed. After such review, the Commission may decide to maintain, amend or withdraw the draft [Protocols 1 and 2].

**3.4.2** Any legislative act adopted jointly by the European Parliament and the Council shall be governed by the ordinary legislative procedure.

The ordinary legislative procedure comprises the steps described below.

The Commission shall submit a proposal to the European Parliament and the Council.

### First reading

The European Parliament shall adopt its position at first reading and communicate it to the Council.

If the Council approves the European Parliament's position, the act concerned shall be adopted in the wording which corresponds to the position of the European Parliament.

If the Council does not approve the European Parliament's position, it shall adopt its position at first reading and communicate it to the European Parliament.

The Council shall inform the European Parliament fully of the reasons which led it to adopt its position at first reading. The Commission shall inform the European

Parliament fully of its position.

*Second reading*

If, within three months of such communication, the European Parliament:

- approves the Council's position at first reading or has not taken a decision, the act concerned shall be deemed to have been adopted in the wording which corresponds to the position of the Council;

- rejects, by a majority of its component members, the Council's position at first reading, the proposed act shall be deemed not to have been adopted;

- proposes, by a majority of its component members, amendments to the Council's position at first reading, the text thus amended shall be forwarded to the Council and to the Commission, which shall deliver an opinion on those amendments.

If, within three months of receiving the European Parliament's amendments, the Council, acting by a qualified majority:

- approves all those amendments, the act in question shall be deemed to have been adopted;

- does not approve all the amendments, the President of the Council, in agreement with the President of the European Parliament, shall within six weeks convene a meeting of the Conciliation Committee.

The Council shall act unanimously on the amendments on which the Commission has delivered a negative opinion.

*Conciliation*

The Conciliation Committee, which shall be composed of the members of the Council or their representatives and an equal number of members representing the European Parliament, shall have the task of reaching agreement on a joint text, by a qualified majority of the members of the Council or their representatives and by a majority of the members representing the European Parliament within six weeks of its being convened, on the basis of the positions of the European Parliament and the Council at second reading.

The Commission shall take part in the Conciliation Committee's proceedings and shall take all necessary initiatives with a view to reconciling the positions of the European Parliament and the Council.

If, within six weeks of its being convened, the Conciliation Committee does not approve the joint text, the proposed act shall be deemed not to have been adopted.

*Third reading*

If, within that period, the Conciliation Committee approves a joint text, the European Parliament, acting by a majority of the votes cast, and the Council, acting by a qualified majority, shall each have a period of six weeks from that approval in which to adopt the act in question in accordance with the joint text. If they fail to do so, the proposed act shall be deemed not to have been adopted.

The periods of three months and six weeks referred to above shall be extended by a maximum of one month and two weeks respectively at the initiative of the European Parliament or the Council. [EC 251/TFEU 294]

**3.4.3** In certain special cases, a legislative act may be submitted to the ordinary legislative procedure on the initiative of a group of Member States, on a recommendation by the European Central Bank, or at the request of the Court of Justice. In those cases the provisions relating to the involvement of the Commission are not applicable. However, the European Parliament and the Council shall communicate the proposed act to the Commission with their positions at first and second readings. The European Parliament or the Council may request the opinion of the Commission throughout the procedure, which the Commission may also deliver on its own initiative. It may also, if it deems it necessary, take part in the Conciliation Committee. [TFEU 289 (new) & EC 251/TFEU 294]

**3.4.4** Any legislative act that is required by any Treaty provision to be adopted by a special legislative procedure shall be adopted by either the Council or the European Parliament with the participation of the other, (or by a joint action in the case of the adoption of the Union's budget [EC 272/TFEU 314]) as specified in such provision. [TFEU 289 (new)]

Acts adopted by a special legislative procedure do not require a proposal from the Commission unless specified in the relevant provision. [TFEU 289]

**3.4.5** The budget of the European Union shall be adopted by the European Parliament and the Council in accordance with the budgetary procedure laid down in the Treaties. [EC 272 (2) – (10)/TFEU 314]

**3.4.6** Where the Treaties do not specify the type of act to be adopted, the institutions shall select it on a case-by-case basis, in compliance with the applicable procedures and with the principle of proportionality.

**3.4.7** When considering draft legislative acts, the European Parliament and the Council shall refrain from adopting acts not provided for by the relevant legislative procedure in the area in question. [EC 253/TFEU 296]

**3.4.8** The European Parliament, the Council and the Commission shall consult each other and by common agreement make arrangements for their cooperation. To that end, they may, in compliance with the Treaties, conclude inter-institutional agreements which may be of a binding nature. [EC 253/TFEU 296]

## Section 3.5 Delegated and Implementing acts

**3.5.1** A legislative act may delegate to the Commission the power to adopt non-legislative acts of general application to supplement or amend certain non-essential elements of the legislative act.

The objectives, content, scope and duration of the delegation of power shall be explicitly defined in the legislative acts. The essential elements of an area shall be reserved for the legislative act and accordingly shall not be the subject of a delegation of power.

Legislative acts shall explicitly lay down the conditions to which the delegation is subject; these conditions may be as follows:

- the European Parliament or the Council may decide to revoke the delegation;

- the delegated act may enter into force only if no objection has been expressed by the European Parliament or the Council within a period set by the legislative act.

The adjective "delegated" shall be inserted in the title of delegated acts. [TFEU 290 (new)]

**3.5.2.** Where uniform conditions for implementing legally binding Union acts are needed, those acts shall confer implementing powers on the Commission, or, in duly justified specific cases, on the Council.

For the purposes of the above paragraph the European Parliament and the Council shall lay down in advance the rules and general principles concerning mechanisms for control by Member States of the Commission's exercise of implementing powers.

The word "implementing" shall be inserted in the title of implementing acts. [TFEU 291 (new)]

**3.5.3** Member States shall participate in the preparation of delegated acts and decisions of the Commission. [TFEU 290 (new) & Legislation]

**ARTICLE 4**
**EXECUTIVE POWERS**

**Section 4.1 The European Council**

**4.1.1** The European Council shall consist of the Heads of State or Government of the Member States, together with its President and the President of the Commission.

**4.1.2** The European Council shall meet twice every six months, convened by its President. When the agenda so requires, the members of the European Council may decide each to be assisted by a minister and, in the case of the President of the Commission, by a member of the Commission. When the situation so requires, the President shall convene a special meeting of the European Council.

**4.1.3** Except where the Treaties provide otherwise, decisions of the European Council shall be taken by consensus.

**4.1.4** The European Council shall elect its President, by a qualified majority, for a term of two and a half years, renewable once. In the event of an impediment or serious misconduct, the European Council can end the President's term of office in accordance with the same procedure.

**4.1.5** The President of the European Council shall

- chair it and drive forward its work;

- ensure the preparation and continuity of the work of the European Council in cooperation with the President of the Commission, and on the basis of the work of the General Affairs Council;

- endeavour to facilitate cohesion and consensus within the European Council;

- present a report to the European Parliament after each of the meetings of the European Council;

- represent the Union at his or her level and in that capacity without prejudice to the powers of the High Representative.

**4.1.6** The President of the European Council shall not hold a national office. [TEU 15 (new)]

**4.1.7** The European Council shall:

- provide the Union with the necessary impetus for its development and shall define the general political directions and priorities thereof;

- with respect to foreign, security and defence matters, identify the strategic interests and objectives of the Union [TEU 22 (new)] and together with the Council, implement a common foreign and security policy; [old TEU 11/new TEU 24],

- appoint a High Representative of the Union for Foreign Affairs and Security Policy to carry out that policy; [TEU 18 (new)]

- propose to the European Parliament its candidate for President of the Commission;

- appoint the Commission as approved by the European Parliament; [TEU 17 (new)] and

- have such further policy making or executive powers as are specified in the Treaties. [Summary]

## Section 4.2 The Council

**4.2.1** Except as expressly provided otherwise in the Treaties, the provisions of Section 3.2 shall apply where the Council exercises the responsibilities set out below. [Summary]

**4.2.2** In connection with the common foreign and security policy the Council shall

- where the international situation requires operational action by the Union, adopt the necessary decisions; [old TEU 14/new TEU 28]

- adopt decisions which shall define the approach of the Union to a particular matter of a geographical or thematic nature; [old TEU 15/new TEU 29]

- have the further policy-making and executive powers specified in the Treaty on European Union relating to crisis management, defence policy, humanitarian and other interventions, permanent structured cooperation among certain Member States in defence matters, and the European Defence Agency [old TEU 17, 28, 47/new TEU 38 – 42 and TEU 43-46 (new)]

**4.2.3** With respect to international agreements addressing matters falling within the competence of the Union, the Council shall authorize the opening of negotiations, adopt negotiating directives, authorize the signing of agreements and conclude them. [TFEU 218]

**4.2.4** The Council shall establish an External Action Service to assist the High Representative [TEU 27 (new)]

**4.2.5** The Council shall carry out policy-making and coordinating functions as laid down in the Treaties. [TEU 16 (new)]. For these purposes and subject to applicable Treaty provisions, the Council has the power to adopt the acts described in paragraph 2.4.1 and has the rulemaking powers described in paragraph 3.5.2. [Summary]

Where the Council acts on a proposal from the Commission, it may amend that proposal only by acting unanimously, except in certain specified cases [EC 250/TFEU 293]

**4.2.6** In the context of economic and monetary policy, the Council shall in particular have the power to:

- adopt broad guidelines for the coordination of the policies of the Member States; [TFEU 5 (new) & EC 99/TFEU 121]

- take measures to assist any Member State experiencing difficulties in the supply of certain products;

- provide financial assistance to any Member State that is in difficulties or is seriously threatened with severe difficulties caused by natural disasters or exceptional occurrences beyond its control; [EC 100/TFEU 122]

- take coercive measures against Member States with an excessive government deficit; [EC 104/TFEU 126]

- adopt supervisory and directional measures specific to those Member States whose currency is the euro; provided that only members of the Council representing Member States whose currency is the euro shall take part in the vote; [TFEU 136 (new)] and

- adopt measures with respect to Member States who have a derogation from the use of the euro, including termination of such derogation. [EC 121(1), 122(2) 2d sentence & 125(5)/TFEU 140]

**4.2.7** The Council is responsible for determining the system of own resources of the Union. However, if a category of resources is added or eliminated, the Council's decision shall not enter into force until it is approved by the Member States in accordance with their respective constitutional requirements. [EC 269/TFEU 311]

**4.2.8** The Council, by common accord with the President-elect of the Commission, shall adopt and propose to the European Parliament the list of the other persons for appointment as members of the Commission. They shall be selected, on the basis of the suggestions made by Member States. [TEU 17]

**Section 4.3 The Commission**

**4.3.1** The Commission appointed between 1 December 2009 and 31 October 2014, shall consist of one national of each Member State, including its President and the High Representative of the Union for Foreign Affairs and Security Policy who shall be one of its Vice-Presidents.

As from 1 November 2014, the Commission shall consist of a number of members, including its President and the High Representative of the Union for Foreign Affairs and Security Policy, corresponding to two thirds of the number of Member States, unless the European Council, acting unanimously, decides to alter this number.

The members of the Commission shall be chosen from among the nationals of the Member States on the basis of a system of strictly equal rotation between the Member States, reflecting the demographic and geographical range of all the Member States.

The Commission is appointed as described in paragraphs 3.1.9. 4.1.7 and 4.2.7.

**4.3.2** The Commission's term of office shall be five years.

**4.3.3** A member of the Commission shall resign if the President so requests. Subject to a procedure in the TEU, the High Representative of the Union for Foreign Affairs and Security Policy shall resign if the President so requests.

**4.3.4** If a motion of censure by the European Parliament is carried, the members of the Commission shall resign as a body and the High Representative of the Union for Foreign Affairs and Security Policy shall resign from the duties that he carries out in the Commission.

**4.3.5** In carrying out its responsibilities, the Commission shall be completely independent. The members of the Commission shall neither seek nor take instructions from any Government or other institution, body, office or entity. They shall refrain from any action incompatible with their duties or the performance of their tasks.

**4.3.6** The President of the Commission is elected as provided in paragraphs 3.1.9 and 4.1.7.

The President of the Commission shall:

- lay down guidelines within which the Commission is to work;

- decide on the internal organisation of the Commission, ensuring that it acts consistently, efficiently and as a collegiate body;

- appoint Vice-Presidents, other than the High Representative of the Union for Foreign Affairs and Security Policy, from among the members of the Commission.

**4.3.7** The Commission shall

- promote the general interest of the Union and take appropriate initiatives to that end;

- ensure the application of the Treaties, and of measures adopted by the institutions pursuant to them;

- oversee the application of Union law under the control of the Court of Justice of the European Union;

- execute the budget and manage programmes;

- exercise coordinating, executive and management functions, as laid down in the Treaties; and

- initiate the Union's annual and multiannual programming with a view to achieving interinstitutional agreements. [TEU 17 (new)]

For the above purposes and subject to applicable Treaty provisions, the Commission has the power to adopt the acts described in paragraph 2.4.1 and has the rulemaking powers described in section 3.5 [Summary]

**4.3.8** The Commission shall ensure the Union's external representation in matters not relating to the common foreign and security policy. [TEU 18 (new)] However, negotiations relating to any international agreement shall be led by a person appointed by the Council taking into account whether the predominant nature of the subject matter relates to the common foreign and security policy or to other matters within the competence of the Union, on the recommendation of the High Representative or the Commission respectively. [EC 300/TFEU218]

**4.3.9** The Commission has the sole authority to make proposals for legislative acts except where the Treaties provide otherwise. Other acts shall be adopted on the basis of a Commission proposal where the Treaties so provide. [TEU 17 (new)]

### Section 4.4 The European Central Bank

**4.4.1** The Governing Council of the European Central Bank shall comprise the members of the Executive Board of the European Central Bank and the Governors of the national central banks of the Member States whose currency is the euro.

The Executive Board shall comprise the President, the Vice-President and four other members. Their term of office shall be eight years and shall not be renewable.

**4.4.2** The European Central Bank, together with the national central banks, shall constitute the European System of Central Banks (ESCB).

**4.4.3** The European Central Bank shall be independent in the exercise of its powers and in the management of its finances.

**4.4.4** The primary objective of the ESCB shall be to maintain price stability. Without prejudice to that objective, it shall support the general economic policies in the Union in order to contribute to the achievement of the latter's objectives.

**4.4.5** The European Central Bank alone may authorise the issue of the euro. The European Central Bank, together with the national central banks of the Member States whose currency is the euro, which constitute the Eurosystem, shall conduct the monetary policy of the Union [EC 108/TFEU 130 and TFEU 282 (new)] and has the powers necessary to fulfill this role [Summary/Protocol 4].

It shall be consulted by other institutions on any proposed Union act, and by national authorities regarding any draft legislative provision, in its fields of competence. [EC 105/TFEU 127]

It shall ensure the fulfilment by national central banks of obligations under the Treaties and has the same powers as the Commission to bring enforcement action before the Court of Justice. [TFEU 271]

### Section 4.5 The Court of Auditors

**4.5.1** The Members of the Court of Auditors shall be appointed for a term of six years.

A Member of the Court of Auditors may be deprived of his office or of his right to a pension or other benefits in its stead only if the Court of Justice, at the request of the Court of Auditors, finds that he no longer fulfils the requisite conditions or meets the obligations arising from his office.

**4.5.2** The Court of Auditors shall examine the accounts of all revenue and expenditure of the Union. It shall also examine the accounts of all revenue and expenditure of all bodies, offices or agencies set up by the Union in so far as the relevant constituent instrument does not preclude such examination.

The Court of Auditors shall provide the European Parliament and the Council with a statement of assurance as to the reliability of the accounts and the legality and regularity of the underlying transactions

**4.5.3** The Court of Auditors shall draw up an annual report after the close of each financial year. It shall be forwarded to the other institutions of the Union and shall be published, together with the replies of these institutions to the observations of the Court of Auditors, in the *Official Journal of the European Union.*

The Court of Auditors may also, at any time, submit observations, particularly in the form of special reports, on specific questions and deliver opinions at the request of one of the other institutions of the Union.

It shall adopt its annual reports, special reports or opinions by a majority of its Members. [EC 247/TFEU 286]

### Section 4.6 The High Representative

**4.6.1** With respect to his or her positions, the High Representative of the Union for Foreign Affairs and Security Policy (the "High Representative") shall

-    take part in the work of the European Council; [TEU 15 (new)]

-    serve as one of the Vice-Presidents of the Commission; and

-    chair the Council when considering foreign affairs [TEU 27 (new)]

**4.6.2** With respect to responsibilities, the High Representative shall:

-    contribute through his or her proposals towards the preparation of the common foreign and security policy;

- when the European Council or the Council has defined a common approach of the Union on any matter of foreign and security policy of general interest in order to determine a common approach, coordinate his or her activities with the Ministers for Foreign Affairs of the Member States within the Council; [TEU 32 (new)]

- ensure implementation of the decisions adopted by the European Council and the Council; [TEU 27 (new)]

- conduct the Union's common foreign and security policy [TEU 18 (new)] and put it into effect; the same shall apply to the common security and defence policy; [TEU 24 (new)]

- ensure the consistency of the Union's external action;

- be responsible within the Commission for responsibilities incumbent on it in external relations and for coordinating other aspects of the Union's external action; [TEU 17 &18 (new)]

- organize coordination with the Member States in international organizations; [TEU 34 (new) and TFEU 220 (new)]

- regularly consult with the European Parliament; [TEU 37 (new)]

- represent the Union in foreign affairs [TEU 27 (new)] and have responsibility for Union delegations; [TFEU 221 (new)]

- undertake other specific responsibilities set out in the Treaties. [Summary]

### Section 4.7 The Member States

**4.7.1** The Member States shall take any appropriate measure, general or particular, to ensure fulfilment of the obligations arising out of the Treaties or resulting from the acts of the institutions of the Union. [EC 10/TEU 4]

**4.7.2** Member States shall adopt all measures of national law necessary to implement legally binding Union acts. [TFEU 291 (new)]

**4.7.3** With respect to external and security matters, the Member States shall

- support the Union's external and security policy actively and unreservedly in a spirit of loyalty and mutual solidarity and shall comply with the Union's action in this area;

- work together to enhance and develop their mutual political solidarity and refrain from any action which is contrary to the interests of the Union or likely to impair its effectiveness as a cohesive force in international relations; [old TEU 11/new TEU 24]

- (acting together with the High Representative) put into effect the common foreign and security policy using national and Union resources; [old TEU 13/new TEU 26]

- ensure that their own national policies conform to the Union positions with respect to foreign, security and defence; [old TEU 14 & 15/new TEU 28 & 29] and

- coordinate their action in international organisations and at international conferences and uphold the Union's positions in such forums. [TEU 34]

**4.7.4** Member States shall avoid excessive government deficits. [EC 104/TFEU 126]

### Section 4.8 The European Ombudsman

**4.8.1** The Ombudsman shall be elected after each election of the European Parliament for the duration of its term of office. The Ombudsman shall be eligible for reappointment. The Ombudsman may be dismissed by the Court of Justice at the request of the European Parliament if he no longer fulfils the conditions required for the performance of his duties or if he is guilty of serious misconduct.

**4.8.2** The Ombudsman shall be completely independent in the performance of his duties. In the performance of those duties he shall neither seek nor take instructions from any Government, institution, body, office or entity. The Ombudsman may not, during his term of office, engage in any other occupation, whether gainful or not.

**4.8.3** The European Ombudsman shall be empowered to receive complaints from any citizen of the Union or any natural or legal person residing or having its registered office in a Member State concerning instances of maladministration in the activities of the Union institutions, bodies, offices or agencies, with the exception of the Court of Justice of the European Union acting in its judicial role. He or she shall examine such complaints and report on them.

**4.8.4** In accordance with his duties, the Ombudsman shall conduct inquiries for which he finds grounds, either on his own initiative or on the basis of complaints submitted to him direct or through a Member of the European Parliament, except where the alleged facts are or have been the subject of legal proceedings. Where the Ombudsman establishes an instance of maladministration, he shall refer the matter to the institution, body, office or agency concerned, which shall have a period of three months in which to inform him of its views. The Ombudsman shall then forward a report to the European Parliament and the institution, body, office or agency concerned. The person lodging the complaint shall be informed of the outcome of such inquiries.

The Ombudsman shall submit an annual report to the European Parliament on the outcome of his inquiries. [TFEU 24 and 228]

### Section 4.9 Executive Enforcement Powers

**4.9.1** Acts of the Council, the Commission or the European Central Bank which impose a pecuniary obligation on persons other than States, shall be enforceable. Enforcement shall be governed by the rules of civil procedure in force in the State in the territory of which it is carried out. [EC 256/TFEU 299]

**4.9.2** If the Commission considers that a Member State has failed to fulfil an obligation under the Treaties, it shall deliver a reasoned opinion on the matter after giving the State concerned the opportunity to submit its observations.

If the State concerned does not comply with the opinion within the period laid down by the Commission, the latter may bring the matter before the Court of

Justice of the European Union. [EC 226/TFEU 258]

**4.9.3** If, after giving notice to the parties concerned to submit their comments, the Commission finds that aid granted by a State or through State resources is not compatible with the internal market, or that such aid is being misused, it shall decide that the State concerned shall abolish or alter such aid within a period of time to be determined by the Commission.

If the State concerned does not comply with this decision within the prescribed time, the Commission or any other interested State may refer the matter to the Court of Justice of the European Union direct. [EC 88/TFEU 108]

**4.9.4** Subject to Union law, the Commission may conduct searches, require the submission of evidence, seek explanations and impose fines on natural or legal persons pursuant to any decision adopted in enforcement of the rules on competition. [EC 83/TFEU 103/legislation]

**4.9.5** The Council may impose fines and other financial and non-financial penalties on any Member State for failure to comply with deficit reduction measures recommended to it by the Council. [EC 104/TFEU 126]

**4.9.6** The European Central Bank may impose fines on undertakings for failure to comply with its regulations [EC 110/TFEU 132/Protocol 4, art 34] and other financial remedies on Central Banks with respect to failure to maintain minimum reserves. [Protocol 4, art 19]

**ARTICLE 5**
**JUDICIAL POWERS**

### Section 5.1 The Court of Justice of the European Union

**5.1.1** The Court of Justice of the European Union shall include the Court of Justice, the General Court and specialised courts.

The Court of Justice shall consist of one judge from each Member State. It shall be assisted by Advocates-General.

The General Court shall include at least one judge per Member State.

The Judges and Advocates-General of the Court of Justice and the members of the General Court shall be appointed by common accord of the governments of the Member States for a term of six years.

**5.1.2** The Court of Justice shall ensure that in the interpretation and application of the Treaties the law is observed. [TEU 19] Acts of the Institutions, bodies, offices and agencies of the Union may be annulled by the Court of Justice of the European Union on grounds of lack of competence, infringement of an essential procedural requirement, infringement of the Treaties or of any rule of law relating to their application, or misuse of powers. [EC 230/TFEU 263]

**5.1.3** The Court of Justice of the European Union shall, in accordance with the Treaties:

- rule on actions brought by a Member State, an institution or a natural or legal person;

- give preliminary rulings, at the request of courts or tribunals of the Member States, on the interpretation of Union law or the validity of acts adopted by the institutions;

- rule in other cases provided for in the Treaties. [TEU 19 (new)]

Except as otherwise provided in connection with actions concerning individuals, the Court of Justice of the European Union shall not have jurisdiction with respect to the provisions relating to the common foreign and security policy nor with respect to acts adopted on the basis of those provisions. [TFEU 275 (new)]

If a question is raised in any proceeding for a preliminary ruling with regard to a person in custody, the Court of Justice of the European Union shall act with the minimum of delay. [TFEU 267]

**5.1.4** Every Member State and institution of the Union has the right to bring an action in the Court of Justice of the European Union within the scope of that court's jurisdiction. [EC 230/TFEU 263]

A natural or legal person may institute proceedings:

- for the annulment of an act addressed to that person or which is of direct and individual concern to that person, and against a regulatory act which is of direct concern to that person and does not entail implementing measures; [EC 230/TFEU 263]

- to seek adoption of decisions that are required to be addressed to them by any Union institution; [EC 232/TFEU 265] and

- to seek compensation for damage suffered as a result of Union acts in accordance with general principles common to the Member States. [EC 235 and 288/TFEU 268 and 340]

Annulment proceedings provided for above shall be instituted within two months of the publication of the measure, or of its notification to the plaintiff, or, in the absence thereof, of the day on which it came to the knowledge of the latter, as the case may be. [EC 230/TFEU 263]

An action seeking the adoption of an act shall be admissible only if the institution, body, office or agency concerned has first been called upon to act. If, within two months of being so called upon, the institution, body, office or agency concerned has not defined its position, the action may be brought within a further period of two months. [EC 232/TFEU 265]

**5.1.5** Actions brought before the Court of Justice of the European Union shall not have suspensory effect. The Court may, however, if it considers that circumstances so require, order that application of the contested act be suspended. [EC 242/TFEU 278]

The Court of Justice of the European Union may in any cases before it prescribe any necessary interim measures. [EC 243/TFEU 279]

**5.1.6** Any party may, in proceedings in which an act of general application adopted by an institution, body, office or agency of the Union is at issue, plead the invalidity of that act in order to invoke before the Court of Justice of the European Union (including in any proceeding referred to it by the courts of the Member States) the inapplicability of that act. [EC 241/TFEU 277]

**5.1.7** If the Court of Justice finds that there is an infringement of Union law by any Member State in proceedings brought before it by the Commission, it may impose a lump sum or penalty payment on the Member State concerned not exceeding the amount specified by the Commission. [EC 227/TFEU 260]

**5.1.8** The Court of Justice of the European Union shall have such jurisdiction with regard to penalties as may be provided for in any regulations adopted jointly by the European Parliament and the Council, and by the Council, pursuant to the provisions of the Treaties. [EC 230/TFEU 263]

**5.1.9** With respect to defaulting witnesses the Court of Justice and the General Court shall have the powers generally granted to courts and tribunals and may impose pecuniary penalties under conditions laid down in its Rules of Procedure. [Protocol 3, art. 27]

**5.1.10** The Court of Justice has the power to remove the Ombudsman as described in paragraph 4.9.1

**5.1.11** An appeal may be brought before the Court of Justice, within two months of the notification of the decision appealed against, against final decisions of the General Court and decisions of that Court disposing of the substantive issues in part only or disposing of a procedural issue concerning a plea of lack of competence or inadmissibility. [Protocol 3, art 56]

An appeal to the Court of Justice shall be limited to points of law. It shall lie on the grounds of lack of competence of the General Court, a breach of procedure before it which adversely affects the interests of the appellant as well as the infringement of Union law by the General Court. [Protocol 3 art 58].

### Section 5.2 The courts of the Member States

**5.2.1** The Courts of the Member States shall:

- give full force and effect to any applicable Union regulations [EC 249/TFEU 288] and to judgments of the Court of Justice of the European Union; [EC 244 and 256/TFEU 280 and 299]

- act in accordance with the obligations of the Member States set out in paragraph 4.7.1 to enforce the rights and obligations of natural or legal persons as described in Article 8; [*ECJ*]

- provide remedies sufficient to ensure effective legal protection in the fields covered by Union law. [TEU 19 (new)/*ECJ*]

**5.2.2** Where a question as to the interpretation or validity of any Union act is raised before any court or tribunal of a Member State, that court or tribunal may, if it considers that a decision on the question is necessary to enable it to give judgment, request the Court of Justice to give a ruling thereon.

Where any such question is raised in a case pending before a court or tribunal of a Member State against whose decisions there is no judicial remedy under national law, that court or tribunal shall bring the matter before the Court. [EC 234/TFEU 267]

## ARTICLE 6
## THE UNION'S COMPETENCES

### Section 6.1 General Principles

**6.1.1** The Union shall act only within the limits of the competences conferred upon it by the Member States in the Treaties to attain the objectives set out therein. Competences not conferred upon the Union in the Treaties remain with the Member States. [TEU 4 (new) and old TEU 5/new TEU 5]

**6.1.2** When the Treaties confer on the Union a competence shared with the Member States in a specific area, the Union and the Member States may legislate and adopt legally binding acts in that area. The Member States shall exercise their competence to the extent that the Union has not exercised its competence. The Member States shall again exercise their competence to the extent that the Union has decided to cease exercising its competence. [TFEU 2 (new)]

**6.1.3** The scope of and arrangements for exercising the Union's competences shall be determined by the provisions of the Treaties relating to each area. [TFEU 2 (new)]

**6.1.4** The use of Union competences is governed by the principles of subsidiarity and proportionality.

Subsidiarity entails that, in areas which do not fall within its exclusive competence, the Union shall act only if and in so far as the objectives of the proposed action cannot be sufficiently achieved by the Member States, either at central level or at regional and local level, but can rather, by reason of the scale or effects of the proposed action, be better achieved at Union level.

Proportionality entails that the content and form of Union action shall not exceed what is necessary to achieve the objectives of the Treaties. [EC 5/TEU 5/Protocol 2]

**6.1.5** When the Treaties confer on the Union exclusive competence in a specific area, only the Union may legislate and adopt legally binding acts, the Member States being able to do so themselves only if so empowered by the Union or for the implementation of Union acts. [TFEU 2 (new)]

**6.1.6** If action by the Union should prove necessary, within the framework of the policies defined in the Treaties, to attain one of the objectives set out in the Treaties, and the Treaties have not provided the necessary powers, the Council shall adopt the appropriate measures.

This competence cannot serve as a basis for attaining objectives pertaining to the common foreign and security policy.

Such measures shall not entail harmonisation of Member States' laws or regulations in cases where the Treaties exclude such harmonisation. [EC 308/ TFEU 352]

## Section 6.2 Fundamental Rights

**6.2.1** The Union may adopt rules designed to prohibit discrimination on grounds of nationality. [EC 12/TFEU 18]

**6.2.2** Within the scope of application of the Treaties, the Union may take appropriate action to combat discrimination based on sex, racial or ethnic origin, religion or belief, disability, age or sexual orientation. [EC 13/TFEU 19]

## Section 6.3 Foreign, security and defence policies

**6.3.1** The Union shall have competence to define and implement a common foreign and security policy, including the progressive framing of a common defence policy. [TFEU 2] The Union's competence in this regard shall cover all areas of foreign policy and all questions relating to the Union's security. [old TEU 11/new TEU 24]. In this connection, the Union may conclude agreements with one or more States or international organizations. [old TEU 24/new TEU 37]

**6.3.2** The common security and defence policy shall be an integral part of the common foreign and security policy. It shall provide the Union with an operational capacity drawing on civilian and military assets. The Union may use them on missions outside the Union for peace-keeping, conflict prevention and strengthening international security in accordance with the principles of the United Nations Charter. The performance of these tasks shall be undertaken using capabilities provided by the Member States. [old TEU 17/new TEU 42]

**6.3.3** The adoption of legislative acts in this context shall be excluded. [old TEU 11 and 23/new TEU 24 and 31] However, the High Representative shall regularly consult the European Parliament on the main aspects and the basic choices of the common foreign and security policy and common defense policy and inform it of how those policies evolve. [old TEU 21/new TEU 36]

**6.3.4** National security remains the sole responsibility of each Member State. [TEU 4 (new)]

## Section 6.4 Currency

The activities of the Union and the Member States shall include a single currency, the euro, and the definition and conduct of a single monetary policy and exchange-rate policy the primary objective of both of which shall be to maintain price stability. [EC 4/TFEU 119]

## Section 6.5 The Union's Finances

**6.5.1** The Union shall provide itself with the means necessary to attain its objectives and carry through its policies.

Without prejudice to other revenue, the budget shall be financed wholly from the Union's own resources. [EC 269/TFEU 311]

**6.5.2** Overdraft facilities or any other type of credit facility with the European Central Bank or with the central banks of the Member States (hereinafter referred to as "national central banks") in favour of Union institutions, bodies, offices or agencies shall be prohibited. [EC 101/TFEU 123]

**6.5.3** The Union shall not be liable for or assume the commitments of central governments, regional, local or other public authorities, other bodies governed by public law, or public undertakings of any Member State, without prejudice to mutual financial guarantees for the joint execution of a specific project. [EC 103/TFEU 125]

### Section 6.6 Exclusive Union Competences

**6.6.1** The Union shall have exclusive competence in the following areas [TFEU 3]:

- customs union; [EC 25-27/TFEU 30-32]

- the establishing of the competition rules necessary for the functioning of the internal market; [EC 81-89/TFEU 101-109]

- monetary policy for the Member States whose currency is the euro; [EC 105-110/TFEU 127-133]

- the conservation of marine biological resources under the common fisheries policy; [EC 32/TFEU 38]

- common commercial policy. [EC 131 &133/TFEU 206 & 207]

**6.6.2** The Union shall also have exclusive competence for the conclusion of an international agreement when its conclusion is provided for in a legislative act of the Union or is necessary to enable the Union to exercise its internal competence, or in so far as its conclusion may affect common rules or alter their scope. [TFEU 3 and 216 (new) and *ECJ*]

### Section 6.7 Shared Competences

**6.7.1** The Union shall share competence with the Member States where the Treaties confer on it a competence which does not relate to the areas referred to in Sections 6.6 or 6.8. [TFEU 4 (new)]

Shared competence between the Union and the Member States applies in the following principal areas:

- internal market; [old TEU 2/new TEU 3, EC 14/TFEU 26, EC 95 & 95/TFEU 114 & 115, EC 40/TFEU 46, EC 47/TFEU 53, EC 52/TFEU 59]

- social policy regarding equal treatment for men and women in employment; [EC 141/TFEU 157]

- economic, social and territorial cohesion; [EC 158-162/TFEU 174-178]

- agriculture and fisheries, excluding the conservation of marine biological resources; [EC 32-38/TFEU 38-44]

- environment; [EC 174-176/TFEU 191-193]

- consumer protection; [EC 153/TFEU 169]

- transport; [EC 70-80/TFEU 90-100]

- trans-European networks; [EC 154-156/TFEU 170-172]

- energy; [TFEU 194 (new)]

- area of freedom, security and justice; [old TEU 29-42 & EC 61-69/TFEU 67-89]

- common safety concerns in public health matters, for specified aspects [EC 152 paras 4 & 5/TFEU 168 paras 4 & 5]

**6.7.2** In the areas of research, technological development and space, the Union shall have competence to carry out activities, in particular to define and implement programmes; however, the exercise of that competence shall not result in Member States being prevented from exercising theirs. [TFEU 4 (new) and EC163-173/ TFEU 179-190]

**6.7.3** In the areas of development cooperation and humanitarian aid, the Union shall have competence to carry out activities and conduct a common policy; however, the exercise of that competence shall not result in Member States being prevented from exercising theirs. [TFEU 4 (new), EC 181a/TFEU 212 and TFEU 213 & 214 (new)]

**6.7.4** The Union shall adopt legislative acts for the creation of European intellectual property rights to provide uniform protection of intellectual property rights throughout the Union and for the setting up of centralised Union-wide authorisation, coordination and supervision arrangements. This shall include language arrangements for the European intellectual property rights. [TFEU 118 (new)] Pending such action, the protection of intellectual property rights shall remain within the competence of the Member States, subject to applicable restrictions imposed by Union law. [Summary]

### Section 6.8 Union competences of co-ordination or support

**6.8.1** The Union shall have the competence to adopt measures, in particular broad guidelines for the economic policies of the Member States. [EC 5 and 99/TEU 5 and TFEU 121]

**6.8.2** The Union shall take measures to ensure coordination of the employment policies of the Member States, in particular by defining guidelines for these policies. [EC 125-130/TFEU 145-150]

**6.8.3** The Union may take initiatives to ensure coordination of Member States' social policies. [TFEU 5 and EC 136-140 & 142-148/TFEU 151-156 & 158-161]

**6.8.4** In certain areas and under the conditions laid down in the Treaties, the Union shall have competence to carry out actions to support, coordinate or supplement the actions of the Member States, without thereby superseding their competence in these areas. [TFEU 6 (new)]. The areas of such action shall, at European level, be:

- protection and improvement of human health; [EC 152/TFEU 168 (excluding paras 4 & 5)]

- industry; [EC 157/TFEU 173]

- culture; [EC 151/TFEU 167]

- tourism; [TFEU 195 (new)]

- education, vocational training, youth and sport; [EC 149 & 150/TFEU 65 & 166]

- civil protection; [TFEU 196 (new)]

- administrative cooperation. [TFEU 197 (new)]

**6.8.5** Legally binding acts of the Union adopted on the basis of the provisions of the Treaties relating to these areas shall not entail harmonisation of Member States' laws or regulations. [TFEU 2 (new)]

## ARTICLE 7
## TREATY LIMITATIONS ON THE EXERCISE OF MEMBER STATE COMPETENCES

### Section 7.1 Purpose

The purpose of this Article 7 is to describe limitations imposed by the Treaty on the Functioning of the European Union on the Member States in the exercise of their retained competences. Such limitations are the foundations of the internal market described in paragraph 1.5.3. Further limitations on the competences of the Member States are implicit in the provisions of other articles, in particular article 8, which includes limitations intended to assure the freedom of movement for workers and others exercising an economic activity as an integral element of citizenship rights. [Summary]

### Section 7.2 Measures affecting the free movement of goods

**7.2.1** Customs duties on imports and exports and charges having equivalent effect shall be prohibited between Member States. This prohibition shall also apply to customs duties of a fiscal nature [TFEU 30] and shall apply to products originating in Member States and to products coming from third countries which are in free circulation in Member States. [EC 25/TFEU 30]

**7.2.2** Quantitative restrictions on imports and exports and all measures having equivalent effect shall be prohibited between Member States. [EC 28 and 29/TFEU 34 and 35]

**7.2.3** The prohibition in paragraph 7.2.2 shall not preclude prohibitions or restrictions on imports, exports or goods in transit justified on grounds of public morality, public policy or public security; the protection of health and life of humans, animals or plants; the protection of national treasures possessing artistic, historic or archaeological value; or the protection of industrial and commercial property. Such prohibitions or restrictions shall not, however, constitute a means of arbitrary discrimination or a disguised restriction on trade between Member States. [EC 30/TFEU 36]

**7.2.4** The prohibition in paragraph 7.2.2 extends to any measure, applicable to both domestic goods and imports lawfully manufactured and marketed in another Member State, that specifies the requirements to be met by, or disproportionately impedes access to the market for, such imports, unless such measure pursues an overriding objective in the general interest (including any objective described in paragraph 7.2.3) subject to the conditions set out in Section 7.6. *[ECJ]*

**7.2.5** Member States shall adjust any State monopolies of a commercial character so as to ensure that no discrimination regarding the conditions under which goods are procured and marketed exists between nationals of Member States. [EC 31/TFEU 37] This requirement entails that Member States shall not maintain or create any such monopoly with respect to the importation of any goods. *[ECJ]*

**7.2.6** No Member State shall impose, directly or indirectly, on the products of other Member States any internal taxation of any kind in excess of that imposed directly or indirectly on similar domestic products.

Furthermore, no Member State shall impose on the products of other Member States any internal taxation of such a nature as to afford indirect protection to other products. [EC 90/TFEU 110]

### Section 7.3 Measures affecting the provision of services

**7.3.1** Within the framework of this section, restrictions on freedom to provide services (except transport services) within the Union shall be prohibited in respect of nationals of Member States who are established in a Member State other than that of the person for whom the services are intended. [EC 49/TFEU 56] This prohibition also extends to any private regulatory body (as such term is defined in paragraph 8.5.2). *[ECJ]*

Where the service provider performs a service in the Member State of the service recipient, the host Member State may apply the requirements governing the provision of such service that are also imposed on its own nationals. [EC 50/TFEU 57].

**7.3.2** The prohibition in paragraph 7.3.1 extends to any measure described in the second part of paragraph 7.3.1 or that indirectly affects the provision of services, if such measure is liable to prohibit, impede or render less attractive the lawful activities of a provider of such services to recipients in, or nationals of, other Member States, unless such measure pursues an overriding objective in the general interest, subject to the conditions set out in Section 7.6.

**7.3.3** The prohibition in paragraph 7.3.1 shall not apply to any Member State measure that provides for special treatment of non-nationals on grounds of public policy, public security or public health. [EC 46/TFEU 52]; or to any measure that relates to activities which in that State are connected, even occasionally, with the exercise of official authority. [EC 49/TFEU 56]

**7.3.4** With respect to transport services within the Union no Member State may, unless the Council has unanimously adopted a measure granting a derogation, make the various provisions governing the subject on 1 January 1958 or, for acceding States, the date of their accession less favourable in their direct or indirect effect on carriers of other Member States as compared with carriers who are nationals of that State. [EC 72/TFEU 92]

## Section 7.4 Measures affecting the freedom to establish a business

**7.4.1** Within the framework of this section, restrictions on the freedom of establishment of nationals of a Member State in the territory of another Member State shall be prohibited. Such prohibition shall also apply to restrictions on the setting-up of agencies, branches or subsidiaries by nationals of any Member State established in the territory of any Member State. Freedom of establishment shall include the right to take up and pursue activities as self-employed persons and to set up and manage undertakings. [EC 43/TFEU 49]

**7.4.2** The host Member State may require persons exercising the right described in paragraph 7.4.1 to comply with the conditions laid down for its own nationals with respect to the particular activity in question.

**7.4.3** The prohibition in paragraph 7.4.1 extends to any measure that applies without distinction to nationals and non-nationals, unless such measure pursues an overriding objective in the general interest, subject to the conditions set out in Section 7.6. Such objective includes any purpose served by Member States' regulation of trades, professions, businesses or legal entities to the extent that such regulation has not yet been liberalized through Union legislation. [EC 43/TFEU 49 and *ECJ*]

**7.4.4** The prohibition in paragraph 7.4.1 shall not apply to any Member State measure that provides for special treatment of non-nationals on grounds of public policy, public security or public health. [EC 46/TFEU 52]; or to any measure relating to activities which in that State are connected, even occasionally, with the exercise of official authority. [EC 45/TFEU 51]

## Section 7.5 Measures affecting the free movement of capital and payments

**7.5.1** All restrictions on the movement of capital between Member States and between Member States and third countries shall be prohibited.

**7.5.2** All restrictions on payments between Member States and between Member States and third countries shall be prohibited. [EC 56/TFEU 63]

**7.5.3** The prohibitions in paragraphs 7.5.1 and 7.5.2 shall be without prejudice to the application to third countries of any restrictions which exist on 31 December 1993 under national or Union law adopted in respect of the movement of capital to or from third countries involving direct investment — including in real estate — establishment, the provision of financial services or the admission of securities to capital markets. In respect of restrictions existing under national law in Bulgaria, Estonia and Hungary, the relevant date shall be 31 December 1999. [EC 57/TFEU 64]

**7.5.4** The prohibitions in paragraphs 7.4.1 and 7.4.2 shall be without prejudice to the right of any Member State to apply the relevant provisions of that State's tax law which distinguish between taxpayers who are not in the same situation with regard to their place of residence or with regard to the place where their capital is invested or is intended to prevent infringements of national law and regulations, in particular in the field of taxation and the prudential supervision of financial institutions, or to lay down procedures for the declaration of capital movements for purposes of administrative or statistical information. Such measures and procedures shall not constitute a means of arbitrary discrimination or a disguised restriction on the free movement of capital and payments. [EC 58/TFEU 65]

**7.5.5** Subject to paragraph 7.5.4, any Member State measure that affects the movement of capital or payments falls within the prohibitions of paragraphs 7.5.1 or 7.5.2, unless its purpose constitutes an overriding objective in the general interest subject to the conditions set out in Section 7.6. [*ECJ*]

### Section 7.6 General principles governing measures that apply without distinction to domestic and interstate circumstances

Where a Member State is permitted to adopt any measure on condition that it pursues an overriding objective in the general interest, that condition will be satisfied only if the measure:

- is within the competence of the Member States;

- is appropriate to such objective;

- does not exceed what is necessary to achieve the objective;

- is not otherwise in breach of Union law.

### Section 7.7 Mutual Recognition

In the case of goods and services, the third condition set out in Section 7.6 will not be satisfied where the measure imposes a duty that is already safeguarded by the Member State where the goods are first placed on the market or where the supplier of the services is established. In any such case, the Member State into which such goods are imported or in which such services are received shall not impose its own requirements to the extent that they address the same duty. [*ECJ*]

### Section 7.8 State Aids

No Member State shall implement or modify any financial aid to any business within its territory that could affect trade between Member States unless such aid has first been notified to, or previously approved by, the Commission. [EC 88/TFEU 108]

### Section 7.9 Public undertakings and exclusive concessions

**7.9.1** In the case of public undertakings and undertakings to which Member States grant special or exclusive rights, Member States shall neither enact nor maintain in force any measure contrary to the rules contained in the Treaties.

**7.9.2** Undertakings entrusted with the operation of services of general economic interest or having the character of a revenue-producing monopoly shall be subject to the rules contained in the Treaties, in particular to the rules on competition, in so far as the application of such rules does not obstruct the performance, in law or in fact, of the particular tasks assigned to them. The development of trade must not be affected to such an extent as would be contrary to the interests of the Union. [EC 86/TFEU 106]

## ARTICLE 8
## RIGHTS AND DUTIES OF THE INDIVIDUAL UNDER UNION LAW

### Section 8.1 Citizenship

**8.1.1** Every person holding the nationality of a Member State shall be a citizen of the Union. Citizenship of the Union shall be additional to and not replace national citizenship. [EC 17/TEU 9 and TFEU 20]

**8.1.2** Citizens of the Union shall enjoy the rights and be subject to the duties provided for in the Treaties. They shall have, *inter alia* the right

- to move and reside freely within the territory of the Member States, subject to the limitations and conditions laid down in the Treaties and by the measures adopted to give them effect [EC 12 and 17/TFEU 18 and 20];

- to vote and to stand as candidates in elections to the European Parliament and in municipal elections in their Member State of residence, under the same conditions as nationals of that State;

- to enjoy, in the territory of a third country in which the Member State of which they are nationals is not represented, the protection of the diplomatic and consular authorities of any Member State on the same conditions as the nationals of that State;

- to petition the European Parliament, to apply to the European Ombudsman, and to address the institutions and advisory bodies of the Union in any of the Treaty languages and to obtain a reply in the same language. [EC 17/TFEU 20, 24 and 227]

These rights shall be exercised in accordance with the conditions and limits defined by the Treaties and by the measures adopted thereunder. [EC 17/TFEU 20]

**8.1.3** With respect to Union citizens who exercise the right of free movement and residence in pursuit of any activity that is within the scope of application of the Treaties, any discrimination on grounds of nationality shall be prohibited. [EC 12/TFEU 18] This prohibition also extends to any measure that indirectly discriminates against non-nationals unless such measure pursues an overriding objective in the general interest, subject to the conditions set out in Section 7.6.

**8.1.4** In the case of workers, free movement shall include the right

- to accept offers of employment actually made;

- to move freely within the territory of Member States for this purpose;

- to stay in a Member State for the purpose of employment in accordance with the provisions governing the employment of nationals of that State laid down by law, regulation or administrative action;

- to remain in the territory of a Member State after having been employed in that State, subject to conditions approved by the Commission. [EC 39/TFEU

45]

-   the right to move to another Member State to seek work. [*ECJ*]

The right of free movement for workers also entails the prohibition of any non-discriminatory measure of a Member State or private regulatory body that indirectly impedes free movement of Union citizens by restricting access to the labour market, unless such measure pursues an overriding objective in the general interest in accordance with the conditions set out in Section 7.6.

The rights of workers described above shall not apply to employment in the public service. [EC 39/TFEU 45]

**8.1.5** Citizens who exercise their right of free movement and residence, but are not workers or self-employed persons, may be required by the host Member State to demonstrate that they have sufficient resources for themselves and their family members not to become a burden on the social assistance system of that Member State. [EC 17/TFEU20/Directive 2004/38].

**8.1.6** Member States may limit the right of free movement and residence on grounds of public policy, public health or public security. [EC 39 and 46/TFEU 45 and 52]

## Section 8.2 Fundamental Rights

**8.2.1** With respect to acts of the Union, individuals have the rights set out in the Charter of Fundamental Rights or otherwise arising under Union law in relation to fundamental rights. Subject to the conditions of Article 5 they may invoke such rights against infringing Union acts. [Summary]

**8.2.2** Individuals may invoke fundamental rights to the extent recognized by Union law in order to have declared inapplicable any conflicting measure adopted by a Member State that infringes a fundamental right falling within the scope of any Union legislative act addressing that right, or that is adopted by a Member State in the context of implementation of Union law. [Old TEU 6/new TEU 6 and *ECJ*]

## Section 8.3 Other Rights under Union law

**8.3.1** Any directly effective provision of Union law may be invoked by individuals in order to have declared inapplicable any conflicting measure adopted by a Member State or by a private regulatory body. [*ECJ*].

**8.3.2** Individuals have the right to invoke any relevant directly applicable Union law in national legal or administrative proceedings. [EC 249/TFEU 288 and *ECJ*]

**8.3.3** Individuals shall be entitled to effective remedies in national courts for infringements of Union law by the Member States in the circumstances described in Section 5.2. [TEU 19 (new), *ECJ*]

**8.3.4** Individuals may challenge the validity of Union acts in the circumstances described in Section 5.1 [Summary]

## Section 8.4 Obligations

**8.4.1** Any directly applicable provision of Union law that by its content and meaning creates obligations for individuals may be enforced against them. [EC 249/TFEU 288]

**8.4.2** If a measure of a Member State or private regulatory body is found to be inapplicable in accordance with paragraph 8.2.2 or 8.3.1, individuals may incur obligations or other legal consequences arising from such inapplicability. [ECJ]

**8.4.3** Any decision addressed to an individual is legally binding on such individual. [EC 249/TFEU 288]

## Section 8.5 Certain Definitions

**8.5.1** The term "individual" means any natural or legal person.

**8.5.2** The term "private regulatory body" means any non-governmental organization that establishes or maintains rules of a general regulatory nature governing an economic activity. [Summary]

# ARTICLE 9
# RELATIONS BETWEEN THE MEMBER STATES

## Section 9.1 Mutual cooperation

Pursuant to the principle of sincere cooperation, the Union and the Member States shall, in full mutual respect, assist each other in carrying out tasks which flow from the Treaties. [TEU 4 (new)]

## Section 9.2 Solidarity

Should a Member State be the object of a terrorist attack or the victim of a natural or man-made disaster, the other Member States shall assist it at the request of its political authorities. To that end, the Member States shall coordinate between themselves in the Council. [TFEU 222 (new)]

## Section 9.3 Coordination of economic and employment policies

**9.3.1** The Member States shall coordinate their economic and employment policies as described below [TFEU 2].

**9.3.2** Member States shall regard their economic policies as a matter of common concern and shall coordinate them within the Council. [EC 99/TFEU 121] Member States shall conduct their economic policies and shall coordinate them in such a way as, in addition, to attain the objective of strengthening the Union's economic, social and territorial cohesion. [EC 158 and 159/TFEU 174 and 175]

**9.3.3** Member States shall avoid excessive government deficits and the Union shall have the competence to apply coercive means to remedy such situations. [EC 104/TFEU 126]

**9.3.4** A Member State shall not be liable for or assume the commitments of central governments, regional, local or other public authorities, other bodies governed by public law, or public undertakings of another Member State, without prejudice to mutual financial guarantees for the joint execution of a specific project. [EC 103/TFEU 125]

### Section 9.4 Duty of co-operation regarding treaty relations with non-member States

The rights and obligations arising from agreements concluded before 1 January 1958 or, for acceding States, before the date of their accession, between one or more Member States on the one hand, and one or more third countries on the other, shall not be affected by the provisions of the Treaties.

To the extent that such agreements are not compatible with the Treaties, the Member State or States concerned shall take all appropriate steps to eliminate the incompatibilities established. Member States shall, where necessary, assist each other to this end and shall, where appropriate, adopt a common attitude.

In applying the agreements referred to in the first paragraph, Member States shall take into account the fact that the advantages accorded under the Treaties by each Member State form an integral part of the establishment of the Union and are thereby inseparably linked with the creation of common institutions, the conferring of powers upon them and the granting of the same advantages by all the other Member States. [EC 307/TFEU 351]

### Section 9.5 Disputes between Member States

**9.5.1** A Member State which considers that another Member State has failed to fulfil an obligation under the Treaties may bring the matter before the Court of Justice of the European Union.

Before a Member State brings an action against another Member State for an alleged infringement of an obligation under the Treaties, it shall bring the matter before the Commission.

The Commission shall deliver a reasoned opinion after each of the States concerned has been given the opportunity to submit its own case and its observations on the other party's case both orally and in writing.

If the Commission has not delivered an opinion within three months of the date on which the matter was brought before it, the absence of such opinion shall not prevent the matter from being brought before the Court. [EC 227/TFEU 259]

Member States shall not submit a dispute concerning the interpretation or application of the Treaties to any method of settlement other than those provided for therein. [EC 292/TFEU 344]

**9.5.2** Member States may by special agreement submit to the Court of Justice a dispute between them which relates to the subject matter of the Treaties. [EC 239/TFEU 273]

Where Member States are in dispute regarding international obligations within the scope of their retained shared competences that may also entail an effect on the Union, they shall submit such dispute to Union procedures where there is any possibility that such tribunal could be required to rule on Union law; and they shall fully consult the Commission in any such case. [*ECJ*]

## § 1.03 FUNDAMENTAL RIGHTS

CHARTER OF FUNDAMENTAL RIGHTS
CHAPTER I
DIGNITY
Article 1
Human dignity

Human dignity is inviolable. It must be respected and protected.

Article 2
Right to life

1. Everyone has the right to life.
2. No one shall be condemned to the death penalty, or executed.

EUROPEAN CONVENTION

CORRESPONDING PROVISIONS

ARTICLE 2

1. Everyone's right to life shall be protected by law. No one shall be deprived of his life intentionally save in the execution of a sentence of a court following his conviction of a crime for which this penalty is provided by law.
PROTOCOL No. 13
ARTICLE 1

The death penalty shall be abolished. No one shall be condemned to such penalty or executed. [Further Articles provide for derogations and reservations. Protocol No. 6 allows for the death penalty in wartime under certain circumstances]

Article 3
Right to the integrity of the person

1. Everyone has the right to respect for his or her physical and mental integrity.
2. In the fields of medicine and biology, the following must be respected in particular:

- the free and informed consent of the person concerned, according to the procedures laid down by law,

- the prohibition of eugenic practices, in particular those aiming at the selection of persons,

- the prohibition on making the human body and its parts as such a source of financial gain,

| CHARTER OF FUNDAMENTAL RIGHTS | EUROPEAN CONVENTION |
|---|---|
| - the prohibition of the reproductive cloning of human beings. | |

### Article 4

| Prohibition of torture and inhuman or degrading treatment or punishment | Article 3 |
|---|---|
| No one shall be subjected to torture or to inhuman or degrading treatment or punishment. | No one shall be subjected to torture or to inhuman or degrading treatment or punishment. |

### Article 5

| Prohibition of slavery and forced labour | Article 4 |
|---|---|
| 1. No one shall be held in slavery or servitude. | 1. No one shall be held in slavery or servitude. |
| 2. No one shall be required to perform forced or compulsory labour. | 2. No one shall be required to perform forced or compulsory labour. |
| | For the purpose of this article the term forced or compulsory labour' shall not include: |
| 3. Trafficking in human beings is prohibited. | (a) any work required to be done in the ordinary course of detention imposed according to the provisions of Article 5 of this Convention or during conditional release from such detention; |
| | (b) any service of a military character or, in case of conscientious objectors in countries where they are recognized, service exacted instead of compulsory military service; |
| | (c) any service exacted in case of an emergency or calamity threatening the life or well-being of the community; |
| | (d) any work or service which forms part of normal civic obligations. |

### CHAPTER II
### FREEDOMS
### Article 6

| Right to liberty and security | ARTICLE 5 |
|---|---|
| Everyone has the right to liberty and security of person. | Everyone has the right to liberty and security of person. |
| | No one shall be deprived of his liberty save in the following cases and in accordance with a procedure prescribed by law: |
| | (a) the lawful detention of a person after conviction by a competent court; |

| CHARTER OF FUNDAMENTAL RIGHTS | EUROPEAN CONVENTION |
|---|---|

EUROPEAN CONVENTION

(b) the lawful arrest or detention of a person for non-compliance with the lawful order of a court or in order to secure the fulfilment of any obligation prescribed by law;

(c) the lawful arrest or detention of a person effected for the purpose of bringing him before the competent legal authority of reasonable suspicion of having committed and offence or when it is reasonably considered necessary to prevent his committing an offence or fleeing after having done so;

(d) the detention of a minor by lawful order for the purpose of educational supervision or his lawful detention for the purpose of bringing him before the competent legal authority;

(e) the lawful detention of persons for the prevention of the spreading of infectious diseases, of persons of unsound mind, alcoholics or drug addicts, or vagrants;

(f) the lawful arrest or detention of a person to prevent his effecting an unauthorized entry into the country or of a person against whom action is being taken with a view to deportation or extradition.

2. Everyone who is arrested shall be informed promptly, in a language which he understands, of the reasons for his arrest and the charge against him.

3. Everyone arrested or detained in accordance with the provisions of paragraph 1(c) of this article shall be brought promptly before a judge or other officer authorized by law to exercise judicial power and shall be entitled to trial within a reasonable time or to release pending trial. Release may be conditioned by guarantees to appear for trial.

## CHARTER OF FUNDAMENTAL RIGHTS

## EUROPEAN CONVENTION

4. Everyone who is deprived of his liberty by arrest or detention shall be entitled to take proceedings by which the lawfulness of his detention shall be decided speedily by a court and his release ordered if the detention is not lawful.

5. Everyone who has been the victim of arrest or detention in contravention of the provisions of this article shall have an enforceable right to compensation.

### Article 7

#### Respect for private and family life

Everyone has the right to respect for his or her private and family life, home and communications.

### Article 8

#### Protection of personal data

1. Everyone has the right to the protection of personal data concerning him or her.

2. Such data must be processed fairly for specified purposes and on the basis of the consent of the person concerned or some other legitimate basis laid down by law. Everyone has the right of access to data which has been collected concerning him or her, and the right to have it rectified.

3. Compliance with these rules shall be subject to control by an independent authority.

### Article 8

1. Everyone has the right to respect for his private and family life, his home and his correspondence.

2. There shall be no interference by a public authority with the exercise of this right except such as is in accordance with the law and is necessary in a democratic society in the interests of national security, public safety or the economic well-being of the country, for the prevention of disorder or crime, for the protection of health or morals, or for the protection of the rights and freedoms of others.

### Article 9

#### Right to marry and right to found a family

The right to marry and the right to found a family shall be guaranteed in accordance with the national laws governing the exercise of these rights.

### Article 12

Men and women of marriageable age have the right to marry and to found a family, according to the national laws governing the exercise of this right.

### PROTOCOL No. 7
#### Article 5

| CHARTER OF FUNDAMENTAL RIGHTS | EUROPEAN CONVENTION |
|---|---|
| | Spouses shall enjoy equality of rights and responsibilities of a private law character between them, and in their relations with their children, as to marriage, during marriage, and in the event of its dissolution. This Article shall not prevent States from taking such measures as are necessary in the interests of the children. |

| Article 10 | Article 9 |
|---|---|
| Freedom of thought, conscience and religion | |
| 1. Everyone has the right to freedom of thought, conscience and religion. This right includes freedom to change religion or belief and freedom, either alone or in community with others and in public or in private, to manifest religion or belief, in worship, teaching, practice and observance. | 1. Everyone has the right to freedom of thought, conscience and religion; this right includes freedom to change his religion or belief, and freedom, either alone or in community with others and in public or private, to manifest his religion or belief, in worship, teaching, practice and observance. |
| 2. The right to conscientious objection is recognised, in accordance with the national laws governing the exercise of this right. | 2. Freedom to manifest one's religion or beliefs shall be subject only to such limitations as are prescribed by law and are necessary in a democratic society in the interests of public safety, for the protection of public order, health or morals, or the protection of the rights and freedoms of others. |

| Article 11 | Article 10 |
|---|---|
| Freedom of expression and information | |
| 1. Everyone has the right to freedom of expression. This right shall include freedom to hold opinions and to receive and impart information and ideas without interference by public authority and regardless of frontiers. | 1. Everyone has the right to freedom of expression. This right shall include freedom to hold opinions and to receive and impart information and ideas without interference by public authority and regardless of frontiers. This article shall not prevent States from requiring the licensing of broadcasting, television or cinema enterprises. |

CHARTER OF FUNDAMENTAL RIGHTS

EUROPEAN CONVENTION

2. The freedom and pluralism of the media shall be respected.

2. The exercise of these freedoms, since it carries with it duties and responsibilities, may be subject to such formalities, conditions, restrictions or penalties as are prescribed by law and are necessary in a democratic society, in the interests of national security, territorial integrity or public safety, for the prevention of disorder or crime, for the protection of health or morals, for the protection of the reputation or the rights of others, for preventing the disclosure of information received in confidence, or for maintaining the authority and impartiality of the judiciary.

## Article 12
### Freedom of assembly and of association

## Article 11

1. Everyone has the right to freedom of peaceful assembly and to freedom of association at all levels, in particular in political, trade union and civic matters, which implies the right of everyone to form and to join trade unions for the protection of his or her interests.

1. Everyone has the right to freedom of peaceful assembly and to freedom of association with others, including the right to form and to join trade unions for the protection of his interests.

2. Political parties at Union level contribute to expressing the political will of the citizens of the Union.

2. No restrictions shall be placed on the exercise of these rights other than such as are prescribed by law and are necessary in a democratic society in the interests of national security or public safety, for the prevention of disorder or crime, for the protection of health or morals or for the protection of the rights and freedoms of others. This article shall not prevent the imposition of lawful restrictions on the exercise of these rights by members of the armed forces, of the police or of the administration of the State.

## Article 13
### Freedom of the arts and sciences

## CHARTER OF FUNDAMENTAL RIGHTS

The arts and scientific research shall be free of constraint. Academic freedom shall be respected.

### Article 14
#### Right to education

1. Everyone has the right to education and to have access to vocational and continuing training.

2. This right includes the possibility to receive free compulsory education.

3. The freedom to found educational establishments with due respect for democratic principles and the right of parents to ensure the education and teaching of their children in conformity with their religious, philosophical and pedagogical convictions shall be respected, in accordance with the national laws governing the exercise of such freedom and right.

### Article 15
#### Freedom to choose an occupation and right to engage in work

1. Everyone has the right to engage in work and to pursue a freely chosen or accepted occupation.

2. Every citizen of the Union has the freedom to seek employment, to work, to exercise the right of establishment and to provide services in any Member State.

3. Nationals of third countries who are authorised to work in the territories of the Member States are entitled to working conditions equivalent to those of citizens of the Union.

### Article 16
#### Freedom to conduct a business

The freedom to conduct a business in accordance with Community law and national laws and practices is recognised.

### Article 17

## EUROPEAN CONVENTION

### PROTOCOL No. 1
#### Article 2

No person shall be denied the right to education. In the exercise of any functions which it assumes in relation to education and to teaching, the State shall respect the right of parents to ensure such education and teaching in conformity with their own religions and philosophical convictions.

### PROTOCOL No. 4
#### Article 1

No one shall be deprived of his liberty merely on the ground of inability to fulfil a contractual obligation.

### PROTOCOL No. 1.

## CHARTER OF FUNDAMENTAL RIGHTS

### Right to property

1. Everyone has the right to own, use, dispose of and bequeath his or her lawfully acquired possessions. No one may be deprived of his or her possessions, except in the public interest and in the cases and under the conditions provided for by law, subject to fair compensation being paid in good time for their loss. The use of property may be regulated by law in so far as is necessary for the general interest.

2. Intellectual property shall be protected.

### Article 18

### Right to asylum

The right to asylum shall be guaranteed with due respect for the rules of the Geneva Convention of 28 July 1951 and the Protocol of 31 January 1967 relating to the status of refugees and in accordance with the Treaty establishing the European Community.

### Article 19

### Protection in the event of removal, expulsion or extradition

1. Collective expulsions are prohibited.

2. No one may be removed, expelled or extradited to a State where there is a serious risk that he or she would be subjected to the death penalty, torture or other inhuman or degrading treatment or punishment.

## EUROPEAN CONVENTION

### Article 1

Every natural or legal person is entitled to the peaceful enjoyment of his possessions. No one shall be deprived of his possessions except in the public interest and subject to the conditions provided for by law and by the general principles of international law.

The preceding provisions shall not, however, in any way impair the right of a State to enforce such laws as it deems necessary to control the use of property in accordance with the general interest or to secure the payment of taxes or other contributions or penalties.

## PROTOCOL NO 4

### Article 3

No one shall be expelled, by means either of an individual or of a collective measure, from the territory of the State of which he is a national.

No one shall be deprived of the right to enter the territory of the State of which he is a national.

### Article 4

Collective expulsion of aliens is prohibited.

## PROTOCOL No. 7

### Article 1

CHARTER OF FUNDAMENTAL RIGHTS

EUROPEAN CONVENTION

1. An alien lawfully resident in the territory of a State shall not be expelled therefrom except in pursuance of a decision reached in accordance with law and shall be allowed: (a) to submit reasons against his expulsion, (b) to have his case reviewed, and (c) to be represented for these purposes before the competent authority or a person or persons designated by that authority.

2. An alien may be expelled before the exercise of his rights under paragraph 1.a, b and c of this Article, when such expulsion is necessary in the interests of public order or is grounded on reasons of national security.

## CHAPTER III
### EQUALITY
#### Article 20
Equality before the law
Everyone is equal before the law.

#### Article 21
Non-discrimination

Article 14

1. Any discrimination based on any ground such as sex, race, colour, ethnic or social origin, genetic features, language, religion or belief, political or any other opinion, membership of a national minority, property, birth, disability, age or sexual orientation shall be prohibited.

2. Within the scope of application of the Treaty on the Functioning of the European Union and of the Treaty on European Union, and without prejudice to the special provisions of those Treaties, any discrimination on grounds of nationality shall be prohibited.

The enjoyment of the rights and freedoms set forth in this Convention shall be secured without discrimination on any ground such as sex, race, colour, language, religion, political or other opinion, national or social origin, association with a national minority, property, birth or other status

PROTOCOL No. 12
Article 1

1. The enjoyment of any right set forth by law shall be secured [rest of paragraph unchanged from Article 14]

## CHARTER OF FUNDAMENTAL RIGHTS

## EUROPEAN CONVENTION

2. No one shall be discriminated against by any public authority on any ground such as those mentioned in paragraph 1.

### Article 22

Cultural, religious and linguistic diversity

The Union shall respect cultural, religious and linguistic diversity.

### Article 23

Equality between men and women

Equality between men and women must be ensured in all areas, including employment, work and pay.

The principle of equality shall not prevent the maintenance or adoption of measures providing for specific advantages in favour of the underrepresented sex.

### Article 24

The rights of the child

1. Children shall have the right to such protection and care as is necessary for their well-being. They may express their views freely. Such views shall be taken into consideration on matters which concern them in accordance with their age and maturity.

2. In all actions relating to children, whether taken by public authorities or private institutions, the child's best interests must be a primary consideration.

3. Every child shall have the right to maintain on a regular basis a personal relationship and direct contact with both his or her parents, unless that is contrary to his or her interests.

### Article 25

The rights of the elderly

CHARTER OF FUNDAMENTAL
RIGHTS

The Union recognises and respects the rights of the elderly to lead a life of dignity and independence and to participate in social and cultural life.

### Article 26

Integration of persons with disabilities

The Union recognises and respects the right of persons with disabilities to benefit from measures designed to ensure their independence, social and occupational integration and participation in the life of the community.

### CHAPTER IV
### SOLIDARITY
### Article 27

Workers' right to information and consultation within the undertaking

Workers or their representatives must, at the appropriate levels, be guaranteed information and consultation in good time in the cases and under the conditions provided for by Union law and national laws and practices.

### Article 28

Right of collective bargaining and action

Workers and employers, or their respective organisations, have, in accordance with Union law and national laws and practices, the right to negotiate and conclude collective agreements at the appropriate levels and, in cases of conflicts of interest, to take collective action to defend their interests, including strike action.

### Article 29

Right of access to placement services

Everyone has the right of access to a free placement service.

### Article 30

EUROPEAN CONVENTION

## CHARTER OF FUNDAMENTAL RIGHTS

### EUROPEAN CONVENTION

Protection in the event of unjustified dismissal

Every worker has the right to protection against unjustified dismissal, in accordance with Union law and national laws and practices.

### Article 31

Fair and just working conditions

1. Every worker has the right to working conditions which respect his or her health, safety and dignity.

2. Every worker has the right to limitation of maximum working hours, to daily and weekly rest periods and to an annual period of paid leave.

### Article 32

Prohibition of child labour and protection of young people at work

The employment of children is prohibited. The minimum age of admission to employment may not be lower than the minimum school-leaving age, without prejudice to such rules as may be more favourable to young people and except for limited derogations.

Young people admitted to work must have working conditions appropriate to their age and be protected against economic exploitation and any work likely to harm their safety, health or physical, mental, moral or social development or to interfere with their education.

### Article 33

Family and professional life

1. The family shall enjoy legal, economic and social protection.

2. To reconcile family and professional life, everyone shall have the right to protection from dismissal for a reason connected with maternity and the right to paid maternity leave and to parental leave following the birth or adoption of a child.

CHARTER OF FUNDAMENTAL RIGHTS

EUROPEAN CONVENTION

### Article 34

Social security and social assistance

1. The Union recognises and respects the entitlement to social security benefits and social services providing protection in cases such as maternity, illness, industrial accidents, dependency or old age, and in the case of loss of employment, in accordance with the rules laid down by Union law and national laws and practices.

2. Everyone residing and moving legally within the European Union is entitled to social security benefits and social advantages in accordance with Union law and national laws and practices.

3. In order to combat social exclusion and poverty, the Union recognises and respects the right to social and housing assistance so as to ensure a decent existence for all those who lack sufficient resources, in accordance with the rules laid down by Union law and national laws and practices.

### Article 35

Health care

Everyone has the right of access to preventive health care and the right to benefit from medical treatment under the conditions established by national laws and practices. A high level of human health protection shall be ensured in the definition and implementation of all Union policies and activities.

### Article 36

Access to services of general economic interest

## CHARTER OF FUNDAMENTAL RIGHTS

The Union recognises and respects access to services of general economic interest as provided for in national laws and practices, in accordance with the Treaty on the Functioning of the European Union, in order to promote the social and territorial cohesion of the Union.

### Article 37
#### Environmental protection

A high level of environmental protection and the improvement of the quality of the environment must be integrated into the policies of the Union and ensured in accordance with the principle of sustainable development.

### Article 38
#### Consumer protection

Union policies shall ensure a high level of consumer protection.

## CHAPTER V
## CITIZENS' RIGHTS
### Article 39
#### Right to vote and to stand as a candidate at elections to the European Parliament

1. Every citizen of the Union has the right to vote and to stand as a candidate at elections to the European Parliament in the Member State in which he or she resides, under the same conditions as nationals of that State.

2. Members of the European Parliament shall be elected by direct universal suffrage in a free and secret ballot.

### Article 40
#### Right to vote and to stand as a candidate at municipal elections

## EUROPEAN CONVENTION

## PROTOCOL No. 1
### Article 3

The High Contracting Parties undertake to hold free elections at reasonable intervals by secret ballot, under conditions which will ensure the free expression of the opinion of the people in the choice of the legislature.

### Article 16

Nothing in Articles 10, 11, and 14 shall be regarded as preventing the High Contracting Parties from imposing restrictions on the political activity of aliens.

## CHARTER OF FUNDAMENTAL RIGHTS

EUROPEAN CONVENTION

Every citizen of the Union has the right to vote and to stand as a candidate at municipal elections in the Member State in which he or she resides under the same conditions as nationals of that State.

### Article 41

#### Right to good administration

1. Every person has the right to have his or her affairs handled impartially, fairly and within a reasonable time by the institutions and bodies of the Union.

2. This right includes:

- the right of every person to be heard, before any individual measure which would affect him or her adversely is taken;

- the right of every person to have access to his or her file, while respecting the legitimate interests of confidentiality and of professional and business secrecy;

- the obligation of the administration to give reasons for its decisions.

3. Every person has the right to have the Union make good any damage caused by its institutions or by its servants in the performance of their duties, in accordance with the general principles common to the laws of the Member States.

4. Every person may write to the institutions of the Union in one of the languages of the Treaties and must have an answer in the same language.

### Article 42

#### Right of access to documents

Any citizen of the Union, and any natural or legal person residing or having its registered office in a Member State, has a right of access to European Parliament, Council and Commission documents.

## CHARTER OF FUNDAMENTAL RIGHTS

### Article 43

#### Ombudsman

Any citizen of the Union and any natural or legal person residing or having its registered office in a Member State has the right to refer to the Ombudsman of the Union cases of maladministration in the activities of the Union institutions or bodies, with the exception of the Court of Justice and the Court of First Instance acting in their judicial role.

### Article 44

#### Right to petition

Any citizen of the Union and any natural or legal person residing or having its registered office in a Member State has the right to petition the European Parliament.

### Article 45

#### Freedom of movement and of residence

1. Every citizen of the Union has the right to move and reside freely within the territory of the Member States.

2. Freedom of movement and residence may be granted, in accordance with the Treaty on the Functioning of the European Union, to nationals of third countries legally resident in the territory of a Member State.

### Article 46

#### Diplomatic and consular protection

## EUROPEAN CONVENTION

### PROTOCOL No. 4

#### Article 2

1. Everyone lawfully within the territory of a State shall, within that territory, have the right to liberty of movement and freedom to choose his residence.

2. Everyone shall be free to leave any country, including his own.

3. No restrictions shall be placed on the exercise of these rights other than such as are in accordance with law and are necessary in a democratic society in the interests of national security or public safety for the maintenance of 'ordre public', for the prevention of crime, for the protection of rights and freedoms of others.

4. The rights set forth in paragraph 1 may also be subject, in particular areas, to restrictions imposes in accordance with law and justified by the public interest in a democratic society.

## CHARTER OF FUNDAMENTAL RIGHTS

Every citizen of the Union shall, in the territory of a third country in which the Member State of which he or she is a national is not represented, be entitled to protection by the diplomatic or consular authorities of any Member State, on the same conditions as the nationals of that Member State.

## CHAPTER VI
### JUSTICE
#### Article 47
Right to an effective remedy and to a fair trial

Everyone whose rights and freedoms guaranteed by the law of the Union are violated has the right to an effective remedy before a tribunal in compliance with the conditions laid down in this Article.

## EUROPEAN CONVENTION

#### Article 13

Everyone whose rights and freedoms as set forth in this Convention are violated shall have an effective remedy before a national authority notwithstanding that the violation has been committed by persons acting in an official capacity.

#### Article 6

1. In the determination of his civil rights and obligations or of any criminal charge against him, everyone is entitled to a fair and public hearing within a reasonable time by an independent and impartial tribunal established by law. Judgement shall be pronounced publicly but the press and public may be excluded from all or part of the trial in the interest of morals, public order or national security in a democratic society, where the interests of juveniles or the protection of the private life of the parties so require, or the extent strictly necessary in the opinion of the court in special circumstances where publicity would prejudice the interests of justice.

## CHARTER OF FUNDAMENTAL RIGHTS

## EUROPEAN CONVENTION

Everyone is entitled to a fair and public hearing within a reasonable time by an independent and impartial tribunal previously established by law. Everyone shall have the possibility of being advised, defended and represented. Legal aid shall be made available to those who lack sufficient resources in so far as such aid is necessary to ensure effective access to justice.[1]

2. Everyone charged with a criminal offence shall be presumed innocent until proved guilty according to law.

3. Everyone charged with a criminal offence has the following minimum rights:

(a) to be informed promptly, in a language which he understands and in detail, of the nature and cause of the accusation against him;

(b) to have adequate time and the facilities for the preparation of his defence;

### Article 48
Presumption of innocence and right of defence

1. Everyone who has been charged shall be presumed innocent until proved guilty according to law.
2. Respect for the rights of the defence of anyone who has been charged shall be guaranteed.

(c) to defend himself in person or through legal assistance of his own choosing or, if he has not sufficient means to pay for legal assistance, to be given it free when the interests of justice so require;

(d) to examine or have examined witnesses against him and to obtain the attendance and examination of witnesses on his behalf under the same conditions as witnesses against him;

(e) to have the free assistance of an interpreter if he cannot understand or speak the language used in court.

### Article 49
Principles of legality and proportionality of criminal offences and penalties

### Article 7

---

[1] See article 6(1)(c) of the Convention

## CHARTER OF FUNDAMENTAL RIGHTS

1. No one shall be held guilty of any criminal offence on account of any act or omission which did not constitute a criminal offence under national law or international law at the time when it was committed. Nor shall a heavier penalty be imposed than that which was applicable at the time the criminal offence was committed. If, subsequent to the commission of a criminal offence, the law provides for a lighter penalty, that penalty shall be applicable.

2. This Article shall not prejudice the trial and punishment of any person for any act or omission which, at the time when it was committed, was criminal according to the general principles recognised by the community of nations.

3. The severity of penalties must not be disproportionate to the criminal offence.

### Article 50

Right not to be tried or punished twice in criminal proceedings for the same criminal offence

No one shall be liable to be tried or punished again in criminal proceedings for an offence for which he or she has already been finally acquitted or convicted within the Union in accordance with the law.

## EUROPEAN CONVENTION

1. No one shall be held guilty of any criminal offence on account of any act or omission which did not constitute a criminal offence under national or international law at the time when it was committed. Nor shall a heavier penalty be imposed than the one that was applicable at the time the criminal offence was committed.

2. This article shall not prejudice the trial and punishment of any person for any act or omission which, at the time when it was committed, was criminal according to the general principles of law recognized by civilized nations.

### PROTOCOL No. 7
### Article 4

1. No one shall be liable to be tried or punished again in criminal proceedings under the jurisdiction of the same State for an offence for which he has already been finally acquitted or convicted in accordance with the law and procedure of that State.

2. The provisions of the preceding paragraph shall not prevent the reopening of the case in accordance with the law and penal procedure of the State concerned, if there is evidence of new or newly discovered facts, or if there has been a fundamental defect in the previous proceedings, which could affect the outcome of the case.

3. No derogation from this Article shall be made under Article 15 of the Convention.

[The Convention contains further provisions relating to appeal that have no counterpart in the Charter.]

| CHARTER OF FUNDAMENTAL RIGHTS | EUROPEAN CONVENTION |
|---|---|

## CHARTER OF FUNDAMENTAL RIGHTS

### CHAPTER VII
### GENERAL PROVISIONS
### Article 51
### Scope

1. The provisions of this Charter are addressed to the institutions and bodies of the Union with due regard for the principle of subsidiarity and to the Member States only when they are implementing Union law. They shall therefore respect the rights, observe the principles and promote the application thereof in accordance with their respective powers.

2. This Charter does not establish any new power or task for the Union, or modify powers and tasks defined by the Treaties.

### Article 52
### Scope of guaranteed rights

1. Any limitation on the exercise of the rights and freedoms recognised by this Charter must be provided for by law and respect the essence of those rights and freedoms. Subject to the principle of proportionality, limitations may be made only if they are necessary and genuinely meet objectives of general interest recognised by the Union or the need to protect the rights and freedoms of others.

2. Rights recognised by this Charter which are based on the Union Treaties shall be exercised under the conditions and within the limits defined by those Treaties.

3. In so far as this Charter contains rights which correspond to rights guaranteed by the Convention for the Protection of Human Rights and Fundamental Freedoms, the meaning and scope of those rights shall be the same as those laid down by the said Convention. This provision shall not prevent Union law providing more extensive protection.

## EUROPEAN CONVENTION

### Article 18

The restrictions permitted under this Convention to the said rights and freedoms shall not be applied for any purpose other than those for which they have been prescribed.

CHARTER OF FUNDAMENTAL RIGHTS

EUROPEAN CONVENTION

### Article 53
#### Level of protection
Nothing in this Charter shall be interpreted as restricting or adversely affecting human rights and fundamental freedoms as recognised, in their respective fields of application, by Union law and international law and by international agreements to which the Union or all the Member States are party, including the European Convention for the Protection of Human Rights and Fundamental Freedoms, and by the Member States' constitutions.

### Article 54
#### Prohibition of abuse of rights
Nothing in this Charter shall be interpreted as implying any right to engage in any activity or to perform any act aimed at the destruction of any of the rights and freedoms recognised in this Charter or at their limitation to a greater extent than is provided for herein.

### Article 17
Nothing in this Convention may be interpreted as implying for any State, group or person any right to engage in any activity or perform any act aimed at the destruction on any of the rights and freedoms set forth herein or at their limitation to a greater extent than is provided for in the Convention

[Note: In the case of the Convention, not all protocols have been ratified by all states. Thus, where a protocol addresses a matter previously appearing in the Convention or an earlier protocol, the earlier language may still apply.]

# Chapter 2

# ORIENTATION

*The materials in this chapter provide historical context and some introductory commentary to the provisions set out in the Template. (Except for § 2.10, Section numbers correspond to Template articles.)*

## § 2.01 FOUNDATIONS OF THE UNION

### [A] Purpose

***The European Coal and Steel Community (ECSC)*** After centuries of competing interests, armed conflict, global rivalries and some of the worst atrocities in the history of mankind, the countries of Europe began in 1950 a political experiment that they hoped would mark a new epoch in their relations with each other and the world. On May 9 of that year, Robert Schumann, French Foreign Minister, announced an extraordinary initiative. He proposed that the coal and steel industries of France and Germany be placed under common sovereignty in the form of a European Coal and Steel Community.

Some cynics would argue that this gesture was nothing more than a recognition of reality rather than a magnanimous offer of reconciliation in the aftermath of World War II. France had occupied the Saarland region of Germany (adjacent to the French region of Alsace-Lorraine) where a significant portion of German coal and steel production was located, with the goal of preventing Germany from once again reviving as a military power based on the basic materials of war. (The occupation ended in 1956 with a plebiscite where the people voted to become a Land within the Federal Republic of Germany.) The United States had, only a year before, supported the establishment of the Federal Republic of Germany with the intent of creating a bulwark against the threat of communism from Stalin's Soviet Union. France was also under pressure to cooperate with the U.S. Marshall Plan initiative, which would benefit all of western Europe through a massive injection of money to rebuild the economy. A condition of this aid was that it had to be administered jointly by the nations in the region.

It is, however, precisely such confluences of external pressures, humanitarian idealism and political reality that are needed to produce dramatic steps such as this. For the idealists this initiative was to be but the first step in the creation of a "United States of Europe." There was much enthusiasm for the idea and as a result, four other countries asked to participate — The Netherlands, Belgium, Luxembourg and Italy. At the time, the UK supported the initiative among these States but remained aloof from participation itself.

Thus, the European Coal and Steel Community (ECSC) came into existence in 1952 pursuant to a Treaty signed by the six west European States. It was set up to provide a regulatory framework for their coal and steel industries. This framework was exceptional in that it was not a mere agency of the States but a new "supranational" body with institutions to which the states transferred their powers within the scope of the Treaty.

The momentum created by the success in realizing the ECSC led quickly to a proposal for a full political and defense union. However, opposing national interests were too strong, and that next step failed to gain the approval of the French Assembly. After some reflection and a conclusion that this had simply been a case of "too far too soon," the participating nations decided to pursue the Community concept with a similar second structure that would cover at least market integration in general. The belief behind this concept was that the creation of a common market among the ECSC states would facilitate over a longer period the foundation for political union in the future. The emulation of the United States as a single vast market and the prosperity it created would convince the peoples of western Europe that they could and should move on to attain political union at some point in the future.

***The European Economic Community (EEC) and the European Atomic Energy Community (EAEC)*** The European Economic Community (EEC) and the European Atomic Energy Community (EAEC) were formed in 1957, building on the earlier model. The essential feature of these Communities was again the creation of a body with powers exercised through Community institutions in the form of a Council of Ministers (comprising representatives of the Member States), a Commission, which was independent, a Court of Justice, and an Assembly, subsequently renamed the European Parliament. The original function of the EEC was not only to create a "common market" among the Member States but also to be a dynamic vehicle leading to an "ever closer union" among them. Over the next 30-plus years, its powers were defined and consolidated in particular by decisions of its Court of Justice, and it thus came to be shaped as a separate sovereign body within the territory, and alongside the Governments, of the Member States. After various stalled efforts, a new impetus for "ever closer union" was provided by the Single European Act of 1986 (SEA), which contained the mechanisms necessary to complete a genuine internal market within the following five years.

***The original European Union*** By 1992, membership of the Communities had increased to 12 States. With the success of the SEA, they now sought to forge ahead with a more broad-ranging union, including the creation of a single currency and political integration in the form of cooperation on justice and home affairs, immigration policy, and foreign and security policy. However, with the exception of the common currency (which necessitated the establishment within the EEC Treaty framework of a new institution, the European Central Bank) they declined initially to use the existing EEC Treaty structure for political integration, in general because they were not willing to concede further powers to the EEC. In particular, they did not wish to use the qualified majority voting system used by the Council of Ministers, nor did they wish to involve the Parliament in their actions. Hence, when they came to tie these various initiatives together in the form of a "European Union", they chose a different model.

The European Union (EU) came into existence in November 1993 upon the entry into force of the Treaty on European Union, or Treaty of Maastricht. In its original form, the EU might be likened to a general partnership among the several Member States. The subject areas in the TEU were largely addressed through intergovernmental processes and not through the more integrationist Community model, although the existing Communities' powers were preserved. The EU could, however, choose to delegate implementation back to the EEC (which was renamed simply the European Community or EC). The Union was described as resting on three "pillars." Within the TEU there were two pillars, Justice and Home Affairs (JHA) and common foreign and security policy (CFSP). The third pillar comprised the European Communities (EC, EAEC and ECSC Treaties).

***Move toward a Constitution for Europe*** The EC Treaty underwent further substantial amendment through the Treaties of Amsterdam and Nice, signed in 1997 and 2001 respectively.

Membership of the EU continued to grow through accession of new Member States, including more recently those that had been part of the former Communist bloc, such that, today, there are 27 Member States.

After the Treaty of Nice in 2002, a general consensus among political leaders of the Union's Member States precipitated the formation of an intergovernmental conference to consider the adoption of a constitution for the Union. Somewhat to the astonishment of many, this led to the signature of a Treaty establishing a Constitution for Europe, one effect of which would have been to consolidate the EC into the EU with the Community model as the predominant element. Although ratified by 18 Member States, this Treaty was voted down in referendums in France and the Netherlands in 2005. This brought the ratification process to a halt.

***The reformed European Union*** In the first half of 2007, the German presidency of the Council introduced a new modified proposal that actually still contained much of the substance of the Constitution Treaty, but, shorn of the outward symbols associated with the "constitution" such as references to a flag and an anthem. This proposal, which took the shape of a reforming treaty that amended the existing treaties rather than replacing them, was approved at the June meeting of heads of state or government in 2007 and signed in Lisbon by all 27 Member States on December 13, 2007 (hence it is now known as the Treaty of Lisbon). After some difficulties in Ireland and the Czech Republic, it was finally ratified by all Member States by October 2009 and came into effect on December 1, 2009.

The Lisbon Treaty had the effect, among other things, of causing the Union to succeed the European Community, which ceased to exist. The EC Treaty was renamed the Treaty on the Functioning of the European Union, and all references in it to the Community became references to the Union, which acquired legal personality, a President (of the European Council) a High Representative for Foreign Affairs and Security Policy, and a foreign diplomatic service of sorts. The EAEC will continue to exist, although there are pressures building for its reform also.

The Treaty of Lisbon effected a substantial rationalization of the existing European organizations. While omitting some of the more symbolic but controversial aspects of the failed Constitution Treaty, it has already been noted that it contained most of the substantive changes envisaged in that document. While much criticized by some as another example of an obsession with internal process and structure while the major issues of the day were neglected, the Lisbon Treaty in truth achieves a number of remarkable objectives.

First, it is now possible to look at the European Union as an integrated constitutional structure. The three pillars have disappeared, and the Union replaces its former self and the European Community. (The EAEC Treaty has nevertheless been amended by a specific Protocol — "Protocol Amending the Treaty establishing the EAEC" — intended to adapt that Treaty to the new rules laid down by the TEU and the TFEU.) Although the CFSP continues to exist outside the parameters of the former Community structures, the European Council with its individual President clearly emerges as a sort of collective "head of state" for the Union. Innovations such as the definition of what constitutes a legislative act make it possible now to identify the Council and European Parliament as the legislature of the Union. Non-legislative acts then fall into the category of policy making and executive activities, while subsidiary rulemaking falls somewhere between the two in much the same way that U.S. Federal Agencies are granted such powers.

Second, the ability to press forward with ever closer union in the political arena will certainly be enhanced through some of the new provisions: for example, the provisions for a simplified revision process; and the facilitative measures for hoped-for EU involvement in defense and security.

Third, the integration of police and justice cooperation in criminal matters (PJCC), which was the renamed JHA, after the transfer of visa and asylum policy to the EC Treaty by the Treaty of Amsterdam, into the renamed Treaty on the Functioning of the European Union means that European integration has definitively broadened beyond the economic sphere into that of the Area of Freedom, Security and Justice (AFSJ). The focus of attention therefore, in terms of future development of the EU, will be across the whole spectrum of domestic affairs. AFSJ is not a new concept (it was first enunciated in the earlier "Tampere declaration" by the European Council), but as a result of the Treaty of Lisbon it now has concrete constitutional form within the institutional structure of the TFEU. Internally, the construction of the AFSJ is the next focus of attention in building an ever closer union.

Fourth, the TFEU now lays out a clear division of competences between the Union and the Member States. While such a division existed *de facto*, the detailed enumeration in the TFEU now legitimizes the categorization of competences in a manner befitting a constitution.

The Treaty of Lisbon does *not* entail that the EU is about to become a European super-state. A federal "superstate" would imply strong executive powers. Such powers, however, continue to reside with the Member States. Only in the legislative branch can we discern a federal structure today. Yet, while the Union has not become a federal state, one might now properly describe it as an "international federation". The term is a suggested designation for a form of association among states where powers are allocated between the Union and the States within defined areas of activity, leaving the States on an equal footing with the Union with respect to the competences they have retained. However, for this to function, it is critical that, like a federal constitution, the Treaties ultimately define the allocation of powers between the federal and state authorities, prevailing in case of conflict. At the very least, it is necessary to spell out what powers are to be exercised by the Union even if the Treaties remain silent as to the powers of the states. This is actually not so different from a conventional federation where the federal constitution may be silent on the extent of state powers — as in the case of the United States. For a discussion of the Union's status, see, for example, M. Avbelj, *Treaty of Lisbon: An ongoing Search for Structural Equilibrium*, 16 COLUM. J. EUR. L. (2009-2010) 523

In conventional nation state federations, powers will be allocated according to whether they require uniform action across the entire territory of the federation or can be safely left to divergent state action. Of course, perception of what these requirements are will vary largely from one system to another because of the particular situation of each country. For example, Germany, with a strong federal constitution, has a civil code that is applicable as federal law throughout Germany. In the United States, the common law equivalent exists at the state level. There are many reasons for this — historical, cultural, geographical. At a minimum it can be expected that the federation will be responsible for external affairs and defense. Without at least these powers, the federation would be at constant risk of disintegration through outside pressures that prise the states apart and cause them to follow their own self-interest. This unfortunately is still the case with the EU, as vividly demonstrated in the aftermath of the 2008 crisis. At the same time, it is clear that the political will to prevent disintegration of monetary union remains very strong.

***Historical Parallels*** The European Union in its post-Lisbon form has come to emulate in some respects the various forms of political organization that characterized continental affairs for centuries. The Holy Roman Empire of the German nation, the German Confederation that succeeded it after it was dissolved in 1806, the North German Federation of 1867 and then the 1871, Second German Empire based on Prussian power, all exhibited various aspects of the structure now visible in Europe. One may note additionally that the German Confederation introduced a Customs Union in 1834 that was intended to pursue the same economic goals as the EEC. Thus, while the Union may seem a very novel structure to those whose history did not share in these arrangements, it has many echoes of the past for the peoples of Germany, Austria, the Low Countries and Central Europe.

Despite these parallels, it must be noted that the Union nonetheless has one absolutely distinctive, novel feature: it is a voluntary union of sovereign states who have willingly surrendered some of their sovereign powers. That was never the case with the Holy Roman Empire or the German Empire, where the constituent states, cities and principalities either never had sovereign powers to surrender or, if they had won them, were at least in some degree then coerced to give them up.

***Other unification initiatives*** Although the European Union is far and away the pre-eminent organization for the promotion of a united Europe, it should not be forgotten that there are other, mostly European-focused organizations that also have played a role, in some cases of quite some significance.

**- Brussels Treaty Organization** This organization was set up as an embryonic defence organization among various west European states excluding Germany. This was the precursor of the **Western European Union** (WEU), which included Germany. This organization was the chosen vehicle in the original TEU for integrating defense policy among the Member States of the European Union. This notion, however, was swept away by the Lisbon Treaty and the WEU has been subsumed into the EU. The Brussels Treaty was terminated in 2010 and the WEU ceased all activity in July 2011.

**- The Council of Europe** The Council of Europe was founded by the Treaty of London in 1949. It is comprised of 47 states including all EU Member States, Russia and most of the republics of the Former Soviet Union. Although it has an Assembly comprised of parliamentarians from its member states and a Committee of Ministers, it is largely a powerless organization. It has, however, sponsored conventions on various matters and promotes relationships between local communities in the member countries. It also has set up various monitoring bodies on issues such as racism and money laundering. Most notable among its achievements was the setting up of the European Court of Human Rights, for which it remains responsible. The Court is discussed further in Chapter 4. The flag and anthem associated with the EU were originally designed for and used by the Council of Europe. Website: www.coe.int. For an interesting assessment of the Council of Europe and its relationship with the European Union, *see* T. Joris and J. Vandenberghe, *The Council of Europe and the European Union: Natural Partners or Uneasy Bedfellows?* 15 COLUM. J. EUR. L. (2008-2009) 1.

**- The European Convention on the Protection of Human Rights and Fundamental Freedoms** *(ECHR)* This Convention was set up by west European states under the aegis of the Council of Europe in 1950 as a treaty that guarantees fundamental human rights to European citizens. It had included a Commission that investigated complaints that may be made when national remedies have been exhausted but now cases are brought directly in the European Court on Human Rights, which is in Strasbourg (France). The Union is required to accede to the ECHR — new TEU 6. Website: www.human-rights-convention.org.

**- EFTA** When the EEC was formed in 1957, the UK spearheaded an alternative organisation for non-member States, called the **European Free Trade Area** or **EFTA**. Most of these states (including, of course, the UK itself) have now joined the EU, leaving only Norway, Iceland and Liechtenstein as members of EFTA. This organization created a free trade area among the members but had none of the supranational or integrationist aspects of the EEC.

**- European Economic Area** Any visitor to Europe will see that the immigration line for nationals of the state includes also EU nationals, nationals of the EEA and Switzerland. The EEA is the European Economic Area comprising the Union plus Norway, Liechtenstein and Iceland, the rump of the membership of EFTA. Much Union legislation applies throughout the EEA, though these three states, as non-members, do not have a formal or direct say in its design.

**- GATT** This is the acronym for the General Agreement on Tariffs and Trade, a multilateral treaty entered into by most western industrialized and developing countries after World War II to promote international trade. The GATT secretariat (in Geneva) has sponsored various "rounds" of significant tariff reductions (the "Dillon", "Kennedy", "Tokyo" and "Uruguay" and "Doha" rounds) (there have been, in total, eight GATT-sponsored rounds). The Uruguay round also introduced sweeping reforms in the area of trade in services and in intellectual property among others, as well as setting up a new body, the World Trade Organization (WTO) to police states' behavior regarding many indirect restrictions on trade.

**- Organization for European Economic Cooperation and Development or OECD** Originally known as the Organization for European Economic Cooperation or OEEC, this body was set up by the states of Western Europe to share out and administer the funds distributed by the United States under the Marshall Aid plan, which was intended to rejuvenate western Europe after the destruction of the war. In 1960 Canada and the United States joined the organization, which was renamed the Organization for Economic Cooperation and Development. It has no legislative powers but does monitor the economies of the various Member States and issues forecasts and acts as a forum for cooperation.

### *A chronology of significant events in European unification after World War II*

| | |
|---|---|
| 1944 | Benelux formed. |
| | Bretton Woods Agreements on system of currency exchange rates. |
| 1946 | Churchill Speech, Zurich, calls for "a kind of United States of Europe". |
| | Bretton Woods agreements establishing a system of fixed exchange rates for currencies becomes effective. World Bank Group comes into existence. |
| 1947 | Marshall Plan commenced — more than $13 billion provided as aid to European States recovering from the effects of World War II. A condition of this aid was that the recipient states work together on its allocation. |
| 1948 | Brussels Treaty Organization created, later to become the Western European Union. |
| | Hague Congress of Europe leads to the formation of the Organization for European Economic Cooperation (OEEC) (now OECD). |
| | General Agreement on Tariffs and Trade signed. |
| 1949 | Formation of Council of Europe. |
| | Establishment of the Federal Republic of Germany. |
| 1950 | Schuman proposal for European Coal and Steel Community (ECSC). |
| | Korean War began, lasting until July 1953. |
| | Pleven Plan — European Defence Community (EDC). |
| | Signature of European Convention for the Protection of Human Rights and Fundamental Freedoms. |
| 1952 | ECSC comes into being. |

NATO Treaty signed.

EDC Treaty signed.

1953    Pleven Plan for European Political Community (EPC) agreed.

1954    French National Assembly rejects EDC and EPC.

1955    Messina Conference of Foreign Ministers of the ECSC Member States.

1956    Spaak report calling for the establishment of a European Economic Community and of a European Atomic Energy Community.

1957    Signature of Treaties of Rome (EEC and EAEC).

1959    Proposal for political union (Plan Fouchet).

Mansholt Plan proposed for the establishment of a Common Agricultural Policy.

1960    Establishment of European Free Trade Area.

1962    Plan Fouchet rejected.

Rejection of United Kingdom's application for membership.

Establishment of principles of agricultural policy.

1964    Agreement on a common policy for grain.

1965    Proposal for own resources (financing of agricultural policy) and majority voting; rejection by France — 7–month boycott — "politique de la chaise vide".

1966    Luxembourg accords purport to give each member state a veto over Community proposed legislation.

1967    Merger of separate Commissions/ECSC High Authority and Councils (Court and Parliament were institutions for three single Communities from the outset).

Britain applies again, with summary rejection by France.

1968    End of the transitional period.

1969    De Gaulle resigns.

Britain reapplies.

Hague summit reaches agreement in principle on enlargement of Community.

1970    Plan Werner (economic and monetary union).

Agreement on own resources for common agricultural policy; more powers to European parliament.

1971    Establishment of regime of "own resources" for the Community.

Bretton Woods fixed exchange rates system collapses when U.S. suspends convertibility of U.S. dollar to gold. Leads to ending of controlled exchange rates.

1972    Member States set up a system based on control of maximum fluctuation of rates of 4.3% around a central dollar exchange rate known as the "Snake in the Tunnel" with only limited success and subsequent narrowing by 1977 to five states as participants with currency values based on a German Mark central exchange rate.

1973    Britain, Ireland and Denmark become members.

1973-1979 Turmoil in the monetary markets and dramatic increases in energy prices prevent significant development of the EC.

1974     Establishment of "European Council," comprising heads of state, originally meeting twice a year for "European Summit". The beginning of broader political cooperation in foreign affairs.

1975     Parliament given a role in budgetary process.

1976     Act of the Council establishing direct elections to the European Parliament.

1977     Parliament, Council and Commission joint declaration on Fundamental Rights.

1979     Creation of the European Monetary System (EMS) and stabilization of exchange rates. UK does not participate. Fluctuations limited to 2.25% (Italy at 6%) around a rate determined by relation to a basket of currencies (the ECU).

         First direct elections to the Parliament.

1981     Greece accedes.

1984     Parliament produces draft "Treaty establishing the European Union".

1986     Spain and Portugal become members.

1987     Single European Act enters into force. Steps taken to liberalize all capital movements; "1992" phenomenon takes hold; pace of mergers and acquisitions, adoption of directives on harmonization, accelerate; governments set up committee to examine establishment of common currency; debate over future political structure of a united Europe begins in earnest.

1989     Court of First Instance established.

         Fall of the Berlin wall and the reunification of Germany.

         Intergovernmental conference set up by European Council meeting in Strasbourg to discuss and propose monetary and political union.

1991     UK joins the EMS.

1992     Signing of the Treaty of Maastricht on Economic, Monetary and Political Union ("TEU"). Sets up the European Union based on three "pillars" (Matters falling within the EC Treaty, Common Foreign and Security Policy and Police and Judicial Co-operation in Criminal Matters.) Also lays the foundations for Economic and Monetary Union.

         Denmark rejects ratification of Treaty of Maastricht in a referendum.

1992     France ratifies Maastricht by referendum; currency crisis causes U.K. and Italy to withdraw from European Monetary System.

1993     Denmark ratifies Treaty following a favorable majority vote in a referendum. Denmark permitted to opt out of provisions on economic and monetary union and on common defense policy and European citizenship.

         U.K. ratifies Treaty after a constitutional challenge to the methods followed to adopt it fails. U.K. permitted to opt out of provisions on economic and monetary union. Germany becomes the last Member State to ratify the Treaty after a challenge before the German Constitutional Court fails. European Union comes into existence.

1994    European Economic Area (EEA) comes into effect. EEA Treaty extends European Union's single market to Austria, Finland, Norway, Sweden, Liechtenstein and Iceland.

European Parliament ratifies the accession treaties of Austria, Finland, Norway, and Sweden. Austria, in a referendum, votes in favor of joining the European Union.

Norway votes against joining the European Union. In earlier referenda, Finland and Sweden had voted to approve membership.

1995    Austria, Finland and Sweden become members of the European Union, bringing the total membership to 15 countries.

"Schengen Group" formed to dismantle border controls, allowing travellers to journey between states without showing passports.

European Currency Unit renamed the "euro" in anticipation of the introduction of the third stage of Monetary Union.

World Trade Organization comes into being.

1997    Treaty of Amsterdam signed, expanding the powers of the Parliament and establishing a social policy chapter for the EC Treaty.

Agreement on Stability and Growth Pact.

1998    Determination of eligibility to participate in the Currency Union.

1999    Euro comes into existence for transfer payments among the 11 eligible Member States (France, Germany, Belgium, Luxembourg, The Netherlands, Italy, Spain, Ireland, Finland, Portugal and Austria).

Treaty of Amsterdam comes into effect.

Tampere Declaration proclaims the start of development of an Area of Freedom Security and Justice as the next initiative toward a unified Europe.

2001    Treaty of Nice signed. Contains provisions to improve and extend weighted majority voting. Also extends functions of the Court of First Instance and permits hearing cases in chambers as the general rule.

Charter of Fundamental Rights proclaimed by the Council, Parliament and Commission Presidents.

European Council meeting at Laeken issues declaration on moving forward with a draft Constitution.

2002    Euro notes and coins placed in circulation in Eurozone and use of former national currencies phased out within six months.

Treaty of Nice ratified in Ireland at second attempt.

ECSC ceases to exist on July 23, 2002.

2003    Treaty of Nice enters into effect.

Signature of Act of Accession of Cyprus, Czech Republic, Estonia, Hungary, Latvia, Lithuania, Malta, Poland, the Slovak Republic and Slovenia.

Intergovernmental Conference starts work on draft Constitution.

Constitution draft presented to European Council, founders on Qualified Majority Voting proposal.

| 2004 | The 10 Member States that signed the 2003 Accession Treaty formally accede. |
|------|---|
| | European Council agrees text of Treaty Establishing a Constitution. |
| | France and Netherlands reject proposed Constitution Treaty in referenda. |
| 2006 | Slovenia joins the eurozone. |
| 2007 | Bulgaria and Romania accede. |
| | Agreement on Treaty of Lisbon, replacing the Treaty establishing a Constitution, signed December 13, 2007. |
| 2008 | Financial crisis hits European banks. Member States take drastic measures to shore up failing institutions. European Commission attempts to assert control based on the State Aids provisions of the EC Treaty. |
| 2009 | Lisbon Treaty comes into effect (December 1) and the EU and EC are merged into a single structure. |
| 2010 | Financial crisis turns into a sovereign debt crisis. |
| 2011 | Greece, Ireland and Portugal receive bailout funds from a new European Stability Facility set up by eurozone governments. Pressure to create a European "economic government", issue common Eurobonds and other measures. |

## [B]  Founding Principles

The avowed purpose of the EEC Treaty was the creation of an ever closer union among the peoples of Europe. This was to be achieved primarily through the creation of a "common market." The language found in the TEU today is a far cry from this modest beginning. The Union is in effect to be the embodiment of democracy and human rights. This is a reflection of the moves toward political union in the first TEU, and of the evolution of the European Parliament into a directly elected legislative body with broad powers to adopt legislation, in conjunction with the Council.

## [C]  Membership (and Related Matters)

***The attraction of membership*** The original six member states of the ECSC, EEC and EAEC were the Federal Republic of Germany, France, The Netherlands, Belgium, Luxembourg and Italy. The chronology above indicates the dates on which states acceded thereafter. It is noteworthy that many of those states had previously had undemocratic regimes, and the Union, with its economic prosperity and dedication to democracy and human rights, offered a powerful incentive for reform in those states. This was true of Greece, which was under a military dictatorship in the early 1970s, Spain and Portugal with their aging fascist regimes and, later on, the countries of central Europe that had only recently broken free of communism and the Soviet yoke.

Other member states had initially had reservations about or legal impediments to joining based on policies of neutrality — Sweden, Finland, Austria and Ireland, but had concluded that the Union was not a military alliance. Ireland is still not a member of NATO, however, because it regards Northern Ireland as territory under occupation of a foreign power and therefore could not be militarily allied with it.

*Territory* The European Union is not a state, and thus does not possess any territory in its own right. Its jurisdiction rests on the territorial sovereignty of the Member States and is in most respects coextensive with it. EC 299/TFEU 355 contains some express detailed provisions relating to the territorial scope of application of the Treaties. Certain territories outside the European Continent are treated as part of Union territory due to their incorporation into the internal structure of a Member state. These are listed in EC 299/TFEU 255 (1).

*Variable integration* There are a number of other forms of integration among Member States that exist and are endorsed by the Treaties:

-   The **Benelux** union, which was a pre-existing Economic Union of Belgium, Netherlands and Luxembourg. It did not entail a monetary union for the three, but there was a monetary union between Belgium and Luxembourg, now superseded by the euro.

-   Regions within Member States. These have representation in the **Committee of the Regions.** See EC 263-265/TFEU 305-307. The Committee must be consulted on some kinds of EU action. The recognition of a particular status for regions of Member States is actually quite significant because it suggests that the central power of Member State governments is yielding to regional interests within them in the context of European Union activity.

-   Since the accession of the UK and Denmark, there has been a continuing friction between states that wish to proceed with unification at a faster pace than others. Although the UK and Denmark have at times shown particular reluctance to endorse new initiatives, other Member States have also asserted objections. Perhaps the most obvious example is the adoption of the euro, which is used by 16 of the 27 Member states. Moreover, there are instances where certain aspects of EU law do not apply: for example, the Charter of Fundamental Rights does not fully apply in the UK; and most of the Schengen arrangement does not fully apply to the UK and Ireland. Descriptions such as a "two-speed Europe" or a Europe of variable geometry have been used to describe this rather peculiar anomaly. In the Treaties, there have been since 1992 specific provisions, known as **Enhanced Cooperation**, that permit Member States to use EU institutions to advance integration beyond the stage reached by the EU as a whole. It may be noted that while the euro appears to be a case of enhanced cooperation, it was from the beginning envisaged as a common currency for the entire Union and the wording of the TFEU continues to treat it this way, recognizing, however, some exceptions.

*External relationships* Many third countries have entered into various forms of agreements with the Union as a result of which some Union law applies in those territories. Perhaps most notable among these arrangements is the **European Economic Area or EEA** This was set up by a Treaty among the EU, the Member

States and former EFTA states in 1994. It now covers the EU plus Liechtenstein, Norway and Iceland. Much EU legislation applies to the EEA. However, the non-EU countries have no direct vote or say in the adoption of EU legislation.

Other countries or territories with special relationships include:

- The **"Overseas countries and territories"** listed in Annex II to the TFEU. These are dependent territories of various Member States. Their special relationship with the Union is described in EC 182-188/TFEU 198-204.

- The **ACP Countries** African, Caribbean and Pacific countries that had special links with a Member State as colonies.

- **Countries having an Association Agreement** An association agreement between the EU and a third country (to which the Member States are usually also parties) may be entered into pursuant to EC 310/TFEU 217. Such an agreement usually provides for import privileges for the third country and other favourable trade arrangements. Association agreements with other European states are usually a prelude to Accession.

*Languages* The ECSC was authentic only in the French version and the working language of the institutions was French. All subsequent treaties were authentic in all official languages and that number has grown to 23 (with some Member States sharing a common language, of course), while Ireland only more recently insisted on adding the Irish language. All legislation is produced in all these official languages but the Court has held that specialized agencies may operate in the more widely known languages only. A major factor holding up the creation of a European Patent is the question of whether patents would be issued in only a few widely spoken languages (English, French, German).

*The Member States in international law* In the Union structure, the Member States have not subordinated their international standing to the point where they have become political units within a single state for purposes of international law. This gives rise to some interesting issues regarding their relations with each other, which technically remain "international." They all maintain embassies in each others' countries and enter into treaties with each other or through multilateral processes that may or may not also involve the Union, depending on the scope of its competences.

## [D]   The Institutions of the Union

*The original structures* The ECSC Treaty had constituted a High Authority as the principal body to administer the Coal and Steel Community. This body stood apart from the Member States and had significant independent rulemaking powers, perhaps the truest example of a "supranational" body. The Treaty also constituted a Council of Ministers and a Court of Justice, as well as an assembly of parliamentarians from the legislatures of the Member States. The model was adopted in modified form by the EEC and EAEC Treaties. Although the High Authority continued to exist, a parallel body, in the form of the Commission, was established under each of the 1957 Treaties to drive the economic integration process and the promotion of atomic energy respectively.

In 1967, the ECSC Council and High Authority and the EEC/EAEC Councils and Commission were merged, retaining their various powers but operating as one body. The Court of Justice and Assembly of the ECSC had already been unified in the EEC/EAEC institutional structures in 1957. Only the institutions were merged, not the Treaties. While the ECSC Treaty has expired, the EAEC Treaty still exists and thus the Council and Commission still act in their capacity under that Treaty or under the TFEU as the subject matter dictates.

Following the successful conclusion of the transitional period, the Member States started to explore the next stages of unification. Such steps necessarily entailed political action. This resulted in the evolution of the European Council.

*Location* The location of the institutions (as shown in the Template) has not been without controversy. The choice of Luxembourg dates back to the foundation of the ECSC, when the High Authority, the Council secretariat and the Court were located there, while the original Assembly was to meet in Strasbourg but was required to hold some plenary sessions in Luxembourg where its secretariat was located. It was a convenient compromise with Luxembourg sitting between the two sponsor states of the ECSC. The choice of Brussels for the EEC/EAEC Commission and Council arose largely out of the willingness of the Brussels government to make buildings available. The Parliament was then given a second seat in Strasbourg to satisfy a French need to have at least one institution on its soil. It started to hold committee meetings in Brussels, however, and has for a long time continued to express a wish to relocate there altogether. However, at the Edinburgh summit in 1992 and as part of the overall agreement on moving forward with political and monetary union, the Member States agreed that its Strasbourg home should be formally ratified. Thus the Parliament today functions in three locations with all the inconvenience and expense that that entails.

## [E]  Objectives of the Treaties

*The internal market* Initially, and as noted above, the ECSC (within its narrow scope) and more generally the EEC aimed to set up a **Common Market**, (EC 2/TFEU repealed). Until the end of the 1970s this was the name by which the original Communities were more generally called in English. The concept connotes a market in goods, services, labor, capital and establishment extending over the territory of all Member States.

A common market represents one stage in economic integration. At the least integrated level are free trade areas, where each country agrees to allow goods from the others to enter free of duties and tariffs. However, goods from third countries are still subject to each country's own tariff system. EFTA and NAFTA are examples of such a structure. Next in level of integration is the customs union, where there is a unified external tariff so that third country goods can circulate freely among all the members once they have cleared the customs of any of the countries. A common market is the next level — where in addition to free movement of goods, the other factors of production — labor, capital, services, businesses, are also free to move without hindrance. Finally, an economic and monetary union comes into existence when the Member States agree to adopt a single currency and a single economic policy for all Member States.

Despite the creation of institutions capable of evolving into federal authorities, the EC Treaty initially made detailed provision only for purely economic matters, and even there focused chiefly on the dismantling of obstacles to trade and movement of people rather than on the transfer of authority to those institutions. General economic policy was left in the hands of the Member States.

The obstacles to trade and movement of peoples may be thought of as "direct" or "indirect." Direct obstacles consist of those laws and regulations that exist solely to restrict exports and imports and the free flow of people, services and money. Indirect obstacles may be found among the myriad laws that serve another purpose (e.g., consumer protection, professional competence or protection from excessive government expenditure) but yet operate to inhibit commerce among the Member States.

With respect to customs duties, former EC 12 provided for a standstill on duties existing at the date of the Treaty, and former EC 13 had provided for progressive abolition over a transitional period. In fact, the phase out of all customs duties was completed ahead of schedule and these transitional provisions became obsolete.

Quota restrictions are taken care of (now) by EC 28-30/TFEU 34-36. As originally intended, these articles were meant to abolish, over the transitional period, the quotas imposed by Member States on imports and exports of goods, essentially by progressively opening up such restrictions until they became unlimited. As will become evident in later chapters of this book, EC 28/TFEU 34 has since taken on a very expanded role and is one of the most influential provisions of the EC Treaty/TFEU in terms of the development of the EU.

The above actions are not, however, enough to remove all direct obstacles. In the first place, internal tax systems, particularly indirect taxes such as sales taxes, may directly penalize imported goods. Thus the Treaty contains a provision, in EC 90/TFEU 110, that prohibits all discriminatory elements of such systems. Note that this does not remove the problems created by the mere differences between such systems that could make it uneconomic to compete with domestic goods. For example, a sales tax may be imposed at various stages of production, resulting in a substantial tax on the various materials going into a product being paid prior to the finished article's exportation to another country, where the aggregate sales tax is much lower. This problem was dealt with through the adoption of a uniform sales tax — value added tax.

The founders also had to contend with the existence of national monopolies that were required to, or in practice did, buy only locally produced products such as cigarettes, matches, alcoholic drinks, and various forms of energy. Often these also had a revenue-producing character (see EC 31/TFEU 37).

The founders were unable to agree on a free "unregulated" market in agricultural goods. As in the United States today, no country in Europe left farmers to the mercy of world markets. This industry is of course extraordinarily vulnerable to swings in supply and demand, and every industrialized country has some form of policy in place designed to even out those swings. Since these policies were very different from one country to another, it was thought vital that the EU should adopt a common policy in this area. Hence, EC 32 through 38/TFEU 38-44 deal with the establishment of a common policy in agriculture.

Finally, as regards goods, however successful the Treaty might have been in removing government restrictions, there was nonetheless a multitude of restrictions in the private sector directly discriminating against out-of-State goods. One of the functions of the competition law provisions found in EC 81-85/TFEU 101-105 was to assure the removal of such "private" restrictions. Thus, although today that policy has primarily the same purpose as U.S. Antitrust Law, the EC Treaty competition provisions serve the additional purpose of breaking down private national barriers to trade.

If restrictions are lifted on the free movement of goods, it then becomes necessary to remove restrictions on the ability to pay for them: in other words, exchange controls must be abolished at least to that extent. This is the function of the original article 106 (deleted by the TEU as no longer necessary as a result of more sweeping measures removing restrictions on the free flow of money and capital under EC 56/TFEU 63).

This then takes care of the interstate restrictions on the movement of goods. However, what of goods entering the market from third countries? There will be a problem if, say, France charges a 10% duty while Germany charges 30%, presumably leading to a distortion of trade in favor of France and encouraging circumvention of the German tariff. To remove this potential distortion one could do two things: either not extend the common market to goods of non-EU origin; or establish a common customs tariff. The former solution applies in so-called free trade areas, such as EFTA or NAFTA. However, there is a problem associated with it: every time the goods cross the frontier between two Member States, there will have to be proof as to the origin of the goods so that duties on non-Member States' goods are properly charged. This means that internal customs frontiers must remain in place. Clearly, this offends against the notion of a "common market"; so the second solution was dictated. EC 25 – 27/TFEU 30-32 therefore set up a common customs tariff, again subject to the phase-in provisions. This tariff has been in operation since 1969. Former EC 10 had provided that goods imported from third countries should be in free circulation: no duties were to be imposed by the Member States once they had entered EU customs territory. See now EC 14/TFEU 26.

The abolition of customs duties and quotas between Member States was achieved during a **Transitional Period.** This ran from the entry into force of the EEC Treaty until July 1969 — during which all customs duties and quotas between Member States were progressively abolished. The Transitional Period was of significance in some of the earlier cases because of consequences that ensued upon its expiry but it is no longer referenced in the EC Treaty/TFEU.

At the same time, a common customs tariff cannot survive without a more general common commercial policy, particularly toward the outside world. This is taken care of now by EC 131-134/TFEU 207-208.

The common market also contemplated the removal of restrictions on the provision of services across national frontiers. Most restrictions relate to the right of a person temporarily to exercise his or her profession in another Member State.

Besides restrictions generally on working in the host state, there is a more fundamental problem: the person may not possess the qualifications required by the host state. The Treaty could not immediately deal with this issue, although, as we shall see, the European Court of Justice has been able to interpret EC 49-50/TFEU 56-57 in a manner that reduces the impact of this difficulty.

As with agriculture in the goods sector, so transport as a service required special attention. See EC 70-80/TFEU 90-100.

In a true common market it is also necessary to ensure that the product or the service can be produced anywhere — which means having the labor and capital in the right place. In other words, it is necessary to guarantee that people — workers and self-employed people — can move freely. The EC Treaty/TFEU deals with the free movement of workers in EC 39-42/TFEU 45-48, specifically addressing immigration, work permit and social security limitations.

The free movement of self-employed persons entails in essence their right to establish their business in a state of which they are not nationals. This is known as the "freedom of establishment." See EC 43–48/TFEU 49-55. Once again, as with services, the problem of differing professional qualifications could not be addressed immediately by the Treaty, even though this clearly represented the greatest hindrance.

So far as capital is concerned, the intention it seems in 1957 was simply to free up movement to the extent necessary to permit exercise of the other freedoms. This at least was as far as the founders could venture politically. Restrictions on the movement of capital could not however survive the advent of the common currency and were thus prohibited after the 1992 TEU (EC 56–60/TFEU 63-67).

From the common market concept it was hoped that further integration, including political integration, would develop. Had the Member States wished to limit themselves purely to trade liberalization (i.e., through the establishment of a free trade area), they could have agreed merely to eliminate tariff barriers on the movement of goods, an action that in itself would not have required the creation of an international legal entity (i.e., the "Community", now succeeded by the Union) or substantial legislative, executive and judicial authorities. The immediate need after the expiry of the transitional period was to create a more genuine market, where indirect obstacles would be eliminated. Perhaps the greatest indirect obstacles to free movement of people were the disparities among the states relating to professional qualifications. The same was true of goods with respect to technical standards.

The glacial pace of efforts in regard to indirect obstacles is what led to the SEA and the 1992 program. This initiative identified a new term, the **single market** (now renamed the **Internal Market**) (EC 14/TFEU 26) intended to reflect a more cohesive market than the term "common market". As a supplement to the formal harmonization process, a new process known as the Open Method of Coordination was introduced at the Lisbon European Council in 2000. It contemplated that the EU institutions would assist the Member States in developing their own policies and coordination across the whole spectrum of governmental activity. It entailed fixing guidelines, establishing quantitative and qualitative criteria and benchmarks, translating these guidelines into national policies by setting specific targets and adopting measures, and periodic monitoring and review. It has met with only mixed success.

*Economic and monetary union* As far back as 1969 the Member States had recognized that a truly common market eventually entailed the same degree of economic and monetary union as exists in the United States. Without it, the market would continue to be subject to distortions arising from currency fluctuations and differing economic goals. However, "EMU" entails the surrender by the Member States of autonomy and sovereignty in the management of the economy and fiscal policy — an area of activity that is closely associated with the role of government. There was, therefore, a political hurdle to overcome.

There was also a practical hurdle. In 1969, the economies of the Member States were substantially different, as were some of the goals of economic policy. Thus, it seemed then that monetary union might have to come first. This, however, would result in tremendous dislocation if introduced without regard to the differing economic conditions. Given the instability of the 1970s, largely arising from the oil price shock of 1973 and the disappearance of fixed exchange rates, EMU was destined, it seemed, to remain a dead letter. Then, in 1979, the introduction of the European Monetary System (EMS) produced a narrow fluctuation band for currency exchange rates that required the Member States to follow the policies of the German Bundesbank, as the authority controlling the single largest component of the European Currency Unit (ECU). This was an "artificial" currency unit consisting of a basket of all Member States' currencies and used for accounting and legislative purposes by the EU, including intervention and similar prices under the Agricultural Policy. It was preceded by the "European Unit of Account" and before that, the "Unit of Account".

The ECU consisted of specific and fixed amounts of Member States currencies. The amount of each currency reflected the country's share of collective Gross National Product and its share of collective trade. The different amounts of national currency within the ECU were used to calculate the relative values of each national currency, on a daily basis.

As already indicated, the TEU of 1992 marked a turning point in respect of at least monetary union. The composition of the ECU basket was frozen on 1 November 1993 when the Treaty on European Union came into effect. The monetary amounts of each currency making up the ECU were irrevocably fixed until the euro was introduced.

The move to a single currency began in mid-1990 with the abolition of exchange controls in most states and the entry of the United Kingdom into the Exchange Rate Mechanism of the European Monetary System. The Maastricht Treaty set out the timetable for the second and third phase of this process. In Stage 2, which began on January 1, 1994, a European Monetary Institute was established, whose governing body comprised Central Bank Governors. The European Monetary Institute (EMI) was totally independent of any other governmental bodies. The EMI established rules, standards and objectives for the Member States so that, over a period of five years, their monetary policy would be coordinated. From January 1, 1994, no Member State was allowed to impose any new restrictions on the free movement of capital except by permission of the Council.

By January 1, 1999 all those Member States (except the United Kingdom, Denmark and Sweden) that had met the budgetary and other monetary preconditions set forth in the "Budgetary Deficit Protocol" and a "Convergence Protocol" irrevocably locked the exchange rates of their currencies as against the ECU. A European System of Central Banks (ESCB), administered by a European Central Bank (ECB), took over responsibility for the single currency, which was named the euro, which replaced the national currencies as an accounting and settlement denomination. In early 2002, the central banks of the participating Member States began issuing euro currency and redeeming the existing national currencies and that process ended in June 2002. Denmark, Sweden and the United Kingdom exercised a specific right not to participate in this third stage.

Today, EC 98–124/TFEU 120-142, together with Protocols on the Statute of the ESCB and Excessive Deficit Procedure, deal with management of monetary policy (in the hands of the European Central Bank). The TFEU also describes a Stability and Growth Pact that is an agreement among all Member States on criteria for economic policy aimed at constraining budget deficits and maintaining price stability. This was considered necessary to support the anti-inflation policy required of the ECB in managing the euro. As the financial crisis of 2008/2009 demonstrated, the Pact was a failure and as of the time of writing, moves are underway to set up a closer form of coordination of economic policy and create a permanent mechanism for intervening to support states that use the euro in times of crisis.

***Area of Freedom, Security and Justice or AFSJ*** This concept was endorsed by the Tampere declaration of 1999. It embraces the provisions that started out in the old TEU relating to Justice and Home Affairs (JHA) — cooperation in criminal justice, asylum and visa policy for third country nationals and free movement for citizens. Asylum and visa policy was placed under the Community by the Treaty of Amsterdam, as were the arrangements under the Schengen Agreement (of 1985 described *infra* § 2.08). After Amsterdam, the JHA provisions were reconstituted as "Police and Justice cooperation in criminal matters" or PJCC. The PJCC provisions were moved into the TFEU by the Lisbon Treaty. The shift into the TFEU means that measures can be adopted based on the procedures in that Treaty including qualified majority voting in the Council and Parliamentary approval. Thus, AFSJ has ceased to be an intergovernmental arrangement and is now fully integrated into the Union's legislative structure.

***Common Foreign and Security Policy*** (***CFSP***) The CFSP came into existence through the original TEU, and was, like JHA and PJCC, a form of intergovernmental cooperation, held outside the legislative and majority-vote decision-making structures of the EC Treaty. It had its own defined forms of action based on unanimity. It also envisaged a process for setting up a common defense policy, at the time based on a plan to use the Western European Union.

CFSP embraces all matters falling within the notion of foreign policy except as regards matters already falling within the scope of the EC/TFEU (this is explained further in Chapters 10 and 12). It is, however, based on a concept of selective action. The Member States retain their foreign policy and national security powers but decide on a case-by-case basis which ones to coordinate within the CFSP.

The Lisbon Treaty left the CFSP in the TEU and thus still standing apart from the EU's normal legislative and decision-making processes described in the TFEU. In fact, the TEU is explicit that there can be no legislative action under the CSFP. However, the special forms of action have been abolished and replaced by the "decision", in other words, a normalized EU form of action. Review by the Court of Justice is, except in certain specific circumstances, excluded.

By virtue of the Lisbon reforms, the EU now has for the first time an official foreign minister in the form of the High Representative, and a form of diplomatic corps known as the External Action Service.

Member States retain their standing in the world community (e.g., diplomatic representation and membership of international organizations) but must use their position to advance any common policies. A national of any Member State is entitled to full consular protection from any of the Member States representatives if that national's own country does not have appropriate representation.

Although the TEU does not yet go very far in extending foreign policy to encompass defense, new TEU 42 describes how a common security and defense policy for the Union will be developed.

## [F]  Autonomy

The doctrine of autonomy applies to EU law rather than the Union itself. Here it may simply be noted that the Union has received certain sovereign powers and that its law must prevail over national law. These are sweeping statements of great significance that are explored in Chapter 3. Clearly this distinguishes the Union from other international organizations in a very pronounced way.

## § 2.02  THE COMPONENTS OF EUROPEAN LAW

### [A]  Constitutional Documents

*Treaties* Over its history, the Union has developed through successive treaties among the Member States. Of these, the two that today represent the constitutional base are the Treaty on European Union and the Treaty on the Functioning of the European Union (TFEU), formerly the Treaty establishing the European Community (EC), itself previously named the Treaty establishing the European Economic Community (EEC). The European Atomic Energy Community treaty (EAEC) continues to exist, as does the EAEC outside the specific structure of the Union. Many of the other treaties listed below were amending Treaties that essentially were spent once they had carried out their amending function. They did, however, mark important stages in the development of the EU and are referred to in the ECJ's decisions. The following treaties were of particular significance:

- **ECSC Treaty or Treaty of Paris** This is the European Coal and Steel Community Treaty dated April 18, 1951, usually cited as "ECSC" as in "article 31

ECSC." It expired in 2002. The immediate goal of the first of the European Community treaties was to place the coal and steel industries of the Member States under a supranational control. These responsibilities have now been subsumed into the TFEU.

- **EAEC Treaty or Euratom Treaty** This is the European Atomic Energy Community Treaty dated March 25, 1957. This Treaty and the EAEC continue to exist as the sole remaining "Community." A number of Member States have called for its updating and improvement, noting that many reforms elsewhere have not been mirrored in this Treaty. For some reflections on this rather neglected Treaty, see Cusak, *A Tale of Two Treaties: An Assessment of the Euratom Treaty in Relation to the EC Treaty*, (2003) CML REV. 117.

- **EEC Treaty** or **Treaty of Rome** The Treaty establishing the European Economic Community, it was signed on March 25, 1957, together with the Convention on Common Institutions, Court statute, German declarations in relation to the former East Germany, and various Protocols. Political goals were still very much in the minds of those who, in 1955, turned their attention to the creation of a common market — seen in essence as an interim step — the groundwork for an eventual political union. The EEC Treaty became simply the Treaty Establishing the European Community (EC Treaty) and was revised and renamed the Treaty on the Functioning of the European Union (TFEU) as result of the Lisbon Treaty.

Since the EAEC and EEC Treaties were both signed in Rome they are sometimes collectively referred to as the "Rome Treaties".

Further Treaties or agreements have now been incorporated into the present provisions of, or effected amendments to, the TEU and TFEU and have ceased to have any independent force:

- **Merger Treaty** Treaty Establishing a single Council and a single Commission of the European Communities, dated April 8, 1965 cited as the Merger Treaty, J.O. 1967 152/1 (July 13, 1967). It has been repealed and its provisions are found in the TFEU.

- **1st Treaty on Budgetary Provisions** This Treaty established the budgetary provisions of the EC and Merger Treaties. The budgetary provisions are now in the TFEU.

- **2nd Budgetary Treaty** This Treaty amending certain financial provisions of the Treaties establishing the European Communities and of the Treaty establishing a Single Commission of the European Communities, dated July 22, 1977 provided for a rebate to the UK. The budgetary provisions are now in the TFEU.

- **Act on Direct Elections** This was a combined Council decision and Act of the Member States dated September 20, 1976, providing for direct elections to the European Parliament starting in 1979.

- **Single European Act or SEA** The Single European Act of February 17 and 28, 1986, (in force July 1987) amended the then EEC Treaty to accelerate the creation of the internal market (the so-called 1992 program). Those amendments have since been superseded by further amending Treaties.

**- Treaty on European Union or Treaty of Maastricht** This Treaty, which came into force in 1993, established the European Union as a structure separate from the European Communities. As a result of the Lisbon Treaty, it now provides for an integrated structure encompassing the former European Community and Union.

**- Treaty of Amsterdam** This amending Treaty was adopted at the Amsterdam European Council on 16 and 17 June 1997 and signed on 2 October 1997 by the Foreign Ministers of the 15 Member States. It entered into force on 1 May 1999. It amended certain provisions of the Treaties, created an EU employment policy, transferred to the Communities some of the areas in the field of justice and home affairs (becoming "justice and criminal matters"), reformed the common foreign and security policy (CFSP), extended qualified majority voting and enabled closer cooperation between Member States. The amendments it introduced have been superseded by subsequent Treaties, most notably the Lisbon Treaty.

**- Treaty of Nice** This amending Treaty was adopted at the Nice European Council in December 2000, signed on February 26, 2001, entered into force on February 1, 2003. It was intended to improve the working of the European institutions before the arrival of 12 new Member States in 2004 and 2007. It limited the size and composition of the Commission, extended qualified majority voting, set up a new weighting of votes within the Council and made the strengthened cooperation arrangements more flexible. The amendments it effected have since been superseded by the Lisbon Treaty. The Declaration on the Future of the Union, annexed to the Treaty, set out the next steps to be taken to deepen the institutional reforms and to make sure that the Treaty of Nice was just one stage in this process.

The **Treaty establishing a Constitution for Europe** This was signed in October 2004 and was intended to merge the EU and the EC into a single EU with legal personality as well as reform the voting system in the Council and amend other institutional matters. Although ratified by 18 Member States, it was defeated in referenda in The Netherlands and France, and was abandoned.

**- Treaty of Lisbon** This amending Treaty replaced the Constitution Treaty and was initially known as the Reform Treaty. (Signed December 13, 2007). Most of the content of the Constitution Treaty reappeared in different form in this Treaty, which amends the EU and EC Treaties rather than replacing them. Only in Ireland was a public referendum required for ratification. The initial referendum failed but a year later the proposition passed by a wide margin and the Treaty entered into effect on December 1, 2009. Since it operated to amend the existing Treaties, it was essentially spent from the moment it became effective.

**- Various Accession Treaties/Acts of Accession** Each Member State not part of the original six signed a Treaty of Accession to which was appended an "Act of Accession". These documents mostly deal with transitional matters, adaptation of legislation and consequential changes to the Institutional arrangements. However, Article 102 of the Act of Accession for the UK, Ireland and Denmark contained an important provision leading to exclusive competence for the EU in the conservation of marine resources. Additionally, the Greenland Treaty of March 13, 1984 provided for the secession of Greenland from the Union (although Denmark remains responsible for foreign affairs).

***The Luxembourg Accords*** This Agreement of January 28 and 29, 1966, concerns decisions involving a vital national interest. It is not officially a legally effective act, merely an understanding among the Member States. Although it is cited not infrequently by Member State Governments as the ultimate protection for their national interests and has probably influenced a preference for unanimity even where qualified majority voting is permitted, it has no legal force in the EU legal order — it is a purely a political understanding.

***The Charter of Fundamental Rights*** This document may rightly be called the first constitutional act of the European Union itself. It was adopted by the institutions by proclamation on December 13, 2007. Unlike the earlier proclamation of the same document at the time of the Treaty of Nice, the 2007 proclamation is given legal force by the TEU as amended by the Lisbon Treaty.

Much of the material in this book concerns what was previously the Treaty establishing the European Community, as the body that has most truly evolved into an autonomous legal system. Case law relating to it will for the most part be just as relevant to the EU as the Community's successor. The ECSC was established for 50 years and disappeared in 2002, with its responsibilities either abandoned or absorbed into the (then) EC. However, some of the early ECSC judicial decisions still have relevance given the similar structure to, and close relationship with, the EC.

***Working with the Treaties*** Some EC Treaty articles were renumbered at various points over the years, while the Treaties of Amsterdam and Lisbon effected a complete renumbering of both the EC and EU Treaties. These changes mean that the article numbering of the post-Lisbon Treaties is completely different from what existed prior to Lisbon, and the same was true of the numbering post-Amsterdam versus the pre-Amsterdam ordering. For ease of reference to the current version of the Treaties, as far as case reports are concerned, the convention has been adopted in this work of placing the *current* (post-Lisbon) numbering in square brackets after the original reference, while all notes and comments refer to the both the pre-Lisbon and post-Lisbon numbering (for example "EC 28/TFEU 34"). For the Treaty on the European Union, this is indicated by "Old TEU" and "New TEU" while for the Treaty on the Functioning of the European Union, reference is to "EC" and "TFEU".

All notes and comments in this book have been recast (except where the context demands otherwise) so as to eliminate allusions to the formal distinctions between the Union and the European Community and between European Union law and the law of the European Communities. Where distinctions need to be drawn, reference is to the subject matter of the TEU or the TFEU, since this distinction *does* remain after entry into force of the Treaty of Lisbon. The term "EU law" is used generically for the law of both the TEU and the TFEU regardless of the former distinctions, and, in the interests of simplicity, the term "EU" is used for both the Union and the former European Community.

## [B]   Legal Acts of the Union

*The basic forms of action available to the Union* The ECSC Treaty had provided that action by the High Authority could be through "decisions", "recommendations" and "opinions". Decisions were actually forms of administrative rulemaking that were directly applicable in all the Member States. The EEC and EAEC Treaties used the term "regulation" in place of the ECSC "decision" and provided also for "directives", "decisions" and "recommendations".

These forms of legal act have survived to the present, although in the Constitution Treaty there had been provision to rename regulations as European laws, a more apt description of their current scope and importance. As already noted, as a result of Lisbon, a formal distinction now exists for the first time between legislative acts and delegated or implementing acts, even though the acts themselves are in both cases still in one of the prescribed designations. In future, subsidiary rules will bear the added designation of "implementing" or "delegated" in their titles. This is a marked improvement from the prior situation although such a distinction existed *de facto*.

EU legislative acts are published in the 23 official languages of the EU. Thus, the Official Journal of the EU (OJ) appears in 23 versions every day. Only regulations and directives are required to be published and appear in the "L" series of the OJ, while decisions, recommendations, and written parliamentary questions appear in the "C" series. Other materials appearing in the "C" series include such matters as may be required as a result of specific procedures in EU legislation, such as notices of proceedings in competition law investigations, European scale invitations to tender etc. Certain notices of European Court proceedings and decisions also are published in the C series.

Citation of the Official Journal L and C Series varies. In this book, usage is: "[Year] OJ L or C issue/page; Translations of issues adopted prior to UK Accession: Special Edition OJ (SE) I or II, + page; French version of Journal: JO (JOCE in French language texts).

- **Regulations** are referenced in full in EU documents by their number, year, relevant Treaty and the institution that adopted it. In this book the reference is abridged to the number and year, e.g., Reg. 1/2003 and it may be assumed that the act was adopted under the EC Treaty/TFEU unless expressly stated otherwise.

- **Directives** are referred to by abbreviated year and number, e.g., Dir. 68/360 until 2000 after which the full year designation is used. (e.g. Directive 2006/123)

- **Decisions** of the Commission or Council are cited by year and number, e.g., Dec. 74/215; (usually by name also in competition cases). The actual date is also often referred to.

So far as "private" or civil/commercial law is concerned, much EU law (outside particular areas such as agriculture) that affects the activities of individuals in their everyday lives and in commercial matters is embodied in directives. This is, of course, because the directive is the primary vehicle for the harmonization and mutual recognition programs of the EU. There is no real equivalent in the U.S. legislative system: much of the body of law contained in directives is either embodied in parallel or exclusive federal legislation (e.g., the Federal Trade Commission's role in consumer protection) or is in fact nonexistent as a body of law in the federal system. In the latter case, in the United States, states may model their laws on the "leading jurisdiction" in order to maintain their competitive position. An example is corporation law, where the Delaware code has provided the model for many other jurisdictions. In other areas, the alignment of state laws has come about through the various commissions on restatement or the establishment of uniform codes, such as the UCC. In yet other areas, states have tended to follow the independently existing federal model (e.g., securities regulation, antitrust).

Thus, what would be federal policy matters in the United States are dealt with through directives in the EU. U.S. federal law in these areas often has a preemptive effect, but directives do not "preempt" national legislation as such: they require it to take a certain form and content. In practice, however, the distinction is not a very tenable one. Application of a federal statute and the enforcement of a directive may have much the same result — contrary state law is unenforceable. The major difference once again is that the issues will be decided ultimately in the courts of the Member States in the European Union, and not in a federal forum.

***Superseded forms of acts*** The EEC Treaty envisioned the use of "**conventions**" in the context of harmonization of civil law outside the specific harmonization scope of the Treaty. Examples are the **Brussels Convention on Jurisdiction and Enforcement of Judgements in Civil and Commercial Matters**, [1978] OJ L304/79). and the **Lugano Convention**, Sept. 16,1988 O.J. 1988, L. 319, 9, which extended the Brussels Convention to Austria, Switzerland, Finland, Iceland, Norway, and Sweden. This form of harmonization no longer exists. In future such measures will take place by regulation or directive, and indeed the Brussels Convention has itself been mostly replaced by Regulation 44/2001 [2001] OJ L 12 (some aspects involved non-member States to which an EU regulation would not of course apply).

In the original TEU, further forms of action were described, with the intent of distinguishing them as intergovernmental and thus outside the Community structure. Acts adopted in these forms of course continue to exist, subject to provisions for their gradual mutation into the standard EU forms of action, but all have been abolished as regards future action. They were as follows:

- **Framework Decisions** (Old TEU 34/new TEU repealed). Used in the context of PJCC.

- **Joint actions** Used in connection with the CFSP.

- **Common positions** (not to be confused with the common position as a step in the EU legislative process), a form of action under PJCC.

- **Conventions** The convention was also recognized in the former TEU 18,21, 22, 27, 34, 36 and 39 in the context of CFSP and PJCC. This was to be a means to provide for coordination in these areas. A convention was adopted by the Council, acting unanimously after consulting the European Parliament, and entered into force when it has been ratified by at least half the Member States. It was rarely used and is now abolished. An example was the **Dublin Convention**, designed to determine which Member State would have responsibility for processing asylum applications under the common European Asylum system now provided for in the EC Treaty/TFEU ([1997] OJ C 254/1).

In a third usage, "Convention" continues to be used in the sense of a process to handle Treaty revisions, though not as the name for any resulting treaty.

## § 2.03   THE LEGISLATURE

### [A]   Evolution of the Legislative Process

Until the SEA, "legislation" was adopted by the Council, and the role of the Parliament had been at best consultative. The SEA introduced the "cooperation procedure" by which the Parliament became entitled to the right to vote on acts in certain defined subject areas. The procedure envisaged in effect a two-chamber structure but the Council had the last word if conciliation between the two chambers failed. The original TEU then introduced a second form of procedure where the Parliament effectively had the last word, known as the 'Co-decision" procedure. Such acts are described as acts of the Council and the Parliament. As a result of Lisbon, the cooperation procedure has been abolished, while the scope of subject matter subject to the co-decision procedure (EC 251/TFEU 194) has been greatly expanded.

### [B]   The Legislative Bodies

*The Council* (EC 202 – 210/TEU 16 and TFEU 237 – 243). The Council, originally known as the Council of Ministers, has always played a pivotal and often solo role in the adoption of what today are called legislative acts.

Since inception, it has consisted of one Minister representing each Member State. However, the minister in question depends on the subject matter of the meeting. TFEU 236 describes the procedure for determining the various Council configurations. These are chaired by the "presidency" with the exception of the Foreign Affairs configuration, which is presided over by the High Representative.

The EU website describes 10 different Council configurations:

General Affairs

Foreign Affairs Economic and Financial Affairs

Justice and Home Affairs (JHA)

Employment, Social Policy, Health and Consumer Affairs

Competitiveness (internal market, industry, research and space)

Transport, Telecommunications and Energy

Agriculture and Fisheries

Environment

Education, youth, culture and sport

Unlike the European Council, which is chaired by the President, an individual, the Presidency of the Council rotates around the Member States at six monthly intervals. Often a Member State's turn in the Presidency is the occasion for it to show its commitment to Europe and six months is long enough in running the Council to produce results. The regular rotation of the Presidency obviates any risk of hegemony. By exception, following Lisbon, the Foreign Affairs configuration is always to be chaired by the High Representative.

At the level below the Council, is **Coreper** (EC 207/TFEU 240) — Comité des Représentants Permanents or Committee of Permanent Representatives — which was formally recognized by the Maastricht Treaty as an integral part of the EC Treaty/TFEU legislative process. It consists of Member States' representatives, who review proposals for legislation and seek to achieve compromises prior to submission of the proposal to the Council. Below Coreper, coordination among the Member States is assured by working parties comprising representatives of the respective ministries. The presiding state in these working parties is the same as that which holds the rotating presidency of the Union.

***The European Parliament*** The European Parliament is directly elected by the people of Europe once every five years. The election process is still largely a matter for each Member State, and it is in many States timed to take place at the same time as national elections. As noted in the Template, it is one of the tasks of the Parliament to draw up a proposal for a uniform system of suffrage, entailing in particular a single system for allocating votes. At present this is still determined State-by-State.

After many years of struggle, the Parliament now has its own statute governing the pay and conditions for Members of the Parliament.

Members of the European Parliament (MEPs) belong to national political parties but are organized into cross border political groupings (unless they choose to be independents). The largest grouping as of 2011 is the European People's Party, a center-right grouping, comprising the Christian Democrat or conservative national parties. One notable absence from this grouping is the contingent of British Conservatives who used to belong to the EPP but have now severed links and allied with some fringe or extreme Euro-sceptic groups from central Europe.

The Parliament's interactions with the Council have a formalized basis in the Treaties but in practical terms there are mechanisms for ensuring a productive dialogue outside those formalities. Various **Inter-institutional Agreements** exist between the Parliament, Council and Commission (see *infra*, Chapter 6).

In addition to the legislative procedures, the Parliament has other powers often associated with a legislature including the election of the President of the Commission (though the candidate is proposed by the European Council), the approval of the Commissioners as a whole, the power of censure over the Commission and consent to international Treaties. It also can ask questions of the other institutions in written form or through parliament "question times."

***The Commission*** Despite the advances in the role of the Parliament, it still does not have the right to initiate legislation, which remains with the Commission.

## § 2.04 EXECUTIVE POWERS

### [A] General Observations

In a sovereign state, the "Executive" comprises the Government, civil service and other agencies. These bodies adopt and implement policy within the powers granted to them by the Constitution or legislation. The Union's executive bodies have mostly policy-making functions, while implementation still resides with the Member States. Even the Commission, often loosely referred to as the "EU's Executive arm" is in significant part a policy-making body although it has varying degrees of implementing powers with respect to the Union's budget, competition policy and other areas.

### [B] The European Council

Political cooperation began as early as 1971 when the Member States began the practice of meeting together several times per year to discuss more general political co-ordination, chiefly on foreign affairs. In 1974, this practice was formalized with the establishment of the "European Council". The first meeting of the European Council was in March 1975 in Dublin. Since then its importance in the workings of the EU has steadily increased. This trend was linked with the growth of the authority of the Heads of State or Government in most of the Member States, either because of the way their constitutions worked or because of how political affairs were conducted. Their personal intervention in EU affairs was therefore a major development. Since 1975 they have provided political impetus or laid down guidelines in areas of prime importance (such as direct elections to Parliament, the European Monetary System, reform of agricultural policy, the accession of new members, completion of the internal market and economic and monetary union).

Today, the European Council is a fully-fledged Institution of the Union and is the top policy-setting body consisting of the Heads of State or Government of the EU Member States (not to be confused with the Council). First mentioned in the EU Treaties in the Single European Act, it finally became an institution of the Union as a result of Lisbon. This was an important step, since it signaled that the Member States now saw their activities within this body as belonging to a separate institutional structure and no longer a "partnership" of sovereign states sitting above and apart from the Union. Lisbon further reinforced this status by creating the office of President of the European Union, thus departing from the former practice of rotating the presidency around the Member States, as still happens with the Council of the EU. There seems to be a widespread misunderstanding of the position of the president. It is really the European Council itself that acts as a sort of collective head of state (though there is no state as such) and the president's role is to coordinate collective action and speak on behalf of the collective will.

## [C]  The Council

This is the exact same body as it is in the legislative context, and its executive role is every bit as important as its legislative one. Its composition, with its variable configurations, seems perhaps more logical with respect to its executive duties where it acts, one might say, like a collective cabinet minister for the portfolio represented by the configuration in which it is meeting. Unlike its legislative function, which, post-Lisbon, is technically open to the public, its executive sessions take place behind closed doors. Again, this would not seem out of place when compared with how government ministers interact with their civil servants on a daily basis in any governmental structure.

## [D]  The Commission

The Commission became a single body for all three Communities in 1967 following the Merger Treaty (including the High Authority of the ECSC). Its underlying task is to promote the goals of the Treaties — to be the engine of European integration and to ensure that European laws are properly implemented by the Member States. It is guaranteed its independence from the Member States and each Commissioner is similarly required to be independent of his or her national allegiance.

In the early years the Commission indeed played a strong role in moving the EEC forward, under the astute guidance of strong Presidents including Mansholt and Hallstein, despite strong counter-pressures from various Member States. In the 1970s it fell victim to the more general economic malaise affecting Europe in the aftermath of the first oil shock in 1973 and was unable to accomplish very much. A sense of "eurosclerosis" set in. However, the SEA and 1992 initiative provided a new boost for its activities, under the presidency of Jacques Delors. Its relative success in achieving the 1992 program, and the invaluable support it was delivered by the ECJ in a series of decisions which will be explored in this casebook, gave it renewed vigor into the 1990s. It also began finally to put real teeth into enforcement of competition policy. Unfortunately there then ensued a very dark period under Jacques Santer, when a series of scandals involving favouritism and misapplication of funds led to the resignation of the entire college of Commissioners. It has now stabilized after various reforms and is once again providing the initiatives needed to sustain and strengthen the Union.

The Commission is a collegiate body and takes decisions by majority vote. It is supported by a substantial staff, though still rather small compared even to the administration of a modestly sized European city. It now also oversees many specialized agencies.

The Commission is often criticized for being elitist and distant from the people. This of course is not its fault, but nor is it really accurate. In the first place, as the agent of executive action, it surely is no more undemocratic than, say, the cabinet of the President of the United States. Ultimately, its president must be approved by the European Parliament, and this has led to a general practice where the Parliament holds hearings on each candidate for Commissioner. Second, it is required to work closely with the representatives of the Member States in the

COREPER structure and also consults the views of many interested parties including industry, trade unions, and NGOs.

## [E]   Specialized Functions

There are other institutions, bodies or officers who also have significant roles in specific areas:

*The Court of Auditors* (EC 246 – 248/TFEU 285-287) This body has played a significant role in uncovering financial abuses within the Commission.

*The European Central Bank or ECB* (EC 105 – 124/TFEU 127-142) The ECB was set up to manage the euro and so came into existence only with the first stage of the conversion of national currencies to the euro in the late 1990s. It is the central authority responsible for setting interest rates for the euro and coordinating management of the euro as a currency. The ECB has the power to administer the European System of Central Banks (ESCB) totally independently of political interference (i.e., on the German model) and has the primary goal of maintaining monetary stability. The ECB played a pivotal role in ensuring liquidity during the 2008-9 financial crisis and the subsequent sovereign debt problems. Its lack of democratic accountability is a matter of concern to some politicians who would like to see it playing a role beyond maintaining the stability of the currency.

*The High Representative* (New TEU 18) This is the person who might generally be thought of as the EU "Foreign Minister". The High Representative brings the Council and the Commission together because that individual chairs both the Council when it is in the Foreign Affairs Configuration, and is a Vice President of the Commission.

*The Ombudsman* This is in origin a Swedish term for an individual appointed to mediate issues between citizens and the government. A description of the role is found in chapter 19, *infra*. For a more detailed account see e.g. T. Alexandros, *The position of the European Ombudsman in the Community system of judicial remedies*, (2007) 32 EL REV. 607.

*Specialized Agencies* These are agencies set up for specific purposes in connection with EU programs. A full list and links to descriptions of these can be found on the EU website. They include the Office for Harmonization in the Internal Market (Trademarks and Designs), the European Chemicals Agency, the European Environment Agency and the European Medicines Agency.

## [F]   The Role of the Member States

The Member States are not EU institutions at all of course, but they play a vital role in the execution of European law, which can only take effect and operate through their governments, civil service, police, judiciary and other governmental bodies. Under new TEU 4 (formerly EC 10) they have a duty to work together in a spirit of sincere cooperation to support the Union.

## § 2.05  JUDICIAL POWERS

### [A]  The Court of Justice of the European Union

***Evolution*** The Court of Justice of the European Union started out as a very modest body under the ECSC, hearing but a few cases a year on rather obscure aspects of the regulatory structure for coal and steel. Even after the formation of the EEC and EAEC it remained a backwater until the *Van Gend* and *Costa* cases (Chapters 4 and 3 respectively). These cases opened up the possibility for private litigants to assert EU law in national courts.

The Court's work gradually expanded, and then came a succession of groundbreaking cases, including *ERTA* (Chapter 12) *Defrenne* (Chapters 4 and 17), *Van Duyn*, (Chapters 5 and 17) *Van Binsbergen* (Chapters 4 and 14) and *Cassis de Dijon* (Chapter 13). The latter finally provided national litigants with the opportunity to challenge a myriad of state laws and regulations that impeded free movement of goods and the concepts embodied in that case found their way into the other "freedoms" so that by the mid-1980s the Court was all but swamped with cases under the preliminary reference procedure. At that time, it also started to open up a broader category of individuals who could have standing to challenge Commission acts (the *Metro* case in Chapter 8), so that its original jurisdiction work began to accelerate as well.

By the late 1980s, the workload of the ECJ made it imperative to create a second court, called the Court of First Instance, (now renamed the General Court) to take over the some of the original jurisdiction of the Court of Justice, which acquired appeal jurisdiction from the CFI's/General Court's decisions. The caseload has since continued to be very heavy and the ECJ, through its preliminary reference jurisdiction has continued to pry open new avenues for asserting EU law in national courts with groundbreaking cases such as the decisions on remedies for individuals against Member States who breach EU Law: *Brasserie du Pecheur/Factortame*, and *Francovich*. (Chapter 9).

The Court's responsibilities are set out in the Template. With respect to original jurisdiction, the CFI/General Court *inter alia* hears cases brought by individuals against Union institutions and also appeals from specialized agency decisions, including the Trademark office, an area that is making the docket increasingly unmanageable. The ECJ hears appeals from the CFI/General Court and has sole jurisdiction under the preliminary reference procedure under EC 234/TFEU 267. It also hears cases where a Member State is a party.

***Judges*** Detailed provisions governing the Court composition and structure are set out in the Statute of the Court of Justice annexed to the Treaties. Both the ECJ and the CFI/General Court may sit in **Chambers** of three or five judges except where a matter of particular importance is being considered. (Statute 16 – 18 (ECJ) and 50 (CFI/General Court) Due to the anticipated expansion arising from the admission of 10 new Member States in 2004, the Treaty of Nice allowed for a "Grand Chamber" to consist of 11 (now 13) judges. The Court itself can decide when a Grand Chamber is required but any Member State or EU institution that is party to proceedings can insist on it. Additionally, the CFI/General Court can sit as single judge for some types of cases.

***Advocates-General*** There are currently eight advocates-general. (Statute 2 – 18) Their role is to prepare an initial opinion providing a context for the case. Their opinions are generally but not always followed by the Court and are often influential in their own right. Their role is not really paralleled in the common law world. They were modeled after the French Commissaire du Gouvernement in the French administrative law system. They do not hold any separate hearings and the parties do not have an opportunity to reply to the opinion. This has led to some suggestion that this might not meet the standards in the Charter for the right to be heard (see further Chapter 19). However, the advocates-general do not participate in the judges' deliberations that lead to the dispositive decision.

The ECJ also originally heard cases regarding matters between civil servants and the various institutions. Since 2006, these are now assigned to a special Civil Service Tribunal.

***Procedure*** Proceedings are mostly by way of written submissions. Judgments are assigned for drafting to one judge — the "Rapporteur." No dissenting judgments are given.

***Case reports*** Cases are assigned a number preceded by a "C-" for ECJ and "T-" for CFI/General Court, thus, e.g. Case C-123/02. Normally the case number is cited preceding the name of the case, but for ease of use in this book it is indicated immediately following the case, followed by the report references. Cases involving an appeal to the ECJ are followed by a "P" suffix.

The EU publishes its cases online within the law database called EUR-Lex. Cases are assigned a CELEX number and can be searched using various prompts from the home page of EUR-Lex. Cases are now reported in all 23 languages.

Official case reports of the Court of Justice of the European Union are found in the European Court Reports (ECR) published by the EU, which today appear in two volumes, I and II, for the ECJ and CFI/General Court respectively. They are identified by year and page, e.g., [2002] ECR I-1002. There is some inconsistency in citation.

Thompson/Sweet and Maxwell publishes its own law reports known as the Common Market Law Reports or CMLR. These are cited as, e.g., [1973] CMLR 233.

Lexis maintains its own electronic report compilation based on CELEX, which contains cases back to approximately 1985.

In this work, pre-1985 cases have been cited using the ECR references, while later cases are referenced to ECR and CELEX-LEXIS. (However, the latter has now been extended to include pre-1985 cases.)

Additionally, this work contains some materials from national courts. These are cited using the relevant national convention.

***Principles of interpretation*** The Court's approach to interpretation of EU Law is extremely controversial among interests that oppose the expansive and teleological techniques employed. The court has tended to proceed by identifying cases that may not in themselves involve factual issues of great moment and using them to establish principles of major importance, to be digested by the legal world and then expanded upon as a doctrine is built up over time. One may summarize the ECJ's role as one of ensuring the effectiveness of Union law, the preservation of the Union's autonomy, and the assurance of a complete system of judicial protection.

For an exploration of this subject see the recent work of L.M. Solan, *Statutory Interpretation in the EU: The Augustinian Approach*, Brooklyn Law School Legal Studies Paper No. 78 (July 2007).

***The Court's workload*** The average time for the handling of a case by the Court of Justice was 16.1 months on average in 2010. The number of new cases (mostly EC 234/TFEU 267 references) before the ECJ rose from 562 in 2009 to 631 in 2010 (a record). The number of cases brought before the CFI/General Court increased from 568 in 2009 to 636 in 2010. The number of staff cases in the Civil Service Tribunal also increased during this period.

## [B]   The Courts of the Member States

While the courts of the Member States are not incorporated into the Union's structure in an organizational sense — they remain wholly national in character — their role in ensuring the effectiveness of Union law can scarcely be overstated. It is these courts that apply Union law as interpreted by the Court of Justice. While Chapter 9 explores this role in more detail, its importance will be evident in the materials throughout this book.

## § 2.06   THE UNION'S COMPETENCES

## [A]   General Principles and Observations

***Comparison with the U.S.*** The Union Treaties define areas of competence for the *Union*. It may be noted that it is indeed the Union rather than the legislature that is recognized here, since the competences may be either legislative or executive but in any event are strictly circumscribed. By contrast, under the U.S. Constitution, legislative powers are expressed to be vested in the Congress. Within the scope of the Constitution and authorizing legislation, *all* executive federal power is vested in the President, although the Constitution does in fact enumerate certain specific powers for that office. The most notable contrast with the EU may be that the U.S. executive branch has sole authority for the conduct of foreign relations. In the Union, the power of the various institutions in this field is strictly circumscribed.

***Principles affecting the exercise of Union competences*** Two principles were adopted in the original TEU primarily to act as a brake on the exercise of Union competences. Subsidiarity acts as a constraint on the exercise of EU competence, not as definition of the boundaries of such competence. Proportionality is a constraint on the scope and content of legislation. However, they are usually linked together.

■ **Subsidiarity** EC 5/TFEU 9-10. The following extract from the EU
  Glossary describes this concept:

The subsidiarity principle is intended to ensure that decisions are taken as
closely as possible to the citizen and that constant checks are made as to
whether action at Community level is justified in the light of the possibilities available at national, regional or local level. Specifically, it is the
principle whereby the Union does not take action (except in the areas which
fall within its exclusive competence) unless it is more effective than action
taken at national, regional or local level. It is closely bound up with the
principles of proportionality and necessity, which require that any action by
the Union should not go beyond what is necessary to achieve the objectives
of the Treaty.

The Edinburgh European Council of December 1992 defined the basic
principles underlying subsidiarity and laid down guidelines for interpreting
Article 5, which enshrines subsidiarity in the EU Treaty. Its conclusions
were set out in a declaration that still serves as the cornerstone of the
subsidiarity principle.

The Treaty of Amsterdam has taken up the approach that follows from this
declaration in a Protocol on the application of the principles of subsidiarity
and proportionality annexed to the EC Treaty. Two of the things this
Protocol introduces are the systematic analysis of the impact of legislative
proposals on the principle of subsidiarity and the use, where possible, of
less binding Community measures.

■ **Proportionality** EC 5/TFEU 9-10. In the context of EU legislation, the
  following extract from the EU Glossary provides a description of this
  concept:

Like the principle of subsidiarity, the principle of proportionality regulates
the exercise of powers by the European Union, seeking to set within
specified bounds the action taken by the institutions of the Union. Under
this rule, the institutions' involvement must be limited to what is necessary
to achieve the objectives of the Treaties. In other words, the extent of the
action must be in keeping with the aim pursued.

This means that when various forms of intervention are available to the
Union, it must, where the effect is the same, opt for the approach that
leaves the greatest freedom to the Member States and individuals.

(Note: The term is also used to describe a basic principle concerning the
relationship of a law and the penalties for its breach.)

## [B]  Fundamental Rights

The TFEU grants authority to the Union to enact laws for the reinforcement of
prohibitions on discrimination on various grounds (See further Chapter 18). This is
the only area where the Union has fundamental rights legislative powers expressly.
This is not surprising since the Charter itself is really a constitutional statement of
such rights and thus unalterable as such.

It is also noteworthy that TEU 7 (Template 1.3.4) grants powers to the Council to suspend voting rights for a Member State that is determined to be in breach of the Union's values (i.e., fundamental rights and democratic government).

## [C]　Foreign Policy

The reference to the common foreign and security policy in article 2 of the TFEU is perhaps rather surprising given the desire of the Member States to ensure that it remains outside the institutional processes of that Treaty. However, the TFEU provisions do seek to lay out a complete description of the Union's competences, so it would have been odd to have made no mention of CFSP at all. Its content and operation, however, are described in the TEU.

## [D]　Finances

(EC 269/TFEU 311). The EU website provides the following description of the Union's financial resources known as "own resources":

> Originally, the Community budget depended on the Member States' financial contributions.

> Under a decision adopted on 21 April 1970, the Member States' contributions were replaced by own resources. These are transfers made by the Member States to the Community budget to cover EU expenditure. The fact that the Community budget is funded from own resources makes the EU financially independent.

> The combined total of all own resources may not currently exceed 1.24% of the aggregate gross national income (GNI) of the Member States. There are four types of own resource:

> - Agricultural duties and sugar levies: these consist mainly of the customs duties on imports from non-Community countries of agricultural produce subject to common organisation of the market and levies on sugar, isoglucose and insulin syrup.

> - Customs duties: these arise from application of the common customs tariff and are collected on imports from third countries at the external borders.

>   These two resources are what are termed the "traditional own resources".

> - The VAT resource: this arises from the application of a uniform percentage rate to the VAT base of each Member State. This rate was reduced to 0.50% in 2004. For all Member States, it is applied to a base capped at 50% of GNP.

> - The resource based on gross national income (the "fourth resource"): introduced in 1988, this is an "additional" resource, because it is set according to the other three sources of budget revenue. A uniform percentage rate is applied to the total GNI of all the Member States, under the budget procedure.

## [E]   Currency

The development and implementation of the euro has been described earlier. Suffice it to point out here that the euro cannot be regarded as the Union's currency, but rather is the common currency of the Member States. It is issued by each state's central bank as a member of the European System of Central Banks, which is controlled by the European Central Bank, thus rendering monetary policy a Union competence. Each Member State has the ability to include its own design on notes and coins, subject to certain requirements and common features, such that euro coins and notes are instantly recognizable as the common currency, whatever state they may have originated in. As noted earlier, although currently 17 Member States have adopted the euro, so other currencies continue to circulate in some Member States, the intent of monetary union is that all Member States would eventually use the same currency.

## [F]   Categories of Competences

Competences specifically arising under the TFEU are now laid out in that Treaty. As a result of Lisbon, it is now possible to classify the competences by the degree to which they are **exclusive** to the Union, **shared** with the Member States or purely **supportive** of the primary competence vested in the Member States. The classification, however, can be a little misleading. Action involving harmonization in the field of the internal market, for example, may start out at a general level, leaving much discretion to the Member States, but then proceed to more and more specificity so that eventually there is no longer any latitude allowed as to how implementation should occur. At point the Union's competence has effectively pre-empted all further State power and is thus de facto exclusive.

These competences can then be further classified by the manner in which they are exercised: common policies; coordination; support; harmonization. The term "common policy" as used in the EC Treaty/TFEU was the term used for policies that superseded individual Member State action ("common" being in effect the adjective derived from "Community") The term was extended to foreign and security policy by the original Treaty on European Union even though that policy was outside the Community structure.

## § 2.07   LIMITS ON THE EXERCISE OF MEMBER STATE COMPETENCES

## [A]   Measures That Interfere With Free Movement of Goods, Services, Capital, or Impede Establishment in Another Member State

***The internal market viewed from a constitutional perspective*** From the earliest days, the Member States were required to abstain from actions that would impair the creation of the common, now internal, market. By reason of the doctrine of direct effect mentioned earlier, these prohibitions can be invoked in the legal systems of the Member States and may also be enforced by Commission action directly against governments in the ECJ.

Over time, the ECJ has elaborated the scope of these prohibitions such that today, it is possible to apply them to Member State measures that are not directed intentionally at restricting the operation of the internal market. Hence they can be viewed as a sort of detailed version of the U.S. dormant commerce clause, a doctrine that prohibits State measures, whatever their purpose, that impose an undue burden on interstate commerce.

***The Freedoms*** The basic prohibitions regarding the preservation of the internal market are still usually described as advancing the specific "freedoms" required to eliminate barriers to economic activity across state borders:

- **Free Movement of Goods** EC 23 – 31/TFEU 28-37. This concept entails the removal of all obstacles relating to the import and export of goods among the Member States.

- **Free Movement of Workers** EC 39 – 42/TFEU 45-48. This concept entails the removal of all obstacles to the movement of EU citizens seeking employment in the EU. Because this freedom is now essentially a more detailed and liberalized aspect of the general rights of citizenship, it is addressed in article 8 of the Template.

- **Freedom to provide services** EC 49 – 55/TFEU 56-62. This is the concept whereby all restrictions on the provision of services by EU citizens across national borders are abolished.

- **Right of Establishment** EC 43 – 48/TFEU 49-55. This is the right for an EU individual or company to set up a business in a state of which he/she/it is not a national.

- **Free movement of capital** EC 56-60/TFEU 63-66. This was the last of the "freedoms" to be liberalized, as a result of provisions in the original TEU in the context of moving towards monetary union. (In this book capital and establishment are considered together, since they obviously are closed linked.)

The scope of all these prohibitions have been developed by the ECJ through many cases over several decades. The Court's approach has been largely consistent although it is not always easy to see where it may be headed with a particular concept in the confines of an individual decision, and very occasionally it has reversed itself. Today however, a number of basic principles are clearly evident from the case law and it these that are addressed in the materials in this casebook as being essentially constitutional in nature given their generality of application.

## [B]   Other Measures

It will be noted that in Article 7 of the Template, there are further prohibitions regarding the exercise of competences of the Member States, including indirect taxation, the granting of state aids, and the operation of state or state sponsored enterprises.

## § 2.08   THE UNION AND THE INDIVIDUAL

### [A]   Citizenship

Under the TFEU, all nationals of Member States share the common status of "European Union citizenship" (as well as their "nationality"). This confers on them the right to move freely among the Member States. The practicalities of ensuring this right are taken care of by the so-called Schengen Agreement or "acquis" (Protocol 2). The following extract from the EU website provides a description of this very important arrangement:

> *On 14th June 1985, the Governments of Belgium, Germany, France, Luxembourg and the Netherlands signed an agreement at Schengen, a small town in Luxembourg, with a view to enabling "(. . .) all nationals of the Member States to cross internal borders freely (. . .)" and to enable the "free circulation of goods and services".*

The five founding countries signed the Convention implementing the Schengen Agreement on 19th June 1990, and were later joined by Italy on 27th November 1990, Spain and Portugal on 25th June 1991, Greece on 6th November 1992, Austria on 28th April 1995 and Denmark, Sweden and Finland on 19th December 1996.

Norway and Iceland also concluded a Co-operation Agreement with the Member States on 19th December 1996 in order to join this Convention.

Subsequently, as of 26th of March 1995, the Schengen acquis was fully applied in Belgium, Germany, France, Luxembourg, Netherlands, Spain and Portugal, in Austria and Italy as of 31st of March 1998 and in Greece as of 26th of March 2000. Finally, as of 25th of March 2001 the Schengen acquis was applicable in full in Norway, Iceland, Sweden, Denmark and Finland.

The Schengen acquis was incorporated into the legal framework of the European Union by means of protocols attached to the Treaty of Amsterdam in 1999. A Council Decision was adopted on 12th May 1999, determining the legal basis for each of the provisions or decisions, which constitute the Schengen acquis, in conformity with the relevant provisions of the Treaty establishing the European Community and the Treaty on European Union.

**Schengen evaluation of new Member States**

Experts from the Member States carried out the so-called "Schengen evaluation" of the new Member States . . . 58 evaluation missions covering data protection, police co-operation, external border controls at land, sea and air borders, and visa policy were undertaken in 2006. In 2007, 15 re-evaluation visits were carried out, together with a new sea and air border evaluation. Nine Schengen Information System evaluation visits were completed.

Although experts from the Commission also participated in these evaluations, the responsibility for evaluation remains with the Council.

This evaluation consisted in particular of verifying that the accompanying measures allowing for the lifting of internal border control are correctly and efficiently applied by the new Member States. Evaluation visits were carried out in the field of external border control, visa, data protection, police cooperation and the Schengen Information System.

*    *    *

Schengen evaluations of EU Member States that are candidates for the lifting of internal border controls are initiated upon request from each Member State concerned, once it considers that it meets all preconditions. It is the responsibility of the States that are already Schengen members to determine that all the preconditions are met and the Council is responsible for carrying out the evaluations.

The (physical) inspection visits are followed by the request to the evaluated State to reply to a questionnaire comprising questions on all fields of the Schengen acquis. Experts (nominated by the Member States), together with a representative of the Commission and of the Secretariat General of the Council carry out inspection visits in order to verify the practical implementation of the acquis in relation to external border checks and surveillance, visas, Schengen Information System, police cooperation and data protection. Each expert group draws up a report, containing a description of the facts, recommendations and conclusions.

Depending on the outcome of the evaluation, the Council decides unanimously (in this context, unanimity includes the Member States fully implementing the Schengen acquis, plus the Member State applying for full implementation) on the date of the lifting of internal border controls or, alternatively, on the need for additional inspections and verifications before stating a date for the lifting of internal border controls.

*    *    *

The total population of the 24 Schengen Member States is 404,921,039 (Estimation: Eurostat 2007).

Although the Schengen Agreements (in fact, Conventions) were originally entered into outside the framework of Union law, the various acts adopted pursuant to them were given EU law status by Decision 1999/436, [1999] OJ L 176/19, while Protocol No. 19 to the TEU and TFEU today governs further steps taken to advance the operation of the Schengen network.

## [B]   Effect of Union Law on Individuals

This is a complex subject. Unlike a conventional federal system, one cannot speak of two tiers of laws both equally applicable to the population within their spheres of application. Only certain forms of Union law have effects on individuals, and in those cases, these effects may be simply to confer rights, or also to impose obligations. Individual rights and obligations derive from the nature of specific provisions of the Treaties and Union acts themselves, and the Template makes reference to "direct effects" and "direct applicability" as part of the description of the components of Union law in Article 2 (explored in chapters 4 and 5, *infra*). The consequences of these attributes for individuals are summarized in an integrated form in article 8 of the Template.

## § 2.09  RELATIONS BETWEEN THE MEMBER STATES

The brevity of this final article of the Template belies the significance of its content. It effectively serves as the counterweight to the description of Union competences and institutions in the preceding articles. By noting duties of cooperation or coordination among the Member States, it confirms that in the key areas of sovereignty — the police power, economic and fiscal matters, and national security — the Member States have not given up any of their inherent powers. As noted, this does not preclude some Union competence (see § 2.06 *supra*) but the role of the Union in this case is to support the efforts of the Member States; the competence itself remains with the latter. If the Union is to take further steps toward a conventional federation, it will have to start assuming powers in these areas. It is difficult to imagine such a step without approval from the population at large. Indeed, the German Constitutional Court has made it clear that Lisbon has pushed the Union as far as it may go within the confines of constitutional provisions allowing the transfer of sovereign powers to international institutions. This is why moves towards an "economic government" for the members of the eurozone are proving highly contentious. It will be fascinating to see how this process may unfold in the coming years.

## § 2.10  FURTHER READING

For a student seeking a basic introductory text, the following may be useful although texts pre-dating the entry into effect of the Treaty of Lisbon may be of limited use.

> FOLSOM, EUROPEAN UNION LAW (7th ed Nutshell series, Thomson/West 2008).

> FOLSOM, PRINCIPLES OF EUROPEAN UNION LAW (Concise Hornbook Series, Thomson/West 2d ed. 2010)

> MATHIJSEN, A GUIDE TO EUROPEAN UNION LAW (9th ed., Sweet and Maxwell, 2007).

Texts specifically addressing EU Constitutional law and comparisons with the U.S. experience include:

> DOUGLAS-SCOTT, THE CONSTITUTIONAL LAW OF THE EUROPEAN UNION (Pearson/ Longman, 2002, 2d edition 2009)

> LENAERTS AND VAN NUFFEL (ed R. Bray), CONSTITUTIONAL LAW OF THE EUROPEAN UNION (3rd edition, Sweet and Maxwell, 2011)

OPPENHEIMER, THE RELATIONSHIP OF COMMUNITY LAW WITH NATIONAL LAW (Cambridge University Press, 2004)

M. TUSHNET (ED.), COMPARATIVE CONSTITUTIONAL FEDERALISM: EUROPE AND AMERICA (Greenwood Press, 1990)

J. Temple Lang, *The Development of European Community Constitutional Law*, 25 INT'L LAWYER 455 (1991)

K. LENAERTS, (ED.), TWO HUNDRED YEARS OF U.S. CONSTITUTIONAL AND 30 YEARS OF EEC TREATY (Kluwer 1988) at p 25

J. Weiler, *The Transformation of Europe*, 100 YALE L.J. 2403 (1991)

R. BARENTS, THE AUTONOMY OF COMMUNITY LAW (Kluwer, 2004)

A. STONE SWEET, THE JUDICIAL CONSTRUCTION OF EUROPE (Oxford University Press, 2004)

A Dyèvre, *The Constitutionalisation of the European Union: Discourse, present, future and facts*, (2005) 30 EL REV. 165.

K. ALTER, THE EUROPEAN COURT'S POLITICAL POWER (Oxford University Press, 2010)

More detailed texts covering a broader range of EU law in English include:

BERMANN, DAVEY, FOX, AND GOEBEL, EUROPEAN UNION LAW (3d edition, Thomson/West, 2010).

Craig and De Burca, EU Law — Text, Cases and Materials, (4th edition, Oxford University Press, 2007).

HARTLEY, FOUNDATIONS OF EUROPEAN UNION LAW (Oxford University Press, new edition 2010)

WETHERILL, CASES AND MATERIALS ON EU LAW (9th ed., Oxford University Press, 2010)

Again, there is a multitude of specialist and general periodicals covering EU matters, in many languages. Some prominent specialist EU journals in English are:

EUROPEAN LAW REVIEW ("EL REV.") (London, Sweet & Maxwell)

COMMON MARKET LAW REVIEW ("CML REV.") (London, Kluwer Law International).

EUROPEAN CONSTITUTIONAL LAW REVIEW (The Hague, TMC Asser Press)

THE COLUMBIA JOURNAL OF EUROPEAN LAW

LEXIS contains a useful collection of EC materials in the European Union Library, using the CELEX LEXIS database mentioned above. CELEX LEXIS cases so far cover the period from 1985 to the present.

The Eur-lex website operated by the EU is accessible by anyone free of charge and contains full reports on most cases decided by the ECJ and the CFI/General Court. The EU itself publishes a vast amount of information on its general website at www.europa.eu.

Many law schools have posted websites to provide guidance on researching EU Law.

# Chapter 3

# THE AUTONOMY OF UNION LAW

## § 3.01 OVERVIEW

*Template* Section 1.6

***Materials in this Chapter*** As the reader proceeds through Article 1 of the Template, the first impression is probably that the European Union appears to be an international organization, perhaps a sort of United Nations for Europe, albeit covering subject matter of a very comprehensive and detailed nature. Section 1.6 brings a surprise. We are suddenly confronted with two remarkable statements: first, that the Union enjoys sovereign powers; and second, that Union law has primacy over national law. These are not features that could even remotely be associated with the United Nations.

Instead, they look more like the fundamental characteristics of a federal system. In such a system, there is a single source of sovereignty, which in a democracy is generally thought to be "the people". The people have chosen to divide their ultimate sovereignty between a federal power and the constituent states. Those two powers exist independently of each other and are typically allocated through a constitution, enacted on behalf of and representing the will of the people.

Do the statements in Template section 1.6 then imply that the Treaties are a form of federal constitution and that the Union is in fact a federation (as that term is used in contemporary practice)? Such a notion does not appear to be borne out by the Treaties. The Union was founded by agreements between sovereign states within the conventions of international law. The Treaties do not proclaim in an unequivocal way that they were an act of the people rather than the Member States. There is still no statement at all in the Treaties that supports the proposition that the Member States (or the people) have transferred sovereign powers to the Union — only that they have *conferred competences* on the Union *to attain objectives they have in common*. The Treaties thus give the impression that the Member States are merely pooling their sovereignty for their own purposes — they have simply chosen to exercise that sovereignty together through the Union as their instrument. Furthermore, the Treaties even today do not contain a clear affirmation of the primacy of Union law (although the rejected Constitution Treaty, signed by all the then Member States, did do so with respect to Union acts). EC 10/TEU 4 certainly imposes duties of sincere cooperation but this obligation seems only to reinforce the impression that the Union is simply a medium for action, and it is the Member States who ultimately are in control.

It is thus to the case law that we must turn to understand how the features described in section 1.6 came to be part of Union law. The materials in § 3.02 consist of the key ECJ cases that have announced the transfer of sovereign rights to the Union and the primacy of Union law. From these cases emerges a clear picture of an autonomous body of law that is embedded in each of the national legal systems.

§ 3.03 contains materials from the courts of the Member States, who have confronted many challenges in trying to accommodate the ECJ's doctrine of supremacy within their own constitutional structures.

§ 3.04 ponders a related question. If Union law has federal characteristics, are the Union and its institutions a form of federal authority as might be familiar to those who live in a federal system? If so, one would not expect them to be subject at all to the jurisdiction of the courts of the Member States. Keep in mind that the federal government of the United States cannot be sued in state court and states cannot be sued by citizens of other states in federal court — Amendment XI to the U.S. Constitution.

*A starting point* This chapter covers the basic principles that form the basis for the autonomy of Union law. It is, however, merely a starting point in that regard. Chapters 4 and 5 address how Union law may be invoked before national courts (the doctrine of "direct effect", without which supremacy would be merely theoretical). Chapter 9 covers the duties of the national courts in upholding and implementing Union law, essentially working out the practical consequences of supremacy. Chapter 11 addresses the scope of Union competences and the extent to which they pre-empt national law. In a more general sense, the autonomy principle is the basis on which all of the materials in this casebook ultimately rest. Thus, the importance of the ECJ's role and indeed also of the role played by the national courts in shaping the Union, as exemplified in this chapter, can scarcely be overstated.

## § 3.02 THE AUTONOMY OF UNION LAW AS DEVELOPED BY THE ECJ

### [A] The Transfer of Sovereign Rights to the Union

### VAN GEND EN LOOS v. NEDERLANDSE ADMINISTRATIE DER BELASTINGEN
Case 26/62, 1963 ECJ CELEX LEXIS 12, [1963] ECR 1
[No paragraph numbering in the original]

[The plaintiff had sought to import a shipment of ureaformaldehyde into the Netherlands from Germany. At the time, customs duties were still in effect as between the two countries (such duties were to be phased out over the Transitional Period). Due to changes in Dutch law, the shipment was subjected to a customs duty that was higher than that previously applied to the same product, in apparent contravention of then article 12 of the EC Treaty, which stated:

Member States shall refrain from introducing between themselves any new customs duties on imports or exports or any charges having equivalent effect, and from increasing those which they already apply in their trade with each other.

The Dutch government pointed out that the duty increase was only an effect of a reclassification of the product under another heading of the Dutch customs tariff, an action it was entitled to take.]

The objective of the EEC Treaty, which is to establish a common market, the functioning of which is of direct concern to interested parties in the Community, implies that this Treaty is more than an agreement which merely creates mutual obligations between the contracting states. This view is confirmed by the preamble to the Treaty which refers not only to governments but to peoples. It is also confirmed more specifically by the establishment of institutions endowed with sovereign rights, the exercise of which affects Member States and also their citizens. Furthermore, it must be noted that the nationals of the States brought together in the Community are called upon to cooperate in the functioning of this Community through the intermediary of the European Parliament and the Economic and Social Committee.

In addition the task assigned to the Court of Justice under article 177 [267], the object of which is to secure uniform interpretation of the Treaty by national courts and tribunals, confirms that the States have acknowledged that Community law has an authority which can be invoked by their nationals before those courts and tribunals. The conclusion to be drawn from this is that the Community constitutes a new legal order of international law for the benefit of which the States have limited their sovereign rights, albeit within limited fields, and the subjects of which comprise not only Member States but also their nationals.

## COSTA v. ENEL
### Case 6/64, [1964] ECR 585
### [No paragraph numbering in the original]

[Mr. Costa (a lawyer) had been a shareholder in an electricity supply company that was nationalized by the Italian government in 1962. He believed this act was unconstitutional and refused to pay his electricity bill of 1,925 Italian lira (about $3). He was prosecuted in a small claims court and in the course of his defense raised arguments that the nationalization was in violation of then EEC Treaty Articles 37 [37], 53, 93 [108] and 102 [117]. (Article 53 was a standstill provision, under which the Member States undertook not to introduce any new restrictions on the right of establishment in their territories of nationals of other Member States, save as otherwise provided in the Treaty.) The Italian court decided to refer these questions to the ECJ under EEC Article 177 (EC 230/TFEU 267).]

As opposed to other international treaties, the Treaty instituting the E.E.C. has created its own order which was integrated with the national order of the Member States the moment the Treaty came into force; as such, it is binding upon them. In fact, by creating a Community of unlimited duration, having its own institutions, its own personality and its own capacity in law, apart from having international standing and more particularly, real powers resulting from a limitation of competence or a transfer of powers from the States to the Community, the Member States, albeit within limited spheres, have restricted their sovereign rights and created a body of law applicable both to their nationals and to themselves.

## NOTES AND QUESTIONS

1. The Court seems to be saying that sovereignty has been divided between the Member States and the Union. Is sovereignty divisible? Or can one make the argument that the Treaties are not purely the act of the signatory states but in some sense were entered into on behalf of the people, the ultimate source of sovereign power, somewhat like the Constitutional Convention establishing the United States?

2. Which features did the Court consider important in determining that the Member States had permanently yielded certain sovereign rights to the (then) European Economic Community? Does the language appearing in TEU 1 (Template section 1.1) that refers to conferral not contradict such a notion?

3. The Court indicates that at least some Treaty provisions may be invoked by individuals in national proceedings against national laws. As noted in the Overview, this concept, usually referred to as "direct effect", is explored as a separate topic in Chapters 4 and 5.

## [B] The Primacy, or Supremacy, of Union Law

### COSTA v. ENEL
Case 6/64, [1964] ECR 585
[No paragraph numbering in the original]

[For the background to this case see the above extract.]

. . . [I]t was . . . submitted that the Milan judge called for an interpretation of the Treaty which was not at all necessary for the solution of the proceedings before him. Since Article 177 [267] is based upon a clear separation of functions between national courts and this Court, it cannot give us power either to investigate the facts of this case or to criticize the reasons and the aims of the request for an authoritative interpretation.

For its part, the Italian Government maintains that the request of the Milan judge is absolutely 'inadmissible' inasmuch as a national court, which is bound to apply a national law, cannot avail itself of Article 177 [267].

The reception, within the laws of each member-State, of provisions having a Community source, and more particularly of the terms and of the spirit of the Treaty, has as a corollary the impossibility, for the member-State, to give preference to a unilateral and subsequent measure against a legal order accepted by them on a basis of reciprocity.

In truth, the executive strength of Community laws cannot vary from one State to the other in favour of later internal laws without endangering the realization of the aims envisaged by the Treaty in Article 5 (2) [TEU 4] and giving rise to a discrimination prohibited by Article 7 [18]. In any case, the obligations undertaken under the Treaty creating the European Community would not be unconditional, but merely potential if they could be affected by subsequent legislative acts of the signatories of the Treaty. Furthermore, whenever the right to legislate unilaterally is allowed to the Member States, it is under a precise and special provision (see for instance Articles 15 [deleted], 93 (3) [108], 223 [346], 224 [347] and 225 [348]).

It is also true that requests for derogation by member-States are subject to a special procedure of authorization (Articles 8 (4) [repealed], 17 (4) repealed], 25 [repealed], 26 [repealed], 73 [repealed], 93 (2) [108], 93 (3) [108] and 226 [repealed]) which would be meaningless if the member-States could exempt themselves from their obligations by means of an ordinary Law. The pre-eminence of Community law is confirmed by Article 189 [288] which prescribes that Community regulations have an 'obligatory' value and are 'directly applicable within each member-State'. Such a provision which, it will be noticed, admits of no reservation, would be wholly ineffective if a member-State could unilaterally nullify its purpose by means of a Law contrary to Community dictates. It follows from all these observations that the rights created by the Treaty, by virtue of their specific original nature, cannot be judicially contradicted by an internal law, whatever it might be, without losing their Community character and without undermining the legal basis of the Community.

The transfer, by member-States, from their national order, in favor of the Community order of the rights and obligations arising from the Treaty, carries with it a clear limitation of their sovereign right upon which a subsequent unilateral law, incompatible with the aims of the Community, cannot prevail. As a consequence, Article 177 [267] should be applied regardless of any national law in those cases where a question of interpretation of the Treaty arises.

## NOTES AND QUESTIONS

1.   How was the supremacy issue relevant to the question of whether there had been a proper reference under then article 177 (EC 234/TFEU 267)?

2.   The U.S. Constitution provides in Article VI that Treaties . . . shall be the supreme Law of the Land; and the Judges in every State shall be bound thereby, anything in the Constitution or Laws of any State to the Contrary notwithstanding." The EEC Treaty however, contained no such "supremacy clause" What then was the basis for the court's conclusion that, in any case of conflict, the Treaty must prevail over the national law of Member States?

3.   In the U.S., according to decisions of the U.S. Supreme Court, in case of conflict between a federal statute and a treaty, the so-called last-in-time rule applies. That is, U.S. courts must give effect to a clearly conflicting federal statute if it is enacted subsequent to the treaty. Many other countries also have adopted the last-in-time approach. Must it be concluded that the European Court of Justice has clearly rejected such an approach with respect to the status of the EU Treaties in the legal systems of the Member States?

4.   In light of the Court's judgment, what precisely is a national court to do if there is in force a conflicting national statute? It may not be able to repeal or annul an act of the national legislature because of constitutional restrictions on judicial review; nor, unless it is the appropriate constitutional court, may it declare the legislation unconstitutional. Did the ECJ's ruling effectively mean it was ruling on the validity of the national law?

**5.** The national court found that EEC 37 (EC 31/TFEU 37) had been violated but on appeal to the Italian Supreme court, the latter held that Costa had no standing to challenge a national law by contesting his electricity bill. Some 20 years later, this position had been definitively reversed by the Italian Constitutional Court so far as EU law is concerned. (See further § 3.03 below.)

**6.** Although it was proposed to include a provision on the primacy or supremacy of EU law in the Treaties as part of the Lisbon reforms, in the end this was simply noted in Declaration No. 17, which reads as follows:

17. Declaration concerning primacy

The Conference recalls that, in accordance with well settled case law of the Court of Justice of the European Union, the Treaties and the law adopted by the Union on the basis of the Treaties have primacy over the law of Member States, under the conditions laid down by the said case law.

The Conference has also decided to attach as an Annex to this Final Act the Opinion of the Council Legal Service on the primacy of EC law as set out in 11197/07 (JUR 260):

"*Opinion of the Council Legal Service of 22 June 2007*

*It results from the case-law of the Court of Justice that primacy of EC law is a cornerstone principle of Community law. According to the Court, this principle is inherent to the specific nature of the European Community. At the time of the first judgment of this established case law (Costa/ENEL, 15 July 1964, Case 6/641 [FN]) there was no mention of primacy in the treaty. It is still the case today. The fact that the principle of primacy will not be included in the future treaty shall not in any way change the existence of the principle and the existing case-law of the Court of Justice.*"

[A footnote reads: "*It follows (. . .) that the law stemming from the treaty, an independent source of law, could not, because of its special and original nature, be overridden by domestic legal provisions, however framed, without being deprived of its character as Community law and without the legal basis of the Community itself being called into question.*"]

## [C]   Effect on National Constitutions and Constitutional Principles

### INTERNATIONALE HANDELSGESELLSCHAFT MBH v. EINFUHR- UND VORRATSSTELLE FÜR GETREIDE UND FUTTERMITTEL
Case 11/70, [1970] ECR 1125

[The German Administrative Court had raised questions regarding the validity of the export certificate system and the deposit of security attached to it ('deposit system') laid down in Council Regulation 120/67 of 13 June 1967 on the common organization of the markets in the cereals sector and in Commission Regulation 473/67 of 21 August 1967 on import and export certificates. The cereals market organization involved intervention through buying-in of cereals to support prices domestically and provisions for refunds on exports that could be sold on the world market only at prices below those supported in the EU. In order to prevent fraud and ensure that product proposed to be exported was in fact exported, the regulation required the exporter to obtain an export certificate and pay a deposit which would be forfeit if the export then did not occur within a specified time frame. The only ground on which the exporter might recover the deposit in the event of non-export was the occurrence of a force majeure event. The German Court was concerned that forfeiture of the entire deposit for what might have been only administrative failures contravened the German Constitution's requirement that penalties for breach of the law should be proportionate to the offence. (Proportionality is dealt with in more detail in chapter 19)]

2 It appears from the grounds of the order referring the matter that the Administrative Court has hitherto refused to admit the validity of the provisions in question and for that reason considers it indispensable to put an end to the existing legal uncertainty. In the view of that court the deposit system is contrary to certain structural principles of the national constitutional law which should be protected in the framework of Community law, such that the primacy of the supranational law should give way before the principles of the German Constitution. More particularly, the deposit system is thought to infringe the principles of freedom of action and disposition, economic liberty and proportionality which follow from Articles 2 (1) and 14 of the German Constitution. The undertaking to import or export arising out of the issue of the certificates, together with the deposit which is attached to them, is thought to constitute an excessive intervention in the freedom of disposition in trade, whereas the purpose of the regulations could be realized by means of interventions which have less heavy consequences.

*    *    *

3 Recourse to legal rules or concepts of national law to judge the validity of instruments promulgated by Community institutions would have the effect of harming the unity and efficacity of Community law. The validity of such instruments can only be judged in the light of Community law. In fact, the law born from the Treaty, the issue of an autonomous source, could not, by its very nature, have the courts opposing to it rules of national law of any nature whatever without losing its Community character and without the legal basis of the Community itself being put in question. Therefore the validity of a Community instrument or its effect within a member-State cannot be affected by allegations that it strikes at either the fundamental rights as formulated in that State's constitution or the principles of a national constitutional structure.

4 An examination should however be made as to whether some analogous guarantee, inherent in Community law, has not been infringed. For respect for fundamental rights has an integral part in the general principles of law of which the Court of Justice ensures respect. The protection of such rights, while inspired by the constitutional principles common to the member-States, must be ensured within the framework of the Community's structure and objectives. We should therefore examine in the light of the doubts expressed by the Administrative Court whether

the deposit system did infringe fundamental rights respect for which must be ensured in the Community legal order.

## NOTES AND QUESTIONS

1.   How did the ECJ deal with the German Court's concerns about potential conflict of the EU Regulation with fundamental rights under the German Constitution? The question at this stage in the development of EU law was how, in the absence (at that time) of any enumeration of fundamental rights at the EU level, was the German Court to implement the ECJ's interpretation. The question was considered in a number of landmark cases in the German Courts (see § 3.03 *infra*). The doubts around the ability of the German Courts to hold that EU law prevails over fundamental rights in the German Constitution continue to reverberate in the German legal system. However, the adoption of the Charter of Fundamental Rights by the Union (on December 12, 2007) and its status as being of equal legal value to the EU Treaties per TEU 6 may finally lay these concerns to rest.

2.   Conflicts with the fundamental rights provisions of State constitutions have also arisen in other Member States. See for example, *Schmidberger*, set out in Chapter 13, where the right of freedom of expression in the Austrian constitution came into apparent conflict with the provisions of the EC Treaty [TFEU] dealing with the free movement of goods, specifically EC 28/TFEU 34.

3.   In the above case, the court upheld the forfeiture requirement, but there have been cases where the challenge to sureties or deposit schemes in other markets has been successful. See, for example, *SA Buitoni v. Fonds d'orientation et de régularisation des marchés agricoles*, Case 122/78, [1979] ECR 677 and *Bela-Mühle Josef Bergmann v. Grows Farm*, Case 114/76 [1977] ECR 1211.

## THE QUEEN v. SECRETARY OF STATE FOR TRANSPORT EX PARTE FACTORTAME LIMITED AND OTHERS
### Case 213/89, 1990 ECJ CELEX LEXIS 426, [1990] ECR I-2433

[Factortame and others were the owners or operators of 95 fishing vessels which were registered in the register of British vessels under the Merchant Shipping Act 1894. 53 of those vessels were originally registered in Spain and flew the Spanish flag, but on various dates as from 1980 they were registered in the British register. The remaining 42 vessels had always been registered in the United Kingdom, but were purchased by the applicants on various dates, mainly since 1983. The applicants were of Spanish nationality and were seeking to take advantage of the fishing quotas allocated to British fishing vessels under the EU's common fisheries policy]

4 The statutory system governing the registration of British fishing vessels was radically altered by Part II of the Merchant Shipping Act 1988 and the Merchant Shipping (Registration of Fishing Vessels) Regulations 1988 (SI 1988, No 1926). It is common ground that the United Kingdom amended the previous legislation in order to put a stop to the practice known as "quota hopping" whereby, according to the United Kingdom, its fishing quotas are "plundered" by vessels flying the British flag but lacking any genuine link with the United Kingdom.

5 The 1988 Act provided for the establishment of a new register in which henceforth all British fishing vessels were to be registered, including those which were already registered in the old general register maintained under the 1894 Act. However, only fishing vessels fulfilling the conditions laid down in Section 14 of the 1988 Act may be registered in the new register.

6 Paragraph 1 of that section provides that, subject to dispensations to be determined by the Secretary of State for Transport, a fishing vessel is eligible to be registered in the new register only if:

"(a) the vessel is British-owned,

(b) the vessel is managed, and its operations are directed and controlled, from within the United Kingdom and;

(c) any charterer, manager or operator of the vessel is a qualified person or company".

According to Section 14(2), a fishing vessel is deemed to be British-owned if the legal title to the vessel is vested wholly in one or more qualified persons or companies and if the vessel is beneficially owned by one or more qualified companies or, as to not less than 75%, by one or more qualified persons. According to Section 14(7) "qualified person" means a person who is a British citizen resident and domiciled in the United Kingdom and "qualified company" means a company incorporated in the United Kingdom and having its principle place of business there, at least 75% of its shares being owned by one or more qualified persons or companies and at least 75% of its directors being qualified persons.

7 The 1988 Act and the 1988 Regulations entered into force on 1 December 1988. However, under Section 13 of the 1988 Act, the validity of registrations effected under the previous Act was extended for a transitional period until 31 March 1989.

8 On 4 August 1989 the Commission brought an action before the Court under Article 169 [258] of the EEC Treaty for a declaration that, by imposing the nationality requirements laid down in Section 14 of the 1988 Act, the United Kingdom had failed to fulfil its obligations under Articles 7 [18], 52 [49] and 221 [55] of the EEC Treaty. That action is the subject of Case 246/89, now pending before the Court. In a separate document, lodged at the Court Registry on the same date, the Commission applied to the Court for an interim order requiring the United Kingdom to suspend the application of those nationality requirements as regards the nationals of other Member States and in respect of fishing vessels which until 31 March 1989 were carrying on a fishing activity under the British flag and under a British fishing licence. By an order of 10 October 1989 in Case 246/89 R Commission v. United Kingdom ((1989) ECR 3125), the President of the Court granted that application. Pursuant to that order, the United Kingdom made an Order in Council amending Section 14 of the 1988 Act with effect from 2 November 1989.

9 At the time of the institution of the proceedings in which the appeal arises, the 95 fishing vessels of the appellants in the main proceedings failed to satisfy one or more of the conditions for registration under Section 14 of the 1988 Act and thus could not be registered in the new register.

10 Since those vessels were to be deprived of the right to engage in fishing as from 1 April 1989, the companies in question, by means of an application for judicial review, challenged the compatibility of Part II of the 1988 Act with Community law. They also applied for the grant of interim relief until such time as final judgment was given on their application for judicial review.

11 In its judgment of 10 March 1989, the Divisional Court of the Queen's Bench Division: (i) decided to stay the proceedings and to make a reference under Article 177 [267] of the EEC Treaty for a preliminary ruling on the issues of Community law raised in the proceedings; and (ii) ordered that, by way of interim relief, the application of Part II of the 1988 Act and the 1988 Regulations should be suspended as regards the applicants.

12 On 13 March 1989, the Secretary of State for Transport appealed against the Divisional Court's order granting interim relief. By judgment of 22 March 1989, the Court of Appeal held that under national law the courts had no power to suspend, by way of interim relief, the application of Acts of Parliament. It therefore set aside the order of the Divisional Court.

13 [The matter was then appealed to the UK's highest court, the House of Lords, which gave judgment on 18 May 1989.] In its judgment it found in the first place that the claims by the appellants in the main proceedings that they would suffer irreparable damage if the interim relief which they sought were not granted and they were successful in the main proceedings were well founded. However, it held that, under national law, the English courts had no power to grant interim relief in a case such as the one before it. More specifically, it held that the grant of such relief was precluded by the old common-law rule that an interim injunction may not be granted against the Crown, that is to say against the government, in conjunction with the presumption that an Act of Parliament is in conformity with Community law until such time as a decision on its compatibility with that law has been given.

14 The House of Lords then turned to the question whether, notwithstanding that rule of national law, English courts had the power, under Community law, to grant an interim injunction against the Crown.

\*   \*   \*

17 It is clear from the information before the Court, and in particular from the judgment making the reference and, as described above, the course taken by the proceedings in the national courts before which the case came at first and second instance, that the preliminary question raised by the House of Lords seeks essentially to ascertain whether a national court which, in a case before it concerning Community law, consider that the sole obstacle which precludes it from granting interim relief is a rule of national law, must disapply that rule.

\*   \*   \*

20 The Court has also held that any provision of a national legal system and any legislative, administrative or judicial practice which might impair the effectiveness of Community law by withholding from the national court having jurisdiction to apply such law the power to do everything necessary at the moment of its application to set aside national legislative provisions which might prevent, even

temporarily, Community rules from having full force and effect are incompatible with those requirements, which are the very essence of Community law . . . .

21 It must be added that the full effectiveness of Community law would be just as much impaired if a rule of national law could prevent a court seised of a dispute governed by Community law from granting interim relief in order to ensure the full effectiveness of the judgment to be given on the existence of the rights claimed under Community law. It follows that a court which in those circumstances would grant interim relief, if it were not for a rule of national law, is obliged to set aside that rule.

22 That interpretation is reinforced by the system established by Article 177 [267] of the EEC Treaty whose effectiveness would be impaired if a national court, having stayed proceedings pending the reply by the Court of Justice to the question referred to it for a preliminary ruling, were not able to grant interim relief until it delivered its judgment following the reply given by the Court of Justice.

23 Consequently, the reply to the question raised should be that Community law must be interpreted as meaning that a national court which, in a case before it concerning Community law, considers that the sole obstacle which precludes it from granting interim relief is a rule of national law must set aside that rule.

## NOTES AND QUESTIONS

1.    This case was one of three involving Factortame. The second case dealt with the underlying issue of EU law that prompted the need for an injunction, while the third case, set out in Chapter 9 (and joined with a case from Germany, *Brasserie du Pêcheur,*) deals with the issue of compensation for breach of EU law by Member States.

2.    What was the specific issue here that caused a problem for the UK courts?

3.    *Factortame* demonstrates how the doctrine of supremacy may have far-reaching consequences for all stages of a proceeding and indeed give rise to the need to create new national law rights to ensure that that doctrine is upheld. But given the substantially different legal procedures that prevail in the various Member States, and particularly between civil law and common law jurisdictions, might there not always be differences that sometimes are to the detriment of the individual, and could this lead to forum shopping?

4.    In *Sanchez-Llamas v. Oregon*, 548 U.S. 331 (2006), the U.S. Supreme Court had to consider article 36(1)(b) of the Vienna Convention on Consular Relations. This article provided that "if a person detained by a foreign country so requests, the competent authorities of the receiving State shall, without delay, inform the consular post of the sending State" of such detention, and "inform the [detainee] of his rights under this sub-paragraph." Article 36(2) specifies: "The rights referred to in paragraph 1 . . . shall be exercised in conformity with the laws and regulations of the receiving State, subject to the proviso . . . that the said laws . . . must enable full effect to be given to the purposes for which the rights accorded under this Article are intended." The majority assumed that the provision was self-executing and could be invoked by a defendant, but concluded that there was no requirement

under the Convention for any specific remedy to be available to a defendant who was not informed of his right to seek consular assistance, and certainly no requirement that the State courts suppress his confession. This did not mean that the invocable right was not without legal force — clearly if the defendant had requested consular assistance and it had been denied, that would have been a different matter. The court's decision was directed to the *scope* of the defendant's rights and the State's obligations entailed in the Convention article. The consequence of the court's decision was to dilute the potential full force of the article. By contrast, within the EU system, cases such as *Factortame* would suggest that the right to have EU law properly applied cannot be abridged as a result of national procedural obstacles. Moreover, as will be seen in Chapter 9, the failure to allow EU law its full effect in all the circumstances may expose the Member States to claims for damages.

## AMMINISTRAZIONE DELLE FINANZE DELLO STATO v. SIMMENTHAL SPA
### Case 106/77, [1978] ECR 629

[At a previous stage of the proceedings in this case, an Italian judge (Pretore) had asked the ECJ some questions designed to help him determine whether veterinary and public health fees levied on imports of beef and veal under the consolidated text of the Italian veterinary and public health laws, the rate of which had last been fixed in December 1970, were compatible with the Treaty and with certain regulations — in particular Council Regulation 805/68 of 27 June 1968 on the common organization of the market in beef and veal. Italy had continued to charge the fees in question on importation of beef and veal from other Member States in violation of the measures introducing the common organization of the beef and veal market, which expressly forbade such charges. Hence the prior references and the conclusions of the Pretore that led to this reference. (ECJ judgment of 15 December 1976 in *Simmenthal S.p.A. v. Italian Minister for Finance* Case 35/76, [1976] ECR 1871).

Based on the answers to those questions, the Pretore then held that the levying of the fees in question was incompatible with the provisions of Community law and ordered the Amministrazione delle Finanze dello Stato (Italian Finance Administration) to repay the fees unlawfully charged, together with interest. The Amministrazione appealed against that order. The Pretore, concluded that the issue before him involved a conflict between certain rules of EU law and a subsequent national law.

He pointed out to the ECJ that to resolve an issue of this kind, according to recently decided cases of the Italian Constitutional Court, the question whether the law in question was unconstitutional under Article 11 of the Constitution had to be referred to the Constitutional Court itself. Thus, the questions he posed to the ECJ were designed to ascertain what consequences flowed from the direct applicability of a provision of EU law in the event of incompatibility with a subsequent legislative provision of a Member State.]

14 Direct applicability in such circumstances means that rules of Community law must be fully and uniformly applied in all the member-States from the date of their entry into force and for so long as they continue in force.

15 The provisions are therefore a direct source of rights and duties for all those affected thereby, whether member-States or individuals, who are parties to legal relationships under Community law.

16 This consequence also concerns any national court whose task it is as an organ of a member-State to protect, in a case within its jurisdiction, the rights conferred upon individuals by Community law.

17 Furthermore, in accordance with the principle of the precedence of Community law, the relationship between provisions of the Treaty and directly applicable measures of the institutions on the one hand and the national law of the member-States on the other is such that those provisions and measures not only by their entry into force render automatically inapplicable any conflicting provision of current national law but — in so far as they are an integral part of, and take precedence in, the legal order applicable in the territory of each of the member-States — also preclude the valid adoption of new national legislative measures to the extent to which they would be incompatible with Community provisions.

18 Indeed any recognition that national legislative measures which encroach upon the field within which the Community exercises its legislative power or which are otherwise incompatible with the provisions of Community law had any legal effect would amount to a corresponding denial of the effectiveness of obligations under-taken unconditionally and irrevocably by member-States pursuant to the Treaty and would thus imperil the very foundations of the Community.

19 The same conclusion emerges from the structure of Article 177 [267] of the Treaty which provides that any court or tribunal of a member-State is entitled to make a reference to the Court whenever it considers that a preliminary ruling on a question of interpretation or validity relating to Community law is necessary to enable it to give judgment.

20 The effectiveness of that provision would be impaired if the national court were prevented from forthwith applying Community law in accordance with the decision or the case law of the Court.

21 It follows from the foregoing that every national court must, in a case within its jurisdiction, apply Community law in its entirety and protect rights which the latter confers on individuals and must accordingly set aside any provision of a national law which may conflict with it, whether prior or subsequent to the Community rule.

22 Accordingly any provision of a national legal system and any legislative, administrative or judicial practice which might impair the effectiveness of Commu-nity law by withholding from the national court having jurisdiction to apply such law the power to do everything necessary at the moment of its application to set aside national legislative provisions which might prevent Community rules from having full force and effect are incompatible with those requirements which are the very essence of Community law.

23 This would be the case in the event of a conflict between a provision of Community law and a subsequent national law if the solution of the conflict were to be reserved for an authority with a discretion of its own, other than the court called

upon to apply Community law, even if such an impediment to the full effectiveness of Community law were only temporary.

24 The first question should therefore be answered to the effect that a national court which is called upon, within the limits of its jurisdiction, to apply provisions of Community law is under a duty to give full effect to those provisions, if necessary refusing of its own motion to apply any conflicting provision of national legislation, even if adopted subsequently, and it is not necessary for the court to request or await the prior setting aside of such provision by legislative or other constitutional means.

25 The essential point of the second question is whether — assuming it to be accepted that the protection of rights conferred by provisions of Community law can be suspended until any national provisions which might conflict with them have been in fact set aside by the competent national authorities — such setting aside must in every case have unrestricted retroactive effect so as to prevent the rights in question from being in any way adversely affected.

26 It follows . . . that national courts must protect rights conferred by provisions of the Community legal order and that it is not necessary for such courts to request or await the actual setting aside by the national authorities empowered so to act of any national measures which might impede the direct and immediate application of Community rules.

## NOTES AND QUESTIONS

1.   Does it follow from the ECJ's ruling that the national court was required to act unconstitutionally *vis-à-vis* Italian law?

2.   The common organization of the market in beef and veal is one component of the common agricultural policy (CAP) — provided for in EC 32-38/TFEU 38-44. As for many of the staple agricultural products, the organization of the beef and veal market is based on a system of intervention in the market place by the authorities of the Member States under authorization from the EU. The intervention mechanism was designed to maintain price levels and therefore income levels for farmers. As in the United States, the need to provide at least some measure of economic stability for farmers had long driven policy in most Member States before the creation of the original Communities. When the EC Treaty was being negotiated, France was adamant that agriculture be included within the common market subject to a common policy to protect the farming industry, which was a much larger factor in the economy than it was in the economies of the other Member States. The CAP is by far the largest consumer of EU funds. (See further, Chapter 11 *infra*.)

3.   The requirement to apply Union law without national constitutional interference also extends to government agencies: See *Larsy v. INASTI*, Case C118/00 [2001] ECR I-5063.

## [D]   Consequences of Applying the Supremacy Doctrine in National Law

## MINISTERO DELLE FINANZE v. IN.CO.GE.'90 SRL, AND OTHERS

Joined Cases C-10/97 TO C-22/97, 1998 ECJ CELEX LEXIS 603, [1998] ECR I-6307

[A series of disputes had arisen between the Italian Ministry of Finance, on the one hand, and IN.CO.GE.'90 and 12 other limited-liability companies (IN.CO.GE.'90 et al.), on the other, relating to the detailed rules governing repayment of the "tassa di concessione governativa" (administrative charge) for entering companies on the register of companies. The registration charge had originally been introduced in 1972. By 1989 the amount had risen to LIT (Italian Lira) 12 million for public limited companies and partnerships limited by shares, LIT 3.5 million for private limited companies and LIT 500 000 for other companies.

In *Ponente Carni and Cispadana Costruzioni v. Amministrazione delle Finanze dello Stato* Joined Cases C-71/91 and C-178/91 [1993] ECR I-1915, the Court had held that Article 10 of Council Directive 69/335/EEC concerning indirect taxes on the raising of capital (OJ, English Special Edition 1969 (II), p. 412) prohibited, subject to the derogating provisions of Article 12, an annual charge due in respect of the registration of capital companies even though the product of that charge contributed to financing the department responsible for keeping the register of companies. The Court also held that Article 12 of Directive 69/335 meant that duties paid by way of fees or dues referred to in Article 12(1)(e) might constitute payment collected by way of consideration for transactions required by law in the public interest such as, for example, the registration of capital companies. The amount of such duties, which might vary according to the legal form taken by the company, was to be calculated according to the cost of the transaction, which might be assessed on a flat-rate basis.

Following that judgment, the registration charge was reduced to LIT 500 000 for all companies and it ceased to be payable annually. IN.CO.GE.'90 et al. successfully applied to the Pretura di Roma for orders enjoining the Ministry of Finance to repay to them the sums which they had paid by way of the registration charge over previous years, but the Ministry of Finance challenged those injunctions by raising two objections alleging, first, that the Pretura di Roma lacked jurisdiction to hear disputes involving tax matters and, second, that the applicants' entitlement to repayment, which, it claimed, was limited to the amounts paid during the three-year period preceding lodgment of their claims, was barred by lapse of time.]

21 It cannot . . . be inferred from the judgment in Simmenthal that the incompatibility with Community law of a subsequently adopted rule of national law has the effect of rendering that rule of national law non-existent. Faced with such a situation, the national court is, however, obliged to disapply that rule, provided always that this obligation does not restrict the power of the competent national courts to apply, from among the various procedures available under national law,

those which are appropriate for protecting the individual rights conferred by Community law. . . .

22 It remains to be considered whether non-application, as the result of a judgment given by the Court, of national legislation which introduced a levy contrary to Community law has the result of depriving that levy retroactively of its character as a charge and thereby divesting of its fiscal nature the legal relationship established when that charge was levied between the national tax authority and the companies liable to pay it.

23 It is settled case-law that the interpretation which, in the exercise of the jurisdiction conferred upon it by Article 177 [267] of the Treaty, the Court gives to a rule of Community law clarifies and defines where necessary the meaning and scope of that rule as it must be or ought to have been understood and applied from the time of its entry into force. It follows that the rule as so interpreted may, and must, be applied by the courts to legal relationships arising and established before the judgment ruling on the request for interpretation, provided that in other respects the conditions enabling an action relating to the application of that rule to be brought before the courts having jurisdiction are satisfied. . . .

24 Further, in terms of that case-law, entitlement to the recovery of sums levied in breach of Community law is a consequence of, and an adjunct to, the rights conferred on individuals by the relevant Community provisions as interpreted by the Court. A Member State is therefore in principle required to repay charges levied in breach of Community law . . .

25 However, in the absence of Community rules governing the matter, such repayment may be claimed only if the substantive and formal conditions laid down by the various national laws are complied with, provided that such conditions are not less favourable than those governing similar domestic actions and do not render virtually impossible or excessively difficult the exercise of rights conferred by Community law . . .

26 Thus, the obligation on the national court to ensure that a domestic charge levied in breach of Community law is refunded must, subject to compliance with the two conditions laid down by the Court in its case-law, be discharged in accordance with the provisions of its national law. It follows that the detailed rules for repayment which are to apply and the classification, for that purpose, of the legal relationship established when that charge was levied between the tax authorities of a Member State and particular companies in that State are matters which fall to be determined under national law.

27 Furthermore, as the Court has recently held, Community law does not in principle preclude the legislation of a Member State from laying down, alongside a limitation period applicable under the ordinary law to actions between private individuals for the recovery of sums paid but not due, special detailed rules governing claims and legal proceedings to challenge the imposition of charges and other levies . . .

28 The possibility thus recognised by the Court of applying those special detailed rules to the repayment of charges and other levies found to be contrary to Community law would be deprived of any effect if, as the Commission argues, the

incompatibility between a domestic levy and Community law necessarily had the effect of depriving that levy of its character as a charge and divesting of its fiscal nature the legal relationship established, when the charge in question was levied, between the national tax authorities and the parties liable to pay it.

29 The answer to the question submitted must therefore be that the obligation on a national court to disapply national legislation introducing a charge contrary to Community law must lead that court, in principle, to uphold claims for repayment of that charge. Such repayment must be ensured in accordance with the provisions of its national law, on condition that those provisions are not less favourable than those governing similar domestic actions and do not render virtually impossible or excessively difficult the exercise of rights conferred by Community law. Any reclassification of the legal relationship established between the tax authorities of a Member State and certain companies in that State when a domestic charge subsequently found to be contrary to Community law was levied is therefore a matter for national law.

## NOTES AND QUESTIONS

**1.** According to the ECJ, what are the consequences of a determination that a national law conflicts with EU law?

**2.** In *Office National des Pensions v. Emilienne Jonkman and Hélène Vercheval and Noelle Permesaen v. Office National des Pensions*, Joined Cases C-231/06 to C-233/06, 2007 ECJ CELEX LEXIS 349, [2006] ECR I-5149, the Court was asked what the national court and Member State government should be required to do in the context of a claim based on gender discrimination contrary to EC 141/TFEU 157:

> 38 [I]t is for the authorities of the Member State concerned to take the general or particular measures necessary to ensure that Community law is complied within that state. While they retain the choice of the measures to be taken, those authorities must in particular ensure that national law is changed so as to comply with Community law as soon as possible and that the rights which individuals derive from Community law are given full effect. 39. In addition, as the Court has repeatedly held in situations of discrimination contrary to Community law, for as long as measures reinstating equal treatment have not been adopted, observance of the principle of equality can be ensured only by granting to persons within the disadvantaged category the same advantages as those enjoyed by persons within the favoured category. In such a situation, a national court must set aside any discriminatory provision of national law, without having to request or await its prior removal by the legislature, and apply to members of the disadvantaged group the same arrangements as those enjoyed by the persons in the other category.

## [E]   The Effects of the Primacy Doctrine on the Position of the Member States in International Law

### YASSIN ABDULLAH KADI AND AL BARAKAAT INTERNATIONAL FOUNDATION v. COUNCIL
Joined Cases C-402/05 P and C-415/05 P, 2008 ECJ EUR-Lex LEXIS 1954, [2008] ECR I-6351

[This case joins appeals from the decisions of the General Court in Case T-306/1 and *Kadi v. Council and Commission*, Case T-315/01 2005 ECJ EUR-Lex LEXIS 673, [2005] ECR II-3649 (based on similar grounds). After the 9/11 attacks in the U.S., the a committee of the UN Security Council had issued rules requiring the member States of the UN to take action freezing the assets of terrorist organizations. In light of the scope of responsibilities of the EU by that time, the EU Member States decided that the freezing of accounts should be by action of the EU Council. This entailed a procedure whereby the Member States first determined from their intelligence services who should be on the list, and this list was then to be forwarded to the Council. The Council then issued regulations formally freezing the assets. Since it would have defeated the purpose if the organizations were given any notice before the regulations went into effect, they were not given any form of hearing before the Council took action. Kadi and others sought to challenge the regulations in the CFI/General Court based on breaches of EU fundamental rights. The CFI/General Court gave a lengthy judgment in which it expressed the view that the EU courts could not stand in the way of the obligations of the Member States under the UN Charter. It therefore declined to review the Council's actions against the standard of EU fundamental rights. Instead, it proceeded to review the actions of the Security Council committee under "Peremptory Principles" (*ius cogens*) of international law and found that there was no breach of such principles.

In the next chapter we shall see that Union law embraces fundamental rights based on general principles common to the Member States and now on the Charter of Fundamental Rights. The ECJ effectively determined in this appeal that the CFI/General Court had erred in finding that the obligations of the Member States under the UN Charter could take precedence over the EU legal system and in particular over the regime of fundamental rights that are an integral part of that legal system.]

280 The Court will now consider the heads of claim in which the appellants complain that the Court of First Instance, in essence, held that it followed from the principles governing the relationship between the international legal order under the United Nations and the Community legal order that the contested regulation, since it is designed to give effect to a resolution adopted by the Security Council under Chapter VII of the Charter of the United Nations affording no latitude in that respect, could not be subject to judicial review of its internal lawfulness, save with regard to its compatibility with the norms of jus cogens, and therefore to that extent enjoyed immunity from jurisdiction.

281 In this connection it is to be borne in mind that the Community is based on the rule of law, inasmuch as neither its Member States nor its institutions can avoid

review of the conformity of their acts with the basic constitutional charter, the EC Treaty, which established a complete system of legal remedies and procedures designed to enable the Court of Justice to review the legality of acts of the institutions . . .

282 It is also to be recalled that an international agreement cannot affect the allocation of powers fixed by the Treaties or, consequently, the autonomy of the Community legal system, observance of which is ensured by the Court by virtue of the exclusive jurisdiction conferred on it by Article 220 EC, [TEU 19] jurisdiction that the Court has, moreover, already held to form part of the very foundations of the Community . . .

283 In addition, according to settled case-law, fundamental rights form an integral part of the general principles of law whose observance the Court ensures. For that purpose, the Court draws inspiration from the constitutional traditions common to the Member States and from the guidelines supplied by international instruments for the protection of human rights on which the Member States have collaborated or to which they are signatories. In that regard, the ECHR has special significance . . .

284 It is also clear from the case-law that respect for human rights is a condition of the lawfulness of Community acts . . . and that measures incompatible with respect for human rights are not acceptable in the Community . . .

285 It follows from all those considerations that the obligations imposed by an international agreement cannot have the effect of prejudicing the constitutional principles of the EC Treaty, which include the principle that all Community acts must respect fundamental rights, that respect constituting a condition of their lawfulness which it is for the Court to review in the framework of the complete system of legal remedies established by the Treaty.

286 In this regard it must be emphasised that, in circumstances such as those of these cases, the review of lawfulness thus to be ensured by the Community judicature applies to the Community act intended to give effect to the international agreement at issue, and not to the latter as such.

287 With more particular regard to a Community act which, like the contested regulation, is intended to give effect to a resolution adopted by the Security Council under Chapter VII of the Charter of the United Nations, it is not, therefore, for the Community judicature, under the exclusive jurisdiction provided for by Article 220 EC, to review the lawfulness of such a resolution adopted by an international body, even if that review were to be limited to examination of the compatibility of that resolution with jus cogens.

288 However, any judgment given by the Community judicature deciding that a Community measure intended to give effect to such a resolution is contrary to a higher rule of law in the Community legal order would not entail any challenge to the primacy of that resolution in international law.

# NOTES AND QUESTIONS

1.   The Union is not a state and cannot therefore be a full member of the United Nations, since membership is reserved for sovereign states. Yet the Union's sovereign powers had been extended to include actions involving the freezing of terrorist assets. This competence depended at the time of this decision on a rather convoluted linkage of various TEU and EC/TFEU provisions, but has since been confirmed in the TFEU by explicit language (EC 60/TFEU 75). The Member States were bound by the UN Security Council Committee actions but had to depend on the Union to carry them out. The CFI/General Court was concerned that if fundamental rights could be asserted at the Union level this might interfere with the duties of the Member States under international law and therefore decided that it could not review the Union's actions. The ECJ rejected the notion that it could not review the Council's actions under EU law. How and why did the Court reach this result? Is this a more satisfactory conclusion to the issue of potential conflict between Union requirements and Member State duties than that reached by the General Court?

2.   Suppose that it were found that an EU regulation that incorporated specific requirements imposed by a UN action (or for that matter, any other body that could take actions binding the Member States) violated principles of EU law in some fashion. This could lead to a breach of obligations imposed on the Member States. Does the ECJ offer any suggestions as to how such a situation might be resolved? Note in this regard that the ECJ explicitly rejects (para 287) the notion that the EU courts have jurisdiction under EC 220/TEU 19 to review the legality of international acts existing outside the EU legal framework.

3.   Did the ECJ endorse the view expressed by the UK elsewhere in the judgment that the UN Charter must prevail over any conflicting provisions of the EU and EC Treaties? Could such an argument be made with respect to a conflict between the UN Charter and the U.S. Constitution or any federal law?

4.   As noted above, the General Court had concluded that it would evaluate the Security Council Resolutions in question and the actions of the Sanctions Committee created by the Security Council, under norms of *jus cogens*, so-called "super norms" or peremptory norms from which no derogation is permitted. The Court cited Article 53 of the Vienna Convention on the Law of Treaties, which defines a peremptory norm of general international law and declares a treaty to be void if it conflicts with a peremptory norm and Article 64, which declares that: "If a new peremptory norm . . . . emerges, any existing treaty which is in conflict with that norm becomes void and terminates." The United States and some other countries involved in the drafting of the Vienna Convention opposed including reference to peremptory norms in the Convention on the ground that to do so would create uncertainty and confusion regarding the validity of treaties. The majority of the states present at the drafting conference decided to include the reference but failed to agree on any examples of *jus cogens* norms. Moreover, the definition of a peremptory norm in Article 53 of the Convention leaves unclear the process whereby it is determined whether the international community of states as a whole has accepted and recognized a particular norm as being one from which no derogation is permitted. At the instance of the United States, Article 66 of the

Convention provides that questions about *jus cogens* are subject to obligatory dispute settlement before the International Court of Justice — the only question that the Vienna Convention so links to the ICJ. Article 66 may only be invoked by a party to the Convention, however, and the United States has never ratified the Convention.

The failure of the drafters of the Vienna Convention to agree on a list of *jus cogens* norms has not been followed by any greater success of the part of state representatives in other forums. For its part, the International Court of Justice, in *Nicaragua v. United States*, asserted that the international prohibition on the use of force was "conspicuous example of a rule of law having the character of *jus cogens.*" *Military and Paramilitary Activities in and Against Nicaragua (Nicaragua v. United States)*, 1986 ICJ 14 (judgment on Merits of June 27). But as Anthony D'Amato has point out, the opinion in the *Nicaragua* case gives no indication as to how the judges reached this conclusion. Anthony D'Amato, *It's a Bird, It's a Plane, It's Jus Cogens*, 6 Conn. J. Int'l Law (1990).

See further, Martin Nettesheim, *U.N. sanctions against individuals — A challenge to the architecture of European Union governance* (2007) 44 CML Rev. 567. For a commentary on the first instance judgment see C. Tomuschat, *Case T-306/01, Ahmed Ali Yusuf and Al Barakaat International Foundation v. Council and Commission; Case T-315/01, Yassin Abdullah Kadi v. Council and Commission'* (2006) 43 CML Rev. 537.

**5.** In *Opinion 1/9, re the Draft Treaty on a European Economic Area*, 1991 ECJ CELEX LEXIS 479, [1991] ECR I-6079 the Court was asked to provide an opinion on the legality under EU law of the referenced draft Treaty (described in Chapter 2). The draft Treaty provided for an alignment of language and interpretation of EU law with the law deriving from the broader EEA Treaty. The ECJ first outlined the essential principle guiding its approach, namely that the EU and the EEA pursue fundamentally different objectives. The EU is a dynamic organization that is constantly moving forward to closer integration, while the EEA is simply a reactive organization. Thus, while the provisions of the two treaties might read identically, there is no guarantee that they will be interpreted the same way going forward. Furthermore, the EEA treaty did not properly recognize the primacy of EU law, but merely provided for national legislatures to assure that national laws should not be contrary to its provisions — which would clearly be inappropriate for the Member States, who were also parties to the EEA Treaty, since EU law goes further than that.

The Court proceeded to examine the Draft EEA Treaty to discover whether the autonomy of the EU system was protected.

It found that a number of the EEA provisions would jeopardize the autonomy of the EU system:

(a) The Treaty provided for an EEA Court that would follow Court of Justice decisions, but this did not apply to future judgments.

(b) The EEA Court had the power implicitly to rule on the division of competences between the EU and the Member States.

(c) The EEA Court had the power to rule on EEA rules that are incorporated directly into the EU legal system and sit alongside the corresponding EU rules. This would contravene the requirement in EC 220/TEU 19 that the ECJ was responsible for interpreting EU law.

(d) The Treaty also provided for EU judges to sit on the EEA Court. The placing of ECJ judges in the EEA Court would require them to take differing approaches to the same rules, which would place them in an impossible position;

(e) The treaty provided for non-binding judgments to be given by the ECJ in response to EFTA Courts seeking interpretation. Here the Court fundamentally objected to the notion that it could serve as an advisory body, a function it considered at odds with its role as a court of law as laid out in the EU Treaties.

In a second Opinion, following changes made to the EEA Treaty based on Opinion 1/91 the Court noted that changes had been made with the goal of preserving the autonomy of the EU legal order:

(a) The revised treaty abandoned the proposal for an EEA Court together with the notion that decisions of the combined court would have identical effects in the EEA and the EU.

(b) The Treaty now established a Joint Committee charged with keeping under review the decisions of the EFTA court and the ECJ (art 105). The Joint Committee's decisions however must not affect the case law of the ECJ. If the Joint Committee could not reconcile conflicting interpretations, there was a further procedure for settling the dispute (art 111). The ECJ was concerned that this might be construed as giving to the Joint Committee the power to give a binding interpretation of EU law, but concluded that it was intended that the Joint Committee could not make a determination that affected the ECJ's case law.

(c) To the extent that the ECJ was asked to give opinions to the Joint committee, although such rulings were not intended to settle the dispute, they would be binding as to the interpretation given, thus not undermining the role of the ECJ as a court.

**6.** Appearing in Chapter 12 is *Opinion 1/76* where the Court had to deal with a somewhat similar issue caused by the participation of the EU and various Member States in an agreement to which Switzerland was also a party, dealing with the administration of laying up fund for inland waterway vessels. The Court ruled the agreement incompatible with the EC Treaty/TFEU for a number of reasons:

(1) Continued participation of the Member States was not compatible with the role of the EU.

(2) The EU's freedom of action was compromised by the transfer of powers to the Board.

(3) The Court's role was compromised.

Similarly, Chapter 9 includes an Opinion of the Court addressing a proposed draft Treaty establishing a European Patent regime. Here, the Court was concerned about the effects the draft treaty might have on the duties of the Member States to interpret and apply Union law.

**7.** Another aspect of the Union's status in international law has now emerged as a result of Lisbon: the Union was given authority to set up its own form of diplomatic corps (the External Action Service). This will exist alongside the representations of the Member States, to represent the Union in matters within its competence. (See Template para. 4.2.4.) The Commission had already had powers in this area, but it may be noted that the Lisbon change entails representation of the *Union*, not a particular institution.

## § 3.03   THE DOCTRINE OF SUPREMACY IN NATIONAL COURTS

### [A]   Acceptance of the ECJ's View of Supremacy?

### ADMINISTRATION DES DOUANES v. SOCIETE CAFES JACQUES VABRE & J. WEIGEL ET CIE SARL
Cour de Cassation (Combined chambers)
[1974] CASS. CH. MIX. 6, [1975] 2 CMLR 336 (COUR DE CASS., CHAMB. COMB., MAY 24, 1975)
(France)

[Jacques Vabre invoked EEC 95 (EC 90/TFEU 110] against a French consumption tax on Dutch coffee imported into France. Under Article 55 of the French Constitution, treaties have the force of law in the national system in priority to national legislation.]

CONCLUSIONS OF THE PROCUREUR GENERAL

If Art. 55 [of the Constitution] referred only to laws prior to a treaty it would have been sufficient if it had provided that "the treaty has the force of law," because it is an absolute principle that subsequent law has precedence over prior law.

An analysis of this provision in the light of the notions of international law which inspired those who drafted the Constitutions of 1946 and 1958 compels us to conclude that the notion of the superiority of a treaty over [national] law makes sense only with regard to laws enacted subsequently to the treaty, because, with regard to prior laws the answer is evident, just as it is evident that the international legal order can be realized and develop only if the States loyally apply the agreements which they have signed, ratified and published.

\*   \*   \*

[The EEC Treaty] establishes the supremacy of Community law in its Article 5 [10] and applies it in a concrete fashion in its Article 189 [288], according to which the regulations are "binding" and are "directly applicable in all Member States"; it deprives the governments, which have signed it, of the power which they possess in classic international law, i.e., to define the sense or the significance of an obscure or ambiguous clause of a diplomatic act. Instead, it entrusts a common European judicial institution with the task of assuring the unity of the interpretation of the

Treaty; it establishes institutions holding powers of their own.

\*    \*    \*

It would be possible for you, in order to assure the pre-eminence of Art. 95 [110] of the Treaty of Rome over the subsequent [national] law, to rely on Art. 55 of the Constitution, but personally, I ask you not to do so but rather to base your decision only on the very nature of the legal order established by the Treaty of Rome.

In fact, if you would limit yourself to deduce the supremacy [of the EEC Treaty] within the French legal system, of Community law over national law, from Art. 55 of our Constitution, you would explain and justify this supremacy with regard to our country. But such a holding would admit that it is a function of our Constitution, and only of our Constitution, that the rank of Community law in our internal legal order [is superior to that of national law.

You would therefore, by implication, furnish a considerable argument to the courts of those Member States which, in the absence of a provision in their constitutions affirming the pre-eminence of treaties, would be tempted to deduce from this the opposite conclusion, as the Italian Constitutional Court did in 1962 when it held that it was a matter of national constitutional law to determine the rank of Community law within the internal order of each Member State.

These are the reasons, gentlemen, for which I ask you not to base your decision on Art. 55 of the Constitution. In this way you would recognize that the transfer of power made by the Member States from their internal legal order in favour of the legal order of the Community — within the limits of the rights and obligations corresponding to the provisions of the Treaty — has as its consequence a definitive limitation of their sovereign rights against which a unilateral and subsequent act, incompatible with the notion of the Community, could not prevail.

This is, by the way, the method which you already employ . . . when you refer a case to the Court of Justice on the basis of Article 177 [267]. In these cases you rely only on this Article of the Treaty and do not refer to any Article of the Constitution or any text of French legislation.

## JUDGMENT OF THE COURT

It is . . . complained that the judgment below invalidated the internal consumption tax established by . . . the Customs Code as a consequence of its incompatibility with the provisions of Article 95 [110] . . .

But the [EEC Treaty], which by virtue of [Article 55] of the Constitution has an authority greater than that of statutes, institutes a separate legal order integrated with that of the Member States. Because of that separateness, the legal order which it has created is directly applicable to the nationals of those States and is binding on their courts. Therefore the [lower court] was correct and did not exceed its powers in deciding that Article 95 [110] of the Treaty was to be applied in the instant case, and not the customs Code, even though the latter was later in date. It follows that the [claim] must be dismissed.

It is also complained that the judgment applied Article 95 [110] of the [EEC

Treaty] when, according to the appeal, Article 55 of the Constitution expressly subjects the authority which it gives to treaties ratified by France to the condition that they should be applied by the other party. The judge at first instance was not therefore able baldly to apply this constitutional provision without investigating whether the State (The Netherlands) from which the product in question was imported has met this condition of reciprocity.

But in the Community legal order the failings of a Member State . . . to comply with the obligations falling on it by virtue of the [EEC Treaty] are subject to the [Member State enforcement] procedure laid down by Article 170 [259] of that Treaty and so the plea of lack of reciprocity cannot be made before the national courts. It follows that this ground must be dismissed.

[The Court also rejected all of the appellant's other grounds for appeal.]

## NOTES AND QUESTIONS

1.  The Constitution of the Fifth Republic (1958) provides:

### Article 54

If the Constitutional Council, on a referral from the President of the Republic, from the Prime Minister, from the President of one or the other Houses, or from sixty Members of the National Assembly or sixty Senators, has held that an international undertaking contains a clause contrary to the Constitution, authorization to ratify or approve the international undertaking involved may be given only after amending the Constitution.

### Article 55

Treaties or agreements duly ratified or approved shall, upon publication, prevail over Acts of Parliament, subject, with respect to each agreement or treaty, to its application by the other party.

Unlike Germany, France does not have a constitutional court as such. Nor, strictly speaking, is there any court in the French judicial system that has the power to declare French legislation unconstitutional. Rather, the Constitutional Council (Conseil Constitutionnel), which is not a court, has the authority, under Articles 61 and 62 of the French Constitution, to review laws *before* they are promulgated by the French Parliament to ascertain whether they conform to the constitution. This review is required for so-called "organic laws," i.e., laws that specify the organization or functions of public powers in developing the principles or rules enunciated in the constitution. Ordinary laws may be reviewed if submitted to the Constitutional Council prior to their promulgation by the President of the Republic, the Prime Minister, the President of the National Assembly, the President of the Senate, or by 60 deputies or 60 senators. If the Constitutional Council decides that the law does not conform to the constitution, it may not be promulgated. The Council's decision is final and not subject to appeal.

The Council of State (Conseil d'Etat) is the central organ of governmental administration. It exercises judicial as well as administrative functions *within the executive branch*. In its judicial capacity, it can review executive and administrative acts. Such review includes determinations of whether these acts conform to the constitution.

The Cour de Cassation is the highest court in the hierarchy of ordinary courts and is to be distinguished from the Council of State, which is not part of the judicial system. Set forth above is a landmark decision of the Cour de Cassation. The proposal of the Procureur Général in *Jacques Vabre* appears much in line with the ECJ's pure "federal" approach, namely, that EU law applies as a result of a concurrent sovereignty with the French Constitution over French territory. Did the Cour de Cassation accept this reasoning?

2.　In *Boisdet*, [1990] Rec. Lebon 250, [1991] 1 CMLR 3, the French court was willing to apply an EU regulation so as to annul a later conflicting French ministerial order relating to the extension of rules on producers of dessert apples. The order was based upon a French statute that permitted such an order, but the court considered the EU regulation controlling. No mention was made of the impact of the French constitution here. It appears that *Boisdet* therefore was decided on the basis that French domestic law was simply inapplicable where it had been preempted by EU law, once again affirming the French courts' willingness to follow the concept expressed by the Procureur in *Vabre* of separate sovereignties in line with the ECJ's approach. Later on, the Conseil Constitutional (Constitutional Council) of France was requested to review the constitutionality of amendments to the French Constitution to enable ratification of the TEU: *Re Ratification of the European Union Treaty*, Case 92-308 DC [1993] 3 CMLR 345. Some remarks in this case, such as the following excerpt, give further support to this view:

> (a) Furthermore, the European Union Treaty does not have the consequence that it alters the legal nature of the European Parliament. The latter is not a sovereign assembly with general powers and is not intended to take part in exercising national sovereignty. The European Parliament belongs to a special legal system which, although integrated into the legal system of the different member-States of the Communities, does not belong to the institutional system of France.

Note that a new Article 88-1 was inserted into the French Constitution to deal with France's ratification of the first TEU and a further change was made to deal with the Lisbon Treaty, so that the provision now reads as follows:

> The Republic shall participate in the European Union constituted by States which have freely chosen to exercise some of their powers in common by virtue of the Treaty on European Union and of the Treaty on the Functioning of the European Union, as they result from the treaty signed in Lisbon on 13 December, 2007.

3.　In Ireland, in *Tate and Robinson v. Minister for Social Welfare and Attorney General*, [1995] 1 Irish reports 425, Carroll, J., in considering the invocability of Directive 79/7 on equal treatment of men and women in social security matters, declared that "We are concerned here with a whole new legal order." He stated further: "I do not accept that the breach of obligation by the State to implement the Directive is a breach of [domestic law] statutory duty. It is . . . . a wrong arising from Community law which has domestic effect and approximates to a breach of Constitutional duty". In another case involving equal treatment, *Murphy v. Bord Telecom Eireann*, [1988] 2 CMLR 753, a preliminary ruling had been obtained by the Irish court that the Irish interpretation of "like work" in the context of the prohibition on sex discrimination in EC 141/TFEU 157 did not conform to the EU interpretation of that term (see on further on this subject, chapter 18 *infra*). The High Court made it very clear that the Irish courts must follow the EU interpretation.

4.    In *Lassagard, Regeringsrattens Arsbok* 1997 No 65 the Swedish Supreme Administrative Court considered an argument that the complainant company had been denied agricultural aid under an EU Regulation because the application was out of time. It was then denied the opportunity to appeal and, in appealing that denial, invoked the principle laid out by the ECJ that national actions implementing EU legislation should be subject to judicial control, a fundamental right recognized as part of EU law. The Supreme Administrative Court accepted this argument and reversed the lower court, thus overturning Swedish procedural law in this regard.

5.    In *Natural Mineral Water Case* GZV 136/94 Europarecht in Fällen p 158, the Austrian Constitutional Court recognized its obligations under EC 10/TEU 4 to interpret national law in accordance with the provisions of directives.

6.    In Belgium, the parliament is given sole final authority to determine the constitutionality of a statute and declare it void. In *Fromagerie "Le Ski"*, [1971] Pasicrisie Belge 886, [1972] CMLR 330, a decision of the Belgian Cour de Cassation, the court held that the Belgian courts may refuse to apply a Belgian statute that conflicts with EU law, and that to do so does not constitute a finding that the statute is annulled.

In this case, the Court of Appeal had declared that "Le Ski" (a company manufacturing yogurt) had grounds for seeking restitution of special duties paid pursuant to a Royal Decree of 1968. The State argued that a law passed subsequently had ratified this Decree and therefore the Court should have enforced the decree. The Court resolved the issue as to whether a later statute could prevail over the earlier EC Treaty as follows:

> Even if assent to a treaty, as required by Article 68(2) of the Constitution, is given in the form of a statute, the legislative power, by giving this assent, is not carrying out a normative function. The conflict which exists between a legal norm established by an international treaty and a norm established by a subsequent statute, is not a conflict between two statutes.

> The rule that a statute repeals a previous statute in so far as there is a conflict between the two, does not apply in the case of a conflict between a treaty and statute.

> In the event of a conflict between a norm of domestic law and a norm of international law which produces direct effects in the internal legal system, the rule established by the treaty shall prevail. The primacy of the treaty results from the very nature of international treaty law.

This is a fortiori the case when a conflict exists, as in the present case, between a norm of internal law and a norm of Community law.

The reason is that the treaties which have created Community law have instituted a new legal system in whose favour the member-States have restricted the exercise of their sovereign powers in the areas determined by those treaties.

Article 12 [25] of the Treaty establishing the European Economic Community is immediately effective and confers on individual persons rights which national courts are bound to uphold.

It follows from all these considerations that it was the duty of the judge to set aside the application of provisions of domestic law that are contrary to this Treaty provision.

Having noted that in the present case the norms of Community law and the norms of domestic law were incompatible, the judgment under attack was able to decide, without infringing the legal provisions set out in the application to this Court, that the effects of the Law of 19 March 1968 had been stopped in so far as it was in conflict with a directly applicable provision of international treaty law. In this respect, the grounds of appeal fail for want of a legal basis.

Without contradicting itself, the judgment was able to declare firstly that "the claim of the appellant [the respondent in the present proceedings] does not lead to a declaration that a law is null and void" and secondly that this claim entails "finding that its effects are stopped." This reasoning, which is attacked, does not suffer from obscurity or contradiction.

In so far as it alleges a violation of Article 97 of the Constitution, this argument fails for want of a legal basis.

In the case of *Orfinger v. Belgian State (Minister for Civil Service), Conseil d'Etat* (Sixth Chamber), Journal des Tribunaux 1997, p 254, the court rationalized the acceptance of the supremacy of EU law on the basis that Belgium could withdraw from the Treaties but so long as it continued to be a signatory, all of the principles and laws of the EU must be applied in Belgium even if the effect is to restrict certain provisions of the Constitution. A similar conclusion was reached by the Italian Court of Cassation in *Talamucci v. Minister of Health* Case 1512/98, Jiust. Civ., 1998, I, p. 1935 where the Court indicated that either EU law must take precedence or, in the event of a serious conflict with the Constitution, Italy could resolve the issue by withdrawing from the EU. The TEU now expressly recognizes the right of withdrawal (TEU 50).

7.   In Case No 384/94 *President of Council of Ministers v. Umbrian Region*, Il Foro Italiano 1994 I p 3289, the Italian Constitutional Court accepted that it had jurisdiction to hear a challenge brought by the Italian Government against a draft law of the Umbrian Region which the Government considered would conflict with EU regulations on vine planting. The purpose of the action was to ensure that the Italian government, as the party responsible for compliance with EU law, was not put in a situation where it would be in breach. This case thus confirms that the

Constitutional Court accepted the principle of responsibility under EC 10/TEU 4. Not every Member State by any means has a procedure for vetting a national or regional law before it becomes law. Could the absence of such a procedure itself be considered a violation of TEU 4?

8.   In *Metten v. Minister of Finance*, Netherlands Council of State (Administrative Law Division, 7 July 1995), Maastricht Journal of European and Comparative Law 1996, p 179, the appellant was an MEP who sought access to EU Council documents. This access was denied by the Dutch Minister based on the confidentiality clause in the EU Council's Rules of Procedure. The Court held that this was a binding obligation that took precedence over national law. The Rules were not adopted in any of the forms laid down in EC 249/TFEU 288, but were nonetheless considered to be applicable in the same way as a regulation.

9.   In Germany, while the supremacy doctrine remains theoretically an unsettled matter, some judges of the Constitutional court have objected to the continued assertions by that court of the ability to appraise EU law in light of the Grundgesetz. Thus, in the *Internationale Handelsgesellschaft* case (the German proceeding) set out below, there is also found the following dissenting passage:

DISSENTING OPINION (Rupp, Hirsh and Wand JJ.)

We regard the reference as inadmissible and therefore cannot concur in the judgement.

\* \* \*

Rules of law which have been issued by organs of the European Communities on the basis of powers transferred to them (secondary Community law) cannot be examined for their compatibility with the norms on fundamental rights in the Constitution.

\* \* \*

The rules of law issued by [the Community] form — together with the provisions of the Treaty and unwritten principles of law — the Community's fund of legal norms. This system of Community law is autonomous and independent of the national legal sphere.

Both legal spheres recognize — each for its own sector — norms dealing with fundamental rights and a legal protection system calculated to enforce these rights.

(a) Fundamental rights are guaranteed not only by the Constitution within the national system of law of the Federal Republic of Germany, but also by the system of law of the European Communities.

\* \* \*

Above all, the essential elements of the principle of the rule of law and fundamental rights are guaranteed at [the] Community level in the case law of the European Court. The principle of proportionality has been recognized by the European Court from the very beginning of its case law as the criterion for the legality of actions of the Community organs. [On] the protection of liberties . . . there is enough . . . case law to permit the statement that fundamental rights are adequately protected at [the] Community level. The European Court has repeatedly emphasized that the observance of fundamental rights belongs to the general legal principles, the upholding of which it is the European Court's duty to ensure. The criteria for this are first and foremost the constitutional traditions of the member States.

The legal system of the European Communities also has at its disposal a legal protection system calculated to enforce these fundamental rights.

It is true that the individual can only appeal to the European Court against acts of the Community organs when he is directly and individually affected by such an act. but in so far as legal rules of the Communities or decisions addressed to the member States require execution by the State organs of the Federal Republic of Germany, the legal remedy provided against the internal State act remains open to the individual. In proceedings of this kind, the German courts also have to examine whether the rules of Community law on which the challenged measure is based are compatible with superior norms of the Community system of law. These superior norms include the fundamental rights and the principles of the rule of law recognized by the European Court. If doubts arise as to whether the rule to be applied is in harmony with the fundamental rights or the principle of the rule of law, the German court may-and in so far as it is acting as a court of final instance indeed must-refer this question to the European Court for a preliminary ruling under Article 177 [267] of the EEC Treaty.

\*　\*　\*

The rules of law issued by [the Community organs] cannot therefore be dependent in their validity and applicability on whether they match the criteria of national law. In content, Community law takes precedence over divergent provisions of national law. This applies not only in relation to norms of simple national law, but also vis-à-vis norms of the national constitutions dealing with fundamental rights.

\*　\*　\*

The "basic structure of the Constitution, on which its identity rests" is not at stake in this process. The question of whether Article 24(1) of the Constitution permits a transfer of sovereign rights which gives Community organs the opportunity to make law binding nationally, entirely untrammelled by being bound by fundamental rights, no longer poses itself today. It is therefore mistaken from the start for the majority of the Court to believe that it has to ward off some "encroachment" on the structures which go to make up the Constitution, and in particular its section dealing with fundamental rights, but binding Community law to the fundamental rights norms of the national Constitution. Nor can such an assumption be founded by reference to the fact that the European Communities do not yet possess any codified catalogue of fundamental rights. In this context, the mode of guaranteeing the fundamental rights is irrelevant, and the assertion that only a codification offers adequate certainty of law does not bear examination . . . The argument that the fundamental rights of the Constitution must also prevail over secondary Community law because the Community still lacks a directly legitimated parliament is not in itself conclusive. The protection of fundamental rights and the democratic principle are not interchangeable inside a democratically constituted community based on the idea of freedom; they complement one another. While the achievement of the democratic principle in the EEC would cause the legislator and the executive to be more deeply concerned with fundamental rights, this would not make the judicial protection of fundamental rights superfluous. The view of the law adopted by the majority of the Court leads, moreover, to unacceptable results. If the applicability of secondary Community law were dependent on its satisfying the fundamental rights norms of a national Constitution, then-since the Member States guarantee fundamental rights to differing extents-the situation could arise where legal rules of the Communities are applicable in some Member States, but not in others. This would result, precisely [in] the field of Community law, in a fragmentation of law. To open up this possibility means exposing a part of European legal unity, endangering the existence of the Community, and negating the basic idea of European unification.

The Bundesverfassungsgericht possesses no jurisdiction to examine rules of Community law against the criteria of the Constitution, in particular of its section on fundamental rights.

*   *   *

The fact that the majority of the Court nonetheless claims this power is an inadmissible trespass on the jurisdiction reserved to the European Court.

## [B]   Conflicts With Fundamental Rights

### INTERNATIONALE HANDELSGESELLSHAFT MBH v. EINFUHR- UND VORRATSSTELLE FÜR GETREIDE UND FUTTERMITTEL (SOLANGE I)
Federal Constitutional Court (2nd Senate)
CASE 2 BVL 52/71, 37 BVERFGE 271, [1974] 2 CMLR 540
(Germany)

[The ECJ's separate judgment in this case and the factual background are set out earlier in this chapter. At the time the only provision in the German constitution, or Grundgesetz (GG) allowing transfer of powers to international bodies was article 24 which states: "The Federation may by legislation transfer sovereign powers to intergovernmental institutions."]

MAJORITY OPINION

[The present case demands] clarification of the relationship between the guarantees of fundamental rights in the Constitution and rules of secondary Community law of the EEC, the execution of which is in the hands of administrative authorities in the Federal Republic of Germany.

This Court — in this respect in agreement with the law developed by the European Court of Justice — adheres to its settled view that the Community law is neither a component part of the national legal system nor international law, but forms an independent system of law flowing from an autonomous legal source.

[I]n principle, the two legal spheres stand independent of and side by side one another in their validity and that, in particular, the competent Community organs, including the European Court of Justice, have to rule on the binding force, construction and observance of Community law, and the competent national organs on the binding force, construction and observance of the constitutional law of the Federal Republic of Germany. The European Court of Justice cannot with binding effect rule on whether a rule of Community law is compatible with the Constitution, nor can the Bundesverfassungsgericht rule on whether, and with what implications, a rule of secondary Community law is compatible with primary Community law. This does not lead to any difficulties as long as the two systems of law do not come into conflict with one another in their substance. There therefore grows forth from the special relationship which has arisen between the Community and its members by the establishment of the Community first and foremost the duty for the competent organs, in particular for the two courts charged with reviewing law — the European Court of Justice and the Bundesverfassungsgericht — to concern themselves in their decisions with the concordance of the two systems of law.

*    *    *

Article 24 of the Constitution deals with the transfer of sovereign rights to inter-State institutions. This cannot be taken literally. Like every constitutional provision of a similar fundamental nature, Article 24 of the Constitution must be understood and construed in the overall context of the whole Constitution. That is, it does not open the way to amending the basic structure of the Constitution, which forms the basis of its identity, without a formal amendment to the Constitution . . . Article 24 of the Constitution . . . nullifies any amendment of the Treaty which would destroy the identity of the valid constitution of the Federal Republic of Germany by encroaching on the structures which go to make it up. And the same would apply to rules of secondary Community law made on the basis of a corresponding interpretation of the valid Treaty and in the same way affecting the structures essential to the Constitution. Article 24 does not actually give authority to transfer sovereign rights, but opens up the national legal system . . . in such a way that the Federal Republic of Germany's exclusive claim to rule is taken back in the sphere of validity of the Constitution and room is given, within the State's sphere of rule to the direct effect and applicability of law from another source.

The part of the Constitution dealing with fundamental rights is an inalienable essential feature of the valid Constitution of the Federal Republic of Germany and one which forms part of the constitutional structure of the Constitution. Article 24 of the Constitution does not without reservation allow it to be subjected to qualifications. In this, the present state of integration of the Community is of crucial importance. The Community still lacks . . . in particular a codified catalogue of fundamental rights, the substance of which is reliably and unambiguously fixed for the future in the same way as the substance of the Constitution . . . As long as this legal certainty, which is not guaranteed merely by the decisions of the European Court of Justice, favourable though these have been to fundamental rights, is not achieved in the course of the further integration of the Community, the reservation derived from Article 24 of the Constitution applies. What is involved is, therefore, a legal difficulty arising exclusively from the Community's continuing integration process, which is still in flux.

\* \* \*

Provisionally, therefore, in the hypothetical case of a conflict between Community law and …; the guarantees of fundamental rights in the Constitution, there arises the question of which system of law takes precedence, that is, ousts the other. In this conflict of norms, the guarantee of fundamental rights in the Constitution prevails as long as the competent organs of the Community have not removed the conflict of norms in accordance with the Treaty mechanism.

From the relationship between Constitution and Community law outlined above, the following conclusions emerge:

In accordance with the Treaty rules on jurisdiction, the European Court of Justice has jurisdiction to rule on the legal validity of the norms of Community law (including the unwritten norms of Community law which it considers exist) and on their construction. It does not, however, decide incidental questions of national law of the Federal Republic of Germany (or in any other Member State) with binding force for this State. Statements in the reasoning of its judgements that a particular aspect of a Community norm accords or is compatible in its substance with a constitutional rule of national law — here, with a guarantee of fundamental rights in the Constitution — constitute non-binding obiter dicta.

\* \* \*

[The] Constitutional Court never rules on the validity or invalidity of a rule of Community law. At most, it can come to the conclusion that such a rule cannot be applied by the authorities or courts of the Federal Republic of Germany in so far as it conflicts with a rule of the Constitution relating to fundamental rights.

\* \* \*

The result is: As long as the integration process has not progressed so far that Community law also receives a catalogue of fundamental rights decided on by a parliament and of settled validity, which is adequate in comparison with the catalogue of fundamental rights contained in the Constitution, a reference by a court in the Federal Republic of Germany to the [German Constitutional Court] following the obtaining of a ruling of the European Court under Article 177 [267] of the Treaty, is admissible and necessary if the German court regards the rule of Community law which is relevant to its decision as inapplicable in the interpretation given by the European Court, because and in so far as it conflicts with one of the fundamental rights in the Constitution.

[The court ruled that the Council regulation did not conflict with the principle of proportionality or any other guarantee of fundamental rights in the German

Constitution.]

## NOTES AND QUESTIONS

**1.** Twelve years after this decision, the German Constitutional Court revisited these issues in *In Re Application of Wünsche Handelsgesellschaft ("Solange II")*, Case 2, BvR 197/83, 73 Bverf GE 339, [1987] 3 CMLR 225 (Federal Constitutional Court, second senate, October 22, 1986). By now, the EU institutions had issued the joint declaration of 5 April 1977 on Human Rights to the effect that "in the exercise of their powers and in pursuance of the aims of the European Communities they will continue to respect these rights". Furthermore, the European Parliament was now a directly elected body. The constitutional court therefore determined that the EU now had in place safeguards comparable to the German Basic Law. Is a set of undefined propositions that can have different meanings in different states comparable to a "bill of rights" enshrined in a constitution? Does this mean that the German Courts accepted the supremacy of EU law over the German Constitution? Suppose the ECJ were to rule unfavorably on an issue (i.e., contrary to the views of the German Constitutional Court)?

In its *European Arrest Warrant* decision, the German Constitutional Court, 2d Senate, Case 2 BvR 2236 (July 18, 2005) actually nullified a German law implementing a Framework Decision adopted under the former TEU regarding extradition between Member States on the basis that it violated the right of German citizens under Article 16 of the *Grundgesetz* not to be extradited. (The Framework Decision as a form of EU action was abolished by the Lisbon Treaty — see further Chapter 5, *infra*). It seems that the Court was more concerned with the manner in which extradition was permitted to occur and thus a revised German law might still have met the requirements of Union Law.

**2.** The conditions set out in *Solange II* were addressed by the German Constitutional Court when confronted in 2000 with some of the multifaceted litigation involving the common organization of the bananas market (See *infra* chapter 8). In the 2000 judgment, the Court concluded that fundamental rights had been appropriately addressed by the ECJ in other bananas litigation (See *T. Port GmbH v. Hauptzollamt Hamburg-Jonas* Joined Cases C-364 and 365/95 [1998] ECR I-1023 and *Germany v. Council* Case C-122/95, 1998 ECR I-973, [1998] ECR I-973) and that the conditions for German constitutional intervention were not triggered.

**3.** Since there is no European court system similar to the U.S. federal court system, in which such issues might ordinarily arise, there has always been some question of enforceability of the Court's rulings. (Yet, it is a sobering thought that the federal authority of the United States was in question for the first 50 years or so of the United States' existence, and it took a civil war to assert federal authority universally. As late as the 1960s the conflict over desegregation required intervention of the national guard to enforce U.S. Supreme Court rulings.) What might happen if the German Court were at some point to rule that the German Government had no authority to agree to Treaty amendments that were held to violate the Basic Law?

**4.**  The *Brunner* case (see further, *infra*) also addressed these concerns in the following passage:

As regards the protection of human rights:

The readiness to accept European integration stated in the Preamble to the Constitution and regulated in Articles 23 and 24 of the Constitution has the consequence that constitutionally relevant encroachments could also come from European institutions, and a protection of basic rights must therefore be guaranteed for the whole of the area to which such measures apply; as a result there is an extension, in particular, of the territorial area to which rights to liberty apply and of the comparative aspects of the application of the rule of equal treatment.

That does not entail a decrease in constitutional standards to a substantial degree. The Federal Constitutional Court by its jurisdiction guarantees that an effective protection of basic rights for the inhabitants of Germany will also generally be maintained as against the sovereign powers of the Communities and will be accorded the same respect as the protection of basic rights required unconditionally by the Constitution, and in particular the Court provides a general safeguard of the essential content of the basic rights. The Court thus guarantees this essential content as against the sovereign powers of the Community as well. Acts done under a special power, separate from national powers of the member-States, exercised by a supra-national organization also affect the holders of basic rights in Germany. They therefore affect the guarantees of the Constitution and the duties of the Constitutional Court, the object of which is the protection of constitutional rights in Germany — in this respect not merely as against German state bodies. However, the Court exercises its jurisdiction on the applicability of secondary Community legislation in Germany in a 'relationship of co-operation' with the European Court, under which that Court guarantees protection of basic rights in any particular case for the whole area of the European Communities, and the Constitutional Court can therefore restrict itself to a general guarantee of the constitutional standards that cannot be dispensed with.

**5.**  The Irish courts have also faced the conflict between EU law and fundamental rights: *Society for the Protection of Unborn Children (Ireland) Ltd v. Grogan*, [1989] IR 753, [1990] 1 CMLR 689 (Dec 19, 1989). (See further Chapter 14 for the ECJ ruling in this case) Article 40.3.3 of the Irish Constitution protects the right to life of unborn children and prohibits abortions. The plaintiff sought to enjoin the publication of information for Irish students as to where they might obtain abortions in England, and the defendants argued that the EU right to personal free movement (and more specifically the right to travel to another Member State), overrode the Irish constitutional provision. Finlay, CJ, stated that he was "quite satisfied that in the instant case where the right sought to be protected is that of a life, there can be no question of a possible or putative right which might exist in European law as a corollary to a right to travel so as to avail of services, counterbalancing the necessity for an interlocutory injunction".

Is this approach one that the ECJ could countenance? What of the built-in exceptions to the right of free movement (EC 46/TFEU 53)? Could EC 295/TFEU 345 be relevant also? (Compare the broad notion of "property" adopted for the purposes of the Fifth and Fourteenth Amendments to the U.S. Constitution).

See also *Attorney General v. X* [1992] 2 CMLR 277 (Supreme Court, March 5, 1992) (Ireland) where a girl was allowed to travel to England for an abortion because the court found there were grounds for believing she would kill herself if not allowed to travel. EU rights were not part of the Court's rationale for refusing an injunction. The basis of any challenge under the Irish Constitution would probably be Article 6, which provides that all governmental powers "derive, under God, from the people [who] . . . decide all questions of national policy, according to the requirements of the common good". Could membership of the EU in fact be argued to be inconsistent with such wording, given the supremacy doctrine established by the ECJ?

At Maastricht, Ireland obtained a protocol to the TEU that nothing in that Treaty "shall affect the application in Ireland of Article 40.3.3. of the constitution."

**6.** In the case of *In re Application of Frau Kloppenburg* case 2 BvR 687/85, 75 BVerfGE 223, [1988] 3 CMLR 1 (Federal Constitutional Court, April 8, 1987), the tables were turned. The German court here overruled a Finance court ruling denying direct effect to a directive on the grounds that the plaintiff's fundamental rights had been infringed by such denial. (Article 101(1) of the Grundgesetz, which guarantees citizens the right to a "lawful judge").

**7.** As a federally organized Member State within the EU, Germany also faces another problem in its relationship with EU law: under its own constitution, the federal government may find itself restricted because of the powers reserved to the states (Länder). In 1986, the Länder objected to the Single European Act because they were not satisfied with the information rights granted under then-current German law and they wanted a substantial say in how the federal government formulates its position in measures proposed to the EC Council of Ministers. They also asserted rights to representation in the Council in the course of Germany's ratification of the Maastricht Treaty at a time when Germany was still dealing with reunification after the collapse of the Berlin wall. The entire controversy surrounding Germany's ratification spawned litigation (see the various extracts from the *Brunner* case, and the insertion of a new article 23 into the German Grundgesetz (Constitution). The rights of the Länder were secured through their participation in the Bundesrat, which is the legislative body at the federal level where the states have their say. The Bundesrat is enabled to appoint a representative to represent their interests along with the federal government, where their essential interests are affected by EU action.

It has been argued, (Professor Eberhard Grabitz (Berlin University Law School)), that the Länder have a constitutional right to participate in EU affairs, based on Article 50 of the Grundgesetz.

Under a 1979 informal agreement, the German federal government and the Länder work together on EU issues. An official from one Land works at the German Embassy in Brussels, and his responsibility is to coordinate the states' cooperation.

A substantial number of matters have been referred to the Länder under this procedure.

**8.** In an echo of the German case, the French Conseil d'Etat in *Société Arcelor Atlantique et Lorraine v. Premier Ministre*, Conseil d'Etat No. 287110, February 8, 2007 considered an argument by Arcelor that the extension of the EU's carbon emissions permit scheme to the steel industry violated the right to equal treatment under the French Constitution. The Conseil d'Etat did refer the question to the ECJ, which held that the EU counterpart of that right was not infringed: *Société Arcelor Atlantique et Lorraine v. Premier Ministre*, Case C127/07, [2008] ECR I-9895.

**9.** For a discussion of how the Constitutional Courts of the Central European Member States are approaching the supremacy issue, see e.g. W. Sadurski, *Solange Chapter 3: Constitutional Courts in Central Europe — Democracy — European Union*, EUI Working Papers law NO 2006/40; and Y. Goldammer and E. Matulionyté, *Analysis and Reflections — The application of European Union law in Lithuania*, (2006) 31 EL REV. 260

## [C]   Restrictions on the Transfer of Sovereignty

### BRUNNER v. EUROPEAN UNION TREATY
Federal Constitutional Court, second senate, October 12, 1993, Cases 2 BvR 2134/92 and 2159/92, [1994] 1 CMLR 57
(Germany)

[The German Constitutional Court was called upon to examine the compatibility of the TEU with the German Constitution. A new article 23 of the constitution had been adopted specifically to enable ratification of the TEU by Germany. (See note 1 below) A number of issues were raised by the plaintiff, including objection to the contemplated adoption of a single European currency and the transfer of further powers to the Union without a corresponding guarantee of democratic processes at the European level. The Court took the view that the TEU could be ratified legally under the constitution but that further transfers of power would have to be reappraised under the constitution. Since the court was considering the TEU and not the EC Treaty as such, the specific issues concerning supremacy, invocability, and direct applicability did not arise and the decision therefore did not necessarily shed further light on them.]

(a) The member-States have established the European Union in order to exercise a part of their functions in common and to that extent to exercise their sovereignty in common. In their resolution made on 11 and 12 December 1992 in Edinburgh the heads of state and government united in the European Council stressed that in the context of the Treaty on the European Union independent and sovereign States have resolved of their own free will to exercise some of their powers in common consistently with the existing Treaties. Accordingly the Union Treaty takes account of the independence and sovereignty of the member-States, since it obliges the Union to respect the national identities of its member-States (Article F(1) [6] of the Union Treaty), it equips the Union and the European Communities only with specific competences and powers in accordance with the principle of limited individual competences. . . . and then establishes the principle of subsidiarity for the Union. . . . as a binding principle of law.

As to the question of where a process of European integration will eventually lead after further amendments to the Treaties, the term 'European Union' may indicate a concern for further integration, but as regards the intended objective the question is ultimately open. In any event the establishment of a 'United States of Europe', in a way comparable to that in which the United States of America became a state, is not at present intended. The new Article 88-1 inserted into the French Constitution in view of the Union Treaty also speaks of member-States which exercise some of their competences in common within the European Union and the European Communities.

The competences and powers which are granted to the European Union and the Communities belonging to it remain essentially the activities of an economic union in so far as they are exercised through the implementation of sovereign rights. The central areas of activity of the European Community in this respect are the customs union and the free movement of goods (Article 3(a) [3(1)(a)] of the E.C. Treaty), the internal market (Article 3(c) [3(1)(c)]), the assimilation of laws to ensure the proper functioning of the common market (Article 3(h)) [3(1)(h)], co-ordination of the member-States' economic policies (Article 3a [4] (1)), and the development of a monetary union. Outside the European Communities, co-operation stays on an inter-governmental basis; that applies particularly in the case of foreign and security policy and the fields of justice and home affairs. . . .

The Federal Republic of Germany, therefore, even after the Union Treaty comes into force, will remain a member of a federation of States, the common authority of which is derived from the member-States and can only have binding effects within the German sovereign sphere by virtue of the German instruction that its law be applied. Germany is one of the 'Masters of the Treaties', which have established their adherence to the Union Treaty concluded 'for an unlimited period' (Article Q) with the intention of long-term membership, but could also ultimately revoke that adherence by a contrary act. The validity and application of European law in Germany depend on the application-of-law instruction of the Accession Act. Germany thus preserves the quality of a sovereign State in its own right and the status of sovereign equality with other States within the meaning of Article 2(1) of the United Nations Charter of 26 June 1945.

(b) The necessary influence of the Bundestag is guaranteed in the first place because, under Article 23(1) of the Constitution, German membership of the European Union, and the further development of the Union through a change in its treaty bases or an extension of its powers all require legislation, which under the conditions of the third sentence of that Article require the qualified majorities of Article 79(2) of the Constitution. In addition, the Bundestag participates in the exercise of German membership rights within the European institutions. It co-operates in the formation of the will of the Federation in these matters in accordance with Article 23(2) and (3) of the Constitution and the Act on the co-operation of the Federal Government and the German Bundestag in European Union matters of 12 March 1993 passed for the implementation of those provisions. These interrelated powers are to be exercised by the Federal Government and the

Bundestag in a spirit of institutional loyalty.

Finally, the Bundestag also influences the European policy of the Federal Government through the latter's responsibility to Parliament (Articles 63 and 67 of the Constitution). This function of initiation and control, which it basically exercises in public proceedings, causes the general public and the political parties to take positions on the government's European policy and thus becomes a factor in the citizen's voting decisions.

## NOTES AND QUESTIONS

1.  Article 23 of the *Grundgesetz (Basic Law)* provides:

(1) With a view to establishing a united Europe, the Federal Republic of Germany shall participate in the development of the European Union that is committed to democratic, social, and federal principles, to the rule of law, and to the principle of subsidiarity, and that guarantees a level of protection of basic rights essentially comparable to that afforded by this Basic Law. To this end the Federation may transfer sovereign powers by a law with the consent of the Bundesrat. The establishment of the European Union, as well as changes in its treaty foundations and comparable regulations that amend or supplement this Basic Law, or make such amendments or supplements possible, shall be subject to paragraphs (2) and (3) of Article 79.

(2) The Bundestag and, through the Bundesrat, the Länder shall participate in matters concerning the European Union. The Federal Government shall keep the Bundestag and the Bundesrat informed, comprehensively and at the earliest possible time.

(3) Before participating in legislative acts of the European Union, the Federal Government shall provide the Bundestag with an opportunity to state its position. The Federal Government shall take the position of the Bundestag into account during the negotiations. Details shall be regulated by a law.

(4) The Bundesrat shall participate in the decision-making process of the Federation insofar as it would have been competent to do so in a comparable domestic matter, or insofar as the subject falls within the domestic competence of the Länder.

(5) Insofar as, in an area within the exclusive competence of the Federation, interests of the Länder are affected, and in other matters, insofar as the Federation has legislative power, the Federal Government shall take the position of the Bundesrat into account. To the extent that the legislative powers of the Länder, the structure of Land authorities, or Land administrative procedures are primarily affected, the position of the Bundesrat shall be given the greatest possible respect in determining the Federation's position consistent with the responsibility of the Federation for the nation as a whole. In matters that may result in increased expenditures or reduced

revenues for the Federation, the consent of the Federal Government shall be required.

(6) When legislative powers exclusive to the Länder are primarily affected, the exercise of the rights belonging to the Federal Republic of Germany as a member state of the European Union shall be delegated to a representative of the Länder designated by the Bundesrat. These rights shall be exercised with the participation and concurrence of the Federal Government; their exercise shall be consistent with the responsibility of the Federation for the nation as a whole.

(7) Details respecting paragraphs (4) through (6) of this Article shall be regulated by a law requiring the consent of the Bundesrat.

How did the Court view the impact of the TEU and EC Treaties? Do you agree with the analysis?

2.   In the Irish case of *Crotty*, the plaintiff had sought to enjoin Ireland's ratification of the Single European Act and succeeded in forcing a referendum on its ratification that delayed the entry into force of the SEA from January 1987 to July 1987. Crotty had argued that once the SEA was in force, he would have been deprived of any ability to challenge the Irish government's act of ratification.

3.   In Denmark, the law implementing the TEU was challenged in the case of *Carlsen and others v. Rasmussen*, Case No 272/1997, 1998 UfR p 800 (Danish Supreme Court). Among the arguments was the assertion that under the Danish Constitution, transfers of sovereignty had to be limited and controlled by the Folketing (Danish Parliament). Article 20 treated such transfers as "delegation" and the transfers should be "to such extent as shall be provided by statute". The presence of EC 308 TFEU 352 was alleged to be a violation of this limitation. The Court examined the ECJ jurisprudence relating to EC 308 TFEU 352 (for which, see *infra*, chapter 10) and concluded that it did not open up unlimited extension of EU powers. The inference of course is that, had it done so, there would have been a valid constitutional objection to the implementing legislation.

In France, the French Constitutional Council was asked by the Government whether the Constitution gave it the power to ratify the Treaty of Amsterdam: *Re Treaty of Amsterdam, 1997, Amending the Treaty on European Union and the Treaties establishing the European Communities* (Dec No 97-394 DC, Journal Officiel de la République Française, 1998, No. 2; Revue du Droit Public, 1998, p 345. The Court concluded that a constitutional revision was required. There could be no objection to this under EU law.

## BLACKBURN v. ATTORNEY GENERAL
### Court of Appeal
### [1971] C.M.L.R. 784,1 W.L.R. 1037 (1971)
### (United Kingdom)

The Master of the Rolls: In this case Mr. Blackburn — as he had done before — has shown eternal vigilance in support of the law. This time he is concerned about the application of Her Majesty's Government to join the Common Market and to sign the Treaty of Rome. He brings two actions against the Attorney General, in which he seeks declarations to the effect that, by signing the Treaty of Rome, Her Majesty's Government will surrender in part the sovereignty of the Crown in Parliament and will surrender it forever. He says that in so doing the Government will be acting in breach of the law. The Attorney-General has applied to strike out the Statement of Claim on the ground that they disclose no reasonable cause of action. The Master and the Judge have struck them out. Mr. Blackburn, with our leave, appeals to this court. He thinks it is important to clear the air.

Much of what Mr. Blackburn says is quite correct. It does appear that if this country should go into the Common Market and sign the Treaty of Rome, it means that we will have taken a step which is irreversible. The sovereignty of these islands will henceforward be limited. It will not be ours alone but will be shared with others. Mr. Blackburn referred us to a decision by the Court of Justice of the European Communities, COSTA v. E.N.E.L., in February 1964, in which the European Court in its judgment said that.

". . . the member-States, albeit within limited spheres, have restricted their sovereign rights and created a body of law applicable both to their nationals and to themselves."

Mr. Blackburn points out that many regulations made by the European Economic Community will become automatically binding on the people of this country, and that all the courts of this country, including the House of Lords, will have to follow the decisions of the European Court in certain defined respects, such as the construction of the Treaty.

I will assume that Mr. Blackburn is right in what he says on those matters. Nevertheless, I do not think these courts can entertain these actions. Negotiations are still in progress for us to join the Common Market. No agreement has been reached. No treaty has been signed. Even if a treaty is signed, it is elementary that these courts take no notice of treaties as such. We take no notice of treaties until they are embodied in laws enacted by Parliament, and then only to the extent that Parliament tells us.

\*   \*   \*

Mr. Blackburn acknowledged the general principle, but he urged that this proposed treaty is in a category by itself, in that it diminishes the sovereignty of Parliament over the people of this country. I cannot accept the distinction. The general principle applies to this treaty as to any other. The treaty-making power of this country rests not in the courts, but in the Crown; that is, Her Majesty acting upon the advice of her Ministers. When her Ministers negotiate and sign a treaty, even a treaty of such paramount importance as this proposed one, they act on behalf of the country as a whole. They exercise the prerogative of the Crown. Their action in so doing cannot be challenged or questioned in these courts.

Mr. Blackburn takes a second point. He says that, if Parliament should implement the Treaty by passing an Act of Parliament for this purpose, it will seek to do the impossible. It will seek to bind its successors. According to the Treaty, once it is signed, we are committed to it irrevocably. Once in the Common Market, we cannot withdraw from it. No Parliament can commit us, says Mr. Blackburn, to that extent. He prays in aid the principle that no Parliament can bind its successors, and that any Parliament can reverse any previous enactment. He refers to what Professor Maitland said about the Act of Union between England and Scotland. Professor Maitland in his Constitutional History of England said:

"We have no irrepealable laws; all laws may be repealed by the ordinary legislature, even the conditions under which the English and Scottish Parliaments agreed to merge themselves in the Parliament of Great Britain."

We have all been brought up to believe that, in legal theory, one Parliament cannot bind another, and that no Act is irreversible. But legal theory does not always march alongside political reality. Take the Statute of Westminster 1931, which takes away the power of Parliament to legislate for the Dominions. Can anyone imagine that Parliament could or would reverse that statute? Take the Acts which have granted independence to the Dominions and territories overseas. Can anyone imagine that Parliament could or would reverse those laws and take away their independence? Most clearly not. Freedom once given cannot be taken away. Legal theory must give way to practical politics. It is as well to remember the remark of Viscount Sankey L.C. in *British Coal Corporation v. The King*:

"The Imperial Parliament could, as matter of abstract law, repeal or disregard Section 4 of the Statute of Westminster. But that is theory and has no relation to reality."

What are the realities here? If Her Majesty's Ministers sign this treaty and Parliament enacts provisions to implement it, I do not envisage that Parliament would afterwards go back on it and try to withdraw from it. But, if Parliament should do so, then I say we will consider that event when it happens. We will then say whether Parliament can lawfully do it or not.

Both sides referred us to the valuable article ("The Basis of Legal Sovereignty") by Professor H. W. R. Wade in which he said that "sovereignty is a political fact for which no purely legal authority can be constituted . . . ". That is true. We must wait to see what happens before we pronounce on sovereignty in the Common Market.

So, while in theory Mr. Blackburn is quite right in saying that no Parliament can bind another, and that any Parliament can reverse what a previous Parliament has done, nevertheless so far as this court is concerned, I think we will wait till that day comes. We will not pronounce upon it today.

A point was raised as to whether Mr. Blackburn has any standing to come before the court. That is not a matter upon which we need rule today. He says that he feels very strongly and that it is a matter in which many persons in this country are concerned. I would not myself rule him out on the ground that he has no standing. But I do rule him out on the ground that these courts will not impugn the treaty-making power of Her Majesty, and on the ground that in so far as Parliament enacts legislation, we will deal with that legislation as and when it arise.

I think the statements of claim disclose no cause of action, and I would dismiss the appeal.

Lord Justice Salmon: While I recognize the undoubted sincerity of Mr. Blackburn's views, I deprecate litigation the purpose of which is to influence political decisions. Such decisions have nothing to do with these courts. These courts are concerned only with the effect of such decisions if and when they have been implemented by legislation. Nor have the courts any power to interfere with the treaty-making power of the Sovereign. As to Parliament, in the present state of the law, it can enact, amend and repeal any legislation it please. The sole power of the courts is to decide and enforce what is the law and not what it should be — now, or in the future.

I agree that this appeal should be dismissed.

Lord Justice Stamp: I agree that the appeal should be dismissed; but I would express no view whatsoever upon the legal implications of this country becoming a party to the Treaty of Rome. In the way Mr. Blackburn put it, I think he confused the division of the powers of the Crown, Parliament and the courts. The Crown enters into treaties; Parliament enacts laws; and it is the duty of this court in proper cases to interpret those laws when made; but it is no part of this court's function or duty to make declarations in general terms regarding the powers of Parliament, more particularly where the circumstances in which the court is asked to intervene are purely hypothetical. Nor ought this court, at the suit of one of Her Majesty's subjects, make declareations regarding the undoubted prerogative power of the Crown to enter into treaties. . . .

## NOTES AND QUESTIONS

1.   In the United Kingdom, EU law was given effect pursuant to an Act of Parliament, the European Communities Act of 1972 (1972 Ch. 68), which provides in relevant part as follows:

2. General implementation of Treaties

(1) All such rights, powers, liabilities, obligations and restrictions from time to time created or arising by or under the Treaties, and all such remedies and procedures from time to time provided for by or under the Treaties, as in accordance with the Treaties are without further enactment to be given legal effect or used in the United Kingdom, shall be recognized and available in law, and be enforced, allowed and followed accordingly; and the expression "enforceable Community right" and similar expressions shall be read as referring to one to which this subsection applies.

(2) Subject to schedule 2 to the Act, at any time after its passing Her Majesty may by Order in Council, and any designated Minister or department may by regulations, make provision —

(a) for the purpose of implementing any Community obligation of the United Kingdom, or enabling any such obligation to be implemented, or of enabling any rights enjoyed or to be enjoyed by the United Kingdom under or by virtue of the Treaties to be exercised; or

(b for the purpose of dealing with matters arising out of or related to any such obligation or rights or the coming into force, or the operation from time to time, of subsection (1) above; and in the exercise of any statutory power or duty, including any power to give directions or to legislate by means of orders, rules, regulations or other subordinate instrument, the person entrusted with the power or duty may have regard to the objects of the Communities and to any such obligation or rights as aforesaid . . .

\*   \*   \*

(4) [A]ny enactment passed or to be passed, other than one contained in this Part of this Act, shall be construed and have effect subject to the foregoing provisions of this section, but except as may be provided by any Act passed after this Act.

3. Decisions on, and proof of, Treaties and Community instruments, etc.

(1) For the purposes of all legal proceedings any question as to the meaning or effect of any of the Treaties, or as to the validity, meaning or effect of any Community instrument, shall be treated as a question of law (and, if not referred to the European Court, be for determination as such in accordance with the principles laid down by any relevant decision of the European Court).

(2) Judicial notice shall be taken of the Treaties, of the Official Journal of the Communities and of any decision of, or expression of opinion by, the European Court on any such question as aforesaid.

**2.**   How does one alter an unwritten constitution to permit what in effect is the overturning of the doctrine of the supremacy of Parliament?

**3.**   The issues raised by the EC Treaty in the context of the Supremacy of Parliament are not necessarily novel. For example, as mentioned in the *Blackburn* case, the Statute of Westminster, dating from 1931, essentially removed the power of Parliament to pass laws for the "Dominions" within the British Empire — such as Australia, Canada and New Zealand. Much the same issue could be said to apply to the "repatriation" of the Canadian Constitution. The U.K. Canada Act of 1982 states: "No Act of the Parliament of the United Kingdom passed after the Constitution Act, 1982 comes into force shall extend to Canada as part of its law". While the U.K. Parliament could repeal this Act, Canada would undoubtedly ignore it and any legislation that purported to apply to Canada. The situation is more complicated in the EU context. This is addressed in the *Thoburn* case, *infra*.

## [D]   Last in Time Rule

### MCCARTHY'S LTD v. SMITH
(English Court of Appeal (Civil Division))
[1979] 3 AN SR 725 [1979] 3 CMLR 44

[Smith had claimed that Mccarthy's, her employer, had discriminated against her in pay in violation of EEC 119 (EC 141/TFEU 157). Mccarthy's on appeal relied on a British statute that was apparently narrower in scope than EC 141/TFEU 157 and would not have permitted recovery.]

Denning MR:

[T]he United Kingdom has passed legislation with the intention of giving effect to the principle of equal pay [under EEC Article 141]. It has done it by the Sex Discrimination Act [of] 1975.

\* \* \*

In construing our statute, we are entitled to look to the Treaty as an aid to its construction; but not only as an aid but as an overriding force. If on close investigation it should appear that our legislation is deficient or is inconsistent with Community law by some oversight of our draftsmen then it is our bounden duty to give priority to Community law. Such is the result of § 2(1) and (4) of the European Communities Act [of] 1972.

I pause here, however, to make one observation on a constitutional point. Thus far I have assumed that our Parliament, whenever it passes legislation, intends to fulfil its obligations under the Treaty. If the time should come when our Parliament deliberately passes an Act with the intention of repudiating the Treaty or any provision in it or intentionally of acting inconsistently with it and says so in express terms, then I should have thought that it would be the duty of our courts to follow the statute of our Parliament. I do not however envisage any such situation. . . . In the present case I assume that the United Kingdom intended to fulfil its obligations under Art. 119 [157].

## THOBURN v. SUNDERLAND CITY COUNCIL; HUNT v. HACKNEY LONDON BOROUGH COUNCIL; HARMAN AND ANOTHER v. CORNWALL COUNTY COUNCIL; COLLINS v. SUTTON LONDON BOROUGH COUNCIL

High Court, Queen's Bench Division [2002] EWHC 195 (Admin), [2003] QB
151
(United Kingdom)

[The defendants in these cases had been prosecuted for offenses under various statutory instruments or orders (secondary legislation made by Government ministers) relating to the requirement to use metric measurements in the sale of non pre-packaged food. For example, Steven Thoburn, a greengrocer in Sunderland had used weighing machines calibrated in pounds and ounces. On 16 February 2000 he was warned by a properly authorized inspector that these machines did not comply with current legislation. He was served with a 28-day notice requiring that the machines be altered so as to yield measurements in metric units. He did not obey the notice. On 31 March 2000 the inspector obliterated the imperial measure stamps on his machines. He continued to use these now unstamped machines to sell loose fruit and vegetables by pound and ounce. He was prosecuted for two offences (there being two relevant machines) under section 11(2) and (3) of the Weights and Measures Act 1985.

The statutory instruments in question in the various prosecutions had in some instances been adopted pursuant to Section 2(2) of the European Communities Act (see Note 1 to the *Blackburn* case, *supra*) and in other instances pursuant to Section 2(2) of the Weights and Measures Act, 1985. Together they were part of the overall scheme designed to implement Council Directive 80/91 on the use of metric measurements as subsequently amended.

Before any amendments section 1 of the 1985 Act had provided in relevant part that

> (1) The yard or the metre shall be the unit of measurement of length and
> the pound or the kilogram shall be the unit of measurement of mass by
> reference to which any measurement involving a measurement of length or
> mass shall be made in the United Kingdom; and-(a) the yard shall be 0.9144
> metre exactly; (b) the pound shall be 0.453 592 37 kilogram exactly.

The principal argument made by the defendants was that Section 1 of the 1985 Act
had impliedly repealed Section 2(2) of the European Communities Act to the extent
that the latter empowered the making of any provision by way of subordinate
legislation, whether so as to amend primary legislation or otherwise, which would be
inconsistent with that section. The regulations amending Section 1 of the 1985 Act
adopted under the powers conferred by the European Communities Act were thus
invalid. In turn, other regulations adopted under the 1985 Act which were part of
the overall scheme and depended on the validity of the amending regulations must
also be considered invalid since they were an integral part of the whole scheme. To
the extent that the argument relating to the implied repeal was actually a valid one,
the question confronted by the court was whether it could apply in the case of a
statute such as the European Communities Act 1972.]


LAWS LJ:

60 The common law has in recent years allowed, or rather created, exceptions to the
doctrine of implied repeal, a doctrine which was always the common law's own
creature. There are now classes or types of legislative provision which cannot be
repealed by mere implication. These instances are given, and can only be given, by
our own courts, to which the scope and nature of parliamentary sovereignty are
ultimately confided. The courts may say-have said-that there are certain circumstances in which the legislature may only enact what it desires to enact if it does so
by express, or at any rate specific, provision. The courts have in effect so held in the
field of European law itself in R v. Secretary of State for Transport, Ex
pFactortame Ltd [1990] 2 AC 85 ("Factortame (No 1)"), and this is critical for the
present discussion. By this means, as I shall seek to explain, the courts have found
their way through the impasse seemingly created by two supremacies, the
supremacy of European law and the supremacy of Parliament.

61 The present state of our domestic law is such that substantive Community rights
prevail over the express terms of any domestic law, including primary legislation,
made or passed after the coming into force of the 1972 Act, even in the face of plain
inconsistency between the two.

*    *    *

62 . . . We should recognise a hierarchy of Acts of Parliament: as it were "ordinary"
statutes and "constitutional" statutes. The two categories must be distinguished on
a principled basis. In my opinion a constitutional statute is one which (a) conditions
the legal relationship between citizen and state in some general, overarching
manner, or (b) enlarges or diminishes the scope of what we would now regard as

fundamental constitutional rights. (a) and (b) are of necessity closely related: it is difficult to think of an instance of (a) that is not also an instance of (b). The special status of constitutional statutes follows the special status of constitutional rights. Examples are Magna Carta 1297 . . . the Bill of Rights 1689 . . . , the Union with Scotland Act 1706 . . . , the Reform Acts which distributed and enlarged the franchise (Representation of the People Acts 1832 . . . 1867 . . . and 1884), the Human Rights Act 1998, the Scotland Act 1998 and the Government of Wales Act 1998. The 1972 Act clearly belongs in this family. It incorporated the whole corpus of substantive Community rights and obligations, and gave overriding domestic effect to the judicial and administrative machinery of Community law. It may be there has never been a statute having such profound effects on so many dimensions of our daily lives. The 1972 Act is, by force of the common law, a constitutional statute.

63 Ordinary statutes may be impliedly repealed. Constitutional statutes may not. For the repeal of a constitutional Act or the abrogation of a fundamental right to be effected by statute, the court would apply this test: is it shown that the legislature's actual-not imputed, constructive or presumed-intention was to effect the repeal or abrogation? I think the test could only be met by express words in the later statute, or by words so specific that the inference of an actual determination to effect the result contended for was irresistible. The ordinary rule of implied repeal does not satisfy this test. Accordingly, it has no application to constitutional statutes. I should add that in my judgment general words could not be supplemented, so as to effect a repeal or significant amendment to a constitutional statute, by reference to what was said in Parliament by the minister promoting the Bill pursuant to Pepper v. Hart [1993] AC 593. A constitutional statute can only be repealed, or amended in a way which significantly affects its provisions touching fundamental rights or otherwise the relation between citizen and state, by unambiguous words on the face of the later statute.

64 This development of the common law regarding constitutional rights, and as I would say constitutional statutes, is highly beneficial. It gives us most of the benefits of a written constitution, in which fundamental rights are accorded special respect. But it preserves the sovereignty of the legislature and the flexibility of our uncodified constitution. It accepts the relation between legislative supremacy and fundamental rights is not fixed or brittle: rather the courts (in interpreting statutes and, now, applying the Human Rights Act 1998) will pay more or less deference to the legislature, or other public decision-maker, according to the subject in hand. Nothing is plainer than that this benign development involves, as I have said, the recognition of the 1972 Act as a constitutional statute.

*     *     *

68 . . . I would recognise for reasons I have given that the common law has in effect stipulated that the principal executive measures of the 1972 Act may only be repealed in the United Kingdom by specific provision, and not impliedly. It might be suggested that it matters little whether that result is given by the law of the EU (as [Prosecution Counsel] submits) or by the law of England untouched by Community law (as I would hold). But the difference is vital to a proper understanding of the relationship between EU and domestic law.

69 In my judgment (as will by now be clear) the correct analysis of that relationship involves and requires these following four propositions. (1) All the specific rights and obligations which EU law creates are by the 1972 Act incorporated into our domestic law and rank supreme: that is, anything in our substantive law inconsistent with any of these rights and obligations is abrogated or must be modified to avoid the inconsistency. This is true even where the inconsistent municipal provision is contained in primary legislation. (2) The 1972 Act is a constitutional statute: that is, it cannot be impliedly repealed. (3) The truth of (2) is derived, not from EU law, but purely from the law of England: the common law recognises a category of constitutional statutes. (4) The fundamental legal basis of the United Kingdom's relationship with the EU rests with the domestic, not the European, legal powers. In the event, which no doubt would never happen in the real world, that a European measure was seen to be repugnant to a fundamental or constitutional right guaranteed by the law of England, a question would arise whether the general words of the 1972 Act were sufficient to incorporate the measure and give it overriding effect in domestic law. But that is very far from this case.

70 I consider that the balance struck by these four propositions gives full weight both to the proper supremacy of Community law and to the proper supremacy of the United Kingdom Parliament. By the former, I mean the supremacy of substantive Community law. By the latter, I mean the supremacy of the legal foundation within which those substantive provisions enjoy their primacy. The former is guaranteed by propositions (1) and (2). The latter is guaranteed by propositions (3) and (4). If this balance is understood, it will be seen that these two supremacies are in harmony, and not in conflict.

## NOTES AND QUESTIONS

1.   What problems arise from relying on a statute of the legislature to give effect to EU law? Is this consistent with the ECJ's views on the priority of EU law? The ECJ has on various occasions objected to national legislation that purports to enact EU regulations that are supposed to be directly applicable in all Member States. Does the UK European Communities Act violate this principle?

2.   Paradoxically, at the day-to-day level, issues of direct applicability and invocability of EU laws made under the Treaties, and in fact the superiority of such laws to national laws (as opposed to the constitution itself) in the UK are more straightforwardly resolved precisely because these doctrines are enshrined in clear language of an Act of Parliament rather than left to court interpretations of more generalized constitutional provisions. In the *Factortame* case set out earlier in this Chapter, the shortcomings of statutory enablement became clear. The ECJ ruled in effect that the UK constitutional doctrine discussed above must not be applied where the result would be to disapply EU law.

As to the revocability of the European Communities Act, when the U.K. House of Lords debated the accession to the European Communities, the Lord Chancellor stated:

But while Parliament's power to repeal the Act applying the [EEC] Treaty remains, and cannot be fettered, I am not implying that it would be right for us to repeal it. The Rome Treaty is not limited in duration, and there is no provision for its termination. Parliament could repeal the Act applying these Treaties; it cannot be prevented from doing so. But it must be recognized that, in International Law, such a step could be justified only in exceptional circumstances.

**3.** In *Thoburn*, prosecution counsel had attempted to bring before the Court the doctrine adopted by the ECJ in *Costa v. ENEL*. How did Laws, LJ, rationalize the supremacy principle with the doctrine of the supremacy of Parliament and the associated principle that Parliament cannot bind itself as to the future? Do you think that the reasoning in this judgment would assure the supremacy of EU law as long as the UK remains a Member State?

The decision by Laws LJ was unsuccessfully challenged in the House of Lords. The challenge included allegations that he had mishandled the case. Subsequently a claim was lodged at the European Court of Human Rights which, in a preliminary proceeding, rejected it. Mr. Thoburn died several days after that decision.

**4.** In the Netherlands, the 1983 Constitution specifically provides that treaties and resolutions of international institutions are binding upon publication, provided by their terms they are capable of having binding effect. (Article 93.) Article 94 provides that Dutch statutes may not be given effect to the extent they conflict with such international acts. While in practice this means the Dutch courts have no difficulty in giving effect to the ECJ's rulings, is this really the solution the ECJ had in mind? Surely EU law is vulnerable to further amendments to the Dutch constitution.

**5.** It is quite surprising that after so many years there is still doubt overall in France as to whether the courts accepted the supremacy of EU law because of the continuing debate over the effect of Article 55 of the Constitution in relation to subsequent conflicting national legislation. The Conseil d'Etat continues to express doubts based on the constitutional provisions regarding the effect of treaties in the French legal system (See *SNIP*, C.E. 3 December 2001, Droit Administratif 2002, No. 55), while the Conseil Constitutionnel and administrative courts appear to have accepted that national legislation and regulation must give way to EU rules in the event of conflict (see Decision 2004-496, June 10, 2004). See C. Richards, *The Supremacy of Community Law before the French Constitutional Court*, (2006) EL REV. 499; and P. CRAIG AND G. DE BURCA (EDS.), THE EVOLUTION OF EU LAW (Oxford University Press, 1999).

## [E] Other Constitutional and Procedural Obstacles

### FACTORTAME LTD. AND OTHERS, APPELLANTS AND SECRETARY OF STATE FOR TRANSPORT, RESPONDENT
[On appeal from R v. SECRETARY OF STATE FOR TRANSPORT, Ex parte FACTORTAME LTD. AND OTHERS]
House of Lords
[1990] 2 AC 85
(United Kingdom)

[The underlying facts of this case are summarized in the ECJ judgment, *supra*. § 3.02. Here Lord Bridge addresses another aspect of the problem confronted by the English courts in granting an injunction prohibiting the implementation of an Act of Parliament.]

But this brings me to what I believe to be the nub of the appeal, in so far as it depends on English law, and to the second critical distinction between the claim to interim relief advanced by the applicants and any claim to interim relief which an English court has ever previously entertained . . . [T]he provisions of Part II of the Act of 1988 require no assistance from the court for their enforcement. Unambiguous in their terms, they simply stand as a barrier to the continued enjoyment by the applicants' vessels of the right to registration as British fishing vessels. In this situation the difficulty which confronts the applicants is that the presumption that an Act of Parliament is compatible with Community law unless and until declared to be incompatible must be at least as strong as the presumption that delegated legislation is valid unless and until declared invalid. But an order granting the applicants the interim relief which they seek will only serve their purpose if it declares that which Parliament has enacted to be the law from 1 December 1988, and to take effect in relation to vessels previously registered under the Act of 1894 from 31 March 1989, not to be the law until some uncertain future date. Effective relief can only be given if it requires the Secretary of State to treat the applicants' vessels as entitled to registration under Part II of the Act in direct contravention of its provisions. Any such order, unlike any form of order for interim relief known to the law, would irreversibly determine in the applicants' favour for a period of some two years rights which are necessarily uncertain until the preliminary ruling of the E.C.J. has been given. If the applicants fail to establish the rights they claim before the E.C.J., the effect of the interim relief granted would be to have conferred upon them rights directly contrary to Parliament's sovereign will and correspondingly to have deprived British fishing vessels, as defined by Parliament, of the enjoyment of a substantial proportion of the United Kingdom quota of stocks of fish protected by the common fisheries policy. I am clearly of the opinion that, as a matter of English law, the court has no power to make an order which has these consequences.

### NOTES AND QUESTIONS

1. The above extract suggests that the difficulty in granting an injunction is not just a question of lack of precedent regarding such a measure against the Crown. What issue does Lord Bridge also highlight?

2.   It will be recalled from *Costa v. ENEL* and the *Simmenthal* case, *supra*, that in Italy, only the Constitutional Court had the power to determine the validity of national legislation. The Constitutional Court, in *SpA Granital v. Amministrazione delle Finanze dello Stato*, Case 170/8, [1984] Il Foro It. 2062, 29 Giru.Cost. I 1098, No. 170, 21 CML REV.. 756, appears to have accepted the supremacy of EC law for all purposes (overriding the requirement that such issues could not be considered by the ordinary courts, which as it may be recalled was the fundamental concern raised by the Italian Government in *Costa v. ENEL*). This notwithstanding, note the reservations expressed in the *Frontini* case, *infra*. A more recent amendment to the Constitution (a new Article 117) has again raised concerns that challenges to national legislation might be possible only in the Constitutional Court: XXTH REPORT ON MONITORING THE APPLICATION OF COMMUNITY LAW, ANNEX VI: APPLICATION OF COMMUNITY LAW BY MEMBER STATE COURTS, COM (2003) 669.

3.   In *Meagher v. Minister For Agriculture and Attorney General* [1994] 1 Irish Reports 347, a different form of constitutional argument was made. The plaintiff had argued that the adoption of regulations to implement a Community Directive was contrary to article 15, s2 of the Irish Constitution because "a power provided by statute to a Minister to make laws by regulation or statutory instrument which included provisions either repealing, amending or modifying other law, including statute law enacted by the Oireachtas (Irish legislature), would constitute an invasion of the sole and exclusive power of making laws vested in the Oireachtas." This, then, might be seen as primarily a challenge based on the breach of principles governing the division of powers between the executive and the legislature enshrined in the Irish Constitution. While the Justices all rejected the argument based on the requirement to implement directives deriving from Ireland's obligations when it acceded to the EEC Treaty, there is no evident acknowledgment that this analysis was independent of the Constitution; the opinions suggest only that the Constitution permitted this result. By contrast, in *Browne v. Attorney General* [2002] IEHC 47 the Court reached the opposite conclusion, namely that a regulation implementing Council Regulation 1239/98 was invalid because under Article 15 it should have been enacted by the Oireachtas.

4.   In the Italian case, *Frontini v. Ministero delle Finanze* case 183, [1974] II Foro It. 314, [1974] 2 CMLR 372 (Constitutional Court, Dec 27, 1973) the plaintiff challenged a 1967 EC Council regulation that increased duties on dairy products. The Italian constitutional court ruled that procedural guarantees under the Italian constitution were inapplicable to EU regulations but at the same time suggested that, in any event, such conflicts were unlikely to arise because of the relatively narrow scope of EU jurisdiction. If, however, a serious conflict were to arise, the Italian court, absent a satisfactory control at the EU level, might have to step in. These issues, it will be recalled, were confronted in the *Costa* and *Simmenthal* case. In *Spa Granital v. Amministrazione delle Finanze dello Stato*, Case 170/84, [1984] II Foro It. 2062, 29 Giur. Cost. I 1098, no. 170, 21 CML REV. 756 p 284 the Italian Constitutional Court seems to have finally dispelled all suggestion that it might retain some overriding powers when questions of EU law are involved.

5.   In an extremely detailed and lengthy *Gauweiler* judgment (421 paragraphs) of 30 June 2009 – 2 BvE 2/08, 2 BvE 5/08, 2 BvR 1010/08, 2 BvR 1022/08, 2 BvR 1259/08 und 2 BvR 182/09, the German Federal Court reviewed the constitutionality

of Germany's proposed ratification of the Lisbon Treaty. Among other considerations, the Court measured the Treaty against the "standard of the right to vote." It noted that the EU is not a sovereign state with its own basis of legitimacy founded on the democratic approval of the people of Europe as a whole. The existence of the European Parliament does not provide this, as the Parliament does not have powers to vote on fundamental social, cultural or political matters and is actually composed of representatives of each Member State rather than the European Union population as a whole. Thus, the EU's democratic basis (as required under the German Constitution) continues to reside with the peoples of each Member State separately.

In the German constitutional structure, it is expressly recognized that Germany may delegate sovereign functions to international bodies (GG 24) and specifically to the EU (GG 23). Thus it is not necessary that all actions taken by the EU be approved by the German legislature. As long as the general area of EU action is clearly delineated it can be approved by appropriate *a priori* enabling legislation.

However, the Lisbon Treaty did contain some provisions that required further authorization from the Germany legislature. First, the mechanism that can cause a shift in the power of the member states (TEU 48 (7)) could not be voted on by the German representative in the European Council under the existing German Constitutional law concerning participation in the EU since it amounted to a revision of the Treaty. Second, certain aspects of the PJCC now transferred to the TFEU could permit the creation of new crimes by vote of the Council (TFEU 83.1 para 3), in essence extending the competence of the EU; and this too would require specific German legislative approval.

The Court went on to find that the new enabling legislation under article 23 of the Grundgesetz had not been sufficiently elaborated and thus would require amendment before ratification could proceed.

In the context of this analysis, and subject to continued adherence to the principle of conferral of powers, (as expressly stated in TEU 5) the Constitutional Court stated that it had no objection to the doctrine of primacy of EU law, and indeed would not have objected to that principle being stated outright in the Treaties as opposed to being alluded to in Declaration No. 17. However, it is still difficult to see that the Constitutional Court's view of supremacy is coextensive with that of the ECJ, since the former continues to reserve the right to review EU acts for compliance with the Grundgesetz.

This decision on the whole was negative with respect to the ability of Germany to proceed beyond the structure of Lisbon into a more complete European Federation. It would seem that Lisbon has reached the high-water mark of what will be acceptable in Germany. But perhaps this is not a bad thing. Any further comprehensive revision of the Treaties would be of such constitutional significance for all Member States that a Europe-wide referendum and (finally) a constitutional endorsement by the people would seem an absolutely necessary step.

For a discussion, see D. Doukas, *The Verdict of the German Federal Constitutional Court on the Lisbon Treaty: Not Guilty, but don't do it again!* (2009) 34 EL REV. 866.

## [F]   Unilateral Determinations on the Scope and Meaning of EU Law

### MINISTRE DE L'INTERIEUR v. COHN-BENDIT
Conseil d'Etat (Assemblée)
[1978] Recueil Lebon 524, [1979] Receuil Dalloz 155, [1980] 1 CMLR 543,
Dec 22, 1978
(France)

According to Article 56 [46] of the Treaty, which does not authorise any European Community body to issue regulations on the subject of public order that would be directly applicable in the Member States, the coordination of legislative and regulatory provisions « creating special rules for foreign nationals in the interest of public order, public safety and public health » is to be accomplished by Council directives adopted on Commission proposal and after consultation of the European Parliament. It appears clearly from Article 189 [288] of the Treaty that, while these directives bind the Member states "as to the result to be achieved," . . . National authorities alone have the authority to choose how to execute the directives and establish for themselves, under national judicial control, the proper means of giving them effect in domestic law. Therefore, irrespective of the provisions they may address to the Member States, directives may not be invoked by nationals of these States in support of legal claims directed against an individual administrative act. It thus follows that M. Cohn-Bendit cannot effectively call upon the administrative s tribunal of Paris to annul the decision of the Minister of the Interior on the ground that it violates the provisions of the Council directive . . . Accordingly, absent any challenge to the regulations adopted by the French Government to implement the council's directive, the answer to M. Cohn-Bendit's lawsuit cannot in any event depend upon an interpretation of the directive. . . . The Minister of the Interior is therefore correct in claiming that the administrative tribunal of Paris improperly referred questions to the Court of Justice on the interpretation of this directive and improperly stayed proceedings pending the decision of that Court . . .

### NOTES AND QUESTIONS

1.   Given the wording of EC 230/TFEU 267, do you think the Conseil d'Etat was right to conclude that it did not need to refer questions to the ECJ? See also the Greek Council of State case, *Katsarou v. DI.KATSA*, Case 3458/1998, Archives of the Council of State, where a majority of the 17-member council decided to interpret TFEU 165 so as to take the question of recognition of a French diploma by a Greek (state) university out of the scope of the Treaty provisions relating to free movement of persons and of Directive 89/48. Having thus interpreted the EU provisions, no reference to the ECJ was necessary. The minority disagreed, arguing that the recognition of the degree was a matter governed by EU law and that therefore a reference to the ECJ was required. Should they have asserted that it was required in any event?

2.   Contrast the Irish case of *Nathan v. Bailey Gibson Ltd, Irish Print Union and Another*, [1998] 2 Irish Reports 164, where the female plaintiff had complained

of indirect discrimination when, as a non-union member, she was denied a position that was to be offered as far as possible only to union members. The Trial Court and the Appeals Court had rejected the complaint. The Irish Supreme Court followed the ECJ's admonition in *Von Colson* (see *infra*, Chapter 9) that it was the duty of the national Courts to interpret national law wherever possible in accordance with the provisions of relevant directives. While the Court clearly understood its duty under EU law, it chose nonetheless not to refer any question to the ECJ. If it had done so, would the ECJ's ruling likely have shed much further light on the subject?

**3.** In *Martinez Perez*, BOE No. 102 27 April 1996, case No 45/1996, the Spanish Constitutional Court rejected an appeal by a Spanish national who was resident in Germany and who had challenged the way his invalidity pension had been calculated by the Spanish authorities because they had not taken into account information relating to his German employment. The lower court had concluded that the authorities had acted properly because the information had not been submitted with a translation into Spanish as required by Article 601 of the Spanish Civil Code. The majority opinion considered this to be "infra-constitutional". Do you think the ECJ would have had a different view?

**4.** In Germany the Constitutional Court has held that failure to refer could violate German due process standards: see, for example, *Re Patented Feedingstuffs*, Case 2 BvR 808/82, [1989] CMLR 902 (2nd Senate, November 9, 1987).

**5.** Reflecting on the materials in this section of the chapter, do you think that the issues that have arisen around the doctrine of EU law supremacy would arise in the context of a perfected federal system such as the United States? If not, why? In terms of the legal effects of a ruling that a law is invalid, is there a difference between issues of unconstitutionality on the one hand and conflicts between federal and state laws on the other? How does this translate in the EU context? See N. MacCormack, Questioning Sovereignty (Oxford University Press, 1999) and P. Kirchhof, *The Balance of Powers between National and European Institutions*, (1999) 5 ELJ 225.

## § 3.04   THE UNION'S INSTITUTIONS IN THE NATIONAL COURTS

### HIGH AUTHORITY OF THE EUROPEAN COAL AND STEEL COMMUNITY v. CONCORDATO OFFICINE ELETTROMECCANICHE MERLINI
#### [1964] CMLR 184
(Italy)

[The Italian Courts were asked by the HA to treat a claim it had against a bankrupt corporation as preferred under Italian law. The Italian court considered this to be a question of Italian law where the issue would be resolved by determining whether the claim was a "tax" or not.]

Under Article 92 of the ECSC Treaty 'the decisions of the High Authority which include a pecuniary obligation on undertakings shall have the enforceability of a

Court judgment. Enforcement on the territory of member States shall be carried out by means of the legal procedure in effect in each State, after the order for enforcement in the form in use in the State on whose territory the decision is to be carried out has been stamped on the decision; this shall be done without more verification than that the decision is authentic. These formalities shall be carried out under the responsibility of a Minister designated for this purpose by each of the Governments. Enforcement may be stayed only by a decision of the Court.'

The fact that the High Authority's decisions are enforceable depends upon the fiscal power of the Community. On the other hand, the fact that execution must be realized through legal proceedings in each member State refers only to the means of execution and not to its substance, which comes from the sovereign power of the Community conferred on it by the Treaty.

These proceedings have nothing in common with proceedings to uphold the nationalization decrees of a foreign State because the High Authority's decision does not come from a foreign State, but from the sovereign power exercised by the Community itself towards the citizens of member-States which is in substance the power of each State exercised through the Community.

*     *     *

Once ascertained that the general levy provided by Article 50 of the Treaty has all the characteristics of a direct taxation, it must be examined whether the claim filed in the bankruptcy of Spa Elettromeccanica Ing Merlini can be considered to rank as preferential.

According to the plaintiff the above claim ranks as preferential under Articles 2752 and 2759 of the Civil Code because the ECSC is a supra-national Community to which all the member-States have transferred a section of their sovereignty including fiscal powers. By joining the ECSC all the member-States have agreed to exercise a part of their sovereignty through the institutions of the Community.

Therefore the financial authority exercised by the ECSC on the undertakings is the same power as that of each State, exercised through the Community. Therefore, according to the Treaty, the decisions of the ECSC are as enforceable as those of the State itself; that is also demonstrated by the enforceable validity of the decisions of the High Authority involving financial obligations. This enforceable validity cannot be explained except on the basis of the presumption that the High Authority's decisions are expressions of the sovereign power of The State.

The Court does not agree with this submission of the plaintiff, with the due respect to the plaintiff's counsel it looks too simple and, above all, conflicts with the view that the ECSC is not a partnership but a sovereign corporation, with full powers, autonomous and exclusive, within the field provided by the Treaty establishing the Community. Following the argument of the plaintiff, the Community would be a free partnership of States and the levies, provided by the Treaty, would be not fiscal taxation but only contributions to a partnership. But this is not so, as the ECSC is a juridical corporation within international law, and this is also accepted within the domestic law of each State.

This means that the Community, while it is composed of the member-States, is, on the other hand, a distinct and autonomous corporation which cannot be identified with them.

It is true that by joining the ECSC each State transfers a part of its sovereignty to the Community, but it is impossible to draw the conclusion that the acts of the ECSC are the acts of each member-State.

The Treaty of the ECSC and the domestic law concerning it are acts of the Italian State, which in this way shows its will to renounce part of its sovereignty on behalf of the Community. But once the Community was formed, it became autonomous and sovereign in its own right and developed its own legislative, executive and judicial activity completely independent of that of the member-States.

Especially when one considers Article 8 of the Treaty, the submission of the plaintiff cannot be accepted. In fact, according to this Article, the Community institutions, once established, belong to the Community itself and not to the member-States. An instance of this is the power to issue decisions against each of the member-States. A further ground is to be found in Article 6 of the Treaty where it is stated that the ECSC is a corporation both within international law and within the domestic law of each of the member-States and therefore can buy personal and real estate and can also be sued.

If there were identity between the Community and the Italian State, as the plaintiff claims, the ECSC would be an institution of the State, meaning therefore for instance that it would appear before the domestic courts through the State solicitor or, when buying or selling estate, would follow the procedure for compulsory purchase valid in Italy.

The ECSC, on the contrary, is a free and autonomous private corporation, under no control from the State institutions and with no obligation to use State solicitors before the domestic court, but employing its own private lawyers.

Therefore the Italian State is in a similar position towards the ECSC as a promoter of a joint stock company towards the company itself, because the company is formed by the will of the promoters and according to the provisions of the articles of association. Once the company is formed it performs its activity independently of the will of each promoter who takes part in the company, but they are not the company, as it is a corporation distinct from the persons of the promoters.

The same applies to the ECSC whose acts and activity do not belong to the Italian State, but to a juridical corporation of which the State is a promoter. The conclusion is that the State does not perform its powers through the Community, but the Community, on the contrary, exercises its powers through the State."

## NOTES AND QUESTIONS

1.  Would you agree with the plaintiff's comment that "the High Authority's decision did not come from a foreign State, but from the sovereign power exercised by the ECSC itself towards the citizens of member-States which is in substance the power of each State exercised through the ECSC"? Did the Court agree with it?

**2.** Would this judgment, when applied to the EU, clearly contradict the notion that the EU is in effect the Member States acting through a common body? Is the analogy with a corporation a good one, do you think? Could it hold true for the EU today?

**3.** See also *Acciaierie San Michele spa (in liquidation) v. High Authority of the ECSC*, Constitutional Court, [1966] I, 1 Giur. It. 193, [1965] I Foro It. 8, [1967] CMLR 160 (Italy. The Italian Court concluded that the ECJ was not a regular Court, because its powers and judgments were only incorporated into Italian law by an ordinary law rather than being part of the Constitutional judicial structure of the Italian state. This would have meant that its judgments could not be enforced in Italy since the court was not recognized as a valid judicial tribunal by the Constitution. The Italian court rejected this notion, noting that the ECJ's authority stemmed from the act of ratification by the Italian State of the ECSC Treaty. The ECJ could not be concerned with what internal arrangements might exist for according court judgments the power of binding decisions. Thus, the decision seems to affirm that the ECSC indeed existed as an autonomous authority. The same logic would seem to extend to the EU. Under what provisions of the TFEU might financial obligations be directly imposed on individuals that would then have to be enforced in national courts?

## MACLAINE WATSON & CO LTD v. DEPARTMENT OF TRADE AND INDUSTRY AND RELATED APPEALS
Court of Appeal, civ. div. April 27, 1988
[1989] 1 CH 72, 253, 286, 309, [1988] 3 All ER 257
(United Kingdom)

[In October 1985 the International Tin Council, a body formed by various sovereign parties and international organizations to stabilize the global tin market announced that it was unable to meet its liabilities and collapsed with debts running into hundreds of millions of UK pounds. Seventeen creditors sued the ITC. Contracts were breached and loans were not repaid, leaving debts of some 140 million pounds. The (then) EC was a party to the Agreement establishing the ITC and was a member of the Council. Counsel for the EEC argued that it should have sovereign immunity, even though the States that were members could not claim that because of the UK's Sovereign Immunity Act.]

The EEC's claim to sovereign immunity

The EEC is a party to the Sixth International Tin Agreement and consequently a member of the ITC. Under the heading 'Membership by intergovernmental organizations' art 56 of the Sixth Agreement provides that any reference to a government or governments 'shall be construed as including a reference to the European Economic Community and to any intergovernmental organization having responsibilities in respect of the negotiation, conclusion and application of international agreements, in particular commodity agreements . . .' For convenience I will continue to refer to the Community as the EEC, and in this section references to 'the Council' are to the EEC Council; not to the ITC.

. . . [EEC] Article 8 (1) [deleted] provided that the common market should be progressively established during a transitional period of 12 years. Article 113 [207] provided that after the end of the transitional period the common commercial policy should be based, inter alia, on the conclusion of trade agreements, and by art 114 [deleted] these were to be concluded by the Council on behalf of the EEC. It was pursuant to these provisions and to a Council Decision of 31 March 1982 that it was decided that the EEC should become a party to the Sixth International Tin Agreement. The EEC joined as a consumer member, and we were told that it did not contribute to the buffer stock. As mentioned in the introduction, with the exception of Maclaine Watson, who only sued the DTI [Department of Trade and Industry], the EEC was sued by all the plaintiffs in these actions as one of the members of the ITC.

\*    \*    \*

The EEC relied on various grounds similar to those relied on by the DTI in respect of their application under RSC Ord 18, r 19. In addition, the EEC relied on a further ground, viz that they were immune in respect of the subject matter of the actions.

\*    \*    \*

The EEC's claim to sovereign immunity is not the same as that raised by the foreign states under the State Immunity Act 1978 with which I have dealt in the foregoing section. It was conceded by counsel on behalf of the EEC that the EEC was not a state and that it could not rely on the 1978 Act. His contention was that the EEC was entitled to sovereign immunity analogous to that of foreign states under the principles of the common law. At the same time, however, he also conceded that the EEC could not be in a better position than the foreign states under the 1978 Act. This concession was presumably based on the qualifications to the doctrine of absolute sovereign immunity at common law . . .

Since I have held that the foreign states were not protected by immunity, because the plaintiffs' claims against them were proceedings relating to exceptions (a) or (b) of s 3(1) of the 1978 Act, it follows that, in my view, the EEC's claim to sovereign immunity does not arise. But we had over two days of argument about it, and it would of course be a matter of considerable importance if the EEC were immune from the jurisdiction of the courts of its Member States. So it is right to deal with this contention. But in my view it is entirely misconceived.

There can be no doubt that the EEC has legal personality in international law. This is provided in the EEC Treaty to which I come shortly, and is therefore part of the law of the Member States. In the case of the United Kingdom the relevant article is incorporated into our law by s 2 of the European Communities Act 1972. No doubt the EEC would also be recognized as a legal entity under the laws of non-Member States, but we are not concerned with this question and I only mention it for the sake of completeness.

Next, there is equally no doubt that the EEC exercises powers and functions which are analogous to those of sovereign states. In particular it has the jus missionis in the sense that it has permanent delegations in many non-Member

States' and receives permanent representatives from many countries, and that all these missions have diplomatic status. Furthermore, apart from the right of legation, the EEC also has the jus tractatus as instanced by the Sixth International Tin Agreement itself, ie the power to conclude or participate in treaties with sovereign states and international organizations. This power has also been widely used. Finally, the EEC enjoys certain sovereign powers to the extent to which these have been ceded to it by its members under the various EEC treaties, and from this cession it has derived its own legislative, executive and judicial organs whose acts and decisions take effect within the Member States. On the other hand, the EEC differs from sovereign states in that it has no sovereignty over territory as such and no nationals or citizens.

Counsels' claim of sovereign immunity for the EEC was based on the possession and exercise of these important powers and functions, analogous to those of sovereign states. And there can of course be no doubt that the international role of the EEC is of outstanding importance and far greater than that of many states whose right to sovereign immunity in our courts is not open to question. But the test of immunity which is under consideration for present purposes does not depend on the international importance of the body which claims it or of the functions which it exercises.

\*   \*   \*

In the present case there has been no recognition of any immunity of the EEC by anyone. It was not suggested that any foreign state, or any foreign courts, have recognized such a claim. Nor has any such recognition been indicated on behalf of the executive organs of the government of the United Kingdom. No certificate about the status of the EEC in this connection was asked for or provided by the Secretary of State for Foreign Affairs. And although the Attorney General was represented in the winding-up and receivership appeals on behalf of the United Kingdom, he has not appeared in support of the EEC's claim to sovereign immunity. Indeed, as counsel for the EEC conceded, this is the first occasion on which any claim to sovereign immunity has been made anywhere on behalf of the EEC. Sovereign states can at least generally be sued in their own courts. But, as forcibly pointed out on behalf of the plaintiffs, if there were any substance in this claim, then the EEC would evidently be immune everywhere. There was no concession that the position in Luxembourg would be any different.

Accordingly, all that remains of this strange submission is the question whether some recognition of the EEC's claim to sovereign immunity is to be derived from any legislative source in this country which it is the function of our courts to interpret. I therefore turn to this aspect, but say at once that the whole of the relevant legislation points in precisely the opposite direction.

\*   \*   \*

Articles 210 [TEU 47] and 211 [335] make it clear that the EEC has legal personality and that it can take part in legal proceedings through the Commission, without any suggestion of any immunity. Article 215 [340] is only consistent with the EEC having contractual liability and at any rate some degree of non-contractual liability. The function of arts 178 [26668 and 269] and 183 [274 and 275] is then to allocate the jurisdictions in which these respective heads of liability can be pursued. Non-contractual liability within the terms of the second paragraph of art 215 [340] is reserved to the Court of Justice, and it may be that it is pursuant to these provisions that Maclaine Watson are suing the EEC in Luxembourg, as we were told. That leaves art 183 [274 and 275] which clearly deals with jurisdiction relating to all other disputes. At first sight it appears to be saying plainly enough that in all cases not covered by the second paragraph of art 215 [340], the courts of the Member States shall have jurisdiction. However, its wording is not as clear as it might be, and counsel for the EEC may well be right in saying that it does not go quite far enough to have this positive effect. There was some discussion and uncertainty about the meaning of the words 'on the ground'. I think that they mean 'on that ground alone'. The purpose was to make it clear that the jurisdiction of the courts of the Member States should not be excluded merely on the ground of the EEC being a party to the dispute, but of course without prejudice to any other ground on which the jurisdiction of the court might be excluded in any given case. Nevertheless, although the article virtually says that the EEC shall have no immunity in the courts of the Member States in cases of disputes not covered by the second paragraph of art 215[340], I agree that it may go too far to treat it as conclusive as though it contained an exhaustive and unequivocal submission to the jurisdiction of the courts of the Member States in all such cases.

But any remaining doubt is then removed by the Treaty provisions which deal specifically with privileges and immunities. Originally the relevant provision was art 218, but this was repealed and replaced by art 28 of the Treaty establishing "a Single Council and a Single Commission of the European Communities" of 8 April 1965, commonly known as the 'Merger Treaty'. The relevant provision in this is as follows:

Article 28

The European Communities shall enjoy in the territories of the member States such privileges and immunities as are necessary for the performance of their tasks, under the conditions laid down in the Protocol annexed to this Treaty . . .' [See now TFEU 343]

If one then turns to the annexed 'Protocol on the Privileges and Immunities of the European Communities', one finds a substantial list of these, applicable to the EEC itself, its officials and other servants, members of the European parliament etc. But there is no suggestion of any jurisdictional immunity whatever. As regards the EEC itself, which is all that we are concerned with, the privileges and immunities follow the same pattern in our International Organizations Act 1968 and the Orders in Council made thereunder, including the 1972 order in the present case. Thus, one finds that the premises and buildings and archives of the EEC are inviolable and that there are far-reaching exemptions from taxes, customs duties etc. But no immunity from any legal process.

# NOTES AND QUESTIONS

**1.** Contrast *Merlini* with the *Maclaine* case: how did the English Court of Appeal view the Community's standing in English legal proceedings? Was this a question of English law or EU law?

**2.** Contrast the situation here with the position under U.S. law. Could the federal government be held accountable in state courts based on its participation in an international commercial contract? In *Maclaine*, might the ECJ have followed the U.S. principle if it had been asked to give an interpretation under EC 230/TFEU 267? (The above decision was unsuccessfully appealed, and settlement was eventually reached. The case did reach the ECJ as an action against the EU for damages (Case 241/87) and the Advocate General gave an opinion: 1989 ECJ CELEX LEXIS 55; [1990] ECR I-1797. However, the case was subsequently settled.)

**3.** EU employees enjoy "privileges and immunities," especially immunity from suit in Member States courts, a term commonly associated with international organizations. In *R v. Manchester Crown Court ex p DPP*, [1994] 1 CMLR 457, a British member of the European Parliament had been prosecuted for dishonestly obtaining checks for expenses. The Crown court judge hearing the case quashed the indictment on the grounds he did not have jurisdiction because this would infringe the sovereignty of the European Parliament and the principles of comity. This decision was ultimately allowed to stand although the House of Lords rebuked the judge for not referring the case to the ECJ. Do you think the judge was right? (See EC 291/TFEU 343 and the Protocol on Privileges and Immunities attached to the Treaties.)

**4.** In *Hurd v. Jones* Case 44/84, [1986] ECR 29, the UK Inland Revenue sought to tax the "European Supplement" and "differential allowance" elements of the income paid to a British national employed at the EU's Culham fusion reactor research facility near Oxford in England. (Hurd was the headmaster of the European School set up to educate children of EU nationals.) Both payments were designed to achieve equality of treatment for nationals from various Member States. The ECJ held that the taxation of these two types of payment would be a violation of EC 10/TEU 4, since it would tend to drain EU resources because the EU would have to gross up the payments to compensate for the tax. However, EC 10/TEU 4 is not directly effective by itself, while EC 12/TFEU 18 cannot be relied on by a national against his own State. Thus while the tax was improper, Hurd lost his appeal.

There appears to be no reference to the "sovereignty of the [then] EC" here as a reason for denying the Member States taxing rights, but is this inconsistent with the concept of such sovereignty as between federal and state authorities? In the United States, the taxation of federal employees by the state where they are resident is accepted. However, the federal authorities do not tax income earned on state and municipal bonds. Why?

**5.** The European Union has the competence to engage in external relations. The question arises, however, as to what this concept covers. Specifically, should the term "external relations" apply not only to relations with non-member states but also to those with Member States? It has been suggested that relationships between the Union and its Member States are best viewed as internal legal relations. The reasoning behind this proposition is that these relations are governed basically by the internal rules of the Union embodied in the underlying treaties and not by the application of general international law norms. This reasoning does not necessarily apply to an international organization such as the United Nations or a regional organization less closely integrated than the European Union. Rather, the definition of the term "external relations" may vary depending on the functions of the particular international organization concerned and on the extent of its structural integration. See further the materials in Chapter 21 and Template article 9.

# Part II

# THE COMPONENTS OF EU LAW

# Chapter 4

# CONSTITUTIONAL DOCUMENTS AND PRINCIPLES

## § 4.01 OVERVIEW

***Template***: Article 2, Sections 2.1-2.3, 2.6, Article 8, sections 8.2-8.4.

***Materials in this Chapter*** This Chapter covers a number of important questions associated with the "primary sources" of Union law, to which all Union legal acts are subject. These primary sources are not all of equal value. Clearly at the top of the hierarchy are the TEU and TFEU. By virtue of their provisions, the Charter of Fundamental Rights and the principles of law common to the Member States are endorsed as equal in status to the Treaties. Although customary international law is also a primary source, it will be seen that it seems to play both a superior role and a subordinate role. The Treaties are subject to the principles of international law but to the extent that they contain conflicting requirements, they will prevail. This is a subject that has particular relevance to the relations between Member States in international law, dealt with in Chapter 21.

§ 4.02 addresses the legal effects of the Treaties in the national legal systems. As noted already in the previous chapter, the doctrine of supremacy would be largely devoid of meaning if Union law could not be invoked by individuals in the national courts (there being no system of Union courts to compare with the federal judiciary in the United States). However, as a matter of first impression it is not obviously the case that the Treaties themselves can be invoked, for two reasons.

First, under national constitutions they may not have the force of law within the domestic legal system. As treaties among sovereign states, they cannot be analogized to a constitutional document in domestic law, such as the United States Constitution.

Second, even if they did have legal force, they might, as a matter of interpretation, still be considered as only creating obligations between the signatory states and not capable of generating rights or obligations for individuals.

As to interpretation, it may be recalled that the ECJ in its *Van Gend* and *Costa* decisions set out in Chapter 3 considered that certain provisions of the Treaties do create rights and obligations for individuals (EC 81 and 82/TFEU 101 and 102) while others could at least be invoked against Member States (the standstill provisions referenced in both those cases.) From this, one might further reason that, if such provisions are capable of being invoked, it should not be possible to undermine this effect by denying the Treaties the force of law, whatever the national constitution might say. If that were not so, widespread differences would result as regards the effect of the Treaties in the various States.

Once again, there is nothing in the Treaties that explicitly speaks to either of these points, so it is to ECJ decisions that we must look for guidance both in terms of rationale and scope. The materials in § 4.02 will illustrate how the Court was able to use a question concerning the interpretation of a Treaty provision (whether it created rights for individuals) to establish also a doctrine of Union law pursuant to which the Treaties should have effect in domestic legal systems *regardless of how they would be treated under national constitutions*. In that regard the Court, noting that the Treaty contained some provisions that were clearly "directly applicable", proceeded to develop a second proposition: that individuals may invoke certain other *non*-directly applicable provisions against Member States, a concept which the Court has usually described in terms of the "direct effect" of certain Treaty provisions.

The difference between direct effect and direct applicability has generated an enormous amount of commentary and attempts at explanation over the years. There have indeed been suggestions that even the ECJ does not always clearly distinguish between them. We suggest that the most satisfactory way of drawing out the distinctions is to focus on how they affect individuals' rights or obligations. Sections 8.3 and 8.4 of the Template attempt to do this. In reading the cases in § 4.02, it is helpful to keep those sections in mind and test them against the Court's rulings.

The materials in § 4.03 deal with what might be viewed as the reverse of § 4.02. They address a situation where national laws are imported into the Union legal order. As may be recalled from Chapter 3, in the *Internationale Handelsgesellschaft* case the ECJ held that Union law encompasses "general principles of law common to the Member States". Primarily this is a reference to fundamental rights. The general principles have now been largely restated in the Charter of Fundamental Rights, which has equal legal value to the Treaties. In future cases, therefore, the Court is likely to pay primary attention to this document rather than the general principles, but the latter remain important in the interpretation of the Treaties, particularly those that do not address fundamental rights. Into this mix there will be injected at some point the European Convention on Human Rights, since the Treaties now require that the Union accede to it.

The materials dwell on a particular feature of EU fundamental rights, from whatever source they are derived, namely the extent of their application. As the Template indicates, they apply to acts of the Union institutions and to any context in which Union law is implemented The materials in this Chapter will provide an outline of that subject, while later chapters will illustrate it in particular subject-matter contexts.

§ 4.04 addresses the role of international law: Union law is subject to international law, at any rate to the extent that this does not conflict directly with the Treaties. This offers a significant contrast with the U.S. legal system, where international law is irrelevant except to the extent that it is incorporated into U.S. legislation or via a Treaty to which the United States is a party.

***Attitudes to treaties in national constitutions*** Under conventional principles of international law relating to the legal effects of treaties, each signatory state has its own methods of rendering treaties part of the internal law of that state. A distinction is drawn in international legal theory and practice between two extremes: monism and dualism. If a state has a pure monist approach, a treaty is considered an integral part of national law as soon as it is ratified by the state, without the necessity of further steps by national institutions at the national level. Under some versions of monism, the national constitution may require that treaties and other forms of international law enjoy supremacy, in case of conflict, over other domestic laws. In contrast, in states having a pure dualist approach, treaties and other forms of international law are considered part of a legal system that is entirely separate from that of national law. They become part of national law only indirectly through the passage of a statute duly enacted by the national legislature. If a treaty is incorporated through the dualist approach, it will, in principle, have no legal effect of its own — the enacting legislation alone will give effect to the intentions of the treaty.

Most European states now have treaty implementation provisions in their constitutions that have at least some monist attributes, although not all of these states accord treaties an equal or superior place within their legal systems. In the United Kingdom, treaties have no force at all unless embodied in or introduced through an Act of Parliament.

***The General Principles of Law*** The importation of the general principles of law of the Member States into the legal system of the EU came about through what used to be article 220 of the EC Treaty and is now incorporated into Article 19 of the TEU. That provision states that the ECJ is required to ensure that the "law is observed." More specifically, as is apparent from the material in Chapter 18, the grounds of review specified in EC 230/TFEU 263 can be interpreted as inclusive of the general principles, while EC 288/TFEU 340 references such general principles explicitly in the context of the non-contractual liability of the EU — probably the closest although still not a very accurate parallel to the importation of state common law into the federal system in the U.S.

***Fundamental Rights*** The primary, though not sole, consequence of the above-mentioned "importation" has been to introduce fundamental rights as an integral part of EU law. As stated already, they are not in themselves an independent and overriding body of law existing, as it were, above the Treaties, but their nature obviously entails that EU law should be subject to them, except where they might conflict with express language in the Treaties. In this regard, later chapters will illustrate in particular how the provisions relating to the internal market and in particular the free movement of goods and services do indeed have the potential to conflict with such principles. With the Charter now apparently of equal value with the Treaties, could this mean that the fundamental concepts of free movement must be attenuated in some way? Creative interpretation usually finds a way to avoid such conflicts but they certainly exist potentially. While on the subject of the Charter we should also note its manner of adoption and what that might signify for the EU legal order. It was incorporated formally into the EU constitutional structure via the Charter of Fundamental Rights adopted by the Union at a ceremony on December 12 2007 (the day prior to the signature of the Lisbon Treaty).

The term "fundamental rights" may be confusing to U.S. lawyers for several reasons. In the first place, U.S. lawyers may distinguish between gradations of rights enshrined in the Constitution and attribute the term "fundamental" only to those that have become applicable also to the states through the Fourteenth Amendment precisely because they are considered so "fundamental" that they are encompassed in the concept of due process. Second, the rights in the Charter may seem in many respects to be more a manifestation of a particular choice of societal structure and somewhat aspirational than the more familiar basic personal rights against the state. Third, many of the Charter's provisions seem to run into each other as, for example, freedom of expression and the right to privacy.

## § 4.02  THE TREATIES

### [A]  The Concept of Direct Effect

## VAN GEND EN LOOS v. NEDERLANDSE ADMINISTRATIE DER BELASTINGEN
Case 26/62, 1963 ECJ CELEX LEXIS 12, [1963] ECR 1
[No paragraph numbering in the original]

[The facts of this case are set out in Chapter 3 but for convenience are repeated and elaborated here.

The plaintiff had sought to import a shipment of ureaformaldehyde into the Netherlands from Germany. At the time, customs duties were still in effect as between the two countries (such duties were to be phased out over the Transitional Period). Due to changes in Dutch law, the shipment was subjected to a customs duty that was higher than that previously applied to the same product, in apparent contravention of then article 12 of the EC Treaty, which stated:

"Member States shall refrain from introducing between themselves any new customs duties on imports or exports or any charges having equivalent effect, and from increasing those which they already apply in their trade with each other."

The Dutch government argued that the duty increase had come about as a result of a reclassification of the product in another heading of the tariff, an action that it was entitled to take. That reclassification occurred after the date of the EEC Treaty.

The Dutch court asked the ECJ whether Article 12 should be interpreted as creating rights for individuals. If it did, then it would be directly applicable in the Dutch legal system by virtue of article 66 (now 94) of the Dutch constitution, as set out in note 1 *infra*. Various intervening Member States also argued that there was no need for individuals to be able to invoke the Treaty on grounds of ensuring its enforcement because it provided in then article 169 (EC 226/TFEU 258) for the Commission to enforce it through a special procedure in the ECJ.]

The first question of the Tariefcommissie is whether Article 12 [deleted] of the Treaty has direct application in national law in the sense that nationals of Member States may on the basis of this article lay claim to rights which the national court must protect.

Although a portion of the judgment appears in Chapter 3, the significance of the case and the relevance of that portion warrant that it be repeated here.]

The objective of the EEC Treaty, which is to establish a common market, the functioning of which is of direct concern to interested parties in the Community, implies that this Treaty is more than an agreement which merely creates mutual obligations between the contracting states. This view is confirmed by the preamble to the Treaty which refers not only to governments but to peoples. It is also confirmed more specifically by the establishment of institutions endowed with sovereign rights, the exercise of which affects Member States and also their citizens. Furthermore, it must be noted that the nationals of the States brought together in the Community are called upon to cooperate in the functioning of this Community through the intermediary of the European Parliament and the Economic and Social Committee.

In addition the task assigned to the Court of Justice under article 177 [267], the object of which is to secure uniform interpretation of the Treaty by national courts and tribunals, confirms that the States have acknowledged that Community law has an authority which can be invoked by their nationals before those courts and tribunals. The conclusion to be drawn from this is that the Community constitutes a new legal order of international law for the benefit of which the States have limited their sovereign rights, albeit within limited fields, and the subjects of which comprise not only Member States but also their nationals.

With regard to the general scheme of the Treaty as it relates to customs duties and charges having equivalent effect it must be emphasized that Article 9, which bases the Community upon a Customs Union, includes as an essential provision the prohibition of these customs duties and charges. This provision is found at the beginning of the part of the Treaty which defines the "Foundations of the Community". It is applied and explained by Article 12 [deleted].

The wording of Article 12 [deleted] contains a clear and unconditional prohibition which is not a positive but a negative obligation. This obligation, moreover, is not qualified by any reservation on the part of States which would make its implementation conditional upon a positive legislative measure enacted under national law. The very nature of this prohibition makes it ideally adapted to produce direct effects in the legal relationship between Member States and their subjects.

The implementation of Article 12 [deleted] does not require any legislative intervention on the part of the States. The fact that under this Article it is the Member States who are made the subject of the negative obligation does not imply that their nationals cannot benefit from this obligation.

In addition, the argument based on articles 169 [258] and 170 [259] of the Treaty put forward by the three governments which have submitted observations to the Court in their statements of case is misconceived. The fact that these Articles of the Treaty enable the Commission and the Member States to bring before the Court a State which has not fulfilled its obligations does not mean that individuals cannot plead these obligations, should the occasion arise, before a national court, any more than the fact that the Treaty places at the disposal of the Commission ways of ensuring that obligations imposed upon those subject to the Treaty are observed, precludes the possibility, in actions between individuals before a national court, of pleading infringements of these obligations.

A restriction of the guarantees against an infringement of Article 12 [deleted] by Member States to the procedures under Articles 169 [258] and 170 [259] would remove all direct legal protection of the individual rights of their nationals. There is the risk that recourse to the procedure under these articles would be ineffective if it were to occur after the implementation of a national decision taken contrary to the provisions of the Treaty.

The vigilance of individuals concerned to protect their rights amounts to an effective supervision in addition to the supervision entrusted by Articles 169 [258] and 170 [259] to the diligence of the Commission and of the Member States.

It follows from the foregoing considerations that, according to the spirit, the general scheme and the wording of the Treaty, Article 12 [deleted] must be interpreted as producing direct effects and creating individual rights which national courts must protect.

## NOTES AND QUESTIONS

1.  Article 66 (see now 94) of The Netherlands Constitution expressly confirmed that international treaties could be a part of Dutch domestic law:

Statutory regulations in force within the Kingdom shall not be applicable if such application is in conflict with provisions of treaties or of resolutions by international institutions that are binding on all persons.

This provision seems to confirm a monist approach (as the term was described in the Overview). International treaties it seems can override even subsequently adopted national legislation. In *Van Gend*, the plaintiffs had invoked the EEC Treaty for that purpose. Why was the issue not then resolved simply on the basis of the Dutch Constitution? What was the precise purpose of the Dutch Court in seeking an interpretation of EEC Article 12?

In considering the above question, it may be helpful to bear in mind the position in the U.S. regarding the way in which treaties become part of internal federal law. Treaties (including international conventions) to which the U.S. is a party become law upon ratification and may or may not have domestic effects. Here, the courts may conclude that a treaty provision is merely in the nature of a contract between the U.S. and another country and is not capable of creating rights for individuals, while other provisions require no action on the part of the legislature to have full force and effect — they are "self-executing." Chief Justice Marshall, in a very early case, *Foster v. Neilson* 27 U.S. (2 Pet.) 253, 314 (1829), described the difference between so-called self- executing treaties and other treaties as follows:

Our constitution declares a treaty to be the law of the land. It is, consequently, to be regarded in courts of justice as equivalent to an act of the legislature, whenever it operates of itself without the aid of any legislative provision. But when the terms of the stipulation import a contract, when either of the parties engages to perform a particular act, the treaty addresses itself to the political, not the judicial department; and the legislature must execute the contract before it can become a rule for the court.

Also of assistance may be the opinion of the Advocate General, whose views differed from those of the Court, as expressed in the following passage [1962 ECJ CELEX LEXIS 33]

The first conclusion we can draw from this analysis is that large parts of the Treaty clearly contain only obligations of Member States, and do not contain rules having a direct internal effect.

It is accordingly within the framework of supranational law that ways of dealing with breaches of the Treaty have been devised. Under Article 169 [258], the Commission gives a Member State which does not fulfil its obligations under the Treaty a time limit within which it can comply with the reasoned opinion of the Commission. Under Article 171 [260] a State in this situation is required to take the necessary measures to comply with the judgment of the Court of Justice. If, for the purpose of Community law, it had been intended to make the direct application of the provisions of the Treaty, in the sense that they are to prevail over national law, a fundamental principle, the procedure for enforcing obedience could have been confined to a declaration of the nullity of measures taken contrary to the provisions of the Treaty. At least the provisions in Article 171 [260], if not also the fixing of a time limit under Article 169 [258], would be superfluous.

If we consider the place which Article 12 [deleted] can occupy in this system, in this range of legal possibilities, it is useful to begin by recalling its wording. It reads as follows:

'Member States shall refrain from introducing between themselves any new customs duties or imports or exports or any charges having equivalent effect and from increasing those which they already apply in their trade with each other.'

It seems to me beyond doubt that the form of words chosen — which moreover no one has called into question — no more precludes the assumption of a legal obligation than does the similar wording of other Articles of the Treaty. To give Article 12 [deleted] a lower legal status would not be in keeping with its importance in the framework of the Treaty. Further, I consider that the implementation of this obligation does not depend on other legal measures of the Community institutions, which allows us in a certain sense to speak of the direct legal effect of Article 12 [deleted].

However, the crucial issue according to the question raised by the Tariefcommissie is whether this direct effect stops at the Governments of the Member States, or whether it should penetrate into the national legal field and lead to its direct application by the administrative authorities and courts of Member States. It is here that the real difficulties of interpretation begin.

In the first place what is remarkable is that the Member States are named as the addressees just as in other provisions which clearly only intend to impose obligations on states (Articles 13 [30], 14 [deleted], 16 [deleted], 27 [deleted] etc). They, the Member States, shall not introduce new customs duties or increase those which they already apply. It must be concluded from this that Article 12 [deleted] does not have in mind administrative practice, that is, the conduct of the national administrative authorities.

But apart from designating those to whom it is addressed, Article 12 [deleted] recalls the wording of other provisions which appear to me beyond any doubt only to lay down obligations for Member States, for they speak expressly of 'obligations' even if only in later paragraphs (see for instance Articles 31 [deleted] and 37 [37]).

In this connexion it is also necessary to mention Article 95 [110] which provides that no Member State shall impose directly or indirectly on the products of other Member States any internal taxation of any kind in excess of that imposed directly or indirectly on similar domestic products and then continues in the third paragraph:

"Member States shall, not later than at the beginning of the second stage, repeal or amend any provisions existing when this Treaty enters into force which conflict with the preceding rules."

It should further be noted that the wording of Article 12 [deleted] does not contain such terms as 'prohibition', 'prohibited', 'inadmissible', 'without effect', which are found in other provisions of the Treaty. It is just when a provision is meant to be applied directly, that is, by the administrative authorities of Member States, that a precise indication of the intended legal effects is indispensable.

But above all we must consider whether, judged by its content, Article 12 [deleted] appears to be adapted for direct application. We must bear in mind that, at least for the time being, Member States still retain to a large degree their legislative powers in customs matters. In certain Member States they lead to formal laws. The direct application of Article 12 [deleted] would thus often take the form of a review of legislative acts by the administrative authorities and the courts of Member States, with the help of the provisions of Article 12 [deleted].

If we look at the object of this provision it appears that, contrary to first impressions, it is very complex. It is therefore scarcely possible for its provisions to be applied in every case without creating problems.

Article 12 [deleted] applies, *inter alia*, to charges having equivalent effect. We have seen recently in another case the difficulties that an exact definition of this concept can entail. Further, Article 12 [deleted] refers to customs duties or charges having equivalent effect applied at a particular moment. In the practice of this Court we have learned that even the term 'applied' can raise considerable difficulties of interpretation. Finally the present proceedings themselves show what problems can be created by a finding of the existence of an increase in applied tariffs based on an alteration of custom nomenclature.

These difficulties emerge all the more clearly when it is realized that in customs law states are not only under a negative duty. Under the Treaty they are required by a continuous series of measures to adapt their customs law and regulations to the development of the Common Market. But if the customs system is continually changing, the supervision of the supplementary standstill provision of Article 12 [deleted] is certainly not easy.

I find it difficult to understand how, in view of this, the Commission can expect that the direct application of Article 12 [deleted] will bring about an increase in legal certainty.

Can it really be assumed that undertakings rely in their commercial operations on a particular interpretation and application of specific provisions of the Treaty or would they not find more reliable guidance in positive national customs provisions?

Even if these arguments alone provide sufficient reasons for rejecting the view that Article 12 [deleted] has direct internal effect, the following additional arguments must be mentioned:

The position of the constitutional laws of the Member States, above all with regard to the determination of the relationship between supranational or international law and subsequent national legislation, is far from uniform. If Article 12 [deleted] is deemed to have a direct internal effect, the situation would arise that breaches of Article 12 [deleted] would render the national customs laws ineffective and inapplicable in only a certain number of Member States. That appears to me to be the case in the Netherlands, the Constitution of which (Article 66) gives international agreements containing generally binding and directly applicable provisions a superior status to that of national law; in Luxembourg (where the courts, in the absence of explicit provisions in the Constitution, have arrived at essentially the same conclusion) and, it may be, in France (perhaps because the relevant Article 55 of the Constitution of 4 October 1958 is not quite clear with regard to later laws and contains moreover a reservation that there must be reciprocal application).

On the other hand, it is certain that the Belgian Constitution does not include any provision dealing with the legal effect of international treaties in relation to national law. They seem, according to the case law of that country, to have the same status as national laws.

Similarly, there is no provision in the text of the Italian Constitution from which the supremacy of international law over national law can be inferred. The case law and the prevailing doctrine do not accord any superior status to treaties, at least in relation to later national laws.

Finally, with regard to German constitutional law, Article 24 of the Basic Law provides that the Federation may by legislation transfer sovereign rights to international institutions. Article 25 provides that the general rules of international law shall form an integral part of Federal law, and shall take precedence over legislation under that law and create rights and duties directly applicable to the inhabitants of the territory of the Federation. However, contrary to the views of certain authors, it cannot be inferred from case law that international treaties have supremacy over later national laws.

The authors of the Treaty were faced with this situation in the field of constitutional law when they drafted the legal texts of the Community. Having regard to this situation it is in my opinion doubtful whether the authors, when dealing with a provision of such importance to customs law, intended to produce the consequences of an uneven development of the law involved in the principle of direct application, consequences which do not accord with an essential aim of the Community.

But neither would a uniform development of the law be guaranteed in those States whose constitutional law gives international agreements precedence over national law.

The Treaty does not provide any machinery to ensure the avoidance of this danger. Article 177 [267] only provides for a right and a duty to refer a question concerning the interpretation of the Treaty to the Court, but not on the other hand a question concerning the compatibility of national with Community law. It is therefore conceivable that national courts might refrain from making a reference to the Court of Justice for a preliminary ruling because they do not see any difficulties of interpretation, and then, however, come to different conclusions in their own interpretation of the Treaty. In this way variations in the application of the law could occur in the courts of the different States as well as in courts of the same State.

After all these considerations which are based upon an examination of the system of the Treaty taken as a whole, upon the wording, the content and the context of the provision to be interpreted, I come to the conclusion that Article 12 [deleted] should be legally classified in the same way as the other rules relating to the customs union. Article 11 [deleted] has a fundamental importance for all of them when it speaks explicitly of 'obligations with regard to customs duties', a phrase which excludes direct internal effect within the meaning of the first question. It is my conviction therefore that question No 1 of the Tariefcommissie should be answered in the negative."

2.   In *Van Gend*, the Court uses the expression "direct effect" and "immediate effect" to describe the characteristics of the Treaty provision in issue. As noted in the Overview, this terminology has been the source of much discussion and, it has to be said, confusion because it obviously is intended to convey something different from "direct applicability", the term explicitly used to describe regulations in EC 249/TFEU 288.

Professor John Jackson has suggested that "direct application expresses the notion that the international treaty instrument has a 'direct' statute-like role in the domestic legal system . . ." John H. Jackson, *Status of Treaties in Domestic Legal Systems: A Policy Analysis*, 86 Am. J. Int'l L. 310 (1992). Jackson distinguishes between direct applicability and "invocability," a concept similar but not identical to "standing." Under his approach, "invocability" refers to the issue of who is entitled to invoke or rely on the treaty norms. "Invocability" would then correspond to the notion of direct effect. Bearing in mind the suggested formulation of the distinction between direct effect and direct applicability in sections 8.3 and 8.4 of the Template, do you think Professor Jackson's analysis is sufficient in the context of EU law?

3.   What would have been the result if the Court had held that EEC 12 did not create rights that could be invoked by individuals?

4.   Note the criteria applied by the Court for determining which provisions of the EC Treaty/TFEU are directly effective. These are summarized in Template paragraph 2.1.6. As regards "direct applicability", are there any other provisions of the EC Treaty/TFEU that might be described as directly applicable? What about EC 230/TFEU 263 (Template para. 5.1.4)?

5.   As in the case of the EC Treaty/TFEU, U.S. court decisions have indicated that individual provisions of a treaty may be invocable and constitute the supreme law of the land even though other provisions of the same treaty are not self-executing and hence non-invocable. See, e.g., *Aguilar v. Standard Oil Co. (New Jersey*, 318 U.S. 724, 738 (1943). Perhaps the best example is the United Nations Charter. Articles 55 and 56, the human rights provisions of the Charter, have been held to be non-self-executing: *Sei Fujii v. California*, 38 Cal. 2d 718, P. 2d 617 (1952). In contrast, the provisions in articles 104 and 105 concerning the legal capacity of the Organization and its privileges and immunities have been held to be self-executing: *Curran v. City of New York*, 77 N.Y.S. 2d 206 (1947).

6.   Notice that the *Van Gend* case preceded *Costa* in time. One may take the view that direct effect is actually the basic principle from which supremacy derives rather than the other way round. For a discussion of this, see M. Dougan, *When worlds collide! Competing visions of the relationship between direct effect and supremacy* (2007) 44 CML Rev. 931. Do you think it matters?

7.   In *Constitutionalism and Pluralism in Marbury and Van Gend*, in M.P. Maduro and L. Azoulai (Eds.), The Past and the Future of EU Law: Revisiting the Classics on the 5th Anniversary of the Rome Treaty (2008), Professor Daniel Halberstam explores how *Marbury v. Madison* and *Van Gend* address the more fundamental balancing of competing claims for ultimate judicial authority within the two systems.

## JOHANNES HENRICUS MARIA VAN BINSBERGEN v. BESTUUR VAN DE BEDRIJFSVERENIGING VOOR DE METAALNIJVERHEID
Case 33/74, [1974] ECR 1299

[Mr. Van Binsbergen, the appellant in a lawsuit in the Netherlands, had entrusted the defence of his interests to a legal representative of Netherlands nationality, a Mr. Kortmann, who was entitled to act for parties before courts and tribunals where representation by an advocaat (roughly equivalent to an attorney admitted to practice in a state in the United States) is not obligatory. Since this legal representative had, during the course of the proceedings, transferred his residence from the Netherlands to Belgium, his capacity to represent the party in question before the Centrale Raad van Beroep was contested on the basis of a provision of Netherlands law under which only persons established in the Netherlands may act as legal representatives before that court. In support of his claim the person concerned invoked the provisions of the Treaty relating to freedom to provide services within the Community. The Court first addressed the scope of the prohibition in EEC 59 (EC 49/TFEU 56). This aspect of the case is addressed in Chapter 14. It then proceeded to consider whether EC 49/TFEU was directly effective (although it may be noted that the referring court asked whether it was directly applicable, a terminology issue that we have already noted.)]

18 The Court is also asked whether the first paragraph of Article 59 [56] and the third paragraph of Article 60 [57] of the EEC Treaty are directly applicable and create individual rights which national courts must protect.

19 This question must be resolved with reference to the whole of the chapter relating to services, taking account, moreover, of the provisions relating to the right of establishment to which reference is made in Article 66 [62].

20 With a view to the progressive abolition during the transitional period of the restrictions referred to in Article 59 [56], Article 63 [deleted] has provided for the drawing up of a 'general programme' — laid down by Council Decision of 18 December 1961 (1962, p. 32) — to be implemented by a series of directives.

21 Within the scheme of the chapter relating to the provision of services, these directives are intended to accomplish different functions, the first being to abolish, during the transitional period, restrictions on freedom to provide services, the second being to introduce into the law of Member States a set of provisions intended to facilitate the effective exercise of this freedom, in particular by the mutual recognition of professional qualifications and the coordination of laws with regard to the pursuit of activities as self-employed persons.

22 These directives also have the task of resolving the specific problems resulting from the fact that where the person providing the service is not established, on a habitual basis, in the State where the service is performed he may not be fully subject to the professional rules of conduct in force in that state.

23 As regards the phased implementation of the chapter relating to services, Article 59 [56], interpreted in the light of the general provisions of Article 8 [deleted] of the Treaty, expresses the intention to abolish restrictions on freedom to provide

services by the end of the transitional period, the latest date for the entry into force of all the rules laid down by the Treaty.

24 The provisions of Article 59 [56], the application of which was to be prepared by directives issued during the transitional period, therefore became unconditional on the expiry of that period.

25 The provisions of that article abolish all discrimination against the person providing the service by reason of his nationality or the fact that he is established in a Member State other than that in which the service is to be provided.

26 Therefore, as regards at least the specific requirement of nationality or of residence, Article 59 [56] and 60 [57] impose a well-defined obligation, the fulfillment of which by the Member States cannot be delayed or jeopardized by the absence of provisions which were to be adopted in pursuance of powers conferred under Articles 63 [deleted] and 66.

27 Accordingly, the reply should be that the first paragraph of article 59 [56] and the third paragraph of article 60 [57] have direct effect and may therefore be relied on before national courts, at least in so far as they seek to abolish any discrimination against a person providing a service by reason of his nationality or of the fact that he resides in a member state other than that in which the service is to be provided.

## NOTES AND QUESTIONS

1. It was not immediately apparent that article 59 (EC 49/TFEU 56) could be directly effective when applying the criteria adopted by the Court in *Van Gend*. The opening phrase "within the framework of the provisions set out below" seemed to suggest that it would require Union legislation to open up the service sector. The original language of the services articles laid out requirements to do so by the end of the transitional period. Almost no action was taken during the transitional period. In *Van Binsbergen*, the Court decided nonetheless that EC 49/TFEU 56 could be considered to be unconditional and sufficiently precise to have direct effect from the end of that period. How did it rationalize the apparent obstacle to direct effect arising from the need for harmonizing legislation, i.e., that the article did not appear to be unconditional?

2. It is possible that a provision can become directly effective over time as the Union adopts rules that eliminate any conditionality. Consider in this context EC 14/TFEU 26. Before the *Schengen* arrangements (described in Chapter 2) had been put in place, the Court had held in *Wijsenbeck* that EC 14/TFEU 26 was not directly effective based on the law as it "stood at the time of the events in question". In light of the Schengen arrangements, could this case be decided differently today?

3. The ability to invoke directly effective provisions is not limited to those for whom the provisions exist: Thus, in *Clean Car Autoservice GesmbH v. Landeshauptmann von Vien*, Case C-350/96, 1998 ECJ CELEX LEXIS 339, 1998 ECR I-2521, Austrian law required that the non-resident owner of a company doing business in Austria was required to appoint a manager who was resident in Austria. Clean Car had applied to the Magistrat der Stadt Wien (Vienna City Council) to register for the trade of maintenance and care of motor vehicles (service station).

When making that application, it stated that it had appointed Mr Rudolf Henssen, a German national residing in Berlin as its manager. It further indicated that Mr Henssen was actively seeking to rent accommodation in Austria and that the declaration relating to his residence there would be forwarded in due course. The Vienna City Council denied Clean Car a business permit because the person appointed as manager did not yet have a residence in Austria. The ECJ made clear that employers were entitled to invoke then article 48 (EC 39/TFEU 45):

18 . . . [I]t must be noted that Article 48 [45](1) states, in general terms, that freedom of movement for workers is to be secured within the Community. Under Article 48 [45](2) and (3), such freedom of movement is to entail the abolition of any discrimination based on nationality between workers of the Member States as regards employment, remuneration and other conditions of work and employment, and to entail the right, subject to limitations justified on grounds of public policy, public security or public health, to accept offers of employment actually made, to move freely within the territory of Member States for that purpose, to stay in a Member State in order to be employed there under the same conditions as nationals of that State and to remain there after such employment.

19 Whilst those rights are undoubtedly enjoyed by those directly referred to — namely, workers — there is nothing in the wording of Article 48 [45] to indicate that they may not be relied upon by others, in particular employers.

20 It must further be noted that, in order to be truly effective, the right of workers to be engaged and employed without discrimination necessarily entails as a corollary the employer's entitlement to engage them in accordance with the rules governing freedom of movement for workers.

21 Those rules could easily be rendered nugatory if Member States could circumvent the prohibitions which they contain merely by imposing on employers requirements to be met by any worker whom they wish to employ which, if imposed directly on the worker, would constitute restrictions on the exercise of the right to freedom of movement to which that worker is entitled under Article 48 [45] of the Treaty.

22 Finally, the above interpretation is corroborated both by Article 2 of Regulation No 1612/68 and by the Court's case-law.

23 It is made explicitly clear in Article 2 of Regulation No 1612/68 that any employer pursuing an activity in the territory of a Member State and any national of a Member State must be able to conclude and perform contracts of employment in accordance with the provisions in force laid down by law, regulation or administrative action, without any discrimination resulting therefrom.

24 . . . [J]ustifications on grounds of public policy, public security or public health, as envisaged in Article 48 [45](3) of the Treaty, may be relied upon not only by Member States in order to justify limitations on freedom of movement for workers under their laws, regulations or administrative provisions but also by individuals in order to justify such limitations under

agreements or other measures adopted by persons governed by private law. Thus, if an employer may rely on a derogation under Article 48 [45](3), he must also be able to rely on the same principles under, in particular, Article 48 [45](1) and (2).

25 In the light of those considerations, the answer to the first question must be that the rule of equal treatment in the context of freedom of movement for workers, enshrined in Article 48 [45] of the Treaty, may also be relied upon by an employer in order to employ, in the Member State in which he is established, workers who are nationals of another Member State.

## [B]   Can Directly Effective Provisions Create Obligations for Individuals?

## UNION ROYALE BELGE DES SOCIETES DE FOOTBALL ASSOCIATION ASBL AND OTHERS v. JEAN-MARC BOSMAN
### Case C-415/93, 1995 ECJ CELEX LEXIS 220, [1995] ECR I-4921

[The Belgian Football Association (URBSFA), in line with international practices and requirements laid down by UEFA and FIFA (European and international football federations), required a (professional) football club to make a payment to another club if the former wished to hire a player whose contract with the latter had come to an end. This arrangement required the issuance of a transfer certificate by URBSFA to the new club. Bosman's contract with a Belgian club had ended and he sought employment with a club in France. URBSFA refused to certify the transfer ostensibly on concerns about the financial standing of the French club. Bosman sued URBSFA and others for damages and claimed (among other things) that the transfer rules infringed his EU right to free movement. The Court addressed several important questions, the first being whether national football associations, being private, fall within the requirements of EC 39/TFEU 45.]

82 . . . Article 48 [45] not only applies to the action of public authorities but extends also to rules of any other nature aimed at regulating gainful employment in a collective manner.

83 The Court has held that the abolition as between Member States of obstacles to freedom of movement for persons and to freedom to provide services would be compromised if the abolition of State barriers could be neutralized by obstacles resulting from the exercise of their legal autonomy by associations or organizations not governed by public law . . .

84 It has further observed that working conditions in the different Member States are governed sometimes by provisions laid down by law or regulation and sometimes by agreements and other acts concluded or adopted by private persons. Accordingly, if the scope of Article 48 [45] of the Treaty were confined to acts of a public authority there would be a risk of creating inequality in its application . . . That risk is all the more obvious in a case such as that in the main proceedings in this case in that . . . the transfer rules have been laid down by different bodies or in different ways in each Member State.

85 UEFA objects that such an interpretation makes Article 48 [45] of the Treaty more restrictive in relation to individuals than in relation to Member States, which are alone in being able to rely on limitations justified on grounds of public policy, public security or public health.

86 That argument is based on an false premise. There is nothing to preclude individuals from relying on justifications on grounds of public policy, public security or public health. Neither the scope nor the content of those grounds of justification is in any way affected by the public or private nature of the rules in question.

87 Article 48 [45] of the Treaty therefore applies to rules laid down by sporting associations such as URBSFA, FIFA or UEFA, which determine the terms on which professional sportsmen can engage in gainful employment.

## NOTES AND QUESTIONS

**1.** Do you find it surprising that EC 39/TFEU 45 can be asserted against private bodies such as the one here? The Court considered that the exceptions to EC 39/TFEU 45 could be invoked by non-governmental bodies. Is this feasible?

**2.** Another interesting feature of *Bosman* is that since the rules applied to clubs, not individuals, the EU competition rules were brought into play. The rules had been condoned by the Commission at an earlier date, action that the ECJ condemned.

## [C]   Direct Applicability (?)

## ROMAN ANGONESE v. CASSA DI RISPARMIO DI BOLZANO SPA.
### Case C-281/98, 2000 ECJ CELEX LEXIS 321, [2000] ECR I-4139

[Mr Angonese, an Italian national whose mother tongue was German applied to take part in a competition for a post with a private banking undertaking in Bolzano, the Cassa di Risparmio.]

6 One of the conditions for entry to the competition was possession of a type-B certificate of bilingualism (in Italian and German) (the Certificate), which used to be required in the province of Bolzano for access to the former carriera di concetto (managerial career) in the public service.

7 According to the file, the Certificate is issued by the public authorities of the province of Bolzano after an examination which is held only in that province. It is usual for residents of the province of Bolzano to obtain the Certificate as a matter of course for employment purposes. Obtaining the Certificate is viewed as an almost compulsory step as part of normal training.

8 The national court has found as a fact that, although Mr Angonese was not in possession of the Certificate, he was perfectly bilingual. With a view to gaining admission to the competition, he had submitted a certificate showing completion of his studies as a draughtsman and certificates attesting to his studies of languages (English, Slovene and Polish) at the Faculty of Philosophy at Vienna University and

had stated that his professional experience included practising as a draughtsman and translating from Polish into Italian.

9 On 4 September 1997, the Cassa de Risparmio informed Mr Angonese that he could not be admitted to the competition because he had not produced the Certificate." Mr Angonese invoked article 48 [45] EC.

\* \* \*

30 It should be noted at the outset that the principle of non-discrimination set out in Article 48 is drafted in general terms and is not specifically addressed to the Member States.

31 Thus, the Court has held that the prohibition of discrimination based on nationality applies not only to the actions of public authorities but also to rules of any other nature aimed at regulating in a collective manner gainful employment and the provision of services. . . .

32 The Court has held that the abolition, as between Member States, of obstacles to freedom of movement for persons would be compromised if the abolition of State barriers could be neutralised by obstacles resulting from the exercise of their legal autonomy by associations or organisations not governed by public . . .

33 Since working conditions in the different Member States are governed sometimes by provisions laid down by law or regulation and sometimes by agreements and other acts concluded or adopted by private persons, limiting application of the prohibition of discrimination based on nationality to acts of a public authority risks creating inequality in its application . . .

34 The Court has also ruled that the fact that certain provisions of the Treaty are formally addressed to the Member States does not prevent rights from being conferred at the same time on any individual who has an interest in compliance with the obligations thus laid down (see Case 43/75 Defrenne v. Sabena [1976] ECR 455, paragraph 31). The Court accordingly held, in relation to a provision of the Treaty which was mandatory in nature, that the prohibition of discrimination applied equally to all agreements intended to regulate paid labour collectively, as well as to contracts between individuals (see Defrenne, paragraph 39).

35 Such considerations must, a fortiori, be applicable to Article 48 of the Treaty, which lays down a fundamental freedom and which constitutes a specific application of the general prohibition of discrimination contained in Article 6 of the EC Treaty (now, after amendment, Article 12 EC). In that respect, like Article 119 of the EC Treaty (Articles 117 to 120 of the EC Treaty have been replaced by Articles 136 EC to 143 EC), it is designed to ensure that there is no discrimination on the labour market.

36 Consequently, the prohibition of discrimination on grounds of nationality laid down in Article 48 of the Treaty must be regarded as applying to private persons as well.

\* \* \*

45 . . . [W]here an employer makes a person's admission to a recruitment

competition subject to a requirement to provide evidence of his linguistic knowledge exclusively by means of one particular diploma, such as the Certificate, issued only in one particular province of a Member State, that requirement constitutes discrimination on grounds of nationality contrary to Article 48 [45] of the EC Treaty.

## NOTES AND QUESTIONS

1.   Noting that the defendant was a commercial bank and not an emanation of the State, how far does EC 39/TFEU 45 extend to create obligations for individuals, do you think? Does it apply to every employer who, for whatever reason, chooses to favor a local resident or national over a non-national?

2.   Could the logic relating to individuals also apply to other provisions that prohibit actions by Member States (TFEU 34, 49, 56, 63)?

## DEFRENNE v. SOCIETE ANONYME BELGE DE NAVIGATION AERIENNE SABENA
### Case 43/75, [1976] ECR 455

[Gabrielle Defrenne, an air hostess, brought action against her employer, Sabena S.A., claiming compensation on the ground that, between 15 February 1963 and 1 February 1966, she suffered as a female worker discrimination in terms of pay as compared with male colleagues who were doing the same work as 'cabin steward'. According to the judgment containing the reference, the parties agreed that the work of an air hostess was identical to that of a cabin steward and in these circumstances the existence of discrimination in pay to the detriment of the air hostess during the period in question was not disputed.]

8 Article 119 [157] pursues a double aim.

9 First, in the light of the different stages of the development of social legislation in the various Member States, the aim of Article 119 [141] is to avoid a situation in which undertakings established in States which have actually implemented the principle of equal pay suffer a competitive disadvantage in intra-Community competition as compared with undertakings established in States which have not yet eliminated discrimination against women workers as regards pay.

10 Secondly, this provision forms part of the social objectives of the Community, which is not merely an economic union, but is at the same time intended, by common action, to ensure social progress and seek the constant improvement of the living and working conditions of their peoples, as is emphasized by the Preamble to the Treaty.

11 This aim is accentuated by the insertion of Article 119 [157] into the body of a chapter devoted to social policy whose preliminary provision, Article 117 [136], marks 'the need to promote improved working conditions and an improved standard of living for workers, so as to make possible their harmonization while the improvement is being maintained'.

12 This double aim, which is at once economic and social, shows that the principle

of equal pay forms part of the foundations of the Community.

13 Furthermore, this explains why the Treaty has provided for the complete implementation of this principle by the end of the first stage of the transitional period.

14 Therefore, in interpreting this provision, it is impossible to base any argument on the dilatoriness and resistance which have delayed the actual implementation of this basic principle in certain Member States.

15 In particular, since Article 119 [157] appears in the context of the harmonization of working conditions while the improvement is being maintained, the objection that the terms of this article may be observed in other ways than by raising the lowest salaries may be set aside.

16 Under the terms of the first paragraph of Article 119 [157] the Member States are bound to ensure and maintain 'the application of the principle that men and women should receive equal pay for equal work'.

17 The second and third paragraphs of the same article add a certain number of details concerning the concepts of pay and work referred to in the first paragraph.

18 For the purposes of the implementation of these provisions a distinction must be drawn within the whole area of application of Article 119 [157] between, first, direct and overt discrimination which may be identified solely with the aid of the criteria based on equal work and equal pay referred to by the article in question and, secondly, indirect and disguised discrimination which can only be identified by reference to more explicit implementing provisions of a Community or national character.

19 It is impossible not to recognize that the complete implementation of the aim pursued by Article 119 [157], by means of the elimination of all discrimination, direct or indirect, between men and women workers, not only as regards individual undertakings but also entire branches of industry and even of the economic system as a whole, may in certain cases involve the elaboration of criteria whose implementation necessitates the taking of appropriate measures at Community and national level.

20 This view is all the more essential in the light of the fact that the Community measures on this question, to which reference will be made in answer to the second question, implement Article 119 [157] from the point of view of extending the narrow criterion of 'equal work', in accordance in particular with the provisions of Convention No 100 on equal pay concluded by the International Labour Organization in 1951, Article 2 of which establishes the principle of equal pay for work 'of equal value'.

21 Among the forms of direct discrimination which may be identified solely by reference to the criteria laid down by Article 119 [157] must be included in particular those which have their origin in legislative provisions or in collective labour agreements and which may be detected on the basis of a purely legal analysis of the situation.

22 This applies even more in cases where men and women receive unequal pay for

equal work carried out in the same establishment or service, whether public or private.

23 As is shown by the very findings of the judgment making the reference, in such a situation the court is in a position to establish all the facts which enable it to decide whether a woman worker is receiving lower pay than a male worker performing the same tasks.

24 In such situation, at least, Article 119 [157] is directly applicable and may thus give rise to individual rights which the courts must protect.

25 Furthermore, as regards equal work, as a general rule, the national legislative provisions adopted for the implementation of the principle of equal pay as a rule merely reproduce the substance of the terms of Article 119 [157] as regards the direct forms of discrimination.

26 Belgian legislation provides a particularly apposite illustration of this point, since Article 14 of Royal Decree No 40 of 24 October 1967 on the employment of women merely sets out the right of any female worker to institute proceedings before the relevant court for the application of the principle of equal pay set out in Article 119 [157] and simply refers to the article.

27 The terms of Article 119 [157] cannot be relied on to invalidate this conclusion.

28 First of all, it is impossible to put forward an argument against its direct effect based on the use in this article of the word 'principle', since, in the language of the Treaty, this term is specifically used in order to indicate the fundamental nature of certain provisions, as is shown, for example, by the heading of the first part of the Treaty which is devoted to 'Principles' and by Article 113 [207], according to which the commercial policy of the Community is to be based on 'uniform principles'.

29 If this concept were to be attenuated to the point of reducing it to the level of a vague declaration, the very foundations of the Community and the coherence of its external relations would be indirectly affected.

30 It is also impossible to put forward arguments based on the fact that Article 119 [157] only refers expressly to 'Member States'.

31 Indeed, as the Court has already found in other contexts, the fact that certain provisions of the Treaty are formally addressed to the Member States does not prevent rights from being conferred at the same time on any individual who has an interest in the performance of the duties thus laid down.

32 The very wording of Article 119 [157] shows that it imposes on States a duty to bring about a specific result to be mandatorily achieved within a fixed period.

33 The effectiveness of this provision cannot be affected by the fact that the duty imposed by the Treaty has not been discharged by certain Member States and that the joint institutions have not reacted sufficiently energetically against this failure to act.

34 To accept the contrary view would be to risk raising the violation of the right to the status of a principle of interpretation, a position the adoption of which would not be consistent with the task assigned to the Court by Article 164 [TEU 19] of the

Treaty.

35 Finally, in its reference to 'Member States', Article 119 [157] is alluding to those States in the exercise of all those of their functions which may usefully contribute to the implementation of the principle of equal pay.

36 Thus, contrary to the statements made in the course of the proceedings this provision is far from merely referring the matter to the powers of the national legislative authorities.

37 Therefore, the reference to 'Member States' in Article 119 [157] cannot be interpreted as excluding the intervention of the courts in direct application of the Treaty.

38 Furthermore it is not possible to sustain any objection that the application by national courts of the principle of equal pay would amount to modifying independent agreements concluded privately or in the sphere of industrial relations such as individual contracts and collective labour agreements.

39 In fact, since Article 119 [157] is mandatory in nature, the prohibition on discrimination between men and women applies not only to the action of public authorities, but also extends to all agreements which are intended to regulate paid labour collectively, as well as to contracts between individuals.

40 The reply to the first question must therefore be that the principle of equal pay contained in Article 119 [157] may be relied upon before the national courts and that these courts have a duty to ensure the protection of the rights which this provision vests in individuals, in particular as regards those types of discrimination arising directly from legislative provisions or collective labour agreements, as well as in cases in which men and women receive unequal pay for equal work which is carried out in the same establishment or service, whether private or public.

\*　\*　\*

The temporal effect of this judgment.

69 The Governments of Ireland and the United Kingdom have drawn the Court's attention to the possible economic consequences of attributing direct effect to the provisions of Article 119 [157], on the ground that such a decision might, in many branches of economic life, result in the introduction of claims dating back to the time at which such effect same into existence.

70 In view of the large number of people concerned such claims, which undertakings could not have foreseen, might seriously affect the financial situation of such undertakings and even drive some of them to bankruptcy.

71 Although the practical consequences of any judicial decision must be carefully taken into account, it would be impossible to go so far as to diminish the objectivity of the law and compromise its future application on the ground of the possible repercussions which might result, as regards the past, from such a judicial decision.

72 However, in the light of the conduct of several of the Member States and the views adopted by the Commission and repeatedly brought to the notice of the circles concerned, it is appropriate to take exceptionally into account the fact that,

over a prolonged period, the parties concerned have been led to continue with practices which were contrary to Article 119 [157], although not yet prohibited under their national law.

73 The fact that, in spite of the warnings given, the Commission did not initiate proceedings under Article 169 [258] against the Member States concerned on grounds of failure to fulfil an obligation was likely to consolidate the incorrect impression as to the effects of Article 119 [157].

74 In these circumstances, it is appropriate to determine that, as the general level at which pay would have been fixed cannot be known, important considerations of legal certainty affecting all the interests involved, both public and private, make it impossible in principle to reopen the question as regards the past.

75 Therefore, the direct effect of Article 119 [157] cannot be relied on in order to support claims concerning pay periods prior to the date of this judgment, except as regards those workers who have already brought legal proceedings or made an equivalent claim.

## NOTES AND QUESTIONS

1.    At the time of the *Defrenne* case, article 119 read as follows:

Article 119. Each Member State shall during the first stage ensure and subsequently maintain the application of the principle that men and women should receive equal pay for equal work. For the purpose of this Article, 'pay' means the ordinary basic or minimum wage of salary and any other consideration, whether in cash or in kind, which the worker receives, directly or indirectly, in respect of his employment from his employer. Equal pay without discrimination based on sex means:

(a) that pay for the same work at piece rates shall be calculated on the basis of the same unit of measurement;

(b) that pay for work at time rates shall be the same for the same job.

In para 24, the Court describes article 119 (EC 141/TFEU 157) as directly applicable. Since it is apparently directed to the Member States rather like a directive, do you think it nonetheless could be directly applicable in the same sense that the term is used in connection with regulations? Note in particular the Court's comment in para 39. Is a statement that the article is directly applicable at odds with its statement in para 75 referring to direct *effect*?

2.    The Court observes that article 119 (EC 141/FEU 157) serves two purposes. What was the significance of this comment?

3.    The Court points out in para 37 that the obligations of the Member States apply to their courts as well as their executive and legislative functions. What was the significance of this conclusion, do you think?

4.    In a second case some two years later, the Court ruled again in the dispute between Ms Defrenne and SABENA, this time regarding the interpretation of EC 141/TFEU 157 in the context of working conditions, holding that the article did not

cover discrimination in anything other than pay: *Gabrielle Defrenne v. Societe anonyme Belge de Navigation Aerienne Sabena* Case 149/77, 1978 ECJ CELEX LEXIS 133, [1978] ECR 1365.

## § 4.03   FUNDAMENTAL RIGHTS

### [A]   General Principles of Law Common to the Member States

### LISELOTTE HAUER v. LAND RHEINLAND — PFALZ
#### Case 44/79, [1979] ECR 3727

[Liselotte Hauer had applied to the competent administrative authority of Land Rheinland-Pfalz for authorisation to plant vines on a plot of land which she owned in the region of Bad Durkheim. That authorisation was refused initially owing to the fact that the plot of land in question was not considered suitable for wine-growing. The applicant lodged an objection against that decision. While proceedings relating to that objection were pending before the competent administrative authority, EC Regulation 1162/76 was enacted and imposed a prohibition for a period of three years on all new planting of vines. Although the Land authority initially considered the property unsuitable for growing vines, as a result of experts' reports on the grapes grown in the same area and taking into account a settlement reached with various other owners of plots of land adjacent to that of the applicant, it concluded that the property could be considered suitable for wine-growing in accordance with minimum requirements laid down by national legislation. Consequently, the authority stated its willingness to grant the authorisation as from the end of the prohibition on new planting imposed by the EU rules. Ms Hauer argued that her property rights guaranteed under the German Constitution had been infringed by the EU regulation.]

15 . . . [F]undamental rights form an integral part of the general principles of the law, the observance of which it ensures; . . . in safeguarding those rights, the Court is bound to draw inspiration from constitutional traditions common to the member-States, so that measures which are incompatible with the fundamental rights recognised by the constitutions of those States are unacceptable in the Community; and that, similarly, international treaties for the protection of human rights on which the member-States have collaborated or of which they are signatories can supply guidelines which should be followed within the framework of Community law. That conception was later recognised by the joint declaration of the European Parliament, the Council and the Commission of 5 April 1977, which, after recalling the case law of the Court, refers on the one hand to the rights guaranteed by the constitutions of the member-States and on the other hand to the European Convention for the Protection of Human Rights and Fundamental Freedoms of 4 November 1950.

16 In these circumstances, the doubts evinced by the Verwaltungsgericht as to the compatibility of the provisions of Regulation 1162/76 with the rules concerning the protection of fundamental rights must be understood as questioning the validity of

the regulation in the light of Community law. In this regard, it is necessary to distinguish between, on the one hand, a possible infringement of the right to property and, on the other hand, a possible limitation upon the freedom to pursue a trade or profession.

*The question of the right to property*

17 The right to property is guaranteed in the Community legal order in accordance with the ideas common to the constitutions of the member-States, which are also reflected in the first Protocol to the European Convention for the Protection of Human Rights.

18 Article 1 of that Protocol provides as follows:

'Every natural or legal person is entitled to the peaceful enjoyment of his possessions. No one shall be deprived of his possessions except in the public interest and subject to the conditions provided for by law and by the general principles of international law.

The preceding provisions shall not, however, in any way impair the right of a State to enforce such laws as it deems necessary to control the use of property in accordance with the general interest or to secure the payment of taxes or other contributions or penalties.'

19 Having declared that persons are entitled to the peaceful enjoyment of their property, that provision envisages two ways in which the rights of a property owner may be impaired, according as the impairment is intended to deprive the owner of his right or to restrict the exercise thereof. In this case it is incontestable that the prohibition on a new planting cannot be considered to be an act depriving the owner of his property, since he remains free to dispose of it or to put it to other uses which are not prohibited. On the other hand, there is no doubt that that prohibition restricts the use of the property. In this regard, the second paragraph of Article 1 of the Protocol provides an important indication in so far as it recognises the right of a State 'to enforce such laws as it deems 'necessary to control the use of property in accordance with the general interest'. Thus the Protocol accepts in principle the legality of restrictions upon the use of property, whilst at the same time limiting those restrictions to the extent to which they are deemed 'necessary' by a State for the protection of the 'general interest'. However, that provision does not enable a sufficiently precise answer to be given to the question submitted by the Verwaltungsgericht.

20 Therefore, in order to be able to answer that question, it is necessary to consider also the indications provided by the constitutional rules and practices of the nine member-States. One of the first points to emerge in this regard is that those rules and practices permit the legislature to control the use of private property in accordance with the general interest. Thus some constitutions refer to the obligations arising out of the ownership of property (German Constitution, Article 14 (2), first sentence), to its social function (Italian Constitution, Article 42 (2)), to the subordination of its use to the requirements of the common good (German Constitution, Article 14 (2), second sentence, and the Irish Constitution, Article 43.2.2°), or of social justice (Irish Constitution, Article 43.2.1°). In all the member-

States, numerous legislative measures have given concrete expression to that social function of the right to property. Thus in all the member-States there is legislation on agriculture and forestry, the water supply, the protection of the environment and town and country planning, which imposes restrictions, sometimes appreciable, on the use of real property.

21 More particularly, all the wine-producing countries of the Community have restrictive legislation, albeit of differing severity, concerning the planting of vines, the selection of varieties and the methods of cultivation. In none of the countries concerned are those provisions considered to be incompatible in principle with the regard due to the right to property.

22 Thus it may be stated, taking into account the constitutional precepts common to the member-States and consistent legislative practices, in widely varying spheres, that the fact that Regulation 1162/76 imposed restrictions on the new planting of vines cannot be challenged in principle. It is a type of restriction which is known and accepted as lawful, in identical or similar forms, in the constitutional structure of all the member-States.

23 However, that finding does not deal completely with the problem raised by the Verwaltungsgericht. Even if it is not possible to dispute in principle the Community's ability to restrict the exercise of the right to property in the context of a common organisation of the market and for the purposes of a structural policy, it is still necessary to examine whether the restrictions introduced by the provisions in dispute in fact correspond to objectives of general interest pursued by the Community or whether, with regard to the aim pursued, they constitute a disproportionate and intolerable interference with the rights of the owner, impinging upon the very substance of the right to property. Such in fact is the plea submitted by the plaintiff in the main action, who considers that only that pursuit of a qualitative policy would permit the legislature to restrict the use of wine-growing property, with the result that she possesses an unassailable right from the moment that it is recognised that her land is suitable for wine growing. It is therefore necessary to identify the aim pursued by the disputed regulation and to determine whether there exists a reasonable relationship between the measures provided for by the regulation and the aim pursued by the Community in this case.

24 The provisions of Regulation 1162/76 must be considered in the context of the common organisation of the market in wine which is closely linked to the structural policy envisaged by the Community in the area in question. The aims of that policy are stated in Regulations (EEC) 816/70 of 28 April 1970 laying down additional provisions for the common organisation of the market in wine, which provides the basis for the disputed regulation, and in Regulation 337/79 of 5 February 1979 on the common organisation of the market in wine, which codifies all the provisions governing the common organisation of the market. Title III of that regulation, laying down 'rules concerning production and for controlling planting', now forms the legal framework in that sphere. Another factor which makes it possible to perceive the Community policy pursued in that field is the Council Resolution of 21 April 1975 concerning new guidelines to balance the market in table wines . . . .

25 Taken as a whole, those measures show that the policy initiated and partially implemented by the Community consists of a common organisation of the market in

conjunction with a structural improvement in the wine-producing sector. Within the framework of the guidelines laid down by Article 39 [39] of the EEC Treaty that action seeks to achieve a double objective, namely, on the one hand, to establish a lasting balance on the wine market at a price level which is profitable for producers and fair to consumers and, secondly, to obtain an improvement in the quality of wines marketed. In order to attain that double objective of quantitative balance and qualitative improvement, the Community rules relating to the market in wine provide for an extensive range of measures which apply both at the production stage and at the marketing stage for wine.

26 In this regard, it is necessary to refer in particular to the provisions of Article 17 of Regulation 816/70, re-enacted in an extended form by Article 31 of Regulation 337/79, which provide for the establishment by the member-States of forecasts of planting and production, co-ordinated within the framework of a compulsory Community plan. For the purpose of implementing that plan measures may be adopted concerning the planting, re-planting, grubbing-up or cessation of cultivation of vineyards.

27 It is in this context that Regulation 1162/76 was adopted. It is apparent from the preamble to that regulation and from the economic circumstances in which it was adopted, a feature of which was the formation as from the 1974 harvest of permanent production surpluses, that regulation fulfils a double function: on the one hand, it must enable an immediate brake to be put on the continued increase in the surpluses; on the other hand, it must win for the Community institutions the time necessary for the implementation of a structural policy designated to encourage high-quality production, whilst respecting the individual characteristics and needs of the different wine-producing regions of the Community, through the selection of land for grape growing and the selection of grape varieties, and through the regulation of production methods.

28 It was in order to fulfil that twofold purpose that the Council introduced by Regulation 1162/76 a general prohibition on new plantings, without making any distinction, apart from certain narrowly defined exceptions, according to the quality of the land. It should be noted that, as regards its sweeping scope, the measure introduced by the Council is of a temporary nature. It is designed to deal immediately with a conjunctural [*Author's note*: meaning "short-term economic"] situation characterised by surpluses, whilst at the same time preparing permanent structural measures.

29 Seen in this light, the measure criticised does not entail any undue limitation upon the exercise of the right to property. Indeed, the cultivation of new vineyards in a situation of continuous over-production would not have any effect, from the economic point of view, apart from increasing the volume of the surpluses; further, such an extension at that stage would entail the risk of making more difficult the implementation of a structural policy at the Community level in the event of such a policy resting on the application of criteria more stringent than the current provisions of national legislation concerning the selection of land accepted for wine growing.

30 Therefore it is necessary to conclude that the restriction imposed upon the use of property by the prohibition on the new planting of vines introduced for a limited

period by Regulation 1162/76 is justified by the objectives of general interest pursued by the Community and does not infringe the substance of the right to property in the form in which it is recognised and protected in the Community legal order.

*The question of the freedom to pursue trade or professional activities*

31 The applicant in the main action also submits that the prohibition on new plantings imposed by Regulation 1162/76 infringes her fundamental rights in so far as its effect is to restrict her freedom to pursue her occupation as a wine-grower.

32 . . . . [A]lthough it is true that guarantees are given by the constitutional law of several member-States in respect of the freedom to pursue trade or professional activities, the right thereby guaranteed, far from constituting an unfettered prerogative, must likewise be viewed in the light of the social function of the activities protected thereunder. In this case, it must be observed that the disputed Community measure does not in any way affect access to the occupation of wine-growing, or the freedom to pursue that occupation on land at present devoted to wine-growing. To the extent to which the prohibition on new plantings affects the free pursuit of the occupation of wine-growing, that limitation is no more than the consequence of the restriction upon the exercise of the right to property, so that the two restrictions merge. Thus the restriction upon the free pursuit of the occupation of wine-growing, assuming that it exists, is justified by the same reasons which justify the restrictions placed upon the use of property.

33 Thus it is apparent from the foregoing that consideration of Regulation 1162/76, in the light of the doubts expressed by the Verwaltungsgericht, has disclosed no factor of such a kind as to affect the validity of that regulation on account of its being contrary to the requirements flowing from the protection of fundamental rights in the Community.

## NOTES AND QUESTIONS

1. How did the Court conclude that fundamental rights are part of the EU legal system? Is the EU principle developed by the Court a clear and distinct EU rule? Is it influenced by the objectives of the Treaty? Is the reliance on the general obligation to assure that the law is observed (EC 220/TEU 19) a justifiable basis for introducing the entire panoply of fundamental rights into the Union legal system?

2. It should be noted that the concept of "general principles" embraces more than just fundamental rights. Such principles may surface in other areas, such as legal privilege (see the *AM&S* case in Chapter 7) and the scope of the right to damages against EU institutions or Member States (Chapters 8 and 9). There are also some principles that permeate all the activities of the Union, both legislative and executive, and of the Member States when implementing Union law: principally those of proportionality and legal certainty, which embraces also the principles of legitimate expectations and non-retroactivity. These do not appear in the enumeration of fundamental rights in the Charter nor do they appear explicitly in the Treaties. They will appear in various subsequent chapters in different contexts, sometimes as principles in themselves (see for example the *Laserdisken* case in

Chapter 6 and the *Alrosa* case in Chapter 7) and sometimes by way of evaluation of other principles, such as the right to property — as indeed happened in *Hauer* itself.

## [B]   The Impact of the Charter of Fundamental Rights

### COMMISSION REPORT ON MONITORING OF COMPLIANCE WITH FUNDAMENTAL RIGHTS
(((COM (2009) 0205)

[In this 2009 report the Commission discusses how new legislative proposals are being evaluated against the requirement to observe fundamental rights, a requirement that is greatly reinforced by the adoption of the Charter.]

In the Reach Regulation, [*Author's note*: this is the Union Regulation regarding the Registration, Evaluation and Approval of Chemicals] an obligation of data sharing among registrants raised issues regarding the right to property. The obligation was considered acceptable in that it was necessary for the protection of the environment and, in particular, designed to avoid repeated testing on animals. These considerations were recorded in the recitals of the regulation.

In the area of agricultural policy, the question of imposing an obligation on Member States to publish a list of beneficiaries of rural development funding was examined. This raised the issue of data protection. Examined against the test of necessity, it was concluded that any interference with data protection was justified by the need to improve the transparency of the Community's action in the area of rural development, to enhance the sound financial management of the public funds involved and to avoid distortion of competition between beneficiaries of rural development measures. These considerations were recorded in the recitals to the Commission act.

A last example comes from the customs area. In the framework of the revision of the Customs Code, a question arose as to giving operators the right to be heard by the customs authorities in procedures relating to the application of customs legislation. It was considered that such a right to be heard was an obligation flowing from the Charter and it is now to be found in Article 16 of the Code.

It is, however, the ever growing importance, in terms of legislative activity, of the area of Justice, Freedom and Security which has, inevitably, brought into sharp focus that the Community and Union are increasingly touching on areas which, very directly, raise fundamental rights issues. In this area, more than any other, the Commission is required to confront delicate and controversial issues pertaining to the necessity and proportionality of possible limitations to fundamental rights.

Given the types of matters covered by the area of Justice, Freedom and Security — the fight against criminality, in particular terrorism, immigration, asylum, border control, to name but a few — it is unsurprising that this policy occupies a pre-eminent place in terms of monitoring the respect for fundamental rights in the Commission's legislative proposals. Citing, only as an example, immigration and asylum policy, a number of delicate questions of respect for fundamental rights can be identified as arising over and over again — the most common being the prohibition of torture and inhuman or degrading treatment or punishment (Article 4 of the Charter), the right to liberty and security (Article 6 of the Charter), the right to respect for family life (Article 7 of the Charter), data protection (Article 8 of the Charter), the right to asylum (Article 18 of the Charter), protection in the event of removal, expulsion or extradition (Article 19 of the Charter), non discrimination (Article 21 of the Charter), the rights of the child (Article 24 of the Charter), the right to an effective remedy and to a fair trial (Article 47 of the Charter).

. . . [M]any of the above issues were reflected in the "asylum package", adopted by the Commission in December 2008. This package provides a particularly suitable "case-study" to demonstrate how the Commission's internal fundamental rights monitoring is applied in practice.

As regards the proposal amending the Reception Conditions Directive, the most sensitive issues raised in terms of respect for fundamental rights were those of the detention of asylum seekers, the right to an effective remedy and the rights of the child. In examining these issues, it was sought to ensure compliance not only with the Charter of Fundamental Rights but also with relevant international standards, in particular the European Convention on Human Rights, the Geneva Convention and the United Nations Convention on the Rights of the Child.

As regards detention, it was considered essential in terms of respect for fundamental rights that the proposal reconfirmed the principle that a person should not be detained solely because he/she is an applicant for international protection. Thereafter, the proposal sets clear parameters for the use of detention in derogation from that principle; in this respect, the proposal takes, as its standard, guidelines from the United Nations High Commissioner for Refugees (UNHCR) on applicable criteria and standards relating to the detention of asylum seekers and Recommendation (2003) 5 of the Council of Europe Committee of Ministers on measures of detention of asylum seekers. Based on these texts, the proposal provides that detention should only be used in exceptional cases and for a limited number of reasons as prescribed by the guidelines. Again, in line with the UNHCR guidelines and the Council of Europe recommendation, the proposal also introduces conditions for detention in order to ensure respect for human dignity in the treatment of detained asylum seekers, and in particular of vulnerable persons. Principally, in this respect, the proposal provides that asylum seekers should not be kept in prison accommodation but in specialized detention facilities, which take into account gender considerations.

In order to ensure compliance with the right to an effective remedy, the proposal introduces a number of procedural guarantees as regards detention. Thus, detention can only be ordered by judicial authorities; where in urgent cases, it is ordered by administrative authorities it must confirmed by judicial authorities within 72 hours. Further, detention should be only for the shortest possible time and, in particular, no longer than is necessary to fulfill administrative procedures. Continued detention has to be reviewed periodically by a judge. A detained asylum seeker is also to be given access to legal assistance or representation which is to be free where the person cannot afford the costs involved. These provisions are essential in ensuring an effective remedy in cases of detention.

As regards the rights of the child, the concern was to ensure that the best interests of the child were an underlying principle. As regards the possible detention of minors, the proposal makes a clear link with the elements which must ground an assessment of the best interests of the child in this respect. In addition, in order to comply with Article 37 of Convention on the Rights of the Child, the proposal provides that the detention of a minor should only be used as a measure of last resort and for the shortest appropriate period of time. Finally, it is forbidden to detain unaccompanied minors.

The proposal to amend the Dublin Regulation also raised issues in relation to detention, effective remedy and the rights of the child. Solutions similar to those in the Reception Conditions proposal were applied. As regards detention, an issue reflecting the specificities of the Dublin system deserves to be underlined, namely, the detention of an asylum-seeker before transfer to another Member State under the Dublin procedure. The proposal envisages that detention can take place where there is a risk of the person absconding and after notification of transfer decisions. This issue required an assessment of necessity and proportionality. Clear parameters have been provided as to when recourse to this possibility was appropriate. These include that the detention decision is based on an individual assessment of each case and that the possibility of alternative less coercive measures such as regular reporting to the authorities, the deposit of a financial guarantee or an obligation to reside at a designated place have to be examined. Further, as regards the decision to detain, procedural safeguards are ensured in terms of a reasoned decision and effective remedies before a judge.

In addition, the right of family unity has been strengthened. Thus, the proposal obliges the reunification of dependent relatives and extends the definition of "family members" as far as minors are concerned, in order to ensure better protection of the "best interests of the child".

In addition, asylum seekers will be reunited with family members who have been granted subsidiary protection.

The main concerns, in terms of compliance with fundamental rights, raised by the proposal to amend the Eurodac Regulation, focused on data protection. In this respect, the proposal aims to ensure better management of the deletion of data from the system and more effective monitoring by the Commission and the European Data Protection Supervisor of access to data in EURODAC by national authorities. Moreover, it is also currently in process of adoption a proposal for a Council decision on requesting comparisons with Eurodac data by Member States' law enforcement authorities and Europol for law enforcement purposes.

However, according to a document annexed to the procedure of adoption of these proposals on 7 October 2009, the European Data Protection Supervisor states in its opinion that he has serious doubts whether these proposals are legitimate on the considerations of necessity, proportionality, legitimacy and respect to the European Convention on Human Rights.

The experience of the asylum package demonstrates that the methodology to monitor the respect of fundamental rights implies not only a procedural element but also a substantive element. The methodology is not an end in itself. Respect for fundamental rights is not simply a mechanism or a procedural obligation; it is a substantive obligation. In underlining its respect for fundamental rights, the Commission has undertaken a substantive adherence. This implies as far as fundamental rights are concerned that the Union must be irreproachable in its legislative activity. In the asylum package, the Commission has sought to deliver on substantive obligations; it has sought to ensure that the starting point is the affirmation of the relevant fundamental right and that, thereafter, any eventual limitation is subject not only to the tests of necessity and proportionality but is also surrounded by safeguards in terms, particularly, of procedures and judicial review.

## [C] The European Convention for the Protection of Human Rights and Fundamental Freedoms

### MARCH 2010 SPEECH BY MR SERHIY HOLOVATY, VICE-CHAIRPERSON OF THE COMMITTEE ON LEGAL AFFAIRS AND HUMAN RIGHTS, COUNCIL OF EUROPE

[Mr Holovaty here discusses the issue of the relationship between the Strasbourg Court of Human Rights (Strasbourg) and the EU Court (Luxembourg).]

For me, the situation is not as complicated as it looks at first sight. In a large measure, this relationship must be perceived as a function undertaken by a specialized human rights court whose role is to exercise external control over the international law obligations of the Union that result from accession to the ECHR. Hence, accession does not threaten the jurisdictional autonomy of the Luxembourg Court. Upon accession, the European Union becomes the 48th "Contracting Party" to the Convention. The Luxembourg Court is then considered by the European Court of Human Rights as a "domestic court", akin to a constitutional or supreme court of any other (States) Party to the Convention. In other words, the ECHR is an instrument of subsidiary protection and the EU institutions, upon accession, will continue to bear primary responsibility in ensuring respect of rights enshrined in the European Convention. It follows that, in a situation in which the EU Charter of Fundamental Rights becomes, de facto, an internal 'Bill of Rights' which sets limitations on the Union's institutions' powers, the ECHR mechanism must be perceived as an external restraint and check on EU activities. Hence, primary responsibility for ensuring respect of human rights within the EU's (autonomous) legal system remains with the Luxembourg Court. The Strasbourg Court is in no sense a higher court than, for instance, Germany's Federal Constitutional Court. The issue is not one of subordination or primacy of courts. The Strasbourg Court must simply ensure "minimum common standards" guaranteed by the European Convention and its protocols.

That said, the artificiality of the present situation must be put right. At present a potential victim, after exhausting domestic and EU remedies, must lodge an application with the Strasbourg Court, not against the perpetrator of the contested EU act, but against one or more EU member states. And if a breach of the Convention is found, there is no guarantee that the victim's situation will be remedied, as the remedy depends on a third party, the European Union.

This is why accession is necessary.

## NOTES AND QUESTIONS

**1.** The TEU requires the Union to accede to the European Convention on Human Rights (ECHR) In fact, though this may yet take awhile, the EU Courts are now beginning to reference ECHR court decisions as part of their reasoning, given that the ECHR reflects the fundamental principles common to Member States that are part of EU law. See in this connection especially the *Matthews* case reproduced in Chapter 17. In *Opinion 2/94* [1996] ECR I-1759 the Court had opined that the Union could not accede to the ECHR, but this has been superseded by the Treaty of Lisbon that authorizes such accession subject to the ratification of all member states of the Council of Europe. When the EU accedes to the convention, it will be bound by the long list of rights set forth in it. Moreover, if the EU accepts the convention's "right of individual petition," EU citizens would be able to file complaints with the European Court of Human Rights against acts of the EU's institutions, and that court would ultimately decide upon the validity of such complaints.

The European Convention on Human Rights is a treaty among sovereign states, including the Member States of the European Union. It has no mechanism similar to EC 234/TFEU 267 and, therefore, there is no means for individuals to invoke it in proceedings before national courts. Consequently, any invocable rights arise purely through the provisions of each country's national law. In France, Italy, Germany, the UK and the Benelux countries, it is part of national law; while in other states it is not. The European Court of Human Rights has held that article 1 of the Convention was intended to make clear that the rights and freedoms guaranteed in the Convention will be directly secured to anyone within the jurisdiction of the contracting states. This intention is reflected in those cases where the Convention has been incorporated into national law but there is no obligation to so incorporate it.

The Convention, while setting out basic principles, also inevitably leaves gaps that need to be filled by interpretative techniques. The Court of Human Rights itself therefore refers to principles generally accepted by the signatory states. See, e.g., *Tyrer* case, judgment of 25 April (1978 Series A: v. 26) p. 15: "[The Convention] is a living instrument which, as the Commission rightly stressed, must be interpreted in the light of present-day conditions." The Convention may be a useful codification of general principles, but the ECJ is still bound to refer to the prevailing legal developments of the Member States.

The Convention adopts a very different approach from that of the U.S. Bill of Rights. While the latter is content to state general principles in a succinct and absolute manner, the Convention tends to state broad rights and then qualify them with various restrictions. These restrictions are themselves subject to limitations; they must be prescribed by a national law, enacted by a legislature enjoying democratic legitimacy; they must have a specific aim such as the protection of public order; and they must be "necessary in a democratic society". In practice, while the Convention is fairly specific in regard to such restrictions, the end result may not be so different from the kind of balancing considerations engaged in by the U.S. Supreme Court.

The Convention (and other principles common to the Member States) does not have the same interpretative effect as the U.S. Bill of Rights: it is impossible to imagine a case under the Convention having the same radical effect as, say, *Brown v. Board of Education*, 347 U.S. 483 (1954). This is due to the lack of direct applicability and uniformity of the Convention and the interplay between contracting states' own constitutions and the Convention's principles.

2.  In *Opinion 2/94*, a number of issues were raised, which will need resolution in the context of accession to the ECHR:

- What will happen to reservations made by individual Member States to the Convention?

- Will there be any cross-reference between the ECHR and the ECJ for interpretative rulings?

- How will the EU be judicially represented in the European Court of Human Rights?

- What will be the status of the EEA Agreement, to which all EU Member States are party?

- Will relevant rulings of the European Court of Human Rights have direct effect in EU Member States?

- Will the institutional aspects of the ECHR (e.g. review by the Council of Europe's Committee of Ministers) conflict with the autonomy of the EU legal system (particularly as the Council membership includes some 20 states that are not Member States of the Union.)

- Will individuals be given the right under EC 230/TFEU 267 to challenge EU acts that affect their rights under the ECHR?

Accession may have unintended consequences. In a 2009 decision, (*Dubus S.A. v. France*) the European Court of Human Rights found that France was in breach of Article 6 § 1 (right to a fair trial) of the European Convention on Human Rights due to the way in which the French Banking Commission investigates and penalizes breaches of French banking law. This procedure has similarities with the procedure used by the Commission in investigating and fining undertakings under EC 81 and 82/TFEU 101 and 102. Conceivably this could lead to changes in that procedure, though probably not the underlying rules themselves. Similar arguments have been presented in a case, pending as of the time of writing, before the General Court: *Saint Gobain Glass France and Others v. Commission.* Case T-56/09 ([2009] OJ C 90/31) See also T. Lock, *EU Accession to the ECHR: Implications for Judicial Review in Strasbourg*, (2010) EL Rev. 777.

## [D]   The Reach and Limits of EU Fundamental Rights

# ELLINIKI RADIOFONIA TILEORASSI ANONIMI ETAIRIA (ERT AE) AND ANOTHER v. DIMOTIKI ETAIRIA PLIROFORISSIS AND SOTIRIOS KOUVELAS AND ` ANOTHER
## Case 260/89, 1991 ECJ CELEX LEXIS 179, [1991] ECR I-2925

[The questions in this case were raised in proceedings between Elliniki Radio-phonia Tileorassi Anonimi Etairia ("ERT"), a Greek radio and television undertak-ing, to which the Greek State had granted exclusive rights for carrying out its activities, and Dimotiki Etairia Pliroforissis ("DEP"), a municipal information company at Thessaloniki, and S Kouvelas, Mayor of Thessaloniki. Notwithstanding the exclusive rights enjoyed by ERT, DEP and the Mayor, in 1989, set up a television station which in that same year began to broadcast television programs.]

3 ERT was established by Law No 1730/1987 . . . According to Article 2(1) of that Law, ERT's object is, without a view to profit, to organize, exploit and develop radio and television and to contribute to the information, culture and entertainment of the Hellenic people. Article 2(2) provides that the State grants to ERT an exclusive franchise, in respect of radio and television, for any activity which contributes to the performance of its task. The franchise includes in particular the broadcasting by radio or television of sounds and images of every kind from Hellenic territory for general reception or by special closed or cable circuit, or any other form of circuit, and the setting up of radio and stations. Under Article 2(3) ERT may produce and exploit by any means radio and television broadcasts. Article 16(1) of the same Law prohibits any person from undertaking, without authorization by ERT, activities for which ERT has an exclusive right.

4 Since it took the view that the activities of DEP and the Mayor of Thessaloniki fell within its exclusive rights, ERT brought summary proceedings before the Thessa-loniki Regional Court in order to obtain, on the basis of Article 16 of Law No 1730/1987, an injunction prohibiting any kind of broadcasting and an order for the seizure and sequestration of the technical equipment. Before that court, DEP and Mr Kouvelas relied mainly on the provisions of Community law and the European Convention on Human Rights.

\*    \*    \*

43 . . . [W]here a Member State relies on the combined provisions of Articles 56 [52] and 66 [62] in order to justify rules which are likely to obstruct the exercise of the freedom to provide services, such justification, provided for by Community law, must be interpreted in the light of the general principles of law and in particular of fundamental rights. Thus the national rules in question can fall under the exceptions provided for by the combined provisions of Articles 56 [52] and 66 [62] only if they are compatible with the fundamental rights the observance of which is ensured by the Court.

44 It follows that in such a case it is for the national court, and if necessary, the Court of Justice to appraise the application of those provisions having regard to all

the rules of Community law, including freedom of expression, as embodied in Article 10 of the European Convention on Human Rights, as a general principle of law the observance of which is ensured by the Court.

45 The reply to the national court must therefore be that the limitations imposed on the power of the Member States to apply the provisions referred to in Articles 66 [62] and 56 [52] of the Treaty on grounds of public policy, public security and public health must be appraised in the light of the general principle of freedom of expression embodied in Article 10 of the European Convention on Human Rights.

## FRIEDRICH KREMZOW v. AUSTRIA
### Case C-299/95, 1997 ECJ CELEX LEXIS 286, [1997] ECR I-2629

[Kremzow, an Austrian judge, had been found guilty of murder in the Austrian courts. Originally he was sentenced to 20 years' imprisonment in a psychiatric hospital and served some 7 years of that sentence, which however was subsequently overturned at a hearing on his appeal without his being present (he had not so requested but the court did not order any representation of its own motion). At that appeal his sentence was increased to life imprisonment, but in an ordinary prison. He sought redress in the European Court of Human Rights which, concluded that, given the gravity of what had been at stake at the hearing, Mr Kremzow ought to have been allowed to defend himself in person in accordance with Article 6(3)(c) of the Convention, notwithstanding his failure to make a request to that effect. Accordingly, the European Court of Human Rights held that Article 6 of the Convention had been violated and awarded Mr Kremzow damages in that respect.

Mr Kremzow brought various proceedings in the Austrian courts for, among other things, damages for the period of his unlawful detention. In his action for damages before the civil courts, Mr Kremzow argued that he had a right to compensation for unlawful detention. The claim was rejected but in a new appeal, Mr Kremzow argued, inter alia, that the later Austrian court proceedings had not rectified the violation of the Convention and that the appeal proceedings before that court should have been resumed for that purpose. He also asked the court to make a reference to the ECJ for a preliminary ruling on whether the national court was bound by the judgment of the European Court of Human Rights, arguing in essence that his imprisonment had deprived him of his right under EC 18/TFEU 21 to move freely within the Union.]

13 Mr Kremzow argues that the Court has jurisdiction to answer the questions referred for a preliminary ruling, inter alia, because he is a citizen of the European Union and, as such, enjoys the right to freedom of movement for persons set forth in Article 8a of the EC Treaty [21] Since any citizen is entitled to move freely in the territory of the Member States without any specific intention to reside, a State which infringes that fundamental right guaranteed by Community law by executing an unlawful penalty of imprisonment must be held liable in damages by virtue of Community law.

16 The appellant in the main proceedings is an Austrian national whose situation is not connected in any way with any of the situations contemplated by the Treaty provisions on freedom of movement for persons. Whilst any deprivation of liberty may impede the person concerned from exercising his right to free movement, the

Court has held that a purely hypothetical prospect of exercising that right does not establish a sufficient connection with Community law to justify the application of Community provisions . . .

17 Moreover, Mr Kremzow was sentenced for murder and for illegal possession of a firearm under provisions of national law which were not designed to secure compliance with rules of Community law . . .

18 It follows that the national legislation applicable in the main proceedings relates to a situation which does not fall within the field of application of Community law.

19 The answer to the national court's questions must therefore be that where national legislation is concerned with a situation which, as in the case at issue in the main proceedings, does not fall within the field of application of Community law, the Court cannot, in a reference for a preliminary ruling, give the interpretative guidance necessary for the national court to determine whether that national legislation is in conformity with the fundamental rights whose observance the Court ensures, such as those deriving in particular from the Convention.

## NOTES AND QUESTIONS

1. Contrast the *ERT* and *Kremzow* cases. How does the ECJ determine whether Union fundamental rights (and now the Charter) apply in any given situation?

## SEDA KÜCÜKDEVECI V SWEDEX GMBH & CO. KG
### Case C-555/07, 2010 ECJ EUR-Lex LEXIS 12, [2010] ECR I-NYR

[Under German law, employees are entitled to a specified notice period if an employer desires to dismiss them. The notice period depends on how long the employee has been employed by them. In calculating the length of employment, they were not required to take into account any employment of an employee between the ages of 18 and 25. This provision was intended to encourage employers to hire younger workers. Ms Kücükdeveci, the plaintiff in this case, argued that this constituted age discrimination contrary to article 6(1) of Directive 2000/78 establishing a framework for equal treatment in employment. However, this directive did not contain any directly effective provisions and thus could not be invoked by the plaintiff in the national court. (The nature of directives and capability to have direct effects are addressed in Chapter 5. The directive may be found in the Documentary Supplement and is addressed further in Chapter 20, *infra.*) The Court concluded that the German law did constitute discrimination on grounds of age, despite the German Government's argument that the law could be justified under the exceptions described in Article 6.]

19. . . . [I]t must first be ascertained, as the referring court suggests, whether the question should be examined by reference to primary European Union law or to Directive 2000/78.

20. In the first place, . . . the Council of the European Union adopted Directive 2000/78 on the basis of Article 13 EC [19], and the Court has held that that directive does not itself lay down the principle of equal treatment in the field of employment

and occupation, which derives from various international instruments and from the constitutional traditions common to the Member States, but has the sole purpose of laying down, in that field, a general framework for combating discrimination on various grounds including age . . .

21. In that context, the Court has acknowledged the existence of a principle of non-discrimination on grounds of age which must be regarded as a general principle of European Union law . . .

22. It should also be noted that Article 6(1) TEU provides that the Charter of Fundamental Rights of the European Union is to have the same legal value as the Treaties. Under Article 21(1) of the charter, '[a]ny discrimination based on — age — shall be prohibited'.

23. For the principle of non-discrimination on grounds of age to apply in a case such as that at issue in the main proceedings, that case must fall within the scope of European Union law.

24. In . . . [T]he allegedly discriminatory conduct adopted in the present case on the basis of the national legislation at issue occurred after the expiry of the period prescribed for the Member State concerned for the transposition of Directive 2000/78, which, for the Federal Republic of Germany, ended on 2 December 2006.

25. On that date, that directive had the effect of bringing within the scope of European Union law the national legislation at issue in the main proceedings, which concerns a matter governed by that directive, in this case the conditions of dismissal.

*　　*　　*

27. It follows that it is the general principle of European Union law prohibiting all discrimination on grounds of age, as given expression in Directive 2000/78, which must be the basis of the examination of whether European Union law precludes national legislation such as that at issue in the main proceedings.

## NOTES AND QUESTIONS

1. With the Charter coming into effect as part of Union law on December 1, 2009, this case is one of the first to address its effects in Union law. It illustrates the first situation described in paragraph 8.2.2 of the Template.

2. Does it seem a little odd that the adoption of a directive that does not have direct effect in national law could result in the application of the Charter to national law with a consequence that the national law has to be declared inapplicable?

## § 4.04    THE ROLE OF INTERNATIONAL LAW IN THE EU LEGAL SYSTEM

### [A]    The Interaction of International Law With EU Laws at the National Level

## ANKLAGEMYNDIGHEDEN v. PETER MICHAEL POULSEN AND DIVA NAVIGATION CORP
### Case C-286/90, 1992 ECJ CELEX LEXIS 197, [1992] ECR I-6019

[Criminal proceedings were brought by the Anklagemyndigheden (Danish Public Prosecutor) against Peter Michael Poulsen (hereinafter "Mr Poulsen") and Diva Navigation Corp. (hereinafter "Diva Navigation"), who were prosecuted on a charge that the crew of the vessel "Onkel Sam", of which Mr Poulsen is the master and Diva Navigation the owner, had retained, transported and stored on board salmon caught in the North Atlantic in contravention of the an EC Regulation. The "Onkel Sam" was registered in Panama and flew the Panamanian flag. It belonged to Diva Navigation, a company governed by Panamanian law, and wholly owned by a Danish national. Mr Poulsen was the master of the vessel; like the rest of the crew, he was Danish and was paid in Denmark. Between voyages, the vessel was normally berthed in a Danish port.

At the beginning of 1990, the "Onkel Sam" caught a quantity of salmon in the North Atlantic outside the waters under the sovereignty and jurisdiction of the Member States. While under way to Poland in order to sell its cargo there, its carburettor became clogged and, in view of the difficult weather conditions, the master decided to head for a Danish port in order to carry out the necessary repairs. While the "Onkel Sam" was moored in that port, it was inspected by the Danish fishery officers, its cargo was seized and then sold on the Danish market, and its master and also its owner were summoned to appear before the Kriminal- og Skifteret to answer a charge that they had contravened Article 6(1)(b) of EC Regulation 3094/86 (the "Regulation").

That Regulation concerned the catching and landing of fish stocks in all maritime waters under the sovereignty or jurisdiction of the Member States and within one of Regions 1 to 8 defined in the Regulation. Article 6(1) of the Regulation provided, with regard to salmon and sea trout, that, even where those fish had been caught outside waters under the sovereignty or jurisdiction of the Member States in Regions 1, 2, 3 and 4, they may not be retained on board, transshipped, landed, transported, stored, sold, displayed or offered for sale, but must be returned immediately to the sea.

Under international law, States are entitled to regulate economic exploitation of an area around their coasts extending out to 200 nautical miles (the exclusive economic zone referred to in the judgment) but are not permitted to interfere with the freedom of navigation. Thus, foreign vessels cannot be interfered with when simply exercising that freedom, States also enjoy full sovereignty over the sea extending 12 nautical miles out from their coastlines. Since the conservation of marine resources became an exclusive EU competence as early as 1979, the rights of the Member States with regard to fishing in their respective exclusive economic zones passed to the EU.]

\*      \*      \*

9 As a preliminary point, it must be observed, first, that the European Community must respect international law in the exercise of its powers and that, consequently, Article 6 abovementioned must be interpreted, and its scope limited, in the light of the relevant rules of the international law of the sea.

\*      \*      \*

11 . . . In the light of the aims of the prohibition laid down in Article 6(1)(b) of the Regulation, this provision must be interpreted so as to give it the greatest practical effect, within the limits of international law.

Nationality of the vessel

12 In its third question, the national court seeks to know whether a vessel registered in a non-member country may be treated, for the purpose of Article 6(1)(b) of the Regulation, as a vessel with the nationality of a Member State on the grounds that there is a genuine link between it and the Member State.

13 In answer to that question, under international law a vessel in principle has only one nationality, that of the State in which it is registered (see in particular Articles 5 and 6 of the Geneva Convention on the High Seas of 29 April 1958 and Articles 91 and 92 of the United Nations Convention on the Law of the Sea).

14 It follows that a Member State may not treat a vessel which is already registered in a non-member country and therefore has the nationality of that country as a vessel flying the flag of that Member State.

15 The fact that the sole link between a vessel and the State of which it holds the nationality is the administrative formality of registration cannot prevent the application of that rule. It was for the State that conferred its nationality in the first place to determine at its absolute discretion the conditions on which it would grant its nationality (see in particular Article 5 of the Geneva Convention on the High Seas of 29 April 1958 and also Article 91 of the United Nations Convention on the Law of the Sea).

16 It follows from these considerations that the answer to the third question must be that a vessel registered in a non-member country may not be treated, for the purpose of Article 6(1)(b) of Council Regulation (EEC) No 3094/86 of 7 October 1986 laying down certain technical measures for the conservation of fishery resources, as a vessel with the nationality of a Member State on the ground that it has a genuine link with that Member State.

\*      \*      \*

Applicability of Article 6 in different sea areas

21 In its fourth question, the national court asks the Court to determine the sea areas in which Article 6(1)(b) of the Regulation is to be applied to a vessel registered in a non-member country.

22 In answer to that question, the abovementioned provision may not be applied to a vessel on the high seas registered in a non-member country, since in principle such a vessel is there governed only by the law of its flag.

23 It is true that in 1982 the European Community signed the abovementioned Convention for the Conservation of Salmon in the North Atlantic. However, that Convention may not be invoked against non-signatory States and cannot, therefore, be applied to vessels registered in those States.

24 As far as the other sea areas are concerned, the Community has the power to adopt rules classifying as illegal the transport and storage in the exclusive economic zone, the territorial sea, inland waters and ports of the Member States of salmon caught within the regions referred to in Article 6(1)(b) of the Regulation.

25 However, the jurisdiction of the coastal State in some of those areas is not absolute. Thus, although the territorial sea falls under the sovereignty of the coastal State, the latter must respect the right of innocent passage through it of vessels flying the flag of other States (Articles 14 to 23 of the Geneva Convention on the Territorial Sea and the Contiguous Zone of 29 April 1958; Articles 17 to 32 of the United Nations Convention on the Law of the Sea). As far as the exclusive economic zone is concerned, the coastal State must in exercising its powers observe in particular freedom of navigation (see Article 58(1) of the United Nations Convention on the Law of the Sea).

26 It follows that Community legislation may not be applied in respect of a vessel registered in a non-member country and sailing in the exclusive economic zone of a Member State, since that vessel enjoys freedom of navigation in that area.

27 Nor may it be applied in respect of such a vessel crossing the territorial waters of a Member State in so far as the vessel is exercising the right of innocent passage in those waters.

28 Conversely, Community legislation may be applied to it when it sails in the inland waters or, more especially, is in a port of a Member State, where it is generally subject to the unlimited jurisdiction of that State.

29 For those reasons, the answer to the fourth question must be that Article 6(1)(b) of Council Regulation (EEC) No 3094/86 of 7 October 1986 laying down certain technical measures for the conservation of fishery resources may in principle be applied to a vessel registered in a non-member country only when that vessel is in the inland waters or in the port of a Member State.

Confiscation of the cargo

30 It is apparent from the order for reference that, in its second question, the national court seeks to ascertain whether it may order the confiscation of a cargo of salmon caught in the areas referred to in Article 6(1)(b) of the Regulation and kept

on board a vessel registered in a non-member country and belonging to a company established in that State, where the cargo is in transit in waters under the jurisdiction of the European Community.

31 The confiscation of a cargo of fish forms part of the panoply of measures that Member States are bound to provide for in order to ensure that Community legislation is observed and to deprive those who contravene it of the financial benefit gained from such contravention. Confiscation is thus an ancillary measure which may be ordered only where there has been an infringement of Community legislation.

32 As is apparent from the answer given to the preceding questions, neither the nationality of the vessel's owner nor the temporary nature of the cargo's presence in waters under Community jurisdiction has any effect on the illegality of the transport.

33 Finally, since the prohibition on transporting and storing salmon caught in the areas mentioned in Article 6(1)(b) of the Regulation can in principle be applied to a vessel registered in a non-member country only when the vessel is in the inland waters or in the port of a Member State, confiscation of the cargo temporarily transported into waters under Community jurisdiction may be ordered only in that situation.

34 Consequently, the answer to the second question must be that the national court may in principle order the confiscation of a cargo of salmon caught in the areas referred to in Article 6(1)(b) of Council Regulation (EEC) No 3094/86 of 7 October 1986 laying down certain technical measures for the conservation of fishery resources, which is in transit in waters under Community jurisdiction and is kept aboard a vessel registered in a non-member country and belonging to a company established in that State, only when that vessel is in the inland waters or in the port of a Member State.

Existence of Community rules on distress

35 In its fifth question, the national court asks whether Community law contains rules concerning compliance with the prohibition contained in Article 6(1)(b) of the Regulation in the case of vessels from non-member countries which have entered a port of a Member State owing to a situation of distress.

36 As to that, none of the regulations adopted by the Council for the purposes of establishing or implementing a Community scheme for the conservation and management of fishery resources contains any provision allowing a vessel in a situation of distress to escape the prohibition.

37 Moreover, the question concerning the legal consequences of the situation of distress does not concern the determination of the sphere of application of Community legislation, but rather the implementation of that legislation by the authorities of the Member States.

38 In those circumstances, it is for the national court to determine, in accordance with international law, the legal consequences which flow, for the purpose of the

abovementioned Article 6, from a situation of distress involving a vessel from a non-member country.

39 Therefore, the answer to the fifth question must be that Community law contains no rules on compliance with the prohibition contained in Article 6(1)(b) of Council Regulation (EEC) No 3094/86 of 7 October 1986 laying down certain technical measures for the conservation of fishery resources, with respect to vessels from non-member countries which have entered a port of a Member State because they are in distress. It is for the national court to determine, in accordance with international law, the legal consequences flowing from such a situation.

## NOTES AND QUESTIONS

1.    Did the Court justify its conclusion that the EU was bound by international law? Is the Court saying that international law is part of the EU legal system?

2.    The ECJ turned back to the national court the question of the interpretation of international law regarding vessels in distress, even though it affected the implementation of EU legislation. What implications might this have? Would anything turn on whether Danish law had a monist or dualist approach to the incorporation of international law in its legal system? Or was the ECJ saying that the Danish court *must* apply international law? If so, would this be because this is mandated by EU legal principles that override national law or was there another reason?

## [B]    Interaction of International Law With Union Law at the Union Level

## RACKE GMBH & CO. v. HAUPTZOLLAMT MAINZ
### Case 162/96, 1998 ECJ CELEX LEXIS 280, [1998] ECR I-3655

[Council Regulation 3300/91 of 11 November 1991 had suspended the trade concessions provided for by the "Cooperation Agreement between the European Economic Community and the Socialist Federal Republic of Yugoslavia" ([1991] OJ L 315/1). Racke had brought proceedings against Hauptzollamt Mainz (Principal Customs Office, Mainz) concerning a customs debt arising on the importation into Germany of certain quantities of wine originating in the Socialist Federal Republic of Yugoslavia. The effect of the suspension of the Agreement was that duty reductions provided for in the agreement were no longer applicable. Racke argued that the Regulation, in suspending the Cooperation Agreement, breached the customary international law principle known as "pacta sunt servanda" (Agreements must be complied with).]

37 It next needs to be examined whether, when invoking in legal proceedings the preferential customs treatment granted to him by Article 22(4) of the Cooperation Agreement, an individual may challenge the validity under customary international law rules of the disputed regulation, suspending the trade concessions granted under that Agreement as from 15 November 1991.

38 In that respect, the Council maintains that the adoption of the disputed

regulation was preceded, logically and legally, by the adoption of Decision 91/586, suspending the application of the Cooperation Agreement on the international level. Adoption of the disputed regulation became necessary in its turn, since the trade concessions provided for in the Agreement had been implemented in the past by an internal Community regulation.

39 The Council submits that, since international law does not prescribe the remedies for breach of its rules, the possible breach of those rules by Decision 91/586 does not necessarily lead to the restoration in force of the Cooperation Agreement and hence, at the Community level, to the invalidity of the disputed regulation by reason of its being contrary to the restored Agreement. Breach of international law might for instance also be penalised by means of damages, leaving the Cooperation Agreement suspended. The Council therefore argues that, in assessing the validity of the disputed regulation, the Court does not need to examine whether suspension of the Cooperation Agreement by Decision 91/586 infringed rules of international law.

40 It is important to note at the outset that the question referred by the national court concerns only the validity of the disputed regulation under rules of customary international law.

41 As far as the Community is concerned, an agreement concluded by the Council with a non-member country in accordance with the provisions of the EC Treaty is an act of a Community institution, and the provisions of such an agreement form an integral part of Community law . . .

42 If, therefore, the disputed regulation had to be declared invalid, the trade concessions granted by the Cooperation Agreement would remain applicable in Community law until the Community brought that Agreement to an end in accordance with the relevant rules of international law.

43 It follows that a declaration of the invalidity of the disputed regulation by reason of its being contrary to rules of customary international law would allow individuals to rely directly on the rights to preferential treatment granted to them by the Cooperation Agreement.

44 For its part, the Commission doubts whether, in the absence of an express clause in the EC Treaty, the international law rules referred to in the order for reference may be regarded as forming part of the Community legal order. Thus, in order to challenge the validity of a regulation, an individual might rely on grounds based on the relationship between him and the Community, but does not, the Commission argues, have the right to rely on grounds deriving from the legal relationship between the Community and a non-member country, which fall within the scope of international law.

45 It should be noted in that respect that . . . the European Community must respect international law in the exercise of its powers. It is therefore required to comply with the rules of customary international law when adopting a regulation suspending the trade concessions granted by, or by virtue of, an agreement which it has concluded with a non-member country.

46 It follows that the rules of customary international law concerning the

termination and the suspension of treaty relations by reason of a fundamental change of circumstances are binding upon the Community institutions and form part of the Community legal order.

47 In this case, however, the plaintiff is incidentally challenging the validity of a Community regulation under those rules in order to rely upon rights which it derives directly from an agreement of the Community with a non-member country. This case does not therefore concern the direct effect of those rules.

48 Racke is invoking fundamental rules of customary international law against the disputed regulation, which was taken pursuant to those rules and deprives Racke of the rights to preferential treatment granted to it by the Cooperation Agreement . . .

49 The rules invoked by Racke form an exception to the pacta sunt servanda principle, which constitutes a fundamental principle of any legal order and, in particular, the international legal order. Applied to international law, that principle requires that every treaty be binding upon the parties to it and be performed by them in good faith (see Article 26 of the Vienna Convention [on the Law of Treaties]).

50 The importance of that principle has been further underlined by the International Court of Justice, which has held that the stability of treaty relations requires that the plea of fundamental change of circumstances be applied only in exceptional cases' . . .

51 In those circumstances, an individual relying in legal proceedings on rights which he derives directly from an agreement with a non-member country may not be denied the possibility of challenging the validity of a regulation which, by suspending the trade concessions granted by that agreement, prevents him from relying on it, and of invoking, in order to challenge the validity of the suspending regulation, obligations deriving from rules of customary international law which govern the termination and suspension of treaty relations.

[The Court concluded that the actual application of the doctrine of pacta sunt servanda is extremely complex due to the many exceptions available which are themselves often based on complex choices. Therefore it declined to review the substance of the Regulation, which involved political choices, and looked only at whether there had been a manifest error of assessment — see further Chapter 8.]

## NOTES AND QUESTIONS

1.  Did the Court accept in principle that EU law may be reviewed by it for compliance with international law? If so, does that mean that international law is a "higher norm" than the Treaties themselves? Suppose that a Treaty provision itself were questioned on the grounds of noncompliance with international law?

2.  How would a U.S. court deal with an argument that a federal law failed to comply with customary international law?

3.  What of multilateral treaties that create "norms" of international law? In *International Fruit Co. NV v. Produktschap voor Groenten en Fruit*, Joined Cases

21-24/72, [1972] ECR 1219, the Court was asked to decide whether, within the meaning of article 177 EEC (EC 234/TFEU 267), the validity of the acts of the institutions of the Union also covers their validity under international law and further, whether Commission Regulations Nos. 459/70, 565/70 and 686/70 — which provided, as safeguard measures, for import restrictions for apples originating in third countries — "are invalid because they are contrary to Article XI of the General Agreement on Tariffs and Trade (GATT)." The GATT was not an agreement to which the original EEC was a party. It was a multilateral agreement to which the Member States were parties, however. The question was essentially whether the EEC could be bound by it as a normative rule of international law:

> 7 Before the incompatibility of a Community measure with a provision of international law can affect the validity of that measure, the Community must first of all be bound by that provision.

*    *    *

> 10 It is clear that at the time when they concluded the treaty establishing the European Economic Community the Member States were bound by the obligations of the General Agreement.

> 11 By concluding a treaty between them they could not withdraw from their obligations to third countries.

> 12 On the contrary, their desire to observe the undertakings of the General Agreement follows as much from the very provisions of the EEC Treaty as from the declarations made by Member States on the presentation of the Treaty to the Contracting Parties of the General Agreement in accordance with the obligation under Article XXIV thereof.

> 13 That intention was made clear in particular by article 110 of the EEC Treaty [206], which seeks the adherence of the Community to the same aims as those sought by the General Agreement, as well as by the first paragraph of article 234 [351] which provides that the rights and obligations arising from agreements concluded before the entry into force of the Treaty, and in particular multilateral agreements concluded with the participation of Member States, are not affected by the provisions of the Treaty.

> 14 The Community has assumed the functions inherent in the tariff and trade policy, progressively during the transitional period and in their entirety on the expiry of that period, by virtue of articles 111 [deleted] and 113 [206] of the Treaty.

> 15 By conferring those powers on the Community, the Member States showed their wish to bind it by the obligations entered into under the General Agreement.

> 16 Since the entry into force of the EEC Treaty and more particularly, since the setting up of the Common External Tariff, the transfer of powers which has occurred in the relations between Member States and the Community has been put into concrete form in different ways within the

framework of the general agreement and has been recognized by the other Contracting Parties.

17 In particular, since that time, the Community, acting through its own institutions, has appeared as a partner in the tariff negotiations and as a party to the agreements of all types concluded within the framework of the General Agreement, in accordance with the provisions of article 114 [deleted] of the EEC Treaty which provides that the tariff and trade agreements "shall be concluded . . . on behalf of the Community".

18 It therefore appears that, in so far as under the EEC Treaty the Community has assumed the powers previously exercised by Member States in the area governed by the General Agreement, the provisions of that agreement have the effect of binding the Community.

The *Racke* case seems to confirm that international Conventions such as the Vienna Convention on the law of treaties mentioned there bind the EU whether or not it is a party to them. However, per *International Fruit*, multilateral treaties such as the GATT require the EU to be a party, or at least bound by some act or behavior demonstrating a willingness to be bound. This seems perhaps a rather difficult distinction. However, international conventions that codify international law (such as the Vienna Convention) can be logically considered to bind non-parties precisely because they do restate customary international law — that is, they do not create specific new or different obligations for States.

# Chapter 5

# LEGAL ACTS OF THE UNION

## § 5.01  OVERVIEW

*Template* Article 2, Sections 2.4 and 2.6 and Article 8, Sections 8.3 and 8.4

*Materials in this chapter* This chapter covers various aspects of binding Union legal acts as designated in EC 249/TFEU 288, namely, regulations, directives and decisions.

§ 5.02 examines the directive from several viewpoints, starting with the extent to which this form of act may be directly effective in a manner similar to certain Treaty provisions. The section also addresses the question as to whether directives may under any circumstances create obligations for individuals, and whether a directive could also be a disguised decision.

§ 5.03 deals with the characteristics of regulations, beginning with the notion of direct applicability and then proceeding to distinguish them from decisions. This exercise had a particular significance under former EC 230, because the language allowing actions for annulment by individuals permitted actions against regulations if they were of direct and individual concern to the applicant *and* were really decisions "in the form of a regulation." Although the Court often used the same test for both, it is also true that, in some instances, even if a regulation actually fulfills the criteria to be considered of direct and individual concern, it might still not be challengeable because of the way the Court has chosen to characterize such measures. Thus, understanding the essential characteristics of regulations as distinguished from decisions remains important.

§ 5.04 looks in particular at what constitutes a decision. In this regard it may be noted that the TFEU does not prescribe any particular formality for this type of act. Unlike regulations, they are not required to be published in the Official Journal. Regulations, by contrast, cannot have any legal effect until so published.

§ 5.05 illustrates the position in Union law of treaties entered into by the Union.

§ 5.06 offers some observations on the nature of ECJ decisions in the context of EC 234/TFEU 267 referrals.

The procedures whereby Union acts become law are addressed in Chapters 6 and 7, while individual standing to challenge Union acts under TFEU 263 is dealt with in Chapter 8.

*Categorization of Union acts* As a result of Lisbon, it is now possible to categorize Union acts having a normative character as legislative, delegated, or implementing, based on the manner of their adoption. All other acts are of an executive character.

The *forms* of acts listed in EC 249/TFEU 288 are not indicative as to which category they belong to. In fact, with the exception of (non-binding) recommendations, each of the forms could potentially be used for any of the categories. Thus, a decision can be a legislative act, while there is at least one explicit instance where a directive is available as an executive act: EC 83/TFEU 106. Any of the forms of legally binding act may or may not be legislative acts depending on how they are adopted and what their purpose is. Decisions may, in terms of their effects and addressees, be anything from major policy guidance when adopted by the European Council all the way to executive acts having precise legal consequences for individuals, as in the case of Commission acts implementing the details of Union policies, such as competition and agriculture.

***Forms of legal act under the old TEU*** It was noted in Chapter 2 that prior to Lisbon, other forms of legal act existed in the TEU. In the case of Police and Justice Cooperation in Criminal Matters (PJCC) these were: common positions, framework decisions, decisions and conventions (old TEU 34), but they had limited legal effects given their location in the TEU. Since, by virtue of Lisbon, PJCC has been moved into the TFEU, it was appropriate that the legal effects of acts adopted while that subject was still part of the TEU should, over time be brought into line with the legal effects of the forms of action available under TFEU 288, which will, of course, be used for future measures in this area. Common positions and yet another form of act, joint actions, were available to the Council as measures under the Common Foreign and Security Policy (CFSP) (old TEU 14 and 15), but since this area remains walled off from the TFEU no changes were required there, although those forms of action have now been replaced by the decision. In PJCC, when it formed part of the TEU, the Commission did not have powers to bring infringement actions under EC 226/TFEU 258, and the ECJ did not automatically have jurisdiction to hear references for interpretation. Under Protocol 36 on transitional provisions, articles 9 et seq., these characteristics will disappear after a transitional period of five years or earlier where the act is amended or replaced, thus assimilating them to acts available under TFEU 288. The United Kingdom has certain rights of opt-out from these changes as more fully set out in Protocol 36, which appears in the Documentary Supplement.

## § 5.02   DIRECTIVES

### [A]   Direct Effect

### VAN DUYN v. HOME OFFICE
Case 41/74, 1974 ECJ CELEX LEXIS 124, [1974] ECR 1337

[This reference to the ECJ by an English court arose out of an action brought against the Home Office by Mrs Van Duyn, a woman of Dutch nationality, who was refused leave to enter the United Kingdom to take up employment as a secretary with the Church of Scientology. Leave to enter was refused in accordance with the policy of the Government of the United Kingdom in relation to that organization, the activities of which it considered to be socially harmful.

The Court considered among other things whether Directive 64/221, implementing the Treaty provisions on the free movement of workers and self employed people also contained provisions that conferred rights on individuals. Specifically, in implementation of the exceptions listed in EC 56/TFEU 52, Article 3(1) of that directive provided that "measures taken on grounds of public policy or public security shall be based exclusively on the personal conduct of the individual concerned."]

11 The United Kingdom observes that, since Article 189 [288] of the Treaty distinguishes between the effects ascribed to regulations, directives and decisions, it must therefore be presumed that the Council, in issuing a directive rather than making a regulation, must have intended that the directive should have an effect other than that of a regulation and accordingly that the former should not be directly applicable.

12 If, however, by virtue of the provisions of Article 189 [288] regulations are directly applicable and, consequently, may by their very nature have direct effects, it does not follow from this that other categories of acts mentioned in that Article can never have similar effects. It would be incompatible with the binding effect attributed to a directive by Article 189 [288] to exclude, in principle, the possibility that the obligation which it imposes may be invoked by those concerned. In particular, where the Community authorities have, by directive, imposed on Member States the obligation to pursue a particular course of conduct, the useful effect [effectiveness] of such an act would be weakened if individuals were prevented from relying on it before their national courts and if the latter were prevented from taking it into consideration as an element of Community law. Article 177 [267], which empowers national courts to refer to the Court questions concerning the validity and interpretation of all acts of the Community institutions, without distinction, implies furthermore that these acts may be invoked by individuals in the national courts. It is necessary to examine, in every case, whether the nature, general scheme and wording of the provisions in question are capable of having direct effects on the relations between Member States and individuals.

13 By providing that measures taken on grounds of public policy shall be based exclusively on the personal conduct of the individual concerned, Article 3 (1) of Directive No 64/221 is intended to limit the discretionary power which national laws generally confer on the authorities responsible for the entry and expulsion of foreign nationals. First, the provision lays down an obligation which is not subject to any exception or condition and which, by its very nature, does not require the intervention of any act on the part either of the institutions of the Community or of Member States. Secondly, because Member States are thereby obliged, in implementing a clause which derogates from one of the fundamental principles of the Treaty in favour of individuals, not to take account of factors extraneous to personal conduct, legal certainty for the persons concerned requires that they should be able to rely on this obligation even though it has been laid down in a legislative act which has no automatic direct effect in its entirety.

## NOTES AND QUESTIONS

1.    Consider the first sentence of para 12 in the above case. This might seem a somewhat arbitrary and tendentious interpretation. Did not the authors of the Treaty intend to draw a clear distinction in EEC Article 189 (EC 249/TFEU 288) between the various types of EU legislation? It is helpful to compare the analysis above with the decision in *Van Gend* relating to Treaty provisions. If Treaty provisions addressing obligations imposed as between Member States can have direct effect in national law, is it not logical to extend the same effect to directives even though only the Member States are bound by them? What do you think of the Court's reasoning?

2.    In this case, the deadline for implementation of the directive had passed. The court has made it clear that directives cannot be invoked before the time limit for their implementation by the authorities of Member States has expired. *Pubblico Ministero v. Ratti*, Case 148/78, [1979] ECR 1629. (See Chapter 11.) However, later cases have indicated a willingness to go beyond this based on EC 10 [TEU 4]. [See Sub-section [C] *infra*]

3.    Even when a Member State has purportedly implemented a directive, it may be invocable. In *Verbond van Nederlandse Ondernemingen (VNO) v. Inspecteur der Invoerrechten en Accijnzen*, Case 51/76 [1977] ECR 113, the Court so ruled, thereby allowing the VNO to invoke the Second VAT Directive despite implementation of its provisions by Dutch authorities. The rationale for the Court's opinion was that, by allowing individuals to invoke the directive, the Community can ensure that Member States have not exceeded the limits of their discretion under the directive.

By thus allowing a state law to be appraised in state courts by reference to the directive it implements, the ECJ has established a relationship between national and EU law that places significantly more importance on the latter than may have originally been contemplated by EC 249/TFEU 288. Clearly national courts will need to look at the texts of both national laws and the directives they implement in any case where an individual litigant raises a question of improper implementation. Member States, faced with this uncertainty over the validity of their own implementing legislation, may be increasingly inclined simply to repeat the text of the directive in their regulations, thus risking incompatibility with pre-existing national legislation. This happened in the United Kingdom, for example, with respect to the Directive on Commercial Agents, where an essentially civil-law concept was grafted onto the common law of contracts.

4.    What was the English court to do as a result of the European Court of Justice ruling in *Van Duyn* — would a significant degree of freedom to apply the ECJ's ruling be incompatible with the uniform application of EU law?

5.    In *Criminal proceedings against Antoine Kortas*, Case C-319/97, 1999 ECJ CELEX LEXIS 313, [1999] ECR I-3143, Mr. Kortas was charged with having sold in his shop, until 15 September 1995, confectionery products imported from Germany and containing a colorant called E 124 or "cochineal red". Under the then Swedish law, the only substances permitted for use as additives were those that had been approved specifically for the food product concerned. However, the relevant

EU directive had not specified this substance as prohibited. Sweden, after accession, had sought a derogation from the directive under then article 100a (EC 95/TFEU 114), but the Commission had failed to respond. (At that time there was no deadline for such response.) Mr Kortas argued that the absence of a prohibition in the directive meant that Swedish law could not be enforced against him. Sweden argued that the derogation procedure ought to be treated as allowing it to continue to ban the substance until the Commission made a decision. This argument was rejected by the Court.

**6.** The Court has held that framework provisions in directives are not directly effective, at least where they impose only a general obligation to adopt a program. See for example *Comitato de coordinamento per la difesa della Cava and others v. Regione Lombardia and Others*, Case C-236/92, 1994 ECJ CELEX LEXIS 116, [1994] ECR I-483; and also Directive 2000/78, addressed in the *Swedex* case in Chapter 4.

## [B] Can Directives Create Obligations for Individuals (Non-Governmental Persons)?

### MARSHALL v. SOUTHAMPTON & SOUTH WEST HAMPSHIRE
### AREA HEALTH AUTHORITY
### Case 152/84, [1986] ECR 723

[The appellant [Marshall] who was born on February 4, 1918, was employed by the respondent, an entity within the UK's National Health Service and therefore a government body. Her employment was terminated when she reached age 62, based on the date of eligibility for a state pension. Male employees became eligible at age 65. Ms. Marshall claimed unfair dismissal based on gender discrimination contrary to Directive 76/207, the directive that extended the prohibition on gender discrimination in employment to aspects other than pay (equal opportunity) as further explained in Chapter 18.]

13 With regard to the argument that a directive may not be relied upon against an individual, it must be emphasized that according to Article 189 of the EEC Treaty [288] the binding nature of a directive, which constitutes the basis for the possibility of relying on the directive before a national court, exists only in relation to "each Member State to which it is addressed." It follows that a directive may not of itself impose obligations on an individual and that a provision of a directive may not be relied upon as such against such a person. It must therefore be examined whether, in this case, the respondent must be regarded as having acted as an individual.

14 In that respect it must be pointed out that where a person involved in legal proceedings is able to rely on a directive as against the State he may do so regardless of the capacity in which the State is acting, whether employer or public authority. In either case, it is necessary to prevent the State from taking advantage of its own failure to comply with Community law.

15 It is for the national court to apply those considerations to the circumstances of each case; the Court of Appeal has, however, stated in the order for referral that the

respondent, Southampton and South West Hampshire Area Health Authority (Teaching), is a public authority.

16 The argument submitted by the United Kingdom that the possibility of relying on provisions of the directive against the respondent qua organ of the State would give rise to an arbitrary and unfair distinction between the rights of State employees and those of private employees does not justify any other conclusion. Such a distinction may easily be avoided if the Member State concerned has correctly implemented the directive in national law.

## NOTES AND QUESTIONS

1.   The ECJ acknowledged that its jurisprudence clearly excluded the right of a private citizen to invoke provisions of a directive against another individual (so-called "horizontal effect") as opposed to the State. The respondent in this case was an emanation of the State and therefore the appellant was held to have the right to invoke the directive against it. Does this make sense in terms of the logic the Court used for limiting the obligations of directives to States? Is there not validity to the argument that there is an artificial difference in rights depending on whether the individual is employed by the State or a private company?

2.   Although the ECJ has consistently denied any "horizontal effect" to directives, (i.e., that they create obligations for private parties) it has invoked EC 10/TEU 4 as a device for imposing a duty on the national courts to interpret national laws as consistent with directives wherever possible. This is dealt with in the *Von Colson* case, Chapter 9.

## CRIMINAL PROCEEDINGS AGAINST SILVIO BERLUSCONI AND OTHERS
Joined Cases C-387/02, C-391/02 and C-403/02, 2005 ECJ CELEX LEXIS 750, [2005] ECR I-3565

[Proceedings were brought against Mr Berlusconi, the Italian Prime Minister, and others alleging breach of the provisions governing false information on companies (false accounting) set out in the Codice civile (the Italian Civil Code'). According to Article 6 of the First Companies Directive:

> Member States shall provide for appropriate penalties in case of: . . . failure to disclose the balance sheet and profit and loss account as required by Article 2(1)(f).

Italy had undertaken a reform of company law in 2002 and a new Article 2621 of the Italian Civil Code, entitled "False notification and unlawful distribution of profits or dividends" was introduced. This had less severe penalties than the previous legislation. The defendants had allegedly committed offences under the old, more severe law, but Italian law contained a principle that where a law has been changed in the meantime, the individual should be prosecuted under whichever legislation was more favorable to that individual. In this case the new legislation would have to be applied. This then raised the issue as to whether that new legislation failed to comply with the standards of Article 6 of the First Companies

Directive in that it did not provide sufficiently serious penalties for breaches of national law implementing this and other companies law directives. The Italian Courts asked whether, if they found the new law to be insufficient, they should set it aside and apply the former, more severe penalties, as a means of giving effect to the requirements of the directive.]

70. The question . . . arises as to whether the principle of the retroactive application of the more lenient penalty applies in the case in which that penalty is at variance with other rules of Community law.

71. It is, however, unnecessary to resolve that question for the purpose of the disputes in the main proceedings as the Community rule in issue is contained in a directive on which the law-enforcement authorities have relied against individuals within the context of criminal proceedings.

72. Admittedly, should the national courts which made the references conclude, on the basis of the replies to be given by the Court, that the new Articles 2621 and 2622 of the Italian Civil Code do not, by reason of certain of their provisions, satisfy the Community law requirement that penalties be appropriate, it would follow, according to the Court's well-established case-law, that the national courts which made the references would be required to set aside, under their own authority, those new articles without having to request or await the prior repeal of those articles by way of legislation or any other constitutional procedure . . .

73. The Court has, however, also consistently ruled that a directive cannot of itself impose obligations on an individual and cannot therefore be relied on as such against that individual . . .

74. In the specific context of a situation in which a directive is relied on against an individual by the authorities of a Member State within the context of criminal proceedings, the Court has ruled that a directive cannot, of itself and independently of a national law adopted by a Member State for its implementation, have the effect of determining or aggravating the liability in criminal law of persons who act in contravention of the provisions of that directive . . .

75. In the situation in the present cases, reliance on Article 6 of the First Companies Directive for the purpose of assessing whether the new Articles 2621 and 2622 of the Italian Civil Code are compatible with that provision could have the effect of setting aside application of the system of more lenient penalties provided for by those articles.

76. It is clear from the decisions for referral that, if the new Articles 2621 and 2622 of the Italian Civil Code were to remain unapplied by reason of their incompatibility with Article 6 of the First Companies Directive, the result could be to render applicable a manifestly more severe criminal penalty, such as that provided for under the former Article 2621 of that code, which was in force at the time when the acts resulting in the prosecutions brought in the cases in the main proceedings were committed.

77. A consequence of that kind would be contrary to the limits which flow from the essential nature of any directive, which, as follows from the case-law cited in paragraphs 73 and 74 of this judgment, preclude a directive from having the effect

of determining or increasing the liability in criminal law of accused persons.

78. In the light of all of the foregoing, the answer to the questions referred for preliminary ruling must be that, in a situation such as that in issue in the main proceedings, the First Companies Directive cannot be relied on as such against accused persons by the authorities of a Member State within the context of criminal proceedings, in view of the fact that a directive cannot, of itself and independently of national legislation adopted by a Member State for its implementation, have the effect of determining or increasing the criminal liability of those accused persons.

## NOTES AND QUESTIONS

1.   Why did the ECJ take the view that the Italian Court was seeking to apply the directive? What would have been the consequence in this case of a determination that the new law failed to comply with the directive?

2.   Silvio Berlusconi served as Italian prime minister from 2001 to 2006 and was until the end of 2011 again Prime Minister. He has been described as Italy's richest man. He founded Fininvest — the basis of a media empire. The criminal proceedings underlying the ECJ case involved accusations that he used the company to create various slush funds for secret and illegal purposes between 1986 and 1989. Proceedings were commenced against him under the laws relating to breach of financial accounting requirements. In 2002, after he became prime minister and the leader of the largest party in the Italian legislature, the latter amended the law to create a much less rigorous definition of false accounting. Additionally, limitation periods that allowed the statute of limitations to continue to run until a final verdict meant that continuing delaying tactics would eventually nullify the prosecution. The case before the ECJ reflected an attempt by the prosecutor to invoke the provisions of the unenacted directive as overriding the Italian legislation as a way of avoiding the less severe penalties of the new law. See A. Biondi, and R. Mastroianni, *Joined Cases C-387/02, C-391/02 and C-403/02, Berlusconi and others* (2006) 43 CML Rev. 553.

## PAOLA FACCINI DORI v. RECREB SRL.
### Case C-91/92 1994 ECJ EUR-Lex LEXIS 103, 1994 ECR I-3325;

[Without having been previously approached by her, Interdiffusion Srl concluded a contract with Miss Faccini Dori at Milan Central Railway Station for an English language correspondence course. Thus the contract was concluded away from Interdiffusion's business premises. Some days later, Miss Faccini Dori informed that company that she was cancelling her order. The company replied on 3 June 1989 that it had assigned its claim to Recreb. On 24 June 1989, Miss Faccini Dori wrote to Recreb confirming that she had cancelled her subscription to the course, indicating inter alia that she relied on the right of cancellation within 7 days as provided for by Directive 85/577 concerning protection of the consumer in respect of contracts negotiated away from business premises. Italy had failed to transpose the directive within the deadline. The ECJ held first that the provision of the directive relied on by Dori was sufficiently precise and unconditional to be considered directly effective.]

20 As the Court has consistently held since its judgment in Case 152/84 Marshall v. Southampton and South-West Hampshire Health Authority [1986] ECR 723, paragraph 48, a directive cannot of itself impose obligations on an individual and cannot therefore be relied upon as such against an individual.

21 The national court observes that if the effects of unconditional and sufficiently precise but untransposed directives were to be limited to relations between State entities and individuals, this would mean that a legislative measure would operate as such only as between certain legal subjects, whereas, under Italian law as under the laws of all modern States founded on the rule of law, the State is subject to the law like any other person. If the directive could be relied on only as against the State, that would be tantamount to a penalty for failure to adopt legislative measures of transposition as if the relationship were a purely private one.

22 . . . [T]he case-law on the possibility of relying on directives against State entities is based on the fact that under Article 189 [288] a directive is binding only in relation to "each Member State to which it is addressed". That case-law seeks to prevent "the State from taking advantage of its own failure to comply with Community law".

23 It would be unacceptable if a State, when required by the Community legislature to adopt certain rules intended to govern the State's relations or those of State entities with individuals and to confer certain rights on individuals, were able to rely on its own failure to discharge its obligations so as to deprive individuals of the benefits of those rights. Thus the Court has recognized that certain provisions of directives on conclusion of public works contracts and of directives on harmonization of turnover taxes may be relied on against the State (or State entities) . . .

24 The effect of extending that case-law to the sphere of relations between individuals would be to recognize a power in the Community to enact obligations for individuals with immediate effect, whereas it has competence to do so only where it is empowered to adopt regulations.

25 It follows that, in the absence of measures transposing the directive within the prescribed time-limit, consumers cannot derive from the directive itself a right of cancellation as against traders with whom they have concluded a contract or enforce such a right in a national court.

## UNILEVER ITALIA SPA v. CENTRAL FOOD SPA
### Case C-443/98, 2000 ECJ CELEX LEXIS 391, [2000] ECR I-7535

[This case concerned Directive 83/189/EEC laying down a procedure for the provision of information in the field of technical standards and regulations (OJ 1983 L 109, p. 8), as amended by Directive 94/10/EC. Unilever Italia SpA (Unilever) had sued Central Food SpA (Central Food) for payment by Central Food for a consignment of olive oil supplied by Unilever which the labeling declared to be of Italian origin. Central Food had defended the claim on the basis that the labeling of the olive oil did not comply with an Italian regulation regarding origin labeling (thus Central Food did not get what it had bargained for in the contract.) Article 8 of the directive required that a draft national regulation within the scope of the directive not be enacted unless first notified to the Commission, while Article 9 of the directive required a delay of 12 months if the Commission indicated that a draft or proposal for Union legislation covering the subject matter of the national law was in process. The Italian regulation was nonetheless enacted. The Commission then specifically warned the Italian government against bringing the law into effect (by publication in the official Gazette) and that failure to comply with the directive would render the Italian law inapplicable. The law was nonetheless published. The Court makes reference to an earlier judgment, CIA Security, which concerned the failure to notify under article 8 of the directive. (The case is described in the following Notes.)]

31 The question from the national court seeks, in essence, to ascertain whether a national court is required, in civil proceedings between individuals concerning contractual rights and obligations, to refuse to apply a national technical regulation which was adopted during a period of postponement of adoption prescribed by Article 9 of Directive 83/189.

* * *

37 . . . [I]t is appropriate, first, to consider whether the legal consequence of failure to fulfil the obligations imposed by Directive 83/189 is the same in relation both to the obligation to observe periods of postponement under Article 9 of Directive 83/189 and to the obligation of notification under Article 8 of Directive 83/189.

38 CIA Security related to a technical regulation which had not been notified in accordance with Article 8 of Directive 83/189. This explains why the operative part of that judgment confines itself to finding that technical regulations which have not been notified in accordance with that article are inapplicable.

39 However, in the statement of the grounds on which that finding was based, the Court also examined the obligations deriving from Article 9 of Directive 83/189. The Court's reasoning shows that, having regard to the objective of Directive 83/189 and to the wording of Article 9 thereof, those obligations must be treated in the same way as those deriving from Article 8 of the same directive.

40 Thus, in paragraph 40 of CIA Security, it was emphasised that Directive 83/189 is designed, by means of preventive control, to protect freedom of movement for goods, which is one of the foundations of the Community, and that, in order for such control to be effective, all draft technical regulations covered by the directive must be notified and, except in the case of those regulations whose urgency justifies an exception, their adoption or entry into force must be suspended during the periods laid down in Article 9.

41 Next, in paragraph 41 of that judgment, the Court held that notification and the period of postponement afford the Commission and the other Member States an opportunity to examine whether the draft regulations in question create obstacles to trade contrary to the EC Treaty or obstacles which were to be avoided through the adoption of common or harmonised measures and also to propose amendments to the national measures envisaged. That procedure also enables the Commission to propose or adopt Community rules regulating the matter dealt with by the envisaged measure.

42 In paragraph 50 of CIA Security the Court indicated that the aim of the directive was not simply to inform the Commission but is also, more generally, to eliminate or restrict obstacles to trade, to inform other States of technical regulations envisaged by a State, to give the Commission and the other Member States time to react and to propose amendments for lessening restrictions to the free movement of goods arising from the envisaged measure and to afford the Commission time to propose a harmonising directive.

43 The Court went on to hold that the wording of Articles 8 and 9 of Directive 83/189 was clear in that they provide a procedure for Community control of draft national regulations, the date of their entry into force being subject to the Commission's agreement or lack of opposition.

44 Although, in paragraph 48 of CIA Security, after reiterating that the aim of Directive 83/189 was to protect freedom of movement for goods by means of preventive control and that the obligation to notify was essential for achieving such Community control, the Court found that the effectiveness of such control would be that much greater if the directive were interpreted as meaning that breach of the obligation to notify constituted a substantial procedural defect such as to render the technical regulations in question inapplicable to individuals, it follows from the considerations set out in paragraphs 40 to 43 of this judgment that breach of the obligations of postponement of adoption set out in Article 9 of Directive 83/189 also constitutes a substantial procedural defect such as to render technical regulations inapplicable.

45 It is therefore necessary to consider, secondly, whether the inapplicability of technical regulations adopted in breach of Article 9 of Directive 83/189 can be invoked in civil proceedings between private individuals concerning contractual rights and obligations.

46 First, in civil proceedings of that nature, application of technical regulations adopted in breach of Article 9 of Directive 83/189 may have the effect of hindering the use or marketing of a product which does not conform to those regulations.

47 That is the case in the main proceedings, since application of the Italian rules is liable to hinder Unilever in marketing the extra virgin olive oil which it offers for sale.

48 Next, it must be borne in mind that, in CIA Security, the finding of inapplicability as a legal consequence of breach of the obligation of notification was made in response to a request for a preliminary ruling arising from proceedings between competing undertakings based on national provisions prohibiting unfair trading.

49 Thus, it follows from the case-law of the Court that the inapplicability of a technical regulation which has not been notified in accordance with Article 8 of Directive 83/189 can be invoked in proceedings between individuals for the reasons set out in paragraphs 40 to 43 of this judgment. The same applies to non-compliance with the obligations laid down by Article 9 of the same directive, and there is no reason, in that connection, to treat disputes between individuals relating to unfair competition, as in the CIA Security case, differently from disputes between individuals concerning contractual rights and obligations, as in the main proceedings.

50 Whilst it is true . . . that a directive cannot of itself impose obligations on an individual and cannot therefore be relied on as such against an individual (see Case C-91/92 Faccini Dori 1994 ECR I-3325, paragraph 20), that case-law does not apply where non-compliance with Article 8 or Article 9 of Directive 83/189, which constitutes a substantial procedural defect, renders a technical regulation adopted in breach of either of those articles inapplicable.

51 In such circumstances, and unlike the case of non-transposition of directives with which the case-law cited by those two Governments is concerned, Directive 83/189 does not in any way define the substantive scope of the legal rule on the basis of which the national court must decide the case before it. It creates neither rights nor obligations for individuals.

52 In view of all the foregoing considerations, the answer to the question submitted must be that a national court is required, in civil proceedings between individuals concerning contractual rights and obligations, to refuse to apply a national technical regulation which was adopted during a period of postponement of adoption prescribed in Article 9 of Directive 83/189.

## NOTES AND QUESTIONS

1. In *CIA Security International SA v. Signalson SA and Securitel SPRL*, Case C-194/94, 1996 ECJ CELEX LEXIS 219, [1996] ECR I-2201 referred to in the above case, the plaintiff had sued the defendant for defamation after the defendant had claimed that the plaintiff's product did not comply with Belgian law. However, the law in question was a technical regulation that should have been notified to the Commission under Directive 83/189. The Belgian government had failed to do so and thus was in breach of the directive. The defendant could not therefore argue that his assertion was true, because the Belgian law with which the plaintiff was alleged to be out of compliance was inapplicable. Thus, in that case, as in the Unilever case, the consequence of the non-compliance of a national law with the directive was that it could be invoked in proceedings between individuals and that legal consequences would ensue for the party seeking to rely on the national law.

There have been other instances where the invocability of the directive against the state has had legal effects on other private parties (sometimes referred to as a "triangular effect"). For example, in *Panagis Pafitis v. Trapeza Kentrikis Ellados AE*, Case 441/93, 1996 ECJ CELEX LEXIS 48, [1996] ECR I-1347, the original shareholders in a bank had brought suit against new shareholders after the bank had increased its capital without a shareholders' resolution. Due to the bank's debt situation, the increase had been ordered by the Governor of the Bank of Greece and the administrator of TKE Bank, subsequently ratified by legislation. Those measures were taken pursuant to Presidential Decree No 861/1975. A Directive required that a resolution was required for public limited liability companies to increase their capital, and the Greek court asked whether this included banks, and specifically banks that were in financial distress. The ECJ confirmed that it did. Consequently, the decision to increase the capital, being contrary to the directive, was invalid. The question of the direct effect or invocability of the directive was not addressed by the Court, but it seems to have been assumed that it could be invoked against the decision to increase the capital that had emanated from the Central

Bank, even though the actual lawsuit was between private parties.

**2.** Do cases such as *CIA* and *Unilever* deal with a materially different situation as regards consequences for individuals as compared with *Marshall, Berlusconi* and *Recreb*? Or is the difference between direct effect (invocability against the State) and direct applicability (creating obligations for individuals) illusory? Bear in mind that in any case where the Court declares a State measure inapplicable by its interpretation of a directive, there are likely to be legal consequences or obligations for other individuals. (In *Unilever* it meant that Central Food could not refuse to pay based on the alleged non-compliance with labelling laws by Unilever.) Consider whether perhaps the ECJ is trying to avoid putting the national courts in a position where they have to "legislate" the provisions of a directive into national law as opposed simply to declaring a conflicting national provision inapplicable.

## [C]   Effects of Directives Before Their Implementation Deadline

### INTER-ENVIRONNEMENT WALLONIE ASBL v. REGION WALLONNE
Case C-129/96, 1997 ECJ CELEX LEXIS 571, [1997] ECR I-7411

[Inter-Environnement Wallonie maintained that a new regional law of the Wallonia region of Belgium had infringed, in particular, Article 11 of Directive 75/442, as amended, and Article 3 of Directive 91/689, inasmuch as the Wallonia law excluded from the permit system the operations of setting up and running an installation intended specifically for the collection, pre-treatment, disposal or recovery of toxic or dangerous waste, where that installation forms an integral part of an industrial production process.]

42 . . . [I]n accordance with current practice, Directive 91/156 itself laid down a period by the end of which the laws, regulations and administrative provisions necessary for compliance are to have been brought into force.

43 Since the purpose of such a period is, in particular, to give Member States the necessary time to adopt transposition measures, they cannot be faulted for not having transposed the directive into their internal legal order before expiry of that period.

44 Nevertheless, it is during the transposition period that the Member States must take the measures necessary to ensure that the result prescribed by the directive is achieved at the end of that period.

45 Although the Member States are not obliged to adopt those measures before the end of the period prescribed for transposition, it follows from the second paragraph of Article 5 [TEU 4] in conjunction with the third paragraph of Article 189 [288] of the Treaty and from the directive itself that during that period they must refrain from taking any measures liable seriously to compromise the result prescribed.

46 It is for the national court to assess whether that is the case as regards the national provisions whose legality it is called upon to consider.

47 In making that assessment, the national court must consider, in particular, whether the provisions in issue purport to constitute full transposition of the directive, as well as the effects in practice of applying those incompatible provisions and of their duration in time.

48 For example, if the provisions in issue are intended to constitute full and definitive transposition of the directive, their incompatibility with the directive might give rise to the presumption that the result prescribed by the directive will not be achieved within the period prescribed if it is impossible to amend them in time.

49 Conversely, the national court could take into account the right of a Member State to adopt transitional measures or to implement the directive in stages. In such cases, the incompatibility of the transitional national measures with the directive, or the non-transposition of certain of its provisions, would not necessarily compromise the result prescribed.

50 The answer to the first question must therefore be that the second paragraph of Article 5 [TEU 4] and the third paragraph of Article 189 [288] of the EEC Treaty, and Directive 91/156, require the Member States to which that directive is addressed to refrain, during the period laid down therein for its implementation, from adopting measures liable seriously to compromise the result prescribed.

## NOTES AND QUESTIONS

1.  Does the Court's ruling here contradict the basic tenet that it is not possible to invoke a directive until its time for implementation has passed?

2.  Is the Member State's obligation only to not take measures that could impede the objectives of the directive? What of day-to-day implementation of existing law through executive action? Must the authorities refer to the directive in making decisions even before the directive is required to be implemented? What about the national courts?

## [D]   Can Directives Be Disguised Decisions?

### GOVERNMENT OF GIBRALTAR v. COUNCIL
298/89, 1993 ECJ CELEX LEXIS 13, [1993] ECR I-3605

[The Government of Gibraltar sought to annul Council Directive 89/463 amending Council Directive 83/416 the aim of which was to establish an EU program for the authorization by the Member States of scheduled inter-regional air services between those States in order to promote the development of the intra-EU network. The directive related in particular to the authorization procedure to be followed, the possible grounds for refusal and the arrangements for approving the tariffs charged. Gibraltar was initially excluded from the application of the directive, to its apparent detriment. Since the Government of Gibraltar is no an organ of a Member State, for the purposes of EC 230/TFEU 263, it had to be treated as a "natural or legal person." The latter does not have the right to challenge acts of the institutions unless they are of direct and individual concern. At the time, EC 230 also required that the act challenged be a "decision."]

15 . . . [T]he term "decision" used in Article 230 [263](2) of the Treaty has the technical meaning employed in Article 189 [288], and that the criterion for distinguishing between a measure of a legislative nature and a decision within the meaning of that latter article must be sought in the general "application" or otherwise of the measure in question.

16 It should also be noted that even though a directive is in principle binding only on the parties to whom it is addressed, namely the Member States, it is normally a form of indirect regulatory or legislative measure. Moreover, the Court has already had occasion to classify a directive as a measure of general application . . .

17 Furthermore, the Court has consistently held that the general application, and thus the legislative nature, of a measure is not called in question by the fact that it is possible to determine more or less precisely the number or even the identity of the persons to whom it applies at any give time, as long as it is established that such application takes effect by virtue of an objective legal or factual situation defined by the measure in question in relation to its purpose . . .

18 Lastly, the Court has already recognized that, where an instrument contains limitations or derogations which are temporary . . . they form an integral part of the provisions as a whole within they are found and, in the absence of any misuse of powers, are of the same general nature as those provisions.

19 In the present case, there is no dispute as to Directive 89/463 being of general application, save as regards Article 2(2), and the directive does indeed concern all scheduled inter-regional air services in the Community and it modifies the system for the authorization of such services by the Member States.

20 The provision under challenge suspends the application of that new system to services to or from Gibraltar until the arrangements in the Joint Declaration made by the Foreign Ministers of Spain and the United Kingdom on 2 December 1987 comes into operation. It thus affects equally all air carriers wishing to operate a direct inter-regional air service between another Community airport and Gibraltar airport and, more generally, all those using the latter airport. It therefore applies to objectively defined situations.

21 Furthermore, it should be noted that Gibraltar airport is not the only airport to have been temporarily excluded from the territorial scope of the directive. Other airports (those in the Greek islands and in the Atlantic islands comprising the autonomous region of the Azores, as well as Oporto airport) have already been temporarily exempted from its application, by virtue of Directive 83/416 of 25 July 1983 and Directive 86/216 of 26 May 1986, cited above, for technical or economic reasons, such as the insufficiency of air traffic or the continuing development of the airport infrastructure.

22 Directive 89/463 justifies the suspension of its application to Gibraltar airport by reference to the agreement in the Joint Declaration made by the Foreign Ministers of Spain and the United Kingdom on 2 December 1987. This constitutes a finding that there is an obstacle of an objective nature to implementation of its directive,

having regard to its aims. In view of the differences between Spain and the United Kingdom, discussed at length by the applicant itself, concerning sovereignty over the territory on which Gibraltar airport is situated and the operational problems resulting from those differences, the development of air services between that airport and the other airports within the Community is conditional on the implementation of the co-operation arrangements agreed between those two States.

23 In those circumstances, Article 2(2) of Directive 89/463 cannot be regarded as constituting a decision within the meaning of Article 173 [263] (2) but on the contrary is of the same general nature as that directive.

24 It follows that the application is inadmissible and must therefore be dismissed, without there being any need to consider the other submissions made in support of the objection of inadmissibility.

## NOTES AND QUESTIONS

1. The plaintiff in this case was seeking to argue that a provision in a directive that addressed its particular situation specifically constituted a decision. Why?

2. The applicant's argument that a specific provision of a directive could be treated as a decision was firmly rejected by the Court. This does not rule out the possibility however that a whole directive could be a disguised decision. The General Court has contemplated such a possibility. See *Union Européenne de l'artisanat et des petites et moyennes entreprises v. Council* Case T-135/96, 1998 ECJ CELEX LEXIS 144, [1998] ECR II-2335.

3. There have been other cases involving the issue of the status of Gibraltar, which remains a colony of the United Kingdom with a certain degree of internal autonomy. Spain has been particularly concerned about moves toward democracy and independence for Gibraltarians since this would undermine its long-running attempt to recover the territory. See in particular the ECHR Court's judgment in the *Matthews* case set out in chapter 17. By contrast with Gibraltar, there are territories within the EU that have an independent status: Andorra (Spain), Monaco (France), the Vatican and San Marino (Italy). The Channel Islands and the Isle of Man are represented by the United Kingdom but have a great deal of internal autonomy and only certain provisions of the Treaties apply to them by virtue of the UK Act of Accession. Many other small territories scattered around the world are also either in principle fully a part of the EU, as for example the French metropolitan territories in the Caribbean, South America and the Indian Ocean, the Portuguese territory of the Azores, and the Spanish islands of Madeira and the Canary Islands or, at the other extreme, excluded altogether from the scope of EU Territory (as for example the Faroe Islands and the Danish territory of Greenland (Greenland had originally been included but Denmark agreed to its withdrawal after a referendum). See generally, EC 299/TFEU 349 and 355.

## § 5.03 REGULATIONS

### [A]   The Nature of Direct Applicability

### AMSTERDAM BULB BV v. PRODUKTSCHAP VOOR SIERGEWASSEN

Case 50-76, 1977 ECJ EUR-Lex LEXIS 75, [1977] ECR 00137

[The Dutch Government had authorized regulations concerning minimum export prices for plant bulbs. In part, these regulations reflected regulations adopted by the Council in the context of the common organization of the market in bulbs.]

3 In addition to the provisions which are identical to those contained in the Community regulations the national rules contain [other] provisions . . .

4 . . . [T]he direct application of a Community regulation means that its entry into force and its application in favour of or against those subject to it are independent of any measure of reception into national law.

5 By virtue of the obligations arising from the Treaty the Member States are under a duty not to obstruct the direct effect inherent in regulations and other rules of Community law.

6 Strict compliance with this obligation is an indispensable condition of simultaneous and uniform application of Community regulations throughout the Community.

7 Therefore, the Member States may neither adopt nor allow national organizations having legislative power to adopt any measure which would conceal the Community nature and effects of any legal provision from the persons to whom it applies.

### NOTES AND QUESTIONS

Does the above judgment indicate that Member States may not introduce national legislation that repeats Union regulations even if it is identical to the Union law? If so, why is this so important?

### [B]   Regulations as Normative Acts (i.e., Distinguished From Decision)

### CONFEDERATION NATIONALE DES PRODUCTEURS DE FRUITS ET LEGUMES v. COUNCIL

Joined Cases16 & 17/62, [1962] ECR 471

[The applicant sought to annul Council Regulation 23, in particular article 9.]

I — as to admissibility

1. Under the terms of the second paragraph of article 173 [263] of the EEC Treaty, any natural or legal person may institute proceedings against an act of the

commission or the council only if that act constitutes either a decision addressed to that person or a decision which, although in the form of a regulation or a decision addressed to another person, is of direct and individual concern to the former. It follows that such a person is not entitled to make an application for annulment of regulations adopted by the Council or the Commission.

The Court admits that the system thus established by the Treaties of Rome lays down more restrictive conditions than does the ECSC Treaty for the admissibility of applications for annulment by private individuals. However, it would not be appropriate for the court to pronounce on the merits of this system which appears clearly from the text under examination.

The court is unable in particular to adopt the interpretation suggested by one of the applicants during the oral procedure, according to which the term 'decision', as used in the second paragraph of article 173 [263], could also cover regulations. Such a wide interpretation conflicts with the fact that article 189 [288] makes a clear distinction between the concept of a 'decision' and that of a 'regulation'. It is inconceivable that the term 'decision' would be used in article 173 [263] in a different sense from the technical sense as defined in article 189 [288]. It follows from the foregoing considerations that the present applications should be dismissed as inadmissible if the measure in dispute constitutes a regulation.

In examining this question, the Court cannot restrict itself to considering the official title of the measure, but must first take into account its object and content.

2. Under the terms of article 189 [288] of the EEC Treaty, a regulation shall have general application and shall be directly applicable in all Member States, whereas a decision shall be binding only upon those to whom it is addressed. The criterion for the distinction must be sought in the general 'application' or otherwise of the measure in question.

The essential characteristics of a decision arise from the limitation of the persons to whom it is addressed, whereas a regulation, being essentially of a legislative nature, is applicable not to a limited number of persons, defined or identifiable, but to categories of persons viewed abstractly and in their entirety. Consequently, in order to determine in doubtful cases whether one is concerned with a decision or a regulation, it is necessary to ascertain whether the measure in question is of individual concern to specific individuals.

In these circumstances, if a measure entitled by its author a regulation contains provisions which are capable of being not only of direct but also of individual concern to certain natural or legal persons, it must be admitted, without prejudice to the question whether that measure considered in its entirety can be correctly called a regulation, that in any case those provisions do not have the character of a regulation and may therefore be impugned by those persons under the terms of the second paragraph of article 173 [263].

3. In this case the measure in dispute was entitled by its author a 'regulation'.

However, the applicants maintain that the disputed provision is in fact 'a decision in the form of a regulation'. It is possible without doubt for a decision also to have a very wide field of application. However, a measure which is applicable to objectively determined situations and which involves immediate legal consequences in all Member States for categories of persons viewed in a general and abstract manner cannot be considered as constituting a decision, unless it can be proved that it is of individual concern to certain persons within the meaning of the second paragraph of article 173 [263].

In this particular case, the disputed provision involves immediate legal consequences in all Member States for categories of persons viewed in a general and abstract manner. In fact, article 9 of the measure in dispute — the provision particularly at issue in the present dispute — abolishes, for certain products and subject to certain time limits, quantitative restrictions on imports and measures having equivalent effect. It involves in addition the requirement that Member States shall dispense with recourse to the provisions of article 44 [deleted] of the Treaty, in particular with regard to the right temporarily to suspend or reduce imports. Consequently, the said article eliminates the restrictions on the freedom of traders to export or import within the Community.

## COMAFRICA SPA AND DOLE FRESH FRUIT EUROPE LTD & CO. v. COMMISSION
### Case T-139/01, 2005 ECJ CELEX LEXIS 37, [2005] ECR II-409

[At issue here were two regulations implementing a revised common organization of the market in bananas. The first attempt (in 1993) at such an organization had been challenged in the WTO by the USA and Ecuador and was the subject of much controversy over many years in the courts of the EU and the Member States. After the disputes were settled the EU in 1998 introduced a regime which would eventually be based on a "first come, first served" system of import licenses. However, there were to be transitional arrangements whereby import licenses would be allocated to "traditional operators" and "newcomers" for a period of time. Their entitlements would be determined by "reference quantities" supplied by the Member States and then adjusted if necessary by the Commission using a co-efficient. The applicants, traditional operators, challenged the implementing Commission regulations, 896/2001 and 1121/2001. Regulation 896 laid down a general procedure for allocating quotas, while Regulation 1121 provided for certain adjustments to quotas after applications had been received.]

97. . . . . [T]he applicants dispute the legislative nature of Regulation No 1121/2001 . . .

98. First, they insist that that regulation only applies to a fixed and closed class of legal persons to which they belong.

99. It is true that Regulation No 1121/2001 in fact applies only to operators who submitted a written application to the relevant national authorities in the past, that is, by 11 May 2001 at the latest; any application made after that date cannot be taken into account. Moreover, Regulation No 1121/2001 applies only to operators who satisfy a number of procedural and substantive conditions.

100. However, it is settled case-law that the general scope of a measure is not called in question by the fact that it is possible to determine the number or even the identity of the persons to whom it applies at a given moment with a greater or lesser

degree of precision as long as it is established that it is applied by virtue of an objective legal or factual situation defined by the measure in relation to the objective of the latter . . .

101. That is indeed the case here. Regulation No 1121/2001 seeks in general terms to ensure the proper implementation of the rules for the management of the tariff quota regime set up by Regulation No 896/2001. That regime is based on a division of the tariff quotas between two categories of operator, namely traditional and non-traditional operators and on separate management rules for A and B tariff quotas, on the one hand, and for the C tariff quota on the other. The purpose of Regulation No 1121/2001 is to make an overall adjustment of the reference quantities sought by the traditional operators A/B and by the traditional operator C to the available quantities of the A/B and C tariff quotas. Thus, in respect of traditional operators A/B, Article 1(1) of that regulation sets an adjustment coefficient of 1.07883 to be applied to their individual reference quantity because the sum of the reference quantities applied for under Article 4(1) of Regulation No 896/2001 turned out to be lower than the available quantities of the tariff quotas.

\*     \*     \*

105. As already stated at paragraph 101 above, Regulation No 1121/2001 was adopted in the light, not of the specific situation of traditional operators A/B, but of an objective factual situation, namely the fact that the sum of the reference quantities notified globally to the Commission by the Member States pursuant to Article 5(1) of Regulation No 896/2001 was less than the available amount of the tariff quotas . . .

106. It must be concluded from the foregoing that the contested regulations are legislative in nature and of general application.

## NOTES AND QUESTIONS

1.    How has the Court distinguished between regulations and decisions? Are the *Comafrica* and *Confédération* decisions consistent?

2.    In *ComAfrica*, do you think the Court was correct to treat Regulation 1121/2001 as a regulation? Despite the language changes between EC 230 and TFEU 263 (Template 5.1.4), does *ComAfrica* suggest that it remains necessary or relevant to determine whether an act is really a regulation or, on the contrary, is a bundle of individual decisions?

3.    The common organization of the market in bananas was originally set up by regulation 404/93. It did away with the previous national market structures where, in some cases, imports to certain Member States had largely derived from the ACP countries that had previously been their colonies. The common organization set up import tariffs and quotas that were intended to protect ACP production. The structure was particularly damaging to German importers and many challenges were brought within the German court system, leading to one case where the Tax Court was prepared to ignore the EU legislation on the grounds that it violated German Fundamental Rights. These arrangements were challenged in the WTO by the USA and Ecuador. In 1997, the WTO panel and subsequently the appeals body

upheld these complaints, particularly those to the effect that the EU system of import licences and compensation for losses caused by natural disasters was incompatible with WTO rules. The system was then reformed in 1998 and again in 2001, with the latest round of changes coming into effect on January 1 2007 whereby a tariff only system replaced the previous quota/tariff system.

The applicants had also challenged the earlier legislation and the CFI/General Court had found the measures in that instance to be disguised decisions. The determination was overturned on appeal to the ECJ: *France v. Comafrica SPA and Dole Fresh Fruit Europe Ltd & Co* Case C-73/97P, 1999 ECJ CELEX LEXIS 237, [1999] ECR I-185.

## § 5.04 DECISIONS

### [A] Direct Effect of Decisions Addressed to Member States

### GRAD v. FINANZAMT TRAUNSTEIN
Case 9/70, [1970] ECR 825

[The German Court (Finanzgericht) had asked whether Article 4 of Council Decision of 13 May 1965, addressed to Germany, on the harmonization of certain provisions affecting competition in transport by rail, road and inland waterway (OJ Special Edition 1965, p. 67) produced direct effects in the legal relationships between the Member States and those subject to their jurisdiction in such a way that these provisions create invocable rights.]

3 The question concerns the combined effect of provisions contained in a decision and a directive. According to Article 189 [288] of the EEC Treaty a decision is binding in its entirety upon those to whom it is addressed. Furthermore, according to this article a directive is binding, as to the result to be achieved, upon each Member State to which it is addressed, but leaves to the national authorities the choice of form and methods.

4 The German Government in its observations defends the view that by distinguishing between the effects of regulations on the one hand and of decisions and directives on the other, Article 189 [288] precludes the possibility of decisions and directives producing the effects mentioned in the question, which are reserved to regulations.

5 However, although it is true that by virtue of Article 189 [288], regulations are directly applicable and therefore by virtue of their nature capable of producing direct effects, it does not follow from this that other categories of legal measures mentioned in that article can never produce similar effects. In particular, the provision according to which decisions are binding in their entirety on those to whom they are addressed enables the question to be put whether the obligation created by the decision can only be invoked by the Community institutions against the addressee or whether such a right may possibly be exercised by all those who have an interest in the fulfillment of this obligation. It would be incompatible with the binding effect attributed to decisions by Article 189 [288] to exclude in principle the possibility that persons affected may invoke the obligation imposed by a

decision. Particularly in cases where, for example, the Community authorities by means of a decision have imposed an obligation on a Member State or all the Member States to act in a certain way, the effectiveness ("l'effet utile") of such a measure would be weakened if the nationals of that State could not invoke it in the courts and the national courts could not take it into consideration as part of Community law. Although the effects of a decision may not be identical with those of a provision contained in a regulation, this difference does not exclude the possibility that the end result, namely the right of the individual to invoke the measure before the courts, may be the same as that of a directly applicable provision of a regulation.

6 Article 177 [267], whereby the national courts are empowered to refer to the Court all questions regarding the validity and interpretation of all acts of the institutions without distinction, also implies that individuals may invoke such acts before the national courts. Therefore, in each particular case, it must be ascertained whether the nature, background and wording of the provision in question are capable of producing direct effects in the legal relationships between the addressee of the act and third parties.

7 The Council Decision of 13 May 1965 addressed to all the Member States is based in particular on Article 75 [91] of the Treaty which empowers the Council to lay down 'common rules', 'the conditions under which non-resident carriers may operate' and 'any other appropriate provision' to implement a common transport policy. The Council therefore has extensive freedom in the choice of the measures to adopt. The decision in question, taken as a whole, lays down the objectives to be achieved within the context of a policy of harmonizing national provisions and the timetable for their realization. In view of these objectives the first paragraph of Article 4 of the decision provides that once a common system of turnover tax has been adopted by the Council and brought into force in the Member States, the latter shall apply that system, in a manner to be determined, to the carriage of goods by rail, road and inland waterway. The second paragraph of that article provides that this common system of turnover tax shall, in so far as the carriage of goods by road, by rail and by inland waterway is subject to specific taxes instead of to the turnover tax, replace such specific taxes.

8 Thus this provision imposes two obligations on the Member States: first, to apply the common system of turnover tax to the carriage of goods by rail, road and inland waterway by a given date, and secondly to replace the specific taxes referred to by the second paragraph by this system no later than the date when it has been brought into force. This second obligation obviously implies a prohibition on introducing or reintroducing such taxes so as to prevent the common system of turnover tax from applying concurrently in the field of transport with additional tax systems of the like nature.

9 It is apparent from the file submitted by the Finanzgericht that the question relates in particular to the second obligation. The second obligation is by its nature mandatory and general, although the provision leaves open the determination of the date on which it becomes effective. It thus expressly prohibits the Member States from applying the common system of turnover tax concurrently with specific taxes levied instead of turnover taxes. This obligation is unconditional and sufficiently

clear and precise to be capable of producing direct effects in the legal relationships between the Member States and those subject to their jurisdiction.

10 The date on which this obligation becomes effective was laid down by the Council Directives on the harmonization of the legislation concerning turnover taxes which fixed the latest date by which the Member States must introduce into their legislation the common system of value-added tax. The fact that this date was fixed by a directive does not deprive this provision of any of its binding force. Thus the obligation created by the second paragraph of Article 4 of the Decision of 13 May 1965 was perfected by the First Directive. Therefore this provision imposes on the Member States obligations — in particular the obligation not to apply as from a certain date the common system of value-added tax concurrently with the specific taxes mentioned — which are capable of producing direct effects in the legal relationships between the Member States and those subject to their jurisdiction and of creating the right for the latter to invoke these obligations before the courts.

## NOTES AND QUESTIONS

1.  *Grad* raises the general question of the extent to which decisions may be enforceable against the addressee by affected third parties. What were the particular characteristics of this Decision that made it invocable against a Member State?

2.  Given the normative effect of a decision addressed to all Member States, is it possible to argue that such an act is not a "decision" in the same sense as one addressed to a particular State or individual? Could it be viewed as a disguised regulation? What would be the consequence of such a determination, specifically as to horizontal effects?

## [B]  Other Executive Acts Having Legal Effects

### AIR FRANCE v. COMMISSION
Case T-3/93, 1994 ECJ CELEX LEXIS 183, [1994] ECR II-121

[Under the EU "Merger Regulation" mergers, acquisitions and other business combinations must be approved by the Commission before they are put into effect if they have a "Community dimension", which depends on the size and location of the parties' revenues. British Airways had agreed to acquire another UK air carrier, Dan Air, but had not notified the transaction to the Commission under the Merger Regulation because it was not considered to be of a "Community dimension" (for further references to merger control and the new Merger Regulation — Regulation 139/2004 — see further Chapters 7 and 11). A statement by the spokesman for Sir Leon Brittan, the Commissioner responsible for competition matters was reported in the following terms by the Europe press agency (Agence Europe):

> The proposed concentration between British Airways and Dan Air (disputed by interested third parties in Great Britain) is not considered of Community dimension as one of the quantitative thresholds fixed by the EC regulation on the prior control of mergers is not reached, stated a spokesman for the European Commission on Friday.

The regulation, according to which the Commission may authorise or impede a merger, stipulates in particular that 'the total turnover achieved individually in the Community by at least two of the companies concerned'should be greater than 250 M ecus per year. This amount is not achieved by the regional European airline Dan Air, either within the Community or at world level. The Commission cannot, therefore, intervene. In the name of subsidiarity, it is up to the British Mergers and Monopolies Commission (MMC) to take a position on the project. Sir Leon Brittan's spokesman stated that the Commission, in its preliminary calculations, did not take into account Dan Air charter flight business because, as a prerequisite for merger with the British number one in air transport, Dan Air (affiliate to the holding company Davis & Newman) should give up this line of business. The merger regulation clearly stipulates on this that 'only the turnover concerning the parties which are the object of the transaction are taken into consideration.

The merger agreement was submitted to the competent British authorities responsible for the control of concentrations, namely the Secretary of State for Trade and Industry who subsequently announced that the national authorities had decided not to block the merger. The Commission argued that its determination of non-Community dimension was not a "decision" as contemplated by EC 230/TFEU 263 but was merely a preliminary act. In its view a decision in the legal sense would only come about when the parties had filed a notification of the merger on the correct form (CO) thus enabling the Commission to evaluate it to see whether it was of Community dimension.

The CFI/General Court decision was not appealed]

43 The Court observes in limine that, according to the case-law of the Court of Justice, "in order to ascertain whether the measures in question are acts within the meaning of Article 173 [263] it is necessary . . . to look to their substance. . . . Any measure the legal effects of which are binding on, and capable of affecting the interests of, the applicant by bringing about a distinct change in his legal position is an act or decision which may be the subject of an action under Article 173 [263] for a declaration that it is void" . . .

44 In order to assess, in the light of that case-law, whether the statement in issue constitutes an act against which an action for annulment may be brought, it is necessary, therefore, to examine the extent to which the statement produces legal effects. From that standpoint the Court considers that the contested statement produces legal effects in a number of respects.

45 The Court considers that the contested act produced, first, a series of legal effects with regard to Member States. Having regard to its general scheme, the application of the Regulation in principle precludes the application of any other rules, in particular national laws which also have as their object the review of transactions involving concentrations between undertakings and which in the event of the Regulation being inapplicable in principle apply to such transactions. Which national laws are potentially applicable to a given transaction depends on the location of the undertakings which are parties to the transaction and of the markets

and activities to which it relates. In the present case, the effect of the statement by the Commissioner responsible for competition matters, by which he publicly declared the Regulation to be inapplicable to the transaction in issue, was to confirm beyond all doubt the competence of the Member States whose territory was more particularly concerned having regard to the location of the undertakings which were parties to the transaction and the air services involved, namely the United Kingdom and the French Republic, to appraise the concentration in the light of their own national laws relating to the review of such concentrations. Moreover, one of the aforesaid Member States did in fact examine the transaction under its national law. The United Kingdom, which has intervened in support of the form of order sought by the defendant, itself contends that the present action is admissible, correctly pointing out that the statement of the Secretary of State dated 2 November 1992 was made possible by the contested statement of 30 October 1992 publicly declaring the Regulation to be inapplicable to the transaction.

46 Furthermore, the contested act produced effects in relation to any Member State whose territory is affected, directly or indirectly, by the transaction. Once the Commission has publicly declared, as in the present case, that a given concentration does not have a Community dimension, that removes any uncertainty as to the fulfilment of the conditions governing the application, by one or more Member States, of Article 22(3) of the Regulation. The Court notes that, here again, the provisions in question have, for the first time since the Regulation came into force, actually been applied by a Member State, in this instance the Kingdom of Belgium. Moreover, as the applicant has pointed out, the request made by the Kingdom of Belgium was in fact submitted within the time-limit of one month from the date of the contested statement, as laid down by the said provisions.

47 Next, the Court considers that the contested act also produced legal effects with regard to the undertakings which were parties to the concentration. As is confirmed, moreover, by the letters sent to the applicant by the Commissioner responsible for competition matters before the present action was brought, the effect of such a statement was to absolve the undertakings involved in the transaction from the obligation to notify it to the Commission pursuant to Article 4(1) of the Regulation. It should in particular be noted that, since by virtue of Article 7(1) of the Regulation the notification of a concentration with a Community dimension has in principle suspensory effect, a public announcement to the undertakings involved in a transaction that they do not have to notify it is tantamount, from the standpoint of the Community law on concentrations, to permitting its immediate completion. It follows that, under Community law, the effect of the contested statement was to make it possible for BA to proceed forthwith with the acquisition of Dan Air.

48 Furthermore, the applicant is correct in its assertion that, in the circumstances of this case, the defendant institution is bound by the terms of the contested statement. Having regard to the difficulty of reversing an operation such as the one at issue in this case, such an operation cannot be satisfactorily completed in a situation in which the undertakings concerned are faced with legal uncertainty.

\*     \*     \*

51 The Court considers, therefore, that the effects of the contested statement are

exactly the same, for the undertakings which were parties to the proposed transaction, as would be the effects of a Commission decision, issued after the transaction had been notified and duly brought before it, in which it found that the transaction did not have a "Community dimension" for the purposes of Article 6(1)(a) of the Regulation. For Member States and third parties, particularly direct competitors of the undertakings which were parties to the transaction, the effects are at least the same as those resulting from a formal decision by the Commission, likewise adopted pursuant to that provision of the Regulation. It is not contested that such a decision would be capable of forming the subject-matter of an action for annulment before the Court.

52 Consequently, the Commission's argument that it could find that a transaction did not have a "Community dimension" only in the circumstances laid down in Article 6(1)(a) of the Regulation, that is to say following notification of the transaction, cannot be upheld. The legal effects of the contested statement are thus adequately established at this stage in the Court's reasoning, whether the effects are those produced in relation to the undertakings directly involved in the concentration, Member States or third parties.

53 Moreover, the Court considers to be unfounded the Commission's contention that, in order for the contested statement to be accepted as being a decision, the Commission would have to be regarded as having acted "on its own initiative". The Court considers that acceptance that the contested statement embodies an action-able decision amounts to no more than recognition of the fact that the Commission, acting on the basis of the opinion expressed by the MTF in response to the request made to it by BA, publicly stated that the Regulation was not applicable to the transaction in question. Since the Regulation, whose application cannot depend merely upon the wishes of the parties, empowers the Commission to examine certain concentrations, the Court considers that, contrary to the Commission's contentions, the latter must necessarily have the power to verify its own competence in relation to a given transaction, regardless of whether that transaction was notified, and to find, as in the present case, that the Regulation is not applicable to a given transaction.

54 It follows that the first part of the objection of inadmissibility raised by the Commission must be rejected.

The form of the act

55 According to the Commission, a further reason why the contested act is not in the nature of a decision is its form; it is not addressed to any person identified by name and does not represent the communication of a decision adopted by it, but simply expresses an opinion on the interpretation of the Regulation. Moreover, given that it was made orally, the communication, which was intended for the general public, was not such as to be the subject of notification under Article 191 [297] of the EEC Treaty. Furthermore, the applicant was unable — and for obvious reasons — to produce the alleged decision by the Commission as an annex to its application, contrary to the provisions of Article 19 of the Protocol on the Statute of the Court of Justice of the EEC.

\*     \*     \*

57 The Court observes in limine that, as is apparent from the case-law of the Court of Justice, "the choice of form cannot change the nature of the measure" . . . and "the form in which such acts or decisions are cast is, in principle, immaterial as regards the question whether they are open to challenge under (Article 173 [263])" . . . It is in the light of that case-law that the merits of the second part of the objection of inadmissibility raised by the defendant must be examined.

58 The Court notes that the contested act is in an unusual form, inasmuch as, first, it is apparent from the inquiry into the case, and in particular from the Commission's answers to the written questions put by the Court, that no written document exists apart from the transcription published by certain press agencies such as Agence Europe, and secondly, the very wide publicity given to the statement tends, by its very form, to assimilate it to an act of general application rather than a decision of an individual nature. However, as regards the fact that the act is not in written form, it has been consistently held, for example in the cases previously cited (see paragraph 43 above), that the right to bring proceedings takes into account, first of all, the contents of the act and whether it produces legal effects which affect the applicant personally. Furthermore, the Court of Justice has previously held to be admissible actions brought against acts which take an unusual form, such as a purely verbal decision . . . In the present case, the terms of the statement, far from being contested by the institution, were on the contrary amply confirmed by it both in the course of the correspondence which took place prior to the bringing of this action and in the course of these proceedings. As regards the nature of the publicity given to the act, it should be noted that this was independent of the act itself, has no bearing on its legality and affects only the date from which the time allowed for bringing an action against it starts to run.

59 Consequently, the Court considers that it must reject both the argument that the applicant has been unable to annex to its application a copy of the contested statement and the argument that the contested statement, not having been properly notified to the undertakings involved in the concentration, has not yet started to produce effects since, as already stated, for the purposes of determining this dispute, the contested statement certainly produced effects on third parties.

## NOTES AND QUESTIONS

1. In *BASF and Others v. Commission (PVC decision)*, Joined Cases T-79/89, T-84/89, T-85/89, T-86/89, T-89/89, T-91/89, T-92/89, T-94/89, T-96/89, T-98/89, T-102/89 and T-104/89, 1992 ECJ CELEX LEXIS 27, [1992] ECR II-315, the Commission, acting as a collegiate body, had adopted a decision finding infringement of EC 81/TFEU 101 on the basis of the full English, French and German texts — the three "working languages" for that particular investigation. However, a Dutch and an Italian company were also involved. The draft decision was formally presented to the Commission for decision without the versions drafted in the latter two languages The Commission approved the draft proposed Decision based on the first three languages and the Commissioner for Competition was delegated formally to "adopt" the other language versions. The CFI/General Court concluded that there had been such a serious breach of the rules requiring collegiate adoption of the

decision that it must be declared "inexistent". The ECJ overruled that decision on appeal but still annulled the Decision. How can one reconcile the CFI/General Court's and ECJ's judgments, requiring as they did the utmost compliance with formalities, with the conclusion of the court in the *Air France* case that a mere press release could constitute notice of an act that appeared to be a de facto decision?

**2.** In *Infront WM AG v. Commission*, Case T-33/01, 2005 ECJ CELEX LEXIS 691, [2005] ECR II-5897, Directive 89/552 as amended provided the legal framework for television broadcasting in the common market. Its primary objective was to facilitate the free movement of television broadcasts within the EU by laying down minimum rules with which the Member States were required to ensure that television broadcasters under their jurisdiction comply. Article 3a of the directive provided that:

> 1. Each Member State may take measures in accordance with Community law to ensure that broadcasters under its jurisdiction do not broadcast on an exclusive basis events which are regarded by that Member State as being of major importance for society in such a way as to deprive a substantial proportion of the public in that Member State of the possibility of following such events via live coverage or deferred coverage on free television. If it does so, the Member State concerned shall draw up a list of designated events, national or non-national, which it considers to be of major importance for society. It shall do so in a clear and transparent manner in due and effective time. In so doing the Member State concerned shall also determine whether these events should be available via whole or partial live coverage, or where necessary or appropriate for objective reasons in the public interest, whole or partial deferred coverage.

> 2. Member States shall immediately notify to the Commission any measures taken or to be taken pursuant to paragraph 1. Within a period of three months from the notification, the Commission shall verify that such measures are compatible with Community law and communicate them to the other Member States. It shall seek the opinion of the Committee established pursuant to Article 23a. It shall forthwith publish the measures taken in the Official Journal and at least once a year the consolidated list of the measures taken by Member States.

> 3. Member States shall ensure, by appropriate means, within the framework of their legislation that broadcasters under their jurisdiction do not exercise the exclusive rights purchased by those broadcasters following the date of publication of this Directive in such a way that a substantial proportion of the public in another Member State is deprived of the possibility of following events which are designated by that other Member State in accordance with the preceding paragraphs via whole or partial live coverage or, where necessary or appropriate for objective reasons in the public interest, whole or partial deferred coverage on free television as determined by that other Member State in accordance with paragraph 1.

Infront WM AG was involved in the acquisition, management and marketing of television broadcasting rights for sporting events and typically purchased such rights from the organiser of the sporting event concerned. It then sold the rights acquired in this way to broadcasters.

Through a series of transactions, Infront contracted with the Fédération Internationale de Football Association (FIFA) to acquire the worldwide (excluding the USA) exclusive broadcasting rights to the final-stage matches ("the finals") of the 2002 and 2006 FIFA World Cup.

As required by Article 3a(2) of the directive, the United Kingdom notified the Commission on 25 September 1998 of the measures taken pursuant to Article 3a(1). Those measures included the list of events of major importance for society designated by that Member State. After some back and forth, the Commission eventually indicated that it did not intend to object to the UK measures.

Infront objected that the list drawn up by the United Kingdom could not be approved because it was incompatible with both Article 3a of the directive and other provisions of EU law. It alleged inter alia in that letter that the list in question was not drawn up pursuant to a clear and transparent procedure, that it included events that were not of major importance for United Kingdom society and that the national and EU consultation procedures were marred by serious deficiencies, and it criticized the retroactive nature of the relevant legislation.

After failing to convince the Commission to change its mind, a proceeding was started with the intention of having the Commission's non-objection annulled. The Commission argued *inter alia* that its action was not a "decision" and therefore could not be challenged by the applicant under EC 230/TFEU 263. The CFI/General Court, consistent with other cases, ruled that any act of an EU institution that changes the legal position of a person or Member State is a legally binding act that permits it to be reviewed by the EU courts. In this case, the conclusions communicated by the Commission to the UK had the effect of validating the UK's list, thus triggering a binding mutual recognition mechanism requiring the other Member States to ensure that broadcasters under their jurisdiction did not circumvent the measures adopted by the United Kingdom. EC 249/TFEU 288 only mentions certain specific instruments, so one might conclude that all "other acts" must be "decisions" — as the CFI/General Court did here. (While the Commission's letter was found to be a "decision" the plaintiff still had to demonstrate that it was of direct and individual concern to it, because it was addressed to another person (the UK). This aspect of the case is dealt with in Chapter 8. The case was unsuccessfully appealed by the Commission: *Commission v. Infront WM AG*, Case C-125/06 P. 2008 ECJ EUR-Lex LEXIS 2345, 2008 ECR I-1451.)

**3.** As the *Air France* case demonstrates, it does not necessarily follow that merely because an act of the EU bears a label other than a decision, directive, or regulation, it has no binding effect or is immune from challenge under TFEU 263. What test has the court applied in determining whether an act of the EU has a legal effect? In the Court's view, does this mean that such acts are "decisions"?

## [C]  "Non-existent" Acts

# CONSORZIO COOPERATIVE D'ABRUZZO v. COMMISSION
## Case 15/85, 1987 ECJ CELEX LEXIS 135, [1987] ECR 1005

[In three successive decisions, the Commission had granted, and then reduced, the amount of a grant of a contribution from the guidance section of the European Agricultural Guidance and Guarantee Fund (EAGGF) towards a project described as "construction of a regional centre for the processing of grape must and for the bottling of wine in the municipality of Frisa (Chieti)". The Consorzio sought *inter alia* the annulment of the third decision of 30 October 1984 reducing the grant. The Commission argued among other things that the second decision (of April 7, 1982) awarding the larger amount of the grant was non-existent due to internal mistakes that led to the adoption of the wrong draft.]

8 It must be emphasized at once that an error consisting in the adoption of a draft other than that which has passed through the various stages of the preparatory procedure cannot invalidate the measure adopted except in so far as it has resulted in objective irregularities. In this case, the only objective irregularities relied upon by the Commission are the infringement of the internal rules for establishing the maximum contribution available from the EAGGF and the fact that the Commission granted a contribution of a different amount from that on which the management committee had given a favourable opinion, without communicating the measure concerned to the council as required by article 22 (3) of Council Regulation No. 355/77.

9 It is necessary to consider whether those two irregularities, on the assumption that they are proven and that they both constitute legal defects, are, as the Commission maintains, such as to render the decision of 7 April 1982 non-existent. If they are not, and the decision of 7 April 1982 is merely vitiated by illegality, the decision of 31 October 1984 would have to be described as a decision withdrawing an earlier measure. It would then be necessary to ascertain whether such withdrawal was contrary to the principles of legal certainty and of the protection of legitimate expectations, which are relied upon by the Consorzio in its third submission.

10 With regard to the argument that the decision of 7 April 1982 is non-existent, it is necessary to point out that under Community law, as under the national laws of the various Member States, an administrative measure, even though it may be irregular, is presumed to be valid until it has been properly repealed or withdrawn by the institution which adopted it. If a measure is deemed to be non-existent, the finding may be made, even after the period for instituting proceedings has expired, that the measure has not produced any legal effects. For reasons of legal certainty which are evident, that classification must consequently be restricted under Community law, as under the national legal systems which provide for it, to measures which exhibit particularly serious and manifest defects.

11 Without there being any need even to consider the gravity of the two irregularities alleged by the Commission, it is sufficient to state that neither of them is manifest. Neither irregularity could be detected by reading the decision. The

internal rules for establishing the maximum contribution available from the EAGGF under Council Regulation No. 355/77 have not been published. Hence, apart from the Commission officials responsible for the proper application of those rules, no one was in a position to ascertain by reading the Decision of 7 April 1982 whether or not those rules had been infringed. The same holds true for the irregularity consisting in the discrepancy between the draft decision submitted to the management committee and the decision adopted on 7 April 1982. Accordingly, the Decision of 7 April 1982 cannot be classified as non-existent.

[The Court proceeded to annul the third decision on the grounds that the principle of legitimate expectations had been breached.]

## NOTES AND QUESTIONS

1. What is the legal consequence of finding that an act is nonexistent?

2. Given the Court's analysis in this case, how would you define the circumstances in which an act would be considered nonexistent? Note also the *BASF* case mentioned in the notes to the *Air France* case, *supra*.

3. In *Société des Usines à tubes de la Sarre v. High Authority*, Joined Cases 1 and 14/57, [1957 and 1958] ECR 105, the dispatch of a letter out of time was held not to nullify the character of the "opinion" that it contained.

4. In *Commission v. Greece*, Case 226/87, 1988 ECJ CELEX LEXIS 412, [1988] ECR 3611, the Commission sought a declaration that Greece was in breach of the EC Treaty by failing to take within the prescribed time-limit the measures necessary to comply with Commission Decision 85/276 of 24 April 1985 concerning the insurance in Greece of public property and loans granted by Greek State-owned banks. Greece argued that Decision 85/276 was unlawful as it infringed the fundamental principle of the division of powers between the EU and the Member States and therefore lacked "any legal basis in the Community legal order." The Court stated:

> . . . [T]hat objection could be upheld only if the measure at issue contained such particularly serious and manifest defects that it could be deemed non-existent . . . . However, the arguments put forward by the Hellenic Republic contain no precise factor of such a kind as to permit the Commission's decision to be so described. Indeed, it itself considered that the decision of 24 April 1985 was not non-existent when it stated, throughout the pre-litigation stage, that it intended to comply with that decision.

5. There seems to be more than one type of application of the putative concept of "non-existent". In *Conzorzio*, the argument was invoked to avoid judicial review. Arguably in the *Greece* case above, and certainly in a later decision, *People's Mojahedin Organization of Iran v. Council*, Case T-256/07, 2008 ECJ EUR-Lex LEXIS 1959, [2008] ECR II-1951, a finding of nonexistence actually depended on a Court ruling that the act was an egregious violation of law. This is something of a puzzle: a nonexistent act could not be challenged under TFEU 267 because it is not an act. But to establish that, one first has to be able to bring an annulment action,

thus assuming that there is an act to be challenged.

## [D] Procedural Acts Preceding a Decision

## INTERNATIONAL BUSINESS MACHINES CORPORATION v. COMMISSION
### Case 60/81, [1981] ECR 2639

[A letter, signed by the Commission's Director General for Competition, was sent to IBM informing IBM that the Commission had initiated against the company a procedure under Article 3 of (former) Regulation No. 17, which was the original act implementing EEC articles 85 and 86 (EC 81 and 82/TFEU 101 and 102 regarding the enforcement of rules prohibiting anti-competitive, or antitrust, conduct. Together with the letter IBM received a statement of objections. The Director General for Competition requested the company to reply in writing within a specified period and stated that it would be given an opportunity later to explain its point of view orally in the course of a hearing. Although Regulation 17 has been repealed and replaced by Regulation 1/2003, the provisions regarding the initiation of proceedings by the Commission are in relevant respects unchanged.]

3 IBM took the view that the measures of which it had been notified in the letter of 19 December 1980 were vitiated by a number of defects and requested the Commission to withdraw the statement of objections and terminate the procedure. The Commission refused to do so and IBM then brought the present action for a declaration that the measures in question were void.

4 IBM's action is based on the submission that the measures which it challenges do not meet the minimum legal criteria which have been laid down for such measures, and that defects in the content of the statement of objections, the inadequacy of the time-limits laid down and the Commission's reservation of the right to raise further objections at a later date have made it impossible for IBM to raise a defence. In addition, IBM considers that the measures impugned amount to an unlawful exercise of its powers by the Commission inasmuch as they have not been the subject of a collegiate decision adopted by all the members of the Commission together although there has been no corresponding delegation of power and, in law, there could not be one, at least without due publication or notification. Finally, IBM maintains that the measures in question offend against the international legal principles of comity between nations and non-interference in internal affairs, principles which ought to have been taken into consideration by the Commission before it adopted the measures in question because the conduct of IBM which is the subject of complaint occurred in the main outside the Community, in particular in the United States of America where it is also the subject of legal proceedings.

\* \* \*

9 [A]ccording to the consistent case-law of the Court any measure the legal effects of which are binding on, and capable of affecting the interests of, the applicant by bringing about a distinct change in his legal position is an act or decision which may be the subject of an action under Article 173 EC [263] for a declaration that it is void. However, the form in which such acts or decisions are cast is, in principle,

immaterial as regards the question whether they are open to challenge under that article.

10 In the case of acts or decisions adopted by a procedure involving several stages, in particular where they are the culmination of an internal procedure, it is clear from the case-law that in principle an act is open to review only if it is a measure definitively laying down the position of the Commission or the Council on the conclusion of that procedure, and not a provisional measure intended to pave the way for the final decision.

11 It would be otherwise only if acts or decisions adopted in the course of the preparatory proceedings not only bore all the legal characteristics referred to above but in addition were themselves the culmination of a special procedure distinct from that intended to permit the Commission or the Council to take a decision on the substance of the case.

12 Furthermore, it must be noted that whilst measures of a purely preparatory character may not themselves be the subject of an application for a declaration that they are void, any legal defects therein may be relied upon in an action directed against the definitive act for which they represent a preparatory step.

13 The effects and the legal character of the initiation of an administrative procedure pursuant to the provisions of Regulation No. 17 and of the notification of objections as provided for in Article 2 of Regulation No. 99/63 must be determined in the light of the purpose of such acts in the context of the Commission's administrative procedure in matters of competition, detailed rules for which have been laid down in the above-mentioned regulations.

14 The procedure was designed to enable the undertakings concerned to communicate their views and to provide the Commission with the fullest information possible before it adopted a decision affecting the interests of an undertaking. Its purpose is to create procedural guarantees for the benefit of the latter and, as may be seen in the 11th recital in the preamble to Regulation No. 17, to ensure that the undertakings have the right to be heard by the Commission.

15 That is why in accordance with Article 19 (1) of Regulation No. 17 and in order to guarantee observance of the rights of the defence, it is necessary to ensure that the undertaking concerned has the right to submit its observations on conclusion of the inquiry on all the objections which the Commission intends to raise against it in its decision and, therefore, to inform it of those objections in the document which is provided for in Article 2 of Regulation No. 99/63. That is why, too, in order to remove any doubt as to the procedural position of the undertaking in question, initiation of the procedure under the above-mentioned provisions is clearly marked by an act manifesting the intention to take a decision.

16 In support of its submission that the application is admissible IBM relies on a number of effects arising from the initiation of a procedure and from communication of the statement of objections.

17 Some of those effects amount to no more than the ordinary effects of any procedural step and, apart from the procedural aspect, do not affect the legal position of the undertaking concerned. That is so, in particular, of the interruption

of the time-limit brought about both by the initiation of a procedure and by the communication of the statement of objections by virtue of Regulation (EEC) No. 2988/74 of the Council of 26 November 1974 concerning limitation periods in proceedings and the enforcement of sanctions under the rules of the European Economic Community relating to transport and competition . . . The same is true as regards the fact that the acts in question are necessary stages to be accomplished by the Commission pursuant to the provisions of Regulation No. 17 before it is able to impose a fine or a periodic penalty payment on the undertaking concerned, and the fact that the acts oblige the undertaking concerned to put up a defence in administrative proceedings.

18 Other effects relied on by IBM do not adversely affect the interests of the undertaking concerned. One such is the fact that initiation of a procedure under Article 9 (3) of Regulation No. 17 puts an end to the jurisdiction of the authorities in the Member States — a result which did not in fact occur in this instance as there were no national proceedings, and which essentially results in protecting the undertaking concerned from parallel proceedings brought by the authorities of the Member States. Another such effect is the fact that communication of the statement of objections is recognized as crystallizing the Commission's position, which means in effect that the Commission is prevented, pursuant to Article 4 of Regulation No. 99/63, from relying in its decision, in the absence of a fresh statement of objections, on the existence of any objections other than those on which the undertaking has been given an opportunity to make known its views, though it does not prevent the Commission from withdrawing its objections and thereby altering its standpoint in favour of the undertaking.

19 A statement of objections does not compel the undertaking concerned to alter or reconsider its marketing practices and it does not have the effect of depriving it of the protection hitherto available to it against the application of a fine, as is the case when the Commission informs an undertaking, pursuant to Article 15 (6) of Regulation No. 17, of the results of the preliminary examination of an agreement which has been notified by the undertaking. Whilst a statement of objections may have the effect of showing the undertaking in question that it is incurring a real risk of being fined by the Commission, that is merely a consequence of fact, and not a legal consequence which the statement of objections is intended to produce.

20 An application for a declaration that the initiation of a procedure and a statement of objections are void might make it necessary for the Court to arrive at a decision on questions on which the Commission has not yet had an opportunity to state its position and would as a result anticipate the arguments on the substance of the case, confusing different procedural stages both administrative and judicial. It would thus be incompatible with the system of the division of powers between the Commission and the Court and of the remedies laid down by the Treaty, as well as the requirements of the sound administration of justice and the proper course of the administrative procedure to be followed in the Commission.

21 It follows from the foregoing that neither the initiation of a procedure nor a statement of objections may be considered, on the basis of their nature and the legal effects they produce, as being decisions within the meaning of Article 173 EC [263] of the EEC Treaty which may be challenged in an action for a declaration that they

are void. In the context of the administrative procedure as laid down by Regulations No. 17 and No. 99/63, they are procedural measures adopted preparatory to the decision which represents their culmination.

22 In support of its submission that the application is admissible IBM relies further on the special circumstances of the case and on the nature and implications of the submissions which it puts forward on the substance of its case, claiming that a judicial review ought to be made available at an early stage in this case both in accordance with the principles of international law in such matters and pursuant to general principles flowing from the laws of the Member States. The present application is intended to establish that the administrative procedure was wholly unlawful from the beginning under the rules of Community law and international law, particularly those concerning the power to initiate such procedures. Any continuation of that administrative procedure is unlawful, it claims, and the fact that IBM may subsequently have the final decision declared void is not sufficient to give it effective legal protection.

23 It is not necessary for the purposes of this case to decide whether, in exceptional circumstances, where the measures concerned lack even the appearance of legality, a judicial review at an early stage such as that envisaged by IBM may be considered compatible with the system of remedies provided for in the Treaty, because the circumstances referred to by the applicant in this case are in any event not such as would make it possible to regard the action as admissible.

24 Moreover, in this instance adequate legal protection for IBM does not require that the measures in question be subject to immediate review. If, on the conclusion of the administrative procedure and after any observations which IBM may submit in the course of it have been examined, the Commission were to adopt a decision which affects IBM's interests, that decision will, in accordance with Article 173 EC [263] of the EEC Treaty, be subject to judicial review in the course of which it will be permissible for IBM to advance all the appropriate arguments. It will then be for the Court to decide whether anything unlawful has been done in the course of the administrative procedure and if so whether it is such as to affect the legality of the decision taken by the Commission on the conclusion of the administrative procedure.

## NOTES AND QUESTIONS

1. In light of the arguments of IBM and the Court's statements, is it possible that a "statement of objections" might in certain circumstances be open to review?

2. Plaintiffs have been frustrated on occasion when they have sought to bring actions under EC 230/TFEU 263 because the Court has found that there had in fact been a prior decision *not* to act, which should have been the subject of the challenge. The Court has shown flexibility in interpreting the time limit where it was not initially clear to the applicant that the Commission had reached a final decision, as for example where a decision was addressed to a Member State that failed to make clear to the applicant that a final decision had been reached: *Top Hit HolzVertrieb v. Commission*, Case 378/87, 1989 ECJ CELEX LEXIS 177, [1989] ECR 1359.

# REYNOLDS TOBACCO AND OTHERS v. COMMISSION
## Case C-131/03 P, 2006 ECJ CELEX LEXIS 442, [2006] ECR I-7795

[This was an appeal from the CFI [General Court]. The appellants asked the Court to set aside the judgment of the CFI/General Court in which it dismissed as inadmissible their applications for annulment of two decisions of the Commission adopting the principle of bringing a civil action against the appellants in the Eastern District of New York, relating to the attempt to suppress smuggling of cigarettes into the EU. The appellants made five points in their plea seeking to overturn a first instance judgment denying them standing.]

54 . . . [O]nly measures the legal effects of which are binding on, and capable of affecting the interests of, the applicant by bringing about a distinct change in his legal position are acts or decisions which may be the subject of an action for annulment . . .

55. Therefore . . . it is not only preparatory acts which fall outside the scope of the judicial review provided for in Article 230 EC [263] but any act not producing legal effects which are binding on and capable of affecting the interests of the individual, such as confirmatory measures and implementing . . .

56. Accordingly, the Court of First Instance did not err in law by inferring from the fact that the contested decisions did not produce binding legal effect for the purposes of Article 230 EC [263] that they could not be the subject of an action without restricting the scope of that approach to preparatory acts.

\*     \*     \*

58. . . . [A]lthough the commencement of proceedings constitutes an indispensable step for the purpose of obtaining a binding judgment it does not per se determine definitively the obligations of the parties to the case, so that, *a fortiori*, the decision to bring legal proceedings does not in itself alter the legal position in question.

59. The question whether the contested decisions are subject to review by the Community courts is irrelevant in that regard.

\*     \*     \*

61. . . [T]he commencement of legal proceedings before any court necessarily entails the application by the court of its own procedural rules, which cannot therefore be viewed as a legal effect, for the purposes of Article 230 EC [263], of the decision to bring an action.

62. It must be added that whether the Commission's contested decisions can be categorised as legal acts which are open to challenge for the purposes of the case-law set out in paragraph 54 of this judgment cannot be dependent on the fact that if the Commission had commenced legal proceedings before a court in a Member State a reference for a preliminary ruling under Article 234 EC would have been possible in the context of those proceedings.

\*     \*     \*

66. . . . [I]f, like any act of a Community institution, the contested decisions carry an incidental implication that the institution in question has adopted a position as to

its competence to adopt them, that adoption of a position cannot itself be viewed as a binding legal effect for the purposes of Article 230 EC [263], as interpreted in the case-law.

## NOTES AND QUESTIONS

Why was the Court so keen to establish that the decision to bring civil proceedings in the United States was not a "decision" in the EU legal sense? Do you think the reasoning withstands close scrutiny?

## [E]   Acts Relating to the Internal Organization of an Institution

### JEAN-CLAUDE MARTINEZ, CHARLES DE GAULLE, FRONT NATIONAL AND EMMA BONINO AND OTHERS v. PARLIAMENT
Joined Cases T-222/99, T-327/99 and T-329/99, 2001 ECJ CELEX LEXIS 468, [2001] ECR II-2823

[A group of European Parliament members from various political factions notified the President of the Parliament, pursuant to Rule 29(4), of the formation of the Technical Group of Independent Members — Mixed Group) (referred to in the case by the French initials, "the TDI Group"), the declared purpose of which was to ensure that all Members are able to exercise their parliamentary mandates in full. Essentially, while being independent members, they wished to enjoy the same privileges as politically aligned groups, such as allocation of speaking time. The presidents of the other political groups, taking the view that the condition relating to political affinities provided for in Rule 29(1) of the Parliament's Rules of Procedure was not satisfied in this case, requested that the question be referred to the Parliament's Committee on Constitutional Affairs for an interpretation of that provision and that the Members concerned be deemed to be non-attached pending a ruling from that Committee. The Commission determined that the TDI Group did not meet the conditions of the Rule and proposed adding an interpretative note which read as follows:

> The formation of a group which openly rejects any political character and all political affiliation between its Members is not acceptable within the meaning of this Rule.

The addition was approved by the Parliament in plenary session on September 14, 1999. The CFI/General Court first dismissed an argument that there had been no act that was capable of challenge, and then proceeded to examine whether it had jurisdiction to rule on a matter internal to the Parliament.

(The plaintiffs unsuccessfully appealed the decision of the CFI/General Court: Case C-488/01 P.2003 ECJ EUR-Lex LEXIS 1873, [2003] ECR I-13355).]

49 . . . [T]he first paragraph of Article 173 EC [263] provides that the Community judicature is to review the legality of acts of the Parliament intended to produce

legal effects in regard to third parties.

50 In the present case, the act of 14 September 1999 was adopted in plenary session by a majority of the Members of the Parliament. For the purposes of the examination as to admissibility, that act must be regarded as an act of the Parliament itself . . .

51 Next, it should be emphasised that for a claim for the annulment of an act of the Parliament to be admissible the first paragraph of Article 173 EC [263] requires, in the light of the case-law, that a distinction be drawn between two categories of acts.

52 Acts of the Parliament which relate only to the internal organisation of its work cannot be challenged in an action for annulment . . . That first class of measures includes acts of the Parliament which either do not have legal effects or have legal effects only within the Parliament as regards the organisation of its work and are subject to review procedures laid down in its Rules of Procedure . . .

53 The second class comprises acts of the Parliament which produce or are intended to produce legal effects in regard to third parties or, in other words, acts going beyond the internal organisation of the work of the institution. Those acts are open to challenge before the Community judicature . . . .).

54 The Parliament contends that the act of 14 September 1999 comes within the first category and cannot therefore be challenged in an action for annulment. The applicants maintain that it belongs to the second category, so that their actions for annulment must be declared admissible.

55 In that connection, it should be recalled that the present applications seek annulment of the act of 14 September 1999 whereby the Parliament decided to adopt the general interpretation of Rule 29(1) proposed by the Committee on Constitutional Affairs and the view expressed by it on the conformity with that Rule of the statement of formation of the TDI Group and to declare the non-existence ex tunc of that group (see paragraph 46 above).

56 It is true that the purpose of the rules of procedure of a Community institution is to organize the internal functioning of its services in the interests of good administration. The rules laid down have therefore as their essential purpose to ensure the smooth conduct of the procedure . . .

57 Nevertheless, that alone does not preclude an act of the Parliament such as that of 14 September 1999 from having legal effects in regard to third parties . . . and thus from being capable of forming the subject-matter of an action for annulment brought before the Community judicature under Article 173 EC [263].

58 Accordingly, it is for the Court of First Instance to determine whether the act of 14 September 1999 may be regarded as producing or being intended to produce legal effects going beyond the internal organisation of the work of the Parliament.

59 The act of 14 September 1999 deprives the Members who declared the formation of the TDI Group of the opportunity of organising themselves by means of that group in a political group within the meaning of Rule 29, with the result that those Members are deemed to be non-attached under Rule 30. As is clear from the matters mentioned at paragraphs 3 and 4 above, those Members are placed, in

carrying out their mandate, in a different situation to that linked to membership of a political group from which they would have benefited had the act of 14 September 1999 not been adopted.

60 The act of 14 September 1999 therefore affects the conditions under which the parliamentary functions of the Members concerned are exercised, and thus produces legal effects in their regard.

61 Elected under Article 1 of the Act of 20 September 1976 concerning the election of the representatives of the Assembly by direct universal suffrage . . . as representatives of the peoples of the States brought together in the Community, the [complainant] Members . . . must, in regard to an act emanating from the Parliament and producing legal effects as regards the conditions under which the electoral mandate is exercised, be regarded as third parties within the meaning of the first paragraph of Article 173 EC [263], irrespective of the position which they personally adopted at the plenary session on 14 September 1999 on the occasion of the vote on the interpretative note to Rule 29(1) proposed by the Committee on Constitutional Affairs.

62 Under those circumstances the act of 14 September 1999 cannot be deemed merely to be an act confined to the internal organisation of the work of the Parliament. Moreover, it should be noted that it is not subject to any verification procedure under the Rules of Procedure. Accordingly . . . it must be open to review by the Community judicature under the first paragraph of Article 173 EC [263].

## NOTES AND QUESTIONS

1.   Is it possible clearly to define why the CFI/General Court did not consider the issue here to be an internal matter?

2.   Given the Constitutional separation of powers, one would be very surprised if the U.S. Supreme Court thought it was entitled to intervene in a matter relating to the internal proceedings of Congress. Since there is no such formal rule in the EU, there was no such objection of principle in this case. However, does it seem appropriate in the broader sense that the CFI/General Court should deem fit to assume jurisdiction over the organization of a democratically elected body? And does EC 230/TFEU 263 have to be stretched to give it that jurisdiction?

3.   By its terms EC 230 EC/TFEU 263 originally referred only to "acts of the Council and the Commission." Nonetheless, the Court had held that acts of the Parliament also were subject to challenge under EC 230/TFEU 263. The rationale of the Court was that, although the EC Treaty in its original form had granted Parliament only powers of consultation and political control, the authority of Parliament had now been expanded to include actions that have legal force with respect to third parties. Thus, according to the Court, EC 230/TFEU 263 should be interpreted as including at least certain acts of Parliament within its coverage. See e.g., *Luxembourg v. European Parliament*, Case 23/81, [1983] ECR 255. The Maastricht Treaty amended what was then EC 173 (EC 230/TFEU 263) to expressly allow actions against the Parliament in respect of acts intended to produce legal effects *vis-à-vis* third parties.

## [F]   Acts Not Adopted by Institutions

### DIR INTERNATIONAL FILM SRL AND OTHERS v. COMMISSION
Joined CasesT-369/84 and T-85/95, 1998 ECJ CELEX LEXIS 23, [1998] ECR II-357

[The applicants sought annulment of, first, the letters from the European Film Distribution Office (EFDO) to the applicants adjourning the procedure in relation to applications for loans under the action programme to promote the development of the European audiovisual industry (MEDIA) for the distribution of two films and/or of the measure whereby the Commission instructed EFDO to take those decisions; and, secondly, the measure of 5 December 1994 whereby EFDO rejected the applications for loans and/or the measure whereby the Commission instructed EFDO to adopt that measure. The Court addressed the question whether the action was admissible given that the applicants were seeking annulment of actions taken by a private body (the EFDO) which was administering the loan program under contract to the Commission. (The CFI/General Court's judgment was partially overruled on appeal on other grounds: see *DIR International Film Srl, and others v. Commission*, Case C-164/98 P. 2000 ECJ EUR-Lex LEXIS 1187,[2000] ECR I-447).]

52 Under Article 7(1) of Decision 90/685, the Commission is responsible for the implementation of the MEDIA programme. Moreover, the judgment in Case 9/56 Meroni v. High Authority 1957 and 1958 ECR 133 shows that delegation of powers coupled with a freedom to make assessments implying a wide discretionary power is not permissible. In accordance with those principles, the relevant agreement between the Commission and EFDO on the financial implementation of the MEDIA programme (see paragraphs 5 and 6 above) makes any decision in that area subject in practice to the prior agreement of the Commission's representatives. In that respect, the Commission has explained that, before each meeting of the EFDO Selection Committee, the Commission's services were informed by the latter of all the applications lodged and, after examining the applications, the Commission officials responsible made their views known (see above, paragraph 9).

53 The Court therefore considers that EFDO's decisions on funding applications submitted under the MEDIA programme are imputable to the Commission, and that the latter is therefore responsible for their content and may be called upon to defend them in court.

54 In this case, the Commission essentially determined the content of the disputed letters and decision, even if the statement of reasons in the latter does not exactly follow the wording proposed by the Commission.

55 The Court finds, therefore, that the disputed letters and decision may in principle form the subject-matter of an action against the Commission before the Community judicature.

# NOTES AND QUESTIONS

1.  The Commission was held responsible here since it had delegated powers to the EFDO. Note that the CFI/General Court nonetheless did not hold the delegation illegal. Similar conclusions have been reached in challenges to Commission regulations implementing Council regulations, where the applicant was permitted to bring suit against the Council. How far might this doctrine go? For example, consider whether a private party could sue the Commission or Council for the acts of a Member State on the basis that the latter was administering an EU regulation.

2.  Note the new language in TFEU 263. Would this enable a private party to sue the delegee directly now?

## § 5.05  TREATIES

### A. RACKE GMBH & CO. v. HAUPTZOLLAMT MAINZ
Case 162/96, 1998 ECJ CELEX LEXIS 280, [1998] ECR I-3655

[For the facts of this case see the extract in Chapter 4. It will be recalled that Racke had asserted rights under a Cooperation Agreement with Yugoslavia which had been suspended. Racke challenged the suspension on the grounds that the suspension breached a rule of customary international law rule (*Pacta sunt servanda*). For this argument to result in a change in the legal situation for Racke, it was necessary to establish that (assuming the suspension was not legitimate), Racke could have invoked provisions of the Cooperation Agreement as being directly effective in EU law.]

30 It therefore needs to be examined first whether Article 22(4), which, as the purpose of the quota regulations cited in the order for reference demonstrates, applies to the main proceedings in this case, is capable of conferring rights to preferential customs treatment directly upon individuals.

31 The Court has consistently held that a provision of an agreement concluded by the Community with non-member countries must be regarded as being directly applicable when, regard being had to its wording and the purpose and nature of the agreement itself, the provision contains a clear and precise obligation which is not subject, in its implementation or effects, to the adoption of any subsequent measure
. . .

32 In order to determine whether the provision contained in Article 22(4) of the Cooperation Agreement meets those criteria, it is necessary first to examine its wording.

33 By its very wording, that provision requires Community measures to implement it in order to enable the annual Community tariff quota to be opened in accordance with the detailed rules laid down by Article 2(1) and (2) of the Additional Protocol, the Community having no discretion as to the adoption of those measures. The Community is obliged to carry out, within a certain period, an exact calculation of customs duties in accordance with those provisions.

34 It follows that, as regards the preferential customs treatment for which it makes provision, Article 22(4) of the Cooperation Agreement is capable of conferring rights upon which individuals may rely before national courts.

35 That finding is, moreover, borne out by examination of the purpose and nature of the agreement of which Article 22(4) forms part.

36 The aim of the Cooperation Agreement is to promote the development of trade between the contracting parties and progressively to remove barriers affecting the bulk of their trade. After the end of the first stage of that liberalisation, on 30 June 1985, the Additional Protocol established the further trade arrangements. It is in that context that Article 22(4), as amended by Article 4 of the Additional Protocol, lays down in respect of certain wines a Community tariff quota within which dismantling of customs duties on importation into the Community is to take place.

## NOTES AND QUESTIONS

1.   In the *Racke* case (para 31) the ECJ referred to the question as to whether the Cooperation Agreement contained "directly applicable" provisions. It seems that what the Court meant by that was whether there were provisions that did not require any EU implementing legislation such that they could be immediately part of EU law. This terminology might seem a little confusing as it sounds more like "direct effect" as that term was developed in the *Van Gend* and *Van Duyn* cases.

However, in this case, only Union law was at issue. The concepts of direct applicability and direct effect as discussed in cases such as *Van Duyn* by contrast had to do with the effects of Union law in *national* law, that is, one level down. *Racke* concerned a situation analogous to that arising under the United States Constitution. At the Union level, treaties concluded by the Council are binding on the institutions and the Member States. The Court has made clear on many occasions that the act of concluding an agreement is a Union act (See *R.& V. Haegeman v. Belgium*, Case 181/73, 1974 ECJ EUR-Lex LEXIS 66 [1974] ECR 449) and that the agreement becomes Union law as a result. The Union approach to treaties is thus "monist" — no separate act is required to "enact" it into EU law, as would be the case in a dualist system. However, as in the United States, just because treaties are "directly applicable" does not entail that all of their provisions can be invoked by individuals. It becomes a question of interpretation as to whether they produce direct effects on which individuals may rely. Recall the *Foster v. Neilson* case in Chapter 4. According to the 1987 Restatement of the Foreign Relations Law of the United States (Third), section 111(4), a treaty is considered not to be self-executing "(a) if the agreement manifests an intention that it shall not become effective as domestic law without the enactment of implementing legislation, (b) if the Senate in giving consent to a treaty, or Congress by resolution, requires implementing legislation, or (c) if implementing legislation is constitutionally required."

Taking into account the *Racke* decision and the above Restatement provision, how do you think the EU position compares with the position in the U.S. as regards the effects of treaties on individuals?

2.   Recall that in Chapter 4 it was observed that the EU can be bound by treaties such as the GATT even if it is not formally a party to them, provided that

it shows an intention to be bound. (*International Fruit*). In such a case there would be no EU act concluding or implementing the treaty. (See also, e.g., *Germany v. Council (Bananas)*, Case C-280/93, 1994 ECJ CELEX LEXIS 385, [1994] ECR I-4973.) Although even this feature did not deter the Court from considering the GATT to be part of EU law, the ECJ was unwilling to find that any provisions of the GATT were actually directly applicable. This conclusion might be compared with *EEC Seed Crushers' and Oil Processors' Federation (FEDIOL) v. Commission*, Case 70/87, 1989 ECJ CELEX LEXIS 106, [1991] ECR 1781, where the applicant brought an action to challenge the Commission's decision not to initiate a procedure to examine certain practices of Argentina concerning the export of soya cake under Article 3(5) of Regulation 2641/84 on the strengthening of the Common Commercial Policy with regard to protection against illicit commercial practices. The complaint by the applicant was rejected by the Commission. The applicant argued that the practices were contrary to certain provisions of the GATT. The Commission argued that the complaint was inadmissible, the GATT provisions not being invocable. The Court rejected the Commission's position on the basis that the GATT provisions were referred to by Article 2(1) of the Regulation insofar as it referred to principles of international law. This was enough to enable the court to interpret the GATT provisions as an integral part of a directly applicable Union act, i.e., the Regulation.

3. In *Polydor Ltd. v. Harlequin Record Shops Ltd.*, Case 270/80, [1982] ECR 329, and *HZA Mainz v. Kupferberg*, Case 104/81, [1982] ECR 3641, the ECJ held that reciprocal direct effect in the other party's legal system was not essential for a treaty to be directly applicable in Union law.

4. Suppose a national court were to consider a treaty entered into by a Member State as well as the Union (a "mixed agreement", discussed in Chapter 12) to be directly applicable and have direct effect in *national* law. Presumably, if that treaty were considered not to create invocable rights in Union law, so that a provision of Union law against which it was invoked would be fully effective, then, if that Union rule conflicted with the position in the national system, the Union rule would have to prevail. Is it acceptable in such a case that the national court would have to apply a rule that might cause the Member State to breach its international law obligation?

5. Given the changes introduced by the WTO agreement, especially those related to safeguards and dispute settlement, the question arose whether the Court would find that the WTO agreement could have direct effect. In *Portugal v. Council* Case C-149/96, 1999 ECJ CELEX LEXIS 88, [1998] ECR I-7379, the Court found it did not have such effects.

## § 5.06   JUDICIAL DECISIONS

### DA COSTA EN SCHAAKE NV, JACOB MEIJER NV, HOECHST-HOLLAND NV v. NETHERLANDS INLAND REVENUE ADMINISTRATION
Joined Cases 28-30/62, [1963] ECR 31
[No paragraph numbering appears in the original]

[The Commission had intervened in this case claiming that a request under EEC 177 (EC 234/TFEU 267) should be rejected for lack of substance, since the questions on which an interpretation was requested from the Court in the present case were decided by the judgment in *Van Gend*, which covered identical questions raised in a similar case.]

A distinction should be made between the obligation imposed by the third paragraph of Article 177 [267] upon national courts or tribunals of last instance and the power granted by the second paragraph of article 177 [267] to every national court or tribunal to refer to the court of the Communities a question on the interpretation of the Treaty. Although the third paragraph of Article 177 [267] unreservedly requires courts or tribunals of a Member State against whose decisions there is no judicial remedy under national law — like the Tariefcommissie — to refer to the Court every question of interpretation raised before them, the authority of an interpretation under article 177 [267] already given by the Court may deprive the obligation of its purpose and thus empty it of its substance. Such is the case especially when the question raised is materially identical with a question which has already been the subject of a preliminary ruling in a similar case.

## NOTES AND QUESTIONS

1.   This case was an important one in that it established that a judgment under EC 234/TFEU 267 should be regarded as having the force of law generally and not just for the resolution of the case in the main proceedings of the national court that referred it. This is not to say, however, that the Court was condoning a policy of avoiding references. It has discouraged national courts from taking the view that a question is so clear that it does not require an interpretation. This is addressed further in Chapter 9.

2.   The EC 234/TFEU 267 procedure only permits interpretation. As such the Court is not invited to apply its ruling to the facts of the case as raised in the national courts and it would be misleading to compare the court's views on the effects of its decisions with the common law doctrine of *stare decisis*. What exactly does the Court say about the authority of its decisions? How does this approach compare with a common law approach based on the notion of binding precedent?

3.   The Court very rarely overrules prior decisions, but this is due to its desire for consistency rather than any common law concept of binding precedent. Usually such overrulings are found necessary only where significant issues of principle are at stake. For example, it will be seen in Chapter 13 that the Court changed course (or at least believed it had) in its approach to EC 28/TFEU34 as it related to rules

establishing general trading rules (the *Torfaen* and *Keck* cases). In Chapter 17, *infra*, another example appears: *Metock and Others v. Minister for Justice, Equality and Law Reform* Case C-127/08, 2008 ECJ EUR-Lex LEXIS 2889, [2008] ECR I-6241. Here, the Court examined its previous case law regarding the rights of persons to reside in an EU Member State who had come from a non-Member State and subsequently acquired citizenship by marriage to an EU citizen who herself was not a national of the state where she resided. Directive 2004/38 generally requires that the latter person is entitled to reside with his spouse as a family member of an EU citizen who is exercising EU citizenship rights, but the Directive's language referred to his "accompanying" his spouse. The court had previously ruled that the Directive did not require that Member States' laws grant residence rights where the person had only acquired citizenship after marriage (and had not therefore accompanied his spouse when she moved to the state of residence). The Irish law in *Metock* implemented this exception by requiring prior lawful residence in another Member State and in *Secretary of State for the Home Department v. Akrich*, Case C-109/01, 2003 ECJ EUR-Lex LEXIS 1651, [2001] ECR I-9607, the Court had upheld such a condition. In *Metock*, it expressly overruled that conclusion.

**4.** When the Court interprets a provision of EU law in a way that causes a Member State law to be inapplicable (as being in conflict with the EU provision), that law must be considered always to have been inapplicable: it does not become so merely because of the Court's judgment: *Procureur de la République v. Waterkeyn*, Cases 314 – 316/81, [1982] ECR 4337. The Court does however have the power to limit retroactivity, as was illustrated in the *Defrenne* case. The latter decision might be taken to suggest that the Court is indeed making law rather than interpreting it, but the reverse is actually true — the Court's power to limit temporal effect is by way of exception to the general rule, for otherwise the Court would not need to pronounce on the temporal effect at all. This aspect also illustrates the nature of Union law as a code-based system. The answer will always be found in the language of written provisions, and the Court is not engaging in the fiction to which common lawyers resort to deny that law is being made by the courts. ("The common law is not a brooding omnipresence in the sky, but the articulate voice of some sovereign or quasi sovereign that can be identified; although some decisions with which I have disagreed seem to me to have forgotten the fact." *Southern Pacific Company v. Jensen*, 244 U.S. 205, 222 (1917) (Holmes, J., dissenting)).

# Part III

# THE UNION'S LEGISLATIVE, EXECUTIVE AND JUDICIAL FUNCTIONS

# Chapter 6

# LEGISLATIVE AND RULEMAKING PROCESSES

## § 6.01  OVERVIEW

***Template*** Article 3

***Materials in this Chapter*** The materials in this Chapter address the legislative and rulemaking processes under the EC Treaty/TFEU. Under the TEU, legislative action under the Common Foreign and Security Policy is prohibited. The European Council and the Council act only by executive decision in that area.

Until Lisbon, the term "legislation" was commonly used but it was not clear what it covered. There were two forms of act that required involvement of both the Parliament and the Council: the "cooperation procedure" and the "co-decision" procedure (discussed further *infra*). The Council also had powers to adopt normative acts, with varying degrees of participation by the Parliament. All of these acts are now confirmed as "legislative" (and the cooperation procedure has been replaced in all cases by the co-decision procedure). The Lisbon Treaty also clarified the status of delegates and implementing rulemaking powers and processes. The latter are technically executive acts since they are excluded from the definition of legislative acts. However, the reference to them in the Template is found in Article 3 of the Template, on the Union's Legislature, because the grant of such powers is made on a case-by-case basis by legislative acts.

- ***Judicial Control*** It is perhaps rather surprising that there should be much relevant case law regarding the respective roles of the institutions in the legislative process at least, since the subject matter seems to be largely political in nature. It is scarcely conceivable for example that, in the United States, one House of Congress would sue the other in the courts — such an action would surely compromise the separation of powers and open up the possibility of the judiciary to insert itself into the legislative process. (Compare, in this connection *United States v. Nixon*, 418 U.S. 683, 94 S. Ct. 3090, 41 L. Ed 2d 1039 (1974). In the EU, this is precisely what happens and with some frequency. This is because the Union exercises its competences according to a huge variety of defined processes, all of which are governed by the TFEU or Union acts and require differing types and levels of involvement on the part of the Institutions and sometimes other bodies — such as the Committee of the Regions. EC 230/TFEU 263 specifically permits actions by one institution against another. The Institutions pay close attention to their powers and privileges and will assert them when necessary in the ECJ.

As a matter of first impression, one might conclude that the original European Communities were conceptualized as exercising a form of delegated power; thus, essentially, being an administrative body. Indeed, much of the language in the original EEC Treaty and even in the current TFEU relating to the role of the ECJ is reminiscent of French public law — that is, law relating to governmental administration. Moreover, the oddity of the Council as a legislative body, where the actual composition depends on the subject matter under discussion, might tend to reinforce the notion that the EU is merely an agent of the Member States.

Such a conclusion however would be incorrect. The notion of "conferred competences" itself implies that the Union has degrees of latitude of action within its areas of responsibility. The existence of qualified majority voting in the Council entails that Member States in the minority are nonetheless bound by its actions. This can scarcely be reconciled with the notion that the Union or the Council is their agent. Moreover, the Parliament's role, massively expanded from where it started out, adds the voice of the peoples of Europe to the process, which may be at odds with the position of the Member States in the Council. Thus, a real federal/state division of competences exists, even if the Union's powers are "conferred", and it is vital that there be a judicial means for resolving disputes, in much the same way that the judicial review doctrine in the United States functions. It is appropriate to maintain judicial control over all aspects of the Union's activities under the TFEU to ensure that the EU does not exceed its conferred powers, while, through the reference process of EC 234/TFEU 267, the Court can also assert discipline over the actions of the Member States within the scope of *their* competences. One might then conclude that the control exercised by the EU Courts lies somewhere between the constitutional model and administrative procedure depending on the subject matter. See in this regard, D. Curtin and D. O'Keefe (eds.), Constitutional Adjudication in European Community and National Law (Butterworths (Ireland), 1992.

***Legislative Acts*** The Constitution Treaty had substituted the term "European law" for "regulation" and "framework law" for "directive" in the context of legislation involving the Council and Parliament. Regrettably, this clarification was lost in the Treaty of Lisbon but the underlying reality has not changed. Note the differences between legislative acts adopted according to the "ordinary legislative procedure" and those adopted pursuant to "a special legislative procedure".

The distinction between ordinary and special procedures is essentially a question of whether an act is adopted by the Council and the Parliament (ordinary) or whether the act is adopted only by the Council (or occasionally the Parliament) with some involvement of the other institution, usually in the form of a required consultation (special). In this regard, note that TEU 48 provides for so-called "bridging" provisions aimed at extending the scope of qualified-majority voting and the ordinary legislative procedure to some policy areas that are today submitted to special legislative procedures. This provision makes it possible to switch from special legislative procedures to the ordinary legislative procedure without passing through the Inter Governmental Conference mechanism requiring ratification by all Member States. The clause allows the European Council, acting unanimously after obtaining Parliament's approval, to authorize application of the ordinary legislative procedure for any legal basis under the Treaty covering policy areas, provided that no national parliament makes known its opposition within six months.

***The EU Legislature*** As with everything else about the constitutional structure of the EU, the "legislature" of the EU is neither fish nor fowl. On the one hand, as noted above, it is subjected to judicial control where every action it takes has to follow whatever the prescribed procedure is for that action and can be questioned in Court. Moreover, generally speaking, neither the Council nor the Parliament can initiate legislation. On the other hand, at least the Parliament has a growing and independent legitimacy as a democratic institution at the European level. The Member States, ever conscious of what this could entail, have been cautious in permitting expansion of its powers and responsibilities but they have come anyway.

***Evolution of the Parliament*** The flexibility of the institutions with regard to the actual margin of discretion left to them by the Treaty is most noticeable when looking at the European Parliament. Indeed, the European Parliament has managed to evolve both thanks to and in spite of the actual constrained powers that the Treaties had granted to it, and has over time wrung from the Member States significant powers and rights for itself.

**- The budget** The first significant grant of powers to the Parliament occurred with the Budgetary Powers Treaty of 1975. The Parliament was permitted to amend compulsory spending (that is, spending on matters required by Union law, chiefly the common agricultural policy), although it could be overridden by the Council; and it could amend or even increase "discretionary spending." These powers were ultimately backed up by the power to reject the whole budget "for important reasons." The first directly elected Parliament did so for the first time in 1980 in an attempt to reform spending growth.

**- Constitutional** The Parliament won the right in 1987 to have its President address the European Council (not then an EU institution, of course). In 2001 it participated in the Convention on the Future of Europe and now has the right to participate in Conventions on future treaty changes. Moreover, as already noted elsewhere, in 2007 it participated along with the Council and Commission in what might be called the first Constitutional Act of the Union itself: the Proclamation of the Charter of Fundamental Rights. Admittedly there had been a similar proclamation in 2000 at the Nice European Council, but the difference this time was that the Charter was then given legal force by the Lisbon Treaty amendments to the TEU.

National politicians now regularly address the Parliament, as do visiting foreign leaders (Reagan, Obama). It has gradually increased its rights of veto over treaties.

**- Appointment/censure of the Commission** During the 1980s, consultation on the choice of the Commission President was introduced outside the formal Treaty procedures. The old TEU of 1992 introduced the right for the Parliament to give its opinion on the choice of President and to vote on the Commission as a whole. In the next following appointment, Jacques Santer, the nominated President, announced he would stand down if he did not receive a favourable opinion, thus conceding significant power to the Parliament. Today the Parliament has the formal right to vote on the candidate for President proposed by the European Council and the right to consent to the rest of the Commission as a whole (proposed by the Council by common accord with the President of the Commission). This entails in practice confirmation hearings for all commissioners. In 2007 two proposed commissioners were given an unfavourable reception, with the consequence that the proposal was withdrawn and a revised one then submitted.

**- Independent statute for MEPs** MEPs were originally compensated in accordance with their respective national practices, a highly objectionable situation that led to attempts to even out the differences through expense allowances, which was viewed very unfavourably by the public and the press. After a very long battle, Parliament finally got its own governing statute that treats MEPS equally regardless of the practices of the country they come from (2007).

**- Co-legislator** The Parliament started with purely consultative powers. As noted above, it gained budgetary powers in the 1970s but did not gain powers to participate in legislation as a second chamber until the SEA of 1986. Initially these powers were ultimately subject to override by the Council, (the "co-operation procedure"). With the old TEU of 1992 it gained powers of co-decision in some areas (enabling it ultimately to block legislation). Over time, as the scope of its powers has increased, the political significance of legislation has also increased. Thus, in 1996, when considering legislation regulating takeover bids, the Parliament found itself embroiled in a truly political and ideological issue leading to substantial amendments to the original Commission proposal. By the Treaty of Amsterdam its powers were significantly extended, and that treaty also removed the procedural requirement for Commission backing for Parliament amendments. Co-decision powers were extended to 38 policy areas. Nice added another seven, and then with the Treaty of Lisbon a further 43 areas were added, while the cooperation procedure was completely abolished. Parliament also has the power to require the Commission to consider drawing up legislative proposals and it also can act on Citizens' petitions.

(For an excellent account of these developments pre-Lisbon, see J PIESTLEY, SIX BATTLES THAT SHAPED THE EUROPEAN PARLIAMENT (John Harper Publishing, 2008)

***Cooperation among institutions*** One might conclude from the above comments that the institutions are constantly locked in internecine feuding about the scope of their powers and privileges. At times this has been true, but the institutions also have learned how to work with each other with considerable flexibility while observing the rigour of the law.

***Separation of Powers*** To what extent do the TEU and TFEU set up a system of checks and balances based on the separation of powers? Some separation might be evident from the nature of the Institutions and their roles. Thus, the role of the European Council is clearly "executive" or policy making. The Commission's rulemaking and administrative powers can be considered consistent with executive responsibilities but its formal position as initiator of legislation goes beyond the optional character of the President's right in the United States to propose legislation. The European Parliament is clearly only a legislative body, but the pivotal role of the Council is both legislative and executive. For further discussion, see K. Lenaerts, *Some Reflections on the Separation of Powers in the European Community* (1991) 28 CML REV. 11. On the other hand, the Council serves as both a legislative and an executive/policy making body. One may also observe that the Member States in fulfilling their duties to implement EU law might be considered a part of the executive function of the EU. In the U.S., while it is not unusual for the States to be delegated the role of enforcing federal law (as for example in the area of environmental policy) the States cannot be required to become instruments of federal policy: *Printz v. United States*, 521 U.S. 898 (1997). As M.P. Maduro has pointed out, in the EU the involvement of the Member States has led to effects on the separation of powers within their own constitutional orders.

## § 6.02 SEPARATION OF POWERS?

### FRANCE, ITALY AND UNITED KINGDOM v. COMMISSION
(TRANSPARENCY DIRECTIVE)
Joined Cases 188 and 190/80, [1982] ECR 2545

[The plaintiffs, various Member States, sought the annulment of Directive 80/723 (June 25, 1980, O.J. 1980, L195) on the transparency of financial relations between the Member States and public undertakings. The directive was adopted by the Commission under then EC 90 (EC 86/TFEU 106 (3)). The purpose of the directive was to enable identification of the financial structure of cooperatives and other entities which are to a greater or lesser extent controlled or owned by governments of the Member States, thus facilitating discovery of the extent of aid given to such entities, and the consequential application of EC 88 and 89/TFEU 108 and 109] to them. Various claims for the invalidity of the directive were made, one of which was that the Commission had no power to adopt the directive as this violated the division of powers between Institutions.]

4 According to the United Kingdom, by adopting the contested directive the Commission committed a breach of the very principles which govern the division of powers and responsibilities between the Community institutions. It is clear from the Treaty provisions governing the institutions that all original law-making power is vested in the Council, whilst the Commission has only powers of surveillance and implementation. That division of powers is confirmed by the specific enabling rules in the Treaty, virtually all of which reserve to the Council the power to adopt regulations and directives. The same division of responsibilities is to be found in particular in the rules on competition. Those provisions themselves confer functions of surveillance on the Commission, whereas it can legislate only within the limits of a specific and express power delegated to it by a measure of the Council.

5 Again according to the United Kingdom, the provisions of the Treaty which exceptionally confer on the Commission the power to issue directives must be interpreted in the light of the foregoing considerations. Commission directives are not of the same nature as those adopted by the Council. Whereas the latter may contain general legislative provisions which may, where appropriate, impose new obligations on Member States, the aim of the former is merely to deal with a specific situation in one or more Member States. As for Article 90 [106] (3), such a limited aim is suggested by the very wording of the provision, which states that the Commission is to "address" appropriate directives or decisions to Member States.

6 There is, however, no basis for that argument in the Treaty provisions governing the institutions. According to Article 4 [TEU 17], the Commission is to participate in carrying out the tasks entrusted to the Community on the same basis as the other institutions, each acting within the limits of the powers conferred upon it by the

Treaty. Article 155 [see now 288] provides, in terms which are almost identical to those used in Article 145 [repealed] to describe the same function of the Council, that the Commission is to have its own power of decision in the manner provided for in the Treaty. Moreover, the provisions of the chapter which lays down general rules concerning the effects and content of measures adopted by the institutions, in particular those of Article 189 [288], do not make the distinction drawn by the United Kingdom between directives which have general application and others which lay down only specific measures. According to the first paragraph of that article, the Commission, just as the Council, has the power to issue directives in accordance with the provisions of the Treaty. It follows that the limits of the powers conferred on the Commission by a specific provision of the Treaty are to be inferred not from a general principle, but from an interpretation of the particular wording of the provision in question, in this case Article 90 [106], analyzed in the light of its purpose and its place in the scheme of the Treaty.

7 In that regard, it is not possible to draw any conclusions from the fact that most of the other specific provisions of the Treaty which provide a power to adopt general measures confer that power on the Council, acting on a proposal from the Commission. Nor can any distinction be drawn between provisions providing for the adoption of directives according to whether they use the word "issue" or "address". According to Article 189 [288], the directives as well as decisions, both of the Council and of the Commission, are addressed to parties which, in so far as directives are concerned, are necessarily Member States. In the case of a provision providing for the adoption of both directives and decisions addressed to Member States, the word "address" therefore simply constitutes the most appropriate common expression.

## NOTES AND QUESTIONS

1. Why would the Member States want to challenge the power of the Commission to issue directives? What arguments did they make?

2. Was the directive issued by the Commission different in nature from those issued by the Council?

3. The EU has not had to confront the very difficult questions faced in the U.S. by the Constitution's attempt to separate the three branches of government. To a large extent the powers of the Commission to make rules in implementation of Council/Council and Parliament legislation are expressly set out. Moreover the Commission has the power to adopt the same types of acts as the Council (at least as regards regulations and decisions). In the United States, for a long time there was a lively debate as to whether the legislature could delegate lawmaking powers. This culminated in two famous Supreme Court decisions dealing with New Deal legislation — *Panama Refining Co. v. Ryan*, 293 U.S. 388 (1935), and *A.L.A. Schechter Poultry Corp. v. United States*, 295 U.S. 495 (1935) — where the delegations to the executive were found to be unconstitutional. The status of these cases and of the "non-delegation" doctrine is today uncertain but clearly much federal activity falls into this category. A parallel in the EU might be found in *ACF Chemiefarma NY v. Commission*, Case 41/69, 1970 ECJ EUR-Lex LEXIS 50, [1970] ECR 661, the applicant alleged that Regulation 17/62, where the original regulation adopted by the Council under EC 83/TFEU 102 establishing procedures

and powers for the enforcement of the competition rules in EC 81 and 82/TFEU 101 and 102, had improperly delegated powers to the Commission. The Regulation permitted the Commission to issue procedural rules for investigating suspected violations, holding hearings and fining violators. The Court rejected the challenge on the basis that then EEC Article 155 permitted it to confer implementing powers on the Commission. (See now TFEU 291).

## § 6.03   LEGISLATIVE BODIES AND PROCEDURES

### [A]   The European Parliament

## MATTHEWS v. UNITED KINGDOM
(App. no. 24833/94), EUROPEAN COURT OF HUMAN RIGHTS (1998)
28 EHRR 361, [1999] ECHR 24833/94

[Gibraltar was reluctantly ceded to Great Britain by Spain in the 1713 Treaty of Utrecht and became a colony in 1830. In a referendum held in 1967, Gibraltarians voted overwhelmingly to remain a British dependency. The subsequent granting of autonomy in 1969 by the UK led to Spain's closing the border and severing all communication links. After many years of negotiations, in September 2006 a three-way agreement was signed. A new noncolonial constitution came into effect in 2007, but the UK retains responsibility for defense, foreign relations, internal security, and financial stability. Gibraltar thus remains a dependent territory of the United Kingdom. It forms part of Her Majesty the Queen's Dominions, but not part of the United Kingdom. The United Kingdom parliament has the ultimate authority to legislate for Gibraltar, but in practice exercises it rarely.

The EU Treaties apply to Gibraltar by virtue of EC 299 (4)/TFEU 355(3), which provides that they apply to the European territories for whose external relations a member State is responsible. Gibraltar was excluded from certain parts of the EC Treaty/TFEU by virtue of the UK Treaty of Accession. Relevant EU legislation becomes part of Gibraltar law in the same way as in other parts of the Union: regulations are directly applicable, and directives and other legal acts of the EU which call for domestic legislation are transposed by domestic primary or secondary legislation. Although Gibraltar is not part of the United Kingdom in domestic terms, by virtue of a declaration made by the United Kingdom government at the time of the entry into force of the British Nationality Act 1981, the term "nationals" and derivatives used in the EC Treaty/TFEU includes British Dependent Territories citizens. However, Gibraltarians did not have the right to vote in European Elections. The UK excluded this right in the Act establishing Direct Elections of 1976 to avoid a diplomatic issue with Spain.

Matthews claimed before the European Commission on Human Rights (a body since abolished) and in the European Court of Human Rights that this exclusion violated her democratic rights under Protocol No 1 Article 3 of the European Convention on Human Rights. Note that the case was heard after the institution of the co-decision procedure but the cooperation procedure was still predominant.]

The [U.K.] Government contended that the European Parliament continued to lack both of the most fundamental attributes of a legislature: the power to initiate legislation and the power to adopt it. They were of the opinion that the only change to the powers and functions of the European Parliament since the Commission last considered the issue . . . — the procedure under Article 189b [294] of the EC Treaty — offered less than even a power of co-decision with the Council, and in any event applied only to a tiny proportion of the Community's legislative output.

The applicant took as her starting-point in this respect that the European Commission of Human Rights had found that the entry into force of the Single European Act in 1986 did not furnish the European Parliament with the necessary powers and functions for it to be considered as a "legislature" . . . She contended that the Maastricht Treaty increased those powers to such an extent that the European Parliament was now transformed from a mere advisory and supervisory organ to a body which assumed, or assumed at least in part, the powers and functions of legislative bodies within the meaning of Article 3 of Protocol No. 1.

* * *

48. In determining whether the European Parliament falls to be considered as the "legislature", or part of it, in Gibraltar for the purposes of Article 3 of Protocol No. 1, the Court must bear in mind the sui generis nature of the European Community, which does not follow in every respect the pattern common in many States of a more or less strict division of powers between the executive and the legislature. Rather, the legislative process in the EC involves the participation of the European Parliament, the Council and the European Commission.

The Court must ensure that "effective political democracy" is properly served in the territories to which the Convention applies, and in this context, it must have regard not solely to the strictly legislative powers which a body has, but also to that body's role in the overall legislative process.

Since the Maastricht Treaty, the European Parliament's powers are no longer expressed to be "advisory and supervisory". The removal of these words must be taken as an indication that the European Parliament has moved away from being a purely consultative body, and has moved towards being a body with a decisive role to play in the legislative process of the European Community. . . .

The European Parliament's role in the Community legislative process depends on the issues concerned (see paras 15-16 above).

Where a regulation or directive is adopted by means of the consultation procedure (for example under Articles 99 [113] or 100 [115] of the EC Treaty) the European Parliament may, depending on the specific provision, have to be consulted. In such cases, the European Parliament's role is limited. Where the EC Treaty requires the procedure set out in Article 189c [repealed] to be used, the European Parliament's position on a matter can be overruled by a unanimous Council. Where the EC Treaty requires the Article 189b [294] procedure to be followed, however, it is not open to the Council to pass measures against the will of the European Parliament. Finally, where the so-called "assent procedure" is used (as referred to in the first paragraph of Article 138b [repealed in part, 225] of the EC Treaty), in relation to matters such as the accession of new member States and the conclusion of certain types of international agreements, the consent of the European Parliament is needed before a measure can be passed.

In addition to this involvement in the passage of legislation, the European Parliament also has functions in relation to the appointment and removal of the European Commission. Thus, it has a power of censure over the European Commission, which can ultimately lead to the European Commission having to resign as a body (Article 144 [234]); its consent is necessary for the appointment of the European Commission (Article 158 [TEU 17]); its consent is necessary before the budget can be adopted (Article 203 [313, 314]); and it gives a discharge to the European Commission in the implementation of the budget, and here has supervisory powers over the European Commission (Article 206 [319]).

Further, whilst the European Parliament has no formal right to initiate legislation, it has the right to request the European Commission to submit proposals on matters on which it considers that a Community act is required (Article 138b [225]).

As to the context in which the European Parliament operates, the Court is of the view that the European Parliament represents the principal form of democratic, political accountability in the Community system. The Court considers that whatever its limitations, the European Parliament, which derives democratic legitimation from the direct elections by universal suffrage, must be seen as that part of the European Community structure which best reflects concerns as to "effective political democracy".

Even when due allowance is made for the fact that Gibraltar is excluded from certain areas of Community activity . . . , there remain significant areas where Community activity has a direct impact in Gibraltar. Further, . . . measures taken under Article 189b [294] of the EC Treaty and which affect Gibraltar relate to important matters such as road safety, unfair contract terms and air pollution by emissions from motor vehicles and to all measures in relation to the completion of the internal market.

The Court thus finds that the European Parliament is sufficiently involved in the specific legislative processes leading to the passage of legislation under Articles 189b [294] and 189c [repealed] of the EC Treaty, and is sufficiently involved in the general democratic supervision of the activities of the European Community, to constitute part of the "legislature" of Gibraltar for the purposes of Article 3 of Protocol No. 1.

## JOINT DISSENTING OPINION OF JUDGES FREELAND AND JUNGWIERT

[I]t is in our view intrinsic to the notion of a "legislature" that the body concerned should have the power to initiate legislation and to adopt it (subject, in the case of some national Constitutions, to the requirement of the assent of the head of State). If this power is lacking, the fact that the body may have other powers often exercisable by national legislatures (for example, powers in relation to censure of the executive or to the budget) is not enough to remedy the deficiency. The existence of such other powers may enhance the body's entitlement to be styled as a parliament and its role in promoting an "effective political democracy". But the facts that it is so styled and has such a role are not to be regarded as requiring it to be treated as a "legislature" unless it has in itself the necessary legislative power.

\* \* \*

[A]s matters stand (and stood at the time of the 1994 elections) . . . Parliament has not in our view reached a stage where it can of itself properly be regarded as constituting a legislature. To borrow the words of Professor Dashwood in his inaugural address at the University of Cambridge in November 1995, "the Community has no legislature, but a legislative process in which the different political institutions have different parts to play". In fact, of the institutions of the Community it is the Council of Ministers which performs the functions most closely related to those of a legislature at national level.

## NOTES AND QUESTIONS

1. What would you consider to be the deciding factors in the majority and minority opinions in this case in their respective conclusions regarding the standing of the European Parliament as a "legislature" within the terms of the ECHR protocol? In particular, what do you think of the assertion that the ability to initiate legislation is an indispensable element of a true legislature? Note in this regard that in the Template, the Commission is described as an element of the legislative process as regards the initiation of legislation. If one looked at the "legislature" as comprising all three institutions, does the issue of initiation go away?

2. Could the Council be considered an embryonic "Senate" and the Parliament a "House of Representatives" given their methods of selection? Note that these procedures owe a lot to the procedures for consultation and approval in the German parliamentary system, as between the Bundesrat (representatives of the Länder (states)) and the Bundestag (elected for specific constituencies). For appraisals of the Council and Parliament see, e.g., M. WESTLAKE AND D. GALLOWAY, THE COUNCIL OF THE EUROPEAN UNION (3rd Edition, Harper, 2004); and D. JUDGE AND D. EARNSHAW, THE EUROPEAN PARLIAMENT (Palgrave, 2003); R. CORBETT, F. JACOBS AND M SHACKLE-TON, THE EUROPEAN PARLIAMENT (6th edition, Harper 2005).

3. What is the significance of the requirement that legislative measures under the ordinary procedure must be initiated only on a proposal from the Commission? What is the difference between a proposal and a recommendation in this context? Why is the Commission involved in the EC 251/TFEU 294 procedure?

4. In the maze of different procedures it is often easy to lose sight of the need to maintain democratic control over all types of legislation. There has been a continuing and vigorous debate over whether the EU suffers from a democratic deficit. One aspect of this debate is the level of involvement of national parliaments in EU legislation. It may, of course, be argued that the national legislatures should not have a place in the procedure anyway — any more than one would expect the legislatures of the states in the United States to have such a place in federal procedures. However, the unique structure of the EU and the absence of direct democratic accountability of the Council, the emphasis on subsidiarity, and the general remoteness of the Commission, were factors in the decision of the drafters

of the Lisbon Treaty to increase the role of national parliaments. Some Member States had already set up general types of committees of their legislatures to deal with this, notably Belgium and Germany, where regionalist or federalist pressures require such consultation. Further to the protocol on the European Parliament and National Parliaments (which was first introduced as a Declaration annexed to the Maastricht Treaty), the Lisbon Treaty introduced also a Protocol on Subsidiarity that foresees greater involvement of the national parliaments in the EU legislative process. This greater involvement of national parliaments is enshrined in new TEU 12, and EC 308/TFEU 352 (amended).

Scrutiny by national parliaments should not be overlooked, but there were inherent weaknesses because the national legislatures did not have any formal place in the procedures. In the United Kingdom, for example, it was often difficult to schedule debates on the less politically sensitive issues, and those that took place might be late at night and quite short. MPs did not always have the necessary information to ask useful questions and there was no clear line of communication back to the Minister who had the responsibility to pursue the matter before the Council. It remains to be seen how the application of these new provisions introduced by Lisbon will solve these problems.

5.　EC 207/TFEU 240 provides that a "committee consisting of the Permanent Representatives of the Member States shall be responsible for preparing the work of the Council and for carrying out the tasks assigned to it by the Council." The committee is not elected and represents largely the views of national civil servants and their political masters.

6.　The cooperation procedure has been abolished by the Lisbon Treaty and the ordinary legislative procedure is now the co-decision procedure, provided for in TFEU 294. What do you think might have triggered the abolition of the cooperation procedure? What might be the consequences? What does it say of the position of the European Parliament within the EU?

7.　Article 3 of the Template lays out the co-decision procedure. It implies a process that seems to envisage lively public debate. The truth, however, is rather different. Under a Joint Declaration on practical arrangements for this procedure ([1999] OJ C 148/1), updated in 2007 ([2007] OJ C 145/2), the institutions have agreed wherever possible to seek agreement at the first reading. This leads to an impression of a "stitch-up" among the general public and is hardly conducive to the resolution of the democratic deficit so often complained of at the Union level. This practice is reinforced by a system of "trilogues" involving the three institutions that again essentially seek to resolve differences behind closed doors. One might, of course, make the same observations about the U.S. Congress in some respects, but there is intense public scrutiny around the outcomes, a feature scarcely present in the Union structure.

## [B]   The Council

## PARLIAMENT v. COUNCIL AND COMMISSION
### (AID TO BANGLADESH)
Joined Cases 181/91 and 248/91, 1993 ECJ CELEX LEXIS 139, [1993] ECR I-3685

2 In the course of an ordinary session of the Council held at Brussels on 13 and 14 May 1991 under the chairmanship of Jacques F. Poos, the Minister of Foreign Affairs of the Grand Duchy of Luxembourg, a decision was taken to grant special aid to Bangladesh. Item 12 of the minutes of that meeting described the decision as follows:

"The Member States meeting in the Council have decided on the basis of a Commission proposal to grant special aid of ECU 60 million to Bangladesh under a Community action.

The distribution amongst the Member States will be based on GNP.

The aid will be integrated into the Community's general action plan for Bangladesh.

It will be provided either directly by the Member States, or by means of an account administered by the Commission.

The Commission will coordinate the whole of the special aid of ECU 60 million."

That decision was the subject of a press release entitled "Aid for Bangladesh-Council conclusions." (reference 6004/91, Press 60-c).

3 Following that decision the Commission opened a special account with Banque Bruxelles Lambert, and invited the Member States to transfer their contributions to it. Only Greece took up that suggestion; the other Member States paid their contributions directly within the framework of bilateral aid.

4 In its action brought against the Council the Parliament seeks the annulment of the decision to grant special aid to Bangladesh (hereinafter "the contested act").

5 By separate document, the Council raised an objection of inadmissibility under Article 91 of the Rules of Procedure on the ground that the contested act was not an act of the Council within the meaning of Article 173 [263] of the Treaty. By decision of 15 June 1992 the Court joined that objection to the substance of the case.

\*     \*     \*

9 The Council claims that the Court should declare the application brought against it inadmissible on the ground that the contested act was adopted, not by the Council, but by the Member States, and thus cannot be the subject of an action for annulment under Article 173 [263] of the Treaty.

10 Parliament submits, on the other hand, that in view of its title, "Council conclusions", and the fact that it was adopted at the 1487th session of the Council, which was attended by, among others, all the Ministers of Foreign Affairs of the Member States, the contested act constitutes an act of the Council. It argues that, by adopting that act, the Council infringed the prerogatives conferred on Parlia-

ment by Article 203 [314] of the Treaty in budgetary matters.

11 In order to decide this point it must be pointed out first that under Article 173 [263] the Court's function is to "review the legality of acts of the Council and the Commission other than recommendations or opinions".

12 It is clear from the wording of that provision that acts adopted by representatives of the Member States acting, not in their capacity as members of the Council, but as representatives of their governments, and thus collectively exercising the powers of the Member States, are not subject to judicial review by the Court. . . . [I]t makes no difference in this respect whether such an act is called an "act of the Member States meeting in the Council" or an "act of the representatives of the Governments of the Member States meeting in the Council".

13 However, the Court has consistently held that an action for annulment is available in the case of all measures adopted by the institutions, whatever their nature or form, which are intended to have legal effects (Case 22/70 Commission v. Council 1971 ECR 263).

14 Consequently, it is not enough that an act should be described as a "decision of the Member States" for it to be excluded from review under Article 173 [263] of the Treaty. In order for such an act to be excluded from review, it must still be determined whether, having regard to its content and all the circumstances in which it was adopted, the act in question is not in reality a decision of the Council.

15 It follows that the assessment of the admissibility of the application is bound up with the assessment to be made of the complaints levelled against the contested act.

16 Before considering those complaints, it should be pointed out that the Community does not have exclusive competence in the field of humanitarian aid, and that consequently the Member States are not precluded from exercising their competence in that regard collectively in the Council or outside it.

17 In support of its application, Parliament relies firstly on the reference made in the contested act to the Commission's proposal. In its opinion, that reference shows that, in view of the procedure which led to the act's adoption, it was the Council, not the Member States, which acted in this case.

18 That argument is not conclusive. Not all proposals from the Commission necessarily constitute proposals within the meaning of Article 149 [293] of the Treaty. Their legal character must be assessed in the light of all the circumstances in which they were made. They may just as well constitute mere initiatives taken in the form of informal proposals.

19 Secondly, Parliament observes that, according to the description of the act, the special aid was to be administered by the Commission. According to the fourth indent of Article 155 [repealed] of the Treaty, however, powers of implementation may be conferred on the Commission only by a decision of the Council.

20 That argument cannot be accepted either. The fourth indent of Article 155 [repealed] of the Treaty does not prevent the Member States from entrusting the Commission with the task of coordinating a collective action undertaken by them on the basis of an act of their representatives meeting in the Council.

21 Thirdly, Parliament submits that the contested act requires the special aid to be distributed among the Member States according to GNP, which, in its view, constitutes a typically Community concept.

22 It is sufficient to state in response to that argument that nothing in the Treaty precludes the Member States from making use outside the Community context of criteria taken from the budgetary provisions for allocating the financial obligations resulting from decisions taken by their representatives.

23 Fourthly, Parliament submits that, in view of the fact that in the future the implementation of the contested act will be subjected to the supervision of the Court of Auditors and Parliament, in accordance with Articles 206a and 206b [as amended, 319] of the Treaty respectively, the act is manifestly a Community act.

24 As can be seen from the Council minutes, quoted above, the contested decision leaves it to the Member States to choose whether to pay their contribution by way of bilateral aid or through an account administered by the Commission. Since the contested act does not require the use of the Community budget for the part of the aid to be administered by the Commission, the budget entry made by the latter cannot have any bearing on how the act is categorized.

25 It follows from the whole of the foregoing that the contested act is not an act of the Council but an act taken by the Member States collectively. The application brought by Parliament against the Council must therefore be declared inadmissible.

## NOTES AND QUESTIONS

1. One would expect, in a federal system, that acts of the constituent states acting together could not have the force of law except as recognized by the federal Constitution. Yet, until the advent of the European Union, "resolutions," and various other "acts" of representatives of the governments of the Member States" had been adopted from time to time. As pointed out, these "acts of the representatives," unlike decisions of the Council, do not originate from an institution of the EU, but from a diplomatic conference, although the latter has the same composition as the Council. Because of this distinction, the rules of the Treaties regarding the way in which decisions of the EU Institutions are taken, their legal effects, implementation and judicial review cannot apply to "acts of the representatives." They are therefore not EU acts. Rather, the validity of the acts of the representatives is governed by general international law. According to the Court, does this mean that they are in any sense part of EU law?

2. In *France v. United Kingdom*, Case 141/78, [1979] ECR 2923, the ECJ considered a resolution of the Council at the 1976 Hague Summit as being a more specific statement of the Member States' obligations under EC10/TEU 4. The United Kingdom had brought certain measures regarding fisheries into force without consulting the Commission as required by the resolution. This did not mean that the resolution had the force of law, however. It was merely a reflection of the duties of the Member States under EC 10/TEU 4. See also *Defrenne v. Société Anonyme Belge de Navigation Aérienne Sabena*, Case 43/75, [1976] ECR 455, where the Court states that "the Resolution [of a Conference of Ministers in 1961 to defer application of Article 119 [157]) was ineffective to make any valid

modification on the time limit fixed by the Treaty."

3. Note that the Member States have adopted "Acts" in connection with accession of new Member States; and also with respect to direct elections to the Parliament. These are appended either to a decision of the Member States or to the respective Treaty of Accession.

4. Note that in some areas, the Council may vote minus some Member States and by special majorities). Is such selective application of general legislation consistent with a unified federal system?

5. As noted in Chapter 2, *supra*, during an earlier phase of the EU's history, when France thought that certain vital national interests were being overridden by Community legislation, it boycotted Council meetings for a period of time "la politique de la chaise vide"). In an effort to resolve the crisis, the then member-States agreed to a de facto compromise known as the Luxembourg Accord of 28 and 29 January 1966, which read in part as follows:

Majority Voting Procedure.

I.     Where, in the case of decisions which may be taken by majority vote on a proposal of the Commission, very important interests of one or more partners are at stake, the Members of the Council will endeavor, within a reasonable time, to reach solutions which can be adopted by all the Members of the Council while respecting their mutual interests and those of the Community, in accordance with Art. 2 of the Treaty.

II.     With regard to the preceding paragraph, the French delegation considers that where very important interests are at stake the discussion must be continued until unanimous agreement is reached.

III.     The six delegations note that there is a divergence of views on what should be done in the event of a failure to reach complete agreement.

IV.     The six delegations nevertheless consider that this divergence does not prevent the Community's work being resumed in accordance with the normal procedure."

(Extracts from the Council Statement appearing in the Bulletin of the EEC, March 1996, pp 8-10)

Examining the Accord in light of the Treaties, do you think that it has any legal effect in the EU system? In light of an increasing number of decisions taken by majority voting and the increased role of the Parliament, is it fair to say it has been abandoned, or might it still have some force? Could one argue that reliance on the Accords, and general obstructive behaviour by a Member State in the Council, might violate EC 10/TEU 4?

Note also Declaration 7 on Article 16(4) of the TEU and Article 238(2) of the TFEU which required the Council to adopt a decision on the coming into effect of the Lisbon Treaty in the following terms:

## Section 1

## Provisions to be applied from 1 November 2014 to 31 March 2017

## Article 1

From 1 November 2014 to 31 March 2017, if members of the Council, representing:

(a) at least three quarters of the population, or

(b) at least three quarters of the number of Member States

necessary to constitute a blocking minority resulting from the application of Article 16(4), first subparagraph, of the Treaty on European Union or Article 238(2) of the Treaty on the Functioning of the European Union, indicate their opposition to the Council adopting an act by a qualified majority, the Council shall discuss the issue.

## Article 2

The Council shall, in the course of these discussions, do all in its power to reach, within a reasonable time and without prejudicing obligatory time limits laid down by Union law, a satisfactory solution to address concerns raised by the members of the Council referred to in Article 1.

## Article 3

To this end, the President of the Council, with the assistance of the Commission and in compliance with the Rules of Procedure of the Council, shall undertake any initiative necessary to facilitate a wider basis of agreement in the Council. The members of the Council shall lend him or her their assistance.

## Section 2

## Provisions to be applied as from 1 April 2017

## Article 4

As from 1 April 2017, if members of the Council, representing:

(a) at least 55% of the population, or

(b) at least 55% of the number of Member States

necessary to constitute a blocking minority resulting from the application of Article 16(4), first subparagraph, of the Treaty on European Union or Article 238(2) of the Treaty on the Functioning of the European Union, indicate their opposition to the Council adopting an act by a qualified majority, the Council shall discuss the issue.

### Article 5

The Council shall, in the course of these discussions, do all in its power to reach, within a reasonable time and without prejudicing obligatory time limits laid down by Union law, a satisfactory solution to address concerns raised by the members of the Council referred to in Article 4.

### Article 6

To this end, the President of the Council, with the assistance of the Commission and in compliance with the Rules of Procedure of the Council, shall undertake any initiative necessary to facilitate a wider basis of agreement in the Council. The members of the Council shall lend him or her their assistance.

## [C]  Interaction between Institutions

### PARLIAMENT v. COUNCIL
#### (TRANSPORT INFRASTRUCTURE COSTS)
Case C-21/94, 1995 EC [114] J CELEX LEXIS 430, [1995] ECR I-1827

[The Parliament brought this action to annul a directive relating to the charging of transport infrastructure costs to heavy goods vehicles ([1998] OJ C 79, p. 8), which eventually adopted by the Council after making some amendments following the consultation with the Parliament.

The Parliament alleged that the Council's failure to consult it a second time before adopting the directive in question constituted an infringement of its right to take part in the EU legislative process. It claimed that reconsultation was required where the text adopted by the Council has been substantially amended in comparison with the Commission's proposal.]

17 It must first of all be borne in mind that due consultation of the Parliament in the cases provided for by the Treaty constitutes an essential formal requirement breach of which renders the measure concerned . . . The effective participation of the Parliament in the legislative process of the Community, in accordance with the procedures laid down by the Treaty, represents an essential factor in the institutional balance intended by the Treaty. Such power reflects the fundamental democratic principle that the people should take part in the exercise of power through the intermediary of a representative assembly . . .

18 The duty to consult the European Parliament in the course of the legislative procedure, in the cases provided for by the Treaty, implies the requirement that the Parliament should be reconsulted whenever the text finally adopted, viewed as a whole, departs substantially from the text on which the Parliament has already been consulted, except where the amendments essentially correspond to the wish of the Parliament itself . . .

19 The Court must therefore consider whether or not the amendments referred to by the Parliament affect the actual substance of the text, viewed as a whole.

20 It should be borne in mind that the Commission proposal on which the Parliament gave its opinion provided that the Council should adopt as soon as possible appropriate measures aimed at introducing a harmonized system of road charging which shall include vehicle taxes, excise duty on fuel and charges (user charges and tolls) for the use of certain types of road infrastructure and shall take infrastructure and external costs, including environmental costs, into account' (Article 9(1)). The Commission was to submit to the Council, before 1 January 1998, a report and proposals aimed at achieving the objective set out in paragraph 1. Acting on the proposals, the Council shall, by 31 December 1998, adopt a harmonized system which shall enter into force as of 30 June 1999 at the latest' (Article 9(3)).

21 In contrast, the directive provides that no later than 31 December 1997 the Commission is to present a report to the Council on implementation of the directive, accompanied if necessary . . . by proposals for establishing cost-charging arrangements based on the principle of territoriality, in which national borders will not play a predominant role' (Article 12).

22 As the Advocate General pointed out in paragraph 49 of his Opinion, it is apparent from a comparison between the Commission's initial proposal and the directive not only that the Council is no longer obliged to adopt a harmonized system by 31 December 1998 at the latest, but also that the Commission is no longer required to submit, in the report to be presented to the Council, proposals for establishing cost-charging arrangements based on the principle of territoriality. Those amendments go to the very essence of the system introduced and must be classified as substantial.

23 It is, moreover, not disputed that those amendments do not correspond to any wish expressed by Parliament.

24 Nevertheless, the Council believes that even if the text finally adopted, viewed as a whole, did depart substantially from the text on which the Parliament had been consulted, it was not required to reconsult that institution provided that, as in this case, the Council was sufficiently well informed as to the opinion of the Parliament on the essential points at issue.

25 That argument must be rejected.

26 Proper consultation of the Parliament in the cases provided for by the Treaty constitutes one of the means enabling it to play an effective role in the legislative process of the Community (see, in particular, the judgment in Case C-316/91 Parliament v. Council 1994 ECR I-625, paragraph 17); to accept the Council's argument would result in seriously undermining that essential participation in the maintenance of the institutional balance intended by the Treaty and would amount to disregarding the influence that due consultation of the Parliament can have on adoption of the measure in question.

27 Since the abovementioned amendments, which affect the scheme of the proposal as a whole, are in themselves enough to require reconsultation of the Parliament, it is not necessary to consider the other arguments put forward by the Parliament.

28 Consequently, the fact that the Parliament was not consulted for a second time

during the legislative procedure laid down in Articles 75 [91] and 99 [113] of the EEC Treaty constitutes an infringement of essential formal requirements as a result of which the measure at issue must be annulled.

Preservation of the effects of the directive

29 In its defence, the Council, supported by the German Government, has asked the Court, if it should annul the directive, to order that the effects of the directive should be preserved until the Council has adopted new legislation.

30 In its reply, the Parliament indicated that it had no objection to such a request, which in fact seemed to it to be justified on important grounds of legal certainty. In its observations on the statements in intervention of the German Government and of the United Kingdom, the Parliament did however suggest that the Court should order the Council to adopt new legislation within a period to be fixed by the Court in order to prompt that institution to resume as quickly as possible the procedure for the proper replacement of the directive.

31 . . . [T]he need to avoid discontinuity in the programme for the harmonization of transport taxation and important considerations of legal certainty, comparable with those arising where certain regulations are annulled, justify the Court in exercising the power expressly conferred on it by the second paragraph of Article 174 [264] of the EC Treaty when it annuls a regulation and in stating which of the effects of the contested directive must be preserved . . .

32 In the particular circumstances of this case, all the effects of the annulled directive should be preserved provisionally until the Council has adopted a new directive.

33 The request of the Parliament that the Court should impose on the Council a time-limit within which the latter must adopt a new directive cannot be upheld. The Court does not have jurisdiction to issue such an order in the context of its review of the legality of an act under Article 173 [263] of the Treaty. The fact none the less remains that the Council is under a duty to put an end within a reasonable period to the infringement it has committed.

## NOTES AND QUESTIONS

1.  This case centers on the interesting question as to what level of alteration to a proposal will trigger a requirement that Parliament be re-consulted. How did the Court analyze this question?

2.  Was the decision to preserve the effects of the directive in question consistent with the statements of the court that the consultation procedure is an essential element of the process designed to ensure that the people of Europe can participate in the legislative process? Does the Court's decision in this regard actually add to legal certainty? Does this imply that the consultation procedure is essentially a waste of time?

3.  Somewhat parallel situations may arise in the U.S. in administrative rulemaking procedures, where public hearings may be required.

4. For similar cases, see, for example, *Parliament v. Council (Visas)*, Case C-392/95, 997 ECJ CELEX LEXIS 326, [1997] ECR I-3213, concerning a regulation for the determination of third countries whose nationals must be in possession of visas when crossing the external borders of the Member States; and *Germany v. Council (Bananas)* Case C-280/93, 1994 ECJ CELEX LEXIS 385, [1994] ECR I-4973, regarding the common organization of the market in bananas where the court stated that consultation of the European Parliament, where that is provided for, means that a fresh consultation should take place whenever the text finally adopted, taken as a whole, differs in essence from the text on which the Parliament has already been consulted, except in cases where the amendments substantially correspond to the wishes of the Parliament itself.

5. In *SA Roquette Freres v. Council*, Case 138/79, [1980] ECR 3333, the ECJ noted that the consultation provided for in various Treaty provisions "is the means which allows the Parliament to play an actual part in the legislative process of the EU. Such power represents an essential factor in the institutional balance intended by the Treaty. Although limited, it reflects at Community level the fundamental democratic principle that the peoples should take part in the exercise of power through the intermediary of a representative assembly. Due consultation of the Parliament in the cases provided for by the Treaty therefore constitutes an essential formality disregard of which means that the measure concerned is void. In that respect it is pertinent to point out that observance of that requirement implies that the Parliament has expressed its opinion. It is impossible to take the view that the requirement is satisfied by the Council's simply asking for the opinion." Could the Parliament nonetheless expand its right of "consultation" to exercise more power?

6. Under EC 254/TFEU 297, regulations must be published in the Official Journal of the EU and enter into force on the date specified in them or, if no date is indicated, on the twentieth day following their publication. According to the court, "in general the principle of legal certainty . . . precludes an EU measure from taking effect from a point in time before its publication, it may exceptionally be otherwise where the purpose to be achieved so demands and where the legitimate expectations of those concerned are duly respected." (*Tunnel Refineries Ltd. v. Council*, Case 114/81 [1982] ECR 3189 at 3206.) EC 254/TFEU 297 requires that directives and decisions be notified to their addressees and take effect upon such notification. However, irregularities in the notification procedure are extraneous to the measure and therefore do not invalidate it. *Imperial Chemical Industries Ltd. v. Council*, Case 48/69, [1972] ECR 619 at 652.

7. In *Skoma-Lux sro v. Celní ředitelství Olomouc*, Case 161/06, [2007] ECR I-10841 the Court interpreted article 58 of the Act of Accession of the 10 new Member States ([2003] OJ L 236/17) to preclude the enforcement of EU law in the new states until the legislation in question had been translated into the additional official languages.

8. The duty of consultation is a two-way street. The Parliament cannot complain about actions taken before it gives its final opinion if it has unduly delayed that opinion or put itself in a position where it cannot be given in a timely manner: *Parliament v. Council (Generalised Preferences)* Case C-65/93 [1995] ECR I-643. If

the Parliament could indefinitely delay action by simply not providing its opinion, this would amount to a power of veto.

**9.** The Institutions have worked out some basic ground rules for their interaction, as set out in the *Interinstitutional Agreement on Better Law-Making* [2003] OJ C 321/1. The provisions of the *Framework Agreement between the Commission and the Parliament* of which an excerpt appears in § 6.06 *infra* are intended to complement the above *Interinstitutional Agreement*. The Council was annoyed that the Commission and the Parliament chose to enter into this further agreement without its involvement. Other interinstitutional agreements (IIAs) are:

- IIA on common guidelines for the **quality of drafting** of Community legislation

- IIA on an accelerated working method for official **codification** of legislative texts

- IIA on a structured use of the **recasting** technique for legal acts.

**10.** The Institutions also need to work with many third parties to obtain information and opinions. Lobbyists play a key role in this process. Much has been written about the development of lobbying efforts at both the Commission and the Parliament. As with the Washington environment, the power of the lobbyists is strong, particularly since both Commission employees and MEPs are remote from day-to-day contact with the population as a whole. Influence at the Parliament tends to be focused on the various standing committees where legislation is assigned and debated much as in the U.S. Congress. The small size of the Commission staff means that often only one person may be the "expert" on a particular subject matter. He or she will look outside for help (this is an integral part of the process). See J. M. Alonso Vizcaino, D. Obradovic, *Good governance requirements concerning the participation of interest groups in EU consultations* (2006) 43 CML Rev. 1049; and S. Mazey and J. Richardson, *Pressure Groups and Lobbying in the EC*, in Juliet Lodge (Ed.), The European Community and the Challenge of the Future (St Martin's Press, 1993).

The Commission and the Parliament have tried to regulate the activities of lobbyists by requiring their registration and by adopting a Code of Conduct of interest representatives in order to make the whole process more transparent. The European Commission launched its online register of interest representatives in June 2008 and adopted on 27 May 2008 a *Communication relating to the European Transparency Initiative: A framework for relations with interest representatives (Register and Code of Conduct)* (COM (2008) 323). The Communication also includes information on the Register for interest representatives with which the Code is closely connected.

**11.** For other detailed accounts of the legislative process, see, e.g., K. Neunreither and A. Wiener (eds.), European Integration after Amsterdam, Institutional Dynamics and Prospects for Democracy (Oxford University Press, 2000); P. Craig and C. Harlow (Eds.), Lawmaking in the European Union (Kluwer, 1998).

## § 6.04   LEGAL STANDARDS FOR LEGISLATIVE ACTS AND RULEMAKING

### [A]   The Requirement to State Reasons and the Legal Basis for Legislation

## THE QUEEN v. SECRETARY OF STATE FOR HEALTH, EX PARTE BRITISH AMERICAN TOBACCO (INVESTMENTS) LTD AND IMPERIAL TOBACCO LTD.
Case C-491/01, 2002 ECJ CELEX LEXIS 628, [2002] ECR I-11453

[Proceedings had been brought in the UK courts by British American Tobacco (Investments) Ltd and Imperial Tobacco Ltd, seeking permission to apply for judicial review of "the intention and/or obligation" of the United Kingdom Government to transpose Directive 2001/37 on tobacco advertising into national law. As will be seen in Chapter 11, a prior attempt at harmonizing tobacco advertising was annulled by the Court. The Court was asked a number of questions by the national court relating to the legal basis of the Directive.]

[Was EC 95/TFEU 114 a valid basis?]

58. It is necessary to consider here whether Article 95 EC [114] is an appropriate legal basis for the Directive and, if it is, to establish whether recourse to Article 133 EC [207] as a second legal basis is either necessary or possible in the circumstances.

59. As a preliminary point, the case-law concerning Article 100a(1) of the EC Treaty (now, after amendment, Article 95 [114](1) EC) must be borne in mind.

60. First of all . . . the measures referred to in that provision are intended to improve the conditions for the establishment and functioning of the internal market and must genuinely have that object, actually contributing to the elimination of obstacles to the free movement of goods or to the freedom to provide services, or to the removal of distortions of competition.

61. Also . . . while recourse to Article 95 EC [114] as a legal basis is possible if the aim is to prevent the emergence of future obstacles to trade resulting from multifarious development of national laws, the emergence of such obstacles must be likely and the measure in question must be designed to prevent them . . .

62. Finally, provided that the conditions for recourse to Article 95 EC [114] as a legal basis are fulfilled, the Community legislature cannot be prevented from relying on that legal basis on the ground that public health protection is a decisive factor in the choices to be made (see, to that effect, the tobacco advertising judgment, paragraph 88). Moreover, the first subparagraph of Article 152(1) EC provides that a high level of human health protection is to be ensured in the definition and implementation of all Community policies and activities, and Article 95 [114] (3) EC explicitly requires that, in achieving harmonisation, a high level of protection of human health should be guaranteed.

63. It is to be determined, in light of those principles, whether the conditions for

recourse to Article 95 EC [114] as a legal basis have, in the case of the Directive, been satisfied.

* * *

67. . . . [H]aving regard to the fact that the public is increasingly conscious of the dangers to health posed by consuming tobacco products, it is likely that obstacles to the free movement of those products would arise by reason of the adoption by the Member States of new rules reflecting that development and intended more effectively to discourage consumption of those products by means of warnings and information appearing on their packaging or to reduce the harmful effects of tobacco products by introducing new rules governing their composition.

68. That analysis is confirmed by the content of the recitals in the preamble to the Directive and by the observations submitted during the procedure.

69. It is apparent from the seventh recital in the preamble to the Directive that several Member States were contemplating adopting measures establishing maximum carbon monoxide yields for cigarettes if such measures were not taken at Community level.

70. Similarly, the ninth recital in the preamble to the Directive states that differences had emerged between the laws of the Member States on the limitation of the maximum nicotine yield of cigarettes. Observations submitted during the procedure show that three Member States had already introduced such limitations and that several others were thinking of doing so. Even if it is accepted that, having regard to the levels at which they were set and to the biochemical link between tar and nicotine, those limitations did not in practice form an obstacle to the marketing of cigarettes which complied with the requirements relating to the maximum tar yield permitted under Community law, the fact nevertheless remains that for Member States to set specific maximum yields for nicotine creates a risk that the subsequent lowering of those maximum yields may entail the creation of obstacles to trade.

71. Furthermore, the 13th recital in the preamble to the Directive mentions negotiations for the drafting of a World Health Organisation Framework Convention on Tobacco Control, including the definition of internationally applicable standards for tobacco products.

72. In addition, the 19th and 22nd recitals in the preamble to the Directive refer to the fact that different Member States have different laws with regard to the presentation of warnings and indications of yields of harmful substances on the one hand and the ingredients and additives used in the manufacture of tobacco products on the other.

73. Lastly, the written procedure reveals that one Member State had adopted provisions regulating the use of certain of the descriptive terms mentioned in the 27th recital in the preamble to the Directive and referred to in Article 7.

74. . . . Article 13(1), which guarantees the free movement of products which comply with its requirements. By forbidding the Member States to prevent, on grounds relating to the matters harmonised by the Directive, the import, sale or consumption of tobacco products which do comply, that provision gives the Directive

its full effect in relation to its object of improving the conditions for the functioning of the internal market.

75. It follows that the Directive genuinely has as its object the improvement of the conditions for the functioning of the internal market and that it was, therefore, possible for it to be adopted on the basis of Article 95 EC [114], and it is no bar that the protection of public health was a decisive factor in the choices involved in the harmonising measures which it defines.

*   *   *

[Was the choice of a secondary basis, namely EC 133/TFEU 207, legitimate?]

93. As a preliminary point, it must be borne in mind that, according to settled case-law, in the context of the organisation of the powers of the Community the choice of a legal basis for a measure must rest on objective factors which are amenable to judicial review. Those factors include in particular the aim and the content of the measure . . .

94. If examination of a Community act shows that it has a twofold purpose or twofold component and if one of these is identifiable as main or predominant, whereas the other is merely incidental, the act must be founded on a sole legal basis, that is, the one required by the main or predominant purpose or component . . . Exceptionally, if it is established that the act simultaneously pursues a number of objectives, indissociably linked, without one being secondary and indirect in relation to the other, such an act may be founded on the various corresponding legal bases . . .

95. In light of the principles set out in the two paragraphs above and having regard to the conclusion in paragraph 91 above, it must be concluded that the Directive could not simultaneously have Articles 95 EC [114] and 133 EC [207] for a legal basis.

96. Without there being any need to consider whether, in its provisions affecting tobacco products exported to non-member countries, the Directive also pursued an objective linked to the implementation of the common commercial policy under Article 133 EC [207], that objective is in any event secondary in relation to the aim and content of the Directive as a whole, which is primarily designed to improve the conditions for the functioning of the internal market.

97. It follows that Article 95 EC [114] constitutes the only appropriate legal basis for the Directive and that it is incorrect for it to cite Article 133 EC [207] also as a legal basis.

98. However, that incorrect reference to Article 133 EC [207] as a second legal basis for the Directive does not of itself mean that the latter is invalid. Such an error in the legal basis relied on for a Community measure is no more than a purely formal defect, unless it gave rise to irregularity in the procedure applicable to the adoption of that act . . .

*   *   *

[Whether recourse to the twofold legal basis of Articles 95 EC [114] and 133 EC

[207] vitiates the procedure in adopting the Directive by reason of the application of two legislative procedures incompatible one with the other, and whether that renders the Directive invalid.]

103. . . . [I]t must be established whether the legislative procedure which was actually followed when the Directive was adopted, on the bases of Articles 95 EC [114] and 133 EC [207], satisfies the requirements of the legislative procedure applicable when a Community act is adopted on the basis of Article 95 EC [114] alone.

104. Article 95 [114] (1) EC provides that measures enacted on its basis are to be adopted in accordance with the co-decision procedure referred to in Article 251 EC and after consulting the Economic and Social Committee.

105. It is common ground that that procedure was followed in the instant case when the Directive was adopted.

106. Furthermore, adding Article 133 EC [207] to Article 95 EC [114] as a second legal basis for the Directive did not prejudice the substance of the co-decision procedure followed in this case.

107. Article 133(4) EC provides that, in exercising the powers conferred upon it by that provision, the Council is to act by a qualified majority.

108. Accordingly, the fact that the procedure laid down for the adoption of acts on that second legal basis was followed did not entail an obligation on the part of the Council to act unanimously in any event, it being borne in mind that in the co-decision procedure laid down in Article 251 EC [294], it is in principle to act by qualified majority, except where it approves the amendments to the common position which have been made by the Parliament and on which the Commission has delivered a negative opinion, in which case it must act unanimously.

109. In those circumstances, . . . the distinction between those cases in which the Council acts by qualified majority and those in which it must act unanimously, which forms the essential point of the legislative procedure, has not in the circumstances of the case been in any way compromised by the simultaneous reference to the two legal bases mentioned in the Directive.

110. The argument that application of the co-decision procedure in the adoption of a measure concerning the common commercial policy is contrary to the separation of powers between institutions intended by the Treaty is in any event without any bearing in the circumstances since, as paragraph 97 above makes clear, the Directive is not an act which must be adopted on the basis of Article 133 EC [207].

111. It follows from the foregoing considerations relating to Question 1(b) that recourse to the twofold legal basis of Articles 95 EC [114] and 133 EC [207] has not vitiated the procedure for adopting the Directive and that the latter is not invalid on that account.

## NOTES AND QUESTIONS

1. What is the Court's view about using more than one legal basis for an act? (See also: *Commission v. Council (Rotterdam Convention)*, Case C-94/03, 2005 ECJ CELEX LEXIS 506, [2006] ECR I-1 and *Commission v. Parliament and Council (Regulation 304/2003 on dangerous chemicals)*, Case C-178/03, 2006 ECJ CELEX LEXIS 986, [2006] ECR I-107.

2. The requirement that the legal basis in the EC Treaty/TFEU be cited has become very important. Why might this be so? How did the Court go about its analysis here as to which was the correct legal basis for the regulations in question?

3. In *Parliament v. Council (Regulation on Shipments of Waste)*, Case 187/93, 1994 ECJ CELEX LEXIS 380, [1994] ECR I-2857, the Parliament sought to annul the choice of EC 175/TFEU 192 for Regulation 259/93 [1993] OJ L 301, but the ECJ upheld the Council's decision on the ground that the regulation specifically addressed environmental policy objectives rather than the completion of the internal market. Given the overlap of the provisions regarding environmental matters, such disputes may become common. Could the choice of a particular basis for legislation be influenced by the composition of the Council adopting the measure (e.g., environmental ministers vs. foreign ministers)? Is there not a danger here that the varying composition of the Council, coupled with legislative developments under different articles, will lead to inherent conflicts between EU laws?

4. Under EC 253/TFEU 296 regulations, directives, and decisions adopted by the Council or the Commission must state the reasons on which they are based and refer to any proposals or opinions that were required to be obtained in accordance with the Treaty. This article is designed to ensure that the decision-making procedures required by the Treaty have been followed. As stated by the European Court of Justice in *British-American Tobacco Ltd. et al. v. Commission* Joined Cases 142/84 and 156/84 1987 ECJ CELEX LEXIS 17, [1987] ECR 4487, "the extent of the duty to provide a statement of reasons prescribed in Article 253 [296] of the Treaty depends on the nature of the measure in question and on the circumstances in which it was adopted." At a minimum, the statement must set forth its reasoning clearly and unambiguously to allow interested parties to know the reasons for the measure involved and the court to exercise its supervisory authority. Failure to do so constitutes an infringement of an essential procedural requirement, which is one of the grounds for annulment under EC 230/TFEU 263. In various opinions the court had indicated that the statement must set forth the facts on which the measure is based, as well as the arguments that were decisive for adoption of the measure. See, e.g., *Geitling Selling Agency for Ruhr Coal et. al. v. High Authority*, Case 2/56, [1957 and 1958] ECR 3 at 15 and *Timex Corporation v. Council and Commission*, Case 264/82, [1985] ECR 849, *Germany v. Commission (Regional Aids)*, Case 248/84, 1987 ECJ CELEX LEXIS 24, [1987] ECR 4013.

5. Where a measure is in fact based on more than one Treaty article and the procedures for adoption differ, both procedures must be followed: see *European Parliament v. Council (International Fund For Ireland)* Case C-166/07, 2009 ECJ EUR-Lex LEXIS 1504, [2009] ECR I-7135.

## [B]  Retroactivity, Legitimate Expectations and Legal Certainty

### OPENBAAR MINISTERIE (PUBLIC PROSECUTOR) v. DANIEL BOUT and BVI BOUT EN ZONEN
#### 1982 ECJ EUR-Lex LEXIS 173, [1982] ECR 00381

[The defendants in this criminal action were prosecuted under Belgian fisheries law for violating regulations regarding net mesh sizes and ship tonnage limitations. At the time EU regulations had not yet been introduced, but it had already been held by the Court that conservation of marine resources was an EU exclusive competence. The defendants argued that Belgium had lost competence to adopt its own regulation, which would then open up the possibility that any subsequent EU regulation would have to be retroactive. When subsequently a regulation on this subject was adopted (Regulation 2527/80), its requirements were less restrictive than the Belgian law, so the defendants indeed argued that the regulation could be considered retroactive.]

13 The [national court] raises the issue whether [Regulation 2527/80] . . . must be interpreted as having retroactive effect. . . . Substantive rules of Community law must be interpreted, in order to ensure respect for the principles of legal certainty and the protection of legitimate expectation, as applying to situations existing before their entry into force only in so far as it clearly follows from their terms, objectives or general scheme that such an effect must be given to them.

14 By virtue of article 22 of [Regulation 2527/80], that regulation entered into force on 1 October 1980. There is nothing in the regulation, or in subsequent regulations extending its validity, to justify the conclusion that it is intended to apply to situations existing prior to that date.

### NOTES AND QUESTIONS

1.  Is it perhaps surprising that the Court did not rule out altogether the idea that an EU act could have retroactive effect?

2.  Retroactivity and legitimate expectations are both aspects of the more general principle sometimes invoked on its own that legislation should not create a situation where private citizens are not able to determine what the law is or how it is to be applied to them (the principle of legal certainty). This principle does not mean that legislation is invalid because it contains broad provisions requiring interpretation. Rather, it is applied to situations where it is not clear whether a law will or can be applied or not. This will be illustrated in the *French Seamen* and *Jacques Pistre* cases, in Chapters 7 and 13 respectively.

3.  It should be noted that these principles also apply to Member States in the course of implementation of EU law (see, *e.g.*, the *Marks and Spencer* case in Chapter 9) and to Union executive acts. See in regard to the latter, *Embassy Limousines & Services v. Parliament*, Case T-203/96, 1998 ECJ CELEX LEXIS 163, [1998] ECR II-4239, where a company had been encouraged to believe it had won a tender to provide limousine services to the Parliament and incurred expense

based on this encouragement only to be told that the whole tender invitation process was annulled. The Court stated:

> 86 It follows from the foregoing that the Parliament, first, induced on the part of the applicant a legitimate expectation by encouraging it to take a risk which went beyond that normally run by tenderers in a tendering procedure and, secondly, failed to inform the applicant of an important change in the conduct of the tendering procedure.

The principle of legitimate expectations requires that where parties reasonably rely on any position taken by the Union and suffer a detriment due to a breach of the trust they have placed in that position, the action giving rise to that detriment may be invalid. See, for example, *Mulder v. Minister van Landbouw en Visserij*, Case C-120/86, [1988] ECR 2321. This concept was used in a rather unusual way to invalidate a regulation imposing customs duties on Austrian goods that was adopted only a month before the EEA came into existence (Austria at that point not being an EU Member State, but about to be a member of the EEA). Under the terms of the EEA Treaty, which of course was already signed at that point, any new customs duties would have been illegal as between the EU and Austria from the date it entered into force: *Opel Austria GmbH v. Council*, 1997 ECJ CELEX LEXIS 21, [1997] ECR II-39.

## § 6.05  ADVICE AND CONSENT

### PARLIAMENT v. COUNCIL (MAURITANIA)
Case C-189/97, 1999 ECJ CELEX LEXIS 267, [1999] ECR I-4741

[The European Parliament sought to have annulled Council Regulation (EC) No 408/97 of 24 February 1997 on the conclusion of an Agreement on cooperation in the sea fisheries sector between the European Community and Mauritania (the "contested regulation"). The Council's action was based on EC 228 (3)/TFEU 218 (6)(b). It should be noted that at the time the general rule was that Parliament should be consulted and only exceptionally was its assent required. After Lisbon there is no longer a hierarchy of rules and indeed agreements requiring "consent" are now listed first in TFEU 218(6)(a).]

20 The Parliament maintains . . . that by requiring its assent for the conclusion of agreements with important budgetary implications, that provision is intended to safeguard its internal powers as a constituent part of the budgetary authority. In the light of that objective, it proposes that, in determining whether an agreement has important budgetary implications, the criteria to be taken into account should include the fact that expenditure under the agreement is spread over several years, the relative share of such expenditure in relation to expenditure of the same kind under the budget heading concerned, and the rate of increase in expenditure under the agreement in question in relation to the financial section of the previous agreement.

21 The Parliament goes on to state that the fisheries agreement with Mauritania undoubtedly satisfies those three criteria. First, it makes provision for financial compensation split into five annual tranches, the amounts of which vary between

ECU 51 560 000 and ECU 55 160 000. Second, that financial compensation represents, for each of the years in question, more than 20% of the appropriations entered under the budget heading concerned (heading B7-8000, International fisheries agreements'). Finally, the financial outlay in favour of the Islamic Republic of Mauritania has increased more than fivefold in relation to the previous agreement, or has more than doubled if only the year 1995, which included exceptional supplementary compensation, is used as the point of reference.

22 The Council, supported by the Spanish Government, contends that the second subparagraph of Article 228 (3) [218 (6)(a)] of the Treaty must be strictly interpreted, since it constitutes a derogation from the rule laid down by the first subparagraph, whereby the Council is to conclude agreements after consulting the Parliament.

23 The Council considers, in that respect, that the criteria put forward by the Parliament are inoperative. First, the fact that expenditure is spread over several years is not decisive, because the budget is, by definition, annual. Nor is the extent of the financial impact of the agreement in relation to expenditure of the same kind under the budget heading in question significant, given that budgetary nomenclature is capable of being altered under the budget procedure and that the amount of available appropriations may always be adapted by means of transfers or supplementary budgets. Finally, the rate of increase in expenditure is not very revealing, since a high rate may very well correspond to minimal expenditure.

24 The Council therefore maintains that, in order to assess whether an agreement has important budgetary implications, it is necessary to refer to the overall budget of the Community, and that it did not act in a manifestly erroneous and arbitrary manner in seeking merely an opinion of the Parliament for a fisheries agreement under which annual expenditure amounted to 0.07% of that budget.

25 In the context of the organisation of powers in the Community, the choice of a legal basis for a measure must be based on objective factors which are amenable to judicial review . . .

26 In order to assess whether an agreement has important budgetary implications within the meaning of the second subparagraph of Article 228(3) [218 (6)(a)] of the Treaty, the Council has referred to the overall budget of the Community. It should be pointed out, however, that appropriations allocated to external operations of the Community traditionally account for a marginal fraction of the Community budget. Thus, in 1996 and 1997, those appropriations, grouped under subsection B7, External operations', barely exceeded 5% of the overall budget. In those circumstances, a comparison between the annual financial cost of an agreement and the overall Community budget scarcely appears significant, and to apply such a criterion might render the relevant wording of the second subparagraph of Article 228 (3) [218(6)(a)] of the Treaty wholly ineffective.

27 The Council maintains, however, that the criterion upon which it relies does not have the effect of excluding the use of that legal basis altogether. In support of that view, it cites the Agreement on cooperation in the sea fisheries sector between the European Community and the Kingdom of Morocco (OJ 1997 L 30, p. 5), the financial implications of which, amounting to 0.15% of the Community budget

annually, it acknowledged were important.

28 The Council has not, however, explained in any way how such a small percentage could render the financial implications of an agreement important, when the scarcely more insignificant figure of 0.07% is said to be insufficient in that respect.

29 As regards the three criteria proposed by the Parliament, the Court finds that the first of them may indeed contribute towards characterising an agreement as having important budgetary implications. Relatively modest annual expenditure may, over a number of years, represent a significant budgetary outlay.

30 The second and third criteria put forward by the Parliament do not, however, appear to be relevant. In the first place, budget headings, which can moreover be altered, vary substantially in importance, so that the relative share of the expenditure under the agreement may be large in relation to appropriations of the same kind entered under the budget heading concerned, even though the expenditure in question is small. Moreover, the rate of increase in expenditure under the agreement may be high in comparison with that arising from the previous agreement, whilst the amounts involved may still be small.

31 . . . [A] comparison between the annual financial cost of an international agreement and the overall budget scarcely appears significant. However, comparison of the expenditure under an agreement with the amount of the appropriations designed to finance the Community's external operations, grouped under subsection B7 of the budget, enables that agreement to be set in the context of the budgetary outlay approved by the Community for its external policy. That comparison thus offers a more appropriate means of assessing the financial importance which the agreement actually has for the Community.

32 Where, as in this case, a sectoral agreement is involved, the above analysis may, in appropriate cases, and without excluding the possibility of taking other factors into account, be complemented by a comparison between the expenditure entailed by the agreement and the whole of the budgetary appropriations for the sector in question, taking the internal and external aspects together. Such a comparison makes it possible to determine, from another angle and in an equally consistent context, the financial outlay approved by the Community in entering into that agreement. However, since the sectors vary substantially in terms of their budgetary importance, that examination cannot result in the financial implications of an agreement being found to be important where they do not represent a significant share of the appropriations designed to finance the Community's external operations.

33 In this case, the fisheries agreement with Mauritania was concluded for five years, which is not a particularly lengthy period. Moreover, the financial compensation for which it makes provision is split into annual tranches the amounts of which vary between ECU 51 560 000 and ECU 55 160 000. In respect of previous budgetary years, those amounts, whilst exceeding 5% of expenditure on fisheries, represent barely more than 1% of the whole of the payment appropriations allocated for external operations of the Community, a proportion which, whilst far from negligible, can scarcely be described as important. In those circumstances, if the Council had taken that comparison into account, it would also have been entitled

to take the view that the fisheries agreement with Mauritania did not have important budgetary implications for the Community within the meaning of the second subparagraph of Article 228 (3) [218(6)(a)] of the Treaty.

34 Furthermore, the scope of that provision, as set out in the Treaty, cannot, despite what the Parliament suggests, be affected by the extent of the powers available to national parliaments when approving international agreements with financial implications.

35 It follows from all the foregoing considerations that the Council was right to conclude the fisheries agreement with Mauritania on the basis, inter alia, of the first subparagraph of Article 228 (3) [218(6)(b)] of the Treaty. This action must therefore be dismissed.

## NOTES AND QUESTIONS

1.    This case is an example perhaps of how political compromise in the drafting of provisions that create greater powers for the Parliament can sometimes lead to questionable results. Does this suggest a problem in terms of how legislative powers are allocated among the institutions? Was the Court's method of analyzing the question raised any more logical than the Parliament's, do you think?

2.    How important did the Court consider the Parliament's argument to be that there should be an analogy with powers of the Member States' legislatures to vote on international agreements? [para 34] Is the limitation of Parliament's role to one of protecting its internal prerogatives appropriate? What of the role of the Council (particularly if it is perceived as a sort of upper House)? By analogy with the U.S., would that not then be the more appropriate body to ratify treaties? Note however that under EC 300/TFEU 218 the Council does not merely ratify, it is the institution that actually concludes agreements.

3.    The Commission and the Parliament have worked out a modus operandi with respect to how they interact in regard to international agreements, as described in the *framework agreement on relations between the European Parliament and the European Commission* (November 2010) in the following terms:

(ii) **International agreements and enlargement**

23. Parliament shall be immediately and fully informed at all stages of the negotiation and conclusion of international agreements, including the definition of negotiating directives. The Commission shall act in a manner to give full effect to its obligations pursuant to Article 218 TFEU, while respecting each Institution's role in accordance with Article 13(2) TEU . . .

24. The information referred to in point 23 shall be provided to Parliament in sufficient time for it to be able to express its point of view if appropriate, and for the Commission to be able to take Parliament's views as far as possible into account. This information shall, as a general rule, be provided to Parliament through the responsible parliamentary committee and, where appropriate, at a plenary sitting. In duly justified cases, it shall be provided to more than one parliamentary committee.

Parliament and the Commission undertake to establish appropriate procedures and safeguards for the forwarding of confidential information from
the Commission to Parliament, . . .

25. The two Institutions acknowledge that, due to their different institutional roles, the Commission is to represent the European Union in
international negotiations, with the exception of those concerning the
Common Foreign and Security Policy and other cases as provided for in the
Treaties.

Where the Commission represents the Union in international conferences,
it shall, at Parliament's request, facilitate the inclusion of a delegation of
Members of the European Parliament as observers in Union delegations,
so that it may be immediately and fully informed about the conference
proceedings. The Commission undertakes, where applicable, to systematically inform the Parliament delegation about the outcome of negotiations.

Members of the European Parliament may not participate directly in these
negotiations. Subject to the legal, technical and diplomatic possibilities,
they may be granted observer status by the Commission. In the event of
refusal, the Commission will inform Parliament of the reasons therefor.

In addition, the Commission shall facilitate the participation of Members of
the European Parliament as observers in all relevant meetings under its
responsibility before and after negotiation sessions.

26. Under the same conditions, the Commission shall keep Parliament
systematically informed about, and facilitate access as observers for
Members of the European Parliament forming part of Union delegations
to, meetings of bodies set up by multilateral international agreements
involving the Union, whenever such bodies are called upon to take decisions
which require the consent of Parliament or the implementation of which
may require the adoption of legal acts in accordance with the ordinary
legislative procedure.

27. The Commission shall also give Parliament's delegation included in
Union delegations to international conferences access to use all Union
delegation facilities on these occasions, in line with the general principle of
good cooperation between the institutions and taking into account the
available logistics.

The President of Parliament shall send to the President of the Commission
a proposal for the inclusion of a Parliament delegation in the Union
delegation no later than 4 weeks before the start of the conference,
specifying the head of the Parliament delegation and the number of
Members of the European Parliament to be included. In duly justified
cases, this deadline can exceptionally be shortened.

The number of Members of the European Parliament included in the
Parliament delegation and of supporting staff shall be proportionate to the
overall size of the Union delegation.

28. The Commission shall keep Parliament fully informed of the progress of accession negotiations and in particular on major aspects and developments, so as to enable it to express its views in good time through the appropriate parliamentary procedures.

29. When Parliament adopts a recommendation on matters referred to in point 28, pursuant to Rule 90(4) of its Rules of Procedure, and when, for important reasons, the Commission decides that it cannot support such a recommendation, it shall explain the reasons before Parliament, at a plenary sitting or at the next meeting of the relevant parliamentary committee.

## § 6.06    IMPLEMENTING AND DELEGATED RULEMAKING PROCEDURES

### REGULATION 182/2011 OF THE EUROPEAN PARLIAMENT AND OF THE COUNCIL OF 16 FEBRUARY 2011 LAYING DOWN THE RULES AND GENERAL PRINCIPLES CONCERNING MECHANISMS FOR CONTROL BY MEMBER STATES OF THE COMMISSION'S EXERCISE OF IMPLEMENTING POWERS
[2011] OJ L 055/13

Whereas:

(1) Where uniform conditions for the implementation of legally binding Union acts are needed, those acts (hereinafter "basic acts") are to confer implementing powers on the Commission, or, in duly justified specific cases and in the cases provided for in Articles 24 and 26 of the Treaty on European Union, on the Council.

(2) It is for the legislator, fully respecting the criteria laid down in the Treaty on the Functioning of the European Union ("TFEU"), to decide in respect of each basic act whether to confer implementing powers on the Commission in accordance with Article 291(2) of that Treaty.

(3) Hitherto, the exercise of implementing powers by the Commission has been governed by Council Decision 1999/468/EC.

(4) The TFEU now requires the European Parliament and the Council to lay down the rules and general principles concerning mechanisms for control by Member States of the Commission's exercise of implementing powers.

\*    \*    \*

## Article 1

### Subject-matter

This Regulation lays down the rules and general principles governing the mechanisms which apply where a legally binding Union act (hereinafter a "basic act") identifies the need for uniform conditions of implementation and requires that the adoption of implementing acts by the Commission be subject to the control of Member States.

## Article 2

### Selection of procedures

1. A basic act may provide for the application of the advisory procedure or the examination procedure, taking into account the nature or the impact of the implementing act required.

2. The examination procedure applies, in particular, for the adoption of:

(a) implementing acts of general scope;

(b) other implementing acts relating to:

(i) programmes with substantial implications;

(ii) the common agricultural and common fisheries policies;

(iii) the environment, security and safety, or protection of the health or safety, of humans, animals or plants;

(iv) the common commercial policy;

(v) taxation.

3. The advisory procedure applies, as a general rule, for the adoption of implementing acts not falling within the ambit of paragraph 2. However, the advisory procedure may apply for the adoption of the implementing acts referred to in paragraph 2 in duly justified cases.

## Article 3

### Common provisions

1. The common provisions set out in this Article shall apply to all the procedures referred to in Articles 4 to 8.

2. The Commission shall be assisted by a committee composed of representatives of the Member States. The committee shall be chaired by a representative of the Commission. The chair shall not take part in the committee vote.

3. The chair shall submit to the committee the draft implementing act to be adopted

by the Commission.

Except in duly justified cases, the chair shall convene a meeting not less than 14 days from submission of the draft implementing act and of the draft agenda to the committee. The committee shall deliver its opinion on the draft implementing act within a time limit which the chair may lay down according to the urgency of the matter. Time limits shall be proportionate and shall afford committee members early and effective opportunities to examine the draft implementing act and express their views.

4. Until the committee delivers an opinion, any committee member may suggest amendments and the chair may present amended versions of the draft implementing act.

The chair shall endeavour to find solutions which command the widest possible support within the committee. The chair shall inform the committee of the manner in which the discussions and suggestions for amendments have been taken into account, in particular as regards those suggestions which have been largely supported within the committee.

5. In duly justified cases, the chair may obtain the committee's opinion by written procedure. The chair shall send the committee members the draft implementing act and shall lay down a time limit for delivery of an opinion according to the urgency of the matter. Any committee member who does not oppose the draft implementing act or who does not explicitly abstain from voting thereon before the expiry of that time limit shall be regarded as having tacitly agreed to the draft implementing act.

Unless otherwise provided in the basic act, the written procedure shall be terminated without result where, within the time limit referred to in the first subparagraph, the chair so decides or a committee member so requests. In such a case, the chair shall convene a committee meeting within a reasonable time.

6. The committee's opinion shall be recorded in the minutes. Committee members shall have the right to ask for their position to be recorded in the minutes. The chair shall send the minutes to the committee members without delay.

7. Where applicable, the control mechanism shall include referral to an appeal committee.

The appeal committee shall adopt its own rules of procedure by a simple majority of its component members, on a proposal from the Commission.

Where the appeal committee is seised, it shall meet at the earliest 14 days, except in duly justified cases, and at the latest 6 weeks, after the date of referral. Without prejudice to paragraph 3, the appeal committee shall deliver its opinion within 2 months of the date of referral.

A representative of the Commission shall chair the appeal committee.

The chair shall set the date of the appeal committee meeting in close cooperation with the members of the committee, in order to enable Member States and the Commission to ensure an appropriate level of representation. By 1 April 2011, the Commission shall convene the first meeting of the appeal committee in order to adopt its rules of procedure.

Article 4

Advisory procedure

1. Where the advisory procedure applies, the committee shall deliver its opinion, if necessary by taking a vote. If the committee takes a vote, the opinion shall be delivered by a simple majority of its component members.

2. The Commission shall decide on the draft implementing act to be adopted, taking the utmost account of the conclusions drawn from the discussions within the committee and of the opinion delivered.

Article 5

Examination procedure

1. Where the examination procedure applies, the committee shall deliver its opinion by the majority laid down in Article 16(4) and (5) of the Treaty on European Union and, where applicable, Article 238(3) TFEU, for acts to be adopted on a proposal from the Commission. The votes of the representatives of the Member States within the committee shall be weighted in the manner set out in those Articles.

2. Where the committee delivers a positive opinion, the Commission shall adopt the draft implementing act.

3. Without prejudice to Article 7, if the committee delivers a negative opinion, the Commission shall not adopt the draft implementing act. Where an implementing act is deemed to be necessary, the chair may either submit an amended version of the draft implementing act to the same committee within 2 months of delivery of the negative opinion, or submit the draft implementing act within 1 month of such delivery to the appeal committee for further deliberation.

4. Where no opinion is delivered, the Commission may adopt the draft implementing act, except in the cases provided for in the second subparagraph. Where the Commission does not adopt the draft implementing act, the chair may submit to the committee an amended version thereof.

Without prejudice to Article 7, the Commission shall not adopt the draft implementing act where:

(a) that act concerns taxation, financial services, the protection of the health or safety of humans, animals or plants, or definitive multilateral safeguard measures;

(b) the basic act provides that the draft implementing act may not be adopted where no opinion is delivered; or

(c) a simple majority of the component members of the committee opposes it.

In any of the cases referred to in the second subparagraph, where an implementing act is deemed to be necessary, the chair may either submit an amended version of that act to the same committee within 2 months of the vote, or submit the draft implementing act within 1 month of the vote to the appeal committee for further deliberation.

5. By way of derogation from paragraph 4, the following procedure shall apply for the adoption of draft definitive anti-dumping or countervailing measures, where no opinion is delivered by the committee and a simple majority of its component members opposes the draft implementing act.

The Commission shall conduct consultations with the Member States. 14 days at the earliest and 1 month at the latest after the committee meeting, the Commission shall inform the committee members of the results of those consultations and submit a draft implementing act to the appeal committee. By way of derogation from Article 3(7), the appeal committee shall meet 14 days at the earliest and 1 month at the latest after the submission of the draft implementing act. The appeal committee shall deliver its opinion in accordance with Article 6. The time limits laid down in this paragraph shall be without prejudice to the need to respect the deadlines laid down in the relevant basic acts.

## Article 6

### Referral to the appeal committee

1. The appeal committee shall deliver its opinion by the majority provided for in Article 5(1).

2. Until an opinion is delivered, any member of the appeal committee may suggest amendments to the draft implementing act and the chair may decide whether or not to modify it.

The chair shall endeavour to find solutions which command the widest possible support within the appeal committee.

The chair shall inform the appeal committee of the manner in which the discussions and suggestions for amendments have been taken into account, in particular as regards suggestions for amendments which have been largely supported within the appeal committee.

3. Where the appeal committee delivers a positive opinion, the Commission shall adopt the draft implementing act.

Where no opinion is delivered, the Commission may adopt the draft implementing act.

Where the appeal committee delivers a negative opinion, the Commission shall not adopt the draft implementing act.

4. By way of derogation from paragraph 3, for the adoption of definitive multilateral safeguard measures, in the absence of a positive opinion voted by the majority provided for in Article 5(1), the Commission shall not adopt the draft measures.

5. By way of derogation from paragraph 1, until 1 September 2012, the appeal committee shall deliver its opinion on draft definitive anti-dumping or countervailing measures by a simple majority of its component members.

Article 7

Adoption of implementing acts in exceptional cases

By way of derogation from Article 5(3) and the second subparagraph of Article 5(4), the Commission may adopt a draft implementing act where it needs to be adopted without delay in order to avoid creating a significant disruption of the markets in the area of agriculture or a risk for the financial interests of the Union within the meaning of Article 325 TFEU.

In such a case, the Commission shall immediately submit the adopted implementing act to the appeal committee. Where the appeal committee delivers a negative opinion on the adopted implementing act, the Commission shall repeal that act immediately. Where the appeal committee delivers a positive opinion or no opinion is delivered, the implementing act shall remain in force.

Article 8

Immediately applicable implementing acts

1. By way of derogation from Articles 4 and 5, a basic act may provide that, on duly justified imperative grounds of urgency, this Article is to apply.

2. The Commission shall adopt an implementing act which shall apply immediately, without its prior submission to a committee, and shall remain in force for a period not exceeding 6 months unless the basic act provides otherwise.

3. At the latest 14 days after its adoption, the chair shall submit the act referred to in paragraph 2 to the relevant committee in order to obtain its opinion.

4. Where the examination procedure applies, in the event of the committee delivering a negative opinion, the Commission shall immediately repeal the implementing act adopted in accordance with paragraph 2.

5. Where the Commission adopts provisional anti-dumping or countervailing measures, the procedure provided for in this Article shall apply. The Commission shall adopt such measures after consulting or, in cases of extreme urgency, after informing the Member States. In the latter case, consultations shall take place 10 days at the latest after notification to the Member States of the measures adopted by the Commission.

Article 9

Rules of procedure

1. Each committee shall adopt by a simple majority of its component members its own rules of procedure on the proposal of its chair, on the basis of standard rules to be drawn up by the Commission following consultation with Member States. Such standard rules shall be published by the Commission in the Official Journal of the

European Union.

In so far as may be necessary, existing committees shall adapt their rules of procedure to the standard rules.

2. The principles and conditions on public access to documents and the rules on data protection applicable to the Commission shall apply to the committees.

## Article 10

### Information on committee proceedings

1. The Commission shall keep a register of committee proceedings which shall contain:

(a) a list of committees;

(b) the agendas of committee meetings;

(c) the summary records, together with the lists of the authorities and organisations to which the persons designated by the Member States to represent them belong;

(d) the draft implementing acts on which the committees are asked to deliver an opinion;

(e) the voting results;

(f) the final draft implementing acts following delivery of the opinion of the committees;

(g) information concerning the adoption of the final draft implementing acts by the Commission; and

(h) statistical data on the work of the committees.

2. The Commission shall also publish an annual report on the work of the committees.

3. The European Parliament and the Council shall have access to the information referred to in paragraph 1 in accordance with the applicable rules.

4. At the same time as they are sent to the committee members, the Commission shall make available to the European Parliament and the Council the documents referred to in points (b), (d) and (f) of paragraph 1 whilst also informing them of the availability of such documents.

5. The references of all documents referred to in points (a) to (g) of paragraph 1 as well as the information referred to in paragraph 1(h) shall be made public in the register.

Article 11

Right of scrutiny for the European Parliament and the Council

Where a basic act is adopted under the ordinary legislative procedure, either the European Parliament or the Council may at any time indicate to the Commission that, in its view, a draft implementing act exceeds the implementing powers provided for in the basic act. In such a case, the Commission shall review the draft implementing act, taking account of the positions expressed, and shall inform the European Parliament and the Council whether it intends to maintain, amend or withdraw the draft implementing act.

Article 12

Repeal of Decision 1999/468/EC

Decision 1999/468/EC is hereby repealed.

The effects of Article 5a of Decision 1999/468/EC shall be maintained for the purposes of existing basic acts making reference thereto.

## NOTES AND QUESTIONS

As the regulation above states, it adopts new rules relating to *implementing* measures by the Commission following the changes introduced by Lisbon. An implementing measure involves a quasi-legislative activity since it entails policy choices, albeit within a limited scope. By contrast, as described in TFEU 290, a delegated measure is supposed to amend or supplement non-essential elements of the underlying legislation and may be regarded as purely executive (indeed, TFEU 290 expressly states that they are "non-legislative" thus, perhaps rather oddly, implying that implementing measures are legislative, which however would be inconsistent with the terminology elsewhere in the TFEU).

1.    Delegated acts as a category were introduced by Lisbon. Prior to Lisbon, the comitology procedures embodied in earlier decisions (see note 3 below) encompassed both implementing and delegated acts. The latter were covered by the "regulatory procedure with scrutiny" introduced in 2006. Since any form of procedural oversight has been abolished by this Regulation, delegated measures may be adopted by the Commission without the procedures described in the above regulation, but authorizing legislation will lay down tight constraints including the possibility of revoking individual measures. Moreover, the delegated powers can be revoked at any time.

The first delegated acts under Art. 290 TFEU were adopted by the Commission in September 2010 to supplement Directive 2010/30/EU on labeling and standard product information of the consumption of energy and other resources by energy-related products. The delegation can be revoked and is subject to sunset provisions and the Parliament has rights to be informed and object to proposed acts. For a discussion of delegated legislation under TFEU 290, see B Driessen, *Delegated legislation after the Treaty of Lisbon: An Analysis of Article 290 TFEU*, (2010) E.L. REV. 837.

Implementing rules by contrast are to be subject to the above regulation and thus to involvement of the Member States. It seems that the differences between the two types of act is not a fundamental conceptual matter but really reflects a choice by the legislator as to how rulemaking should be done.

It seems then that the difference between the two types of acts is not a fundamental conceptual issue but really a choice by the legislator as to how rulemaking for implementation of EU acts should proceed.

**2.**   Why are the Member States involved in the implementing process? Why is the Parliament only involved to the extent necessary to monitor whether the implementation measures might exceed the grant of powers in the underlying legislation? How is this procedure compatible with democratic principles?

**3.**   This regulation evolved out of earlier Decisions that set up procedures for consulting the Member States on implementing and delegated acts, known as "Comitology." This approach embodied in the first comitology decision of 1987 was the subject of much criticism by the Parliament, which had raised three major objections:

1.   it was extremely bureaucratic, involving hundreds of Member State civil servants;

2.   the Parliament had no role in the procedure;

3.   There was too much influence on the part of the Member States.

A 1999 revised Comitology Decision brought the Parliament into the process for the Regulatory Procedure, though, as indicated, in a very limited manner.

Under Dec. 1999/468, there were several different procedures:

- An *advisory procedure* (article 3) which required the Commission to take the utmost account of an advisory committee appointed for the purpose.

- A *management procedure* (article 4) generally was used in agriculture — the Council could override a Commission act with its own decision, where the Commission adopted a decision that was not in accordance with the Committee's recommendation.

- A *regulatory procedure* (article 5). If this was specified as the required procedure, then the Commission could adopt the measure if in accordance with the opinion of the committee but if not, then it had to be referred to the Council and the Parliament had to be notified. The Parliament gave its opinion to the Council if it considered that the act exceeds the implementing powers under the original act. The Council could then enact or reject the proposal (regardless of the Parliament's opinion) within three months. If it rejected it, the Commission has to start the process again; but if the Council didn't adopt or reject the original proposal, then that proposal was adopted by the Commission.

■   A *regulatory procedure with scrutiny.* If this was specified in the underlying act, then the Commission could act if in accordance with the Committee's opinion, but otherwise had to refer to the Council. In both variants, the Parliament had a formal right to be consulted. This was designed to mirror the EC 251/TFEU 294 procedure for implementation of acts themselves adopted under that procedure. The Parliament had the power to block the measure but if it did not then it would be adopted by the Commission or the Council as the case may be.

The examination procedure in the 2011 regulation essentially replaces the management and regulatory procedures of Dec. 1999/468. Note that there is no longer any role for either the Council or the Parliament in the examination procedure unless an issue of excess of powers arises.

**4.** Outside the formal structure, since 1987 the Parliament had sought to ensure that the procedures allowing for the greatest Commission autonomy were adopted and had sought also to increase its supervision over the Commission. The so-called informal Plumb-Delors Agreement provided for the Commission to transmit most implementing measures to the Parliament at the same time as they were sent to the relevant committee. This practice has now been formalized in the above regulation but overall the Parliament still has limited powers here.

**5.** The committee procedure for implementing acts might be contrasted with the situation in various Member States where implementing rules may have to be brought to the national legislature for approval. The failure to allow for more democracy in this process is one reason why critics still allege a "democratic deficit" within the Union structure. While it is possible to lobby or otherwise seek to influence the contents of such rules, they are still far from the transparent procedures existing in various Member States or in the United States, where federal agencies are required to lay out proposed rules and call for comments from the public. Perhaps in Europe, were such procedures more open, the sort of bad press the EU often gets for adopting apparently nonsensical rules (the shape of bananas, the content of sausages etc.) could be avoided? Might the new regulation actually have made the situation worse?

**6.** Note that the Council also may receive implementing powers. However, this is supposed to be only in exceptional cases. Why might this be?

**7.** As of 2009 there were more than 266 committees responsible for implementing activities.

# Chapter 7

# EXECUTIVE POWERS

## § 7.01  OVERVIEW

*Template* Article 4, in particular sections 4.3, 4.7 and 4.9.

***Nature of the Union's "executive" branch*** It will be evident from the Template that the Union does not possess an "executive branch" equivalent to the role of the President in the United States. Chiefly, this is exemplified by the absence of a "government" of the Union. Although the European Council might be characterized as a collective "head of state", there is no "state".

It has been noted already (Chapter 2) that the functions of the various bodies described in Article 4 of the Template are clearly executive in nature, taking the form of policy-making activities that are then implemented at various levels by Union institutions and the Member States. One might therefore conceptualize the Union's executive branch as basically a three-tier structure.

The top tier consists of the European Council and the Council of the EU. These bodies formulate policies that translate into executive decisions requiring action by other bodies. The next tier down consists of Union institutions and bodies that have implementing powers. The Council itself has such powers but chiefly it is the Commission that has this role, and increasingly, specialized agencies also have quite detailed implementation responsibilities. The third tier consists of the civil service and other government agencies of the Member States.

**- The top tier: The European Council and the Council** The top tier of the executive branch is almost purely political in nature and therefore by and large lies outside the scope of a law casebook. However, one may note that these political bodies can in some cases take decisions that have direct legal effects on individuals and in that respect such decisions may be subject to scrutiny by the Court of Justice of the EU. This is evident, for example, in the actions taken to freeze the bank accounts of suspected terrorist groups after 9/11. In this regard, it may be noted that the ECJ now has jurisdiction to review the legality of acts adopted by the European Council (TFEU 263, amending EC 230). However, the ECJ still does not have jurisdiction with respect to the CFSP in general nor with respect to the acts adopted under it (TFEU 275 and TEU 24).

Although the European Council is perhaps most commonly associated with foreign policy, its role is much broader—it sets the political direction for the Union across the board. It has thus played a high-profile role in seeking a solution to the Euro crisis.

**- The second tier: The Commission** The second tier, by contrast, is largely administrative and thus becomes subject to judicial control in much the same manner as executive agencies of the United States government.

Increasingly, the activities of the specialized agencies are also now generating legal issues. Indeed, the CFI/General Court is in danger of becoming swamped by the volume of challenges to the decisions of such bodies.

Other areas of the Union's administrative activities, while of great political or economic importance, are again somewhat peripheral to a law casebook. For example, the Commission has responsibility for implementing the Union's multiplicity of programs under the aegis of the seven-year financial framework and annual budget. The Commission is responsible for preparing and administering an annual budget of well over €130 billion, and a significant percentage of that is still spent on maintaining the agricultural policy. The budget-setting process is a highly politicized issue, pitting the Parliament against the Member States.

The second tier also embraces the administration of the external relations of the Union. At the implementation level, the Union's External Action Service has now been established, though its responsibilities are still being mapped out. There is an embryonic military capability (about 200 personnel) that has the responsibility to define areas of EU military intervention in support of the political decisions taken by the European Council and to liaise with NATO and the Member States in taking concrete actions. This can result in the deployment of the forces of the Member States under the Union flag. The interventions in the Balkan states are a dramatic illustration of this aspect. Again, most of this activity so far at least does not generally trigger legal issues but is politically highly charged. For further reading, see N. NUGENT, THE GOVERNMENT AND POLITICS OF THE EUROPEAN UNION (6th Edition, Oxford University Press, 2006).

The Commission's role under EC 300/TFEU 218 appears to be very much that of a civil service function rather than an executive in the governmental sense, i.e., it negotiates on the basis of a mandate from the Council, rather than setting the policy itself, and it is the Council that both sets the policy and concludes the agreement. Is the Council therefore also to be regarded as part of the executive function here? Does it then play the role of both executive and legislature?

Under EC 111/TFEU 219, the EC 300/TFEU 218 procedure may not apply in relation to negotiations with third countries on exchange rate matters. In this area the Council is permitted to assume the negotiating role. As with the move to independent agencies for internal matters mentioned earlier, the effect is once again to limit the Commission's role. As a result of Lisbon, the roles of the Commission in the TFEU and of the High Representative and President of the European Council under the CFSP have become a somewhat complex interplay of forces. Chiefly it should be noted that the High Representative is supposed to represent the Union in CFSP matters where the position is responsible to the European Council and the Council, while in TFEU matters the High Representative is a Vice President of the Commission and therefore answerable to the Commission President. What sort of issues could this raise? How does the President of the European Council fit into this picture? (For descriptions of their roles, see Constitutional Template, Article 4.)

Also of great importance now is another executive body, the European Central Bank. It is independent of the other Institutions and of the Member States and economic cooperation within the Union. Its remit is above all to preserve the value of the euro. Again, this is a politically sensitive area. The independence of the Bank from an administrative standpoint has given rise to issues with the Commission, which asserts control over ethical conduct by the Bank's staff through "OLAF" ("Office de Lutte Anti-Fraude", or Anti-fraud office).

In addition to the Commission itself, there are now some 22 specialized agencies and six executive agencies administering specific programs (see Regulation 58/2003 [2003] OJ L 11/1). The specialized agencies may or may not exercise significant powers: for example, the Office for Harmonization of the Internal Market and the Union Plant Variety Office issues "Union" trademarks, while at the other end of the spectrum the European Institute for Gender Equality is largely a forum for exchanging and gathering information.

**- The third tier: The Member States** The third tier implicates Union law through the Commission's responsibility to ensure its correct implementation. In that regard, EC 226/TFEU 258 is the principal procedure, but not the only one. For example, the actions available under the provisions on state aids also provide avenues for ensuring Member State compliance. The Commission's role here is often delicate. It is not a question of simply firing off lawsuits every time a Member State appears to be in breach. Rather, the Commission uses its powers here to steer Member State action in directions that help shape the EU as a whole. The Commission thus has a wide discretion to prioritize and temper its engagement here and might justly be viewed as exercising more of a "leadership" than an "enforcement" prerogative. It brokers compliance between two legislative bodies — the EU on the one hand and the Member State governments on the other — and so its role is primarily an executive one, although clearly backed up by a quasi-judicial component.

It has been observed that the administrations of the Member States increasingly play a "double-hatted" role, being both an integral part of the State apparatus but also in a sense acting as part of a pan-European agency when applying rules derived from the Union: D Curtin and M. Egeberg, *Tradition and Innovation: Europe's Accumulated Executive Order*, (2008) 31 West European Politics, 639, at pp 649-650.

***Principles governing the Commission's activities*** A number of general principles shape the way the Commission functions.

**- Financial controls** Like any government agency, the Commission has responsibility for administering public money and is subject to audit and legal requirements to enforce its duties. The Court of Auditors frequently finds numerous irregularities that never seem to be fully explained and the Parliament, which gives the discharge to the Commission on its execution of the budget, always seems to find concerns. Matters, however, have improved from the low in the 1990s when widespread fraud, lack of control over grants to third parties, and more general misuse of position resulted in the resignation of the entire Commission under then President Santer after publication of an extremely damning report by a Committee of Independent Experts, *First Report on Allegations Regarding Fraud, Misman-*

*agement and Nepotism in the European Commission*, March 15, 1999. One result of these findings was the establishment of the above mentioned "OLAF" unit. This body operates independently and, where appropriate, in close concertation with the authorities of the Member States.

- **Independence** It was a fundamental tenet of the original European Treaties that the High Authority of the ECSC and the Commission under the EEC and EAEC Treaties was to be entirely independent of the Member States in order to represent the driving force of European integration. (The ECB has a similar status with respect to monetary policy.) Today, the role of the Commission is clearly more nuanced. Much of its original mandate has been achieved although there are certainly many imperfections still to be resolved. At the same time, with the broadening of the Union's competences into areas of political sensitivity, it may seem rather anachronistic that the Commission, through its power of initiation of legislation, should continue to be appointed and not elected. As a practical reality, such rigid demarcations are never possible, and the Commission has increasingly to take into account whatever is the predominant political force in the Parliament. One might also keep in mind that in the United States, only the President and Vice President are elected, while the President's cabinet, which exercises enormous power, is appointed. Thus, the democratic deficit here is in the manner of the election of the President of the Commission. He is proposed by the European Council and the European Parliament has only the power to accept or reject the nominee. This obviously contrasts with the direct election of the U.S. President (although one may note that technically this happens through the Electoral College).

The independence principle has on occasion surfaced in the European Court. For example, in *France v. Commission (Guidelines on Regulatory Cooperation)*, Case C-233/02, 2004 ECJ CELEX LEXIS 151, [2004] ECR I-2759, France sought annulment of the decision by which the Commission concluded an agreement with the United States of America titled "Guidelines on Regulatory Cooperation and Transparency", *inter alia* on the grounds that the agreement fettered the Commission's right of initiative with respect to proposals for legislation. The Guidelines dealt with mechanisms to aid cooperation in drafting of technical regulatory measures but were non-binding and thus did not restrict the Commission's power of initiative.

- **Collegiate responsibility** There have been a number of Court judgments that have shaped the ability of the Commission to delegate its powers to individual Commissioners or civil servants. For example, In *Akzo Chemie BV and Akzo Chemie UKLtd v. Commission*, Case 5/85, 1986 ECJ CELEX LEXIS 257, [1986] ECR 2585, the Commission had adopted a decision requiring Akzo to submit to an investigation under the Competition rules. One of the grounds on which the decision was challenged was violation of the principle that Commission decisions should be made by the whole Commission, and could not be delegated to an individual Commissioner. The Court stated:

> 30 [I]t must first be pointed out that that principle is to be traced to Article 17 of the Merger Treaty according to which 'the Commission shall act by a majority of the number of members provided for in article 10. A meeting of

the Commission shall be valid only if the number of members laid down in its rules of procedure is present'. The principle of collegiate responsibility thus laid down is founded on the equal participation of the members of the Commission in the adoption of decisions and it follows from that principle, in particular, that decisions should be the subject of a collective deliberation and that all the members of the college of Commissioners bear collective responsibility on the political level for all decisions adopted.

31 It is also necessary to describe, particularly from the point of view of the system of delegations of authority, the measures adopted by the Commission in order to prevent the rule requiring collective deliberation from having a paralysing effect on the full Commission.

32 In the first place, on 23 July 1975, the Commission introduced into its provisional Rules of Procedure a new Article 27 according to which subject to the principle of collegiate responsibility being respected in full the Commission may empower its members to take, in its name and subject to its control, clearly defined "measures of management or administration" (Official Journal, 1975 L 199, p. 43).

33 In the second place, on the same date, the Commission adopted an internal decision laying down the principles and conditions on which delegations of authority would be granted. According to the information supplied by the Commission in reply to a question put to it by the court, that decision established certain procedural guarantees in order to ensure that the decisions adopted pursuant to a delegation of authority complied with the principle of collegiate responsibility. Thus, decisions delegating authority must be adopted at meetings of the Commission and such delegations may only be made to designated persons for designated categories of everyday measures of management or administration. Furthermore, the person to whom authority has been delegated may adopt a decision only if all the departments concerned are in agreement and only if he is satisfied that the decision does not need, for whatever reason, to be considered by the full Commission. Finally, all decisions adopted under a delegation of authority are transmitted on the day following their adoption to all the members of the Commission and to all departments.

34 In the third place, in the particular sphere of competition law, the member of the Commission responsible for competition matters was granted, by Decision of 5 November 1980, the power to adopt in the name of the Commission certain procedural measures provided for in Regulation No. 17. He may decide alone to initiate the procedure, on his own, to seek information from undertakings and to order an undertaking to submit to an investigation under Article 14 (3) of Regulation No. 17.

35 With regard to the compatibility of that system with the principle of collegiate responsibility, it should be pointed out that in its judgment of 17 January 1984 (Joined Cases 43 and 63/82, VBVB and VBBB v. Commission, (1984) ECR 19), the most recent decision on that point, the court decided that the Commission could, within certain limits and subject to certain conditions, authorize its members to adopt certain decisions in its name

without the principle of collegiate responsibility which governed its functioning being impaired by such authorization. Two considerations underlie
that settled case-law.

36 On the one hand, such a system of delegation of authority does not have
the effect of divesting the Commission of powers by conferring on the
member to whom authority is delegated powers to act his own right.
Decisions adopted under a delegation of authority are adopted in the name
of the Commission, which is fully responsible for them, and may be the
subject of an application for annulment under the same conditions as if they
had been considered by the full Commission. Moreover, the Commission
has set up machinery making it possible to reserve for the full Commission
certain measures which could be adopted under a delegation of authority.
Finally, it has retained the right to reconsider the decisions granting
delegations of authority.

37 On the other hand, limited to specific categories of measures of
management or administration, and thus excluding by definition decisions
of principle, such a system of delegations of authority appears necessary,
having regard to the considerable increase in the number of decisions which
the Commission is required to adopt, to enable it to perform its duties. The
need to ensure that the decision-making body is able to function corresponds to a principle inherent in all institutional systems and which is set
out in particular in Article 16 of the Merger Treaty, according to which "the
Commission shall adopt its rules of procedure so as to ensure that both it
and its departments operate."

In *Hoechst v. Commission*, Joined Cases 46/87 and 227/88, 1989 ECJ CELEX
LEXIS 104, [1989] ECR 2859, a further point was raised in this regard. The
company had initially refused to submit to an investigation under Article 14 of
former Regulation 17/62 relating to a suspected violation of EU competition law.
One of the issues raised by Hoechst was whether the delegation could be proper
where the result of the failure of the company to comply with it led to the imposition
of a periodic fine. The ECJ stated:

    44 It is common ground that the contested decision ordering the
    investigation was adopted by the so-called delegation procedure, provided
    for by the Commission Decision of 5 November 1980, empowering the
    Member of the Commission with responsibility for competition to adopt a
    decision under Article 14(3) of Regulation No 17 on behalf of and under the
    responsibility of the Commission ordering undertakings to submit to
    investigations. In its judgment of 23 September 1986 in Case 5/85 AKZO
    Chemie v. Commission ((1986) ECR 2585), the Court has already held that
    that decision delegating authority did not infringe the principle of collegiate
    responsibility enshrined in Article 17 of the Merger Treaty.

    45 However, the applicant considers it necessary for the Court to re-
    examine the lawfulness of that delegation procedure which the applicant
    regards as incompatible with the principle nulla poena sine lege. It claims
    that the Commission, by a mere internal administrative measure, has
    modified the constituent elements of an infringement in respect of which a

fine may be imposed under Article 15 of Regulation No 17 because, with effect from the abovementioned decision of 5 November 1980, such an infringement is constituted by a refusal to submit to an investigation ordered by a single Member of the Commission and not, as previously, by the Commission as a collegiate body.

46 In that regard, it should be pointed out that although it is correct that the conditions under which a fine may be imposed under Article 15 of Regulation No 17 cannot be amended by a decision of the Commission, it was neither the purpose nor the effect of the abovementioned decision delegating authority to make such an amendment. In so far as the system of delegation of authority for decisions ordering investigations does not infringe the principle of collegiality, the decisions adopted by virtue of such delegation must be regarded as decisions of the Commission within the meaning of Article 15 of Regulation No 17.

In reality, the collegiality principle is rather difficult to sustain given the President's powers, particular after Lisbon. The President decides on the portfolio allocation and can reshuffle it and, under TEU 17, now has the power to require the resignation of any member of the Commission other than the High Representative (who can be dismissed by the same procedure by which he or she is appointed).

See further, S Lefevre, *Rules of procedure do matter: The legal status of the institutions' power of self-organisation*, (2006) 30 EL Rev. 802.

***Materials in this Chapter*** The materials in this Chapter cover two subjects within the scope of executive powers that are of particular legal interest.

§ 7.02 addresses the principles and procedures governing the Commission's administration of the competition law under EC 81 and 82/TFEU 101 and 102. (The aspect of competition policy addressing State aids is covered elsewhere).

The substance of the EU's competition policy is outside the scope of this casebook. It is a vast and complex subject on a scale now comparable to the body of law in the United States known as antitrust law (dating back to the Sherman Act of 1893). Like U.S. antitrust law, EU competition law has had phases of development that reflect in many respects the gradual maturing of the Union itself.

Although the competition policy provisions were embodied in the EEC Treaty and thus technically effective from 1957 (originally articles 85 and 86), it was only in 1962 that the first regulation dealing with enforcement procedures was adopted: Regulation 17/62. Somewhat surprisingly, this regulation remained in place for 40 years, although by the end of that period it was clearly failing to meet modern needs. It provided that the Commission should be the sole administrative body with responsibility for enforcing EU competition policy. This was the right approach in the early years because the Commission was able to mark out its policy approach in a coordinated and measured way.

The Commission began by deploying its powers primarily toward breaking down barriers to trade between Member States that existed because of licensing, sales and distribution practices. The competition provisions were viewed by many at the time as the equivalent in the private sector of the Treaty provisions regarding the removal of governmental obstacles to trade (customs duties and quantitative restrictions). This policy direction entailed much focus on what are called "vertical restraints" (as illustrated in the *Grundig* case appearing in Chapter 11), where manufacturers used distribution and intellectual property licensing to perpetuate national markets and exclude foreign competition. For example, since trademarks existed at the State level (unlike the United States), it was possible to grant exclusive rights on a country by country basis, thus preventing inter-State trade in goods. Over this period, a good deal was accomplished both in terms of eliminating the restrictive effects of such agreements and delineating acceptable practices through a series of block exemption regulations under EC 81/TFEU 101.

It was not until the 1980s that a change of direction emerged as the Commission began to focus on the core prohibitions of traditional antitrust or competition law, namely agreements among competitors to fix prices or share markets. Through a rather painful process of decision-making and critical review by the ECJ, the Commission gradually built up both competence and confidence. During the 1990s the Commission was able to introduce a leniency program that dramatically increased its enforcement capability by encouraging parties to come forward and report violations with the offer of immunity from, or reduced exposure to, fines. In the first decade of the twenty-first century and with further modifications to the leniency program, the Commission started to increase the size of fines significantly, assisted at this point by published fining guidelines. It is now not uncommon in the larger cases to see fines of hundreds of millions of euros imposed on each participant in a price-fixing conspiracy.

From an administrative point of view, Regulation 17/62, while assuring exclusive competence to the Commission created a serious build-up of problems over time — see note 2 under § 7.02 [E] *infra*. However, as the years passed, the Member States gradually modernized their national competition laws such that it became easier to align EU and national policy. This enabled a sweeping overhaul of the EU enforcement structure resulting in Regulation 1/2003. While the basic procedures for investigating and deciding on infringements remains, the Member States now have authority to take similar actions on behalf of the EU at the national level alongside their own similar laws. This enables the Commission, with its relatively modest staff, to focus on matters of policy and key matters particularly for the purpose of establishing precedents and guidance.

In addition to the two regulations mentioned, the Union adopted a merger control regime in 1989, to permit the pre-approval or rejection of "concentrations" (acquisitions, mergers or other combinations including joint ventures) that were of "Community dimension". This is commented on further in Chapter 11.

There is a huge quantity of literature dealing generally with the competition law of the EU. The most well-established work in English is C. Bellamy and G. Child, Common Market Law of Competition, ed P. Roth QC and V. Rose (6th edition, Oxford University Press,2007). See also C. Harding and J. Joshua, Regulating Cartels in Europe: A Study of Legal Control of Corporate Delinquency (Oxford University Press, 2003).

For administrative aspects of the competition rules under Regulation 17/62 see C-D Ehlerman, *The European Administration and the Public Administration of*

*Member States with regard to Competition Law,* [1995] ECLR; A. Haslam-Jones, *A Comparative Analysis of the Decision Making Process: Competition Matters in Member States of the European Union, the European Commission and the United States* [1995] 3 ELCR 154.

Section 7.02 covers the administrative aspects of the competition law, including the role of the Member States, the procedure leading up to a decision of infringement, and the imposition of fines or other remedies. The EU process here will look rather unfamiliar to U.S. readers, given the apparent combination of the roles of investigator, prosecutor and judge performed by the Commission. This section can be read in conjunction with Chapter 19, where the materials, while addressing in general the right to good administration as described in the Charter of Fundamental Rights, are largely derived from the area of competition policy enforcement.

Chapter 11 will address jurisdictional aspects of the competition law.

Section 7.03 looks at the role of the Commission in enforcing the correct implementation of Union law by the Member States. Given 50 years of existence of the Communities and now the EU, it is not surprising that light has been shed on the many different ways in which Member States have failed to comply, either intentionally or negligently, with their duties under the Treaties. This chapter does not attempt to do justice to the vast jurisprudence in this area. Rather, the materials have been chosen to illustrate some key principles that have arisen in the context of direct enforcement by the Commission. What is the nature of the duty? Can a Member State plead "force majeure" or lack of reciprocity? How do national rights and procedures dovetail with EU requirements? Do the Member States have "rights of the defence" like individuals? What remedies are available to compel compliance?

This unique procedure is a reflection in particular of the role of the directive. It might be observed that so far as the Union is concerned, the duty of the Member States is one of implementation, so essentially an executive function. But for the Member States the action required is legislative or at least rulemaking in character. This dichotomy is particularly evident when Member States encounter practical or political difficulties in adopting the required legislation. From the Union's point of view, this is a failure of the Member States' implementation duty. Thus, such difficulties are not an excuse, any more, say, than practical obstacles encountered by the U.S. executive branch in implementing federal legislation would be legally excusable.

## § 7.02 ENFORCEMENT OF COMPETITION LAW

### [A] Enforcement Authorities

### TFEU PROVISIONS

#### Article 101

#### (ex Article 81 TEC)

1. The following shall be prohibited as incompatible with the internal market: all agreements between undertakings, decisions by associations of undertakings and concerted practices which may affect trade between Member States and which have as their object or effect the prevention, restriction or distortion of competition within the internal market, and in particular those which:

(a) directly or indirectly fix purchase or selling prices or any other trading conditions;

(b) limit or control production, markets, technical development, or investment;

(c) share markets or sources of supply;

(d) apply dissimilar conditions to equivalent transactions with other trading parties, thereby placing them at a competitive disadvantage;

(e) make the conclusion of contracts subject to acceptance by the other parties of supplementary obligations which, by their nature or according to commercial usage, have no connection with the subject of such contracts.

2. Any agreements or decisions prohibited pursuant to this Article shall be automatically void.

3. The provisions of paragraph 1 may, however, be declared inapplicable in the case of:

– any agreement or category of agreements between undertakings,

– any decision or category of decisions by associations of undertakings,

– any concerted practice or category of concerted practices,

which contributes to improving the production or distribution of goods or to promoting technical or economic progress, while allowing consumers a fair share of the resulting benefit, and which does not:

(a) impose on the undertakings concerned restrictions which are not indispensable to the attainment of these objectives;

(b) afford such undertakings the possibility of eliminating competition in respect of a substantial part of the products in question.

*Article 102*

(ex Article 82 TEC)

Any abuse by one or more undertakings of a dominant position within the internal market or in a substantial part of it shall be prohibited as incompatible with the internal market in so far as it may affect trade between Member States.

Such abuse may, in particular, consist in:

(a)   directly or indirectly imposing unfair purchase or selling prices or other unfair trading conditions;

(b)   limiting production, markets or technical development to the prejudice of consumers;

(c)   applying dissimilar conditions to equivalent transactions with other trading parties, thereby placing them at a competitive disadvantage;

(d)   making the conclusion of contracts subject to acceptance by the other parties of supplementary obligations which, by their nature or according to commercial usage, have no connection with the subject of such contracts.

*Article 103*

(ex Article 83 TEC)

1. The appropriate regulations or directives to give effect to the principles set out in Articles 101 and 102 shall be laid down by the Council, on a proposal from the Commission and after consulting the European Parliament.

2. The regulations or directives referred to in paragraph 1 shall be designed in particular:

(a)   to ensure compliance with the prohibitions laid down in Article 101(1) and in Article 102 by making provision for fines and periodic penalty payments;

(b)   to lay down detailed rules for the application of Article 101(3), taking into account the need to ensure effective supervision on the one hand, and to simplify administration to the greatest possible extent on the other;

(c)   to define, if need be, in the various branches of the economy, the scope of the provisions of Articles 101 and 102;

(d)   to define the respective functions of the Commission and of the Court of Justice of the European Union in applying the provisions laid down in this paragraph;

(e)   to determine the relationship between national laws and the provisions contained in this Section or adopted pursuant to this Article.

\*     \*     \*

*Article 105*

(ex Article 85 TEC)

1. Without prejudice to Article 104, the Commission shall ensure the application of the principles laid down in Articles 101 and 102. On application by a Member State or on its own initiative, and in cooperation with the competent authorities in the Member States, which shall give it their assistance, the Commission shall investigate cases of suspected infringement of these principles. If it finds that there has been an infringement, it shall propose appropriate measures to bring it to an end.

2. If the infringement is not brought to an end, the Commission shall record such infringement of the principles in a reasoned decision. The Commission may publish its decision and authorise Member States to take the measures, the conditions and details of which it shall determine, needed to remedy the situation.

3. The Commission may adopt regulations relating to the categories of agreement in respect of which the Council has adopted a regulation or a directive pursuant to Article 103(2)(b).

# REGULATION 1/2003
## [2003] OJ L1/1

Article 4

Powers of the Commission

For the purpose of applying Articles 81 [101] and 82 [102] of the Treaty, the Commission shall have the powers provided for by this Regulation.

Article 5

Powers of the competition authorities of the Member States

The competition authorities of the Member States shall have the power to apply Articles 81 [101] and 82 [102] of the Treaty in individual cases. For this purpose, acting on their own initiative or on a complaint, they may take the following decisions:

-   requiring that an infringement be brought to an end,

-   ordering interim measures,

-   accepting commitments,

-   imposing fines, periodic penalty payments or any other penalty provided for in their national law.

Where on the basis of the information in their possession the conditions for prohibition are not met they may likewise decide that there are no grounds for action on their part.

\*   \*   \*

Article 11

Cooperation between the Commission and the competition authorities of the
Member States

1. The Commission and the competition authorities of the Member States shall
apply the Community competition rules in close cooperation.

2. The Commission shall transmit to the competition authorities of the Member
States copies of the most important documents it has collected with a view to
applying Articles 7, 8, 9, 10 and Article 29(1). At the request of the competition
authority of a Member State, the Commission shall provide it with a copy of other
existing documents necessary for the assessment of the case.

3. The competition authorities of the Member States shall, when acting under
Article 81 [101] or Article 82 [102] of the Treaty, inform the Commission in writing
before or without delay after commencing the first formal investigative measure.
This information may also be made available to the competition authorities of the
other Member States.

4. No later than 30 days before the adoption of a decision requiring that an
infringement be brought to an end, accepting commitments or withdrawing the
benefit of a block exemption Regulation, the competition authorities of the Member
States shall inform the Commission. To that effect, they shall provide the Commission with a summary of the case, the envisaged decision or, in the absence thereof,
any other document indicating the proposed course of action. This information may
also be made available to the competition authorities of the other Member States.
At the request of the Commission, the acting competition authority shall make
available to the Commission other documents it holds which are necessary for the
assessment of the case. The information supplied to the Commission may be made
available to the competition authorities of the other Member States. National
competition authorities may also exchange between themselves information necessary for the assessment of a case that they are dealing with under Article 81 [101]
or Article 82 [102] of the Treaty.

5. The competition authorities of the Member States may consult the Commission
on any case involving the application of Community law.

6. The initiation by the Commission of proceedings for the adoption of a decision
under Chapter III shall relieve the competition authorities of the Member States of
their competence to apply Articles 81 [101] and 82 [102] of the Treaty. If a
competition authority of a Member State is already acting on a case, the
Commission shall only initiate proceedings after consulting with that national
competition authority.

Article 12

Exchange of information

1. For the purpose of applying Articles 81 [101] and 82 of the Treaty the Commission and the competition authorities of the Member States shall have the power to provide one another with and use in evidence any matter of fact or of law, including confidential information.

2. Information exchanged shall only be used in evidence for the purpose of applying Article 81 [101] or Article 82 of the Treaty and in respect of the subject-matter for which it was collected by the transmitting authority. However, where national competition law is applied in the same case and in parallel to Community competition law and does not lead to a different outcome, information exchanged under this Article may also be used for the application of national competition law.

3. Information exchanged pursuant to paragraph 1 can only be used in evidence to impose sanctions on natural persons where:

- the law of the transmitting authority foresees sanctions of a similar kind in relation to an infringement of Article 81 [101] or Article 82 of the Treaty or, in the absence thereof,

- the information has been collected in a way which respects the same level of protection of the rights of defence of natural persons as provided for under the national rules of the receiving authority. However, in this case, the information exchanged cannot be used by the receiving authority to impose custodial sanctions.

Article 13

Suspension or termination of proceedings

1. Where competition authorities of two or more Member States have received a complaint or are acting on their own initiative under Article 81 [101] or Article 82 [102] of the Treaty against the same agreement, decision of an association or practice, the fact that one authority is dealing with the case shall be sufficient grounds for the others to suspend the proceedings before them or to reject the complaint. The Commission may likewise reject a complaint on the ground that a competition authority of a Member State is dealing with the case.

2. Where a competition authority of a Member State or the Commission has received a complaint against an agreement, decision of an association or practice which has already been dealt with by another competition authority, it may reject it.

## Article 14

### Advisory Committee

1. The Commission shall consult an Advisory Committee on Restrictive Practices and Dominant Positions prior to the taking of any decision under Articles 7, 8, 9, 10, 23, Article 24(2) and Article 29(1).

2. For the discussion of individual cases, the Advisory Committee shall be composed of representatives of the competition authorities of the Member States. For meetings in which issues other than individual cases are being discussed, an additional Member State representative competent in competition matters may be appointed. Representatives may, if unable to attend, be replaced by other representatives.

3. The consultation may take place at a meeting convened and chaired by the Commission, held not earlier than 14 days after dispatch of the notice convening it, together with a summary of the case, an indication of the most important documents and a preliminary draft decision. In respect of decisions pursuant to Article 8, the meeting may be held seven days after the dispatch of the operative part of a draft decision. Where the Commission dispatches a notice convening the meeting which gives a shorter period of notice than those specified above, the meeting may take place on the proposed date in the absence of an objection by any Member State. The Advisory Committee shall deliver a written opinion on the Commission's preliminary draft decision. It may deliver an opinion even if some members are absent and are not represented. At the request of one or several members, the positions stated in the opinion shall be reasoned.

4. Consultation may also take place by written procedure. However, if any Member State so requests, the Commission shall convene a meeting. In case of written procedure, the Commission shall determine a time-limit of not less than 14 days within which the Member States are to put forward their observations for circulation to all other Member States. In case of decisions to be taken pursuant to Article 8, the time-limit of 14 days is replaced by seven days. Where the Commission determines a time-limit for the written procedure which is shorter than those specified above, the proposed time-limit shall be applicable in the absence of an objection by any Member State.

5. The Commission shall take the utmost account of the opinion delivered by the Advisory Committee. It shall inform the Committee of the manner in which its opinion has been taken into account.

6. Where the Advisory Committee delivers a written opinion, this opinion shall be appended to the draft decision. If the Advisory Committee recommends publication of the opinion, the Commission shall carry out such publication taking into account the legitimate interest of undertakings in the protection of their business secrets.

7. At the request of a competition authority of a Member State, the Commission shall include on the agenda of the Advisory Committee cases that are being dealt with by a competition authority of a Member State under Article 81 [101] or Article 82 [102] of the Treaty. The Commission may also do so on its own initiative. In either

case, the Commission shall inform the competition authority concerned.

A request may in particular be made by a competition authority of a Member State in respect of a case where the Commission intends to initiate proceedings with the effect of Article 11(6).

The Advisory Committee shall not issue opinions on cases dealt with by competition authorities of the Member States. The Advisory Committee may also discuss general issues of Community competition law.

## Article 15

### Cooperation with national courts

1. In proceedings for the application of Article 81 [101] or Article 82 [102] of the Treaty, courts of the Member States may ask the Commission to transmit to them information in its possession or its opinion on questions concerning the application of the Community competition rules.

2. Member States shall forward to the Commission a copy of any written judgment of national courts deciding on the application of Article 81 [101] or Article 82 [102] of the Treaty. Such copy shall be forwarded without delay after the full written judgment is notified to the parties.

3. Competition authorities of the Member States, acting on their own initiative, may submit written observations to the national courts of their Member State on issues relating to the application of Article 81 [101] or Article 82 [102] of the Treaty. With the permission of the court in question, they may also submit oral observations to the national courts of their Member State. Where the coherent application of Article 81 [101] or Article 82 [102] of the Treaty so requires, the Commission, acting on its own initiative, may submit written observations to courts of the Member States. With the permission of the court in question, it may also make oral observations. For the purpose of the preparation of their observations only, the competition authorities of the Member States and the Commission may request the relevant court of the Member State to transmit or ensure the transmission to them of any documents necessary for the assessment of the case.

4. This Article is without prejudice to wider powers to make observations before courts conferred on competition authorities of the Member States under the law of their Member State.

## NOTES AND QUESTIONS

1.   Regulation 1/2003 replaced Regulation 17/62. As noted above, Regulation 17/62 was considerably different in its approach in that it expressly reserved application of EU competition law to the Commission, including the power to take decisions to grant exemptions under EC 81/TFEU 101 (3). Do you think the new arrangements represent a shift of power away from the Commission? Do they suggest a weakening or strengthening of enforcement?

2.   Does the role given to the Member States authorities to administer EU law

undermine the system of legal protection in the EU legal order? Consider that, under EC 230/TFEU 263, a party to national proceedings cannot challenge a decision of the national authorities directly in the EU Court. Are there other ways to enlist the latter's involvement? (The role of the national courts in EU competition law is addressed in Chapter 9).

**3.** As noted in the Overview, the Commission is also entrusted with the administration of the "Merger Regulation" under which it has the power to review proposed joint ventures, mergers and acquisitions having a "Community dimension" prior to their going into effect. The first basic procedural regulation was Regulation 4064/89, [1989] O.J. L395/1. This has now been superseded by Regulation 139/2004 [2004] OJ L14/1, implemented by Commission Regulation 802/2004, [2004] OJ L 133.

## [B] Complaints

### AUTOMEC SRL v. COMMISSION
#### Case T-24/90, 1992 ECJ CELEX LEXIS 66, [1992] ECR II-2223

[The Commission had declined to act on a complaint notified by the plaintiff under former regulation 17 relating to certain alleged anticompetitive practices by the German based car maker BMW. The complaint procedure is continued in Regulation 1/2003. For relevant current provisions in Regulation 1/2003 see Article 7 and in Regulation 773/2004 see articles 2 and 5-9.]

79 [A]lthough the Commission cannot be compelled to conduct an investigation, the procedural safeguards provided for by Article 3 of Regulation No 17 and Article 6 of Regulation No 99/63 oblige it nevertheless to examine carefully the factual and legal particulars brought to its notice by the complainant in order to decide whether they disclose conduct of such a kind as to distort competition in the common market and affect trade between Member States . . .

80 Where, as in this case, the Commission has decided to close the file on a complaint without carrying out an investigation, the review of legality which the Court must undertake focuses on whether or not the contested decision is based on materially incorrect facts or is vitiated by an error of law, a manifest error of appraisal or misuse of powers.

81 It is for the Court to verify, in the light of those principles, first, whether the Commission carried out the examination of the complaint which was required of it by evaluating, with all due care, the factual and legal particulars adduced by the applicant in his complaint and, secondly, whether the Commission has given a proper statement of reasons for closing the file on the complaint on the basis of its power to "apply different degrees of priority in dealing with the examination of alleged infringements brought to its notice", on the one hand, and in the light of the Community interest in the case as a priority criterion, on the other.

82 In this connection the Court finds in the first place that the Commission carried out a careful examination of the complaint, during which it not only took account of the factual and legal particulars adduced in the complaint itself, but also conducted an informal exchange of views and information with the applicant and its lawyers.

It was only after it had apprised itself of the further particulars given by the applicant on that occasion and of the observations submitted in response to the letter sent pursuant to Article 6 of Regulation No 99/63 that the Commission rejected the complaint. Therefore, having regard to the factual and legal particulars set out in the complaint, the Commission carried out an appropriate examination thereof and cannot be accused of lack of diligence.

83 Secondly, as regards the statement of reasons in the contested decision closing the file, the Court points out in the first place that the Commission is entitled to apply different degrees of priority in dealing with the complaints submitted to it.

84 The next point to consider is whether it is legitimate, as the Commission has argued, to refer to the Community interest in a case as a priority criterion.

85 In this connection, it should be borne in mind that, unlike the civil courts, whose task is to safeguard the individual rights of private persons in their relations inter se, an administrative authority must act in the public interest. Consequently, the Commission is entitled to refer to the Community interest in order to determine the degree of priority to be applied to the various cases brought to its notice. This does not amount to removing action by the Commission from the scope of judicial review, since, in view of the requirement to provide a statement of reasons laid down by Article 190 [296] of the Treaty, the Commission cannot merely refer to the Community interest in the abstract. It must set out the legal and factual considerations which led it to conclude that there was insufficient Community interest to justify investigation of the case. It is therefore by reviewing the legality of those reasons that the Court can review the Commission's action.

86 In order to assess the Community interest in further investigation of a case, the Commission must take account of the circumstances of the case, and in particular of the legal and factual particulars set out in the complaint referred to it. The Commission should in particular balance the significance of the alleged infringement as regards the functioning of the common market, the probability of establishing the existence of the infringement and the scope of the investigation required in order to fulfil, under the best possible conditions, its task of ensuring that Articles 85 [101] and 86 [102] are complied with.

87 In that context, it is necessary to consider whether the Commission was right in this case to conclude that there was insufficient Community interest in further investigation of the case, on the ground that the applicant, who had already brought proceedings in the Italian courts concerning the termination of the distribution agreement, could also submit to those courts the question whether BMW Italia's distribution system was compatible with Article 85 [101](1) of the Treaty.

88 In that regard, it should be observed that, in reaching that conclusion, the Commission did not merely state that as a general rule it ought not to proceed with a case simply on the ground that the national courts had jurisdiction. Related disputes between Automec and BMW Italia concerning the latter's distribution system had already been brought before the national courts and the applicant did not deny that the Italian courts were already apprised of the contractual relations between BMW Italia and its distributors. In the particular circumstances of the case, reasons pertaining to procedural economy and the sound administration of

justice militate in favour of the case being considered by the courts to which related questions had already been referred.

89 However, in order to assess the legality of the contested decision closing the file, it necessary to determine whether, in referring the complainant undertaking to the national courts, the Commission failed to take account of the extent of the protection which national courts can provide in respect of the applicant's rights under Article 85 [101] (1) of the Treaty.

90 In this connection, it should be observed that Article 85 [101](1) and Article 86 [102] [102] produce direct effects in relations between individuals and confer rights on the individuals concerned which the national courts must safeguard (see the judgment of the Court of Justice in BRT, cited above). The power to apply those provisions is vested concurrently in the Commission and the national courts . . . That conferral of competence is moreover characterized by the duty of sincere cooperation between the Commission and the national courts, arising under Article 5 of the EEC Treaty [TEU 4] . . .

91 It is therefore necessary to consider whether the Commission was entitled to rely upon such cooperation in order to ensure that the question of the compatibility of BMW Italia's distribution system with Article 85 [101](1) of the EEC Treaty was assessed.

92 To that end, the Italian courts can examine, first, whether the system involves restrictions of competition within the meaning of Article 85 [101](1). In the event of doubt, they may seek a preliminary ruling from the Court of Justice. If they find that there has been a restriction of competition contrary to Article 85 [101](1), they must go on to consider whether the system qualifies for block exemption under Regulation No 123/85. That question also falls within their jurisdiction . . . [*Authors' note*: block exemptions are referenced later in this chapter]. If there is any doubt as to the validity or the interpretation of the regulation, the national court may also make a reference to the Court of Justice for a preliminary ruling under Article 177 [267] of the Treaty. In each case the national court is in a position to give a ruling on the conformity of the distribution system with Article 85 [101](1) of the Treaty.

93 Although the national courts do not have the power to order any infringement found by them to be brought to an end and to impose fines on the undertakings responsible, as the Commission can, it is nevertheless for the national courts to apply Article 85 [101](2) of the Treaty in relations between individuals. In making express provision for that civil sanction, the Treaty presupposes that national law gives the national courts the power to safeguard the rights of undertakings which have been subjected to anti-competitive practices.

94 In this case, the applicant has not produced any evidence from which it might be inferred that Italian law provides no legal remedy enabling the Italian courts to safeguard the applicant's rights in a satisfactory manner.

95 A further point to note is that the existence in the present case of an exemption regulation. assuming that it applies. Was a factor which the Commission was entitled to take into account in order to assess the Community public interest in carrying out an investigation into a distribution system of that kind. As the

Commission has rightly observed, the main aim of a regulation on block exemption is to restrict the notification and individual examination of the distribution agreements in use in the sector of activity concerned. Moreover, the existence of such a regulation facilitates the application of competition law by the national courts.

96 Consequently, in referring the applicant to the national courts, the Commission did not fail to take into account the extent of the protection which those courts can afford to the applicant's rights under Article 85 [101](1) and (2) of the Treaty.

97 It follows from the whole of the foregoing that the Court's examination of the contested decision has not disclosed any error of law or of fact or any manifest error of assessment. Accordingly, the plea alleging that Community law, in particular Article 155 [211] of the Treaty, Article 3 of Regulation No 17 and Article 6 of Regulation No 99/63, has been infringed is unfounded.

98 Furthermore, it follows necessarily from the foregoing considerations that the statement of reasons in the contested decision is sufficient because the applicant has been able duly to assert its rights before the Court, and the Court has been able to carry out its review of legality.

## UNION FRANCAISE DE L'EXPRESS (UFEX), FORMERLY SYNDICAT FRANÇAIS DE L'EXPRESS INTERNATIONAL (SFEI), DHL INTERNATIONAL AND SERVICE CRIE v. COMMISSION AND MAY COURIER.
### Case C-119/97 P, 1999 ECJ CELEX LEXIS 250, [1999] ECR I-1341

[The Court of First Instance had dismissed the plaintiffs' application for annulment of a Commission decision rejecting the complaint brought by them under EC 82/TFEU 102 of the EC Treaty. They had complained about certain practices of the French Post Office as having been in breach of EC 82/TFEU 102 and had brought proceedings in the French courts against the Post Office.]

88 The Commission, entrusted by Article 89 [105] (1) of the EC Treaty with the task of ensuring application of the principles laid down in Articles 85 [101] and 86 [102], is responsible for defining and implementing the orientation of Community competition policy . . . In order to perform that task effectively, it is entitled to give differing degrees of priority to the complaints brought before it.

89 The discretion which the Commission has for that purpose is not unlimited, however.

90 First, the Commission is under an obligation to state reasons if it declines to continue with the examination of a complaint.

91 Since the reasons stated must be sufficiently precise and detailed to enable the Court of First Instance effectively to review the Commission's use of its discretion to define priorities . . . the Commission must set out the facts justifying the decision and the legal considerations on the basis of which it was adopted . . .

92 Second, when deciding the order of priority for dealing with the complaints brought before it, the Commission may not regard as excluded in principle from its

purview certain situations which come under the task entrusted to it by the Treaty.

93 In this context, the Commission is required to assess in each case how serious the alleged interferences with competition are and how persistent their consequences are. That obligation means in particular that it must take into account the duration and extent of the infringements complained of and their effect on the competition situation in the Community.

94 If anti-competitive effects continue after the practices which caused them have ceased, the Commission thus remains competent under Articles 2, 3(g) and 86 [102] of the Treaty to act with a view to eliminating or neutralising them . . .

95 In deciding to discontinue consideration of a complaint against those practices on the ground of lack of Community interest, the Commission therefore cannot rely solely on the fact that practices alleged to be contrary to the Treaty have ceased, without having ascertained that anti-competitive effects no longer continue and, if appropriate, that the seriousness of the alleged interferences with competition or the persistence of their consequences has not been such as to give the complaint a Community interest.

96 In the light of the above considerations, it must be concluded that, by holding, without ascertaining that the anti-competitive effects had been found not to persist and, if appropriate, had been found not to be such as to give the complaint a Community interest, that the investigation of a complaint relating to past infringements did not correspond to the task entrusted to the Commission by the Treaty but served essentially to make it easier for the complainants to show fault in order to obtain damages in the national courts, the Court of First Instance took an incorrect view of the Commission's task in the field of competition.

## NOTES AND QUESTIONS

1.  Are the two cases above consistent? What reasons might justify the Commission's decision not to take action?

2.  What was the significance of the Court's remarks in paragraph 96 regarding the duty of the Commission?

3.  In *Roger Tremblay and Others v. Syndicat des Exploitants des Lieux de Loisirs*, Case T-5/93, 1995 ECJ CELEX LEXIS 44, [1995] ECR II-185 (appeal dismissed in Case C-91/95 P, 1996 ECJ EUR-Lex LEXIS 500, [1996] ECR I-5547) the Commission had received numerous applications under Regulation 17, for a finding that Société des Auteurs, Compositeurs et Editeurs de Musique ("SACEM"), the society which manages copyright in musical works in France, had infringed EU competition rules. All of the parties were located in France. The Commission rejected the complaints and told the parties they could pursue their claims in the French courts. (The case was unsuccessfully appealed to the ECJ on other points) The applicants claimed that if they were forced to rely only on proceedings in the French courts, they would suffer a detriment because the French courts were not in the same position as the Commission to obtain evidence or otherwise enforce the rules as the Commission could. The Court considered that "where the effects of the infringements alleged in a complaint are essentially

confined to the territory of one Member State and where proceedings have been brought before the courts and competent administrative authorities of that Member State by the complainant against the body against which the complaint was made, the Commission is entitled to reject the complaint through lack of any sufficient Community interest in further investigation of the case, provided however that the rights of the complainant or of its members can be adequately safeguarded, in particular by the national courts."

To what extent does the *Automec* case (and the *Tremblay* case above) suggest that the Commission can decline to act in cases that concern facts arising in only one Member State? What remedies did it expect the parties would have in the national courts? Are the national courts in the same position as the Commission to gather relevant evidence? Suppose the French courts misunderstood the law?

4.   In the United States, criminal prosecutors as well as federal agencies enjoy a very wide measure of discretion in determining which cases to pursue. Most do not have structures that set rules and procedures for the exercise of that discretion (an exception being the NLRB). By contrast, in Germany, at least for criminal prosecutions, once a file has been opened, the prosecutor is required to pursue the case and may only discontinue it if a formal determination is made to close the file based on written reasoning.

5.   The Commission has introduced, via a "Settlement Notice" published [2008] OJ C 167/1 a system of "plea bargaining" in competition matters. The legal ramifications of this new approach remain to be worked out, particularly as regards the procedure leading to a decision as described in this Chapter. The full text of the "Procedure" described in the Notice is set out below.

## [C]   Investigations

## REGULATION 1/2003
[2003] OJ L1/1

Article 18

Requests for information

1. In order to carry out the duties assigned to it by this Regulation, the Commission may, by simple request or by decision, require undertakings and associations of undertakings to provide all necessary information.

2. When sending a simple request for information to an undertaking or association of undertakings, the Commission shall state the legal basis and the purpose of the request, specify what information is required and fix the time-limit within which the information is to be provided, and the penalties provided for in Article 23 for supplying incorrect or misleading information.

3. Where the Commission requires undertakings and associations of undertakings to supply information by decision, it shall state the legal basis and the purpose of the request, specify what information is required and fix the time-limit within which it

is to be provided. It shall also indicate the penalties provided for in Article 23 and indicate or impose the penalties provided for in Article 24. It shall further indicate the right to have the decision reviewed by the Court of Justice.

4. The owners of the undertakings or their representatives and, in the case of legal persons, companies or firms, or associations having no legal personality, the persons authorised to represent them by law or by their constitution shall supply the information requested on behalf of the undertaking or the association of undertakings concerned. Lawyers duly authorised to act may supply the information on behalf of their clients. The latter shall remain fully responsible if the information supplied is incomplete, incorrect or misleading.

5. The Commission shall without delay forward a copy of the simple request or of the decision to the competition authority of the Member State in whose territory the seat of the undertaking or association of undertakings is situated and the competition authority of the Member State whose territory is affected.

6. At the request of the Commission the governments and competition authorities of the Member States shall provide the Commission with all necessary information to carry out the duties assigned to it by this Regulation.

## Article 19

### Power to take statements

1. In order to carry out the duties assigned to it by this Regulation, the Commission may interview any natural or legal person who consents to be interviewed for the purpose of collecting information relating to the subject-matter of an investigation.

2. Where an interview pursuant to paragraph 1 is conducted in the premises of an undertaking, the Commission shall inform the competition authority of the Member State in whose territory the interview takes place. If so requested by the competition authority of that Member State, its officials may assist the officials and other accompanying persons authorised by the Commission to conduct the interview.

## Article 20

### The Commission's powers of inspection

1. In order to carry out the duties assigned to it by this Regulation, the Commission may conduct all necessary inspections of undertakings and associations of undertakings.

2. The officials and other accompanying persons authorised by the Commission to conduct an inspection are empowered:

(a) to enter any premises, land and means of transport of undertakings and associations of undertakings;

(b) to examine the books and other records related to the business, irrespective of the medium on which they are stored;

(c) to take or obtain in any form copies of or extracts from such books or records;

(d) to seal any business premises and books or records for the period and to the extent necessary for the inspection;

(e) to ask any representative or member of staff of the undertaking or association of undertakings for explanations on facts or documents relating to the subject-matter and purpose of the inspection and to record the answers.

3. The officials and other accompanying persons authorised by the Commission to conduct an inspection shall exercise their powers upon production of a written authorisation specifying the subject matter and purpose of the inspection and the penalties provided for in Article 23 in case the production of the required books or other records related to the business is incomplete or where the answers to questions asked under paragraph 2 of the present Article are incorrect or misleading. In good time before the inspection, the Commission shall give notice of the inspection to the competition authority of the Member State in whose territory it is to be conducted.

4. Undertakings and associations of undertakings are required to submit to inspections ordered by decision of the Commission. The decision shall specify the subject matter and purpose of the inspection, appoint the date on which it is to begin and indicate the penalties provided for in Articles 23 and 24 and the right to have the decision reviewed by the Court of Justice. The Commission shall take such decisions after consulting the competition authority of the Member State in whose territory the inspection is to be conducted.

5. Officials of as well as those authorised or appointed by the competition authority of the Member State in whose territory the inspection is to be conducted shall, at the request of that authority or of the Commission, actively assist the officials and other accompanying persons authorised by the Commission. To this end, they shall enjoy the powers specified in paragraph 2.

6. Where the officials and other accompanying persons authorised by the Commission find that an undertaking opposes an inspection ordered pursuant to this Article, the Member State concerned shall afford them the necessary assistance, requesting where appropriate the assistance of the police or of an equivalent enforcement authority, so as to enable them to conduct their inspection.

7. If the assistance provided for in paragraph 6 requires authorisation from a judicial authority according to national rules, such authorisation shall be applied for. Such authorisation may also be applied for as a precautionary measure.

8. Where authorisation as referred to in paragraph 7 is applied for, the national judicial authority shall control that the Commission decision is authentic and that the coercive measures envisaged are neither arbitrary nor excessive having regard to the subject matter of the inspection. In its control of the proportionality of the coercive measures, the national judicial authority may ask the Commission, directly or through the Member State competition authority, for detailed explanations in particular on the grounds the Commission has for suspecting infringement of

Articles 81 [101] and 82 [102] of the Treaty, as well as on the seriousness of the suspected infringement and on the nature of the involvement of the undertaking concerned. However, the national judicial authority may not call into question the necessity for the inspection nor demand that it be provided with the information in the Commission's file. The lawfulness of the Commission decision shall be subject to review only by the Court of Justice.

Article 21

Inspection of other premises

1. If a reasonable suspicion exists that books or other records related to the business and to the subject-matter of the inspection, which may be relevant to prove a serious violation of Article 81 [101] or Article 82 [102] of the Treaty, are being kept in any other premises, land and means of transport, including the homes of directors, managers and other members of staff of the undertakings and associations of undertakings concerned, the Commission can by decision order an inspection to be conducted in such other premises, land and means of transport.

2. The decision shall specify the subject matter and purpose of the inspection, appoint the date on which it is to begin and indicate the right to have the decision reviewed by the Court of Justice. It shall in particular state the reasons that have led the Commission to conclude that a suspicion in the sense of paragraph 1 exists. The Commission shall take such decisions after consulting the competition authority of the Member State in whose territory the inspection is to be conducted.

3. A decision adopted pursuant to paragraph 1 cannot be executed without prior authorisation from the national judicial authority of the Member State concerned. The national judicial authority shall control that the Commission decision is authentic and that the coercive measures envisaged are neither arbitrary nor excessive having regard in particular to the seriousness of the suspected infringement, to the importance of the evidence sought, to the involvement of the undertaking concerned and to the reasonable likelihood that business books and records relating to the subject matter of the inspection are kept in the premises for which the authorisation is requested. The national judicial authority may ask the Commission, directly or through the Member State competition authority, for detailed explanations on those elements which are necessary to allow its control of the proportionality of the coercive measures envisaged.

However, the national judicial authority may not call into question the necessity for the inspection nor demand that it be provided with information in the Commission's file. The lawfulness of the Commission decision shall be subject to review only by the Court of Justice.

4. The officials and other accompanying persons authorised by the Commission to conduct an inspection ordered in accordance with paragraph 1 of this Article shall have the powers set out in Article 20(2)(a), (b) and (c). Article 20(5) and (6) shall apply mutatis mutandis.

Article 22

Investigations by competition authorities of Member States

1. The competition authority of a Member State may in its own territory carry out any inspection or other fact-finding measure under its national law on behalf and for the account of the competition authority of another Member State in order to establish whether there has been an infringement of Article 81 [101] or Article 82 [102] of the Treaty. Any exchange and use of the information collected shall be carried out in accordance with Article 12.

2. At the request of the Commission, the competition authorities of the Member States shall undertake the inspections which the Commission considers to be necessary under Article 20(1) or which it has ordered by decision pursuant to Article 20(4). The officials of the competition authorities of the Member States who are responsible for conducting these inspections as well as those authorised or appointed by them shall exercise their powers in accordance with their national law.

If so requested by the Commission or by the competition authority of the Member State in whose territory the inspection is to be conducted, officials and other accompanying persons authorised by the Commission may assist the officials of the authority concerned.

# REGULATION 773/2004
[2004] OJ L 123/27

Article 3

Power to take statements

1. Where the Commission interviews a person with his consent in accordance with Article 19 of Regulation (EC) No 1/2003, it shall, at the beginning of the interview, state the legal basis and the purpose of the interview, and recall its voluntary nature. It shall also inform the person interviewed of its intention to make a record of the interview.

2. The interview may be conducted by any means including by telephone or electronic means.

3. The Commission may record the statements made by the persons interviewed in any form. A copy of any recording shall be made available to the person interviewed for approval. Where necessary, the Commission shall set a time-limit within which the person interviewed may communicate to it any correction to be made to the statement.

## Article 4

### Oral questions during inspections

1. When, pursuant to Article 20(2)(e) of Regulation (EC) No 1/2003, officials or other accompanying persons authorised by the Commission ask representatives or members of staff of an undertaking or of an association of undertakings for explanations, the explanations given may be recorded in any form.

2. A copy of any recording made pursuant to paragraph 1 shall be made available to the undertaking or association of undertakings concerned after the inspection.

3. In cases where a member of staff of an undertaking or of an association of undertakings who is not or was not authorised by the undertaking or by the association of undertakings to provide explanations on behalf of the undertaking or association of undertakings has been asked for explanations, the Commission shall set a time-limit within which the undertaking or the association of undertakings may communicate to the Commission any rectification, amendment or supplement to the explanations given by such member of staff. The rectification, amendment or supplement shall be added to the explanations as recorded pursuant to paragraph 1.

## NOTES AND QUESTIONS

As regards the production of files and information, the Commission does not go to the lengths experienced in the United States where the FTC or the Justice Department issues subpoenas for production of documents. However, Commission requests can be quite burdensome and place the obligation on the parties addressed to turn over responsive documents, with fines being imposable if it should transpire that they are discovered not to have done so. Does the role of the Commission as "prosecutor" and "judge" accord with common notions of "justice"?

## AM & S EUROPE LIMITED v. COMMISSION
### Case 155/79, 1982 ECJ CELEX LEXIS 15, [1982] ECR 1575

[Australian Mining & Smelting Europe (AM & S) sought annulment of a Commission decision that required it to produce for examination by officers of the Commission all the documents for which legal privilege was claimed.]

18 [The rules relating to obtaining information] do not exclude the possibility of recognizing, subject to certain conditions, that certain business records are of a confidential nature. Community law, which derives from not only the economic but also the legal interpenetration of the Member States, must take into account the principles and concepts common to the laws of those states concerning the observance of confidentiality, in particular, as regards certain communications between lawyer and client. That confidentiality serves the requirements, the importance of which is recognized in all of the Member States, that any person must be able, without constraint, to consult a lawyer whose profession entails the giving of independent legal advice to all those in need of it.

19 As far as the protection of written communications between lawyer and client is concerned, it is apparent from the legal systems of the Member States that, although the principle of such protection is generally recognized, its scope and the criteria for applying it vary, as has, indeed, been conceded both by the applicant and by the parties who have intervened in support of its conclusions.

20 Whilst in some of the Member States the protection against disclosure afforded to written communications between lawyer and client is based principally on a recognition of the very nature of the legal profession, inasmuch as it contributes towards the maintenance of the rule of law, in other Member States the same protection is justified by the more specific requirement (which, moreover, is also recognized in the first-mentioned states) that the rights of the defence must be respected.

21 Apart from these differences, however, there are to be found in the national laws of the Member States common criteria inasmuch as those laws protect, in similar circumstances, the confidentiality of written communications between lawyer and client provided that, on the one hand, such communications are made for the purposes and in the interests of the client's rights of defence and, on the other hand, they emanate from independent lawyers, that is to say, lawyers who are not bound to the client by a relationship of employment.

22 Viewed in that context Regulation No. 17 must be interpreted as protecting, in its turn, the confidentiality of written communications between lawyer and client subject to those two conditions, and thus incorporating such elements of that protection as are common to the laws of the Member States.

23 As far as the first of those two conditions is concerned, in Regulation No. 17 itself, in particular in the eleventh recital in its preamble and in the provisions contained in article 19, care is taken to ensure that the rights of the defence may be exercised to the full, and the protection of the confidentiality of written communications between lawyer and client is an essential corollary to those rights. In those circumstances, such protection must, if it is to be effective, be recognized as covering all written communications exchanged after the initiation of the administrative procedure under Regulation No. 17 which may lead to a decision on the application of articles 85 [101] and 86 [102] of the Treaty or to a decision imposing a pecuniary sanction on the undertaking. It must also be possible to extend it to earlier written communications which have a relationship to the subject-matter of that procedure.

24 As regards the second condition, it should be stated that the requirement as to the position and status as an independent lawyer, which must be fulfilled by the legal adviser from whom the written communications which may be protected emanate, is based on a conception of the lawyer's role as collaborating in the administration of justice by the courts and as being required to provide, in full independence, and in the overriding interests of that cause, such legal assistance as the client needs. The counterpart of that protection lies in the rules of professional ethics and discipline which are laid down and enforced in the general interest by institutions endowed with the requisite powers for that purpose. Such a conception reflects the legal traditions common to the Member States and is also to be found in legal order of the Community, as is demonstrated by article 17 of the Protocols

on the Statutes of the Court of Justice of the EEC and the EAEC, and also by article 20 of the Protocol on the Statute of the Court of Justice of the ECSC.

25 Having regard to the principles of the Treaty concerning freedom of establishment and the freedom to provide services the protection thus afforded by Community law, in particular in the context of Regulation No. 17, to written communications between lawyer and client must apply without distinction to any lawyer entitled to practise his profession in one of the Member States, regardless of the Member State in which the client lives.

26 Such protection may not be extended beyond those limits, which are determined by the scope of the common rules on the exercise of the legal profession as laid down in council directive 77/249/EEC of 22 March 1977 (OJ l 78, p.17), which is based in its turn on the mutual recognition by all the Member States of the national legal concepts of each of them on this subject.

27 In view of all these factors it must therefore be concluded that although Regulation No. 17, and in particular article 14 thereof, interpreted in the light of its wording, structure and aims, and having regard to the laws of the Member States, empowers the Commission to require, in the course of an investigation within the meaning of that Article, production of the business documents the disclosure of which it considers necessary, including written communications between lawyer and client, for proceedings in respect of any infringements of articles 85 [101] and 86 [102] of the Treaty, that power is, however, subject to a restriction imposed by the need to protect confidentiality, on the conditions defined above, and provided that the communications in question are exchanged between an independent lawyer, that is to say one who is not bound to his client by a relationship of employment, and his client.

28 Finally, it should be remarked that the principle of confidentiality does not prevent a lawyer's client from disclosing the written communications between them if he considers that it is in his interests to do so.

(c) The procedures relating to the application of the principle of confidentiality

29 If an undertaking which is the subject of an investigation under article 14 of Regulation No. 17 refuses, on the ground that it is entitled to protection of the confidentiality of information, to produce, among the business records demanded by the Commission, written communications between itself and its lawyer, it must nevertheless provide the Commission's authorized agents with relevant material of such a nature as to demonstrate that the communications fulfil the conditions for being granted legal protection as defined above, although it is not bound to reveal the contents of the communications in question.

30 Where the Commission is not satisfied that such evidence has been supplied, the appraisal of those conditions is not a matter which may be left to an arbitrator or to a national authority. Since this is a matter involving an appraisal and a decision which affect the conditions under which the Commission may act in a field as vital to the functioning of the common market as that of compliance with the rules on competition, the solution of disputes as to the application of the protection of the confidentiality of written communications between lawyer and client may be sought only at community level.

31 In that case it is for the Commission to order, pursuant to article 14 (3) of Regulation No. 17, production of the communications in question and, if necessary, to impose on the undertaking fines or periodic penalty payments under that regulation as a penalty for the undertaking's refusal either to supply such additional evidence as the Commission considers necessary or to produce the communications in question whose confidentiality, in the Commission's view, is not protected in law.

32 The fact that by virtue of article 185 [242] of the EEC Treaty any action brought by the undertaking concerned against such decisions does not have suspensory effect provides an answer to the Commission's concern as to the effect of the time taken by the procedure before the court on the efficacy of the supervision which the Commission is called upon to exercise in regard to compliance with the Treaty rules on competition, whilst on the other hand the interests of the undertaking concerned are safeguarded by the possibility which exists under articles 185 [242] and 186 [243] of the Treaty, as well as under article 83 of the Rules of Procedure of the Court, of obtaining an order suspending the application of the decision which has been taken, or any other interim measure.

[The Court went on to determine that most of the documents were protected and annulled the decision.]

# NOTES AND QUESTIONS

1.   Does the doctrine described by the Court resemble the concept of privilege as it exists in common law jurisdictions, or is it something different? Consider in particular the underlying basis for according the confidentiality. Consider also the fact that in civil law jurisdictions there is no general discovery of documents in civil litigation. Would this tend to suggest that legal privilege is unnecessary in that context?

2.   The Court expressly denied privilege to in-house lawyer communications. What reasons justified this? Does it make sense in terms of encouraging corporations to comply or come forward with leniency applications?

In *Akzo Nobel Chemicals Ltd and Akcros Chemicals Ltd v. Commission* Joined Cases T-125 and 253/03, 2007 ECJ CELEX LEXIS 555, [2007] ECR II-3523 the Court confirmed that the Commission cannot look at documents for which privilege is (properly) claimed during a dawn raid; documents may be privileged if drawn up for the purposes of seeking external legal advice (this is an extension of the *AM&S* doctrine); and no privilege extends to communications between business people and their in-house counsel.

3.   Note that in Regulation 1/2003, the Commission has received increased powers of investigation — for it is now permitted to ask a much broader range of questions during a surprise inspection and to carry out inspections of private homes and cars of a company's directors, managers and staff members. In addition, the Commission may seal business premises. The Commission will also have the ability to impose significantly higher financial penalties on companies deemed to be non-cooperating. Surprise inspections are clearly vital to effective enforcement because the ability to prove a violation is largely dependent on securing documents before they are destroyed. Such investigations without warrants have provoked

reactions based on alleged due process violations in the U.S., but again there is a recognition that sometimes this is the only way to secure evidence.

In *Roquette Frères S.A. v. Directeur Général de la Concurrence, de la Consommation et de la Répression des fraudes, and Commission*, Case C-94/00, 2002 ECJ CELEX LEXIS 270, [2002] ECR I-9011, the Commission had adopted a decision requiring Roquette to submit to an onsite inspection under article 14 of Regulation 17/62. The French Competition Order required that the search be authorized by a judge and in this case an authorization order was granted. Roquette submitted to the inspection but then challenged the order. The CFI/General Court gave the following guidance in the dispositive part of the judgment:

2. Community law requires the Commission to ensure that the national court in question has at its disposal all the information which it needs in order to carry out the review which it is required to undertake. In that regard, the information supplied by the Commission must in principle include:

- a description of the essential features of the suspected infringement, that is to say, at the very least, an indication of the market thought to be affected and of the nature of the suspected restrictions of competition;

- explanations concerning the manner in which the undertaking at which the coercive measures are aimed is thought to be involved in the infringement in question;

- detailed explanations showing that the Commission possesses solid factual information and evidence providing grounds for suspecting such infringement on the part of the undertaking concerned;

- as precise as possible an indication of the evidence sought, of the matters to which the investigation must relate and of the powers conferred on the Community investigators; and

- in the event that the assistance of the national authorities is requested by the Commission as a precautionary measure, in order to overcome any opposition on the part of the undertaking concerned, explanations enabling the national court to satisfy itself that, if authorisation for the coercive measures were not granted on precautionary grounds, it would be impossible, or very difficult, to establish the facts amounting to the infringement.

3. On the other hand, the national court may not demand that it be provided with the evidence in the Commission's file on which the latter's suspicions are based.

4. Where the national court considers that the information communicated by the Commission does not fulfil the requirements referred to in point 2 of this operative part, it cannot, without violating Article 14(6) of Regulation No 17 and Article 5 of the EC Treaty (now Article 10 EC [TEU 4]), simply dismiss the application brought before it. In such circumstances, it is required as rapidly as possible to inform the Commission, or the national authority which has brought the latter's request before it, of the difficulties

encountered, where necessary by asking for any clarification which it may need in order to carry out the review which it is to undertake. Not until any such clarification is forthcoming, or the Commission fails to take any practical steps in response to its request, may the national court in question refuse to grant the assistance sought on the ground that, in the light of the information available to it, it is unable to hold that the coercive measures envisaged are not arbitrary or disproportionate to the subject-matter of those measures.

5. The information to be provided by the Commission to the national court may be contained either in the investigation decision itself or in the request made to the national authorities under Article 14(6) of Regulation No 17, or indeed in an answer — even one given orally — to a question put by that court.

Is there any inference in the above guidance that national constitutional principles have any part to play in the national court's decision whether to authorize a search? Given that the purpose of the search is to find evidence, why did the Court require that, nonetheless, the Commission have a certain level of information already in order to justify the search? Why couldn't the parties who are subjected to a raid simply challenge the Commission's actions under EC 230/TFEU 263? More generally, why is it necessary to have resort to national rules at all in connection with an EU action such as this?

For comparisons with the U.S. standards on searches, particularly warrantless searches, as part of regulatory enforcement, see for example, *Camara v. Municipal Court*, 387 U.S. 523 (1967), *See v. Seattle*, 387 U.S. 541 (1967), *Frank v. Maryland*, 359 U.S. 360 (1959), *Colonnade Catering Corp. v. United States*, 397 U.S. 72 (1970), *United States v. Biswell*, 406 U.S. 311 (1972), *Marshall v. Barlow's, Inc.*, 436 U.S. 307 (1978), *Donovan v. Dewey*, 452 U.S. 594 (1981) and *New York v. Burger*, 482 U.S. 691 (1987).

## [D]   Initiation of Proceedings and Process Leading to a Decision

## TOKAI CARBON CO. LTD (T-71/03), INTECH EDM BV (T-74/ 03), INTECH EDM AG (T-87/03) AND SGL CARBON AG (T-91/ 03) v. COMMISSION
Joined Cases T-71/03, T-74/03, T-87/03 and T-91/03, 2005 ECJ CELEX LEXIS 803, [2005] ECR II-10

[The applicants had been found to have infringed EC 81/TFEU 101 and sought annulment under EC 230/TFEU 263 in the CFI/General Court. One argument they made was that the statement of objections issued by the Commission that initiated the proceeding leading to the contested decision was improper. For relevant provisions relating to the procedure relating to the Statement of Objections see now Regulation 1/2003, articles 27 and 28, and Regulation 773/2004 articles 2 and 10-16.]

138. According to settled case-law, the statement of objections must be couched in terms which, even if succinct, are sufficiently clear to enable the parties concerned

properly to identify the conduct complained of by the Commission and to enable them properly to defend themselves, before the Commission adopts a final decision. That obligation is satisfied where the decision does not allege that the persons concerned have committed infringements other than those referred to in the statement of objections and only takes into consideration facts on which the persons concerned have had the opportunity of making known their views . . .

139. More specifically, as regards the calculation of the fines, it is also settled case-law that the Commission satisfies its obligation to respect the right of undertakings to be heard where it expressly states, in the statement of objections, that it is going to consider whether it is appropriate to impose fines on the undertakings and also indicates the main factual and legal criteria capable of giving rise to a fine, such as the gravity and the duration of the alleged infringement and the fact that the infringement was committed intentionally or negligently'. In doing so it gives them the necessary details to enable them to defend themselves not merely against the finding of an infringement but also against the imposition of fines . . .

140. Thus, so far as concerns the determination of the amount of the fines, the rights of defence of the undertakings are guaranteed before the Commission through their opportunity to make submissions on the duration, the gravity and the forseeability of the anti-competitive nature of the infringement . . .

141. By contrast, where it has indicated the elements of fact and of law on which it would base its calculation of the fines, the Commission is under no obligation to explain the way in which it would use each of those elements in determining the level of the fine. To give indications as regards the level of the fines envisaged, before the undertakings have been invited to submit their observations on the allegations against them, would be to anticipate the Commission's decision and would thus be inappropriate . . .

## NOTES AND QUESTIONS

1.    What, according to the Court, are the minimum legal requirements regarding the contents of a statement of objections under EC 81/TFEU 101?

2.    As to "burden of proof" and "standard of proof", note the comments of A-G Sir Gordon Slynn in *Musique Diffusion Française and Others v. Commission*, Joined Cases 100-103/80, [1983] ECR 1825:

Once a finding has been made that a concerted practice exists, since it is the applicant who is claiming that the Commission's decision should be annulled, the burden of proving the illegality of the decision falls, in general and in the first instance, on the applicant. This follows from a principle of law recognised in all Member States, that the legal burden of proving the facts essential to an assertion normally lies on the party asserting it. On the other hand, the allegations of facts made by the Commission in a decision must be such as to warrant the conclusion drawn from them. If they do not warrant that conclusion, the decision may be annulled, even in the absence of any evidence adduced by the applicants.

**3.** For a U.S. parallel of sorts regarding the requirements of statements of objections to set out all the facts and reasoning upon which the decision is based, see *Bowen v. Georgetown University Hospital*, 488 U.S. 204 (1988) where the agency put forward an interpretation argument for the first time only in the litigation, not in its prior decision-making process.

Many detailed issues have been raised in the ECJ and now the CFI/General Court based on inadequate reasoning (i.e., the Commission's decision failed adequately to state the grounds on which its decision was based) or on failure to observe proper procedures. The Court of First Instance/General Court has been particularly critical of the Commission's procedures, and as a consequence, a number of important decisions have been annulled for procedural deficiencies.

**4.** The *AM&S* case dealt with legal privilege and the extent to which the Commission could seize and use documents that were confidential due to such privilege. By contrast, the confidentiality provisions in article 16 of Regulation 773 and article 28 of Regulation 1 address the *handling* of documents by the authorities. This is clearly a very sensitive area, and it is routine practice for parties to seek business secrets status for information supplied or obtained. Serious consequences can ensue if the Commission fails to secure confidentiality, as was evident in the *Adams* case (*Adams v. Commission*, Joined Cases145/83 and 53/84, [1985] ECR 3651). Mr. Adams had sued for compensation based on alleged negligence by the Commission in leaking his identity as an informant who had provided certain documents to the Commission regarding anticompetitive practices by his employer, Hoffman LaRoche. LaRoche, through various means (including visits and phone calls by their attorney, Dr. Alder, to the Commission) came to the conclusion that Mr. Adams was responsible for providing the documents. The revelation of his identity led *inter alia* to his arrest, detention and conviction in Switzerland for violation of Swiss Business Secret Legislation. The Court found the Commission liable.

The competition rules are not the only area where the issue of confidentiality arises. In *Timex Corp. v. Council and Commission*, Case 264/82, [1985] ECR 849, the issue arose in the context of Article 7(4) of Regulation 3017/79, which deals with "anti-dumping" procedures. (In an anti-dumping procedure duties may be imposed on goods from third countries that are being sold in the Community at prices less than home market prices, or a deemed equivalent, and cause injury to EU industry.) Article 7(4) allowed a complainant (i.e., an EU based company) to "inspect all information made available to the Commission by any party to an investigation . . . provided that it is relevant to the defence of [its] interests and not confidential within the meaning of Article 8 . . ." (Article 8(3) provides that "information will ordinarily be considered to be confidential if its disclosure is likely to have a significantly adverse effect upon the supplier or the source of such information.")

## [E]   Clearance and Exemptions

### REGULATION 1/2003
[2003] OJ L1/1

Article 10

Finding of inapplicability

Where the Community public interest relating to the application of Articles 81 [101] and 82 [102] of the Treaty so requires, the Commission, acting on its own initiative, may by decision find that Article 81 [101] of the Treaty is not applicable to an agreement, a decision by an association of undertakings or a concerted practice, either because the conditions of Article 81 [101](1) of the Treaty are not fulfilled, or because the conditions of Article 81 [101] (3) of the Treaty are satisfied.

The Commission may likewise make such a finding with reference to Article 82 [102] of the Treaty.

Article 29

Withdrawal in individual cases

1. Where the Commission, empowered by a Council Regulation, such as Regulations 19/65/EEC, (EEC) No 2821/71, (EEC) No 3976/87, (EEC) No 1534/91 or (EEC) No 479/92, to apply Article 81[101](3) of the Treaty by regulation, has declared Article 81[101](1) of the Treaty inapplicable to certain categories of agreements, decisions by associations of undertakings or concerted practices, it may, acting on its own initiative or on a complaint, withdraw the benefit of such an exemption Regulation when it finds that in any particular case an agreement, decision or concerted practice to which the exemption Regulation applies has certain effects which are incompatible with Article 81[101](3) of the Treaty.

2. Where, in any particular case, agreements, decisions by associations of under-takings or concerted practices to which a Commission Regulation referred to in paragraph 1 applies have effects which are incompatible with Article 81[101](3) of the Treaty in the territory of a Member State, or in a part thereof, which has all the characteristics of a distinct geographic market, the competition authority of that Member State may withdraw the benefit of the Regulation in question in respect of that territory.

## NOTES AND QUESTIONS

1.   The procedure under Regulation 17 for seeking an exemption, or alterna-tively a "negative clearance", entailed notifying an agreement to the Commission. The notification of the agreement had the effect of suspending fines for acting pursuant to the agreement from the date of the notification, so it became common

practice to file a notification to create a degree of immunity. How does the new regulation change this?

2.   Under Regulation 17/62, the Commission had taken to issuing "comfort letters", which it could process more quickly without having to go through the entire procedure leading to a decision. See *Procureur de la Republique et. al v. Giry et al.*, Joined Cases 253/78 and 1-3/79 [1980] ECR 2327. This process was a rather unsatisfactory solution to deal with the vast number of notifications. The Commission did not routinely publish its comfort letters and tended to limit itself to a press release, if that, at the time the file had been closed. There are probably many commercial arrangements in place today that relied on Commission statements, however brief, regarding their legal standing. Would a party still be able to rely on public statements relating to such letters under the new Regulation? What about press releases and notices concerning more general pronouncements of Commission policy?

## [F]   Fines

### REGULATION 1/2003
[2003] OJ L1/1

Article 23

Fines

1. The Commission may by decision impose on undertakings and associations of undertakings fines not exceeding 1% of the total turnover in the preceding business year where, intentionally or negligently:

(a) they supply incorrect or misleading information in response to a request made pursuant to Article 17 or Article 18(2);

(b) in response to a request made by decision adopted pursuant to Article 17 or Article 18(3), they supply incorrect, incomplete or misleading information or do not supply information within the required time-limit;

(c) they produce the required books or other records related to the business in incomplete form during inspections under Article 20 or refuse to submit to inspections ordered by a decision adopted pursuant to Article 20(4);

(d) in response to a question asked in accordance with Article 20(2)(e),

- they give an incorrect or misleading answer,

- they fail to rectify within a time-limit set by the Commission an incorrect, incomplete or misleading answer given by a member of staff, or

- they fail or refuse to provide a complete answer on facts relating to the subject-matter and purpose of an inspection ordered by a decision adopted pursuant to Article 20(4);

(e) seals affixed in accordance with Article 20(2)(d) by officials or other accompanying persons authorised by the Commission have been broken.

2. The Commission may by decision impose fines on undertakings and associations of undertakings where, either intentionally or negligently:

(a) they infringe Article 81[101] or Article 82[102] of the Treaty; or

(b) they contravene a decision ordering interim measures under Article 8; or

(c) they fail to comply with a commitment made binding by a decision pursuant to Article 9.

For each undertaking and association of undertakings participating in the infringement, the fine shall not exceed 10% of its total turnover in the preceding business year.

Where the infringement of an association relates to the activities of its members, the fine shall not exceed 10% of the sum of the total turnover of each member active on the market affected by the infringement of the association.

3. In fixing the amount of the fine, regard shall be had both to the gravity and to the duration of the infringement.

4. When a fine is imposed on an association of undertakings taking account of the turnover of its members and the association is not solvent, the association is obliged to call for contributions from its members to cover the amount of the fine.

Where such contributions have not been made to the association within a time-limit fixed by the Commission, the Commission may require payment of the fine directly by any of the undertakings whose representatives were members of the decision-making bodies concerned of the association.

After the Commission has required payment under the second subparagraph, where necessary to ensure full payment of the fine, the Commission may require payment of the balance by any of the members of the association which were active on the market on which the infringement occurred.

However, the Commission shall not require payment under the second or the third subparagraph from undertakings which show that they have not implemented the infringing decision of the association and either were not aware of its existence or have actively distanced themselves from it before the Commission started investigating the case.

The financial liability of each undertaking in respect of the payment of the fine shall not exceed 10% of its total turnover in the preceding business year.

5. Decisions taken pursuant to paragraphs 1 and 2 shall not be of a criminal law nature.

Article 24

Periodic penalty payments

1. The Commission may, by decision, impose on undertakings or associations of undertakings periodic penalty payments not exceeding 5% of the average daily turnover in the preceding business year per day and calculated from the date appointed by the decision, in order to compel them:

(a) to put an end to an infringement of Article 81[101] or Article 82[102] of the Treaty, in accordance with a decision taken pursuant to Article 7;

(b) to comply with a decision ordering interim measures taken pursuant to Article 8;

(c) to comply with a commitment made binding by a decision pursuant to Article 9;

(d) to supply complete and correct information which it has requested by decision taken pursuant to Article 17 or Article 18(3);

(e) to submit to an inspection which it has ordered by decision taken pursuant to Article 20(4).

2. Where the undertakings or associations of undertakings have satisfied the obligation which the periodic penalty payment was intended to enforce, the Commission may fix the definitive amount of the periodic penalty payment at a figure lower than that which would arise under the original decision. Article 23(4) shall apply correspondingly.

CHAPTER VII

LIMITATION PERIODS

Article 25

Limitation periods for the imposition of penalties

1. The powers conferred on the Commission by Articles 23 and 24 shall be subject to the following limitation periods:

(a) three years in the case of infringements of provisions concerning requests for information or the conduct of inspections;

(b) five years in the case of all other infringements.

2. Time shall begin to run on the day on which the infringement is committed. However, in the case of continuing or repeated infringements, time shall begin to run on the day on which the infringement ceases.

3. Any action taken by the Commission or by the competition authority of a Member State for the purpose of the investigation or proceedings in respect of an

infringement shall interrupt the limitation period for the imposition of fines or periodic penalty payments. The limitation period shall be interrupted with effect from the date on which the action is notified to at least one undertaking or association of undertakings which has participated in the infringement. Actions which interrupt the running of the period shall include in particular the following:

(a) written requests for information by the Commission or by the competition authority of a Member State;

(b) written authorisations to conduct inspections issued to its officials by the Commission or by the competition authority of a Member State;

(c) the initiation of proceedings by the Commission or by the competition authority of a Member State;

(d) notification of the statement of objections of the Commission or of the competition authority of a Member State.

4. The interruption of the limitation period shall apply for all the undertakings or associations of undertakings which have participated in the infringement.

5. Each interruption shall start time running afresh. However, the limitation period shall expire at the latest on the day on which a period equal to twice the limitation period has elapsed without the Commission having imposed a fine or a periodic penalty payment. That period shall be extended by the time during which limitation is suspended pursuant to paragraph 6.

6. The limitation period for the imposition of fines or periodic penalty payments shall be suspended for as long as the decision of the Commission is the subject of proceedings pending before the Court of Justice.

Article 26

Limitation period for the enforcement of penalties

1. The power of the Commission to enforce decisions taken pursuant to Articles 23 and 24 shall be subject to a limitation period of five years.

2. Time shall begin to run on the day on which the decision becomes final.

3. The limitation period for the enforcement of penalties shall be interrupted:

(a) by notification of a decision varying the original amount of the fine or periodic penalty payment or refusing an application for variation;

(b) by any action of the Commission or of a Member State, acting at the request of the Commission, designed to enforce payment of the fine or periodic penalty payment.

4. Each interruption shall start time running afresh.

5. The limitation period for the enforcement of penalties shall be suspended for so long as:

(a) time to pay is allowed;

(b) enforcement of payment is suspended pursuant to a decision of the Court of Justice.

# THE FINING GUIDELINES AND THE LENIENCY NOTICE
### (Summary reproduced from the EU's website)

*Fining Guidelines* [introduced September 2006]:

The new guidelines refine the method used by the Commission, imposing stiffer fines on firms that violate the provisions of the Treaty establishing the European Community (EC Treaty) prohibiting cartels and other restrictive business practices (Article 81 [101]) and abuses of dominant position (Article 82 [102]).

The new guidelines introduce four main changes to enhance the deterrent effect of the fines imposed by the Commission. These are a basic amount for simply committing the infringement, an amount related to the value of sales involved in the infringement, a closer correlation between the fine and the duration of the infringement and higher fines in the event of re-offending.

## Basic amount of the fine

The basic amount is calculated as a percentage of the value of the sales connected with the infringement, multiplied by the number of years the infringement has been taking place.

The percentage of the value of sales is determined according to the gravity of the infringement (nature, combined market share of all the parties concerned, geographic scope, etc.) and may be as much as 30%.

The Commission then adds to this initial calculation a further amount that is applied to all cartel cases and, at the Commission's discretion, to certain other types of infringement. This will be between 15 and 25% of the value of annual sales, irrespective of the duration of the infringement. This is intended to deter firms from engaging in illegal practices in the first place.

## Adjustments to the basic amount

The basic amount, calculated according to the method described above, may then be adjusted by the Commission, downwards if it finds that there are mitigating circumstances, or upwards in the event of aggravating circumstances.

Firms that commit similar infringements again will now be fined more heavily. The Commission will penalise re-offending, taking into account not only its own earlier decisions but also rulings by national authorities. Firms that re-offend could now face a 100% increase in their fine for each subsequent infringement."

*Leniency Notice*:

"The notice concerns secret cartels between firms aimed at:

- fixing prices;

- fixing production or sales quotas;

- market sharing, including rigged invitations to tender;

- restricting imports or exports.

These are among the most serious restrictions of competition as they inevitably lead to price increases and reduced choice for the consumer.

## Immunity from fines

The Commission will grant a firm participating in a cartel complete immunity from a fine if it is the first to provide information and evidence of the existence of the cartel, on condition that the firm:

- provides all the evidence and information available concerning the alleged cartel;

- cooperates fully, on a continuous basis and expeditiously with the Commission throughout the administrative procedure;

- ends its involvement in the suspected infringement as soon as it submits evidence of the infringement;

- has not coerced other firms to take part in the infringement.

## Reduced fines

A firm that does not meet the conditions for complete immunity may, however, be eligible for a reduced fine if it is able:

- to provide significant proof: the proof must represent added value as regards the evidence already in the Commission's possession;

- to terminate its involvement in the illegal activity as soon as it submits evidence thereof.

The first firm wishing to cooperate with the Commission and meeting the conditions described above will benefit from a reduction of between 50% and 30%, the second firm will benefit from a reduction of between 30% and 20%, whilst firms subsequently joining in will be granted a maximum reduction of 20%.

However, the reduction in the fine will also be in proportion to the quality of the information and the date on which it was supplied, as well as to the extent of cooperation with the Commission throughout the procedure.

**Applications for leniency**

Firms wishing to benefit from leniency in a cartel case should apply in writing to the Directorate-General for Competition . . . which undertakes to treat all information confidentially. If the application for immunity or for a reduction in fines is viewed favourably by the Commission, the firm concerned undertakes to supply all the evidence immediately. The evidence must be presented in hypothetical terms.

If the conditions of the notice are satisfied, the Commission may decide to grant conditional immunity to the firm in question. As regards the application for a reduction in the fine, evidence is not taken into account until the Commission has taken a position on any existing application for conditional immunity relating to the same suspected infringement. If necessary, the Commission will verify the added value of the information supplied and will then announce the amount of the reduction.

It should be noted, however, that a firm benefiting from immunity or a reduction in fines is not protected from the consequences in civil law of its involvement in the infringement.

# NOTES AND QUESTIONS

1.   The introduction of the Leniency Program parallels similar policies adopted in the United States. It has dramatically increased the number of successful Commission investigations. At the same time, the Fining Guidelines have put corporations on notice that the consequences of violating the competition law will be extremely serious.

2.   Note that in *BASF AG and UCB SA v. Commission*, Joined Cases T-101/05 and T-111/05, 2007 ECJ EUR-Lex LEXIS 2397, [2008] ECR II-4949, the Court of First Instance/General Court for the first time, when reviewing the decision in an EC 230/TFEU 263 action, *increased* a fine imposed by the Commission. The increase was small and was intended to correct a technical defect found in the decision. However, the Court has a general power to increase fines and could conceivably in the future raise the fine based on a view that the Commission had simply been too lenient. This power may serve at the very least to constrain annulment claims that are based on flimsy grounds. The same case also provides some detailed on guidance on the specific issue as to whether there was one continuous or several separate cartels. A single infringement can be found based either on the legal characterization of the anti-competitive conduct or on the personal nature of the liability for the infringement. In the first category, the description of the conduct may be broad enough to capture an evolution over time so that the conduct may change but still be caught. The latter category seems to capture the instance where an undertaking knowingly participates at some stage in a cartel and is then held responsible for the entirety of the conduct from beginning to end.

3.   One consequence of introducing the guidelines has been to introduce a form of retroactive effect, because the parties to a cartel would not have known what the penalties could be when they engaged in the illegal conduct. Does it seem right that

companies should be faced with much heavier fines than they had reason to believe they would face when they engaged in the illegal conduct? Could this create issues under the Charter of Fundamental Rights?

**4.** For the approach in U.S. administrative law practice, one might compare *Atchison, T. and S.F. Ry. v. Wichita Bd of Trade*, 412 U.S. 800 (1973) and *Shaw's Supermarkets Inc. v. NLRB* 884 F. 2d 34 (1st Cir. 1989). Generally the U.S. Courts have been unwilling, as in Europe, to hold agencies to precedent in a formalistic way, but, again as in Europe, may require at least a reasoned explanation for the change of course.

**5.** There are risks for companies that take advantage of the leniency program. It does require that the amnesty or leniency applicant provide significant information to the Commission and therefore there is a risk that an applicant will cause an investigation to start and then be found not to benefit from the leniency. It could also spark an investigation in the U.S. (and vice versa) and could create issues for the parties *vis à vis* their exposure to civil actions under U.S. antitrust law, where triple damages are available.

**6.** It might seem implicit in the leniency procedure that the party seeking this protection, having received credit for its cooperation, will not seek to challenge the final Commission decision. However, this did happen in *Schunk GmbH and Schunk Kohlenstoff-Technik GmbH v. Commission*, Case T-69/04, 2008 ECJ EUR-Lex LEXIS 2236, [2008] ECR II-2567, forcing the Commission to file a sort of counterclaim, despite the absence of any procedure in the Court's Rules covering this.

## SUMITOMO CHEMICAL CO. LTD, AND SUMIKA FINE CHEMICALS CO. LTD v. COMMISSION
### Case T-22/02 and T-23/02, 2005 ECJ CELEX LEXIS 468, [2005] ECR II-4065

[The applicants in this case, inter alia, challenged the Commission's decision regarding an infringement of Article 81 [101] in that it dealt with conduct that had already ceased. The statute of limitations under Regulation 2988/74 [1974] OJ 319/1 had expired as regards the ability of the Commission to impose a fine, but there is no statute of limitations as regards finding of an infringement. The Court's judgment was unsuccessfully appealed to the ECJ in *Sumitomo Metal Industries Ltd (C-403/04 P) and Nippon Steel Corp. v. Commission* Joined cases C-403/04 P and C-405/04 P, 2007 ECJ EUR-Lex LEXIS 3314, [2007] ECR I-00729.]

130 . . . [I]t has already been noted in paragraph 37 of the present judgment that the cessation of an infringement of the competition rules before the adoption of a decision by the Commission is not in itself a factor precluding the exercise of the Commission's power to find that infringement since the Court of Justice has held that the Commission can adopt a decision declaring conduct which had already been terminated by the undertaking concerned to be an infringement, provided however that the institution has a legitimate interest in so doing . . .

131 Moreover . . . whilst, under the system established by Regulation No 17, the Commission's power to find an infringement arises only implicitly, that is to the

extent that the express powers to order cessation of the infringement and to impose fines necessarily implies it . . . such an implied power is nevertheless not solely dependent on the exercise by the institution of those express powers. Accordingly, the fact that the Commission no longer has the power to impose fines on persons committing an infringement on account of the expiry of the limitation period referred to in Article 1(1) of Regulation No 2988/74 does not in itself preclude the adoption of a decision finding that that past infringement has been committed.

132 As regards the applicants' arguments set out in paragraphs 115 to 118 above, the question which they raise is not in fact whether the Commission had the competence to find, by means of a decision, the past infringements alleged to have been committed by the applicants, but whether, in the present case, the Commission had a legitimate interest in adopting a decision finding those infringements . . . By those arguments, the applicants therefore in essence criticise the way in which that competence was exercised in the present case.

133 The Court must point out that it is not clear from the Decision that the Commission did in fact consider whether or not it had such an interest.

134 When questioned on this point at the hearing, the defendant relied upon paragraph 651 of the Decision, which they claim sets out the Commission's finding that it was appropriate to adopt a decision finding an infringement against the applicants, which, in its opinion, amounts essentially to saying that there was a legitimate interest in so doing.

135 However, it must be found that by asserting in that paragraph that '[t]he rules on limitation periods concern exclusively the imposition of fines or penalties' and that '[t]hey have no bearing on the entitlement of the Commission to investigate cartel cases and to adopt as appropriate prohibition decisions', the defendant merely replies to and rejects the argument raised by the applicants to the effect that, assuming the infringements in question are established, they could no longer be the subject of a decision because they were time-barred. It cannot be inferred from that assertion that the Commission also considered whether it had a legitimate interest in adopting a decision finding infringements which the applicants had already brought to an end.

136 It follows from the foregoing that, as it failed to consider, when adopting the Decision, whether the finding of the infringements against the applicants was justified by a legitimate interest, the Commission committed an error of law justifying the annulment of the Decision in so far as it concerns the applicants.

137 Moreover, the defendant has not demonstrated to the Court the existence in the present case of such a legitimate interest. It is true that the defendant stated to the Court that, in addition to the interest of clarifying a legal situation, which was accepted as being legitimate in the circumstances of the case giving rise to the judgment in *GVL* v. *Commission*, other interests could in the present case justify the adoption of the Decision against the applicants, namely the need to promote exemplary behaviour on the part of the undertakings, the interest in discouraging any repeat infringement, given the particularly serious nature of the infringements in question, and the interest in enabling the injured parties to bring matters before the national civil courts.

138 It must, however, be found that the defendant merely sets out in generic terms three premisses, without demonstrating, by reference to the particular circumstances of the present case relating to the very serious and extensive infringements alleged against the applicants, that those premisses are established and consequently establish its legitimate interest in adopting against the applicants a decision finding those infringements. The Commission has not specifically explained to the Court why the gravity and geographic scale of the infringements in question made it necessary to find, by the Decision, infringements which had come to an end in the particular case of the applicants. Further, it has adduced no evidence whatsoever of the risk of recidivism on the part of the applicants. Moreover, the defendant has not given any indication, relating to the particular circumstances of the present case, of legal proceedings undertaken or even capable of being envisaged by third parties injured by the infringements.

139 Furthermore, the applicants challenged the legitimacy of the interests referred to by the defendant before the Court, submitting that the statement of objections had been sufficiently dissuasive in their case, that there was no genuine danger of a return to the anti-competitive practices in question and that the desire to assist in the bringing of proceedings before national courts was in itself debateable. The defendant has not responded in detail to those objections so as to establish the legitimate interest alleged.

## NOTES AND QUESTIONS

This case deals with a different element of the Commission's discretion, namely the extent to which it can find infringement for which it cannot impose a fine due to the expiry of the statute of limitations. Does it make sense to operate a limitation period that applies only to the ability to impose fines and not to the finding of infringement? What was the CFI's/General Court's view on this?

### [G]   Other Forms of Remedy

## REGULATION 1/2003
### [2003] OJ L1/1

Article 7

Finding and termination of infringement

1. Where the Commission, acting on a complaint or on its own initiative, finds that there is an infringement of Article 81[101] or of Article 82[102] of the Treaty, it may by decision require the undertakings and associations of undertakings concerned to bring such infringement to an end. For this purpose, it may impose on them any behavioural or structural remedies which are proportionate to the infringement committed and necessary to bring the infringement effectively to an end. Structural remedies can only be imposed either where there is no equally effective behavioural remedy or where any equally effective behavioural remedy would be more

burdensome for the undertaking concerned than the structural remedy. If the Commission has a legitimate interest in doing so, it may also find that an infringement has been committed in the past.

2. Those entitled to lodge a complaint for the purposes of paragraph 1 are natural or legal persons who can show a legitimate interest and Member States.

## Article 8

### Interim measures

1. In cases of urgency due to the risk of serious and irreparable damage to competition, the Commission, acting on its own initiative may by decision, on the basis of a prima facie finding of infringement, order interim measures.

2. A decision under paragraph 1 shall apply for a specified period of time and may be renewed in so far this is necessary and appropriate.

## Article 9

### Commitments

1. Where the Commission intends to adopt a decision requiring that an infringement be brought to an end and the undertakings concerned offer commitments to meet the concerns expressed to them by the Commission in its preliminary assessment, the Commission may by decision make those commitments binding on the undertakings. Such a decision may be adopted for a specified period and shall conclude that there are no longer grounds for action by the Commission.

2. The Commission may, upon request or on its own initiative, reopen the proceedings:

(a) where there has been a material change in any of the facts on which the decision was based;

(b) where the undertakings concerned act contrary to their commitments; or

(c) where the decision was based on incomplete, incorrect or misleading information provided by the parties.

## COMMISSION v. ALROSA COMPANY LTD
### Case C-441/07P, 2010 ECJ EUR-Lex LEXIS 686, [2010] ECR I-NYR

[The Commission had launched an investigation into the number one producer and supplier of diamonds, De Beers. De Beers had a supply agreement with Alrosa, a Russian company and the number two producer and supplier of diamonds. De Beers and Alrosa notified their agreement to the Commission under Regulation 17/62 (in 2002, before Regulation 1/2003 came into force). The Commission then opened two sets of proceedings under Regulation 1/2003. The first was based on EC 81/TFEU 101, investigating both De Beers and Alrosa. The second investigated a possible abuse of a dominant position by De Beers contrary to EC 82/TFEU 102. De Beers and Alrosa proposed joint commitments in 2004 to the Commission which entailed a reduction and eventual elimination of the sales of rough diamonds by Alrosa to De Beers. The Commission however, acting under article 9 of Regulation 1/2003, rejected the joint commitment and proceeded to accept a commitment from De Beers alone prohibiting *all* purchases of diamonds by it from Alrosa. The CFI/General Court found that that decision (2006/520) was disproportionate and annulled it. The Commission appealed.]

8. By the judgment under appeal, the General Court annulled the contested decision. Its reasoning may be summarised as follows.

9. In paragraph 126 of the judgment under appeal, the General Court held that 'the [contested decision was] vitiated by an error of assessment which, moreover, [was] manifest. It [was] clear from the circumstances of the case that other, less onerous, solutions than the permanent prohibition of transactions between De Beers and Alrosa were possible in order to achieve the aim pursued by the [contested decision], that their determination presented no particular difficulties of a technical nature and that the Commission could not relieve itself of the duty to consider such solutions'.

10. In paragraph 128 of the judgment, the General Court stated that, prima facie, the most appropriate solution would therefore have been to prohibit the parties from entering into any agreement allowing De Beers to reserve to itself the whole, or even a material part, of Alrosa's production exported outside the CIS, without it being necessary to prohibit all purchases by De Beers of diamonds produced by Alrosa.

11. In paragraph 129 of the judgment, the General Court found that the Commission had failed to explain in what way the joint commitments did not address the concerns expressed in its preliminary assessment. In paragraph 132 it concluded that those joint commitments, which the Commission admittedly was under no obligation to take into account, none the less represented a less onerous measure than the measure which it decided to make binding.

12. It found, in paragraph 156 of the judgment under appeal, that Alrosa was right to argue, first, that the prohibition on all trading relations between De Beers and itself for an indefinite period manifestly went beyond what was necessary in order to achieve the targeted objective and, second, that other solutions existed that were proportionate to that objective. It said that, in making use of the procedure allowing commitments offered by an undertaking concerned to be made binding, the Commission was not relieved of its duty to apply the principle of proportionality, which required in this case that there should be an appraisal in concreto of the viability of those intermediate solutions. It accordingly held, in paragraph 157 of the judgment, that Alrosa's plea alleging infringement of Article 9(1) of Regulation No 1/2003 and of the principle of proportionality was well founded and that the contested decision should be annulled on that ground alone.

*   *   *

[The appeal]

34. Under Article 9 of Regulation No 1/2003, where the Commission intends to adopt a decision requiring an infringement to be brought to an end, it may make the commitments offered by the undertakings concerned binding if they meet the competition concerns expressed in its preliminary assessment.

35. This is a new mechanism introduced by Regulation No 1/2003 which is intended to ensure that the competition rules laid down in the EC Treaty [TFEU] are applied effectively, by means of the adoption of decisions making commitments, proposed by the parties and considered appropriate by the Commission, binding in order to provide a more rapid solution to the competition problems identified by the Commission, instead of proceeding by making a formal finding of an infringement. More particularly, Article 9 of the regulation is based on considerations of procedural economy, and enables undertakings to participate fully in the procedure, by putting forward the solutions which appear to them to be the most appropriate and capable of addressing the Commission's concerns.

36. . . . [A]lthough Article 9, unlike Article 7 of Regulation No 1/2003, does not expressly refer to proportionality, the principle of proportionality, as a general principle of European Union law, is none the less a criterion for the lawfulness of any act of the institutions of the Union, including decisions taken by the Commission in its capacity of competition authority.

37. That being so, in the examination of acts of the Commission, whether in the context of Article 7 or of Article 9 of Regulation No 1/2003, the questions always arise, first, of the precise extent and limits of the obligations which flow from the observance of that principle and, second, of the limits of judicial review.

38. The specific characteristics of the mechanisms provided for in Articles 7 and 9 of Regulation No 1/2003 and the means of action available under each of those provisions are different, which means that the obligation on the Commission to ensure that the principle of proportionality is observed has a different extent and content, depending on whether it is considered in relation to the former or the latter article.

39. Article 7 of Regulation No 1/2003 expressly indicates the extent to which the principle of proportionality applies in situations covered by that article. In accordance with Article 7(1) of the regulation, the Commission may impose on the undertakings concerned any behavioural or structural remedies which are proportionate to the infringement committed and necessary to bring the infringement effectively to an end.

40. Article 9 of that regulation, by contrast, provides merely that in proceedings under that provision, as follows from recital 13 in the preamble to the regulation, the Commission is not required to make a finding of an infringement, its task being confined to examining, and possibly accepting, the commitments offered by the undertakings concerned in the light of the problems identified by it in its preliminary assessment and having regard to the aims pursued.

41. Application of the principle of proportionality by the Commission in the context of Article 9 of Regulation No 1/2003 is confined to verifying that the commitments

in question address the concerns it expressed to the undertakings concerned and that they have not offered less onerous commitments that also address those concerns adequately. When carrying out that assessment, the Commission must, however, take into consideration the interests of third parties.

42. Judicial review for its part relates solely to whether the Commission's assessment is manifestly incorrect.

43. In the judgment under appeal, the General Court proceeded from the proposition that the application of the principle of proportionality has the same effect in relation to decisions taken under Article 7 of Regulation No 1/2003 as in relation to those taken under Article 9 of that regulation.

44. . . . [T]he General Court held that it would be contrary to the scheme of Regulation No 1/2003 for a decision which would, under Article 7(1) of the regulation, have to be regarded as disproportionate to the infringement that had been established to be taken by having recourse to the procedure laid down under Article 9(1) in the form of a commitment that is made binding.

45. That conclusion is not correct.

46. Those two provisions of Regulation No 1/2003, as noted in paragraph 38 above, pursue different objectives, one of them aiming to put an end to the infringement that has been found to exist and the other aiming to address the Commission's concerns following its preliminary assessment.

47. There is therefore no reason why the measure which could possibly be imposed in the context of Article 7 of Regulation No 1/2003 should have to serve as a reference for the purpose of assessing the extent of the commitments accepted under Article 9 of the regulation, or why anything going beyond that measure should automatically be regarded as disproportionate. Even though decisions adopted under each of those provisions are in either case subject to the principle of proportionality, the application of that principle none the less differs according to which of those provisions is concerned.

48. Undertakings which offer commitments on the basis of Article 9 of Regulation No 1/2003 consciously accept that the concessions they make may go beyond what the Commission could itself impose on them in a decision adopted under Article 7 of the regulation after a thorough examination. On the other hand, the closure of the infringement proceedings brought against those undertakings allows them to avoid a finding of an infringement of competition law and a possible fine.

49. Moreover, the fact that the individual commitments offered by an undertaking have been made binding by the Commission does not mean that other undertakings are deprived of the possibility of protecting the rights they may have in connection with their relations with that undertaking.

50. It must therefore be concluded that the Commission is right to submit that in the judgment under appeal the General Court wrongly considered that the application of the principle of proportionality must be assessed, in the case of decisions taken under Article 9 of Regulation No 1/2003, by reference to the way in which it is assessed in connection with decisions taken under Article 7 of that regulation despite the different concepts underlying those two provisions.

## NOTES AND QUESTIONS

**1.** Until the successful appeal, the *Alrosa* case was one of only a few examples where a challenge based on proportionality had succeeded. The ECJ, however, rejected the CFI/General Court's analysis on that subject based on the particular wording of articles 7 and 9 of Regulation 1/2003. What was the ECJ's objection to the General Court's approach? Do you think it is reasonable for the Commission to endorse a commitment from the party under investigation (here, De Beers) that has serious repercussions for third parties (here, Alrosa)? What do you think the Court had in mind in paragraph 49?

**2.** For a comparative U.S. case regarding proportionality as the term is used in Article 7 of Regulation 1/2003, see *Jacob Siegel Co. v. FTC*, 327 U.S. 608 (1946), where the company was ordered to abandon an allegedly deceptive brand name by the FTC. The Court thought there might have been an appropriate, less harsh remedy, and remanded the case.

**3.** The Court proceeded to determine what scope of review was open to the Court to review the discretion exercised by the Commission in deciding that the joint commitment was insufficient and that the commitment to refrain from buying any diamonds from Alrosa was correct. This aspect of the case appears in Chapter 8.

## [H]  Settlement Procedure

### COMMISSION NOTICE ON THE CONDUCT OF SETTLEMENT PROCEDURES
[2008] OJ C 167/1

[This Notice reflects a bold initiative by the Commission to speed up and simplify the procedures described above where the parties are willing to admit to a violation of the competition rules. After an explanatory introduction, the Notice lays out the procedure involved.]

### 2. PROCEDURE

5. The Commission retains a broad margin of discretion to determine which cases may be suitable to explore the parties' interest to engage in settlement discussions, as well as to decide to engage in them or discontinue them or to definitely settle. In this regard, account may be taken of the probability of reaching a common understanding regarding the scope of the potential objections with the parties involved within a reasonable timeframe, in view of factors such as number of parties involved, foreseeable conflicting positions on the attribution of liability, extent of contestation of the facts. The prospect of achieving procedural efficiencies in view of the progress made overall in the settlement procedure, including the scale of burden involved in providing access to non-confidential versions of documents from the file, will be considered. Other concerns such as the possibility of setting a precedent might apply. The Commission may also decide to discontinue settlement discussions if the parties to the proceedings coordinate to distort or destroy any

evidence relevant to the establishment of the infringement or any part thereof or to the calculation of the applicable fine. Distortion or destruction of evidence relevant to the establishment of the infringement or any part thereof may also constitute an aggravating circumstance within the meaning of point 28 of the Commission Guidelines on the method of setting fines . . . and may be regarded as lack of cooperation within the meaning of points 12 and 27 of the Leniency Notice. The Commission may only engage in settlement discussions upon the written request of the parties concerned.

6. While parties to the proceedings do not have a right to settle, should the Commission consider that a case may, in principle, be suitable for settlement, it will explore the interest in settlement of all parties to the same proceedings.

7. The parties to the proceedings may not disclose to any third party in any jurisdiction the contents of the discussions or of the documents which they have had access to in view of settlement, unless they have a prior explicit authorization by the Commission. Any breach in this regard may lead the Commission to disregard the undertaking's request to follow the settlement procedure. Such disclosure may also constitute an aggravating circumstance, within the meaning of point 28 of the Guidelines on fines and may be regarded as lack of cooperation within the meaning of points 12 and 27 of the Leniency Notice.

### 2.1. Initiation of proceedings and exploratory steps regarding settlement

8. Where the Commission contemplates the adoption of a decision pursuant to Article 7 and/or Article 23 of Regulation (EC) No 1/2003, it is required in advance to identify and recognize as parties to the proceedings the legal persons on whom a penalty may be imposed for an infringement of Article 81[101] of the Treaty.

9. To this end, the initiation of proceedings pursuant to Article 11(6) of Regulation (EC) No 1/2003 in view of adopting such a decision can take place at any point in time, but no later than the date on which the Commission issues a statement of objections against the parties concerned. Article 2(1) of Regulation (EC) No 773/2004 further specifies that, should the Commission consider it suitable to explore the parties' interest in engaging in settlement discussions, it will initiate proceedings no later than the date on which it either issues a statement of objections or requests the parties to express in writing their interest to engage in settlement discussions, whichever is the earlier.

10. After the initiation of proceedings pursuant to Article 11(6) of Regulation (EC) No 1/2003, the Commission becomes the only competition authority competent to apply Article 81[101] of the Treaty to the case in point.

11. Should the Commission consider it suitable to explore the parties' interest to engage in settlement discussions, it will set a time-limit of no less than two weeks pursuant to Articles 10a(1) and 17(3) of Regulation (EC) No 773/2004 within which parties to the same proceedings should declare in writing whether they envisage engaging in settlement discussions in view of possibly introducing settlement submissions at a later stage. This written declaration does not imply an admission by the parties of having participated in an infringement or of being liable for it.

12. Whenever the Commission initiates proceedings against two or more parties within the same undertaking, the Commission will inform each of them of the other legal entities which it identifies within the same undertaking and which are also concerned by the proceedings. In such a case, should the concerned parties wish to engage in settlement discussions, they must appoint joint representatives duly empowered to act on their behalf by the end of the time-limit referred to in point 11. The appointment of joint representatives aims solely to facilitate the settlement discussions and it does not prejudge in any way the attribution of liability for the infringement amongst the different parties.

13. The Commission may disregard any application for immunity from fines or reduction of fines on the ground that it has been submitted after the expiry of the time-limit referred to in point 11.

## 2.2. Commencing the settlement procedure: settlement discussions

14. Should some of the parties to the proceedings request settlement discussions and comply with the requirements referred to in points 11 and 12, the Commission may decide to pursue the settlement procedure by means of bilateral contacts between the Commission Directorate-General for Competition and the settlement candidates.

15. The Commission retains discretion to determine the appropriateness with each undertaking. In line with Article 10a(2) of Regulation (EC) No 773/2004, this includes determining, in view of the progress made overall in the settlement procedure, the order and sequence of the bilateral settlement discussions as well as the timing of the disclosure of information, including the evidence in the Commission file used to establish the envisaged objections and the potential fine Information will be disclosed in a timely manner as settlement discussions progress.

16. Such an early disclosure in the context of settlement discussions pursuant to Article 10a(2) and Article 15(1a) of Regulation (EC) No 773/2004 will allow the parties to be informed of the essential elements taken into consideration so far, such as the facts alleged, the classification of those facts, the gravity and duration of the alleged cartel, the attribution of liability, an estimation of the range of likely fines, as well as the evidence used to establish the potential objections. This will enable the parties effectively to assert their views on the potential objections against them and will allow them to make an informed decision on whether or not to settle. Upon request by a party, the Commission services will also grant it access to non-confidential versions of any specified accessible document listed in the case file at that point in time, in so far as this is justified for the purpose of enabling the party to ascertain its position regarding a time period or any other aspect of the cartel.

17. When the progress made during the settlement discussions leads to a common understanding regarding the scope of the potential objections and the estimation of the range of likely fines to be imposed by the Commission, and the Commission takes the preliminary view that procedural efficiencies are likely to be achieved in view of the progress made overall, the Commission may grant a final time-limit of at least 15 working days for an undertaking to introduce a final settlement submission pursuant to Articles 10a(2) and 17(3) of Regulation (EC) No 773/2004.

The time-limit can be extended following a reasoned request. Before granting such time-limit, the parties will be entitled to have the information specified in point 16 disclosed to them upon request.

18. The parties may call upon the Hearing Officer at any time during the settlement procedure in relation to issues that might arise relating to due process. The Hearing Officer's duty is to ensure that the effective exercise of the rights of defence is respected.

19. Should the parties concerned fail to introduce a settlement submission, the procedure leading to the final decision in their regard will follow the general provisions, in particular Articles 10(2), 12(1) and 15(1) of Regulation (EC) No 773/2004, instead of those regulating the settlement procedure.

## 2.3. Settlement submissions

20. Parties opting for a settlement procedure must introduce a formal request to settle in the form of a settlement submission. The settlement submission provided for in Article 10a(2) of Regulation (EC) No 773/2004 should contain:

(a) an acknowledgement in clear and unequivocal terms of the parties' liability for the infringement summarily described as regards its object, its possible implementation, the main facts, their legal qualification, including the party's role and the duration of their participation in the infringement in accordance with the results of the settlement discussions;

(b) an indication of the maximum amount of the fine the parties foresee to be imposed by the Commission and which the parties would accept in the framework of a settlement procedure;

(c) the parties' confirmation that, they have been sufficiently informed of the objections the Commission envisages raising against them and that they have been given sufficient opportunity to make their views known to the Commission;

(d) the parties' confirmation that, in view of the above, they do not envisage requesting access to the file or requesting to be heard again in an oral hearing, unless the Commission does not reflect their settlement submissions in the statement of objections and the decision;

(e) the parties' agreement to receive the statement of objections and the final decision pursuant to Articles 7 and 23 of Regulation (EC) No 1/2003 in an agreed official language of the European Community.

21. The acknowledgments and confirmations provided by the parties in view of settlement constitute the expression of their commitment to cooperate in the expeditious handling of the case following the settlement procedure. However, those acknowledgments and confirmations are conditional upon the Commission meeting their settlement request, including the anticipated maximum amount of the fine.

22. Settlement requests cannot be revoked unilaterally by the parties which have provided them unless the Commission does not meet the settlement requests by reflecting the settlement submissions first in a statement of objections and ultimately, in a final decision (see in this regard points 27 and 29). The statement of

objections would be deemed to have endorsed the settlement submissions if it reflects their contents on the issues mentioned in point 20(a). Additionally, for a final decision to be deemed to have reflected the settlement submissions, it should also impose a fine which does not exceed the maximum amount indicated therein.

## 2.4. Statement of objections and reply

23. Pursuant to Article 10(1) of Regulation (EC) No 773/2004, the notification of a written statement of objections to each of the parties against whom objections are raised is a mandatory preparatory step before adopting any final decision. Therefore, the Commission will issue a statement of objections also in a settlement procedure.

24. For the parties' rights of defence to be exercised effectively, the Commission should hear their views on the objections against them and supporting evidence before adopting a final decision and take them into account by amending its preliminary analysis, where appropriate. The Commission must be able not only to accept or reject the parties' relevant arguments expressed during the administrative procedure, but also to make its own analysis of the matters put forward by them in order to either abandon such objections because they have been shown to be unfounded or to supplement and reassess its arguments both in fact and in law, in support of the objections which it maintains.

25. By introducing a formal settlement request in the form of a settlement submission prior to the notification of the statement of objections, the parties concerned enable the Commission to effectively take their views into account already when drafting the statement of objections, rather than only before the consultation of the Advisory Committee on Restrictive Practices and Dominant Positions (hereinafter the 'Advisory Committee') or before the adoption of the final decision.

26. Should the statement of objections reflect the parties'settlement submissions, the parties concerned should within a time-limit of at least two weeks set by the Commission in accordance with Articles 10a(3) and 17(3) of Regulation (EC) No 773/2004, reply to it by simply confirming (in unequivocal terms) that the statement of objections corresponds to the contents of their settlement submissions and that they therefore remain committed to follow the settlement procedure. In the absence of such a reply, the Commission will take note of the party's breach of its commitment and may also disregard the party's request to follow the settlement procedure.

27. The Commission retains the right to adopt a statement of objections which does not reflect the parties'settlement submission. If so, the general provisions in Articles 10(2), 12(1) and 15(1) of Regulation (EC) No 773/2004 will apply. The acknowledgements provided by the parties in the settlement submission would be deemed to be withdrawn and could not be used in evidence against any of the parties to the proceedings. Hence, the parties concerned would no longer be bound by their settlement submissions and would be granted a time-limit allowing them, upon request, to present their defence anew, including the possibility to access the file and to request an oral hearing.

## 2.5. Commission decision and settlement reward

28. Upon the parties' replies to the statement of objections confirming their commitment to settle, Regulation (EC) No 773/2004 allows the Commission to proceed, without any other procedural step, to the adoption of the subsequent final decision . . .

29. The Commission retains the right to adopt a final position which departs from its preliminary position expressed in a statement of objections endorsing the parties'settlement submissions, either in view of the opinion provided by the Advisory Committee or for other appropriate considerations in view of the ultimate decisional autonomy of the Commission to this effect. However, should the Commission opt to follow that course, it will inform the parties and notify to them a new statement of objections in order to allow for the exercise of their rights of defence in accordance with the applicable general rules of procedure. It follows that the parties would then be entitled to have access to the file, to request an oral hearing and to reply to the statement of objections. The acknowledgments provided by the parties in the settlement submissions would be deemed to have been withdrawn and could not be used in evidence against any of the parties to the proceedings.

30. The final amount of the fine in a particular case is determined in the decision finding an infringement pursuant to Article 7 and imposing a fine pursuant to Article 23 of Regulation (EC) No 1/2003.

31. In line with the Commission's practice, the fact that an undertaking cooperated with the Commission under this Notice during the administrative procedure will be indicated in the final decision, so as to explain the reason for the level of the fine.

32. Should the Commission decide to reward a party for settlement in the framework of this Notice, it will reduce by 10% the amount of the fine to be imposed after the 10% cap has been applied having regard to the Guidelines on the method of setting fines imposed pursuant to Article 23(2)(a) of Regulation (EC) No 1/2003 (1). Any specific increase for deterrence (2) used in their regard will not exceed a multiplication by two.

33. When settled cases involve also leniency applicants, the reduction of the fine granted to them for settlement will be added to their leniency reward.

## 3. GENERAL CONSIDERATIONS

34. This Notice applies to any case pending before the Commission at the time of or after its publication in the Official Journal of the European Union.

35. Access to settlement submissions is only granted to those addressees of a statement of objections who have not requested settlement, provided that they commit — together with the legal counsels getting access on their behalf — not to make any copy by mechanical or electronic means of any information in the settlement submissions to which access is being granted and to ensure that the information to be obtained from the settlement submission will solely be used for the purposes of judicial or administrative proceedings for the application of the Community competition rules at issue in the related proceedings. Other parties

such as complainants will not be granted access to settlement submissions.

36. The use of such information for a different purpose during the proceeding may be regarded as lack of cooperation within the meaning of points 12 and 27 of the Leniency Notice. Moreover, if any such use is made after the Commission has already adopted a prohibition decision in the proceedings, the Commission may, in any legal proceedings before the Community Courts, ask the Court to increase the fine in respect of the responsible undertaking. Should the information be used for a different purpose, at any point in time, with the involvement of an outside counsel, the Commission may report the incident to the bar of that counsel, with a view to disciplinary action.

37. Settlement submissions made under this Notice will only be transmitted to the competition authorities of the Member States pursuant to Article 12 of Regulation (EC) No 1/2003, provided that the conditions set out in the Network Notice (3) are met and provided that the level of protection against disclosure awarded by the receiving competition authority is equivalent to the one conferred by the Commission.

38. Upon the applicant's request, the Commission may accept that settlement submissions be provided orally. Oral settlement submissions will be recorded and transcribed at the Commission's premises. In accordance with Article 19 of Regulation (EC) No 1/2003 and Articles 3(3) and 17(3) of Regulation (EC) No 773/2004 undertakings making oral settlement submissions will be granted the opportunity to check the technical accuracy of the recording, which will be available at the Commission's premises and to correct the substance of their oral settlement submissions and the accuracy of the transcript without delay.

39. The Commission will not transmit settlement submissions to national courts without the consent of the relevant applicants, in line with the provisions in the Commission Notice on the co-operation between the Commission and the courts of the EU Member States in the application of Articles 81[101] and 82[102] EC.

40. The Commission considers that normally public disclosure of documents and written or recorded statements (including settlement submissions) received in the context of this Notice would undermine certain public or private interests, for example the protection of the purpose of inspections and investigations, within the meaning of Article 4 of Regulation (EC) No 1049/2001 of the European Parliament and of the Council of 30 May 2001 regarding public access to European Parliament, Council and Commission documents (1), even after the decision has been taken.

41. Final decisions taken by the Commission under Regulation (EC) No 1/2003 are subject to judicial review in accordance with Article 230 of the Treaty. Moreover, as provided in Article 229 of the Treaty and Article 31 of Regulation (EC) No 1/2003, the Court of Justice has unlimited jurisdiction to review decisions on fines adopted pursuant to Article 23 of Regulation (EC) No 1/2003.

## NOTES AND QUESTIONS

**1.** The settlement procedure here allows for an expedited process where the Commission decides it would be appropriate and the parties under investigation admit to wrongdoing. Does this sound like plea bargaining or is it something much less? Why, do you think, does the procedure not allow a more general ability to settle any case, even where the party initially denies wrongdoing?

**2.** Given its very limited scope, is it likely that settlements will happen with any frequency? Surely a mere 10 percent off (whatever the fine turns out to be) is scarcely enough incentive?

## [I]   International Cooperation Among Antitrust Enforcement Bodies

### FRANCE v. COMMISSION
#### (COMPETITION LAW ENFORCEMENT COOPERATION)
#### Case 327/91, 1994 ECJ CELEX LEXIS 26, [1994] ECR I-3641

[France sought a declaration that the Agreement signed on 23 September 1991 by the Commission and the Government of the United States of America regarding the application of their competition laws (hereinafter 'the Agreement') was void. The Agreement had been signed in Washington by the Attorney General and by the President of the Federal Trade Commission, on behalf of the Government of the United States, of the one part, and by the Vice-President of the Commission on behalf of the Commission.]

5 The purpose of the Agreement is to promote cooperation and coordination and lessen the possibility or impact of differences between the parties in the application of their competition laws.

6 To that end, it provides for notification by each party to the other of measures taken by it in the enforcement of its competition laws which may affect important interests of the other party . . . the exchange of information concerning various matters of mutual interest relating to the application of competition laws . . . coordination of enforcement activities . . . and reciprocal consultation procedures . . .

7 In addition, Article V. of the Agreement provides for cooperation regarding anti-competitive activities in the territory of one party that adversely affect important interests of the other ('positive comity'). In such circumstances, the party whose important interests are affected may notify the other party and request that that party's competition authorities take enforcement measures against the anti-competitive activities carried out on its territory. With a view to avoiding conflicts, Article VI provides that each party is to seek to take into account the important interests of the other party when deciding on enforcement measures ('traditional comity').

Confidentiality of information is ensured by Article VIII, which allows the parties to refrain from providing information to each other if its disclosure is prohibited by law or is incompatible with important interests of the party possessing such information.

8 Article IX provides that 'nothing in this Agreement shall be interpreted in a manner inconsistent with the existing laws, or as requiring any change in the laws, of the United States of America or the European Communities or of their respective States or Member States'.

9 Article X lays down the form to be taken by communications and notifications, which may be effected by oral, telephonic, written or facsimile communication.

10 Lastly, under Article XI(1) the Agreement is to enter into force upon signature and, in accordance with Article XI(2), it is to remain in force until 60 days after the date on which either party notifies the other party in writing that it wishes to terminate the Agreement. Under paragraph (3), the operation of the Agreement is to be reviewed not more than 24 months from the date of its entry into force.

11 The Agreement has not been published in the Official Journal of the European Communities.

*    *    *

18 The French Government puts forward three pleas in support of its application. The first plea alleges that the Commission was not competent to conclude such an agreement, the second that there is no statement of reasons for the Agreement and that the principle of legal certainty has been contravened, and the third that Community competition law has been infringed . . .

19 Article 228 [218](1) of the EEC Treaty, in the version in force at the time of the events material to this case, provided as follows:

'Where this Treaty provides for the conclusion of agreements between the Community and one or more States or an international organization, such agreements shall be negotiated by the Commission. Subject to the powers vested in the Commission in this field, such agreements shall be concluded by the Council, after consulting the European Parliament where required by this Treaty.'

20 The French Republic argues that that provision expressly reserves to the Council the power to conclude international agreements. Consequently, by concluding the Agreement, the Commission, which is empowered merely to conduct negotiations in that field, exceeded its powers.

21 The Commission contends that the Agreement in fact constitutes an administrative agreement which it is competent to conclude. In view of the nature of the obligations which it lays down, failure to perform the Agreement would result, not in an international claim capable of giving rise to liability on the part of the Community, but merely in termination of the Agreement.

22 The Commission further points out that, in any event, Article IX of the Agreement, cited above, precludes the parties from interpreting its provisions in a manner inconsistent with their own laws (and, moreover, as regards the European Communities, with the laws of the Member States) or as requiring any change in their own laws.

23 As the Court has already found, the Agreement produces legal effects.

24 Next, it is the Community alone, having legal personality pursuant to Article 210 [TEU 47] of the Treaty, which has the capacity to bind itself by concluding agreements with a non-member country or an international organization.

25 There is no doubt, therefore, that the Agreement is binding on the European Communities. It falls squarely within the definition of an international agreement concluded between an international organization and a State, within the meaning of Article 2(1)(a)(i) of the Vienna Convention of 21 March 1986 on the Law of Treaties between States and International Organizations or between International Organizations. In the event of non-performance of the Agreement by the Commission, therefore, the Community could incur liability at international level.

26 That being so, the question is whether the Commission was competent under Community law to conclude such an agreement.

*    *    *

[The Court then considered a technical argument by the Commission based on the French language terminology in the Treaty which it rejected.]

40 The Commission's final argument against the French Government's plea is that its power to conclude international agreements is all the more clear-cut in the present case, since the EEC Treaty has conferred on it specific powers in the field of competition.

*    *    *

That argument cannot be accepted either. Even though the Commission has the power, internally, to take individual decisions applying the rules of competition, a field covered by the Agreement, that internal power is not such as to alter the allocation of powers between the Community institutions with regard to the conclusion of international agreements, which is determined by Article 228 [218] of the Treaty.

## NOTES AND QUESTIONS

1.    The backdrop to this case is a history of friction between national antitrust authorities over their respective competencies and the so-called extraterritorial application of (especially U.S.) antitrust law. A mutual desire to avoid such clashes and to provide a framework for cooperation among national antitrust authorities resulted in new agreements between the United States and several other countries and the (then) European Community calling for, *inter alia*, notification prior to the commencement of litigation. See A. D. Ham, *International Cooperation in the Antitrust Field and in Particular the Agreement between the United States of America and the Commission of the European Communities*, (1993) 30 CML REV. 571.

2.    Do you agree with the Court's decision here? Is the institutional balance within the Union more important than the effect such a decision might have on the credibility of the Union *vis-à-vis* third countries? Following this ruling, the

Commission approached the Council for authorization to negotiate a letter agreement, and the Council gave this in December 1994.

## § 7.03  SUPERVISING THE IMPLEMENTATION OF UNION LAW BY THE MEMBER STATES

### [A]  The Scope of the Duty

### COMMISSION v. FRANCE
#### (FRENCH SEAMEN)
Case 167/73, [1974] ECR 359

[The Commission brought proceedings under EC 226/TFEU 258 to establish that France was infringing the EC Treaty due to the maintenance in place of Article 3(2) of Ministerial Order of 21 November 1960 which provided that employment on the bridge and in the engine and wireless rooms on board merchant ships of French fishing vessels or pleasure cruisers was reserved to persons of French nationality, and employment generally was so limited in the ratio of three to one.]

4 In so far as it applies to nationals of other Member States, Article 3 (2), according to the Commission, is incompatible with Article 48 [45] of the Treaty, under which freedom of movement for workers entails the abolition of any discrimination based on nationality between workers of the Member States as regards employment, remuneration and other conditions of work and employment.

5 The continuance of the provision in question is likewise said to be incompatible with Regulation No 1612/68 and, in particular, with Article 4 thereof under which provisions laid down by law, regulation or administrative action of Member States which restrict by number or percentage the employment of foreign nationals in any undertaking, branch of activity or region, or at a national level, shall not apply to nationals of the other Member States.

6 The Government of the French Republic contends that the Commission has not established a legal interest because, in spite of the continuance of the provision in question, there is no discrimination in its application between French nationals and those of other Member States, taking into account that the directions given verbally to the naval authorities requires that the 'nationals of the Community shall be treated as French nationals', so that these nationals are not 'obliged to comply with any formalities nor to suffer any delay in obtaining the right to employment by way of exemption'.

\*      \*      \*

34 In challenging the legal interest of the Commission the Government of the French Republic has also sought to deny that a default exists in the case in question solely as a result of the maintenance in the national legal system of the law in dispute without taking into consideration the application which is made of it in practice.

35 A correct assessment of the legal position should have led the French authorities

to find that since the provisions of Article 48 [45] and of Regulation No 1612/68 are directly applicable in the legal systems of every Member State and Community law has priority over national law, these provisions give rise, on the part of those concerned, to rights which the national authorities must respect and safeguard and as a result of which all contrary provisions of internal law are rendered inapplicable to them.

*    *    *

40 It appears both from the argument before the Court and from the position adopted during the parliamentary proceedings that the present state of affairs is that freedom of movement for workers in the sector in question continues to be considered by the French authorities not as a matter of right but as dependent on their unilateral will.

41 It follows that although the objective legal position is clear, namely, that Article 48 [45] and Regulation No 1612/68 are directly applicable in the territory of the French Republic, nevertheless the maintenance in these circumstances of the wording of the Code du Travail Maritime gives rise to an ambiguous state of affairs by maintaining, as regards those subject to the law who are concerned, a state of uncertainty as to the possibilities available to them of relying on Community law.

42 This uncertainty can only be reinforced by the internal and verbal character of the purely administrative directions to waive the application of the national law.

43 The free movement of persons, and in particular workers, constitutes, as appears both from Article 3 (c) of the Treaty and from the place of Articles 48 [45] to 51 [48] in part two of the Treaty, one of the foundations of the Community.

*    *    *

46 It thus follows from the general character of the prohibition on discrimination in Article 48 [45] and the objective pursued by the abolition of discrimination that discrimination is prohibited even if it constitutes only an obstacle of secondary importance as regards the equality of access to employment and other conditions of work and employment.

47 The uncertainty created by the maintenance unamended of the wording of Article 3 of the Code du Travail Maritime constitutes such an obstacle.

48 It follows that in maintaining unamended, in these circumstances, the provisions of Article 3 (2) of the Code du Travail Maritime as regards the nationals of other Member States, the French Republic has failed to fulfil its obligations under Article 48 of the Treaty and Article 4 of Regulation No 1612/68 of the Council of 15 October 1968.

## NOTES AND QUESTIONS

1.   In the above case, the French Government was found to be in default of EU law although it was established French practice to treat nationals of all other Member States as if they were French nationals. Moreover, the French Government recognized that EC 39/TFEU 45 and Regulation 1612/68 were directly

366 EXECUTIVE POWERS CH. 7

applicable and that it was therefore under an obligation to set aside and not apply any provisions of national law contrary to them. Nonetheless, the ECJ ruled against France. On what basis? See also *Commission v. Italy (Repayment of taxes)*, Case 104/86, 1988 ECJ CELEX LEXIS 132, [1988] ECR 1799.

2.   Similar situations have arisen in relation to the implementation of directives, where a Member State has failed to adopt precise legislation but has relied instead on informal ministerial orders that do not have the force of law. Could the Member State's action be challenged on the basis of the ECJ's decision in *French Seamen*? Consider in particular the peculiar nature of direct effect (invocability) as it applies to directives.

3.   Violations of Treaty rules are usually the result of failure by the legislatures of the Member States to introduce the correct legislation in implementation of directives. However, there is no reason why EC 226/TFEU 258 actions should not be brought also where at least the immediate cause of the failure is the judicial branch of the government. The *Defrenne* case in Chapter 4 and the *Köbler* case in Chapter 9 might be considered examples of this feature.

4.   The question has been posed as to whether EC10/TEU 4 could be construed as imposing a general obligation on Member States to impose criminal penalties for breach of EU law by individuals. There are certainly cases where directives or regulations have required such imposition as for example for breach of accounting requirements in the context of company law harmonization (see the *Berlusconi* case in Chapter 5), or laws relating to fish conservation measures (see for example the case against France set out in Chapter 7, where the failure adequately to enforce EU rules led to a penalty imposed on France), but it does not appear that the ECJ has been willing so far to refer solely to EC10/TEU 4 as creating such an obligation. See *Criminal proceedings against Paul Vandevenne, Marc Wilms, Jozef Mesotten and Wilms Transport NV*, Case C-7/90, 1991 ECJ CELEX LEXIS 370, [1991] ECR I-2911:

> 11 [W]hen a Community regulation does not provide any specific penalty in case of breach but refers on this matter to national provisions, the Member States retain a discretion as to the choice of penalties. However, under Article 5 [TEU 4] of the EEC Treaty, which requires the Member States to take all measures necessary to guarantee the application and effectiveness of Community law, they must ensure that infringements of a Community regulation are penalized under conditions, both procedural and substantive, which are analogous to those applicable to infringements of national law of a similar nature and importance and which, in any event, make the penalty effective, proportionate and dissuasive.

> 12 It follows that neither Article 5 [TEU 4] of the Treaty nor Article 17(1) of Regulation No 3820/85 requires a Member State to introduce into its national law a specific system of criminal liability, such as the criminal liability of legal persons, in order to ensure compliance with the obligations imposed by Article 15 of the regulation.

## [B]   The Commission's Discretion to Take Action Under EC 226/TFEU 258

### STAR FRUIT COMPANY SA v. COMMISSION
Case 247/87, 1989 ECJ CELEX LEXIS 140, [1989] ECR 291

[Star Fruit Company, which specialized in the importation and exportation of fresh bananas, sought a declaration that the Commission had failed to commence proceedings against the French Republic under EC 226/TFEU 258.]

2 The applicant considers that the system for supplying the banana market in France is incompatible with Article 30 [34] et seq. EEC and with Article 2 of the Lome Convention of 28 February 1975 . . . It therefore requested the Commission, by letter of 17 April 1987, to commence proceedings under Article 169 [258] EEC against the French Republic in order to determine that the system in question is incompatible with the aforementioned provisions, to call upon that member-State to abolish import quotas on bananas originating in non-member States which are in free circulation in the other Member States of the Community and to pay it compensation for the damage which it has allegedly suffered as a result of the impossibility of fulfilling the orders of its French customers and the loss of goods resulting from the import bans applied by the member-State in question.

*   *   *

9 It appears that the applicant has not even identified the act adopted by the Commission against which the action is directed. Consequently, the application is inadmissible in so far as it is based on Article 173 [263] (2) EEC.

10 In so far as it is based on Article 175 [265](3) of the Treaty, the purpose of the application is to obtain a declaration that in not commencing against the French Republic proceedings to establish its breach of obligations the Commission infringed the Treaty by failing to take a decision.

11 However, it is clear from the scheme of Article 169 [258] of the Treaty that the Commission is not bound to commence the proceedings provided for in that provision but in this regard has a discretion which excludes the right for individuals to require that institution to adopt a specific position.

12 It is only if it considers that the member-State in question has failed to fulfil one of its obligations that the Commission delivers a reasoned opinion. Furthermore, in the event that the State does not comply with the opinion within the period allowed, the institution has in any event the right, but not the duty, to apply to the Court of Justice for a declaration that the alleged breach of obligations has occurred.

13 It must also be observed that in requesting the Commission to commence proceedings pursuant to Article 169 [258] the applicant is in fact seeking the adoption of acts which are not of direct and individual concern to it within the meaning of Article 173 [263] (2) and which it could not therefore challenge by means of an action for annulment in any event.

14 Consequently, the applicant cannot be entitled to raise the objection that the

Commission failed to commence proceedings against the French Republic pursuant to Article 169 [258] of the Treaty.

15 It follows that the application is inadmissible in its entirety.

## NOTES AND QUESTIONS

1.  The *Star Fruit* case emphasizes a very significant point, namely that the Commission cannot be compelled by a private party to take action under EC 226/TFEU 258 and that it has complete discretion in that regard. On what legal basis is the private action precluded? Suppose a Member State or another Institution complained of inaction?

2.  In continental Member States, public prosecutors may be under a duty to bring prosecutions where they have reasonable grounds to believe that a crime has been committed by a particular individual. This contrasts with the Anglo-American tradition where public prosecutors generally have wide discretionary powers. Although an individual litigant may not have the right to force action by the Commission, does this necessarily imply that the Commission enjoys an absolute discretion?

See also *Asociacion Profesional de Empresorias de Pesca Comunitarios v. European Community*, Case 207/86, 1988 ECJ CELEX LEXIS 158, [1988] ECR 21. A duty to bring enforcement actions would impose an intolerable burden on the Commission, particularly as directives involve more and more widespread and detailed application. A good example would be the public procurement directives concerning Member State bidding procedures for government contracts, where *de minimis* breaches of the rules by Member States are commonplace.

3.  Having failed in its action before the European Court of Justice, what, if any, alternative remedies might Star Fruit have had?

## COMMISSION v. ITALY
### (MINIMUM PRICES)
### Case 7/61, [1961] ECR 317
### [No paragraph numbering appears in the original]

[The Commission sought a judgment that Italy had failed to comply with EU law but in the meantime appropriate legislation had been introduced.]

The correspondence between the parties . . . shows that the Italian Government finally complied with the Commission's point of view and, as from 1 July 1961, instituted a scheme of minimum prices for some of the products concerned, whilst re-establishing complete freedom of importation for the others.

It is incumbent on the Court to examine whether the conclusions in the application no longer have any purpose, so that there is no point in proceeding to judgment.

It follows from the terms of Article 171 [260] of the Treaty that the purpose of the action is to obtain the judgment of the Court, to the effect that a Member State has failed to fulfil an obligation under the Treaty.

It is for the Court to say whether the failure has occurred, without having to examine whether, subsequent to the bringing of the action, the State in question took the measures necessary to bring the infringement to an end.

It is true that the second paragraph of Article 169 [258] gives the Commission the right to bring the matter before the Court only if the State concerned does not comply with the Commission's opinion within the period laid down by the Commission, the period being such as to allow the State in question to regularize its position in accordance with the provisions of the Treaty.

However, if the Member State does not comply with the opinion within the prescribed period, there is no question that the Commission has the right to obtain the Court's judgment on that Member State's failure to fulfil the obligations flowing from the Treaty.

In the present case, although it recognizes that the Italian Government finally respected its obligations, albeit after the expiry of the period referred to above, the Commission retains an interest in obtaining a decision on the issue whether the failure occurred.

The action cannot be declared lacking in purpose.

## NOTES AND QUESTIONS

1.   Why would the Commission have an interest in bringing proceedings where the failure complained of has already been terminated? Note that this case arose during the first years of the [then] Community's existence.

2.   The Commission also has extensive powers, indeed obligations, of "surveillance" over the activities of the Member States within the scope of the EC Treaty, including economic and monetary affairs.

### [C]   Do the Member States Have "Rights of the Defense"?

### COMMISSION v. BELGIUM
(MINERVAL)
Case 293/85, 1988 ECJ CELEX LEXIS 35, [1988] ECR 305

[The Commission alleged that Belgium had: "(a) failed, in section 16(1) of the Act of 21 June 1985 on education . . . to exempt nationals of other Member States who had come to Belgium for the sole purpose of studying in (public) Belgian universities from the supplementary enrolment fee (known as the 'minerval'); (b) authorized the rectors of universities, in section 16(2) of that Act, to refuse to enrol such students; (c) made it impossible in practice, in section 59(2) of that Act, for nationals of other Member States who had come to Belgium for the sole purpose of following a non-university course of higher education, whether technical, professional or specialized secondary training, to benefit from the exemption from the 'minerval' owing to the fact that such exemption was linked to the grant of the right of residence, and made grant of exemption from that 'minerval' to students from other Member States subject to the additional requirement of proof that they had adequate means of support, as followed from section 59(2) of that Act; and (d) restricted the possibility of obtaining reimbursement of 'minervals' wrongly paid under EU law solely to EU nationals who had brought legal proceedings before 13 February 1985, the date on which the judgment in *Gravier v. City of Liège*, Case 293/83, [1985] ECR 593 was delivered (see further Chapter 17).

10 The Kingdom of Belgium has raised an objection of inadmissibility against the Commission's application complaining that in the pre-litigation procedure preceding the application to the Court the Commission did not comply with the basic procedural safeguards laid down in Article 169 [258] EEC. It considers that the period of eight clear days for replying to the letter of formal notice and the period of 15 days to comply with the reasoned opinion were too short and were not permissible in view of the complexity of the matter and the scope of the amendments that had to be made to the relevant rules in order to bring them into line with Community law.

11 The Commission agrees that the periods allowed were short but it points out that they were not absolute time-limits and that replies supplied after the expiry of those periods would have been taken into account. Short periods were fixed because of the impending start of the 1985 academic year and because the Kingdom of Belgium had been aware of the Commission's position since 25 June 1985 at the latest. Immediately before the adoption of the Belgian Act in question the Commission was concerned by the conditions which were going to govern the access of Community students to Belgian vocational training establishments at the start of the academic year and which were contrary to Community law. From the outset, the Commission wanted the pre-litigation procedure to be conducted in such a way that the matter could be brought before the Court in time for it to order interim measures safeguarding the rights of students before the registration procedures were closed.

12 In the alternative, the Commission points out that the Kingdom of Belgium in fact had more than a month to reply to the letter of formal notice before the reasoned opinion was sent. Furthermore, over one month elapsed before the application and request for interim measures were lodged with the Court.

13 It should be pointed out first that the purpose of the prelitigation procedure is to give the member-State concerned an opportunity, on the one hand, to comply with its obligations under Community law and, on the other, to avail itself of its right to defend itself against the complaints made by the Commission.

14 In view of that dual purpose the Commission must allow member-States a reasonable period to reply to the letter of formal notice and to comply with a reasoned opinion, or, whether appropriate, to prepare their defence. In order to determine whether the period allowed is reasonable, account must be taken of all the circumstances of the case. Thus very short periods may be justified in particular circumstances, especially where there is an urgent need to remedy a breach or where the member-State concerned is fully aware of the Commission's views long before the procedure starts.

## NOTES AND QUESTIONS

The issue raised in this case might be regarded as a form of procedural due process and suggests the further question: should a Member State be entitled to all the procedural protections afforded individuals (e.g., a right to a fair hearing, confidentiality of business secrets, etc.)? If the rules being developed by the Court in that regard derive from the constitutional protections for individuals *against* the state, and from the European Convention on Human Rights, how could they then also apply in favor of states? Or was the Court really applying a different set of considerations?

## [D]   Remedies

### COMMISSION v. FRANCE
#### (FISHERIES INSPECTIONS)
#### Case C-304/02, 2005 ECJ CELEX LEXIS 322, [2005] ECR I-6263

[*Following is an abbreviated version of the Court's description of the events leading to this action.* Starting in 1982 the Council had established certain control measures for fishing activities by vessels of the Member States (these were the measures that were still pending at the time of the *Rogers v. Dartheney* decision in chapter 11). The measures included an EU system for the technical monitoring of conservation and resource management measures, structural measures, measures concerning the common organization of the market, and certain provisions relating to the effectiveness of sanctions to be applied in cases where the abovementioned measures were not observed. Each Member State was required to adopt, in accordance with EU rules, appropriate measures to ensure the effectiveness of the system and to place sufficient means at the disposal of its competent authorities to enable them to perform their tasks of inspection and control. Thus, Article 2(1) of Regulation No 2847/93 stated:

> In order to ensure compliance with all the rules in force concerning conservation and control measures, each Member State shall, within its territory and within maritime waters subject to its sovereignty or jurisdiction, monitor fishing activity and related activities. It shall inspect fishing vessels and investigate all activities thus enabling verification of the implementation of this Regulation, including the activities of landing, selling, transporting and storing fish and recording landings and sales.

Article 31(1) and (2) of Regulation No 2847/93 provided:

> 1. Member States shall ensure that the appropriate measures be taken, including of [sic] administrative action or criminal proceedings in conformity with their national law, against the natural or legal persons responsible where common fisheries policy have [sic] not been respected, in particular following a monitoring or inspection carried out pursuant to this Regulation.

> 2. The proceedings initiated pursuant to paragraph 1 shall be capable, in accordance with the relevant provisions of national law, of effectively

depriving those responsible of the economic benefit of the infringements or of producing results proportionate to the seriousness of such infringements, effectively discouraging further offences of the same kind.

The technical measures laid down by those regulations concerned, inter alia, the minimum mesh size for nets, the prohibition on attaching to nets certain devices by means of which the mesh is obstructed or diminished, and the prohibition on offering for sale fish of less than the minimum size (undersized fish') except for catches representing only a limited percentage of the overall catch (by-catches').

In case C-64/88 *Commission v. France*, the Court found France had failed to maintain adequate controls in relation to the minimum mesh size for nets the attachment to nets of devices prohibited by the Community rules (paragraphs 16 and 17 of the judgment); It had also failed to fulfil control obligations in relation to by-catches and compliance with the technical measures of conservation prohibiting the sale of undersized fish; and had failed to take action in respect of infringements.

The Commission in late 1991 requested the French authorities to inform it of the measures taken to comply with the judgment in Case C-64/88 *Commission v. France*. In January 1992 the French authorities replied that they intended to do their utmost to comply with the Community provisions. In the course of a number of visits to French ports the Commission inspectors found that the situation had improved, but noted that the French authorities' controls were inadequate in several respects including failure to comply with the Community rules in the measuring of the minimum mesh size of nets; inadequate controls, enabling undersized fish to be offered for sale; and laxness on the part of the French authorities in taking action in respect of infringements. The Commission warned the French authorities of the possibility of fines and gave France two months to take all the measures necessary in order to comply with the earlier judgment.

During this period, inspection visits were made to French ports. On the basis of reports drawn up after [various ports], the Commission staff reached the conclusion that two problems remained, namely inadequate controls enabling undersized fish to be offered for sale and the laxness on the part of the French authorities in taking action in respect of infringements. The Commission thus concluded that the earlier judgment had not been complied with as regards the two matters mentioned above. The Commission indicated that, in this context, it regarded as particularly serious the fact that public documents relating to sales by auction officially use the code 00 in clear breach of Council Regulation (EC) No 2406/96 of 26 November 1996 laying down common marketing standards for certain fishery products' (OJ 1996 L 334, p. 1). In their response of 1 August 2000, the French authorities essentially contended that since the last inspection report national fisheries control had undergone significant change. An internal reorganization had taken place, with the establishment of a fisheries control unit', which subsequently became a fisheries control task force', and the means of control had been strengthened, including the provision of patrol boats and of a system for the on-screen surveillance of vessels' positions and the circulation of instructions for the use of control staff. Yet, in an inspection visit from 18 to 28 June 2001 to the communes Guilvinec, Lesconil, Saint-Guenole and Loctudy, the Commission's inspectors recorded poor controls, the presence of undersized fish and the offering for sale of those fish under the code 00'.

The French authorities then sent to the Commission a copy of an instruction addressed to the regional and departmental maritime directorates, enjoining them to put an end to use of the code 00' by 31 December 2001 and to apply from that date the statutory penalties to economic operators not complying with the instruction. The French authorities referred to an increase since 1998 in the number of proceedings for infringement of the rules on minimum sizes and to the deterrent effect of the penalties imposed. They also informed the Commission of the adoption in 2001 of a general fisheries control plan, which laid down priorities, including implementation of a hake recovery plan and strict control of compliance with minimum sizes. The Commission however decided that France was still not compliant. Further inspections were undertaken and it was concluded that the number of cases of undersized fish being offered for sale had decreased in Brittany but problems remained on the Mediterranean coast with regard to bluefin tuna, and that inspections on landing were infrequent.

The Commission asked for the reports and sets of statistics relating to implementation of the various measures for the general organization of fisheries control to which the French Government had referred. After being requested by the Court to indicate the number of inspections at sea and on land which the French authorities had carried out since the bringing of the present action with a view to ensuring compliance with the rules relating to the minimum size of fish, the number of infringements recorded and the action taken by the courts in respect of those infringements, on 30 January 2004 the French Government lodged fresh statistics. They showed that the number of inspections, findings of infringement and convictions was lower in 2003 than in 2002. The French Government stated that the decrease in inspections at sea was due to the mobilization of French vessels to fight the pollution caused by the shipwrecking of the oil tanker Prestige and that inspections on land had decreased because the discipline of fishermen had improved. It explained that the decrease in the number of convictions was due to the effects of a law granting an amnesty, while pointing out that the average amount of the fines imposed had increased.]

Financial penalties for the breach of obligations

75. To punish the failure to comply with the judgment in Case C-64/88 Commission v. France, the Commission suggested that the Court should impose a daily penalty payment on the French Republic from delivery of the present judgment until the day on which the breach of obligations is brought to an end. In light of the particular features of the breach that has been established, the Court considers that it should examine in addition whether imposition of a lump sum could constitute an appropriate measure.

The possibility of imposing both a penalty payment and a lump sum

\*    \*    \*

80. The procedure laid down in Article 228 [260](2) EC has the objective of inducing a defaulting Member State to comply with a judgment establishing a breach of obligations and thereby of ensuring that Community law is in fact applied. The

measures provided for by that provision, namely a lump sum and a penalty payment, are both intended to achieve this objective.

81. Application of each of those measures depends on their respective ability to meet the objective pursued according to the circumstances of the case. While the imposition of a penalty payment seems particularly suited to inducing a Member State to put an end as soon as possible to a breach of obligations which, in the absence of such a measure, would tend to persist, the imposition of a lump sum is based more on assessment of the effects on public and private interests of the failure of the Member State concerned to comply with its obligations, in particular where the breach has persisted for a long period since the judgment which initially established it.

82. That being so, recourse to both types of penalty provided for in Article 228 [260](2) EC is not precluded, in particular where the breach of obligations both has continued for a long period and is inclined to persist.

83. This interpretation cannot be countered by reference to the use in Article 228 [260](2) EC of the conjunction or' to link the financial penalties capable of being imposed. As the Commission and the Danish, Netherlands, Finnish and United Kingdom Governments have submitted, that conjunction may, linguistically, have an alternative or a cumulative sense and must therefore be read in the context in which it is used. In light of the objective pursued by Article 228 [260] EC, the conjunction or' in Article 228 [260](2) EC must be understood as being used in a cumulative sense."

\*   \*   \*

98. On the basis of the method of calculation which it has set out in its communication 97/C 63/02 of 28 February 1997 on the method of calculating the penalty payments provided for pursuant to Article 228 [260] of theEC Treaty (OJ 1997 C 63, p. 2), the Commission suggested that the Court should impose on the French Republic a penalty payment of EUR 316 500 for each day of delay by way of penalty for non-compliance with the judgment in Case C-64/88 Commission v. France, from the date of delivery of the judgment in the present case until the day on which the judgment in Case C-64/88 Commission v. France has been complied with.

99. The Commission considers that an order imposing a penalty payment is the most appropriate instrument for putting an end as soon as possible to the infringement which has been established and that, in the present case, a penalty payment of EUR 316 500 for each day of delay fits the seriousness and duration of the infringement, due regard being had to the need to make the penalty effective. That sum is calculated by multiplying a uniform basic amount of EUR 500 by a coefficient of 10 (on a scale of 1 to 20) for the seriousness of the infringement, by a coefficient of 3 (on a scale of 1 to 3) for the duration of the infringement and by a coefficient of 21.1 (based on the gross domestic product of the Member State in question and the weighting of votes in the Council of the European Union), which is deemed to reflect the ability to pay of the Member State concerned.

100. The French Government submits that there is no reason to impose a penalty payment because it has brought the breach of obligations to an end and, in the

alternative, that the amount of the penalty payment requested is disproportionate.

101. It points out that, so far as the seriousness of the infringement is concerned, in Case C-387/97 Commission v. Greece the Commission suggested a coefficient of 6, although the breach of obligations compromised public health and no measure had been taken with a view to complying with the previous judgment, two factors which are absent here. Accordingly, the coefficient of 10 suggested by the Commission in the present case is not acceptable.

102. The French Government also maintains that the measures required to comply with the judgment in Case C-64/88 Commission v. France were unable to produce immediate effects. Given the inevitable time-lag between the adoption of the measures and their impact becoming perceptible, the Court cannot take into account the whole of the period passing between delivery of the first judgment and that of the forthcoming judgment.

103. As to those submissions, while it is clear that a penalty payment is likely to encourage the defaulting Member State to put an end as soon as possible to the breach that has been established . . . In exercising its discretion, it is for the Court to set the penalty payment so that it is appropriate to the circumstances and proportionate both to the breach that has been established and to the ability to pay of the Member State concerned . . .

104. In that light, and as the Commission has suggested in its communication of 28 February 1997, the basic criteria which must be taken into account in order to ensure that penalty payments have coercive force and Community law is applied uniformly and effectively are, in principle, the duration of the infringement, its degree of seriousness and the ability of the Member State to pay. In applying those criteria, regard should be had in particular to the effects of failure to comply on private and public interests and to the urgency of getting the Member State concerned to fulfil its obligations . . .

105. As regards the seriousness of the infringement and, in particular, the effects of failure to comply on private and public interests, it is to be remembered that one of the key elements of the common fisheries policy consists in rational and responsible exploitation of aquatic resources on a sustainable basis, in appropriate economic and social conditions. In this context, the protection of juvenile fish proves decisive for reestablishing stocks. Failure to comply with the technical measures of conservation prescribed by the common policy, in particular the requirements regarding the minimum size of fish, therefore constitutes a serious threat to the maintenance of certain species and certain fishing grounds and jeopardises pursuit of the fundamental objective of the common fisheries policy.

106. Since the administrative measures adopted by the French authorities have not been implemented in an effective manner, they cannot reduce the seriousness of the breach established.

107. Having regard to those factors, the coefficient of 10 (on a scale of 1 to 20) is therefore an appropriate reflection of the degree of seriousness of the infringement.

108. As regards the duration of the infringement, suffice it to state that it is considerable, even if the starting date be that on which the Treaty on European

Union entered into force and not the date on which the judgment in Case C-64/88 Commission v. France was delivered . . . Accordingly, the coefficient of 3 (on a scale of 1 to 3) suggested by the Commission appears appropriate.

109. The Commission's suggestion of multiplying a basic amount by a coefficient of 21.1 based on the gross domestic product of the French Republic and on the number of votes which it has in the Council is an appropriate way of reflecting that Member State's ability to pay, while keeping the variation between Member States within a reasonable range . . .

110. Multiplying the basic amount of EUR 500 by the coefficients of 21.1 (for ability to pay), 10 (for the seriousness of the infringement) and 3 (for the duration of the infringement) gives a sum of EUR 316 500 per day.

111. As regards the frequency of the penalty payment, account should, however, be taken of the fact that the French authorities have adopted administrative measures which could serve as a framework for implementation of the measures required to comply with the judgment in Case C-64/88 Commission v. France. Nevertheless, it is not possible for the necessary adjustments to previous practices to be instantaneous or their impact to be perceived immediately. It follows that any finding that the infringement has come to an end could be made only after a period allowing an overall assessment to be made of the results obtained.

112. Having regard to those considerations, the penalty payment must be imposed not on a daily basis, but on a half-yearly basis.

## NOTES AND QUESTIONS

1.    What criteria were used for setting the level of fines?

2.    Are penalties an adequate remedy for all types of breaches?

3.    See also *Commission v. Hellenic Republic*, Case C-387/97, 2000 ECJ CELEX LEXIS 99, [2000] ECR I-5047, where, in a judgment more than four years previous to this action (Case 45/91), the Greek government had been found in breach of Directive 75/442 concerning the disposal of toxic and hazardous waste. Essentially, a site close to the river Kouroupitos in the area of Chania had been used to dump waste that had then found its way into the river. Despite repeated communications from the Commission and assurances given as to plans to close the dump, the Court determined that Greece had not implemented the necessary measures to comply.

4.    For a discussion of the EC 226/TFEU 258 procedure, see C. Harlow and R. Rawlings, *Accountability and Law Enforcement: The Centralized EU Infringement Procedure*, (2006) 31 EL REV. 447. As regards penalties, see P. Wenneras, *A New Dawn for Commission Enforcement under Arts 226 and 228 EC: General and Persistent (GAP) Infringements, Lump Sums, and Penalty Payments* (2006) 43 CML REV. 31. For commentary on the Court's role, see I. Kilbey, *The Interpretation of Article 260 TFEU (Ex 228 EC)* EL REV. 2010.

5.    Keep in mind that the Commission has the power to impose remedies under the State aid provisions. These remedies may require the private parties who

received illegal aid to repay it. At first sight it seems unreasonable to expect them to bear the burden of the State's breach. The rationale for this seems to be that they would be able to challenge the Commission's decision against the illegal aid. The parties might then be able to claim damages, presumably from the Member State concerned, citing *Fives Lille Cail v. High Authority*, Joined Cases 19,21/60, 2, 3/61, [1961] ECR 296.

# Chapter 8

# JUDICIAL PROTECTION

## § 8.01  OVERVIEW

*Template* Article 8, section 8.1

***The concept of Judicial Protection*** In relation to original jurisdiction, the temptation may be to think of the ECJ as exercising a power of judicial review like the United States Supreme Court, but the analogy is rather misleading. In the EU system, the ECJ started out as a court that bore much more resemblance to a French administrative court. Its duty was to provide judicial protection against wrongful acts of Union institutions. Yet, with the growth of Union competences and the formalization in the post-Lisbon TFEU of the Union's legislative powers, the role of the EU Court is clearly much more than just a check on administrative power.

In that regard, since the ECJ can review legislative acts as well as executive acts or secondary rulemaking, it runs the risk of straying into the political arena. It is not surprising that it has tried to stay clear of reviewing legislative acts. It has avoided this, both by interpreting individual standing in a very limited way as regards actions by individuals, and by declining to review political choices inherent in legislative acts where individual standing is recognized.

By contrast, it has been a severe taskmaster in reviewing Union executive acts, in the main meaning acts of the Commission. This is where the notion of "judicial protection" diverges from "judicial review". The ECJ has seen its mission to be to provide a complete system of judicial control over such acts to protect individual citizens from acts of maladministration. (Case 294/83 *Les Verts v. Parliament* [1986] ECR 1339). The analogy in the U.S. is the U.S. Administrative Procedure Act of 1946, Pub. L. 79-404, 60 Stat. 237 ("APA"). This Act describes procedures to be followed in the making of individual decisions and the establishment of rules under delegated powers. They may frequently grant powers of a judicial nature. (Most U.S. specialized agencies have both rulemaking and judicial powers.) Thus, the scope of review by the courts, while sometimes also applying underlying "constitutionality" considerations, will likely focus on specifics such as whether: (a) power was properly delegated by the legislature; (b) officials have acted within the scope of the delegated power and used their powers for the purpose for which they were granted; (c) specified procedures have been followed; (d) decisions involving a judicial act have complied with due process requirements, such as the right to a fair hearing and to an impartial judge.

***Materials in this Chapter*** In this Chapter, the materials focus mostly on the procedural and jurisdictional aspects of the original jurisdiction of the Court of

Justice:

- **Actions for annulment** This topic covers three issues. First, the **standing** of individuals in the European Courts to challenge Union acts: With respect to actions for annulment, the interpretation given by the ECJ and more recently the CFI/General Court to the conditions laid down in EC 230/TFEU 263 with respect to challenge by private parties of legislative and regulatory acts, and to challenge by third parties of decisions addressed to others, have proven to be controversial and at times confusing. Bodies of law have arisen based on the subject matter being challenged, to whom an act is addressed, and, more generally, underlying policy reasons for restricting or opening up the possibility of challenge in given areas. After 50 years of jurisprudence one can discern an underlying policy that discourages actions against legislative acts by private parties but is more accepting of challenges to executive acts by parties to whom such acts are not addressed but who might be considered to be directly and individually concerned by them.

Second, the **scope of Review:** While the Court can review acts against a very broad set of legal standards, it has drawn certain boundaries as to what is actually reviewable.

Third, the **effects of annulment:** what elements are annulled and how may the defects be corrected?

-       **Actions to require the adoption of an act** For individuals, this form of challenge has proven to be of very limited usefulness due to lack of standing.

-       **The "plea of illegality"** A way of raising the illegality of an act in a subsequent case involving implementation based on that act.

-       **Claims for damages** Claims for damages may also to be considered an aspect of judicial control. The provisions of EC 235 and 288/TFEU 268 and 340 are best seen as a second form of judicial protection for individuals who have been adversely affected by some form of maladministration or wrongdoing in the course of decision- or rule-making, whether or not they also have a right to have the act annulled. Similarities may be found in the United States in the context of actions for breach of civil rights legislation: *Butz v. Economou*, 438 U.S. 478 (1978). See also *Newport v. Fact Concerts*, 453 U.S. 247 (1980); *Middlesex County Sewerage Authority et al. v. National Sea Clammers*, 453 U.S. 1 (1981). A suit may succeed even if the officials acted in good faith: *Owen v. City of Independence*, 445 U.S. 622 (1980).

***Evolution of the text of EC 230/TFEU 263*** Until Lisbon, the language of EC 230 had remained unchanged since 1957 as regards the standing of individuals although broadening changes were made with respect to the categories of acts and institutions that could be reviewed. Lisbon, however, did update the language relating to individuals to reflect the evolution of the jurisprudence and also effected other changes:

- ■   In paragraph 1, TFEU 263 extends both the types of bodies whose acts may be challenged (European Council and other "bodies, offices or agencies") and the type of acts that can be challenged (any act intended to produce legal effects vis à vis third parties). The change in the type of acts that may be challenged by individuals reflects the development of the ECJ's case law in that regard (as indicated already in Chapter 3) so does not change the law as it has so developed.

- In paragraph 3 the Committee of the Regions is given the power to challenge acts in order to protect its prerogatives (this means, to ensure that it is properly consulted per the Treaty rules)

- In paragraph 4, the reference to "decision" has been changed to "act". This also reflects development of case law.

- The language that previously referenced "decisions in the form of regulations" has been eliminated but now we have an additional category called the "regulatory act which is of direct concern to them and does not entail implementing measures". The terms "regulatory act" and "implementing measures" will require clarification by the Courts and other institutions.

***Grounds of review*** Chapter 19 illustrates the criteria the Court may apply when reviewing executive acts, but in reality the cases scattered throughout this book are illustrations of these criteria. The specific enumerated grounds in EC 230/TFEU 263 are indeed not often referred to by the Courts at all — they have for all intents and purposes been subsumed under the obligation to ensure, pursuant to EC 220/TEU 19, that the "law is observed" and the more general ground of review in EC 230/TFEU 263 regarding "any rule of law relating to [the Treaty's] application". As observed in Chapter 4, this has permitted the wholesale importation of fundamental rights based on principles common to the Member States as embodied in the European Convention on Human Rights.

Much has been written about the Court of Justice and its procedure. See, e.g., D. Edward, *How the Court of Justice Works* (1995) 20 EL Rev. 539; A. Ward, Judicial Review and the Rights of Private Parties in EU Law (2nd Edition, Oxford University Press, 2007); H. Schermers, Judicial Protection in the European Union (6th edition, Kluwer, 2002); G. De Burca and J.H.H. Weiler (Eds.), The European Court of Justice (Oxford University Press, 2001).

***The ECJ as an Appeals court*** The materials in this chapter do not cover the role of the ECJ as an appeals court specifically, but there are illustrations both here and in other chapters of the contrasts between the approach of the ECJ and the CFI/General Court when the ECJ has overruled a CFI/General Court judgment in part or wholly. The absence of any dissenting opinions in the judgments of the CFI/General Court (true of the ECJ too, of course) makes it more difficult perhaps for parties to see where they might have an opportunity to appeal a point successfully. Sometimes a close vote might provide real encouragement to appeal, as appears to have been the case in the *Microsoft* decision in 2007, where, according to a Bloomberg report, the CFI/General Court judges apparently voted 7-6 against Microsoft. If Microsoft had known this, would it have been more inclined to appeal? (It didn't.)

## § 8.02 ACTIONS BY INDIVIDUALS FOR ANNULMENT OF UNION ACTS

### [A] Challenges to Decisions Addressed to Another Person — Direct Concern

### TOEPFER ET AL. v. COMMISSION
Joined Cases106 and 107/63, [1965] ECR 405
[No paragraph numbering appears in the original]

[During the transitional period, and before quotas and customs duties on goods from other Member States had been abolished, the applicants had, on October 1, 1963, requested a license to import maize from France. The German government denied them a license, as was possible in principle under EEC regulations allowing protective measures. However, such a decision required confirmation by the Commission, which the Commission gave on October 4. However, on 1 October 1963 the Commission took a decision fixing new free-at-frontier prices for maize imported into Germany as from 2 October, so that the danger which the protective measures were to guard against no longer existed as from that date. Therefore, the only persons affected by the said measures were importers who had applied for an import licence on 1 October 1963, and it was clear that the number and identity of these importers had already become fixed and ascertainable before 4 October, when the contested decision was made. Thus, the Commission was in a position to know that its decision affected the interests and the position of only the importers who had applied for licenses on October 1, the last day when protective measures could apply.]

According to the terms of Article 22 of Regulation No 19, when a Member State has given notice of the protective measures provided for in paragraph (1) of the said Article, the Commission shall decide within four working days of the notification whether the measures are to be retained, amended or abolished.

The last sentence of the second paragraph of Article 22 provides that the Commission's decision shall come into force immediately.

Therefore a decision of the Commission amending or abolishing protective measures is directly applicable and concerns interested parties subject to it as directly as the measures which it replaces.

It would be illogical to say that a decision to retain protective measures had a different effect, as the latter type of decision does not merely give approval to such measures, but renders them valid.

Therefore decisions made under the third and fourth subparagraphs of Article 22 (2) are of direct concern to the interested parties.

## NOTES AND QUESTIONS

**1.** The Court here defines "direct concern" in the context of a decision addressed to a Member State. Until Lisbon, EC 230 had referenced a right for individuals to challenge decisions addressed "to another person" if they were of direct and individual concern to such individuals. What general understanding of the term "direct concern" can be derived from the Court's approach?

**2.** The *Toepfer* case illustrates another aspect of the phenomenon peculiar to the EU structure that on the whole sets it apart from the United States, i.e., rulemaking and decisions by the Member States in the course of implementation of EU rules, sanctioned by "decisions" of the Commission.

**3.** The Commission action in this case was a "decision" but the Commission may be empowered both to enact regulations or take decisions addressed to Member States in substantially similar areas of activity. Might this then mean that applicants could be placed at a disadvantage simply by the choice of legislative measure?

## COMITE CENTRAL D'ENTREPRISE DE LA SOCIETE GENERALE DES GRANDES SOURCES AND OTHERS v. COMMISSION
Case T-96/92, 1995 ECJ CELEX LEXIS 27, [1995] ECR II-1213

[European company laws require that larger companies have one or more works councils that comprise representatives of management and workers and which must be consulted on significant matters including sale of a business. The Commission had decided to approve Nestle's acquisition of the Perrier Group under (former) Regulation 4064/89 — the first merger control regulation (or "control of concentrations") — subject to the condition that certain businesses be divested. The plaintiffs here, various works councils of the companies to be acquired brought an action for the annulment of the decision. In order to show direct concern they argued that both their legal rights as works councils per se were directly affected, and that additionally, the legal rights of the employees they represented were directly affected.

In the course of the judgment the court makes reference to Directive 77/187 [1977] OJ L 61/26 on transfers of undertakings. This directive requires that when a business is sold, the contracts of employment, compensation and benefits of the employees transfer and may not be altered by the new owner by reason of the transaction.

This decision of the CFI/General Court was not appealed.]

38 With respect, in the second place, to the question whether the contested Decision is of direct concern to the applicants, it must be stated to begin with that the concentration in question cannot prejudice the own rights of the representatives of the employees of the undertakings concerned. Contrary to the applicants' assertions, even supposing that the concentration brings about a reduction in the resources of the various applicant councils following job losses as alleged, that circumstance cannot in any event be regarded as adversely affecting those councils'

own rights. They have no interest in the maintenance of the undertakings' workforce specifically in order to guard against any reduction in their funds, the level of which is based on the level of the payroll. The employees' representative organizations can assert rights of their own only in relation to the functions and privileges given to them, under the applicable legislation, in an undertaking with a particular structure. In that respect, moreover, it follows essentially from Article 5 of Directive 77/187/EEC that, in the event of a transfer of an undertaking, the safeguarding of the own rights of the employees' representative organizations and the protective measures enjoyed by the employees' representatives are to be ensured in accordance with the laws, regulations and administrative provisions of the Member States. It follows from the above considerations that only a decision which may have an effect on the status of the employees' representative organizations or on the exercise of the prerogatives and duties given them by the legislation in force can affect such organizations' own interests. That cannot be the case with a decision authorizing a concentration.

39 Moreover, with respect to the prejudice allegedly caused by the Decision to the consultative functions of the applicant councils within their undertakings, with reference for example to decisions relating to the concentration itself, the restructuring or alleged job losses, it must be noted that Regulation No 4064/89 lays down rules for the review of concentrations from the point of view of Community competition law without prejudice to the exercise by the representatives of the employees of the undertakings concerned of all the rights they have under the applicable national law. Regulation No 4064/89 expressly confirms, moreover, in the thirty-first recital that it "in no way detracts from the collective rights of employees as recognized in the undertakings concerned".

40 It must be stated further that the argument that the contested Decision directly prejudices the interests of the Perrier employees, in so far as it entails, according to the applicants, the abolition of jobs and the loss of collective benefits, does not withstand examination either. It must be stated in this respect that the legislation intended to safeguard the rights of the employees, in particular in the event of a concentration, prevents the realization of a concentration in itself entailing the alleged consequences for the level and conditions of employment in the undertakings in question, as will be shown in the following paragraphs. Such effects are thus produced only if measures which are independent of the concentration itself are first adopted, by the undertakings in question acting alone or by the social partners, as the case may be, in conditions strictly defined by the applicable rules. Bearing in mind in particular the bargaining power of the various social partners, the possibility of such measures being adopted is not entirely theoretical, which means that the employees' representatives cannot be regarded as directly concerned by the decision authorizing the concentration . . .

41 On this point, it follows clearly from the applicable legislation that job losses and changes in the social benefits given to the Perrier group employees either by their individual contracts or, within the group of undertakings which are signatories thereto, by the collective agreement of 14 March 1989 to which the applicants refer, are not inevitable following a concentration. Article 3 of Directive 77/187/EEC provides for the transfer to the transferee of the transferor's rights and obligations arising from a contract of employment or from an employment relationship existing

on the date of the transfer of the undertaking. Moreover, the first subparagraph of Article 4(1) of that directive provides that "the transfer of an undertaking . . . shall not in itself constitute grounds for dismissal by the transferor or the transferee".

42 In this respect it must also be noted that the annulment of the Commission's Decision, in so far as that Decision authorizes the concentration in question by making its declaration of compatibility subject inter alia to the requirement for Nestle to sell certain undertakings belonging to the Perrier group, would not constitute a safeguard against all measures involving job losses adopted in accordance with the law. In that connection, the fact that Article 4 of Directive 77/187/EEC goes on to state that it "shall not stand in the way of dismissals that may take place for economic, technical or organizational reasons entailing changes in the workforce" confirms that such dismissals can in no case follow directly from a concentration, but require the adoption of independent measures subject to identical rules to those which apply where there is no concentration.

43 Similarly, with respect more particularly to the assertions as to the loss of the social benefits enjoyed by the Pierval employees, it must be stated that Directive 77/187/EEC provides, in the first subparagraph of Article 3(2), that "following the transfer . . . the transferee shall continue to observe the terms and conditions agreed in any collective agreement on the same terms applicable to the transferor under that agreement, until the date of termination or expiry of the collective agreement or the entry into force or application of another collective agreement".

\*     \*     \*

44 It follows from all the above points that current individual contracts are all transferred to the new company.

\*     \*     \*

45 It follows that in the present case the acquisition of Perrier by Nestle, accompanied by the sale by Nestle of some of the Perrier group's brand names and sources to a third party, does not in itself entail any direct consequences for the rights which the Perrier employees derive from their contracts or employment relationship. In the absence of any direct causal link between the alleged attack on those rights and the Commission's decision making authorization of the concentration subject inter alia to the transfer of certain brand names and sources, the persons concerned must have an appropriate legal remedy available for the defence of their legitimate interests not at the stage of the review of the lawfulness of the said decision, but at the stage of the measures which are the immediate origin of the adverse effects thus alleged, and which may be adopted by the undertakings or in certain cases by the social partners concerned without any intervention by the Commission. It is at the stage of the adoption of such measures, review of which is within the jurisdiction of the national courts, that the safeguards intervene which are given to employees by the provisions of national law and of Community law such as, in particular, Directive 77/187/EEC . . .

46 For all the above reasons, the applicants cannot be regarded as directly concerned by the contested decision, without prejudice to the guarantee of the procedural rights given them by Regulation No 4064/89 in the administrative

procedure. It must be noted that as a general rule where a regulation gives procedural rights to third persons, they must have a remedy available for the protection of their legitimate interests, in accordance with settled case-law . . . On this point, it must be stated in particular that the right of specified third persons to be properly heard, on application by them, during the administrative procedure can in principle be given effect to by the Community judicature only at the stage of review of the lawfulness of the Commission's final decision. It follows that, although in the present case the considerations set out above make it apparent that in substance the final decision is not of direct concern to the applicants, they must nevertheless be recognized as being entitled to bring proceedings against that decision for the specific purpose of examining whether the procedural guarantees which they were entitled to assert, during the administrative procedure, under Article 18 of Regulation No 4064/89 have been infringed, as they allege. Only if the Court were to find a clear breach of those guarantees, such as to prejudice the applicants' right to make an effective statement of their position, if they have applied to do so, during the administrative procedure, would the Court have to annul the decision on the ground of breach of essential procedural requirements. In the absence of such a substantial breach of their procedural rights, the mere fact that the applicants claim, before the Community judicature, that those rights have been infringed during the administrative procedure cannot make the application admissible in so far as it is based on pleas alleging breach of substantive rules of law, given that, as the Court has already established above, the applicants' legal position is not directly affected by the wording of the Decision. Only if the latter condition was fulfilled would the applicants be entitled, under Article 173 EC [263] of the Treaty, to ask the Court to examine the statement of reasons in, and the substantive lawfulness of, the Decision.

## NOTES AND QUESTIONS

**1.** Discuss how the Court applied the criteria for establishing direct concern here.

**2.** For other cases involving challenges to decisions by the Commission under the former merger regulation, see, for example, *Air France v. Commission*, Case T-3/93, 1994 ECJ CELEX LEXIS 183, [1994] ECR II-121 — an extract of which appears in Chapter 5 — where the plaintiff challenged the Commission's decision that it did not have power under the "Merger Regulation" to intervene in the takeover of Dan Air by British Airways. The CFI/General Court considered this decision affected Air France directly because it could have commented on the takeover if the Merger Regulation had applied. Furthermore, it was individually concerned because of the unique effects the merger had on it. By contrast in *Zunis Holding and Others v. Commission*, Case T-83/92, 1993 ECJ CELEX LEXIS 230, [1993] ECR II-1169, shareholders in a company where another shareholder had increased its holding were found not to be individually concerned by the Commission's decision that the increase did not give that shareholder a "decisive influence" over the decision-making of the company.

**3.** See also *INFRONT WM AG v. Commission*, Case T-33/01, 2005 ECJ CELEX LEXIS 691, [2005] ECR II-5897, which is explained in Chapter 5.

## [B]   Challenges to Decisions Addressed to Another Person — Individual Concern

### TOEPFER ET AL. v. COMMISSION
Joined Cases 106 and 107/63, [1965] ECR 405
[No paragraph numbering appears in the original]

[The facts of this case are set out in the extract appearing earlier in this chapter.]

(p 411)

It is clear from the fact that on 1 October 1963 the Commission took a decision fixing new free-at-frontier prices for maize imported into the Federal Republic as from 2 October, that the danger which the protective measures retained by the Commission were to guard against no longer existed as from this latter date.

Therefore the only persons concerned by the said measures were importers who had applied for an import license during the course of the day of 1 October 1963. The number and identity of these importers had already become fixed and ascertainable before 4 October, when the contested decision was made. The Commission was in a position to know that its decision affected the interests and the position of the said importers alone.

The factual situation thus created differentiates the said importers, including the applicants, from all other persons and distinguishes them individually just as in the case of the person addressed.

Therefore the objection of inadmissibility which has been raised is unfounded and the applications are admissible.

### PLAUMANN & CO. v. COMMISSION
Case 25/62, [1963] ECR 95
[No paragraph numbering appears in the original]

[The applicant challenged a Commission decision addressed to Germany refusing to authorize Germany to suspend in part customs duties applicable to mandarins and clementines imported from third countries.]

Persons other than those to whom a decision is addressed may only claim to be individually concerned if that decision affects them by reason of certain attributes which are peculiar to them or by reason of circumstances in which they are differentiated from all other persons and by virtue of these factors distinguishes them individually just as in the case of the person addressed. In the present case the applicant is affected by the disputed Decision as an importer of clementines, that is to say, by reason of a commercial activity which may at any time be practiced by any person and is not therefore such as to distinguish the applicant in relation to the contested Decision as in the case of the addressee.

For these reasons the present action for annulment must be declared inadmissible.

## NOTES AND QUESTIONS

1.  How did the situations of the applicants in *Plaumann* and *Toepfer* differ?

2.  In *Spijker v. Commission*, Case 231/82 [1983] ECR 2559, the Court held that the applicant failed to establish individual concern. There the Commission had addressed a decision to the three Benelux countries banning the import of Chinese manufactured brushes. Applicant was the only importer of such brushes in the Benelux countries. Nonetheless, the Court held he was unable to challenge the Commission's decision because the decision allowed the measures taken by national authorities to take effect only for the period subsequent to that for which the applicant had applied for license. The applications he had already submitted were not affected by the measures; they applied only to future transactions, and there was a theoretical possibility that other traders could be equally affected.

## METRO SB-GROβMÄRKTE GMBH & C. KG v. COMMISSION
### Case 26/76, [1977] ECR 1875

[Metro sought the annulment of a Commission Decision under article 85 (EC 81/TFEU 101) determining that the selective distribution system established by the undertaking Schwarzwalder Apparate-Bau-Anstalt August Schwer and Soehne GmbH ("SABA") for distributing its electronic equipment for the leisure market did not fall within article 81 [101](1); and also a subsequent decision refusing to review the earlier decision.]

6 Since the contested decision was not addressed to Metro it is necessary to consider whether it is of direct and individual concern to it.

Metro is a so-called self-service wholesale trading undertaking having some 30 establishments in the Federal Republic of Germany and in certain other Member States.

This form of distribution, which means that Metro competes in particular with specialist wholesalers, consists in obtaining from producers wholesale supplies of a wide range of foodstuffs (food department) and other products (non-food department) in order to resell them, principally to retailers, who will themselves resell the products, but also to commercial or industrial undertakings or small businesses which wish to apply the goods purchased for commercial purposes and, lastly, to private customers termed 'institutional consumers', although it should be noted that this latter practice forms the subject-matter of dispute between the parties.

Metro distributes these products through the so-called 'cash and carry' system whereby purchasers serve themselves in sales areas where the goods are stored in such a way that they may be removed easily by the customers themselves, are displayed simply and are paid for in cash, which results in lower prices and makes it possible to operate satisfactorily on lower profit margins than those of the traditional wholesale trade.

This form of marketing is thus characterized both by special sales methods and by the nature of the customers sought by the wholesaler.

8 When the applicant applied to SABA for recognition as a wholesaler for the distribution of electronic equipment for the leisure market SABA refused because the applicant would not agree to a number of conditions to which SABA subjects the grant of the status of a SABA wholesaler and which, the applicant maintains, are not compatible with the structure of the self-service wholesale trade as Metro engages in it.

Specific instances of this are the prohibition on SABA wholesalers regarding the supply of SABA equipment to trade consumers, that is to say to dealers or small businesses outside the trade in electrical goods but using the equipment purchased for commercial purposes within their business, likewise the prohibition on supplies to 'institutional' consumers and the obligations imposed upon wholesalers under the cooperation agreements linking them with SABA.

The intervener SABA, on the other hand, maintains that those conditions are compatible with Metro's business activity and that its refusal to appoint the latter as wholesaler stems instead from Metro's sales policy, which is intended to combine in one unit the roles of wholesaler and retailer and to which SABA cannot agree in view of the structure of its distribution system whereby a clear distinction is maintained between those two operations in accordance, as SABA maintains, with the requirements of Federal German legislation.

9 Since the defendant refused to appoint the applicant, on 7 and 9 November 1973 the latter lodged with the Commission, in accordance with Article 3 (2) (b) of Regulation No 17, a request for a finding that the distribution system established by SABA was contrary to Articles 85 [101] and 86 [102] of the Treaty and that SABA should be required to terminate that system.

*    *    *

12 Since Metro considered that the distribution system [eventually] approved [by the Commission] retained features unlawfully preventing its appointment as a SABA wholesaler it lodged this application.

13 The abovementioned facts establish that the contested decision was adopted in particular as the result of a complaint submitted by Metro and that it relates to the provisions of SABA's distribution system, on which SABA relied and continues to rely as against Metro in order to justify its refusal to sell to the latter or to appoint it as a wholesaler, and which the applicant had for this reason impugned in its complaint.

It is in the interests of a satisfactory administration of justice and of the proper application of Articles 85 [81] and 86 [82] that natural or legal persons who are entitled, pursuant to Article 3 (2) (b) of Regulation No 17, to request the Commission to find an infringement of Articles 85 [81] and 86 [82] should be able, if their request is not complied with either wholly or in part, to institute proceedings in order to protect their legitimate interests.

In those circumstances the applicant must be considered to be directly and individually concerned, within the meaning of the second paragraph of Article 173 EC [263], by the contested decision and the application is accordingly admissible.

## NOTES AND QUESTIONS

**1.** In holding that Metro was directly and individually concerned, what criteria did the Court apply?

**2.** The decision in this case was addressed to another individual, contrasting with the *Plaumann/Toepfer* cases where it was addressed to a Member State. In terms of reconciling *Metro* with these earlier cases, is this a relevant distinction? How else might the cases be reconciled, if at all? What are the differences between them?

**3.** In *Kruidvat BVBA v. Commission*, Case C-70/97 P, 1998 ECJ CELEX LEXIS 617, [1998] ECR I-7183, a member of a trade association who had worked with the association in support of a complaint to the Commission regarding anticompetitive practices arising from a distribution network of luxury perfumes was held not to have standing under EC 230/TFEU 263. The court cited Kruidvat's failure to make a complaint itself and that it had not applied for admission to the network. It was the trade association that had responded to a Commission request for comments. Kruidvat sought annulment of a Commission decision approving the network, but the Court held that the action was inadmissible. It noted that:

> 48 In that regard, it should be recalled that in Articles 173 [263] and 184 [277], on the one hand, and in Article 177 [267], on the other, the Treaty established a complete system of legal remedies and procedures designed to permit the Court of Justice to review the legality of measures adopted by the institutions . . .

> 49 In this case, whilst Kruidvat could not bring an application for the annulment of the Decision, it remained able . . . to plead before national courts, adjudicating in accordance with Article 177 [267] of the Treaty, that the Decision was unlawful.

Is this a satisfactory outcome for the applicant? How realistic is the EC 234/TFEU 267 procedure in such cases?

## KWEKERIJ GEBROEDERS VAN DER KOOY BV ET AL. v. COMMISSION
### Joined Cases 67-68/85 and 70/85, [1988] ECR 219

[Kwekerij Gebroeders van der Kooy BV, a limited liability company, JW van Vliet, a market gardener, and the Landbouwschap, a body governed by public law and the Netherlands sought the annulment of Commission Decision 85/215/EEC which had determined that a preferential tariff charged to glasshouse growers for natural gas in the Netherlands was incompatible with article 92 (EC 87/TFEU 107). The Landbouwschap was an industry association that had responsibility for negotiating the tariff.]

15 . . . The contested decision is of concern to the [individual growers] . . . solely by virtue of their objective capacity as growers established in the Netherlands and qualifying for the preferential gas tariff on the same footing as any other grower in the same circumstances. With regard to them, therefore, the decision is a measure of general application covering situations which are determined objectively, and

entails legal effects for categories of persons envisaged in a general and abstract manner. Thus the contested decision cannot be regarded as being of individual concern to the applicants.

16 For those reasons, the application in Case 67/85 must be declared inadmissible.

\* \* \*

18 The Commission maintains that, even on the assumption that the Landbouwschap acted as the growers' representative in the tariff negotiations with Gasunie, a body set up to promote the collective interests of a category of persons cannot be considered to be directly and individually concerned for the purposes of Article 173 EC [263](2) by a measure affecting the general interests of that category. See the judgments of the Court of 18 March 1975 in case 72/74 Union Syndicale v. Council ((1975)) ECR 401 and 28 March 1982 in case135/81 Groupement des Agences de Voyages v. Commission ((1982)) ECR 3799).

\* \* \*

19 The objection cannot be upheld.

20 First of all, contrary to the Commission's assertion, the Landbouwschap acts as the representative of growers' organizations in regard to gas tariffs.

21 Although the Landbouwschap cannot be considered to be directly and individually concerned by Decision 85/215 as a recipient of the contested aid, it is none the less true that, as the Landbouwschap rightly argues, its position as negotiator of gas tariffs in the interests of the growers is affected by Decision 85/215.

22 Furthermore, in that capacity the Landbouwschap has taken an active part in the procedure under Article 93 [108](2) by submitting written comments to the Commission and by keeping in close contact with the responsible officials throughout the procedure.

23 Lastly, the Landbouwschap is one of the parties to the contract which established the tariff disallowed by the Commission, and in that capacity is mentioned several times in Decision 85/215. In that capacity it was also obliged, in order to give effect to the decision, to commence fresh tariff negotiations with Gasunie and to reach a new agreement.

24 It must therefore be concluded that in the circumstances of this case the Landbouwschap was entitled to bring proceedings under Article 173 EC [263](2) for the annulment of Commission Decision 85/215.

25 It follows that the objection of inadmissibility raised by the Commission in Case 68/85 must be rejected.

## NOTES AND QUESTIONS

1.   In *Kwekerij*, the ECJ held that the growers' applications were inadmissible but that the Landbouwschap's application was admissible. Why did the Court consider that the individual growers were not individually concerned? Is it necessary that all the parties so affected be definitively identified? Wouldn't it be

possible to determine the "closed class" simply by virtue of who would be affected by the tariff as of the date of the decision? Why was the Association's position different?

2.   In *Bundesverband der Nahrungsmittel- und Speiseresteverwertung eV and Josef Kloh v. European Parliament and Council*, Case T-391/02, 2004 ECJ CELEX LEXIS 363, [2004] ECR II-1447, (a case that actually concerned a challenge to a legislative act) the CFI/General Court summarized the jurisprudence of the Courts that has developed with respect to when an association of undertakings may be granted standing in as limited to three kinds of circumstances: where a legal provision expressly grants it a series of procedural powers; where the association itself is distinguished individually because its own interests as an association are affected, in particular because its negotiating position has been affected by the measure whose annulment is being sought; and where it represents the interests of undertakings that would themselves be entitled to bring proceedings. [This case was not appealed.]

3.   Given the narrow circumstances where an association might be granted standing, the Court has rejected most applications by organizations claiming to represent a general interest group: see, for example, *Congrès national du Kurdistan (KNK) v. Council*, Case T-206/02, 2005 ECJ CELEX LEXIS 106, [2005] ECR II-523.

## [C]   Challenges to Legislative and Regulatory Acts

### ALLIED CORPORATION v. COMMISSION
Joined Cases 239/82, 275/82 [1984] ECR 1005

[Allied and other plaintiffs sought annulment of Commission Regulation 1976/82 of 19 July 1982 imposing a provisional anti-dumping duty on imports of certain chemical fertilizer originating in the U.S. One of the plaintiffs, Demufert, was an importer rather than a (non EU) exporter. A product is to be considered as being dumped if its export price to the EU is less than a comparable price for the like product, in the ordinary course of trade, as established for the exporting country. The duty is intended to make up the difference between the exporting country price and the imported EU price.]

7 The Commission raises an objection of inadmissibility against the application lodged by Demufert. The Commission contends that Demufert, in its capacity as an independent importer, has no locus standi, under the provisions of the second paragraph of Article 173 EC [263] of the EEC Treaty, to apply for a declaration that two regulations whose validity is contested are void. According to the Commission, the anti-dumping duty imposed by the regulations at issue — which merely supplement Regulation No. 349/81 imposing a definitive anti-dumping duty — is of concern to Demufert only in its objective capacity as an importer. As such, Demufert does not therefore according to the consistent case-law of the Court . . . meet the requirement, stipulated by the second paragraph of Article 173 EC [263], that the measures in question should be of direct and individual concern to it.

8 As far as the other applicants are concerned, the Commission merely expresses

doubts as regards the admissibility of their applications. In the first place, it concedes that there is a very specific reference to the applicants in question both in Regulation No. 349/81 and in the contested regulations, which were adopted following the withdrawal of the undertakings given individually by those applicants. The Commission also acknowledges that, in their capacity as producers and exporters, those undertakings are not guaranteed legal protection in the Member States of the Community and since the sole factor which gives rise to the collection of anti-dumping duty is importation, the applicants may bring an action before the Court only through undertakings which import their products. Secondly, however, the Commission maintains that the sole effect of the contested regulations is to bring the applicants, following the withdrawal of their undertakings, within the scope of the general system established by Regulation No. 349/81, a measure which is in substance unquestionably a regulation inasmuch as it applies to all imports of the product in question originating in the United States. From the point of view of avoiding a needless duplication of legal remedies, the Commission considers it undesirable to make available a means of redress parallel to the proceedings which may be instituted in the national courts against the collection of anti-dumping duty in the wake of complaints by importers. Finally, the Commission draws attention to the "unusual" consequences which would follow if the applications were declared admissible, since the effect of such a declaration would be to ascribe a dual character to anti-dumping measures, inasmuch as the same measures would have to be classified as "decisions" in relation to certain undertakings and as "regulations" in relation to all the other undertakings.

9 During the oral procedure, the Commission, after indicating once again its opposition to the admissibility of Demufert's application, informed the Court that, on balance, it was in favor of the admissibility of direct actions brought by undertakings from non-member countries and, in any event, of those brought by the applicant undertakings on the ground that they were expressly mentioned in the statement of the reasons for, and in the provisions of, the contested measures. The Commission considers that such an approach would have a beneficial effect on the interests of Community undertakings in non-member countries in the event of the initiation of anti-dumping proceedings against them, particularly in the United States of America where the means of redress are to a large extent available to undertakings from other countries. The Commission takes the view that, in the interests of reciprocity, it is appropriate to provide similar guarantees under the judicial system of the Community.

10 The questions of admissibility raised by the Commission must be resolved in the light of the system established by Regulation No. 3017/79 and, more particularly, of the nature of the anti-dumping measures provided for by that regulation, regard being had to the provisions of the paragraph of Article 173 EC [263] of the EEC Treaty.

11 Article 13 (1) of Regulation No. 3017/79 provides that "anti-dumping or countervailing duties, whether provisional or definitive, shall be imposed by regulation". Although it is true that, in the light of the criteria set out in the second paragraph of Article 173 EC [263], such measures are, in fact, as regards their nature and their scope, of a legislative character, inasmuch as they apply to all the traders concerned, taken as a whole, the provisions may none the less be of direct

and individual concern to those producers and exporters who are charged with practicing dumping. It is clear from Article 2 of Regulation No. 3017/79 that anti-dumping duties may be imposed only on the basis of the findings resulting from investigations concerning the production prices and export prices of undertakings which have been individually identified.

12 It is thus clear that measures imposing anti-dumping duties are liable to be of direct and individual concern to those producers and exporters who are able to establish that they were identified in the measures adopted by the Commission or the Council or were concerned by the preliminary investigations.

13 As the Commission has rightly stated, to acknowledge that undertakings which fulfil those requirements have a right of action, in accordance with the principles laid down in the second paragraph of Article 173 EC [263], does not give rise to a risk of duplication of means of redress since it is possible to bring an action in the national courts only following the collection of an anti-dumping duty which is normally paid by an importer residing within the Community. There is no risk of conflicting decisions in this area since, by virtue of the mechanism of the reference for a preliminary ruling under Article 177 [267] of the EEC Treaty, it is for the Court of Justice alone to give a final decision on the validity of the contested regulations.

14 It follows that the applications lodged by Allied, Kaiser and Transcontinental are admissible. All three applicants gave an undertaking under Article 10 of Regulation No. 3017/79, they were accordingly referred to individually in Article 2 of Regulation No. 349/81 and, after withdrawing their undertakings, their individual circumstances formed the subject-matter of the two regulations contested in the applications.

15 However, the position is different in the case of Demufert, since that applicant is an importer established in one of the Member States and is not referred to in any of the measures which are contested in the applications before the Court. As such, therefore, Demufert is concerned by the effects of the contested regulations only in so far as it comes objectively within the scope of the provisions of those regulations. The uncontested fact that Demufert acted as importing agent for Allied does not alter that conclusion. . . . [I]n the present case the existence of dumping has been established, as is stated in the tenth recital in the preamble to regulation No. 349/81, by reference to the export prices of American producers and not by reference to the retail price charged by European importers, with the result that the findings relating to the existence of dumping are not of direct concern to Demufert, whereas they are of direct concern to the producers and exporters. It must be pointed out that, in so far as it was compelled to pay anti-dumping duties, it is open to the applicant to bring an action in the competent national court in the context of which it can put forward its arguments against the validity of the regulations at issue.

16 It follows that the application submitted by Demufert must be declared inadmissible.

# CODORNIU SA v. COUNCIL
## Case 309/89, 1994 ECJ CELEX LEXIS 4, [1994] ECR I-1853

[Cordorniu sought the annulment of Article 1(2)(c) of Council Regulation (EEC) No 2045/89 of 19 June 1989 amending Regulation (EEC) No 3309/85 laying down general rules for the description and presentation of sparkling wines and aerated sparkling wines. As a result of these regulations, the name "cremant" was restricted to producers in certain parts of France and Luxembourg. Codorniu, a Spanish producer which owned the trademark "Grand Cremant de Cordorniu" was thus prohibited from using its mark for its Spanish origin product.]

14 In support of its objection of inadmissibility the Council states that it did not adopt the contested provision on the basis of the circumstances peculiar to certain producers but on the basis of a choice of wine-marketing policy in relation to a particular product. The contested provision reserves the use of the term 'crémant' to quality sparkling wines psr manufactured under specific conditions in certain Member States. It thus constitutes a measure applicable to an objectively determined situation which has legal effects in respect of categories of persons considered in a general and abstract manner.

15 According to the Council, Codorniu is concerned by the contested provision only in its capacity as a producer of quality sparkling wines psr using the term 'crémant', like any other producer in an identical situation. Even if when that provision was adopted the number or identity of producers of sparkling wines using the term 'crémant' could theoretically be determined, the measure in question remains essentially a regulation inasmuch as it applies on the basis of an objective situation of law or fact defined by the measure in relation to its objective.

16 Codorniu alleges that the contested provision is in reality a decision adopted in the guise of a regulation. It has no general scope but affects a well-determined class of producers which cannot be altered. Such producers are those who on 1 September 1989 traditionally designated their sparkling wines with the term 'crémant'. For that class has no general scope. Furthermore, the direct result of the contested provision will be to prevent Codorniu from using the term 'Gran Cremant' which will involve a loss of 38% of its turnover. The effect of that damage is to distinguish it, within the meaning of the second paragraph of Article 173 EC [263] of the Treaty, from any other trader. Codorniu alleges that the Court has already recognized the admissibility of an action for annulment brought by a natural or legal person against a regulation in such circumstances . . . .

17 Under the second paragraph of Article 173 EC [263] of the Treaty the institution of proceedings by a natural or legal person for a declaration that a regulation is void is subject to the condition that the provisions of the regulation at issue in the proceedings constitute in reality a decision of direct and individual concern to that person.

18 As the Court has already held, the general applicability, and thus the legislative nature, of a measure is not called in question by the fact that it is possible to determine more or less exactly the number or even the identity of the persons to whom it applies at any given time, as long as it is established that it applies to them

by virtue of an objective legal or factual situation defined by the measure in question in relation to its purpose . . .

19 Although it is true that according to the criteria in the second paragraph of Article 173 EC [263] of the Treaty the contested provision is, by nature and by virtue of its sphere of application, of a legislative nature in that it applies to the traders concerned in general, that does not prevent it from being of individual concern to some of them.

20 Natural or legal persons may claim that a contested provision is of individual concern to them only if it affects them by reason of certain attributes which are peculiar to them or by reason of circumstances in which they are differentiated from all other persons . . .

21 Codorniu registered the graphic trade mark 'Gran Cremant de Codorniu' in Spain in 1924 and traditionally used that mark both before and after registration. By reserving the right to use the term 'crémant' to French and Luxembourg producers, the contested provision prevents Codorniu from using its graphic trade mark.

22 It follows that Codorniu has established the existence of a situation which from the point of view of the contested provision differentiates it from all other traders.

23 It follows that the objection of inadmissibility put forward by the Council must be dismissed.

## NOTES AND QUESTIONS

**1.** What general principles regarding the notion of "direct and individual concern" in the context of challenges to regulations might be drawn from these cases?

**2.** *Codorniu* expands the scope of individual concern. How did the Court justify allowing the challenge mounted by plaintiffs to a regulation that it admitted applied to an objective situation?

**3.** Constrast *Union de Pequenos Agricultores v. Council*, Case C-50/00, 2002 ECJ CELEX LEXIS 257, [2002] ECR I-6677, in which the Court stated:

35 Thus, under Article 173 EC [263] of the Treaty, a regulation, as a measure of general application, cannot be challenged by natural or legal persons other than the institutions, the European Central Bank and the Member States . . .

36 However, a measure of general application such as a regulation can, in certain circumstances, be of individual concern to certain natural or legal persons and is thus in the nature of a decision in their regard . . . That is so where the measure in question affects specific natural or legal persons by reason of certain attributes peculiar to them, or by reason of a factual situation which differentiates them from all other persons and distinguishes them individually in the same way as the addressee . . .

Here the Court did acknowledge that the regulation must be in the nature of a decision so far as the applicants were concerned, but essentially applied the direct and individual concern criteria to determine that it was. Thus it seems to have evolved a different test to the one seen in the earlier cases (see Chapter 5). In Chapter 5, we saw that the Court had tended to characterize a measure as a regulation even if it actually applied to an identifiable and finite number of persons, if it was intended to apply objective situations. If this approach had been taken in *Codorniu* it would have been fatal to the applicant's standing because the applicant at that time still had to demonstrate that the act was in fact a decision. However, the Court effectively ignored this requirement.

See also *Extramet v. Council*, Case C-358/89, 1992 ECJ CELEX LEXIS 59, [1991] ECR I-2501, in the context of anti-dumping measures.

In *Sofrimport SARL v. Commission*, Case 152/88, 1992 ECJ CELEX LEXIS 14, [1990] ECR I-2477, the applicants, who were fruit importers, were seeking to annul a number of Commission regulations suspending the issuance of import licenses from Chile and fixing quantities of such imports from third countries. Under one of the regulations, the Commission was required to take into account, when exercising its powers under the regulations, the "special position of products in transit" when the regulations came into force. The Court held that applicants, who had goods in transit when the contested regulations came into force, were individually concerned. In the Court's view, such persons constituted a restricted group that could not be expanded after the measure at issue came into effect.

## COMMISSION v. JEGO-QUERE & CIE SA
### Case C-263/02 P, 2004 ECJ CELEX LEXIS 157, [2004] ECR I-3425

[In December 2000, the Commission and the Council, having been alerted by the International Council for the Exploration of the Sea (ICES), and noting the urgent need to establish a plan for the recovery of the stock of hake, had adopted Regulation 1162/2001, the principal aim of which was to reduce catches of juvenile hake immediately. This regulation applied to fishing vessels operating in the areas defined by it. It imposed minimum mesh sizes for those vessels, varying according to the areas concerned, for the different net fishing techniques employed, irrespective of the type of fish which the vessel is seeking to catch. Jego-Quéré sought the annulment of the Regulation in the CFI/General Court, which declared the action admissible on the grounds that there was no national procedure allowing a State court challenge, so that the applicants would have been completely denied a remedy. (Case T-177/01 *Jego Quéré v. Commission* 2002 ECR II-2365). The Commission sought on appeal to have that ruling overturned.]

29. It should be noted that individuals are entitled to effective judicial protection of the rights they derive from the Community legal order, and the right to such protection is one of the general principles of law stemming from the constitutional traditions common to the Member States. That right has also been enshrined in Articles 6 and 13 of the ECHR . . .

30. By Articles 230 EC [263] and Article 241 EC [274], on the one hand, and by Article 234 [267], on the other, the Treaty has established a complete system of legal remedies and procedures designed to ensure review of the legality of acts of the

institutions, and has entrusted such review to the Community Courts. Under that system, where natural or legal persons cannot, by reason of the conditions for admissibility laid down in the fourth paragraph of Article 173 EC [263], directly challenge Community measures of general application, they are able, depending on the case, either indirectly to plead the invalidity of such acts before the Community Courts under Article 241 EC [277] or to do so before the national courts and ask them, since they have no jurisdiction themselves to declare those measures invalid, to make a reference to the Court of Justice for a preliminary ruling on validity (see Union de Pequenos Agricultores v. Council, paragraph 40).

31. Thus it is for the Member States to establish a system of legal remedies and procedures which ensure respect for the right to effective judicial protection . . .

32. In that context, in accordance with the principle of sincere cooperation laid down in Article 10 EC [TEU 4], national courts are required, so far as possible, to interpret and apply national procedural rules governing the exercise of rights of action in a way that enables natural and legal persons to challenge before the courts the legality of any decision or other national measure relative to the application to them of a Community act of general application, by pleading the invalidity of such an act (see Union de Pequenos Agricultores v. Council, paragraph 42).

33. However, it is not appropriate for an action for annulment before the Community Court to be available to an individual who contests the validity of a measure of general application, such as a regulation, which does not distinguish him individually in the same way as an addressee, even if it could be shown, following an examination by that Court of the particular national procedural rules, that those rules do not allow the individual to bring proceedings to contest the validity of the Community measure at issue. Such an interpretation would require the Community Court, in each individual case, to examine and interpret national procedural law. That would go beyond its jurisdiction when reviewing the legality of Community measures . . .

34. Accordingly, an action for annulment before the Community Court should not on any view be available, even where it is apparent that the national procedural rules do not allow the individual to contest the validity of the Community measure at issue unless he has first contravened it.

35. In the present case, it should be pointed out that the fact that Regulation No 1162/2001 applies directly, without intervention by the national authorities, does not mean that a party who is directly concerned by it can only contest the validity of that regulation if he has first contravened it. It is possible for domestic law to permit an individual directly concerned by a general legislative measure of national law which cannot be directly contested before the courts to seek from the national authorities under that legislation a measure which may itself be contested before the national courts, so that the individual may challenge the legislation indirectly. It is likewise possible that under national law an operator directly concerned by Regulation No 1162/2001 may seek from the national authorities a measure under that regulation which may be contested before the national court, enabling the operator to challenge the regulation indirectly.

36. Although the condition that a natural or legal person can bring an action

challenging a regulation only if he is concerned both directly and individually must be interpreted in the light of the principle of effective judicial protection by taking account of the various circumstances that may distinguish an applicant individually, such an interpretation cannot have the effect of setting aside the condition in question, expressly laid down in the Treaty. The Community Courts would otherwise go beyond the jurisdiction conferred by the Treaty (see Union de Pequenos Agricultores v. Council, paragraph 44).

37. That applies to the interpretation of the condition in question set out at paragraph 51 of the contested judgment, to the effect that a natural or legal person is to be regarded as individually concerned by a Community measure of general application that concerns him directly if the measure in question affects his legal position, in a manner which is both definite and immediate, by restricting his rights or by imposing obligations on him.

38. Such an interpretation has the effect of removing all meaning from the requirement of individual concern set out in the fourth paragraph of Article 173 EC [263].

39. It follows from the above that the Court of First Instance erred in law. Accordingly, the second plea in law must be declared to be well founded.

## NOTES AND QUESTIONS

1. The CFI/General Court thought that it should allow actions to ensure effective judicial protection, in any event where it was not possible or at least undesirable to encourage a party to take illegal actions in order to set up a case for challenging the measure in the courts of a Member State. The following excerpt from the CFI/General Court judgment lays out that Court's approach:

43 It is therefore necessary to consider whether, in a case such as this, where an individual applicant is contesting the lawfulness of provisions of general application directly affecting its legal situation, the inadmissibility of the action for annulment would deprive the applicant of the right to an effective remedy.

44 In that regard, it should be recalled that, apart from an action for annulment, there exist two other procedural routes by which an individual may be able to bring a case before the Community judicature — which alone have jurisdiction for this purpose — in order to obtain a ruling that a Community measure is unlawful, namely proceedings before a national court giving rise to a reference to the Court of Justice for a preliminary ruling under Article 234 EC [267] and an action based on the non-contractual liability of the Community, as provided for in Article 235 EC [268] and the second paragraph of Article 288 EC [340].

45 However, as regards proceedings before a national court giving rise to a reference to the Court of Justice for a preliminary ruling under Article 234 EC, it should be noted that, in a case such as the present, there are no acts of implementation capable of forming the basis of an action before national courts. The fact that an individual affected by a Community measure may

be able to bring its validity before the national courts by violating the rules it lays down and then asserting their illegality in subsequent judicial proceedings brought against him does not constitute an adequate means of judicial protection. Individuals cannot be required to breach the law in order to gain access to justice . . .

46 The procedural route of an action for damages based on the non-contractual liability of the Community does not, in a case such as the present, provide a solution that satisfactorily protects the interests of the individual affected. Such an action cannot result in the removal from the Community legal order of a measure which is nevertheless necessarily held to be illegal. Given that it presupposes that damage has been directly occasioned by the application of the measure in issue, such an action is subject to criteria of admissibility and substance which are different from those governing actions for annulment, and does not therefore place the Community judicature in a position whereby it can carry out the comprehensive judicial review which it is its task to perform. In particular, where a measure of general application, such as the provisions contested in the present case, is challenged in the context of such an action, the review carried out by the Community judicature does not cover all the factors which may affect the legality of that measure, being limited instead to the censuring of sufficiently serious infringements of rules of law intended to confer rights on individuals . . .

47 On the basis of the foregoing, the inevitable conclusion must be that the procedures provided for in, on the one hand, Article 234 EC [267] and, on the other hand, Article 235 EC [268] and the second paragraph of Article 288 EC [340] can no longer be regarded, in the light of Articles 6 and 13 of the ECHR and of Article 47 of the Charter of Fundamental Rights, as guaranteeing persons the right to an effective remedy enabling them to contest the legality of Community measures of general application which directly affect their legal situation.

48 It is true that such a circumstance cannot constitute authority for changing the system of remedies and procedures established by the Treaty, which is designed to give the Community judicature the power to review the legality of acts of the institutions. In no case can such a circumstance allow an action for annulment brought by a natural or legal person which does not satisfy the conditions laid down by the fourth paragraph of Article 173 EC [263] to be declared admissible . . .

49 However . . . , there is no compelling reason to read into the notion of individual concern, within the meaning of the fourth paragraph of Article 173 EC [263], a requirement that an individual applicant seeking to challenge a general measure must be differentiated from all others affected by it in the same way as an addressee.

50 In those circumstances, and having regard to the fact that the EC Treaty established a complete system of legal remedies and procedures designed to permit the Community judicature to review the legality of measures adopted by the institutions . . . the strict interpretation, applied until now,

of the notion of a person individually concerned according to the fourth paragraph of Article 173 EC [263], must be reconsidered.

51 In the light of the foregoing, and in order to ensure effective judicial protection for individuals, a natural or legal person is to be regarded as individually concerned by a Community measure of general application that concerns him directly if the measure in question affects his legal position, in a manner which is both definite and immediate, by restricting his rights or by imposing obligations on him. The number and position of other persons who are likewise affected by the measure, or who may be so, are of no relevance in that regard

The line of reasoning seeks to reject the ECJ's insistence on effective judicial remedies but the General Court had concluded that the availability of national remedies was insufficient. How did the ECJ deal with that argument? What do you think drove the ECJ to revert to the narrow interpretation it had started with in *Toepfer*?

2. For an interesting development in the U.S. on *locus standi*, see the case of *Massachusetts v. EPA*, 549 U.S. 497 (2007), concerning standing to challenge the EPA, with regard to its duty to regulate greenhouse gas emissions from automobiles. The majority opinion, written by Justice John Paul Stevens, indicated that only one petitioner needs to have standing to authorize review. States should be afforded a "special solicitude" to claim standing as sovereign entities representing a multitude of interests. In the words of Justice Stevens:

That Massachusetts does in fact own a great deal of the 'territory alleged to be affected' only reinforces the conclusion that its stake in the outcome of this case is sufficiently concrete to warrant the exercise of federal judicial power.

Note that in the EU system, Member States automatically have standing to challenge any Union act.

## § 8.03 THE SCOPE OF REVIEW

### UNITED KINGDOM v. COUNCIL
#### (WORKING TIME)
#### Case C-84/94, 1996 ECJ CELEX LEXIS 194, [1996] ECR I-5755

[Under its developing social policy, the EU had adopted a directive that limited the number of hours anyone could work per week. The UK, in the course of its extensive attack on the directive, challenged it on grounds that it breached both the principles of proportionality and subsidiarity.]

58 [T]he Council must be allowed a wide discretion in an area which, as here, involves the legislature in making social policy choices and requires it to carry out complex assessments. Judicial review of the exercise of that discretion must therefore be limited to examining whether it has been vitiated by manifest error or misuse of powers, or whether the institution concerned has manifestly exceeded the limits of its discretion.

59 So far as concerns the first condition, it is sufficient that . . . the measures on the organization of working time which form the subject-matter of the directive, save for that contained in the second sentence of Article 5, contribute directly to the improvement of health and safety protection for workers within the meaning of Article 118a [138], and cannot therefore be regarded as unsuited to the purpose of achieving the objective pursued.

60 The second condition is also fulfilled. Contrary to the view taken by the applicant, the Council did not commit any manifest error in concluding that the contested measures were necessary to achieve the objective of protecting the health and safety of workers.

## NOTES AND QUESTIONS

1.  As noted in the Overview, examples of the Court's approach to the scope of its review are found throughout this book. This case is included here merely to illustrate the classic statement of the Court's views on its powers of review and particularly its ability to review the exercise of discretion by EU lawmaking bodies. It essentially is determining that that exercise is not itself justiciable by the Court. Is that a justified position, given the grounds of review set out in EC 230/TFEU 263? Many other cases have confirmed this approach. Does this approach overall suggest that the Court is more of an administrative tribunal than a constitutional court? See F. Jacobs, *Is The Court of Justice of the European Communities a Constitutional Court?* in D. CURTIN AND D. O'KEEFFE (EDS.), CONSTITUTIONAL ADJUDICATION IN EUROPEAN COMMUNITY AND NATIONAL LAW (Butterworths (Ireland) 1992); A. STONE SWEET, THE JUDICIAL CONSTRUCTION OF EUROPE (Oxford University Press, 2004).

2.  In the United States, judicial review of the substantive discretionary elements of rulemaking by administrative agencies is not common. See *Citizens to Preserve Overton Park, Inc. v. Volpe*, 401 U.S. 402 (1971) and *United States v. Nova Scotia Food Prods. Corp.*, 568 F.2d 240 (2d Cir. 1977). However, substantive objections may be dressed up as procedural issues. See, for example, *Udall v. FPC*, 387 U.S. 428 (1967).

## COMMISSION v. ALROSA COMPANY LTD
### Case C-441/07P, 2010 ECJ EUR-Lex LEXIS 686, [2010] ECR I-NYR

[The facts of this case are set out in Chapter 7. Here, the ECJ considers the scope of its review in relation to the finding by the CFI/General Court that it had jurisdiction to review the Commission's evaluation of economic factors in determining what remedy to order.]

59. It should be recalled that the Commission examined the joint commitments [originally offered by De Beers and Alrosa] after inviting third parties to submit observations and finding that the results of that public consultation were negative. From that it concluded that those commitments were not sufficient.

60. To answer the Commission's complaint and ascertain whether the General Court really did, as the Commission submits, infringe the discretion it has in connection

with accepting commitments under Article 9 of Regulation No 1/2003, the extent of that discretion should first be defined.

61. Since the Commission is not required itself to seek out less onerous or more moderate solutions than the commitments offered to it, . . . its only obligation in the present case in relation to the proportionality of the commitments was to ascertain whether the joint commitments offered in the proceedings initiated under Article 81 EC [101] were sufficient to address the concerns it had identified in the proceedings initiated under Article 82 EC [102].

62. . . . [T]he Commission concluded, after taking note of the results of the market test it had conducted, that the joint commitments were not appropriate for resolving the competition problems it had identified.

63. The General Court could have held that the Commission had committed a manifest error of assessment only if it had found that the Commission's conclusion was obviously unfounded, having regard to the facts established by it.

64. However, the General Court made no such finding.

65. Instead it examined other less onerous solutions for the purpose of applying the principle of proportionality, including possible adjustments of the joint commitments, in paragraphs 128, 129 and 137 to 153 of the judgment under appeal.

66. In paragraphs 129 to 136 of the judgment under appeal, the General Court expressed its own differing assessment of the capability of the joint commitments to eliminate the competition problems identified by the Commission, before concluding in paragraph 154 that alternative solutions that were less onerous for the undertakings than a complete ban on dealings existed in the present case.

67. By so doing, the General Court put forward its own assessment of complex economic circumstances and thus substituted its own assessment for that of the Commission, thereby encroaching on the discretion enjoyed by the Commission instead of reviewing the lawfulness of its assessment.

68. That error of the General Court in itself justifies setting aside the judgment under appeal.

\*   \*   \*

[The Court, having set aside the General Court's judgment, then proceeded to give its own judgment as permitted under article 61 of the Statute of the Court.]

120. . . . It follows from all the considerations set out in this judgment that in adopting the contested decision the Commission did not make an error of law or a manifest error of assessment or breach the principle of proportionality. Alrosa has not succeeded in showing that the individual commitments offered by De Beers and made binding by the Commission manifestly went beyond what was necessary to address the concerns identified by the Commission in its preliminary assessment.

## NOTES AND QUESTIONS

The EU courts have tended to be more willing to review the discretionary elements of an act where the enabling regulation actually severely circumscribes the extent of that discretion. This emerges in particular from the cases relating to damages (*infra*, this Chapter) and matters involving infringement of fundamental rights (*infra*, Chapter 19, and specifically the cases dealing with proportionality.) As will be seen further in Chapter 19, the scope of review is considerably expanded when dealing with administrative decisions involving individuals because these are quasi-judicial in nature and evidentiary burdens and standards must be met. See, for example, *Commission v. Tetra Laval*, Case C-12/03P, 2005 ECJ CELEX LEXIS 48, [2005] ECR I-987, where the ECJ, on an appeal from the CFI/General Court, stated:

38. . . . [T]he Court of First Instance correctly set out the tests to be applied when carrying out judicial review of a Commission decision on a concentration . . . [T]he Court stated that the basic provisions of the Regulation, in particular Article 2, confer on the Commission a certain discretion, especially with respect to assessments of an economic nature, and that, consequently, review by the Community Courts of the exercise of that discretion, which is essential for defining the rules on concentrations, must take account of the margin of discretion implicit in the provisions of an economic nature which form part of the rules on concentrations.

39. Whilst the Court recognises that the Commission has a margin of discretion with regard to economic matters, that does not mean that the Community Courts must refrain from reviewing the Commission's interpretation of information of an economic nature. Not only must the Community Courts, inter alia, establish whether the evidence relied on is factually accurate, reliable and consistent but also whether that evidence contains all the information which must be taken into account in order to assess a complex situation and whether it is capable of substantiating the conclusions drawn from it. Such a review is all the more necessary in the case of a prospective analysis required when examining a planned merger with conglomerate effect.

Do you think that the above paragraphs are consistent with the Court's views as expressed in *Alrosa* with regard to the scope of review that the European Court should apply?

## § 8.04 SCOPE AND EFFECTS OF ANNULMENT

## NTN TOYO BEARING COMPANY LIMITED AND OTHERS v. COUNCIL
### Case 240/84, 1987 ECJ CELEX LEXIS 474, [1987] ECR 1809

[NTN sought annulment of Council Regulation No 2089/84 of 19 July 1984 imposing a definitive anti-dumping duty on imports of ball-bearings originating in Japan and Singapore.]

4 The Council considers that the application is admissible only in so far as it is concerned with the anti-dumping duty imposed on the applicant. The Council observes that the contested measure is a regulation and therefore only those of its provisions which are of direct and individual concern to the applicant may be contested in an application for a declaration of nullity.

5 . . . [M]easures imposing anti-dumping duties, adopted pursuant to Council Regulation (EEC) No 3017/79 of 20 December 1979 on protection against dumped or subsidized imports from countries not members of the European Economic Community . . . are liable to be of direct and individual concern, within the meaning of the second paragraph of Article 173 EC [263] of the Treaty, to those producers and exporters who are able to establish that they were identified in the measures adopted by the Commission or the Council or were concerned by the preliminary investigations. The Council does not deny that the contested regulation is liable to be of direct and individual concern to NTN, which is expressly named therein.

6 However, it should be noted that the contested regulation does not lay down general rules which apply to a whole group of traders without distinguishing between them but imposes different anti-dumping duties on a series of manufacturers or exporters of small ball-bearings established in Japan and Singapore who are expressly named, and also on other undertakings which are not named but which pursue the same activities in those same countries. Under those circumstances it must be concluded that NTN is individually concerned only by those provisions of the contested regulation which impose on it a specific anti-dumping duty and determine the amount thereof, and not by those provisions which impose anti-dumping duties on other undertakings.

7 It follows from the foregoing that the objection of inadmissibility raised by the Council must be upheld and the application dismissed as inadmissible in so far as it seeks a declaration that Regulation No 2089/84 is void in its entirety. It is, however, necessary to declare the application admissible and to examine its merits in so far as it seeks a declaration that those provisions of the contested regulation which are of concern exclusively to NTN are void.

## NOTES AND QUESTIONS

1. In *NTN*, the Court considered the plaintiff's claim inadmissible insofar as it sought to annul the entire regulation, but admissible insofar as the regulation directly and individually concerned the particular plaintiff. What was the effect on the scope of annulment?

2. Suppose the regulation's scheme is seriously impaired by its "partial validity". How might the issuing institution remedy the situation? In *Sofrimport SARL v. Commission*, Case 152/88, 1992 ECJ CELEX LEXIS 14, [1990] ECR I-2477, the Court had occasion to review the basis for challenges to regulations having to do with the market in fruit and vegetables and in particular measures dealing with products in transition:

15 Since the application for annulment is admissible only insofar as it concerns the position of products in transit, only the third of those

submissions, the only one which challenges the application of protective measures to those products, should be examined.

16 Under the first subparagraph of Article 3(3) of Regulation 2707/72, 'the measures provided for in paragraph 1 shall take account of the special position of products in transit of the Community.' The effect of that provision is to enable an importer whose goods are in transit to rely on a legitimate expectation that in the absence of an overriding public interest no suspensory measures will be applied against him.

17 The Commission submits first that it adequately protected traders whose goods were in transit by extending the period of validity of import licenses from 30 to 40 days, by Regulation 871/88. That argument cannot be upheld. It is sufficient to observe that the specific protection provided by Article 3(3) of Regulation 2707/72 concerns goods not covered by a license.

18 The Commission goes on to argue that a reasonably careful trader could have expected that it might at any time take protective measures once it had expressly reserved that possibility in Article 3(3) of Regulation 346/88. Simply to inform traders of the possibility of protective measures cannot, however, be regarded as sufficient. In order to meet the requirements of the special protection provided for in Article 3(3) of Regulation 2707/72, the measure should also have indicated the situations in which the public interest might justify the application of protective measures with regard to goods in transit.

19 It must be held that the Commission has not in this case demonstrated the existence of any overriding public interest justifying the application of suspensory measures with regard to goods in transit.

20 Consequently, the Commission has failed to fulfill its obligations under Article 3(3) of Regulation 2707/72.

21 Regulations 962/88, 984/88 and 1040/88 must therefore be declared void insofar as they concern products in transit towards the Community; for the rest, the application for annulment must be dismissed.

## ROGER TREMBLAY, HARRY KESTENBERG AND SYNDICAT DES EXPLOITANTS DE LIEUX DE LOISIRS (SELL) v. COMMISSION
### Case T-224/95, 1997 ECJ CELEX LEXIS 97, [1997] ECR II-2215

[The plaintiffs had asked the Commission to find that Articles 85 and 86 [EC 81 and 82/TFEU 101 and 102] of the EEC Treaty had been infringed by a group of discotheque operators called BEMIM (Bureau Europeen des Medias de l'Industrie Musicale) of which Roger Tremblay and Harry Kestenberg, individual operators of discotheques, were members at that time. That application cited the Societe des Auteurs, Compositeurs et Editeurs de Musique (hereinafter SACEM'), the society which manages copyright in musical works in France. Between 1979 and 1988 the Commission also received similar complaints from other complainants. This was a second case involving the same basic issues. The first is referred to in Chapter 7.

This second case was brought because the applicants believed the Commission had failed to take the necessary actions to comply with the Court's first decision, in which it found that the Commission had failed to take the necessary procedural steps in responding to the applicants' request for action to be taken against third parties under EC 82/TFEU 102. It was not appealed.]

72 When the Court of First Instance annuls an act of an institution, it is required, under Article 176 [266] to take the measures necessary to comply with the Court's judgment. In that connection, both Community courts have held that, in order to comply with their judgments and to implement them fully, the institution is required to observe not only the operative part of the judgment but also the grounds which led to the judgment and constitute its essential basis, inasmuch as they are necessary to determine the exact meaning of what is stated in the operative part. It is those grounds which, on the one hand, identify the precise provision held to be illegal and, on the other, indicate the specific reasons which underlie the finding of illegality contained in the operative part and which the institution concerned must take into account when replacing the annulled measure . . .

73 In the present case, the applicants contend, first of all, that the Commission disregarded the judgment in Tremblay I, which, in their view, required it to conduct an inquiry. However, it follows from the operative part and grounds of that judgment that the Court of First Instance partially annulled the earlier Commission decision of 12 November 1992 for breach of Article 190 [296] of the Treaty on the ground that it did not apprise the applicants of the reasons justifying rejection of their complaints in so far as these concerned market partitioning. That conclusion did not therefore imply that the Court of First Instance was requesting the Commission to conduct investigations or, a fortiori, that it was giving it some kind of direction to take action in that regard, which is something which it does not have power to do in the context of its review of legality . . . Moreover, since in this judgment . . . . the Court has found that the Commission has now satisfied its obligation under Article 190 [296] of the Treaty to state reasons for its decision in regard to the allegation of market partitioning, the argument that the judgment in Tremblay I has been disregarded and that Article 176 of the Treaty has therefore been infringed cannot avail the applicant.

## NOTES AND QUESTIONS

The applicants here alleged that the annulment of the Commission's decision declining to take action under EC 86/TFEU 106 required the Commission then to take such action, at least in terms of carrying out an investigation. However, the Court disagreed. How would you summarize the Court's view as to the Commission's duty in this regard?

## § 8.05   ACTIONS BY INDIVIDUALS TO REQUIRE THE ADOPTION OF AN ACT

### LORD BETHELL v. COMMISSION
Case 246/81, [1982] ECR 2277

3 Lord Bethell who was a member of the European Parliament and Chairman of the Freedom of the Skies Campaign, had for some time past been engaged in action against agreements and concerted practices which, he alleges, existed between airlines operating scheduled flights as regards passenger fares in Europe. He complained to the Commission for failing to take action but the Commission declined to act, pointing out that in most cases the final fixing of air fares was the sole responsibility of the Member States so that there was in principle no ground to scrutinize the activity of companies on the basis of Article 85 [EC 81/TFEU 101]. However, bearing in mind the special relationships existing between the States and the companies, the Commission would examine the subject further from the point of view of the state aid articles and that most scheduled airlines were in a dominant position within the Common Market. After emphasizing the difficulty and complexity of an analysis intended to establish the abusive nature of air fares, the Director General informed the applicant of certain future steps proposed by the Commission.

Lord Bethell was not satisfied with that answer and brought an action based, as stated above, on Article 175 [EC 232/TFEU 265] or, in the alternative, on Article 173 [EC 230/TFEU 265].

*   *   *

11 In the words of the second paragraph of Article 173 EC [263], any natural or legal person may, under the conditions laid down in that article, institute proceedings "against a decision addressed to that person or against a decision which, although in the form of a regulation or a decision addressed to another person, is of direct and individual concern to the former".

12 According to the third paragraph of Article 175 [265], any natural or legal person may, under the conditions laid down in that article, complain to the Court that an institution of the Community "has failed to address to that person any act other than a recommendation or an opinion".

13 It appears from the provisions quoted that the applicant, for his application to be admissible, must be in a position to establish either than he is the addressee of a measure of the Commission having specific legal effects with regard to him, which is, as such, capable of being declared void, or that the Commission, having been duly called upon to act in pursuance of the second paragraph of Article 175 [265], has failed to adopt in relation to him a measure which he was legally entitled to claim by virtue of the rules of Community law.

14 In reply to a question from the Court the applicant stated that the measure to which he believed himself to be entitled was "a response, an adequate answer to his complaint saying either that the Commission was going to act upon it or saying that it was not and, if not, giving reasons". Alternatively the applicant took the view that the letter addressed to him on 17 July 1981 by the Director General for Competition

was to be described as an act against which proceedings may be instituted under the second paragraph of Article 173 EC [263].

15 The principal question to be resolved in this case is whether the Commission had, under the rules of Community law, the right and the duty to adopt in respect of the applicant a decision in the sense of the request made by the applicant to the Commission in his letter of 13 May 1981. It is apparent from the content of that letter and from the explanations given during the proceedings that the applicant is asking the Commission to undertake an investigation with regard to the airlines in the matter of the fixing of air fares with a view to a possible application to them of the provisions of the Treaty with regard to competition.

16 It is clear therefore that the applicant is asking the Commission, not to take a decision in respect of him, but to open an inquiry with regard to third parties and to take decisions in respect of them. No doubt the applicant, in his double capacity as a user of the airlines and a leading member of an organization of users of air passenger services, has an indirect interest, as other users may have, in such proceedings and their possible outcome, but he is nevertheless not in the precise legal position of the actual addressee of a decision which may be declared void under the second paragraph of Article 173 EC [263] or in that of the potential addressee of a legal measure which the Commission has a duty to adopt with regard to him, as is the position under the third paragraph of Article 175 [265].

17 It follows that the application is inadmissible from the point of view of both Article 175 [265] and Article 173 EC [263].

## NOTES AND QUESTIONS

1. What test did the Court apply here to determine standing to bring an action under EC 232/TFEU 265? Given the nature of that test, does it seem likely that in practical terms EC 232/TFEU 265 will be largely unused? Or could there be circumstances where EC 230/TFEU 263 is not available to the applicant?

2. In the United States, review of inaction is possible under the APA, 5 U.S.C.A. Sect. 551 (13). However, while standing to bring actions relating to Agency inaction is not the barrier that it is in Europe, the Courts have tended to be very reluctant to require action, as compared with review of action taken: See, for example, *Heckler v. Chaney*, 470 U.S. 821 (1985) where the court held that an agency's refusal to initiate an enforcement proceeding was "presumptively unreviewable". Where review has been granted, the courts have then tended to focus on the same issue as surfaces in the context of standing in the European Courts. Thus, they will insist that some specific action be required, rather than a generalized rulemaking action: see, for example, *Norton v. Southern Utah Wilderness Allliance*, 542 U.S. (2004)

## COMMISSION v. T-MOBILE AUSTRIA GMBH
### Case C-141/02 P, 2005 ECJ CELEX LEXIS 728, [2005] ECR I-1283

[max.mobil (which had become T-Mobile Austria by the time this appeal was lodged) had requested the Commission to find that Austria had infringed the combined provisions of EC 82 and 86 (TFEU 102 and 106), by deciding not to take action against Austria after the Austrian authorities had allegedly unlawfully conferred advantages on its competitor, Mobilkom, in the allocation of frequencies. The CFI/General Court had declared the action admissible.]

16. The Court of First Instance first pointed out, in paragraph 48 of the judgment under appeal, that the diligent and impartial treatment of a complaint is justified by the right to sound administration of individual situations, which is one of the general principles that are common to the constitutional traditions of the Member States and which is set out in Article 41(1) of the Charter of Fundamental Rights of the European Union proclaimed at Nice on 7 December 2000 (OJ 2000 C 364, p. 1) (the Charter of Fundamental Rights').

17. The Court of First Instance went on, in paragraphs 49 and 51 of the judgment under appeal, to state that the obligation to undertake a diligent and impartial examination of a complaint has been imposed on the Commission in the areas coming under Articles 85 and 86 of the EC Treaty (now Articles 81 EC [101] and 82 EC [102]), in addition to those coming under Article 92 of the EC Treaty (now, after amendment, Article 87 EC [107]) and Article 93 of the EC Treaty (now Article 88 EC [108]). The Court of First Instance took the view that Article 90 [106] of the Treaty had to be interpreted in the same way as the Treaty provisions on competition, which expressly grant procedural rights to complainants. It took the view that max.mobil was in a situation comparable to that referred to in Article 3 of Regulation No 17 . . .

18. The Court of First Instance concluded by pointing out, in paragraphs 52 and 53 of the judgment under appeal, that the existence of an obligation to undertake a diligent and impartial examination was justified by the general duty of supervision to which the Commission is subject. That had to apply without distinction in the context of Articles 85 [101], 86 [102], 90 [106], 92 [107] and 93 [108] of the EC Treaty, even though the precise manner in which such obligations are discharged varies according to the specific areas to which they apply and, in particular, to the procedural rights expressly conferred by the Treaty or by secondary Community law in those areas on the persons concerned. Consequently, the Commission's argument, first, that Article 90 [106](3) of the Treaty did not extend to individuals and, second, that the protection of individuals was ensured by the obligations directly imposed on Member States was irrelevant.

19. In paragraph 54 of the judgment under appeal, the Court of First Instance drew a distinction between the procedures set out in Article 90 [106](3) of the Treaty and in Article 169 [258] of the EC Treaty (now Article 226 EC [258]). According to that Court, whereas under Article 169 [258] of the Treaty the Commission may' commence Treaty-infringement proceedings against a Member State, Article 90 [106](3) of the same Treaty provides, by contrast, that the Commission is to adopt the appropriate measures where necessary'. Those words indicate that the Commission must undertake a diligent and impartial examination of complaints, on completion of which it exercises its discretion as to whether there are grounds for conducting an investigation and, if there are, to decide whether to take measures against the Member State or States concerned. In contrast to the position regarding its decisions to commence Treaty-infringement proceedings under Article 169 [258] of the Treaty, the Commission's power to act on a complaint

pursuant to Article 90 [106](3) of that Treaty, although discretionary, is none the less subject to judicial review . . .

20. While the Commission enjoys a wide discretion both in relation to the action which it considers necessary to be taken and in relation to the means appropriate for that purpose . . . the Court of First Instance pointed out, in paragraphs 55 to 57 of the judgment under appeal, that, in so far as the Commission is required to undertake a diligent and impartial examination of a complaint, compliance with that obligation does not, however, mean that its decision on whether or not to take action pursuant to that complaint can avoid being amenable to the same judicial review as that in cases where infringements have been established in the areas covered by Articles 85 [101] and 86 [102] of the Treaty . . . The Court of First Instance stated further that such judicial review is also one of the general principles that are common to the constitutional traditions of the Member States, as is confirmed by Article 47 of the Charter of Fundamental Rights.

21. In order to respect the discretion of the Commission in a case where the contested measure is a Commission decision not to use the power conferred on it by Article 90 [106](3) of the Treaty, the role of the Community judicature must, in the view of the Court of First Instance, be limited to a circumscribed review in which it checks that the contested measure includes a statement of reasons which reflects due consideration of the relevant aspects of the case, that the facts are materially accurate, and that the assessment of those facts is not vitiated by any manifest error.

\*   \*   \*

68. . . . [I]ndividuals may, in certain circumstances, be entitled to bring an action for annulment against a decision which the Commission addresses to a Member State on the basis of Article 90 [106](3) of the Treaty if the conditions laid down in the fourth paragraph of Article 173 EC [263] of the EC Treaty (now, following amendment, the fourth paragraph of Article 230 [263]) are satisfied.

69. It follows, however, from the wording of Article 90 [106](3) of the Treaty and from the scheme of that article as a whole that the Commission is not obliged to bring proceedings within the terms of those provisions, as individuals cannot require the Commission to take a position in a specific sense.

70. The fact that max.mobil has a direct and individual interest in annulment of the Commission's decision to refuse to act on its complaint is not such as to confer on it a right to challenge that decision. The letter by which the Commission informed max.mobil that it was not intending to bring proceedings against the Republic of Austria cannot be regarded as producing binding legal effects, with the result that it is not a challengeable measure that is capable of being the subject of an action for annulment.

71. Nor can max.mobil claim a right to bring an action pursuant to Regulation No 17, which is not applicable to Article 90 [106] of the Treaty.

72. That finding is not at variance with the principle of sound administration or with any other general principle of Community law. No general principle of Community law requires that an undertaking be recognised as having standing before the

Community judicature to challenge a refusal by the Commission to bring proceedings against a Member State on the basis of Article 90 [106] (3) of the Treaty.

73. The max.mobil company did not therefore have standing to bring an action before the Court of First Instance challenging the Commission's decision to refuse to pursue and sanction an alleged infringement of the rules on competition resulting from the decision by the Austrian Government not to draw a distinction between the amount of the fee charged to max.mobil and that charged to its competitor, Mobilkom, for the operation of their mobile telephony networks.

74. It must accordingly be held that the Court of First Instance erred in declaring the action brought by max.mobil against the contested measure to be admissible.

## NOTES AND QUESTIONS

1. In *Bundesverband der Bilanzbuchhalter e.V. v. Commission*, Case C-107/95 P., 1997 ECJ CELEX LEXIS 225; 1997 ECR I-947, (which was cited in the above case) the Court had stated that: "The possibility cannot be ruled out that exceptional situations might exist where an individual or, possibly, an association constituted for the defence of the collective interests of a class of individuals has standing to bring proceedings against a refusal by the Commission to adopt a decision pursuant to its supervisory functions under Article 90 [106] (1) and (3)." The T-Mobile judgment reflected a rather pragmatic acceptance by the ECJ that the Member States would have been exceptionally annoyed to discover that private parties could force the Commission to act against them. Why, though, did the ECJ also object even to the very limited scope of review suggested by the CFI/General Court?

It is clear that generally the ECJ has denied private parties the right to have the Commission take action under EC 86/TFEU 106(3). In *Netherlands, Koninklijke PTT Nederland NV and PTT Post BV v. Commission (Express Delivery Services)*, Joined Cases C-48/90 and 66/90, 1992 ECJ CELEX LEXIS 144, [1992] ECR I-13 the Court indicated one exception — where the Commission had declared that a Dutch law granting an exclusive franchise to the Dutch Post Office (PTT) infringed inter alia, EC 90 (EC 86/TFEU 106] (1). The Court held that these undertakings were the direct beneficiaries of the State measure at issue and that they are expressly named in the Postal Law, that the contested decision related directly to them and that the economic consequences of that decision directly affected them. However, this is clearly a different situation from the one arising in cases such as max.mobil.

2. In practice, EC 232/TFEU 265 has proved largely ineffective for private litigants because the article requires that the act requested be one that the EU institution is required to address to them. Once again, where executive decisions are involved concerning individuals, such as in competition cases under EC 81 and 82/TFEU 101 and 102, a complaint of inaction under EC 232/TFEU 265 *can be* successfully invoked. See the CFI/General Court decision in *Ladbroke Racing (Deutschland) GmbH v. Commission*, Case T-74/92, 1995 ECJ CELEX LEXIS 26, [1995] ECR II-115, [this case was not appealed although a subsequent related dispute on other issues was successfully appealed in favor of the Commission] The

CFI/General Court considered that the applicant (Ladbroke) did have standing to complain of a failure of the Commission to act on a complaint under (former) Regulation 17/62 referencing EC 82/TFEU 102. The Commission had already initiated a review of the conduct in question under EC 81/TFEU 101 and did not respond specifically to the EC 82/TFEU 102 issue. The CFI/General Court held that it should have and that the complainant had standing to assert EC 232/TFEU 265.

**3.** As the title to this section indicates, in practice the distinction between EC 230/TFEU 263 and EC 232/TFEU 265 might seem blurred. There is, after all, always a "decision" somewhere in the process, even if the decision is purely an internal conclusion not to take any action. However, such a decision, remaining purely internal, and not communicated outside the institution (e.g., the implied decision in the *Ladbroke* case, see Note 2 above) is not dispositive of the applicant's legal position, but only preparatory to the taking of a formal decision. The rationale is that such a decision could always be revisited until it is communicated to the applicant. Thus, using EC 230/TFEU 263 in this context is inappropriate — EC 232/TFEU 265 is the correct basis for a challenge if the applicant has a right to a response that is not forthcoming.

It follows that, by contrast, where a decision not to act *is* communicated to the applicant, it may become challengeable under EC 230/TFEU 263, as long as it has a legal effect on the applicant. This is well illustrated by *Athinaiki*, Case C-521/06 P, 2008 ECJ EUR-Lex LEXIS 2077, [2008] ECR I-5829, where the applicant sought an annulment of a conclusion to take no action under article EC 88(3)/TFEU 108(3)) that was notified to the applicant by the Commission (the applicant having complained). The CFI/General Court had concluded that the applicant's action was not admissible since the action was merely preparatory to any decision under EC 88(2)/TFEU 108(2)) (following the *IBM* approach — see Chapter 5 *supra*). The ECJ disagreed, however, and held that the Commission's action had the legal effect of halting the process and thus deprived the applicant of any rights under EC 88(2)/TFEU 108(2)).

**4.** The question of whether an act is a decision or not is not an entirely theoretical argument. If a decision does have a dispositive effect, and the applicant continues to wait for what it believes is some further act that never ensues, it may be barred by the two-month time limit if it eventually challenges a failure to act based on EC 232/TFEU 265).

**5.** For a review of the state of *locus standi* generally, see C Koch, *Locus standi of private applicants under the EU Constitution: Preserving gaps in the protection of individuals' right to an effective remedy*, (2005) 30 EL Rev. 511.

## § 8.06   THE PLEA OF ILLEGALITY

### SIMMENTHAL S.P.A. v. COMMISSION
Case 92/78, [1979] ECR 777

[Italian agricultural intervention authorities had solicited bids for the purchase of beef, and applicant Simmenthal had submitted one. Before the Italian authorities ruled on the bid, the Commission addressed a decision (78/258) to the Member States that fixed maximum quantities and minimum prices for beef sales by national intervention agencies. Simmenthal's bid was then rejected by the Italian authorities on the ground that it fell outside the allowable limits. In its EC 230/TFEU 263 action to annul the decision, Simmenthal invoked EC 241/TFEU 277 to challenge both regulations and "notices of invitation to tender" that formed the basis for the guidelines set forth in the Commission's decision. The Court held that the Decision itself was of direct and individual concern to the Applicant.]

34 While the applicant formally challenges Commission Decision No 78/258 it has at the same time criticized, in reliance on article 184 [277] of the EEC Treaty, certain aspects of the "linking" system in the form in which it has been implemented pursuant to the new Article 14 of Regulation No 805/68, by Regulation No 2900/77 and No 2901/77 and also by the notices of invitations to tender of 13 January 1978.

\* \* \*

37 [T]here are grounds for questioning whether Article 184 [277] applies to the notices of invitations to tender of 13 January 1978 when according to its wording it only provides for the calling in question of "regulations".

38 These notices are general acts which determine in advance and objectively the rights and obligations of the traders who wish to participate in the invitations to tender which these notices make public.

39 . . . Article 184 [277] of the EEC Treaty gives expression to a general principle conferring upon any party to proceedings the right to challenge, for the purpose of obtaining the annulment of a decision of direct and individual concern to that party, the validity of previous acts of the institutions which form the legal basis of the decision which is being attacked, if that party was not entitled under Article 173 EC [263] of the Treaty to bring a direct action challenging those acts [and] by which it was thus affected without having been in a position to ask that they be declared void.

40 The field of application of the said article must therefore include acts of the institutions which, although they are not in the form of a regulation, nevertheless produce similar effects and on those grounds may not be challenged under Article 173 EC [263] by natural or legal persons other than Community institutions and Member States.

41 This wide interpretation of Article 184 [277] derives from the need to provide those persons who are precluded by the second paragraph of Article 173 EC [263] from instituting proceedings directly in respect of general acts with the benefit of a judicial review of them at the time when they are affected by implementing decisions which are of direct and individual concern to them.

42 The notices of invitations to tender of 13 January 1978 in respect of which the applicant was unable to initiate proceedings are a case in point, seeing that only the decision taken in consequence of the tender which it had submitted in answer to a specific invitation to tender could be of direct and individual concern to it.

43 There are therefore good grounds for declaring that the applicant's challenge during the proceedings under Article 184 [277], which relates not only to the above-mentioned regulations but also to the notices of invitations to tender of 13 January 1978, is admissible, although the latter are not in the strict sense measures laid down by regulation.

[Turning to the merits of the case, the Court held that the regulations and notices were invalid, annulled the Commission's decision that was based on them, and remanded the matter to the Commission and the Italian authorities.]

## NOTES AND QUESTIONS

1.   What did this case say about the scope of a party's ability to invoke EC 241/TFEU 277?

2.   Note that in *Simmenthal* the Court of Justice opines that EC 241/TFEU 277 of the EC Treaty "gives expression to a general principle conferring upon any party to proceedings the right to challenge [acts of the Community] if that party was not entitled under EC 230 EC/TFEU 263 of the Treaty to bring a direct action challenging those acts [and] by which it was thus affected without having been in a position to ask that they be declared void." It appears that a Member State that had standing to challenge an act and chose not to, loses the right to invoke EC 241/TFEU 277. Thus, in *National Farmers Union v. Secrétariat Général du Gouvernement*, Case C-241/01 2002 ECJ CELEX LEXIS 606, [2002] ECR I-9079, the Court ruled that a Member State that was an addressee of various Commission Decisions and that had not challenged the legality of those decisions within the time limit laid down by the fifth paragraph of Article 173 EC [263] did not have standing subsequently before a national court to invoke their unlawfulness in order to dispute the merits of an action brought against it. (This may also be the case for individuals who have a right to seek annulment — see Chapter 9, *infra*.)

However, it may also be the case that in exceptional circumstances a Member State could invoke EC 241/TFEU 277 if the defects in the legislation in question are extremely serious — see *Commission v. Greece*, Case 226/87 *infra*.

3.   EC 241/TFEU 277 can also be invoked in national proceedings (*University of Hamburg*, Case 216/82, [1983] ECR 2787) against national action based on an EU decision or regulation, but in this case it may be more a question of applying the general rule that the validity of EU legislation is in any event challengeable in the national courts because the matter has to be referred to the ECJ under EC 234/TFEU 267. See also *Hessische Knappschaft v. Maison Singer et Fils*, Case 44/65 [1965] ECR 970.

4.   For an analysis of the plea of illegality, see, e.g., M. Vogt, *Indirect Judicial Protection in EC Law: The Case of the Plea of Illegality*, (2006) 31 EL REV. 364.

## § 8.07 CLAIMS FOR DAMAGES AGAINST EU INSTITUTIONS

### [A] An Autonomous Cause of Action

## MERKUR-AUßENHANDELS-GMBH v. COMMISSION
### Case 43/72, [1973] ECR 1055

[Merkur sought compensation for the damage it suffered owing to the Commission's failure to fix compensatory amounts, as envisaged by Article 1 of Regulation No 974/71 of the Council of 12 May 1971 (OJ L 106, p. 1), for exports of products processed from barley for the period from 12 May to 2 August 1971.]

2 Thereby, it is alleged, the Commission infringed both the above Regulation and the rule against discrimination contained in Article 40 of the EEC Treaty, and these infringements involve the Community in liability under the second paragraph of Article 215 [340] of the Treaty.

The infringements arise either from the fact that Regulation No 1014/71 of 17 May 1971. . . . in force during the period referred to above, made no provision for compensatory amounts on exports of products processed from barley, or from the fact that the Commission did not give retrospective effect to Regulation No 1687/71 of 30 July 1971. . . . which came into force on 2 August 1971 and provided for the amounts to be granted on these products.

Admissibility

3 While it has made no formal objection on the point, the Commission has expressed doubt as to whether a claim for damages can be admissible, as the Court has already decided, when, by challenging the legality of a Community regulation, it seeks a financial result, identical or similar to that which would arise from the annulment of the regulation, although an application by the applicant for such an annulment would not itself be admissible.

4 However, the action for damages provided for in Articles 178 [268] and 215 [340] of the Treaty was included as an autonomous form of action, with a particular purpose to fulfil within the system of actions, and subject to conditions on its use by its specific nature.

Such an action differs from an application for annulment in that its end is not the cancellation of a particular measure but compensation for damage caused by an institution in the performance of its duties.

The action for damages seeks only recognition that a right to compensation exists and, therefore, satisfaction solely for the benefit of the applicant.

5 The Commission then maintains that the applicant should be sent back to pursue its claim before the administrative and judicial authorities in the Federal Republic of Germany, on the grounds that the event giving rise to the present dispute was the refusal by the competent customs office in that Member State to grant the applicant compensatory amounts on the exports it had made to third countries.

If such a procedure were followed it would result in a reference to the Court under Article 177 [267] of the Treaty from the German courts of the question of the validity of Regulations Nos 1014/71 and 1687/71.

6 But the Court already has the case before it and within its jurisdiction, and is therefore bound to see whether or not these regulations are tainted with the alleged irregularities.

It would not be in keeping with the proper administration of justice and the requirements of procedural efficiency to compel the applicant to have recourse to national remedies and thus to wait for a considerable length of time before a final decision on his claim is made.

7 The action is therefore admissible.

## NOTES AND QUESTIONS

1. Does this case support an action under EC 235/TFEU 268 if the underlying purpose is to achieve the same result as if the act in question had been annulled? Why might that be objectionable?

2. What is the consequence of an award under EC 235/TFEU 268? Is the act complained of still enforceable against other parties?

3. The same issue arose in the *Tillack* case set out below regarding a complaint against the Commission's anti-fraud agency, OLAF (see Chapter 7) where the court reiterated its position in the following terms:

> 96 In relation to the claim for damages regarding OLAF's 'complaint', the Commission also submits that that claim is inadmissible since it is closely linked to an action for annulment which itself is inadmissible.

> 97 In that regard, the action to establish liability is an autonomous form of action, with a particular purpose to fulfil within the system of legal remedies and subject to conditions of use dictated by its specific purpose. Although actions for annulment and for failure to act seek a declaration that a legally binding measure is unlawful or that such a measure has not been taken, an action to establish liability seeks compensation for damage resulting from a measure or from unlawful conduct, attributable to a Community institution or body . . .

> 98 Thus, individuals who, by reasons of the conditions as to admissibility laid down under the fourth paragraph of Article 173 EC [263], cannot contest directly certain Community acts or measures, none the less have the opportunity of putting in issue conduct lacking the features of a decision, which accordingly cannot be challenged by way of an action for annulment, by bringing an action for non-contractual liability under Article 235 EC and the second paragraph of Article 288 EC, where such conduct is of such a nature as to entail liability for the Community . . .

> 99 Therefore, the admissibility of the action for damages brought by the applicant seeking compensation for the non-material harm which he

allegedly suffered as a result of the misconduct which OLAF is accused of must be considered independently of the action for annulment.

# SA BIOVILAC NV v. EUROPEAN ECONOMIC COMMUNITY
## Case 59/83, [1984] ECR 4057

[Since 1978 Biovilac had manufactured and marketed Kulactic and since 1980 Bioblanca, two basic feedingstuffs for piglets and poultry made from whey. It sought compensation for the damage which it allegedly suffered as a result of the enactment and implementation of certain Commission regulations. The alleged damage — an appreciable reduction in the sales of its products since November 1982 and a drastic reduction in those sales since 1 March 1983 — was alleged to be caused by those regulations.]

5 In the Commission's view, the applicant ought to have brought its action for damages in the national courts since it is directed above all against measures which the national authorities adopted in implementation of Community law, namely the sales of skimmed-milk powder at reduced prices by the intervention agencies.

6 It must be observed with regard to that objection that in its application the applicant does not challenge the measures adopted by the national authorities to implement Community law but the Commission's measures themselves since it is clear from its arguments that it complains that . . . the establishment of the scheme [under the regulation] by the Commission caused the damage for which it claims compensation.

7 It follows from the above observations that the Court has jurisdiction in this case and that it must therefore examine the question whether the enactment of those regulations may give rise to liability on the part of the Community by virtue of its legislative action. The objection of inadmissibility based upon the failure to have recourse to national remedies must therefore be rejected.

## NOTES AND QUESTIONS

1. On what grounds could the Commission argue that the plaintiffs ought to have sought a remedy in national law before instituting proceedings in the Court of Justice?

2. The joint liability issue first arose in *Kampffmeyer v. Commission*, Joined Cases 5, 7, 13-24/66, [1967] ECR 245. As will be seen in Chapter 11, *infra*, much of the actual implementation of the agricultural policy has been left in the hands of the Member States' authorities. In this case the German Government had taken safeguard measures that the Commission had upheld but that the Court in another case had ruled illegal. The Court accepted that the Commission's acts were wrongful but stated that before determining the damage for which the EU should be held liable, it was necessary for the national court to have the opportunity to give judgment on any liability on the part of Germany. This being the case, final judgment could not be given before the applicants had produced the decision of the national court on the matter.

The plaintiffs were in fact sent backward and forward between the national courts and the ECJ for over seven years before the German court gave judgment in their favor.

The essential problem here was that both the Member States and the EU were responsible. This can arise where the EU has failed to take steps it should have taken to prevent a breach by a Member State, and where the Member State faithfully implements an illegal EU act. (See, e.g., *R. and V. Haegeman Sprl v. Commission*, Case 96/71 [1972] ECR 1005.

A somewhat related issue has also arisen in the context of EC 230/TFEU 263. In *Rau v. BALM*, Joined Cases 133-136/85, 1987 ECJ CELEX LEXIS 146, [1987] ECR 2289, the Court considered what should happen where actions could be brought under EC 230 and 234/TFEU 263 and 267 at the same time:

> 9 [T]he possibility of bringing a direct action under the second paragraph of Article 173 EC [263] of the EEC Treaty against a decision adopted by a Community institution does not preclude the possibility of bringing an action in a national court against a measure adopted by a national authority for the implementation of that decision on the ground that the latter decision is unlawful".

## [B]    Tort Liability?

### CLAUDE SAYAG AND S.A. ZURICH v. JEAN-PIERRE LEDUC, DENISE THONNON AND S.A. LA CONCORDE
#### Case 9/69, [1969] ECR 329

[This case arose under the EAEC Treaty involving identical provisions to those in the then EEC Treaty. The plaintiff was injured as a result of an accident that occurred while an EAEC official was driving his private car on EAEC business and was in possession of a "travel order".]

4 This gives rise to the first question whether, while not acting in his official capacity within the meaning of Article 11 of the Protocol on the Privileges and Immunities annexed to the EAEC Treaty, such an official may be considered to be acting in the performance of his duties within the meaning of the second paragraph of Article 188 of that Treaty.

5 As regards non-contractual liability, the Treaty subjects the Community to rules forming part of the Community legal system and which impose on it a uniform system in compensating for damage caused by its institutions and by its servants in the performance of their duties.

6 The Treaty ensures the uniform application of this system and the independence of the institutions of the Community by giving the Court of Justice jurisdiction in disputes in this matter.

7 By referring at one and the same time to damage caused by the institutions and to that caused by the servants of the Community, Article 188 indicates that the Community is only liable for those acts of its servants which, by virtue of an internal

and direct relationship, are the necessary extension of the tasks entrusted to the institutions.

8 In the light of the special nature of this legal system, it would not therefore be lawful to extend it to categories of acts other than those referred to above.

9 A servant's use of his private car for transport during the performance of his duties does not satisfy the conditions set out above.

10 A reference to a servant's private car in a travel order does not bring the driving of such car within the performance of his duties, but is basically intended to enable any necessary reimbursement of the travel expenses involved in the use of this means of transport to be made in accordance with the standards laid down for this purpose.

11 Only in the case of force majeure or in exceptional circumstances of such overriding importance that without the servant's using private means of transport the Community would have been unable to carry out the tasks entrusted to it, could such use be considered to form part of the servant's performance of his duties, within the meaning of the second paragraph of Article 188 of the Treaty.

12 It follows from the above that the driving of a private car by a servant cannot in principle constitute the performance of his duties within the meaning of the second paragraph of Article 188 of the EAEC Treaty.

## NOTES AND QUESTIONS

**1.** In *Sayag*, the Court determined that article 188(2) of the EAEC Treaty, which is identical to EC 288/TFEU 340 (2), did not cover an event that in the U.S. would be considered a government tort. Why not? What is the purpose of EC 288/TFEU 340?

**2.** After the Court's decision in *Sayag*, what, if any, remedies are available to Mr. Leduc and Mr. van Hassan to recover damages for their injuries suffered during the accident caused by Mr. Sayag? Are these remedies satisfactory?

**3.** Is there any equivalent in the United States to the concept embodied in EC 288/TFEU 340? Given the manner in which judicial review arises in the U.S. system, could damages be obtained against a federal agency or the U.S. Congress for unconstitutional acts? What, for example, of the internment of persons of Japanese origin during World War II?

### ISMERI EUROPA SRL v. COURT OF AUDITORS
Case T-277/97, 1999 ECJ CELEX LEXIS 131, [1999] ECR II-1825

[Aid from the European Union to Mediterranean non-member States was granted within the framework of the "MED" Programs. They were designed so as to make it possible to develop decentralised cooperation. Under those programmes, partners from Member States of the European Union and from the Mediterranean basin which form networks of four to eight members amongst themselves were entrusted with the realisation of a project planned by themselves. Since it lacked sufficient own resources to enable it to manage the MED programs itself, the

Commission subcontracted their administration and financial management to the Agence pour les Réseaux Transmediterranéens (Agency for Trans-Mediterranean Networks — ARTM), a non-profit-making organisation established by it under Belgian law specifically for this task. The technical monitoring functions were contracted out to Technical Assistance Bureaux (BATs), which were usually consultancy firms, including the applicant. The Court of Auditors published a report in which it described a number of serious shortcomings on the part of Ismeri, which, as a result, lost its contract. One of the arguments made by Ismeri was that the report was defamatory.]

108 The Court notes that, under the first subparagraph of Article 188c [287](2) of the Treaty, the Court of Auditors is required to examine whether all revenue has been received and all expenditure incurred by the Community in a lawful and regular manner and whether financial management has been sound. Under paragraph 4 of that provision, it is to submit its observations either in the annual report or in the form of special reports.

109 Actuated by the concern to ensure that its tasks are properly carried out, the Court of Auditors may exceptionally, and in particular where there is a serious malfunction affecting the lawfulness and regularity of revenue and expenditure or the requirements of sound financial management, make a full report on the facts established and give the names of any third parties directly involved. The naming of those involved is all the more necessary where anonymity may give rise to confusion or cast doubt on their identity, which is liable to harm the interests of those concerned by the investigation of the Court of Auditors but not implicated by its critical assessments.

110 In those circumstances, the assessments made concerning third parties are fully subject to review by the Court of First Instance. They may constitute maladministration and thus give rise, where appropriate, to non-contractual liability on the part of the Community, if either the facts reported are not substantively correct or the interpretation placed on facts which are substantively correct is erroneous or one-sided.

## NOTES AND QUESTIONS

1.   Cases such as *Ismeri* and *Sayag* might be thought to raise the question as to whether it will be necessary to develop an EU concept of tort for matters such as negligence and defamation. But is this how the Court sees it? Is tort even the right concept to apply here?

## [C]   Claims Arising From Legislative or Regulatory Acts

### HOLTZ & WILLEMSEN GMBH v. COUNCIL AND COMMISSION
Case 153/73, [1974] ECR 675

[The applicant sought compensation for the damage caused to it by the unlawful acts of the Council and Commission in that, within the framework of the common organization of the market in oils and fats established by Regulation No 136/66, an additional subsidy was introduced by Regulation No 876/67 which was renewed from year to year and limited to colza and rape seed harvested in the Community and processed in Italy. The subsidy had been introduced on a temporary basis to alleviate hardship incurred by Italian mills as a result of the introduction of the common organization of the oils and fats market due to the cost advantages enjoyed by French oil producers who were now free to sell in Italy. The applicant, operating in Germany, sought damages representing the amount which it would have received during the years 1969 to 1972 if the additional subsidy had been granted to all the Community oil mills on the basis of the sole criterion of their distance from the production areas. It was argued that the Regulations in question constituted an infringement of the rule prohibiting any discrimination contained in the first paragraph of Article 7 (EC 12/TFEU 18) [1] and the second paragraph of Article 40 (3) of the EEC Treaty (EC 34/TFEU 40).]

6 The applicant bases its action in the first place on the fact that the additional subsidy granted to Italian oil mills constitutes discrimination on grounds of nationality and infringes the first paragraph of Article 7 [18] of the Treaty.

The applicant states that, under the second paragraph of Article 40 [34] (3) of the Treaty, which applies the general principle set out in Article 7 [18] to agricultural policy, if different treatment had been accorded to the Italian oil mills, not by reason of their nationality but because of their distance from the production areas, it should have enjoyed the same subsidy as the oil mills in northern Italy.

The applicant does not base its action on the fact that the Council and the Commission have respectively decided and proposed additional subsidy for Italian oil mills, but on the fact that this rule does not apply equally to it.

7 Under the second paragraph of Article 215 [340] of the Treaty and the general principles to which this provision refers, Community responsibility depends on the coincidence of a set of conditions as regards the unlawfulness of the acts alleged against the institutions, the fact of damage, and the existence of a direct link in the chain of causality between the wrongful act and the damage complained of.

Since it relates to a legislative act which involves the choice of economic policy, the Community is not liable for any damage suffered by individuals as a consequence of this act under the provisions of Article 215 [340], second paragraph, of the Treaty, unless a sufficiently flagrant violation of a superior rule of law for the protection of the individual has occurred.

8 Regulation No 136/66/EEC of the Council of 22 September 1966, which entered

into force on 1 October 1966, has applied since 1 July 1967 to colza and rape seed and to oil produced therefrom.

This Regulation aims, by means of a system of basic intervention prices and derived intervention prices, at alleviating the burden of transport costs to the oil mills for the seeds of colza products in the various areas.

9 Since difficulties arose in Italy on the opening of the inter-Community frontiers on the coming into force of Regulation No 136/66, in particular from the fact the colza oil produced in France was available on the Italian market at prices considerably lower than those of oil produced in Italy, the Italian Government requested authority from the Commission to bring in protective measures under Article 226 [258] of the Treaty.

10 On the Commission rejecting this request by Decision dated 11 October 1967, the Council, by Regulation No 876/67, issued under Article 36 of Regulation No 136/66, introduced an 'additional subsidy' amounting to 0.675 u.a. per 100 kg of seed for 'colza and rape seed harvested in the Community which is sent during the course of the 1967/68 marketing year to an oil mill in Italian territory' in order to be processed.

Regulation No 876/67 justifies the grant of additional subsidy on the ground that 'pending a more thorough examination of the causes of the difficulties (encountered in Italy in the oil seed crushing industry) and of production conditions in the Community, the said difficulties can be lessened during the present marketing year by the grant of (such) a subsidy'.

11 This subsidy was repeated for the 1968/69 to 1973/74 marketing years by Regulations of the Council.

\*     \*     \*

12 The defendants have stated that the difficulties which these rules aim at lessening are caused in particular by the fact that transport costs of 100 kg of colza seed from France to Italy are higher than that of the 41 kg of oil which they contain, so that in spite of the system introduced by Regulation No 136/66 to offset the transport costs of seed, French oil could come onto the Italian market at a lower price than that of oil produced in the country from seed harvested in France.

13 The additional subsidy in question is thus intended to compensate for the disadvantages in competition caused to the Italian mills far from the Community production areas by the structure of the common organization of the market.

\*     \*     \*

14 Although it is incumbent upon the institutions responsible to seek with all due diligence the causes of such difficulties and to adapt the regulations on the common organization of the markets as soon as possible to remedy the defects revealed, they are at liberty, in the meantime, to take provisional measures, which are limited to those Member States in which the market has been more particularly affected.

15 Such would appear to have been the case with regard to Regulation No 876/67 and the Regulations which re-enacted it.

Although the explanation given by the defendants, according to which the introduction of French oils at prices very much less than the cost price of Italian oil mills was due to the difference in transport costs of the oil processed in France in relation to that from colza seed from French centers of production, is not altogether satisfactory, it is however apparent that the institution of the common organization of the markets in oils and fats has produced a new situation prejudicial to the Italian market in oil products.

The Council could therefore issue a provisional measure intended to lessen the difficulties limited to the Italian oil mills.

16 The applicant has not claimed that at the time comparable difficulties had arisen on the German market, in particular in so far as it is concerned.

17 Although the Council has therefore not infringed Article 40 (3) [34(2)] of the Treaty, it must nevertheless be admitted that the provisional nature inherent in such a measure risks disappearing as soon as it has succeeded in excluding for any length of time undertakings of a Member State from the common organization of the market.

18 Having regard to the nature of the problems involved, by putting an end to the measures after the 1973/74 marketing year, the Council has respected their provisional nature.

The action is therefore not valid in law and must be rejected.

## NOTES AND QUESTIONS

1. As indicated in the above case, the ECJ has determined that in cases where the act complained of results from the exercise of a discretionary power by an EU institution, damages are only available where there has been a breach of a "superior rule of law or the protection of the individual." What does this mean?

2. The applicant in the above case had asserted a breach of the principle of non-discrimination on the basis of EC12/TFEU 18 and EC 34/TFEU 40. Did the Court consider that the principles contained in those provisions were not superior rules of law by the Court? Or did it conclude that the principle had not been breached? What was the significance of the reference to the transitional nature of the measure complained of?

3. There must also be a causal link between the act complained of and the damage. Does it follow that this link should arise specifically out of the breach of the superior rule of law?

## DORSCH CONSULT INGENIEURGESELLSCHAFT MBH v. COUNCIL AND COMMISSION
### Case C-237/982000 ECJ EUR-Lex LEXIS 1002;2000 ECR I-04549

[*Following is an abbreviated version of the Court's summary of the facts.* In 1975, Dorsch Consult had concluded with the Ministry of Works and Housing of the Republic of Iraq (hereinafter "the Iraqi Ministry") a contract for services relating to the organisation and supervision of works on the construction of Iraqi Expressway No 1. The contract, which was for a minimum period of six years, was subsequently renewed several times for the purposes of execution and supervision of the abovementioned works. Outstanding debts owed to the applicant by the Iraqi authorities at the beginning of 1990 for services rendered under the abovementioned contract were acknowledged in two letters, dated 5 and 6 February 1990, from the Iraqi Ministry to an Iraqi bank, Rafidian Bank, directing it to transfer the sums due to the applicant to the latter's bank account.

As a consequence of the invasion of Kuwait, the UN Security Council adopted certain resolutions imposing an embargo on trade with Iraq. Consequently, the EU Council adopted Regulation No. 2340/90. Article 1 prohibited as from 7 August 1990 the introduction into the territory of the Community of all commodities or products originating in, or coming from, Iraq or Kuwait and the export to those countries of all commodities or products originating in, or coming from, the Community. Article 2 prohibited as from 7 August 1990 (a) all activities or commercial transactions, including all operations connected with transactions which have already been concluded or partially carried out, the object or effect of which is to promote the export of any commodity or product originating in, or coming from, Iraq or Kuwait; (b) the sale or supply of any commodity or product, wherever it originates or comes from, to any natural or legal person in Iraq or Kuwait or to any other natural or legal person for the purposes of any commercial activity carried out in or from the territory of Iraq or Kuwait; and (c) any activity the object or effect of which is to promote such sales or supplies.

On 16 September 1990 the "Higher Revolutionary Council of the Republic of Iraq", referring to "arbitrary decisions by certain governments", adopted with retroactive effect from 6 August 1990 Law No 57 on protection of Iraqi property, interests and rights in Iraq and elsewhere (hereinafter "Law No 57"). Article 7 of that Law froze all property and assets and income from them held at the material time by the governments, undertakings, companies and banks of those States which had adopted "arbitrary decisions" against Iraq.

Not having received payment from the Iraqi authorities of the sums acknowledged as due, Dorsch Consult asked the Council and the Commission to compensate it for the damage suffered as a result of those debts having become irrecoverable through application of Law No 57, since that Law had been adopted in response to the adoption by the Community of Regulation No 2340/90. The Council denied liability.

Dorsch Consult asked the CFI/General Court to hold the Community liable, principally, on the basis of the principle of the Community's liability for lawful acts, because its property rights had been infringed in a way equivalent to an expropriation and, in the alternative, on the basis of the principle of liability for an unlawful act, the unlawful act having consisted in this case in the failure by the Community legislature, when adopting that regulation, to establish a procedure for compensating economic operators for the loss caused by that regulation. The claim failed in the CFI/General Court, and Dorsch Consult appealed to the ECJ.]

17 It should be pointed out at the outset that the Court of First Instance has rightly pointed out . . . that it is settled law of the Court of Justice that if the Community is to incur non-contractual liability as a result of a lawful or unlawful act, it is

necessary in any event to prove that the alleged damage is real and that a causal link exists between that act and the alleged damage . . .

18 The Court of First Instance also rightly considered that it is clear from the relevant case-law that, in the event of the principle of Community liability for a lawful act being recognised in Community law, a precondition for such liability would in any event be the existence of unusual and special damage . . .

19 It follows that the Community cannot incur non-contractual liability in respect of a lawful act, as in the present case, unless the three conditions referred to in the two preceding paragraphs, namely the reality of the damage allegedly suffered, the causal link between it and the act on the part of the Community institutions, and the unusual and special nature of that damage, are all fulfilled.

## NOTES AND QUESTIONS

**1.** This case might be seen as an illustration of the so-called "Equality of burden" concept, where a lawful act may give rise to compensation by the authorities if it places an unfair burden on particular individuals. Although it appears at first sight to be an unfamiliar concept in Anglo-American jurisprudence, does it actually have an approximate counterpart in U.S. law? Does the Court reject the proposition that such claims might be made in EU law?

**2.** The *Dorsch* judgment does not allude specifically to a principle of EU law that a party that is asked to bear a special burden incurred through adoption of a lawful act should be entitled to compensation. Does the ECJ in effect accept that principle? If the act has such a consequence, why not treat it as unlawful?

**3.** In *FIAMM and FIAMM Technologies v. Council and Commission*, Joined Cases C-120/06 P and C-121/06 P, 2008 ECJ EUR-Lex LEXIS 2138, [2008] ECR I-6513, the ECJ appears to have rejected the notion of undue burden as a ground for compensation where the act in question is not unlawful.

**4.** In practice, the question of damages in the case of legal acts may well be of little importance. If the issue mainly revolves around the "unfair burden" concept, individuals might be better off arguing that the act violates fundamental rights relating to equality of treatment or deprivation of property, such that the acts would in fact be considered illegal, if they meet the test generally applied to regulatory acts, as set out in section [B] above.

## [D]   Claims Arising From Executive Decisions

### COMMISSION v. CAMAR SRL AND TICO SRL
Case C-312/00 P, 2002 ECJ CELEX LEXIS 338, [2002] ECR I-11355

[This is one of many legal proceedings in the history of the EU's ill-fated attempt to set up a common organization in bananas and then to adjust that organization to implement the GATT Uruguay Round agreements. Prior to these agreements, bananas had been imported based on member-State quota schemes. For countries with historic ties to African, Caribbean or Pacific nations (the ACP nations) — for example, France, Italy and the United Kingdom — their supplies had come almost exclusively from those countries. Under the Uruguay agreements, the EU was required to open up its markets to non traditional sources. It therefore introduced a common organization of the market with transitional measures to protect existing traders and producers. (Regulation 404/93 [1993] OJ L 47/1).

Under this regime, zero tariff quotas were granted to importers by categories — with Category A covering imports from non-traditional sources while Category B covered traditional (ACP) sources, which were based on historic levels of imports. Imports in excess of these quotas would be subject to a customs duty. The transitional regime included some safeguards in the case where there might be a disruption of supply from any of the ACP countries. Article 30 of Regulation 404, provided for the adoption of measures to

> to assist the transition from arrangements existing before the entry into force of this Regulation to those laid down by this Regulation, and in particular to overcome difficulties of a sensitive nature, the Commission, acting in accordance with the procedure laid down in Article 27, shall take any transitional measures it judges necessary.

Camar had been set up in 1983 to import bananas into Italy from Somalia (a traditional source). After the startup of the common organization, it suffered severe supply disruptions due to the civil war and then climatic variations occasioned by the fluctuations in the El Nino current. It appealed to the Commission for assistance (specifically the right to import replacement supplies from other countries at a zero tariff) but the Commission rejected the requests (inter alia the decision of July 17, 1997). It did so, it appears, based on an interpretation by the ECJ in a previous case (T-Port) of Article 30 to the effect that the provision could only be applied where the existence of the enterprise was threatened. The applicant was particularly aggrieved after seeing the Commission grant relief to various Caribbean nations that had suffered devastation from various hurricanes. Among other claims, Camar sought in case 260/97 compensation for what it considered a breach by the Commission of its duty under article 30. It argued that under the previous Italian scheme it would have been able to receive assistance, so its losses were a direct result of the less flexible nature of the common organization under regulation 404. It further argued that the Commission was incorrect to base its conclusions on whether or not Camar's continued existence was threatened.

The CFI/General Court annulled the Commission's decisions and awarded compensation. It found that the Commission had committed a manifest error of judgement in concluding that Camar would be unable to deal with the crisis it faced unless Article 30 were applied, annulled the decision and awarded damages. The illegality of the decision, the CFI/General Court concluded, was enough to justify a damage award under EC 235/TFEU 268. The Commission appealed (with the Council intervening).]

52. As for the Council's ground of appeal complaining that the Court of First Instance based itself, in order to hold the Commission liable, on its case-law according to which, in the field of administrative action, any infringement of the law constitutes illegality that is capable of rendering the Community liable, it is appropriate to point out that the system of rules which the Court has worked out in relation to the non-contractual liability of the Community takes into account, inter

alia, the complexity of the situations to be regulated, difficulties in the application or interpretation of the texts and, more particularly, the margin of discretion available to the author of the act in question . . .

53. It is appropriate to point out also that, Community law confers a right to reparation where three conditions are met: the rule of law infringed must be intended to confer rights on individuals; the breach must be sufficiently serious; and there must be a direct causal link between the breach of the obligation resting on the author of the act and the damage sustained by the injured parties . . .

54. As to the second condition, the decisive test for finding that a breach of Community law is sufficiently serious is whether the Community institution concerned manifestly and gravely disregarded the limits on its discretion . . . Where that institution has only considerably reduced, or even no, discretion, the mere infringement of Community law may be sufficient to establish the existence of a sufficiently serious breach . . .

55. It follows from the foregoing that the decisive test for determining whether there has been such an infringement is not the individual nature of the act in question, but the discretion available to the institution when it was adopted.

56. In those circumstances, it must be held that the Court of First Instance made an error of law when it held that the Commission's liability could arise from the mere illegality of the Decision on 17 July 1997, without taking account of the discretion which the Commission enjoyed in the adoption of that measure.

57. However, it should be pointed out that where the grounds of a judgment of the Court of First Instance disclose an infringement of Community law but the operative part of the judgment is shown to be well founded for other legal reasons, the appeal must be dismissed . . .

58. At paragraph 145 of the contested judgment, the Court of First Instance held that . . . the Commission has a broad discretion when assessing whether transitional measures are necessary on the basis of Article 30 of Regulation No 404/93.

59. Furthermore, as is apparent from paragraph 18 of this judgment, the Court of First Instance concluded, at paragraph 149 of the contested judgment, both that the Commission had committed a manifest error of appraisal in considering that Camar was capable of overcoming the difficulties caused by the transition from the Italian national arrangements to the Community system by relying on the operation of the market, and that the only way that Camar could deal with the difficulties it faced was for the Commission to adopt transitional measures as provided for in Article 30 of Regulation No 404/93.

60. Such manifest and grave disregard, by the Commission, of the limits placed on its discretion is a sufficiently serious infringement of Community law, within the meaning of the case-law cited at paragraphs 53 and 54 of this judgment, and is therefore such as to render the Community liable.

61. Since it has not been disputed that the other conditions essential to the non-contractual liability of the Community are satisfied in this case, the Court of First Instance correctly upheld the claim for compensation against the Commission in Case T-260/97.

## NOTES AND QUESTIONS

**1.** Was there a breach of a "superior rule of law" here, or has the Court changed its criteria for awarding compensation in cases involving the exercise of discretion as compared with *Holtz & Willemsen*?

**2.** The cases mentioned by the Court as justifying the possibility of compensation for the mere breach of EU law were cases involving actions against Member States or referenced such cases. In *Dillenkofer* (cited in the judgment), for example, Germany had failed altogether to enact legislation to implement a directive. The Court stated that:

> Failure to take any measure to transpose a directive in order to achieve the result it prescribes within the period laid down for that purpose constitutes per se a serious breach of EU law and consequently gives rise to a right of reparation for individuals suffering injury if the result prescribed by the directive entails the grant to individuals of rights whose content is identifiable and a causal link exists between the breach of the State's obligation and the loss and damage suffered.

**3.** For a more detailed analysis of this subject, see C. Hilson, *The Role of Discretion in EC Law on Non-Contractual Liability*, (2005) 42 CML Rev. 677.

## [E]    Claims Based on Maladministration

### HANS-MARTIN TILLACK v. COMMISSION
Case T-193/04, 2006 ECJ CELEX LEXIS 553, [2006] ECR II-3995

[The applicant was a journalist employed by the German magazine Stern. He had obtained certain documents from OLAF (the anti-fraud unit of the Commission) which disclosed the existence of possible irregularities in a number of the Commission's services (the van Buitenen memorandum'). OLAF began in internal investigation regarding the leak. It subsequently published a press release indicating that it could not be ruled out that the applicant had bribed an official of the Commission to obtain the documents. The applicant refused to disclose his sources and lodged a complaint with the Ombudsman who, after investigation, concluded that OLAF had committed an act of maladministration and was of the opinion that OLAF, which had accepted his draft recommendation, had not implemented it adequately. In those circumstances, he took the view that a critical remark on his part could constitute adequate reparation for the complainant. OLAF forwarded information concerning suspicions of breach of professional secrecy and bribery to the judicial authorities in Brussels (Belgium) and Hamburg (Germany), referring to Article 10(2) of Regulation No 1073/1999 (the "OLAF complaint"). These authorities both opened investigations into alleged corruption and, in the case of the Belgian judicial authorities, for breach of professional secrecy. On 19 March 2004, on the instructions of the investigating judge responsible for the case, the Belgian police carried out a search at the applicant's home and office and seized or sealed professional documents and personal belongings. After various further steps, the applicant eventually sought annulment of an OLAF decision to turn over the file to the Belgian and German authorities and also sought compensation under EC

288/TFEU 340. The action for annulment was dismissed as non-admissible but the applicant pressed a case for damages.]

121 As a preliminary point, the protection of family life, the freedom of the press, the principle of the presumption of innocence and the right to a fair trial, which are fundamental rights, confer rights on individuals which are enforced by the Community Courts. In that regard, the applicant alleges two instances of misconduct of OLAF which, being distinct from one another, must be examined separately.

122 First, as regards the application for damages for the harm allegedly suffered as a result of OLAF's 'complaint', it has been found that it was the task of the judicial authorities to decide what action should be taken in respect of the information forwarded by OLAF on the basis of Article 10(2) of Regulation No 1073/1999, even though that forwarding of information is in no way binding upon them (see paragraph 70 above). Consequently, the conduct of the national judicial authorities, which decided, in the context of their own prerogatives, to initiate legal proceedings and then to carry out investigations, caused the harm allegedly suffered by the applicant.

123 In addition, the applicant does not explain how forwarding information, which is confidential in nature and in respect of which a breach of confidentiality is not alleged, to national judicial authorities could harm his professional reputation and standing in professional circles.

124 It follows that the applicant has not established the existence of a sufficiently direct causal link between the forwarding of the information by OLAF to the Belgian judicial authorities pursuant to Article 10(2) of Regulation No 1073/1999 and the damage claimed.

125 The condition requiring a causal link between the damage alleged and OLAF's conduct in order for the Community to incur non-contractual liability not having been satisfied in this case, the action for damages relating to OLAF's 'complaint' must be dismissed without it being necessary to examine the other conditions governing that liability.

126 Second, as regards the application for damages to make good the damage allegedly resulting from OLAF's press releases, the applicant refers to the draft recommendation of the Ombudsman of 10 June 2003 and the latter's recommendation of 20 November 2003, holding that there had been maladministration, and infers that the press release of 27 March 2002 constitutes 'as such', an 'unlawful administrative act' and that the press release of 30 September 2003 represents a new instance of maladministration, which, by reiterating the allegations made in the earlier press release, also infringes the principle of proportionality.

127 In that regard, first, the principle of sound administration, which is the only principle alleged to have been breached in this context, does not, in itself, confer rights upon individuals . . . . except where it constitutes the expression of specific rights such as the right to have affairs handled impartially, fairly and within a reasonable time, the right to be heard, the right to have access to files, or the obligation to give reasons for decisions, for the purposes of Article 41 of the Charter of fundamental rights of the European Union, proclaimed on 7 December 2000 inNice (OJ 2000 C 364, p. 1), which is not the case here.

128 For the sake of completeness, the classification as an 'act of maladministration' by the Ombudsman does not mean, in itself, that OLAF's conduct constitutes a sufficiently serious breach of a rule of law within the meaning of the case-law. In the institution of the Ombudsman, the Treaty has given citizens of the Union, and more particularly officials and other servants of the Community, an alternative remedy to that of an action before the Community Courts in order to protect their interests. That alternative non-judicial remedy meets specific criteria and does not necessarily have the same objective as judicial proceedings . . .

129 Also, in view of the autonomy granted to OLAF by Regulation No 1073/1999 and of the general objective of press releases of providing information to the public, OLAF enjoys discretion as regards the appropriateness and content of its press releases in respect of its investigatory activities.

130 In addition, it is apparent from an examination of the wording of the press release of 27 March 2002 that the only passage which could possibly be deemed prejudicial is worded as follows:

'According to information received by [OLAF], a journalist has received a number of documents relating to the so-called "van Buitenen affair". It is not inconceivable that payment may have been made to somebody within OLAF (or possibly another EU institution) for these documents. . . .'

131 Even supposing that those with knowledge of the case could make the connection with the applicant, those allegations, formulated in a hypothetical way, without indicating the applicant's name or the name of the magazine for which he worked, do not constitute a manifest and grave disregard, by OLAF, of the limits of its discretion. Furthermore, it was *Stern* itself which, in its press release of 28 March 2002, cited the applicant's name. The applicant's identity, in relation to OLAF's investigations, was thus not revealed by OLAF but by his employer *Stern* magazine. Therefore, the damage that the applicant allegedly suffered to his professional reputation and standing in professional circles, in respect of that publication, cannot be attributed to OLAF. Consequently, the press release in dispute does not amount to a sufficiently serious breach of Community law by OLAF.

132 For its part, OLAF's press release of 30 September 2003, which was published following the European Ombudsman's draft recommendation of 18 June 2003, seeks to tone down the allegations contained in the press release of 27 March 2002. It thus states:

'. . . OLAF's enquiries have not yet been completed, but to date, [OLAF] has not obtained proof that such a payment was made.' Therefore, that press release does not constitute a sufficiently serious breach of a rule of law any more than the previous one.

133 The same conclusion must be drawn in relation to the statement of the OLAF spokesman which was cited in the *European Voice* magazine of 4 April 2002, according to which OLAF 'had prima facie evidence that a payment might have been made', since the cautiousness of the words used does not establish the existence of a sufficiently serious breach of Community law. As for the statement of

the Director of OLAF on Stern TV on 24 March 2004, the applicant does not provide any means of verifying its content.

134 Moreover, the applicant does not develop any legal arguments in his application which make it possible to assess how exactly the publication of the press releases and other public statements by OLAF could be classified as a 'sufficiently serious breach' of a rule of law.

135 It follows from the above that the applicant has failed to show the existence of a sufficiently serious breach of Community law attributable to OLAF capable of causing him harm. Therefore, his claim for damages in relation to the press releases and OLAF's other public statements must be dismissed without its being necessary to assess whether the applicant has actually suffered the damage alleged and the extent of that damage.

## NOTES AND QUESTIONS

1.   Does the Court apply the same test to cases of alleged maladministration as it does to cases involving discretionary acts of legislation or implementation of policy?

2.   In *Stanley George Adams v. Commission*, Joined Cases 145/83 and 53/84, [1985] ECR 3651 (as already observed in Chapter 7), Adams had claimed compensation for the wrongful disclosure of his identity as an informant in proceedings under EC 81/TFEU 101. Such an act would not, of course, result necessarily in quantifiable loss, but justice certainly required a pecuniary remedy. He had, however, failed to take certain steps that would have assisted in the Commission in protecting that identity and the Court held that his contribution to the damage he suffered must be taken into account:

> 53 It must therefore be concluded that in principle the Community is bound to make good the damage resulting from the discovery of the applicant's identity by means of the documents handed over to Roche by the Commission. It must however be recognised that the extent of the Commission's liability is diminished by reason of the applicant's own negligence. The applicant failed to inform the Commission that it was possible to infer his identity as the informant from the documents themselves, although he was in the best position to appreciate and to avert that risk. Nor did he ask the Commission to keep him informed of the progress of the investigation of Roche, and in particular of any use that might be made of the documents for that purpose. Lastly, he went back to Switzerland without attempting to make any inquiries in that respect, although he must have been aware of the risks to which his conduct towards his former employer had exposed him with regard to Swiss legislation.
>
> 54 Consequently, the applicant himself contributed significantly to the damage which he suffered. In assessing the conduct of the Commission on the one hand and that of the applicant on the other, the Court considers it equitable to apportion responsibility for that damage equally between the two parties.

55 It follows from all the foregoing considerations that the Commission must be ordered to compensate the applicant to the extent of one half of the damage suffered by him as a result of the fact that he was identified as the source of information regarding Roche's anti-competitive practices. For the rest, however, the application must be dismissed. The amount of the damages is to be determined by agreement between the parties or, failing such agreement, by the Court.

3.   Mr. Tillack subsequently brought a case against Belgium in the European Court of Human Rights and won. He was awarded €10,000 in damages and €30,000 in costs. The Court held that the protection of his sources as a journalist fell within article 10 ECHR.

# Chapter 9

## EU LAW IN THE NATIONAL COURTS

### § 9.01  OVERVIEW

***Template*** Article 5 paragraph 5.1.3, Section 5.2 and Article 8, Section 8.2

***The materials in this Chapter*** The national courts play a critical role in the EU constitutional structure. Their function is described by the ECJ in its 2011 Opinion on the draft Treaty setting up a Unified Patent Litigation System. This decision appears at the end of this Chapter, since it provides a rather convenient summing-up of the various aspects of EU law dealt with in the sections preceding it.

The Chapter begins by looking at the preliminary reference procedure laid out in EC 234/TFEU 267. At first it might seem rather odd to treat this as part of an examination focused on the courts of the Member States. Yet it will be clear from the cases included here that the issues all have to do with how EU law issues are dealt with in the national courts. What are the boundaries of the right or duty to refer? What constitutes a national court or tribunal? While the ECJ admittedly reserves to itself the answer to these questions, it does so in the context of its role as an integral part of national proceedings that implicate EU law.

The next section addresses the statement in EC 10/TEU 4 regarding the so-called "duty of sincere co-operation" that is imposed on the Member States. As noted in Chapter 2, this is one of the underlying principles of the EU constitutional structure that manifests itself in different ways. Here it arises in the context of the duty of the national courts as a branch of government, a phenomenon that was observed already in the *Defrenne* case in Chapter 4, *supra*. This doctrine has allowed questions of interpretation of EU laws to be referred even though the provisions are not directly effective and thus cannot be invoked by individuals. As such, whether or not the national courts then choose to interpret national law consistently with EU law requirements, the doctrine provides a further avenue for the ECJ to provide uniform interpretation of EU rules.

Section 9.04 is a lengthy section that addresses the aspects of the requirement, originally formulated by the ECJ and now enshrined in the TFEU, that national courts must provide effective remedies for persons legitimately asserting EU rights. The materials here illustrate a feature of the EU legal order that is extremely complex and difficult to rationalize. The ECJ's approach has been, overall, to make sure that national procedures do not place those asserting EU rights in a worse position than those asserting national rights. Yet there are limits to this doctrine. The ECJ has been concerned with ensuring that the total absence of procedures, or the existence of procedural obstacles, does not prevent the assertion of EU rights. Since all of this takes place within the confines of national law, there are clearly circumstances where the ability ultimately to invoke EU rights will vary from one state to another. The ECJ's attempts to set uniform ground rules has so far failed to bring any clarity to the situation except at a level of abstraction that essentially leaves all of the practical questions unanswered. Thus, each case must be decided on its facts.

***The Importance of the Preliminary Reference*** Without the pivotal role of the ECJ in assuring a base level of uniformity in the interpretation of EU law through the EC 234/TFEU 267 reference procedure, it is difficult to imagine that the EEC would scarcely have developed beyond a rather loose association of bickering states. This point has already been well illustrated in previous chapters. However, it should be noted that the ECJ was not alone here. It is evident that in various ways the courts of the Member States, and litigants seeking to establish firm foundations for Union law through those courts, have been just as vital to the evolution of the Union. Mr. Costa, of *Costa v. ENEL* fame, was a lawyer who used his $3 dispute with the electricity company to engineer a reference that established the supremacy of EU law. As will be seen in § 9.02, the ECJ has not generally been willing to reject references even where it appears that the national proceedings were being used to obtain an ECJ ruling where the underlying dispute did not really manifest any differences between the parties. In similar vein, the ECJ, while cautious about situations where the law of one Member State is brought into question in the courts of another state, has not sought to discourage such references. Again, in determining whether a national body is a "court or tribunal", it has been willing to accept references from bodies that play what is really a regulatory role, particularly where that role implicates important concepts of EU law.

The Court also has not discouraged references even where it appears that the questions on which it is asked to rule have been answered in previous decisions. The Court has pointed out that one should be careful about assuming that a previous ruling can be applied automatically to a different factual situation in another Member State. At the same time, within the national systems, the notion that every time an EU law is invoked, the national court should refer, is surely unworkable. Clearly established principles can be applied without any need for interpretation: thus, for example, it is not questioned that customs duties on goods entering from another Member State are prohibited. If a litigant were to assert otherwise, the national court would seem perfectly justified in rejecting that assertion and proceeding to apply the law. What needs to be guarded against rather, is any suggestion that the national courts can simply choose not to refer a genuine question of EU law because they think they know the answer; or that it would unduly delay the case; or that this should be left to the highest court to resolve. It is of course true that the reference procedure can introduce a delay of perhaps 18 months; but this seems inherent in any federally tiered system. In the United States, an issue of constitutionality may take a different route, proceeding upward by appeal, but the proceedings leading to a final result may be just as protracted.

The reference procedure has the merit of eliminating the need for the national courts to study rulings of courts of other Member States. Lord Denning MR, head of the UK Court of Appeal during the early days of the UK's membership of the EEC had suggested just such a possibility in the *Bulmer v. Bollinger* case (1974 Ch.

49). Actually, this suggestion does not seem unreasonable on its face; but the difficulties of trying to understand quite different contexts, procedures and substantive laws, not to mention language difficulties, make such an exercise more appropriate for academics than judges. The notion also raises an evidential question: would a decision, say, of a German Tax Court be a matter of fact or law if introduced into argument in an English court? Unlike typical foreign law questions, the EU law element, wherever considered, is the law of both countries. It is surely best to stay well away from such issues.

Lord Denning had also offered some more general guidance in the *Bulmer* case on when lower courts ought to refer. However, it was already clear that this is a discretion enjoyed by each individual court and cannot be overridden by higher court directives: see *Rheinmühlen-Düsseldorf v. Einfuhr- und Vorratsstelle für Getreide und Futtermittel* Case 166/73, 1974 ECJ EUR-Lex LEXIS 60, [1974] ECR 33:

> 3 The provisions of article 177 [267] are absolutely binding on the national judge and, in so far as the second paragraph is concerned, enable him to refer a case to the court of justice for a preliminary ruling on interpretation or validity.

> This Article given national courts the power and, where appropriate, imposes on them the obligation to refer a case for a preliminary ruling, as soon as the judge perceives either of his own motion or at the request of the parties that the litigation depends on a point referred to in the first paragraph of article 177.

> 4 It follows that national courts have the widest discretion in referring matters to the court of justice if they consider that a case pending before them raises questions involving interpretation, or consideration of the validity, of provisions of Community law, necessitating a decision on their part.

> It follows from these factors that a rule of national law whereby a court is bound on points of law by the rulings of a superior court cannot deprive the inferior courts of their power to refer to the court questions of interpretation of Community law involving such rulings.

> It would be otherwise if the questions put by the inferior court were substantially the same as questions already put by the superior court.

> On the other hand the inferior court must be free, if it considers that the ruling on law made by the superior court could lead it to give a judgment contrary to Community law, to refer to the court questions which concern it.

> If inferior courts were bound without being able to refer matters to the court, the jurisdiction of the latter to give preliminary rulings and the application of Community law at all levels of the judicial systems of the member states would be compromised.

> 5 The reply must therefore be that the existence of a rule of domestic law whereby a court is bound on points of law by the rulings of the court

superior to it cannot of itself take away the power provided for by article 177 [267] of referring cases to the court.

EC 234/TFEU 267 also allows the Court to rule on the validity of EU laws. Does this imply that the courts of the Member States also have that power? It is obvious that if national courts were able to question the validity of EU laws themselves, a somewhat chaotic situation could arise where those laws were effective in some states and not others, while the effects of the rulings themselves might also differ. In the United States, by contrast, it is not uncommon for federal courts in different districts or circuits to adopt opposing rulings, or for state courts to take differing positions on federal constitutional issues, but eventually the matter can be settled in the Supreme Court. There would be no such assurance in the EU system because the ECJ does not have the power to quash state court decisions. Thus, while the preliminary reference procedure recognizes that the validity of EU law is an appropriate question, the ECJ has been firm in its position that it alone can make that determination and also rule on the consequences.

It should be kept in mind that references relating to measures within the scope of Treaty provisions on police and justice cooperation in criminal matters do not allow the Court to rule on the validity or proportionality of executive measures taken by the authorities of the Member States in the exercise of the police power (TFEU 276).

***The notion of the "effectiveness" of EU law*** This topic provides a pointed reminder that the EU does not enjoy a federal system where state law and federal law are matters for different court systems. The need to apply EU law in the national courts has caused the ECJ to develop a doctrine of "effectiveness" that is simply not needed in a conventional federal system. This doctrine imposes ground rules on the national courts to ensure that litigants' EU rights can be asserted. This includes not only the "equivalency" doctrine mentioned above, but in some cases the elimination of obstacles and even the creation of new forms of action. Moreover, national courts in some contexts may have the duty to raise EU law issues even if the litigants have not. This aspect seems quite alien to U.S. lawyers. It is simply not part of the structure that constitutional issues or clashes between federal and state law are the responsibility of the courts unless the litigants choose to raise those issues. One can assume that federal law is safely in the hands of federal authorities, including the federal courts and will be fully effective as and when invoked. For a review of the concept, see A Arnull, *The Principle of Effective Judicial Protection in EU Law: An Unruly Horse?* (1911) EL REV. 51

It is clear that issues regarding the reference procedure are closely connected with the effectiveness doctrine. This is particularly evident in considering whether a national court that has made a reference to the ECJ should suspend the application of national law thought to be in conflict with EU law. In the context of the reference procedure, this looks like a matter solely for the national court. Yet if the failure to suspend national law were to lead to irreparable harm to the litigants' EU rights, then it impinges on the effectiveness of EU law.

## § 9.02   THE EC 234/TFEU 267 REFERRAL

### [A]   Is a Ruling "Necessary to Enable [the National Court] to Give Judgment"?

### FOGLIA v. NOVELLO
Case 104/79, [1980] ECR 745

[Proceedings were brought in Italy (the "court" being the Pretura di Bra) concerning the costs incurred by the plaintiff, Mr Foglia a wine-dealer in the Piedmont province of Italy in the dispatch to Menton, France of some cases of Italian liqueur wines which he sold to the defendant, Mrs Novello. Mrs. Novello had agreed in the purchase contract to bear French taxes unless these were improperly levied under EC 90/TFEU 110.]

3 The file on the case shows that the contract of sale between Foglia and Novello stipulated that Novello should not be liable for any duties which were claimed by the Italian or French authorities contrary to the provisions on the free movement of goods between the two countries or which were at least not due. Foglia adopted a similar clause in his contract with the Danzas undertaking to which he entrusted the transport of the cases of liqueur wine to Menton; that clause provided that Foglia should not be liable for such unlawful charges or charges which were not due.

4 The order making the reference finds that the subject-matter of the dispute is restricted exclusively to the sum paid as a consumption tax when the liqueur wines were imported into French territory. The file and the oral argument before the Court of Justice have established that that tax was paid by Danzas to the French authorities, without protest or complaint; that the bill for transport which Danzas submitted to Foglia and which was settled included the amount of that tax and that Mrs Novello refused to reimburse the latter amount to Foglia in reliance on the clause on unlawful charges or charges which were not due expressly included in the contract of sale.

5 In the view of the Pretura the defences advanced by Novello entail calling in question the validity of French legislation concerning the consumption tax on liqueur wines in relation to Article 95 [110] of the EEC Treaty.

6 The attitude of Foglia in the course of the proceedings before the Pretura may be described as neutral. Foglia has in fact maintained that he could not in any case be liable for the amount corresponding to the French consumption tax since, if it was lawfully charged, it should have been borne by Novello whilst Danzas would be liable if it were unlawful.

7 This point of view prompted Foglia to request the national court to increase the scope of the proceedings and to summon Danzas as a third party having an interest in the action. The court nevertheless considered that before it could give a ruling on that request it was necessary to settle the problem whether the imposition of the consumption tax paid by Danzas was in accordance with the provisions of the EEC Treaty or not.

8 The parties to the main action submitted a certain number of documents to the

Pretura which enabled it to investigate the French legislation concerning the taxation of liqueur wines and other comparable products. The court concluded from its investigation that such legislation created a "serious discrimination" against Italian liqueur wines and natural wines having a high degree of alcoholic strength by means of special arrangements made for French liqueur wines termed "natural sweet wines" and preferential tax treatment accorded certain French natural wines with a high degree of alcoholic strength and bearing a designation of origin. On the basis of that conclusion the court formulated the questions which it has submitted to the Court of Justice.

9 In their written observations submitted to the Court of Justice the two parties to the main action have provided an essentially identical description of the tax discrimination which is a feature of the French legislation concerning the taxation of liqueur wines; the two parties consider that that legislation is incompatible with Community law. In the course of the oral procedure before the Court Foglia stated that he was participating in the procedure before the Court in view of the interest of his undertaking as such and as an undertaking belonging to a certain category of Italian traders in the outcome of the legal issues involved in the dispute.

10 It thus appears that the parties to the main action are concerned to obtain a ruling that the French tax system is invalid for liqueur wines by the expedient of proceedings before an Italian court between two private individuals who are in agreement as to the result to be attained and who have inserted a clause in their contract in order to induce the Italian court to give a ruling on the point. The artificial nature of this expedient is underlined by the fact that Danzas did not exercise its rights under French law to institute proceedings over the consumption tax although it undoubtedly had an interest in doing so in view of the clause in the contract by which it was also bound and moreover of the fact that Foglia paid without protest that undertaking's bill which included a sum paid in respect of that tax.

11 The duty of the Court of Justice under Article 177 [267] of the EEC Treaty is to supply all courts in the Community with the information on the interpretation of Community law which is necessary to enable them to settle genuine disputes which are brought before them. A situation in which the Court was obliged by the expedient of arrangements like those described above to give rulings would jeopardize the whole system of legal remedies available to private individuals to enable them to protect themselves against tax provisions which are contrary to the Treaty.

12 This means that the questions asked by the national court, having regard to the circumstances of this case, do not fall within the framework of the duties of the Court of Justice under Article 177 [267] of the Treaty.

13 The Court of Justice accordingly has no jurisdiction to give a ruling on the questions asked by the national court.

## NOTES AND QUESTIONS

**1.** One could have the impression that the *Foglia* case, in the eyes of the ECJ, raised a question as to whether, in U.S. parlance, there was a genuine "case or controversy" before the national court. Is that how the Court saw it?

In a second reference (Case 244/80, part of which is excerpted below in connection with another issue), the national Court explained that there was in fact a form of proceeding for a declaratory judgment involved for which the interpretation was necessary. The ECJ then laid out in detail what the duties of the national court and the ECJ are in connection with determining the propriety of the reference in the following terms:

> 14. . . . [A]rticle 177 [267] is based on cooperation which entails a division of duties between the national courts and the court of justice in the interest of the proper application and uniform interpretation of Community law throughout all the Member States.

> 15. With this in view it is for the national court — by reason of the fact that it is seised of the substance of the dispute and that it must bear the responsibility for the decision to be taken — to assess, having regard to the facts of the case, the need to obtain a preliminary ruling to enable it to give judgment.

> 16 In exercising that power of appraisal the national court, in collaboration with the Court of Justice, fulfils a duty entrusted to them both of ensuring that in the interpretation and application of the Treaty the law is observed. Accordingly the problems which may be entailed in the exercise of its power of appraisal by the national court and the relations which it maintains within the framework of article 177 [267] with the Court of Justice are governed exclusively by the provisions of Community law.

> 17 In order that the Court of Justice may perform its task in accordance with the Treaty it is essential for national courts to explain, when the reasons do not emerge beyond any doubt from the file, why they consider that a reply to their questions is necessary to enable them to give judgment.

> 18 It must in fact be emphasized that the duty assigned to the court by article 177 [267] is not that of delivering advisory opinions on general or hypothetical questions but of assisting in the administration of justice in the Member States. It accordingly does not have jurisdiction to reply to questions of interpretation which are submitted to it within the framework of procedural devices arranged by the parties in order to induce the court to give its views on certain problems of Community law which do not correspond to an objective requirement inherent in the resolution of a dispute. A declaration by the court that is has no jurisdiction in such circumstances does not in any way trespass upon the prerogatives of the national court but makes it possible to prevent the application of the procedure under article 177 [267] for purposes other than those appropriate for it.

19 Furthermore, it should be pointed out that, whilst the Court of Justice must be able to place as much reliance as possible upon the assessment by the national court of the extent to which the questions submitted are essential, it must be in a position to make any assessment inherent in the performance of its own duties in particular order to check, as all courts must, whether it has jurisdiction. Thus the court, taking into account the repercussions of its decisions in this matter, must have regard, in exercising the jurisdiction conferred upon it by article 177 [267], not only to the interests of the parties to the proceedings but also to those of the Community and of the Member States. Accordingly it cannot, without disregarding the duties assigned to it, remain indifferent to the assessments made by the courts of the Member States in the exceptional cases in which such assessments may affect the proper working of the procedure laid down by article 177 [267].

20 The spirit of cooperation which must govern the performance of the duties assigned by article 177 [267] to the national courts on the one hand and the Court of Justice on the other requires the latter to have regard to the national court's proper responsibilities, it implies at the same time that the national court, in the use which it makes of the facilities provided by article 177 [267], should have regard to the proper function of the Court of Justice in this field.

21 The reply to the first question must accordingly be that whilst, according to the intended role of article 177 [267], an assessment of the need to obtain an answer to the questions of interpretation raised, regard being had to the circumstances of fact and of law involved in the main action, is a matter for the national court it is nevertheless for the Court of Justice, in order to confirm its own jurisdiction, to examine, where necessary, the conditions in which the case has been referred to it by the national court.

The Court did not consider that the Pretore's new submission introduced any new fact that would cause the Court to change its mind from the first decision, but invited the national court to submit any new circumstances that might yet cause a change of mind. No further reference was made, however.

2.    Compare the two following cases with *Foglia*.

In *Werner Mangold v. Rudiger Helm*, Case C-144/04, 2005 ECJ CELEX LEXIS 607, [2005] ECR I-9981, the German Government had argued that the underlying dispute in the national court was "fictitious", since there was some evidence that the case had been deliberately contrived to challenge the German "Harz" law (the TzBfG) under which persons aged over 52 could be offered fixed term contracts of employment, thus enabling the employer to avoid the considerable burdens associated with obligations to regular employees:

32. At the hearing the admissibility of the reference for a preliminary ruling was challenged by the Federal Republic of Germany, on the grounds that the dispute in the main proceedings was fictitious or contrived. Indeed, in the past Mr Helm has publicly argued a case identical to Mr Mangold's, to the effect that Paragraph 14(3) of the TzBfG is unlawful.

\* \* \*

38. . . . . [I]n the case in the main proceedings, it hardly seems arguable that the interpretation of Community law sought by the national court does actually respond to an objective need inherent in the outcome of a case pending before it. In fact, it is common ground that the contract has actually been performed and that its application raises a question of interpretation of Community law. The fact that the parties to the dispute in the main proceedings are at one in their interpretation of Paragraph 14(3) of the TzBfG cannot affect the reality of that dispute.

In *Skatteverket v. Gourmet Classic Ltd*, Case C-458/06, 2008 ECJ EUR-Lex LEXIS 2496, [2008]ECR I-4207, the Regeringsrätten (Swedish Supreme Administrative Court) asked the ECJ for an interpretation of article 20 of Directive 92/83 regarding the harmonization of the structures of excise duties on alcohol and alcoholic beverages. Gourmet Classic had obtained a preliminary opinion from the Skatterättsnämnden (Swedish Revenue Law Commission) that cooking wine was exempted under the Swedish implementing legislation. One member of the Commission, however, had taken the position that cooking wine was outside the scope of that legislation altogether. The Skatteverket (Swedish tax administration) had confirmed the preliminary opinion. There was clearly no dispute between the parties in the national proceedings (Gourmet presumably having been satisfied with the ruling from the Commission) but the Skatteverket asked the Supreme Administrative Court for confirmation of the preliminary opinion. There was therefore no "case or controversy" between the parties. However the ECJ accepted jurisdiction, based on the following rationale:

26. While the spirit of cooperation which must prevail in the exercise of the functions assigned by Article 234 EC [267] to the national courts, on the one hand, and the Community judicature, on the other, requires the Court of Justice to have regard to the particular responsibilities of the national court, it implies at the same time that the national court, in the use which it makes of the possibilities offered by that article, must have regard to the particular function entrusted to the Court of Justice in this field, which is to assist in the administration of justice in the Member States and not to deliver advisory opinions on general or hypothetical questions . . .

27. With regard to the main proceedings, the Court has already held that, in the case of an appeal, the purpose of the procedure before the Regeringsrätten is to review the legality of an opinion which, once it becomes definitive, binds the tax authorities and serves as the basis for the assessment to tax if and to the extent to which the person who applied for the opinion continues with the action envisaged in his application and that, in those circumstances, the Regeringsrätten must be held to be carrying out a judicial function . . .

28. The fact that the Skatteverket confirmed the preliminary opinion of the Skatterättsnämnden does not affect the judicial nature of the main proceedings.

29. In addition, in the main proceedings, the referring court asks the Court of Justice a question concerning the interpretation of a provision of Community law, namely the first indent of Article 20 of Directive 92/83, and it considers that a preliminary ruling on that point is necessary in order to review the legality of the preliminary opinion of the Skatterättsnämnden. The Court is therefore not being asked to deliver an advisory opinion on a hypothetical question.

30. According to the order for reference, the Regeringsrätten has unlimited jurisdiction in this connection, independently of the submissions of the parties.

31. Moreover, since there is no judicial remedy under national law against the decisions of the Regeringsrätten, that court is obliged, under the third paragraph of Article 234 EC [267], to bring the matter before the Court of Justice.

32. Consequently, as already stated in paragraph 23 of this judgment, in proceedings such as the main proceedings, it is only by referring a question to the Court for a preliminary ruling that the objective pursued by that provision can be attained, that is to ensure the proper application and uniform interpretation of Community law in all the Member States and to prevent a body of national case-law that is not in accordance with the rules of Community law from coming into existence in the Member State concerned.

    **3.**    Where it is clear that the parties' intent is to have a national law declared illegal, (and there is no dispute as to the meaning of the EU act), the national court is still free to refer but it must give a convincing reason why the interpretation is necessary: *Plato Plastik Robert Frank GmbH v. Caropack Handelsgesellschaft mbH*, Case 341/01, 2004 ECJ EUR-Lex LEXIS 678, [2004] ECR I-4883.

## SALONIA v. POIDOMANI
### Case 126/80, 1981 ECJ EUR-Lex LEXIS 165, [1981] ECR 1563.

[A dispute had arisen between the holder of a licence issued by the administrative authorities for the retail selling of newspapers and periodicals in general and the proprietors of the warehouses for the distribution of newspapers and periodicals in Ragusa, concerning the refusal of the latter in 1978 to deliver newspapers and periodicals to the said licence-holder. The warehouse proprietors contended that they were under no obligation to supply newspapers and periodicals to holders of a retail-selling licence issued by the administrative authorities since such a licence affords licence-holders no more than a possibility of being supplied. They maintained that at the time the distribution system for newspapers and periodicals in Italy was governed by a national agreement between the Italian Federation of Newspapers Publishers and the United Federation of Trade Union of Newsagents and that the plaintiff in the main action did not meet the requirements of article 2 of that agreement. They emphasized in this connexion that under that provision, in communes with over 2 500 inhabitants, publishers might supply their publications for sale only to holders of a licence issued by an inter-regional joint committee which entitled them to receive from the distributors publications intended for sale.

Although none of the parties raised a question of EU law in the proceedings, the Italian court believed that the national agreement might have infringed article 85 (EC 81/TFEU 101).]

5 The defendants in the main action allege that in the present case, the Court has not been validly seised, under Article 177 [267] of the Treaty, of a request for a preliminary ruling. They maintain, in the first place, that the questions referred to the Court bear no relation to the real subject-matter of the dispute since neither the plaintiff nor the defendants have relied on any rule of Community law in support of their arguments. They contend, moreover, that the questions submitted relate to an agreement to which none of the parties to the case is a signatory. Finally, they point out that the interpretation of the Treaty sought by the national court serves no useful purpose since the national agreement . . . was no longer in force when the facts giving rise to the action occurred and it could not therefore at that time constitute the legal basis for the refusal on the part of the newspaper distributors to supply the plaintiff.

6 . . . [A]rticle 177 [267] of the Treaty, which is based on a distinct separation of functions between national courts and the Court of Justice, does not allow the latter to criticize the reasons for the reference. Consequently, a request from a national court may be rejected only if it is quite obvious that the interpretation of Community law or the examination of the validity of a rule of Community law sought by that court bears no relation to the actual nature of the case or to the subject-matter of the main action.

7 However, that is not so in this case. In the first place, the fact that the parties to the main action failed to raise a point of Community law before the national court does not preclude the latter from bringing the matter before the Court of Justice. In providing that reference for a preliminary ruling may be submitted to the court where "a question is raised before any court or tribunal of a member state", the second and third paragraphs of Article 177 [267] of the Treaty are not intended to restrict this procedure exclusively to cases where one or other of the parties to the main action has taken the initiative of raising a point concerning the interpretation or the validity of Community law, but also extend to cases where a question of this kind is raised by the national court or tribunal itself which considers that a decision thereon by the court of justice is "necessary to enable it to give judgment."

8 Similarly, the fact that neither the plaintiff nor the defendants to the main action are parties to the national agreement forming the subject-matter of the questions on the interpretation of the Treaty referred to the Court of Justice by the national court does not call in question the court's jurisdiction since the application of Article 177 [267] of the Treaty is subject to the sole requirement that national courts must be provided with all the relevant elements of Community law which are necessary to enable them to give judgment.

9 Finally, although it is true that the agreement in question was repudiated by one of the parties . . . with the result that it was no longer in force at the time when the facts giving rise to the case occurred, or when the main action was commenced, . . . nevertheless the defendants in the main action themselves did not rule out, in their oral argument, the possibility that certain clauses of the agreement might have continued to be applied in practice . . . Furthermore, it is clear from the order

referring the matter to the Court that in the main action the defendants had relied on the provisions of the above-mentioned national agreement . . . in order to have the application dismissed.

10 For those reasons, the objection raised by the defendants in the main action must be dismissed.

## NOTES AND QUESTIONS

1.    The *Salonia* case addresses a different aspect: must the ECJ accept jurisdiction where the issue appears to have nothing to do with the resolution of the national proceedings? The plaintiffs had not raised an EU law argument and so the defendants had not had any opportunity prior to the reference to make any argument regarding the possible effects of EC 81/TFEU 101. Does it seem appropriate in such circumstances that the ECJ should nonetheless be willing to accept the reference? Or is this not its concern?

2.    There have been quite a few references over the years in which it was argued that an interpretation of EU law was not necessary to enable the national court to give judgment.

For example, in *Massam Dzodzi v. Belgian State*, Joined Cases C-297/88 and C-197/89, 1990 ECJ EUR-Lex LEXIS 476, [1990] ECR I-3763. the national court was of the view that a Belgian immigration law, while implementing EU law, also intended to put spouses of nationals in the same position as spouses of nationals from other Member States in terms of rights of entry and residence and legal remedies, so as to avoid "reverse discrimination" against Belgian nationals. The national court sought interpretation of Regulation 1251/70 and Directive 64/221 (dealing with entry and residence) even though these EU measures did not apply to a State's own nationals. The ECJ concluded that it could still accept the reference even though the proceedings in the national court concerned a situation that was "purely internal" to Belgium and the Belgian law was not required by the EU legislation to protect Belgian nationals or their spouses. Only indirectly could the EU provisions be considered relevant, on the basis that the Belgian law had put such individuals on the same footing as EU nationals.

In *Manuel José Lourenço Dias v. Director da Alfândega do Porto* Case C-343/90, 1992 ECJ CELEX LEXIS 219, [1992] ECR I-4673, Dias was prosecuted for failing to pay a motor vehicle tax. The national court referred a whole series of detailed questions to the ECJ, but the Portuguese Government maintained that most of them had nothing to do with the resolution of the case. The Court stated:

> 18 . . . [T]he Court considers that it cannot give a preliminary ruling on a question raised in a national court where, inter alia, the interpretation requested relates to measures not yet adopted by the Community institutions . . . the procedure before the court making the reference for a preliminary ruling has already been terminated . . . or the interpretation of Community law or the examination of the validity of a rule of Community law sought by the national court bears no relation to the actual nature of the case or to the subject-matter of the main action . . .

19 It should also be borne in mind that, in order to enable the Court to provide a useful interpretation of Community law, it is appropriate that, before making the reference to the Court, the national court should establish the facts of the case and settle the questions of purely national law . . . By the same token, it is essential for the national court to explain the reasons why it considers that a reply to its questions is necessary to enable it to give judgment . . .

20 With this information in its possession, the Court is in a position to ascertain whether the interpretation of Community law which is sought is related to the actual nature and subject-matter of the main proceedings. If it should appear that the question raised is manifestly irrelevant for the purposes of deciding the case, the Court must declare that there is no need to proceed to judgment.

In a more recent case, the Court has also accepted jurisdiction where a reference is made regarding the interpretation of a directive, the deadline for transposition of which has not yet arrived (such that in principle it is not yet relevant to the application of national law): *VTB-VAB NV v. Total Belgium NV and Galatea BVBA v. Sanoma Magazines Belgium* Joined Cases C-261 and C-299/07, 2009 ECJ EUR-Lex LEXIS 296, [2009] ECR I-2949, though here, as may be recalled from Chapter 5, (*Interenvironnement Wallonie*) the ECJ has held that Member States are under an obligation to refrain from taking actions that could frustrate the purpose of the directive, so there is an EU legal issue raised by questions regarding its interpretation in such circumstances.

Cases such as these suggest that the Court is not normally disposed to reject a reference on grounds that EU law is not in issue in the national proceedings, thus expanding its ability to provide guidance. Could this be objectionable on the basis that it might circumvent the limitations implicit in the "direct effect" doctrine addressed in chapters 4 and 5?

## SRL CILFIT AND LANIFICIO DI GAVARDO SPA v. MINISTRY OF HEALTH
### Case 283/81, [1982] ECR 3415

[In this reference, the national court asked a question on the interpretation of the third paragraph of EC 234/TFEU 267 itself.]

7 [The] obligation to refer a matter to the Court of Justice is based on co-operation, established with a view to ensuring the proper application and uniform interpretation of Community law in all the Member States, between national courts, in their capacity as courts responsible for the application of Community law, and the Court of Justice. More particularly, the third paragraph of Article 177 [267] seeks to prevent the occurrence within the Community of divergences in judicial decisions on questions of Community law. The scope of that obligation must therefore be assessed, in view of those objectives, by reference to the powers of the national courts, on the one hand, and those of the Court of Justice, on the other, where such a question of interpretation is raised within the meaning of Article 177 [267]. In this connexion, it is necessary to define the meaning for the purposes of Community law

of the expression "where any such question is raised" in order to determine the circumstances in which a national court or tribunal against whose decisions there is no judicial remedy under national law is obliged to bring a matter before the Court of Justice.

\*     \*     \*

9 Article 177 [267] does not constitute a means of redress available to the parties to a case pending before a national court or tribunal. Therefore the mere fact that a party contends that the dispute gives rise to a question concerning the interpretation of Community law does not mean that the court or tribunal concerned is compelled to consider that a question has been raised within the meaning of Article 177 [267]. On the other hand, a national court or tribunal may, in an appropriate case, refer a matter to the Court of Justice of its own motion.

10 Secondly, . . . the courts or tribunals referred to in the third paragraph have the same discretion as any other national court or tribunal to ascertain whether a decision on a question of Community law is necessary to enable them to give judgment. Accordingly, those courts or tribunals are not obliged to refer to the Court of Justice a question concerning the interpretation of Community law raised before them if that question is not relevant, that is to say, if the answer to that question, regardless of what it may be, can in no way affect the outcome of the case.

11 If, however, those courts or tribunals consider that recourse to Community law is necessary to enable them to decide a case, Article 177 [267] imposes an obligation on them to refer to the Court of Justice any question of interpretation which may arise.

\*     \*     \*

13 It must be remembered in this connexion that in its judgment of 27 March 1963 in Joined Cases 28 to 30/62 (Da Costa v. Nederlandse Belastingadministratie [1963] ECR 31) the Court ruled that: "Although the third paragraph of Article 177 [267] unreservedly requires courts or tribunals of a Member State against whose decisions there is no judicial remedy under national law . . . to refer to the Court every question of interpretation raised before them, the authority of an interpretation under Article 177 [267] already given by the Court may deprive the obligation of its purpose and thus empty it of its substance. Such is the case especially when the question raised is materially identical with a question which has already been the subject of a preliminary ruling in a similar case."

14 The same effect . . . may be produced where previous decisions of the Court have already dealt with the point of law in question, irrespective of the nature of the proceedings which led to those decisions, even though the questions at issue are not strictly identical.

15 However, it must not be forgotten that in all such circumstances national courts and tribunals, including those referred to in the third paragraph of Article 177 [267], remain entirely at liberty to bring a matter before the Court of Justice if they consider it appropriate to do so.

16 Finally, the correct application of Community law may be so obvious as to leave

no scope for any reasonable doubt as to the manner in which the question raised is to be resolved. Before it comes to the conclusion that such is the case, the national court or tribunal must be convinced that the matter is equally obvious to the courts of the other Member States and to the Court of Justice. Only if those conditions are satisfied, may the national court or tribunal refrain from submitting the question to the Court of Justice and take upon itself the responsibility for resolving it.

17 However, the existence of such a possibility must be assessed on the basis of the characteristic features of Community law and the particular difficulties to which its interpretation gives rise.

18 To begin with, it must be borne in mind that Community legislation is drafted in several languages and that the different language versions are all equally authentic. An interpretation of a provision of Community law thus involves a comparison of the different language versions.

19 It must also be borne in mind, even where the different language versions are entirely in accord with one another, that Community law uses terminology which is peculiar to it. Furthermore, it must be emphasized that legal concepts do not necessarily have the same meaning in Community law and in the law of the various Member States.

20 Finally, every provision of Community law must be placed in its context and interpreted in the light of the provisions of Community law as a whole, regard being had to the objectives thereof and to its state of evolution at the date on which the provision in question is to be applied.

21 In the light of all those considerations, the answer to the question submitted by the Corte Suprema di Cassazione must be that the third paragraph of Article 177 [267] of the EEC Treaty is to be interpreted as meaning that a court or tribunal against whose decisions there is no judicial remedy under national law is required, where a question of Community law is raised before it, to comply with its obligation to bring the matter before the Court of Justice, unless it has established that the question raised is irrelevant or that the Community provision in question has already been interpreted by the Court or that the correct application of Community law is so obvious as to leave no scope for any reasonable doubt. The existence of such a possibility must be assessed in the light of the specific characteristics of Community law, the particular difficulties to which its interpretation gives rise and the risk of divergences in judicial decisions within the Community.

## NOTES AND QUESTIONS

1. In this case the ECJ appeared to accept the possibility that cases in the national courts that involve EU law issues may not need to be referred even by a final appeal court if the EU law in question is so clear that it does not require interpretation. This is generally referred to as the *acte clair* doctrine. However, the ECJ set forth some considerations that the national courts must take into account before deciding not to refer. Do the Court's limitations leave much real possibility for the national courts to decline a reference or, on the contrary, do they leave national courts with too much discretion to decline a reference? Note that the ECJ was considering here a case where apparently the issue in question had been the

subject of prior references. But suppose the issue were one of first impression. Would the national court still be "entitled" to rely on the *acte clair* doctrine?

2.   Note that it is for the national court to make the decision to refer — the parties themselves have no right to require a reference. However, suppose a court of final appeal refuses a reference: how might the parties get such a decision overturned? Are there any EU procedures open to them?

3.   Is the doctrine of *acte clair* satisfactory in a system where the EU legal order exists as an autonomous body of law within the national legal orders?*Acte clair*, after all, has the effect of containing the consideration of EU law issues entirely within the national court system.

4.   The German Constitutional Court has considered that a failure by another court to refer a matter to the ECJ may itself constitute a breach of German constitutional law: *Re Value Added Tax Exception*, Case 2 BSR 876/85 [1988] NUW 2173, [1989] 1 CMLR 113 (second senate, first chamber, November 4, 1987). Why would national constitutional law be relevant? Does this mean that litigants in Germany have better protection than in other Member States, where perhaps no such constitutional protection exists? Might this encourage forum shopping? Is it right that litigants have greater rights under EU law in some countries? Perhaps this is not so different from the situation that can sometimes prevail in the United States where federal circuits disagree.

5.   For a general work on EC 234/TFEU 267 referrals, see D. Anderson and M. Demetriou, References to the European Court (2nd Edition, Sweet and Maxwell, 2002). For an example of Member State guidance (UK) as well as the ECJ Guidance, see http://www.hmcourts-service.gov.uk/cms/801.htm. See also J. Komarek, *Federal Elements in the Community Judicial System: Building Coherence in the Community Legal System*, (2005) CML Rev. 9.

## FOGLIA v. NOVELLO (No. 2)
### Case 244/80, [1981] ECR 3045

[The underlying facts were the same as in *Foglia v. Novello (No. 1)*]

23 The third question concerns circumstances in which, in proceedings between individuals before a court of a Member State, a dispute arises as to the compatibility with Community law of the legislation of a Member State other than that of the State in which that court is situated. The Pretore has submitted in this connexion the question whether in such a case the Member State whose legislation is at issue may be joined in the proceedings instituted before the court in question.

24 The reply on this point must be that in the absence of provisions of Community law in the matter, the possibility of taking proceedings before a national court against a Member State other than that in which that court is situated depends both on the laws of the latter and on the principles of international law.

25 In the fourth question the Pretore has asked whether the protection provided for individuals by the procedure under Article 177 [267] is different, or indeed diminished, when such a question is raised in proceedings between individuals as

opposed to proceedings between an individual and the administration.

26 In answer to the question thus raised it must be emphasized that all individuals whose rights are infringed by measures adopted by a Member State which are contrary to Community law must have the opportunity to seek the protection of a court possessed of jurisdiction and that such a court, for its part, must be free to obtain information as to the scope of the relevant provisions of Community law by means of a procedure under Article 177 [267]. In principle the degree of protection afforded by the courts therefore must not differ according to whether such a question is raised in proceedings between individuals or in an action to which the State whose legislation is challenged is a party in one form or another.

27 Nevertheless, as the Court has stated in its reply set out above to the first question it is for the Court of Justice to appraise the conditions in which a case is referred to it by a national court in order to confirm that it has jurisdiction. In that connexion the question whether the proceedings are between individuals or are directed against the State whose legislation is called in question is not in all circumstances irrelevant.

28 On the one hand it must be pointed out that the court before which, in the course of proceedings between individuals, an issue concerning the compatibility with Community law of legislation of another Member State is brought is not necessarily in a position to provide for such individuals' effective protection in relation to such legislation.

29 On the other hand, regard being had to the independence generally ensured for the parties by the legal systems of the Member States in the field of contract, the possibility arises that the conduct of the parties may be such as to make it impossible for the State concerned to arrange for an appropriate defence of its interests by causing the question of the invalidity of its legislation to be decided by a court of another Member State. Accordingly, in such procedural situations it is impossible to exclude the risk that the procedure under Article 177 [267] may be diverted by the parties from the purposes for which it was laid down by the Treaty.

30 The foregoing considerations as a whole show that the Court of Justice for its part must display special vigilance when, in the course of proceedings between individuals a question is referred to it with a view to permitting the national court to decide whether the legislation of another Member State is in accordance with Community law.

31 The reply to the fourth question must accordingly be that in the case of preliminary questions intended to permit the national court to determine whether provisions laid down by law or regulation in another Member State are in accordance with Community law the degree of legal protection may not differ according to whether such questions are raised in proceedings between individuals or in an action to which the State whose legislation is called in question is a party, but that in the first case the Court of Justice must take special care to ensure that the procedure under Article 177 [267] is not employed for purposes which were not intended by the Treaty.

# NOTES AND QUESTIONS

**1.** In this second *Foglia* case, the Court addressed, *inter alia*, the issue as to whether it would be appropriate to question a Member State law in the courts of another Member State. What was the Court's view? Since the Court only interprets EU law, should it be concerned at all about this question? Is it appropriate that it should be giving directions to the courts of the Member States on caution in this area?

**2.** Once the ECJ had given its second ruling, what was the national court to do, faced as it still was with the resolution of the matter, and particularly the determination of the lawfulness of the French legislation?

**3.** Some critics of the judgments in the *Foglia* cases suggest that they may hinder the EU in fulfilling some of its most fundamental goals. What might be the basis for such a proposition? Do you agree with it?

See also *Kommanditgesellschaft in Firma Eau de Cologne & Parfumerie-Fabrik, Glockengasse n. 4711 v. Provide Srl.*, Case C-150/88, 1989 ECJ CELEX LEXIS 358, [1989] ECR 3891, where the Court made it very clear that merely because proceedings in a court of one Member State involve the compatibility of the laws of another Member State (in this case, Italy) with EU law, this does not mean that the Court does not have jurisdiction to provide the interpretation requested. The Italian government had raised objections to the Court's assuming jurisdiction.

> 12 Those objections must be dismissed. First, the documents before the Court do not allow any doubt as to the genuineness of the dispute in the main proceedings or, therefore, the propriety of the request for a preliminary ruling. Secondly, the Court has consistently held . . . that, when ruling on questions intended to permit the national court to determine whether national provisions are in accordance with Community law, the Court may provide the criteria for the interpretation of Community law which will enable the national court to solve the legal problem with which it is faced. The same is true when it is to be determined whether the provisions of a Member State other than that of the court requesting the ruling are compatible with Community law.

Looking at this statement, is it clear why the Court feels no concern about its jurisdiction in such cases? Have the concerns expressed in *Foglia No 2* now disappeared? Contrast *Bacardi-Martini SAS and Cellier des Dauphins v. Newcastle United Football Co. Ltd.*, Case C-318/00 [2003] ECR I-905. The national law in issue was a French statute that prohibited showing advertisements for alcoholic drinks on television (the "Loi Evin"). Bacardi had contracted with an advertising company called Dorna to display ads at Newcastle's stadium. Newcastle arranged for a UEFA cup match between it and the French club Metz to be broadcast on a French television station. It then learned shortly before the match that the Bacardi ads were going to be shown as part of that broadcast and sought to interfere in the contract between Dorna and Bacardi to get the ads removed. In fact they were not removed but Dorna took action to ensure that they were shown only for several seconds at a time instead of the 30-second slots that Bacardi had paid for. Bacardi then sued Newcastle for interfering in its contract and argued, among other things, that the French law was invalid as a breach of EC 49/TFEU 56 (free movement of services), which then would have removed any justification Newcastle would have had for interfering. However, the ECJ was not satisfied that the validity of the law would have made any difference to Newcastle's position and sent the case back to the English High Court for further explanation as to why its ruling was really necessary for the resolution of the case. The Court gave the following guidance:

44 In order that the Court may perform its task in accordance with the Treaty, it is essential for national courts to explain, when the reasons do not emerge beyond any doubt from the file, why they consider that a reply to their questions is necessary to enable them to give judgment . . . Thus the Court has held that it is essential that the national court should give at the very least some explanation of the reasons for the choice of the Community provisions which it requires to be interpreted and of the link it establishes between those provisions and the national legislation applicable to the dispute . . .

45 Moreover, the Court must display special vigilance when, in the course of proceedings between individuals, a question is referred to it with a view to permitting the national court to decide whether the legislation of another Member State is in accordance with Community law (*Foglia*, paragraph 30).

46 In the present case, as the questions referred are intended to enable the national court to assess the compatibility with Community law of the legislation of another Member State, the Court must be informed in some detail of that court's reasons for considering that an answer to the questions is necessary to enable it to give judgment.

47 It appears from the High Court's account of the legal context that it has to apply English law in the main proceedings. It nevertheless considers that the issue of the legality of the Loi Évin provisions is central to resolution of the proceedings before [it]. It does not, however, state positively that an answer to that question is necessary to enable it to give judgment.

48 On being requested by the Court to explain more fully the basis on which Newcastle could rely on the Loi Évin, the High Court has essentially confined itself to repeating the defendant's argument that it could reasonably anticipate that a failure to give instructions to remove the advertisements in the stadium would result in a breach of French law.

49 On the other hand, the High Court has not said whether it itself considered that Newcastle could reasonably suppose that it was obliged to comply with the French legislation, and there is nothing else to that effect before the Court.

50 The United Kingdom Government has contended that the premiss for concluding that the questions referred are material could be the existence of an obligation on the part of Newcastle, in terms of its contract with CSI for the broadcast of the Newcastle-Metz match by a French television

station, to comply with the French legislation. On this point, it suffices to state that the national court has not mentioned the existence of any such contractual obligation.

51 Furthermore, . . . even if the national court were to consider that Newcastle could reasonably suppose that compliance with the French legislation required it to intervene in the contracts in question, it is not clear why that would no longer be the case if the provision with which Newcastle wished to ensure compliance turned out to be contrary to Article 59 [56] of the Treaty.

52 The order for reference contains no information on this point either.

53 In those circumstances, the conclusion must be that the Court does not have the material before it to show that it is necessary to rule on the compatibility with the Treaty of legislation of a Member State other than that of the court making the reference.

54 The questions referred to the Court for a preliminary ruling are therefore inadmissible."

4.    From a U.S. perspective, a somewhat analogous situation might be found in the Eleventh Amendment to the effect that individual citizens may not sue a State in federal court.

## [B]   "Before Any Court or Tribunal of a Member State"

### PRETORE DI SALO v. PERSONS UNKNOWN
Case 14/86, 1987 ECJ CELEX LEXIS 357, [1987] ECR 2545

[The Italian Pretore di Salo referred to the Court for a preliminary ruling under EC 234/TFEU 267 a question on the interpretation of Council Directive 78/659 of 18 July 1978 on the quality of fresh waters needing protection or improvement in order to support fish life.]

2 Those questions were raised in criminal proceedings against persons unknown concerning certain offences contrary to a number of legislative provisions relating to the protection of waters.

3 The proceedings were initiated following a report submitted by an anglers' association as a result of the death of many fish in the River Chiese, due essentially to the many dams placed in the river for hydro-electric and irrigation purposes, which were said to cause significant and sudden changes in the water level. Other anglers' associations had already submitted reports on the same matters and on the discharge of noxious substances into the same river, but it had been decided that no action was to be taken on those reports.

*    *    *

6 Without expressly arguing that the Court does not have jurisdiction to reply to the questions referred to it, the Italian Government draws the Court's attention to the nature of the functions performed in this case by the Pretore, which are both those of a public prosecutor and those of an examining magistrate. The Pretore carries

out preliminary investigations in his capacity as public prosecutor and, where these disclose no grounds for continuing the proceedings, makes an order accordingly in the place of an examining magistrate. That order is not a judicial act because it cannot acquire the force of res judicata or create an irreversible procedural situation and because no reasons need be given for it, whereas Article 111 of the Italian Constitution imposes an obligation to state reasons in the case of judicial acts.

7 It must be observed that the Pretori are judges who, in proceedings such as those in which the questions referred to the Court in this case were raised, combine the functions of a public prosecutor and an examining magistrate. The Court has jurisdiction to reply to a request for a preliminary ruling if that request emanates from a court or tribunal which has acted in the general framework of its task of judging, independently and in accordance with law, cases coming within the jurisdiction conferred on it by law, even though certain functions of that court or tribunal in the proceedings which give rise to the reference for a preliminary ruling are not, strictly speaking, of a judicial nature.

8 At the hearing, the Italian Government also maintained that, having regard to the present stage of the proceedings, at which the facts have not been sufficiently established and those who may be responsible have not yet been identified, a reference for a preliminary ruling is premature.

9 The Commission considers that the reference for a preliminary ruling is inadmissible because in criminal proceedings against persons unknown it is possible that a decision may never be given on the substance of the case. All that is required for that to be the case is for those responsible never to be identified. At the hearing, the Commission also relied on another argument in support of the proposition that the Court does not have jurisdiction: if, after the Court's decision, the persons responsible were identified, they would be prevented from defending before the Court the interpretation of Community law most in conformity with their interests. That would constitute a violation of the right to a fair hearing.

10 . . . [I]f the interpretation of Community law is to be of use to the national court, it is essential to define the legal context in which the interpretation requested should be placed. In that perspective, it might be convenient in certain circumstances for the facts of the case to be established and for questions of purely national law to be settled at the time when the reference is made to the Court of Justice so as to enable the latter to take cognizance of all the matters of fact and law which may be relevant to the interpretation of Community law which it is called upon to give.

11 . . . [T]hose considerations do not in any way restrict the discretion of the national court, which alone has a direct knowledge of the facts of the case and of the arguments of the parties, which will have to take responsibility for giving judgment in the case and which is therefore in the best position to appreciate at what stage of the proceedings it requires a preliminary ruling from the Court of Justice. The decision at what stage in proceedings a question should be referred to the Court of Justice for a preliminary ruling is therefore dictated by considerations of procedural economy and efficiency to be weighed only by the national court and not by the Court of Justice.

12 It should also be pointed out that the Court has consistently held that the fact that judgments delivered on the basis of references for a preliminary ruling are binding on the national courts does not preclude the national court to which such a judgment is addressed from making a further reference to the Court of Justice if it considers it necessary in order to give judgment in the main proceedings. Such a reference may be justified when the national court encounters difficulties in understanding or applying the judgment, when it refers a fresh question of law to the Court, or again when it submits new considerations which might lead the Court to give a different answer to a question submitted earlier . . .

13 It follows that where the accused are identified after the reference for a preliminary ruling and if one of the above mentioned conditions arises, the national court may once again refer a question to the Court of Justice and thereby ensure that due respect is given to the right to a fair hearing.

14 In those circumstances, the objections raised by the Commission and the Italian Government concerning the jurisdiction of the Court must be rejected.

## NOTES AND QUESTIONS

1.    Here the Court rejected arguments that it did not have jurisdiction. On what grounds? Was there not some merit to the arguments regarding the premature nature of the reference?

2.    In *Ignacio Pedro Santesteban Goicoechea*, Case C-296/08 PPU, 2008 ECJ EUR-Lex LEXIS 2137, [2008] ECR I-6307, the question was raised as to whether the referring Court, the Chambre de l'instruction (Indictment Division) of the Cour d'appel de Montpellier (Court of Appeal, Montpellier) was a "court" within the meaning of EC 234/TFEU 267. Although such bodies do exercise administrative functions at a preliminary stage in judicial proceedings, the Court looks at whether the body in question qualifies as a court or tribunal by taking into account a number of factors, such as whether the body is established by law, whether it is permanent, whether its jurisdiction is compulsory, whether its procedure is *inter partes*, whether it applies rules of law and whether it is independent (see *Synetairismos Farmakopoion Aitolias & Akarnanias (Syfait) and Others v. GlaxoSmithKline plc and GlaxoSmithKline AEVE*, Case C-53/03, 2005 ECJ EUR-Lex LEXIS 483, [2005] ECR I-4609.) A national court may refer a question to the Court only if there is a case pending before it and if it is called on to give judgment in proceedings intended to lead to a decision of a judicial nature. It held that it is not disputed that the indictment divisions of courts of appeal satisfy the above conditions. These factors would clearly serve to distinguish its judicial function from its administrative and investigative duties. This distinction was not at all clear in the *Pretore di Salo* case. Perhaps the Court would have decided differently in that decision based on these later, more developed criteria.

3.    It may be noted also that in civil law jurisdictions, the courts may be called upon to exercise some administrative functions. The ECJ declines to hear references from such courts because the ECJ's role is to assist in the judicial function only. For an example, see *Standesamt Stadt Niebüll*, Case C-96/04, 2006 ECJ EUR-Lex LEXIS 1966, [2006] ECR I-3561, where a German Court refused to

recognize a double-barreled name (mother's and father's names) for a German child that had been approved by the Danish authorities while the parents were resident in Denmark. (German law does not allow such double-barreled names.) However, the ECJ will accept a reference from an appeals court dealing with a challenge to a lower court's decision exercising an administrative role, since at this point the appeals court *is* exercising a judicial function: *Cartesio Oktató és Szolgáltató bt*, Case C-210/06, 2008 ECJ EUR-Lex LEXIS 2112, [2008] ECR I-9641. The Court has also declined to hear references from authorities exercising quasi-judicial functions that are, however, not part of an independent judiciary. For example, in *Synetairismos Farmakopoion Aitolias & Akarnanias (Syfait) and Others v. GlaxoSmithKline plc and GlaxoSmithKline AEVE*, Case C-53/03, 2005 ECJ CELEX LEXIS 220, 2005 ECR I-4609, the Greek Competition Commission (Epitropi Antagonismou) was determined not to be a court or tribunal. The Court cited a number of reasons:

30. It should be noted, first of all, in this regard that the Epitropi Antagonismou is subject to the supervision of the Minister for Development. Such supervision implies that that minister is empowered, within certain limits, to review the lawfulness of the decisions adopted by the Epitropi Antagonismou.

31. Next, whilst it is true that the members of the Epitropi Antagonismou enjoy personal and operational independence and are bound in the exercise of their duties only by the law and their conscience within the meaning of Law No 703/1977, it nevertheless remains that there are no particular safeguards in respect of their dismissal or the termination of their appointment. That system does not appear to constitute an effective safeguard against undue intervention or pressure from the executive on the members of the Epitropi Antagonismou . . .

32. It should also be noted that under Article 8C(1)(b) and (d) of Law No 703/1977, the President of the Epitropi Antagonismou is responsible for the coordination and general policy of the secretariat, is the immediate superior of the personnel of that secretariat and exercises disciplinary power over them.

33. It should be noted in this regard that the Tribunales Economico-Administrativos (Economic and Administrative Courts) (Spain) were found by the Court, in paragraphs 39 and 40 of the Gabalfrisa judgment, to be third parties in relation to the departments of the tax authority responsible for the management, clearance and recovery of VAT, particularly given the separation of functions between them. However, in so far as there is an operational link between the Epitropi Antagonismou, a decision-making body, and its secretariat, a fact-finding body on the basis of whose proposal it adopts decisions, the Epitropi Antagonismou is not a clearly distinct third party in relation to the State body which, by virtue of its role, may be akin to a party in the course of competition proceedings.

34. Lastly, it should be noted that a competition authority such as the Epitropi Antagonismou is required to work in close cooperation with the Commission of the European Communities and may, pursuant to Article

11(6) of Council Regulation (EC) No 1/2003 of 16 December 2002 on the implementation of the rules on competition laid down in Articles 81 [101] and 82 [102] of the Treaty (OJ 2003 L 1, p. 1), be relieved of its competence by a decision of the Commission. It should moreover be noted in this context that Article 11(6) of Regulation No 1/2003 essentially maintains the rule in Article 9(3) of Council Regulation No 17 of 6 February 1962, First Regulation implementing Articles 81 and 82 of the Treaty (OJ, English Special Edition, 1959-1962 p. 87), that the competition authorities of the Member States are automatically relieved of their competence where the Commission initiates its own proceedings (see in that connection the 17th recital in the preamble to Regulation No 1/2003).

The rationale in this case seems logical enough, but consider whether the Court might not also have had in mind the effect on the structure of Regulation 1/2003 if had it decided that the Greek Commission were a court or tribunal. What might those effects have been? (See Chapter 7 *supra* and Regulation 1/2003 in the Documentary Supplement.)

## NORDSEE DEUTSCHE HOCHSEEFISCHEREI GMBH v. REEDEREI MOND HOCHSEEFISCHEREI NORDSTERN AG & CO. KG AND REEDEREI FRIEDRICH BUSSE HOCHSEEFISCHEREI NORDSTERN AG & CO. KG
### Case 102/81, [1982] ECR 1095

[A dispute had arisen concerning the performance of a contract entered into in 1973 by a number of German shipbuilders. The contract concerned a joint project for building 13 factory-ships for fishing and its purpose was to apportion equally among the contracting parties all financial aid received by them from the EAGGF (Guidance and Guarantee Fund), so that one thirteenth of the total amount of aid granted would be allotted for each ship to be built. By mutual agreement the parties to the contract had previously submitted applications to the Fund for aid for the construction of nine ships. Of those nine applications the Commission finally accepted only six, the others being either withdrawn or rejected. One of the undertakings participating in the building programme sought payment from two of the other undertakings of the amounts to which it was entitled under the contract. The dispute was submitted for arbitration, as the contract of 1973 contained a clause stating that in the event of disagreement between the parties on any question arising from the contract a final decision was to be given by an arbitrator, all recourse to the ordinary courts being excluded. In accordance with that clause the arbitrator was appointed by the Chamber of Commerce of Bremen after it had become apparent that the parties to the dispute could not agree on the appointment of an arbitrator.]

5 During the arbitration hearing the respondents claimed that the 1973 contract was void in so far as it arranged for aid from the Fund to go to the building of ships in respect of which the Commission had not granted such aid. They took the view that aid from the Fund was linked to completion of a specific project and could not therefore validly be transferred by the recipient to a different project.

6 The arbitrator was of the opinion that under German law the validity of a contract

to share aid from the Fund depended on whether such sharing amounted to an irregularity under the relevant Community regulations. Considering that a decision on the point was necessary in order to allow him to make his award he referred the matter to the Court for a preliminary ruling.

Applicability of Article 177 [267]

7 Since the arbitration tribunal which referred the matter to the Court for a preliminary ruling was established pursuant to a contract between private individuals the question arises whether it may be considered as a court or tribunal of one of the Member States within the meaning of Article 177 [267] of the Treaty.

*    *    *

10 It is true . . . that there are certain similarities between the activities of the arbitration tribunal in question and those of an ordinary court or tribunal inasmuch as the arbitration is provided for within the framework of the law, the arbitrator must decide according to law and his award has, as between the parties, the force of res judicata, and may be enforceable if leave to issue execution is obtained. However, those characteristics are not sufficient to give the arbitrator the status of a "court or tribunal of a Member State" within the meaning of Article 177 [267] of the Treaty.

11 The first important point to note is that when the contract was entered into in 1973 the parties were free to leave their disputes to be resolved by the ordinary courts or to opt for arbitration by inserting a clause to that effect in the contract. From the facts of the case it appears that the parties were under no obligation, whether in law or in fact, to refer their disputes to arbitration.

12 The second point to be noted is that the German public authorities are not involved in the decision to opt for arbitration nor are they called upon to intervene automatically in the proceedings before the arbitrator. The Federal Republic of Germany, as a Member State of the Community responsible for the performance of obligations arising from Community law within its territory pursuant to Article 5 [TEU 4] and Articles 169 [258] to 171 [260] of the Treaty, has not entrusted or left to private individuals the duty of ensuring that such obligations are complied with in the sphere in question in this case.

13 It follows from these considerations that the link between the arbitration procedure in this instance and the organization of legal remedies through the courts in the Member State in question is not sufficiently close for the arbitrator to be considered as a "court or tribunal of a Member State" within the meaning of Article 177 [267].

14 . . . Community law must be observed in its entirety throughout the territory of all the Member States . . . [I]f questions of Community law are raised in an arbitration resorted to by agreement the ordinary courts may be called upon to examine them either in the context of their collaboration with arbitration tribunals, in particular in order to assist them in certain procedural matters or to interpret the law applicable, or in the course of a review of an arbitration award — which may be more or less extensive depending on the circumstances — and which they may be

required to effect in case of an appeal or objection, in proceedings for leave to issue execution or by any other method of recourse available under the relevant national legislation.

15 It is for those national courts and tribunals to ascertain whether it is necessary for them to make a reference to the Court under Article 177 [267] of the Treaty in order to obtain the interpretation or assessment of the validity of provisions of Community law which they may need to apply when exercising such auxiliary or supervisory functions.

16 It follows that in this instance the Court has no jurisdiction to give a ruling.

## NOTES AND QUESTIONS

1. What reasons did the Court give for declining jurisdiction in this case? The ECJ noted that the parties were free to opt for the regular courts or arbitration and chose arbitration. Suppose arbitration had been mandatory, i.e., mandatory under German Legislation or, for example, a trade association rule. Would the Court have ruled the same way? See in this regard *C. Broekmeulen v. Huisarts Registratie Commissie*, Case 246/80, 1981 ECJ EUR-Lex LEXIS 212, 1981 ECR 2311, where the appeal body of the organization in the Netherlands responsible for certifying doctors was considered to be a tribunal as intended by EC 234/TFEU 267. As with the *Foglia* and *Greek Competition Commission* cases discussed above, one could perhaps discern an ulterior reason for the Court's decision: if the appeal body were not able to refer questions, important issues relating to EU law on mutual recognition of professional qualifications might not be able to reach the Court.

2. Is there a policy argument for or against excluding commercial arbitrations from the "courts" or "tribunals" that can make EC 234/TFEU 267 references? Is it significant that private arbitration is an increasingly prevalent form of dispute resolution in Europe? Would it make a difference if the arbitrator were required to apply considerations other than purely legal ones?

3. Suppose parties with no connections with the European Union were to choose, say, German law as the governing law of their contract. If a dispute goes to the national court for decision, should the ECJ accept jurisdiction in the event of a reference?

4. For further discussion see G. Anagnostaras, *Analysis and Reflections — Preliminary problems and jurisdiction uncertainties: The admissibility of questions referred by bodies performing quasi-judicial functions*, (2006) 30 EL REV. 878.

## [C] Rulings on the Validity of EU Acts

## FIRMA FOTO-FROST v. HAUPTZOLLAMT LUEBECK-OST
### Case 314/85, 1987 ECJ CELEX LEXIS 200, [1987] ECR 4199

[This case arose before the reunification of the Federal Republic of Germany and the German Democratic Republic. Foto-Frost, an importer, exporter and wholesaler of photographic goods sought annulment of a notice issued by the Hauptzollamt (Principal Customs Office) Lübeck-Ost for the post-clearance recovery of import duties following a Commission decision addressed to what was then West Germany or Bundesrepublik on 6 May 1983 in which it was held that it was not permissible to waive the recovery of import duties in the case in question.

The operations to which the recovery of duties related were Foto-Frost's importation into the Federal Republic of Germany and release for free circulation there of prismatic binoculars originating in the German Democratic Republic. Foto-Frost purchased the binoculars from traders in Denmark and the United Kingdom, which dispatched them to it under the Community external transit procedure from customs warehouses in Denmark and the Netherlands. FotoFrost contended that the importation related to German internal trade. Under Treaty protocols, trade between the former German Democratic Republic and the Bundesrepublik was treated as German internal trade and not trade with a third country. The question posed to the ECJ was whether the national court had jurisdiction to declare the underlying Commission decision invalid.]

12 Article 177 [267] confers on the Court jurisdiction to give preliminary rulings on the interpretation of the Treaty and of acts of the Community institutions and on the validity of such acts. The second paragraph of that Article provides that national courts may refer such questions to the Court and the third paragraph of that Article puts them under an obligation to do so where there is no judicial remedy under national law against their decisions.

13 In enabling national courts against whose decisions there is a judicial remedy under national law to refer to the Court for a preliminary ruling questions on interpretation or validity, Article 177 [267] did not settle the question whether those courts themselves may declare that acts of Community institutions are invalid.

14 Those courts may consider the validity of a Community act and, if they consider that the grounds put forward before them by the parties in support of invalidity are unfounded, they may reject them, concluding that the measure is completely valid. By taking that action they are not calling the existence of the Community measure in question.

15 On the other hand, those courts do not have the power to declare acts of the Community institutions invalid. . . . The main purpose of the powers accorded to the Court by Article 177 [267] is to ensure that Community law is applied uniformly by national courts. That requirement of uniformity is particularly imperative when the validity of a Community act is in question. Divergences between courts in the Member States as to the validity of Community acts would be liable to place in jeopardy the very unity of the Community legal order and detract from the requirements of legal certainty.

16 The same conclusion is dictated by consideration of the necessary coherence of the system of judicial protection established by the Treaty. In that regard it must be observed that requests for preliminary rulings, like actions for annulment, constitute means for reviewing the legality of acts of the Community institutions. . . . [I]n Articles 173 [263] and 184 [241], on the one hand, and in Article 177 [267], on the other, the Treaty established a complete system of legal remedies and

procedures designed to permit the Court of Justice to review the legality of measures adopted by the institutions'.

17 Since Article 173 [263] gives the Court exclusive jurisdiction to declare void an act of a Community institution, the coherence of the system requires that where the validity of a Community act is challenged before a national court the power to declare the act invalid must also be reserved to the Court of Justice.

18 It must also be emphasized that the Court of Justice is in the best position to decide on the validity of Community acts. Under Article 20 of the Protocol on the Statute of the Court of Justice of the EEC, Community institutions whose acts are challenged are entitled to participate in the proceedings in order to defend the validity of the acts in question. Furthermore, under the second paragraph of Article 21 of that Protocol the Court may require the Member States and institutions which are not participating in the proceedings to supply all information which it considers necessary for the purposes of the case before it.

19 It should be added that the rule that national courts may not themselves declare Community acts invalid may have to be qualified in certain circumstances in the case of proceedings relating to an application for interim measures; however, that case is not referred to in the national court's question.

20 The answer to the first question must therefore be that the national courts have no jurisdiction themselves to declare that acts of Community institutions are invalid.

## NOTES AND QUESTIONS

1. Why are Member States' courts prohibited from pronouncing on the invalidity of EU law? In the United States, the state courts may declare a federal statute unconstitutional. Is there a significant difference between the position of the European Court of Justice and that of the U.S. Supreme Court in this regard? See in this regard 28 U.S.C. sec. 1257, which states:

> (a) Final judgments or decrees rendered by the highest court of a State in which a decision could be had, may be reviewed by the Supreme Court by writ of certiorari where the validity of a treaty or statute of the United States is drawn in question or where the validity of a statute of any State is drawn in question on the ground of its being repugnant to the Constitution, treaties, or laws of the United States, or where any title, right, privilege, or immunity is specially set up or claimed under the Constitution or the treaties or statutes of, or any commission held or authority exercised under, the United States.

2. Note that the Court in *Foto-Frost* expressly stated that a national court is permitted to reject a party's challenge to the validity of an EU action and declare the action valid. What is the Court's rationale for reaching this conclusion? Do you find it convincing?

3. In *Zuckerfabrik Süderdithmarschen AG v. Hauptzollamt Itzehoe*, Joined Cases C-143/88 and C-92/89, 1991 ECJ CELEX LEXIS 26, [1991] ECR I-415, the Court ruled that a national court may, on an interim basis, suspend a domestic

measure based on an EU regulation that is alleged to be invalid. The Court indicated, however, that such action by a national court would be permissible only if the following conditions are met: (a) the national court has serious doubts regarding the validity of the EU measures; (b) it requests the Court of Justice to issue a preliminary ruling on the validity of the measure; (c) the matter is urgent and the applicant is likely to suffer serious and irreparable damage if relief is refused; and (d) due account is taken of the interest of the EU and the need to ensure the effectiveness of EU law. Has the Court's decision in *Süderdithmarschen* undermined or strengthened the EU legal order? Is its decision consistent with its earlier decisions establishing the supremacy of EU law that conflicts with national law?

## TWD TEXTILWERKE DEGGENDORF GMBH v. GERMANY
### Case 188/92, 1994 ECJ CELEX LEXIS 113, [1994] ECR I-833,

[TWD had received a subsidy from the German government which the Commission had subsequently reviewed and found to be in violation of EC 86/TFEU 106. The Federal Minister for Economic Affairs forwarded to TWD for information a copy of the relevant decision, Decision 86/509, and pointed out that it could bring an action against that decision under Article 230 of the Treaty. Neither Germany nor TWD challenged the decision before the Court of Justice. Subsequently, and well after the expiry of the two month time limit for an EC 230/TFEU 263 challenge, the German Government revoked the certificate approving eligibility for the subsidy and demanded the repayment of the subsidy. TWD appealed the revocation. It will be recalled from chapter 8 that the Court has made it clear that the plea of illegality is not available to a Member State that had standing to bring an EC 230/TFEU 263 action. The question therefore arose whether this doctrine would also preclude a national court from allowing a private party to assert invalidity.]

10 The issue before the national court is whether or not, in the factual and legal circumstances of the main proceedings, the applicant is time-barred from pleading the unlawfulness of the Commission's decision in support of an action brought against the administrative act by which the national authority, in implementation of the Commission's decision, revoked the certificates which formed the legal basis for the aid which it had received.

11 The national court emphasizes that the Commission's decision was not challenged by the applicant in the main proceedings, the recipient of the aid with which the decision was concerned, although a copy of that decision had been sent to it by the Federal Ministry of Economic Affairs and that Ministry had explicitly informed it that it could bring an action against that decision before the Court of Justice.

12 The question submitted to the Court must be answered in the light of those circumstances.

13 It is settled law that a decision which has not been challenged by the addressee within the time-limit laid down by Article 173 [263] of the Treaty becomes definitive as against him . . .

14 The undertaking in receipt of individual aid which is the subject-matter of a Commission decision adopted on the basis of Article 93 [107] of the Treaty has the

right to bring an action for annulment under the second paragraph of Article 173 [263] of the Treaty even if the decision is addressed to a Member State. . . . By virtue of the third paragraph of that article, the expiry of the time-limit laid down in that provision has the same time-barring effect vis-à-vis such an undertaking as it does vis-à-vis the Member State which is the addressee of the decision.

15 It is settled law that a Member State may no longer call in question the validity of a decision addressed to it on the basis of Article 93 [107] (2) of the Treaty once the time-limit laid down in the third paragraph of Article 173 [263] of the Treaty has expired . . .

16 That case-law, according to which it is impossible for a Member State which is the addressee of a decision taken under the first paragraph of Article 93 [107](2) of the Treaty to call in question the validity of the decision in the proceedings for non-compliance provided for in the second paragraph of that provision, is based in particular on the consideration that the periods within which applications must be lodged are intended to safeguard legal certainty by preventing Community measures which involve legal effects from being called in question indefinitely.

17 It follows from the same requirements of legal certainty that it is not possible for a recipient of aid, forming the subject-matter of a Commission decision adopted on the basis of Article 93 [107] of the Treaty, who could have challenged that decision and who allowed the mandatory time-limit laid down in this regard by the third paragraph of Article 173 [263] of the Treaty to expire, to call in question the lawfulness of that decision before the national courts in an action brought against the measures taken by the national authorities for implementing that decision.

18 To accept that in such circumstances the person concerned could challenge the implementation of the decision in proceedings before the national court on the ground that the decision was unlawful would in effect enable the person concerned to overcome the definitive nature which the decision assumes as against that person once the time-limit for bringing an action has expired.

19 It is true that in its judgment in Joined Cases 133 to 136/85 Rau v. BALM [1987] ECR 2289, on which the French Government relies in its observations, the Court held that the possibility of bringing a direct action under the second paragraph of Article 173 [263] of the EEC Treaty against a decision adopted by a Community institution did not preclude the possibility of bringing an action in a national court against a measure adopted by a national authority for the implementation of that decision, on the ground that the latter decision was unlawful.

20 However, as is clear from the Report for the Hearing in those cases, each of the plaintiffs in the main proceedings had brought an action before the Court of Justice for the annulment of the decision in question. The Court did not therefore rule, and did not have to rule, in that judgment on the time-barring effects of the expiry of time-limits. It is precisely that issue with which the question referred by the national court in this case is concerned.

21 This case is also distinguishable from Case 216/82 Universität Hamburg v. Hauptzollamt Hamburg-Kehrwieder [1983] ECR 2771.

22 In the judgment in the case the Court held that a plaintiff whose application for

duty-free admission had been rejected by a decision of a national authority taken on the basis of a decision of the Commission addressed to all the Member States had to be able to plead, in proceedings brought under national law against the rejection of his application, the illegality of the Commission's decision on which the national decision adopted in his regard was based.

23 In that judgment that Court took into account the fact that the rejection of the application by the national authority was the only measure directly addressed to the person concerned of which it had necessarily been informed in good time and which it could challenge in the courts without encountering any difficulty in demonstrating its interest in bringing proceedings. It held that in those circumstances the possibility of pleading the unlawfulness of the Commission's decision derived from a general principle of law which found its expression in Article 184 [249] of the EEC Treaty, namely the principle which confers upon any party to proceedings the right to challenge, for the purpose of obtaining the annulment of a decision of direct and individual concern to that party, the validity of previous acts of the institutions which form the legal basis of the decision which is being attacked, if that party was not entitled under Article 173 [263] of the Treaty to bring a direct action challenging those acts by which it was thus affected without having been in a position to ask that they be declared void . . .

24 In the present case, it is common ground that the applicant in the main proceedings was fully aware of the Commission's decision and of the fact that it could without any doubt have challenged it under Article 173 [263] of the Treaty.

25 It follows from the foregoing that, in factual and legal circumstances such as those of the main proceedings in this case, the definitive nature of the decision taken by the Commission pursuant to Article 93 [107] of the Treaty vis-à-vis the undertaking in receipt of the aid binds the national court by virtue of the principle of legal certainty.

26 The reply to be given to the first question must therefore be that the national court is bound by a Commission decision adopted under Article 93 [107](2) of the Treaty where, in view of the implementation of that decision by the national authorities, the recipient of the aid to which the implementation measures are addressed brings before it an action in which it pleads the unlawfulness of the Commission's decision and where that recipient of aid, although informed in writing by the Member State of the Commission's decision, did not bring an action against that decision under the second paragraph of Article 173 [263] of the Treaty, or did not do so within the period prescribed.

## NOTES AND QUESTIONS

1. It is certainly one thing to greatly restrict the ability of a Member State to plead illegality when it had the opportunity to bring an EC 230/TFEU 263 action. But is it fair to demand the same thing of a private party? What problems are created for the national courts by the *TWD* ruling? Might they be required to examine for themselves whether a party was directly and individually concerned under EC 230/TFEU 263? See in this regard, *R. v. Intervention Board for*

*Agricultural Produce ex parte Accrington Beef Co. Ltd*, Case C-241/95, 1996 ECJ CELEX LEXIS 509, 1996 ECR I-6699.

2. The full implications of allowing challenges to validity of Community legislation through the EC 234/TFEU 267 procedure are far from being worked through by the ECJ at this point. *Textilwerke*, however indicates that the Court is willing to restrict such challenges.

3. Note that challenges under EC 234/TFEU 267 must go to the ECJ while challenges under EC 230/TFEU 263 go to the CFI/General Court. Does this create any problems?

4. See also *Nachi Europe GmbH v. Hauptzollamt Krefeld*, Case C-239/99, 2001 ECJ CELEX LEXIS 672, [2001] ECR I-1197.

## § 9.03 THE DUTY OF SINCERE COOPERATION (EC 10/TEU 4)

### VON COLSON & KAMANN v. LAND NORDRHEIN-WESTFALEN
### Case 14/83, [1984] ECR 1891

[Two qualified social workers, Sabine von Colson and Elisabeth Kamann were denied employment by the Land Nordrhein-Westfalen in a prison that handled exclusively male prisoners. The authorities cited problems and risks connected with the appointement of female candidates and for those reasons appointed instead male candidates who were however less well-qualified. The Labor Court (Arbeitsgericht) of Hamm held that there had been discrimination and took the view that under German law the only sanction for discrimination in recruitment was compensation for "Vertrauensschaden", or the loss incurred by candidates who are victims of discrimination as a result of their belief that there would be no discrimination in the establishment of the employment relationship. The relevant legal provision states that the employer is liable for "damages in respect of the loss incurred by the worker as a result of his reliance on the expectation that the establishment of the employment relationship would not be precluded by such a breach" (of the principle of equal treatment). This provision was intended to implement Council Directive no 76/207. Consequently the Labor Court found that it could order the reimbursement only of the travel expenses incurred by the plaintiff Von Colson in pursuing her application for the post (DM 7.20) and that it could not allow the plaintiffs' other claims. The plaintiffs asserted that this provision infringed article 6 of Directive 76/207 the same provision as in *Marshall* (see chapter 5).]

22 It is impossible to establish real equality of opportunity without an appropriate system of sanctions. That follows not only from the actual purpose of the directive but more specifically from article 6 thereof which, by granting applicants for a post who have been discriminated against recourse to the courts, acknowledges that those candidates have rights of which they may avail themselves before the courts.

23 Although, . . . full implementation of the directive does not require any specific

form of sanction for unlawful discrimination, it does entail that that sanction be such as to guarantee real and effective judicial protection. Moreover it must also have a real deterrent effect on the employer. It follows that where a Member State chooses to penalize the breach of the prohibition of discrimination by the award of compensation, that compensation must in any event be adequate in relation to the damage sustained.

24 In consequence it appears that national provisions limiting the right to compensation of persons who have been discriminated against as regards access to employment to a purely nominal amount, such as, for example, the reimbursement of expenses incurred by them in submitting their application, would not satisfy the requirements of an effective transposition of the directive.

25 The nature of the sanctions provided for in the Federal Republic of Germany in respect of discrimination regarding access to employment and in particular the question whether the rule in paragraph 611a (2) of the Bürgerliches Gesetzbuch excludes the possibility of compensation on the basis of the general rules of law were the subject of lengthy discussion before the court. The German government maintained in the oral procedure that that provision did not necessarily exclude the application of the general rules of law regarding compensation. It is for the national court alone to rule on that question concerning the interpretation of its national law.

26 However, the Member States' obligation arising from a directive to achieve the result envisaged by the directive and their duty under article 5 [TEU 4] the Treaty to take all appropriate measures, whether general or particular, to ensure the fulfilment of that obligation, is binding on all the authorities of Member States including, for matters within their jurisdiction, the courts. It follows that, in applying the national law and in particular the provisions of a national law specifically introduced in order to implement directive no 76/207, national courts are required to interpret their national law in the light of the wording and the purpose of the directive in order to achieve the result referred to in the third paragraph of article 189 [288].

27 On the other hand, as the above considerations show, the directive does not include any unconditional and sufficiently precise obligation as regards sanctions for discrimination which, in the absence of implementing measures adopted in good time may be relied on by individuals in order to obtain specific compensation under the directive, where that is not provided for or permitted under national law.

28 It should, however, be pointed out to the national court that although directive no 75/207/EEC, for the purpose of imposing a sanction for the breach of the prohibition of discrimination, leaves the Member States free to choose between the different solutions suitable for achieving its objective, it nevertheless requires that if a Member States chooses to penalize breaches of that prohibition by the award of compensation, then in order to ensure that it is effective and that it has a deterrent effect, that compensation must in any event be adequate in relation to the damage sustained and must therefore amount to more than purely nominal compensation such as, for example, the reimbursement only of the expenses incurred in connection with the application. It is for the national court to interpret and apply the legislation adopted for the implementation of the directive in conformity with

the requirements of community law, in so far as it is given discretion to do so under national law.

## NOTES AND QUESTIONS

1. Assuming that national courts perceive themselves as having discretion under their own constitutional rules to interpret domestic law in such a way as to comply with EU law, how, if at all, might the Court's decision in *Von Colson* allow a plaintiff in national courts to circumvent some of the limitations on the invocability of directives indicated in its decision in *Marshall* (see Chapter 5, *supra*)? For further consideration of EU law relating to gender discrimination, see Chapter 18 *infra*. The interpretation requirement may apply to any national law that might come into conflict with Union law: see *Marleasing SA v. La Comercial Internacional de Alimentacion SA*. Case 106/89, 1990 ECJ EUR-Lex LEXIS 398, 1990 ECR I-4135.

2. In *Kolpinghuis Nijmegen BV*, Case 80/86, 1987 ECJ CELEX LEXIS 381, [1987] ECR 3969, criminal proceedings had been brought against Kolpinghuis for breach of EEC Directive 80/777 on water purity, which had not yet been implemented by the Dutch authorities. The Court held that the obligation of national courts to interpret domestic law to comply with EU law was "limited by the general principles of law which form part of Community law and in particular the principles of legal certainty and non-retroactivity." Does this set a limit to the scope of EC 10//TEU 4?

3. EC 10/TEU 4 became a central feature of the Court's efforts to secure compliance with EU law in the courts of the Member States. It was in particular the basis for a doctrine that the authorities of the Member States may be held liable for compensation to individuals for failures to implement EU laws (now enshrined in TEU 19, addressed in the next section). This is a different and much broader doctrine than was evident in the *Von Colson* decision, which was addressed only to the adequacy of state law with respect to compensation mandated by a directive. EC 10/TEU 4 may also be considered in a more general sense the Treaty provision underpinning the doctrine of mutual recognition, addressed in Chapters 13 and 14. The doctrine also applies to EU Institutions: see for example *Parliament v. Council*, Case C-65/93, 1995 ECJ CELEX LEXIS 558, [1995] ECR I-643.

4. For a helpful discussion of the role of EC 10/TEU 4, see J. Temple Lang, *Community Constitutional Law: Art. 5 EEC Treaty* (1990) CML REV. 645 and a follow-up article, Temple Lang, *The duties of co-operation of national authorities and courts under Art 10 E.C.: two more reflections* (2001) EL REV. 84. See also S. Drake, *Twenty years after Von Colson: The impact of 'indirect effect' on the protection of the individual's Community rights*, (2005) 30 EL REV. 329.

## § 9.04   TEU 19: "EFFECTIVE LEGAL PROTECTION"

### [A]   The General Principle of Equivalence to National Protection

### UNIBET (LONDON) LTD AND UNIBET (INTERNATIONAL) LTD v. JUSTITIEKANSLERN
Case C-432/05, 2007 ECJ CELEX LEXIS 153, [2007] ECR I-2271

[Unibet, a British company, purchased advertising space in a number of different Swedish media with a view to promoting its gaming services on the internet. In accordance with the Law on Lotteries, Sweden took a number of measures, including obtaining injunctions and commencing criminal proceedings, against those media which had agreed to provide Unibet with advertising space. No administrative action or criminal proceedings were brought against Unibet, which however brought an action against Sweden in the High Court (Högsta domstolen) seeking (a) a declaration that it has the right, pursuant to EC49 EC 49/TFEU 56, to promote its gaming and betting services in Sweden, (b) compensation for the damage suffered as a result of that prohibition on promotion, and (c) a declaration that the prohibition and the measures and sanctions for breach thereof did not apply to it.]

37 It is to be noted at the outset that, according to settled case-law, the principle of effective judicial protection is a general principle of Community law stemming from the constitutional traditions common to the Member States, which has been enshrined in Articles 6 and 13 of the European Convention for the Protection of Human Rights and Fundamental Freedoms . . . paragraph 61) and which has also been reaffirmed by Article 47 of the Charter of fundamental rights of the European Union, proclaimed on 7 December 2000 inNice (OJ 2000 C 364, p. 1).

38 Under the principle of cooperation laid down in Article 10 EC [TEU 4], it is for the Member States to ensure judicial protection of an individual's rights under Community law . . .

39 It is also to be noted that, in the absence of Community rules governing the matter, it is for the domestic legal system of each Member State to designate the courts and tribunals having jurisdiction and to lay down the detailed procedural rules governing actions for safeguarding rights which individuals derive from Community law . . .

40 Although the EC Treaty has made it possible in a number of instances for private persons to bring a direct action, where appropriate, before the Community Court, it was not intended to create new remedies in the national courts to ensure the observance of Community law other than those already laid down by national law . . .

41 It would be otherwise only if it were apparent from the overall scheme of the national legal system in question that no legal remedy existed which made it possible to ensure, even indirectly, respect for an individual's rights under Community law . . .

42 Thus, while it is, in principle, for national law to determine an individual's standing and legal interest in bringing proceedings, Community law nevertheless requires that the national legislation does not undermine the right to effective judicial protection . . . It is for the Member States to establish a system of legal remedies and procedures which ensure respect for that right . . .

43 In that regard, the detailed procedural rules governing actions for safeguarding an individual's rights under Community law must be no less favourable than those governing similar domestic actions (principle of equivalence) and must not render practically impossible or excessively difficult the exercise of rights conferred by Community law (principle of effectiveness) . . .

44 Moreover, it is for the national courts to interpret the procedural rules governing actions brought before them, such as the requirement for there to be a specific legal relationship between the applicant and the State, in such a way as to enable those rules, wherever possible, to be implemented in such a manner as to contribute to the attainment of the objective, referred to at paragraph 37 above, of ensuring effective judicial protection of an individual's rights under Community law.

45 It is in the light of those considerations that the answer must be given to the first question referred by the Högsta domstolen.

46 According to that court, Swedish law does not provide for a self-standing action which seeks primarily to dispute the compatibility of a national provision with higher-ranking legal rules.

47 In that regard . . . the principle of effective judicial protection does not require it to be possible, as such, to bring a free-standing action which seeks primarily to dispute the compatibility of national provisions with Community law, provided that the principles of equivalence and effectiveness are observed in the domestic system of judicial remedies.

48 Firstly, it is apparent from the order for reference that Swedish law does not provide for such a free-standing action, regardless of whether the higher-ranking legal rule to be complied with is a national rule or a Community rule.

49 However, with regard to those two categories of legal rules, Swedish law permits individuals to obtain an examination of that question of compatibility in proceedings before the ordinary courts or before the administrative courts by way of a preliminary issue.

50 It is also apparent from the order for reference that the court which is to determine that question is required to disapply the contested provision if it considers that it conflicts with a higher-ranking legal rule, regardless of whether it is a national or a Community rule.

51 In that examination, it is only where a provision adopted by the Swedish Parliament or Government is manifestly in conflict with a higher-ranking legal rule that such a provision is to be disapplied. . . . [T]hat condition does not apply, on the other hand, where the higher-ranking rule in question is a rule of Community law.

52 Therefore, as was observed by all the governments which submitted observations and by the Commission, it is clear that the detailed procedural rules governing

actions brought under Swedish law for safeguarding an individual's rights under Community law are no less favourable than the rules governing actions for safeguarding an individual's rights under national provisions.

53 It is necessary, secondly, to establish whether the effect of the indirect legal remedies provided for by Swedish law for disputing the compatibility of a national provision with Community law is to render practically impossible or excessively difficult the exercise of rights conferred by Community law.

54 In that regard, each case which raises the question whether a national procedural provision renders the application of Community law impossible or excessively difficult must be analysed by reference to the role of that provision in the procedure, its progress and its special features, viewed as a whole, before the various national instances . . .

55 It is apparent from the order for reference that Swedish law does not prevent a person, such as Unibet, from disputing the compatibility of national legislation, such as the Law on Lotteries, with Community law but that, on the contrary, there exist various indirect legal remedies for that purpose.

56 Thus, firstly, the Högsta domstolen states that Unibet may obtain an examination of whether the Law on Lotteries is compatible with Community law in the context of a claim for damages before the ordinary courts.

57 It is also clear from the order for reference that Unibet brought such a claim and that the Högsta domstolen found it to be admissible.

58 Consequently, where an examination of the compatibility of the Law on Lotteries with Community law takes place in the context of the determination of a claim for damages, that action constitutes a remedy which enables Unibet to ensure effective protection of the rights conferred on it by Community law.

59 It is for the Högsta domstolen to ensure that the examination of the compatibility of that law with Community law takes place irrespective of the assessment of the merits of the case with regard to the requirements for damage and a causal link in the claim for damages.

60 Secondly, the Högsta domstolen adds that, if Unibet applied to the Swedish Government for an exception to the prohibition on the promotion of its services in Sweden, any decision rejecting that application could be the subject of judicial review proceedings before the Regeringsrätten, in which Unibet would be able to argue that the provisions of the Law on Lotteries are incompatible with Community law. Where appropriate, the competent court would be required to disapply the provisions of that law that were considered to be in conflict with Community law.

61 It is to be noted that such judicial review proceedings, which would enable Unibet to obtain a judicial decision that those provisions are incompatible with Community law, constitute a legal remedy securing effective judicial protection of its rights under Community law . . .

62 Moreover, the Högsta domstolen states that if Unibet disregarded the provisions of the Law on Lotteries and administrative action or criminal proceedings were brought against it by the competent national authorities, it would have the

opportunity, in proceedings brought before the administrative court or an ordinary court, to dispute the compatibility of those provisions with Community law. Where appropriate, the competent court would be required to disapply the provisions of that law that were considered to be in conflict with Community law.

63 In addition to the remedies referred to at paragraphs 56 and 60 above, it would therefore be possible for Unibet to claim in court proceedings against the administration or in criminal proceedings that measures taken or required to be taken against it were incompatible with Community law on account of the fact that it had not been permitted by the competent national authorities to promote its services in Sweden.

64 In any event, it is clear from paragraphs 56 to 61 above that Unibet must be regarded as having available to it legal remedies which ensure effective judicial protection of its rights under Community law. If, on the contrary, as mentioned at paragraph 62 above, it was forced to be subject to administrative or criminal proceedings and to any penalties that may result as the sole form of legal remedy for disputing the compatibility of the national provision at issue with Community law, that would not be sufficient to secure for it such effective judicial protection.

65 Accordingly, the answer to the first question must be that the principle of effective judicial protection of an individual's rights under Community law must be interpreted as meaning that it does not require the national legal order of a Member State to provide for a free-standing action for an examination of whether national provisions are compatible with Article 49 EC [56], provided that other effective legal remedies, which are no less favourable than those governing similar domestic actions, make it possible for such a question of compatibility to be determined as a preliminary issue, which is a task that falls to the national court.

*Question 2*

66 By its second question, the Högsta domstolen essentially asks whether the principle of effective judicial protection of an individual's rights under Community law requires it to be possible in the legal order of a Member State to obtain interim relief suspending the application of national measures until the competent court has given a ruling on whether those measures are compatible with Community law.

67 As a preliminary point, it must be pointed out that a court seised of a dispute governed by Community law must be in a position to grant interim relief in order to ensure the full effectiveness of the judgment to be given on the existence of the rights claimed under Community law . . .

68 Under the national law set out in the order for reference, the purpose of applications for such relief can only be to provide interim protection of the rights the applicant asserts in the substantive action, as is apparent from paragraph 9 above.

69 In the action in the main proceedings, it is not disputed that Unibet made two applications for interim relief, the first in connection with an application for a declaration, and the second in connection with a claim for damages.

70 With regard to the first of those applications for interim relief, it is apparent from

the order for reference that the application for a declaration was considered to be inadmissible, under national law, at first instance and on appeal. Whilst upholding that interpretation of national law, the Högsta domstolen none the less has doubts concerning the requirements of Community law in that regard, which led it to ask the first question referred for a preliminary ruling (see paragraphs 36 to 65 above).

71 According to the answer to the first question, the principle of effective judicial protection of an individual's rights under Community law does not require the national legal order of a Member State to provide for a free-standing action for an examination of whether national provisions are compatible with Community law, provided that other legal remedies make it possible for such an issue of compatibility to be determined as a preliminary issue, which is a task that falls to the national court.

72 Where it is uncertain under national law, applied in accordance with the requirements of Community law, whether an action to safeguard respect for an individual's rights under Community law is admissible, the principle of effective judicial protection requires the national court to be able, none the less, at that stage, to grant the interim relief necessary to ensure those rights are respected.

73 However, the principle of effective judicial protection of an individual's rights under Community law does not require it to be possible in the legal order of a Member State to obtain interim relief from the competent national court in the context of an application that is inadmissible under the law of that Member State, provided that Community law, as interpreted in accordance with paragraph 71 above, does not call into question that inadmissibility.

74 With regard to the application for interim relief made in connection with the claim for damages, it is apparent from the order for reference and from other documents in the case-file that that claim was considered to be admissible.

75 As the Advocate General stated at point 74 of her Opinion and as was noted at paragraph 67 above, the national court seised of a dispute governed by Community law must be able to grant interim relief in order to ensure the full effectiveness of the judgment to be given on the existence of the rights claimed under Community law.

76 Consequently, where the competent national court examines, in the context of the claim for damages, whether the Law on Lotteries is compatible with Community law, it must be able to grant the interim relief sought, provided that such relief is necessary, which it is a matter for the national court to determine, in order to ensure the full effectiveness of the judgment to be given on the existence of the rights claimed under Community law.

77 It follows from the foregoing that the answer to the second question must be that the principle of effective judicial protection of an individual's rights under Community law must be interpreted as requiring it to be possible in the legal order of a Member State for interim relief to be granted until the competent court has given a ruling on whether national provisions are compatible with Community law, where the grant of such relief is necessary to ensure the full effectiveness of the judgment to be given on the existence of such rights.

*Question 3*

78 By its third question, the Högsta domstolen asks essentially whether, having regard to the principle of effective judicial protection of an individual's rights under Community law, and where the compatibility of national provisions with Community law is being challenged, the grant of interim relief to suspend the application of such provisions, until the competent court has given a ruling on whether those provisions are compatible with Community law, is governed by the criteria laid down by the national law applicable before the competent court or by Community criteria.

79 It is clear from established case-law that the suspension of enforcement of a national provision based on a Community regulation in proceedings pending before a national court, whilst it is governed by national procedural law, is in all Member States subject to conditions which are uniform and analogous with the conditions for an application for interim relief brought before the Community Court . . . However, the case in the main proceedings is different from those giving rise to those judgments in that Unibet's application for interim relief does not seek to suspend the effects of a national provision adopted in accordance with a Community regulation where the legality of that regulation is contested, but rather the effects of national legislation where the compatibility of that legislation with Community law is contested.

80 Therefore, in the absence of Community rules governing the matter, it is for the domestic legal system of each Member State to determine the conditions under which interim relief is to be granted for safeguarding an individual's rights under Community law.

81 Accordingly, the grant of interim relief to suspend the application of national provisions until the competent court has given a ruling on whether those provisions are compatible with Community law is governed by the criteria laid down by the national law applicable before that court.

82 However, those criteria cannot be less favourable than those applying to similar domestic actions (principle of equivalence) and must not render practically impossible or excessively difficult the interim judicial protection of rights conferred by Community law (principle of effectiveness).

83 The answer to the third question must therefore be that the principle of effective judicial protection of an individual's rights under Community law must be interpreted as meaning that, where the compatibility of national provisions with Community law is being challenged, the grant of any interim relief to suspend the application of such provisions until the competent court has given a ruling on whether those provisions are compatible with Community law is governed by the criteria laid down by the national law applicable before that court, provided that those criteria are no less favourable than those applying to similar domestic actions and do not render practically impossible or excessively difficult the interim judicial protection of those rights.

# NOTES AND QUESTIONS

1. The ECJ in this case attempts to set out a comprehensive summary of the principles applicable to effective enforcement of EU law in national courts. Taking into account the cases already reviewed in prior chapters (particularly the *Factortame* case in Chapter 3), how would you summarize the Court's approach? For a discussion of the relationship between supremacy and effectiveness, see M. Ross, *Effectiveness in the European legal order(s): Beyond supremacy to constitutional proportionality?* (2006) 31 EL REV. 476.

2. Under no circumstances may national procedures be used to deprive a citizen of EU rights where the Member State's default is the cause of the denial of a remedy: *Theresa Emmott v. Minister for Social Welfare and Attorney General* Case C-208/90, 1991 ECJ CELEX LEXIS 424, [1991] ECR I-4269. Mrs. Emmott sought retroactive payment of a disability benefit to which she believed she was entitled under Directive 79/7. (The directive had not been implemented in Ireland within the deadline.) When she applied for it, she was told she would have to wait until another case on referral to the ECJ was decided: *Cotter and McDermott v. Minister for Social Welfare*, Case C-377/89, 1991 ECJ CELEX LEXIS 234, [1991] ECR I-1155. As soon as that judgment had been delivered, Mrs. Emmott entered into correspondence with the Minister for Social Welfare with a view to obtaining the claimed benefit. She was then confronted with an argument by the Government that the time limit for making the claim had passed. The ECJ made it clear that Mrs Emmott could not be prevented from asserting her EU rights.

## [B] The Obligation of the National Court to Raise EU Law Issues of its Own Motion

### JEROEN VAN SCHIJNDEL AND JOHANNES NICOLAAS CORNELIS VAN VEEN v. STICHTING PENSIOENFONDS VOOR FYSIOTHERAPEUTEN

Joined Cases C-430/93 and C-431/93, 1995 ECJ CELEX LEXIS 225, [1995] ECR I-4705

[Mr van Veen and Mr van Schijndel, who exercised the profession of physiotherapist in the Netherlands as employees, applied for exemption from compulsory membership of an occupational pension scheme for physiotherapists, the Pension Fund Foundation for Physiotherapists. Under the Fund's rules (which were sanctioned by the Government), membership in this scheme was compulsory but there was an exception that allowed physiotherapists to join an alternative scheme where the pension insurance arrangements applied to "all members of the profession employed by the company". The Fund refused exemption on the ground that the pension scheme which the two physiotherapists had joined by entering into contractual arrangements with the insurance company Delta Lloyd was not applicable to all members of the profession in the service of the employer concerned ("the collectivity requirement"). It therefore directed Mr van Veen and Mr van Schijndel to continue to pay the contributions payable under the pension scheme. Mr van Veen and Mr van Schijndel challenged the Fund's decisions, the former before the Kantonrechter (Cantonal Court) at Breda and the latter before the Kantonrechter at Tilburg, on the ground that the collectivity requirement had no basis in either the pension scheme regulations of the Fund or in the Dutch law (WVD). No issue of compatibility with EU law was raised in the initial judgments including appeals.]

10 Mr van Veen and Mr van Schijndel applied to the Hoge Raad [Supreme court] to have [the prior] judgments quashed. For the first time in the proceedings they contended in particular that the Breda Rechtbank should have considered, "if necessary of its own motion", the question of the compatibility of compulsory Fund membership with higher-ranking rules of Community law, in particular Article 3(f) [repealed] the second paragraph of Article 5 [TEU 4], Articles 85 [101] and 86 [102] and Article 90 [106], as well as Articles 52 to 58 [49 to 55] and 59 to 66 [56-62] of the EEC Treaty. In their view, the requirement in question could render ineffective the competition rules applicable to providers of pension insurance and to individual members of the profession by imposing or promoting the conclusion of contracts incompatible with Community competition rules or reinforcing their effects. Furthermore, the Fund could not meet market demand, or at any rate demand for equivalent pension insurance on more attractive terms.

11 The Hoge Raad has found that in support of their plea in cassation Mr van Veen and Mr van Schijndel are relying on various facts and circumstances which were not established by the Breda Rechtbank or relied on by them in support of their claims before the lower courts. In Netherlands law, a plea in cassation by its nature excludes new arguments unless on pure points of law, that is to say that they do not require an examination of facts. Furthermore, even though Article 48 of the Netherlands Code of Civil Procedure requires courts to raise points of law, if necessary, of their own motion, the principle of judicial passivity in cases involving civil rights and obligations freely entered into by the parties entails that additional pleas on points of law cannot require courts to go beyond the ambit of the dispute defined by the parties themselves nor to rely on facts or circumstances other than those on which a claim is based.

*     *     *

13 The competition rules mentioned by the national court are binding rules, directly applicable in the national legal order. Where, by virtue of domestic law, courts or tribunals must raise of their own motion points of law based on binding domestic rules which have not been raised by the parties, such an obligation also exists where binding Community rules are concerned . . .

14 The position is the same if domestic law confers on courts and tribunals a discretion to apply of their own motion binding rules of law. Indeed, pursuant to the principle of cooperation laid down in Article 5 [TEU 4] of the Treaty, it is for national courts to ensure the legal protection which persons derive from the direct effect of provisions of Community law . . .

15 The reply to the first question must therefore be that, in proceedings concerning civil rights and obligations freely entered into by the parties, it is for the national court to apply Articles 3(f) [repealed], 85 [101], 86 [102] and 90 [106] of the Treaty even when the party with an interest in application of those provisions has not relied

on them, where domestic law allows such application by the national court . . .

16 . . . [T]the Hoge Raad seeks [additionally] to ascertain whether such an obligation also exists where, in order to apply of its own motion the aforementioned Community rules, the court would have to abandon the passive role assigned to it by going beyond the ambit of the dispute defined by the parties themselves and/or by relying on facts and circumstances other than those on which the party to the proceedings with an interest in application of the provisions of the Treaty bases his claim.

17 In the absence of Community rules governing the matter, it is for the domestic legal system of each Member State to designate the courts and tribunals having jurisdiction and to lay down the detailed procedural rules governing actions for safeguarding rights which individuals derive from the direct effect of Community law. However, such rules must not be less favourable than those governing similar domestic actions nor render virtually impossible or excessively difficult the exercise of rights conferred by Community law.

\*    \*    \*

19 For the purposes of applying those principles, each case which raises the question whether a national procedural provision renders application of Community law impossible or excessively difficult must be analysed by reference to the role of that provision in the procedure, its progress and its special features, viewed as a whole, before the various national instances. In the light of that analysis the basic principles of the domestic judicial system, such as protection of the rights of the defence, the principle of legal certainty and the proper conduct of procedure, must, where appropriate, be taken into consideration.

20 In the present case, the domestic law principle that in civil proceedings a court must or may raise points of its own motion is limited by its obligation to keep to the subject-matter of the dispute and to base its decision on the facts put before it.

21 That limitation is justified by the principle that, in a civil suit, it is for the parties to take the initiative, the court being able to act of its own motion only in exceptional cases where the public interest requires its intervention. That principle reflects conceptions prevailing in most of the Member States as to the relations between the State and the individual; it safeguards the rights of the defence; and it ensures proper conduct of proceedings by, in particular, protecting them from the delays inherent in examination of new pleas.

22 In those circumstances, . . . Community law does not require national courts to raise of their own motion an issue concerning the breach of provisions of Community law where examination of that issue would oblige them to abandon the passive role assigned to them by going beyond the ambit of the dispute defined by the parties themselves and relying on facts and circumstances other than those on which the party with an interest in application of those provisions bases his claim.

## NOTES AND QUESTIONS

1.   How would you summarize the ECJ's approach to the question as to when or whether a national court must raise supremacy issues of its own motion? Does it perhaps fall a little short of what one might have expected?

2.   Given the absence of a federal court system in the EU, and the voluntary nature of EC 230/TFEU 267 with respect to references to the ECJ except for courts of last resort, the ECJ's approach highlights a possible weakness in the supremacy doctrine. Given the reference to national procedural rules, does this approach mean that EU law is likely to be applied unevenly in the various Member States?

3.   In *Germany v. Arcor*, Case C-392/04, 2006 ECJ CELEX LEXIS 500, [2006] ECR I-8559, the ECJ clarified that the obligation to raise supremacy issues has to be balanced by the application of the principle of legal certainty. Thus, a matter that has been finally disposed of by an administrative act confirmed by a national court judgment may only be re-opened if this is permitted by state law, the applicant acted promptly and time limits for doing so have not expired. See in this regard also *Kühne & Heitze* Case C-453/00, 2004 ECJ CELEX LEXIS 14, [2004] ECR I-837; and *Kapferer v. Schlanck and Schick*, Case C-234/04 2006 ECJ CELEX LEXIS 254, [2006] ECR I-2585.

4.   The *Van Schijndel* and *Factortame* cases are illustrative of the tensions that have arisen in according supremacy and effectiveness to EU law in national legal systems. The various ramifications of this are explored in more depth in Chapter 9, *infra*.

5.   The ECJ's views in *van Schijndel* might be compared with the position on own motion requirements in the European Court. In *Ireland and others v. Commission*, Joined Cases T-50/06, T-56/06, T-62/06 and T-69/06, 2007 ECJ EUR-Lex LEXIS 2714, [2007] ECR II-172, the CFI/General Court had held that the Commission had failed to give proper reasons for its decision and annulled it on that sole ground, but did so without the parties having themselves raised the issue. While the General Court could and indeed was required to do so if it believed that there had been an infringement of an essential procedural requirement, it should have reopened the procedure to allow the parties to make arguments. Failure to make provision to hear such arguments violated fundamental rights relating to the right to be heard and to a fair trial.

## OCEANO GRUPO EDITORIAL SA v. ROCIO MURCIANO QUINTERO), AND SALVAT EDITORES SA v. JOSE M. SANCHEZ ALCON PRADES JOSE LUIS COPANO BADILLO AND OTHERS
Joined cases C-240/98 to C-244/98, 2000 ECJ CELEX LEXIS 308, [2000] ECR I-4941

[This case concerned Council Directive 93/13/EEC on unfair terms in consumer contracts ([1993] OJ L 95/29) (the "Directive"). Each of the defendants, all resident in Spain, had entered into a contract for the purchase by instalments of an encyclopaedia for personal use. The plaintiffs were the sellers of the encyclopaedias.

The contracts contained a term conferring jurisdiction on the courts in Barcelona, a city in which none of the defendants in the main proceedings was domiciled but where the plaintiffs in those proceedings had their principal place of business. The purchasers did not pay the sums due on the agreed dates, and the sellers brought actions in the Juzgado de Primera Instancia No 35 de Barcelona to recover the sums. Notice of the claims was not served on the defendants since the Barcelona court had doubts as to whether it had jurisdiction over the actions in question. The Spanish Supreme Court had held on several occasions that such jurisdiction clauses were unfair. The Barcelona court asked the ECJ whether EU law required that it determine of its own motion whether an unfair term was void.]

25 As to the question of whether a court seised of a dispute concerning a contract between a seller or supplier and a consumer may determine of its own motion whether a term of the contract is unfair, it should be noted that the system of protection introduced by the Directive is based on the idea that the consumer is in a weak position vis-a-vis the seller or supplier, as regards both his bargaining power and his level of knowledge. This leads to the consumer agreeing to terms drawn up in advance by the seller or supplier without being able to influence the content of the terms.

26 The aim of Article 6 of the Directive, which requires Member States to lay down that unfair terms are not binding on the consumer, would not be achieved if the consumer were himself obliged to raise the unfair nature of such terms. In disputes where the amounts involved are often limited, the lawyers' fees may be higher than the amount at stake, which may deter the consumer from contesting the application of an unfair term. While it is the case that, in a number of Member States, procedural rules enable individuals to defend themselves in such proceedings, there is a real risk that the consumer, particularly because of ignorance of the law, will not challenge the term pleaded against him on the grounds that it is unfair. It follows that effective protection of the consumer may be attained only if the national court acknowledges that it has power to evaluate terms of this kind of its own motion.

27 Moreover . . . the system of protection laid down by the Directive is based on the notion that the imbalance between the consumer and the seller or supplier may only be corrected by positive action unconnected with the actual parties to the contract. That is why Article 7 of the Directive, paragraph 1 of which requires Member States to implement adequate and effective means to prevent the continued use of unfair terms, specifies in paragraph 2 that those means are to include allowing authorised consumer associations to take action in order to obtain a decision as to whether contractual terms drawn up for general use are unfair and, if need be, to have them prohibited, even if they have not been used in specific contracts.

28 . . . [I]t is hardly conceivable that, in a system requiring the implementation of specific group actions of a preventive nature intended to put a stop to unfair terms detrimental to consumers' interests, a court hearing a dispute on a specific contract containing an unfair term should not be able to set aside application of the relevant term solely because the consumer has not raised the fact that it is unfair. On the contrary, the court's power to determine of its own motion whether a term is unfair must be regarded as constituting a proper means both of achieving the result sought by Article 6 of the Directive, namely, preventing an individual consumer

from being bound by an unfair term, and of contributing to achieving the aim of Article 7, since if the court undertakes such an examination, that may act as a deterrent and contribute to preventing unfair terms in contracts concluded between consumers and sellers or suppliers.

29 It follows from the above that the protection provided for consumers by the Directive entails the national court being able to determine of its own motion whether a term of a contract before it is unfair when making its preliminary assessment as to whether a claim should be allowed to proceed before the national courts.

## NOTES AND QUESTIONS

1.   Can this case be reconciled with the *Van Schijndel* approach regarding the requirement for a Court to raise an EU issue of its own motion? Or does this case address a situation that cannot be compared with the situation in *Van Schijndel*? In thinking about this question, consider the following cases.

In *Kühne & Heitz*, Case C-453/00, 2003 ECJ EUR-Lex LEXIS 2096, [2004] ECR I-837 the ECJ had laid down certain principles regarding the circumstances under which a national court or authority should reopen a case so as to properly take account of a subsequent ruling on the EU act in question:

The principle of cooperation arising from EC 10/TEU 4 imposes on an administrative body an obligation to review a final administrative decision, where an application for such review is made to it, in order to take account of the interpretation of the relevant provision given in the meantime by the Court where:

- under national law, it has the power to reopen that decision;

- the administrative decision in question has become final as a result of a judgment of a national court ruling at final instance;

- that judgment is, in the light of a decision given by the Court subsequent to it, based on a misinterpretation of Community law which was adopted without a question being referred to the Court for a preliminary ruling under [the third paragraph of EC 234/ TFEU 267]; and

- the person concerned complained to the administrative body immediately after becoming aware of that decision of the Court.

In *Willy Kempter KG v. HZA Hamburg-Jonas* Case C-2/06, 2008 ECJ EUR-Lex LEXIS 590, [2008] ECR I-411, the issue centered on the third criterion, where the issue was that no question as to the meaning of EU law had ever been raised in the proceedings that led to a final judgment. The ECJ held that the ruling should be reopened to ensure that EU law (as subsequently interpreted) was properly applied and drew a distinction between cases such as this and those where an EU law claim, subsequently raised by a party in an appeal, was not raised in the litigation as originally pled by the parties.

In *Petersbroeck, Van Campentiout e Lie SCS v. Belgian State*, Case C-312/93, 1995 ECJ CELEX LEXIS 190, [1995] ECR I-4599, Belgium contended that an EU law argument in a tax appeal case was a new plea that was inadmissible because it had been raised outside the time-limit laid down by the Code des Impôts sur les Revenus (Income Tax Code, in the version applicable at the material time. Under those provisions, pleas that had not been raised in the complaint nor considered of his own motion by the Director could be raised by the appellant taxpayer either in the appeal document or by notice in writing to the Registry of the Cour d' Appel, subject to a limitation period of 60 days with effect from the lodging by the Director of a certified true copy of the contested decision together with all the documents relating to the taxpayer's objection. It appears that, under Belgian case law, a plea is new for the purposes of the abovementioned provisions if it raises for the first time an issue that in its object, nature or legal basis differs from those already before the Director. The ECJ held that a national procedural rule that precludes a national court from considering of its own motion whether domestic law is compatible with EU law is contrary to EU law. The effect of the Belgian provision was to preclude the national court from hearing the EU law argument. The ECJ held that the rule could not be used to preclude the ability of the national court to do so, explaining its ruling in the following terms:

> 14 . . . [E]ach case which raises the question whether a national procedural provision renders application of Community law impossible or excessively difficult must be analysed by reference to the role of that provision in the procedure, its progress and its special features, viewed as a whole, before the various national instances. In the light of that analysis the basic principles of the domestic judicial system, such as protection of the rights of the defence, the principle of legal certainty and the proper conduct of procedure, must, where appropriate, be taken into consideration.

> 15 In the present case, according to domestic law, a litigant may no longer raise before the Cour d' Appel a new plea based on Community law once the 60-day period with effect from the lodging by the Director of a certified true copy of the contested decision has elapsed.

> 16 Whilst a period of 60 days so imposed on a litigant is not objectionable per se, the special features of the procedure in question must be emphasized.

> 17 First of all, the Cour d' Appel is the first court which can make a reference to the Court of Justice since the Director before whom the first-instance proceedings are conducted is a member of the fiscal authorities and, consequently, is not a court or tribunal within the meaning of Article 177 of the Treaty [267] . . .

> 18 Secondly, the limitation period whose expiry prevented the Cour d' Appel from examining of its own motion the compatibility of a measure of domestic law with Community law started to run from the time when the Director lodged a certified true copy of the contested decision. That meant, in this case, that the period during which new pleas could be raised by the appellant had expired by the time the Cour d' Appel held its hearing so that

the Cour d' Appel was denied the possibility of considering the question of compatibility.

19 Thirdly, it seems that no other national court or tribunal in subsequent proceedings may of its own motion consider the question of the compatibility of a national measure with Community law.

20 Finally, the impossibility for national courts or tribunals to raise points of Community law of their own motion does not appear to be reasonably justifiable by principles such as the requirement of legal certainty or the proper conduct of procedure.

2.    Even if under both national and EU law a national court has the power and the duty (in principle) to raise issues of EU law where the parties have not done so, it is not obliged to do so where the result would be to put the plaintiff in a worse position than if it had not brought the action at all. This is an application of a fundamental procedural right found in some jurisdictions known as *"reformatio in peius"*: *Heemskert BV, Firma Schaap v. Productschap Vee en Vlees*, Case C-455/06, 2008 ECJ EUR-Lex LEXIS 2189, [2008] ECR I-8763. It sheds an interesting light on the interplay of fundamental rights and the need to ensure that EU law is properly applied.

## [C]  Interplay with National Evidentiary and Procedural Rules

## AMMINISTRAZIONE DELLE FINANZE DELLO STATO v. SPA SAN GIORGIO
### Case 199/82, [1983] ECR 3595

[This was a national court proceeding that involved the same kind of issue that resulted in a Commission action against Italy. The Italian government had imposed inspection charges on imports that had been ruled contrary to EU law. Parties then sought to recover the improper charges and were confronted with an evidential rule that required them to prove that they had suffered loss with the presumption being that the charges had been passed along to their customers.]

11 In essence the first question asks whether a Member State may make repayment of national charges levied contrary to the requirements of Community law conditional upon proof that those charges have not been passed on to other persons:

where repayment is subject to rules of evidence which render the exercise of rights which the national courts are under a duty to protect virtually impossible; and

where the same restrictive conditions do not apply to the repayment of any other national tax, charge or duty wrongly levied.

12 In that connection it must be pointed out in the first place that entitlement to the repayment of charges levied by a Member State contrary to the rules of Community law is a consequence of, and an adjunct to, the rights conferred on individuals by the Community provisions prohibiting charges having an effect equivalent to customs

duties or, as the case may be, the discriminatory application of internal taxes. Whilst it is true that repayment may be sought only within the framework of the conditions as to both substance and form, laid down by the various national laws applicable thereto, the fact nevertheless remains, as the court has consistently held, that those conditions may not be less favourable than those relating to similar claims regarding national charges and they may not be so framed as to render virtually impossible the exercise of rights conferred by Community law.

*   *   *

13 However, as the Court has also recognized in previous decisions . . . Community law does not prevent a national legal system from disallowing the repayment of charges which have been unduly levied where to do so would entail unjust enrichment of the recipients. There is nothing in Community law therefore to prevent courts from taking account, under their national law, of the fact that the unduly levied charges have been incorporated in the price of the goods and thus passed on to the purchasers. Thus national legislative provisions which prevent the reimbursement of taxes, charges, and duties levied in breach of community law cannot be regarded as contrary to community law where it is established that the person required to pay such charges has actually passed them on to other persons.

14 On the other hand, any requirement of proof which has the effect of making it virtually impossible or excessively difficult to secure the repayment of charges levied contrary to community law would be incompatible with Community law. That is so particularly in the case of presumptions or rules of evidence intended to place upon the taxpayer the burden of establishing that the charges unduly paid have not been passed on to other persons or of special limitations concerning the form of the evidence to be adduced, such as the exclusion of any kind of evidence other than documentary evidence. Once it is established that the levying of the charge is incompatible with community law, the court must be free to decide whether or not the burden of the charge has been passed on, wholly or in part, to other persons.

15 In a market economy based on freedom of competition, the question whether, and if so to what extent, a fiscal charge imposed on an importer has actually been passed on in subsequent transactions involves a degree of uncertainty for which the person obliged to pay a charge contrary to Community law cannot be systematically held responsible.

16 The national court also asks the Court of Justice whether rules restricting the repayment of charges levied contrary to Community law are compatible with the principles of the EEC Treaty when they are not applied identically to every national tax, charge or duty. In that regard it refers to the judgments in which, after stating that the extent to which it is possible to contest charges unlawfully claimed or to recover charges unduly paid differs in the various Member States, and even within a single Member State, according to the type of tax or charge in question . . . the Court emphasized that individuals who seek to enforce rights by virtue of provisions of Community law may not be treated less favourably than persons who pursue similar claims on the basis of domestic law.

17 It must be pointed out in that regard that the requirement of non-discrimination laid down by the Court cannot be construed as justifying legislative measures

intended to render any repayment of charges levied contrary to Community law virtually impossible, even if the same treatment is extended to taxpayers who have similar claims arising from an infringement of national tax law. The fact that rules of evidence which have been found to be incompatible with the rules of Community law are extended, by law, to a substantial number of national taxes, charges and duties or even to all of them is not therefore a reason for withholding the repayment of charges levied contrary to Community law.

18 The reply to the first question must therefore be that a Member State cannot make the repayment of national charges levied contrary to the requirements of Community law conditional upon the production of proof that those charges have not been passed on to other persons if the repayment is subject to rules of evidence which render the exercise of that right virtually impossible, even where the repayment of other taxes, charges or duties levied in breach of national law is subject to the same restrictive conditions.

## MARKS & SPENCER PLC v. COMMISSIONERS OF CUSTOMS & EXCISE
### Case C-62/00, 2002 ECJ CELEX LEXIS 262, [2002] ECR I-6325

[Marks & Spencer, the UK-based retailer, made a claim for repayment of an amount of VAT that had initially been paid as a result of an incorrect interpretation of the Sixth Council Directive (77/388) on Value Added Tax. The UK had however introduced a 3 year time limit on claims for reimbursement which applied even to claims already made and this had the effect of depriving M&S of the full refund. The Court began by confirming that the directive had been correctly implemented by the UK following the change in the UK rules to correct the previous mistake. However, this fact did not mean that the directive was now no longer relevant. If individuals were deprived of the right to recover sums incorrectly charged, they could still invoke the directive as long as the directive had directly effective provisions, which was the case here.]

43 The United Kingdom Government maintains that the principle of the protection of legitimate expectations is not relevant in a dispute such as that in the main proceedings. It submits that determination of the procedural rules governing claims for the recovery of overpayments of VAT is entirely a matter of domestic law, subject only to observance of the Community-law principles of equivalence and effectiveness. If the principle of the protection of legitimate expectations were applicable in the dispute in the main proceedings, the only expectation would be that individuals are entitled to have their claims dealt with in accordance with the procedural rules of national law, which happened in the present case.

44 In that connection, the Court has consistently held that the principle of the protection of legitimate expectations forms part of the Community legal order and must be observed by the Member States when they exercise the powers conferred on them by Community directives (see, to that effect, Case 316/86 Krucken 1988 ECR 2213, paragraph 22, Joined Cases C-31/91 to C-44/91 Lageder and Others 1993 ECR I-1761, paragraph 33, Case C-381/97 Belgocodex 1998 ECR I-8153, paragraph 26, and Case C-396/98 Schlossstrasse 2000 ECR I-4279, paragraph 44).

45 The Court has held, in particular, that a legislative amendment retroactively depriving a taxable person of a right to deduction he has derived from the Sixth Directive is incompatible with the principle of the protection of legitimate expectations (Schlossstrasse, cited above, paragraph 47).

46 Likewise, in a situation such as that in the main proceedings, the principle of the protection of legitimate expectations applies so as to preclude a national legislative amendment which retroactively deprives a taxable person of the right enjoyed prior to that amendment to obtain repayment of taxes collected in breach of provisions of the Sixth Directive with direct effect.

47 In the light of all those considerations, the reply to the question referred must be that national legislation retroactively curtailing the period within which repayment may be sought of sums paid by way of VAT collected in breach of provisions of the Sixth Directive with direct effect, such as those in Article 11A(1), is incompatible with the principles of effectiveness and of protection of legitimate expectations.

## NOTES AND QUESTIONS

1.   In *San Giorgio*, does the Court adhere to the principle of equivalence to national rights and remedies or does it insist on an EU-specific override of the national procedure (and if so, to what extent)?

2.   In *Marks & Spencer*, we again see coming into play the general principles of law described in Chapter 3 that pervade all of EU Law. The application of EU principles resulted in a conclusion that the retroactive nature of the time limitation was invalid. This was because the Court was concerned to make sure that affected individuals were accorded their full rights under the Sixth Directive in circumstances where they had originally been the subject of an incorrect interpretation. Suppose, however, that the denial of a refund was due to incompetence or a mistake not involving the interpretation of EU law. Would the retroactivity of the legislation in that case be valid? Does it make sense to hold it invalid for some purposes and not others? Or might it be concluded that all aspects of legislation implementing a Directive are subject to EU standards? What implications might this have for the constitutional structures of the Member States? How far might this doctrine be carried?

3.   The principle of legitimate expectations was first recognized by the Court in *Töpfer*, Case 112/77, [1978] ECR 1019. Successful appeals based on this principle are scarce in the ECJ case law since the ECJ has always refused the application of this principle *contra legem*, meaning that it will not apply the principle if it leads to a decision contrary to EU Law. It is therefore not a form of "fundamental right" but rather a principle governing the interpretation and implementation of EU law.

## [D] The Principle of Effectiveness in the Context of Civil Actions Between Private Parties

### COURAGE LTD v. BERNARD CREHAN AND BERNARD CREHAN v. COURAGE LTD AND OTHERS
Case C-453/99, 2001 ECJ CELEX LEXIS 755, [2001] ECR I-6297

[In 1991 Mr Crehan had concluded two 20-year leases with IEL imposing an obligation to purchase beer from Courage. The rent, subject to a five-year upward-only rent review, was to be the higher of the rent for the immediately preceding period or the best open market rent obtainable for the residue of the term on the other terms of the lease. The tenant had to purchase a fixed minimum quantity of specified beers and IEL agreed to procure the supply of specified beer to the tenant by Courage at the prices shown in the latter's price list. In 1993, Courage, the plaintiff in the main proceedings, brought an action for the recovery from Mr Crehan of the sum of GBP 15 266 for unpaid deliveries of beer. Mr Crehan contested the action on its merits, contending that the beer tie was contrary to (then) Article 85 (EC 81/TFEU 101) of the Treaty and automatically void under EC 81/TFEU 101 (2). Courage argued that under English law a party to an illegal contract could not invoke that invalidity in order to claim damages from the counterparty. Crehan also asserted a counterclaim in damages based on the illegal conduct of Courage. For relevant provisions now in Regulation 1/2003, see articles 6, 15 and 16 in the Documentary Supplement.)]

24 It follows from the foregoing considerations that any individual can rely on a breach of Article 85 [101](1) of the Treaty before a national court even where he is a party to a contract that is liable to restrict or distort competition within the meaning of that provision.

25 As regards the possibility of seeking compensation for loss caused by a contract or by conduct liable to restrict or distort competition, it should be remembered from the outset that, in accordance with settled case-law, the national courts whose task it is to apply the provisions of Community law in areas within their jurisdiction must ensure that those rules take full effect and must protect the rights which they confer on individuals . . .

26 The full effectiveness of Article 85 [101] of the Treaty and, in particular, the practical effect of the prohibition laid down in Article 85 [101](1) would be put at risk if it were not open to any individual to claim damages for loss caused to him by a contract or by conduct liable to restrict or distort competition.

27 Indeed, the existence of such a right strengthens the working of the Community competition rules and discourages agreements or practices, which are frequently covert, which are liable to restrict or distort competition. From that point of view, actions for damages before the national courts can make a significant contribution to the maintenance of effective competition in the Community.

28 There should not therefore be any absolute bar to such an action being brought by a party to a contract which would be held to violate the competition rules.

29 However, in the absence of Community rules governing the matter, it is for the

domestic legal system of each Member State to designate the courts and tribunals having jurisdiction and to lay down the detailed procedural rules governing actions for safeguarding rights which individuals derive directly from Community law, provided that such rules are not less favourable than those governing similar domestic actions (principle of equivalence) and that they do not render practically impossible or excessively difficult the exercise of rights conferred by Community law (principle of effectiveness) . . .

30 In that regard, the Court has held that Community law does not prevent national courts from taking steps to ensure that the protection of the rights guaranteed by Community law does not entail the unjust enrichment of those who enjoy them . . .

31 Similarly, provided that the principles of equivalence and effectiveness are respected . . . Community law does not preclude national law from denying a party who is found to bear significant responsibility for the distortion of competition the right to obtain damages from the other contracting party. Under a principle which is recognised in most of the legal systems of the Member States and which the Court has applied in the past . . . a litigant should not profit from his own unlawful conduct, where this is proven.

32 In that regard, the matters to be taken into account by the competent national court include the economic and legal context in which the parties find themselves and, as the United Kingdom Government rightly points out, the respective bargaining power and conduct of the two parties to the contract.

33 In particular, it is for the national court to ascertain whether the party who claims to have suffered loss through concluding a contract that is liable to restrict or distort competition found himself in a markedly weaker position than the other party, such as seriously to compromise or even eliminate his freedom to negotiate the terms of the contract and his capacity to avoid the loss or reduce its extent, in particular by availing himself in good time of all the legal remedies available to him.

34 . . . [A] contract might prove to be contrary to Article 85 [101](1) of the Treaty for the sole reason that it is part of a network of similar contracts which have a cumulative effect on competition. In such a case, the party contracting with the person controlling the network cannot bear significant responsibility for the breach of Article 85 [101], particularly where in practice the terms of the contract were imposed on him by the party controlling the network.

35 Contrary to the submission of Courage, making a distinction as to the extent of the parties' liability does not conflict with the case-law of the Court to the effect that it does not matter, for the purposes of the application of Article 85 [101] of the Treaty, whether the parties to an agreement are on an equal footing as regards their economic position and function . . . That case-law concerns the conditions for application of Article 85 [101] of the Treaty while the questions put before the Court in the present case concern certain consequences in civil law of a breach of that provision.

36 Having regard to all the foregoing considerations, the questions referred are to be answered as follows:

- a party to a contract liable to restrict or distort competition within the meaning of

Article 85 [101] of the Treaty can rely on the breach of that article to obtain relief from the other contracting party;

- Article 85 [101] of the Treaty precludes a rule of national law under which a party to a contract liable to restrict or distort competition within the meaning of that provision is barred from claiming damages for loss caused by performance of that contract on the sole ground that the claimant is a party to that contract;

- Community law does not preclude a rule of national law barring a party to a contract liable to restrict or distort competition from relying on his own unlawful actions to obtain damages where it is established that that party bears significant responsibility for the distortion of competition.

## NOTES AND QUESTIONS

**1.**  How did the ECJ justify the right of a party to a contract to bring a claim for damages under EC 81/TFEDU 101 (2) against the other party where both had been in breach of EU law by entering into it in the first place?

**2.**  Courage had argued that EC 81/TFEU 101 makes no reference to differences in bargaining power and the ECJ agreed. The ECJ nonetheless refers to the notion of the inherent differences in bargaining power between the parties, in the context of a civil action. Does that mean, then, that EU law has two different meanings? Is English contract law also in some way affected by this ruling?

**3.**  Note that the contract in this case did not involve in and of itself an effect on trade between Member States as required by EC 81/TFEU 101. This issue, and the cases referred to that support EU jurisdiction in such circumstances, are discussed in Chapter 11.

## VINCENZO MANFREDI v. LLOYD ADRIATICO ASSICURAZIONI SPA, ANTONIO CANNITO v. FONDIARIA SAI SPA AND NICOLO TRICARICO AND PASQUALINA MURGOLO v. ASSITALIA SPA

Joined Cases C-295/04 to C-298/04, 2006 ECJ CELEX LEXIS 348, [2006] ECR I-6619

[Manfedi had sought recovery of excessive premiums for insurance policies allegedly arising out of an anticompetitive agreement among Italian insurers. Various procedural difficulties were encountered under Italian law including the statute of limitations and rules regarding quantum and heads of damage.]

77. . . . [I]n the absence of Community rules governing the matter, it is for the domestic legal system of each Member State to lay down the detailed procedural rules governing actions for safeguarding rights which individuals derive directly from Community law, provided that such rules observe the principles of equivalence and effectiveness.

78. A national rule under which the limitation period begins to run from the day on which the agreement or concerted practice was adopted could make it practically impossible to exercise the right to seek compensation for the harm caused by that

prohibited agreement or practice, particularly if that national rule also imposes a short limitation period which is not capable of being suspended.

79. In such a situation, where there are continuous or repeated infringements, it is possible that the limitation period expires even before the infringement is brought to an end, in which case it would be impossible for any individual who has suffered harm after the expiry of the limitation period to bring an action.

80. It is for the national court to determine whether such is the case with regard to the national rule at issue in the main proceedings.

81. . . .I]n the absence of Community rules governing the matter, it is for the domestic legal system of each Member State to prescribe the limitation period for seeking compensation for harm caused by an agreement or practice prohibited under Article 81 EC [101], provided that the principles of equivalence and effectiveness are observed.

82. In that regard, it is for the national court to determine whether a national rule which provides that the limitation period for seeking compensation for harm caused by an agreement or practice prohibited under Article 81 EC [101] begins to run from the day on which that prohibited agreement or practice was adopted, particularly where it also imposes a short limitation period that cannot be suspended, renders it practically impossible or excessively difficult to exercise the right to seek compensation for the harm suffer.

*   *   *

89. In accordance with settled case-law, the national courts whose task it is to apply the provisions of Community law in areas within their jurisdiction must ensure that those rules take full effect and must protect the rights which they confer on individuals . . .

90. As was pointed out in paragraph 60 of this judgment, the full effectiveness of Article 81 EC [101] and, in particular, the practical effect of the prohibition laid down in Article 81(1) EC [101] would be put at risk if it were not open to any individual to claim damages for loss caused to him by a contract or by conduct liable to restrict or distort competition.

91. Indeed, the existence of such a right strengthens the working of the Community competition rules and discourages agreements or practices, frequently covert, which are liable to restrict or distort competition. From that point of view, actions for damages before the national courts can make a significant contribution to the maintenance of effective competition in the Community . . .

92. As to the award of damages and the possibility of an award of punitive damages, in the absence of Community rules governing the matter, it is for the domestic legal system of each Member State to set the criteria for determining the extent of the damages, provided that the principles of equivalence and effectiveness are observed.

93. In that respect, first, in accordance with the principle of equivalence, it must be possible to award particular damages, such as exemplary or punitive damages, pursuant to actions founded on the Community competition rules, if such damages

may be awarded pursuant to similar actions founded on domestic law . . .

94. However, it is settled case-law that Community law does not prevent national courts from taking steps to ensure that the protection of the rights guaranteed by Community law does not entail the unjust enrichment of those who enjoy them . . .

95. Secondly, it follows from the principle of effectiveness and the right of any individual to seek compensation for loss caused by a contract or by conduct liable to restrict or distort competition that injured persons must be able to seek compensation not only for actual loss (damnum emergens) but also for loss of profit (lucrum cessans) plus interest.

96. Total exclusion of loss of profit as a head of damage for which compensation may be awarded cannot be accepted in the case of a breach of Community law since, especially in the context of economic or commercial litigation, such a total exclusion of loss of profit would be such as to make reparation of damage practically impossible . . .

97. As to the payment of interest . . . an award made in accordance with the applicable national rules constitutes an essential component of compensation.

98. . . . [I]n the absence of Community rules governing that field, it is for the domestic legal system of each Member State to set the criteria for determining the extent of the damages for harm caused by an agreement or practice prohibited under Article 81 EC [101], provided that the principles of equivalence and effectiveness are observed.

99. Therefore, first, in accordance with the principle of equivalence, if it is possible to award specific damages, such as exemplary or punitive damages, in domestic actions similar to actions founded on the Community competition rules, it must also be possible to award such damages in actions founded on Community rules. However, Community law does not prevent national courts from taking steps to ensure that the protection of the rights guaranteed by Community law does not entail the unjust enrichment of those who enjoy them.

100. Secondly, it follows from the principle of effectiveness and the right of individuals to seek compensation for loss caused by a contract or by conduct liable to restrict or distort competition that injured persons must be able to seek compensation not only for actual loss (damnum emergens) but also for loss of profit (lucrum cessans) plus interest.

## NOTES AND QUESTIONS

1.  The Court references the need for no less favorable treatment for EU-based actions. The issues addressed in the above case are probably just the tip of the iceberg in terms of the complexities involved in fashioning a right of action here that draws on some form of modified national procedure. What other issues could you identify? Suppose, for example, that a Member State decides to introduce a formal EU-law based procedure and allows triple damages. Could these lead to forum shopping? Would the ECJ have to lay down EU standards for jurisdiction? Again, suppose a Member State were to introduce criminal penalties specifically for violations of EC 81 or 82/TFEU 101 or 102. What sort of EU issues might this raise?

Is it really feasible to leave such matters to national law? See T. Eilmansberger, *The Green Paper on Damages Actions for Breach Of The EC Antitrust Rules and Beyond: Reflections on the Utility and Feasibility of Stimulating Private Enforcement Through Legislative Action* (2007), 44 CML REV. 431-478; and A. Riley and J. Peysner, *Analysis and Reflections — Damages in EC antitrust actions: Who pays the piper?* (2007) 31 EL REV. 748.

**2.**   In *Cartel Damage Claims ("CDC") v. Dyckerhoff AG*, the German Supreme Court (Bundesgerichtshof, "BGH") KZR 42/08 decided in its judgment of April 7, 2009 that actions based on damages claims assigned to a single plaintiff are permissible under German law — this has obvious parallels with U.S. class actions, where plaintiffs can opt into the class. CDC was set up in Belgium specifically to aggregate claims in competition law matters and in this case successfully sued six German cement producers based on such claims.

**3.**   The Commission has issued detailed guidance to the national courts regarding co-operation with the Commission: *Commission Notice on the Co-operation between the Commission and the Courts of the EU Member States in the application of articles 81 and 82 ec [101 and 102]* (2004/c 101/04). The provision of information to the Courts could prejudice the parties' position unnecessarily if the Commission provided the statement of objections to a national court, which then would reach a conclusion based on the allegations in it, whether or not they were substantiated. The Notice seeks to deal with this situation.

**4.**   One of the problems identified in Europe with regard to civil claims for violations of EC 81 or 82/TFEU 101 or 102 is whether the leniency program described in Chapter 7 operated by the Commission could precipitate civil claims, thus discouraging leniency applications. The question has come up in the context of the Commission's push to encourage such claims. What effect do you think the introduction of a robust civil claims procedure in a Member State might have on the effectiveness of the leniency program?

**5.**   Outside the arena of competition law, the involvement of the Commission in national court proceedings is part of a notable trend in directives enacted since 1990 to introduce conciliation procedures where disputes arise between individuals and governments or "emanations of a government", such as state-mandated monopolies.

## § 9.05   EFFECTIVE LEGAL PROTECTION — ACTIONS FOR DAMAGES

### [A]   The Basic Principles

### FRANCOVICH v. ITALY
Joined Cases 6 & 9/90, 1991 ECJ CELEX LEXIS 369, [1991] ECR I-5357

[Directive 80/987 required that employees in Member States enjoy a minimum level of protection in the event of insolvency of their employers. Under the directive specific guarantees were to be provided for the payment of unpaid remuneration. Italy failed to take any action to implement the directive. In response to this failure the Commission had brought proceedings against Italy before the Court of Justice, and the Court had ruled that Italy had breached EU Law. In a national court, certain employees, owed arrears of salary by their employers who had become insolvent, sued the Italian state for damages for failing to implement the directive. The national court referred several questions to the Court of Justice for a preliminary ruling. After first holding that the directive in question was not directly effective since the guarantor institutions were not identified, the Court turned to the issue of Italy's possible liability in damages to the workers for its failure to implement the directive.]

29 The national court thus raises the issue of the existence and scope of a State's liability for loss and damage resulting from breach of its obligations under Community law.

30 That issue must be considered in the light of the general system of the Treaty and its fundamental principles.

(a) The existence of State liability as a matter of principle

31 It should be borne in mind at the outset that the EEC Treaty has created its own legal system, which is integrated into the legal systems of the Member States and which their courts are bound to apply. The subjects of that legal system are not only the Member States but also their nationals. Just as it imposes burdens on individuals, Community law is also intended to give rise to rights which become part of their legal patrimony. Those rights arise not only where they are expressly granted by the Treaty but also by virtue of obligations which the Treaty imposes in a clearly defined manner both on individuals and on the Member States and the Community institutions . . .

32 Furthermore, it has been consistently held that the national courts whose task it is to apply the provisions of Community law in areas within their jurisdiction must ensure that those rules take full effect and must protect the rights which they confer on individuals . . .

33 The full effectiveness of Community rules would be impaired and the protection of the rights which they grant would be weakened if individuals were unable to obtain redress when their rights are infringed by a breach of Community law for which a Member State can be held responsible.

34 The possibility of obtaining redress from the Member State is particularly indispensable where, as in this case, the full effectiveness of Community rules is subject to prior action on the part of the State and where, consequently, in the absence of such action, individuals cannot enforce before the national courts the rights conferred upon them by Community law.

35 It follows that the principle whereby a State must be liable for loss and damage caused to individuals as a result of breaches of Community law for which the State can be held responsible is inherent in the system of the Treaty.

36 A further basis for the obligation of Member States to make good such loss and damage is to be found in Article 5 [TEU 4] of the Treaty, under which the Member States are required to take all appropriate measures, whether general or particular, to ensure fulfilment of their obligations under Community law. Among these is the

obligation to nullify the unlawful consequences of a breach of Community law . . .

37 It follows from all the foregoing that it is a principle of Community law that the Member States are obliged to make good loss and damage caused to individuals by breaches of Community law for which they can be held responsible.

(b) The conditions for State liability

38 Although State liability is thus required by Community law, the conditions under which that liability gives rise to a right to reparation depend on the nature of the breach of Community law giving rise to the loss and damage.

39 Where, as in this case, a Member State fails to fulfil its obligation under the third paragraph of Article 189 [288] of the Treaty to take all the measures necessary to achieve the result prescribed by a directive, the full effectiveness of that rule of Community law requires that there should be a right to reparation provided that three conditions are fulfilled.

40 The first of those conditions is that the result prescribed by the directive should entail the grant of rights to individuals. The second condition is that it should be possible to identify the content of those rights on the basis of the provisions of the directive. Finally, the third condition is the existence of a causal link between the breach of the State's obligation and the loss and damage suffered by the injured parties.

41 Those conditions are sufficient to give rise to a right on the part of individuals to obtain reparation, a right founded directly on Community law.

42 Subject to that reservation, it is on the basis of the rules of national law on liability that the State must make reparation for the consequences of the loss and damage caused. In the absence of Community legislation, it is for the internal legal order of each Member State to designate the competent courts and lay down the detailed procedural rules for legal proceedings intended fully to safeguard the rights which individuals derive from Community law . . .

43 Further, the substantive and procedural conditions for reparation of loss and damage laid down by the national law of the Member States must not be less favourable than those relating to similar domestic claims and must not be so framed as to make it virtually impossible or excessively difficult to obtain reparation . . .

44 In this case, the breach of Community law by a Member State by virtue of its failure to transpose Directive 80/987 within the prescribed period has been confirmed by a judgment of the Court. The result required by that directive entails the grant to employees of a right to a guarantee of payment of their unpaid wage claims. As is clear from the examination of the first part of the first question, the content of that right can be identified on the basis of the provisions of the directive.

45 Consequently, the national court must, in accordance with the national rules on liability, uphold the right of employees to obtain reparation of loss and damage caused to them as a result of failure to transpose the directive.

46 The answer to be given to the national court must therefore be that a Member

State is required to make good loss and damage caused to individuals by failure to transpose Directive 80/987.

# NOTES AND QUESTIONS

1.    What rationale does the Court offer for determining that Member States can be liable to compensate individuals for breach of Treaty obligations?

2.    In *Commission v. United Kingdom*, Case 383/92 1994 ECJ CELEX LEXIS 148, [1994] ECR I-2479, the European Court of Justice ruled that the United Kingdom was in breach of Directive 75/129 on the approximation of the laws of Member States relating to collective redundancies [employee layoffs] of February 17, 1975, in not requiring consultations with employees unrepresented by a trade union who had been dismissed for reasons unrelated to their job performance. The UK had violated EC 10/TEU 4 in failing to provide for effective sanctions against an employer who fails to comply with the obligation to inform and consult workers' representatives as required by the directive. Could employees dismissed prior to this decision without the required consultation sue the UK government for damages? Exactly what damage would be suffered? Is there a sufficient causal connection?

If it is possible to obtain damages in certain circumstances against a Member State, ought it also to be possible to obtain an injunction requiring the state to implement? Is a state court competent to make such an order? Is not EC 226/TFEU 258 designed for this purpose?

3.    For a review of the law after *Francovich*, see M-P F Granger, *National applications of Francovich and the construction of a European administrative jus commune* (2007) 32 ECR 157.

4.    It should be borne in mind that damages may not be the only way in which private parties may seek to enforce EU law against Member States. For example, national courts are required, if requested by private plaintiffs, to enforce the State aid provisions by ordering the repayment of illegally granted aids. The Commission in 1995 first issued a *Cooperation Notice* on state aids, which was replaced by a new Notice in 2008 renamed "*Commission Notice on the Enforcement of State Aid Law by National Courts*". The purpose of the new Notice is to provide solid legal encouragement to parties who believe they have been disadvantaged by illegal aids granted to others. This is likely to be a fruitful source of litigation, particularly in light of the extraordinary measures taken by Member States to deal with the 2008/9 financial crisis. Although many of these measures were "approved" by the Commission, it remains to be seen whether what may have been approved is vastly exceeded by what may actually be granted over time by the Member States.

## BRASSERIE DU PECHEUR SA v. BUNDESREPUBLIK DEUTSCHLAND AND THE QUEEN v. SECRETARY OF STATE FOR TRANSPORT, EX PARTE: FACTORTAME LTD AND OTHERS

Joined Cases C-46/93 and C-48/93, 1996 ECJ CELEX LEXIS 589, [1996] ECR I-1029

[The *Factortame* case first came to the ECJ in the context of a reference on the question whether the UK Courts were bound to give interim relief even though English law would have prevented this. This aspect of the *Factortame* litigation is set out in Chapter 3. The case then proceeded to the question of damages against the UK government. A similar case claiming damages for breach of EC 28/TFEU 34 by Germany for, in effect, preventing the import of beer that failed to meet the Reinheitsgebot (purity law) by prohibiting the use of the term "Bier" (beer) for such products. The two cases were heard together as they raised the same fundamental question as to whether the parties could claim damages against Member States for breach of directly effective (invocable) EU law. Several governments contended that Member States are required to make good loss or damage caused to individuals only where the provisions breached are not directly effective. Thus, they argued, in *Francovich* the Court simply sought to fill a lacuna in the system for safeguarding rights of individuals.]

20 The Court has consistently held that the right of individuals to rely on the directly effective provisions of the Treaty before national courts is only a minimum guarantee and is not sufficient in itself to ensure the full and complete implementation of the Treaty . . . The purpose of that right is to ensure that provisions of Community law prevail over national provisions. It cannot, in every case, secure for individuals the benefit of the rights conferred on them by Community law and, in particular, avoid their sustaining damage as a result of a breach of Community law attributable to a Member State. . . . [T]he full effectiveness of Community law would be impaired if individuals were unable to obtain redress when their rights were infringed by a breach of Community law.

21 This will be so where an individual who is a victim of the non-transposition of a directive and is precluded from relying on certain of its provisions directly before the national court because they are insufficiently precise and unconditional, brings an action for damages against the defaulting Member State for breach of the third paragraph of Article 189 [288] of the Treaty. In such circumstances, which obtained in the case of Francovich and Others, the purpose of reparation is to redress the injurious consequences of a Member State's failure to transpose a directive as far as beneficiaries of that directive are concerned.

22 It is all the more so in the event of infringement of a right directly conferred by a Community provision upon which individuals are entitled to rely before the national courts. In that event, the right to reparation is the necessary corollary of the direct effect of the Community provision whose breach caused the damage sustained.

23 In this case, it is undisputed that the Community provisions at issue, namely Article 30 [34] of the Treaty in Case C-46/93 and Article 52 [49] in Case C-48/93,

have direct effect in the sense that they confer on individuals rights upon which they are entitled to rely directly before the national courts. Breach of such provisions may give rise to reparation.

24 The German Government further submits that a general right to reparation for individuals could be created only by legislation and that for such a right to be recognized by judicial decision would be incompatible with the allocation of powers as between the Community institutions and the Member States and with the institutional balance established by the Treaty.

25 It must, however, be stressed that the existence and extent of State liability for damage ensuing as a result of a breach of obligations incumbent on the State by virtue of Community law are questions of Treaty interpretation which fall within the jurisdiction of the Court.

26 In this case, as in Francovich and Others, those questions of interpretation have been referred to the Court by national courts pursuant to Article 177 [267] of the Treaty.

27 Since the Treaty contains no provision expressly and specifically governing the consequences of breaches of Community law by Member States, it is for the Court, in pursuance of the task conferred on it by Article 164 [TEU 19] of the Treaty of ensuring that in the interpretation and application of the Treaty the law is observed, to rule on such a question in accordance with generally accepted methods of interpretation, in particular by reference to the fundamental principles of the Community legal system and, where necessary, general principles common to the legal systems of the Member States.

28 Indeed, it is to the general principles common to the laws of the Member States that the second paragraph of Article 215 [340] of the Treaty refers as the basis of the non-contractual liability of the Community for damage caused by its institutions or by its servants in the performance of their duties.

29 The principle of the non-contractual liability of the Community expressly laid down in Article 215 [340] of the Treaty is simply an expression of the general principle familiar to the legal systems of the Member States that an unlawful act or omission gives rise to an obligation to make good the damage caused. That provision also reflects the obligation on public authorities to make good damage caused in the performance of their duties.

30 In any event, in many national legal systems the essentials of the legal rules governing State liability have been developed by the courts.

31 In view of the foregoing considerations, the Court held in Francovich and Others . . . that the principle of State liability for loss and damage caused to individuals as a result of breaches of Community law for which it can be held responsible is inherent in the system of the Treaty.

32 It follows that that principle holds good for any case in which a Member State breaches Community law, whatever be the organ of the State whose act or omission was responsible for the breach.

33 In addition, in view of the fundamental requirement of the Community legal

order that Community law be uniformly applied . . . the obligation to make good damage caused to individuals by breaches of Community law cannot depend on domestic rules as to the division of powers between constitutional authorities.

34 . . . [I]n international law a State whose liability for breach of an international commitment is in issue will be viewed as a single entity, irrespective of whether the breach which gave rise to the damage is attributable to the legislature, the judiciary or the executive. This must apply a fortiori in the Community legal order since all State authorities, including the legislature, are bound in performing their tasks to comply with the rules laid down by Community law directly governing the situation of individuals.

35 The fact that, according to national rules, the breach complained of is attributable to the legislature cannot affect the requirements inherent in the protection of the rights of individuals who rely on Community law and, in this instance, the right to obtain redress in the national courts for damage caused by that breach.

36 Consequently, the reply to the national courts must be that the principle that Member States are obliged to make good damage caused to individuals by breaches of Community law attributable to the State is applicable where the national legislature was responsible for the breach in question.

*Conditions under which the State may incur liability for acts and omissions of the national legislature contrary to Community law (second question in Case C-46/93 and first question in Case C-48/93)*

37 By these questions, the national courts ask the Court to specify the conditions under which a right to reparation of loss or damage caused to individuals by breaches of Community law attributable to a Member State is, in the particular circumstances, guaranteed by Community law.

38 Although Community law imposes State liability, the conditions under which that liability gives rise to a right to reparation depend on the nature of the breach of Community law giving rise to the loss and damage (Francovich and Others, paragraph 38).

39 In order to determine those conditions, account should first be taken of the principles inherent in the Community legal order which form the basis for State liability, namely, first, the full effectiveness of Community rules and the effective protection of the rights which they confer and, second, the obligation to cooperate imposed on Member States by Article 5 [TEU 4] of the Treaty . . .

40 In addition, as the Commission and the several governments which submitted observations have emphasized, it is pertinent to refer to the Court's case-law on non-contractual liability on the part of the Community.

41 First, the second paragraph of Article 215 [340] of the Treaty refers, as regards the non-contractual liability of the Community, to the general principles common to the laws of the Member States, from which, in the absence of written rules, the Court also draws inspiration in other areas of Community law.

42 Second, the conditions under which the State may incur liability for damage

caused to individuals by a breach of Community law cannot, in the absence of particular justification, differ from those governing the liability of the Community in like circumstances. The protection of the rights which individuals derive from Community law cannot vary depending on whether a national authority or a Community authority is responsible for the damage. 43 The system of rules which the Court has worked out with regard to Article 215 [340] of the Treaty, particularly in relation to liability for legislative measures, takes into account, inter alia, the complexity of the situations to be regulated, difficulties in the application or interpretation of the texts and, more particularly, the margin of discretion available to the author of the act in question.

44 Thus, in developing its case-law on the non-contractual liability of the Community, in particular as regards legislative measures involving choices of economic policy, the Court has had regard to the wide discretion available to the institutions in implementing Community policies.

45 The strict approach taken towards the liability of the Community in the exercise of its legislative activities is due to two considerations. First, even where the legality of measures is subject to judicial review, exercise of the legislative function must not be hindered by the prospect of actions for damages whenever the general interest of the Community requires legislative measures to be adopted which may adversely affect individual interests. Second, in a legislative context characterized by the exercise of a wide discretion, which is essential for implementing a Community policy, the Community cannot incur liability unless the institution concerned has manifestly and gravely disregarded the limits on the exercise of its powers . . .

46 That said, the national legislature, like the Community institutions, does not systematically have a wide discretion when it acts in a field governed by Community law. Community law may impose upon it obligations to achieve a particular result or obligations to act or refrain from acting which reduce its margin of discretion, sometimes to a considerable degree. This is so, for instance, where, as in the circumstances to which the judgment in Francovich and Others relates, Article 189 [288] of the Treaty places the Member State under an obligation to take, within a given period, all the measures needed in order to achieve the result required by a directive. In such a case, the fact that it is for the national legislature to take the necessary measures has no bearing on the Member State's liability for failing to transpose the directive.

47 In contrast, where a Member State acts in a field where it has a wide discretion, comparable to that of the Community institutions in implementing Community policies, the conditions under which it may incur liability must, in principle, be the same as those under which the Community institutions incur liability in a comparable situation.

48 In the case which gave rise to the reference in Case C-46/93, the German legislature had legislated in the field of foodstuffs, specifically beer. In the absence of Community harmonization, the national legislature had a wide discretion in that sphere in laying down rules on the quality of beer put on the market.

49 As regards the facts of Case C-48/93, the United Kingdom legislature also had a wide discretion. The legislation at issue was concerned, first, with the registration

of vessels, a field which, in view of the state of development of Community law, falls within the jurisdiction of the Member States and, secondly, with regulating fishing, a sector in which implementation of the common fisheries policy leaves a margin of discretion to the Member States.

50 Consequently, in each case the German and United Kingdom legislatures were faced with situations involving choices comparable to those made by the Community institutions when they adopt legislative measures pursuant to a Community policy.

51 In such circumstances, Community law confers a right to reparation where three conditions are met: the rule of law infringed must be intended to confer rights on individuals; the breach must be sufficiently serious; and there must be a direct causal link between the breach of the obligation resting on the State and the damage sustained by the injured parties.

52 Firstly, those conditions satisfy the requirements of the full effectiveness of the rules of Community law and of the effective protection of the rights which those rules confer.

53 Secondly, those conditions correspond in substance to those defined by the Court in relation to Article 215 [340] in its case-law on liability of the Community for damage caused to individuals by unlawful legislative measures adopted by its institutions.

54 The first condition is manifestly satisfied in the case of Article 30 [34] of the Treaty, the relevant provision in Case C-46/93, and in the case of Article 52 [49], the relevant provision in Case C-48/93. Whilst Article 30 [34] imposes a prohibition on Member States, it nevertheless gives rise to rights for individuals which the national courts must protect . . .

55 As to the second condition, as regards both Community liability under Article 215 [340] and Member State liability for breaches of Community law, the decisive test for finding that a breach of Community law is sufficiently serious is whether the Member State or the Community institution concerned manifestly and gravely disregarded the limits on its discretion.

56 The factors which the competent court may take into consideration include the clarity and precision of the rule breached, the measure of discretion left by that rule to the national or Community authorities, whether the infringement and the damage caused was intentional or involuntary, whether any error of law was excusable or inexcusable, the fact that the position taken by a Community institution may have contributed towards the omission, and the adoption or retention of national measures or practices contrary to Community law.

57 On any view, a breach of Community law will clearly be sufficiently serious if it has persisted despite a judgment finding the infringement in question to be established, or a preliminary ruling or settled case-law of the Court on the matter from which it is clear that the conduct in question constituted an infringement.

58 While, in the present cases, the Court cannot substitute its assessment for that of the national courts, which have sole jurisdiction to find the facts in the main proceedings and decide how to characterize the breaches of Community law at

issue, it will be helpful to indicate a number of circumstances which the national courts might take into account.

59 In Case C-46/93 a distinction should be drawn between the question of the German legislature's having maintained in force provisions of the Biersteuergesetz concerning the purity of beer prohibiting the marketing under the designation "Bier" of beers imported from other Member States which were lawfully produced in conformity with different rules, and the question of the retention of the provisions of that same law prohibiting the import of beers containing additives. As regards the provisions of the German legislation relating to the designation of the product marketed, it would be difficult to regard the breach of Article 30 [34] by that legislation as an excusable error, since the incompatibility of such rules with Article 30 [34] was manifest in the light of earlier decisions of the Court, in particular Case 120/78 Rewe-Zentral 1979 ECR 649 ("Cassis de Dijon") and Case 193/80 Commission v. Italy 1981 EC [101] R 3019 ("vinegar"). In contrast, having regard to the relevant case-law, the criteria available to the national legislature to determine whether the prohibition of the use of additives was contrary to Community law were significantly less conclusive until the Court's judgment of 12 March 1987 in Commission v. Germany, cited above, in which the Court held that prohibition to be incompatible with Article 30 [28].

60 A number of observations may likewise be made about the national legislation at issue in Case C-48/93.

61 The decision of the United Kingdom legislature to introduce in the Merchant Shipping Act 1988 provisions relating to the conditions for the registration of fishing vessels has to be assessed differently in the case of the provisions making registration subject to a nationality condition, which constitute direct discrimination manifestly contrary to Community law, and in the case of the provisions laying down residence and domicile conditions for vessel owners and operators.

62 The latter conditions are prima facie incompatible with Article 52 [43] of the Treaty in particular, but the United Kingdom sought to justify them in terms of the objectives of the common fisheries policy. In the judgment in Factortame II, . . . the Court rejected that justification.

63 In order to determine whether the breach of Article 52 [43] thus committed by the United Kingdom was sufficiently serious, the national court might take into account, inter alia, the legal disputes relating to particular features of the common fisheries policy, the attitude of the Commission, which made its position known to the United Kingdom in good time, and the assessments as to the state of certainty of Community law made by the national courts in the interim proceedings brought by individuals affected by the Merchant Shipping Act.

64 Lastly, consideration should be given to the assertion made by Rawlings (Trawling) Ltd, the 37th claimant in Case C-48/93, that the United Kingdom failed to adopt immediately the measures needed to comply with the Order of the President of the Court of 10 October 1989 in Commission v. United Kingdom, cited above, and that this needlessly increased the loss it sustained. If this allegation which was certainly contested by the United Kingdom at the hearing, should prove correct, it should be regarded by the national court as constituting in itself a

manifest and, therefore, sufficiently serious breach of Community law.

65 As for the third condition, it is for the national courts to determine whether there is a direct causal link between the breach of the obligation borne by the State and the damage sustained by the injured parties.

66 The aforementioned three conditions are necessary and sufficient to found a right in individuals to obtain redress, although this does not mean that the State cannot incur liability under less strict conditions on the basis of national law.

67 . . . [S]ubject to the right to reparation which flows directly from Community law where the conditions referred to in the preceding paragraph are satisfied, the State must make reparation for the consequences of the loss and damage caused in accordance with the domestic rules on liability, provided that the conditions for reparation of loss and damage laid down by national law must not be less favourable than those relating to similar domestic claims and must not be such as in practice to make it impossible or excessively difficult to obtain reparation . . .

68 In that regard, restrictions that exist in domestic legal systems as to the non-contractual liability of the State in the exercise of its legislative function may be such as to make it impossible in practice or excessively difficult for individuals to exercise their right to reparation, as guaranteed by Community law, of loss or damage resulting from the breach of Community law.

69 In Case C-46/93 the national court asks in particular whether national law may subject any right to compensation to the same restrictions as apply where a law is in breach of higher-ranking national provisions, for instance, where an ordinary Federal law infringes the Grundgesetz of the Federal Republic of Germany.

70 While the imposition of such restrictions may be consistent with the requirement that the conditions laid down should not be less favourable than those relating to similar domestic claims, it is still to be considered whether such restrictions are not such as in practice to make it impossible or excessively difficult to obtain reparation.

71 The condition imposed by German law where a law is in breach of higher-ranking national provisions, which makes reparation dependent upon the legislature's act or omission being referable to an individual situation, would in practice make it impossible or extremely difficult to obtain effective reparation for loss or damage resulting from a breach of Community law, since the tasks falling to the national legislature relate, in principle, to the public at large and not to identifiable persons or classes of person.

72 Since such a condition stands in the way of the obligation on national courts to ensure the full effectiveness of Community law by guaranteeing effective protection for the rights of individuals, it must be set aside where an infringement of Community law is attributable to the national legislature.

73 Likewise, any condition that may be imposed by English law on State liability requiring proof of misfeasance in public office, such an abuse of power being inconceivable in the case of the legislature, is also such as in practice to make it impossible or extremely difficult to obtain effective reparation for loss or damage resulting from a breach of Community law where the breach is attributable to the national legislature.

74 Accordingly, the reply to the questions from the national courts must be that, where a breach of Community law by a Member State is attributable to the national legislature acting in a field in which it has a wide discretion to make legislative choices, individuals suffering loss or injury thereby are entitled to reparation where the rule of Community law breached is intended to confer rights upon them, the breach is sufficiently serious and there is a direct causal link between the breach and the damage sustained by the individuals.

## NOTES AND QUESTIONS

1. In terms of the justification for holding Member States responsible to compensate for breaches of EU law, how does this case differ from *Francovich*?

2. The ECJ made a point of assimilating damages claims against Member States with EC 288/TFEU 340 actions against EU institutions. What difficulties might need to be worked out with regard to this approach?

3. What if the national legal system does not permit such claims? Might it be necessary for a Member State to have to reorganize or at least modify its justice system in order to ensure that rights of appeal are available so as to prevent final judgments from being entered in infringement of EU law? Could a failure to make such adjustments itself constitute an infringement? Consider in this regard *Dorsch Consult Ingenieurgesellschaft mbH v. Bundesbaugesellschaft Berlin mbH*, Case C-54/96, 1997 ECJ CELEX LEXIS 549, [1997] ECR I-4961, where the Court had to consider the appropriateness of an appeals procedure relating to the award of public procurement contracts where the relevant Directive, 92/50, had not yet been transposed into national law. The Court held that:

> [I]n order to observe the requirement that domestic law must be interpreted in conformity with Directive 92/50 and the requirement that the rights of individuals must be protected effectively, the national court must determine whether the relevant provisions of its domestic law allow recognition of a right for individuals to bring an appeal in relation to awards of public service contracts. In circumstances such as those arising in the present case, the national court must determine in particular whether such a right of appeal may be exercised before the same bodies as those established to hear appeals concerning the award of public supply contracts and public works contracts.

In *Bourgoin SA and others v. Ministry of Agriculture, Fisheries and Food*, [1986] 1 QB 716, [1986] 1 CMLR 267, and before the *Brasserie du Pecheur* decision, the English Court of Appeal had been faced with a claim for damages for breach of EC 28/TFEU 34. The judgments provide a long and interesting analysis of the issues created by the possibility of such claims. Lord Justice Parker, for example, thought that such claims should only exist where they would also exist for a failure by the UK government, such as for wilful misfeasance, where the purpose was to protect individuals and discourage government abuse.

The above observations are in all likelihood symptomatic of the kinds of difficulties national courts will have to deal with, as they try to integrate this ruling into their national legal systems. Judicial remedies in English common law have evolved over several centuries as part of an overall development in the relationship between courts and government. In civil law systems, public and administrative law has its own standing independent of the civil, criminal and commercial court systems. Blending EU law into these very different approaches and achieving uniformity of approach across the entire EU looks like a huge task that will take many years of references to clarify.

## [B]   Culpability — Margin of Choice for the Member State

## WALTER RECHBERGER, RENATE GREINDL, HERMANN HOFMEISTER AND OTHERS v. AUSTRIA
### Case C-140/97, 1999 ECJ CELEX LEXIS 256, [1999] ECR I-3499

[*Following is an abbreviated version of the Court's summary of the facts.* The plaintiffs sought damages from the Austrian government for failure to transpose Council Directive 90/314/EEC of 13 June 1990 on package travel, package holidays and package tours (OJ 1990 L 158, p. 59) properly into national law, which prevented the plaintiffs from obtaining the reimbursement of money they had paid to a travel organizer who became insolvent. Article 7 of the Directive provides that the organizer of the package tour or holiday is to provide "sufficient evidence of security for the refund of money paid over and for the repatriation of the consumer in the event of insolvency". Austria introduced legislation by regulation to implement the directive but the regulation covered trips booked after January 1 1995 with a travel date after May 1, 1995. The Directive however required the implementing legislation to be in effect as of January 1 1995.

Paragraph 3(2) of the Regulation provided that the value of the guarantee should be no less than 5% of the organizer's business turnover in the corresponding quarter of the previous calendar year. In the first year of business, the amount of cover was to be based on the estimated turnover from the intended activity. If the travel organizer received deposits from customers of more than 10% of the price of the trip or if he received the balance of the price more than ten days prior to departure, the amount covered was to be at least 10% of the reference value mentioned in the preceding sentence.

The plaintiffs were subscribers to the daily newspaper Neue Kronenzeitung. In November 1994 they received a letter from the publisher informing them that, to thank subscribers for their loyalty, the newspaper had arranged for the travel organizer Arena-Club-Reisen to offer them by way of gift (save for airport taxes) a four or seven day trip to one of four European destinations.

Subscribers who accepted the offer received a confirmation of their booking from the travel organizer and were required to pay the organizer a deposit of 10% of the relevant charges, the balance being payable no later than ten days before the scheduled departure date.

The offer proved to be far more successful than the travel organizer had anticipated, and this caused the organizer logistical and financial difficulties which led it to apply, on 4 July 1995, for bankruptcy proceedings to be initiated against it. The advertising campaign organized by Neue Kronenzeitung was subsequently held by the Austrian Supreme Court to be incompatible with national competition law.

The plaintiffs booked their trips between 19 November 1994 and 12 April 1995. Some of them were to travel alone, others in the company of one, two or three persons. They all paid the whole of the travel costs in advance. However, the trips, which were to take place between 10 April and 23 July 1995 according to the individual bookings, were cancelled for a number of reasons.

For three of the plaintiffs in the main action who made bookings in 1994 no guarantee was provided since the Regulation only applied to package travel booked after 1 January 1995. Two of the three registered their claims as creditors in the organizing company's insolvency, but although they were admitted as creditors they failed to obtain any settlement from the available assets in the estate. The payments of another three of the plaintiffs who booked their trips after 1 January 1995 and were to leave after 1 May 1995 were in principle covered by a guarantee issued in accordance with the Regulation. However, the bank guarantee of 4,000,000 Austrian Schillings issued by the travel organizer was insufficient to reimburse the travel costs they had paid, the final level of cover being only 25.38% of the amount paid.]

50 According to the case-law of the Court, a breach is sufficiently serious where, in the exercise of its legislative powers, an institution or a Member State has manifestly and gravely disregarded the limits on the exercise of its powers. Factors which the competent court may take into consideration include the clarity and precision of the rule breached . . .

51 In the present case it must be held that neither Article 7 nor any other provision of the Directive may be interpreted as conferring a right upon the Member States to limit the application of Article 7 to trips taken on a date later than the time-limit prescribed for transposition of the Directive. The Member State in question here enjoyed no margin of discretion as to the entry into force, in its own law, of the provisions of Article 7. That being so, the limitation of the protection prescribed by Article 7 to trips with a departure date of 1 May 1995 or later is manifestly incompatible with the obligations under the Directive and thus constitutes a sufficiently serious breach of Community law.

52 The fact that the Member State has implemented all the other provisions of the Directive does not alter that finding.

53 In view of the foregoing the answer to the fourth question must be that transposition of Article 7 of the Directive in a way that limits the protection prescribed by that provision to trips with a departure date four months or more after the expiry of the period prescribed for transposing the Directive constitutes a sufficiently serious breach of Community law, even where the Member State has implemented all the other provisions of the Directive.

\* \* \*

67 By its sixth question the national court is essentially asking whether, where there is a direct causal link between the conduct of the State which has only partially transposed the directive and the loss or damage suffered by individuals, that causal link might not render that State liable if it shows that there was

imprudent conduct on the part of the travel organiser or that exceptional or unforeseeable events occurred.

68 The plaintiffs in the main action maintain that unlawful conduct on the part of the travel organiser or any other third party cannot exempt the Member State concerned from liability. The question concerning exceptional and unforeseeable increase in risk is irrelevant in the present case since a substantial increase in turnover can never be unforeseeable and provision for it should in any event have been made by the national legislature.

69 The Republic of Austria argues that, in any event, there is no direct causal link between late or incomplete transposition of Article 7 of the Directive and the loss or damage suffered by consumers if the date and scope of the implementing measures can have contributed to the occurrence of the loss or damage only as a result of a chain of wholly exceptional and unforeseeable events.

70 According to the United Kingdom and Swedish Governments, it is for the national court to determine, according to the principles applicable under its national law, whether, in any given case, there is a direct causal link between, on the one hand, a Member State's failure to transpose Article 7 within the prescribed period or to do so adequately and, on the other hand, the loss or damage suffered by the consumer, such as to render the Member State liable and to require it to reimburse the unsecured sums in full.

71 According to the Commission, that causal link should be held to exist even when the organiser's insolvency and its extent are to be attributed to wholly exceptional and unforeseeable causes.

72 In this connection, it should be observed that, . . . it is for the national courts to determine whether there is a direct causal link between the breach of the obligation resting on the State and the damage sustained by the injured parties.

73 In the present case, it should first be observed that the national court found that there was such a direct causal link between the conduct of the Member State which had failed to transpose the Directive in full and the damage sustained by the individuals.

74 Next, it should be pointed out that Article 7 of the Directive imposes an obligation of result, namely to guarantee package travellers the refund of money paid over and their repatriation in the event of the travel organiser's bankruptcy. Such a guarantee is specifically aimed at arming consumers against the consequences of the bankruptcy, whatever the causes of it may be.

75 In those circumstances, the Member State's liability for breach of Article 7 of the Directive cannot be precluded by imprudent conduct on the part of the travel organiser or by the occurrence of exceptional and unforeseeable events.

76 Such circumstances, in as much as they would not have presented an obstacle to the refund of money paid over or the repatriation of consumers if the guarantee system had been implemented in accordance with Article 7 of the Directive, are not such as to preclude the existence of a direct causal link.

77 Consequently, the answer to the sixth question must be that once a direct causal

link has been established a Member State's liability for breach of Article 7 of the Directive cannot be precluded by imprudent conduct on the part of the travel organiser or by the occurrence of exceptional or unforeseeable events.

## NOTES AND QUESTIONS

1.    The ECJ gives guidance here on what constitutes a sufficiently serious and manifest breach. What conclusions might be drawn from the Court's analysis of this point? Is there a general principle to be found here? Can the Court's ruling be reconciled with its case law under EC 288/TFEU 340 regarding acts involving discretionary powers?

2.    The Court considers the causal nexus to the damage to be a matter for determination by the State courts. Is this a satisfactory level of guidance? Could this result in disparities between Member States? Does the Court's ruling itself violate the principle of legal certainty?

3.    For a contrasting case, see *R. v. HM Treasury ex parte British Telecommunications* Case C-392/93, 1996 ECJ CELEX LEXIS 44, [1996] ECR I-1631, where the UK had failed properly to implement the utilities directive. The UK transposition had preempted the power of utility companies to decide which services were within the scope of the EU rules relating to public procurement. The UK, though mistaken, was held not to be liable for damages.

## [C]    Fault and Damages Criteria

### BRASSERIE DU PECHEUR SA v. BUNDESREPUBLIK DEUTSCHLAND AND THE QUEEN v. SECRETARY OF STATE FOR TRANSPORT, EX PARTE: FACTORTAME LTD AND OTHERS
Joined Cases C-46/93 and C-48/93, 1996 ECJ CELEX LEXIS 589, [1996] ECR I-1029

[See chapter 3 and the earlier excerpt in this chapter for the facts of these cases]

74 . . . [T]he State must make good the consequences of the loss or damage caused by the breach of Community law attributable to it, in accordance with its national law on liability. However, the conditions laid down by the applicable national laws must not be less favourable than those relating to similar domestic claims or framed in such a way as in practice to make it impossible or excessively difficult to obtain reparation.

75 By its third question, the Bundesgerichtshof essentially seeks to establish whether, pursuant to the national legislation which it applies, the national court is entitled to make reparation conditional upon the existence of fault (whether intentional or negligent) on the part of the organ of the State to which the infringement is attributable.

76 As is clear from the case-file, the concept of fault does not have the same content in the various legal systems.

77 Next, it follows from the reply to the preceding question that, where a breach of Community law is attributable to a Member State acting in a field in which it has a wide discretion to make legislative choices, a finding of a right to reparation on the basis of Community law will be conditional, inter alia, upon the breach having been sufficiently serious.

78 So, certain objective and subjective factors connected with the concept of fault under a national legal system may well be relevant for the purpose of determining whether or not a given breach of Community law is serious . . .

79 The obligation to make reparation for loss or damage caused to individuals cannot, however, depend upon a condition based on any concept of fault going beyond that of a sufficiently serious breach of Community law. Imposition of such a supplementary condition would be tantamount to calling in question the right to reparation founded on the Community legal order.

80 Accordingly, the reply to the question from the national court must be that, pursuant to the national legislation which it applies, reparation of loss or damage cannot be made conditional upon fault (intentional or negligent) on the part of the organ of the State responsible for the breach, going beyond that of a sufficiently serious breach of Community law.

*The actual extent of the reparation (question 4(a) in Case C-46/93 and the second question in Case C-48/93)*

81 By these questions, the national courts essentially ask the Court to identify the criteria for determination of the extent of the reparation due by the Member State responsible for the breach.

82 Reparation for loss or damage caused to individuals as a result of breaches of Community law must be commensurate with the loss or damage sustained so as to ensure the effective protection for their rights.

83 In the absence of relevant Community provisions, it is for the domestic legal system of each Member State to set the criteria for determining the extent of reparation. However, those criteria must not be less favourable than those applying to similar claims based on domestic law and must not be such as in practice to make it impossible or excessively difficult to obtain reparation.

84 In particular, in order to determine the loss or damage for which reparation may be granted, the national court may inquire whether the injured person showed reasonable diligence in order to avoid the loss or damage or limit its extent and whether, in particular, he availed himself in time of all the legal remedies available to him.

85 Indeed, it is a general principle common to the legal systems of the Member States that the injured party must show reasonable diligence in limiting the extent of the loss or damage, or risk having to bear the damage himself . . .

86 The Bundesgerichtshof asks whether national legislation may generally limit the obligation to make reparation to damage done to certain, specifically protected

individual interests, for example property, or whether it should also cover loss of profit by the claimants. It states that the opportunity to market products from other Member States is not regarded in German law as forming part of the protected assets of the undertaking.

87 Total exclusion of loss of profit as a head of damage for which reparation may be awarded in the case of a breach of Community law cannot be accepted. Especially in the context of economic or commercial litigation, such a total exclusion of loss of profit would be such as to make reparation of damage practically impossible.

88 As for the various heads of damage referred to in the Divisional Court's second question, Community law imposes no specific criteria. It is for the national court to rule on those heads of damage in accordance with the domestic law which it applies, subject to the requirements set out in paragraph 83 above.

89 As regards in particular the award of exemplary damages, such damages are based under domestic law, as the Divisional Court explains, on the finding that the public authorities concerned acted oppressively, arbitrarily or unconstitutionally. In so far as such conduct may constitute or aggravate a breach of Community law, an award of exemplary damages pursuant to a claim or an action founded on Community law cannot be ruled out if such damages could be awarded pursuant to a similar claim or action founded on domestic law.

90 Accordingly, the reply to the national courts must be that reparation by Member States of loss or damage which they have caused to individuals as a result of breaches of Community law must be commensurate with the loss or damage sustained. In the absence of relevant Community provisions, it is for the domestic legal system of each Member State to set the criteria for determining the extent of reparation. However, those criteria must not be less favourable than those applying to similar claims or actions based on domestic law and must not be such as in practice to make it impossible or excessively difficult to obtain reparation. National legislation which generally limits the damage for which reparation may be granted to damage done to certain, specifically protected individual interests not including loss of profit by individuals is not compatible with Community law. Moreover, it must be possible to award specific damages, such as the exemplary damages provided for by English law, pursuant to claims or actions founded on Community law, if such damages may be awarded pursuant to similar claims or actions founded on domestic law.

## NOTES AND QUESTIONS

1. The German Government had argued that some form of tortious fault standard (negligence or wilful default) should be an element in the assessment of liability. What was the ECJ's view?

2. How would you describe the Court's minimum standards for determining damages?

## [H]    Who Is Responsible?

## SALOMONE HAIM v. KASSENZAHNARZTLICHE VEREINIGUNG NORDRHEIN
### Case C-424/97, 2000 ECJ CELEX LEXIS 103, [2000] ECR I-5123

[Salomone Haim, an Italian dental practitioner, brought a claim against the Kassenzahnarztliche Vereinigung Nordrhein (Association of Dental Practitioners of Social Security Schemes in Nordrhein, the KVN), a public-law body, in order to obtain compensation for the loss of earnings which he claims to have suffered as a result of the breach of EU law by the KVN. He had brought an earlier case regarding other aspects of his treatment, but in this case essentially, the breach consisted in applying a requirement that for dental practitioners to be reimbursed by the social security scheme administered by the KVN, they should have a sufficient knowledge of the German language. Mr Haim suffered a loss of earnings due to his disqualification in this regard.]

27 . . . [I]t is for each Member State to ensure that individuals obtain reparation for loss and damage caused to them by non-compliance with Community law, whichever public authority is responsible for the breach and whichever public authority is in principle, under the law of the Member State concerned, responsible for making reparation . . .

28 Member States cannot, therefore, escape that liability either by pleading the internal distribution of powers and responsibilities as between the bodies which exist within their national legal order or by claiming that the public authority responsible for the breach of Community law did not have the necessary powers, knowledge, means or resources.

29 However . . . there is nothing to suggest that reparation for loss and damage caused to individuals by national measures taken in breach of Community law must necessarily be provided by the Member State itself in order for its obligations under Community law to be fulfilled.

30 As regards Member States with a federal structure, the Court has held that, if the procedural arrangements in the domestic system enable the rights which individuals derive from the Community legal system to be effectively protected and it is not more difficult to assert those rights than the rights which they derive from the domestic legal system, reparation for loss and damage caused to individuals by national measures taken in breach of Community law need not necessarily be provided by the federal State in order for the Community law obligations of the Member State concerned to be fulfilled . . .

31 That is also true for those Member States, whether or not they have a federal structure, in which certain legislative or administrative tasks are devolved to territorial bodies with a certain degree of autonomy or to any other public-law body legally distinct from the State. In those Member States, reparation for loss and damage caused to individuals by national measures taken in breach of Community law by a public-law body may therefore be made by that body.

32 Nor does Community law preclude a public-law body, in addition to the Member

State itself, from being liable to make reparation for loss and damage caused to individuals as a result of measures which it took in breach of Community law.

33 It is well settled that, subject to the existence of a right to obtain reparation which is founded directly on Community law where the conditions for Member State liability for breach of Community law are met, it is on the basis of rules of national law on liability that the State must make reparation for the consequences of the loss and damage caused, with the proviso that the conditions for reparation of loss and damage laid down by national legislation must not be less favourable than those relating to similar domestic claims and must not be so framed as to make it in practice impossible or excessively difficult to obtain reparation . . .

## NOTES AND QUESTIONS

1.    Does the *Haim* case suggest that the State might devolve its obligations to compensate on other (non-State) bodies?

2.    See also *Fantask A/S E.A. v. Industriministeriet*, Case C-188/95, 1997 ECJ CELEX LEXIS 253, [1997] ECR I-6783; and R Davis, *Analysis and Reflections — Liability in damages for a breach of Community law: Some reflections on the question of who to sue and the concept of 'the state'*, (2006) 31 EL REV. 69.

## GERHARD KÖBLER v. AUSTRIA
### Case C-224/01, 2003 ECJ CELEX LEXIS 403, [2003] ECR I-10239

[Mr Köbler had been denied a length of service increment because, in computing the length of service requirement of 15 years, no account had been taken of periods of service in universities in other Member States. He argued that this amounted to indirect discrimination contrary to EU law. The claim had been denied by the Austrian Courts who decided that the increment was a loyalty bonus, (that is, specifically designed as a retention scheme) and there was no further appeal possible. He brought an action for compensation for breach of EU law. The original court deciding his claim had decided not to make a reference under EC 234/TFEU 267, based on a mistaken belief that the ECJ had previously clearly ruled that a "loyalty bonus" did not interfere with a worker's free movement rights contrary to EC 39/TFEU 45.]

31. The Court has . . . held that that [the compensation principle] applies to any case in which a Member State breaches Community law, whichever is the authority of the Member State whose act or omission was responsible for the breach . . .

32. In international law a State which incurs liability for breach of an international commitment is viewed as a single entity, irrespective of whether the breach which gave rise to the damage is attributable to the legislature, the judiciary or the executive. That principle must apply a fortiori in the Community legal order since all State authorities, including the legislature, are bound in performing their tasks to comply with the rules laid down by Community law which directly govern the situation of individuals . . .

33. In the light of the essential role played by the judiciary in the protection of the rights derived by individuals from Community rules, the full effectiveness of those

rules would be called in question and the protection of those rights would be weakened if individuals were precluded from being able, under certain conditions, to obtain reparation when their rights are affected by an infringement of Community law attributable to a decision of a court of a Member State adjudicating at last instance.

34. It must be stressed, in that context, that a court adjudicating at last instance is by definition the last judicial body before which individuals may assert the rights conferred on them by Community law. Since an infringement of those rights by a final decision of such a court cannot thereafter normally be corrected, individuals cannot be deprived of the possibility of rendering the State liable in order in that way to obtain legal protection of their rights.

35. Moreover, it is, in particular, in order to prevent rights conferred on individuals by Community law from being infringed that under the third paragraph of Article 234 EC [267] a court against whose decisions there is no judicial remedy under national law is required to make a reference to the Court of Justice.

36. Consequently, it follows from the requirements inherent in the protection of the rights of individuals relying on Community law that they must have the possibility of obtaining redress in the national courts for the damage caused by the infringement of those rights owing to a decision of a court adjudicating at last instance . . .

37. Certain of the governments which submitted observations in these proceedings claimed that the principle of State liability for damage caused to individuals by infringements of Community law could not be applied to decisions of a national court adjudicating at last instance. In that connection arguments were put forward based, in particular, on the principle of legal certainty and, more specifically, the principle of res judicata, the independence and authority of the judiciary and the absence of a court competent to determine disputes relating to State liability for such decisions.

38. In that regard the importance of the principle of res judicata cannot be disputed . . . In order to ensure both stability of the law and legal relations and the sound administration of justice, it is important that judicial decisions which have become definitive after all rights of appeal have been exhausted or after expiry of the time-limits provided for in that connection can no longer be called in question.

39. However, it should be borne in mind that recognition of the principle of State liability for a decision of a court adjudicating at last instance does not in itself have the consequence of calling in question that decision as res judicata. Proceedings seeking to render the State liable do not have the same purpose and do not necessarily involve the same parties as the proceedings resulting in the decision which has acquired the status of res judicata. The applicant in an action to establish the liability of the State will, if successful, secure an order against it for reparation of the damage incurred but not necessarily a declaration invalidating the status of res judicata of the judicial decision which was responsible for the damage. In any event, the principle of State liability inherent in the Community legal order requires such reparation, but not revision of the judicial decision which was responsible for the damage.

40. It follows that the principle of res judicata does not preclude recognition of the principle of State liability for the decision of a court adjudicating at last instance.

41. Nor can the arguments based on the independence and authority of the judiciary be upheld.

42. As to the independence of the judiciary, the principle of liability in question concerns not the personal liability of the judge but that of the State. The possibility that under certain conditions the State may be rendered liable for judicial decisions contrary to Community law does not appear to entail any particular risk that the independence of a court adjudicating at last instance will be called in question.

43. As to the argument based on the risk of a diminution of the authority of a court adjudicating at last instance owing to the fact that its final decisions could by implication be called in question in proceedings in which the State may be rendered liable for such decisions, the existence of a right of action that affords, under certain conditions, reparation of the injurious effects of an erroneous judicial decision could also be regarded as enhancing the quality of a legal system and thus in the long run the authority of the judiciary.

44. Several governments also argued that application of the principle of State liability to decisions of a national court adjudicating at last instance was precluded by the difficulty of designating a court competent to determine disputes concerning the reparation of damage resulting from such decisions.

45. In that connection, given that, for reasons essentially connected with the need to secure for individuals protection of the rights conferred on them by Community rules, the principle of State liability inherent in the Community legal order must apply in regard to decisions of a national court adjudicating at last instance, it is for the Member States to enable those affected to rely on that principle by affording them an appropriate right of action. Application of that principle cannot be compromised by the absence of a competent court.

46. According to settled case-law, in the absence of Community legislation, it is for the internal legal order of each Member State to designate the competent courts and lay down the detailed procedural rules for legal proceedings intended fully to safeguard the rights which individuals derive from Community law . . .

47. Subject to the reservation that it is for the Member States to ensure in each case that those rights are effectively protected, it is not for the Court to become involved in resolving questions of jurisdiction to which the classification of certain legal situations based on Community law may give rise in the national judicial system . . .

48. It should be added that, although considerations to do with observance of the principle of res judicata or the independence of the judiciary have caused national legal systems to impose restrictions, which may sometimes be stringent, on the possibility of rendering the State liable for damage caused by mistaken judicial decisions, such considerations have not been such as absolutely to exclude that possibility. Indeed, application of the principle of State liability to judicial decisions has been accepted in one form or another by most of the Member States . . . even if subject only to restrictive and varying conditions.

49. It may also be noted that, in the same connection, the ECHR and, more particularly, Article 41 thereof enables the European Court of Human Rights to order a State which has infringed a fundamental right to provide reparation of the damage resulting from that conduct for the injured party. The case-law of that court shows that such reparation may also be granted when the infringement stems from a decision of a national court adjudicating at last instance . . .

50. It follows from the foregoing that the principle according to which the Member States are liable to afford reparation of damage caused to individuals as a result of infringements of Community law for which they are responsible is also applicable where the alleged infringement stems from a decision of a court adjudicating at last instance. It is for the legal system of each Member State to designate the court competent to adjudicate on disputes relating to such reparation.

## NOTES AND QUESTIONS

1.   How did the ECJ deal with the point raised here that the original salary claim was *res judicata*?

2.   There seem to be serious internal constitutional issues raised here regarding the independence of the judiciary. How did the ECJ resolve this, if at all?

3.   What do you think it would take to hold a Member State accountable in damages for a failure of its courts to make a reference? Note that in the above case, the ECJ went on to decide that the failure was either manifest or sufficiently serious.

4.   Could the ECJ's ruling here imply that a court of first instance in a Member State could be asked to rule on the propriety of a judgment by the highest court in the land?

5.   For another case concerning liability for the conduct of national courts, see *Traghetti del Mediterraneo* Case C-173/03, 2006 ECJ CELEX LEXIS 270, [2006] ECR I-5177, where the ECJ emphasised that attempts by a Member State to limit liability for wrongful judgments to situations where there was intentional fault and serious misconduct will be considered a violation of EU law. See also G. Anagnostaras, *Analysis and Reflections — Erroneous judgments and the prospect of damages: The scope of the principle of governmental liability for judicial breaches* (2006), 31 EL Rev. 735.

## § 9.06   THE CONSTITUTIONAL POSITION OF THE NATIONAL COURTS IN THE EU

### OPINION 1/09
Compatibility of a the draft agreement for the creation of a unified patent litigation system with the Treaties
[2011] ECR NYR

[The court was asked give an opinion under TFEU 218 on the compatibility of an international treaty that would have set up a unified European patent litigation system. Among other things, the envisaged agreement would establish a European and Community Patents Court ('the PC') composed of a court of first instance, comprising a central division and local and regional divisions, and a court of appeal, that court having jurisdiction to hear appeals brought against decisions delivered by the court of first instance.]

64. Since the draft agreement establishes, in essence, a new court structure, it is appropriate to bear in mind, first, the fundamental elements of the legal order and judicial system of the European Union, as designed by the founding Treaties and developed by the case-law of the Court, in order to assess whether the creation of the PC is compatible with those elements.

65. It is apparent from the Court's settled case-law that the founding treaties of the European Union, unlike ordinary international treaties, established a new legal order, possessing its own institutions, for the benefit of which the States have limited their sovereign rights, in ever wider fields, and the subjects of which comprise not only Member States but also their nationals. [T]he essential characteristics of the European Union legal order thus constituted are in particular its primacy over the laws of the Member States and the direct effect of a whole series of provisions which are applicable to their nationals and to the Member States themselves . . . .

66. As is evident from Article 19(1) TEU, the guardians of that legal order and the judicial system of the European Union are the Court of Justice and the courts and tribunals of the Member States.

67. Moreover, it is for the Court to ensure respect for the autonomy of the European Union legal order thus created by the Treaties . . .

68. It should also be observed that the Member States are obliged, by reason, inter alia, of the principle of sincere cooperation, set out in the first subparagraph of Article 4(3) TEU, to ensure, in their respective territories, the application of and respect for European Union law . . . Further, pursuant to the second subparagraph of Article 4(3) TEU, the Member States are to take any appropriate measure, general or particular, to ensure fulfilment of the obligations arising out of the Treaties or resulting from the acts of the institutions of the European Union. In that context, it is for the national courts and tribunals and for the Court of Justice to ensure the full application of European Union law in all Member States and to ensure judicial protection of an individual's rights under that law . . .

69. The national court, in collaboration with the Court of Justice, fulfils a duty

entrusted to them both of ensuring that in the interpretation and application of the Treaties the law is observed . . .

70. The judicial system of the European Union is moreover a complete system of legal remedies and procedures designed to ensure review of the legality of acts of the institutions . . .

71. As regards the characteristics of the PC, it must first be observed that that court is outside the institutional and judicial framework of the European Union. It is not part of the judicial system provided for in Article 19(1) TEU. The PC is an organisation with a distinct legal personality under international law.

72. In accordance with Article 15 of the draft agreement, the PC is to be vested with exclusive jurisdiction in respect of a significant number of actions brought by individuals in the field of patents. That jurisdiction extends, in particular, to actions for actual or threatened infringements of patents, counterclaims concerning licences, actions for declarations of non-infringement, actions for provisional and protective measures, actions or counterclaims for revocation of patents, actions for damages or compensation derived from the provisional protection conferred by a published patent application, actions relating to the use of the invention before the granting of the patent or to the right based on prior use of the patent, actions for the grant or revocation of compulsory licences in respect of Community patents, and actions for compensation for licences. To that extent, the courts of the contracting States, including the courts of the Member States, are divested of that jurisdiction and accordingly retain only those powers which are not subject to the exclusive jurisdiction of the PC.

73. It must be added that, in accordance with Article 14a of the draft agreement, the PC, in carrying out its tasks, has the duty to interpret and apply European Union law. The draft agreement confers on that court the main part of the jurisdiction *ratione materiae* held, normally, by the national courts, to hear disputes in the Community patent field and to ensure, in that field, the full application of European Union law and the judicial protection of individual rights under that law.

74. As regards an international agreement providing for the creation of a court responsible for the interpretation of its provisions, the Court has, it is true, held that such an agreement is not, in principle, incompatible with European Union law. The competence of the European Union in the field of international relations and its capacity to conclude international agreements necessarily entail the power to submit itself to the decisions of a court which is created or designated by such agreements as regards the interpretation and application of their provisions . . . .

75. Moreover, the Court has stated that an international agreement concluded with third countries may confer new judicial powers on the Court provided that in so doing it does not change the essential character of the function of the Court as conceived in the EU and FEU Treaties . . .

76. The Court has also declared that an international agreement may affect its own powers provided that the indispensable conditions for safeguarding the essential character of those powers are satisfied and, consequently, there is no adverse effect on the autonomy of the European Union legal order . . .

77. However, the judicial systems under consideration in the abovementioned Opinions were designed, in essence, to resolve disputes on the interpretation or application of the actual provisions of the international agreements concerned. Further, while providing particular powers to the courts of third countries to refer cases to the Court for a preliminary ruling, those systems did not affect the powers of the courts and tribunals of Member States in relation to the interpretation and application of European Union law, nor the power, or indeed the obligation, of those courts and tribunals to request a preliminary ruling from the Court of Justice and the power of the Court to reply.

78. By contrast, the international court envisaged in this draft agreement is to be called upon to interpret and apply not only the provisions of that agreement but also the future regulation on the Community patent and other instruments of European Union law, in particular regulations and directives in conjunction with which that regulation would, when necessary, have to be read, namely provisions relating to other bodies of rules on intellectual property, and rules of the FEU Treaty concerning the internal market and competition law. Likewise, the PC may be called upon to determine a dispute pending before it in the light of the fundamental rights and general principles of European Union law, or even to examine the validity of an act of the European Union.

79. As regards the draft agreement submitted for the Court's consideration, it must be observed that the PC:

— takes the place of national courts and tribunals, in the field of its exclusive jurisdiction described in Article 15 of that draft agreement,

— deprives, therefore, those courts and tribunals of the power to request preliminary rulings from the Court in that field,

— becomes, in the field of its exclusive jurisdiction, the sole court able to communicate with the Court by means of a reference for a preliminary ruling concerning the interpretation and application of European Union law and

— has the duty, within that jurisdiction, in accordance with Article 14a of that draft agreement, to interpret and apply European Union law.

80. While it is true that the Court has no jurisdiction to rule on direct actions between individuals in the field of patents, since that jurisdiction is held by the courts of the Member States, nonetheless the Member States cannot confer the jurisdiction to resolve such disputes on a court created by an international agreement which would deprive those courts of their task, as 'ordinary' courts within the European Union legal order, to implement European Union law and, thereby, of the power provided for in Article 267 TFEU, or, as the case may be, the obligation, to refer questions for a preliminary ruling in the field concerned.

81. The draft agreement provides for a preliminary ruling mechanism which reserves, within the scope of that agreement, the power to refer questions for a preliminary ruling to the PC while removing that power from the national courts.

82. It must be emphasised that the situation of the PC envisaged by the draft agreement would differ from that of the Benelux Court of Justice which was the subject of Case C-337/95 *Parfums Christian Dior* [1997] ECR I-6013, paragraphs

21 to 23. Since the Benelux Court is a court common to a number of Member States, situated, consequently, within the judicial system of the European Union, its decisions are subject to mechanisms capable of ensuring the full effectiveness of the rules of the European Union.

83. It should also be recalled that Article 267 TFEU, which is essential for the preservation of the Community character of the law established by the Treaties, aims to ensure that, in all circumstances, that law has the same effect in all Member States. The preliminary ruling mechanism thus established aims to avoid divergences in the interpretation of European Union law which the national courts have to apply and tends to ensure this application by making available to national judges a means of eliminating difficulties which may be occasioned by the requirement of giving European Union law its full effect within the framework of the judicial systems of the Member States. Further, the national courts have the most extensive power, or even the obligation, to make a reference to the Court if they consider that a case pending before them raises issues involving an interpretation or assessment of the validity of the provisions of European Union law and requiring a decision by them . . .

84. The system set up by Article 267 TFEU therefore establishes between the Court of Justice and the national courts direct cooperation as part of which the latter are closely involved in the correct application and uniform interpretation of European Union law and also in the protection of individual rights conferred by that legal order.

85. It follows from all of the foregoing that the tasks attributed to the national courts and to the Court of Justice respectively are indispensable to the preservation of the very nature of the law established by the Treaties.

86. In that regard, the Court has stated that the principle that a Member State is obliged to make good damage caused to individuals as a result of breaches of European Union law for which it is responsible applies to any case in which a Member State infringes European Union law, whichever is the authority of the Member State whose act or omission was responsible for the breach, and that principle also applies, under specific conditions, to judicial bodies . . .

87. It must be added that, where European Union law is infringed by a national court, the provisions of Articles 258 TFEU to 260 TFEU provide for the opportunity of bringing a case before the Court to obtain a declaration that the Member State concerned has failed to fulfil its obligations . . .

88. It is clear that if a decision of the PC were to be in breach of European Union law, that decision could not be the subject of infringement proceedings nor could it give rise to any financial liability on the part of one or more Member States.

89. Consequently, the envisaged agreement, by conferring on an international court which is outside the institutional and judicial framework of the European Union an exclusive jurisdiction to hear a significant number of actions brought by individuals in the field of the Community patent and to interpret and apply European Union law in that field, would deprive courts of Member States of their powers in relation to the interpretation and application of European Union law and the Court of its powers to reply, by preliminary ruling, to questions referred by those courts and,

consequently, would alter the essential character of the powers which the Treaties confer on the institutions of the European Union and on the Member States and which are indispensable to the preservation of the very nature of European Union law.

## NOTES AND QUESTIONS

1.    This Opinion provides a rather useful summary of the constitutional position of the Courts of the Member States in the Union's legal order. In what way was that position threatened by the Patent Court envisaged by the Treaty? What specific aspects of the proposed court were of particular concern?

2.    Does the Opinion suggest that a specialist Patent Court for a European Patent system is not possible under any circumstances? How might the court's objections be overcome?

# Part IV

# EUROPEAN UNION COMPETENCES

# Chapter 10

## UNION COMPETENCES — GENERAL THEMES

### § 10.01  OVERVIEW

*Template*: Article 6, Section 6.1

*Materials in this Chapter*: This chapter provides some general observations on the subject of Union Competences and includes materials illustrating the principles set out in Template section 6.

*Union Competences after Lisbon*  As already noted in Chapter 2, the Treaty of Lisbon introduced new language in revised articles 2-6 of the TFEU that create three categories of competence: Exclusive competence, shared powers, and supporting action. This language does not really change the status quo but rather attempts to restate it in clear constitutional terms. Thus, article 3 lays out precisely those areas where the EU has exclusive competence:

- Customs Union

- EU level competition policy

- Monetary policy for Member States using the euro

- Conservation of marine biological resources

- Common commercial policy

Such exclusivity also applies when concluding treaties that affect internal legislation. It should be emphasized that as a factual matter none of this is radically new. For example, as will be evident from the *Rogers* case in Chapter 11, the concept of exclusivity in the area of conservation of marine resources already has a history dating back to 1979, while Chapter 12 will illustrate that treaty-making powers affecting internal EU regulation were first held to be exclusive (within certain limits) as far back as the early 1970s.

*Division between the TEU and the TFEU*  There remains a division of powers based on the content of the TEU and the TFEU (and EAEC) Treaties respectively. It is evident that the provisions of the CFSP in the TEU at the basic level identify this as an area where the EU is, in a realistic sense, a medium for intergovernmental cooperation. Once policy direction has been set, however, implementing steps may draw in the institutions of the EU acting under powers granted by either the TEU or the TFEU. An example of this in the area of CFSP is the body of regulations relating to freezing of assets that were the subject matter of the *Kadi/Al Barakaat* case appearing in Chapter 3. What initially started out as something requiring the kind of intergovernmental cooperation envisaged by the

CFSP led to regulations issued under the powers granted in the then EC Treaty, with the consequence that that particular subject matter has now transferred into the latter's integrationalist structure.

***Types of power conferred on the EU.*** Although the TFEU does not grant generalized commerce powers, unlike the U.S. Constitution, such powers exist through more specific grants. Three types may be identified.

First, there are provisions that actually set out the policy choices inherent in such powers *in the Treaty itself.* See, for example, articles EC 25/TFEU 30 through EC 27/TFEU 32 mandating the creation of a Common Customs Tariff, and articles EC 81/TFEU 101 through EC 86/TFEU 106 on competition policy.

Second, some provisions grant framework powers to the EU. The first type is to be found in articles that reference "common" policy. Articles EC 32/TFEU 38 through EC 37/TFEU 43 set out the requirements for a "common" agricultural policy and "common" provisions are to be found relating to transport, (EC 70/TFEU 90 — EC 80/100) and external commercial policy (articles EC 131/TFEU 206 — EC 134/TFEU 207). These are areas where it was expected that the EU would become the legislator in lieu of the Member States, though this has not always worked out, as the materials in Chapter 11 will show.

Third, and perhaps most significantly over the longer term, there are various provisions conferring powers to harmonize national laws relating to the establishment and functioning of the internal market. These may be found in their most general form in articles EC 94/TFEU 115 and EC 95/TFEU 114, but specific areas are also dealt with in other places, such as articles EC 47/TFEU 53 and EC 52/TFEU 59. It is this type of action that most resembles the more general scope of the U.S. Commerce Clause.

Initially, one might be surprised to learn that harmonization provisions involve conferral of legislative competence at all. The grant of powers to harmonize suggests that the EU's role is not envisaged as extending beyond attempts to align national regulation. However, this would be to misunderstand completely the nature of EU action. The fact is that whenever the EU acts under these powers, it is at the very least circumscribing the powers of the Member States because such action has *binding and superior legal effects* (as illustrated in Chapters 3 and 5, *supra*). Thus, to a greater or lesser degree such action reduces the scope of discretionary action on the part of the Member States. The harmonization provisions might therefore be seen as a form of gradual transfer of powers, all the time replacing State discretion with EU action.

***Subsidiarity and proportionality*** As EU action has gathered pace, there has been a correspondingly strong counteraction by the Member States who have become concerned that they are losing power in areas where they expected to remain sovereign. This has led to the inclusion of provisions in the Treaties proclaiming that the EU must be bound by the twin principles of subsidiarity and proportionality. These themes are developed further in this chapter.

***Parallels and contrasts with the U.S.*** The exercise of powers in the EU, mentioned above, suggests similarities to the doctrine of preemption in the U.S. For any given area of action, the question can be asked as to whether the Constitution or federal legislation intend that federal powers should be exclusive, and that therefore there is no scope for the exercise of that power at the State level. Or is there continuing power to act for as long as the Federal authority has not done so? And when it does, does the mere act of doing so, even if not complete, entirely preempt state action? Or can one take a more pragmatic view based on intention?

The U.S. Supreme Court has over time defined the following tests for this exercise:

- Was there an expressed intent to pre-empt?

- Did Congress intend to "occupy a field" in a given area because the "federal regime" is so pervasive?

- Is compliance with both federal and state regulations impossible?

- Does a state law interfere with the proper and complete execution of the federal purpose?

Similar questions can be asked when considering the effects of the exercise of harmonization powers in the EU. Whether termed "preemption" or something else, the result of such exercise is that the Member States may no longer legislate so as to compromise the full effect of the EU legislation. The conferral of exclusive powers in a given area might be considered the most extreme form of preemption, since essentially the power to legislate is removed from the Member States altogether, even if a corresponding exercise of EU power has not yet occurred. Again, this point is illustrated by the *Rogers* case set out in Chapter 11.

For discussion of the relationship of the primacy of EU law and the notion of preemption, see Robert Schütze, '*Supremacy without pre-emption? The very slowly emergent doctrine of Community pre-emption*' (2006) 43 CML REV. 1023.

Even in the case of exclusive powers, however, the Treaty may permit continued action at the State level. This is exemplified by the approach taken to competition law (EC 81 and 82/TFEU 101 and 102). Here, the Member States can still legislate and conduct *national* competition policy but are subject to jurisdictional constraints on the application of that policy. (The same situation pertains in the United States with regard to antitrust law.) The result is that the Member States cannot take decisions that would exceed those constraints. It follows that the scope of application of State competition legislation itself must be read subject to such constraints, even if not explicit, but the legitimacy of such laws is otherwise unaffected.

A second parallel may be found in the issues that arise over the jurisdictional basis for the exercise of federal/EU powers. When Congress enacts legislation founded on the Commerce Clause, it is frequently necessary to determine whether that legislation actually deals with interstate and foreign commerce, in other words, the scope of the power. Judges' views on this have reflected the ebb and flow of federal power from a political standpoint. In the more recent past it seemed that the effect on such commerce has needed to be only relatively minimal to justify federal action. On the other hand, it is noteworthy that the U.S. Supreme Court has set constitutional limits on federal legislative jurisdiction. See, e.g., *New York v. United States*, 521 U.S. 898 (1997) (declaring it unconstitutional for the federal government to "commandeer" state legislative or administrative powers); *United States v. Lopez*, 514 U.S. 549 (1995) (Federal Gun-Free Zones Act making it a federal offense to possess a firearm on school grounds or within 1000 feet of any school is unconstitutional because in excess of Congress's power to legislate under the Interstate Commerce Clause).

In the EU, the tension between federation and State manifests itself in the form of "subsidiarity" and "proportionality." These concepts are explored in § 10.02 of this Chapter.

A third point of similarity with the U.S. might appear to be the general grant of powers to enact legislation where the Treaties, and the U.S. Constitution respectively, do not grant express powers — so-called necessary and proper powers. In the case of the TFEU, this grant is found in EC 308/TFEU 352. This concept also is explored in § 10.03 of this Chapter.

Other aspects of the division of powers in the EU/EC might be thought to present more of a contrast than a parallel, even if still finding some echoes, with the U.S. system.

Perhaps the greatest contrast can be found in the strength of the powers accorded to the "federal" authorities in the two systems. It was observed at the beginning of this chapter that in a national federal system such as the United States, matters such as foreign relations and defense can be expected to be assigned entirely to the federal authorities; while in many internal matters the constituent states might have considerable freedom of action. On the whole, it is true to say that the EU largely reflects the opposite situation. Despite the TEU provisions on CFSP, the general conduct of foreign affairs and defense, as an executive matter at least, and except as regards commercial matters, is still primarily in the hands of the Member States. Restrictions on barriers to the internal market, on the other hand, including such matters as controls on state subsidies, are prohibited in some respects to a much greater degree than is the case in the United States.

It should be acknowledged, however, that foreign policy and defense are increasingly being seen as requiring EU action and have been progressively elaborated as part of the Union structure. As the Member States have become more comfortable with the involvement of the Union they have been willing to start moving control into the EU institutional structure. An example would be policy relating to immigration from outside the EU.

The restricted nature of EU power entails a second contrast with the U.S. In the U.S., the power to conduct foreign policy is vested in the executive branch under the Constitution and has an existence independent of the division of internal powers. The individual states accepted that that authority resided with the President. As remarked above, such power moves to the EU through action of the European Council on a piecemeal basis.

A third contrast is the feature now called "enhanced cooperation". It entails the right of groups of Member States to pursue integration at a different speed than others, thus resulting in legislative activity that may only affect those states, involving the exclusion of other Member States from the process to a greater or lesser degree. This multi-speed integration process is now formally embedded in the TEU (Articles 43 – 45) and EC Treaty/TFEU provisions that entitle the participating Member States to make use of EU Institutions.

An example of how this procedure works can be seen in the decision to move forward with a unitary patent protection proposal:

(Official EU Website: http://europa.eu/scadplus/leg/en/lvb/l26056.htm)

### Proposal for a Council Decision authorising enhanced cooperation in the area of the creation of unitary patent protection Adoption of the Council Decision 2 March 2011 2010/0384 (NLE) 6524/11

3. On 4 December 2009, the Council adopted conclusions on an "Enhanced patent system for Europe" and a general approach on the proposal for a Regulation on the EU Patent (change from the "Community" to "EU" patent due to the entry into force of the Lisbon Treaty on 1 December 2009). However, the translation arrangements for the EU patent remained out of the scope of these Council conclusions due to the change of the legal basis for the creation of the EU patent under the Lisbon Treaty.

4. On 2 July 2010, the Commission submitted to the Council a proposal for a Council Regulation on the translation arrangements for the EU patent 5, in accordance with Article 118(2) of the Treaty on the Functioning of the European Union (TFEU).

5. Having witnessed all its efforts to reach a unanimous agreement on this proposal fail, the Belgian Presidency, supported by the majority of delegations, concluded at the end of the extraordinary Competitiveness Council on 10 November 2010 that insurmountable difficulties existed making a decision on the translation arrangements requiring unanimity impossible now and in the foreseeable future and that the objectives of the proposed Regulations to establish unitary patent protection in the entire European Union could not be attained within a reasonable period by applying the relevant provisions of the Treaties. This conclusion was confirmed at the Competitiveness Council meeting on 10 December 2010.

6. In the light of these developments, twelve Member States addressed formal requests to the Commission indicating that they wish to establish enhanced cooperation in the area of the creation of unitary patent protection and that the Commission should submit a proposal to the Council to that end.

7. On 16 December 2010, the Commission submitted to the Council a proposal for a Council Decision authorising enhanced cooperation in the area of the creation of unitary patent protection.

8. In the meantime, thirteen more Member States have decided to participate in the envisaged enhanced cooperation, thus bringing the total number of participating Member States to twenty-five.

9. On 7 February 2011, the Permanent Representatives Committee reached agreement on the draft Council Decision contained in 5538/11 and proposed

to the Council to transmit a request to the European Parliament for its consent.

10. On 14 February 2011, the Council decided to request the European Parliament's consent on the draft Council Decision contained in 5538/11, in accordance with Article 329(1) of TFEU.

11. On 15 February 2011, the European Parliament gave its consent to proceed with the enhanced cooperation as set out in the draft Decision contained in 5538/11.

12. At the meeting of the Permanent Representatives Committee on 23 February 2011, it was noted that all delegations except Italy and Spain are supportive of the draft Council Decision as contained in 5538/11 and of the statements set out in the addendum to this Note.

13. Recalling their joint statement at the Competitiveness Council on 10 December 20107, Italy and Spain consider that the proposed enhanced cooperation is unacceptable on both procedural and substantive grounds. These delegations question the fulfilment of the conditions imposed by the Treaties for the launching of enhanced cooperation in this case and they reserve the right to initiate legal actions against it. They affirm also that the impact of the envisaged enhanced cooperation on the efforts to set up a single patent jurisdiction has not been sufficiently assessed in the absence of the opinion of the European Court of Justice on the draft Treaty for the creation of a single patent litigation system.

14. Both the Commission and the Council Legal Service pointed out that there is no legal impediment to go ahead with the enhanced cooperation, given that this does not cover the new patent jurisdiction envisaged in the draft international agreement referred to the Court of Justice for opinion. [For which see Chapter 9 *supra*.]

15. The Council Legal Service has pointed out that a Member State referred to in the Council's decision authorising the enhanced cooperation as one of the Member States participating in the enhanced cooperation in question would be entitled to withdraw as long as no substantive act related to the enhanced cooperation has been adopted.

One could perhaps draw a parallel here with the actions of groups of states in the U.S. that have come together to enact parallel legislation on global warming and air quality. However, unlike the situation in the EU, such initiatives do not call the underlying constitutional basis of the federal system into question, because they are not sponsored through tinkering with the basic constitutional documents.

Finally, it is a unique feature of the EU system that there exist, within the Member States themselves, varying degrees of federalist structures. This has led on occasion to friction between states and federation powers regarding the onward conferral of powers by the federal government to the EU. This has been a feature of Germany's relationship with the Union and the EU for a long time, given Germany's pronounced federal structure. However, as other distinct components of the Member States, such as Scotland in the UK, or the Belgian regions, gain more autonomy, one can expect to see increasing tensions between them and the continuing desire of the governments of the States to maintain control of relationships with the EU and other Member States.

# § 10.02   SUBSIDIARITY AND PROPORTIONALITY

## [A]   Texts

### THE "LAEKEN DECLARATION" OF DEC 14/15 2001

[This is the declaration that led to the convening of the "Constitutional Convention" (Bull. EU 2001-12 Annex I)]

Citizens often hold expectations of the European Union that are not always fulfilled. And vice versa — they sometimes have the impression that the Union takes on too much in areas where its involvement is not always essential. Thus the important thing is to clarify, simplify and adjust the division of competence between the Union and the Member States in the light of the new challenges facing the Union. This can lead both to restoring tasks to the Member States and to assigning new missions to the Union, or to the extension of existing powers, while constantly bearing in mind the equality of the Member States and their mutual solidarity.

A first series of questions that needs to be put concerns how the division of competence can be made more transparent. Can we thus make a clearer distinction between three types of competence: the exclusive competence of the Union, the competence of the Member States and the shared competence of the Union and the Member States? At what level is competence exercised in the most efficient way? How is the principle of subsidiarity to be applied here? And should we not make it clear that any powers not assigned by the Treaties to the Union fall within the exclusive sphere of competence of the Member States? And what would be the consequences of this?

The next series of questions should aim, within this new framework and while respecting the 'acquis communautaire', to determine whether there needs to be any reorganisation of competence. How can citizens' expectations be taken as a guide here? What missions would this produce for the Union? And, vice versa, what tasks could better be left to the Member States? What amendments should be made to the Treaty on the various policies? How, for example, should a more coherent common foreign policy and defence policy be developed? Should the Petersberg tasks be updated? Do we want to adopt a more integrated approach to police and criminal law cooperation? How can economic policy coordination be stepped up? How can we intensify cooperation in the field of social inclusion, the environment, health and food safety? But then, should not the day-to-day administration and implementation of the Union's policy be left more emphatically to the Member States and, where their constitutions so provide, to the regions? Should they not be provided with guarantees that their spheres of competence will not be affected?

Lastly, there is the question of how to ensure that a redefined division of competence does not lead to a creeping expansion of the competence of the Union or to encroachment upon the exclusive areas of competence of the Member States and, where there is provision for this, regions. How are we to ensure at the same time that the European dynamic does not come to a halt? In the future as well, the Union must continue to be able to react to fresh challenges and developments, and must be able to explore new policy areas. . . .

# PROTOCOL ON THE APPLICATION OF THE PRINCIPLES OF SUBSIDIARITY AND PROPORTIONALITY
## [2007] OJ C 306/150

[Protocol annexed to the Treaty on European Union, to the Treaty on the Functioning of the European Union and, where applicable, to the Treaty establishing the European Atomic Energy Community.]

### Article 1

Each institution shall ensure constant respect for the principles of subsidiarity and proportionality, as laid down in Article 5 of the Treaty on European Union.

### Article 2

Before proposing legislative acts, the Commission shall consult widely. Such consultations shall, where appropriate, take into account the regional and local dimension of the action envisaged. In cases of exceptional urgency, the Commission shall not conduct such consultations. It shall give reasons for its decision in its proposal.

### Article 3

For the purposes of this Protocol, "draft legislative acts" shall mean proposals from the Commission, initiatives from a group of Member States, initiatives from the European Parliament, requests from the Court of Justice, recommendations from the European Central Bank and requests from the European Investment Bank for the adoption of a legislative act.

### Article 4

The Commission shall forward its draft legislative acts and its amended drafts to national Parliaments at the same time as to the Union legislator.

The European Parliament shall forward its draft legislative acts and its amended drafts to national Parliaments.

The Council shall forward draft legislative acts originating from a group of Member States, the Court of Justice, the European Central Bank or the European Investment Bank and amended drafts to national Parliaments.

Upon adoption, legislative resolutions of the European Parliament and positions of the Council shall be forwarded by them to national Parliaments.

## Article 5

Draft legislative acts shall be justified with regard to the principles of subsidiarity and proportionality. Any draft legislative act should contain a detailed statement making it possible to appraise compliance with the principles of subsidiarity and proportionality. This statement should contain some assessment of the proposal's financial impact and, in the case of a directive, of its implications for the rules to be put in place by Member States, including, where necessary, the regional legislation. The reasons for concluding that a Union objective can be better achieved at Union level shall be substantiated by qualitative and, wherever possible, quantitative indicators. Draft legislative acts shall take account of the need for any burden, whether financial or administrative, falling upon the Union, national governments, regional or local authorities, economic operators and citizens, to be minimised and commensurate with the objective to be achieved.

## Article 6

Any national Parliament or any chamber of a national Parliament may, within eight weeks from the date of transmission of a draft legislative act, in the official languages of the Union, send to the Presidents of the European Parliament, the Council and the Commission a reasoned opinion stating why it considers that the draft in question does not comply with the principle of subsidiarity. It will be for each national Parliament or each chamber of a national Parliament to consult, where appropriate, regional parliaments with legislative powers.

If the draft legislative act originates from a group of Member States, the President of the Council shall forward the opinion to the governments of those Member States.

If the draft legislative act originates from the Court of Justice, the European Central Bank or the European Investment Bank, the President of the Council shall forward the opinion to the institution or body concerned.

## Article 7

1. The European Parliament, the Council and the Commission, and, where appropriate, the group of Member States, the Court of Justice, the European Central Bank or the European Investment Bank, if the draft legislative act originates from them, shall take account of the reasoned opinions issued by national Parliaments or by a chamber of a national Parliament.

Each national Parliament shall have two votes, shared out on the basis of the national Parliamentary system. In the case of a bicameral Parliamentary system, each of the two chambers shall have one vote.

2. Where reasoned opinions on a draft legislative act's non-compliance with the principle of subsidiarity represent at least one third of all the votes allocated to the national Parliaments in accordance with the second subparagraph of paragraph 1,

the draft must be reviewed. This threshold shall be a quarter in the case of a draft legislative act submitted on the basis of Article 76 of the Treaty on the Functioning of the European Union on the area of freedom, security and justice.

After such review, the Commission or, where appropriate, the group of Member States, the European Parliament, the Court of Justice, the European Central Bank or the European Investment Bank, if the draft legislative act originates from them, may decide to maintain, amend or withdraw the draft. Reasons must be given for this decision.

3. Furthermore, under the ordinary legislative procedure, where reasoned opinions on the non-compliance of a proposal for a legislative act with the principle of subsidiarity represent at least a simple majority of the votes allocated to the national Parliaments in accordance with the second subparagraph of paragraph 1, the proposal must be reviewed. After such review, the Commission may decide to maintain, amend or withdraw the proposal.

If it chooses to maintain the proposal, the Commission will have, in a reasoned opinion, to justify why it considers that the proposal complies with the principle of subsidiarity. This reasoned opinion, as well as the reasoned opinions of the national Parliaments, will have to be submitted to the Union legislator, for consideration in the procedure:

(a)   before concluding the first reading, the legislator (the European Parliament and the Council) shall consider whether the legislative proposal is compatible with the principle of subsidiarity, taking particular account of the reasons expressed and shared by the majority of national Parliaments as well as the reasoned opinion of the Commission;

(b)   if, by a majority of 55% of the members of the Council or a majority of the votes cast in the European Parliament, the legislator is of the opinion that the proposal is not compatible with the principle of subsidiarity, the legislative proposal shall not be given further consideration.

*Article 8*

The Court of Justice of the European Union shall have jurisdiction in actions on grounds of infringement of the principle of subsidiarity by a legislative act, brought in accordance with the rules laid down in Article 263 of the Treaty on the Functioning of the European Union by Member States, or notified by them in accordance with their legal order on behalf of their national Parliament or a chamber thereof.

In accordance with the rules laid down in the said Article, the Committee of the Regions may also bring such actions against legislative acts for the adoption of which the Treaty on the Functioning of the European Union provides that it be consulted.

*Article 9*

The Commission shall submit each year to the European Council, the European Parliament, the Council and national Parliaments a report on the application of Article 5 of the Treaty on European Union. This annual report shall also be forwarded to the Economic and Social Committee and the Committee of the Regions.

## NOTES AND QUESTIONS

1.　According to the principle of subsidiarity, the Union should confine itself to taking action where it is required at the Union level, while leaving the Member States free to deal with the local impact. The concept should in no way be assumed to be the equivalent of "states rights", which is a jurisdictional approach to the division of powers. On the contrary, subsidiarity implies that where the EU does have jurisdiction, it should refrain from going beyond what is necessary at that level.

2.　Despite the wording of paragraph (13) of the Amsterdam Protocol, do you consider that the concept of subsidiarity is ultimately justiciable or is it really a political statement?

3.　Should subsidiarity color a national court's approach when considering compliance of national legislation with EU law?

4.　Does the new power of control of national Parliaments of the respect of the principle of subsidiarity and proportionality seem efficient to you? Does this endorse the political nature of the concept of subsidiarity? As to the role of national parliaments in the process, see, e.g., P. Kiiver, *The Early Warning System for the Principle of Subsidiarity: the National Parliament as Conseil d'Etat for Europe*, (2011) EL REV. 98

5.　For an appraisal of subsidiarity, see, e.g., A. ESTELLA, THE EU PRINCIPLE OF SUBSIDIARITY AND ITS CRITIQUE (Oxford University Press, 2002).

## [B]　Judicial Consideration of Subsidiarity

## THE QUEEN v. SECRETARY OF STATE FOR HEALTH, EX PARTE BRITISH AMERICAN TOBACCO (INVESTMENTS) LTD AND IMPERIAL TOBACCO LTD
### Case C-491/01, 2002 ECJ CELEX LEXIS 628, [2002] ECR I-11453

[The plaintiffs had sought permission in the English High Court to apply for judicial review of "the intention and/or obligation" of the United Kingdom Government to transpose into national law Directive 2001/37 on the approximation of the laws, regulations and administrative provisions of the Member States concerning the manufacture, presentation and sale of tobacco products (OJ 2001 L 194, p. 26). Previously, the Council had adopted certain other directives on tobacco. Council Directive 89/622/EEC dealt with the labelling of tobacco products and the prohibition of the marketing of certain types of tobacco for oral use (OJ 1989 L 359, p. 1).

This directive had been adopted on the basis of EC 95/TFEU 114. It established *inter alia* a general warning to be carried on the unit packaging of all tobacco products, together with additional warnings exclusively for cigarettes and, from 1992, extended the requirement for additional warnings to other tobacco products Directive 90/239/EEC set the maximum limits for the tar yield of cigarettes marketed in theMember States at 15 milligrams per cigarette with effect from 31 December 1992 and at 12 milligrams per cigarette from 31 December 1997. The directive at issue in this case was adopted on the basis of EC95 EC/TFEU 114 and EC 133/TFEU 207 and was aimed at recasting Directives 89/622 and 90/239 by amending and adding to their provisions. Both prior directives were repealed in the process.]

6. According to the second and third recitals in the preamble to the Directive, there are still substantial differences between the Member States' laws, regulations and administrative provisions on the manufacture, presentation, and sale of tobacco products which impede the functioning of the internal market, and those barriers ought to be eliminated by approximating the rules applicable in that area.

7. In the words of the fourth recital in the preamble to the Directive:

"In accordance with Article 95 [114] (3) of the Treaty, a high level of protection in terms of health, safety, environmental protection and consumer protection should be taken as a basis, regard being had, in particular, to any new developments based on scientific facts; in view of the particularly harmful effects of tobacco, health protection should be given priority in this context."

\* \* \*

74. The claimants in the main proceedings maintain that the principle of subsidiarity is applicable to measures relating to the internal market such as the Directive and that, when the latter was adopted, the Community legislature left that principle wholly out of account or, in any event, failed to take it properly into account. If it had done so, it would have had to reach the conclusion that there was no need to adopt the Directive, since harmonised rules had already been established by Directives 89/622 and 90/239 for the purpose of eliminating barriers to trade in tobacco products. Furthermore, they argue that no evidence has been adduced to show that the Member States could not adopt the measures of public health protection they considered necessary.

175. The Belgian Government and the Parliament maintain that the principle of subsidiarity does not apply to the Directive, inasmuch as that principle is applicable only in those areas in which the Community does not have exclusive competence, whereas the Directive, being adopted for the purpose of attaining the internal market, comes within one of those areas of exclusive competence. In any event, even if it were accepted that that principle applied to the Directive, it was complied with in the circumstances, since the action undertaken could not have been satisfactorily achieved at Member State level.

176. The United Kingdom, French, Netherlands and Swedish Governments, and the Council and Commission, submit that the principle of subsidiarity is applicable in the present case and was complied with by the Directive. The United Kingdom and French Governments and the Commission observe in particular that the consider-

ations set out in paragraphs 30 to 34 of Netherlands v. Parliament and Council, cited above, may be applied to the circumstances of this case and prompt the conclusion that the Directive is valid with regard to the principle of subsidiarity. According to the Netherlands Government and the Commission, where the conditions for the use of Article 95 [114] EC have been satisfied, the conditions for Community action under the second paragraph of Article 5 EC [5] are also satisfied, since it is clear that no Member State acting alone can take the necessary measures to prevent any divergence between the laws of the Member States having an impact on trade.

Findings of the Court

177. The principle of subsidiarity is set out in the second paragraph of Article 5 EC [5], according to which, in areas which do not fall within its exclusive competence, the Community is to take action only if and in so far as the objectives of the proposed action cannot be sufficiently achieved by the Member States and can therefore, by reason of the scale or effects of the proposed action, be better achieved at Community level.

178. Article 3 of the protocol on the application of the principles of subsidiarity and proportionality, annexed to the Treaty establishing the European Community, states that the principle of subsidiarity does not call into question the powers conferred on the Community by the Treaty as interpreted by the Court.

179. It is to be noted, as a preliminary, that the principle of subsidiarity applies where the Community legislature makes use of Article 95 [114] EC, inasmuch as that provision does not give it exclusive competence to regulate economic activity on the internal market, but only a certain competence for the purpose of improving the conditions for its establishment and functioning, by eliminating barriers to the free movement of goods and the freedom to provide services or by removing distortions of competition (see, to that effect, the tobacco advertising judgment, paragraphs 83 and 95).

180. As regards the question whether the Directive was adopted in keeping with the principle of subsidiarity, it must first be considered whether the objective of the proposed action could be better achieved at Community level.

181.[T]he Directive's objective is to eliminate the barriers raised by the differences which still exist between the Member States' laws, regulations and administrative provisions on the manufacture, presentation and sale of tobacco products, while ensuring a high level of health protection, in accordance with Article 95(3) EC [114].

182. Such an objective cannot be sufficiently achieved by the Member States individually and calls for action at Community level, as demonstrated by the multifarious development of national laws in this case.

183. It follows that, in the case of the Directive, the objective of the proposed action could be better achieved at Community level.

184. Second, the intensity of the action undertaken by the Community in this instance was also in keeping with the requirements of the principle of subsidiarity in that, as paragraphs 122 to 141 above make clear, it did not go beyond what was necessary to achieve the objective pursued.

185. It follows from the foregoing conclusions concerning Question 1(f) that the Directive is not invalid by reason of infringement of the principle of subsidiarity.

## NOTES AND QUESTIONS

**1.** What do you think of the Belgian Government's and Parliament's argument that the principle of subsidiarity may differ or not even be applicable depending on the area of law involved and the degree to which powers have been transferred to the EU?

**2.** In the United States, federal jurisdiction depends heavily on the presence of interstate commerce, and maintaining the proper balance of power between the states and the federal government is of the utmost importance. For a comparative discussion of EU subsidiarity and U.S. federalism, see George Bermann, *Taking Subsidiarity Seriously: Federalism in the European Community and the United States*, 94 Colum. L. Rev. 331 (1994)

## [C]   Judicial Consideration of Proportionality

### UNITED KINGDOM v. COUNCIL
#### (WORKING TIME DIRECTIVE)
#### Case C-84/94, 1996 ECJ CELEX LEXIS 194, [1996] ECR I-5755

[This text is from the same case that appears in Chapter 8, in that context addressing the scope of review that the ECJ is willing to undertake. Here the substance of the UK's position regarding compliance with the proportionality principles is discussed.]

2 The directive was adopted on the basis of Article 118a [154] of the Treaty, which provides as follows:

> 1. Member States shall pay particular attention to encouraging improvements, especially in the working environment, as regards the health and safety of workers, and shall set as their objective the harmonization of conditions in this area, while maintaining the improvements made.

> 2. In order to help achieve the objective laid down in the first paragraph, the Council, acting in accordance with the procedure referred to in Article 189c [repealed] and after consulting the Economic and Social Committee, shall adopt by means of directives minimum requirements for gradual implementation, having regard to the conditions and technical rules obtaining in each of the Member States.

> Such directives shall avoid imposing administrative, financial and legal constraints in a way which would hold back the creation and development of small and medium-sized undertakings.

> 3. The provisions adopted pursuant to this article shall not prevent any Member State from maintaining or introducing more stringent measures for the protection of working conditions compatible with this Treaty.

3 The directive, in accordance with Article 1 thereof, lays down minimum health and safety requirements for the organization of working time, and applies to all sectors of activity, both public and private, within the meaning of Article 2 of Council Directive 89/391/EEC of 12 June 1989 on the introduction of measures to encourage improvements in the safety and health of workers at work (OJ 1989 L 183, p. 1), with the exception of air, rail, road, sea, inland waterway and lake transport, sea fishing, other work at sea and the activities of doctors in training.

\*    \*    \*

51 First, [the UK] argues, not all measures which may "improve" the level of health and safety protection of workers constitute minimum requirements. In particular, those consisting in global reductions in working time or global increases in rest periods, whilst having a certain beneficial effect on the health or safety of workers, do not constitute "minimum requirements" within the meaning of Article 118a [154].

52 Second, a provision cannot be regarded as a "minimum requirement" if the level of health and safety protection of workers which it establishes can be attained by measures that are less restrictive and involve fewer obstacles to the competitiveness of industry and the earning capacity of individuals. In the applicant's submission, neither the Commission's proposals nor the directive provide any explanation as to why the desired level of protection could not have been achieved by less restrictive measures, such as, for example, the use of risk assessments if working hours exceeded particular norms.

53 Third, the conclusion that the measures envisaged will in fact improve the level of health or safety protection of workers must be based on reasonable grounds. In its view, the present state of scientific research in the area concerned falls far short of justifying the contested measures.

54 Fourth, a measure will be proportionate only if it is consistent with the principle of subsidiarity. The applicant argues that it is for the Community institutions to demonstrate that the aims of the directive could better be achieved at Community level than by action on the part of the Member States. There has been no such demonstration in this case.

55 The argument of non-compliance with the principle of subsidiarity can be rejected at the outset. It is said that the Community legislature has not established that the aims of the directive would be better served at Community level than at national level. But that argument, as so formulated, really concerns the need for Community action, which has already been examined in paragraph 47 of this judgment.

56 Furthermore, as is clear from paragraph 17 of this judgment, the applicant bases its argument on a conception of "minimum requirements" which differs from that in Article 118a [154]. That provision does not limit Community action to the lowest common denominator, or even to the lowest level of protection established by the various Member States, but means that Member States are free to provide a level of protection more stringent than that resulting from Community law, high as it may be.

57 As regards the principle of proportionality, the Court has held that, in order to

establish whether a provision of Community law complies with that principle, it must be ascertained whether the means which it employs are suitable for the purpose of achieving the desired objective and whether they do not go beyond what is necessary to achieve it.

58 As to judicial review of those conditions, however, the Council must be allowed a wide discretion in an area which, as here, involves the legislature in making social policy choices and requires it to carry out complex assessments. Judicial review of the exercise of that discretion must therefore be limited to examining whether it has been vitiated by manifest error or misuse of powers, or whether the institution concerned has manifestly exceeded the limits of its discretion.

59 So far as concerns the first condition, it is sufficient that the measures on the organization of working time which form the subject-matter of the directive, save for that contained in the second sentence of Article 5, contribute directly to the improvement of health and safety protection for workers within the meaning of Article 118a [154], and cannot therefore be regarded as unsuited to the purpose of achieving the objective pursued.

60 The second condition is also fulfilled. Contrary to the view taken by the applicant, the Council did not commit any manifest error in concluding that the contested measures were necessary to achieve the objective of protecting the health and safety of workers.

61 In the first place, Article 4, which concerns the mandatory rest break, applies only if the working day is longer than six hours. Moreover, the relevant details, particularly the duration of the break and the terms on which it is granted, are to be laid down in collective agreements or agreements between the two sides of industry or, failing that, by national legislation. Finally, that provision may be the subject of several derogations, relating either to the status of the worker (Article 17(1)) or to the nature or characteristics of the activity pursued (Article 17(2), points 2.1 and 2.2), to be implemented by means of collective agreements or agreements concluded between the two sides of industry at national or regional level (Article 17(3)).

62 Second, the minimum uninterrupted weekly rest period of twenty-four hours provided for by the first sentence of Article 5, plus the eleven hours' daily rest referred to in Article 3, may be the subject of the same derogations as those authorized in relation to Article 4, referred to above. Further derogations relate to shift work activities and activities involving periods of work split up over the day (Article 17(2), point 2.3). In addition, the reference period of seven days may be extended to fourteen days (Article 16(1)).

63 Third, as regards Article 6(2), which provides that the average working time for each seven-day period is not to exceed forty-eight hours, Member States may lay down a reference period not exceeding four months (Article 16(2)), which may in certain cases be extended to six months for the application of Article 17(2), points 2.1 and 2.2, and 17(3) (Article 17(4), first sentence), or even to twelve months (Article 17(4), second sentence). Article 18(1)(b)(i) even authorizes Member States, under certain conditions, not to apply Article 6.

64 Fourth, in relation to Article 7 concerning paid annual leave of four weeks, Article

18(1)(b)(ii) authorizes Member States to allow a transitional period of three years, during which workers must be entitled to three weeks' paid annual leave.

65 Finally, as to the applicant's argument that adoption of the contested directive was unnecessary since Directive 89/391 already applies to the areas covered by the contested directive, it is sufficient to note that Directive 89/391, as stated in Article 1 thereof, merely lays down, in order to encourage improvements in the health and safety of workers at work, general principles, as well as general guidelines for their implementation, concerning the prevention of occupational risks, the protection of health and safety, the elimination of risk and accident factors, and the provision of information to, consultation, participation and training of workers and their representatives. It is not therefore apt to achieve the objective of harmonizing minimum rest periods, rest breaks and a maximum limit to weekly working time, which form the subject-matter of the contested directive.

66 It follows that, in taking the view that the objective of harmonizing national legislation on the health and safety of workers, while maintaining the improvements made, could not be achieved by measures less restrictive than those that are the subject-matter of the directive, the Council did not commit any manifest error.

67 In the light of all the foregoing considerations, the plea of breach of the principle of proportionality must also be rejected.

## NOTES AND QUESTIONS

1.   Does the above extract shed any further light on the distinction between the concepts of subsidiarity and proportionality?

2.   Does the Court give its own view as to whether the directive was proportional? Given the Court's reasoning here, do you think it is very likely that it will ever decide that legislation is void due to a breach of the proportionality principle?

## GERMANY v. PARLIAMENT AND COUNCIL
### (DEPOSIT GUARANTEE SCHEMES)
### Case C-233/94, 1997 ECJ CELEX LEXIS 55, [1997] ECR I-2405

[Germany sought annulment of Directive 94/19/EC on deposit-guarantee schemes ([1994] OJ L 135/5,) [a system designed to assure the safety of bank deposits, covered in the use by the FDIC] and, in the alternative, for annulment of the second subparagraph of Article 4(1), Article 4(2), and the second sentence of the first subparagraph of Article 3(1) of the Directive].

2 The Directive was adopted on the basis of the first and third sentences of Article 57 [53](2) of the EC Treaty, in accordance with the procedure referred to in Article 189b [294] of the Treaty. In the Council, the Federal Republic of Germany voted against its adoption.

5 Article 3 of the Directive provides as follows:

1. Each Member State shall ensure that within its territory one or more deposit-guarantee schemes are introduced and officially recognized. Except in the circumstances envisaged in the second subparagraph and in paragraph 4, no credit

institution authorized in that Member State pursuant to Article 3 of Directive 77/780/EEC may take deposits unless it is a member of such a scheme.

A Member State may, however, exempt a credit institution from the obligation to belong to a deposit-guarantee scheme where that credit institution belongs to a system which protects the credit institution itself and in particular ensures its liquidity and solvency, thus guaranteeing protection for depositors at least equivalent to that provided by a deposit-guarantee scheme, and which, in the opinion of the competent authorities, fulfils the following conditions:

- the system must be in existence and have been officially recognized when this Directive is adopted,

- the system must be designed to prevent deposits with credit institutions belonging to the system from becoming unavailable and have the resources necessary for that purpose at its disposal,

- the system must not consist of a guarantee granted to a credit institution by a Member State itself or by any of its local or regional authorities,

- the system must ensure that depositors are informed in accordance with the terms and conditions laid down in Article 9.

4. Where national law permits, and with the express consent of the competent authorities which issued its authorization, a credit institution excluded from a deposit-guarantee scheme may continue to take deposits if, before its exclusion, it has made alternative guarantee arrangements which ensure that depositors will enjoy a level and scope of protection at least equivalent to that offered by the officially recognized scheme.'

6 Article 4 provides that:

1. Deposit-guarantee schemes introduced and officially recognized in a Member State in accordance with Article 3(1) shall cover the depositors at branches set up by credit institutions in other Member States.

Until 31 December 1999 neither the level nor the scope, including the percentage, of cover provided shall exceed the maximum level or scope of cover offered by the corresponding guarantee scheme within the territory of the host Member State.

2. Where the level and/or scope, including the percentage, of cover offered by the host Member State guarantee scheme exceeds the level and/or scope of cover provided in the Member State in which a credit institution is authorized, the host Member State shall ensure that there is an officially recognized deposit-guarantee scheme within its territory which a branch may join voluntarily in order to supplement the guarantee which its depositors already enjoy by virtue of its membership of its home Member State scheme.

The scheme to be joined by the branch shall cover the category of institution to which it belongs or most closely corresponds in the host Member State.

3. Member States shall ensure that objective and generally applied conditions are established for branches' membership of a host Member State's scheme in accordance with paragraph 2. Admission shall be conditional on fulfilment of the

relevant obligations of membership, including in particular payment of any contributions and other charges. Member States shall follow the guiding principles set out in Annex II in implementing this paragraph.

4. If a branch granted voluntary membership under paragraph 2 does not comply with the obligations incumbent on it as a member of a deposit-guarantee scheme, the competent authorities which issued the authorization shall be notified and, in collaboration with the guarantee scheme, shall take all appropriate measures to ensure that the aforementioned obligations are complied with.

If those measures fail to secure the branch's compliance with the aforementioned obligations, after an appropriate period of notice of not less than 12 months the guarantee scheme may, with the consent of the competent authorities which issued the authorization, exclude the branch. Deposits made after the date of exclusion shall continue to be covered by the voluntary scheme until the dates on which they fall due. Depositors shall be informed of the withdrawal of the supplementary cover.

5. The Commission shall report on the operation of paragraphs 2, 3 and 4 no later than 31 December 1999 and shall, if appropriate, propose amendments thereto.'

7 Article 7 then provides as follows:

1. Deposit-guarantee schemes shall stipulate that the aggregate deposits of each depositor must be covered up to ECU 20 000 in the event of deposits' being unavailable.

Until 31 December 1999 Member States in which, when this Directive is adopted, deposits are not covered up to ECU 20 000 may retain the maximum amount laid down in their guarantee schemes, provided that this amount is not less than ECU 15 000.

2. Member States may provide that certain depositors or deposits shall be excluded from guarantee or shall be granted a lower level of guarantee. Those exclusions are listed in Annex I.

3. This Article shall not preclude the retention or adoption of provisions which offer a higher or more comprehensive cover for deposits. In particular, deposit-guarantee schemes may, on social considerations, cover certain kinds of deposits in full.

. . .

8 Articles 8 to 10 lay down the conditions for the implementation of the deposit-guarantee scheme.

\* \* \*

50 The German Government claims that, even in the case of harmonization measures, the Community legislature must remain within the discretion available to it, which is limited, in particular, by the principle of proportionality. That principle has not been complied with in the present case.

51 The German Government states that the export prohibition laid down in the second subparagraph of Article 4(1) of the Directive is, in principle, incompatible with Article 52 of the Treaty since it restricts the right of establishment. Branches are deprived of an element of competition as against the national banks of the host

Member State to such an extent that, in certain cases, financial institutions may even be forced for that reason to refrain from establishing a network of branches in another Member State.

52 According to the German Government, the export prohibition is not necessary in order to achieve the objective of the Directive, namely to prevent the market disturbances which arise if customers withdraw their deposits from their national credit institutions in order to transfer them to the branches of approved credit institutions in other Member States, since there are alternatives to that prohibition which would result in a less severe disturbance to the business of credit institutions. It would thus, for example, have been possible to insert a protective provision for the benefit of credit institutions in the Member States where the protection of depositors is less extensive authorizing intervention only where a disturbance in a Member State is imminent.

54 In response to those arguments it must be recalled that the Court has held that, in order to establish whether a provision of Community law complies with the principle of proportionality, it must be ascertained whether the means which it employs are suitable for the purpose of achieving the desired objective and whether they do not go beyond what is necessary to achieve it.

55 In assessing the need for the measure in question, it should be emphasized that the Community legislature was seeking to regulate an economically complex situation. Before the adoption of the Directive, deposit-guarantee schemes did not exist in all the Member States; moreover, most of them did not cover depositors with branches set up by credit institutions authorized in other Member States. The Community legislature therefore needed to assess the future, uncertain effects of its action. In so doing, it could choose between the general prevention of a risk and the establishment of a system of specific protection.

56 In such a situation the Court cannot substitute its own assessment for that of the Community legislature. It could, at most, find fault with its legislative choice only if it appeared manifestly incorrect or if the resultant disadvantages for certain economic operators were wholly disproportionate to the advantages otherwise offered.

57 According to the 14th recital in the preamble to the Directive, the Parliament and the Council chose to avoid, from the very beginning, any market disturbance resulting from the offer by branches of some credit institutions of higher cover than that offered by credit institutions authorized by the host Member State. Since the possibility of such a disturbance could not be wholly ruled out, it follows that the Community legislature has shown to the requisite legal standard that it was pursuing a legitimate objective. Moreover, the restriction constituted by the export prohibition on the activities of the credit institutions concerned is not manifestly disproportionate.

58 It follows that the plea of infringement of the principle of proportionality must also be rejected. 59 On those grounds, the application for annulment of the second subparagraph of Article 4(1) of the Directive must be rejected.

Article 4(2)

60 According to the German Government, the obligation under Article 4(2) of the Directive to include branches in the host Member State's guarantee scheme in order to supplement the guarantee provided in the home Member State is contrary to the principle of supervision by the home Member State and to the principle of proportionality.

\* \* \*

66 According to the German Government, Article 4(2) of the Directive is contrary to the principle of proportionality because the measure which it enacts is not indispensable to the attainment of the objective pursued.

67 The German Government claims that the deposit-guarantee schemes of the host Member State should assume responsibility for the difference between the lower cover provided in the home Member State and the higher cover granted in the host Member State, and even, in certain cases, for the entire guarantee.

68 The supplementary guarantee therefore contains considerable risks for the deposit-guarantee schemes of the host Member State, since they are required to compensate depositors even though the host State is no longer in a position adequately to supervise the liquid assets and solvency of the branch and, therefore, to foresee or prevent the possible insolvency of a branch of a foreign institution. Those risks are in no way removed by the fact that, in accordance with the guiding principles set out in Annex II to the Directive, each guarantee scheme can require the provision of all relevant information and has the right to verify such information with the home Member State's competent authorities. No provision requires the supervisory authorities of the home Member State to provide the necessary information.

70 The Court notes that, according to the 13th recital, Article 4(2) of the Directive seeks to remedy the disadvantages resulting from disparities in compensation and different conditions of competition, within the same territory, between national institutions and branches of institutions from other Member States. Moreover, in the 16th recital, the Community legislature states that the cost of funding guarantee schemes should be taken into account and that it would appear reasonable to set the harmonized minimum guarantee level at ECU 20 000. Article 7 of the Directive provides for the possibility of derogating from that minimum amount until 31 December 1999; until that date the security does not have to exceed ECU 15 000.

71 It is clear from those recitals and those provisions that the Community legislature did not wish to impose an excessive burden on home Member States which did not yet have deposit-guarantee schemes or which had only schemes providing for a lower guarantee. In those circumstances, it could not require them to bear the risk associated with an additional cover resulting from a political decision of a particular host Member State. The alternative solution proposed by the German Government, namely compulsory supplementary cover by the schemes of the home Member State, would not therefore have achieved the intended aim.

72 Moreover, . . . the obligation imposed on the host State is subject to various conditions that are intended to ease its task. Thus, under Article 4(3), the host Member State may require branches wishing to join one of its guarantee schemes

to pay a contribution and, by virtue of point (a) of Annex II to the Directive, require the home State to provide information on those branches. Furthermore, Article 4(4) of the Directive aims to ensure compliance with the obligations incumbent on such a branch as a member of the deposit-guarantee scheme. It follows from these various provisions that Article 4(2) does not have the effect of causing an excessive burden for the guarantee schemes of host Member States.

73 In view of all the foregoing considerations, the plea of infringement of the principle of proportionality must be rejected.

74 It follows that the application for annulment of Article 4(2) of the Directive must also be rejected.

The second sentence of the first subparagraph of Article 3(1)

75 The German Government claims that the membership obligation arising from the second sentence of the first subparagraph of Article 3(1) of the Directive is contrary to the third subparagraph of Article 3b of the Treaty and to the general principle of proportionality.

76 First of all, the German Government claims that the principle of proportionality laid down in the third subparagraph of Article 3b[TEU 5] of the Treaty was specifically set out, in particular, in the conclusions of the European Council in Edinburgh relating to that provision, which provide that, when adopting legislative measures, the Community will endeavour to take account of well-established national practices and that the measures adopted by the Community must offer to the Member States alternative solutions to achieve the objectives pursued.

77 However, according to the German Government, when drawing up the second sentence of the first subparagraph of Article 3(1) of the Directive, the Parliament and the Council did not take account of the scheme existing in Germany as a well-established national practice' within the meaning of the guidelines of the European Council. Since 1976 there has been a deposit-guarantee fund of the Association of German Banks, membership of which is voluntary and which has always functioned effectively.

78 Likewise, the obligation under the Directive to join a scheme does not leave any room for the Member States to adopt different approaches' in regard to the application of the Directive, such as a voluntary deposit-guarantee scheme. The German Government considers that, since voluntary membership constitutes an advantage for credit institutions at a competitive level, they would join a deposit-guarantee scheme without being compelled to do so by the State. Thus, in Germany in October 1993 only five institutions, whose deposits are slight overall, had remained outside such a scheme.

79 Finally, the membership obligation imposes an excessive burden on the credit institutions. As is proved by the German scheme, depositors can be protected by other less restrictive measures, such as the obligation on a bank to inform its clients of its membership of a deposit-guarantee scheme.

80 Without it being necessary to determine the precise legal value of the conclusions of the European Council in Edinburgh on which the German Government relies in this context, it should be pointed out, first of all, that when the Community

legislature harmonizes legislation all well-established national practices' cannot be respected.

81 Second, it appears that in the present case the Federal Republic of Germany is the sole Member State to invoke the voluntary membership of a deposit-guarantee scheme as such a practice.

82 Third, it is common ground that the Community legislature considered it to be necessary to ensure a harmonized minimum level of deposit-guarantee, wherever those deposits were located within the Community. Having regard to that requirement and to the fact that in some Member States there was no deposit- guarantee scheme, the legislature cannot be criticized for having provided for an obligation to join a scheme, despite the proper functioning of a voluntary membership scheme in Germany.

83 Finally, the German Government itself accepts that in October 1993 only five credit institutions out of 300 were not members of a deposit-guarantee scheme. The membership obligation therefore merely compels those few credit institutions to join and consequently cannot be considered to be excessive.

84 On those same grounds, the legislature cannot be criticized for not having provided for an alternative approach to compulsory membership, such as an obligation to inform customers of any membership of a scheme. That obligation would not have made it possible to achieve the objective of ensuring a harmonized minimum level of guarantee for all deposits.

85 Consequently, the application for annulment of the second sentence of the first subparagraph of Article 3(1) of the Directive must be rejected.

86 It follows from all the above considerations that the application must be dismissed.

## NOTES AND QUESTIONS

Does this case suggest that proportionality has more than one meaning?

## § 10.03    IMPLIED POWERS AND THE ROLE OF EC 308/TFEU 352

### SPAIN v. COUNCIL
### (PATENTS FOR MEDICINAL PRODUCTS).
### Case C-350/92, 1995 ECJ CELEX LEXIS 38, [1995] ECR I-1985

[The Spanish Government challenged the system set up by an EU regulation to grant certificates for medicinal products aimed at ensuring that a patentee of a such a product enjoys patent protection for a period long enough to recover the investment in research and development, given that there is often significant time lag between when an application for a patent is made and the eventual authorization to place the product on the market. There were two grounds of challenge, the first of which was that the [then] Community did not have the power to enact legislation with respect to patents.]

12 The Kingdom of Spain, supported by the Hellenic Republic, argues first that, in the allocation of powers between the Community and the Member States, the latter have not surrendered their sovereignty in industrial property matters, as is demonstrated by the combined provisions of Articles 36 [36] and 222 [345] of the Treaty.

13 Citing the case-law of the Court, Spain argues that the Community has no power to regulate substantive patent law, and may harmonize only those aspects relating to the exercise of industrial property rights which are capable of having an effect upon the achievement of the general objectives laid down in the Treaty. Such action may not take the form of a new industrial property right which, by its nature, content and effects, alters the basic concept in force under the national legal systems of each of the Member States. The duration of a patent is its most important feature, since it intrinsically affects the balance in time between the rights and obligations of its holder, whether legal or economic in character.

14 The Council, supported by the French Republic and the Commission, argues from the case-law that the purpose of Article 36 [36] of the Treaty is not to reserve certain matters for the exclusive competence of Member States. As for Article 222 [345] of the Treaty, its purpose is to allow general freedom to Member States in the organization of their property regimes, but it cannot completely prohibit Community intervention in the property rights of individuals, without paralysing the powers of the Community.

15 The case-law has not excluded the possibility of the Community determining by legislation the conditions and rules regarding the protection conferred by industrial property rights, should such action prove necessary in pursuing its objectives. In any event, the creation of the supplementary certificate does not in any way affect the substance of the rights of the holder of the basic patent. It is a mechanism for correcting the shortcomings of the system for protecting pharmaceutical research, which arise from the need to obtain marketing authorization in order to make use of the innovation.

16 In the light of those arguments, the Court must examine whether Articles 222 [345] and 36 [36] of the EEC Treaty reserve the power to regulate substantive patent law for the national legislature, thereby excluding any Community action in the matter.

17 In that respect, the Court held in its judgment in Commission v. United Kingdom that, as Community law stands, the provisions on patents have not yet been the subject of unification at Community level or in the context of approximation of laws, and that, in those circumstances, it is for the national legislature to determine the conditions and rules regarding the protection conferred by patents.

18 However, it added that the provisions of the Treaty, and in particular Article 222 [345], which provides that the Treaty does not in any way prejudice the rules in Member States governing the system of property ownership, cannot be interpreted as reserving to the national legislature, in relation to industrial and commercial property, the power to adopt measures which would adversely affect the principle

of free movement of goods within the common market as provided for and regulated by the Treaty.

19 Thus, far from endorsing the argument that rules concerning the very existence of industrial property rights fall within the sole jurisdiction of the national legislature, the Court was anticipating the unification of patent provisions or harmonization of the relevant national legislation.

20 The Court followed similar reasoning in relation to Article 36 [36] of the Treaty. That provides, in particular, that the provisions of Articles 30 to 34 shall not preclude prohibitions or restrictions justified on grounds of the protection of industrial and commercial property, but that such prohibitions or restrictions shall not constitute a means of arbitrary discrimination or a disguised restriction on trade between Member States.

21 In its judgment in Case 35/76 Simmenthal v. Italian Minister for Finance 1976 ECR 1871, paragraph 14, the Court held that Article 36 [36] is not designed to reserve certain matters to the exclusive jurisdiction of Member States but permits national laws to derogate from the principle of the free movement of goods to the extent to which such derogation is and continues to be justified for the attainment of the objectives referred to in that article.

22 It follows that neither Article 222 [345] nor Article 36 [36] of the Treaty reserves a power to regulate substantive patent law to the national legislature, to the exclusion of any Community action in the matter.

23 The Court has, moreover, confirmed in Opinion 1/94 (1994 ECR I-5267, paragraph 59) that, at the level of internal legislation, the Community is competent, in the field of intellectual property, to harmonize national laws pursuant to Articles 100 [115] and 100a [95114] and may use Article 235 [352] as the basis for creating new rights superimposed on national rights, as it did in Council Regulation (EC) No 40/94 of 20 December 1993 on the Community trade mark (OJ 1994 L 11, p. 1).

24 The first submission by the Kingdom of Spain must therefore be dismissed.

## NOTES AND QUESTIONS

1.   On what basis did the court conclude that the EU had the power to issue the contested regulation? Does the above case support the presence of implied powers within the TFEU as regards areas of internal legislation? (Note that implied powers do exist for external relations within the scope of the Treaty — see Chapter 12).

2.   Note that as a result of Lisbon, the Union does now possess competence to legislate in this area. *See* Template para. 6.7.4.

## COMMISSION v. COUNCIL
### (ERASMUS)
### Case 242/87, 1989 ECJ CELEX LEXIS 413, [1989] ECR 1425

[The Commission brought an action for the annulment of Council Decision 87/327/EEC adopting the European Community Action Scheme for the Mobility of University Students (ERASMUS).

The decision took as its legal basis Article 128 (EC150/TFEU 166] and article 235 (EC 308/TFEU 253) of the EC Treaty and Council Decision 63/266 laying down general principles for implementing a common vocational training policy. The language of article 128 has since been modified but it still addresses specifically only vocational training.]

6 . . . [I]t follows from the very wording of Article 235 [352] that its use as the legal basis for a measure is justified only where no other provision of the Treaty gives the Community institutions the necessary power to adopt the measure in question.

7 The Commission maintains that the Council had the power to adopt the contested decision on the sole basis of Article 128 [166] of the Treaty and Decision 63/266. According to the Council and the intervening governments, the additional reference to Article 235 [352] was necessary, first, because the measures planned under the Erasmus programme go beyond the powers conferred on the Council by Article 128 [166] in the area of vocational training and, secondly, because the subject-matter of that programme exceeds the scope of vocational training within the meaning of that article. It is therefore necessary to examine the various arguments put forward to justify recourse to Article 235 [352] with those two points in mind.

(a) The powers of the Council in the area of vocational training

8 Whereas the Commission considers that Article 128 [166] of the EEC Treaty constitutes the proper legal basis for the adoption of operational measures for implementing the common vocational training policy, the Council and the intervening governments maintain that that provision of the Treaty allows for the development of that policy at an embryonic stage only. They believe that the provision in question is of a programmatic rather than instrumental character and provides for a division of powers between the Member States and the Community institutions. They assert that while it is for the Council to define the criteria with which the Member States are obliged to comply when implementing the vocational training policy, it is not within the Council's power, on the basis of that same provision, to specify Community action of the kind planned in the Erasmus programme.

9 In the face of those divergent views, it should be recalled that Article 128 [166] provides that "the Council shall, acting on a proposal from the Commission and after consulting the Economic and Social Committee, lay down general principles for implementing a common vocational training policy capable of contributing to the harmonious development both of the national economies and of the common market". As the Commission has rightly pointed out, the fact that the implementation of a common vocational training policy is provided for precludes any interpretation of that provision which would mean denying the Community the means of action needed to carry out that common policy effectively.

10 The Court has already noted that the common vocational training policy referred to in Article 128 [151] of the Treaty is gradually being established. The abovementioned Decision 63/266, which constitutes the point of departure for that process of gradual implementation, is based on the idea that the task of implementing the general principles of the common vocational training policy is one for the Member States and the Community institutions working in cooperation.

11 From an interpretation of Article 128 [166] based on that conception it follows that the Council is entitled to adopt legal measures providing for Community action in the sphere of vocational training and imposing corresponding obligations of cooperation on the Member States. Such an interpretation is in accordance with the wording of Article 128 [166] and also ensures the effectiveness of that provision.

*    *    *

13 Under the system governing Community powers, the powers of the institutions and the conditions on their exercise derive from various specific provisions of the Treaty, and the differences between those provisions, particularly as regards the involvement of the European Parliament, are not always based on consistent criteria.

14 It must, however, be added that among the provisions of the Treaty relied upon in support of the Council's position, Article 57 [53] is certainly relevant in defining the scope of Article 128 [166]. Article 57 [53] provides specifically for the adoption of directives for the mutual recognition of diplomas, certificates and other evidence of formal qualifications and for the coordination of national provisions concerning the taking up and pursuit of activities as self-employed persons. It follows that that type of measure, even if it concerns the area of vocational training, does not fall under Article 128 [166].

15 However, the scope of that provision as a general basis for the adoption of measures relating to vocational training policy cannot be limited by the fact that specific action in the sphere of vocational training is envisaged in particular in Article 41 [41] of the Treaty in the context of the common agricultural policy and in Article 125 [164] in connection with aid granted by the European Social Fund.

19 In the light of the foregoing, it must be held that the measures envisaged under the Erasmus programme do not exceed the limits of the powers conferred on the Council by Article 128 [166] of the Treaty in the area of vocational training. The decision in question provides for Community information projects and promotional activity and imposes on Member States obligations of cooperation.

20 Although it is true that Action 3 of the programme concerns "measures to promote mobility though the academic recognition of diplomas and periods of study", examination of the various measures provided for in this part of the programme shows that they are designed merely to prepare for and encourage the recognition envisaged; that recognition itself is not the subject-matter of the action. The nature of the action is thus sufficient to show that it does not fall under the exclusive scope of application of Article 57 [53] of the Treaty.

21 It follows from the foregoing that the Council was empowered to enact the contested measure on the basis of Article 128 [166] of the Treaty, subject to examination of the question whether that measure exceeded the scope of vocational training.

(b) The scope of vocational training

22 While the Commission considers that the programme in question concerns vocational training alone, the Council and the intervening governments believe that

it goes beyond that field in several respects.

23 They claim in the first place that the Erasmus programme is applicable to all university studies, a large part of which do not constitute vocational training.

24 As the Court has consistently held, any form of education which prepares for a qualification for a particular profession, trade or employment or which provides the necessary skills for such a profession, trade or employment is vocational training, whatever the age and the level of training of the pupils or students, even if the training programme includes an element of general education.

25 . . . [T]he Court has already stated that, in general, university studies fulfil those criteria and the only exceptions are certain courses of study which, because of their particular nature, are intended for persons wishing to improve their general knowledge rather than prepare themselves for an occupation.

26 It also follows from that judgment that studies do not cease to constitute vocational training where they do not directly provide the required qualification for a particular profession but provide specific training and skills, or in the case of university education, they are divided into different stages which must be regarded as a single unit, where it is not possible to make a distinction between one stage which does not constitute vocational training and a second which does.

27 It follows that in general the studies to which the contested programme applies fall within the sphere of vocational training, and only in exceptional cases will the action planned under the programme be found to be applicable to university studies which, because of their particular character, are outside that sphere. The mere possibility of the latter cannot justify the conclusion that the contested programme goes beyond the scope of vocational training and that therefore the Council was not empowered to adopt it pursuant to Article 128 [166] of the Treaty.

28 It was maintained, secondly, that certain objectives of the contested programme, in particular that of "strengthening the interaction between citizens in different Member States with a view to consolidating the concept of a people's Europe" (Article 2(iv) of the contested decision) exceeded the scope of vocational training.

29 In that regard it must be pointed out, first, that the Court has already held that there is a special link between the common vocational training policy and the free movement of persons and, secondly, that the perfectly legitimate aim that the development of a common policy should be in keeping with the general objectives of the Community, such as the achievement of a people's Europe, cannot lead to a change in the proper legal basis of measures which fall objectively under the common policy in question.

30 Thirdly, it was asserted that the contested decision affected the organization of education inasmuch as it is intended to set up a European network for university cooperation (Action 1 of the programme).

31 The Court has already held . . . that although educational and training policy is not as such included in the spheres which the Treaty has entrusted to the Community institutions, it does not follow that the exercise of powers transferred to the Community is in some way limited if it is of such a nature as to affect the measures taken in the execution of a policy such as that of education and training.

32 According to the terms of Action 1, set out in the annex to the contested decision, the European university network will be composed of those universities which have chosen to conclude certain agreements for exchanges of students and teachers. Although it is true that it is for the Community to set up the network, universities may only participate on the basis of the provisions governing their status and organization, which are not affected by the programme in question. Consequently that argument cannot be accepted.

33 It was also maintained that recourse to Article 235 [352] of the Treaty was necessary because the programme in question included some aspects falling within the sphere of research.

34 It is clear that scientific research is characteristically one of the proper functions of a university. Not only does a proportion of university staff devote its time exclusively to research but research constitutes in principle an essential element in the work of most university teachers and of some students, for example those studying for a doctorate or similar qualification.

35 Any interpretation of the contested decision to the effect that it did not concern the scientific research work of universities would lead to a considerable limitation on the scope of certain objectives of the Erasmus programme, in particular that of "((promoting)) broad and intensive cooperation between universities in all Member States" and that of "((harnessing)) the full intellectual potential of the universities in the Community by means of increased mobility of teaching staff, thereby improving the quality of the education and training provided by the universities with a view to securing the competitiveness of the Community in the world market" (Article 2(ii) and (iii)).

36 Consequently, in the absence of any express reservation in the contested decision as regards scientific research, it must be held that at least some of the initiatives planned are aimed at the spheres of both research and vocational training. That is especially true of Action 1 (" Establishment and operation of a European university network "), which provides in particular for "support for teaching staff and university administrators to visit other Member States, to enable them to prepare programmes of integrated study with universities of these Member States and to exchange experience on the latest developments in their area of expertise", and support to encourage greater mobility for teaching staff (paragraphs 3 and 4). Moreover, Article 130G of the Treaty, added by the Single European Act, sets out, among other activities to be carried out by the Community in pursuing the objectives laid down in the new title of the Treaty on research and technological development, the stimulation of training and mobility of researchers in the Community.

*     *     *

37 It follows that inasmuch as the contested decision concerns not only the sphere of vocational training but also that of scientific research, the Council did not have the power to adopt it pursuant to Article 128 [166] alone and thus was bound, before the Single European Act entered into force, to base the decision on Article 235 [352] as well. The Commission's first submission that the legal basis chosen was unlawful must therefore be rejected.

## NOTES AND QUESTIONS

1. In the above case, how was EC 308/TFEU 352 used? Did it actually extend the powers of the Union?

2. It might be thought that EC 308/352 is the equivalent of the "necessary and proper" clause in the U.S. Constitution. The "necessary and proper" clause has been interpreted as not granting *new* powers to the United States — it is necessarily tied to the existing scope of U.S. power. In the landmark case of *McCulloch v. Maryland* 17 U.S. (4 Wheat.) 316, 4 L. Ed. 579 (1819), the Supreme Court gave the necessary and proper clause of the United States Constitution an expansive reading as creating implied powers and establishing the legitimate role of the federal government in dealing with national problems. Rather than interpreting the clause as a limitation of Congress's enumerated powers, the Court ruled it was an express recognition of the need to provide additional law-making power for the execution of the enumerated powers.

For its part, the ECJ has generally interpreted article EC 308/TFEU 352 so as to limit its utilization by the Council to those (relatively rare) situations where there is truly no basis for Council action elsewhere in the Treaty. In the past, the concern of the ECJ in interpreting and applying article 308 has *not* been the scope of "constitutional" limits on EU power, but rather that the delicate balance of power between the "legislative" organs of the EU — the Council the Commission and Parliament — be maintained. Joseph Weiler noted in *The transformation of Europe*, 100 Yale L.J. 2403, 2445-46 (1991) as follows:

> In a variety of fields, including, for example, conclusion of international Agreements, the granting of emergency food aid to third countries, and creation of new institutions, the Community made use of Article 235 [352] in a manner that was simply not consistent with the narrow interpretation of the Article as a codification of the implied powers doctrine in its instrumental sense. Only a truly radical and "creative" reading of the Article could explain and justify its usage as, for example, the legal basis for granting emergency food aid to non-associated states. But this wide reading in which all the institutions partook, meant that it would become virtually impossible to find an activity which could not be brought within the objectives of the Treaty.

However, this "expansive" interpretation may no longer be in fashion. See for example, the Court's opinion regarding accession to the ECHR, *Opinion 2/94*, 1996 ECJ CELEX LEXIS 619, [1996] ECR I-1759), where article EC 308/TFEU 352 was held not to grant powers to act in areas not otherwise covered by or within the scope of the EC Treaty/TFEU.

3. Professor Weiler, in *The Division of Competences in the European Union*, EP DG for Research Working Document Political series w-26, suggested that article EC 308/TFEU 352 could be used for the basis for a common defense policy since the EU couldn't function if it were occupied. What would you say to that argument? Consider articles 4 and 5 TEU introduced by the Treaty of Lisbon. Note also that EC 308 was modified by Lisbon to its present form in TFEU 352.

# Chapter 11

# INTERNAL COMPETENCES

## § 11.01 OVERVIEW

***Template***: Article 6, Sections 6.2-6.8

***Materials in this Chapter***: This chapter explores the different kinds of competences conferred on the EU with respect to internal affairs. The materials illustrate how exclusive and shared competences operate, particularly in terms of the effects on the Member States. A detailed description of every competence and the substance of the policies or programs adopted by the Union are not covered. These vary, at one extreme, from being a subject worthy of separate legal study (such as competition law), to areas of interest to specialists only (customs or conservation of marine resources), through to matters of interest mainly in the political sphere. It should be emphasized again that competences are conferred on the Union rather than on the Union's legislative bodies as such, thus such competences may be executive or legislative depending on the specific provisions.

***Fundamental Rights*** Although the Charter of Fundamental Rights is now an integral part of the primary law of the Union, the Treaties do not grant any powers to it in this field except to legislate against discrimination, and then only within the scope of application of the Treaties. (This notion is considered specifically in Chapter 17, *infra*.) The inability to legislate on fundamental rights is not surprising if such rights are supposed to be part of the constitutional structure, just as they are in the U.S. Constitution. It is interesting to note perhaps that the right to legislate against discrimination is an independent one in the Union, while in the United States, it had to be justified under the Commerce Clause.

***Currency*** This is addressed under exclusive powers, *infra*.

***Union Finances*** The power to raise taxes and borrow money is clearly a critical element of a state's sovereign power, not only in the obvious sense that other essential state functions depend on it, but also because it is used to manage the economy as a whole. The Union itself has no fiscal powers (one may however recall from the *Meroni* case in Chapter 3 that the levy system that applied under the ECSC as an exception), and is dependent on transfers from the Member States, through the mechanism of "own resources" already outlined Chapter 2, *supra*. An interesting perspective on how this compares with the earlier years of federal states is found in the THE EUROPEAN COMMUNITY'S BUDGET, published by the EU in 1986:

> Parallels in history
>
> Disputes constantly rage in the Community between the Member States, or between the institutions (Parliament, Council and Commission) involved

in the decision-making process, or sometimes between the two, about respective roles in distributing and redistributing funds and about shares of the Community cake. This is by no means as unusual as it is often made out to be, and the situation certainly does not deserve the fuss made of it in the press. Not only are disputes of this kind the order of the day in federal or newly-federations. This is something which all States founding a federation or confederation have experienced from the start, and had to learn to live with. The United States, Switzerland, the Federal Republic of Germany, Canada and Australia are all good examples.

A group of independent experts set up by the Commission to study the role of public finance in European integration, under the chairmanship of Sir Donald MacDougall made a detailed analysis of the five federations listed above, together with three contrasting examples of centrally-managed Community States (France, Italy and the United Kingdom). The MacDougall report is an impressive contribution to understanding this subject. It was published in two volumes by the Commission in April 1977.

In the United States, it took the central government and Congress-formed by the Confederation of 1781 — more than 80 years (until after the Civil War) to institute own resources other than revenue from customs duties. Even today, 'revenue sharing' between the Federal Government in Washington and the individual states remains a source of constant frictions in American domestic policy.

In Switzerland. . . . , the cantons jealously defend their sovereignty in tax matters. Fiscal adjustment between the different levels of government is frequently, and hotly, debated in Switzerland.

The specific problems of federation and the practical experience of the Federal Republic of Germany are in many ways illuminating for the development of financial relations between the community and its Member States:

The federal German State, which emerged as a customs federation in 1867 from the German customs union formed in 1834, and became a political entity with the founding of the German Empire in 1871, did not become a fully-fledged customs union until 1888. Until 1913, and in some respects even until Erzberger's finance reform in 1919-20, it remained dependent on matricular contributions from its Member States ('the hanger-on of the constituent states', as Bismarck called it). This led to the development of a 'fiscal federation'. The federation did not receive full customs power until the Basic Law was adopted in Bonn in 1949.

The Union nonetheless does have some limited scope to intervene in taxation matters in order to protect the internal market, but there is no competence to harmonize income tax regimes. In this regard, the European Commission issued a Communication dated May 23, 2001 on 'tax policy in the European Union — Priorities for the years ahead' (COM (2001) 260) and stressed that harmonization on taxation at the EU level is not a priority as long as Member States respect EU rules. Therefore, Member States are competent to set up their own tax systems.

The European Commission aims at creating incentives to encourage coordination of national policies in order to eliminate tax obstacles to all form of cross-border economic activity (see Communication 'Removing cross border tax obstacles for EU citizens' of December 20, 2010, COM/2010/769).

Insofar as indirect taxation may affect the functioning of the internal market, the Union's powers in this area fall within the scope of that particular shared competence. The EU Member States must respect EU rules on fair tax competition, non-discrimination, and state aids as well as EU Directives relating to those areas. Moreover, Articles EC 90/TFEU 110 to EC 93/TFEU 113 allow the EU legislator to harmonize legislation concerning turnover taxes, excise duties and other forms of indirect taxation to the extent that such harmonization is necessary to ensure the establishment and the functioning of the internal market and to avoid distortion of competition. Thus, according to Directive 2006/112 — which is a recast of a 1977 directive — Member States must in principle apply a minimum tax rate of 15 percent to all the supplies of goods and services except for some specific goods. This obligation for Member States to set a minimum 15% VAT threshold slightly limits the Member States'sovereignty for setting a competitive internal fiscal policy.

EU Member States have also agreed on a Code of Conduct for business taxation that is designed to detect measures that unduly affect the location of business activity in the EU by being targeted merely at non-residents and by providing them with a more favourable tax treatment than that which is generally available in the Member State concerned.

Although the Union is dependent on transfers from the Member States for its revenue (other than income arising from its executive functions, such as collection of fines for breach of the competition rules) the availability of transferred funds is guaranteed by the Treaties and thus the Union is able to determine its own spending budget. (This was discussed in Chapter 6.)

***Exclusive Competences — Competition Policy*** The framers of the EEC Treaty made a policy choice to include a competition law regime in the Treaty itself. The Council has exclusive power to adopt rules of implementation, pursuant to which the Commission has been granted overall enforcement powers. One may note that this is one of the few areas where, while the Parliament has to be consulted, the provisions of EC 83/TFEU 103 do not speak of acting by a special legislative procedure, thus rendering the rulemaking executive in character.

In the U.S., the equivalent laws (antitrust) were adopted under the more general powers of the Commerce Clause more than 100 years after the ratification of the Constitution. While there are several U.S. statutes dealing with this subject, the Sherman Act, Sections 1 and 2, is the law most comparable to articles EC 81/TFEU 101 and EC 82/TFEU 102.

Competition, or antitrust, law prohibits agreements and unilateral behavior that prevents or damages competition in the market place. Agreements among competitors to fix prices and share markets, and abuses of monopoly or dominant positions are the behaviors most associated with this area of law. Enforcement has steadily increased over the last 20 years and is now a global phenomenon, with many countries following to a greater or lesser degree the EU approach.

From a constitutional standpoint, what is of interest here is the scope of EU competition law and its relationship with national laws in that area and indeed other policy areas. Articles EC 81/TFEU 101 and EC 82/TFEU 102 are different in several major ways from the other provisions of the Treaty. First and foremost, they are addressed to, and primarily are intended to impose obligations on, private citizens, not Member States. They thus constitute a form of directly applicable legislation that is clearly invocable even between individuals. The presence of these articles was, it may be recalled, in the mind of the ECJ as it reasoned its way to invocability of other Treaty provisions (*Van Gend en Loos*) and supremacy (*Costa v. ENEL*): the Treaty does create obligations for individuals who should therefore have rights against the Member States to ensure that the states observe their duties.

Although articles EC 81/TFEU 101 and EC 82/TFEU 102 establish an EU policy on competition, they do not preclude competence of the Member States to administer national competition policies within their own territory. Originally, the Council granted the Commission certain exclusive rights in the administration of the EU Competition law, including the grant of exemptions under EC 81(3)/TFEU 101. The burden of administration, however, began to obstruct the priority activities required of the Commission and thus, through Regulation 1/2003, a new scheme was introduced whereby the national competition authorities were granted the ability to administer the law, while article EC 81(3)/TFEU 101 became self-applying. As the materials will illustrate, this new scheme raises potentially many questions in terms of the relationship between EU and the Member States. Increasingly also, a form of preemptive effect is becoming evident in terms of how the EU law affects and limits other policies of the Member States.

While it is certainly the case that the drafters of the EEC Treaty intended these provisions to assure a viable market-based economy for the EU, it was already noted in Chapter 7 that they also had very much in mind the detrimental effect that anti-competitive behavior among private citizens could have on the formation of a common market. This was particularly true of so-called vertical restraints — restrictions arising from relationships with distributors and licensees. It was true also though of the "hardcore" antitrust behavior in the form of price-fixing cartels and monopolies, that often had the consequence (and indeed the intent) of protecting national industry from foreign competition. Unlike U.S. antitrust law, therefore, EU competition law has in the past had the very important additional purpose of breaking down "private" restrictions on interstate trade. It might be considered the private sector equivalent of such articles as EC 28/TFEU 34, EC 43/49 and EC 49/TFEU 56. This manifested itself in much activity over the first 30 years since the foundation of the EC, which gave the appearance (and probably the reality) that the Commission was less interested in pursuing traditional antitrust activity and more concerned with the promotion of the common market.

It is safe to say that this approach has now changed. The pursuit of hardcore cartels — price fixing and market sharing — has, particularly since the implementation of Reg. 1/2003, become the backbone of competition policy. That regulation, by co-opting the authorities of the Member States into the enforcement of EU law, has provided a great deal more legitimacy to the program within the Member States. Moreover, Member States themselves have been strengthening their own laws and increasing their enforcement, in some cases even with the introduction of criminal penalties.

***Exclusive competences — monetary policy for Member States whose currency is the euro*** The uniqueness and perhaps oddity of the approach to monetary policy in the EU reflects the differing views of the Member States to the process of ever closer union probably more than any other aspect of the Union's structure. As of the time of writing, 17 Member States have adopted the euro, 10 have not, but in most cases would aspire eventually to do so. A few (the UK, Denmark and Sweden) have taken the view that, though they might qualify for membership already, their commitment to national sovereignty is too strong to give up power in this highly sensitive area.

For eurozone members, powers to conduct monetary policy are entirely vested in the European Central Bank (ECB) and the System of Central Banks. The Union has no powers of legislation to govern the ECB, the conduct of which is constrained by the goals set out in the Treaties. This rigidity has proven of some difficulty when confronting the financial crisis that began in 2008 and continues to weigh on the Union. The only possibility for modifications of the Bank's duty lies in changes to the Treaties themselves. .

***Other exclusive competences*** Somewhat in contrast with competition policy and eurozone monetary policy, where the Commission or the ECB respectively is the "enforcer in chief", exclusive powers in the other enumerated areas exist to enact legislation or set policy, while enforcement remains a matter for the Member States. For example, the common customs tariff is determined at the Union level, but the collection of customs duties remains in the hands of the Member States. The same is true of the policy relating to the conservation of marine resources. The common commercial policy is something of a mixture, since commercial treaties are negotiated by the Commission and executed by the Council, while much of the day-to-day implementation of concomitant internal aspects remain in the hands of the Member States. Since this policy is principally an aspect of foreign affairs, it is addressed separately in Chapter 12 *infra*.

***Shared Competences*** The notion of shared competences embraces many variants in terms of the scope of the Union competence. At one end of the scale, some provisions authorize the Union to adopt a common policy (e.g., agriculture, immigration and transport). Others, such as those relating to the internal market, grant powers of harmonization. At the other end of the spectrum, measures relating to criminal law grant only powers to further cooperation between Member States.

***Shared Competences — Agriculture and fisheries (except conservation of marine resources)*** The agricultural sector of the economy had long been treated as requiring special protection by the governments of the original six Member States of the EEC and this was true also to varying degrees of all other Member States. If agricultural goods were to be included within the common market, then these varying systems of protection would have to be aligned. The choice was to make agriculture a "common policy" where the original EEC would assume a significant degree of exclusive competence in terms of overall policy decisions and implementing legislation. This does not imply that the Member States are deprived of authority in areas not covered by the common policy or at a level of intervention that does not interfere with the common policy. Thus, agricultural policy is not designated as an exclusive competence by the 3 and 4 TFEU. The central question addressed by the materials in this Chapter is that of understanding the extent to which the States can continue to adopt their own rules where they might impinge on the EU's policy.

Most agricultural production is subject to a common policy that is based on intervention in the internal marketplace to maintain prices at agreed levels and external protection in the form of levies on goods from third countries; necessary, of course, to avoid undercutting the internal price support mechanisms. See the factual description of the CAP in Chapter 2, *supra*. For a more detailed account, see A. GREER, AGRICULTURAL POLICY IN EUROPE (Manchester University Press, 2005).

There are now some 20 markets covered by basic regulations that have some or many of the features described in the above excerpt. A structural and guidance fund for long-term reform had been set up in and was most recently updated by Regulation 1257/1999, [1999] OJ L 160/80. The separate market organization regulations were brought together in Regulation 1234/2007, [2007] OJ L 299/1, effective January 1, 2008.

***Shared competences — the Internal Market*** This is by far the most active field for EU legislation, but the powers here are quite different from common policies. Here the EC Treaty/TFEU envisages harmonization of national laws as a general principle and not the substitution of Member State legislative powers by the Union.

Until the 1980s harmonization proceeded in a piecemeal manner and the results were largely insignificant. Attempts to write detailed standards for very narrow areas got bogged down for years and were often outdated by the time they were enacted (if ever). In the field of services, progress was even slower. However, the decisions of the ECJ (to be explored in Part V) that expanded the scope of the articles defining and restricting State powers contributed importantly to a change of direction. This resulted first in a concentrated program to unblock stalled initiatives (the so-called single market initiative embodied in the SEA with its stated 1992 target). This was accompanied by a change of underlying approach, based on the notion of setting broad standards across multiple industries, resulting in broad-brush directives. A concomitant development relied on the doctrine of mutual recognition, whereby, rather than harmonizing legislation, the EU chose to focus on getting rid of multiple burdens on industry by requiring Member States to recognize equivalent standards in other States. Again, this was in no small way due to the continued development of the jurisprudence of the ECJ.

The result is that harmonization efforts have tended to result in broader principles governing the freedom of Member States to regulate, akin perhaps to some forms of legislation in the United States where federal laws with broad goals are implemented under Federal guidance by the States (environmental legislation being such an example). This change of direction might appear to have resulted in a slowdown in the developing scope of EU powers. The opposite is really the case. The decisions that are made in setting broader standards are themselves statements of policy and thus reflect a move to overall EU preemption of the larger political choices. The heated debates both in EU legislative bodies and the Member States around the scope of the directives relating to financial services introduced in

2006 ("MIFID") (as further described below) and to mutual recognition of qualifications (the Bolkestein directive) are good examples of this. Perhaps this can best be characterized as EU regulation by proxy, with the Member States' role largely reduced to executive implementation and rulemaking. Such powers, however, still require a reasoned justification that they are necessary for the goals stated in EC 94 and 95/TFEU 114 and 113. This is explored in section 3 of this Chapter.

The broader approach described above is not necessarily a valid solution for all areas. For example, where the mere existence of different regulations continues to impede the formation of the internal market, the EU might choose to move in the converse direction, so that it may be expected that over time EU regulation may eventually replace national laws altogether.

An example of this is the more than 800-page Regulation 1907/2006 [2006] OJ L 396/1 on the Registration, Evaluation, Authorization and Restriction of Chemicals (REACH), which imposes an EU system of regulation on the sale and use of chemicals, superseding the legislation of the Member States after many years of progressive harmonization of laws relating to the safety of chemicals (as, for example, was in issue in the case of *Ratti, infra,*). The REACH regulation was adopted on the basis of EC 95/TFEU 114. The regulation, which sets up a European Chemicals Agency to administer REACH, is a far cry from the historic concept of harmonization, and if TFEU 114 is indeed to be used for such types of legislation, this certainly suggests that the EU in fact has broad latent powers of regulation.

Another example can be seen in the field of trademarks. Unlike the United States Constitution, which expressly grants to the U.S. Congress the power to register trademarks, no such power has historically existed in the EU — the Treaties themselves did not grant any *express* powers to the Union relating to intellectual property. This has, however, changed with the entry into force of the Treaty of Lisbon, but in any event the Union had already established a regulation relating to Union trademarks together with an agency to manage this system. More and more such agencies or coordinating authorities are springing up.

In contrast to competition policy, the EC Treaty/TFEU did not confer any specific powers on the EU with respect to *other* forms of market conduct regulation, notably financial services and capital markets. The need for EU intervention in this area has of course evolved as the common market took shape, as capital movements were liberalized, and as the world moved to a global marketplace. Hence by the 1990s it was becoming increasingly obvious that national regulation was no longer sufficient to deal with cross border activities. The EU has now adopted a sweeping directive on Markets in Financial Instruments ("MIFID") which was to be implemented before November 1, 2007. This directive was adopted pursuant to the harmonization provisions of the EC Treaty/TFEU.

***Shared competences — economic, social and regional cohesion*** The EC Treaty/ TFEU provides for EU action involving funding for sectors, regions and various social goals. An EU policy on regional aids had been developing for a number of years, beginning in the mid-1970s. In addition, the 'Structural' portion of the former European Agricultural Guidance and Guarantee Fund (EAGGF or FEOGA, its French acronym), plus the "Social Fund" and the "Regional Development Fund", have had a long history and have been transformed over the years reflecting changes in overall policy direction. From the beginning, the European Investment Bank was assigned the role of providing or guaranteeing loans at favorable rates for European infrastructure projects.

Obviously, policies under which such funds operate must be closely coordinated with aids granted by the Member States and approved by the Commission. In this regard, governmental assistance at the EU level combined with State aids becomes a significant element of policy, which perhaps seems at odds with EC 87-89/TFEU 107-109. The key factor, of course, is that the decisions on financial assistance by the Union are taken at the EU level and are by definition compatible with EU objectives even if they favor certain regions and industries. There is no doubt that countries such as Ireland have benefited greatly from EU policy permitting national aids on the basis that Ireland is a special region of the EU.

Altogether then, the EU does have significant powers to intervene in the economy through various mechanisms ranging from the detailed market organizations within the framework of the agricultural policy, to special funds with particular goals, to more general support for Member State programs.

***Shared Competences — The Area of Freedom, Security and Justice (AFSJ)*** It is a significant achievement for the EU that the Union has been able to acquire powers in this area and that those powers are now built into the integrationist framework of the TFEU.

The process of movement from the TEU to the EC Treaty/TFEU began with the Treaty of Amsterdam, which moved visa and asylum policy over. Developing alongside this were the specific measures taken by the Schengen countries. These were eventually assumed into the EU structure via a Protocol, No 19. Thus there are two parallel sources of legitimation for measures in the immigration and asylum field. The Court has been clear that those relating specifically to Schengen arrangements are adopted under the Protocol: See, e.g., *United Kingdom v. Council*, Case C-137/05 [2007] ECR I – 11593. Police and Judicial Cooperation in Criminal Matters (PJCC) were moved into the TFEU by the Lisbon Treaty.

Competences regarding the AFSJ vary from adopting a common policy (as for immigration from outside the Union) to powers to "develop cooperation" in police and justice matters. The TFEU articles that confer competence on the Union in this respect do not, notably (and consistent with the core provisions of the internal market), impose a specific duty on the Member States to cooperate with each other. Their duty (when legislated by the Union) is thus owed to the Union, and only to each other pursuant to the more general duty of cooperation found in EC 10/TEU 4.

***Powers of coordination and support*** The competences in this area vary by subject matter. The TFEU is deliberately specific about the nature of the competence. With a few exceptions, the role of the Union is to encourage cooperation between the Member States, although the Treaty provisions do not always lay down a duty of cooperation for the States.

In the areas of economic and employment policy, the Treaty imposes a duty on the Member States to cooperate with each other (see Chapter 21 *infra* and article

9 of the Template).

Notwithstanding the above, it is clear that the Member States have given up some of the conventional instruments used by governments to stimulate growth or prevent overheating in the economy such as import controls, various forms of exchange rate controls, including limits on capital flows in and out of the country, and manipulation of interest rates through the mechanism of the national central bank. All of these instruments are still widely used outside the EU, in particular in still-developing countries such as China and India. Under the EC Treaty provisions dealing with the constitution of the European System of Central Banks and the European Central Bank (ECB), the ECB was given complete independence and assigned the task of controlling inflation through use of interest rates.

Following the banking crisis in 2008/9 that preceded the sovereign debt crisis in Europe, the Union created a new regulatory body, the European Banking Authority — see Regulation 1093/2010 [2010] OJ 331/12 and Directive 2010/78 [2010] OJ 331/120. Given the absence of Union competences with respect to economic policy in general, these measures were adopted on the basis of EC 95/TFEU 114. As a practical matter, they do, of course, make inroads into the competences of the national authorities in the field of economic and monetary policy, especially with respect to those States participating in the euro.

For response to the sovereign debt crisis, see also Chapter 21 *infra*.

## § 11.02   EXCLUSIVE POWERS — EU COMPETITION LAW

*[NOTE: Relevant provisions of the TFEU are set out in Chapter 7, supra.]*

### [A]   Internal Jurisdiction — the Effect on Trade

#### ETABLISSEMENTS CONSTEN SARL AND GRUNDIG-VERKAUFS-GMBH v. COMMISSION
Joined Cases 56 and 58/64, [1966] ECR 299
[No paragraph numbering appears in the original]

[Grundig, a German manufacturer of electrical appliances, had granted Consten sole distribution rights in France, along with an exclusive licence to use Grundig's "GINT" trademark. UNEF, another French company, began importing Grundig products into France that had been purchased in Germany. Consten brought trademark infringement proceedings in the course of which it became evident that EU competition law would be relevant. Grundig notified the agreements to the EU Commission under then article 85 (EC 81/TFEU 101). This case was brought to challenge the Commission's adverse decision.]

The applicants submit that the prohibition in Article 85 [101] (1) applies only to so-called horizontal agreements. The Italian Government submits furthermore that sole distributorship contracts do not constitute 'agreements between undertakings' within the meaning of that provision, since the parties are not on a footing of equality. With regard to these contracts, freedom of competition may only be protected by virtue of Article 86 [82] of the Treaty.

Neither the wording of Article 85 [101] nor that of Article 86 [102] gives any ground for holding that distinct areas of application are to be assigned to each of the two Articles according to the level in the economy at which the contracting parties operate. Article 85 [101] refers in a general way to all agreements which distort competition within the Common Market and does not lay down any distinction between those agreements based on whether they are made between competitors operating at the same level in the economic process or between non-competing persons operating at different levels. In principle, no distinction can be made where the Treaty does not make any distinction.

Furthermore, the possible application of Article 85 [101] to a sole distributorship contract cannot be excluded merely because the grantor and the concessionnaire are not competitors inter se and not on a footing of equality. Competition may be distorted within the meaning of Article 85 [101] (1) not only by agreements which limit it as between the parties, but also by agreements which prevent or restrict the competition which might take place between one of them and third parties. For this purpose, it is irrelevant whether the parties to the agreement are or are not on a footing of equality as regards their position and function in the economy. This applies all the more, since, by such an agreement, the parties might seek, by preventing or limiting the competition of third parties in respect of the products, to create or guarantee for their benefit an unjustified advantage at the expense of the consumer or user, contrary to the general aims of Article 85 [101].

It is thus possible that, without involving an abuse of a dominant position, an agreement between economic operators at different levels may affect trade between Member States and at the same have as its object or effect the prevention, restriction or distortion of competition, thus falling under the prohibition of Article 85 [101] (1).

In addition, it is pointless to compare on the one hand the situation, to which Article 85 [101] applies, for a producer bound by a sole distributorship agreement to the distributor of his products with on the other hand that of a producer who includes within his undertaking the distribution of his own products by some means, for example, by commercial representatives, to which Article 85 [101] does not apply. These situations are distinct in law and, moreover, need to be assessed differently, since two marketing organizations, one of which is integrated into the manufacturer's undertaking whilst the other is not, may not necessarily have the same efficiency. The wording of Article 85 [101] causes the prohibition to apply, provided that the other conditions are met, to an agreement between several undertakings. Thus it does not apply where a sole undertaking integrates its own distribution network into its business organization. It does not thereby follow, however, that the contractual situation based on an agreement between a manufacturing and a distributing undertaking is rendered legally acceptable by a simple process of economic analogy — which is in any case incomplete and in contradiction with the said Article. Furthermore, although in the first case the Treaty intended in Article 85 [101] to leave untouched the internal organization of an undertaking and to render it liable to be called in question, by means of Article 86 [102], only in cases where it reaches such a degree of seriousness as to amount to an abuse of a dominant position, the same reservation could not apply when the impediments to competition result from agreement between two different undertakings which then as a general rule simply require to be prohibited.

Finally, an agreement between producer and distributor which might tend to restore the national divisions in trade between Member States might be such as to frustrate the most fundamental objectives of the Community. The Treaty, whose preamble and content aim at abolishing the barriers between States, and which in several provisions gives evidence of a stern attitude with regard to their reappearance, could not allow undertakings to reconstruct such barriers. Article 85 [101] (1) is designed to pursue this aim, even in the case of agreements between undertakings placed at different levels in the economic process.

* * *

The applicants and the German Government maintain that the Commission has relied on a mistaken interpretation of the concept of an agreement which may affect trade between Member States and has not shown that such trade would have been greater without the agreement in dispute.

The defendant replies that this requirement in Article 85 [101] (1) is fulfilled once trade between Member States develops, as a result of the agreement, differently from the way in which it would have done without the restriction resulting from the agreement, and once the influence of the agreement on market conditions reaches a certain degree. Such is the case here, according to the defendant, particularly in view of the impediments resulting within the Common Market from the disputed agreement as regards the exporting and importing of the Grundig products to and from France.

The concept of an agreement 'which may affect trade between Member States' is intended to define, in the law governing cartels, the boundary between the areas respectively covered by Community law and national law. It is only to the extent to which the agreement may affect trade between Member States that the deterioration in competition caused by the agreement falls under the prohibition of Community law contained in Article 85 [101]; otherwise it escapes the prohibition.

In this connexion, what is particularly important is whether the agreement is capable of constituting a threat, either direct or indirect, actual or potential, to freedom of trade between Member States in a manner which might harm the attainment of the objectives of a single market between States. Thus the fact that an agreement encourages an increase, even a large one, in the volume of trade between States is not sufficient to exclude the possibility that the agreement may 'affect'such trade in the abovementioned manner. In the present case, the contract between Grundig and Consten, on the one hand by preventing undertakings other than Consten from importing Grundig products into France, and on the other hand by prohibiting Consten from re-exporting those products to other countries of the Common Market, indisputably affects trade between Member States. These limitations on the freedom of trade, as well as those which might ensue for third parties from the registration in France by Consten of the GINT trade mark, which Grundig places on all its products, are enough to satisfy the requirement in question.

Consequently, the complaints raised in this respect must be dismissed.

* * *

The applicants and the German Government maintain that since the Commission restricted its examination solely to Grundig products the decision was based upon a false concept of competition and of the rules on prohibition contained in Article 85 [101] (1), since this concept applies particularly to competition between similar products of different makes; the Commission, before declaring Article 85 [101] (1) to be applicable, should, by basing itself upon the 'rule of reason', have considered the economic effects of the disputed contract upon competition between the different makes. There is a presumption that vertical sole distributorship agreements are not harmful to competition and in the present case there is nothing to invalidate that presumption. On the contrary, the contract in question has increased the competition between similar products of different makes.

The principle of freedom of competition concerns the various stages and manifestations of competition. Although competition between producers is generally more noticeable than that between distributors of products of the same make, it does not thereby follow that an agreement tending to restrict the latter kind of competition should escape the prohibition of Article 85 [101] (1) merely because it might increase the former.

Besides, for the purpose of applying Article 85 [101] (1), there is no need to take account of the concrete effects of an agreement once it appears that it has as its object the prevention, restriction or distortion of competition.

Therefore the absence in the contested decision of any analysis of the effects of the agreement on competition between similar products of different makes does not, of itself, constitute a defect in the decision.

It thus remains to consider whether the contested decision was right in founding the prohibition of the disputed agreement under Article 85 [101] (1) on the restriction on competition created by the agreement in the sphere of the distribution of Grundig products alone. The infringement which was found to exist by the contested decision results from the absolute territorial protection created the said contract in favour of Consten on the basis of French law. The applicants thus wished to eliminate any possibility of competition at the wholesale level in Grundig products in the territory specified in the contract essentially by two methods.

First, Grundig undertook not to deliver even indirectly to third parties products intended for the area covered by the contract. The restrictive nature of that undertaking is obvious if it is considered in the light of the prohibition on exporting which was imposed not only on Consten but also on all the other sole concessionnaires of Grundig, as well as the German wholesalers. Secondly, the registration in France by Consten of the GINT trade mark, which Grundig affixes to all its products, is intended to increase the protection inherent in the disputed agreement, against the risk of parallel imports into France of Grundig products, by adding the protection deriving from the law on industrial property rights. Thus no third party could import Grundig products from other Member States of the Community for resale in France without running serious risks.

The defendant properly took into account the whole distribution system thus set up by Grundig. In order to arrive at a true representation of the contractual position the contract must be placed in the economic and legal context in the light of which it was concluded by the parties. Such a procedure is not to be regarded as an unwarrantable interference in legal transactions or circumstances which were not the subject of the proceedings before the Commission.

The situation as ascertained above results in the isolation of the French market and makes it possible to charge for the products in question prices which are sheltered from all effective competition. In addition, the more producers succeed in their efforts to render their own makes of product individually distinct in the eyes of the consumer, the more the effectiveness of competition between producers tends to diminish. Because of the considerable impact of distribution costs on the aggregate cost price, it seems important that competition between dealers should also be stimulated. The efforts of the dealer are stimulated by competition between distributors of products of the same make. Since the agreement thus aims at isolating the French market for Grundig products and maintaining artificially, for products of a very well-known brand, separate national markets within the Community it is therefore such as to distort competition in the Common Market.

It was therefore proper for the contested decision to hold that the agreement constitutes an infringement of Article 85 [101] (1). No further considerations, whether of economic data (price differences between France and Germany, representative character of the type of appliance considered, level of overheads borne by Consten) or of the criteria upon which the Commission relied in its comparisons between the situations of the French and German markets, and no possible favorable effects of the agreement in other respects, can in any way lead, in the face of abovementioned restrictions, to a different solution under Article 85 [101] (1).

## NOTES AND QUESTIONS

1.   In this case the court laid down the basic criteria for determining whether there is an effect on interstate trade. It rapidly became clear following this decision that, as in the United States, it is not necessary that an agreement relate specifically to trade between two states for there to be an effect on interstate trade. In light of *Grundig*, is the requirement for such an effect in your view purely a jurisdictional one (as in the U.S.) or is it also substantive? Should it be substantive if EC 81/TFEU 101 is also intended to promote the achievement of the common market, or is the goal met simply by focusing on the anti-competitive nature of the agreements under review?

2.   The *Grundig* case establishes the principle that EU competition law applies to "vertical arrangements" as well as "horizontal ones" (i.e., it applies to arrangements between suppliers and customers as well as to those between competitors). This decision had as much, if not more, to do with promoting the common market as it did with promoting competition. In what ways did the arrangement in issue here restrict competition? Is there not much to be said for the case that the exclusive distributorship actually promoted competition by supporting the penetration of *Grundig* products in the French market? Why did the Court reject this argument?

**3.** The Court and the Commission have consistently followed the technique adopted in *Grundig* of first establishing the broadest possible scope of application for EC 81 and 82/TFEU 101 and 102 and then setting guidelines as to conduct that will be considered acceptable as a matter of policy. This policy manifests itself through individual decisions establishing infringements or exemptions and through regulations establishing exemptions for categories of agreements — including the type of exclusive distributorship at issue in *Grundig*. However, while such policy tolerates some restrictions on competition, any aspects of arrangements covered by such policies that tend to partition the common market along national lines are strictly forbidden.

In the U.S., the evaluation of vertical agreements that restrict competition in a narrow technical sense is based on a "rule of reason". This means that they are not illegal unless, on an overall evaluation of their effects they can be considered to be harmful to consumers. A limited form of "rule of reason" had also developed in the EU, pursuant to which some agreements could be considered acceptable under EC 81/TFEU 101 (1) even though they restrict competition in a technical sense. This approach first surfaced in *Metro v. Commission*, Case 26/76, [1977] ECR 1875, (appearing also in Chapter 8) where a distribution system for electronic appliances operated by the German company SABA was intended to promote SABA products as high-quality goods with professional sales and after sales support. Thus, SABA refused to admit Metro, as a wholesale supermarket, to its network. This exclusionary practice meant that SABA's products were not subject to intra-brand competition. The ECJ held that in certain cases, price competition might be secondary to other forms of competition (here, on quality) and the absence of such price competition might not then automatically bring the agreements within EC 81(1)/TFEU 101. Many parties have argued that the rule of reason could extend to many other cases. For example, a joint venture between two companies that enabled them to undertake a project that neither could do on its own might be considered justified under this "rule of reason." It may also be argued that in such cases the inability to undertake the project simply means there is no competition to restrict.

Under the system introduced by Regulation 1/2003, exemptions under EC 81/TFEU 101 (3) can exist without a Commission decision. Given the rationale for such exemptions expressed in article EC 81/TFEU 101 (3), these cannot be equated with the rule of reason as it exists in the U.S. but nonetheless the underlying foundation for these exemptions is that agreements falling within them are on balance beneficial.

**4.** While EC 82/TFEU 102 contains a similar reference to the requirement for an effect on trade between Member States, the dominant position need only be in a substantial part of the common market, and the Court has held that this may consist of a position within one Member State or even part of one Member State only: see *Suiker Unie v. Commission*, Joined Cases 40-48, 50, 54-56, 111, 113-114/73, [1975] ECR 1663, where the Court stated:

> For the purpose of determining whether a specific territory is large enough to amount to a substantial part of the common market within the meaning of Article 82 [102] of the Treaty the pattern and volume of the production

and consumption of the said product as well as the habits and economic opportunities of vendors and purchasers must be considered.

In this case, the ECJ held that each of the Belgium-Luxembourg and Southern German sugar markets was a "substantial part" of the common market. In *Port of Genoa*, Case C-179/90, 1991 ECJ CELEX LEXIS 414, [1991] ECR I-5889, a single port was held to be a substantial part of the market because of the high volume of shipping:

> 15 As regards the definition of the market in question, it may be seen from the order for reference that it is that of the organization on behalf of third persons of dock work relating to ordinary freight in the Port of Genoa and the performance of such work. Regard being had in particular to the volume of traffic in that port and its importance in relation to maritime import and export operations as a whole in the Member State concerned, that market may be regarded as constituting a substantial part of the common market.

## VINCENZO MANFREDI v. LLOYD ADRIATICO ASSICURAZIONI SPA, ANTONIO CANNITO v. FONDIARIA SAI SPA AND NICOLO TRICARICO AND PASQUALINA MURGOLO v. ASSITALIA SPA

Joined Cases C-295/04 to C-298/04, 2006 ECJ CELEX LEXIS 348, [2006] ECR I-6619

[The Plaintiffs sought various forms of relief including recovery of the increase in the cost of premiums as a result of the alleged violations of EC 81/TFEU 101 through the sharing of premium information by insurers. This practice had already been declared unlawful by the Italian competition authority. Several questions were raised as to the requirements of EU law with respect to the EU right to claim damages as previously laid down in the *Crehan* case which, together with another extract of this case, appears in Chapter 9 *supra*.]

42. For an agreement, decision or practice to be capable of affecting trade between Member States, it must be possible to foresee with a sufficient degree of probability, on the basis of a set of objective factors of law or of fact, that they may have an influence, direct or indirect, actual or potential, on the pattern of trade between Member States in such a way as to cause concern that they might hinder the attainment of a single market between Member States. Moreover, that influence must not be insignificant.

43. Thus, an effect on intra-Community trade is normally the result of a combination of several factors which, taken separately, are not necessarily decisive.

44. In that regard it should be stated, as the Advocate General rightly pointed out in paragraph 37 of his Opinion, that the mere fact that the participants in a national arrangement also include undertakings from other Member States is an important element in the assessment, but, taken alone, it is not so decisive as to permit the conclusion that the criterion of trade between Member States being affected has been satisfied.

45. On the other hand, the fact that an agreement, decision or concerted practice relates only to the marketing of products in a single Member State is not sufficient to exclude the possibility that trade between Member States might be affected. An agreement, decision or concerted practice extending over the whole of the territory of a Member State has, by its very nature, the effect of reinforcing the partitioning of markets on a national basis, thereby holding up the economic interpenetration which the Treaty is designed to bring about.

46. Further, in the case of services, the Court has already held that an influence on the pattern of trade between Member States may consist in the activities in question being conducted in such a way that their effect is to partition the common market and thereby restrict freedom to provide services, which constitutes one of the objectives of the Treaty.

47. It is for the national court to determine whether, in the light of the characteristics of the national market at issue, there is a sufficient degree of probability that the agreement or concerted practice at issue in the main proceedings may have an influence, direct or indirect, actual or potential, on the sale of civil liability auto insurance policies in the relevant Member State by operators from other Member States and that that influence is not insignificant.

48. However, when giving a preliminary ruling the Court may, where appropriate, provide clarification designed to give the national court guidance in its interpretation.

49. In that regard, according to the case-law of the Court, since the market concerned is susceptible to the provision of services by operators from other Member States, the members of a national price cartel can retain their market share only if they defend themselves against foreign competition.

50. The national court's decision indicates that the AGCM observed that the market for civil liability auto insurance premiums has considerable barriers to entry which have arisen primarily due to the need to set up an efficient distribution network and a network of centres for the settlement of accident claims throughout Italy. However, the national court also points out that insurance companies from other Member States but with activities in Italy also took part in the agreement ruled unlawful by the AGCM. It therefore appears that the market concerned is susceptible to the provision of services by insurance companies from other Member States, although such barriers make the provision of those services more difficult.

51. In such circumstances, it is a matter, in particular, for the national court to examine whether the mere existence of the agreement or concerted practice was capable of having a deterrent effect on insurance companies from other Member States without activities in Italy, in particular by enabling the coordination and fixing of civil liability auto insurance premiums at a level at which the sale of such insurance by those companies would not be profitable (see, to that effect, British Sugar, cited above, paragraphs 29 and 30).

52. The answer to the first question in Joined Cases C-295/04 to C-298/04 must therefore be that an agreement or concerted practice, such as that at issue in the main proceedings, between insurance companies, consisting of a mutual exchange of information that makes possible an increase in civil liability auto insurance

premiums not justified by market conditions, which infringes national rules on the protection of competition, may also constitute an infringement of EC 81/TFEU 101 if, in the light of the characteristics of the national market at issue, there is a sufficient degree of probability that the agreement or concerted practice at issue may have an influence, direct or indirect, actual or potential, on the sale of those insurance policies in the relevant Member State by operators established in other Member States and that that influence is not insignificant.

## NOTES AND QUESTIONS

**1.** Is the test proposed by the Court something that a national court could determine, particularly where the effect can be only potential?

**2.** See also *Van den Bergh Foods Ltd v. Commission*, Case T-65/98, 2003 ECJ CELEX LEXIS 4, [2003] ECR II-4653.

**3.** Where the parties are all situated in one Member State, this will not take the agreement out of EC 81/TFEU 101 (1), *Cementhandelaaren v. Commission*, Case 8/72, [1972] ECR 977, but the lack of physical means to conduct trade between Member States in a given product may mean that there cannot be an effect on trade. See *Electricity Industry in England and Wales*, [1994] OJ C 15/15. See also the Commission Notice on this subject, which in its full version attempts to deal with all such questions in considerable depth. While there may be circumstances such as the electricity case where an agreement is incapable of affecting trade between Member States due to a physical impediment — e.g., gas or electricity that cannot flow because of the absence of connecting pipelines, there could, however, still be such an effect to the extent the product competes with not-in-kind products (e.g., gas and heating oil) if there is in fact interchangeability of use.

## [B]  Appreciable Effect on Trade Between Member States and Appreciable Effect on Competition

### FRANZ VÖLK v. ETABLISSEMENTS J. VERVAECKE
#### Case 5/69, [1969] ECR 295

[Völk had granted Vervaecke exclusive distribution rights in Belgium and Luxemborg. However, Völk's share of the market in its home territory-Germany-was tiny — not exceeding 0.5% for any of his products. The national court asked whether the disputed contract fell within the prohibition set out in Article 85 [EC 81/TFEU 101](1) and whether regard must be had to the proportion of the market which the plaintiff had actually acquired or which he had endeavored to acquire in the Member States, in particular in Belgium and in Luxembourg, the sales zone within which the defendant enjoyed absolute protection.]

2/4 Although the Court is not entitled within the framework of sub-paragraph (a) of the first paragraph of Article 177 [267] to apply the Treaty to a particular case, it may nevertheless derive from the wording of the decision referring the matter the questions which relate exclusively to the interpretation of the Treaty. The question raised relates to agreements which are characterized by the fact that a producer who has granted a distributor the exclusive right of sale of his products for certain countries in the Common Market has undertaken to protect the distributor against deliveries which might be made in those countries by third parties and has obtained from the distributor an undertaking not to sell competing products. The question is thus reduced to whether, in deciding whether such agreements fall within the prohibition set out in Article 85 [101](1) of the Treaty, regard must be had to the proportion of the market which the grantor controls or endeavors to obtain in the territory ceded.

5/7 If an agreement is to be capable of affecting trade between Member States it must be possible to foresee with a sufficient degree of probability on the basis of a set of objective factors of law or of fact that the agreement in question may have an influence, direct or indirect, actual or potential, on the pattern of trade between Member States in such a way that it might hinder the attainment of the objectives of a single market between States. Moreover the prohibition in Article 85 [101](1) is applicable only if the agreement in question also has as its object or effect the prevention, restriction or distortion of competition within the Common Market. Those conditions must be understood by reference to the actual circumstances of the agreement. Consequently an agreement falls outside the prohibition in Article 85 [101] when it has only an insignificant effect on the markets, taking into account the weak position which the persons concerned have on the market of the product in question. Thus an exclusive dealing agreement, even with absolute territorial protection, may, having regard to the weak position of the persons concerned on the market in the products in question in the area covered by the absolute protection, escape the prohibition laid down in Article 85 [101](1).

## COMMISSION NOTICE ON AGREEMENTS OF MINOR IMPORTANCE WHICH DO NOT APPRECIABLY RESTRICT COMPETITION UNDER EC 81/TFEU 101(1) OF THE TREATY ESTABLISHING THE EUROPEAN COMMUNITY (DE MINIMIS)
[2001] OJ C 368/7
[Partial extract with footnotes omitted]

1. Article 81 [101] (1) prohibits agreements between undertakings which may affect trade between Member States and which have as their object or effect the prevention, restriction or distortion of competition within the common market. The Court of Justice of the European Communities has clarified that this provision is not applicable where the impact of the agreement on intra-Community trade or on competition is not appreciable.

2. In this notice the Commission quantifies, with the help of market share thresholds, what is not an appreciable restriction of competition under Article 81 [101] of the EC Treaty. This negative definition of appreciability does not imply that agreements between undertakings which exceed the thresholds set out in this notice appreciably restrict competition. Such agreements may still have only a negligible effect on competition and may therefore not be prohibited by Article 81 [101].

3. Agreements may in addition not fall under Article 81(1) [101] because they are not capable of appreciably affecting trade between Member States. This notice does not deal with this issue. It does not quantify what does not constitute an appreciable effect on trade. It is however acknowledged that agreements between small and medium-sized undertakings, as defined in the Annex to Commission Recommendation 96/280/EC, are rarely capable of appreciably affecting trade between Member States. Small and medium-sized undertakings are currently defined in that recommendation as undertakings which have fewer than 250 employees and have either an annual turnover not exceeding EUR 40 million or an annual balance-sheet total not exceeding EUR 27 million.

4. In cases covered by this notice the Commission will not institute proceedings either upon application or on its own initiative. Where undertakings assume in good faith that an agreement is covered by this notice, the Commission will not impose fines. Although not binding on them, this notice also intends to give guidance to the courts and authorities of the Member States in their application of Article 81 [101].

5. This notice also applies to decisions by associations of undertakings and to concerted practices.

6. This notice is without prejudice to any interpretation of Article 81 [101] which may be given by the Court of Justice or the Court of First Instance of the European Communities.

## II

7. The Commission holds the view that agreements between undertakings which affect trade between Member States do not appreciably restrict competition within the meaning of Article 81(1) [101]:

> (a) if the aggregate market share held by the parties to the agreement does not exceed 10% on any of the relevant markets affected by the agreement, where the agreement is made between undertakings which are actual or potential competitors on any of these markets (agreements between competitors); or

> (b) if the market share held by each of the parties to the agreement does not exceed 15% on any of the relevant markets affected by the agreement, where the agreement is made between undertakings which are not actual or potential competitors on any of these markets (agreements between non-competitors).

In cases where it is difficult to classify the agreement as either an agreement between competitors or an agreement between non-competitors the 10% threshold is applicable.

8. Where in a relevant market competition is restricted by the cumulative effect of agreements for the sale of goods or services entered into by different suppliers or distributors (cumulative foreclosure effect of parallel networks of agreements having similar effects on the market), the market share thresholds under point 7 are reduced to 5%, both for agreements between competitors and for agreements between non-competitors. Individual suppliers or distributors with a market share

not exceeding 5% are in general not considered to contribute significantly to a cumulative foreclosure effect. A cumulative foreclosure effect is unlikely to exist if less than 30% of the relevant market is covered by parallel (networks of) agreements having similar effects.

9. The Commission also holds the view that agreements are not restrictive of competition if the market shares do not exceed the thresholds of respectively 10%, 15% and 5% set out in point 7 and 8 during two successive calendar years by more than 2 percentage points.

10. In order to calculate the market share, it is necessary to determine the relevant market. This consists of the relevant product market and the relevant geographic market. When defining the relevant market, reference should be had to the notice on the definition of the relevant market for the purposes of Community competition law. The market shares are to be calculated on the basis of sales value data or, where appropriate, purchase value data. If value data are not available, estimates based on other reliable market information, including volume data, may be used.

11. Points 7, 8 and 9 do not apply to agreements containing any of the following hardcore restrictions:

(1) as regards agreements between competitors as defined in point 7, restrictions which, directly or indirectly, in isolation or in combination with other factors under the control of the parties, have as their object:

(a) the fixing of prices when selling the products to third parties;

(b) the limitation of output or sales;

(c) the allocation of markets or customers;

(2) as regards agreements between non-competitors as defined in point 7, restrictions which, directly or indirectly, in isolation or in combination with other factors under the control of the parties, have as their object:

(a) the restriction of the buyer's ability to determine its sale price, without prejudice to the possibility of the supplier imposing a maximum sale price or recommending a sale price, provided that they do not amount to a fixed or minimum sale price as a result of pressure from, or incentives offered by, any of the parties;

(b) the restriction of the territory into which, or of the customers to whom, the buyer may sell the contract goods or services, except the following restrictions which are not hardcore:

- the restriction of active sales into the exclusive territory or to an exclusive customer group reserved to the supplier or allocated by the supplier to another buyer, where such a restriction does not limit sales by the customers of the buyer,

- the restriction of sales to end users by a buyer operating at the wholesale level of trade,

- the restriction of sales to unauthorised distributors by the members of a selective distribution system, and

- the restriction of the buyer's ability to sell components, supplied for the purposes of incorporation, to customers who would use them to manufacture the same type of goods as those produced by the supplier;

(c) the restriction of active or passive sales to end users by members of a selective distribution system operating at the retail level of trade, without prejudice to the possibility of prohibiting a member of the system from operating out of an unauthorised place of establishment;

(d) the restriction of cross-supplies between distributors within a selective distribution system, including between distributors operating at different levels of trade;

(e) the restriction agreed between a supplier of components and a buyer who incorporates those components, which limits the supplier's ability to sell the components as spare parts to end users or to repairers or other service providers not entrusted by the buyer with the repair or servicing of its goods;

(3) as regards agreements between competitors as defined in point 7, where the competitors operate, for the purposes of the agreement, at a different level of the production or distribution chain, any of the hardcore restrictions listed in paragraph (1) and (2) above.

## NOTES AND QUESTIONS

1.    According to *Völk*, is the "minor impact" of an agreement to be assessed by reference to the effect on competition or the effect on trade between Member States?

2.    How does the notion of an "agreement of minor importance" relate, if at all, to the notion of the "effect on trade between Member States"? See in this regard the following extract from the Commission Notice on the appreciable effect on trade, [2004] OJ C 101 [footnotes omitted]:

52. The Commission holds the view that in principle agreements are not capable of appreciably affecting trade between Member States when the following cumulative conditions are met:

(a) The aggregate market share of the parties on any relevant market within the Community affected by the agreement does not exceed 5%, and

(b) In the case of horizontal agreements, the aggregate annual Community turnover of the undertakings concerned in the products covered by the agreement does not exceed 40 million euro. In the case of agreements concerning the joint buying of products the relevant turnover shall be the parties' combined purchases of the products covered by the agreement.

In the case of vertical agreements, the aggregate annual Community turnover of the supplier in the products covered by the agreement does not exceed 40 million euro. In the case of licence agreements the relevant turnover shall be the aggregate turnover of the licensees in the products incorporating the licensed technology and the licensor's own turnover in such products. In cases involving agreements concluded between a buyer and several suppliers the relevant turnover shall be the buyer's combined purchases of the products covered by the agreements.

The Commission will apply the same presumption where during two successive calendar years the above turnover threshold is not exceeded by more than 10% and the above market threshold is not exceeded by more than 2 percentage points. In cases where the agreement concerns an emerging not yet existing market and where as a consequence the parties neither generate relevant turnover nor accumulate any relevant market share, the Commission will not apply this presumption. In such cases appreciability may have to be assessed on the basis of the position of the parties on related product markets or their strength in technologies relating to the agreement.

53. The Commission will also hold the view that where an agreement by its very nature is capable of affecting trade between Member States, for example, because it concerns imports and exports or covers several Member States, there is a rebuttable positive presumption that such effects on trade are appreciable when the turnover of the parties in the products covered by the agreement calculated as indicated in paragraphs 52 and 54 exceeds 40 million euro. In the case of agreements that by their very nature are capable of affecting trade between Member States it can also often be presumed that such effects are appreciable when the market share of the parties exceeds the 5% threshold set out in the previous paragraph. However, this presumption does not apply where the agreement covers only part of a Member State (see paragraph 90 below).

54. With regard to the threshold of 40 million euro (cf. paragraph 52 above), the turnover is calculated on the basis of total Community sales excluding tax during the previous financial year by the undertakings concerned, of the products covered by the agreement (the contract products). Sales between entities that form part of the same undertaking are excluded.

55. In order to apply the market share threshold, it is necessary to determine the relevant market. This consists of the relevant product market and the relevant geographic market. The market shares are to be calculated on the basis of sales value data or, where appropriate, purchase value data. If value data are not available, estimates based on other reliable market information, including volume data, may be used.

56. In the case of networks of agreements entered into by the same supplier with different distributors, sales made through the entire network are taken into account.

57. Contracts that form part of the same overall business arrangement constitute a single agreement for the purposes of the NAAT-rule. Undertakings cannot bring themselves inside these thresholds by dividing up an agreement that forms a whole from an economic perspective.

# STERGIOS DELIMITIS v. HENNINGER BRAU AG
## Case C-234/89, 1991 ECJ CELEX LEXIS 170, [1991] ECR I-935

[Henninger had entered into a contract with Delimitis (the "publican") to let a public house to him. Clause 6 of the contract required the publican to obtain supplies of draft, bottled and canned beer from the brewery, and soft drinks from the brewery's subsidiaries. The range of products in question was determined on the basis of the current price lists of the brewery and its subsidiaries. However, the publican was permitted to purchase beers and soft drinks offered by undertakings established in other Member States.

Under Clause 6 the publican had to purchase a minimum quantity of 132 hectolitres of beer a year. If he bought less, he was required to pay a penalty for non-performance.

The contract also permitted the sale of other beer above this limit. The contract was terminated by Delimitis. The brewery considered that he still owed it some money, comprising rent, a lump sum penalty for failure to observe the minimum purchasing requirement and miscellaneous costs. The brewery deducted that amount from his deposit which had been paid by the publican. Delimitis raised the argument in defense that the contract was unenforceable under para (2) of then Article 85 (EC 81/TFEU101).]

15 [I]n the present case it is necessary to analyse the effects of a beer supply agreement, taken together with other contracts of the same type, on the opportunities of national competitors or those from other Member States, to gain access to the market for beer consumption or to increase their market share and, accordingly, the effects on the range of products offered to consumers.

16 In making that analysis, the relevant market must first be determined. The relevant market is primarily defined on the basis of the nature of the economic activity in question, in this case the sale of beer. Beer is sold through both retail channels and premises for the sale and consumption of drinks. From the consumer's point of view, the latter sector, comprising in particular public houses and restaurants, may be distinguished from the retail sector on the grounds that the sale of beer in public houses does not solely consist of the purchase of a product but is also linked with the provision of services, and that beer consumption in public houses is not essentially dependent on economic considerations. The specific nature of the public house trade is borne out by the fact that the breweries organize specific distribution systems for this sector which require special installations, and that the prices charged in that sector are generally higher than retail prices.

17 It follows that in the present case the reference market is that for the distribution of beer in premises for the sale and consumption of drinks.

18 Secondly, the relevant market is delimited from a geographical point of view. It should be noted that most beer supply agreements are still entered into at a national level. It follows that, in applying the Community competition rules, account is to be taken of the national market for beer distribution in premises for the sale and consumption of drinks.

19 In order to assess whether the existence of several beer supply agreements

impedes access to the market as so defined, it is further necessary to examine the nature and extent of those agreements in their totality, comprising all similar contracts tying a large number of points of sale to several national producers.

20 The existence of a bundle of similar contracts, even if it has a considerable effect on the opportunities for gaining access to the market, is not, however, sufficient in itself to support a finding that the relevant market is inaccessible, inasmuch as it is only one factor, amongst others, pertaining to the economic and legal context in which an agreement must be appraised. The other factors to be taken into account are, in the first instance, those also relating to opportunities for access.

21 In that connection it is necessary to examine whether there are real concrete possibilities for a new competitor to penetrate the bundle of contracts by acquiring a brewery already established on the market together with its network of sales outlets, or to circumvent the bundle of contracts by opening new public houses. For that purpose it is necessary to have regard to the legal rules and agreements on the acquisition of companies and the establishment of outlets, and to the minimum number of outlets necessary for the economic operation of a distribution system. The presence of beer wholesalers not tied to producers who are active on the market is also a factor capable of facilitating a new producer's access to that market since he can make use of those wholesalers's sales networks to distribute his own beer.

22 Secondly, account must be taken of the conditions under which competitive forces operate on the relevant market. In that connection it is necessary to know not only the number and the size of producers present on the market, but also the degree of saturation of that market and customer fidelity to existing brands, for it is generally more difficult to penetrate a saturated market in which customers are loyal to a small number of large producers than a market in full expansion in which a large number of small producers are operating without any strong brand names. The trend in beer sales in the retail trade provides useful information on the development of demand and thus an indication of the degree of saturation of the beer market as a whole. The analysis of that trend is, moreover, of interest in evaluating brand loyalty. A steady increase in sales of beer under new brand names may confer on the owners of those brand names a reputation which they may turn to account in gaining access to the public-house market.

23 If an examination of all similar contracts entered into on the relevant market and the other factors relevant to the economic and legal context in which the contract must be examined shows that those agreements do not have the cumulative effect of denying access to that market to new national and foreign competitors, the individual agreements comprising the bundle of agreements cannot be held to restrict competition within the meaning of Article 85(1) [101] of the Treaty. They do not, therefore, fall under the prohibition laid down in that provision.

24 If, on the other hand, such examination reveals that it is difficult to gain access to the relevant market, it is necessary to assess the extent to which the agreements entered into by the brewery in question contribute to the cumulative effect produced in that respect by the totality of the similar contracts found on that market. Under the Community rules on competition, responsibility for such an effect of closing off the market must be attributed to the breweries which make an

appreciable contribution thereto. Beer supply agreements entered into by breweries whose contribution to the cumulative effect is insignificant do not therefore fall under the prohibition under Article 85 [101] (1)].

25 In order to assess the extent of the contribution of the beer supply agreements entered into by a brewery to the cumulative sealing-off effect mentioned above, the market position of the contracting parties must be taken into consideration

26 The contribution of the individual contracts entered into by a brewery to the sealing-off of that market also depends on their duration. If the duration is manifestly excessive in relation to the average duration of beer supply agreements generally entered into on the relevant market, the individual contract falls under the prohibition under Article 85 [101] (1). A brewery with a relatively small market share which ties its sales outlets for many years may make as significant a contribution to a sealing-off of the market as a brewery in a relatively strong market position which regularly releases sales outlets at shorter intervals.

27 The reply to be given to the first three questions is therefore that a beer supply agreement is prohibited by Article 85(1) [101] of the EEC Treaty, if two cumulative conditions are met. The first is that, having regard to the economic and legal context of the agreement at issue, it is difficult for competitors who could enter the market or increase their market share to gain access to the national market for the distribution of beer in premises for the sale and consumption of drinks. The fact that, in that market, the agreement in issue is one of a number of similar agreements having a cumulative effect on competition constitutes only one factor amongst others in assessing whether access to that market is indeed difficult. The second condition is that the agreement in question must make a significant contribution to the sealing-off effect brought about by the totality of those agreements in their economic and legal context. The extent of the contribution made by the individual agreement depends on the position of the contracting parties in the relevant market and on the duration of the agreement.

The compatibility with Article 85(1) [101] of a beer supply agreement containing an access clause

28 A beer supply agreement containing an access clause differs from the other beer supply agreements normally entered into inasmuch as it authorizes the reseller to purchase beer from other Member States. Such access mitigates, in favour of the beers of other Member States, the scope of the prohibition on competition which in a classic beer supply agreement is coupled with the exclusive purchasing obligation. The scope of the access clause must be assessed in the light of its wording and its economic and legal context.

29 As far as its wording is concerned, it should be noted that the clause affords only very limited access if it is regarded as solely authorizing the reseller himself to purchase competing beers in other Member States. However, the degree of access is greater if it also permits the reseller to sell beers imported from other Member States by other undertakings.

30 As far as its economic and legal context is concerned, it should be pointed out that where, as in this case, one of the other clauses stipulates that a minimum quantity of the beers envisaged in the agreement must be purchased, it is necessary to

examine what that quantity represents in relation to the sales of beer normally achieved in the public house in question. If it appears that the stipulated quantity is relatively large, the access clause ceases to have any economic significance and the prohibition on selling competing beers regains its full force, particularly when under the agreement the obligation to purchase minimum quantities is backed by penalties.

31 If the interpretation of the wording of the access clause or an examination of the specific effect of the contractual clauses as a whole in their economic and legal context shows that the limitation on the scope of the prohibition on competition is merely hypothetical or without economic significance, the agreement in question must be treated in the same way as a classic beer supply agreement. Accordingly, it must be assessed under Article 85(1) [101] of the Treaty in the same way as beer supply agreements in general.

32 The position is different where the access clause gives a national or foreign supplier of beers from other Member States a real possibility of supplying the sales outlet in question. An agreement containing such a clause is not in principle capable of affecting trade between Member States within the meaning of Article 85(1) [101], with the result that it escapes the prohibition laid down in that provision.

33 The reply to the Oberlandesgericht's fourth question should therefore be that a beer supply agreement which permits the reseller to buy beer from other Member States is not such as to affect trade between States provided that the permission corresponds to a real possibility for a national or foreign supplier to supply the reseller with beers from other Member States.

## NOTES AND QUESTIONS

1.  In *Brasserie de Haecht*, referenced in the above case, the ECJ had held that where the market is characterized by a network of very similar exclusive purchasing contracts between the same suppliers and many purchasers (typically, breweries/pubhouses and gasoline suppliers/service station dealers), these agreements must be viewed as a whole, meaning that any one of these agreements may be void under EC 81/TFEU 101). In what ways does the *Delimitis* decision shed further light on this analysis?

2.  Is the Court's approach to networks of agreements justifiable as a matter of interpretation of EC 81/TFEU 101?

## [C]  Extraterritorial Reach

### A AHLSTROM OY AND OTHERS v. COMMISSION
Joined Cases 89/85, 104/85, 114/85, 116-117/85 and 25-129/85, [1988] ECR 5193

[The Plaintiffs including Ahlstrom, a Finnish company had appealed a Commission decision finding that they had operated a cartel in wood pulp. At the time Finland was not a Member State.]

2 The alleged infringements consisted of: concertation between those producers on prices announced each quarter to customers in the Community and on actual transaction prices charged to such customers; price recommendations addressed to its members by the Pulp, Paper and Paperboard Export Association of the United States (formerly named Kraft Export Association and hereinafter referred to as "KEA"), an association of a number of United States producers; and, as regards Fincell, the common sales organization of some 10 Finnish producers, the exchange of individualized data concerning prices with certain other wood pulp producers within the framework of the Research and Information Centre for the European Pulp and Paper Industry which is run by the trust company Fides of Switzerland.

3 [T]he Commission set out the grounds which in its view justify the Community's jurisdiction to apply Article 85 [101] of the Treaty to the concertation in question. It stated first that all the addressees of the decision were either exporting directly to purchasers within the Community or were doing business within the Community through branches, subsidiaries, agencies or other establishments in the Community. It further pointed out that the concertation applied to the vast majority of the sales of those undertakings to and in the Community. Finally it stated that two-thirds of total shipments and 60% of consumption of the product in question in the Community had been affected by such concertation.

4 As regards specifically the Finnish undertakings and their association, Fincell, the Commission stated . . . that the Free Trade Agreement between the Community and Finland (Official Journal 1973, L 328, p. 1) contains "no provision which prevents the Commission from immediately applying Article 85 [101] (1) of the EEC Treaty where trade between Member States is affected".

6 All the applicants which have made submissions regarding jurisdiction maintain first of all that by applying the competition rules of the Treaty to them the Commission has misconstrued the territorial scope of Article 85 [101]. They note that in its judgment of 14 July 1972 in Case 48/69 ICI v. Commission ((1972)) ECR 619 the Court did not adopt the "effects doctrine" but emphasized that the case involved conduct restricting competition within the common market because of the activities of subsidiaries which could be imputed to the parent companies.

7 The applicants which are members of the KEA further submit that the application of Community competition rules to them is contrary to public international law in so far as it is in breach of the principle of non-interference. They maintain that in this case the application of Article 85 [101] harmed the interest of the United States in promoting exports by United States undertakings as recognized in the Webb Pomerene Act of 1918 under which export associations, like the KEA, are exempt from United States anti-trust laws.

\*   \*   \*

Incorrect assessment of the territorial scope of Article 85 [101] of the Treaty and incompatibility of the decision with public international law

(a) The individual undertakings

11 In so far as the submission concerning the infringement of Article 85 [101] of the Treaty itself is concerned, it should be recalled that that provision prohibits all agreements between undertakings and concerted practices which may affect trade between Member States and which have as their object or effect the restriction of competition within the common market.

12 It should be noted that the main sources of supply of wood pulp are outside the Community, in Canada, the United States, Sweden and Finland and that the market therefore has global dimensions. Where wood pulp producers established in those countries sell directly to purchasers established in the Community and engage in price competition in order to win orders from those customers, that constitutes competition within the common market.

13 It follows that where those producers concert on the prices to be charged to their customers in the Community and put that concertation into effect by selling at prices which are actually coordinated, they are taking part in concertation which has the object and effect of restricting competition within the common market within the meaning of Article 85 [101] of the Treaty.

14 Accordingly, it must be concluded that by applying the competition rules in the Treaty in the circumstances of this case to undertakings whose registered offices are situated outside the Community, the Commission has not made an incorrect assessment of the territorial scope of Article 85 [101].

15 The applicants have submitted that the decision is incompatible with public international law on the grounds that the application of the competition rules in this case was founded exclusively on the economic repercussions within the common market of conduct restricting competition which was adopted outside the Community.

16 It should be observed that an infringement of Article 85 [101], such as the conclusion of an agreement which has had the effect of restricting competition within the common market, consists of conduct made up of two elements, the formation of the agreement, decision or concerted practice and the implementation thereof. If the applicability of prohibitions laid down under competition law were made to depend on the place where the agreement, decision or concerted practice was formed, the result would obviously be to give undertakings an easy means of evading those prohibitions. The decisive factor is therefore the place where it is implemented.

17 The producers in this case implemented their pricing agreement within the common market. It is immaterial in that respect whether or not they had recourse to subsidiaries, agents, sub-agents, or branches within the Community in order to make their contacts with purchasers within the Community.

18 Accordingly the Community's jurisdiction to apply its competition rules to such conduct is covered by the territoriality principle as universally recognized in public international law.

19 As regards the argument based on the infringment of the principle of non-interference, it should be pointed out that the applicants who are members of

KEA have referred to a rule according to which where two States have jurisdiction to lay down and enforce rules and the effect of those rules is that a person finds himself subject to contradictory orders as to the conduct he must adopt, each State is obliged to exercise its jurisdiction with moderation. The applicants have concluded that by disregarding that rule in applying its competition rules the Community has infringed the principle of non-interference.

20 There is no need to enquire into the existence in international law of such a rule since it suffices to observe that the conditions for its application are in any event not satisfied. There is not, in this case, any contradiction between the conduct required by the United States and that required by the Community since the Webb Pomerene Act merely exempts the conclusion of export cartels from the application of United States anti-trust laws but does not require such cartels to be concluded.

22 As regards the argument relating to disregard of international comity, it suffices to observe that it amounts to calling in question the Community's jurisdiction to apply its competition rules to conduct such as that found to exist in this case and that, as such, that argument has already been rejected.

23 Accordingly it must be concluded that the Commission's decision is not contrary to Article 85 [101] of the Treaty or to the rules of public international law relied on by the applicants.

## NOTES AND QUESTIONS

1.  To what extent does the above decision recognize the extraterritorial application of EU competition law? International law recognizes the right of a state to assume jurisdiction over conduct that has effects within its territory (the so-called "effects" doctrine). However, it is maintained by many that the parties involved must have at least *intended* their conduct to take effect within the state. Does the ECJ appear to embrace this doctrine in the above case? In your view is this a matter of substantive law or merely a question of enforcement?

2.  This was not the first decision having to do with the subject of extraterritorial jurisdiction, although there had been relatively few cases previously, the most notable being *Imperial Chemical Industries Ltd. v. Commission*, Case 48/69, [1972] ECR 619 where, on this subject the ECJ stated:

> 125 The applicant, whose registered office is outside the Community, argues that the commission is not empowered to impose fines on it by reason merely of the effects produced in the common market by actions which it is alleged to have taken outside the Community.

> 126 Since a concerted practice is involved, it is first necessary to ascertain whether the conduct of the applicant has had effects within the Common Market.

> 127 It appears from what has already been said that the increases at issue were put into effect within the Common Market and concerned competition between producers operating within it.

128 Therefore the actions for which the fine at issue has been imposed constitute practices carried on directly within the common market.

129 It follows from what has been said in considering the submission relating to the existence of concerted practices, that the applicant company decided on increases in the selling prices of its products to users in the common market, and that these increases were of a uniform nature in line with increases decided upon by the other producers involved.

130 By making use of its power to control its subsidiaries established in the community, the applicant was able to ensure that its decision was implemented on that market.

131 The applicant objects that this conduct is to be imputed to its subsidiaries and not to itself.

132 The fact that a subsidiary has separate legal personality is not sufficient to exclude the possibility of imputing its conduct to the parent company.

133 Such may be the case in particular where the subsidiary, although having separate legal personality, does not decide independently upon its own conduct on the market, but carries out, in all material respects, the instructions given to it by the parent company.

134 Where a subsidiary does not enjoy real autonomy in determining its course of action in the market, the prohibitions set out in article 85 [101] (1) may be considered inapplicable in the relationship between it and the parent company with which it forms one economic unit.

135 In view of the unity of the group thus formed, the actions of the subsidiaries may in certain circumstances be attributed to the parent company.

136 It is well-known that at the time the applicant held all or at any rate the majority of the shares in those subsidiaries

137 The applicant was able to exercise decisive influence over the policy of the subsidiaries as regards selling prices in the common market and in fact used this power upon the occasion of the three price increases in question.

138 In effect the telex messages relating to the 1964 increase, which the applicant sent to its subsidiaries in the Common Market, gave the addressees orders as to the prices which they were to charge and the other conditions of sale which they were to apply in dealing with their customers.

139 In the absence of evidence to the contrary, it must be assumed that on the occasion of the increases of 1965 and 1967 the applicant acted in a similar fashion in its relations with its subsidiaries established in the Common Market.

140 In the circumstances the formal separation between these companies, resulting from their separate legal personality, cannot outweigh the unity of their conduct on the market for the purposes of applying the rules on competition.

141 It was in fact the applicant undertaking which brought the concerted practice into being within the Common Market.

142 The submission as to lack of jurisdiction raised by the applicant must therefore be declared to be unfounded.

Has there been an evolution in the Court's approach between *ICI* and the *Woodpulp* cases? Again, does the *ICI* case suggest support for the "effects" doctrine?

3. The classic case on the "effects" doctrine is *United States v. Aluminum Company of America*, 148 F.2d 416 (2d Cir. 1945). In that case, a prosecution by the U.S. Government under section 1 of the Sherman Act, one of the defendants was Aluminum Limited ("Limited"), a Canadian corporation formed to take over properties of the Aluminum Company of America (Alcoa) outside the United States. Not quite half of each company's shares were owned by the same group of individuals. The government alleged that both Limited and Alcoa had participated in a foreign cartel, called the Alliance. The court, however, concluded that Alcoa was not a party to the Alliance and "did not join in any violation of § 1 of the Act, so far as concerned foreign commerce."

Turning to the issue of whether Limited violated the Act, Judge Learned Hand suggested that this depended upon the nature of the Alliance. Created in 1931 pursuant to an agreement among a French corporation, two German companies, one Swiss company, one British company, and Limited, the Alliance was a Swiss corporation. Under an agreement concluded in 1936, each shareholder was to have a fixed free quota of the production of aluminum for every share it held, but as its production exceeded the sum of its quotas, it was to pay a royalty, graduated progressively in proportion to its excess; and these royalties were divided among the shareholders in proportion to their shares. Although the agreement was silent as to imports of aluminum into the United States, when the question arose, all the shareholders agreed that such imports should be included in the quotas.

Judge Hand ruled that jurisdiction would lie if the agreement was intended to affect imports into the United States and there was in fact some effect on them. Judge Hand greatly aided the government's case when he held that once the government had proved an intent to affect imports, the burden of proof shifted to Limited to demonstrate that there was no such effect.

Foreign reaction to *Alcoa*, as well as that of some commentators, was sharp. The decision has been criticized as an "exorbitant" exercise of U.S. antitrust jurisdiction over foreign defendants and transactions. Others have strongly defended the decision. For a suggestion that the criticism of *Alcoa* is based on a misreading of Judge Hand's opinion, see ALAN C. SWAN AND JOHN F. MURPHY, THE REGULATION OF INTERNATIONAL BUSINESS AND ECONOMIC RELATIONS 2d ed. 889-894 (LexisNexis, 1999).

4. Attempts to enforce U.S. antitrust law have generated much controversy over the years; some countries (such as Switzerland) have laws on business secrecy that are invoked to prevent disclosure of documents in that country in proceedings in the U.S. Courts. Other countries have in the past enacted "blocking" statutes that aimed specifically to prohibit compliance with U.S. court orders.

5.   Note that the EU and U.S. have agreed on exchange of information antitrust matters. (See *France v. Commission* Case 327/91, Chapter 7, *supra.* France successfully challenged the Commission's power to conclude this agreement; as indicated there, the Council became involved and gave its approval and an agreement is now in place). There has been interesting discussion around the idea of an international antitrust enforcement agency. What EU legal problems might arise with such a concept?

## [D]  EU Competition Law Interaction with National Competition Laws

### REGULATION 1/2003
### [2003] OJ L1/1

Article 3

Relationship between Articles 81 [101] and 82 [102] of the Treaty and national competition laws

1. Where the competition authorities of the Member States or national courts apply national competition law to agreements, decisions by associations of undertakings or concerted practices within the meaning of Article 81(1) of the Treaty which may affect trade between Member States within the meaning of that provision, they shall also apply Article 81 [101] of the Treaty to such agreements, decisions or concerted practices. Where the competition authorities of the Member States or national courts apply national competition law to any abuse prohibited by Article 82 [102] of the Treaty, they shall also apply Article 82 [102] of the Treaty.

2. The application of national competition law may not lead to the prohibition of agreements, decisions by associations of undertakings or concerted practices which may affect trade between Member States but which do not restrict competition within the meaning of Article 81 [101](1) of the Treaty, or which fulfil the conditions of Article 81 [101](3) of the Treaty or which are covered by a Regulation for the application of Article 81 [101](3) of the Treaty. Member States shall not under this Regulation be precluded from adopting and applying on their territory stricter national laws which prohibit or sanction unilateral conduct engaged in by undertakings.

3. Without prejudice to general principles and other provisions of Community law, paragraphs 1 and 2 [see previous section] do not apply when the competition authorities and the courts of the Member States apply national merger control laws nor do they preclude the application of provisions of national law that predominantly pursue an objective different from that pursued by Articles 81 [101] and 82 [102] of the Treaty.

# NOTES AND QUESTIONS

**1.** Does Regulation 1/2003 help to define the relationship of national and EU competition law?

**2.** The regulation specifically allows, indeed requires, that any application of national competition law to a set of circumstances to which EC 81 or 82/TFEU 101 or 102 are applicable should involve also the application of the latter. Could this lead to two separate sanctions (one national, one Union) for the same conduct? In *Walt Wilhelm and others v. Bundeskartellamt*, Case 14/68 [1968] ECR 1, the Court stated in this regard:

> 11 The possibility of concurrent sanctions need not mean that the possibility of two parallel proceedings pursuing different ends is unacceptable. Without prejudice to the conditions and limits indicated in the answer to the first question, the acceptability of a dual procedure of this kind follows in fact from the special system of the sharing of jurisdiction between the Community and the Member States with regard to cartels. If, however, the possibility of two procedures being conducted separately were to lead to the imposition of consecutive sanctions, a general requirement of natural justice, such as that expressed at the end of the second paragraph of Article 90 of the ECSC Treaty, demands that any previous punitive decision must be taken into account in determining any sanction which is to be imposed. In any case, so long as no regulation has been issued under Article 87 [103] (2)(e), no means of avoiding such a possibility is to be found in the general principles of Community law; this leaves intact the reply given to the first question.

Is the regulation consistent with the Court's conclusion on this point?

**3.** The U.S. federal courts have consistently held that Congress intended the federal anti-trust laws to supplement rather than preempt state anti-trust laws. State anti-trust law is seen as playing an important role in dealing with local interests: *Salveson v. Western States Bankcard Ass'n*, 731 F.2d 1423 (9th Cir. 1984); *Redwood Theaters Inc. v. Festival Enterprises Inc.*, 908 F. 2d 477 (9th Cir. 1990); *Exxon Corp. v. Governor of Maryland*, 437 U.S. 117 (1978).

**4.** There is also potential for conflict between policy decisions to exempt under EC 81/TFEU 101 (3) and EC 82/TFEU 102: see *Tetra Pak Rausing S.A. v. Commission*, Case T-51/89, 1990 ECJ CELEX LEXIS 207, [1990] ECR II-309, in which the Commission found that Tetra Pak, by acquiring, through its purchase of the Liquipak Group, the exclusivity of the patent license granted by the National Research and Development Council to Novus Corp., a company in the Liquipak group, was in breach of EC82/TFEU 102 from the date of that acquisition until the exclusivity came to an end. The exclusive license in question, which qualified for block exemption under Commission Regulation No. 2349/84, related to a new process for packaging long-life milk. Although Tetra Pak informed the Commission in the course of the administrative procedure that it was abandoning all claims to exclusivity in the license, the Commission considered that a finding of infringement should be made by formal decision with a view, *inter alia*, to clarifying its position on the relevant point of law. Since the point raised was unprecedented, no fine was imposed on Tetra Pak. The Court stated:

33 [T]he applicant stresses that the grant of exemption, coupled with the Commission's power to withdraw the benefit of the exemption, gives undertakings a legitimate expectation that they will not be found to have infringed Articles 85 [101] and 86 [102] so long as the Commission has not taken a decision to withdraw the exemption.

34 The applicant considers, contrary to the Commission, that legal certainty cannot be secured by the undertaking applying for negative clearance. The need to make such an application would undermine the efficacy of the block exemption, one of whose primary functions is to enable undertakings to conclude and implement agreements without consulting the Commission. The fact that negative clearance does not afford the same degree of certainty as exemption is shown by the inclusion amongst agreements exempted under Regulation No 2349/84, cited above, of certain agreements which would not normally fall within Article 85(1) [101]. The Commission justified that solution on the ground of the need for legal certainty for the undertakings concerned (paragraph 18 of the preamble and Article 2 of the regulation). More specifically the applicant points out that an application for negative clearance does not preclude the imposition of a fine in respect of conduct subsequent to the application but prior to the decision finding the infringement (Commission Decision 85/79/EEC of 14 December 1984, John Deere, Official Journal 1985 L 35, p. 58, point 38). Furthermore, the applicant continues, the agreement may be unenforceable in national courts pending the Commission's investigation. Finally, negative clearance is not binding on national courts.

35 The Commission argues, to the contrary, that the block-exemption system, including the rules prompted by considerations of legal certainty for undertakings, is concerned only with application of Article 85 [101]. Article 86 [102] establishes a prohibition which applies from the date on which the infringement is committed and, as the Court pointed out in Hoffmann-La Roche, legal certainty can be ensured as regards the application of that provision by an application for negative clearance under Article 2 of Regulation No 17, cited above.

36 The Court of Justice has consistently endorsed the principles of legal certainty and legitimate expectation, by virtue of which the effect of Community legislation must be clear and predictable for those who are subject to it.

37 The question therefore is whether the application of Article 86 [102] becomes unpredictable whenever an agreement fulfils the conditions for block exemption. This Court accepts that, apart from considerations of administrative simplification, one of the main purposes of block exemption is to secure legal certainty for the parties to an agreement as regards the validity of that agreement under Article 85 [101] so long as the Commission has not withdrawn the benefit of block exemption. But that does not discharge undertakings in a dominant position from the obligation to comply with Article 86 [102]. On the contrary, the Court of Justice held in

Case 322/81 Michelin v. Commission 1983 ECR 3461 that any undertaking in a dominant position has "a special responsibility not to allow its conduct to impair genuine undistorted competition on the common market" (paragraph 57). Accordingly, an undertaking cannot rely on the alleged unpredictability of the application of Article 86 in order to escape the prohibition there laid down.

38 In any event, as far as the present case is concerned, although the requirements of legal certainty could not prevent Article 86 being applied to the applicant's acquisition of the exclusive licence, they did none the less prompt the Commission to mitigate the consequences of the infringement for the applicant. The Commission took into account "the fact that the contraventions . . . were relatively novel" by not imposing a fine on the applicant (paragraph 2 of point 62 of the Decision).

**5.**   Note also that the regulation regarding merger control (Council Regulation 139/2004 of 20 January 2004) on the control of concentrations between undertakings) also contains complex provisions relating to the division of responsibilities between the EU and the Member States.

# § 11.03   EXCLUSIVE POWERS — CONSERVATION OF MARINE RESOURCES

## LIEUTENANT COMMANDER A. G. ROGERS v. H. B. L. DARTHENAY
### Case 87/82, [1983] ECR 1579

[The Plymouth Magistrates' Court (UK) (the lowest rung of the criminal court system in the UK)) referred to the Court of Justice for a preliminary ruling four questions on the interpretation of Regulation No. 2527/80 of 28 September 1980 laying down technical measures for the conservation of fishery resources. The questions arose in the course of a prosecution brought by Lieutenant Commander Rogers, Royal Navy, for the Ministry of Agriculture, against the master of a French fishing boat called the "Christine Marie", Mr Darthenay, regarding infringement of UK secondary legislation laying down measures relating to boats and methods of fishing.]

3 Article 7 of Regulation No. 2527/80, the validity of which was extended by subsequent regulations until 31 October 1981, provides:

"No device shall be used by means of which the mesh in any part of a fishing net is obstructed or otherwise effectively diminished. This provision does not exclude the use of the devices referred to in the detailed implementing rules to be adopted in accordance with the procedure laid down in Article 20."

4 According to Article 20, detailed rules for the implementation of the regulation are to be adopted in accordance with the procedure laid down in Articles 31 (2) and 32 of Council Regulation No. 100/76 of 29 January 1976 on the common organization of the market in fishery products . . . Article 31 sets up a Management Committee for Fishery Products which delivers an opinion in accordance with Article 32 (1) and (2).

Article 32 (3) authorizes the Commission, or in some cases the Council, to adopt the appropriate measures. In the event, no detailed implementing rules were adopted before the end of the period of validity of Regulation No. 2527/80.

5 During that period the British Government issued Statutory Instrument No. 1994 of 1980, Article 8 of which provides:

"(1) A trawl, Danish seine or similar net carried

(a) in any British fishing boat registered in the United Kingdom, or

(b) in any waters adjacent to the United Kingdom and within British fishery limits by a fishing boat not registered in the United Kingdom and registered in any country

shall not have attached to it a device having the effect of obstructing or diminishing the mesh in contravention of Article 7 of the Council Regulation.

(2) Notwithstanding paragraph (1) of this article, any canvas, netting or other material may be attached to the underside of the cod-end of a net for the purpose of preventing or reducing wear and tear, if it is fastened to the cod-end only along the forward and lateral edges of such canvas, netting or other material."

6 On 5 August 1981, the fishing boat "Christine Marie" was fishing within British fishery limits and using, as was stated by the national court, "a trawl, Danish Seine or similar net having attached to it (on the top of the cod-end) a device, a second piece of net".

7 In the course of the prosecution the accused contended that Article 7 of Regulation No. 2527/80 did not apply to him on the grounds, first, that the exceptions provided for by the second sentence of Article 7 had not been adopted by the Community at the material time and secondly that, since the Member States were no longer entitled to exercise any power of their own in the matter of conservation measures in their territorial waters, the United Kingdom did not have the power to adopt measures such as those contained in Article 8 (2) of Statutory Instrument No. 1994 of 1980.

\* \* \*

9 The first question [referred by the Magistrate] asks whether Article 7 of Regulation No. 2527/80 can have effect even though the detailed implementing measures provided for in the second sentence of that article were not adopted by the competent Community authorities.

10 The purpose of Regulation No. 2527/80 is to ensure the protection of fishing stocks and also a balanced exploitation of the resources of the sea in the interests both of fishermen and of consumers. It follows that the prohibition laid down in the first sentence of Article 7 of the regulation constitutes an essential provision for the achievement of the objective pursued, since without that prohibition there would be no effective conservation measure at Community level.

11 Moreover, that first sentence of Article 7 of Regulation No. 2527/80 is an independent and perfectly clear provision, creating a prohibition with immediate effect which cannot depend upon the adoption of the detailed implementing rules

provided for in the second sentence of Article 7.

12 The expression "detailed implementing rules" used in the second sentence of Article 7 refers to the determination of certain fishing attachments the use of which appears to be compatible with the prohibition laid down in the first sentence and not to implementing measures necessary to ensure the full effect of that prohibition. Consequently, the fact that the detailed implementing rules referred to in Article 7 have not been adopted cannot in any event prevent the prohibition laid down in the first sentence of that article from taking full effect.

13 The answer to the first question should therefore be that the prohibition in Article 7 of Regulation No. 2527/80 takes full effect even though the detailed implementing rules provided for in the second sentence of that article have not been adopted.

*   *   *

15 In the third question the national court, having established that the detailed implementing rules provided for in the second sentence of Article 7 have not been adopted, refers to the law applicable in this case. In that regard it must be borne in mind that since the expiry on 1 January 1979 of the transitional period provided for in Article 102 of the Act of Accession the power to adopt, as part of the common fisheries policy, measures to conserve the resources of the sea vests fully and finally in the Community.

16 Consequently, it is necessary first to examine whether Article 7 may be interpreted in such a way that, even in the absence of the detailed implementing rules provided for in the second sentence, it is possible to infer directly from that provision whether and on what conditions the use of devices for the protection of nets is permitted.

17 In this regard it should be noted that until the end of the transitional period the use of devices for the protection of fishing nets was permitted under the rules and practice of several Member States and that Article 7 does not intend to substitute for such a possibility a general prohibition on the use of all, even protective, devices.

18 Such an interpretation would in fact be contrary to the purpose of Article 7, the first sentence of which, although it lays down a general prohibition, nevertheless does not exclude the use of certain devices. It is true that the aim of the first sentence of Article 7, which is to protect fishing stocks, requires that the mesh of fishing nets may not be obstructed or diminished; however, that requirement must be qualified inasmuch as account should be taken of the fact that fishermen need to use certain types of device in order to protect their fishing nets.

19 It would therefore be contrary to the scheme of Regulation No. 2527/80 if such protection of fishing nets could not be taken into consideration simply because detailed implementing rules have not been adopted.

20 That is also clear from the terms of Article 7. Indeed, the beginning of the second sentence ("This provision does not exclude the use of the devices . . .") and also the expression "detailed implementing rules", used to qualify the provisions to be adopted, show clearly that all the rules, including therefore the permission to use devices for the protection of nets, must have immediate effect and that the essential

task of the Commission and the Management Committee was merely to give formal expression to that permission in implementing legislation.

21 In the absence of such legislation, it is for the competent courts to fill the resulting lacuna in a manner which is consistent with the aim of protecting fishing stocks and which also takes into account the fact that protection of fishing nets should be permitted.

## NOTES AND QUESTIONS

1.   Does the ECJ take the view in *Rogers* that EU law has "occupied the field"? What specifically caused the Court to take the view that Member States could not adopt legislation in this particular area?

2.   In the *Rogers* case, note that the issue arose in a magistrate's court. What guidance did the magistrates receive as to how they should apply conservation policy here? Were they entitled to regard the UK legislation as irrelevant or, on the contrary, highly relevant to determining the scope of the right to use protective devices for fishing nets?

3.   The Court has held that where the Member States continue to have responsibilities in an area of exclusive competence (such as Fisheries), they can do so only by means of a specific authorization: *Donckerwolcke*, Case 41/76, [1976] ECR 1921 at para 32. The exclusive competence in the case of fisheries was actually explicitly conferred by Article 102 of the Act of Accession of the UK, Denmark and Ireland.

4.   For a parallel case to *Rogers v. Darthenay*, see *Commission v. United Kingdom* Case 804/79 [1981] ECR 2403. A common Fisheries policy was adopted finally in 1983, reformed by a series of measures from 1999 to 2002; See Regulation 104/2000 [2000] OJ L17/22; also Regulation 2371/2002 [2002] OJ L358/59. A guidance and guarantee fund similar to that for agriculture is now governed by Reg. 1263/1999 [1999] OJ L161/54.

5.   For a discussion of exclusive competences, see R. Schütze, *Dual federalism constitutionalised: The emergence of exclusive competences in the EC legal order*, (2007) 32 EL Rev. 3.

## § 11.04   SHARED POWERS — AGRICULTURE AND FISHERIES

### [A]   Preemption?

## PIGS MARKETING BOARD v. RAYMOND REDMOND
### Case 83/78, [1978] ECR 2347

[Northern Ireland had introduced regulations setting up a Pigs Marketing Board which was granted exclusive rights to purchase pigs from producers who had to be registered with the Board. Redmond had transported 75 bacon pigs without being covered by an authorization from the board and was being prosecuted following a complaint by the board to the resident magistrate, Armagh, for a breach of the regulations.]

11 The defendant argued in his defence before the resident magistrate that the provisions of the Pigs Marketing Scheme and the movement of pigs regulations under which he was charged were incompatible with the provisions of Community law, in particular with the regulations on the common organization of the market in pigmeat and the provisions of the treaty with regard to competition.

\* \* \*

51 It follows from the foregoing that the decisive questions for the solution of the case before the resident magistrate concern the compatibility with the provisions relating to the free movement of goods and the common organization of the market in pigmeat of a market system laid down by the legislation of a Member State and managed by a body which has power, thanks to the compulsory powers vested in it, to control the sector of the market in question by measures such as subjecting the marketing of the goods to a requirement that the producer shall be registered with the body in question, the prohibition of any sale otherwise than to that body or through its agency, on the conditions determined by it, and the prohibition of any unauthorized transport of the goods in question.

\* \* \*

56 . . . [O]nce the Community has, pursuant to Article 40 [40] of the Treaty, legislated for the establishment of the common organization of the market in a given sector, Member States are under an obligation to refrain from taking any measure which might undermine or create exceptions to it.

57 With a view to applying that statement in the case of the pigs marketing scheme it should be borne in mind that the common organization of the market in pigmeat, like the other common organizations, is based on the concept of an open market to which every producer has free access and the functioning of which is regulated solely by the instruments provided for by that organization.

58 Hence any provisions or national practices which might alter the pattern of imports or exports or influence the formation of market prices by preventing producers from buying and selling freely within the state in which they are established, or in any other Member State, in conditions laid down by Community rules and from taking advantage directly of intervention measures or any other measures for regulating the market laid down by the common organization are incompatible with the principles of such organization of the market.

60 Any intervention by a Member State or by its regional or subordinate authorities in the market machinery apart from such intervention as may be specifically laid down by the Community Regulation runs the risk of obstructing the functioning of the common organization of the market and of creating unjustified advantages for certain groups of producers or consumers to the prejudice of the economy of other Member States or of other economic groups within the Community.

61 In this respect it is impossible to accept the Board's argument to the effect that its price policy is dependent upon market trends and accordingly does not perturb

the formation of prices according to the regulation.

62 Indeed this situation by no means excludes the fact that the national provisions in dispute have the effect of placing producers in a position of complete dependence on the board and forbidding them access to the market in the conditions laid down by the treaty and the common organization set up by virtue of the Treaty.

63 In this respect account be taken of article 2 of Regulation No 2759/75 which lays down a series of measures intended to encourage action by trade and joint trade organizations to facilitate the adjustment of supply to market requirements by reason in particular of a better organization of production, processing or marketing of the products in question.

64 However, that provision makes possible the institution of such measures only within the framework of a Community procedure intended to guarantee that the general interests of the community are safeguarded and that the objectives laid down by article 39 [39] of the Treaty are observed.

65 The questions referred to the court by the Resident Magistrate should therefore be answered to the effect that a marketing system on a national or regional scale set up by the legislation of a Member State and administered by a body which, by means of compulsory powers vested in it, is empowered to control the sector of the market in question or a part of it by measures such as subjecting the marketing of the goods to a requirement that the producer shall be registered with the body in question, the prohibition of any sale otherwise than to that body or through its agency on the conditions determined by it, and the prohibition of all transport of the goods in question otherwise than subject to the authorization of the body in question are to be considered as incompatible with the requirements of articles 30 [34] and 34[35] of the EEC Treaty and of Regulation No 2759/75 on the common organization of the market in pigmeat.

## NOTES AND QUESTIONS

1. Does this case suggest that common organizations of markets within the framework of the Common Agricultural Policy (CAP) preempt national legislation regulating such markets? Note in particular the references to articles EC 28/TFEU 34 and EC 29/TFEU 35. Do those references suggest an alternative approach?

2. For a case involving direct interference with the intervention mechanisms, see *Commission v. Greece*, Case C-61/90, 1992 ECJ CELEX LEXIS 149, 1992 ECR I-2407. In *P.J. Van der Hulst's Zonen v. Produktschap voor Siegewassen*, Case 51/74, [1975] ECR 79, Van der Hulst's cultivated and sold flower bulbs. It objected to payment of certain sums claimed from it as levies under Dutch law, chargeable on bulbs of the 1972 season. These levies were a "surplus" levy and a "trade" levy in the bulb sector.

The effect of the regulations governing the surplus levy was that every purchaser in possession of a trade card issued by the trade organization in the ornamental plants sector benefited from a reduction on the selling price and that every seller was obliged to pay the levy upon the sale of bulbs to a purchaser, including every foreign purchaser, not in possession of the card, the allowance and the levy being of the same amount. The levy was not charged in cases where the bulb producer used the bulbs for flower growing on his own premises and, for a certain time in 1973, this also applied in the case of a purchaser in possession of a trade card who used the bulbs himself for flower growing. The revenue from the levy was paid into a fund whose main purpose was to finance the purchase of bulbs that were submitted for destruction because they had not fetched on the market the minimum price fixed by the fund.

The Court's answer was as follows:

18 The second question asks the Court to rule whether Article 40 [40] of the Treaty and Article 1 of Regulation (EEC) No 234/68 or any other provision or general principle of Community law mean that, as regards the sector defined in Article 1 of Regulation (EEC) No 234/68, Dutch bodies having legislative capacity are no longer permitted to make any market-regulatory provisions such as that contained in the 'Regulation — Surplus Levy' and in the 'Regulation — Trade Levy' except for the purpose of carrying into effect the provisions of Regulation (EEC) No 234/68 or any other provisions of Community law.

19 Article 40 [40] (2) of the Treaty provides that a common organization of agricultural markets shall be established taking the form of common rules on competition, compulsory coordination of the various national market organizations, or a European market organization.

20 Under Article 40 [40] (3) the common organization established in one or other of these forms may include all measures required to attain the objectives of the common agricultural policy, in particular regulation of prices, aids for the production and marketing of the various products, storage and carry-over arrangements, and common machinery for stabilizing imports or exports.

21 Article 1 of Regulation No 234/68 provides that the common organization of the market established thereunder shall comprise common quality standards and a trading system in the sector concerned.

22 Article 12 of the Regulation provides that the Council shall add further provisions to the Regulation as may be required in the light of experience.

23 The second recital of the preamble to Regulation No 234/68 states that the production of live trees and other plants, bulbs, roots and the like, cut flowers and ornamental foliage is of particular importance to the agricultural economy of certain regions of the Community and declares the need to promote the rational marketing of such production and to ensure stable market conditions.

24 As regards bulbs in particular, it is not disputed that exports from the Netherlands represent more than 90% of the total exports from Member States.

25 Once the Community has, pursuant to Article 40 [40] of the Treaty, legislated for establishment of a common organization of the market in a

given sector, Member States are under an obligation to refrain from taking any measure which might undermine or create exceptions to it.

26 For this reason it is first of all necessary to consider whether a set of regulations such as those under review is compatible with Regulation No 234/68 having regard not only to the express provisions of the legislation but also to its aims and objects.

27 Regulation No 234/68 contains no reference, either in positive or in negative terms, to the compatibility or otherwise of national regulations, present or future, with the common market organization established by its provisions.

28 Consideration must therefore by given to the question whether the existence of a national intervention mechanism, such as that established by the Netherlands regulations, is of such a nature as to undermine the aims and objects of Regulation No 234/68.

29 When the volume of national production is of such magnitude in the Common Market as that of bulb production in the Netherlands, a mechanism of this kind can be of value in promoting the rational marketing of production and ensuring stable market conditions not only in the Member State concerned but also throughout the Community.

30 It is still necessary, however, to study not only the national intervention mechanism as a whole but also its constituent parts, especially the quality standards which must be satisfied by products to qualify for intervention, in their relationship to the quality standards fixed by the Community for the marketing of the products.

31 In this connexion national quality standards which are less demanding than Community standards may tend to encourage the production of unmarketable bulbs.

32 If the extra cost which this imposes on the fund financing the intervention is covered by the levy and thus distributed among the marketed products, including exports, this militates against the aim pursued by the common organization of the market and the regulations are to that extent incompatible with it.

Could the Court have considered that articles EC 28/TFEU 34 or EC 29/TFEU 35 were relevant here? Do you think there has been a change in approach compared with the *Redmond* case? In particular, does the ECJ's approach seem similar to the approach that might be adopted in the United States with respect to federal preemption? Should one approach this topic from the point of view of the supremacy of EU law over national laws, or is it a question of the application of EC 10/TEU 4? Are these approaches in fact the same? Note also in this connection the Court's remarks in *Commission v. France (Milk Substitutes)*, Case 216/84, 1988 ECJ CELEX LEXIS 3, [1988] ECR 793:

18 As for the French Government's argument that the prohibition on the marketing of milk substitutes in France is consonant with the Common Agricultural Policy, it must first be observed that milk products are subject

to a common organization of the market, which is designed to stabilize the milk market, inter alia, by means of intervention measures. It appears from the established case law of the Court that once the Community has established a common market organization in a particular sector, the Member States must refrain from taking any unilateral measure which consequently falls within the competence of the Community. It is therefore for the Community and not for a Member State to seek a solution to this problem in the context of the Common Agricultural Policy.

19 In this connection, it must be added that, even if they support a common policy of the Community, national measures may not conflict with one of the fundamental principles of the Community — in this case that of the free movement of goods — unless they are justified by reasons recognized by Community law.

## [B] Interaction with National Policies in Other Areas

### R (ON THE APPLICATION OF MILK MARQUE LTD AND ANOTHER) (DAIRY INDUSTRY FEDERATION, THIRD PARTY) v. COMPETITION COMMISSION AND OTHERS
Case C-137/00, 2003 ECJ CELEX LEXIS 78, [2003] ECR I-7975

[The UK Competition authority had concluded that, under UK competition law, Milk Marque, a farmer's co-operative, had a monopoly position in the supply of milk in the UK and had abused that position, *inter alia* by engaging in practices that kept the price of milk above where it would have been under normal competitive conditions.]

46 Milk Marque and the NFU submit that it is clear from the Court's case-law that the national authorities are not competent to apply national competition law, such as the FTA or the CA, in a sector covered by a common organisation of the market. They consider that the Community legislation establishing the common organisation of the market in milk and milk products is exhaustive and confers exclusive competence on the Community.

47 The Community's exclusive competence precludes the Member States or their emanations from adopting measures which seek to fix, directly or indirectly, a uniform producer price for milk. Furthermore, the national measures do not need to relate directly to prices for them to infringe the exclusive competence of the Community. The Court has recognised that even measures outside the agricultural sector may infringe the exclusive competence conferred on the Community.

48 As regards the main proceedings, Milk Marque and the NFU submit that the measures adopted by the Secretary of State constitute unilateral action by the State with a view to affecting price formation and the marketing of milk in a market covered by a common organisation. The aim of the measures is to bring about a fall in average milk prices. According to them, that objective was pursued notwithstanding that the Milk Marque producer price has consistently been significantly below the target price set by the Community. In other words, the national measures seek to establish a producer price at a level that is even lower than the target price.

49 Furthermore, the implementation of those measures has as its object and effect the reduction of producer prices and consumer prices to a level which the national authorities have unilaterally determined to be in the national public interest, irrespective of what is in the Community public interest.

50 Finally, Milk Marque and the NFU submit that activities undertaken in the context of a common organisation of the market are subject to the application of competition law only by virtue of the first paragraph of Article 36 EC [42], which acknowledges that the common agricultural policy takes precedence over the objectives of the Treaty in the field of competition, and of Regulation No 26. The parallel application of national and Community competition law would produce conflicts because the operation of Community competition law must take account of the objectives of the common agricultural policy and accordingly subjects agricultural cooperatives to the regime established by Regulation No 26. The operation of national competition law, on the other hand, is not so limited and allows for the adoption of measures which cannot lawfully be taken under Regulation No 26.

51 The United Kingdom Government argues that, if the Community had wished to exclude the application of national competition law from the agricultural sector, it could have made use of a mechanism which has always been available to it. Community regulations and directives could have been adopted under Article 83[103](2)(e) EC. However, notwithstanding the existence of that mechanism, no relevant regulation or directive has been adopted. National competition law is therefore, in principle, fully capable of applying to the agricultural sector.

52 With regard to the argument that the EC Treaty has effected a complete transfer of competence from national authorities to the Community in relation to the common agricultural policy as a whole and the objectives set out in Article 33 EC [39] in particular, the United Kingdom Government observes that a common organisation of a market cannot exist in a vacuum, divorced from the national laws and measures that are necessary to give it effect. The United Kingdom Government points out, as an example, that the application of national criminal law in a sector covered by a common organisation of the market may not only be permitted but required as a matter of Community law.

53 In the same way, Community competition law does not constitute a complete code because it applies only if there is an effect on trade between Member States. To exclude the application of national competition law, and thereby to allow no control in circumstances where there is no effect on inter-State trade, would be to allow even seriously anti-competitive agreements and abuses of power, such as those identified in the Competition Commission's report.

54 The Dairy Industry Federation (hereinafter the DIF) submits that the relevant Community rules do not preclude the application of national competition law in all circumstances relating to the manner in which producers of milk organise themselves into cooperatives and conduct themselves in regard to the sale and processing of their milk. Referring to the Court's case-law, it submits that the adoption of measures on the basis of national law is precluded by the existence of Community legislation only where the adoption of such measures would prejudice the full and uniform application of Community law or the effects of measures taken or to be taken to implement it.

55 The Commission infers . . . that no provision in Community law precludes Article 82 [102] EC from being applied in the normal way in the agricultural sector. By the same token, there is nothing to preclude Member States from applying analogous provisions of national law in that sector.

56 According to the Commission, in the main proceedings, the application of the FTA to Milk Marque could not in any way jeopardise the application of the Community competition rules, as the Commission has not initiated any steps against Milk Marque under those rules.

Findings of the Court

57. It must first of all be observed that the maintenance of effective competition on the market for agricultural products is one of the objectives of the common agricultural policy and the common organisation of the relevant markets.

58. Whilst art 36 EC [42] has conferred on the Council of the European Union responsibility for determining the extent to which the Community competition rules are applicable to the production of and trade in agricultural products, in order to take account of the particular position of the markets for those products that provision nevertheless establishes the principle that the Community competition rules are applicable in the agricultural sector.

59. That conclusion is also confirmed both by the first recital in the preamble to Regulation 26/62 and by the court's case law, according to which the common organisations of the market are based on the concept of an open market to which every producer has free access under effective conditions of competition.

60. In addition, the importance of competition in the context of the common organisation of the market in milk and milk products is seen clearly in art 25(3)(a) of Regulation 804/68, which provides that, where a Member State is authorised to grant to a national organisation the special rights provided for in art 25(1), it must ensure that the exercise of those rights 'does not affect competition in the agricultural sector more than is absolutely necessary'.

61. As the common organisations of the markets in agricultural products are therefore not a competition-free zone, it must be pointed out that, in accordance with settled case law, Community competition law and national competition law apply in parallel, since they consider restrictive practices from different points of view. Whereas arts 81[101] and 82 EC [102] regard them in the light of the obstacles which may result from trade between Member States, national law proceeds on the basis of the considerations peculiar to it and considers restrictive practices only in that context.

62. The argument advanced by Milk Marque and the NFU to the effect that that case law cannot be transposed to the common organisation of the market in milk and milk products cannot be upheld.

63. Admittedly, in a sector covered by a common organisation of the market, a fortiori where that organisation is based on a common price system, the Member States are under an obligation to refrain from taking any measures which might undermine or create exceptions to it. In particular, Member States can no longer

take action, through national provisions taken unilaterally, affecting the machinery of price formation at the production and marketing stages established under the common organisation.

64. However, having regard to the fact that, as is clear from paras 57 to 60 of this judgment, the maintenance of effective competition is one of the objectives of the common organisation of the market in milk and milk products, it must be observed that any measure adopted by the authorities of a Member State in application of national competition law cannot be regarded, by its very nature, as undermining or creating exceptions to the functioning of the common organisation of the market. Moreover, national measures which seek to eliminate a distortion of competition which is the result of abuse of the powerful position enjoyed by an agricultural co-operative on the national market cannot a priori be regarded as measures affecting the machinery of price formation established under the common organisation at Community level, within the meaning of the case law cited at para 63 of this judgment.

65. Next, if arts 32 [38] to 38 EC [44] and Regulation 26/62 and Regulation 804/68 were interpreted as meaning that, in the sector governed by the common organisation of the market in milk and milk products, the competence of the authorities of the Member States to act in application of their national competition law is wholly excluded, there would be no means, in that sector, of eliminating distortions of competition where there is no Community dimension.

66. Finally, given that the scope of the Community competition rules is not the same as the scope of national competition rules, the mere fact that in art 36 EC [42] and Regulation 26/62 the Community legislature has endeavoured to reconcile the objectives of the common agricultural policy with Community competition policy does not necessarily mean that any application of national competition law conflicts with art 36 EC [42] and Regulation 26/62.

67. Having regard to those considerations, it must be concluded that arts 32 [38] to 38 EC [44] and Regulation 26/62 and Regulation 804/68 must be interpreted as meaning that, in the sector governed by the common organisation of the market in milk and milk products, the national authorities in principle retain jurisdiction to apply their national competition law to a milk producers' co-operative in a powerful position on the national market.

68. It is thus necessary, secondly, to consider the limits of that jurisdiction and whether they are exceeded by the adoption of measures such as those at issue in the main proceedings.

*    *    *

80. It must first of all be observed that . . . where there is a regulation establishing the common organisation of the market in a given sector the Member States are under an obligation to refrain from taking any measures which might undermine or create exceptions to it.

81. Secondly, it is also clear from settled case law that, even in regard to the competition rules of the Treaty, art 36 EC [42] gives precedence to the objectives of the common agricultural policy over those in relation to competition policy.

82. With regard to measures such as those at issue in the main proceedings, it is common ground that they do not undermine an express provision of the rules establishing the common organisation of the market in milk and milk products.

83. The question then arises as to whether such measures, in the light of the means employed to implement them, produce effects which are likely to impede the functioning of the mechanisms provided for by the common organisation concerned.

84. As is clear from the documents before the court, the purpose of the national measures at issue in the main proceedings is to reduce the market power of Milk Marque and its ability to increase the price of milk charged by member producers beyond levels judged to be competitive, and to do so in the interests of both producers and consumers.

85. . . . [T]he essential aim of the machinery of the common organisation of the market in milk and milk products is to achieve price levels at the production and wholesale stages which take into account both the interests of Community production as a whole in the relevant sector and those of consumers and which guarantee market supplies without encouraging overproduction.

86. In consequence, the objectives of that common organisation cannot be compromised by national measures such as those at issue in the main proceedings since they do not as such affect the fixing of prices but rather seek to safeguard the proper working of the machinery for setting prices in order to achieve price levels which serve the interests of both producers and consumers.

87. With regard, in particular, to the question whether national measures such as those at issue in the main proceedings infringe the relevant Community legislation because the milk price of Milk Marque producers was lower than the target price laid down by Regulation 1190/97 before the national authorities took action, it must be observed that that fact alone is not sufficient to render those measures unlawful under Community law.

88. First of all, this sort of price guideline is a political objective at Community level and is not a guarantee to all producers in every Member State that they will earn an income corresponding to the target price.

89. Secondly, given that . . . the maintenance of effective competition is one of the objectives of the common organisation of the market in milk and milk products, art 3(1) of Regulation 804/68 cannot be interpreted as meaning that producers of milk have the right to seek to earn an income corresponding to the target price by any means, including those that may constitute abuses or be anti-competitive.

90. The arguments advanced by Milk Marque and the NFU, however, seem to imply that the Competition Commission in its report and the Secretary of State in the subsequent decisions adopted by him failed to have regard to the fact that one of the objectives of the common agricultural policy is to ensure a fair standard of living for the agricultural community, in particular, by increasing the individual earnings of persons engaged in agriculture, and gave too much weight to the objective of ensuring that supplies reach consumers at reasonable prices.

91. In that connection, it must be observed that, in pursuing the various aims laid down in art 33 [39] EC, the Community institutions have a permanent duty to

reconcile the individual aims. Although that duty to reconcile any contradictions means that no single aim may be pursued in isolation in such a way as to make the achievement of the others impossible, the Community institutions may allow one of them temporary priority in order to satisfy the demands of the economic or other conditions in light of which their decisions are made.

92. Whilst it is true that that case law has been developed in relation to acts by the Community institutions in the area of the common organisation of the agricultural markets, the fact remains that it may be applied by analogy to acts of the national authorities in the exercise of their jurisdiction in the area of national competition policy. Given that, as is clear from paras 80 and 81 of this judgment, in the course of those acts, the national authorities are under an obligation to respect the objectives of the common agricultural policy as set out in art 33 EC [39], they must also ensure that any contradictions between those objectives are reconciled.

93. In this case, in order to reply to the question whether the Competition Commission's report and the decisions of the Secretary of State reconciled, in an acceptable manner, the various objectives laid down in art 33 EC [39] or whether in fact they had the effect of favouring the objective of ensuring reasonable prices in supplies to consumers to the point of rendering the realisation of the other objectives impossible, a thorough investigation is required in particular into the situation in the milk market in the United Kingdom during the relevant period and into the effects on that market of the application of the measures at issue. Since such an investigation necessarily involves the finding of facts in the main proceedings, it is for the national court to undertake it.

94. Having regard to all of those considerations, the reply to the first question must be that arts 32 [38] to 38 EC [44] and Regulation 26/62 and Regulation 804/68 must be interpreted as meaning that, in the sector governed by the common organisation of the market in milk and milk products, the national authorities in principle retain jurisdiction to apply national competition law to a milk producers' co-operative in a powerful position on the national market.

Where the national competition authorities act in the sector governed by the common organisation of the market in milk and milk products, they are under an obligation to refrain from adopting any measure which might undermine or create exceptions to that common organisation.

Measures taken by national competition authorities in the sector governed by the common organisation of the market in milk and milk products may not, in particular, produce effects which are such as to impede the working of the machinery provided for by that common organisation. However, the mere fact that the prices charged by a dairy co-operative were already lower than the target price for milk before those authorities intervened is not sufficient to render the measures taken by them in relation to that co-operative in application of national competition law unlawful under Community law.

Furthermore, such measures may not compromise the objectives of the common agricultural policy as set out in art 33(1) EC [39]. The national competition authorities are under an obligation to ensure that any contradictions between the various objectives laid down in art 33 EC [39] are reconciled where necessary, without giving any one of them so much weight as to render the achievement of the others impossible.

## NOTES AND QUESTIONS

1. The arguments of the plaintiffs here suggested that a common organization of the market under the agricultural policy could be viewed as completely occupying the field, thus excluding any legislation that might impinge upon it. This would be a very broad form of preemption. Consider the UK government's reply. How did the Court reconcile the enforcement of national competition law with the common organization?

2. The Commission argued that the structure of the EU market organization works to promote competition. Do you agree?

## DE SAMVIRKENDE DANSKE LANDBOFORENINGER v. MINISTRY OF FISCAL AFFAIRS
### Case 297/82, [1983] ECR 3299

[This case concerned the interaction of the common agricultural policy (CAP) with social and taxation policies of a Member State (Denmark). It arose at a time when the CAP was under severe strain from fluctuating interest rates. Intervention prices were fixed in ECU (q.v. Chapter 2) which was simply a basket of currencies, with each national currency comprising a portion of the basket based on its GDP. As the Danish Krone dropped in value against the overall basket, the intervention price in ECU became higher when translated into that currency, which would have artificially inflated farmers' incomes. Although EU law sought to counteract this effect by a system of monetary compensation amounts (described in Note 1) the Danish government did not wish to use this option and chose instead to impose additional taxes on income.]

2 [A]t the end of 1979, the Danish Government adopted an economic programme which, in order to reduce the adverse balance of payments and to improve the employment situation, provided in particular for the growth in income for all sectors of society to be checked and for the burdens thereby imposed upon the population to be fairly shared. Since the devaluation of the Danish krone formed an essential part of that plan, devaluation was effected on [28] November 1979 to the extent of 4.76% against the other currencies in the European Monetary System. However, the Danish Government wished the central rate for the Danish krone to correspond to the agricultural conversion rate in relation to the European Currency Unit [ECU], in order to avoid the introduction of monetary compensatory amounts. Therefore on 3 December 1979 the Council, at the request of the Danish Government, devalued the representative rate of the Danish krone by 4.63% against the ECU in the agricultural sector. (Council Regulation No. 2717/79 Official Journal, L 309, p1.)]

*    *    *

3 That devaluation resulted in an increase in agricultural prices expressed in Danish kroner, which ought under normal circumstances to have brought about a signifi-

cant increase in income for Danish agriculture. In order to offset that increase in income, which was regarded as inconsistent with the provisions of the above-mentioned programme, the Danish Government submitted on 4 December 1979 a draft Law concerning land tax on agricultural property. The Law was adopted by the Folketing [Danish Parliament] on 21 December 1979, confirmed on 28 December 1979 and promulgated as Law No. 541.

4 The tax, which operated only during 1980, was assessed by reference to the value of property determined on the basis of a general assessment of the commercial value of the land, without taking into account the amount or nature of the agricultural production actually obtained from it.

5 The Samvirkende Danske Landboforeninger [Federation of Danish Farmers' Associations], acting on behalf of three farmers who owned their land and who challenged the validity of the tax, brought an action before the Ostre Landsret, claiming that the Land tax Law in respect of agricultural property was to be regarded as incompatible with the spirit and conditions for implementation of the EEC Treaty and of the Common Agricultural Policy, in so far as its object and effect were, on the one hand, to neutralize the effects of a measure enacted by the European Communities and, on the other, to thwart the purpose of the devaluation, which was to increase the income of Danish agriculture.

\* \* \*

7 It is clear from the order for reference that the proceeds of the tax were paid into the Treasury without being assigned to any specific purpose, and it is common ground between the parties that the tax did not affect price formation, the free movement of goods or indeed the quantity of products available on the market and that it did not have the effect of a customs duty or a charge having equivalent effect. It follows that the compatibility with Community law of the tax measure in question must be assessed solely by reference to Articles 39 [39] to 43 [43] of the Treaty and to the common general principles which govern the organization of the markets.

8 Although the parties to the main action express different opinions as to the precise reasons for which the Danish Government introduced the tax measure in question and as to the exact effects of that measure, they are agreed that it is part of an income policy intended to apportion the tax burden among the various sectors of the working population. As the Danish, French and Italian Governments and the Commission correctly argue, . . . , nothing in the common organization of markets is opposed, in principle, to such a national policy. According to Article 39 [39] (2) (c) of the Treaty, in working out the Common Agricultural Policy account is to be taken of "the fact that in the Member States agriculture constitutes a sector closely linked with the economy as a whole". The Common Agricultural Policy was not intended, therefore, to shield those engaged in agriculture from the effects of a national incomes policy. Moreover, the fixing of common prices within the framework of the common organization of markets does not serve to guarantee to agricultural producers a net price independently of any taxation imposed by the national authorities, and the very wording of Article 39 [39] (1) (b) shows that the increase in individual earnings of persons engaged in agriculture is envisaged as being primarily the result of the structural measures described in subparagraph (a).

9 According to the plaintiff in the main action, however, the particular circumstances in which the national measure in question was adopted render it incompatible with Community law. In fact, the acknowledged aim of the tax introduced by Law No. 541 in reducing the income of Danish farmers was to neutralize the sole effect sought by a Community measure, in this instance the Council regulation of 3 December 1979 which devalued the Danish krone against the European Currency Unit [ECU] in order to increase the income of those same farmers. Thus the Danish Parliament encroached upon a power transferred to the Community authorities.

10 That argument cannot be accepted. Indeed it is clear from the preamble to the Council regulation of 3 December 1979 that it was adopted not in order to ensure higher net income for Danish farmers, but solely in order to avoid the introduction in Denmark of monetary compensatory amounts. That aim was in no way affected by the introduction of the contested land tax. Moreover, as the Commission correctly observes, there could be no real neutralization of the effect of the Council regulation unless the increase in agricultural prices expressed in Danish kroner and resulting from that regulation could not be achieved. The land tax introduced by Law No. 541 clearly did not have that result: its effect was solely to absorb part of the revenue obtained by agricultural producers from the sale of their products, after the law of supply and demand and the common price system had taken normal effect.

11 Nevertheless, the methods used to implement a national incomes policy which includes, among other persons, agricultural producers would be incompatible with the Treaty and with the rules on the common organization of markets if those methods interfered with the functioning of the machinery employed by those organizations in order to achieve their ends. The real problem posed by the land tax in question in relation to those rules is therefore whether that land tax produced such effect.

12 . . . [I]t is for the national court to decide whether the tax of which it is required to take cognizance has in fact had effects which obstruct the working of the machinery established by the common organizations of markets. With a view to the decision which has to be made in that respect by the national court it is, however, possible to identify certain features of Community law and to deduce certain criteria for assessment.

23 The essential aim of the machinery of the common organizations of the market is to achieve price levels at the production and whole-sale stages which take into account both the interests of Community production as a whole in the relevant sector and those of consumers, and which guarantee market supplies without encouraging over-production.

14 Those aims might be jeopardized, in the first place, by national tax measures exerting an appreciable influence, even if unintentionally, on price levels on the market. However, there is less risk of such an effect on price formation where it is a question not of a charge on agricultural production but of a land tax applied to agricultural land as a whole and assessed without taking into account the amount or nature of the agricultural production actually obtained.

15 Secondly, it should be noted that, as the plaintiff in the main action argued before

the Court and as the Commission acknowledged, tax measures exerting directly or indirectly an appreciable effect on the structure of agricultural holdings and consequently on the nature and volume of supplies on the agricultural markets, might also jeopardize the aims pursued by the common organizations of the market.

16 In that regard it is clear that the risk of such an effect on the structure of agricultural production depends in particular on the following features of the rate of the tax, whether it is temporary or permanent, whether or not it affects all agricultural property, whether or not there is a direct link between the amount of the tax and the income of each producer and whether or not the proceeds of the tax were assigned to a specific purpose and if so, what that purpose was.

## NOTES AND QUESTIONS

1.   Monetary compensatory amounts (MCAs), were designed to counter the adverse effects of changes in exchange rates on prices for agricultural products in the various Member States. The following extract from The European Community's Budget, Periodical 1/1986 describes how MCAs operated and why they were needed:

Difficulties with currencies and monetary compensation

The introduction of the European Monetary System (EMS) and the ECU in 1979 brought to an end the period of uncertainty caused by currency upheavals and fluctuating exchange rates that began when the convertibility of the U.S. dollar in gold was suspended in August 1971. The Community had to try and solve the particularly complicated problems of mathematics, conversion and evaluation which resulted and experimented with such things as the 'snake in the tunnel' (1972) and block floating ('the snake') from 1973. Its task was made more difficult by the fact that France in particular had to withdraw from the snake on a number of occasions.

In the agricultural sector, a system of compensation at frontiers (monetary compensatory amounts — MCAs) had to be introduced to cope with these problems. This was necessary as the common prices for about 80% of agricultural products are uniformly expressed in ECU. Any change in exchange rates or adjustment of central rates therefore has a direct effect on the market organization prices which have to be converted into each national currency. Revaluation decreases and devaluation increases the guaranteed support prices in the country involved. The system of monetary compensatory amounts was introduced in May 1971 to mitigate these effects which jeopardize the unity of the common market. Under the system, representative rates ('green' rates) were introduced which differ from the official exchange rates. Discussions of the monetary compensatory amounts caused major problems in the annual farm price negotiations, since, with the change in the value of the green rates, the price increases had different effect on prices in the individual countries. Prices went up more in countries with a weak currency and negative MCAs and less in countries with a strong currency and positive MCAs. The system of agricultural MCAs is extremely complicated. A much simplified example will show what is involved:

The Community price for market organization product X has been fixed at a uniform 100 ECU. At the time this corresponded in national currencies to DM 235 or FF670. Revaluation of the German mark and devaluation of the French franc changed these amounts to DM 225 and FF 690. The guaranteed producer prices would therefore fall by DM 10 in the Federal Republic and rise by FF 20 in France. Representative green rates of DM 230 and FF 680 would therefore be fixed for the remainder of the marketing year. In cross-border trade in agricultural products there would have to be positive compensation of DM 5 and negative compensation of FF 10 to neutralize in the agricultural sector the effect of the change in central rates which had been made deliberately as a result of economic policy.

This system of MCAs also proved to be a considerable burden on the Community budget. Although, because positive MCAs increased revenue and negative MCAs increased expenditure, only the balances were of significance, they still represented a cost of one-tenth or more of total Guarantee expenditure. In addition, there were the uncertainties arising from the impossibility of forecasting currency trends when drawing up the preliminary draft budget.

1992 saw the start of an attempt to eliminate surpluses in anticipation of the arrival of the 10 new member-States of central and eastern Europe. Prices would be steered more towards world market levels. MCAs were replaced in 1992 by a scheme that would introduce direct aid where loss of income occurred as a result of lost income: Regulation 3813/92, OJ 1992 L387/1 andRegulation 2799/98 OJ 1998 L349/1.

**2.**   Do you think the Danish Court received clear guidance here on how the Danish tax measure and Danish incomes policy were to be appraised in the context of the EC agricultural policy? Was it possible for the national court to make this judgment before evidence as to the actual effects of the tax became available?

## § 11.05   SHARED POWERS — THE INTERNAL MARKET

### [A]   The Scope of Harmonization Powers

## TFEU PROVISIONS

*Article 26*

(ex Article 14 TEC)

1. The Union shall adopt measures with the aim of establishing or ensuring the functioning of the internal market, in accordance with the relevant provisions of the Treaties.

2. The internal market shall comprise an area without internal frontiers in which the free movement of goods, persons, services and capital is ensured in accordance with the provisions of the Treaties.

3. The Council, on a proposal from the Commission, shall determine the guidelines and conditions necessary to ensure balanced progress in all the sectors concerned.

## *Article 53*

### (ex Article 47 TEC)

1. In order to make it easier for persons to take up and pursue activities as self-employed persons, the European Parliament and the Council shall, acting in accordance with the ordinary legislative procedure, issue directives for the mutual recognition of diplomas, certificates and other evidence of formal qualifications and for the coordination of the provisions laid down by law, regulation or administrative action in Member States concerning the taking-up and pursuit of activities as self-employed persons.

2. In the case of the medical and allied and pharmaceutical professions, the progressive abolition of restrictions shall be dependent upon coordination of the conditions for their exercise in the various Member States.

## *Article 114*

### (ex Article 95 TEC)

1. Save where otherwise provided in the Treaties, the following provisions shall apply for the achievement of the objectives set out in Article 26. The European Parliament and the Council shall, acting in accordance with the ordinary legislative procedure and after consulting the Economic and Social Committee, adopt the measures for the approximation of the provisions laid down by law, regulation or administrative action in Member States which have as their object the establishment and functioning of the internal market.

2. Paragraph 1 shall not apply to fiscal provisions, to those relating to the free movement of persons nor to those relating to the rights and interests of employed persons.

3. The Commission, in its proposals envisaged in paragraph 1 concerning health, safety, environmental protection and consumer protection, will take as a base a high level of protection, taking account in particular of any new development based on scientific facts. Within their respective powers, the European Parliament and the Council will also seek to achieve this objective.

*       *       *

*Article 115*

Without prejudice to Article 114, the Council shall, acting unanimously in accordance with a special legislative procedure and after consulting the European Parliament and the Economic and Social Committee, issue directives for the approximation of such laws, regulations or administrative provisions of the Member States as directly affect the establishment or functioning of the internal market.

*Article 168*

(ex Article 152 TEC)

1. A high level of human health protection shall be ensured in the definition and implementation of all Union policies and activities.

\* \* \*

5. The European Parliament and the Council, acting in accordance with the ordinary legislative procedure and after consulting the Economic and Social Committee and the Committee of the Regions, may also adopt incentive measures designed to protect and improve human health and in particular to combat the major cross-border health scourges, measures concerning monitoring, early warning of and combating serious cross-border threats to health, and measures which have as their direct objective the protection of public health regarding tobacco and the abuse of alcohol, excluding any harmonisation of the laws and regulations of the Member States.

## GERMANY v. PARLIAMENT AND COUNCIL
### (TOBACCO ADVERTISING DIRECTIVE)
### C-376/98, 2000 ECJ CELEX LEXIS 366, [2000] ECR I-8419

[Germany sought to annul Directive 98/43/EC of the European Parliament and of the Council of 6 July 1998 on the approximation of the laws, regulations and administrative provisions of the Member States relating to the advertising and sponsorship of tobacco products [1992] OJ L 213/9.]

\* \* \*

76 The Directive is concerned with the approximation of laws, regulations and administrative provisions of the Member States relating to the advertising and sponsorship of tobacco products. The national measures affected are to a large extent inspired by public health policy objectives.

77 The first indent of Article 129 [168](4) of the Treaty excludes any harmonisation of laws and regulations of the Member States designed to protect and improve human health.

78 But that provision does not mean that harmonising measures adopted on the basis of other provisions of the Treaty cannot have any impact on the protection of human health. Indeed, the third paragraph of Article 129 [168] (1) provides that

health requirements are to form a constituent part of the Community's other policies.

79 Other articles of the Treaty may not, however, be used as a legal basis in order to circumvent the express exclusion of harmonisation laid down in Article 129(4) [168] of the Treaty.

80 In this case, the approximation of national laws on the advertising and sponsorship of tobacco products provided for by the Directive was based on Articles 100a[114], 57[53](2) and 66[62] of the Treaty.

81 Article 100a [114](1) of the Treaty empowers the Council, acting in accordance with the procedure referred to in Article 189b [repealed] . . . and after consulting the Economic and Social Committee, to adopt measures for the approximation of the provisions laid down by law, regulation or administrative action in Member States which have as their object the establishment and functioning of the internal market.

82 Under Article 3 (c) [repealed] of the EC Treaty . . . , the internal market is characterised by the abolition, as between Member States, of all obstacles to the free movement of goods, persons, services and capital. Article 7a of the EC Treaty [26] . . . which provides for the measures to be taken with a view to establishing the internal market, states in paragraph 2 that that market is to comprise an area without internal frontiers in which the free movement of goods, persons, services and capital is ensured in accordance with the provisions of the Treaty.

83 Those provisions, read together, make it clear that the measures referred to in Article 100a[114](1) of the Treaty are intended to improve the conditions for the establishment and functioning of the internal market. To construe that article as meaning that it vests in the Community legislature a general power to regulate the internal market would not only be contrary to the express wording of the provisions cited above but would also be incompatible with the principle embodied in Article 3b of the EC Treaty (now Article 5 TFEU) that the powers of the Community are limited to those specifically conferred on it.

84 Moreover, a measure adopted on the basis of Article 100a [114] of the Treaty must genuinely have as its object the improvement of the conditions for the establishment and functioning of the internal market. If a mere finding of disparities between national rules and of the abstract risk of obstacles to the exercise of fundamental freedoms or of distortions of competition liable to result therefrom were sufficient to justify the choice of Article 100a[114] as a legal basis, judicial review of compliance with the proper legal basis might be rendered nugatory. The Court would then be prevented from discharging the function entrusted to it by Article 164 of the EC Treaty (now Article 220 TFEU) of ensuring that the law is observed in the interpretation and application of the Treaty.

85 So, in considering whether Article 100a [114] was the proper legal basis, the Court must verify whether the measure whose validity is at issue in fact pursues the objectives stated by the Community legislature.

86 It is true, . . . cited above, that recourse to Article 100a[114] as a legal basis is possible if the aim is to prevent the emergence of future obstacles to trade resulting

from multifarious development of national laws. However, the emergence of such obstacles must be likely and the measure in question must be designed to prevent them.

87 The foregoing considerations apply to interpretation of Article 57[53](2) of the Treaty, read in conjunction with Article 66[62] thereof, which expressly refers to measures intended to make it easier for persons to take up and pursue activities by way of services. Those provisions are also intended to confer on the Community legislature specific power to adopt measures intended to improve the functioning of the internal market.

88 Furthermore, provided that the conditions for recourse to Articles 100a [114], 57[53](2) and 66 [62] as a legal basis are fulfilled, the Community legislature cannot be prevented from relying on that legal basis on the ground that public health protection is a decisive factor in the choices to be made. On the contrary, the third paragraph of Article 129 [168](1) provides that health requirements are to form a constituent part of the Community's other policies and Article 100a [114](3) expressly requires that, in the process of harmonisation, a high level of human health protection is to be ensured.

89 It is therefore necessary to verify whether, in the light of the foregoing, it was permissible for the Directive to be adopted on the basis of Articles 100a[114], 57[53](2) and 66[62] of the Treaty.

The Directive

90 In the first recital in the preamble to the Directive, the Community legislature notes that differences exist between national laws on the advertising and sponsorship of tobacco products and observes that, as a result of such advertising and sponsorship transcending the borders of the Member States, the differences in question are likely to give rise to barriers to the movement of the products which serve as the media for such activities and the exercise of freedom to provide services in that area, as well as to distortions of competition, thereby impeding the functioning of the internal market.

91 According to the second recital, it is necessary to eliminate such barriers, and, to that end, approximate the rules relating to the advertising and sponsorship of tobacco products, whilst leaving Member States the possibility of introducing, under certain conditions, such requirements as they consider necessary in order to guarantee protection of the health of individuals.

92 Article 3(1) of the Directive prohibits all forms of advertising and sponsorship of tobacco products and Article 3(4) prohibits any free distribution having the purpose or the effect of promoting such products. However, its scope does not extend to communications between professionals in the tobacco trade, advertising in sales outlets or in publications published and printed in third countries which are not principally intended for the Community market (Article 3(5)).

93 The Directive also prohibits the use of the same names both for tobacco products and for other products and services as from 30 July 1998, except for products and services marketed before that date under a name also used for a tobacco product,

whose use is authorised under certain conditions (Article 3(2)). With effect from 30 July 2001, tobacco products must not bear the brand name, trade-mark, emblem or other distinctive feature of any other product or service, unless the tobacco product has already been traded under that brand name, trade-mark, emblem or other distinctive feature before that date (Article 3(3)(a)).

94 Pursuant to Article 5, the Directive is not to preclude Member States from laying down, in accordance with the Treaty, such stricter requirements concerning the advertising or sponsorship of tobacco products as they deem necessary to guarantee the health protection of individuals.

95 It therefore necessary to verify whether the Directive actually contributes to eliminating obstacles to the free movement of goods and to the freedom to provide services, and to removing distortions of competition.

Elimination of obstacles to the free movement of goods and the freedom to provide services

96 It is clear that, as a result of disparities between national laws on the advertising of tobacco products, obstacles to the free movement of goods or the freedom to provide services exist or may well arise.

97 In the case, for example, of periodicals, magazines and newspapers which contain advertising for tobacco products, it is true, as the applicant has demonstrated, that no obstacle exists at present to their importation into Member States which prohibit such advertising. However, in view of the trend in national legislation towards ever greater restrictions on advertising of tobacco products, reflecting the belief that such advertising gives rise to an appreciable increase in tobacco consumption, it is probable that obstacles to the free movement of press products will arise in the future.

98 In principle, therefore, a Directive prohibiting the advertising of tobacco products in periodicals, magazines and newspapers could be adopted on the basis of Article 100a[114] of the Treaty with a view to ensuring the free movement of press products, on the lines of Directive 89/552, Article 13 of which prohibits television advertising of tobacco products in order to promote the free broadcasting of television programmes.

99 However, for numerous types of advertising of tobacco products, the prohibition under Article 3(1) of the Directive cannot be justified by the need to eliminate obstacles to the free movement of advertising media or the freedom to provide services in the field of advertising. That applies, in particular, to the prohibition of advertising on posters, parasols, ashtrays and other articles used in hotels, restaurants and cafes, and the prohibition of advertising spots in cinemas, prohibitions which in no way help to facilitate trade in the products concerned.

100 Admittedly, a measure adopted on the basis of Articles 100a[114], 57[53](2) and 66[55] of the Treaty may incorporate provisions which do not contribute to the elimination of obstacles to exercise of the fundamental freedoms provided that they are necessary to ensure that certain prohibitions imposed in pursuit of that purpose are not circumvented. It is, however, quite clear that the prohibitions mentioned in

the previous paragraph do not fall into that category.

101 Moreover, the Directive does not ensure free movement of products which are in conformity with its provisions.

102 Contrary to the contentions of the Parliament and Council, Article 3(2) of the Directive, relating to diversification products, cannot be construed as meaning that, where the conditions laid down in the Directive are fulfilled, products of that kind in which trade is allowed in one Member State may move freely in the other Member States, including those where such products are prohibited.

103 Under Article 5 of the Directive, Member States retain the right to lay down, in accordance with the Treaty, such stricter requirements concerning the advertising or sponsorship of tobacco products as they deem necessary to guarantee the health protection of individuals.

104 Furthermore, the Directive contains no provision ensuring the free movement of products which conform to its provisions, in contrast to other directives allowing Member States to adopt stricter measures for the protection of a general interest (see, in particular, Article 7(1) of Council Directive 90/239/EEC of 17 May 1990 on the approximation of the laws, regulations and administrative provisions of the Member States concerning the maximum tar yield of cigarettes (OJ 1990 L 137, p. 36) and Article 8(1) of Council Directive 89/622/EEC of 13 November 1989 on the approximation of the laws, regulations and administrative provisions of the Member States concerning the labelling of tobacco products (OJ 1989 L 359, p. 1)).

105 In those circumstances, it must be held that the Community legislature cannot rely on the need to eliminate obstacles to the free movement of advertising media and the freedom to provide services in order to adopt the Directive on the basis of Articles 100a[114], 57[53](2) and 66[62] of Treaty.

Elimination of distortion of competition

106 In examining the lawfulness of a directive adopted on the basis of Article 100a[114] of the Treaty, the Court is required to verify whether the distortion of competition which the measure purports to eliminate is appreciable.

107 In the absence of such a requirement, the powers of the Community legislature would be practically unlimited. National laws often differ regarding the conditions under which the activities they regulate may be carried on, and this impacts directly or indirectly on the conditions of competition for the undertakings concerned. It follows that to interpret Articles 100a [114], 57[53](2) and 66[62] of the Treaty as meaning that the Community legislature may rely on those articles with a view to eliminating the smallest distortions of competition would be incompatible with the principle, already referred to in paragraph 83 of this judgment, that the powers of the Community are those specifically conferred on it.

108 It is therefore necessary to verify whether the Directive actually contributes to eliminating appreciable distortions of competition.

109 First, as regards advertising agencies and producers of advertising media, undertakings established in Member States which impose fewer restrictions on

tobacco advertising are unquestionably at an advantage in terms of economies of scale and increase in profits. The effects of such advantages on competition are, however, remote and indirect and do not constitute distortions which could be described as appreciable. They are not comparable to the distortions of competition caused by differences in production costs, such as those which, in particular, prompted the Community legislature to adopt Council Directive 89/428/EEC of 21 June 1989 on procedures for harmonising the programmes for the reduction and eventual elimination of pollution caused by waste from the titanium dioxide industry (OJ 1989 L 201, p. 56).

110 It is true that the differences between certain regulations on tobacco advertising may give rise to appreciable distortions of competition. As the Commission and the Finnish and United Kingdom Governments have submitted, the fact that sponsorship is prohibited in some Member States and authorised in others gives rise, in particular, to certain sports events being relocated, with considerable repercussions on the conditions of competition for undertakings associated with such events.

111 However, such distortions, which could be a basis for recourse to Article 100a[114] of the Treaty in order to prohibit certain forms of sponsorship, are not such as to justify the use of that legal basis for an outright prohibition of advertising of the kind imposed by the Directive.

112 Second, as regards distortions of competition in the market for tobacco products, irrespective of the applicant's contention that such distortions are not covered by the Directive, it is clear that, in that sector, the Directive is likewise not apt to eliminate appreciable distortions of competition.

113 Admittedly, as the Commission has stated, producers and sellers of tobacco products are obliged to resort to price competition to influence their market share in Member States which have restrictive legislation. However, that does not constitute a distortion of competition but rather a restriction of forms of competition which applies to all economic operators in those Member States. By imposing a wide-ranging prohibition on the advertising of tobacco products, the Directive would in the future generalise that restriction of forms of competition by limiting, in all the Member States, the means available for economic operators to enter or remain in the market.

114 In those circumstances, it must be held that the Community legislature cannot rely on the need to eliminate distortions of competition, either in the advertising sector or in the tobacco products sector, in order to adopt the Directive on the basis of Articles 100a [114], 57 [53](2) and 66 [62] of the Treaty.

115 In view of all the foregoing considerations, a measure such as the directive cannot be adopted on the basis of Articles 100a [114], 57 [53](2) and 66[62] of the Treaty.

116 In those circumstances, the pleas alleging that Articles 100a [114], 57 [53](2) and 66[55] do not constitute an appropriate legal basis for the Directive must be upheld.

117 As has been observed in paragraphs 98 and 111 of this judgment, a directive prohibiting certain forms of advertising and sponsorship of tobacco products could

have been adopted on the basis of Article 100a [114] of the Treaty. However, given the general nature of the prohibition of advertising and sponsorship of tobacco products laid down by the Directive, partial annulment of the Directive would entail amendment by the Court of provisions of the Directive. Such amendments are a matter for the Community legislature. It is not therefore possible for the Court to annul the Directive partially.

118 Since the Court has upheld the pleas alleging that the choice of Articles 100a[114], 57[53](2) and 66[62] as a legal basis was inappropriate, it is unnecessary to consider the other pleas put forward by the applicant. The Directive must be annulled in its entirety.

## NOTES AND QUESTIONS

**1.** In the above case the ECJ annulled the directive based on arguments relating to the legal basis. What was the Court's reasoning?

**2.** Why was it not open to the Member States to "fix" the problem with the directive by simply agreeing among themselves to adopt national legislation outside the EU framework?

It seems odd that the Court would have taken what appears to be an "anti-European" position. For a critical appraisal of the Court's approach, see DERRICK WYATT, COMMUNITY COMPETENCE TO REGULATE THE INTERNAL MARKET, Oxford Legal Studies Research Paper 9/2007.

For discussions of the scope of the harmonization competence, see S. Vogenauer and S. Weatherill, *The European Community's competence for a comprehensive harmonisation of contract law — An empirical analysis*, (2006) 30 EL REV. 821; and G. Davies, *Can selling arrangements be harmonised?* (2005) 30 EL REV. 370.

## [B]   Preemptive Effects of Harmonization

### COMMISSION v. UNITED KINGDOM
(DIM — DIP)
Case 60/86, 1988 ECJ CELEX LEXIS 120, [1988] ECR 3921

[The Commission asked the ECJ to declare that the UK was in breach of Council Directive 76/756/EEC of 27 July 1976 on the approximation of the laws of the Member States relating to the installation of lighting and light-signalling devices on motor vehicles and their trailers, by prohibiting the use of motor vehicles manufactured after 1 October 1986 and put into service after 1 April 1987 which were not equipped with "dim-dip lighting" (essentially, what are known in the U.S. as "daytime running lamps").]

2. A dim-dip device as referred to in the application is defined by the Road Vehicles Lighting Regulations 1984 (Statutory Instrument 1984 No 821) (hereinafter referred to as "the national regulations") as "a device which satisfies the requirements laid down in Part I of Schedule 3 to the national regulations. Under those requirements, whenever the obligatory front lamps of the motor vehicle are

switched on and either the engine is running or the ignition switch is in the driving position the dim-dip device will switch on automatically and simultaneously either the dipped-beam headlamps at a reduced intensity or two separate "town lamps". It is clear from the documents before the Court that the dim-dip lighting device may either be physically separate from the other devices or be incorporated in them.

3 Regulation 16 of the national regulations in question prohibits the use on the roads of the United Kingdom of any motor vehicle put into service after 1 April 1987 and manufactured after 1 October 1986 which is not equipped with such a lighting device.

4 Directive 76/756/EEC on the installation of lighting and light — signalling devices on motor vehicles is one of the separate directives envisaged by the framework directive, namely Council Directive 70/156/EEC of 6 February 1970 on the approximation of the laws of the Member States relating to the type-approval of motor vehicles and their trailers (Official Journal 1970 L 42, p.1). Article 2 (1) of Directive 76/756/EEC, as amended by Council Directive 83/276/EEC of 26 May 1983 (Official Journal 1983 L 151, p. 47), provides as follows:

"No Member State may:

refuse, in respect of a type of vehicle, to grant EEC type-approval or national type-approval, or refuse or prohibit the sale, registration, entry into service or use of vehicles,

on grounds relating to the installation on the vehicles of the lighting and light-signalling devices, whether mandatory or optional, listed in Items 1.5.7 to 1.5.20 of Annex I if these devices are installed in accordance with the requirements set out in Annex I."

5 Reference is made to the Report for the Hearing for a fuller account of the national legislation, the course of the procedure and the submissions and arguments of the parties, which are mentioned or discussed hereinafter only in so far as is necessary for the reasoning of the Court.

6 The Commission maintains that by virtue of Article 2 (1) of Directive 76/756/EEC it is not possible to prohibit the use of a motor vehicle on grounds connected with the installation of lighting and light-signalling devices if such devices are installed in the vehicle in question in accordance with the requirements set out in Annex I to the directive. It states that the obligation not to refuse type-approval and the obligation not to prohibit the use of motor vehicles are intended to be complementary and are drafted in such a way that the technical requirements are exactly the same.

7 The United Kingdom, on the other hand, relies on a literal interpretation of Article 2 (1) of Directive 76/756/EEC and maintains that the words "these devices" can refer only to the devices listed in Items 1.5.7 to 1.5.20 of Annex I to the directive. It takes the view that Directive 76/756/EEC does not contain an exhaustive harmonization of the requirements relating to the installation of lighting and light-signalling devices with the result that the Member States have the power to lay down additional requirements such as the installation of dim-dip lighting devices.

8 It must be pointed out in the first place that the fourth recital in the preamble to

the framework directive, namely Directive 70/156/EEC on the approximation of the laws of the Member States relating to the type-approval of motor vehicles and their trailers, states that "the harmonized technical requirements applicable to individual parts and characteristics of a vehicle should be specified in separate directives". In addition, Directive 70/156/EEC envisages the introduction of a Community type-approval procedure for each vehicle type in order that compliance with the harmonized technical requirements can be checked once specifications for all the individual parts and characteristics of the vehicle have been laid down in separate directives. Such a procedure has not yet been introduced because specifications relating to some individual parts and characteristics of the vehicle have not been laid down in any separate directive. However, in the mean time and as a transitional measure, Directive 70/156/EEC provides that type-approval may be granted on the basis of the Community requirements "as and when separate directives relating to the various vehicle parts and characteristics enter into force, national requirements remaining applicable in respect of parts and characteristics still not covered by such directives" (seventh recital and Article 10).

9 As has already been stated, Directive 76/756/EEC is the separate directive, within the meaning of Directive 70/156/EEC, which specifies the harmonized technical requirements applicable to the installation of lighting and light-signalling devices on motor vehicles and their trailers. Whilst the third recital in the preamble to Directive 76/756/EEC states that common requirements for the construction of lighting and light-signalling devices are to be the subject of further special directives, that is not the case as regards the installation of such devices. The wording of Article 2 (1), which refers to "the lighting and light-signalling devices, whether mandatory or optional", listed in Annex I, implies that Annex I lists all the lighting and light-signalling devices which were considered to be necessary or acceptable on motor vehicles (Items 1.5.1 to 1.5.6 specify solely certain ways of fixing these types of lamps).

10 It is clear from the documents before the Court that the reason for which dim-dip devices were not included in the provisions, even as optional devices, is that the technical committee of national experts did not consider them acceptable given the state of technical progress at the time. In addition, it was not considered appropriate to adapt Directive 76/756/EEC, after its entry into force, so as to take account of technical progress in accordance with the procedure laid down in Article 13 of Directive 70/156/EEC and Article 5 of Directive 76/756/EEC, by bringing dim-dip devices within the scope of the latter directive.

11 Such an interpretation of the exhaustive nature of the list of lighting and light-signalling devices set out in Annex I to the directive is consistent with the purpose of Directive 70/156/EEC which is to reduce, and even eliminate, hindrances to trade within the Community resulting from the fact that mandatory technical requirements differ from one Member State to another (see the first and second recitals in the preamble to Directive 70/156/EEC). In the context of Directive 76/756/EEC that objective is reflected in the obligation imposed on the Member States to adopt the same requirements "either in addition to or in place of their existing rules" (second recital).

12 It follows that the Member States cannot unilaterally require manufacturers who

have complied with the harmonized technical requirements set out in Directive 76/756/EEC to comply with a requirement which is not imposed by that directive, since motor vehicles complying with the technical requirements laid down therein must be able to move freely within the common market.

13 It must therefore be declared that, by prohibiting, in breach of Council Directive 76/756/EEC of 27 July 1976, the use of motor vehicles manufactured after 1 October 1986 and put into service after 1 April 1987 which are not equipped with a dim-dip device, the United Kingdom has failed to fulfil its obligations under Community law.

# PUBBLICO MINISTERO v. RATTI
## Case 148/78, [1979] ECR 1629

[This case concerned Directives No 73/173/EEC of 4 June 1973 on the classification, packaging and labeling of dangerous preparations (solvents) and No 77/728/EEC of 7 November 1977 on the classification, packaging and labeling of paints, varnishes, printing inks, adhesives and similar products.]

2 [The referred] questions are raised in the context of criminal proceedings against the head of an undertaking which produces solvents and varnishes, on a charge of having infringed certain provisions of the Italian Law No 245 of 5 March 1963. . . . which require manufacturers of products containing benzene, toluene and xylene to affix to the containers of those products labels indicating, not only the fact that those substances are present, but also their total percentage and, separately, the percentage of benzene.

3 As far as solvents are concerned, that legislation ought, at the material time, to have been amended in order to comply with Directive No 73/173 of 4 June 1973, the provisions of which Member States were supposed to incorporate into their internal legal orders by 8 December 1974 at the latest, an obligation which the Italian Government has not fulfilled.

4 That amendment would have resulted in the repeal of the provision of the Italian Law, which the accused is charged with contravening and would consequently have altered the conditions for applying the criminal sanctions contained in the law in question.

5 As regards the packaging and labelling of varnishes, Directive No 77/728 of 7 November 1977 had, at the material time, been adopted by the Council, but by virtue of Article 12 thereof Member States have until 9 November 1979 to bring into force the laws, regulations and administrative provisions necessary to comply therewith.

6 The incorporation of the provisions of that directive into the internal Italian legal order must likewise result in the repeal of the provisions of the Italian law which the accused is charged with contravening.

7 As regards the packaging and labelling of both the solvents and the varnishes produced by his undertaking, the accused complied, in the one case, with the provisions of Directive No 73/173 (solvents), which the Italian Government had failed to incorporate into its internal legal order, and, in the other case, with the

provisions of Directive No 77/728 (varnishes), which Member States must implement by 9 November 1979.

* * *

A — The interpretation of Directive No 73/173

9 This directive was adopted pursuant to Article 100 of the Treaty and Council Directive No 67/548/EEC of 27 June 1967 . . . amended on 21 May 1973 . . . on dangerous substances, in order to ensure the approximation of the laws, regulations and administrative provisions of the Member States on the classification, packaging and labelling of dangerous preparations (solvents).

10 That directive proved necessary because dangerous substances and preparations were subject to rules in the Member States which displayed considerable differences, particularly as regards labelling, packaging and classification according to the degree of risk presented by the said products.

11 Those differences constituted a barrier to trade and to the free movement of goods and directly affected the establishment and functioning of the market in dangerous preparations such as solvents used regularly in industrial, farming and craft activities, as well as for domestic purposes.

12 In order to eliminate those differences the directive made a number of express provisions concerning the classification, packaging and labelling of the products in question . . .

13 As regards Article 8, to which the national court referred in particular, and which provides that Member States may not prohibit, restrict or impede on the grounds of classification, packaging or labelling the placing on the market of dangerous preparations which satisfy the requirements of the directive, although it lays down a general duty, it has no independent value, being no more than the necessary complement of the substantive provisions contained in the aforesaid articles and designed to ensure the free movement of the products in question.

14 The Member States were under a duty to implement Directive No 73/173, in accordance with Article 11 thereof, within 18 months of its notification.

15 All the Member States were so notified on 8 June 1973.

16 The period of 18 months expired on 8 December 1974 and up to the time when the events material in the case occurred the provisions of the directive had not been implemented within the Italian internal legal order.

17 In those circumstances the national court, finding that "there was a manifest contradiction between the Community rules and internal Italian law", wondered "which of the two sets of rules should take precedence in the case before the court".

* * *

25 [T]he national court asks, essentially, whether, in incorporating the provisions of the directive on solvents into its internal legal order, the State to which it is addressed may prescribe "obligations and limitations which are more precise and

detailed than, or at all events different from, those set out in the directive", requiring in particular information not required by the directive to be affixed to the containers.

26 The combined effect of Articles 3 to 8 of Directive No 73/173 is that only solvents which "comply with the provisions of this directive and the annex thereto" may be placed on the market and that Member States are not entitled to maintain, parallel with the rules laid down by the said directive for imports, different rules for the domestic market.

27 Thus it is a consequence of the system introduced by Directive No 73/173 that a Member State may not introduce into its national legislation conditions which are more restrictive than those laid down in the directive in question, or which are even more detailed or in any event different, as regards the classification, packaging and labelling of solvents and that this prohibition on the imposition of restrictions not provided for applies both to the direct marketing of the products on the home market and to imported products.

28 The second question submitted by the national court must be answered in that way.

29 In the third question the national court asks whether the duty to indicate on the container of the solvent offered for sale that it contains benzene, toluene and xylene, specifying the total percentage of those substances and, separately that of benzene, pursuant to Article 8 of Law No 245 of 5 March 1963, may be considered incompatible with the said directive.

30 Article 8 of Italian Law No 245 of 5 March 1963 lays down a duty, "where solvents contain benzene, toluene or xylene, to affix to the containers offered for sale a label mentioning the presence of those substances in the solvents, the total percentage of those substances and, separately, the percentage of benzene . . .".

31 However, Article 5 of Directive No 73/173 requires in all cases that packages indicate clearly and indelibly the presence of substances classified as toxic under Article 2, such as benzene, and also that they show, but only in certain cases, the presence of substances classified as harmful, such as toluene and xylene in a concentration higher than 5%.

32 On the other hand no indication of the percentage, separate or in the aggregate, of those substances is required.

33 Thus the answer to the national court must be that Directive No 73/173 must be interpreted as meaning that it is not permissible for national provisions to prescribe that containers shall bear a statement of the presence of ingredients of the products in question in terms going beyond those laid down by the said directive.

34 The fourth question is drafted as follows:

"Do the said national provisions, which are applicable without distinction to all goods placed on the domestic market, nevertheless constitute an obstacle, a prohibition or a restriction on trade in and the free movement of such goods, even if such provisions were enacted for the purpose of ensuring greater protection for the physical safety of users of the products in question?"

35 This question is an allusion to Article 30 [42] of the Treaty which permits exceptions to the free movements of goods to the extent to which they are justified on grounds of public security or the protection of health and life of humans and animals.

36 When, pursuant to Article 100[113] of the Treaty, Community directives provide for the harmonization of measures necessary to ensure the protection of the health of humans and animals and establish Community procedures to supervise compliance therewith, recourse to Article 30[42] ceases to be justified and the appropriate controls must henceforth be carried out and the protective measures taken in accordance with the scheme laid down by the harmonizing directive.

37 Directive No 73/173 provides that where a Member State established that a dangerous preparation, although satisfying the requirements of that directive, presents a health or safety risk, it may have recourse, temporarily and subject to the supervision of the Commission, to a protective measure provided for in Article 9 of the directive in accordance with the procedure laid down in that article.

38 It follows that national provisions going beyond those laid down in Directive No 73/173 are compatible with Community law only if they have been adopted in accordance with the procedures and formalities prescribed in Article 9 of the said directive.

## NOTES AND QUESTIONS

1.   Identify the reasons that led the Court to conclude that the directives in the *Dim-dip* and *Ratti* cases were intended to be exhaustive and thereby deny any right to a Member State to enforce stricter rules. Does this mean that EU law has "preempted" national law in this area? Note that the judgment in the "dim-dip" case even denies the UK the right to prohibit the use of motor vehicles without "dim-dip" lights on UK manufactured cars intended to be sold only in the UK.

2.   As noted by the Court, the imposition of minimum standards lays open the possibility that a state will treat products made and packaged in its territory less favorably than products imported from a Member State where the minimum standard has been permitted. This seems entirely in keeping with the concept of mutual recognition. See *Criminal proceedings against Jacqueline Brandsma* C-293/94, 1996 ECR I-3159 (discussed in Chapter 13, *infra*). Would it in your view be likely to have any effect on trade between Member States — in other words, could the directive actually exacerbate rather than resolve obstacles to trade created by these particular national differences?

## [C]   Conferral of Responsibilities on the EU in the Context of Harmonized Laws

### GERMANY v. COUNCIL
#### (CONSUMER SAFETY DIRECTIVE)
#### Case 359/92, 1994 ECJ CELEX LEXIS 138, [1994] ECR I-3681

[Directive 92/59 was adopted under article 100a (EC 95/TFEU 114) of the Treaty for the purpose of ensuring that consumer products placed on the internal market of the EU did not in general present a risk to the consumer under normal conditions of use or, at least, involve only a very low level of risk.

Article 9 provided as follows:

If the Commission becomes aware, through notification given by the Member States or through information provided by them, in particular under Article 7 or Article 8, of the existence of a serious and immediate risk from a product to the health and safety of consumers in various Member States and if:

(a) one or more Member States have adopted measures entailing restrictions on the marketing of the product or requiring its withdrawal from the market, such as those provided for in Article 6(1)(d) to (h);

(b) Member States differ on the adoption of measures to deal with the risk in question;

(c) the risk cannot be dealt with, in view of the nature of the safety issue posed by the product and in a manner compatible with the urgency of the case, under the other procedures laid down by the specific Community legislation applicable to the product or category of products concerned; and

(d) the risk can be eliminated effectively only by adopting appropriate measures applicable at Community level, in order to ensure the protection of the health and safety of consumers and the proper functioning of the common market,

the Commission, after consulting the Member States and at the request of at least one of them, may adopt a decision, in accordance with the procedure laid down in Article 11, requiring Member States to take temporary measures from among those listed in Article 6(1)(d) to (h).]

12 The Federal Republic of Germany based its application for annulment on two pleas in law. First, it claimed that Article 9 of the directive had no legal base. Second, it claimed that the article was contrary to the principle of proportionality. The Council and the Commission contended, for their part, that neither of those two pleas in law was well founded.

\*   \*   \*

19 Article 100a (5) [114] of the Treaty provides: "The harmonization measures . . . shall, in appropriate cases, include a safeguard clause authorizing the Member States to take, for one or more of the non-economic reasons referred to in Article

36 [36], provisional measures subject to a Community control procedure."

20 That article only concerns supervision, by the Community authorities, of measures taken by the Member States. The purpose of Article 9 of the directive, however, is not to introduce a control procedure of that kind. It sets out a Community procedure for the coordination of national measures with respect to a product, in order to ensure that it may circulate freely throughout the Community without danger to the consumer.

21 Secondly, the question arises whether Article 100a [114](1) of the Treaty, supplemented by the third indent of Article 145, constitutes an appropriate legal base for Article 9 of the directive, as the Council and the Commission contend.

22 . . . [F]or the purposes of implementing the objectives set out in Article 8a of the EEC Treaty (now Article 7a [26] of the EC Treaty), Article 100a [114](1) of the Treaty empowers the Council to adopt, in accordance with the procedure laid down therein, measures which have as their object the abolition of barriers to trade arising from differences between the provisions laid down by law, regulation or administrative action in Member States.

23 However, the harmonization effected by the directive is of a particular type, which the Council, by reference to the terms used in the third recital in the preamble to the directive, describes as "horizontal" harmonization.

24 According to the fourth recital in the preamble, the directive establishes at Community level "a general safety requirement for any product placed on the market that is intended for consumers or likely to be used by consumers". In accordance with that "general safety requirement" (see Title II), producers are obliged, first, to place only safe products on the market; second, to provide consumers with the relevant information to enable them to assess the risks inherent in a product throughout the normal or reasonably foreseeable period of its use, where such risks are not immediately obvious without adequate warnings, and to take precautions against those risks; and third, to adopt measures commensurate with the characteristics of the products which they supply, to enable them to be informed of risks which those products might present and to take appropriate action including, if necessary, withdrawing the product in question from the market to avoid those risks. Distributors are required to act with due care in order to help to ensure compliance with the general safety requirement (Article 3 of the directive).

25 The directive requires Member States to adopt the necessary laws, regulations and administrative provisions to make producers and distributors comply with their obligations under it in such a way that products placed on the market are safe. In particular, Member States must establish or nominate authorities to monitor the compliance of products with the obligation to place only safe products on the market and arrange for such authorities to have the necessary powers to take the appropriate measures incumbent upon them under the directive, including the possibility of imposing suitable penalties in the event of failure to comply with the obligations deriving from it (Article 5 of the directive).

26 Under Article 6 of the directive, Member States must, for the purposes of Article 5, have the necessary powers, acting in accordance with the degree of risk and in

conformity with the Treaty, and in particular with Articles 30 [34] and 36 [36] thereof, to adopt appropriate measures to attain, inter alia, the objectives laid down in Article 6(1)(a) to (h).

27 However, Articles 7 and 8 of the directive entrust the Commission with the task of supervising measures taken by Member States which are likely to hinder trade.

28 Under Article 7, Member States must inform the Commission of measures which restrict the placing of a product or product batch on the market or require its withdrawal from the market, such as those provided for in Article 6(1)(d) to (h), specifying their reasons for adopting them.

29 Under Article 8, Member States must as a matter of urgency inform the Commission of emergency measures which they have adopted or decided to adopt in order to prevent, restrict or impose specific conditions on the possible marketing or use, within their territory, of a product or product batch by reason of a serious and immediate risk presented by the said product or product batch to the health and safety of consumers. Member States may also pass on to the Commission any information in their possession regarding the existence of a serious and immediate risk before deciding to adopt the measures in question.

30 Under the scheme established by the directive, it is possible, even likely, that differences may exist between the measures taken by Member States. As the eighteenth recital in the preamble states, such differences may "entail unacceptable disparities in consumer protection and constitute a barrier to intra-Community trade".

31 Under that scheme, the nineteenth recital in the preamble to the directive indicates, it may also be necessary to cope with serious product-safety problems which affect or could affect, in the immediate future, all or a large part of the Community and which, in view of the nature of the safety problem posed by the product and of its urgency, cannot be dealt with effectively under the procedures laid down in the specific rules of Community law applicable to the products or category of products in question.

32 The Community legislature therefore considered it necessary, in order to cope with a serious and immediate risk to the health and safety of consumers, to provide for an adequate mechanism allowing, in the last resort, for the adoption of measures applicable throughout the Community, in the form of decisions addressed to the Member States (see the twentieth recital in the preamble to the directive).

33 For that purpose, Article 9 of the directive empowers the Commission, on the basis of the information received, to act in cases where a product placed on the market puts in serious and immediate jeopardy the health and safety of consumers in a number of Member States and those States differ with respect to the measures adopted or planned with regard to that product, that is to say, where such measures do not provide the same level of protection and thereby prevent the product from moving freely within the Community. Article 9 provides that, to the extent that effective protection can be ensured only by action at Community level and no other procedure specifically applicable to the product can be used, the Commission may adopt a decision requiring Member States to take temporary measures from among those listed in Article 6(1)(d) to (h).

34 As is apparent from the eighteenth, nineteenth and twentieth recitals of the preamble to the directive and from the structure of Article 9, the purpose of that provision is to enable the Commission to adopt, as promptly as possible, temporary measures applicable throughout the Community with respect to a product which presents a serious and immediate risk to the health and safety of consumers, so as to ensure compliance with the objectives of the directive. The free movement of goods can be secured only if product safety requirements do not differ significantly from one Member State to another. A high level of protection can be achieved only if dangerous products are subject to appropriate measures in all the Member States.

35 Such action must be taken by the Commission in close cooperation with the Member States. For one thing, decisions taken at Community level may be adopted by the Commission only after consulting the Member States and at the request of a Member State. For another, such measures may be adopted by the Commission only if they are in accordance with the opinion of a committee composed of the Member States' representatives and a Commission representative. Otherwise the measure must be adopted by the Council within a specified period. Lastly, those decisions are addressed only to Member States. The twentieth recital in the preamble to the directive states that such decisions are not of direct application to traders in the Community and must be incorporated in a national measure.

36 Thus, in the circumstances set out in Article 9, action by the Community authorities is justified by the fact that, in the terms used in Article 9(d), "the risk can be eliminated effectively only by adopting appropriate measures at Community level, in order to ensure the protection of the health and safety of consumers and the proper functioning of the Common Market".

37 Such action is not contrary to Article 100a [114](1) of the Treaty. The measures which the Council is empowered to take under that provision are aimed at "the establishment and functioning of the internal market". In certain fields, and particularly in that of product safety, the approximation of general laws alone may not be sufficient to ensure the unity of the market. Consequently, the concept of "measures for the approximation" of legislation must be interpreted as encompassing the Council's power to lay down measures relating to a specific product or class of products and, if necessary, individual measures concerning those products.

38 So far as concerns the argument that the power thus conferred on the Commission goes beyond that which, in a federal state such as the Federal Republic of Germany, is enjoyed by the Bund in relation to the Länder, it must be borne in mind that the rules governing the relationship between the Community and its Member States are not the same as those which link the Bund with the Länder. Furthermore, the measures taken for the implementation of Article 100a [114] of the Treaty are addressed to Member States and not to their constituent entities. Nor do the powers conferred on the Commission by Article 9 of the directive have any bearing upon the division of powers within the Federal Republic of Germany.

39 Accordingly the legal base of the powers delegated to the Commission by Article 9 of the directive is Article 100a [114](1) of the Treaty.

# NOTES AND QUESTIONS

1.  It appears from the above case that the German government believed that the Council may have "circumvented" the EC 95/TFEU 114 provisions relating to harmonization (i.e., to the effect that the directive provided for actions going beyond harmonization). How did the Court deal with the arguments raised by Germany? Is it implicit in Germany's argument that EC 95/TFEU 114 only allows directives?

2.  The Commission has also been assigned responsibilities under other directives. For example, Articles 9-11 of Directive 92/13 [1992] OJ L 76/14 introduced a conciliation procedure applicable to procurement in the water/energy, transport and telecommunications sectors. The Commission can be requested by a private party to appoint a conciliator to mediate between such party and the government entity in question. The conciliator makes a report to the Commission. Is the involvement of the Commission even to this limited extent consistent with the notion of a "directive"?

## [D]   EU Involvement and Special Agencies — An Example: Trademarks

### COUNCIL REGULATION (EC) No 40/94
### (UNION TRADEMARK)
### [1994] OJ L11

Article 1 Community trade mark

1. A trademark for goods or services which is registered in accordance with the conditions contained in this Regulation and in the manner herein provided is hereinafter referred to as a 'Community trade mark'.

2. A Community trade mark shall have a unitary character. It shall have equal effect throughout the Community: it shall not be registered, transferred or surrendered or be the subject of a decision revoking the rights of the proprietor or declaring it invalid, nor shall its use be prohibited, save in respect of the whole Community. This principle shall apply unless otherwise provided in this Regulation.

Article 2

Office

An Office for Harmonization in the Internal Market (trade marks and designs), hereinafter referred to as 'the Office', is hereby established.

\*   \*   \*

## Article 13

### Exhaustion of the rights conferred by a Community trade mark

1. A Community trade mark shall not entitle the proprietor to prohibit its use in relation to goods which have been put on the market in the Community under that trade mark by the proprietor or with his consent.

2. Paragraph 1 shall not apply where there exist legitimate reasons for the proprietor to oppose further commercialization of the goods, especially where the condition of the goods is changed or impaired after they have been put on the market.

## Article 14

### Complementary application of national law relating to infringement

1. The effects of Community trade marks shall be governed solely by the provisions of this Regulation. In other respects, infringement of a Community trade mark shall be governed by the national law relating to infringement of a national trade mark in accordance with the provisions of Title X.

2. This Regulation shall not prevent actions concerning a Community trade mark being brought under the law of Member States relating in particular to civil liability and unfair competition.

3. The rules of procedure to be applied shall be determined in accordance with the provisions of Title X.

\*   \*   \*

## Article 16

### Dealing with Community trade marks as national trade marks

1. Unless Articles 17 to 24 provide otherwise, a Community trade mark as an object of property shall be dealt with in its entirety, and for the whole area of the Community, as a national trade mark registered in the Member State in which, according to the Register of Community trade marks, (a) the proprietor has his seat or his domicile on the relevant date; or (b) where subparagraph (a) does not apply, the proprietor has an establishment on the relevant date.

2. In cases which are not provided for by paragraph 1, the Member State referred to in that paragraph shall be the Member State in which the seat of the Office is situated.

As regards the procedure for levy of execution in respect of a Community trade mark, the courts and authorities of the Member States determined in accordance with Article 16 shall have exclusive jurisdiction. On request of one the parties, levy of execution shall be entered in the Register and published.

\*   \*   \*

## Article 25

### Filing of applications

1. An application for a Community trade mark shall be filed, at the choice of the applicant, (a) at the Office; or (b) at the central industrial property office of a Member State or at the Benelux Trade Mark Office. An application filed in this way shall have the same effect as if it had been filed on the same date at the Office.

2. Every filing that is equivalent to a regular national filing under the national law of the State where it was made or under bilateral or multilateral agreements shall be recognized as giving rise to a right of priority.

\*   \*   \*

## Article 32

### Equivalence of Community filing with national filing

A Community trade mark application which has been accorded a date of filing shall, in the Member States, be equivalent to a regular national filing, where appropriate with the priority claimed for the Community trade mark.

\*   \*   \*

## Article 34

### Claiming the seniority of a national trade mark

1. The proprietor of an earlier trade mark registered in a Member State, including a trade mark registered in the Benelux countries, or registered under international arrangements having effect in a Member State, who applies for an identical trade mark for registration as a Community trade mark for goods or services which are identical with or contained within those for which the earlier trade mark has been registered, may claim for the Community trade mark the seniority of the earlier trade mark in respect of the Member State in or for which it is registered.

2. Seniority shall have the sole effect under this Regulation that, where the proprietor of the Community trade mark surrenders the earlier trade mark or allows it to lapse, he shall be deemed to continue to have the same rights as he would have had if the earlier trade mark had continued to be registered.

3. The seniority claimed for the Community trade mark shall lapse if the earlier trade mark the seniority of which is claimed is declared to have been revoked or to be invalid or if it is surrendered prior to the registration of the Community trade mark.

\*   \*   \*

## Article 63

### Actions before the Court of Justice

1. Actions may be brought before the Court of Justice against decisions of the Boards of Appeal on appeals.

2. The action may be brought on grounds of lack of competence, infringement of an essential procedural requirement, infringement of the Treaty, of this Regulation or of any rule of law relating to their application or misuse of power.

## NOTES AND QUESTIONS

**1.** The Trademark Regulation is based on EC 308/TFEU 352. Why could it not be based on the harmonization provisions of the Treaty?

**2.** What exactly is a "Community trade mark"? Does it equate in any way to a stand-alone trademark such as might be registered in the U.S. trademark office? What does this say about the scope of EU powers in this area?

**3.** One may contrast the success of the Trademark regime with the still-faltering effort on patents as described in the following summary provided by the EU.

# § 11.06   SHARED POWERS — CIVIL AND CRIMINAL LAW

# TFEU PROVISIONS

*Article 81*

(ex Article 65 TEC)

1. The Union shall develop judicial cooperation in civil matters having cross-border implications, based on the principle of mutual recognition of judgments and of decisions in extrajudicial cases. Such cooperation may include the adoption of measures for the approximation of the laws and regulations of the Member States.

\*   \*   \*

*Article 82*

(ex Article 31 TEU)

1. Judicial cooperation in criminal matters in the Union shall be based on the principle of mutual recognition of judgments and judicial decisions and shall include

the approximation of the laws and regulations of the Member States in the areas referred to in paragraph 2 and in Article 83.

\* \* \*

*Article 83*

(ex Article 31 TEU)

1. The European Parliament and the Council may, by means of directives adopted in accordance with the ordinary legislative procedure, establish minimum rules concerning the definition of criminal offences and sanctions in the areas of particularly serious crime with a cross-border dimension resulting from the nature or impact of such offences or from a special need to combat them on a common basis.

These areas of crime are the following: terrorism, trafficking in human beings and sexual exploitation of women and children, illicit drug trafficking, illicit arms trafficking, money laundering, corruption, counterfeiting of means of payment, computer crime and organised crime.

On the basis of developments in crime, the Council may adopt a decision identifying other areas of crime that meet the criteria specified in this paragraph. It shall act unanimously after obtaining the consent of the European Parliament.

2. If the approximation of criminal laws and regulations of the Member States proves essential to ensure the effective implementation of a Union policy in an area which has been subject to harmonisation measures, directives may establish minimum rules with regard to the definition of criminal offences and sanctions in the area concerned. Such directives shall be adopted by the same ordinary or special legislative procedure as was followed for the adoption of the harmonisation measures in question, without prejudice to Article 76.

3. Where a member of the Council considers that a draft directive as referred to in paragraph 1 or 2 would affect fundamental aspects of its criminal justice system, it may request that the draft directive be referred to the European Council. In that case, the ordinary legislative procedure shall be suspended. After discussion, and in case of a consensus, the European Council shall, within four months of this suspension, refer the draft back to the Council, which shall terminate the suspension of the ordinary legislative procedure.

Within the same timeframe, in case of disagreement, and if at least nine Member States wish to establish enhanced cooperation on the basis of the draft directive concerned, they shall notify the European Parliament, the Council and the Commission accordingly. In such a case, the authorisation to proceed with enhanced cooperation referred to in Article 20(2) of the Treaty on European Union and Article 329(1) of this Treaty shall be deemed to be granted and the provisions on enhanced cooperation shall apply.

\* \* \*

*Article 85*

(ex Article 31 TEU)

1. Eurojust's mission shall be to support and strengthen coordination and cooperation between national investigating and prosecuting authorities in relation to serious crime affecting two or more Member States or requiring a prosecution on common bases, on the basis of operations conducted and information supplied by the Member States' authorities and by Europol.

In this context, the European Parliament and the Council, by means of regulations adopted in accordance with the ordinary legislative procedure, shall determine Eurojust's structure, operation, field of action and tasks. These tasks may include:

    (a)    the initiation of criminal investigations, as well as proposing the initiation of prosecutions conducted by competent national authorities, particularly those relating to offences against the financial interests of the Union;

    (b)    the coordination of investigations and prosecutions referred to in point (a);

    (c)    the strengthening of judicial cooperation, including by resolution of conflicts of jurisdiction and by close cooperation with the European Judicial Network.

These regulations shall also determine arrangements for involving the European Parliament and national Parliaments in the evaluation of Eurojust's activities.

2. In the prosecutions referred to in paragraph 1, and without prejudice to Article 86, formal acts of judicial procedure shall be carried out by the competent national officials.

*Article 86*

1. In order to combat crimes affecting the financial interests of the Union, the Council, by means of regulations adopted in accordance with a special legislative procedure, may establish a European Public Prosecutor's Office from Eurojust. The Council shall act unanimously after obtaining the consent of the European Parliament.

In the absence of unanimity in the Council, a group of at least nine Member States may request that the draft regulation be referred to the European Council. In that case, the procedure in the Council shall be suspended. After discussion, and in case of a consensus, the European Council shall, within four months of this suspension, refer the draft back to the Council for adoption.

Within the same timeframe, in case of disagreement, and if at least nine Member States wish to establish enhanced cooperation on the basis of the draft regulation concerned, they shall notify the European Parliament, the Council and the Commission accordingly. In such a case, the authorisation to proceed with enhanced cooperation referred to in Article 20(2) of the Treaty on European Union and Article 329(1) of this Treaty shall be deemed to be granted and the provisions on enhanced cooperation shall apply.

2. The European Public Prosecutor's Office shall be responsible for investigating, prosecuting and bringing to judgment, where appropriate in liaison with Europol, the perpetrators of, and accomplices in, offences against the Union's financial interests, as determined by the regulation provided for in paragraph 1. It shall exercise the functions of prosecutor in the competent courts of the Member States in relation to such offences.

3. The regulations referred to in paragraph 1 shall determine the general rules applicable to the European Public Prosecutor's Office, the conditions governing the performance of its functions, the rules of procedure applicable to its activities, as well as those governing the admissibility of evidence, and the rules applicable to the judicial review of procedural measures taken by it in the performance of its functions.

4. The European Council may, at the same time or subsequently, adopt a decision amending paragraph 1 in order to extend the powers of the European Public Prosecutor's Office to include serious crime having a cross-border dimension and amending accordingly paragraph 2 as regards the perpetrators of, and accomplices in, serious crimes affecting more than one Member State. The European Council shall act unanimously after obtaining the consent of the European Parliament and after consulting the Commission.

## Article 87

### (ex Article 30 TEU)

1. The Union shall establish police cooperation involving all the Member States' competent authorities, including police, customs and other specialised law enforcement services in relation to the prevention, detection and investigation of criminal offences.

\* \* \*

## Article 88

### (ex Article 30 TEU)

1. Europol's mission shall be to support and strengthen action by the Member States' police authorities and other law enforcement services and their mutual cooperation in preventing and combating serious crime affecting two or more Member States, terrorism and forms of crime which affect a common interest covered by a Union policy.

\* \* \*

*Article 89*

(ex Article 32 TEU)

The Council, acting in accordance with a special legislative procedure, shall lay down the conditions and limitations under which the competent authorities of the Member States referred to in Articles 82 and 87 may operate in the territory of another Member State in liaison and in agreement with the authorities of that State. The Council shall act unanimously after consulting the European Parliament.

## NOTES AND QUESTIONS

1.   In what ways do the above provisions grant executive authority to the Union? Does this mean that the Union is acquiring police powers?

2.   Is the structure of these provisions consistent with the notion of a federal organization, or do they actually suggest that in this area, at least, the Union is moving toward some form of unitary government?

3.   As was evident with the internal market, and in particular from cases such as *Internationale Handelsgesellschaft* in Chapter 3, *supra)* the powers granted to the Union here enable it to adopt legislation that could be in conflict with national constitutions. So far, while Union measures have not been challenged directly, state implementing action has been, specifically as regards the implementation of the Framework Decision creating the "European Arrest Warrant". (Framework Decision 2002/584/JHA [2001] OJ L 190/1 The implementing legislation in Germany was held to be unconstitutional, as written, as it potentially allowed extradition contrary to conditions laid down in article 16 (2) of the Grundgesetz (Basic Law) with respect to how the requesting state (in this case, Spain) dealt with the matter: *Re Constitutionality of German Law implementing the Framework Decision on the European Arrest Warrant* [2006] 1 CMLR 16. Understandably, this led to significant tension between Germany and Spain. The Polish Constitutional Tribunal also found that the implementing Polish legislation was unconstitutional: Case P105, *Re Enforcement of European Arrest Warrant (Polish Constitutional Tribunal,* [2006] 1 CMLR 36.

# Chapter 12

# EXTERNAL RELATIONS COMPETENCES

## § 12.01 OVERVIEW

***Template***: Article 6, 6.3 and 6.6

***Materials in this Chapter***: The materials in this chapter examine, from a legal standpoint, the competences of the Union to conduct external relations granted pursuant to the TFEU. The significance of this is explained in the following paragraphs.

***Context*** The ability of states to engage in relations with other states on the basis of equality is perhaps the first characteristic of sovereignty that springs to mind if we conceptualize the world as comprised of nation-states each existing as a subject of international law. This implies that each state is free to engage in any activity in its relations with others, mirroring all of its internal sovereign powers and encompassing also its defense or sometimes regrettably its offensive capabilities. Quite clearly, such a notion is merely a paradigm and scarcely is able to explain the complexities of the modern world. This is particularly exemplified in the case of the European Union. Here, the Member States, while still sovereign powers, have conceded a considerable amount of competence to the European Union, which thus acts like a sovereign state (including, now, its own version of a diplomatic service), yet it is not one at all.

***The Union's external relations dichotomy*** From a legal perspective, the Union's competence to conduct external relations falls into two categories. Section 6.3 of the Template describes what appears to be a potentially limitless power of the Union to conduct foreign affairs (the Common Foreign and Security Policy or CFSP). It even references the development of a common Union defense. However, though the Template indeed lists these as Union competences, it will be noted that they are granted pursuant to the TEU. The institutional, lawmaking and executive powers described in the TFEU do not apply to them. They are thus of a different order altogether from the enumeration of competences in the TFEU, reminiscent in fact of the pre-Lisbon "pillar" structure described in Chapter 2. In practice this segregation means that they still reside, in reality, in the realm of inter-governmental cooperation. The Member States choose areas where they desire to act together in the name of the Union, but otherwise remain free to behave like sovereign states.

The Template notes that national security remains entirely a matter for the Member States, yet at the same time it reflects the Treaty provisions that envisage the development of a common defense. At present this does not imply that the Union would have its own standing military. A common defense will be built on coordination of national capabilities. Such a development is already under way, with some 200 personnel now seconded to Brussels to work on projects of common interest. This includes liaison with NATO.

How, then, does the EU differ from NATO? NATO is an alliance under a treaty that expressly declares that an attack on one member is to be regarded as an attack on all. It functions through secondment of a certain portion of national defense forces to a central organization. However, the reality is that each state is free to choose what it might contribute to any particular mission.

The concept of an EU defense force, while also built on secondment of national resources, operates on a quite different premise. Here, it is acting in the name of the *Union*, not an alliance of states, and is intended to carry out a *Union* policy. Thus, in the not inconsiderable number of missions already undertaken (including, for example, peacekeeping in Bosnia and Kosovo), the national forces have indeed been Union forces acting under a unitary Union command.

In contrast with the CFSP, the powers of the Union under the TFEU are exclusive — that is to say, the Member States now no longer have any authority to pursue their own policies or take their own action. Such exclusive powers are either granted expressly by the TFEU (the common commercial policy) or arise as a result of the exercise of the Union's internal competences, whether or not such competences are internally exclusive.

This dichotomy of competences is in some respects now rather blurred as a result of the powers granted to the various Union institutions to determine and execute policies. The TFEU structure gives a significant role to the Commission, which is, however, excluded from representing the Union under the CFSP. At the same time, the Union's High Representative for external affairs serves as a representative of the European Council (under CFSP) and as a Vice President of the Commission for TFEU affairs. Clearly the intent was to provide consistency of approach (it is after all, one Union). But the combination of roles here should not obscure the separate and distinct legal bases for the Union's competences.

***Comparison with the United States*** In the United States, external relations and defense are the responsibility of the federal government. This is true for all subject matter and all activities related to foreign affairs — even those areas that are, on a domestic level, within the primary or exclusive competence of the constituent states. If it were not, there would be no way of handling such issues internationally, given that the individual states do not have international legal personality. Only the federal authority has the *capacity* to act internationally.

General external relations and particularly treaty-making power are conferred on the federal government through the grant of this power to the President. Because the President was regarded as the successor to the power previously exercised by the British Crown, the foreign relations power of that office is necessarily unfettered except as might be otherwise expressly prescribed by the Constitution. The states must abstain from any action that might compromise the federal external relations power.

This state of affairs, however, leads to a quandary. If the President has unfettered power to negotiate and conclude international treaties as part of that office's external relations power, and such treaties are themselves expressed by the U.S. Constitution to be the supreme law of the land (subject of course to ratification by the Senate), can a Treaty have internal effects that could not, under the Constitution, be enacted domestically? What of the Tenth Amendment, which reserves to the states powers not expressly granted to the federal government? Here it could be argued that if the internal power lies with the states, the federal government cannot usurp it by the device of entering into international obligations that require internal implementation outside the scope of its internal attribution of powers. Yet this is not so. Consider in this regard the Supreme Court's well-known decision in *State of Missouri v. Holland*, 252 U.S. 416, 40 S. CT. 382, 64 L. ED. 641, (1920):

Justice Holmes:

> This is a bill in equity brought by the State of Missouri to prevent a game warden of the United States from attempting to enforce the Migratory Bird Treaty Act of July 3, 1918, c. 128, 40 Stat. 755, and the regulations made by the Secretary of Agriculture in pursuance of the same. The ground of the bill is that the statute is an unconstitutional interference with the rights reserved to the States by the Tenth Amendment, and that the acts of the defendant done and threatened under that authority invade the sovereign right of the State and contravene its will manifested in statutes. The State also alleges a pecuniary interest, as owner of the wild birds within its borders and otherwise, admitted by the Government to be sufficient, but it is enough that the bill is a reasonable and proper means to assert the alleged quasi sovereign rights of a State.

> \*    \*    \*

> On December 8, 1916, a treaty between the United States and Great Britain was proclaimed by the President. It recited that many species of birds in their annual migrations traversed certain parts of the United States and of Canada, that they were of great value as a source of food and in destroying insects injurious to vegetation, but were in danger of extermination through lack of adequate protection. It therefore provided for specified close seasons and protection in other forms, and agreed that the two powers would take or propose to their law-making bodies the necessary measures for carrying the treaty out. 39 Stat. 1702.

> \*    \*    \*

> It is unnecessary to go into any details, because, as we have said, the question raised is the general one whether the treaty and statute are void as an interference with the rights reserved to the States.

> To answer this question it is not enough to refer to the Tenth Amendment, reserving the powers not delegated to the United States, because by Article II, section 2, the power to make treaties is delegated expressly, and by Article VI treaties made under the authority of the United States, along with the Constitution and laws of the United States made in pursuance thereof, are declared the supreme law of the land. If the treaty is valid

there can be no dispute about the validity of the statute under Article I, section 8, as a necessary and proper means to execute the powers of the Government. The language of the Constitution as to the supremacy of treaties being general, the question before us is narrowed to an inquiry into the ground upon which the present supposed exception is placed.

It is said that a treaty cannot be valid if it infringes the Constitution, that there are limits, therefore, to the treaty-making power, and that one such limit is that what an act of Congress could not do unaided, in derogation of the powers reserved to the States, a treaty cannot do. An earlier act of Congress that attempted by itself and not in pursuance of a treaty to regulate the killing of migratory birds within the States had been held bad in the District Court. *United States v. Shauver*, 214 F. 154, 1914 U.S. Dist. LEXIS 1795 (E.D. Ark. 1914); *United States v. McCullagh*, 221 Fed. Rep. 288. Those decisions were supported by arguments that migratory birds were owned by the States in their sovereign capacity for the benefit of their people, and that under cases like Geer v. Connecticut, 161 U.S. 519, this control was one that Congress had no power to displace. The same argument is supposed to apply now with equal force.

Whether the two cases cited were decided rightly or not they cannot be accepted as a test of the treaty power. Acts of Congress are the supreme law of the land only when made in pursuance of the Constitution, while treaties are declared to be so when made under the authority of the United States. It is open to question whether the authority of the United States means more than the formal acts prescribed to make the Convention. We do not mean to imply that there are no qualifications to the treaty-making power; but they must be ascertained in a different way. It is obvious that there may be matters of the sharpest exigency for the national well being that an act of Congress could not deal with but that a treaty followed by such an act could, and it is not lightly to be assumed that, in matters requiring national action, "a power which must belong to and somewhere reside in every civilized government" is not to be found. *Andrews v. Andrews*, 188 U.S. 14, 33. What was said in that case with regard to the powers of the States applies with equal force to the powers of the nation in cases where the States individually are incompetent to act.

\*   \*   \*

The treaty in question does not contravene any prohibitory words to be found in the Constitution. The only question is whether it is forbidden by some invisible radiation from the general terms of the Tenth Amendment. We must consider what this country has become in deciding what that Amendment has reserved.

The State as we have intimated founds its claim of exclusive authority upon an assertion of title to migratory birds, an assertion that is embodied in statute. No doubt it is true that as between a State and its inhabitants the State may regulate the killing and sale of such birds, but it does not follow that its authority is exclusive of paramount powers. To put the claim of the State upon title is to lean upon a slender reed. Wild birds are not in the possession of anyone; and possession is the beginning of ownership. The whole foundation of the State's rights is the presence within their jurisdiction of birds that yesterday had not arrived, tomorrow may be in another State and in a week a thousand miles away. If we are to be accurate we cannot put the case of the State upon higher ground than that the treaty deals with creatures that for the moment are within the state borders, that it must be carried out by officers of the United States within the same territory, and that but for the treaty the State would be free to regulate this subject itself.

As most of the laws of the United States are carried out within the States and as many of them deal with matters which in the silence of such laws the State might regulate, such general grounds are not enough to support Missouri's claim. Valid treaties of course "are as binding within the territorial limits of the States as they are elsewhere throughout the dominion of the United States." Baldwin v. Franks, 120 U.S. 678, 683. No doubt the great body of private relations usually fall within the control of the State, but a treaty may override its power.

*   *   *

Here a national interest of very nearly the first magnitude is involved. It can be protected only by national action in concert with that of another power. The subject-matter is only transitorily within the State and has no permanent habitat therein. But for the treaty and the statute there soon might be no birds for any powers to deal with. We see nothing in the Constitution that compels the Government to sit by while a food supply is cut off and the protectors of our forests and our crops are destroyed. It is not sufficient to rely upon the States. The reliance is vain, and were it otherwise, the question is whether the United States is forbidden to act. We are of opinion that the treaty and statute must be upheld.

The judgment in *State of Missouri v. Holland*, though not unambiguous, confirms a general principle that the U.S. government can indeed enter into treaties *and* implement them in the United States even if it could not have taken similar action by congressional legislation.

As noted above, the opposite is true for the EU. It has only conferred powers, and beyond that, the Member States continue to have competence. The provisions addressing the execution of the Union's competences in this area, TFEU 218 (which has changed significantly from its predecessor, EC 300) provides for a procedure for the negotiation and conclusion of treaties by the EU. According to TFEU 218, the Union's powers as described are limited to the extent that they may overlap with the CFSP, but otherwise today the article implicitly acknowledges the provisions of both the common commercial policy and of TFEU 3 and 216.

**Recognition of the Union by other States** Both the Member States and (per TEU 47) the Union have the necessary *legal personality* under their domestic law and international law to enter into treaties and otherwise participate in international affairs. There is now no state or organization that refuses to recognize that capacity. However, any international organization that allows only Sovereign States to be members (the United Nations being the classic example) cannot admit the Union to full membership. This creates particular issues for the Union and its Member States, given the scope of Union powers — See further Chapter 21, *infra*.

## § 12.02   EXCLUSIVE COMPETENCE — EC 133/TFEU 207

### [A]   Scope

### OPINION 1/75
### (LOCAL COST STANDARD)
### [1975] ECR 1355

[No paragraph numbering appears in the original text]

[The ECJ had been requested to provide an opinion on the legality under the EC Treaty of the EU's entering into the OECD Understanding on a Local Cost Standard in connection with export credits.]

Articles 112 [repealed] and 113 [207] of the Treaty must be borne in mind in formulating a reply to this question.

The first of these provisions provides that:

"Member States shall, before the end of the transitional period, progressively harmonize the systems whereby they grant aid for exports to third countries, to the extent necessary to ensure that competition between undertakings of the Community is not distorted."

Since there is no doubt that the grant of export credits falls within the system of aids granted by Member States for exports, it is already clear from Article 112 [repealed] that the subject-matter of the standard laid down in the Understanding in question relates to a field in which the provisions of the Treaty recognize a Community power.

Furthermore, Article 113 [207] of the Treaty lays down, in paragraphs (1) and (2), that:

'. . . the common commercial policy shall be based on uniform principles, particularly in regard to . . . export policy. . . .'

The field of the common commercial policy, and more particularly that of export policy, necessarily covers systems of aid for exports and more particularly measures concerning credits for the financing of local costs linked to export operations. In fact, such measures constitute an important element of commercial policy, that concept having the same content whether it is applied in the context of the international action of a State or to that of the Community.

Directives concerning credit insurance, adopted by the Council towards the end of 1970 and the beginning of 1971 expressly recognize the important role played by export credits in international trade, as a factor of commercial policy.

For these reasons the subject-matter covered by the standard contained in the Understanding in question, since it forms part not only of the sphere of the system of aids for exports laid down at Article 112 of the Treaty but also, in a more general way, of export policy and, by reason of that fact, of the sphere of the common commercial policy defined in Article 113 [207] of the Treaty, falls within the ambit of the Community's powers.

In the case of the measures necessary to implement the principles laid down in the abovementioned provisions, particularly those covered by Article 113 [207] of the Treaty, concerning the common commercial policy, the Community is empowered, pursuant to the powers which it possesses, not only to adopt internal rules of Community law, but also to conclude agreements with third countries pursuant to Article 113 [207] (2) and Article 114 [repealed] of the Treaty.

A commercial policy is in fact made up by the combination and interaction of internal and external measures, without priority being taken by one over the others. Sometimes agreements are concluded in execution of a policy fixed in advance, sometimes that policy is defined by the agreements themselves.

Such agreements may be outline agreements, the purpose of which is to lay down uniform principles. Such is the case with the Understanding on local costs: it does not have a specific content adapted to particular export credit transactions; it merely lays down a standard, sets out certain exceptions, provides, in exceptional circumstances, for derogations and, finally, lays down general provisions. Furthermore, the implementation of the export policy to be pursued within the framework of a common commercial policy does not necessarily find expression in the adoption of general and abstract rules of internal or Community law. The common commercial policy is above all the outcome of a progressive development based upon specific measures which may refer without distinction to 'autonomous' and external aspects of that policy and which do not necessarily presuppose, by the fact that they are linked to the field of the common commercial policy, the existence of a large body of rules, but combine gradually to form that body.

2. The exclusive nature of the Community's powers

The reply to this question depends, on the one hand, on the objective of the Understanding in question and, on the other hand, on the manner in which the common commercial policy is conceived in the Treaty.

At Nos I and II the Understanding itself defines the transactions to which the common standard applies, and those which, on the other hand, are excluded from its field of application because they are directed to specifically military ends or because they have been entered into with developing countries.

It is to be understood from this definition that the subject-matter of the standard, and therefore of the Understanding, is one of those measures belonging to the common commercial policy prescribed by Article 113 [207] of the Treaty.

Such a policy is conceived in that article in the context of the operation of the Common Market, for the defence of the common interests of the Community, within which the particular interests of the Member States must endeavour to adapt to each other.

Quite clearly, however, this conception is incompatible with the freedom to which the Member States could lay claim by invoking a concurrent power, so as to ensure that their own interests were separately satisfied in external relations, at the risk of compromising the effective defence of the common interests of the Community.

In fact any unilateral action on the part of the Member States would lead to disparities in the conditions for the grant of export credits, calculated to distort competition between undertakings of the various Member States in external markets. Such distortion can be eliminated only by means of a strict uniformity of credit conditions granted to undertakings in the Community, whatever their nationality.

It cannot therefore be accepted that, in a field such as that governed by the Understanding in question, which is covered by export policy and more generally by the common commercial policy, the Member States should exercise a power concurrent to that of the Community, in the Community sphere and in the international sphere. The provisions of Articles 113 [207] and 114 [repealed] concerning the conditions under which, according to the Treaty, agreements on commercial policy must be concluded show clearly that the exercise of concurrent powers by the Member States and the Community in this matter is impossible.

To accept that the contrary were true would amount to recognizing that, in relations with third countries, Member States may adopt positions which differ from those which the Community intends to adopt, and would thereby distort the institutional framework, call into question the mutual trust within the Community and prevent the latter from fulfilling its task in the defence of the common interest.

It is of little importance that the obligations and financial burdens inherent in the execution of the agreement envisaged are borne directly by the Member States. The 'internal' and 'external' measures adopted by the Community within the framework of the common commercial policy do not necessarily involve, in order to ensure their compatibility with the Treaty, a transfer to the institutions of the Community of the obligations and financial burdens which they may involve: such measures are solely concerned to substitute for the unilateral action of the Member States, in the field under consideration, a common action based upon uniform principles on behalf of the whole of the Community.

\* \* \*

Accordingly, THE COURT gives the following opinion:

The Community has exclusive power to participate in the Understanding on a Local Cost Standard referred to in the request for an opinion.

## NOTES AND QUESTIONS

1. What was the Court's rationale for determining that article 113 (EC 133/TFEU 207) granted *exclusive* powers in this case? What were the internal consequences?

**2.** In *Re Territorial Sea: Commission v. United Kingdom*, Case C-146/89, 1991 ECJ CELEX LEXIS 150, [1991] ECR I-3533, the ECJ held that the United Kingdom was precluded from altering the size of its territorial waters by unilaterally altering its baselines (which close off bays and river estuaries and establish the point from which the territorial sea is measured) even though under international law it has the right to do so as a sovereign state. Here the issue was one of conflict with internal EU competence regarding the conservation of marine resources. (See the *Rogers* case in Chapter 11, *supra*.)

# OPINION 1/94
## (AGREEMENT ESTABLISHING THE WORLD TRADE ORGANIZATION)
### 1994 ECJ CELEX LEXIS 459, [1994] ECR I-5627

[The Commission had submitted a request for an opinion regarding competence of the Union under the various agreements comprised within the multiplicity of agreements setting up the World Trade Organization (WTO). The WTO Agreement established a common institutional framework for the conduct of trade relations among its members in matters related to the agreements and legal instruments annexed to it, embodying the results of the Uruguay Round multilateral trade negotiations. In this extract, the Court considered the extent to which EC 133/TFEU 207 granted competence to the Union to conclude the General Agreement on Trade in Services (the "GATS" agreement.]

35 The Commission's main contention is that the conclusion of both GATS and TRIPs falls within the exclusive competence conferred on the Community in commercial policy matters by Article 113 [207] of the EC Treaty. That point of view has been vigorously disputed, as to its essentials, by the Council, by the Member States which have submitted observations and by the European Parliament, which has been permitted, at its request, to submit observations. It is therefore appropriate to begin by examining the Commission's main contention, with reference to GATS and to TRIPs respectively.

## A. GATS

36 Relying essentially on the non-restrictive interpretation applied by the Court's case-law to the concept of the common commercial policy . . . the links or overlap between goods and services, the purpose of GATS and the instruments used, the Commission concludes that services fall within the common commercial policy, without any need to distinguish between the different modes of supply of services and, in particular, between the direct, cross-frontier supply of services and the supply of services through a commercial presence in the country of the person to whom they are supplied. The Commission also maintains that international agreements of a commercial nature in relation to transport (as opposed to those relating to safety rules) fall within the common commercial policy and not within the particular title of the Treaty on the common transport policy.

37 It is appropriate to consider, first, services other than transport and, subsequently, the particular services comprised in transport.

38 As regards the first category, it should be recalled at the outset that in Opinion 1/75 the Court, which had been asked to rule on the scope of Community competence as to the arrangements relating to a local cost standard, held that 'the field of the common commercial policy, and more particularly that of export policy, necessarily covers systems of aid for exports and more particularly measures concerning credits for the financing of local costs linked to export operations' ([1975] ECR 1362). The local costs in question concerned expenses incurred for the supply of both goods and services. Nevertheless, the Court recognized the exclusive competence of the Community, without drawing a distinction between goods and services.

39 In its Opinion 1/78 . . . the Court rejected an interpretation of Article 113 [207] 'the effect of which would be to restrict the common commercial policy to the use of instruments intended to have an effect only on the traditional aspects of external trade'. On the contrary, it considered that 'the question of external trade must be governed from a wide point of view', as is confirmed by 'the fact that the enumeration in Article 113 [207] of the subjects covered by commercial policy . . . is conceived as a non-exhaustive enumeration' (Opinion 1/78, cited above, paragraph 45).

40 The Commission points out in its request for an opinion that in certain developed countries the services sector has become the dominant sector of the economy and that the global economy has been undergoing fundamental structural changes. The trend is for basic industry to be transferred to developing countries, whilst the developed economies have tended to become, in the main, exporters of services and of goods with a high value-added content. The Court notes that this trend is borne out by the WTO Agreement and its annexes, which were the subject of a single process of negotiation covering both goods and services.

41 Having regard to this trend in international trade, it follows from the open nature of the common commercial policy, within the meaning of the Treaty, that trade in services cannot immediately, and as a matter of principle, be excluded from the scope of Article 113 [207], as some of the Governments which have submitted observations contend.

42 In order to make that conclusion more specific, however, one must take into account the definition of trade in services given in GATS in order to see whether the overall scheme of the Treaty is not such as to limit the extent to which trade in services can be included within Article 113 [207].

43 Under Article I(2) of GATS, trade in services is defined, for the purposes of that agreement, as comprising four modes of supply of services: (1) cross-frontier supplies not involving any movement of persons; (2) consumption abroad, which entails the movement of the consumer into the territory of the WTO member country in which the supplier is established; (3) commercial presence, i.e. the presence of a subsidiary or branch in the territory of the WTO member country in which the service is to be rendered; (4) the presence of natural persons from a WTO member country, enabling a supplier from one member country to supply services within the territory of any other member country.

44 As regards cross-frontier supplies, the service is rendered by a supplier

established in one country to a consumer residing in another. The supplier does not move to the consumer's country; nor, conversely, does the consumer move to the supplier's country. That situation is, therefore, not unlike trade in goods, which is unquestionably covered by the common commercial policy within the meaning of the Treaty. There is thus no particular reason why such a supply should not fall within the concept of the common commercial policy.

45 The same cannot be said of the other three modes of supply of services covered by GATS, namely, consumption abroad, commercial presence and the presence of natural persons.

46 As regards natural persons, it is clear from Article 3 of the Treaty [repealed], which distinguishes between 'a common commercial policy' in paragraph (b) and 'measures concerning the entry and movement of persons' in paragraph (d), that the treatment of nationals of non-member countries on crossing the external frontiers of Member States cannot be regarded as falling within the common commercial policy. More generally, the existence in the Treaty of specific chapters on the free movement of natural and legal persons shows that those matters do not fall within the common commercial policy.

*　*　*

## B. TRIPs

54 The Commission's argument in support of its contention that the Community has exclusive competence under Article 113 [207] is essentially that the rules concerning intellectual property rights are closely linked to trade in the products and services to which they apply.

55 It should be noted, first, that Section 4 of Part III of TRIPs, which concerns the means of enforcement of intellectual property rights, contains specific rules as to measures to be applied at border crossing points. . . . [T]hat section has its counterpart in the provisions of Council Regulation (EEC) No 3842/86 of 1 December 1986 laying down measures to prohibit the release for free circulation of counterfeit goods (OJ 1986 L 357, p. 1). Inasmuch as that regulation concerns the prohibition of the release into free circulation of counterfeit goods, it was rightly based on Article 113 [207] of the Treaty: it relates to measures to be taken by the customs authorities at the external frontiers of the Community. Since measures of that type can be adopted autonomously by the Community institutions on the basis of Article 113 [207] of the EC Treaty, it is for the Community alone to conclude international agreements on such matters.

56 However, as regards matters other than the provisions of TRIPs on the release into free circulation of counterfeit goods, the Commission's arguments cannot be accepted.

57 Admittedly, there is a connection between intellectual property and trade in goods. Intellectual property rights enable those holding them to prevent third parties from carrying out certain acts. The power to prohibit the use of a trade mark, the manufacture of a product, the copying of a design or the reproduction of a book, a disc or a videocassette inevitably has effects on trade. Intellectual

property rights are moreover specifically designed to produce such effects. That is not enough to bring them within the scope of Article 113 [207]. Intellectual property rights do not relate specifically to international trade; they affect internal trade just as much as, if not more than, international trade.

58 . . . [T]he primary objective of TRIPs is to strengthen and harmonize the protection of intellectual property on a worldwide scale. The Commission has itself conceded that, since TRIPs lays down rules in fields in which there are no Community harmonization measures, its conclusion would make it possible at the same time to achieve harmonization within the Community and thereby to contribute to the establishment and functioning of the common market.

59 It should be noted here that, at the level of internal legislation, the Community is competent, in the field of intellectual property, to harmonize national laws pursuant to Articles 100 [115] and 100a [114] and may use Article 235 [352] as the basis for creating new rights superimposed on national rights, as it did in Council Regulation (EC) No 40/94 of 20 December 1993 on the Community trade mark (OJ 1994 L 11, p. 1). Those measures are subject to voting rules (unanimity in the case of Articles 100 [94] and 235 [352]) or rules of procedure (consultation of the Parliament in the case of Articles 100 [94] and 235 [352], the joint decision-making procedure in the case of Article 100a [114]) which are different from those applicable under Article 113 [207].

60 If the Community were to be recognized as having exclusive competence to enter into agreements with non-member countries to harmonize the protection of intellectual property and, at the same time, to achieve harmonization at Community level, the Community institutions would be able to escape the internal constraints to which they are subject in relation to procedures and to rules as to voting.

61 Institutional practice in relation to autonomous measures or external agreements adopted on the basis of Article 113 [207] cannot alter this conclusion.

62 The Commission cites three cases in which, by virtue of the 'new commercial policy instrument' (Council Regulation (EEC) No 2641/84 of 17 September 1984 on the strengthening of the common commercial policy with regard in particular to protection against illicit commercial practices (OJ 1984 L 252, p. 1), which was itself based on Article 113 [207] of the Treaty), procedures were opened to defend the Community's intellectual property interests: Commission Decision 87/251/EEC of 12 March 1987 on the initiation of an international consultation and disputes settlement procedure concerning a United States measure excluding imports of certain aramid fibres into the United States of America (OJ 1987 L 117, p. 18); notice of initiation of an 'illicit commercial practice' procedure concerning the unauthorized reproduction of sound recordings inIndonesia (OJ 1987 C 136, p. 3); notice of initiation of an examination procedure concerning an illicit commercial practice, within the meaning of Council Regulation (EEC) No 2641/84, consisting of piracy of Community sound recordings inThailand (OJ 1991 C 189, p. 26).

63 The measures which may be taken pursuant to that regulation in response to a lack of protection in a non-member country of intellectual property rights held by Community undertakings (or to discrimination against them in that field) are unrelated to the harmonization of intellectual property protection which is the

primary objective of TRIPs. According to Article 10(3) of Regulation No 2641/84, cited above, those measures are: the suspension or withdrawal of any concession resulting from commercial policy negotiations; the raising of existing customs duties or the introduction of any other charge on imports; and the introduction of quantitative restrictions or any other measures modifying import or export conditions in trade with the non-member country concerned. All those measures fall, by their very nature, within the ambit of commercial policy.

64 The Commission also relies on measures adopted by the Community in relation to Korea within the framework of Council Regulation (EEC) No 4257/88 of 19 December 1988 applying generalized tariff preferences for 1989 in respect of certain industrial products originating in developing countries (OJ 1988 L 375, p. 1). Since Korea had discriminated between its trading partners as regards protection of intellectual property (see the nineteenth recital in the preamble to the regulation), the Community suspended the generalized tariff preferences in respect of its products (Article 1(3) of the regulation).

65 That argument is no more convincing than the preceding one. Since the grant of generalized preferences is a commercial policy measure . . . so too is their suspension. That does not in any way show that the Community has exclusive competence pursuant to Article 113 [207] to conclude an agreement with non-member countries to harmonize the protection of intellectual property worldwide.

66 In support of its argument, the Commission has also cited provisions relating to the protection of intellectual property in certain agreements with non-member countries concluded on the basis of Article 113 [207] of the Treaty.

67 It should be noted that those provisions are extremely limited in scope . . .

68 The fact that the Community and its institutions are entitled to incorporate within external agreements otherwise falling within the ambit of Article 113 [207] ancillary provisions for the organization of purely consultative procedures or clauses calling on the other party to raise the level of protection of intellectual property does not mean that the Community has exclusive competence to conclude an international agreement of the type and scope of TRIPs.

*        *        *

71 In the light of the foregoing, it must be held that, apart from those of its provisions which concern the prohibition of the release into free circulation of counterfeit goods, TRIPs does not fall within the scope of the common commercial policy.

## NOTES AND QUESTIONS

1.   To what extent does EC133/TFEU 207 apply to services and intellectual property? Why might the Member States have objected to that? What was the relevance of the reference to the treatment of this subject matter internally within the EC Treaty/TFEU?

2.   In *Criminal proceedings against Peter Leifer, Reinhold Otto Krauskopf and Otto Holzer*, Case C-83/94, 1995 ECJ CELEX LEXIS 452, [1995] ECR I-3231,

charges had been brought against the defendants alleging that they had delivered plant, plant parts and chemical products to Iraq from 1984 to 1988 without having the necessary export licences. The Court was asked to consider whether export controls relating to dual use goods fell exclusively within the scope of EC133/TFEU 207. Dual use goods are those that are designed for and can be used for both military and commercial purposes. The Court stated:

> 9 Implementation of such a common commercial policy requires a non-restrictive interpretation of that concept, so as to avoid disturbances in intra-Community trade by reason of the disparities which would then exist in certain sectors of economic relations with non-member countries (see Opinion 1/78 of the Court 1979 ECR 2871, paragraph 45).

> 10 So, national rules whose effect is to prevent or restrict the export of certain products fall within the scope of the common commercial policy within the meaning of Article 113 [207] of the Treaty.

> 11 The fact that the restriction concerns dual-use goods does not affect that conclusion. The nature of those products cannot take them outside the scope of the common commercial policy.

It would thus appear that the ECJ is willing to override Member State prerogatives with respect to national security in the interests of preserving the unity of EU trade policy. The regulation in question here, Council Regulation (EEC) No 2603/69, establishing common rules for exports (OJ, English Special Edition 1969 (II), p. 590, did provide, however, that Member States might adopt national measures restricting the export of dual use goods to non-member countries pursuant to EC 296/TFEU 346 (1)(b) or EC 297/TFEU 347, or on the basis of Article 11 of the regulation.

**3.** For an account of the World Trade Organization, see P.F.J. MACRORY, A.E. APPLETON AND M.G. PLUMMER (EDS.), THE WORLD TRADE ORGANIZATION (Springer, 2005).

## [B]  Interaction with Member State Competences

### OPINION 1/78
### (INTERNATIONAL AGREEMENT ON NATURAL RUBBER)
### [1979] ECR 2871

[The Commission had asked the Court to give its opinion on the compatibility with the EC Treaty of the draft International Agreement on Natural Rubber which was the subject of negotiations in the United Nations Conference on Trade and Development (hereinafter referred to as "UNCTAD"), and, more particularly, whether the Community was competent to conclude the agreement in question. The Natural Rubber agreement included provision for intervention in the natural rubber market through the medium of a buffer stock, which required funding by the parties to the agreement. At the time of the Opinion, the Member States and the Community were still discussing options as to how they would subscribe this cost.]

36 As the Council has indicated, the problem of competence which has been

submitted to the Court must be examined from two aspects. The first question is whether the agreement envisaged, by reason of its subject-matter and objectives, comes within the concept of common commercial policy referred to in Article 113 [207] of the Treaty. The second question — but only if the first question is answered in the affirmative — is whether, by reason of certain specific arrangements or special provisions of the agreement concerning matters coming within the powers of the Member States, the participation of the latter in the agreement is necessary.

The Court will consider first the general aspects concerning the subject- matter and objectives of the agreement.

37 The central question raised by the Commission's request is whether the international agreement on rubber comes as a whole or at least in essentials within the sphere of the "common commercial policy" referred to in Article 113 [207] of the Treaty. It is common ground that the agreement envisaged is closely connected with commercial policy. The difference of views relates to the extent of the sphere of application of Article 113 [207] so that it remains uncertain whether that provision entirely covers the subject-matter of the agreement in question.

*   *   *

[The Court here described the extensive links between the proposed agreements and commercial policy and then went on to consider the more problematic presence of other aspects.]

(b) The agreement's links with general economic policy

47 In its arguments the Council has raised the problem of the interrelation within the structure of the Treaty of the concepts of "economic policy" and "commercial policy". In certain provisions economic policy is indeed considered primarily as a question of national interest . . . In other provisions economic policy is envisaged as being a matter of common interest as is the case with Articles 103 [120] to 116 [126], which are grouped together in a title devoted to the "economic policy" of the Community. The chapter devoted to the common commercial policy forms part of that title.

48 The considerations set out above already form to some extent an answer to the arguments relating to the distinction to be drawn between the spheres of general economic policy and those of the common commercial policy since international co-operation, inasmuch as it does not belong to commercial policy, would be confused with the domain of general economic policy. If it appears that it comes, at least in part, under the common commercial policy, as has been indicated above, it follows clearly that it could not, under the name of general economic policy, be withdrawn from the competence of the Community.

49 Having regard to the specific nature of the provisions relating to commercial policy in so far as they concern relations with non-member countries and are founded, according to Article 113 [207], on the concept of a common policy, their scope cannot be restricted in the light of more general provisions relating to economic policy and based on the idea of mere co-ordination. Consequently, where the organization of the Community's economic links with non- member countries

may have repercussions on certain sectors of economic policy such as the supply of raw materials to the Community or price policy, as is precisely the case with the regulation of international trade in commodities, that consideration does not constitute a reason for excluding such objectives from the field of application of the rules relating to the common commercial policy. Similarly, the fact that a product may have a political importance by reason of the building up of security stocks is not a reason for excluding that product from the domain of the common commercial policy.

*     *     *

V — Problems raised by the financing of the agreement and by other specific provisions

52 Consideration must still be given, having regard to what has been stated above as regards correspondence between the objective and purposes of the agreement envisaged and the concept of common commercial policy, whether the detailed arrangements for financing the buffer stock, or certain specific clauses of the agreement, concerning technological assistance, research programmes, the maintenance of fair conditions of labor in the rubber industry and consultations relating to national tax policies which may have an effect on the price of rubber lead to a negation of the Community's exclusive competence.

53 As regards the question of financing, the Council and those of the governments which have supported its views state that since those negotiating the agreement have opted for financing by means of public funds, the finances of the Member States will be involved in the execution of the agreement so that it cannot be accepted that such undertakings should be entered into without their participation. The Commission, for its part, takes the view that the question of competence precedes that of financing and that the question of Community powers cannot therefore be made dependent on the choice of financial arrangements.

*     *     *

56 The Court takes the view that the fact that the agreement may cover subjects such as technological assistance, research programmes, labor conditions in the industry concerned or consultations relating to national tax policies which may have an effect on the price of rubber cannot modify the description of the agreement which must be assessed having regard to its essential objective rather than in terms of individual clauses of an altogether subsidiary or ancillary nature. This is the more true because the clauses under consideration are in fact closely connected with the objective of the agreement and the duties of the bodies which are to operate in the framework of the International Natural Rubber Organization which it is planned to set up. The negotiation and execution of these clauses must therefore follow the system applicable to the agreement considered as a whole.

57 With regard to the system of financing it should be borne in mind in the first place that, in its recommendation to the Council on 5 October 1978 under Article 113 [207], the Commission had proposed that the application of the financial clauses of the agreement on natural rubber should be effected by the Community itself with

a direct contribution from the Community budget. Whilst accepting that this method of financing would be possible having regard to the financial provisions of the EEC Treaty, the Council expressed its preference for financing by the Member States. However, no formal decision has yet been taken on this question. Moreover, there is no certainty as regards the attitude of the various Member States on this particular question and its implications for the apportionment of the financial burdens.

58 Having regard to the uncertainty which exists as regards the final solution to be adopted for this problem, the Court feels bound to have regard to two possible situations: one in which the financial burdens envisaged by the agreement would be entered in the Community budget and one in which the burdens would be directly charged to the budgets of the Member States. The Court itself is in no position, within the limits of the present proceedings, to make any choice between the two alternatives.

59 In the first case no problem would arise as regards the exclusive powers of the Community to conclude the agreement in question. As has been indicated above, the mechanism of the buffer stock has the purpose of regulating trade and from this point of view constitutes an instrument of the common commercial policy. It follows that Community financing of the charges arising would have to be regarded as a solution in conformity with the Treaty.

60 The facts of the problem would be different if the second alternative were to be preferred. It cannot in fact be denied that the financing of the buffer stock constitutes an essential feature of the scheme for regulating the market which it is proposed to set up. The extent of and the detailed arrangements for the financial undertakings which the Member States will be required to satisfy will directly condition the possibilities and the degree of efficiency of intervention by the buffer mechanism whilst the decisions to be taken as regards the level of the central reference price and the margins of fluctuation to be permitted either upwards or downwards will have immediate repercussions on the use of the financial means put at the disposal of the International Rubber Council which is to be set up and on the extent of the financial means to be put at its disposal. Furthermore sight must not be lost of the fact that the financial structure which it is proposed to set up will make necessary, as is mentioned in the documents submitted to the Court and reflecting the most recent stage of negotiations, co-ordination between the use of the specific financial means put at the disposal of the future International Rubber Council and those which it might find in the Common Fund which is to be set up. If the financing of the agreement is a matter for the Community the necessary decisions will be taken according to the appropriate Community procedures. If on the other hand the financing is to be by the Member States that will imply the participation of those States in the decision-making machinery or, at least, their agreement with regard to the arrangements for financing envisaged and consequently their participation in the agreement together with the Community. The exclusive competence of the Community could not be envisaged in such a case.

*     *     *

VII — Concluding remarks

63 It follows from all the foregoing considerations that the envisaged International Natural Rubber Agreement, in spite of the special features which distinguish it from classical trade and tariff agreements, comes under the commercial policy as it is envisaged in Article 113 [207] of the EEC Treaty.

The consequences of that finding as regards the exclusive powers of the Community to negotiate and conclude the agreement envisaged might nevertheless be modified having regard to the option still to be exercised with regard to the arrangements for financing the machinery of the buffer stock in the event of the financial burden's being directly assumed by the Member States.

## NOTES AND QUESTIONS

1.    The above case highlights the difficulties of defining "commercial policy" particularly given its overlap with other areas such as general economic policy, which were still within the competence of the Member States. Did the ECJ consider that the EC had exclusive competence notwithstanding these difficulties? How did it resolve the "overlapping" competences issue?

2.    The above opinion recognized that the agreement in question might require the participation of both the Member States and the EU. Does it matter that there is a clear designation in any such agreement as to whether the Member States are responsible or the EU? How would third parties to the Natural Rubber Agreement know who should be responsible for the various obligations? Could they hold the EU and the Member States jointly liable?

## [C]    Relationship with Other EC/TFEU Internal Competences

### OPINION 1/94
(AGREEMENT    ESTABLISHING    THE    WORLD    TRADE ORGANIZATION)
1994 ECJ CELEX LEXIS 459, [1994] ECR I-5627

[See the first extract from this case for the background. Here the Court addressed how the Common Commercial Policy under EC 133/TFEU207 related to other competences in the Treaty.]

29 As regards the Agreement on Agriculture [part of the WTO suite of agreements], it is true that Article 43 [43] has been held to be the appropriate legal basis for a directive laying down uniform rules on the conditions under which products may be marketed, not only in intra-Community trade but also when they originate from non-member countries . . . However, that directive was intended to achieve one or more of the common agricultural policy objectives laid down in Article 39 [39] of the Treaty. That is not the case as regards the Agreement on Agriculture annexed to the WTO Agreement. The objective of the Agreement on Agriculture is to establish, on a worldwide basis, 'a fair and market-oriented agricultural trading system' . . . The fact that the commitments entered into under that Agreement require internal

measures to be adopted on the basis of Article 43 [43] of the Treaty does not prevent the international commitments themselves from being entered into pursuant to Article 113 [207] alone.

30 The Council further contends that, for the same reasons as were put forward in relation to the Agreement on Agriculture, it will also be necessary to rely on Article 43 [43] of the EC Treaty as the basis for its decision to conclude the Agreement on the Application of Sanitary and Phytosanitary Measures.

31 That contention must be rejected. The Agreement on the Application of Sanitary and Phytosanitary Measures is confined, as stated in its preamble, to 'the establishment of a multilateral framework of rules and disciplines to guide the development, adoption and enforcement of sanitary and phytosanitary measures in order to minimize their negative effects on trade'. Such an agreement can be concluded on the basis of Article 113 [207] alone.

32 According to the Netherlands Government, the joint participation of the Community and the Member States in the WTO Agreement is justified, since the Member States have their own competence in relation to technical barriers to trade by reason of the optional nature of certain Community directives in that area, and because complete harmonization has not been achieved and is not envisaged in that field.

33 That argument cannot be accepted. The Agreement on Technical Barriers to Trade, the provisions of which are designed merely to ensure that technical regulations and standards and procedures for assessment of conformity with technical regulations and standards do not create unnecessary obstacles to international trade (see the preamble and Articles 2.2 and 5.1.2 of the Agreement), falls within the ambit of the common commercial policy.

34 It follows that the Community has exclusive competence, pursuant to Article 113 [207] of the EC Treaty, to conclude the Multilateral Agreements on Trade in Goods.

## NOTES AND QUESTIONS

1.    Given the very specific provisions regarding agricultural policy in the Treaty, is it perhaps surprising that the Court nonetheless concluded that agricultural issues fell within EC 133/TFEU 207? Alternatively, is the argument that EC 133/TFEU 207 did not apply because of EC 37/TFEU 43 rather doubtful, given that agriculture is an area where clearly the EU does have the power to act internally?

2.    Where EC 133/TFEU 207 might be a basis for external action, but the action predominantly concerns another subject covered elsewhere in the EC/TFEU, then that other area becomes the sole ground for the action: *Opinion 2/00, (Cartagena Protocol)*, 2001 ECJ CELEX LEXIS 364, [2001] ECR I-9713. This case concerned the signature by the Union and the Member States of the Convention on Biological Diversity. The Court was asked for an Opinion regarding the correct legal basis for the action on behalf of the European Community. The issue was whether it fell under the Environmental Policy provisions (EC 174 et seq./TFEU 191 et seq.) or the Common Commercial Policy. If the latter were the correct basis, then the Member States should not have been parties to the Convention, because the CCP

is an exclusive competence of the EU. In this case, although the Convention addressed trade in Living modified organisms, the Court held that EC 175/TFEU 192 was the appropriate legal basis for conclusion of the Protocol on behalf of the EU.

## § 12.03  EXCLUSIVE COMPETENCES UNDER TFEU 3 AND 216

### [A]  Effect on Common Rules or Alteration of their Scope

### COMMISSION v. COUNCIL
(AETR/ERTA)
Case 22/70, [1971] ECR 263

[The Member States, under the auspices of the United Nations Economic Commission for Europe, had negotiated and concluded a European Agreement concerning the work of crews of vehicles engaged in international road transport (AETR). The Commission took the view that they did not have the competence to do so.]

2 As a preliminary objection, the Council has submitted that the application is inadmissible on the ground that the proceedings in question are not an act the legality of which is open to review under the first paragraph of Article 173 [263] of the Treaty.

3 To decide this point, it is first necessary to determine which authority was, at the relevant date, empowered to negotiate and conclude the AETR.

4 The legal effect of the proceedings differs according to whether they are regarded as constituting the exercise of powers conferred on the Community, or as acknowledging a coordination by the Member States of the exercise of powers which remained vested in them.

5 To decide on the objection of inadmissibility, therefore, it is necessary to determine first of all whether, at the date of the proceedings in question, power to negotiate and conclude the AETR was vested in the Community or in the Member States.

1 — The initial question

6 The Commission takes the view that Article 75 [91] of the Treaty, which conferred on the Community powers defined in wide terms with a view to implementing the common transport policy, must apply to external relations just as much as to domestic measures in the sphere envisaged.

7 It believes that the full effect of this provision would be jeopardized if the powers which it confers, particularly that of laying down 'any appropriate provisions', within the meaning of subparagraph (1) (c) of the article cited, did not extend to the conclusion of agreements with third countries.

8 Even if, it is argued, this power did not originally embrace the whole sphere of transport, it would tend to become general and exclusive as and where the common policy in this field came to be implemented.

9 The Council, on the other hand, contends that since the Community only has such powers as have been conferred on it, authority to enter into agreements with third countries cannot be assumed in the absence of an express provision in the Treaty.

10 More particularly, Article 75 [91] relates only to measures internal to the Community, and cannot be interpreted as authorizing the conclusion of international agreements.

11 Even if it were otherwise, such authority could not be general and exclusive, but at the most concurrent with that of the Member States.

12 In the absence of specific provisions of the Treaty relating to the negotiation and conclusion of international agreements in the sphere of transport policy — a category into which, essentially, the AETR falls — one must turn to the general system of Community law in the sphere of relations with third countries.

13 Article 210 [TEU 47] provides that 'The Community shall have legal personality'.

14 This provision, placed at the head of Part Six of the Treaty, devoted to 'General and Final Provisions', means that in its external relations the Community enjoys the capacity to establish contractual links with third countries over the whole field of objectives defined in Part One of the Treaty, which Part Six supplements.

15 To determine in a particular case the Community's authority to enter into international agreements, regard must be had to the whole scheme of the Treaty no less than to its substantive provisions.

16 Such authority arises not only from an express conferment by the Treaty — as is the case with Articles 113 [207] and 114 [deleted] for tariff and trade agreements and with Article 238 [310] for association agreements — but may equally flow from other provisions of the Treaty and from measures adopted, within the framework of those provisions, by the Community institutions.

17 In particular, each time the Community, with a view to implementing a common policy envisaged by the Treaty, adopts provisions laying down common rules, whatever form these may take, the Member States no longer have the right, acting individually or even collectively, to undertake obligations with third countries which affect those rules.

18 As and when such common rules come into being, the Community alone is in a position to assume and carry out contractual obligations towards third countries affecting the whole sphere of application of the Community legal system.

19 With regard to the implementation of the provisions of the Treaty the system of internal Community measures may not therefore be separated from that of external relations.

20 Under Article 3 (e), the adoption of a common policy in the sphere of transport is specially mentioned amongst the objectives of the Community.

21 Under Article 5 [TEU 4] the Member States are required on the one hand to take

all appropriate measures to ensure fulfillment of the obligations arising out of the Treaty or resulting from action taken by the institutions and, on the other, hand, to abstain from any measure which might jeopardize the attainment of the objectives of the Treaty.

22 If these two provisions are read in conjunction, it follows that to the extent to which Community rules are promulgated for the attainment of the objectives of the Treaty, the Member States cannot, outside the framework of the Community institutions, assume obligations which might affect those rules or alter their scope.

23 According to Article 74 [90], the objectives of the Treaty in matters of transport are to be pursued within the framework of a common policy.

24 With this in view, Article 75 [91](1) directs the Council to lay down common rules and, in addition, 'any other appropriate provisions'.

25 By the terms of subparagraph (a) of the same provision, those common rules are applicable 'to international transport to or from the territory of a Member State or passing across the territory of one or more Member States'.

26 This provision is equally concerned with transport from or to third countries, as regards that part of the journey which takes place on Community territory.

27 It thus assumes that the powers of the Community extend to relationships arising from international law, and hence involve the need in the sphere in question for agreements with the third countries concerned.

28 Although it is true that Articles 74 [90] and 75 [91] do not expressly confer on the Community authority to enter into international agreements, nevertheless the bringing into force, on 25 March 1969, of Regulation No 543/69 of the Council on the harmonization of certain social legislation relating to road transport (OJ L 77, p. 49) necessarily vested in the Community power to enter into any agreements with third countries relating to the subject-matter governed by that regulation.

29 This grant of power is moreover expressly recognized by Article 3 of the said regulation which prescribes that: 'The Community shall enter into any negotiations with third countries which may prove necessary for the purpose of implementing this regulation'.

30 Since the subject-matter of the AETR falls within the scope of Regulation no 543/69, the Community has been empowered to negotiate and conclude the agreement in question since the entry into force of the said regulation.

31 These Community powers exclude the possibility of concurrent powers on the part of Member States, since any steps taken outside the framework of the Community institutions would be incompatible with the unity of the Common Market and the uniform application of Community law.

32 This is the legal position in the light of which the question of admissibility has to be resolved.

# NOTES AND QUESTIONS

**1.** The ECJ's decision in this case was very controversial at the time, recognizing as it did a sort of creeping competence in external affairs to match internal powers. But which internal powers are sufficient to trigger the complementary external powers?

**2.** Why was article 113 (EC 133/TFEU 207) considered inapplicable here?

**3.** To the extent that the Member States continue to have capacity under international law, in what ways do the EC Treaty/TFEU and now also the TEU restrict their ability to act independently quite apart from the express and implied powers of the EU?

**4.** What procedure for negotiation and conclusion of agreements should apply when the EU acts under implied powers?

**5.** In the ERTA case, Advocate General Dutheillet De Lamothe expressed his opposition to the possibility of following the model in U.S. Supreme Court cases that developed the concept of "implied" powers for the federal government, especially the President. *Missouri v. Holland*, set forth above, is perhaps the classic example of such a case. Other examples include *United States v. Curtiss-Wright Export Corporation*, 299 U.S. 304(1936), which sets forth an expansive (and controversial) view of the President's "inherent" foreign affairs powers, and *Dames & Moore v. Regan*, 453 U.S. 654 (1981), which held that the President had authority to terminate claims against Iran in U.S. courts as part of the hostage settlement agreement with Iran. See also *Commission v. Council*, Case C-25/94, 1996 ECJ CELEX LEXIS 187, [1996] ECR I-1469.

## OPINION 1/94
### (AGREEMENT ESTABLISHING THE WORLD TRADE ORGANIZATION)
### 1994 ECJ CELEX LEXIS 459, [1994] ECR I-5627

[See the first extract above for the background. In this extract of the WTO case, the Commission had argued that variants of the AETR/ERTA doctrine (now the third basis for exclusive jurisdiction listed in TFEU 216) justified the conferral of exclusive competence on the Union on its harmonization competence with respect to GATS and TRIPs.]

78 The Commission asserted at the hearing that the Member States' freedom to conduct an external policy based on bilateral agreements with non-member countries will inevitably lead to distortions in the flow of services and will progressively undermine the internal market.

79 In reply to that argument, suffice it to say that there is nothing in the Treaty which prevents the institutions from arranging, in the common rules laid down by them, concerted action in relation to non-member countries or from prescribing the approach to be taken by the Member States in their external dealings.

\*   \*   \*

81 Unlike the chapter on transport, the chapters on the right of establishment and

on freedom to provide services do not contain any provision expressly extending the competence of the Community to 'relationships arising from international law'. One cannot therefore infer from those chapters that the Community has exclusive competence to conclude an agreement with non-member countries to liberalize first establishment and access to service markets, other than those which are the subject of cross-border supplies within the meaning of GATS, which are covered by Article 113 [207].

*    *    *

87 . . . [T]he Commission refers to Articles 100a [114] and 235 [352] of the Treaty as the basis of exclusive external competence.

88 As regards Article 100a, [114] it is undeniable that, where harmonizing powers have been exercised, the harmonization measures thus adopted may limit, or even remove, the freedom of the Member States to negotiate with non-member countries. However, an internal power to harmonize which has not been exercised in a specific field cannot confer exclusive external competence in that field on the Community.

89 Article 235 [352] cannot in itself vest exclusive competence in the Community at international level. Save where internal powers can only be effectively exercised at the same time as external powers, internal competence can give rise to exclusive external competence only if it is exercised. This applies *a fortiori* to Article 235 [352].

90 Although the only objective expressly mentioned in the chapters on the right of establishment and on freedom to provide services is the attainment of those freedoms for nationals of the Member States of the Community, it does not follow that the Community institutions are prohibited from using the powers conferred on them in that field in order to specify the treatment which is to be accorded to nationals of non-member countries. Numerous acts adopted by the Council on the basis of Articles 54 [50] and 57 [53](2) of the Treaty contain provisions in that regard. The Commission has listed them in response to a question from the Court.

*    *    *

95 Whenever the Community has included in its internal legislative acts provisions relating to the treatment of nationals of non-member countries or expressly conferred on its institutions powers to negotiate with non-member countries, it acquires exclusive external competence in the spheres covered by those acts.

96 The same applies in any event, even in the absence of any express provision authorizing its institutions to negotiate with non-member countries, where the Community has achieved complete harmonization of the rules governing access to a self-employed activity, because the common rules thus adopted could be affected within the meaning of the AETR judgment if the Member States retained freedom to negotiate with non-member countries.

97 That is not the case in all service sectors, however, as the Commission has itself acknowledged.

98 It follows that competence to conclude GATS is shared between the Community

and the Member States.

## B. TRIPs

99 In support of its claim that the Community has exclusive competence to conclude TRIPs, the Commission relies on the existence of legislative acts of the institutions which could be affected within the meaning of the AETR judgment if the Member States were jointly to participate in its conclusion, and, as with GATS, on the need for the Community to participate in the agreement in order to achieve one of the objectives set out in the Treaty (the 'Opinion 1/76 doctrine'), as well as on Article 100a [114] and 235 [352].

100 The relevance of the reference to Opinion 1/76 is just as disputable in the case of TRIPs as in the case of GATS: unification or harmonization of intellectual property rights in the Community context does not necessarily have to be accompanied by agreements with non-member countries in order to be effective.

101 Moreover, Articles 100a [114] and 235 [352] of the Treaty cannot in themselves confer exclusive competence on the Community, as stated above.

102 It only remains, therefore, to consider whether the subordinate legislative acts adopted in the Community context could be affected within the meaning of the AETR judgment if the Member States were to participate in the conclusion of TRIPs, as the Commission maintains.

103 Suffice it to say on that point that the harmonization achieved within the Community in certain areas covered by TRIPs is only partial and that, in other areas, no harmonization has been envisaged.

104 Some of the Governments which have submitted observations have argued that the provisions of TRIPs relating to the measures to be adopted to secure the effective protection of intellectual property rights, such as those ensuring a fair and just procedure, the rules regarding the submission of evidence, the right to be heard, the giving of reasons for decisions, the right of appeal, interim measures and the award of damages, fall within the competence of the Member States. If that argument is to be understood as meaning that all those matters are within some sort of domain reserved to the Member States, it cannot be accepted. The Community is certainly competent to harmonize national rules on those matters, in so far as, in the words of Article 100 [115] of the Treaty, they 'directly affect the establishment or functioning of the common market'. But the fact remains that the Community institutions have not hitherto exercised their powers in the field of the 'enforcement of intellectual property rights', except in Regulation No. 3842/86 laying down measures to prohibit the release for free circulation of counterfeit goods.

105 It follows that the Community and its Member States are jointly competent to conclude TRIPs.

# NOTES AND QUESTIONS

**1.** In the *WTO* decision, do you think there has been a change in the Court's approach compared with *ERTA*?

**2.** Why should the exercise of harmonizing powers justify the conferral of exclusive competence on the EU in external matters? Do not the Member States remain heavily involved in the law-making and execution process in such areas? In what circumstances does internal harmonization give rise to the creation of external relations powers of the EU?

**3.** What view of EC 308/TFEU 352 is expressed by the Court in the context of external relations?

## COMMISSION v. BELGIUM
### (OPEN SKIES)
### Case C-471/98, 2002 ECJ CELEX LEXIS 37, [2002] ECR I-9681

[Belgium had individually negotiated, initialled and concluded, in 1995, and applied an open skies' agreement with the U.S. in the field of transport. This agreement liberalized air travel and amended prior agreements going back to 1930 on the subject between the two countries. In relation to U.S.-Belgium travel it covered the same ground, to one degree or another, as Community regulations relating to *intra-* EU air travel. The Commission argued that both the conclusion of the 1995 agreement and Belgium's failure to rescind prior agreements were breaches of Belgium's overriding obligations under EC 10/TEU 4.

With respect to intra-EU air travel, the Council had adopted three packages of measures, in 1987, 1990 and 1992 respectively, designed to ensure freedom to provide services in the air-transport sector and to apply the EU's competition rules in that sector. The legislation adopted in 1992, the third package, comprised Regulations Nos 2407/92, 2408/92 and 2409/92.

Regulation No 2407/92, concerned requirements for the *granting and maintenance of operating licences* by Member States in relation to air carriers established in the EU.

Regulation No 2408/92, concerned *access for EU air carriers to intra-EU air routes.* An EU air carrier was defined as an air carrier with a valid operating licence granted in accordance with Regulation No 2407/92.

Regulation No 2409/92, laid down the criteria and procedures to be applied for the *establishment of fares and rates on air services* for carriage wholly within the EU. The regulation did not apply to fares and rates charged by air carriers other than EU air carriers nor to fares and rates established by public service obligation.

In addition to Regulations Nos 2407/92, 2408/92 and 2409/92, enacted in 1992, the EU legislature adopted other measures in relation to air transport, in particular Regulations Nos 2299/89 and 95/93.

Regulation No 2299/89 applied to *computerised reservation systems* (CRSs) to the extent that they contained air transport products when offered for use and/or used in the territory of the EU, irrespective of the status or nationality of the system vendor, the source of the information used or the location of the relevant central data processing unit, or the geographical location of the airports between which air carriage takes place. However this regulation did not apply in respect of a parent carrier of a third country to the extent that its CRS outside the territory of the EU did not offer EU air carriers equivalent treatment to that provided under the Regulation and under Commission Regulation (EEC) No 83/91.

Regulation No 95/93 also applied to air carriers from non-member countries but required reciprocity from the non-member country systems.

Member States were to inform the Commission of any serious difficulties encountered, in law or in fact, by EU air carriers in obtaining slots at airports in third countries.]

55 The Commission charges the Kingdom of Belgium with having infringed the external competence of the Community by entering into the disputed commitments. It maintains in that respect that that competence arises, first, from the necessity, within the meaning of Opinion 1/76 of 26 April 1977 (1977 ECR 741), of concluding an agreement containing such commitments at Community level, and, second, from the fact that the disputed commitments affect, within the meaning of the judgment in Case 22/70 Commission v. Council 1971 ECR 263 (the 'AETR' judgment), the rules adopted by the Community in the field of air transport.

* * *

88 . . . [W]hilst Article 84 [100](2) of the Treaty does not establish an external Community competence in the field of air transport, it does make provision for a power for the Community to take action in that area, albeit one that is dependent on there being a prior decision by the Council.

89 It was, moreover, by taking that provision as a legal basis that the Council adopted the third package' of legislation in the field of air transport.

90 The Court has already held, in paragraphs 16 to 18 and 22 of the AETR judgment, that the Community's competence to conclude international agreements arises not only from an express conferment by the Treaty but may equally flow from other provisions of the Treaty and from measures adopted, within the framework of those provisions, by the Community institutions; that, in particular, each time the Community, with a view to implementing a common policy envisaged by the Treaty, adopts provisions laying down common rules, whatever form these may take, the Member States no longer have the right, acting individually or even collectively, to undertake obligations towards non-member countries which affect those rules or distort their scope; and that, as and when such common rules come into being, the Community alone is in a position to assume and carry out contractual obligations towards non-member countries affecting the whole sphere of application of the Community legal system.

91 Since those findings imply recognition of an exclusive external competence for the Community in consequence of the adoption of internal measures, it is appropriate to ask whether they also apply in the context of a provision such as Article 84 [100] (2) of the Treaty, which confers upon the Council the power to decide whether, to what extent and by what procedure appropriate provisions may

be laid down' for air transport, including, therefore, for its external aspect.

92 If the Member States were free to enter into international commitments affecting the common rules adopted on the basis of Article 84 [100] (2) of the Treaty, that would jeopardise the attainment of the objective pursued by those rules and would thus prevent the Community from fulfilling its task in the defence of the common interest.

93 It follows that the findings of the Court in the AETR judgment also apply where, as in this case, the Council has adopted common rules on the basis of Article 84 [100](2) of the Treaty.

94 It must next be determined under what circumstances the scope of the common rules may be affected or distorted by the international commitments at issue and, therefore, under what circumstances the Community acquires an external competence by reason of the exercise of its internal competence.

95 According to the Court's case-law, that is the case where the international commitments fall within the scope of the common rules. . . . or in any event within an area which is already largely covered by such rules . . . In the latter case, the Court has held that Member States may not enter into international commitments outside the framework of the Community institutions, even if there is no contradiction between those commitments and the common rules . . .

96 Thus it is that, whenever the Community has included in its internal legislative acts provisions relating to the treatment of nationals of non-member countries or expressly conferred on its institutions powers to negotiate with non-member countries, it acquires an exclusive external competence in the spheres covered by those acts . . .

97 The same applies, even in the absence of any express provision authorising its institutions to negotiate with non-member countries, where the Community has achieved complete harmonisation in a given area, because the common rules thus adopted could be affected within the meaning of the AETR judgment if the Member States retained freedom to negotiate with non-member countries . . .

98 On the other hand . . . any distortions in the flow of services in the internal market which might arise from bilateral open skies' agreements concluded by Member States with non-member countries do not in themselves affect the common rules adopted in that area and are thus not capable of establishing an external competence of the Community.

99 There is nothing in the Treaty to prevent the institutions arranging, in the common rules laid down by them, concerted action in relation to non-member countries or to prevent them prescribing the approach to be taken by the Member States in their external dealings . . .

100 It is in the light of those considerations that it falls to be determined whether the common rules relied on by the Commission in the present action are capable of being affected by the international commitments entered into or confirmed by the Kingdom of Belgium in 1995.

101 It is undisputed that the commitments in question comprise an exchange of . . .

rights by virtue of which an airline designated by the United States of America has the right to transport passengers between the Kingdom of Belgium and another Member State of the European Union on flights the origin or destination of which is in the United States of America. The Commission's first argument is that that commitment, particularly when viewed in the context of the combined effect produced by all the bilateral commitments of that type contracted by Member States with the United States of America, in that it allows American carriers to use intra-Community routes without complying with the conditions laid down by Regulation No 2407/92, affects both that regulation and Regulation No 2408/92.

102 That argument must be rejected.

103 As is clear from the title and Article 3(1) of Regulation No 2408/92, that regulation is concerned with access to intra-Community air routes for Community air carriers alone, these being defined by Article 2(b) of that regulation as air carriers with a valid operating licence granted by a Member State in accordance with Regulation No 2407/92. That latter regulation, as may be seen from Articles 1(1) and 4 thereof, defines the criteria for the granting by Member States of operating licences to air carriers established in the Community which, without prejudice to agreements and Conventions to which the Community is a contracting party, are owned directly or through majority ownership by Member States and/or nationals of Member States and are at all times effectively controlled by such States or such nationals, and also the criteria for the maintenance in force of those licences.

104 It follows that Regulation No 2408/92 does not govern the granting of traffic rights on intra-Community routes to non-Community carriers. Similarly, Regulation No 2407/92 does not govern operating licences of non-Community air carriers which operate within the Community.

105 Since the international commitments in issue do not fall within an area already covered by Regulations Nos 2407/92 and 2408/92, they cannot be regarded as affecting those regulations for the reason put forward by the Commission.

106 Moreover, the very fact that those two regulations do not govern the situation of air carriers from non-member countries which operate within the Community shows that, contrary to what the Commission maintains, the third package' of legislation is not complete in character.

107 The Commission next submits that the discrimination and distortions of competition arising from the international commitments at issue, viewed on the basis of their effect combined with that produced by the corresponding international commitments entered into by other Member States, affect the normal functioning of the internal market in air transport.

108 However . . . that kind of situation does not affect the common rules and is therefore not capable of establishing an external competence of the Community.

109 The Commission maintains, finally, that the Community legislation on which it relies contains many provisions relating to non-member countries and air carriers of those countries. That applies in particular, it maintains, to Regulations Nos 2409/92, 2299/89 and 95/93.

110 In that regard, it should be noted, first, that, according to Article 1(2)(a) of

Regulation No 2409/92, that regulation does not apply to fares and rates charged by air carriers other than Community air carriers, that restriction however being stated to be without prejudice to paragraph 3' of the same article. Under Article 1(3) of Regulation No 2409/92, only Community air carriers are entitled to introduce new products or fares lower than the ones existing for identical products.

111 It follows from those provisions, taken together, that Regulation No 2409/92 has, indirectly but definitely, prohibited air carriers of non-member countries which operate in the Community from introducing new products or fares lower than the ones existing for identical products. By proceeding in that way, the Community legislature has limited the freedom of those carriers to set fares and rates, where they operate on intra-Community routes by virtue of the fifth-freedom rights which they enjoy. Accordingly, to the extent indicated in Article 1(3) of Regulation No 2409/92, the Community has acquired exclusive competence to enter into commitments with non-member countries relating to that limitation on the freedom of non-Community carriers to set fares and rates.

112 It follows that, since the entry into force of Regulation No 2409/92, the Kingdom of Belgium has no longer been entitled, despite the renegotiation of the 1980 Agreement, to enter on its own into or maintain in force international commitments concerning the fares and rates to be charged by carriers of non-member countries on intra-Community routes.

113 A commitment of that type arises from Article 12 of the 1980 Agreement, as amended in 1995. The Kingdom of Belgium has thus infringed the Community's exclusive external competence resulting from Article 1(3) of Regulation No 2409/92.

114 The Belgian Government's argument that that commitment, in so far as it establishes the principle of the freedom to determine prices and limits the intervention of the contracting parties in the determination of prices to specific anomalous situations ('predatory' or discriminatory prices, prices which are unreasonably high due to abuse of a dominant position or artificially low due to State aid), does not contradict Regulation No 2409/92, which is likewise founded on the principle of free determination of prices, cannot disturb the finding in the preceding paragraph. The failure of the Kingdom of Belgium to fulfil its obligations lies in the fact that it was not authorised to enter into such a commitment on its own or to maintain it in force when renegotiating the 1980 Agreement, even if the substance of that commitment does not conflict with Community law.

115 Secondly, it follows from Articles 1 and 7 of Regulation No 2299/89 that, subject to reciprocity, that regulation also applies to nationals of non-member countries, where they offer for use or use a CRS in Community territory.

116 By the effect of that regulation, the Community thus acquired exclusive competence to contract with non-member countries the obligations relating to CRSs offered for use or used in its territory.

## NOTES AND QUESTIONS

1.  In *Opinion 1/03 (Lugano Convention)*, [2006] ECR I-1145, the Court tried to clarify the perhaps rather confusing state of affairs that had arisen as a result of its apparent retreat from the *ERTA* doctrine in the *Open Skies* case, in the following words:

122. . . . . [T]he Court has found there to be exclusive Community competence in particular where the conclusion of an agreement by the Member States is incompatible with the unity of the common market and the uniform application of Community law (ERTA, paragraph 31), or where, given the nature of the existing Community provisions, such as legislative measures containing clauses relating to the treatment of nationals of non-member countries or to the complete harmonisation of a particular issue, any agreement in that area would necessarily affect the Community rules within the meaning of the ERTA judgment . . .

123. On the other hand, the Court did not find that the Community had exclusive competence where, because both the Community provisions and those of an international convention laid down minimum standards, there was nothing to prevent the full application of Community law by the Member States . . . Similarly, the Court did not recognise the need for exclusive Community competence where there was a chance that bilateral agreements would lead to distortions in the flow of services in the internal market, noting that there was nothing in the Treaty to prevent the institutions from arranging, in the common rules laid down by them, concerted action in relation to non-member countries or from prescribing the approach to be taken by the Member States in their external dealings . . .

124. It should be noted in that context that the Community enjoys only conferred powers and that, accordingly, any competence, especially where it is exclusive and not expressly conferred by the Treaty, must have its basis in conclusions drawn from a specific analysis of the relationship between the agreement envisaged and the Community law in force and from which it is clear that the conclusion of such an agreement is capable of affecting the Community rules.

125. In certain cases, analysis and comparison of the areas covered both by the Community rules and by the agreement envisaged suffice to rule out any effect on the former . . .

126. However, it is not necessary for the areas covered by the international agreement and the Community legislation to coincide fully. Where the test of an "area which is already covered to a large extent by Community rules" . . . is to be applied, the assessment must be based not only on the scope of the rules in question but also on their nature and content. It is also necessary to take into account not only the current state of Community law in the area in question but also its future development, insofar as that is foreseeable at the time of that analysis . . .

127. That that assessment must include not only the extent of the area covered but also the nature and content of the Community rules is also clear from the Court's case-law . . . stating that the fact that both the Community rules and the international agreement lay down minimum standards may justify the conclusion that the Community rules are not affected, even if the Community rules and the provisions of the agreement cover the same area.

128. In short, it is essential to ensure a uniform and consistent application of the Community rules and the proper functioning of the system which they establish in order to preserve the full effectiveness of Community law.

Do these paragraphs in fact clarify the situation? From the *WTO*, *Open Skies* and *Lugano* cases, what principles might now be enumerated to determine whether exclusive competence has passed to the EU?

2.   A number of other cases concerning this subject matter have also been decided. See, for example, *Commission v. Germany*, Case C-476/98, 2002 ECJ CELEX LEXIS 40, [2002] ECR I-9855.

3.   How satisfactory a situation is it when the competence to deal with third countries depends on a rigorous scrutiny of internal measures to determine whether they could be affected by an international agreement? What practical consequences ensue from the Court's rulings?

4.   In *Officier van Justitie v. Cornelis Kramer and Others*, Joined Cases 3, 4 and 6/76, [1976] ECR 1279, the Court had ruled that in the area of conservation of marine biological resources, the Community had exclusive jurisdiction. At the time this case was viewed by some as perhaps preempting Member State action internally, even if no action had yet been taken at the EU level. This is addressed in the *Rogers* case in Chapter 11. (Today this area is specifically declared an exclusive Union competence under TFEU 3.) The Court ruled that as a result of a specific provision in the Act of Accession regarding the UK, Ireland and Denmark, this area was to be considered an EU competence even though the EU had not yet acted. This then required it to address the issue of how existing international obligations under the North Atlantic Fisheries Convention should be performed by the Member States until the EU took over:

44/45 It follows from all these factors that Member States participating in the Convention and in other similar agreements are now not only under a duty not to enter into any commitment within the framework of those Conventions which could hinder the Community in carrying out the tasks entrusted to it by article 102 of the Act of Accession, but also under a duty to proceed by common action within the Fisheries Commission. It further follows therefrom that as soon as the Community institutions have initiated the procedure for implementing the provisions of the said article 102, and at the latest within the period laid down by that article, those institutions and the Member States will be under a duty to use all the political and legal means at their disposal in order to ensure the participation of the Community in the Convention and in other similar agreements.

## [B]  "Necessary to Enable the Union to Exercise Internal Competences"

### OPINION 1/76
### (LAYING UP FUND)
### [1977] ECR 741

[The Commission had asked the Court to give an opinion on an agreement with Switzerland relating to financial support for barge-owners in time of over-capacity on the principal waterways flowing through EU territory — in particular the Rhine.]

1 The object of the system laid down by the draft Agreement and expressed in the Statute annexed thereto is to rationalize the economic situation of the inland waterway transport industry in a geographical region in which transport by inland waterway is of special importance within the whole network of international transport. Such a system is doubtless an important factor in the common transport policy, the establishment of which is included in the activities of the Community laid down in Article 3 of the EEC Treaty [repealed]. In order to implement this policy, Article 75 [91] of the Treaty instructs the Council to lay down according to the prescribed procedure common rules applicable to international transport to or from the territory of one or more Member States. This article also supplies, as regards the Community, the necessary legal basis to establish the system concerned.

2 In this case, however, it is impossible fully to attain the objective pursued by means of the establishment of common rules pursuant to Article 75 [91] of the Treaty, because of the traditional participation of vessels from a third State, Switzerland, in navigation by the principal waterways in question, which are subject to the system of freedom of navigation established by international agreements of long standing. It has thus been necessary to bring Switzerland into the scheme in question by means of an international agreement with this third State.

3 The power of the Community to conclude such an agreement is not expressly laid down in the Treaty. However, the Court has already had occasion to state, most recently in its judgment of 14 July 1976 in Joined Cases 3, 4 and 6/76, Cornelis Kramer and Others, [1976] ECR 1279, that authority to enter into international commitments may not only arise from an express attribution by the Treaty, but equally may flow implicitly from its provisions. The Court has concluded inter alia that whenever Community law has created for the institutions of the Community powers within its internal system for the purpose of attaining a specific objective, the Community has authority to enter into the international commitments necessary for the attainment of that objective even in the absence of an express provision in that connexion.

4 This is particularly so in all cases in which internal power has already been used in order to adopt measures which come within the attainment of common policies. It is, however, not limited to that eventuality. Although the internal Community measures are only adopted when the international agreement is concluded and made enforceable, as is envisaged in the present case by the proposal for a regulation to be submitted to the Council by the Commission, the power to bind the

Community vis-a-vis third countries nevertheless flows by implication from the provisions of the Treaty creating the internal power and in so far as the participation of the Community in the international agreement is, as here, necessary for the attainment of one of the objectives of the Community.

5 In order to attain the common transport policy, the contents of which are defined in Articles 74 [90] and 75 [91] of the Treaty, the Council is empowered to lay down 'any other appropriate provisions', as expressly provided in Article 75 [91] (1)(c). The Community is therefore not only entitled to enter into contractual relations with a third country in this connexion but also has the power, while observing the provisions of the Treaty, to cooperate with that country in setting up an appropriate organism such as the public international institution which it is proposed to establish under the name of the 'European Laying-up Fund for Inland Waterway Vessels'. The Community may also, in this connexion, cooperate with a third country for the purpose of giving the organs of such an institution appropriate powers of decision and for the purpose of defining, in a manner appropriate to the objectives pursued, the nature, elaboration, implementation and effects of the provisions to be adopted within such a framework.

6 A special problem arises because the draft Agreement provides for the participation as contracting parties not only of the Community and Switzerland but also of certain of the Member States. These are the six States which are party either to the revised Convention of Mannheim for the Navigation of the Rhine of 17 October 1868 or the Convention of Luxembourg of 27 October 1956 on the Canalization of the Moselle, having regard to the relationship of the latter to the Rhine Convention. Under Article 3 of the Agreement, these States undertake to make the amendments of the two abovementioned Conventions necessitated by the implementation of the Statute annexed to the Agreement.

7 This particular undertaking, . . . explains and justifies the participation in the Agreement, together with the Community, of the six abovementioned States. Precisely because of that undertaking the obstacle presented by the existence of certain provisions of the Mannheim and Luxembourg Conventions to the attainment of the scheme laid down by the Agreement will be removed. The participation of these States in the Agreement must be considered as being solely for this purpose and not as necessary for the attainment of other features of the system. In fact, under Article 4 of the Agreement, the enforceability of this measure and of the Statute extends to the territories of all the Member States including those who are not party to the agreement; it may therefore be said that, except for the special undertaking mentioned above, the legal effects of the agreement with regard to the Member States result, in accordance with article 228 [218] (2) of the Treaty, exclusively from the conclusion of the latter by the Community. In these circumstances, the participation of the six Member States as contracting parties to the Agreement is not such as to encroach on the external power of the Community. There is therefore no occasion to conclude that this aspect of the draft Agreement is incompatible with the Treaty.

## NOTES AND QUESTIONS

**1.** The rationale for finding that the EU was necessarily involved with the laying-up fund agreement is quite different from that expressed in the *ERTA* case. Here, the EU was attempting to adopt an *internal* policy that required the cooperation of a third party. Did the EU's competence to conclude this Agreement then derive from internal competence as in *ERTA* or in some other way?

**2.** Why were certain Member States permitted to participate in this agreement even though it was within the EU's competence? To what extent might states that did not have any interest in the laying up fund demand to participate in the negotiations or at least send observers?

**3.** With respect to the role of the Member States in the United Nations Security Council when it is taking action on matters within EU competence, does this case mean that the UK and France, as permanent members, must adopt a common stance based on direction from the EU?

## OPINION 1/94
### (AGREEMENT ESTABLISHING THE WORLD TRADE ORGANIZATION)
### 1994 ECJ CELEX LEXIS 459, [1994] ECR I-5627

[For the background to this opinion see the first excerpt from the same case, *supra.* Another argument advanced by the Commission for exclusive competence for the Union as regarded GATS was the rationale in Opinion 1/76.]

85 Opinion 1/76 related to an issue different from that arising from GATS. It concerned rationalization of the economic situation in the inland waterways sector in the Rhine and Moselle basins, and throughout all the Netherlands inland waterways and the German inland waterways linked to the Rhine basin, by elimination of short-term overcapacity. It was not possible to achieve that objective by the establishment of autonomous common rules, because of the traditional participation of vessels from Switzerland in navigation on the waterways in question. It was necessary, therefore, to bring Switzerland into the scheme envisaged by means of an international agreement.

86 That is not the situation in the sphere of services: attainment of freedom of establishment and freedom to provide services for nationals of the Member States is not inextricably linked to the treatment to be afforded in the Community to nationals of non-member countries or in non-member countries to nationals of Member States of the Community.

## NOTES AND QUESTIONS

On what grounds did the Court dismiss the arguments based on *Opinion 1/76*?

## § 12.04   "MIXED AGREEMENTS"

### OPINION 1/94
### (WTO AGREEMENT)
### 1994 ECJ CELEX LEXIS 459, [1994] ECR I-5627

[For the background see the first excerpt from this Opinion, *supra*]

106 At the hearing, the Commission drew the Court's attention to the problems which would arise, as regards the administration of the agreements, if the Community and the Member States were recognized as sharing competence to participate in the conclusion of the GATS and TRIPs agreements. While it is true that, in the negotiation of the agreements, the procedure under Article 113 [207] of the Treaty prevailed subject to certain very minor adjustments, the Member States will, in the context of the WTO, undoubtedly seek to express their views individually on matters falling within their competence whenever no consensus has been found. Furthermore, interminable discussions will ensue to determine whether a given matter falls within the competence of the Community, so that the Community mechanisms laid down by the relevant provisions of the Treaty will apply, or whether it is within the competence of the Member States, in which case the consensus rule will operate. The Community's unity of action vis-à-vis the rest of the world will thus be undermined and its negotiating power greatly weakened.

107 In response to that concern, which is quite legitimate, it must be stressed, first, that any problems which may arise in implementation of the WTO Agreement and its annexes as regards the coordination necessary to ensure unity of action where the Community and the Member States participate jointly cannot modify the answer to the question of competence, that being a prior issue.

108 Next where it is apparent that the subject-matter of an agreement or Convention falls in part within the competence of the Community and in part within that of the Member States, it is essential to ensure close cooperation between the Member States and the Community institutions, both in the process of negotiation and conclusion and in the fulfilment of the commitments entered into. That obligation to cooperate flows from the requirement of unity in the international representation of the Community.

109 The duty to cooperate is all the more imperative in the case of agreements such as those annexed to the WTO Agreement, which are inextricably interlinked, and in view of the cross-retaliation measures established by the Dispute Settlement Understanding. Thus, in the absence of close cooperation, where a Member State, duly authorized within its sphere of competence to take cross-retaliation measures, considered that they would be ineffective if taken in the fields covered by GATS or TRIPs, it would not, under Community law, be empowered to retaliate in the area of trade in goods, since that is an area which on any view falls within the exclusive competence of the Community under Article 113 [207] of the Treaty. Conversely, if the Community were given the right to retaliate in the sector of goods but found itself incapable of exercising that right, it would, in the absence of close cooperation, find itself unable, in law, to retaliate in the areas covered by GATS or TRIPs, those

being within the competence of the Member States.

## NOTES AND QUESTIONS

1. On what grounds did the ECJ require the Member States to cooperate? Is this in conflict with their inherent sovereignty in the areas for which they are competent?

2. For an appraisal of mixed agreements, see J.H.H. Weiler, *The External Legal Relations of Non-Unitary Actors: Mixity and the Federal Principle* in J.H.H. WEILER, THE CONSTITUTION OF EUROPE: DO THE NEW CLOTHES HAVE AN EMPEROR? (Cambridge University Press 1999).

## COMMISSION v. IRELAND
### (NUCLEAR REPROCESSING)
Case C-459/03, 2006 ECJ CELEX LEXIS 238, [2006] ECR I-4635

[The Commission sought a declaration that, by instituting dispute-settlement proceedings against the United Kingdom of Great Britain and Northern Ireland under the United Nations Convention on the Law of the Sea concerning the nuclear waste reprocessing MOX plant located at Sellafield (United Kingdom), Ireland had failed to fulfil its obligations under EC 10/TEU 4 and EC 292 EC/TFEU 344 and Articles 192 EAEC (similar to EC 10/TEU 4 and 193 EAEC (similar to EC 292/TFEU 344). The MOX plant was designed to recycle plutonium from spent nuclear fuel by mixing plutonium dioxide with depleted uranium dioxide and thereby converting it into a new fuel known as MOX, an abbreviation used to designate mixed oxide fuel, intended for use as an energy source in nuclear power stations. Using the broader framework of the Convention, Ireland brought proceedings before the Arbitral Tribunal established under the Convention for the Protection of the Marine Environment of the North-East Atlantic.]

172. . . . The Commission criticises Ireland for having breached Articles 10 EC [TEU 4] and 192 EA by bringing the proceedings before the Arbitral Tribunal without having first informed and consulted the competent Community institutions.

173. This second part of the third head of complaint relates to an alleged omission by Ireland which is distinct from the conduct forming the subject-matter of the first head of complaint. It is for that reason necessary to examine it.

174. The Court has pointed out that, in all the areas corresponding to the objectives of the EC Treaty, Article 10 EC [TEU 4] requires Member States to facilitate the achievement of the Community's tasks and to abstain from any measure which could jeopardise the attainment of the objectives of the Treaty . . . The Member States assume similar obligations under the EAEC Treaty by virtue of Article 192 EA.

175. The Court has also emphasised that the Member States and the Community institutions have an obligation of close cooperation in fulfilling the commitments undertaken by them under joint competence when they conclude a mixed agreement . . .

176. That is in particular the position in the case of a dispute which, as in the present

case, relates essentially to undertakings resulting from a mixed agreement which relates to an area, namely the protection and preservation of the marine environment, in which the respective areas of competence of the Community and the Member States are liable to be closely interrelated, as is, moreover, evidenced by the Declaration of Community competence and the appendix thereto.

177. The act of submitting a dispute of this nature to a judicial forum such as the Arbitral Tribunal involves the risk that a judicial forum other than the Court will rule on the scope of obligations imposed on the Member States pursuant to Community law.

178. Moreover . . . the Commission's services had already contended that the dispute relating to the MOX plant, as referred by Ireland to the arbitral tribunal constituted pursuant to the Convention for the Protection of the Marine Environment of the North-East Atlantic, was a matter falling within the exclusive jurisdiction of the Court.

179. In those circumstances, the obligation of close cooperation within the framework of a mixed agreement involved, on the part of Ireland, a duty to inform and consult the competent Community institutions prior to instituting dispute-settlement proceedings concerning the MOX plant within the framework of the Convention.

180. The same duty of prior information and consultation was also imposed on Ireland by virtue of the EAEC Treaty in so far as that Member State contemplated invoking provisions of that Treaty and measures adopted pursuant to it within the framework of the proceedings which it was proposing to bring before the Arbitral Tribunal.

181. It is common ground that, at the date on which those proceedings were brought, Ireland had not complied with that duty of prior information and consultation.

182. Regard being had to the foregoing, the third head of complaint must be upheld in so far as it seeks a declaration by the Court that, by bringing proceedings under the dispute-settlement system set out in the Convention, without having first informed and consulted the competent Community institutions, Ireland has failed to comply with its duty of cooperation under Articles 10 EC [TEU 4] and 192 EA.

183. The action must accordingly be upheld.

## NOTES AND QUESTIONS

1. Does this case possibly suggest a radical change has actually taken place in the sovereignty of the Member States to act in international law? Could this be extended to broader situations where Member States could be compelled to ratify treaties such as the Convention on the Law of the Seas based on their EU obligations?

2. In *Hermès International v. FHT Marketing Choice BV*, Case C-53/96, 1998 ECJ CELEX LEXIS 258, [1998] ECR I-3603, the ECJ held that it had jurisdiction

to interpret provisions of a mixed agreement that were based on Member States' competence (intellectual property):

> 32 [W]here a provision can apply both to situations falling within the scope of national law and to situations falling within the scope of Community law, it is clearly in the Community interest that, in order to forestall future differences of interpretation, that provision should be interpreted uniformly, whatever the circumstances in which it is to apply (see, to that effect, Case C-130/95 Giloy v. Hauptzollamt Frankfurt am Main-Ost 1997 ECR I-4291, paragraph 28, and Case C-28/95 Leur-Bloem v. Inspecteur der Belastingdienst/Ondernemingen 1997 ECR I-4161, paragraph 34). In the present case, as has been pointed out in paragraph 28 above, Article 50 of the TRIPs Agreement applies to Community trade marks as well as to national trade marks.

See also *Parfums Christian Dior SA v. TUK Consultancy BV and Assco Geruste GmbH and Rob van Dijk v. Wilhelm Layher GmbH & Co. KG and Layher BV*, Joined cases C-300/98 and C-392/98, 2000 ECJ CELEX LEXIS 334, [2000] ECR I-11307.

## § 12.05    SURRENDER OF UNION POWERS TO THE MEMBER STATES

### BULK OIL (ZUG) AG v. SUN INTERNATIONAL LTD AND SUN OIL TRADING CO.
Case 174/84, 1986 ECJ CELEX LEXIS 95, [1986] ECR 559

[The UK operated a policy of prohibiting the export of North Sea oil to non-EEA member-countries. BP, as a producer of North Sea crude, had originally entered into a contract to deliver North Sea crude to Sun, which had a redelivery contract with Bulk Oil. BP refused to deliver it to Sun after it discovered that the destination of the shipment was Israel and Sun then declined to deliver to Bulk Oil which sued for breach of contract.]

20 [T]he national court asks in essence whether Regulation 2603/69 must be interpreted as permitting the implementation of a policy such as that in issue with regard to oil exports.

21 Article 1 of Council Regulation 2603/69 of 20 December 1969 establishing common rules for exports provides that 'the exportation of products from the European Economic Community to third countries shall be free, that is to say, they shall not be subject to any quantitative restriction, with the exception of those restrictions which are applied in conformity with the provisions of this Regulation'. Article 10 states that 'until such time as the Council, acting by a qualified majority on a proposal from the Commission, shall have introduced common rules in respect of the products listed in the Annex to this Regulation, the principle of freedom of export from the Community as laid down in Article 1 shall not apply to those products'. The products listed in the annex include, under headings 27.09 and 27.10, crude oil and petroleum oils.

22 Bulk submits that Article 113 [207] of the Treaty and Regulation 2603/69 preclude a member-State from adopting and maintaining, without specific authorization, a policy prohibiting the exportation of oil to certain non-member countries, including Israel.

23 On the basis of an analysis of the judgments of the Court in the area of common commercial policy Bulk argues that in that field the Community has exclusive competence, and a member-State may adopt a measure only if specifically authorized to do so by the Community. The common commercial policy covers measures restricting exports to non-member countries, whether these are quantitative restrictions or measures having equivalent effect. The United Kingdom Government's policy was a measure of commercial policy intended to regulate exports of crude oil to non-member countries and it directly influenced the conduct of undertakings. The Community did not specifically authorize the United Kingdom policy.

24 In Bulk's view, Article 10 of Regulation 2603/69 does not amount to such authorization. It is clear from an analysis of the preamble to Regulation 2603/69 and of the provisions of that regulation taken as a whole that Article 10 only derogated from the principle of freedom to export to non-member countries laid down in Article 1 with regard to certain products in order to prevent the old national export restrictions relating to the products listed in the annex from becoming invalid at the end of the transitional period. Those provisions were not intended to give, nor did they have the effect of giving, Member States a free hand to introduce new restrictions on exports, even for a product included in the annex to the regulation. Exports of crude oil therefore remained within the field of application of Regulation 2603/69 and thus of the common commercial policy, as is confirmed, moreover, by the adoption of the Council Regulation 1934/82 of 12 July 1982, which amended Regulation 2603/69 and established new rules for exports of crude oil.

25 Bulk infers from that that if, contrary to Bulk's submissions, the Council had purported to allow the Member States a free hand to impose new export restrictions on any product listed in the annex to Regulation 2603/69, such a provision would be void as incompatible with the Treaty and in particular Article 113 [207].

26 Referring to well-established case law of the Court, Sun, the United Kingdom and the Commission are agreed that the Community alone has the power to legislate with regard to exports to non-member countries. In the sphere of commercial policy, therefore, the principle remains that Member States may adopt national measures only if specifically authorized to do so by the Community institutions.

27 They consider, however, that Regulation 2603/69 is a measure implementing Article 113 [207] with regard to exports to non-member countries. Although Article 1 of the regulation lays down the general principle that such exports should be free, Article 10 clearly states that that principle of freedom of export does not apply to the products listed in the annex to the regulation, including oil. Regulation 2603/69 therefore permitted Member States which had imposed quantitative restrictions on exports of one of the products listed in the annex to alter those restrictions and adopt new ones until such time as the Council should adopt common rules for those products, as envisaged by Article 10 of the regulation.

28 According to these parties that argument is supported by an analysis of Council Regulation 1934/82, referred to above, which was intended, according to its preamble, to 'clarify' the scope of Articles 1 and 10 of Regulation 2603/69. Article 1 of Regulation 1934/82 provides that the principle of freedom of export from the Community does not apply, for all the Member States, to a single product, crude oil, 'in view in particular of the international commitments entered into by certain Member States.' Under that regulation, therefore, all the Member States, whether or not they have restricted exports of oil in the past, are free to do so and were already free to do so under Regulation 2603/69.

29 It should be recalled that according to Article 113 [207](1) of the Treaty the common commercial policy is to be based on uniform principles, particularly in regard to changes in tariff rates, the conclusion of tariff and trade arrangements, the achievement of uniformity in measures of liberalization, export policy and measures to protect trade.

30 Furthermore, as the Court stated in its Opinion of 11 November 1975 (Opinion 1/75 ([1975] ECR 1355, [1976] 1 CMLR 85), 'it cannot be accepted that in a field covered by export policy and more generally by the common commercial policy the Member States should exercise a power concurrent to that of the Community, in the Community sphere and in the international sphere . . . To accept that the contrary were true would amount to recognizing that, in relations with third countries, Member States may adopt positions which differ from those which the Community intends to adopt, and would thereby distort the institutional framework, call into question the mutual trust within the Community and prevent the latter from fulfilling its task in the defence of the common interest.'

31 . . . [S]ince full responsibility in the matter of commercial policy was transferred to the Community by Article 113 [207](1) measures of commercial policy of a national character are only permissible after the end of the transitional period by virtue of specific authorization by the Community.

32 Article 1 of Regulation 2603/69 lays down the general rule that exports from the Community to non-member countries are free, that is to say, not subject to quantitative restrictions, with the exception of those applied in accordance with the provisions of that regulation. Article 10 of the regulation limits the scope of that principle on a transitional basis with regard to certain products, until such time as the Council shall have established common rules applicable to them; it provides that the principle of freedom of export from the Community does not apply to the products listed in the annex, including oil.

33 . . . Article 10 of Regulation 2603/69 and the annex to that regulation constitute a specific authorization permitting the Member States to impose quantitative restrictions on exports of oil to non-member countries, and there is no need to distinguish in that regard between previously existing quantitative restrictions and those which are subsequently introduced.

34 With regard to Bulk's argument that such an interpretation of Article 10 of Regulation 2603/69 would mean that that provision was void on grounds of incompatibility with Article 113 [207] of the Treaty, it should indeed be recalled that in its Opinion of 4 October 1979 (Opinion 1/78 ([1979] ECR 2871, [1979] 3 CMLR

639) the Court stated that 'where the organization of the Community's economic links with non-member countries may have repercussions on certain sectors of economic policy such as the supply of raw materials to the Community or price policy, as is precisely the case with the regulation of international trade in commodities, that consideration does not constitute a reason for excluding such objectives from the field of application of the rules relating to the common commercial policy. Similarly, the fact that a product may have a political importance by reason of the building-up of security stocks is not a reason for excluding that product from the domain of the common commercial policy.'

35 It should be pointed out, however, that in that Opinion the Court was concerned only with the prohibition of a general exclusion, as a matter of principle, of certain products from the field of application of the common commercial policy and not with the Council's discretion to exclude, on a transitional basis, certain products from the common rules on exports.

36 Having regard to the discretion which it enjoys in an economic matter of such complexity, in this case the Council could, without contravening Article 113 [207], provisionally exclude a product such as oil from the common rules on exports to non-member countries, in view in particular of the international commitments entered into by certain Member States and taking into account the particular characteristics of that product, which is of vital importance for the economy of a State and for the functioning of its institutions and public services.

37 The answer to the second part of the first question must therefore be that Council Regulation 2603/69 of 20 December 1969 establishing common rules for exports does not prohibit a member-State from imposing new quantitative restrictions or measures having equivalent effect on its exports of oil to non-member countries.

## NOTES AND QUESTIONS

1.  In *Sun*, the court seemed to accept that the EU could authorize Member States to take measures of external commercial policy even though covered by EC 133/TFEU 207. Is such an authorization to be considered a transfer back of sovereign power or are the Member States acting as delegees of the EU? What might the consequences be for third party countries dealing with the EU? Suppose the Member States adopt different approaches? How can this approach be reconciled with the principles justifying exclusive competence? What is the effect of including those principles in the Treaty itself (following Lisbon)?

2.  An argument was also made that is analogous to that which arises in connection with the scope of directives, i.e., whether and to what extent the EU intended to occupy the field. How did the Court deal with this issue in the context of external relations?

3.  Note that in *ERTA*, the Member States were authorized to continue negotiations even though competence lay with the EU. On what basis were they allowed to do so? Is there an element of political realism in the ECJ's approach?

# TREATY LIMITATIONS ON THE EXERCISE OF MEMBER STATE COMPETENCES

# Chapter 13

# MEASURES AFFECTING THE FREE MOVEMENT OF GOODS

## § 13.01 OVERVIEW

***Template*** Article 7, Sections 7.1, 7.2 and 7.6

***General comment on Part V*** The TFEU contains provisions that *limit* the powers of the Member States to regulate commerce insofar as those powers would interfere with the achievement of the internal market (echoes here of the interstate trade jurisdictional requirement of the U.S. Constitution.) Chief among these are the provisions that seek to prohibit restrictions on the free movement of goods and services, on the establishment of persons seeking to conduct a business in another Member State and on the movement of capital and payments. The free movement of workers is also usually included in this category but that subject is addressed in the context of citizenship in Chapter 17, for reasons explained in that chapter.

***Materials in this Chapter*** This chapter examines the Treaty provisions regarding the prohibition of Member State measures that restrict the free movement of goods. The EC Treaty/TFEU addresses three types of restriction: customs duties and measures having equivalent effect; quantitative restrictions and measures having equivalent effect; and indirect taxation. The cases will illustrate the scope of these provisions, but mostly focus on quantitative restrictions where the jurisprudence has had a profound effect on the development of the Union.

***Comparison with the U.S. dormant commerce clause*** The explicit provisions in the TFEU limiting State powers have parallels with the doctrine in the U.S. known as the *dormant commerce clause.* This holds that the grant of powers to Congress to regulate interstate and foreign commerce does not simply confer powers on the U.S. Congress. It also implicitly limits the powers of the various States to make laws that create an undue burden on interstate commerce. It was by no means clear at the time that the grant of federal powers would necessarily preclude state action in this area. The absence of any separate enumeration of state powers in the Commerce Clause might explain why, in Article I, Section 10. Clause 2 of the U.S. Constitution, the framers of the Constitution thought it necessary to include at least some precise restrictions on the states' powers to impose customs duties on interstate trade. Under the previous Confederation, the imposition of customs, duties, etc. had been a constant source of friction between the states and was a primary motivator for the construction of a more powerful federation. Even under the new Constitution, a limitation on the States going beyond measures directed at interstate commerce was not initially an accepted proposition.

Since the primary purpose of the original EEC Treaty was to create a common market it is not surprising that it contained express provisions limiting the powers of the Member States in the field of (what was then) international trade. These provisions may be viewed as concrete manifestations of the U.S. dormant commerce clause doctrine and have developed well beyond what the original drafters of the EEC Treaty may have envisioned, as did the equivalent U.S. Constitutional provision on commerce powers.

***Duties and quantitative restrictions*** When the original EEC was formed, the most obvious manifestation of Member States' rules affecting "interstate commerce" in goods was the practice of imposing import tariffs and quotas on foreign goods and services. It was hardly surprising, then, that specific attention was given to the elimination of what were direct and purposeful obstacles to trade.

Turning then to "quantitative restrictions", EC 28/TFEU 34 might at first sight be interpreted as a narrow provision, dealing only with overt restrictions on imports. But, given the reference to "measures equivalent", it could also be very broad — indeed, covering almost any legislation or regulation at state level that has the potential, even if very indirectly, to affect trade between Member States in any way. Thus it could have an impact on rules directed at how products are made, delivered, sold or used such as, for example, labeling requirements for parts; technical standards for tractors; authorization of pharmaceutical and agricultural products; minimum or maximum content rules for alcoholic drinks; purity standards and pesticide residue levels for foodstuffs; safety standards; and designations of origin or quality.

Beyond this, legislation that implements state policies on matters not directed specifically to the sale of products or services may also have an effect on interstate trade, as, for example, rules in implementation of environmental policy, health care programs, working conditions, national security, education, housing and taxation. What is notable, of course, is that the laws in these areas are unlikely to be directed at imports as such. If one accepts that they nonetheless fall within the scope of EC 28/TFEU 34, then some sort of evaluation will be required as to their legitimacy, since it would be politically impossible to hold them automatically contrary to the Treaty without wrecking legitimate policies in unrelated areas.

The evolution of the case law with respect to this provision has followed a rather tortuous route that reflects on the one hand the desire of the Court to use it as a far-reaching means for removing national barriers to trade, while on the other hand recognizing the need to allow the Member States to continue to manage their internal affairs and recognizing their right to differ from one another in their approaches.

***The impact of EC 28 and 30/TFEU 34 and 36 on intellectual property rights*** The unifying characteristic of intellectual property rights is that they grant exclusivity to their owners. The existence of such rights at national level within the European Union meant that such exclusivity is asserted at the Member State level, with the result that goods manufactured and sold in one state may not be imported into another state if they infringe the owner's rights in the importing state. Such rights are clearly capable of falling within the definition of measures equivalent to quantitative restrictions on imports under EC 28/TFEU 34. However, EC 30/TFEU

36 provides a specific exemption for "industrial and commercial property" provided (as with the other exemptions) that restrictions on imports resulting from such rights do not "constitute a means of arbitrary discrimination or a disguised restriction on trade between Member States." The ECJ's interpretation of this provision was a major contribution to the removal of barriers to trade caused by the continued existence of national intellectual property rights.

***Indirect taxation*** The Treaty prohibits discrimination in the imposition of sales and use taxes and excise taxes as between domestic and imported goods. However, as with quantitative restrictions, indirect taxation may create a burden for imports simply because the rates or method of application differ from one State to another. In the United States, this remains the case today and undoubtedly leads to some distortion in trade. In the EU, the approach was to adopt at a very early stage under the harmonization provisions of the EC Treaty/TFEU a uniform system of taxation known as Value Added Tax or VAT. This is explained later on in this Chapter.

## § 13.02 CUSTOMS DUTIES

### INTERZUCCHERI v. DITTA REZZANO
#### Case 105/76, [1977] ECR 1029

[Council Regulation 1009/67/EEC on the common organization of the market in sugar, which came into force on July 1, 1968 applied, inter alia, to white and raw beet sugar and cane sugar and also to sugar beet and sugar cane. Under Article 34 of the Regulation, Italy was, for 1974/75, authorized to grant "adaptation subsidies" to the sugar industry. The Comitato Interministeriale dei Prezzi (Interdepartmental Committee on Prices, "the CIP") established the Cassa Conguaglio Zucchero (Sugar Equalization Fund) financed by a sovrapprezzo (surcharge) on every quantity and type of white sugar, whether home-produced or imported. Interzuccheri S.p.A. sold 10,000 kilograms of sugar to Ditta Rezzano e Cavassa for a sum of 5,100,000 lire including the surcharge of 70 lire per kilogram. Ditta Rezzano refused to pay the amount corresponding to the surcharge, claiming that it was contrary to EC law. The plaintiff company thereupon brought proceedings before the Pretore of Recco with a view to obtaining an order that the defendant pay the sum in question.]

7 Article 9 [28] of the Treaty . . . prohibits the imposition of customs duties on imports or all charges having equivalent effect in trade between Member States. Likewise Article 20 (2) of Regulation no. 1009/67/EEC and Article 21 (2) of Regulation (EEC) no. 3330/74 prohibit, save as otherwise provided in those regulations or by derogation determined by the Council, the levying of any customs duty or charge having equivalent effect.

8 . . . [T]he prohibitions contained in Articles 9 [28] and 13 [deleted] are aimed at any tax demanded at the time or by reason of importation and which, being imposed specifically on imported products to the exclusion of the similar domestic product, results in the same restrictive consequences on the free movement of goods as a customs duty by altering the cost price of that product. On the other hand, the fact

that a charge is applied without distinction to domestic products as well as to products from other Member States gives rise to the question whether the taxation at issue falls within the prohibition in articles 9 [28] and 13 [deleted] or the rule against discrimination in matters of internal taxation laid down by article 95 [110].

9 One and the same scheme of taxation cannot, under the system of the Treaty, belong simultaneously to both the categories mentioned, having regard to the fact that the charges referred to in articles 9 [28] and 13 [deleted] must simply be abolished whilst, for the purpose of applying internal taxation, article 95 [110] provides solely for the elimination of any form of discrimination, direct or indirect, in the treatment of the domestic products of a Member State and of products originating in other Member States. Financial charges within a general system of internal taxation applying systematically to domestic and imported products according to the same criteria are not to be considered as charges having equivalent effect.

10 The situation would be different only if such a duty, which is limited to particular products, had the sole purpose of financing activities for the specific advantage of the taxed domestic products so as to make good, wholly or in part, the fiscal charge imposed upon them. Such a fiscal device would in fact only appear to be a system of internal taxation and accordingly could by reason of its protective character be termed a charge having an effect equivalent to customs duties so as to bring articles 9 [28] and 13 [deleted] and the provisions of the regulations quoted into operation. Such a definition would nevertheless imply a clearly established connexion between, on the one hand, the collection of a fiscal duty levied without distinction on the products in question, whether domestic or imported, and, on the other hand, the advantage which enures only for the benefit of the domestic products by reason of the proceeds of that same duty.

11 It is therefore for the national court to establish the existence or otherwise of this connexion and to take into account, in the circumstances, the fact that, according to the information on the file, it appears that the revenue produced by the imposition of the contested charge benefits beet-producers as well as the processing industry in such a way that sugar, as a product distinct from beet, only receives less than half of the funds collected.

12 It follows from the foregoing that the answer to the first question must be that a duty falling within a general system of internal taxation applying to domestic products as well as to imported products according to the same criteria can constitute a charge having an effect equivalent to a customs duty on imports only if it has the sole purpose of financing activities for the specific advantage of the taxed domestic product; if the taxed product and the domestic product benefiting from it are the same; and if the charges imposed on the domestic product are made good in full.

# COMMISSION v. DENMARK
## (GROUNDNUTS)
### Case 158/82, [1983] ECR 3573

[*Following is abbreviated version of the Court's summary of the facts.* Denmark prohibited the sale or assignment of groundnuts and groundnut products in which aflatoxin is detected in significant quantities. The importation into Denmark of such products from other Member States (as well as from non-member countries) was subject to a systematic health inspection including the taking of samples and laboratory analysis. However, the Director of the Statens Levnedsmiddelinstitut [State Foodstuffs Institute] could approve a certificate of analysis drawn up by a foreign laboratory made on the basis of a sample taken and analyzed in that country.

The health inspection was carried out by a private Danish laboratory designated by the Director of the Statens Levnedsmiddelinstitut. The importer was required to pay the laboratory a charge for carrying out the inspection, the purpose of which is to establish that the consignment of groundnuts concerned did not contain aflatoxin, a substance dangerous to human health and produced by certain kinds of fungus.

The fungi produce a considerable quantity of a toxic substance called aflatoxin when the necessary conditions of temperature and humidity occur together. They therefore present a potential risk of contamination in food products and in particular, for climatic reasons, in those coming from tropical and subtropical regions. According to the Danish Government, groundnuts and groundnut products in particular constituted the group of products with the highest risk of contamination by aflatoxin and for which the risk materializes the most often. Since aflatoxin is one of the most virulent of carcinogenic substances, even in very small quantities, the Danish Government is of the view that not even the slightest contamination of foodstuffs by aflatoxin may be tolerated. It considered that the inspections were justified on health grounds. Since Denmark itself did not grow groundnuts they were imported principally from Germany, the United Kingdom and the Netherlands, apart from direct imports from the United States, the East Indies and China. The Danish Government stated that there were no compulsory inspections of the same nature in other Member States.

The charges for sampling and analysis to be paid to Danish laboratories for carrying out the inspections, which were payable by the importer, were not fixed by the State but by the laboratories themselves without its being necessary for them to obtain the approval of the authorities, and were to be paid directly to the laboratory.]

18 The Court has consistently held that any pecuniary charge, whatever its designation or mode of application, which is imposed unilaterally on goods by reason of the fact that they cross a frontier, and which is not a customs duty in the strict sense, constitutes a charge having an effect equivalent to a customs duty within the meaning of Articles 9 [28], 12 [30], 13 [deleted] and 16 [deleted] of the Treaty, even if it is not imposed on behalf of the State.

19 The only exception is where the charge in question represents payment for a service rendered to the importer, of a sum in proportion to the service, or if it forms

part of a general system of internal charges applied systematically in accordance with the same criteria to both national products and imported or exported products.

20 The Danish Government conceded in the course of the proceedings that the charge at issue was not in the nature of payment for a service rendered to the importer. It maintained, however, that it was a charge forming part of a general system of internal taxation.

21 In that regard it may be observed that there is a well-established line of authority to the effect that a charge on importation does not constitute internal taxation under Article 95 [110] unless it forms part of a general system applicable systematically to categories of products in accordance with objective criteria irrespective of the origin of the products.

22 As the Danish Government rightly emphasizes, the Court has indeed recognized that a charge which is imposed on products imported from another Member State, even where there is no identical or similar national product, does not, by that fact alone, constitute a charge having an effect equivalent to a customs duty and may constitute internal taxation within the meaning of Article 95 [110] of the Treaty if it fulfills the above conditions.

23 However, examination of the facts relied on before the Court by the Danish Government in support of its argument that Article 95 [110] applies does not permit the conclusion that the charge at issue forms part of a general system of internal taxation.

24 The Danish Government concedes that the group of products which is affected by the disputed charge and which is defined by the risk of the products' being contaminated by aflatoxin comprises solely groundnuts, groundnut products and Brazil nuts. Such a limited number of products cannot fall within the concept of "whole classes of . . . products" a concept which implies a much larger number of products determined by general and objective criteria.

25 With regard to the Danish Government's argument that the general approach followed in the legislation applicable in Denmark is that the taxpayer is responsible for general health inspection costs while the costs of laboratory analyses necessitated by special health inspections for certain foodstuffs are borne by the undertakings concerned, it should be emphasized that a distinction between general inspection and so-called "special" inspections does not in itself constitute a sufficiently precise and, above all, objective criterion to form the basis for a general system of internal taxes within the meaning of the decisions of the Court of Justice cited above. The Danish Government has not shown that the two types of inspections are objectively distinguishable, for example on the basis of their technical approach. Moreover, in a number of cases even general inspection requires laboratory analyses similar to those carried out in the context of special inspections.

26 With regard to the products covered by the Orders based on Article 41 of the Law on foodstuffs, it appears from the file that they comprise on the one hand food products subject to inspection to determine whether certain nutrients have in fact been added and on the other products considered to be potentially harmful because of certain risks they present, namely groundnuts and Brazil nuts. The difference

regarding the nature, the character and the purpose of the inspections envisaged for each of those two groups prevents the fees levied on groundnuts and Brazil nuts from being regarded as forming part of the same system as those levied for the checking of additives.

27 The Danish Government has thus failed to show that the charge in dispute meets the conditions for it to be regarded as part of a general system of internal taxation.

## NOTES AND QUESTIONS

1. In *Interzuccheri* the Court had to give guidance on whether the sovraprezzo charge in issue amounted to a form of taxation covered by EC 90 EC/TFEU 110. Why? What difference did the Court consider this would make in terms of the validity of the charge? Looking at the two cases above, what are the criteria that should be used to determine whether a charge is part of an internal taxation system?

2. In the *Groundnuts* case, why could Denmark not have found a legal basis for justifying the cost of inspection on the basis that it represented a legitimate charge for inspection similar to the qualification in Article I Section 10 of the U.S. Constitution? The latter recognized the authority of the States to levy charges to cover "inspection costs". In the EU issues have frequently arisen as to whether such charges on imported goods amount to customs duties. Generally, the ECJ has held that where a charge is justified as part of an internal system, the size of the charge should bear a reasonable relationship to the cost of the inspection or other activity. For example, a charge levied to cover the costs of collecting a value added tax payment will not be a duty unless it is clearly out of proportion to the cost of doing so. See *Donner v. Netherlands*, Case 39/82, [1983] ECR 19, *Commission v. Belgium*, Case 132/82, [1983] ECR 1649.

Compare U.S. cases such as *Portland Pipe Line Corp. v. Environmental Improvement Commission*, 307 A.2d 1 (Me. 1973), in which the Supreme Court of Maine upheld a state regulatory enactment designed to fix responsibility and compensation for oil spills occurring in Maine waters. The State regulation imposed an annual license fee per barrel of oil transferred over coastal waters of the State. The fee was used to create a revolving fund to cover clean-up costs of spills, and research and development concerning environmental damage due to the transfer of oil in those waters. One of the challenges to the state regulation was a challenge based on Article I, Section 10, clause 2 of the U.S. Constitution. The Court rejected this challenge on two grounds (307 A.2d at 36):

> First, the license fee is not imposed "on Imports or Exports". Because the transfer fee is imposed on an activity related the importation of oil [i.e. off-loading] rather than on the property imported, the fee is not sufficiently direct to be "on Imports" under Article 1, Section 10, Clause 2.

> Second, the license fee is not a duty or impost since the overall effect of the Act is the establishment of a regulatory scheme for controlling oil pollution which is essentially to protect the public interest and affords benefits to those subject to the license fee.

In this connection, compare Case C–173/05 in Note 5 *infra.*

**3.** The elimination of customs duties on goods originating in other Member States was a primary objective of the EC Treaty. Similarly, the establishment of a customs union (i.e., the establishment of a common external tariff) was spelled out in considerable detail (former EEC articles 9-29). Both objectives were achieved ahead of the Treaty schedule.

**4.** One of the major problems encountered by the confederation preceding the U.S. Constitution was the impairment of trade and commerce resulting from the imposition of customs and similar duties. C.W. Wright, in ECONOMIC HISTORY OF THE UNITED STATES (McGraw Hill, 1949) has described how the imposition of duties and controls on goods from other colonies was a constant source of friction prior to independence. After 1776, the states of the confederation continued to impose such burdens, and indeed Massachusetts increased duties on some products and banned others altogether in 1786 as part of a protectionist scheme for its shipbuilding industry.

**5.** Cases on customs duties have become rarer as the internal market has matured and Member States came to understand their responsibilities under the Treaty. However, occasionally new cases do appear. For example, in *Commission v. Italy*, Case C-173/05, [2007] ECR NYR, the Commission claimed that a law adopted by the Sicilian region of Italy that imposed an "environmental tax" on gas pipelines, was in breach of EC 23/TFEU 28, EC 25/TFEU 30 EC 26/TFEU 31 and EC133/TFEu 207 and Articles 4 and 9 of the Cooperation Agreement between the European Economic Community and the People's Democratic Republic of Algeria of 1976. This agreement contained identical provisions on free movement of goods to that in the EC Treaty/TFEU, but the tax also triggered the TFEU directly due to its application of the rules to goods in transit, as established by the Court in the *SIOT* case. The Court stated:

35 It is common ground that, in the present case, an environmental tax has been introduced by the Sicilian Law, aimed at financing investments intended to reduce and prevent the risks for the environment arising from the presence of gas pipelines containing methane gas in the Sicilian Region. The transport and distribution of the methane gas in question are carried out using gas pipelines classified as 'type 1 pipelines' for the purposes of the Ministerial Order of 24 November 1984, which are connected to the trans-Mediterranean pipelines which transport such gas from Algeria.

36 Under Article 6(3) of the Sicilian Law, the chargeable event giving rise to the environmental tax is ownership of the gas pipelines, containing the gas, which cross the Sicilian Region's territory.

37 On this point, in its observations, the Italian Government asserts that the disputed tax does not target the goods, but only the transport infrastructure. By the Italian Government's own admission, however, the disputed tax is payable only if the gas is actually present in the infrastructure.

38 Nor does the Italian Government deny that the only facilities which fulfil the taxation conditions laid down in the Sicilian Law are those connected to

the trans-Mediterranean gas pipelines which transport natural gas from Algeria.

39 Accordingly, the Court finds that the tax introduced by the Sicilian Law is a fiscal charge levied on goods imported from a non-member country, namely Algerian methane gas, for the purpose of distribution and consumption of that gas in Italy or of the transit thereof towards other Member States.

40 . . . [S]uch a tax on goods imported from a non-member country, in this case the People's Democratic Republic of Algeria, is contrary to both Articles 23 EC [28] and 133 EC [207] and Article 9 of the Cooperation Agreement.

41 The Court further notes that, in so far as the Algerian gas which is taxed under the Sicilian Law is imported into Italy and subsequently exported to other Member States, the disputed tax is likely to affect intra-Community trade, contrary to Article 25 [30] EC.

42 Lastly, regarding the Italian Government's argument to the effect that the Commission's action is unfounded because the disputed tax was introduced with the sole aim of protecting the environment, in the light of, inter alia, the requirements of the precautionary principle, the Court notes that charges having equivalent effect to customs duties are prohibited irrespective of the purpose for which they were introduced and the destination of the revenue from them . . .

## § 13.03   INDIRECT TAXATION

### [A]   Discrimination Against Imported Products

### HUMBLOT v. DIRECTEUR DES SERVICES FISCAUX
#### Case 112/84, [1985] ECR 1367

[Mr. Humblot sought repayment of a special tax imposed by the French government on certain vehicles. There were two different types of tax due annually on motor vehicles. First, a differential tax to which cars rated at 16 CV (fiscal horsepower) or less were subject and secondly a special tax on vehicles rated at more than 16 CV. The amount of differential tax payable increased progressively and uniformly with the power rating for tax purposes, but the special tax was levied at a single and considerably higher rate. In 1981 Mr. Humblot became the owner of a car rated at 36 CV. Before he could put the vehicle on the road Mr. Humblot had to pay the special tax, which, at that time, amounted to 5,000 FF. After paying that sum Mr. Humblot brought a complaint before the tax administration with a view to obtaining a refund of the difference between that sum and the highest rate of the differential tax (at the time 1,100 FF). His complaint was rejected and he brought an action against French tax authorities where he argued that the imposition of the special tax was contrary to EEC articles 30 and 95 (EC 28/TFEU34 and EC90/TFEU 110).]

7 It appears from the documents in the case that the essence of the question is whether Article 95 [110] prohibits the charging on cars exceeding a given power rating for tax purposes of a special fixed tax the amount of which is several times the highest amount of the progressive tax payable on cars of less than the said power rating for tax purposes, where the only cars subject to the special tax are imported, in particular from other Member States.

8 In his observations submitted to the court Mr Humblot points out that the special tax affects imported vehicles only, since no French car is rated for tax purposes at more than 16 cv. Mr Humblot argues that nevertheless vehicles of 16 cv or less and vehicles exceeding 16 cv are completely comparable as regards their performance, price and fuel consumption. As a result, he contends that the French State, by subjecting imported vehicles alone to a special tax much greater in amount than the differential tax, has created discrimination contrary to article 95 [110] of the Treaty.

9 For its part, the French Government considers that the special tax is contrary neither to the first nor to the second paragraph of article 95 [110]. It argues that the special tax is charged solely on luxury vehicles, which are not similar, within the meaning of the first paragraph of article 95 [110], to cars liable to the differential tax. Moreover, whilst the French Government concedes that some vehicles rated at 16 cv or less and others rated at more than 16 cv are in competition and so subject to the second paragraph of article 95 [110], it maintains that the special tax is not contrary to that provision, since it has not been shown that the tax has the effect of protecting domestic products. It argues that there is no evidence that a consumer who may have been dissuaded from buying a vehicle of more than 16 cv will purchase a car of French manufacture of 16 cv or less.

10 The Commission considers that the special tax is contrary to the first paragraph of article 95 [110] of the Treaty. It argues that all cars, irrespective of their power rating for tax purposes, are similar within the meaning of the case-law of the court. That being so, it is no longer possible for a Member State to create discrimination between imported and domestically-produced vehicles. The only exception is where a Member State taxes products differently — even identical products — on the basis of neutral criteria consistent with objectives of economic policy which are compatible with the Treaty, whilst avoiding discrimination between domestic and imported products. The Commission contends, however, that the criterion adopted by France in this instance, namely power rating for tax purposes, is not geared to an economic policy objective, such as heavier taxation of luxury products or vehicles with high fuel consumption. Accordingly, the Commission considers that the special tax, which is almost five times the highest rate of differential tax, affects imported vehicles only and does not pursue an economic policy objective compatible with the Treaty, is contrary to the first paragraph of article 95 [110] of the Treaty.

11 The United Kingdom government considers that vehicles of more than 16 cv are in a competitive relationship with some cars with a lower power rating for tax purposes, from which it follows that the special tax is contrary to the second paragraph of article 95 [110] of the Treaty since it diverts consumers from imported cars to French prestige models.

12 It is appropriate in the first place to stress that as Community law stands at present the Member States are at liberty to subject products such as cars to a

system of road tax which increases progressively in amount depending on an objective criterion, such as the power rating for tax purposes, which may be determined in various ways.

13 Such a system of domestic taxation is, however, compatible with article 95 [110] only in so far as it is free from any discriminatory or protective effect.

14 That is not true of a system like the one at issue in the main proceedings. Under that system there are two distinct taxes: a differential tax which increases progressively and is charged on cars not exceeding a given power rating for tax purposes and a fixed tax on cars exceeding that rating which is almost five times as high as the highest rate of the differential tax. Although the system embodies no formal distinction based on the origin of products it manifestly exhibits discriminatory or protective features contrary to article 95 [110], since the power rating determining liability to the special tax has been fixed at a level such that only imported cars, in particular from other Member States, are subject to the special tax whereas all cars of domestic manufacture are liable to the distinctly more advantageous differential tax.

15 In the absence of considerations relating to the amount of the special tax, consumers seeking comparable cars as regards such matters as size, comfort, actual power, maintenance costs, durability, fuel consumption and price would naturally choose from among cars above and below the critical power rating laid down by French law. However, liability to the special tax entails a much larger increase in taxation than passing from one category of car to another in a system of progressive taxation embodying balanced differentials like the system on which the differential tax is based. The resultant additional taxation is liable to cancel out the advantages which certain cars imported from other member states might have in consumers' eyes over comparable cars of domestic manufacture, particularly since the special tax continues to be payable for several years. In that respect the special tax reduces the amount of competition to which cars of domestic manufacture are subject and hence is contrary to the principle of neutrality with which domestic taxation must comply.

16 In the light of the foregoing considerations the question raised by the national court for a preliminary ruling should be answered as follows: article 95 [110] of the EEC Treaty prohibits the charging on cars exceeding a given power rating for tax purposes of a special fixed tax the amount of which is several times the highest amount of the progressive tax payable on cars of less than the said power rating for tax purposes, where the only cars subject to the special tax are imported, in particular from other Member States.

## NOTES AND QUESTIONS

1. Which paragraph of EC 90/TFEU 110 was the Court considering in this case, and why? Compare *Humblot* with the Court's statement in *Commission v. Italian Republic*, 200/85, 1986 ECJ CELEX LEXIS 322, [1986] ECR 3953:

> 2 Differential taxation on diesel-engined cars on the basis of cubic capacity as a result of which the higher rate of value-added tax applies exclusively to imported cars is not discriminatory and does not have a protective effect

within the meaning of article 95 [110] of the treaty where most models of imported diesel-engined cars fall within the category taxed at the normal rate, only one model falls within the category taxed at the higher rate and, if regard is had not only to diesel-engined cars, the higher rate is levied not only on imported cars but also on domestically manufactured cars.

After *Humblot*, the French Government subsequently revised the tax rules by replacing the FF5,000 tax with nine specific tax bands. This scheme was also found discriminatory: *Feldain v. Directeur des Services Fiscaux*, Case 433/85, [1987] ECR 2397 where the Court concluded that:

19 In view of the foregoing considerations, it must be stated that a system of road tax in which one tax band comprises more power ratings for tax purposes than the others, with the result that the normal progression of the tax is restricted in such a way as to afford an advantage to top-of-the-range cars of domestic manufacture, and in which the power rating for tax purposes is calculated in a manner which places vehicles imported from other member states at a disadvantage has a discriminatory or protective effect within the meaning of article 95 [110] of the Treaty.

**2.**    In the United States, most states impose sales and use taxes on the final sale to the consumer. The situation is described in the following excerpt from STEIN, HAY, WAELBROECK, EUROPEAN COMMUNITY LAW AND INSTITUTIONS IN PERSPECTIVE (Bobbs Merrill 1976), pages 381-82:

In the United States, indirect taxes are mostly State rather than federal. Such taxes take various forms, but the most common indirect taxes are sales, 'use,' and 'privilege' taxes, which are generally exacted according to the destination principle. State taxation of articles in interstate commerce has been upheld by the United States Supreme Court, but only in those instances in which the particular tax was found not to violate either the Commerce Clause or Due Process Clause of the Federal Constitution.

\*    \*    \*

Since these taxes are collected according to the destination principle, collecting them may be a nearly insurmountable problem for the taxing State, unless the item being taxed is subject to some type of licensing system (such as all States have for motor vehicles), which would bring the transaction to the attention of the authorities in the taxing State (State of destination).

Take the following example: Smith, a resident of State A, goes to State B and purchases a color television set, upon which he pays no tax. He brings the set back to State A, which imposes a use tax on color television sets. Unless State A has some way of learning of Smith's purchase, it has no way of imposing the use tax on the set. Any attempt by State A to fashion a statute that would impose a duty upon the merchant in State B to collect the tax for State A would violate both Due Process (no taxable nexus) and the commerce Clause (unreasonable burden on interstate commerce).

However, where a taxpayer purchases goods outside a State which are then delivered to him across State lines, it appears that no successful constitutional objection can be raised to the imposition of a use tax by the taxpayer's own State in which the goods are used, (if it learns of the transaction, as mentioned above) even though the taxpayer then uses the goods in interstate commerce. The rationale for this view, based upon the destination principle and what seems to be a narrow, technical view of the Commerce Clause, is that the articles have come to rest, and interstate commerce has ended; therefore, the use tax is a local, intrastate event.

State excise taxes are frequently imposed on motor fuel, cigarettes and alcohol (*ad valorem*). In addition, there are some specific rates in some states, usually in the form of business license taxes. These may or may not be insignificant as a cost of doing business.

In 1982, the percentage of total state revenue supplied by sales taxes averaged 30 percent. With the removal of federal support in many areas, this percentage is likely to be higher today. Sales taxes are favored as a means of raising additional revenue since they are relatively easy to collect and enforce. They are also more popular with the public.

Use taxes on automobiles, boats and planes are enforced against individuals through the required registration of these items. If goods are purchased in State A for delivery in State B, and the seller has a business nexus with State B, the seller will be liable for sales tax to the latter state. State auditors are entitled to call for production of out-of-state business records. Moreover, state auditors are free to visit or even locate in other states for the purpose of auditing businesses operating within their states. Some 20 Western/Midwestern and Southern states have offices in New York City for the purposes of auditing Eastern Seaboard activities.

Mail order business has, since the Supreme Court decision in *National Bellas Hess v. Department of Revenue of State of Illinois*, 386 U.S. 753 (1967), been exempt from state taxation where there is a lack of nexus with the delivery state. However, in *Quill Corp. v. North Dakota by and through Heitkamp*, 112 S. Ct. 1904 (1992), the Court overruled *Bellas Hess* insofar as that decision was based on the due process clause of the Fifth Amendment but affirmed its basis in the dormant commerce clause doctrine. This may give a new impetus to controversial efforts in Congress to pass legislation that would permit the state of delivery to impose a use tax. Prior to the Court's ruling in *Quill*, opponents argued, *inter alia*, that Congress could not adopt such legislation consistently with the due process clause. The commerce clause, of course, poses no such barriers for Congress.

Generally, enforcement and control is carried out by auditors. In addition, a body known as the Multistate Tax Commission carries out nationwide audits for some 20 states. This Commission is not popular in some states due to this tendency to undermine state authority. There are also reciprocal agreements between states dealing with the sharing of information. Clearly, the relatively small differences in rates between states in the United States has not caused distortions of trade as between neighboring states, although the *Bellas Hess* decision may have done much to further the cause of mail order. In the Union, the situation was and is dramatically more complex. At the outset, each of the original six member states levied a profusion of taxes on transaction, many of them having a distinctive discriminator element against foreign imports.

The federal courts have shown remarkable tolerance of state taxes that might be considered to have an effect on interstate trade: see for example, *Complete Auto Transit mc. v. Brady*, 430 U S. 274 (1977). In this case the Supreme Court held that a tax will not be considered an impermissible burden on interstate commerce by the activity if it:

- has a substantial nexus with the taxing state;

- is fairly apportioned;

- does not discriminate against interstate commerce;

- is fairly related to the services supplied by the states.

See also *Commonwealth Edison Co. v. Montana*, 453 U.S. 609 (1981).

In Europe, prior to the creation of the European Community, many of the taxes were levied at various stages of production, as discussed in the following excerpt from Stein, Hay, Waelbroeck, *op. cit.* at 377, 379-81:

> Before the introduction of the VAT by the EEC, the tax systems of the EEC members were characterized by high rate sales taxes in the form of multi-stage, cumulative turnover taxes, which were levied at each stage of the production and distribution process (hence the descriptive term 'cascade tax'). France was the sole exception, since it had adopted a value added tax in 1954. One consequence of the cascade tax system was that there were acute differences in tax treatment in favor of vertically-integrated industries, due to the phenomenon of 'pyramiding': at each stage the tax was built into the price: thus the more stages which applied their markup on price plus tax and then added their own tax, the more pyramided and swollen the tax became. Thus, the tax was viewed as having anti-competitive and discriminatory effects. But its most serious inadequacy from the Community viewpoint was that, since it was based upon the principle of taxation upon destination (i.e., that all products to be used at the same destination should be taxed at the same rate, regardless of where they are produced), the cascade tax required the imposition of compensatory taxes on imported goods and repayments ('drawbacks') on the exported goods between Member States (Arts. 96-97 of the EEC Treaty), which could be used for protectionist purposes, and which also, since they required a 'tax frontier,' were not compatible, with the goal of establishing a 'frontier-free' common internal market.

*     *     *

> Because of the above-described difficulties in the systems of indirect taxation in existence in the Member States at the time of the creation of the EEC, the Commission almost immediately began an intensive study of the problem of tax harmonization under Art. 99 [115], culminating in the Neumark Report, issued in 1962, which recommended, inter alia, that each Member State of the EEC adopt a value-added tax. The final decision to

adopt the VAT in place of the cascade tax is embodied in two 1967 directives of the Council.

The VAT system has now been adopted in all Member States [including all 'new' members].

Since the national VAT systems vary greatly, the Commission took a significant step toward harmonization by proposing the "Sixth Directive, "which would call for a uniform basis of tax assessment among EEC members.

\* \* \*

As adopted by the EEC members, the value added tax achieves the effect of a retail tax on personal (as opposed to business) consumption, and thus avoids the pyramiding effect of the cascade turnover tax, since at each stage the taxes paid are kept separate from the cost of goods at that stage and are subtracted from it. The result is that the VAT is passed along from stage to stage and is ultimately paid by the consumer.

For example, suppose that a 10% value added tax is imposed upon a steel product as it progresses from iron ore in the mine to the final transaction, when a finished product incorporating the steel is sold over the counter to a consumer. First, the mining company would bring an X amount of ore out of the ground and sell it to a steel mill for, let us say, $50.00. Assuming for the sake of simplicity that the ore cost nothing to take out of the ground and furthermore, that the mine had no capital investment, the "value added" at the time of the sale to the steel mill would be the entire $50.00, and the steel mill would pay 10% of that sum, $5.00, to the mining company in value added tax, which the mining company would in turn pay into the national treasury of the country involved.

The steel mill would then process the ore and sell the steel to a manufacturer for say, $150. At the time of this transaction, the manufacturer would pay the steel mill $13.00 in value added tax. But the steel mill would only pass on to the treasury $10.00 representing 10% of the value added by the steel mill. The other $5.00 received from the manufacturer would compensate the steel mill for the tax it paid on the iron ore.

In turn, the manufacturer would shape the steel into an appliance and sell it to a retailer for say, $300, collecting $30.00 from the retailer in value added tax, $15.00 of which would go to the treasury; the other $15.00 it would keep as compensation for the tax it paid to the steel mill.

The retailer would then sell the appliance to a consumer for say, $500, and the consumer would pay the retailer $50.00 in value added tax, $20.00 of which the retailer would remit to the treasury, the other $30.00 being compensation for the tax he paid to the manufacturer.

Thus, although the value added tax is collected at each stage in the production-distribution process, it is not pyramided, but rather is passed on to the next stage, until it reaches the consumer, who, having no one to pass the tax onto, pays the entire amount of the VAT. The amount of the VAT is indicated on the invoice for each transaction in the process. This facilitates tax collection which is another significant advantage in countries where tax evasion has traditionally been a serious problem".

Other taxes, such as excise taxes on vehicles or alcohol, continue to exist alongside VAT and are frequently contested on the grounds that they discriminate against out of state goods.

3.    In the application of article EC90/TFEU 110(1), suppose there is some objective policy behind a taxing scheme: could this render any discriminatory side effects legitimate? In *Chemial Farmaceutici v. DAF SpA*, Case 140/79, [1981] ECR 1, the Italian government attempted to favor, through a tax system, ethyl alcohol obtained through fermentation in preference to the manufactured (synthetic) equivalent. The underlying purpose was to discourage the use of ethylene (derived from crude oil) so that it would be reserved for more economically important purposes. It was also true, however, that Italy was not a significant producer of the synthetic product. The Court stated:

14 [I]n its present stage of development Community law does not restrict the freedom of each Member State to lay down tax arrangements which differentiate between certain products on the basis of objective criteria, such as the nature of the raw materials used or the production process employed. Such differentiation is compatible with Community law if it pursues economic policy objectives which are themselves compatible with the requirements of the Treaty and its secondary law and if the detailed rules are such as to avoid any form of discrimination, direct or indirect, in regard to imports from other Member States or any form of protection of competing domestic products.

15 Differential taxation such as that which exists in Italy for denatured synthetic alcohol on the one hand and denatured alcohol obtained by fermentation on the other satisfies these requirements. It appears in fact that that system of taxation pursues an objective of legitimate industrial policy in that it is such as to promote the distillation of agricultural products as against the manufacture of alcohol from petroleum derivatives. That choice does not conflict with the rules of Community law or the requirements of a policy decided within the framework of the Community.

16 The detailed provisions of the legislation at issue before the national court cannot be considered as discriminatory since, on the one hand, it is not disputed that imports from other Member States of alcohol by fermentation qualify for the same tax treatment as Italian alcohol produced by fermentation and, on the other hand, although the rate of tax prescribed for synthetic alcohol results in restraining the importation of synthetic alcohol originating in other Member States, it has an equivalent economic effect in the national territory in that it also hampers the establishment of profitable production of the same product in Italian industry.

What differences exist between the *Chemial* case and *Humblot* that resulted in a different interpretation by the Court? In *Commission v. Greece* Case C-132/88 [1990] ECR I-1567, higher horsepower cars were more highly taxed than lower

horsepower cars. An argument that this was motivated by social policy considerations, i.e. that it constituted an indirect tax on wealth, was accepted by the Court.
What does this suggest by way of comparison with other EC Treaty free movement
provisions? The Court also held that the Commission had not proven that the Greek
tax incited consumers to buy domestic cars rather than intermediate or low
horsepower imports.

Note that the Court refers to "the present stage of development [of Community
law]". What further developments might cause the Court to reach a different
conclusion?

4. In *Gaston Schul Douane-Expediteur v. Inspecteur der Invoerrechten en
Accijnzen, Roosendaal*, Case 15/81, [1982] ECR 1409, the Court found that it was
incompatible with EC 90/TFEU 110 for a Member State to charge VAT on the
importation of secondhand goods from another Member State by a private party
while the sale of such goods within the Member State was not liable to VAT. This was
because no account was taken of the residual element of VAT paid in the member
state from which the goods had been exported, which was still contained in the value
of the goods on importation. Would the *Gaston Schul* reasoning apply to importation by private parties of goods that have been bought in normal commerce and on
which VAT has been paid?

5. In *Ákos Nádasdi and Ilona Németh v. Vám- és Pénzügyörség Dél-Alföldi
Regionális Parancsnoksága* Joined Cases C-290 and 333/05, 2006 ECJ CELEX
LEXIS 572, [2006] ECR I-10115, the Court found that because Hungarian
registration duty on imported used cars was the same as on used domestic cars,
discrimination existed under EC 90/TFEU 110 because the domestic vehicles bore
the duty when originally sold as new. Hence the tax on imported vehicles did not
take account of depreciation in value.

## [B]  Indirect Protection Between Products

### JOHN WALKER AND SONS LTD v. MINISTERIUM FOR
### SKATTER OG AFGIFTER
Case 243/84, [1986] ECR 875

[Danish law applied differential excise taxes as between Scotch whisky and fruit
wine based liqueurs. Fruit wine of the liqueur type of an alcoholic strength not
exceeding 20 percent by volume was subject to a specific duty calculated per liter of
the product. Scotch whisky, however, like other spirits, as well as fruit wine of the
liqueur type of an alcoholic strength exceeding 20 percent by volume and grape
wine of the liqueur type exceeding 23 percent by volume were subject to duty
consisting of a specific duty imposed per liter of pure ethyl alcohol and a duty
proportionate to the highest selling price charged by wholesalers.]

4 The order for reference indicates that John Walker & Sons Ltd., the plaintiff in
the main proceedings, produces Scotch whisky of an alcoholic strength of 40 percent
by volume which it markets, among other countries, in Denmark. In 1982 it
instituted proceedings against the Danish Ministry for Fiscal Affairs before the
Ostre Landsret for a declaration that taxation which differentiates between Scotch

whisky and fruit wine of the liquor type, Danish products which it regards as either similar to, or in competition with, Scotch whisky, is contrary to Article 95 [110] of the EEC Treaty.

\* \* \*

11 In order to determine whether products are similar within the terms of the prohibition laid down in the first paragraph of Article 95 [110] it is necessary to consider . . . . whether they have similar characteristics and meet the same needs from the standpoint of consumers. The Court endorsed a broad interpretation of the concept of similarity in its judgments of February 27, 1980, in Case No. 168/78 Commission v. France [1980] E.C.R. 347, and July 15, 1982, in Case No. 216/81 Cogis v. Amministrazione delle Finanze dello Stato [1982] E.C.R. 2701, and assessed the similarity of the products not according to whether they were strictly identical, but according to whether their use was similar and comparable. Consequently, in order to determine whether products are similar it is necessary first to consider certain objective characteristics of both categories of beverages, such as their origin, the method of manufacture and their organoleptic properties, in particular taste and alcohol content, and secondly to consider whether or not both categories of beverages are capable of meeting the same needs from the standpoint of consumers.

12 It should be noted that the two categories of beverages exhibit manifestly different characteristics. Fruit wine of the liqueur type is a fruit-based product obtained by natural fermentation, whereas Scotch whisky is a cereal-based product obtained by distillation. The organoleptic properties of the two products are also different. As the Court held inREWE (supra), the fact that the same raw material, for example alcohol, is to be found in the two products is not sufficient reason to apply the prohibition contained in the first paragraph of Article 95 [110]. For the products to be regarded as similar, that raw material must also be present in more or less equal proportions in both products. In that regard, it must be pointed out that the alcoholic strength of Scotch whisky is 40 percent by volume, whereas the alcoholic strength of fruit wine of the liqueur type, to which the Danish tax legislation applies, does not exceed 20 percent by volume.

13 The contention that Scotch whisky may be consumed in the same way as fruit wine of the liqueur type, as an apéritif diluted with water or with fruit juice, even if it were established, would not be sufficient to render Scotch whisky similar to fruit wine of the liqueur type, whose intrinsic characteristics are fundamentally different.

14 The answer to the first question must therefore be that the first paragraph of Article 95 [110] of the EEC Treaty must be interpreted as meaning that products such as Scotch whisky and fruit wine of the liqueur type may not be regarded as similar products.

The second paragraph of Article 95 [110] of the EEC Treaty

15 In its second question the national court seeks to ascertain whether, if they are not similar products, Scotch whisky and fruit wine of the liqueur type are to be regarded as competing products and, if so, whether taxation that differentiates between the two products, of the kind imposed by the aforesaid Danish legislation,

is to be regarded as incompatible with the second paragraph of Article 95 [110] of the EEC Treaty.

\* \* \*

19 The second paragraph of Article 95 [110] of the EEC Treaty provides that no Member State may impose on the products of other Member States any internal taxation of such a nature as to afford indirect protection to other domestic products.

20 The provision therefore pursues the general aim of guaranteeing fiscal neutrality and seeks to ensure that the Member States do not discriminate against products originating in other Member States by favoring domestic products under their national tax legislation, thereby creating barriers to the free movement of goods between the Member States.

21 It is clear from the documents forwarded by the national court and from the observations submitted to the Court of Justice that the product which bears the lightest tax burden is manufactured almost exclusively in Denmark and that whisky, which is exclusively an imported product, is taxed not as such but as an alcoholic beverage included in the tax category of spirits — that is to say, beverages with a high alcohol content — which comprises other products, the vast majority of which are Danish.

22 In order to enable the national court to determine whether, in those circumstances, the differential taxation imposed by the Danish tax system constitutes an infringement of the second paragraph of Article 95 [110], it is necessary to recall that the Court of Justice has consistently held (see in particular the judgment of March 15, 1983, in Case No. 319/81, Commission v. Italy [1983 ECR. 601 that Community law at its present stage of development does not restrict the freedom of each Member State to lay down tax arrangements which differentiate between certain products on the basis of objective criteria, such as the nature of the raw materials used or the production processes employed. Such differentiation is compatible with Community law if it pursues objectives of economic policy which are themselves compatible with the requirements of the Treaty and its secondary legislation, and if the detailed rules are such as to avoid any form of discrimination, direct or indirect, in regard to imports from other Member States or any form of protection of competing domestic products.

23 Accordingly, without there being any need to ascertain whether there exists a competitive relationship between Scotch whisky and fruit wine of the liqueur type, the answer to the second question must be that at the present stage of its development Community law, and in particular the second paragraph of Article 95 [110] of the EEC Treaty, does not preclude the application of a system of taxation which differentiates between certain beverages on the basis of objective criteria. Such a system does not favor domestic producers if a significant proportion of domestic production of alcoholic beverages falls within each of the relevant tax categories.

# NOTES AND QUESTIONS

**1.** Why did the Court conclude that no "similar products," within the meaning of EC 90/TFEU 110, were present in this case? Retrace the Court's reasoning. How important is it to decide whether a case falls under paragraph 1 or paragraph 2 of EC 90/TFEU 110? Would a determination of an infringement of paragraph (2) necessarily require the Member State to adjust the tax system so that the tax burden is the same as for the "protected" product? A mere difference in taxation between two "dissimilar products" may not be sufficient to conclude that there is a protective effect In *Commission v. Belgium*, Case 356/85, 1987 ECR 3299, a six percent difference in the tax levied on beer compared with wine (wine being taxed at the higher rate) was found not to be protective. The tax was based on cost, so most of the difference in the tax borne was related to that factor and the Court concluded that the relatively minor difference was unlikely to have any protective effect.

**2.** What criteria did the Court use to distinguish between paragraphs (1) and (2) of EC 90/TFEU 110? Under paragraph (2) the need to demonstrate a protective effect may render a tax considerably less likely to be in violation. See *Commission v. Belgium*, Case 356/85, 1987 ECR 3299, where the ECJ held that a national system of taxation in which wines from fresh grapes coming from other Member States are subject to a higher value added tax rate than the rate applied to domestically produced beer is not incompatible with article 90, second paragraph, of the Treaty to the extent that, on the one hand, the difference between the respective prices of wine and beer of comparable quality is so great that the difference between the rates of tax for the two products is not likely to influence the behavior of the consumer and, on the other hand, there is no longer any protective effect indicated in statistics on the comparative development of the consumption of wine on the one hand and the consumption of beer on the other in the Member State in question.

**3.** Note that EC 90/TFEU 110 only applies to taxes on products, and does not therefore apply to matters covered by the Treaty provisions on capital and services.

**4.** Discriminatory taxes have been a recurring problem in the United States, as indicated by the following extract from STEIN, HAY, WAELBROECK, *op. cit.*, at 381, 422-23 [describing the situation in the United States in the mid-1970s]:

> Indirect State taxes which discriminate in favor of local commerce have been held to violate the Commerce Clause. For example, Mississippi imposed a $50.00 per truck "privilege tax" upon trucks operated by a laundry in Memphis, Tennessee, which did business in Mississippi. Local laundries licensed in the State of Mississippi were taxed only $8.00 per truck. The Supreme Court held the tax to be an unlawful discrimination against interstate commerce."

*          *          *

[A] substantial amount of state legislation sets limits on price competition, entry into business and free movement of goods. For example, a number of state statutes permit resale price maintenance, limit entry into certain trades, and make it difficult to sell goods produced in other states.

Using their police power, many state and local governments have instituted regulations that limit or avoid competition. For example, as a health measure, many prohibit the sale of fresh milk that has not been produced in inspected dairies. Since the inspectors travel within a circumscribed area, a milk-shed is established limiting competition to the dairies within the area.

\* \* \*

There are many provisions for administrative supervision over prices of agricultural commodities and foodstuffs, milk, fuels, and gasoline . . . . Some statutes provide that all gasoline prices must be posted publicly, and that there can be no variation from posted prices — a mechanism that prevents gasoline stations from cutting a price to any customer unless they cut prices to all.

Alcoholic beverages are given special treatment. In the liquor "monopoly" states, liquor prices are fixed in the state-operated stores, the only retail sources permitted. A number of other states require that the distillers and importers set the wholesale and retail prices of alcoholic beverages.

\* \* \*

Other regulations have permitted groups of competitors to set prices with government approval. For example, state laws permit rate-setting in the insurance field, as well as price-setting and marketing cooperation by agricultural producers.

A number of states have regulated competition by controlling production. This has been a notable feature in the oil-producing states which have set allowable production quotas through state regulatory agencies.

\* \* \*

Michigan levied a tax of 4 cents a gallon on wine made from home grown grapes and 50 cents on the product made from California grapes. Alabama levied an annual tax of $1,000 on each winery. However, if 75 percent of the materials used were home-grown, the tax was only $25.00.

At one time California declared an embargo on strawberries grown in Louisiana, which state retaliated with an embargo on California citrus.

\* \* \*

A host of labeling statutes and labeling requirements greatly complicate the marketing of certain goods throughout the country. Many types of drugs and other products require tags which are specified by the individual states. Since these label specifications are not uniform, a manufacturer must affix a special label for each of a number of jurisdictions . . . .

By way of some more recent specific examples, in *Bacchus Imports, Ltd v. Dias* 468 U.S. 263, 104 S. Ct. 3049, 82 L. Ed. 2d 200 (1984) Hawaii had imposed a 20 percent excise tax on sales of liquor, but exempted Hawaiian-produced Okolehao and pineapple wine. Hawaii sought to justify the exemptions on the basis that the domestic industries were struggling, but the U.S. Supreme Court concluded that the Commerce Clause created an absolute limitation on discriminatory legislation. The fact that the production of these wines was *de minimis* and therefore the tax probably didn't have any material effect on the competitive position of imported wines was not sufficient to override the Commerce clause limitation. Does this case seem analogous to the *John Walker* case or does it present a different issue? How would such an issue be analyzed in Europe?

Again, the Supreme Court struck down a discriminatory tax in the form of a premium payment on milk sold by distributors that was used to subsidize Massachusetts farmers: *West Lynn Creamery, Inc. v. Healy* 512 U.S. 186, 114 S. Ct. 2205, 129 L. Ed. 2d 157 (1994). The Court pointed out that:

> the "premium payments" are effectively a tax which makes milk produced out of State more expensive. Although the tax also applies to milk produced in Massachusetts. Its effect on Massachusetts producers is entirely (indeed more than) offset by the subsidy provided exclusively to Massachusetts dairy farmers. Like an ordinary tariff, the tax is thus effectively imposed only on out-of-State products . . . .

By contrast, consider *Prudential Ins. Co. v. Benjamin* 328 U.S. 408, 66 S. Ct. 1142, 90 L. Ed. 1342 (1946), where the Supreme Court held that the McCarren Act permitted discriminatory state taxes on insurance and noted that the Commerce Clause "enables Congress not only to promote but also to prohibit interstate commerce". See also *Western & Southern Life Ins. Co v. State Board*, 451 U.S. 648, 101 S. Ct. 2070, 68 L.Ed.2d 514 (1981). Could such a conclusion ever be reached under EU rules? In this connection one might consider the case of *Socridis v. Receveur Principal des Douanes*, C-166/98, 1999 ECJ CELEX LEXIS 572, [1999] ECR I-3791, where a Council Directive (92/84) aimed at a first step towards harmonization of excise taxes on both wine and beer had set a minimum tax rate on beer but set a zero threshold on wine. The French government had significantly increased the excise tax on beer in implementation of the directive:

> 13 Socridis submits that the second paragraph of Article 95 [110] of the Treaty itself contains a requirement of proportionality which applies inter alia to the basis of assessment, to the method of levy and to the rate of taxation. Consequently, by taxing imported beverages more heavily than a competing national beverage a Member State is in breach of that provision of the Treaty in so far as the difference is out of proportion to the differences between the two categories of beverage concerned.

> 14 It argues that the differences in taxation required and motivated by Directives 92/83 and 92/84 manifestly exceed the objective differences between beer and wine.

> 15 Furthermore, fixing the minimum rate of excise duty on wine at zero amounts to authorising the Member States to exonerate wine permanently

from all excise duty. Such an exoneration favours what is an essential product for the States in the south of Europe, where beer represents neither a sector nor a beverage which is of cultural importance. Six Member States apply that minimum, in any event: the Federal Republic of Germany, the Hellenic Republic, the Kingdom of Spain, the Italian Republic and the Grand Duchy of Luxembourg, as well as, since the date of its accession to the Communities, the Republic of Austria.

16 The first point to note is that the general purpose of Article 95 [110] of the Treaty is to guarantee the free movement of goods between the Member States under normal conditions of competition by eliminating all forms of protection which may result in the application of internal taxation which discriminates against products from other Member States and to guarantee that internal taxation is wholly neutral for the purposes of competition between domestic and imported products.

17 In that context, the second paragraph of Article 95 [110] of the Treaty is intended, more specifically, to prevent any form of indirect fiscal protectionism affecting imported products which, although not similar, within the meaning of the first paragraph of Article 95 [110], to domestic products, nevertheless compete with some of them, even if only partially, indirectly or potentially . . .

18 In that connection, only commonly consumed wines, which in general are cheap wines, have enough characteristics in common with beer to constitute an alternative choice for consumers and may therefore be regarded as being in competition with beer for the purposes of the second paragraph of Article 95 [110] of the Treaty . . . Consequently, the ground of invalidity based on that provision relied on by Socridis to challenge the minimum excise duty fixed by Directive 92/84 arises only to the extent that it applies to commonly consumed wines.

19 Next, the Court has consistently held that directives do not infringe the Treaty if they leave the Member States a sufficiently wide margin of appreciation to enable them to transpose them into national law in a manner consistent with the requirements of the Treaty . . .

20 It is common ground that Directives 92/83 and 92/84 merely require Member States to apply a minimum excise duty on beer. Consequently, the Member States retain a sufficiently wide margin of discretion to ensure that the relationship of the taxes on wine and beer excludes any protection for domestic production within the meaning of Article 95 [110] of the Treaty.

21 The plea that Directives 92/83 and 92/84 are invalid because they are incompatible with the second paragraph of Article 95 [110] of the Treaty must therefore be rejected.

The Court makes some rather sweeping assertions about the nature of competition between beer and wine, as well as about cultural differences. What factual bases, if any, does it cite for these?

## § 13.04   OVERALL SCOPE OF EC 28/TFEU 34

### PROCUREUR DU ROI v. BENOIT AND GUSTAVE DASSONVILLE
#### Case 8/74, [1974] ECR 837

[Under Belgian law, an importer wishing to use a designation of origin in connection with imported goods needed to produce a certificate of origin for the products.

In 1970, Gustave Dassonville, a wholesaler in business in France, and his son Benoit Dassonville, who managed a branch of his father's business in Belgium imported into Belgium "Scotch whisky" under the brand names "Johnnie Walker" and "Vat 69," which Gustave Dassonville had purchased from the French importers and distributors of these two brands of whisky. On the bottles, the Dassonvilles affixed, with a view to their sale in Belgium, labels bearing in particular the printed words "British Customs Certificate of Origin," followed by a hand-written note of the number and date of the French excise bond on the permit register. This excise bond constituted the official document which, according to French rules, had to accompany a product bearing a designation of origin. France did not require a certificate of origin for "Scotch whisky."

The Dassonvilles were accused of having committed forgeries or assisted therein by affixing to the bottles the handwritten labels, with fraudulent intent to induce belief that they were in possession, (which they were not) of an official document certifying the origin of the whisky, and made use of forged documents; and of having contravened Belgian law by knowingly importing, selling, displaying for sale, holding in their possession or transporting for the purposes of sale and delivery, whisky bearing a designation duly adopted by the Belgian Government without causing the whisky to be accompanied by an official document (i.e. a Certificate of Origin issued by the British Customs Authorities) certifying its right to such designation.]

5 All trading rules enacted by Member States which are capable of hindering, directly or indirectly, actually or potentially, intra-community trade are to be considered as measures having an effect equivalent to quantitative restrictions.

### NOTES AND QUESTIONS

Consider the definition of a quantitative restriction that appears in the above extract. In referring to direct or indirect, actual or potential hindrances to trade, is this a far-reaching definition? Or does the reference to "trading rules" create a limit? For example, would that term rule out a speed limit imposed on continental trucks (with a left-hand drive) arriving in the UK that was not imposed on UK trucks (with a right-hand drive) if that speed limit was deemed necessary by the UK government for safety reasons? What about non-discriminatory taxes on income that have the effect of reducing demand for goods generally?

## § 13.05   DISCRIMINATION AGAINST IMPORTS

### [A]   Must there Be an Intent to Protect Domestic Products?

### PROCUREUR DU ROI v. BENOIT AND GUSTAVE DASSONVILLE
Case 8/74, [1974] ECR 837

[See the above extract for the facts of this case]

6 In the absence of a Community system guaranteeing for consumers the authenticity of a product's designation of origin, if a Member State takes measures to prevent unfair practices in this connexion, it is however subject to the condition that these measures should be reasonable and that the means of proof required should not act as a hindrance to trade between Member States and should, in consequence, be accessible to all Community nationals.

7 Even without having to examine whether or not such measures are covered by article 36 [36], they must not, in any case, by virtue of the principle expressed in the second sentence of that article, constitute a means of arbitrary discrimination or a disguised restriction on trade between Member States.

8 That may be the case with formalities, required by a Member State for the purpose of proving the origin of a product, which only direct importers are really in a position to satisfy without facing serious difficulties.

9 Consequently, the requirement by a Member State of a certificate of authenticity which is less easily obtainable by importers of an authentic product which has been put into free circulation in a regular manner in another Member State than by importers of the same product coming directly from the country of origin constitutes a measure having an effect equivalent to a quantitative restriction as prohibited by the Treaty.

## NOTES AND QUESTIONS

1.   How was the Belgian law discriminatory against imports in the above case (if at all)? In paragraph 7, the Court did not apparently consider EEC article 36 (EC 30/TFEU 36) to be relevant, yet it seemed to draw on the qualification set out in that article as part of its analysis under EC 28/TFEU 34. How was EC 30/TFEU 36 relevant to that reasoning?

2.   In the U.S. although, under the commerce clause, the federal government has assumed wide powers of regulation in lieu of the states, so as to avoid a multiplicity of different requirements, the states had, under the Twenty-First Amendment retained significant freedom of action in the regulation of the wine industry. In 1990, a 33-state task force set up by the industry reported that it was "time the 50 states stopped treating each other like foreign countries and buried the restless corpse of Prohibition." It asked the National Conference on State Legislatures to standardize licensing, unify state-federal and interstate regulations, and

consider reciprocal shipping agreements between states.

The Task Force pointed out that, with all the various state regulations, often varying significantly, wine was one of the few products where interstate sales were spoken of in terms of "import" and "export."

Many challenges to state regulation in this area have appeared. See in particular, *Granholm v. Heald*, 544 U.S. 460 (2005), where the U.S. Supreme Court ruled that laws in New York and Michigan discriminated against out-of-state wineries in allowing only in-state wineries to ship directly to consumers as a means for preventing minors from obtaining alcohol. The following extract from the Court's judgment provides an interesting echo of the ECJ's balancing test in *Cassis*:

> Concluding that the States' direct-shipment laws are not authorized by the Twenty-first Amendment does not end the inquiry, for this Court must still consider whether either State's regime "advances a legitimate local purpose that cannot be adequately served by reasonable nondiscriminatory alternatives," *New Energy Co. of Ind.* v. *Limbach*, 486 U.S. 269, 278. The States provide little evidence for their claim that purchasing wine over the Internet by minors is a problem. The 26 States now permitting direct shipments report no such problem, and the States can minimize any risk with less restrictive steps, such as requiring an adult signature on delivery. The States' tax evasion justification is also insufficient. Increased direct shipment, whether in or out of state, brings the potential for tax evasion. However, this argument is a diversion with regard to Michigan, which does not rely on in-state wholesalers to collect taxes on out-of-state wines. New York's tax collection objectives can be achieved without discriminating against interstate commerce, *e.g.*, by requiring a permit as a condition of direct shipping, which is what it does for in-state wineries. Both States also benefit from federal laws that supply incentives for wineries to comply with state regulations. Other rationales — facilitating orderly market conditions, protecting public health and safety, and ensuring regulatory accountability — can also be achieved through the alternative of an evenhanded licensing requirement." (pp. 26–29)

Canada and Australia appear to have suffered from the same problems. For example, in Canada, the then prime minister, Brian Mulroney, warned in 1990 that any redistribution of power between the federal government and the country's 10 provinces would have to include removal of inter-provincial trade barriers. Mr. Mulroney maintained that a fundamental principle of the reform process should be a willingness "to tear down the barriers that currently impeded the movement of people, goods and services across the provinces."

Although no customs duties are levied on inter-provincial trade, non-tariff barriers are in many cases as significant as those applying to imports from foreign countries. They include provincial government preferences for local suppliers, restrictive product standards, requirements that certain goods — notably beer — can be sold in a province only if they are produced there. As in the EU today, government procurement at provincial level is also discriminatory against out-of-province goods.

# OPENBAAR MINISTERIE v. VAN TIGGELE
## Case 82/77, [1978] ECR 25

[Van Tiggele in the Netherlands was charged with selling gin below the national minimum price.]

12 For the purposes of the article 30 [34] prohibition it is sufficient that the measures in question are likely to hinder, directly or indirectly, actually or potentially, imports between Member States.

13 Whilst national price-control rules applicable without distinction to domestic products and imported products cannot in general produce such an effect they may do so in certain specific cases.

14 Thus imports may be impeded in particular when a national authority fixes prices or profit margins at such a level that imported products are placed at a disadvantage in relation to identical domestic products either because they cannot profitably be marketed in the conditions laid down or because the competitive advantage conferred by lower cost prices is cancelled out.

15 These are the considerations in the light of which the question submitted must be settled since the present case concerns a product for which there is no common organization of the market.

16 First a national provision which prohibits without distinction the retail sale of domestic products and imported products at prices below the purchase price paid by the retailer cannot produce effects detrimental to the marketing of imported products alone and consequently cannot constitute a measure having an effect equivalent to a quantitative restriction on imports.

17 Furthermore the fixing of the minimum profit margin at a specific amount, and not as a percentage of the cost price, applicable without distinction to domestic products and imported products is likewise incapable of producing an adverse effect on imported products which may be cheaper, as in the present case where the amount of the profit margin constitutes a relatively insignificant part of the final retail price.

18 On the other hand this is not so in the case of a minimum price fixed at a specific amount which, although applicable without distinction to domestic products and imported products, is capable of having an adverse effect on the marketing of the latter in so far as it prevents their lower cost price from being reflected in the retail selling price.

19 This is the conclusion which must be drawn even though the competent authority is empowered to grant exemptions from the fixed minimum price and though this power is freely applied to imported products, since the requirement that importers and traders must comply with the administrative formalities inherent in such a system may in itself constitute a measure having an effect equivalent to a quantitative restriction.

20 The temporary nature of the application of the fixed minimum prices is not a factor capable of justifying such a measure since it is incompatible on other grounds with Article 30 [34] of the Treaty.

## NOTES AND QUESTIONS

**1.** How exactly was the Dutch law in *van Tiggele* discriminatory against imports?

**2.** See also *Tasca*, Case 65/75 [1976] ECR 291, where the Court considered whether a domestic law imposing a maximum selling price respectively was compatible with EC 28/TFEU 34. Tasca was accused in Italy of selling sugar above the permitted national maximum price. While recognizing that a maximum price does not in itself constitute a measure equivalent in effect to a quantitative restriction, the Court advised that it becomes so when fixed at a level high enough to make sale of the imported product difficult if not impossible. In the face of a maximum price, importers of more highly priced goods might have to cut their profit margins or even be forced to sell at a loss.

**3.** The ECJ here suggested that measures applicable without distinction to domestic and imported products usually could not hinder trade within the meaning given to EC 28/TFEU 34 in *Dassonville*. It will be seen in following sections of this chapter that such a statement would not hold true today.

### [B]   Legal Consequences for Measures that Infringe EC 28/TFEU 34

### CRIMINAL PROCEEDINGS AGAINST JACQUES PISTRE, MICHELE BARTHES, YVES MILHAU AND DIDIER OBERTI
Joined Cases C-21/94, C-322/94, C-323/94 AND C-324/94, 1997 ECJ CELEX LEXIS 60, [1997] ECR I-2343

3 The defendants are French nationals who manage companies established in Lacaune in the departement of Tarn in France which manufacture and market cured food products. They are being prosecuted for having marketed in 1991 cooked meat products under a label on which appeared the descriptions denominations "mountain" "montagne" hill country or Monts de Lacaune' when they had not been authorized to make, in relation to those products, specific reference to mountain areas, as required by Article 34 of Law No 85-30 of 9 January 1985 on the development and protection of mountain regions.

41 As regards the second part of the question, the French Government and the Commission point out that the facts in question in the main proceedings are confined to French territory since the prosecutions in question have been brought against French nationals and concern French products marketed on French territory. According to the French Government, the prosecutions do not therefore fall within the ambit of Articles 30 [34] and 36 [36] relating to the free movement of goods between Member States, so that it is not necessary to answer the question whether domestic legislation such as that in question in the main proceedings is compatible with Articles 30 [34] and 36 [36].

42 That argument cannot be accepted.

43 . . . [T]he prohibition laid down in Article 30 [34] of the Treaty covers all trading rules enacted by Member States which are capable of hindering, directly or

indirectly, actually or potentially, intra-Community trade.

44 Accordingly, whilst the application of a national measure having no actual link to the importation of goods does not fall within the ambit of Article 30 [34] of the Treaty . . . Article 30 [34] cannot be considered inapplicable simply because all the facts of the specific case before the national court are confined to a single Member State.

45 In such a situation, the application of the national measure may also have effects on the free movement of goods between Member States, in particular when the measure in question facilitates the marketing of goods of domestic origin to the detriment of imported goods. In such circumstances, the application of the measure, even if restricted to domestic producers, in itself creates and maintains a difference of treatment between those two categories of goods, hindering, at least potentially, intra-Community trade.

46 The French Government points out that the national legislation in question in the main proceedings is not applied by its authorities to products imported from other Member States. Since its entry into force in 1988, no prosecution has been brought with respect to products imported from Member States bearing the indication mountain'. In those circumstances, it cannot be argued that the legislation in question actually constitutes a measure having an effect equivalent to a quantitative restriction within the meaning of Article 30 [34] of the Treaty. The French Government accepts, however, that Article 34 of Law No 85-30 does not expressly exclude from its scope products imported from other Member States, so that imported products bearing indications referring to mountain areas could be held to have been put on the market in breach of the legislation in question if the relevant authorization has not been obtained for them.

47 The French Government adds that, in so far as application of its domestic legislation may constitute an obstacle to free movement of goods, it is justified on grounds relating to consumer protection and fair trading.

48 Since the French Government has accepted that the domestic legislation in question could be applied to products imported from other Member States, it follows, first, that it constitutes an obstacle to intra-Community trade for the purposes of Article 30 [34] of the Treaty.

49 Next, legislation such as that in question in the main proceedings discriminates against goods imported from other Member States in so far as it reserves use of the description mountain' to products manufactured on national territory and made from domestic raw materials . . . .

50 It is clear from Article 2 of Decree No 88-194 and from Articles 3, 4 and 5 of Law No 85-30 that, in order for the description mountain' or specific geographical references to mountain areas to be used in relation to a product, its production, preparation, manufacture and packaging must be carried out in mountain areas situated on French territory. It is thus apparent that the legislation does not enable imported products to fulfil the conditions to which authorization to use the description mountain' is subject.

51 Similarly, grant of the authorization is, according to Article 2 of Decree No

88-194, dependent on the use, in the manufacture of processed products, of raw materials which come from mountain areas situated on French territory. According to that provision, imported products may not therefore be used in the manufacture of processed products bearing the description mountain'.

52 According to settled case-law, domestic legislation of that kind, since it is discriminatory in character, may be justified only on one of the grounds mentioned in Article 36 [36] of the Treaty . . .

53 In the present case, the legislation concerned cannot be justified on any of the grounds listed in Article 36 [36]. Of those grounds, only protection of industrial and commercial property, in the sense of protection of indications of provenance, could be relevant. However, it is clear from paragraph 36 [36] of this judgment that the description mountain', as protected by the domestic legislation in question, cannot be characterized as an indication of provenance.

54 The answer to the second part of the question must therefore be that Article 30 [34] of the Treaty precludes application of domestic rules, such as those laid down by Article 34 of Law No 85-30 and Decree No 88-194, which restrict use of the description mountain' to products manufactured on national territory and prepared from domestic raw materials.

55 In these circumstances, there is no need to examine the question whether and, if so, on what conditions domestic rules similar to those contained in the relevant French legislation but not entailing any discrimination against products imported from other Member States could meet the requirements of Articles 30 [34] and 36 [36] of the Treaty.

## NOTES AND QUESTIONS

1.    In *Pistre*, the French proceedings in question concerned an entirely domestic set of facts. Although the law clearly could have applied to imports in this case, the French Government stated that it had not applied the law in question to imports. Yet the Court declined to rule out the application of EC 28/TFEU 34. How did it arrive at this conclusion? Does the case suggest that once a law is found to be in violation of EC 28/TFEU 34, it is necessarily invalid for all purposes including purely domestic trade?

2.    Compare *Bunting v. Oregon*, 243 U.S. 426 (1917), where the U.S. Supreme Court upheld a state law regulating maximum hours of work in manufacturing, in part because it did not seem directed against interstate commerce.

## [C]   The EC 30/TFEU 36 Exceptions

# ADRIAAN DE PEIJPER, MANAGING DIRECTOR OF CENTRAFARM BV
Case 104/75, [1976] ECR 613

2. [De Peijper was accused] of having infringed the Netherlands public health legislation, on the one hand by supplying pharmacies in that Member State with medicinal preparations which he had imported from the United Kingdom without the consent of the Netherlands authorities and, on the other hand, by failing to have in his possession certain documents connected with these medicinal preparations, namely the 'file' and the 'records' prescribed by the said legislation.

3 Under that legislation 'file' means a document which the importer must keep for 'every pharmaceutical packaging of a pharmaceutical preparation which he imports' and which must contain detailed particulars concerning the said packaging and especially of the quantitative and qualitative composition as well as the method of preparation; these particulars have to be signed and endorsed 'seen and approved' by 'the person who is responsible for the manufacture abroad'.

4 It is the practice for the importer to produce the 'file' to the competent authorities for 'certification' which at the same time authorizes him to market the packaging in the Netherlands so that only an importer who has the 'file' in his possession can obtain this authorization.

5 Under the Netherlands legislation 'records' mean documents which an importer must have in his possession when he supplies a pharmaceutical preparation which he has imported and which establish that the latter has in fact been manufactured and checked in accordance with the particulars on the above mentioned 'file' and relating to the manufacturing formula as well as the rules for checking the preparation and the substances of which this preparation is composed.

6 It appears that the 'file' relates to the product in general whereas the 'records' refer to each specific batch of the product which the importer wishes to place on the market.

7 The accused in the main proceedings does not deny the matters of which he is accused but argues that he could not comply with the rules in question because he was unable to obtain the documents which are at issue in those proceedings.

8 The explanation for this is that the medicinal preparations in question were manufactured by a British producer — belonging to a group whose operational centre is in Switzerland —, that the accused in the main proceedings purchased them from a wholesaler established in the United Kingdom and then imported them 'in parallel' into the Netherlands and finally that the said manufacturer or the representative of the group in the Netherlands refused to give the accused the help which was absolutely necessary if the latter was to obtain possession of the above-mentioned documents.

\*   \*   \*

11 The Court is asked to rule whether national authorities faced with such a

situation adopt a measure equivalent to a quantitative restriction and prohibited by the Treaty when they make the authorization to place a product on the market, for which a parallel importer has applied, conditional upon the production of documents identical with those which the manufacturer or his duly appointed importer has already lodged with them.

\*    \*    \*

15 Health and the life of humans rank first among the property or interests protected by Article 36 [36] and it is for the Member States, within the limits imposed by the Treaty, to decide what degree of protection they intend to assure and in particular how strict the checks to be carried out are to be.

16 Nevertheless it emerges from Article 36 [36] that national rules or practices which do restrict imports of pharmaceutical products or are capable of doing so are only compatible with the Treaty to the extent to which they are necessary for the effective protection of health and life of humans.

17 National rules or practices do not fall within the exception specified in Article 36 [36] if the health and life of humans can as effectively be protected by measures which do not restrict intra-Community trade so much.

18 In particular Article 36 [36] cannot be relied on to justify rules or practices which, even though they are beneficial, contain restrictions which are explained primarily by a concern to lighten the administration's burden or reduce public expenditure, unless, in the absence of the said rules or practices, this burden or expenditure clearly would exceed the limits of what can reasonably be required.

19 The situation described by the national court must be examined in the light of these considerations.

20 For this purpose a distinction must be drawn between on the one hand the documents relating to a medicinal preparation in general, in this case the 'file' prescribed by the Netherlands legislation, and, on the other hand, those relating to a specific batch of this medicinal preparation imported by a particular trader, in this case the 'records' which have to be kept under the said legislation.

21 (a) With regard to the documents relating to the medicinal preparation in general, if the public health authorities of the importing Member State already have in their possession, as a result of importation on a previous occasion, all the pharmaceutical particulars relating to the medicinal preparation in question and considered to be absolutely necessary for the purpose of checking that the medicinal preparation is effective and not harmful, it is clearly unnecessary, in order to protect the health and life of humans, for the said authorities to require a second trader who has imported a medicinal preparation which is in every respect the same, to produce the above-mentioned particulars to them again.

22 Therefore national rules or practices which lay down such a requirement are not justified on grounds of the protection of health and life of humans within the meaning of Article 36 [36] of the Treaty.

23 (b) With regard to the documents relating to a specific batch of a medicinal preparation imported at a time when the public health authorities of the Member

State of importation already, have in their possession a file relating to this medicinal preparation, these authorities have a legitimate interest in being able at any time to carry out a thorough check to make certain that the said batch complies with the particulars on the file.

24 Nevertheless, having regard to the nature of the market for the pharmaceutical product in question, it is necessary to ask whether this objective cannot be equally well achieved if the national administrations, instead of waiting passively for the desired evidence to be produced to them — and in a form calculated to give the manufacturer of the product and his duly appointed representatives an advantage — were to admit, where appropriate, similar evidence and, in particular, to adopt a more active policy which could enable every trader to obtain the necessary evidence.

25 This question is all the more important because parallel importers are very often in a position to offer the goods at a price lower than the one applied by the duly appointed importer for the same product, a fact which, where medicinal preparations are concerned, should, where appropriate, encourage the public health authorities not to place parallel imports at a disadvantage, since the effective protection of health and life of humans also demands that medicinal preparations should be sold at reasonable prices.

26 National authorities possess legislative and administrative methods capable of compelling the manufacturer or his duly appointed representative to supply particulars making it possible to ascertain that the medicinal preparation which is in fact the subject of parallel importation is identical with the medicinal preparation in respect of which they are already informed.

27 Moreover, simple co-operation between the authorities of the Member States would enable them to obtain on a reciprocal basis the documents necessary for checking certain largely standardized and widely distributed products.

28 Taking into account all these possible ways of obtaining information the national public health authorities must consider whether the effective protection of health and life of humans' justifies a presumption of the non-conformity of an imported batch with the description of the medicinal preparation, or whether on the contrary it would not be sufficient to lay down a presumption of conformity with the result that, in appropriate cases, it would be for the administration to rebut this presumption.

29 Given a factual situation such as that described in the first question the answer must therefore be that rules or practices which make it possible for a manufacturer and his duly appointed representatives simply by refusing to produce the 'file' or the 'records' to enjoy a monopoly of the importation and marketing of the product in question must be regarded as being unnecessarily restrictive and cannot therefore come within the exceptions specified in Article 36 [36] of the Treaty, unless it is clearly proved that any other rules or practice would obviously be beyond the means which can reasonably be expected of an administration operating in a normal manner.

## NOTES AND QUESTIONS

1.  How did the Court determine that the Dutch requirements did not arise from a need to protect human health? Could the Court have equally well analyzed the requirements based on their being a "disguised restriction" on trade? If so, why do you think the Court chose not to follow that path?

2.  The Court was clearly troubled that the producer was able to prevent "parallel imports" by refusing the documentation — in effect abusing its position by taking advantage of the Dutch requirement. This theme is developed at length later in relation to the use of national trademark laws — see *infra*. Was this opportunity for abuse in fact a reason for determining that the Dutch law was not justified on health grounds?

## R v. MAURICE DONALD HENN AND JOHN FREDERICK ERNEST DARBY
### Case 34/79, 1980 ECJ CELEX LEXIS 130, [1979] ECR 3795

[The defendants were convicted at Ipswich Crown Court (UK) of a number of offences. Only one of the charges brought against the appellants was relevant to the present reference — that of being "knowingly concerned in the fraudulent evasion of the prohibition of the importation of indecent or obscene articles, contrary to section 42 of the Customs Consolidation Act, 1876, and section 304 of the Customs and Excise Act, 1952."]

The articles involved in the charge against the appellants formed part of a consignment of several boxes of obscene films and magazines which had been brought into the United Kingdom on 14 October 1975 by a lorry which arrived at Felixstowe by ferry from Rotterdam. The charge related to six films and seven magazines, all of Danish origin.]

4 The appellants contended that the United Kingdom had no consistent policy of public morality in regard to indecent or obscene articles. In that respect they pointed to differences in the law applied in the different constituent parts of the United Kingdom. They contended furthermore that a complete prohibition of the importation of indecent or obscene articles resulted in the application to importation of stricter rules than those which applied internally and constituted arbitrary discrimination within the meaning of Article 36 [36] of the Treaty.

5 According to the Agreed Statement of Law accompanying the order seeking the preliminary ruling, it is true that, in this field, the laws of the different parts of the United Kingdom, that is to say, England and Wales, Scotland, northern Ireland and the Isle of Man, differ from each other and that each is derived from a number of different sources, some of which are to be found in the common law and others in statute.

6 According to the same statement, the various laws of the United Kingdom recognize and apply two different and distinct criteria. The first, referred to in the statement as "Standard A", relates to the words "indecent or obscene" which appear in the customs legislation and in certain other legislation and are also used to indicate the ambit of the English common law offence of "outraging public

decency". These words convey, according to the statement, a single idea, that of offending against recognized standards of propriety, "indecent" being at the lower end of the scale, and "obscene" at the upper end.

7 The second criterion, referred to in the statement as "Standard B", relates to the word "obscene" as used alone in the Obscene Publications Acts, 1959 and 1964, (which apply to England and Wales only) and in describing the ambit of certain common law offences in England and Wales, Scotland and Northern Ireland. According to the statement, this word applies to a more restricted class of material, namely that which tends to "deprave and corrupt" those exposed to the material.

8 The Obscene Publications Acts, 1959 and 1964, create certain offences in regard to the publication of obscene articles but exclude from their field of application "obscene articles", as defined therein, if their publication is justified on the ground that it is in the interests of science, literature, art or learning or other objects of general concern.

9 The mere possession, for non-commercial purposes, of articles which offend against either Standard A or Standard B is not a criminal offence in any part of the United Kingdom.

10 The relevant provisions concerning the importation of pornographic articles are section 42 of the Customs Consolidation Act, 1876, and section 304 of the Customs and Excise Act, 1952. They apply throughout the United Kingdom. Put shortly, they provide that indecent or obscene articles are liable for forfeiture and destruction upon arrival in the United Kingdom and that whoever attempts fraudulently to bring such articles into the United Kingdom shall be guilty of an offence. The seventh schedule to the Customs and Excise Act, 1952, provides a procedure for testing before a court the liability of goods to forfeiture.

\* \* \*

16 Each Member State is entitled to impose prohibitions on imports justified on grounds of public morality for the whole of its territory, as defined in Article 227 [299] of the Treaty, whatever the structure of its constitution may be and however the powers of legislating in regard to the subject in question may be distributed. The fact that certain differences exist between the laws enforced in the different constituent parts of a Member State does not thereby prevent that State from applying a unitary concept in regard to prohibitions on imports imposed, on grounds of public morality, on trade with other Member States.

17 The answer to the second and third questions must therefore be that the first sentence of Article 36 [36] upon its true construction means that a Member State may, in principle, lawfully impose prohibitions on the importation from any other Member State of articles which are of an indecent or obscene character as understood by its domestic laws and that such prohibitions may lawfully be applied to the whole of its national territory even if, in regard to the field in question, variations exist between the laws in force in the different constituent parts of the Member State concerned.

\* \* \*

20 According to the second sentence of Article 36 [36] the restrictions on imports referred to in the first sentence may not "constitute a means of arbitrary discrimination or a disguised restriction on trade between Member States".

21 In order to answer the questions which have been referred to the Court it is appropriate to have regard to the function of this provision, which is designed to prevent restrictions on trade based on the grounds mentioned in the first sentence of Article 36 [36] from being diverted from their proper purpose and used in such a way as either to create discrimination in respect of goods originating in other Member States or indirectly to protect certain national products. That is not the purport of a prohibition, such as that in force in the United Kingdom, on the importation of articles which are of an indecent or obscene character. Whatever may be the differences between the laws on this subject in force in the different constituent parts of the United Kingdom, and notwithstanding the fact that they contain certain exceptions of limited scope, these laws, taken as a whole, have as their purpose the prohibition, or at least, the restraining, of the manufacture and marketing of publications or articles of an indecent or obscene character. In these circumstances it is permissible to conclude, on a comprehensive view, that there is no lawful trade in such goods in the United Kingdom. A prohibition on imports which may in certain respects be more strict than some of the laws applied within the United Kingdom cannot therefore be regarded as amounting to a measure designed to give indirect protection to some national product or aimed at creating arbitrary discrimination between goods of this type depending on whether they are produced within the national territory or another Member State.

## NOTES AND QUESTIONS

1.   What was the significance of the argument that the laws within UK territory differed somewhat from one area to another? If there had been no domestic law at all relating to obscenity, would the exception of EC 30/TFEU 36 still have been available?

2.   The Court has generally declined to allow a Member State to rely on EC 30/TFEU 36 as regards public security where the EU has adopted measures that attempt to deal with or take account of a Member State's concerns regarding the subjects listed in the article, or where the security in question is economic in nature. However, see *Campus Oil Ltd. v. Minister for Industry and Energy*, Case 72/83 [1984] ECR 2727, where, the Court found further that the EU rules did not preclude Member State measures based on state security grounds that transcended *"mere"* economic security (in this case assurance of petroleum supplies), even if such economic considerations might have been a primary motivator behind the States' actions:

8 A Member State that is totally . . . dependent on imports for its supplies for petrol products may rely on grounds of public security within the meaning of Article 36 [36] for the purpose of requiring importers to cover a certain proportion of their needs by purchases from a refinery situated in its territory at prices fixed by the competent minister on the basis of the costs incurred in the operation of that refinery, if the production of the refinery cannot be freely disposed of at competitive prices on the market

concerned. The quantities of petrol products must not exceed the minimum supply requirements without which the public security of the state concerned would be affected or the level of production necessary to keep the refinery's production capacity available in the event of a crisis.

# COMMISSION v. FRANCE
## (PROCESSING AIDS FOR FOODSTUFFS)
### Case 333/08, [2010] ECR

[The Commission complained that a French decree-law conflicted with EC 28/TFEU 34 first, by imposing a prior authorisation scheme on processing aids and foodstuffs whose manufacturing process used processing aids from other Member States in which they were legally manufactured and/or marketed; and, in the alternative, by failing to establish, for the purpose of obtaining authorisations for the use of processing aids, a procedure which was sufficiently clear, easily accessible and transparent and which met the requirements of legal certainty.

As referred to in this case, processing aids are substances used in the process of elaborating or manufacturing a foodstuff. Their aim is to obtain a certain technical effect during that process.

Although EU law harmonises certain categories of processing aids, those at stake are not subject to horizontal harmonization at EU level. Therefore, in general, Member States remain free to regulate the use of processing aids while complying with the EC Treaty/TFEU.]

46 In its application, the Commission [objected to] the lack of justification on grounds of protecting public health for the obstacles to the free movement of goods created by the prior authorisation schemes enacted by that legislation.

\*     \*     \*

73 [The] free movement of goods between Member States is a fundamental principle of the Treaty which finds its expression in the prohibition, set out in Article 28 EC [34], of quantitative restrictions on imports between Member States and all measures having equivalent effect.

75 It is undisputed that the prior authorisation scheme laid down by the [French decree] constitutes a measure having equivalent effect to a quantitative restriction within the meaning of Article 28 EC [34].

76 The prior authorisation scheme laid down by that decree makes it more costly and difficult, or, in certain cases, impossible, to market processing aids and foodstuffs in the preparation of which processing aids lawfully manufactured and/or marketed in other Member States have been used.

77 First, that scheme hinders the free movement of processing aids, intended to be used in the preparation of foodstuffs, coming from other Member States where they are lawfully manufactured and/or marketed, in so far as they are subjected to criteria of purity or other characteristics, such as maximum authorised residual doses, established by the French legislation.

78 Second, it hinders the free movement of finished foodstuffs from other Member

States in which the presence, however infinitesimal, of residues of a processing aid not authorised in France can be found, or in which the presence of residues of processing aids authorised in France can be found, where the maximum residual amounts determined by the French authorisation decisions have been exceeded.

79 Third, that prior authorisation scheme hinders the free movement of finished foodstuffs from other Member States whose preparation involved the use of a processing aid not authorised in France, or authorised there but not satisfying the criteria as to purity or other characteristics laid down by the French legislation, or authorised there but used in a different manner from that authorised by the French legislation, even where there are no residues in the finished foodstuff, or residues are present only in the authorised quantities.

80 According to consistent case-law, national legislation making the addition of a nutritive substance to a foodstuff lawfully manufactured and/or marketed in other Member States subject to prior authorisation is not in principle contrary to Community law provided certain conditions are fulfilled.

81 First, such legislation must be accompanied by a procedure allowing economic operators to obtain the entry of that nutritive substance in the national list of authorised substances.

82 Second, an application for the entry of a nutritive substance on the national list of authorised substances may be rejected by the competent national authorities only if that substance poses a genuine threat to public health.

84 It should be noted . . . that [the] differences between nutritive substances voluntarily and intentionally added to foodstuffs and processing aids are not capable of excluding the possibility of a Member State relying, in principle, on Article 30 EC [36] and the objective of protecting public health in order to justify prior authorisation schemes such as those at issue in this case. If such differences existed in relation to substances subject to a prior authorisation scheme, they would be relevant not for determining whether the choice of such a scheme is in principle excluded in Member States but as regards the means of applying the principle of proportionality in relation to the scheme which is applicable to them.

85 As regards the objective of protecting public health, it is for the Member States, in the absence of harmonisation and in so far as doubts subsist in the current state of scientific research, to decide at which level they intend to ensure the protection of the health and life of persons, and whether to require prior authorisation for the marketing of processing aids and foodstuffs in the preparation of which such aids have been used, whilst at the same time taking into account the requirements of the free movement of goods within the Community.

87 Since Article 30 EC [36] contains an exception, which must be narrowly interpreted, to the rule of the free movement of goods within the Community, it is for the national authorities which invoke it to demonstrate in each case, taking account of the results of international scientific research, that their legislation is necessary in order effectively to protect the interests referred to in that provision, and, in particular, that the marketing of the products in question poses a genuine threat to public health.

88 A prohibition on marketing processing aids or foodstuffs in which processing aids have been used which have been lawfully manufactured and/or marketed in other Member States must therefore be based on an in-depth assessment of the risk alleged by the Member State invoking Article 30 EC [36].

89 A decision to prohibit marketing, which indeed constitutes the most restrictive obstacle to trade in products lawfully manufactured and marketed in other Member States, can be adopted only if the real risk alleged for public health appears sufficiently established on the basis of the latest scientific data available at the date of the adoption of such decision. In such a context, the object of the risk assessment to be carried out by the Member State is to appraise the degree of probability of harmful effects on human health from the addition of certain nutrients to foodstuffs and the seriousness of those potential effects.

90 In exercising their discretion relating to the protection of public health, the Member States must comply with the principle of proportionality. The means which they choose must therefore be confined to what is actually necessary to ensure the safeguarding of public health; they must be proportional to the objective thus pursued, which could not have been attained by measures which are less restrictive of intra-Community trade.

92 A correct application of the precautionary principle presupposes, first, identification of the potentially negative consequences for health of the proposed use of processing aids, and, secondly, a comprehensive assessment of the risk to health based on the most reliable scientific data available and the most recent results of international research.

93 Where it proves to be impossible to determine with certainty the existence or extent of the alleged risk because of the insufficiency, inconclusiveness or imprecision of the results of studies conducted, but the likelihood of real harm to public health persists should the risk materialise, the precautionary principle justifies the adoption of restrictive measures, provided they are non-discriminatory and objective.

94 In this case, the French Republic justifies the prior authorisation scheme laid down by its legislation by reference to the potential health risks of certain categories of processing aids.

95 However, if there are risks concerning certain categories of processing aids, the national legislation must be targeted and clearly justified in relation to those categories and must not envisage all processing aids or all foodstuffs in the preparation of which processing aids not entering into those dangerous or suspect categories have been used. It is not sufficient to base justification on potential risks posed by the substances or products subject to authorisation.

96 It is true that a Member State may base justification on the precautionary principle where it proves impossible to determine with certainty the existence or the scope of the alleged risk. However, a correct application of that principle presupposes that the Member State demonstrates the existence of the conditions, referred to in paragraph 92 of this judgment, required for the latter to apply.

97 As regards the prior authorisation scheme laid down by the [French Decree],

there is no demonstration of the existence of those conditions. Even if, as the French Republic claims, in accordance with the precautionary principle the Member State merely has to establish the risk which the use of processing aids may pose, the fact remains that the generalised presumption of a health risk put forward by that Member State in this case is not supported by evidence to explain why the marketing of any foodstuff, in the preparation of which processing aids have been used which have been lawfully manufactured and/or marketed in other Member States, must depend on the entry of the processing aid in question on a positive list established by French legislation, which in turn depends on the conformity of the foodstuff in question with purity criteria, requirements concerning maximum residual doses or conditions for using processing aids laid down by that legislation.

99 . . . [I]n order to comply with the principle of proportionality, the means which the Member States choose must be limited to what is actually necessary in order to safeguard health.

100 Examination of the file concerning the prior authorisation scheme laid down by the [French Decree] shows the latter to be disproportionate in that it systematically prohibits, without prior authorisation, the marketing of any processing aids or of any foodstuffs in the preparation of which processing aids lawfully manufactured and/or marketed in other Member States were used, without making any distinction according to the various processing aids or according to the level of risk which their use might potentially pose for health.

101 By its systematic nature, the [French Decree] does not permit compliance with Community law as regards prior identification of the harmful effects of processing aids and the assessment of the actual risk which they pose for health, both of which require an in-depth, case-by-case assessment of the effects which use of the processing aids in question might produce.

102 Moreover, that scheme systematically hinders the marketing of foodstuffs in the preparation of which processing aids were used if the method of using the latter does not correspond to the method of use prescribed by the French legislation, even in the absence of detectable residues of those processing aids in the final foodstuffs.

103 A Member State cannot justify a systematic and untargeted prior authorisation scheme such as that laid down by the [French Decree] by pleading the impossibility of carrying out more exhaustive prior examinations by reason of the considerable quantity of processing aids which may be used or by reason of the fact that manufacturing processes are constantly changing. As is apparent from Articles 6 and 7 of Regulation No 178/2002, concerning the analysis of risks and the application of the precautionary principle, such an approach does not correspond to the requirements laid down by the Community legislature as regards both Community and national food legislation and designed to achieve the general objective of a high level of health protection.

104 It is true that, as the French Republic has argued, one of the alternative methods less restrictive of free movement suggested by the Commission, namely the mentioning of the processing aids used in the manufacturing process of a foodstuff, is not capable of achieving the objective of protection envisaged by the French legislation concerning processing aids in relation to which a genuine risk to

health has been established. However, this Court must reject the argument of that Member State that such a mention would in any event constitute an infringement of Directive 2000/13. Although Article 6(4)(c)(ii) of that directive shows that processing aids do not constitute ingredients which must compulsorily be mentioned on labelling, in accordance with Article 3(1) of that directive, the Member States may, in accordance with Article 18(1) of that directive, lay down measures on labelling which are justified for reasons of protecting public health.

105 It should also be noted, as the French Republic has pointed out, that the mere fact that one Member State imposes less strict rules than those applicable in another Member State does not mean that the latter are incompatible with Articles 28 EC [30] and 30 EC [36]. However, the absence of a prior authorisation scheme with regard to the use of processing aids in the preparation of foodstuffs in all or nearly all of the other Member States may be relevant when assessing the objective justification put forward in relation to the French legislation, and, particularly, with regard to the assessment of its proportionality.

110 Having regard to the above, the Commission's first head of claim must be regarded as being well founded . . .

## NOTES AND QUESTIONS

1.   How does the ECJ define the scope of the public health exception?

2.   In light of the ECJ's comments in this case, is public health a ground on which Member States can easily rely in order to benefit from the exception laid down in EC 30/TFEU 36?

## [D]   The Effect of EC 30/TFEU 36 on Intellectual Property Rules

### CENTRAFARM BV AND ADRIAAN DE PEIJPER v. WINTHROP BV
Case 16/74, [1974] ECR 1183

[Centrafarm had imported goods in the Netherlands from other Member States that bore Winthrop's trademarks. Under Dutch law, Winthrop was entitled to assert its Dutch trademark to prevent the products being sold in the Netherlands even though it had originally affixed the trademark when the goods were marketed in other Member States.]

3 The Court [is asked] to state whether, under the conditions postulated, the rules in the EEC Treaty concerning the free movement of goods prevent the trade mark owner from ensuring that a product protected by the trade mark is not marketed by others.

4 As a result of the provisions in the Treaty relating to the free movement of goods, and in particular Article 30 [34], quantitative restrictions on imports and all measures having equivalent effect are prohibited between Member States.

5 By Article 36 [36] these provisions shall nevertheless not include prohibitions or

restrictions on imports justified on grounds of the protection of industrial or commercial property.

6 Nevertheless, it is clear from this same Article, in particular its second sentence, as well as from the context, that whilst the Treaty does not affect the existence of rights recognized by the legislation of a Member State in matters of industrial and commercial property, yet the exercise of these rights may nevertheless, depending on the circumstances, be affected by the prohibitions in the Treaty.

7 Inasmuch as it provides an exception to one of the fundamental principles of the Common Market, Article 36 [36] in fact only admits of derogations from the free movement of goods where such derogations are justified for the purpose of safeguarding rights which constitute the specific subject-matter of this property.

8 In relation to trade marks, the specific subject-matter of the industrial property is the guarantee that the owner of the trade mark has the exclusive right to use that trade mark, for the purpose of putting products protected by the trade mark into circulation for the first time, and is therefore intended to protect him against competitors wishing to take advantage of the status and reputation of the trade mark by selling products illegally bearing that trade mark.

9 An obstacle to the free movement of goods may arise out of the existence, within a national legislation concerning industrial and commercial property, of provisions laying down that a trade mark owner's right is not exhausted when the product protected by the trade mark is marketed in another Member State, with the result that the trade mark owner can prevent importation of the product into his own Member State when it has been marketed in another Member State.

10 Such an obstacle is not justified when the product has been put onto the market in a legal manner in the Member State from which it has been imported, by the trade mark owner himself or with his consent, so that there can be no question of abuse or infringement of the trade mark.

11 In fact, if a trade mark owner could prevent the import of protected products marketed by him or with his consent in another Member State, he would be able to partition off national markets and thereby restrict trade between Member States, in a situation where no such restriction was necessary to guarantee the essence of the exclusive right flowing from the trade mark.

12 The question referred should therefore be answered to the effect that the exercise, by the owner of a trade mark, of the right which he enjoys under the legislation of a Member State to prohibit the sale, in that State, of a product which has been marketed under the trade mark in another Member State by the trade mark owner or with his consent is incompatible with the rules of the EEC Treaty concerning the free movement of goods within the Common Market.

\* \* \*

15 The Court [is asked] to state, in substance, whether the trade mark owner can, notwithstanding the answer given to the first question prevent importation of products marketed under the trade mark, given the existence of price differences resulting from governmental measures adopted in the exporting country with a view to controlling prices of those products.

16 It is part of the Community authorities' task to eliminate factors likely to distort competition between Member States, in particular by the harmonization of national measures for the control of prices and by the prohibition of aids which are incompatible with the Common Market, in addition to the exercise of their powers in the field of competition.

17 The existence of factors such as these in a Member State, however, cannot justify the maintenance or introduction by another Member State of measures which are incompatible with the rules concerning the free movement of goods, in particular in the field of industrial and commercial property.

18 The question referred should therefore be answered in the negative.

## NOTES AND QUESTIONS

1.   The Court specifically refers to the *exercise* of trademark rights. However, EC 28 and 30/TFEU 34 and 36 are addressed to Member States, not the owners of the marks, so how does EC 28/TFEU 34 come to be applied? Would not EC 28/TFEU 34 more appropriately apply to the *existence* of such rights (over which Member States have control) or does the Court in fact attribute responsibility for the exercise of the rights to the Member States?

2.   The *Centrafarm* case adopts a doctrine known as "exhaustion of rights", which means that a registered trademark confers on owners the exclusive right to place the product bearing the mark on the market. Thereafter it can be freely traded under that mark. As applied by the Court, this encompasses placing of products on the market by the owner or someone else with his consent even in other Member States where there are separate registrations for the mark under that country's trademark law. Does it also include the placing of products on the markets of non-Member States? How could one logically distinguish the two?

3.   The Court refers to the "specific subject-matter" in the context of industrial property. Is this to be considered an EU concept, which would then mean that "industrial property" would have a meaning independent of that given to it by each Member State?

4.   The doctrine of exhaustion spawned a great many cases testing the various permutations employed by companies to seek continued trademark protection aimed at protecting differential pricing in the various Member States. Today, these issues are largely resolved through the adoption of a directive creating a Union Trademark (actually a bundle of individual State marks) that clearly spells out the exhaustion doctrine. In light of ECJ decisions, that directive specifically does not extend the doctrine to imports into the EU subject to certain caveats. This was challenged in the *Laserdisken* case that appears in Chapter 20.

## CENTRAFARM B.V. v. STERLING DRUG, INC.
### Case 15/74 [1974] ECR 1183

[In this case, Centrafarm had sought to import from the UK into the Netherlands pharmaceutical products manufactured by Sterling Drug's licensee in the U.K. Sterling held a patent for the drugs in both the UK and The Netherlands and asserted its Dutch patent to block the imports from the UK.]

2 In the decision making the reference the Hoge Raad set out as follows the elements of fact and of national law in issue in relation to the questions referred:

- A patentee holds parallel patents in several of the states belonging to the EEC,

- The products protected by those patents are lawfully marketed in one or more of those Member States by undertakings to which the patentee has granted licences to manufacture and/or sell,

- those products are subsequently exported by third parties and are marketed and further dealt in one of those other Member States,

- the patent legislation in the last mentioned state gives the patentee the right to take legal action to prevent products thus protected by patents from being there marketed by others, even where these products were previously lawfully marketed in another country by the patentee or by the patentee's licencee.

3 It appears from the proceedings that the main action is concerned with the rights of a proprietor of parallel patents in several Member States who grants an exclusive licence to sell, but not to manufacture, the patent product in one of those states, while at the same time the patentee does not manufacture the patent product in that same Member State . . .

4 [The question posed by the national court] requires the Court to state whether, under the conditions postulated, the rules in the EEC Treaty concerning the free movement of goods prevent the patentee from ensuring that the product protected by the patent is not marketed by others.

5 As a result of the provisions in the Treaty relating to the free movement of goods and in particular of Article 30 [34], quantitative restrictions on imports and all measures having equivalent effect are prohibited between Member States.

6 By article 36 [36] these provisions shall nevertheless not include prohibitions or restrictions on imports justified on grounds of the protection of industrial or commercial property.

7 Nevertheless, it is clear from this same article, in particular its second sentence, as well as from the context, that whilst the treaty does not affect the existence of rights recognized by the legislation of a member state in matters of industrial and commercial property, yet the exercise of these rights may nevertheless, depending on the circumstances, be affected by the prohibitions in the Treaty.

8 Inasmuch as it provides an exception to one of the fundamental principles of the common market, article 36 [36] in fact only admits of derogations from the free movement of goods where such derogations are justified for the purpose of safeguarding rights which constitute the specific subject matter of this property.

9 In relation to patents, the specific subject matter of the industrial property is the guarantee that the patentee, to reward the creative effort of the inventor, has the exclusive right to use an invention with a view to manufacturing industrial products

and putting them into circulation for the first time, either directly or by the grant of licences to third parties, as well as the right to oppose infringements.

10 An obstacle to the free movement of goods may arise out of the existence, within a national legislation concerning industrial and commercial property, of provisions laying down that a patentee's right is not exhausted when the product protected by the patent is marketed in another member state, with the result that the patentee can prevent importation of the product into his own member state when it has been marketed in another state.

11 Whereas an obstacle to the free movement of goods of this kind may be justified on the ground of protection of industrial property where such protection is invoked against a product coming from a member state where it is not patentable and has been manufactured by third parties without the consent of the patentee and in cases where there exist patents, the original proprietors of which are legally and economically independent, a derogation from the principle of the free movement of goods is not, however, justified where the product has been put onto the market in a legal manner, by the patentee himself or with his consent, in the member state from which it has been imported, in particular in the case of a proprietor of parallel patents.

13 The plaintiff in the main action claims, in this connection, that by reason of divergences between national legislations and practice, truly identical or parallel patents can hardly be said to exist.

14 It should be noted here that, in spite of the divergences which remain in the absence of any unification of national rules concerning industrial property, the identity of the protected invention is clearly the essential element of the concept of parallel patents which it is for the courts to assess.

15 The question referred should therefore be answered to the effect that the exercise, by a patentee, of the right which he enjoys under the legislation of a member state to prohibit the sale, in that state, of a product protected by the patent which has been marketed in another member state by the patentee or with his consent is incompatible with the rules of the EEC Treaty concerning the free movement of goods within the common market.

## NOTES AND QUESTIONS

1. The above case illustrates the Court's view regarding the application of EC 28/TFEU 34 to patents. Are the issues perhaps different as between patents and trademarks (considering the nature of the rights)? Patents do not exist at common law and are therefore perhaps to be regarded as pure privileges granted by the state. Does this make a difference?

2. As long as the patents are owned by different entities, there is no bar to invocation of patent law to bar imports. For example, in *Parke Davis v. Probel*, 24/67, [1968] ECR 55, there were no patents available for pharmaceutical products manufactured in Italy. The products at issue originated there and were then imported into the Netherlands. Dutch patent law was held to properly prevent such importation.

**3.**  Does it seem right that the corollary of this case — i.e., where the owner has himself manufactured the products in a country that does not grant protection — should result in no protection in the importing state? Suppose the owner subsequently assigns the rights in the importing state to a third party?

**4.**  There is a considerable body of law that deals with technology transfers, including a block exemption, under EC 81/TFEU 101. Consideration of this aspect would be beyond the scope of this book. The block exemption does address the issue of abuse of patent licensing to partition the market.

## WARNER BROTHERS INC. v. CHRISTIANSEN
Case 158/86, 1988 ECJ CELEX LEXIS 146, [1988] ECR 2605

3 Warner, the owner in the United Kingdom of the copyright of the film "Never Say Never Again", which it produced in that country, assigned the management of the video production rights in Denmark to Metronome.

4 The video-cassette of the film was on sale in the United Kingdom with Warner's consent. Mr Christiansen, who manages a video shop in Copenhagen, purchased a copy in London with a view to hiring it out in Denmark and imported it into that Member State for that purpose.

5 On the basis of Danish legislation, which enables the author or producer of a musical or cinematographic work to take action to restrain the hiring-out of videograms of that work until such time as he gives his consent, Warner and Metronome obtained an injunction from the Copenhagen City Court prohibiting the defendant from hiring out the video-cassette in Denmark.

\*     \*     \*

8 The national court seeks to ascertain, in essence, whether Articles 30 [34] and 36 [36] of the EEC Treaty preclude the application of national legislation which gives an author the right to make the hiring-out of video-cassettes conditional on his authorization, where those video-cassettes have already been put into circulation with his consent in another Member State whose legislation allows the author to control their initial sale without giving him the right to prohibit them from being hired out.

9 It should be noted that, unlike the national copyright legislation which gave rise to the judgment of 20 January 1981 in Joined Cases 55 and 57/80 (Musik Vertrieb Membran v. GEMA [1981] ECR 147), the legislation which gives rise to the present preliminary question does not enable the author to collect an additional fee on the actual importation of recordings of protected works which are marketed with his consent in another Member State, or to set up any further obstacle whatsoever to importation or resale. The rights and powers conferred on the author by the national legislation in question comes into operation only after importation has been carried out.

10 None the less, it must be observed that the commercial distribution of video-cassettes takes the form not only of sales but also, and increasingly, that of hiring out to individuals who possess video-tape recorders. The right to prohibit such hiring-out in a Member State is therefore liable to influence trade in

video-cassettes in that State and hence, indirectly, to affect intra-Community trade in those products. Legislation of the kind which gave rise to the main proceedings must therefore, in the light of established case-law, be regarded as a measure having an effect equivalent to a quantitative restriction on imports, which is prohibited by Article 30 [34] of the Treaty.

11 Consideration should therefore be given to whether such legislation may be considered justified on grounds of the protection of industrial and commercial property within the meaning of Article 36 [36] — a term which was held by the Court, in its judgment of 6 October 1982 in Case 262/81 (Coditel v. Cine-Vog [1982] ECR 3381), to include literary and artistic property.

12 In that connexion it should first be noted that the Danish legislation applies without distinction to video-cassettes produced in situ and video-cassettes imported from another Member State. The determining factor for the purposes of its application is the type of transaction in video-cassettes which is in question, not the origin of those video-cassettes. Such legislation does not therefore, in itself, operate any arbitrary discrimination in trade between Member States.

13 It should further be pointed out that literary and artistic works may be the subject of commercial exploitation, whether by way of public performance or of the reproduction and marketing of the recordings made of them, and this is true in particular of cinematographic works. The two essential rights of the author, namely the exclusive right of performance and the exclusive right of reproduction, are not called in question by the rules of the Treaty.

14 Lastly, consideration must be given to the emergence, demonstrated by the Commission, of a specific market for the hiring-out of such recordings, as distinct from their sale. The existence of that market was made possible by various factors such as the improvement of manufacturing methods for video-cassettes which increased their strength and life in use, the growing awareness amongst viewers that they watch only occasionally the video-cassettes which they have bought and, lastly, their relatively high purchase price. The market for the hiring-out of video-cassettes reaches a wider public than the market for their sale and, at present, offers great potential as a source of revenue for makers of films.

15 However, it is apparent that, by authorizing the collection of royalties only on sales to private individuals and to persons hiring out video-cassettes, it is impossible to guarantee to makers of films a remuneration which reflects the number of occasions on which the video-cassettes are actually hired out and which secures for them a satisfactory share of the rental market. That explains why, as the Commission points out in its observations, certain national laws have recently provided specific protection of the right to hire out video-cassettes.

16 Laws of that kind are therefore clearly justified on grounds of the protection of industrial and commercial property pursuant to Article 36 [36] of the Treaty.

17 However, the defendant . . . contends that the author is at liberty to choose the Member State in which he will market his work. The defendant in the main proceedings emphasizes that the author makes his choice according to his own interests and must, in particular, take into consideration the fact that the legislation of certain Member States, unlike that of certain others, confers on him an exclusive

right enabling him to restrain the hiring-out of the recording of the work even when that work has been offered for sale with his consent. That being so, a maker of a film who has offered the video-cassette of that film for sale in a Member State whose legislation confers on him no exclusive right of hiring it out (as in the main proceedings) must accept the consequences of his choice and the exhaustion of his right to restrain the hiring-out of that video-cassette in any other Member State.

18 That objection cannot be upheld. It follows from the foregoing considerations that, where national legislation confers on authors a specific right to hire out video-cassettes, that right would be rendered worthless if its owner were not in a position to authorize the operations for doing so. It cannot therefore be accepted that the marketing by a film-maker of a video-cassette containing one of his works, in a Member State which does not provide specific protection for the right to hire it out, should have repercussions on the right conferred on that same film-maker by the legislation of another Member State to restrain, in that State, the hiring-out of that video-cassette.

19 In those circumstances, the answer to be given to the question submitted by the national court is that Articles 30 [34] and 36 [36] of the Treaty do not prohibit the application of national legislation which gives an author the right to make the hiring-out of video-cassettes subject to his permission, when the video-cassettes in question have already been put into circulation with his consent in another Member State whose legislation enables the author to control the initial sale, without giving him the right to prohibit hiring-out.

## NOTES AND QUESTIONS

1.   Some Member States have adopted legislation or allowed quasi-private organizations to adopt rules that allow for further fees to be paid for use even of an "original" work. See *Deutsche Grammophon GmbH v. Metro*, Case 78/70, [1971] ECR 487, where Deutsche Grammophon sought to block the import into Germany of records that it had sold through its French subsidiary in France. Obviously the records were "originals", but German Law had special provisions allowing the restriction of imports. The ECJ held that the law could not be invoked. In the *Christiansen* case, the videocassette was being rented out. Suppose it had been sold instead?

2.   The Advocate-General law thought that the exhaustion of rights doctrine should have applied in this case. Do you agree that the owner in *Christiansen* consented to the hiring out of the video in other Member States when he sold a copy in London? Why did the ECJ think otherwise? See also *Basset v. SACEM* Case 402/85, [1987] ECR 1747.

## § 13.06    NON-DISCRIMINATORY TECHNICAL REQUIREMENTS

### [A]    General Principle

### REWE — ZENTRAL AG v. BUNDESMONOPOLVERWALTUNG FUER BRANNTWEIN
### ("CASSIS DE DIJON")
Case 120/78, [1979] ECR 649

[The principal activity of Rewe-Zentral AG, a central cooperative undertaking, was the importation of goods from other Member States. On September 14, 1976, it requested authorization from the Bundesmonopolverwaltung für Branntwein (Federal Monopoly Administration for Spirits) to import from France, for the purposes of marketing in the Federal Republic of Germany, certain potable spirits, including the liqueur "Cassis de Dijon," containing 15 to 20 percent by volume of alcohol.

The Bundesmonopolverwaltung informed Rewe that authorization to import was not necessary for the importation of spirits into the Federal Republic and at all events the importation of liqueurs was not subject to authorization. However, it informed Rewe that the "Cassis de Dijon" which it intended to import could not be sold in the Federal Republic of Germany, since the Branntweinmonopolgesetz provided that only potable spirits having a wine-spirit content of at least 32 percent may be marketed in that country. Rewe brought an action against that decision before the Verwaltungsgericht (Administrative Court), Darmstadt.]

8 In the absence of common rules relating to the production and marketing of alcohol . . . it is for the Member States to regulate all matters relating to the production and marketing of alcohol and alcoholic beverages on their own territory.

Obstacles to movement within the Community resulting from disparities between the national laws relating to the marketing of the products in question must be accepted in so far as those provisions may be recognized as being necessary in order to satisfy mandatory requirements relating in particular to the effectiveness of fiscal supervision, the protection of public health, the fairness of commercial transactions and the defence of the consumer.

9 The government of the Federal Republic of Germany, intervening in the proceedings, put forward various arguments which, in its view, justify the application of provisions relating to the minimum alcohol content of alcoholic beverages, adducing considerations relating on the one hand to the protection of public health and on the other to the protection of the consumer against unfair commercial practices.

10 As regards the protection of public health the German Government states that the purpose of the fixing of minimum alcohol contents by national legislation is to avoid the proliferation of alcoholic beverages on the national market, in particular alcoholic beverages with a low alcohol content, since, in its view, such products may

more easily induce a tolerance towards alcohol than more highly alcoholic beverages.

11 Such considerations are not decisive since the consumer can obtain on the market an extremely wide range of weakly or moderately alcoholic products and furthermore a large proportion of alcoholic beverages with a high alcohol content freely sold on the German market is generally consumed in a diluted form.

12 The German government also claims that the fixing of a lower limit for the alcohol content of certain liqueurs is designed to protect the consumer against unfair practices on the part of producers and distributors of alcoholic beverages.

This argument is based on the consideration that the lowering of the alcohol content secures a competitive advantage in relation to beverages with a higher alcohol content, since alcohol constitutes by far the most expensive constituent of beverages by reason of the high rate of tax to which it is subject.

13 However, this line of argument cannot be taken so far as to regard the mandatory fixing of minimum alcohol contents as being an essential guarantee of the fairness of commercial transactions, since it is a simple matter to ensure that suitable information is conveyed to the purchaser by requiring the display of an indication of origin and of the alcohol content on the packaging of products.

14 It is clear from the foregoing that the requirements relating to the minimum alcohol content of alcoholic beverages do not serve a purpose which is in the general interest and such as to take precedence over the requirements of the free movement of goods, which constitutes one of the fundamental rules of the Community.

## NOTES AND QUESTIONS

1.    In *Cassis*, the actual facts of the case did not concern the denial of an import license, but rather, internal regulations that prohibited the sale of the product once imported. Could the Court have considered this simply as a direct restriction on imports and thus evaluate it on the basis only of EC 28/TFEU 34? Keeping in mind that the Court's approach was to define the scope of what was meant by a "measure equivalent to a quantitative restriction" ("MEQR") under EC 28/TFEU 34 in the context of non-discriminatory rules, what would you say were the elements of that definition? Was it significant that the imported product here had been both lawfully *produced* and *marketed* in another Member State? Could this then mean that as long as a product has been legally placed on the market somewhere in the EU, it should then be able to circulate everywhere without restriction? Would this not undermine the Court's explicit recognition that the power of regulation remains with the Member States until the EU takes action (through harmonization)?

2.    In the U.S., in the early cases of *Gibbons v. Ogden*, 9 Wheat. 1 (1824), and *Cooley v. Board of Port Wardens*, 12 How. 299 (1851), the issue was primarily whether states could continue to regulate intrastate matters that directly impinged on interstate commerce — in other words, the scope of the commerce clause. Even if a state has the power to regulate trade within its own territory, the U.S. Constitution nonetheless imposes limitations on such regulation insofar as the state laws discriminate against out-of-state residents or goods or otherwise impose a

burden on interstate commerce disproportionate to the purpose of such regulation. See, *e.g., Minnesota v. Barber*, 136 U.S. 313 (1890); *Huron Portland Cement Co. v. City of Detroit*, 362 U.S. 440 (1960). Such cases continue to crop up in a seemingly infinite number of fact patterns — see, for example, *Dean Milk Co. v. City of Madison*, 340 U.S. 349, 71 S. Ct. 295, 95 L. Ed. 329 (1951). Do the *Dassonville* and *Cassis* cases suggest that the ECJ is following the same approach, albeit expressed differently?

**3.** The ECJ has ruled that there is no *de minimis* rule under EC 28/TFEU 34. This contrasts with the requirement developed by the Court in EC 81 and 82/TFEU 101 and 102 that an agreement between private parties that restricts competition must *appreciably* affect trade between Member States. (See further Chapter 7, *supra*). In *Criminal proceedings against Jan van de Haar and Kaveka de Meern BV*, Joined Cases 177 & 178/82, [1984] ECR 1797 it stated:

> 13 It must be emphasized in that connection that Article 30 [34] of the Treaty does not distinguish between measures having an effect equivalent to quantitative restrictions according to the degree to which trade between Member States is affected. If a national measure is capable of hindering imports it must be regarded as a measure having an effect equivalent to a quantitative restriction, even though the hindrance is slight and even though it is possible for imported products to be marketed in other ways.

**4.** The Commission issued a communication following the *Cassis* decision [1980] OJ C 256/2: which reads in part:

> Any product imported from another Member State must in principle be admitted to the territory of the importing Member State if it has been lawfully produced, that is, conforms to rules and processes of manufacture that are customarily and traditionally accepted in the exporting country, and is marketed in the territory of the latter.

> This principle implies that Member States, when drawing up commercial or technical rules liable to affect the free movement of goods, may not take an exclusively national viewpoint and take account only of requirements confined to domestic products. The proper functioning of the common market demands that each Member State also give consideration to the legitimate requirements of the other Member States.

> - Only under very strict conditions does the Court accept exceptions to this principle; barriers to trade resulting from differences between commercial and technical rules are only admissible: — if the rules are necessary, that is appropriate and not excessive, in order to satisfy mandatory requirements (public health, protection of consumers or the environment, the fairness of commercial transactions, etc.);

> - if the rules serve a purpose in the general interest which is compelling enough to justify an exception to a fundamental rule of the Treaty such as the free movement of goods;

> - if the rules are essential for such a purpose to be attained, i.e. are the means which are the most appropriate and at the same time least hinder

trade.

\*    \*    \*

The principles deduced by the Court imply that a Member State may not in principle prohibit the sale in its territory of a product lawfully produced and marketed in another Member State even if the product is produced according to technical or quality requirements which differ from those imposed on its domestic products. Where a product "suitably and satisfactorily" fulfils the legitimate objective of a Member State's own rules (public safety, protection of the consumer or the environment, etc.), the importing country cannot justify prohibiting its sale in its territory by claiming that the way it fulfils the objective is different from that imposed on domestic products.

5.    The grounds for legitimacy of State laws as proposed by the ECJ in *Cassis* apparently cover a somewhat different spectrum than the exceptions listed in EC 30/TFEU 36, which are applicable in the case of discriminatory laws. In the case of non-discriminatory laws such as was in issue in *Cassis*, the sorts of exceptions described in EC 30/TFEU 36 are built into the analysis of whether the law infringes EC 28/TFEU 34 and thus EC 30/TFEU 36 would seem to be irrelevant. Does it seem a little odd that by contrast, a law that is found to be discriminatory against imports benefits from what might be a somewhat narrower range of legitimate purposes than one that is nondiscriminatory?

## [B]    Evaluation — Rules that Failed the General Interest Test

### MINISTERE PUBLIC v. GERARD DESERBAIS
Case 286/86, 1988 ECJ CELEX LEXIS 179, [1988] ECR 4907

[Criminal proceedings had been brought against Gerard Déserbais, the director of a dairy products undertaking, for importing into and marketing in France under the name "Edam" a cheese from the Federal Republic of Germany having a fat content of 34.3%, whereas under French legislation the use of the name "Edam" is restricted to a type of cheese having a minimum fat content of 40%. That legislation was adopted pursuant to the International Convention on the Use of Designations of Origin and Names for Cheeses signed, inter alios, by France, at Stresa on 1 June 1951. Mr Déserbais was found guilty of and fined under the applicable French legislation for the offence of unlawful use of a trade name ("usurpation de dénomination").]

\*    \*    \*

8 The Court is requested to expound, with respect to circumstances such as those of the present case, its previous decisions on the prohibition of measures having equivalent effect within the meaning of Article 30 [34] of the Treaty. According to those decisions, in the absence of common rules on the marketing of the products in question, obstacles to free movement within the Community resulting from disparities in national legislation must be accepted in so far as the national rules,

applying without distinction to domestic and imported products, can be justified as being necessary in order to satisfy imperative requirements relating inter alia to consumer protection and fair trading.

9 In order to reply to the question submitted by the national court, it must be observed in the first place, as is apparent from the order for reference, that the designation "Edam" is not an appellation of origin or an indication of origin, terms which . . . describe products coming from a specific geographical area. It is merely the name under which a type of cheese is sold. Moreover, in the Stresa Convention, the word "Edam" does not appear among the appellations of origin but among the "names" of cheeses.

10 In that connection, the national court starts from the premise that the cheese in question, containing 34% fat, has been lawfully and traditionally produced in the Federal Republic of Germany under the name "Edam" in accordance with the laws and regulations applicable to it there, and that consumers' attention is adequately drawn to that fact by the labelling.

11 It must also be stated that at the present stage of development of Community law there are no common rules governing the names of the various types of cheeses in the Community. Accordingly, it cannot be stated in principle that a Member State may not lay down rules making the use by national producers of a name for a cheese subject to the observance of a traditional minimum fat content.

12 However, it would be incompatible with Article 30 [34] of the Treaty and the objectives of a common market to apply such rules to imported cheeses of the same type where those cheeses have been lawfully produced and marketed in another Member State under the same generic name but with a different minimum fat content. The Member State into which they are imported cannot prevent the importation and marketing of such cheeses where adequate information for the consumer is ensured.

13 The question may arise whether the same rule must be applied where a product presented under a particular name is so different, as regards its composition or production, from the products generally known by that name in the Community that it cannot be regarded as falling within the same category. However, no situation of that kind arises in the circumstances described by the national court in this case.

14 The Netherlands Government points out in this regard that consumer protection and fair trading require observance of international agreements concerning the use of the name of a particular product. Consequently, each Member State could make the right to use the name "Edam" subject to compliance with the requirements laid down by the Stresa Convention and the Codex Alimentarius, drawn up jointly by the Food and Agriculture Organization and the World Health Organization, both of which instruments lay down a minimum fat content of 40% for that type of cheese.

15 It must be observed that the rules of the Codex Alimentarius on the composition of certain foodstuffs are in fact intended to provide guidance for defining the characteristics of those foodstuffs. However, the mere fact that a product does not wholly conform with the standard laid down does not mean that the marketing of it can be prohibited.

16 The Stresa Convention, it should be recalled, was signed before the EEC Treaty entered into force and, of the present Member States, only Denmark, France, Italy and the Netherlands are parties to it.

17 It must also be borne in mind that, as the Court has already held, the purpose of the first paragraph of Article 234 [307] of the Treaty is to lay down, in accordance with the principles of international law, that the application of the Treaty does not affect the duty of the Member State concerned to respect the rights of non-member countries under a prior agreement and to perform its obligations thereunder . . .).

18 Consequently, provided that, as in the present case, the rights of non-member countries are not involved, a Member State cannot rely on the provisions of a pre-existing convention of that kind in order to justify restrictions on the marketing of products coming from another Member State where the marketing thereof is lawful by virtue of the free movement of goods provided for by the Treaty.

19 It must therefore be stated, in reply to the question submitted, that Article 30 [34] et seq. of the Treaty must be interpreted as precluding a Member State from applying national legislation making the right to use the trade name of a type of cheese subject to the observance of a minimum fat content to products of the same type imported from another Member State when those products have been lawfully manufactured and marketed under that name in that Member State and consumers are provided with proper information.

## NOTES AND QUESTIONS

1.    The Court accepted that France was entitled to lay down its own rules and the French law surely seemed a reasonable one in light of its adoption in compliance with the Stresa Convention. So why did the Court reject the rule in such strong terms?

2.    In *Schutzverband Gegen Unwesen In der Wirtsschaft v. Weinvertriebs GmbH*, Case 59/82, [1983] ECR 1217, the Court shed further light on this issue, stating that while the protection of consumers could "justify obstacles to the free movement of goods resulting from disparities in national rules relating to the marketing of products, the discriminatory nature of a national rule excludes the application of that criterion, which concerns only provisions of legislation governing the uniform marketing of national and imported products".

## COMMISSION v. GERMANY
### (BEER PURITY)
Case 178/84, 1987 ECJ CELEX LEXIS 20, [1987] ECR 1227

[The Commission sought a declaration that a German tax law (the Biersteuergesetz) forbidding the use of the term "Bier" except for beer made without additives was contrary to EC 28/TFEU 34.]

31 The German Government's argument that article 10 of the Biersteuergesetz is essential in order to protect German consumers because, in their minds, the designation "Bier" is inseparably linked to the beverage manufactured solely from the ingredients laid down in article 9 of the Biersteuergesetz must be rejected.

32 Firstly, consumers' conceptions which vary from one Member State to the other are also likely to evolve in the course of time within a Member State. The establishment of the common market is, it should be added, one of the factors that may play a major contributory role in that development. Whereas rules protecting consumers against misleading practices enable such a development to be taken into account, legislation of the kind contained in article 10 of the Biersteuergesetz prevents it from taking place . . . [T]he legislation of a Member State must not "crystallize given consumer habits so as to consolidate an advantage acquired by national industries concerned to comply with them".

33 Secondly, in the other Member States of the Community the designations corresponding to the German designation "Bier" are generic designations for a fermented beverage manufactured from malted barley, whether malted barley on its own or with the addition of rice or maize. The same approach is taken in Community law as can be seen from heading no 22.03 of the Common Customs Tariff. The German legislature itself utilizes the designation "Bier" in that way in article 9 (7) and (8) of the Biersteuergesetz in order to refer to beverages not complying with the manufacturing rules laid down in article 9 (1) and (2).

34 The German designation "Bier" and its equivalents in the languages of the other Member States of the community may therefore not be restricted to beers manufactured in accordance with the rules in force in the Federal Republic of Germany.

35 It is admittedly legitimate to seek to enable consumers who attribute specific qualities to beers manufactured from particular raw materials to make their choice in the light of that consideration. However . . . that possibility may be ensured by means which do not prevent the importation of products which have been lawfully manufactured and marketed in other Member States and, in particular, "by the compulsory affixing of suitable labels giving the nature of the product sold". By indicating the raw materials utilized in the manufacture of beer "such a course would enable the consumer to make his choice in full knowledge of the facts and would guarantee transparency in trading and in offers to the public". It must be added that such a system of mandatory consumer information must not entail negative assessments for beers not complying with the requirements of article 9 of the Biersteuergesetz.

36 Contrary to the German Government's view, such a system of consumer information may operate perfectly well even in the case of a product which, like beer, is not necessarily supplied to consumers in bottles or in cans capable of bearing the appropriate details. That is borne out, once again, by the German legislation itself. Article 26 (1) and (2) of the aforementioned regulation implementing the Biersteuergesetz provides for a system of consumer information in respect of certain beers, even where those beers are sold on draught, when the requisite information must appear on the casks or the beer taps.

37 It follows from the foregoing that by applying the rules on designation in article 10 of the Biersteuergesetz to beers imported from other Member States which were manufactured and marketed lawfully in those states the Federal Republic of Germany has failed to fulfil its obligations under Article 30 [34] of the EEC Treaty.

## NOTES AND QUESTIONS

Do you think the Court gave due weight to the arguments regarding the general understanding of the usage of the term "Bier" in Germany? Is labeling the panacea for these sorts of cases? See, for example, H.-C. von Heydebrand u.d. Lasa, *Free Movement of Foodstuffs, Consumer Protection and Food Standards in the European Community: Has the Court of Justice Got it Wrong*? (1991) 16 EL REV. 391.

### [C]   *Cassis* and the Doctrine of Mutual Recognition

## CRIMINAL PROCEEDINGS AGAINST JACQUELINE BRANDSMA
### Case C-293/94, 1996 ECJ CELEX LEXIS 262, [1996] ECR I-3159

[Criminal proceedings had been brought against Mrs Brandsma, in her capacity as the person responsible for the HEMA shop in Turnhout, Belgium, for infringing a Belgian law on the possession, marketing and use of pesticides and plant protection products. Ms Brandsma has been prosecuted for selling a product called "HEMA Tegelreiniger", used to prevent algae from growing on walls and tiles. No application for authorization had been made to the Belgian Ministry of Public Health in respect of this product, but it had an authorization number in the Netherlands, where it was sold in various large stores belonging to the HEMA group.]

3 Considering that the case raised a problem of interpretation of Community law, the national court stayed proceedings and referred the following questions to the Court for a preliminary ruling:

"1. Must a legal provision of a Member State prohibiting pesticides for non-agricultural use which have not been previously authorized by the Minister responsible for public health from being marketed, acquired, offered, put on display or sale, kept, prepared, transported, sold, disposed of for valuable consideration or free of charge, imported or used, be regarded as a quantitative restriction or a measure having equivalent effect within the meaning of Article 30 [34] of the EEC Treaty, where that national provision has the effect that a pesticide for non-agricultural use lawfully marketed in another Member State may not be imported and sold in the first-mentioned Member State unless prior authorization has been obtained from the Minister responsible for public health in the first-mentioned State?

2. If the answer to the first question is in the affirmative and such provision is contrary to Article 30 [34] of the EEC Treaty, may the first-mentioned Member State, in the circumstances set out above, lawfully rely on the exception set out in Article 36 [36] of the EEC Treaty on grounds of protection of public health in order to maintain the provision in question and avoid the application of the prohibition contained in Article 30 [34] of the EEC Treaty?"

4 As far as the first question is concerned, all the parties agree that the Belgian law must be regarded as a measure having an effect equivalent to a quantitative

restriction within the meaning of Article 30 [34] of the Treaty.

5 In this regard, it should be noted that, as the Court has consistently held, legislation such as that applicable in this case constitutes a measure having an effect equivalent to a quantitative restriction within the meaning of Article 30 [34] of the Treaty, since it is capable of hindering, directly or indirectly, actually or potentially, trade between the Member States . . .

6 In these circumstances, the reply to the first question should be that a legal provision of a Member State prohibiting pesticides for non-agricultural use which have not been previously authorized from being marketed, acquired, offered, put on display or sale, kept, prepared, transported, sold, disposed of for valuable consideration or free of charge, imported or used, constitutes a measure having an effect equivalent to a quantitative restriction within the meaning of Article 30 [34] of the Treaty.

7 As far as the second question is concerned, Ms Brandsma avers that the product sold by her has been approved in the Netherlands and satisfies all the requirements of the applicable directives. She cites in this connection Council Directive 67/548/EEC of 27 June 1967 on the approximation of laws, regulations and administrative provisions relating to the classification, packaging and labelling of dangerous substances (OJ, English Special Edition 1967, p. 234), Council Directive 76/769/EEC of 27 July 1976 on the approximation of the laws, regulations and administrative provisions of the Member States relating to restrictions on the marketing and use of certain dangerous substances and preparations (OJ 1976 L 262, p. 201) and Council Directive 78/631/EEC of 26 June 1978 on the approximation of the laws of the Member States relating to the classification, packaging and labelling of dangerous preparations (pesticides) (OJ 1978 L 206, p. 13). Consequently, Article 36 [36] may be relevant only in so far as the requirement for fresh approval goes beyond what is provided for by those directives. Moreover, it would not be permissible under Article 36 [36] of the Treaty for the product in question to be required to be subjected to a fresh approval procedure in Belgium, since public health in that State is sufficiently protected by the grant of authorization in the Netherlands. In addition, counsel for Ms Brandsma made it clear at the hearing that neither HEMA nor his client had lodged any application for approval in respect of the product in Belgium. In any event, the onus is on the Public Prosecutor to establish that the Belgian formality is essential on public health grounds and that the Netherlands approval is insufficient in that regard.

8 The Netherlands, Austrian and Swedish Governments, the United Kingdom and the Commission point out that the product in question comes into the class of biocides, for which there is at present no harmonization directive, but merely a proposal for a directive providing for national approval procedures (OJ 1995 C 261, p. 5).

9 They consider that this case is similar to Case 272/80 Frans-Nederlandse Maatschappij voor Biologische Producten 1981 ECR 3277, and conclude that a national measure requiring prior authorization to market a product is justified on grounds of the protection of public health within the meaning of Article 36 [36] of the Treaty. The United Kingdom and Sweden also mention protection of the environment as a justification.

10 The Court finds that, as Community legislation stands, there is not yet any provision relating to the marketing of biocidal products. . . . [T]he directives relied upon by the defendant in the main proceedings are not relevant with regard to the marketing of a product such as HEMA Tegelreiniger. It will therefore be necessary to determine whether a national provision such as the one applicable in the main proceedings can be justified in the light of the derogations referred to in Article 36 [36] of the Treaty.

11 Since biocidal products are used to combat organisms harmful to human or animal health and organisms liable to damage natural or manufactured products, they inevitably contain dangerous substances. As the Netherlands, Austria, Sweden, the United Kingdom and the Commission have rightly observed, in the absence of harmonizing rules, the Member States are free to decide on their intended level of protection of human health and life and on whether to require prior authorization for the marketing of such products.

12 As the Court held, however, in Frans-Nederlandse Maatschappij voor Biologische Producten, at paragraph 14, whilst a Member State is free to require a product of the type in question, which has already received approval in another Member State, to undergo a fresh procedure of examination and approval, the authorities of the Member States are nevertheless required to assist in bringing about a relaxation of the controls existing in intra-Community trade and to take account of technical or chemical analyses or laboratory tests which have already been carried out in another Member State.

13 The reply to the second question should therefore be that national legislation prohibiting the marketing of a biocidal product containing dangerous substances, such as the product at issue, without prior authorization from the competent authorities is justified under Article 36 [36] of the Treaty, even if that product has already been authorized for sale in another Member State. The competent authorities are not, however, entitled unnecessarily to require technical or chemical analyses or laboratory tests when the same analyses or tests have already been carried out in that other Member State and their results are available to those authorities or may at their request be placed at their disposal.

## NOTES AND QUESTIONS

1.    Although the above case dealt with the exception in EC 30/TFEU 36 and therefore did not as such involve the balancing test in *Cassis*, it seems to confirm that the imposition of testing and approval requirements in the importing State is legitimate as long as they do not require unnecessary duplication of testing already carried out in the exporting state. This may be seen then as a parallel of the "proportionality" test evident in *Cassis* — i.e., does the rule go further than it needs to protect an otherwise legitimate interest? There is thus no reason to suppose that the same logic would not apply to any case analyzed under EC 28/TFEU 34. This proportionality test then underpins a whole framework for a requirement that the importing Member State should take into account the rules of other Member States when applying its own regulations and may often then be required to adapt them so as to give recognition to the rules of the exporting Member State.

For a parallel in the context of the *Cassis* balancing process, see *Radiosistemi Srl v. Prefetto di Genova.*, Case C-388/00 and 429/00, 2002 ECJ CELEX LEXIS 361, [2002] ECR I-5845, where the Court stated:

> 44 It is true that the national type-approval for radio equipment is of such a nature as to be justified by considerations of public security and imperative requirements relating to the proper functioning of the public telecommunications network. It is not disputed, however, that equipment such as that at issue in the main proceedings does in fact comply with the national provisions concerning the proper use of radio frequencies in the Member State of import.

> 45 It is none the less clear from the order for reference that the national provisions only allow traders to establish the compliance of their equipment by affixing the national type-approval stamp. Moreover, such a requirement *is manifestly not proportionate* to the objective contemplated, because it does not allow a trader to establish, in a less burdensome manner, that the equipment meets the national requirements, and because it duplicates checks already carried out in another Member State.

> 46 It follows from the foregoing that national provisions such as those at issue in the main proceedings cannot be justified under either Article 30 [34] [36] EC or by mandatory requirements recognised by the case-law.[Emphasis supplied]

**2.** In *Cassis* itself, the Court had concluded that the law in question did not pass muster as a bona fide mandatory requirement, and thus there was no need to proceed to the further step of determining whether it was proportionate to the objective. Where a State law is prima facie justified, it seems that the question as to whether it is disproportionate to its stated objective is necessarily fact specific. See, for example: *Commission v. Denmark*, Case 302/86, 1988 ECJ CELEX LEXIS 189, [1989] ECR 4607, (System whereby producers were allowed to market only a limited amount of beer and soft drinks in containers that had not been approved by the National Agency was not proportionate to the aim of protection of the environment). The Court has tried on occasion to bring some objectivity to the exercise by referring to international criteria: *The State v. Leon Motte*, Case 247/84, [1985] ECR 3887; and to standards in the exporting Member State: *In re Robertson*, Case 220/81, [1982] ECR 2349.

**3.** One important difference between the EU and the U.S. systems is that the U.S. Federal authorities are competent to carry out market surveillance operations whereas EU authorities are not. Market surveillance is to be understood as the framework system where authorities can directly check on the market (i.e., in warehouses, at distribution level, in outlets or at retailers'stage) whether a product conforms to legislation (with regard to the substances authorized to be included in the product or the labeling requirements it must respect, etc). In the EU, only Member States' authorities are empowered to carry out market surveillance, even for those products that are covered by EU harmonization measures (see Chapter 6). This may inevitably lead to a divergence of interpretations of EU rules between Member States' authorities that may disrupt the free flow of goods within the EU Internal market. Therefore, while it is true to say that the increase of EU decisions that are made in setting broader standards are themselves statements of policy and thus reflect a move to overall EU preemption of the larger political choices (see Chapter 6), it is also true that this trend may (and in practice sometimes does) gravely disrupt the free movement of goods downstream, at the level of market surveillance. In order to mitigate the impact of these divergent interpretations of EU law between EU Member States at the level of market surveillance, the EU legislature has adopted Regulation 765/2008, which sets the requirements Member States' authorities have to follow when carrying out their market surveillance operations. This regulation thus purports to enhance cooperation between Member States with a view to ensuring a more uniform approach regarding national market surveillance programs.

In parallel, the EU legislature also adopted Regulation 764/2008 (appearing below) on mutual recognition that, in contrast to Regulation 765/2008, applies to products which do not fall within any EU harmonised legislation. Regulation 764/2008 thus aims to regulate Member States' rules impacting the marketing of a product when such a product is already lawfully marketed in another Member State. For this purpose, the Regulation reaffirms the principle of mutual recognition of test reports and certificates issued by accredited conformity-assessment bodies located in Member States and lays down a procedure for the application of the principle of mutual recognition in individual cases.

The adoption of both Regulation 764/2008 and Regulation 765/2008 are symptomatic of the remaining hurdles to the free movement of goods, which are mainly due to the absence of an EU market surveillance body.

# REGULATION 764/2008 LAYING DOWN PROCEDURES RELATING TO THE APPLICATION OF CERTAIN NATIONAL TECHNICAL RULES TO PRODUCTS LAWFULLY MARKETED IN ANOTHER MEMBER STATE AND REPEALING DECISION N°3052/95/EC
[2008] OJ L218/21

## CHAPTER 1 SUBJECT MATTER AND SCOPE

### Article 1

#### Subject matter

1. The aim of this Regulation is to strengthen the functioning of the internal market by improving the free movement of goods.

2. This Regulation lays down the rules and procedures to be followed by the competent authorities of a Member State when taking or intending to take a decision, as referred to in Article 2(1), which would hinder the free movement of a product lawfully marketed in another Member State and subject to Article 28 of the Treaty.

3. It also provides for the establishment of Product Contact Points in the Member States to contribute to the achievement of the aim of this Regulation, as set out in paragraph 1.

Article 2

Scope

1. This Regulation shall apply to administrative decisions addressed to economic operators, whether taken or intended, on the basis of a technical rule as defined in paragraph 2, in respect of any product, including agricultural and fish products, lawfully marketed in another Member State, where the direct or indirect effect of that decision is any of the following:

(a) the prohibition of the placing on the market of that product or type of product;

(b) the modification or additional testing of that product or type of product before it can be placed or kept on the market;

(c) the withdrawal of that product or type of product from the market.

For the purposes of point (b) of the first subparagraph, modification of the product or type of product shall mean any modification of one or more of the characteristics of a product or a type of product as listed in point (b)(i) of paragraph 2.

2. For the purposes of this Regulation, a technical rule is any provision of a law, regulation or other administrative provision of a Member State:

(a) which is not the subject of harmonisation at Community level; and

(b) which prohibits the marketing of a product or type of product in the territory of that Member State or compliance with which is compulsory when a product or type of product is marketed in the territory of that Member State, and which lays down either:

(i) the characteristics required of that product or type of product, such as levels of quality, performance or safety, or dimensions, including the requirements applicable to the product or product type as regards the name under which it is sold, terminology, symbols, testing and test methods, packaging, marking or labelling; or

(ii) any other requirement which is imposed on the product or type of product for the purposes of protecting consumers or the environment, and which affects the life-cycle of the product after it has been placed on the market, such as conditions of use, recycling, reuse or disposal, where such conditions can significantly influence the composition, nature or marketing of the product or type of product.

3. This Regulation shall not apply to:

(a) decisions of a judicial nature taken by national courts or tribunals;

(b) decisions of a judicial nature taken by law enforcement authorities in the course of the investigation or prosecution of a criminal offence as regards the terminology, symbols or any material reference to unconstitutional or criminal organisations or offences of a racist or xenophobic nature.

* * *

## CHAPTER 2 PROCEDURE FOR THE APPLICATION OF A TECHNICAL RULE

### Article 4

#### Information on the product

Where a competent authority submits a product or type of product to an evaluation to determine whether or not to adopt a decision as referred to in Article 2(1), it may request from the economic operator identified in accordance with Article 8, with due regard to the principle of proportionality, any of the following in particular:

(a) relevant information concerning the characteristics of the product or type of product in question;

(b) relevant and readily available information on the lawful marketing of the product in another Member State.

### Article 5

#### Mutual recognition of the level of competence of accredited conformity-assessment bodies

Member States shall not refuse certificates or test reports issued by a conformity-assessment body accredited for the appropriate field of conformity-assessment activity in accordance with Regulation (EC) No 765/2008 on grounds related to the competence of that body.

### Article 6

#### Assessment of the need to apply a technical rule

1. Where a competent authority intends to adopt a decision as referred to in Article 2(1), it shall send the economic operator identified in accordance with Article 8 written notice of that intention, specifying the technical rule on which the decision is to be based and setting out technical or scientific evidence to the effect that:

(a) the intended decision is justified on one of the grounds of public interest set out in Article 30 [34] of the Treaty or by reference to other overriding reasons of public interest; and

(b) the intended decision is appropriate for the purpose of achieving the objective pursued and does not go beyond what is necessary in order to attain that objective. Any intended decision shall be based on the characteristics of the product or type of product in question.

The economic operator concerned shall, following receipt of such notice, be allowed at least 20 working days in which to submit comments. The notice shall specify the time limit within which comments may be submitted.

2. Any decision as referred to in Article 2(1) shall be taken and notified to the economic operator concerned and to the Commission within a period of 20 working days from the expiry of the time limit for the receipt of comments from the economic operator referred to in paragraph 1 of this Article. It shall take due account of those comments and shall state the grounds on which it is based, including the reasons for rejecting the arguments, if any, put forward by the operator, and the technical or scientific evidence as referred to in paragraph 1 of this Article.

Where duly justified by the complexity of the issue, the competent authority may, once only, extend the period specified in the first subparagraph by a maximum of 20 working days. That extension shall be duly reasoned and shall be notified to the economic operator before the expiry of the initial period.

Any decision as referred to in Article 2(1) shall also specify the remedies available under the law in force in the Member State concerned and the time limits applying to such remedies. Such a decision may be challenged before national courts or tribunals or other instances of appeal.

3. Where, after giving written notice in accordance with paragraph 1, the competent authority decides not to adopt a decision as referred to in Article 2(1), it shall immediately inform the economic operator concerned accordingly.

4. When the competent authority fails to notify the economic operator of a decision as referred to in Article 2(1) within the period specified in paragraph 2 of this Article, the product shall be deemed to be lawfully marketed in that Member State insofar as the application of its technical rule as referred to in paragraph 1 of this Article is concerned.

Article 7

Temporary suspension of the marketing of a product

1. The competent authority shall not temporarily suspend the marketing of the product or type of product in question, during the procedure laid down in this Chapter, except where either:

(a) under normal or reasonably foreseeable conditions of use, the product or type of product in question poses a serious risk to the safety and health of the users; or

(b) the marketing of the product or type of product in question is generally prohibited in a Member State on grounds of public morality or public security.

2. The competent authority shall immediately notify the economic operator identified in accordance with Article 8 and the Commission of any suspension as referred to in paragraph 1 of this Article. In the cases referred to in paragraph 1(a) of this Article, that notification shall be accompanied by a technical or scientific justification.

3. Any suspension of the marketing of a product pursuant to this Article may be challenged before national courts or tribunals or other instances of appeal.

## Article 8

### Information to the economic operator

References to the economic operators in Articles 4, 6 and 7 shall be considered references:

(a) to the manufacturer of the product, if established in the Community, or the person who has placed the product on the market or requests to the competent authority that the product be placed on the market;

(b) where the competent authority cannot establish the identity and contact details of any of the economic operators referred to in point (a), to the manufacturer's representative, when the manufacturer is not established in the Community or, if there is no representative established in the Community, to the importer of the product;

(c) where the competent authority cannot establish the identity and contact details of any of the economic operators referred to in points (a) and (b), to any professional in the supply chain whose activity may affect any property of the product regulated by the technical rule which is being applied to it;

(d) where the competent authority cannot establish the identity and contact details of any of the economic operators referred to in points (a), (b) and (c), to any professional in the supply chain whose activity does not affect any property of the product regulated by the technical rule which is being applied to it.

## CHAPTER 3 PRODUCT CONTACT POINTS

## Article 9

### Establishment of Product Contact Points

1. Member States shall designate Product Contact Points in their territories and shall communicate their contact details to the other Member States and to the Commission.

2. The Commission shall draw up and regularly update a list of Product Contact Points and publish it in the Official Journal of the European Union. The Commission shall also make that information available through a website.

## Article 10

### Tasks

1. Product Contact Points shall, at the request of, inter alia, an economic operator or a competent authority of another Member State, provide the following information:

(a) the technical rules applicable to a specific type of product in the territory in which those Product Contact Points are established and information as to whether that type of product is subject to a requirement for prior authorisation under the laws of their Member State, together with information concerning the principle of mutual recognition and the application of this Regulation in the territory of that Member State;

(b) the contact details of the competent authorities within that Member State by means of which they may be contacted directly, including the particulars of the authorities responsible for supervising the implementation of the technical rules in question in the territory of that Member State;

(c) the remedies generally available in the territory of that Member State in the event of a dispute between the competent authorities and an economic operator.

2. Product Contact Points shall respond within 15 working days of receiving any request as referred to in paragraph 1.

3. Product Contact Points in the Member State in which the economic operator concerned has lawfully marketed the product in question may provide the economic operator or the competent authority as referred to in Article 6 with any relevant information or observations.

4. Product Contact Points shall not charge any fee for the provision of the information referred to in paragraph 1.

## NOTES AND QUESTIONS

**1.** This Regulation sets out a new procedure aimed at regulating Member States (MS) technical rules impacting the marketing of a product when these products are already lawfully marketed in another Member State. In essence, Regulation 764/2008 provides for procedural protection of economic operators that could be confronted with a decision taken by a Member State prohibiting the marketing of a product on the basis of non-compliance with a Member State technical rule, whereas those products are lawfully marketed in another Member State. What do you think might change following this regulation? Do you think the fact that it is a Regulation might enhance the impact of the substance of the text?

**2.** The basic principle underlying mutual recognition is that there should be competition between the regulatory regimes of Member States that would lead to best practices. How workable is that concept? Suppose the State of origin has imposed *no* requirement in respect of a particular product that the destination State considers should be regulated and indeed imposes a rigorous standard?

**3.** In *Commission v. France (Foie Gras)* Case C-184/96, 1998 ECJ CELEX LEXIS 287, [1998] ECR I-6197 the Court agreed with the Commission's argument that national regulation must contain mutual recognition provisions.

**4.** In line with the new approach to EU legislation based on facilitation of mutual recognition (described in Chapter 5, *supra*), the Parliament and Council adopted Directive 98/34 [1998] OJ L204/37, laying down a procedure for the provision of information in the field of technical standards and regulations (the "Transparency Directive") which requires prior notification to the Commission of new technical standards; and also Decision 3052/95/EC [1995] OJ L321/1 which set out a procedure for the exchange of information on measures that affected the free movement of goods, requiring Member States to notify the Commission of any measure that is intended to prevent free movement.

## § 13.07   THE BOUNDARIES OF EC 28/TFEU 34

### [A]   Measures that Merely Affect the Overall Volume of Trade

### TORFAEN BOROUGH COUNCIL v. B & Q PLC
Case C-145/88, 1989 ECJ CELEX LEXIS 357, [1989] ECR 3851

[B&Q, a DIY chain in the UK, had opened its stores on Sundays in violation of the Shops Act 1950]

5 Before the national court, B & Q submitted that Section 47 of the Shops Act was a measure having an effect equivalent to a quantitative restriction on imports within the meaning of Article 30 [34] of the EEC Treaty and that it was not justified under Article 36 [36] of the EEC Treaty or by virtue of any "mandatory requirement".

6 The Council denied that the ban on Sunday trading constituted a measure having an effect equivalent to a quantitative restriction on the ground that it applied to domestic and imported products alike and did not put imported products at any disadvantage.

7 The national court found that in the instant case the ban on Sunday trading had the effect of reducing B & Q's total sales, that approximately 10% of the goods sold by B & Q came from other Member States and that a corresponding reduction of imports from other Member States would therefore ensue.

*     *     *

10 By its first question the national court seeks to establish whether the concept of measures having an effect equivalent to quantitative restrictions within the meaning of Article 30 [34] of the Treaty also covers provisions prohibiting retailers from opening their premises on Sunday if the effect of the prohibition is to reduce in absolute terms the sales of goods in those premises, including goods imported from other Member States.

11 The first point which must be made is that national rules prohibiting retailers from opening their premises on Sunday apply to imported and domestic products

alike. In principle, the marketing of products imported from other Member States is not therefore made more difficult than the marketing of domestic products.

12 Next, it must be recalled that in its judgment of 11 July 1985 in Joined Cases 60 and 61/84 Cinetheque SA and Others v. Federation nationale des cinemas francais (1985) ECR 2618, the Court held, with regard to a prohibition of the hiring of video-cassettes applicable to domestic and imported products alike, that such a prohibition was not compatible with the principle of the free movement of goods provided for in the Treaty unless any obstacle to Community trade thereby created did not exceed what was necessary in order to ensure the attainment of the objective in view and unless that objective was justified with regard to Community law.

13 In those circumstances it is therefore necessary in a case such as this to consider first of all whether rules such as those at issue pursue an aim which is justified with regard to Community law. As far as that question is concerned, the Court has already stated in its judgment of 14 July 1981 in Case 155/80 Oebel (1981) ECR 1991 that national rules governing the hours of work, delivery and sale in the bread and confectionery industry constitute a legitimate part of economic and social policy, consistent with the objectives of public interest pursued by the Treaty.

14 The same consideration must apply as regards national rules governing the opening hours of retail premises. Such rules reflect certain political and economic choices in so far as their purpose is to ensure that working and non-working hours are so arranged as to accord with national or regional socio-cultural characteristics, and that, in the present state of Community law, is a matter for the Member States. Furthermore, such rules are not designed to govern the patterns of trade between Member States.

15 Secondly, it is necessary to ascertain whether the effects of such national rules exceed what is necessary to achieve the aim in view. As is indicated in Article 3 of Commission Directive 70/50/EEC of 22 December 1969 (Official Journal, English Special Edition 1970 (I), p.17), the prohibition laid down in Article 30 [34] covers national measures governing the marketing of products where the restrictive effect of such measures on the free movement of goods exceeds the effects intrinsic to trade rules.

16 The question whether the effects of specific national rules do in fact remain within that limit is a question of fact to be determined by the national court.

17 The reply to the first question must therefore be that Article 30 [34] of the Treaty must be interpreted as meaning that the prohibition which it lays down does not apply to national rules prohibiting retailers from opening their premises on Sunday where the restrictive effects on Community trade which may result therefrom do not exceed the effects intrinsic to rules of that kind.

## CRIMINAL PROCEEDINGS AGAINST: B. KECK AND D. MITHOUARD

Joined Cases C-267/91 and C-268/91, 1993 ECJ CELEX LEXIS 173, [1993] ECR I-6097

[Keck and Mithouard were prosecuted by French authorities for selling in an unaltered state articles at prices less than their actual cost price.]

3 In their defence Mr Keck and Mr Mithouard contended that a general prohibition on resale at a loss, as laid down by those provisions, is incompatible with Article 30 [34] of the Treaty and with the principles of the free movement of persons, services, capital and free competition within the Community.

4 The Tribunal de Grande Instance, taking the view that it required an interpretation of certain provisions of Community law, stayed both sets of proceedings and referred the following question to the Court for a preliminary ruling:

"Is the prohibition in France of resale at a loss under Article 32 of Order No 86-1243 of 1 December 1986 compatible with the principles of the free movement of goods, services and capital, free competition in the Common Market and non-discrimination on grounds of nationality laid down in the Treaty of 25 March 1957 establishing the EEC, and more particularly in Articles 3 and 7 thereof, since the French legislation is liable to distort competition:

(a) firstly, because it makes only resale at a loss an offence and exempts from the scope of the prohibition the manufacturer, who is free to sell on the market the product which he manufactures, processes or improves, even very slightly, at a price lower than his cost price;

(b) secondly, in that it distorts competition, especially in frontier zones, between the various traders on the basis of their nationality and place of establishment?"

5 Reference is made to the Report for the Hearing for a fuller account of the facts of the case, the procedure and the written observations submitted to the Court, which are mentioned or discussed hereinafter only in so far as is necessary for the reasoning of the Court.

6 It should be noted at the outset that the provisions of the Treaty relating to free movement of persons, services and capital within the Community have no bearing on a general prohibition of resale at a loss, which is concerned with the marketing of goods. Those provisions are therefore of no relevance to the issue in the main proceedings.

7 Next, as regards the principle of non-discrimination laid down in Article 7 [18] of the Treaty, it appears from the orders for reference that the national court questions the compatibility with that provision of the prohibition of resale at a loss, in that undertakings subject to it may be placed at a disadvantage vis-a-vis competitors in Member States where resale at a loss is permitted.

8 However, the fact that undertakings selling in different Member States are subject to different legislative provisions, some prohibiting and some permitting resale at a loss, does not constitute discrimination for the purposes of Article 7 [18] of the Treaty. The national legislation at issue in the main proceedings applies to

any sales activity carried out within the national territory, regardless of the nationality of those engaged in it . . .

9 Finally, it appears from the question submitted for a preliminary ruling that the national court seeks guidance as to the possible anti-competitive effects of the rules in question by reference exclusively to the foundations of the Community set out in Article 3 of the Treaty, without however making specific reference to any of the implementing rules of the Treaty in the field of competition.

10 In these circumstances, having regard to the written and oral argument presented to the Court, and with a view to giving a useful reply to the referring court, the appropriate course is to look at the prohibition of resale at a loss from the perspective of the free movement of goods.

11 By virtue of Article 30 [34], quantitative restrictions on imports and all measures having equivalent effect are prohibited between Member States. The Court has consistently held that any measure which is capable of directly or indirectly, actually or potentially, hindering intra-Community trade constitutes a measure having equivalent effect to a quantitative restriction.

12 National legislation imposing a general prohibition on resale at a loss is not designed to regulate trade in goods between Member States.

13 Such legislation may, admittedly, restrict the volume of sales, and hence the volume of sales of products from other Member States, in so far as it deprives traders of a method of sales promotion. But the question remains whether such a possibility is sufficient to characterize the legislation in question as a measure having equivalent effect to a quantitative restriction on imports.

14 In view of the increasing tendency of traders to invoke Article 30 [34] of the Treaty as a means of challenging any rules whose effect is to limit their commercial freedom even where such rules are not aimed at products from other Member States, the Court considers it necessary to re-examine and clarify its case-law on this matter.

15 It is established by the case-law beginning with "Cassis de Dijon" (Case 120/78 Rewe-Zentral v. Bundesmonopolverwaltung fuer Branntwein 1979 ECR 649) that, in the absence of harmonization of legislation, obstacles to free movement of goods which are the consequence of applying, to goods coming from other Member States where they are lawfully manufactured and marketed, rules that lay down requirements to be met by such goods (such as those relating to designation, form, size, weight, composition, presentation, labelling, packaging) constitute measures of equivalent effect prohibited by Article 30 [34]. This is so even if those rules apply without distinction to all products unless their application can be justified by a public-interest objective taking precedence over the free movement of goods.

16 By contrast, contrary to what has previously been decided, the application to products from other Member States of national provisions restricting or prohibiting certain selling arrangements is not such as to hinder directly or indirectly, actually or potentially, trade between Member States within the meaning of the Dassonville judgment (Case 8/74 1974 ECR 837), so long as those provisions apply to all relevant traders operating within the national territory and so long as they affect in the same

manner, in law and in fact, the marketing of domestic products and of those from other Member States.

17 Provided that those conditions are fulfilled, the application of such rules to the sale of products from another Member State meeting the requirements laid down by that State is not by nature such as to prevent their access to the market or to impede access any more than it impedes the access of domestic products. Such rules therefore fall outside the scope of Article 30 [34] of the Treaty.

18 Accordingly, the reply to be given to the national court is that Article 30 [34] of the EEC Treaty is to be interpreted as not applying to legislation of a Member State imposing a general prohibition on resale at a loss.

## NOTES AND QUESTIONS

1.   The potentially wide sweep of the statements in *Dassonville* and *Cassis* brought into question the validity of trading regulations that only affected interstate trade in goods in general terms. The Court initially seemed willing to appraise such general rules under EC 28/TFEU 34. Thus, in *Cinéthèque v. Fédération Nationale des Cinémas Français* 60 & 61/84, [1985] ECR 2605, the Court reviewed a French law that banned the sale of videos for one year from the date of the release of a film and concluded that it could was objectively justified as a measure to promote cinema-going. See also *Torfaen, supra*. Thus, the ruling in *Keck* marked a distinct change of mind. Note the reference to "selling arrangements" — perhaps a rather awkward translation of the French term "modalités de vente". How does one actually distinguish between "selling arrangements" and rules relating to products? What about legislation that is neither a selling arrangement nor a "trading rule" (as the term was used in *Dassonville*)?

2.   In *Leclerc-Siplec v. T.F.I. Publicité and TFI Publicité*, Case C-412/93, 1995 ECJ CELEX LEXIS 218, [1995] ECR I-179, the ECJ was asked to consider a prohibition on television advertising under French law on distribution activities. The purpose was to protect regional newspapers. Under *Keck*, such a rule would appear to fall outside EC 28/TFEU 34. The Advocate-General in *Leclerc-Siplec* argued that if such a rule has a *substantial* impact on *access to the market*, where the rule does not apply to goods themselves, it falls within EC 28/TFEU 34. See also *R. Hunermund v. Landesapothekerkammer Baden-Württemburg*, Case C-292/92, 1993 ECJ CELEX LEXIS 435, [1993] ECR I-6787.

3.   In *Commission v. Greece (Baby Milk Formula)*, Case C-391/92, 1995 ECJ CELEX LEXIS 40, [1995] ECR I-1621, the Commission had taken Greece to the ECJ for maintaining a law that required that baby formula for children up to the age of five be sold only in pharmacies. Even though the rule necessarily affected only imports because all baby formula was imported, the ECJ nonetheless ruled that this measure was legitimate on the basis of its ruling in *Keck*.

4.   For discussion of the impact of the *Keck* case, see e.g. Chalmers, *Repackaging the Internal Market: The Ramifications of the Keck Judgment*, (1994) EL Rev. 385.

**5.** In *Vereinigte Familiapress Zeitungsverlags- und vertriebs GmbH v. Heinrich Bauer Verlag*, Case C-368/95, 1997 ECJ CELEX LEXIS 316, [1997] ECR I-3689, proceedings were brought by Vereinigte Familiapress Zeitungsverlags- und vertriebs GmbH), an Austrian newspaper publisher, against Heinrich Bauer Verlag, a newspaper publisher established in Germany, for an order that the latter should cease to sell in Austria publications offering readers the chance to take part in games for prizes, in breach of the Gesetz über unlauteren Wettbewerb 1992 (Austrian Law on Unfair Competition). The argument was made by Bauer that the law infringed EC 28/TFEU 34, but the plaintiff countered that the law was justified as protecting the right to free speech. (This is addressed in Chapter 20.) Under *Keck*, the Austrian government argued unsuccessfully that the Court should have treated the Austrian law as a selling arrangement outside the scope of EC 28/TFEU 34 altogether. Would there not have been some merit to such an argument?

See also *Konsumentombudsmannen (KO) v. Gourmet International Products AB (GIP)*, Case 405/98, 2001 ECJ CELEX LEXIS 89, [2001] ECR I-1795, where the Court, in considering an advertising ban on alcoholic beverages in Sweden rejected the notion that just because the ban was general in nature, and might be considered a "selling arrangement" as envisaged by *Keck*, it would necessarily be outside EC 28/TFEU 34:

> 21 Even without its being necessary to carry out a precise analysis of the facts characteristic of the Swedish situation, which it is for the national court to do, the Court is able to conclude that, in the case of products like alcoholic beverages, the consumption of which is linked to traditional social practices and to local habits and customs, a prohibition of all advertising directed at consumers in the form of advertisements in the press, on the radio and on television, the direct mailing of unsolicited material or the placing of posters on the public highway is liable to impede access to the market by products from other Member States more than it impedes access by domestic products, with which consumers are instantly more familiar.

## [B]   Non-Technical Requirements that Have a Discriminatory Effect Against Imports

### COMMISSION v. GERMANY
(LAW ON PHARMACIES)
Case C-141/07, 2008 ECJ EUR-Lex LEXIS 1429, [2008] ECR I-6935.

[The Court considered a Commission complaint regarding article 14 of the German Law on Pharmacies (the "ApoG"). In essence, the rule required dispensaries to be located in the vicinity of the hospitals using them in order to assure emergency supplies. This had the practical effect of excluding supplies by almost all non-German pharmacies. The rule was not directed to imported products as such, indeed it did not concern the products themselves at all. In these circumstances one might have expected that the ECJ might have followed *Keck*, but, as in *Motor Cycle Trailers*, it took a different tack.]

29. The Court of Justice . . . made clear that national provisions restricting or prohibiting certain selling arrangements which, first, apply to all relevant traders operating within the national territory and, second, affect in the same manner, in law and in fact, the marketing of domestic products and those from other Member States are not liable to hinder, directly or indirectly, actually or potentially, trade between Member States within the meaning of the Dassonville line of case-law . . .

30. In the present case, it must be recalled that Paragraph 14 of the ApoG lays down the requirements which external pharmacies must meet if they are to be eligible to supply medicinal products to hospitals in Germany.

31. However, the contested provisions do not concern the characteristics of the medicinal products, but concern solely the arrangements permitting their sale . . . Consequently, they must be regarded as concerning selling arrangements within the meaning of Keck and Mithouard, which is moreover not disputed by the parties to these proceedings.

32. As is made clear in Keck and Mithouard, however, such a selling arrangement can fall outside the prohibition laid down in Article 28 EC only if it satisfies the two conditions stated in paragraph 29 above.

33. As regards the first of those conditions, it is clear that the contested provisions apply indiscriminately to all the operators concerned who carry out their business on German territory, since they apply to all pharmacies which wish to supply medicinal products to German hospitals, whether they are established in Germany or in another Member State.

34. As regards the second of those conditions, it is undisputed that the contested provisions lay down a series of cumulative criteria which in practice require, as the Federal Republic of Germany moreover expressly acknowledges, a degree of geographical proximity between the pharmacy supplying the medicinal products and the hospital for which those products are intended.

35. It follows that the contested provisions are such as to make the supply of medicinal products to German hospitals more difficult and more costly for pharmacies established in Member States other than the Federal Republic of Germany than for pharmacies established in the latter State. Pharmacies established in other Member States, unless they are in a border region and near to the German hospital concerned, which wish to conclude a supply contract with such a hospital must either transfer their dispensary to the vicinity of the hospital concerned or open another pharmacy near to the hospital.

36. Consequently, as regards the supply of medicinal products to German hospitals, those provisions do not affect in the same way products marketed by pharmacies established in the territory of the Federal Republic of Germany and those marketed by pharmacies situated in another Member State.

37. That conclusion cannot be rebutted by the circumstance, relied on by the Federal Republic of Germany, that, in relation to the sale of medicinal products to German hospitals, the contested provisions do not place pharmacies established outside that Member State at any greater disadvantage than pharmacies situated in Germany which have their dispensaries situated at some distance from the hospital

for which the medicinal products are intended.

38. Those provisions cannot cease to be restrictive merely because in one part of the territory of the Member State concerned, namely that part that is distant from the hospital concerned, those provisions affect in the same way the marketing of medicinal products by pharmacies established in Germany and by pharmacies established in other Member States . . .

39. Nor can it be maintained that the marketing of medicinal products from other Member States is no more affected than the marketing of medicinal products from regions of Germany which are remote from the hospital to be supplied. For a national measure to be characterised as discriminatory or protective within the meaning of the rules on the free movement of goods, it is not necessary for it to have the effect of favouring national products as a whole or of placing only imported products at a disadvantage and not national products . . .

40. Equally irrelevant is the circumstance, relied on by the Federal Republic of Germany, that a pharmacy established in another Member State has the opportunity to supply medicinal products to the hospital's internal pharmacy or to an external pharmacy which satisfies the cumulative conditions laid down in the contested provisions.

41 . . . [A]lthough the Community rules on the free movement of goods do not require that it should be possible for hospitals situated in Member States to obtain supplies of medicinal products from external pharmacies, when a Member State provides for such a possibility, it opens that activity to the market and is accordingly bound to comply with the Community rules.

42. The Court must also reject the argument of the Federal Republic of Germany that the contested provisions are not the cause of there being a lesser quantity of medicinal products supplied to German hospitals by pharmacies situated outside that Member State, because, as a general rule, adequate quantities of medicinal products authorised in Germany are not available in such pharmacies.

43. Since the contested provisions are liable to hinder intra-Community trade, they must be considered as a measure having equivalent effect to a quantitative restriction on imports within the meaning of Article 28 EC [34], without it being necessary to prove that they have had an appreciable effect on such trade . . .

44. It follows from all of the foregoing that the contested provisions are liable to hinder intra-Community trade and constitute a measure having equivalent effect to a quantitative restriction on imports prohibited by Article 28 EC [34].

45. In those circumstances, it must be examined whether the contested provisions can be justified on grounds such as those relied on by the Federal Republic of Germany relating to the protection of public health.

## NOTES AND QUESTIONS

1. This case suggests that the ECJ is moving away from an approach that draws a boundary to the scope of EC 28/TFEU34 in the form of a categorization of general selling arrangements versus specific product-related regulation. Does the

approach then suggest a watering down of the *Keck* doctrine? Does the prohibition on discriminatory rules actually place any measure, whether a selling arrangement or any other type of measure, out of the confines of *Keck* such that it ought to be considered in exactly the same way as any rule directed specifically at products?

2.   The concept of effect on access to the market for imports as the determinant in cases involving laws not related to the products themselves has found many supporters, particularly as *Keck* created the risk of overcorrecting the direction that the court was concerned with. The Court appears to be moving in the direction of using that test. See also S. Wetherill, *After Keck: Some Thoughts on How to Clarify the Clarification* (1996) 33 CML Rev. 885; and M. Derlén and J. Lindholm, *Article 28 E.C. and Rules on Use: A Step towards a Workable Doctrine for Measures having Equivalent Effect to Quantitative Restrictions*, 16 Colum. J. Eur. L. (2009-2010) 191.

## [C]   Non-discriminatory Measures Affecting Consumer Behavior

### COMMISSION v. ITALY
### (USE OF TRAILERS WITH MOTOR CYCLES)
### Case 110/05, 2009 ECJ EUR-Lex LEXIS 111, [2009] ECR I-519

[The Commission claimed that Italy was in breach of EC 28/TFEU 34 by maintaining in force Article 56 of the Italian Highway Code, under which only automobiles, trolleybuses (vehicles with an electric motor not authorized on rails which take their energy from an overhead contact line) and automobile tractors (three wheeled motor vehicles intended to tow semi-trailers) are allowed to tow trailers. Thus, there was no market in Italy to speak of for the sale of trailers specifically designed for use with motor-cycles.]

18 The Commission proposes to apply to the first category of rules the criteria set out in paragraph 5 of the judgment in Case 8/74 *Dassonville* [1974] ECR 837 and to consider each case separately. With regard to the second category of rules, once they impose an absolute prohibition on the use of a certain product or a prohibition which permits only limited or exceptional use of it, they constitute, by definition, measures having equivalent effect to quantitative restrictions on imports within the meaning of EC 28/TFEU 34 EC. The Commission considers that it is neither appropriate nor necessary to extend the criteria set out in paragraphs 16 and 17 of the judgment in Joined Cases C-267/91 and C-268/91 *Keck and Mithouard* [1993] ECR I-6097 to rules concerning the use of a product and thereby create an additional category of measures which are not within the scope of ARTICLE 28 [34] EC.

\*   \*   \*

35. . . . [O]bstacles to the free movement of goods which are the consequence of applying, to goods coming from other Member States where they are lawfully manufactured and marketed, rules that lay down requirements to be met by such goods constitute measures of equivalent effect to quantitative restrictions even if those rules apply to all products alike . . .

36. By contrast, the application to products from other Member States of national provisions restricting or prohibiting certain selling arrangements is not such as to hinder directly or indirectly, actually or potentially, trade between Member States for the purposes of the case-law flowing from Dassonville, on condition that those provisions apply to all relevant traders operating within the national territory and that they affect in the same manner, in law and in fact, the marketing of domestic products and of those from other Member States. Provided that those conditions are fulfilled, the application of such rules to the sale of products from another Member State meeting the requirements laid down by that State is not by nature such as to prevent their access to the market or to impede access any more than it impedes the access of domestic products . . .

37. Consequently, measures adopted by a Member State the object or effect of which is to treat products coming from other Member States less favourably are to be regarded as measures having equivalent effect to quantitative restrictions on imports within the meaning of Article 28 EC [34], as are the measures referred to in paragraph 35 of the present judgment. Any other measure which hinders access of products originating in other Member States to the market of a Member State is also covered by that concept.

\*     \*     \*

49. In order to assess whether the Commission's complaint is well founded, it should be pointed out that, although Article 56 of the Highway Code concerns a prohibition on using a motorcycle and a trailer together in Italy, the national provision must be considered, in particular, from the angle of the restriction that it could represent for free movement of trailers. Although it is not disputed that motorcycles can easily be used without a trailer, the fact remains that the latter is of little use without a motor vehicle that may tow it.

50. It is common ground that Article 56 of the Highway Code applies without regard to the origin of trailers.

\*     \*     \*

55. In its reply to the Court's written question, the Commission claimed, without being contradicted by the Italian Republic, that, in the case of trailers specially designed for motorcycles, the possibilities for their use other than with motorcycles are very limited. It considers that, although it is not inconceivable that they could, in certain circumstances, be towed by other vehicles, in particular, by automobiles, such use is inappropriate and remains at least insignificant, if not hypothetical.

56. It should be noted in that regard that a prohibition on the use of a product in the territory of a Member State has a considerable influence on the behaviour of consumers, which, in its turn, affects the access of that product to the market of that Member State.

57. Consumers, knowing that they are not permitted to use their motorcycle with a trailer specially designed for it, have practically no interest in buying such a trailer . . . Thus, Article 56 of the Highway Code prevents a demand from existing in the market at issue for such trailers and therefore hinders their importation.

58. It follows that the prohibition laid down in Article 56 of the Highway Code, to the extent that its effect is to hinder access to the Italian market for trailers which are specially designed for motorcycles and are lawfully produced and marketed in Member States other than the Italian Republic, constitutes a measure having equivalent effect to quantitative restrictions on imports within the meaning of Article 28 EC [34], unless it can be justified objectively.

59. Such a prohibition may be justified on one of the public interest grounds set out in Article 30 EC [36] or in order to meet imperative requirements . . . In either case, the national provision must be appropriate for securing the attainment of the objective pursued and not go beyond what is necessary in order to attain it . . .

[The Court proceeded to find the rule justified on traffic safety grounds]

## ÅKLAGAREN v. PERCY MICKELSSON AND JOAKIM ROOS
### Case 142/05, 2009 ECJ EUR-Lex LEXIS 1429, [2009] ECR I-4273

[P. Mickelsson and J. Roos were prosecuted under Swedish law for failure to comply with a prohibition on the use of personal watercraft as laid down by national regulations on the use of jet-skis (personal watercraft) that implemented Directive 94/25 relating to recreational craft (OJ 1994 L 164, p. 15), as amended by Directive 2003/44/EC of the European Parliament and of the Council of 16 June 2003 (OJ 2003 L 214, p. 18) ('Directive 94/25'). The Swedish legislation was adopted to protect the environment and prohibited the use of personal watercraft on navigable waterways. The defendants argued that such legislation infringed EC 28/TFEU 34.]

25. It is apparent from the file sent to the Court that, at the material time, no waters had been designated as open to navigation by personal watercraft, and thus the use of personal watercraft was permitted on only general navigable waterways. However, the accused in the main proceedings and the Commission of the European Communities maintain that those waterways are intended for heavy traffic of a commercial nature making the use of personal watercraft dangerous and that, in any event, the majority of navigable Swedish waters lie outside those waterways. The actual possibilities for the use of personal watercraft in Sweden are, therefore, merely marginal.

26. Even if the national regulations at issue do not have the aim or effect of treating goods coming from other Member States less favourably, which is for the national court to ascertain, the restriction which they impose on the use of a product in the territory of a Member State may, depending on its scope, have a considerable influence on the behaviour of consumers, which may, in turn, affect the access of that product to the market of that Member State . . .

27. Consumers, knowing that the use permitted by such regulations is very limited, have only a limited interest in buying that product . . .

28. In that regard, where the national regulations for the designation of navigable waters and waterways have the effect of preventing users of personal watercraft from using them for the specific and inherent purposes for which they were intended or of greatly restricting their use, which is for the national court to ascertain, such regulations have the effect of hindering the access to the domestic market in question for those goods and therefore constitute, save where there is a

justification pursuant to Article 30 EC [36] or there are overriding public interest requirements, measures having equivalent effect to quantitative restrictions on imports prohibited by Article 28 EC [34].

29. Moreover, in either case, the national provision must be appropriate for securing the attainment of the objective pursued and not go beyond what is necessary in order to attain it.

30. The Swedish Government maintains that the national regulations are justified by the objective of environmental protection and by the objectives referred to in Article 30 EC. The restriction on the use of personal watercraft to particular waters makes it possible, inter alia, to prevent unacceptable environmental disturbances. The use of personal watercraft has negative consequences for fauna, in particular where such a craft is used for a lengthy period on a small area or driven at great speed. The noise as a whole disturbs people and animals and above all certain protected species of birds. Furthermore, the easy transport of personal watercraft facilitates the spread of animal diseases.

31. It must be pointed out, in that regard, that, according to Article 30 EC, Article 28 EC does not preclude prohibitions or restrictions on imports justified inter alia on grounds of the protection of health and life of humans, animals or plants.

32. Furthermore, according to settled case-law, national measures capable of hindering intra-Community trade may be justified by the objective of protection of the environment provided that the measures in question are proportionate to the aim pursued . . .

33. As the protection of the environment, on the one hand, and the protection of health and life of humans, animals and plants, on the other hand, are, in the present case, closely related objectives, they should be examined together in order to assess whether regulations such as those at issue in the main proceedings are justified.

34. It is not open to dispute that a restriction or a prohibition on the use of personal watercraft are appropriate means for the purpose of ensuring that the environment is protected. However, for the national regulations to be capable of being regarded as justified, it is also incumbent on the national authorities to show that their restrictive effects on the free movement of goods do not go beyond what is necessary to achieve that aim.

35. The Swedish Government maintains that the prohibition on the use of personal watercraft leaves users of those craft with not less than 300 general navigable waterways on the Swedish coast and on the large lakes, which constitutes a very extensive area. Furthermore, the geographical position of those aquatic areas in Sweden precludes measures of a scope different from that of the provisions in the national regulations at issue in the main proceedings.

\*     \*     \*

39. Regulations such as those at issue in the main proceedings may, in principle, be regarded as proportionate provided that, first, the competent national authorities are required to adopt such implementing measures, secondly, those authorities have actually made use of the power conferred on them in that regard and designated the waters which satisfy the conditions provided for by the national regulations and,

lastly, such measures have been adopted within a reasonable period after the entry into force of those regulations.

40. It follows that national regulations such as those at issue in the main proceedings may be justified by the aim of the protection of the environment provided that the above conditions are complied with. It is for the national court to ascertain whether those conditions have been satisfied in the main proceedings.

## NOTES AND QUESTIONS

The above cases concerned national measures regulating the use of goods for the public good (respectively, traffic safety and the protection of the environment). Unlike in the *German Pharmacies* case, the measures could not be considered to have any *de facto* discriminatory effect against imports. So on what basis was the Court able to conclude that in principle they nonetheless fell within EC 28/TFEU34?

## [D]   Rules not Related to Goods at All

### EUGEN SCHMIDBERGER, INTERNATIONALE TRANSPORTE UND PLANZUGE v. AUSTRIA
Case C-112/00, 2003 ECJ CELEX LEXIS 75, [2003] ECR I-5659

[Schmidberger, a German company, operated a number of tractor-trailers that used the A 13 Brenner motorway to transport lumber from Germany to Italy. He alleged that for four days he was prevented from using it and suffered damage due to the closure of the motorway for a demonstration by an environmental group known as Transitforum. The demonstration was lawful under Austrian law and the authorities had taken the action to close the motorway. Schmidberger sued the Austrian government invoking EC 28/TFEU 34. The *Commission v. France* decision mentioned in the judgment is described in Note 3.]

56 It is settled case-law since the judgment in Case 8/74 *Dassonville* [1974] ECR 837, paragraph 5) that those provisions, taken in their context, must be understood as being intended to eliminate all barriers, whether direct or indirect, actual or potential, to trade flows in intra-Community trade . . .

57 In this way the Court held in particular that, as an indispensable instrument for the realisation of a market without internal frontiers, Article 30 [34] does not prohibit only measures emanating from the State which, in themselves, create restrictions on trade between Member States. It also applies where a Member State abstains from adopting the measures required in order to deal with obstacles to the free movement of goods which are not caused by the State . . .

58 The fact that a Member State abstains from taking action or, as the case may be, fails to adopt adequate measures to prevent obstacles to the free movement of goods that are created, in particular, by actions by private individuals on its territory aimed at products originating in other Member States is just as likely to obstruct intra-Community trade as is a positive act . . .

59 Consequently, Articles 30 [34] and 34 [35] of the Treaty require the Member States not merely themselves to refrain from adopting measures or engaging in conduct liable to constitute an obstacle to trade but also, when read with Article 5 [TEU 4] of the Treaty, to take all necessary and appropriate measures to ensure that that fundamental freedom is respected on their territory . . . Article 5 [TEU 4] of the Treaty requires the Member States to take all appropriate measures, whether general or particular, to ensure fulfilment of the obligations arising out of the Treaty and to refrain from any measures which could jeopardise the attainment of the objectives of that Treaty.

60 Having regard to the fundamental role assigned to the free movement of goods in the Community system, in particular for the proper functioning of the internal market, that obligation upon each Member State to ensure the free movement of products in its territory by taking the measures necessary and appropriate for the purposes of preventing any restriction due to the acts of individuals applies without the need to distinguish between cases where such acts affect the flow of imports or exports and those affecting merely the transit of goods.

\*   \*   \*

62 It follows that, in a situation such as that at issue in the main proceedings, where the competent national authorities are faced with restrictions on the effective exercise of a fundamental freedom enshrined in the Treaty, such as the free movement of goods, which result from actions taken by individuals, they are required to take adequate steps to ensure that freedom in the Member State concerned even if, as in the main proceedings, those goods merely pass through Austria en route for Italy or Germany.

63 It should be added that that obligation of the Member States is all the more important where the case concerns a major transit route such as the Brenner motorway, which is one of the main land links for trade between northern Europe and the north of Italy.

64 In the light of the foregoing, the fact that the competent authorities of a Member State did not ban a demonstration which resulted in the complete closure of a major transit route such as the Brenner motorway for almost 30 hours on end is capable of restricting intra-Community trade in goods and must, therefore, be regarded as constituting a measure of equivalent effect to a quantitative restriction which is, in principle, incompatible with the Community law obligations arising from Articles 30 [34] and 34 [35] of the Treaty, read together with Article 5 [TEU 4] thereof, unless that failure to ban can be objectively justified.

Whether the restriction may be justified

65 In the context of its fourth question, the referring court asks essentially whether the purpose of the demonstration on 12 and 13 June 1998 — during which the demonstrators sought to draw attention to the threat to the environment and public health posed by the constant increase in the movement of heavy goods vehicles on the Brenner motorway and to persuade the competent authorities to reinforce measures to reduce that traffic and the pollution resulting therefrom in the highly

sensitive region of the Alps — is such as to frustrate Community law obligations relating to the free movement of goods.

66 However, even if the protection of the environment and public health, especially in that region, may, under certain conditions, constitute a legitimate objective in the public interest capable of justifying a restriction of the fundamental freedoms guaranteed by the Treaty, including the free movement of goods, it should be noted . . . that the specific aims of the demonstration are not in themselves material in legal proceedings such as those instituted by Schmidberger, which seek to establish the liability of a Member State in respect of an alleged breach of Community law, since that liability is to be inferred from the fact that the national authorities did not prevent an obstacle to traffic from being placed on the Brenner motorway.

67 Indeed, for the purposes of determining the conditions in which a Member State may be liable and, in particular, with regard to the question whether it infringed Community law, account must be taken only of the action or omission imputable to that Member State.

68 In the present case, account should thus be taken solely of the objective pursued by the national authorities in their implicit decision to authorise or not to ban the demonstration in question.

69 It is apparent from the file in the main case that the Austrian authorities were inspired by considerations linked to respect of the fundamental rights of the demonstrators to freedom of expression and freedom of assembly, which are enshrined in and guaranteed by the ECHR and the Austrian Constitution.

70 In its order for reference, the national court also raises the question whether the principle of the free movement of goods guaranteed by the Treaty prevails over those fundamental rights.

71 According to settled case-law, fundamental rights form an integral part of the general principles of law the observance of which the Court ensures. For that purpose, the Court draws inspiration from the constitutional traditions common to the Member States and from the guidelines supplied by international treaties for the protection of human rights on which the Member States have collaborated or to which they are signatories. The ECHR has special significance in that respect . . .

72 The principles established by that case-law were reaffirmed in the preamble to the Single European Act and subsequently in Article F.2 of the Treaty on European Union . . . That provision states that [t]he Union shall respect fundamental rights, as guaranteed by the European Convention for the Protection of Human Rights and Fundamental Freedoms signed in Rome on 4 November 1950 and as they result from the constitutional traditions common to the Member States, as general principles of Community law.

73 It follows that measures which are incompatible with observance of the human rights thus recognised are not acceptable in the Community . . .

74 Thus, since both the Community and its Member States are required to respect fundamental rights, the protection of those rights is a legitimate interest which, in principle, justifies a restriction of the obligations imposed by Community law, even

under a fundamental freedom guaranteed by the Treaty such as the free movement of goods.

75 It is settled case-law that where, as in the main proceedings, a national situation falls within the scope of Community law and a reference for a preliminary ruling is made to the Court, it must provide the national courts with all the criteria of interpretation needed to determine whether that situation is compatible with the fundamental rights the observance of which the Court ensures and which derive in particular from the ECHR . . . .

76 In the present case, the national authorities relied on the need to respect fundamental rights guaranteed by both the ECHR and the Constitution of the Member State concerned in deciding to allow a restriction to be imposed on one of the fundamental freedoms enshrined in the Treaty.

77 The case thus raises the question of the need to reconcile the requirements of the protection of fundamental rights in the Community with those arising from a fundamental freedom enshrined in the Treaty and, more particularly, the question of the respective scope of freedom of expression and freedom of assembly, guaranteed by Articles 10 and 11 of the ECHR, and of the free movement of goods, where the former are relied upon as justification for a restriction of the latter.

78 First, whilst the free movement of goods constitutes one of the fundamental principles in the scheme of the Treaty, it may, in certain circumstances, be subject to restrictions for the reasons laid down in Article 36 of that Treaty or for overriding requirements relating to the public interest, in accordance with the Court's consistent case-law since the judgment in Case 120/78 *Rewe-Zentral* (*Cassis de Dijon*) [1979] ECR 649.

79 Second, whilst the fundamental rights at issue in the main proceedings are expressly recognised by the ECHR and constitute the fundamental pillars of a democratic society, it nevertheless follows from the express wording of paragraph 2 of Articles 10 and 11 of the Convention that freedom of expression and freedom of assembly are also subject to certain limitations justified by objectives in the public interest, in so far as those derogations are in accordance with the law, motivated by one or more of the legitimate aims under those provisions and necessary in a democratic society, that is to say justified by a pressing social need and, in particular, proportionate to the legitimate aim pursued . . .

80 Thus, unlike other fundamental rights enshrined in that Convention, such as the right to life or the prohibition of torture and inhuman or degrading treatment or punishment, which admit of no restriction, neither the freedom of expression nor the freedom of assembly guaranteed by the ECHR appears to be absolute but must be viewed in relation to its social purpose. Consequently, the exercise of those rights may be restricted, provided that the restrictions in fact correspond to objectives of general interest and do not, taking account of the aim of the restrictions, constitute disproportionate and unacceptable interference, impairing the very substance of the rights guaranteed . . .

81 In those circumstances, the interests involved must be weighed having regard to all the circumstances of the case in order to determine whether a fair balance was struck between those interests.

83 As regards the main case, it should be emphasised at the outset that the circumstances characterising it are clearly distinguishable from the situation in the case giving rise to the judgment in *Commission* v. *France*, . . . referred to by Schmidberger as a relevant precedent in the course of its legal action against Austria.

84 By comparison with the points of fact referred to by the Court . . . . in *Commission* v. *France*, cited above, it should be noted, first, that the demonstration at issue in the main proceedings took place following a request for authorisation presented on the basis of national law and after the competent authorities had decided not to ban it.

85 Second, because of the presence of demonstrators on the Brenner motorway, traffic by road was obstructed on a single route, on a single occasion and during a period of almost 30 hours. Furthermore, the obstacle to the free movement of goods resulting from that demonstration was limited by comparison with both the geographic scale and the intrinsic seriousness of the disruption caused in the case giving rise to the judgment in *Commission* v. *France*, cited above.

86 Third, it is not in dispute that by that demonstration, citizens were exercising their fundamental rights by manifesting in public an opinion which they considered to be of importance to society; it is also not in dispute that the purpose of that public demonstration was not to restrict trade in goods of a particular type or from a particular source. By contrast, in *Commission* v. *France*, cited above, the objective pursued by the demonstrators was clearly to prevent the movement of particular products originating in Member States other than the French Republic, by not only obstructing the transport of the goods in question, but also destroying those goods in transit to or through France, and even when they had already been put on display in shops in the Member State concerned.

87 Fourth, in the present case various administrative and supporting measures were taken by the competent authorities in order to limit as far as possible the disruption to road traffic. Thus, in particular, those authorities, including the police, the organisers of the demonstration and various motoring organisations cooperated in order to ensure that the demonstration passed off smoothly. Well before the date on which it was due to take place, an extensive publicity campaign had been launched by the media and the motoring organisations, both in Austria and in neighbouring countries, and various alternative routes had been designated, with the result that the economic operators concerned were duly informed of the traffic restrictions applying on the date and at the site of the proposed demonstration and were in a position timeously to take all steps necessary to obviate those restrictions. Furthermore, security arrangements had been made for the site of the demonstration.

88 Moreover, it is not in dispute that the isolated incident in question did not give rise to a general climate of insecurity such as to have a dissuasive effect on intra-Community trade flows as a whole, in contrast to the serious and repeated disruptions to public order at issue in the case giving rise to the judgment in *Commission* v. *France*, cited above.

89 Finally, concerning the other possibilities envisaged by Schmidberger with

regard to the demonstration in question, taking account of the Member States' wide margin of discretion, in circumstances such as those of the present case the competent national authorities were entitled to consider that an outright ban on the demonstration would have constituted unacceptable interference with the fundamental rights of the demonstrators to gather and express peacefully their opinion in public.

90 The imposition of stricter conditions concerning both the site — for example by the side of the Brenner motorway — and the duration — limited to a few hours only — of the demonstration in question could have been perceived as an excessive restriction, depriving the action of a substantial part of its scope. Whilst the competent national authorities must endeavour to limit as far as possible the inevitable effects upon free movement of a demonstration on the public highway, they must balance that interest with that of the demonstrators, who seek to draw the aims of their action to the attention of the public.

91 An action of that type usually entails inconvenience for non-participants, in particular as regards free movement, but the inconvenience may in principle be tolerated provided that the objective pursued is essentially the public and lawful demonstration of an opinion.

92 In that regard, the Republic of Austria submits, without being contradicted on that point, that in any event, all the alternative solutions which could be countenanced would have risked reactions which would have been difficult to control and would have been liable to cause much more serious disruption to intra-Community trade and public order, such as unauthorised demonstrations, confrontation between supporters and opponents of the group organising the demonstration or acts of violence on the part of the demonstrators who considered that the exercise of their fundamental rights had been infringed.

93 Consequently, the national authorities were reasonably entitled, having regard to the wide discretion which must be accorded to them in the matter, to consider that the legitimate aim of that demonstration could not be achieved in the present case by measures less restrictive of intra-Community trade.

## NOTES AND QUESTIONS

1. This case might be perceived as having some similarity with the *Torfaen* and *Keck* cases in that the national measure in issue here had a generalized effect on the overall volume of trade. If that were actually the case, then the ECJ might have been expected to reject an argument based on EC 28/TFEU 34. Since it did not, what was it specifically that differentiated the situation here?

2. The central issue in this case was whether the Austrian Government's action in allowing the demonstration temporarily to impair the free movement of goods was contrary to EC 28/TFEU 34 EC. Did the Court evaluate that action (and by implication the right of free expression) on an objective justification basis (per *Cassis*), or on some inherent constraint embedded at the EU level?

3. In the *Commission v. France* decision mentioned in the above judgment, the Court had found France to be in breach of EC 28/TFEU 34 by failing to take

sufficient action to prevent French farmers from impeding imports of Spanish produce by attacking trucks and shops and blocking roads. That case was distinguished on the basis that while public demonstrations might be an exercise of free speech, the actions of French farmers involved criminal damage and the French government should not have stood by and allowed that to continue unabated over a significant period.

## [E]   Abuse of the *Cassis* Doctrine

## ASSOCIATION DES CENTRES DISTRIBUTEURS EDOUARD LECLERC v. "AU BLE VERT" SARL
### Case 229/83, 1985 ECJ CELEX LEXIS 95, [1985] ECR 1

[A 1981 French Law provided that all publishers or importers of books were required to fix a retail selling price for the books that they publish or import. Where books were published in France are re-imported, the retail selling price fixed by the importer was to be no lower than that fixed by the publisher.

The "Centre Leclerc" supermarkets were retail outlets which initially sold groceries but had extended their activities to, *inter alia*, the sale of books. They had exported books published in France and then reimported them. They were sued for selling below the publisher's price and invoked EC 28/TFEU 34 in defense.]

21 The Commission considers that the legislation in question constitutes a measure equivalent in effect to a quantitative restriction on imports, contrary to Article 30 [34] of the Treaty. It observes that two provisions of the Law of August 10, 1981, are peculiar to imported books, namely: first, the price of imported books is to be fixed by the importer, the principal distributor being deemed for this purpose to be the importer; and, secondly, where books published in France are imported, the retail price is to be no lower than the price fixed by the publisher. In the Commission's view, those two provisions impede imports by making it impossible for importers to charge lower prices and preventing them from penetrating the French market by means of price competition. Leclerc expresses substantially the same view.

22 The French Government argues that legislation of the type at issue is not contrary to Article 30 [34]. In its contention, each Member State remains free to regulate its domestic trade. The restriction on retail price competition does not in any way restrict imports. Imported and domestic books are treated identically in that respect. The principal distributor is responsible for fixing the price of foreign books because he performs a commercial role in the domestic market equivalent to that performed by the publisher in distributing French books. The French Government contends that the provision relating to books published in France and re-imported is vital in order to make the legislation as a whole coherent and to prevent the re-importation of books from being used as a device for circumventing the Law.

23 Article 30 [34] of the EEC Treaty prohibits quantitative restrictions on imports and all measures having equivalent effect in trade between Member States. The Court of Justice has consistently held that under that article any national measure which is capable of hindering intra-Community trade, directly or indirectly, actually

or potentially, is to be considered a measure having an effect equivalent to a quantitative restriction. That would be the case, for instance, where national legislation treated domestic products differently from imported products or disadvantaged, in any manner whatsoever, the marketing of imported products vis-à-vis domestic products.

24 In that regard, two different situations to which the national legislation in question applies must be considered: first, that of books published in another Member State and imported into the Member State concerned, and, secondly, that of books published in the Member State concerned and re-imported, following exportation to another Member State.

25 As regards books published in another Member State and imported into the Member State concerned, a provision whereby the retail price is to be fixed by the importer responsible for complying with the statutory requirement to deposit one copy of each imported book with the authorities, that is to say, the principal distributor, transfers the responsibility for fixing the retail price to a trade at a different stage in the commercial process than the publisher and makes it impossible for any other importer of the same book to charge the retail price in the importing State that he considers adequate in light of the cost price in the State in which it was published. Contrary to the French Government's contention, such a provision does not merely assimilate the rules applying to imported books to those applying to domestic books but creates separate rules for imported books which are liable to impede trade between Member States. Such a provision must therefore be viewed as a measure equivalent in effect to a quantitative restriction on imports, contrary to Article 30 [34] of the EEC Treaty.

26 On the other hand, insofar as the legislation applies to books published in the Member State concerned and re-imported following exportation to another Member State, a provision requiring such books to be sold at the retail price fixed by the publisher does not make a distinction between domestic and imported books. Nevertheless, such a provision discourages the marketing of re-imported books by preventing the importer from passing on in the retail price an advantage resulting from a lower price obtained in the exporting Member State. Accordingly, it constitutes a measure equivalent in effect to a quantitative restriction on imports, contrary to Article 30 [34].

27 However, the above finding is not applicable where it is established that the books in question were exported for the sole purpose of re-importation in order to circumvent legislation of the type at issue.

## NOTES AND QUESTIONS

The *Leclerc* case indirectly raises the question of what is meant by "lawfully manufactured and marketed" in another Member State. There does not seem to have been any question of "manufacturing" here so the issue was purely whether the product had been marketed. What does the court say about this? Is it possible to draw a clear line between what is or is not an abuse?

# Chapter 14

# MEASURES AFFECTING THE FREE MOVEMENT OF SERVICES

## § 14.01  OVERVIEW

*Template* Sections 7.3 and 7.6

***How restrictions on the cross border provision of services can arise*** As in the case of goods, the Treaty places limitations on the Member States to prevent them from creating obstacles to the creation of the internal market with respect to cross-border services. The nature of the most frequently encountered limitations, however, is rather different because they do not address the services themselves (unlike restrictions on goods), but rather the attributes of the persons providing them (or receiving them) (EC 49/TFEU 56 et seq.). Such attributes typically are:

- residence

- nationality

- possession of a business license

- possession of specific qualifications to practice a trade or profession (since these are regulated at the state level)

- personal free movement rights (however, this subject, being closely related to free movement for workers, is covered in Chapter 17, *infra.*)

This is not to say that restrictions cannot arise from the application of laws that *do* affect the services themselves. Often these arise from application of laws relating to other areas of state competence. This is discussed further below.

***Materials in this Chapter***: The Chapter illustrates how EC 49/TFEU 56 has been applied to the various situations described above.

§ 14.02 covers requirements relating to residence or nationality.

§ 14.03 addresses the limitations on free movement arising from the non-discriminatory aspects of national systems of business licenses and qualifications.

§ 14.04 covers cases where the Member State law does in fact relate to the service itself rather than the provider or recipient.

§ 14.05 illustrates how the Treaty provisions on services interact with the fundamental competences of the Member States — police powers, taxation, budgetary matters.

761

§ 14.06 reviews the cases that have defined in different respects the scope and boundaries of application of EC 49/TFEU 56, including its application to the receipt of services.

***The scope of the provisions relating to services***  Given its apparently broad wording, EC 49/TFEU 56 might be thought to prohibit *all* restrictions on the freedom to provide services from out of state, such that Member States cannot restrict them based on any of the attributes listed above. This would entail, for example, that the host state cannot impose a licensing or educational requirement when the service is conducted from another state even though domestic providers would need to meet such a requirement. If one accepts that premise, the logical conclusion would be that out-of-state service providers should be subject only to the rules of the state where they are located.

However, the last paragraph of EC 50/TFEU 57 clearly indicates that out-of-state service providers must comply with host state regulations. This seems virtually to smother the open language of EC 49/TFEU 56. The vast majority of services require a physical presence in the host state (plumbers, lawyers, tour guides, to name but a few of the thousands of trades and professions), but the service providers in such cases apparently then must have a local license and often a local qualification. Does this then mean that EC 49/TFEU 56 is, after all, virtually a dead letter?

The ECJ has firmly rejected such a consequence. It has taken the view that the purpose of the local conditions requirement is actually to protect service providers from discrimination. This did not of course mean that it could simply void all local requirements. However, it has held such requirements to the same standard as it developed in *Cassis*: in the absence of harmonization, such rules are acceptable as long as they serve a legitimate purpose with a proportionate response. In fact, it will be seen that analogies with *Cassis* are pervasive throughout the chapter whether for that reason, or because the measure applies without distinction to domestic and cross border services. The evaluation principle has also been applied to cases where the prohibition on restrictions of services impinges on the fundamental competences of the Member States — police powers, taxation and budgetary matters (government expenditure), where distinctions in treatment between nationals and non-nationals may have to be accepted if the measures creating such distinctions are necessary and proportionate to the exercise of these powers.

***EU Action***  The liberalization of cross border services within the EU really only started in the 1980s, first with ECJ rulings and then with the impulse of the EU legislature. The latter tried to achieve liberalization of services through the adoption of specific pieces of legislation in fields such as transport, financial services, telecommunication, broadcasting and healthcare. In the case of lawyers, Directive 77/249 [1977] OJ L 78/17 on cross border legal services achieved some moderate success, but still contained quite restrictive conditions (See further the notes to the *Lawyers Services* case in this chapter.) The adoption of these specific pieces of legislation clearly aims to explicitly submit some national sensitive industry sectors to the EU rules on the internal market. However, the Council, which represents Member States' interests, often succeeds in substituting, in the final versions of legislation, language that mitigates the impact of the draft originally prepared by the European Commission and supported by the European Parliament. There continues to be intense resistance on the part of trade unions and other organizations and politicians to any notion that local qualifications and licensing rules could in principle be bypassed by those established in another Member state.

For example, obstacles arising from local requirements for business licenses and the like were addressed in a directive of 2006 (the so-called Bolkestein directive, 2006/123). The directive also addressed some establishment issues. The basic principle on which this directive was originally to be based was that duplicate burdens were to be eliminated through the recognition of home state authorization. However, this proved extremely controversial, with fears being voiced that it would compromise many aspects of regulation that supported differing social values in the various States. Indeed, since it was under discussion at the time of the referenda on the Constitutional Treaty, it was invoked as a symbol of how the EU had lost touch with its diverse population. This was manifested in particular by references during the campaign on the referendum in France to the mythical "Polish plumber" who would take away the livelihood of French nationals. In the end, the directive was watered down as regards the principle of home state regulation. The change brings it closer to the existing case law that continues to recognize the right of the host state to regulate subject to prohibitions on nondiscrimination and undue dual burdens. It should be noted that another directive, 2005/36, had already been adopted relating to a general system for the recognition of qualifications for professionals. A summary of this directive appears in Chapter 15.

Similarly, in 2011, the EU legislature adopted a directive on cross border healthcare that enables patients to benefit in some cases from medical care in other Member States. The adoption of this directive was controversial for another reason: it relates to the very politically and financially sensitive field of social security, which falls within Member States' competence. The directive still enables the Member States' authorities to subject patients, in some cases, to a prior authorization regime from their home Member State before being allowed to get treatment in another Member State. (See further the *Muller-Faure* case in this chapter.)

***Comparison with the United States*** As noted in Chapter 13, the United States Supreme Court, under the dormant commerce clause doctrine, has interpreted the Constitution's affirmative grant to Congress of the power to regulate interstate commerce as including a negative implication that, at least to some extent, the states' power under the former Articles of Confederation to interfere with interstate commerce has been limited. Much less frequently, the Court has cited the privileges and immunities clause of the Fourteenth Amendment to protect interstate commercial relationships. This clause, which provides that the "Citizens of each State shall be entitled to all Privileges and Immunities of Citizens in the several States," has as its primary focus the political integration of the United States. It protects the residents of one state from unwarranted discrimination by another within the latter's jurisdiction. It does not, however, apply to corporations, which are not considered "citizens" within the meaning of the clause.

In the U.S. as in Europe, it is often state law that lays down qualification requirements for services — as for example, in law, teaching or insurance. Additionally, business licenses are a matter for the states. Thus, there are similarities to the EU in terms of potential obstacles to the provision of cross-border services in the U.S., and the European cases often have U.S. parallels.

## § 14.02   RESIDENCE AND NATIONALITY

### JOHANNES HENRICUS MARIA VAN BINSBERGEN v. BESTUUR VAN DE BEDRIJFSVERENIGING VOOR DE METAALNIJVERHEID
#### Case 33/74, [1974] ECR 1299

[For the facts of this case see the extract in Chapter 4.]

10 The restrictions to be abolished pursuant to articles 59 [56] and 60 [57] include all requirements imposed on the person providing the service by reason in particular of his nationality or of the fact that he does not habitually reside in the state where the service is provided, which do not apply to persons established within the national territory or which may prevent or otherwise obstruct the activities of the person providing the service.

11 In particular, a requirement that the person providing the service must be habitually resident within the territory of the state where the service is to be provided may, according to the circumstances, have the result of depriving article 59 [56] of all useful effect, in view of the fact that the precise object of that article is to abolish restrictions on freedom to provide services imposed on persons who are not established in the state where the service is to be provided.

12 However, taking into account the particular nature of the services to be provided, specific requirements imposed on the person providing the service cannot be considered incompatible with the treaty where they have as their purpose the application of professional rules justified by the general good — in particular rules relating to organization, qualifications, professional ethics, supervision and liability — which are binding upon any person established in the state in which the service is provided, where the person providing the service would escape from the ambit of those rules being established in another Member State.

13 Likewise, a Member State cannot be denied the right to take measures to prevent the exercise by a person providing services whose activity is entirely or principally directed towards its territory of the freedom guaranteed by article 59 [56] for the purpose of avoiding the professional rules of conduct which would be applicable to him if he were established within that state; such a situation may be subject to judicial control under the provisions of the chapter relating to the right of establishment and not of that on the provision of services.

14 In accordance with these principles, the requirement that persons whose functions are to assist the administration of justice must be permanently established for professional purposes within the jurisdiction of certain courts or tribunals cannot be considered incompatible with the provisions of articles 59 [56] and 60 [57], where such requirement is objectively justified by the need to ensure observance of professional rules of conduct connected, in particular, with the administration of justice and with respect for professional ethics.

15 That cannot, however, be the case when the provision of certain services in a Member State is not subject to any sort of qualification or professional regulation and when the requirement of habitual residence is fixed by reference to the territory of the state in question.

16 In relation to a professional activity the exercise of which is similarly unrestricted within the territory of a particular Member State, the requirement of residence within that state constitutes a restriction which is incompatible with articles 59 [56] and 60 [57] of the Treaty if the administration of justice can satisfactorily be ensured by measures which are less restrictive, such as the choosing of an address for service.

17 It must therefore be stated in reply to the question put to the court that the first paragraph of article 59 [56] and the third paragraph of article 60 [57] of the EEC Treaty must be interpreted as meaning that the national law of a member state cannot, by imposing a requirement as to habitual residence within that state, deny persons established in another member state the right to provide services, where the provision of services is not subject to any special condition under the national law applicable.

## NOTES AND QUESTIONS

**1.** As observed already in Chapter 4, *Van Binsbergen* opened up the path to liberalization of services by declaring then article 59 (EC 49/TFEU 56) to be directly effective. This was a response to the questions posed by the national court. Could the Court have simply reshaped the questions and relied on EC 54/TFEU 61, given that the national rule was clearly a restriction based on residence?

**2.** The qualifying language of the opening phrase of EC 49/TFEU 56 made clear that the last paragraph of EC 50/TFEU 57 prevented EC 49/TFEU 56 from overriding Member State regulation of services as such, but clearly *Van Binsbergen* opened up the possibility for the application of the prohibition where there was no objective justification for the application of a State rule. What happened thereafter was a slow development of a principle similar to that which the court had developed in the context of goods, starting with *Cassis de Dijon*. In the case of services, the last paragraph of EC 50/TFEU 57 was read as an exception to the general prohibition in EC 49/TFEU 56. The Court recognized that the Member States had the right to maintain national regulations, but the purpose of such regulations would have to pursue an overriding objective of general interest, be appropriate to the achievement of that objective and proportionate to it.

## § 14.03　BUSINESS LICENSES AND QUALIFICATIONS

### CRIMINAL PROCEEDINGS AGAINST ALFRED JOHN WEBB
#### Case 279/80, 1981 ECJ CELEX LEXIS 220, [1981] ECR 3305

[Webb, based in the UK, had been prosecuted by the Dutch authorities for providing contract employee services in the Netherlands without authorization from the Minister for Social Affairs.]

4 Article 1 (1) (b) of the [Dutch] Law defines the activity in question as the provision of manpower for another person for hire or reward and otherwise than in pursuance of a contract of employment with that other person, for the performance of work usually carried on in his undertaking.

5 The accused in the main action, Alfred John Webb, who is the manager of a company incorporated under English law and established in the United Kingdom, holds a licence under United Kingdom law for the provision of manpower. The company provides technical staff for the Netherlands in particular. The staff are recruited by the company and made available, temporarily and for consideration, to undertakings located in the Netherlands, no contract of employment being entered into as between such staff and the undertakings. In the case at issue it was established by the court considering the facts that in February 1978 the company had on three occasions, not being in possession of a licence issued by the Netherlands Minister for Social Affairs, supplied workers for undertakings in the Netherlands, for consideration and otherwise than in pursuance of a contract of employment concluded with the latter, for the performance of work usually carried on in those undertakings.

\*    \*    \*

12 The second and third questions ask in substance whether Article 59 [56] of the Treaty precludes a Member State from making the provision of manpower within its territory subject to possession of a licence in the case of an undertaking established in another Member State, in particular when that undertaking holds a licence issued by the latter State.

\*    \*    \*

15 The Federal German Government and the Danish Government maintain that the legislation of the State in which the service is provided must, as a general rule, be applied in toto to any person providing such services whether or not he is established in that State by virtue of the principle of equality and, in particular, the third paragraph of Article 60 [57] of the Treaty, according to which the person providing a service may, in order to do so, pursue his activity in the Member State where the service is provided under the same conditions as are imposed by that State on its own nationals.

16 The principal aim of the third paragraph in Article 60 [57] is to enable the provider of the service to pursue his activities in the Member State where the service is given without suffering discrimination in favour of the nationals of that State. However, it does not mean that all national legislation applicable to nationals of that State and usually applied to the permanent activities of undertakings established therein may be similarly applied in its entirety to the temporary activities of undertakings which are established in other Member States.

17 . . . . [S]pecific requirements imposed on the provider of the services cannot be considered incompatible with the Treaty where they have as their purpose the application of rules governing such activities. However, the freedom to provide services is one of the fundamental principles of the Treaty and may be restricted only by provisions which are justified by the general good and which are imposed

on all persons or undertakings operating in the said State in so far as that interest is not safeguarded by the provisions to which the provider of the service is subject in the Member State of his establishment.

18 It must be noted in this respect that the provision of manpower is a particularly sensitive matter from the occupational and social point of view. Owing to the special nature of the employment relationships inherent in that kind of activity, pursuit of such a business directly affects both relations on the labour market and the lawful interests of the workforce concerned. That is evident, moreover, in the legislation of some of the Member States in this matter, which is designed first to eliminate possible abuse and secondly to restrict the scope of such activities or even prohibit them altogether.

19 It follows in particular that it is permissible for Member States, and amounts for them to a legitimate choice of policy pursued in the public interest, to subject the provision of manpower within their borders to a system of licensing in order to be able to refuse licences where there is reason to fear that such activities may harm good relations on the labour market or that the interests of the workforce affected are not adequately safeguarded. In view of the differences there may be in conditions on the labour market between one Member State and another, on the one hand, and the diversity of the criteria which may be applied with regard to the pursuit of activities of that nature on the other hand, the Member State in which the services are to be supplied has unquestionably the right to require possession of a licence issued on the same conditions as in the case of its own nationals.

20 Such a measure would be excessive in relation to the aim pursued, however, if the requirements to which the issue of a licence is subject coincided with the proofs and guarantees required in the State of establishment. In order to maintain the principle of freedom to provide services the first requirement is that in considering applications for licences and in granting them the Member State in which the service is to be provided may not make any distinction based on the nationality of the provider of the services or the place of his establishment; the second requirement is that it must take into account the evidence and guarantees already furnished by the provider of the services for the pursuit of his activities in the Member State of his establishment.

21 The reply to the second and third questions raised by the Hoge Raad is therefore that Article 59 [56] does not preclude a Member State which requires agencies for the provision of manpower to hold a licence from requiring a provider of services established in another Member State and pursuing such activities on the territory of the first Member State to comply with that condition even if he holds a licence issued by the State in which he is established, provided, however, that in the first place when considering applications for licences and in granting them the Member State in which the service is provided makes no distinction based on the nationality of the provider of the services or his place of establishment, and in the second place that it takes into account the evidence and guarantees already produced by the provider of the services for the pursuit of his activities in the Member State in which he is established.

## NOTES AND QUESTIONS

1.    The Court did not appear to consider the option of requiring the Netherlands simply to recognize the British license as sufficient. Why?

2.    In *Säger v. Dennemeyer*, Case C-76/90, 1991 ECJ CELEX LEXIS 396, [1991] ECR I-4221, at issue was the provision of patent-renewal services in Germany by an English company. In Germany such services were to be provided only by patent agents. The Advocate-General argued that notwithstanding the non-overtly discriminatory intent of the German law, it should be evaluated under EC 49/TFEU 56.

3.    The U.S. "dormant" commerce clause has been held always to forbid per se discrimination, but is more relaxed regarding state regulation that may dispropor- tionately affect out-of-state operators.

## COMMISSION v. GERMANY
### (LAWYERS SERVICES)
Case 427/85, 1988 ECJ CELEX LEXIS 53, [1988] ECR 1123

[The Commission sought a declaration that various rules in a German law of 1980 implementing Directive 77/249 on cross border lawyers'services breached EC 49/TFEU 56 and the directive. Article 5 of the directive requires foreign lawyers to work in conjunction with a German lawyer. The ECJ first upheld the Commission's argument that a rule requiring a foreign lawyer to act in conjunction with a German lawyer in cases where the client was not required to be represented by a lawyer violated the directive. Similarly it upheld the complaint that the rules applying to working in conjunction with a local lawyer were disproportionate in terms of the degree of collaboration required. It then proceeded to consider the argument of the Commission that the German law violated the directive by limiting the foreign attorney's participation in the same way that a German lawyer not admitted to that particular practice would be limited.]

34 [The relevant provision of the 1980 law] must be applied by analogy in cases where representation by lawyers admitted to practise before the judicial authority in question is required. by virtue of the code of civil procedure, such representation is compulsory in civil cases heard by a Landgericht (Regional Court) and the higher courts — (Oberlandesgerichte (Higher Regional Courts) and the Bundesgerich- tshof (Federal Court of Justice) — and by a Familiengericht (Family Court). In so far as representation by a lawyer is compulsory in cases before those courts, that lawyer must therefore be admitted to practise before the court before which the case is brought. A lawyer not so admitted only has the right to present observations in the course of the oral proceedings with the assistance of the duly admitted lawyer; the law of 1980 places the lawyer providing services in the same position.

35 The Commission considers that article 5 of the directive merely allows a requirement to be imposed that the lawyer providing services should act in conjunction with a lawyer admitted to practise before the judicial authority in question, but does not allow the services provided to be restricted to the making of statements during the oral proceedings with the assistance of the duly admitted lawyer, as occurs under the German legislation in all civil proceedings in which more

than a specified amount is involved. The Commission adds that in its opinion the situation of the lawyer providing services is not comparable to that of a German lawyer, since a lawyer providing services in another Member State does not have any establishment there and is not admitted to practise before any judicial authority there.

36 The German Government points out that a German lawyer who is not admitted to practise before the judicial authority in question must also restrict himself to the limited participation provided for in [the German law] of the Bundesrechtsanwaltsordnung and that, consequently, a lawyer providing services is not placed at a disadvantage by comparison with a lawyer established in the federal republic of Germany. The principle of restricting the right to plead to a specific geographical area was introduced in the interests of the proper administration of justice, and the lawyer's connection with a specific locality improves communication between the lawyer and the judicial authority in question and thus facilitates the conduct of the proceedings.

37 The German Government adds that, if the lawyer providing services were placed in the same position as a lawyer admitted to practise before the judicial authority in question, German lawyers would be placed at a disadvantage by comparison with their colleagues established in other Member States. To illustrate this, it refers in particular to the example of the Bundesgerichtshof, the Supreme Federal Court for civil and criminal matters: only a limited group of German lawyers specializing in appeals on points of law is admitted to practise before that court and can thus take all the procedural steps necessary, whereas, according to the Commission's view, any lawyer established in another Member State should have the same rights.

38 It appears that this difference of views is concerned essentially with the question whether the Federal Republic of Germany is entitled to impose upon lawyers providing services the same conditions as it applies to German lawyers not admitted to practise before the court in question. The provisions of the directive do not provide an answer to that question; it must be considered in the light of the principles governing the freedom to provide services deriving from articles 59 [56] and 60 [57] of the Treaty.

39 In that connection, it must be borne in mind that, according to article 59 [56], all restrictions on freedom to provide services are to be abolished, particularly in order to enable a person providing a service to pursue his activity in the state where the service is provided under the same conditions as are imposed by that state on its own nationals, to use the wording of the third paragraph of article 60 [57].

40 The principal aim of those provisions is to enable the provider of the service to pursue his activities in the Member State where the service is given without suffering discrimination in favour of the nationals of that state. . . . [T]hat does not mean that all national legislation applicable to nationals of that state and usually applied to the permanent activities of persons established therein may be similarly applied in its entirety to the temporary activities of persons who are established in other Member States.

41 The rule of territorial exclusivity contained in [the German law] is precisely part of national legislation normally relating to a permanent activity of lawyers

established in the territory of the Member State concerned, all such lawyers having the right to gain admission to practise before one, and sometimes two, German judicial authorities, and to pursue before them all the activities necessary for representation of clients or the defence of their interests. On the other hand, a lawyer providing services who is established in another Member State is not in a position to be admitted to practise before a German court.

42 In those circumstances, it must be stated that the rule of territorial exclusivity cannot be applied to activities of a temporary nature pursued by lawyers established in other Member States, since the conditions of law and fact which apply to those lawyers are not in that respect comparable to those applicable to lawyers established on German territory.

43 However, this finding only applies subject to the obligation of the lawyer providing services to work in conjunction, within the limits and on the conditions described above, with a lawyer admitted to practise before the judicial authority in question.

## NOTES AND QUESTIONS

1.   In the above case, the Court did not deny that the rule in question could be valid for German lawyers. Does this make sense? Could German lawyers assert reverse discrimination? Why was the German requirement here not objectively justifiable?

2.

The Lawyers Services directive at issue in the above case does not do much more than require Member States to allow lawyers from other Member States to act in the host state in their home state capacity giving advice on the home state's laws. If they wish to appear in court they must be introduced *pro hac vice* and (as indicated in the headnote) may be required to work in conjunction with a lawyer qualified in the host state. They are subject to both the home and host states' ethics rules. For other cases interpreting and applying Directive 77/24, see *Commission v. France*, C-294/89, 1991 ECJ CELEX LEXIS 188, [1991] ECR 3591, *Claude Gullung v. Conseils de L'ordre des avocats du barreau de Colmar et de Saverne*, Case 292/86, 1988 ECJ CELEX LEXIS 182, [1988] ECR 111. For an insightful overview of this area, see Goebel, *Lawyers in the European Community: Progress Towards Community-Wide Rights of Practice*, 15 FORDHAM INT'L L.J. 556 (1991-92).

3.

The provision of lawyers'services in other States arises from time to time in the United States. Thus, in *Birbrower, Montalbano, Condon & Frank v. Superior Court*, 17 Cal. 4th 119, 70 Cal. Rptr. 2d 304, 949 P.2d 1 (1998), attorneys of the plaintiff firm, located in New York, had negotiated on behalf of a client in California and filed an arbitration claim. Their client, being unhappy with the size of their fee, sought to avoid it by invoking the State Bar Act of 1927 prohibiting anyone but active members of the California Bar from representing clients in legal matters. Although it was asserted that arbitration proceedings did not amount to practice of law, the Court upheld the prohibition in this case. (California subsequently amended its law to exclude arbitration.) See now Rule 5.5 of the ABA's Model Rules of Professional Conduct that does support the provision of temporary services not involving any form of establishment in the host state.

## JOSEP PEÑARROJA FA v. BUREAU OF THE COUR DE CASSATION
### Joined Cases C-372/09 and C-373/09, [2011] ECR NYR

[Mr Peñarroja Fa, a Spanish national, had applied for initial enrolment, for a period of two years, in the registry of court experts of the Cour d'appel de Paris, as a Spanish-language translator. He lived in Barcelona and, for over twenty years, had pursued the profession of accredited expert translator in Catalonia. After passing a competitive public examination, he was officially appointed to that position by the Spanish Ministry of Foreign Affairs and the Catalonian Government. He invoked Directive 2005/36 on the recognition of professional qualifications. Under Article 1 of that directive, Member States must recognize professional qualifications obtained in one or more other Member States as far as "regulated professions" are concerned as long as it allows the holder of the said qualifications to pursue the same profession there, for access to and pursuit of that profession.

Mr. Fa's application was rejected by a decision of the General Assembly of the Cour d'appel de Paris of 12 November 2008. At the same time, Mr Peñarroja Fa had applied for enrolment as an Spanish-language expert translator in the national register of court experts kept by the *Bureau* of the Cour de cassation. His application was also rejected by a decision of the *Bureau* of 8 December 2008.]

27 [T]he definition of 'regulated profession' is a matter of EU law.

28 Under Article 3(1)(a) of Directive 2005/36, 'regulated profession' means 'a professional activity or group of professional activities, access to which, the pursuit of which, or one of the modes of pursuit of which is subject, directly or indirectly, by virtue of legislative, regulatory or administrative provisions to the possession of specific professional qualifications'.

29 In that regard, it should be noted that Law No 71-498 and Decree No 2004-163 [the relevant French laws] are designed, with a view to protecting litigants and to ensuring the sound administration of justice, to enable the establishment of a register of professionals in various fields of expertise, to which the courts can turn for expert opinions or the performance of other duties in the context of the various procedures relating to cases before them.

30 [T]he sole purpose of those provisions is to facilitate recourse to the services of professionals, whether members of regulated professions or not, and not to lay down rules governing recognition of a particular qualification, a matter which does not fall within the competence of the cours d'appel or of the *Bureau* of the Cour de cassation. Moreover, those courts may lawfully have recourse to experts who are not entered in those registers. Accordingly, those provisions do not, by themselves, establish a 'regulated profession'.

32 Consequently, . . . the duties of court expert translators, as discharged by experts enrolled in a register such as the national register of court experts

maintained by the Cour de cassation, are not covered by the definition of 'regulated profession'set out in Article 3(1)(a) of Directive 2005/36.

\* \* \*

47 [M]r Peñarroja Fa resides in Barcelona, pursues in Catalonia the profession of accredited expert translator and wishes to be enrolled as a translator, in France, in the two registers of court experts at issue in the main proceedings.

48 Since it is not apparent from the documents before the Court whether Mr Peñarroja Fa intends to establish himself on French territory, the question referred to the Court must be examined only in the light of the provisions of the EC Treaty which apply to the freedom to provide services.

49 The French Government argues that national legislation such as that at issue in the main proceedings, concerning both the register of court experts maintained by each cour d'appel and the national register of court experts, does not constitute a restriction on the freedom to provide court expertise services, inter alia because judges may as a general rule appoint any person of their choice who is not entered in the registers of court experts.

50 In that context, it should be noted that Article 49 EC [56] requires not only the elimination of all discrimination on grounds of nationality against providers of services who are established in another Member State, but also the abolition of any restriction — even if it applies to national providers of services and to those of other Member States alike — which is liable to prohibit, to impede or to render less advantageous the activities of a provider of services established in another Member State in which he lawfully provides similar services . . .

51 [E]ven though, under national law, registers of court experts are established 'for the guidance of the judges', they are intended to make it possible for the courts to ensure that the professionals who assist them have the skills and other attributes essential to the quality and efficiency of the public administration of justice.

52 In the light of that objective, it must be held that the establishment of registers of court experts such as those at issue in the main proceedings is likely to influence the choice made by the courts, that is to say, they will tend to appoint experts enrolled in such registers, whom they can assume to have the attributes necessary for assisting them.

53 In consequence, even though there is no formal obligation requiring the courts to appoint only those experts who are enrolled in those registers, the establishment of the registers constitutes a restriction of the freedom to provide the services of a court expert translator.

54 [E]ven in the absence of harmonisation in this area, such a restriction of the freedom to provide services may, where it is applicable to all individuals or undertakings carrying on business in the territory of the host Member State, be justified by an overriding reason in the public interest to the extent that it is appropriate for securing the attainment of the objective which it pursues and does not go beyond what is necessary in order to attain it, and in so far as that interest is not safeguarded by the rules to which such a service provider is subject in the Member State of establishment.

55 Among those overriding reasons in the public interest are the protection of litigants and the sound administration of justice.

57 In that regard, although the protection of litigants and the sound administration of justice may justify the establishment of a register of experts who will be those most often called upon in practice, that register must nevertheless be established on the basis of objective and non-discriminatory factors.

58 It is settled law that national authorities must ensure, inter alia, that qualifications obtained in another Member State are accorded their proper value and duly taken into account.

60 [T]here is no requirement under any statutory or legislative provision to state the reasons for a decision refusing initial enrolment in those registers; that the procedure for enrolment does not involve any act which might come within the scope of the French procedure for accessing administrative documents; and that, when hearing an action contesting a decision refusing enrolment, the Cour de cassation merely confirms that the proper procedure was followed for consideration of the application and, in consequence, does not address issues such as the professional attributes of the candidate.

61 Consequently, it is clear that decisions refusing enrolment of court expert translators in the registers of experts in circumstances such as those of the case before the referring court are not open to effective review by the courts as regards the taking into account of the experience and qualifications obtained and recognised in other Member States.

63 It follows that all decisions must be open to judicial scrutiny enabling their legality under EU law to be reviewed. In order to ensure that such review by the courts is effective, the interested party must be able to obtain the reasons for the decision taken in relation to him, thus enabling that interested party to defend himself under the best possible conditions and to decide, with full knowledge of the relevant facts, whether it is worth applying to the courts.

64 Consequently, in so far as national legislation which constitutes a restriction on the freedom to provide services does not establish mechanisms to ensure effective judicial scrutiny of the taking into account at their proper value of the qualifications of a court expert translator recognised by courts in other Member States, that legislation does not comply with the requirements of article 49 EC [56].

## NOTES AND QUESTIONS

1. Why was the profession at issue here not considered to be a regulated profession? What was the significance of this conclusion?

2. Note the Court's ruling that EC 49/TFEU 56 requires that there be a means to challenge denial of entry into the register. Thus, effectively, the denying authority would have to give reasons for its denial. What sort of reasons might then justify a refusal?

## § 14.04  MEASURES AFFECTING THE SERVICES THEMSELVES

### WOLFF & MULLER GMBH & CO. KG v. JOSE FILIPE PEREIRA FELIX.
### Case C-60/03, 2004 CELEX LEXIS 472, [2004] ECR I-9553

[Under Article 5 of Directive 96/71 concerning the posting of workers in the framework of the provision of services, [1997] OJ L 18/1 the Member States were to take appropriate measures to ensure protection of workers from default under the host country's minimum pay laws. In particular they were to ensure that the workers and/or their representatives have available to them adequate procedures for the enforcement of obligations under this Directive. In fact, under Article 3(1)(c) of the directive, undertakings established in the host state were to be held responsible for ensuring that workers posted to them in their territory enjoy the benefit of the host territory's labor laws including minimum rates of pay. In Germany, this responsibility was imposed by way of a requirement that the host state recipient of the services guarantee minimum wage payments to the workers posted to it (the "AEntG"). Wolff & Muller, a construction undertaking, had subcontracted building work in Germany to a Portuguese company. Pereira, who was a Portuguese national employed by the latter company, sued Wolff and Muller for back wages based on the German minimum wage legislation. The ECJ had to consider whether this guarantee requirement constituted an impediment to the provision of services contrary to Directive 96/71 and EC 49/TFEU 56.]

30. It is apparent from the wording of Article 5 of Directive 96/71 that the Member States have a wide margin of appreciation in determining the form and detailed rules governing the adequate procedures under the second paragraph of Article 5. In applying that wide margin of appreciation they must however at all times observe the fundamental freedoms guaranteed by the Treaty . . . and, thus, in regard to the main proceedings, freedom to provide services.

31. In that regard it should first be recalled that, under settled case-law, Article 49 EC [56] requires not only the elimination of all discrimination on grounds of nationality against providers of services who are established in another Member State, but also the abolition of any restriction, even if it applies without distinction to national providers of services and to those of other Member States, which is liable to prohibit, impede or render less attractive the activities of a provider of services established in another Member State in which he lawfully provides similar services . . .

32. As the Court held, the application of the host Member State's domestic legislation to service providers is liable to prohibit, impede or render less attractive the provision of services by persons or undertakings established in other Member States to the extent that it involves expenses and additional administrative and economic burdens . . .

33. It is for the referring court to determine whether that is the case in the main proceedings concerning liability as guarantor. In that connection it is important to take account of the effect of that measure on the provision of services not only by

subcontractors established in another Member State but also by any general undertakings from that State.

34. It is further clear from settled case-law that, where legislation such as Paragraph 1a of the AEntG, on the supposition that it constitutes a restriction on freedom to provide services, is applicable to all persons and undertakings operating in the territory of the Member State in which the service is provided, it may be justified where it meets overriding requirements relating to the public interest in so far as that interest is not safeguarded by the rules to which the provider of such a service is subject in the Member State in which he is established and in so far as it is appropriate for securing the attainment of the objective which it pursues and does not go beyond what is necessary in order to attain it . . .

35. Overriding reasons relating to the public interest which have been recognised by the Court include the protection of workers . . .

36. However, although it may be acknowledged that, in principle, the application by the host Member State of its minimum-wage legislation to providers of services established in another Member State pursues an objective of public interest, namely the protection of employees . . . the same is true in principle of measures adopted by the host Member State and intended to reinforce the procedural arrangements enabling a posted worker usefully to assert his right to a minimum rate of pay.

37. In fact, if entitlement to minimum rates of pay constitutes a feature of worker protection, procedural arrangements ensuring observance of that right, such as the liability of the guarantor in the main proceedings, must likewise be regarded as being such as to ensure that protection.

38. In regard to the national court's observation that the priority purpose pursued by the national legislature on adoption of Paragraph 1(a) of the AEntG is to protect the national job market rather than remuneration of the worker, it should be pointed out that it is for that court to verify whether, on an objective view, the legislation at issue in the main proceedings secures the protection of posted workers. It is necessary to determine whether those rules confer a genuine benefit on the workers concerned, which significantly augments their social protection. In this context, the stated intention of the legislature may lead to a more careful assessment of the alleged benefits conferred on workers by the measures which it has adopted . . .

39. The referring court has doubts concerning the genuine benefit to posted workers of liability as guarantor owing both to the practical difficulties with which they would be faced in asserting before the German courts their right to pay as against the general undertaking and owing to the fact that that protection would lose its economic value when the actual chance to be gainfully employed in Germany is appreciably reduced.

40. However, as Mr Pereira Felix, the German, Austrian and French Governments and the Commission rightly point out, it is none the less the case that a provision such as Paragraph 1(a) of the AEntG benefits posted workers on the ground that, to the advantage of the latter, it adds to the primary obligant in respect of the minimum rate of pay, namely the employer, a further obligant who is jointly liable

with the first debtor and is generally more solvent. On an objective view a rule of that kind is therefore such as to ensure the protection of posted workers. Moreover, the dispute in the main proceedings itself appears to confirm that Paragraph 1(a) of the AEntG is of protective intent.

41. Inasmuch as one of the objectives pursued by the national legislature is to prevent unfair competition on the part of undertakings paying their workers at a rate less than the minimum rate of pay, a matter which it is for the referring court to determine, such an objective may be taken into consideration as an overriding requirement capable of justifying a restriction on freedom to provide services provided that the conditions mentioned in paragraph 34 hereof are met.

42. Moreover, as the Austrian Government has rightly pointed out in its observations, there is not necessarily any contradiction between the objective of upholding fair competition on the one hand and ensuring worker protection, on the other. The fifth recital in the preamble to Directive 96/71 demonstrates that those two objectives can be pursued concomitantly.

43. Finally, as regards the observations of Wolff and Muller according to which liability as guarantor is disproportionate in relation to the objective pursued, it is in fact clear from the case-law cited at paragraph 34 hereof that, in order to be justified, a measure must be apt to ensure attainment of the objective pursued by it and must not go beyond what is necessary in that connection.

44. It is for the national court to determine that those conditions are met in regard to the objective sought, which is to ensure protection of the worker concerned.

45. In those circumstances the reply to the question referred must be that Article 5 of Directive 96/71, interpreted in the light of Article 49 EC [56], does not preclude, in a case such as that in the main proceedings, a national system whereby, when subcontracting the conduct of building work to another undertaking, a building contractor becomes liable, in the same way as a guarantor who has waived the defence of prior recourse, for the obligation on that undertaking or that undertaking's subcontractors to pay the minimum wage to a worker or to pay contributions to a joint scheme for parties to a collective agreement where the minimum wage means the sum payable to the worker after deduction of tax, social security contributions, payments towards the promotion of employment or other such social insurance payments (net pay), if the safeguarding of workers' pay is not the primary objective of the legislation or is merely a subsidiary objective.

## NOTES AND QUESTIONS

1.  How did the ECJ in this case deal with the argument that the German law created an undue burden on the interstate provision of services, given that it applied to any contractor services in the building sector? Would this decision not have a chilling effect on the provision of cheap labor from the less developed countries of the EU? Is that a good thing?

2.  Could it have been argued that the directive itself was contrary to EC 49/TFEU 56?

**3.** In terms of the social impact of statutes regulating the conduct of trades or professions, compare *Lochner v. New York*, 198 U.S. 45 (1905). Here, the Supreme Court held unconstitutional a statute of New York limiting the number of hours a baker could work a day to 10. The Supreme Court found there to be no good grounds relating to the health of the workers or to their possible exploitation to justify restrictions on the right to freedom of contract as protected by the Fourteenth Amendment, (which of course extends to the states and does not require any interstate commerce connection). In terms of social policy versus freedom of commerce, how would you characterize the ECJ's approach in *Wolff*?

**4.** In *Josef Corsten*, Case C-58/98, 2000 ECJ CELEX LEXIS 268, [2000] ECR I-7919, the Court ruled that in the dispositive part of the judgment that:

> Article 59 [56] of the EC Treaty . . . and Article 4 of Council Directive 64/427/EEC of 7 July 1964 laying down detailed provisions concerning transitional measures in respect of activities of self-employed persons in manufacturing and processing industries falling within ISIC Major Groups 23-40 (Industry and small craft industries) preclude rules of a Member State which make the carrying out on its territory of skilled trade work by providers of services established in other Member States subject to an authorisation procedure which is likely to delay or complicate exercise of the right to freedom to provide services, where examination of the conditions governing access to the activities concerned has been carried out and it has been established that those conditions are satisfied. Furthermore, any requirement of entry on the trades register of the host Member State, assuming it was justified, should neither give rise to additional administrative expense nor entail compulsory payment of subscriptions to the chamber of trades."

## ALPINE INVESTMENTS BV v. MINISTER VAN FINANCIEN
### Case C-384/93, 1995 ECJ CELEX LEXIS 210, [1995] ECR I-1141

[Alpine Investments, a Dutch company specializing in commodities futures, challenged the restriction imposed on it by the Netherlands Ministry of Finance prohibiting it from contacting individuals by telephone without their prior consent in writing in order to offer them various financial services (a practice known as "cold calling").]

4 The parties to a commodities futures contract undertake to buy or sell a specified quantity of a commodity of a given quality at a price and date fixed at the time the contract is concluded. They do not, however, intend actually to take delivery of or to deliver the commodity but contract solely in the hope of profiting from price fluctuations between the time the contract is concluded and the month of delivery. This can be done by entering into a mirror-image transaction on the futures market before the beginning of the month of delivery.

5 Alpine Investments offers three types of service in relation to commodities futures contracts: portfolio management, investment advice and the transmission of clients' orders to brokers operating on commodities futures markets both within and outside the Community. It has clients not only in the Netherlands but also in

Belgium, France and the United Kingdom. It is not however established anywhere outside the Netherlands.

*    *    *

18 First, [the national court] asks whether the fact that the services in question are just offers without, as yet, an identifiable recipient of the service precludes application of Article 59 [56] of the Treaty.

19 The freedom to provide services would become illusory if national rules were at liberty to restrict offers of services. The prior existence of an identifiable recipient cannot therefore be a condition for application of the provisions on the freedom to provide services.

20 The second aspect of the question is whether Article 59 [56] covers services which the provider offers by telephone to persons established in another Member State and which he provides without moving from the Member State in which he is established.

21 In this case, the offers of services are made by a provider established in one Member State to a potential recipient established in another Member State. It follows from the express terms of Article 59 [56] that there is therefore a provision of services within the meaning of that provision.

22 The answer to the first question is therefore that, on a proper construction, Article 59 [56] of the EEC Treaty covers services which the provider offers by telephone to potential recipients established in other Member States and provides without moving from the Member State in which he is established.

The second question

23 The national court's second question asks whether rules of a Member State which prohibit providers of services established in its territory from making unsolicited telephone calls to potential clients established in other Member States in order to offer their services constitute a restriction on freedom to provide services within the meaning of Article 59 [56] of the Treaty.

24 The preliminary observation should be made that the prohibition at issue applies to the offer of cross-border services.

25 In order to reply to the national court's question, three points must be examined in turn.

26 First, it must be determined whether the prohibition against telephoning potential clients in another Member State without their prior consent can constitute a restriction on freedom to provide services. The national court draws the Court's attention to the fact that providers established in the Member States where the potential recipients reside are not necessarily subject to the same prohibition or in any event not on the same terms.

27 A prohibition such as that at issue in the main proceedings does not constitute a restriction on freedom to provide services within the meaning of Article 59 [56] solely by virtue of the fact that other Member States apply less strict rules to

providers of similar services established in their territory . . .

28 However, such a prohibition deprives the operators concerned of a rapid and direct technique for marketing and for contacting potential clients in other Member States. It can therefore constitute a restriction on the freedom to provide cross-border services.

29 Secondly, it must be considered whether that conclusion may be affected by the fact that the prohibition at issue is imposed by the Member State in which the provider is established and not by the Member State in which the potential recipient is established.

30 The first paragraph of Article 59 [56] of the Treaty prohibits restrictions on freedom to provide services within the Community in general. Consequently, that provision covers not only restrictions laid down by the State of destination but also those laid down by the State of origin. As the Court has frequently held, the right freely to provide services may be relied on by an undertaking as against the State in which it is established if the services are provided for persons established in another Member State . . .

31 It follows that the prohibition of cold calling does not fall outside the scope of Article 59 [56] of the Treaty simply because it is imposed by the State in which the provider of services is established.

32 Finally, certain arguments adduced by the Netherlands Government and the United Kingdom must be considered.

33 They submit that the prohibition at issue falls outside the scope of Article 59 [56] of the Treaty because it is a generally applicable measure, it is not discriminatory and neither its object nor its effect is to put the national market at an advantage over providers of services from other Member States. Since it affects only the way in which the services are offered, it is analogous to the non-discriminatory measures governing selling arrangements which, according to the decision in Joined Cases C-267 and 268/91 Keck and Mithouard 1993 ECR I-6097, paragraph 16, do not fall within the scope of Article 30 [34] of the Treaty.

34 Those arguments cannot be accepted.

35 Although a prohibition such as the one at issue in the main proceedings is general and non-discriminatory and neither its object nor its effect is to put the national market at an advantage over providers of services from other Member States, it can none the less, as has been held above (see paragraph 28), constitute a restriction on the freedom to provide cross-border services.

36 Such a prohibition is not analogous to the legislation concerning selling arrangements held in Keck and Mithouard to fall outside the scope of Article 30 of the Treaty.

37 According to that judgment, the application to products from other Member States of national provisions restricting or prohibiting, within the Member State of importation, certain selling arrangements is not such as to hinder trade between Member States so long as, first, those provisions apply to all relevant traders operating within the national territory and, secondly, they affect in the same

manner, in law and in fact, the marketing of domestic products and of those from other Member States. The reason is that the application of such provisions is not such as to prevent access by the latter to the market of the Member State of importation or to impede such access more than it impedes access by domestic products.

38 A prohibition such as that at issue is imposed by the Member State in which the provider of services is established and affects not only offers made by him to addressees who are established in that State or move there in order to receive services but also offers made to potential recipients in another Member State. It therefore directly affects access to the market in services in the other Member States and is thus capable of hindering intra-Community trade in services.

39 The answer to the second question is therefore that rules of a Member State which prohibit providers of services established in its territory from making unsolicited telephone calls to potential clients established in other Member States in order to offer their services constitute a restriction on freedom to provide services within the meaning of Article 59 [56] of the Treaty.

The third question

40 The national court's third question asks whether imperative reasons of public interest justify the prohibition of cold calling and whether that prohibition must be considered to be objectively necessary and proportionate to the objective pursued.

41 The Netherlands Government argues that the prohibition of cold calling in off-market commodities futures trading seeks both to safeguard the reputation of the Netherlands financial markets and to protect the investing public.

42 Financial markets play an important role in the financing of economic operators and, given the speculative nature and the complexity of commodities futures contracts, the smooth operation of financial markets is largely contingent on the confidence they inspire in investors. That confidence depends in particular on the existence of professional regulations serving to ensure the competence and trustworthiness of the financial intermediaries on whom investors are particularly reliant.

43 Although the protection of consumers in the other Member States is not, as such, a matter for the Netherlands authorities, the nature and extent of that protection does none the less have a direct effect on the good reputation of Netherlands financial services.

44 Maintaining the good reputation of the national financial sector may therefore constitute an imperative reason of public interest capable of justifying restrictions on the freedom to provide financial services.

45 As for the proportionality of the restriction at issue, it is settled case-law that requirements imposed on the providers of services must be appropriate to ensure achievement of the intended aim and must not go beyond that which is necessary in order to achieve that objective . . .

46 As the Netherlands Government has justifiably submitted, in the case of cold

calling the individual, generally caught unawares, is in a position neither to ascertain the risks inherent in the type of transactions offered to him nor to compare the quality and price of the caller's services with competitors' offers. Since the commodities futures market is highly speculative and barely comprehensible for non-expert investors, it was necessary to protect them from the most aggressive selling techniques.

47 Alpine Investments argues however that the Netherlands Government's prohibition of cold calling is not necessary because the Member State of the provider of services should rely on the controls imposed by the Member State of the recipient.

48 That argument must be rejected. The Member State from which the telephone call is made is best placed to regulate cold calling. Even if the receiving State wishes to prohibit cold calling or to make it subject to certain conditions, it is not in a position to prevent or control telephone calls from another Member State without the cooperation of the competent authorities of that State.

49 Consequently, the prohibition of cold calling by the Member State from which the telephone call is made, with a view to protecting investor confidence in the financial markets of that State, cannot be considered to be inappropriate to achieve the objective of securing the integrity of those markets.

50 Alpine Investments also argues that a general prohibition of telephone canvassing of potential clients is not necessary for the achievement of the objectives pursued by the Netherlands authorities. Requiring broking firms to tape-record unsolicited telephone calls made by them would suffice to protect consumers effectively. Such rules have moreover been adopted in the United Kingdom by the Securities and Futures Authority.

51 That point of view cannot be accepted. . . . . [T]he fact that one Member State imposes less strict rules than another Member State does not mean that the latter's rules are disproportionate and hence incompatible with Community law.

52 Alpine Investments argues finally that, since it is of a general nature, the prohibition of cold calling does not take into account the conduct of individual undertakings and accordingly imposes an unnecessary burden on undertakings which have never been the subject of complaints by consumers.

53 That argument must also be rejected. Limiting the prohibition of cold calling to certain undertakings because of their past conduct might not be sufficient to achieve the objective of restoring and maintaining investor confidence in the national securities markets in general.

54 In any event, the rules at issue are limited in scope. First, they prohibit only the contacting of potential clients by telephone or in person without their prior agreement in writing, while other techniques for making contact are still permitted. Next, the measure affects relations with potential clients but not with existing clients who may still give their written agreement to further calls. Finally, the prohibition of unsolicited telephone calls is limited to the sector in which abuses have been found, namely the commodities futures market.

55 In the light of the above, the prohibition of cold calling does not appear disproportionate to the objective which it pursues.

56 The answer to the third question is therefore that Article 59 [56] does not preclude national rules which, in order to protect investor confidence in national financial markets, prohibit the practice of making unsolicited telephone calls to potential clients resident in other Member States to offer them services linked to investment in commodities futures.

## NOTES AND QUESTIONS

Would it not be more appropriate to expect the service here to be regulated in the host state? Is there not a danger of conflicting regulations in such cases? How do you explain the Court's willingness to evaluate the measure here, given that the host state regulation exception in EC 49/TFEU 56 was not applicable?

## CODITEL v. CINE VOG FILMS
### Case 62/79, [1980] ECR 881

2 [The] questions [referred] were raised during an action brought by a Belgian cinematographic film distribution company, Ciné Vog Films SA, the respondent before the Cour d'Appel, for infringement of copyright. The action is against a French company, Les Films la Boétie, and three Belgian cable television diffusion companies, which are hereafter referred to collectively as the Coditel companies. Compensation is sought for the damage allegedly caused to Ciné Vog by the reception in Belgium of a broadcast by German television of the film *Le Boucher* for which Ciné Vog obtained exclusive rights in Belgium from Les Films la Boétie.

3 It is apparent from the file that the Coditel companies provide, with the authority of the Belgian administration, a cable television diffusion service covering part of Belgium. Television sets belonging to subscribers to the service are linked by cable to a central aerial having special technical features which enable Belgian broadcasts to be picked up as well as certain foreign broadcasts which the subscriber cannot always receive with a private aerial, and which furthermore improve the quality of the pictures and sound received by the subscribers.

\* \* \*

5 The facts of the case bearing upon the outcome of the dispute were summarised by the Cour d'Appel as follows. By an agreement of 8 July 1969 Les Films la Boétie, acting as the owner of all the proprietary rights in the film *Le Boucher*, gave Ciné Vog the 'exclusive right' to distribute the film in Belgium for seven years. The film was shown in cinemas in Belgium starting on 15 May 1970. However, on 5 January 1971 German television's first channel broadcast a German version of the film and this broadcast could be picked up in Belgium. Ciné Vog considered that the broadcast had jeopardised the commercial future of the film in Belgium. It relied upon this ground of complaint both against Les Films la Boétie, for not having observed the exclusivity of the rights which it had transferred to it, and against the Coditel companies for having relayed the relevant broadcast over their cable diffusion networks.

6 The Cour d'Appel first of all examined the activities of the cable television diffusion companies from the point of view of copyright infringement. It considered

that those companies had made a 'communication to the public' of the film within the meaning of the provisions applying in this field and that, as regards copyright law and subject to the effect thereon of Community law, they therefore needed the authorisation of Ciné Vog to relay the films over their networks. The effects of this reasoning by the Cour d'Appel that the authorisation given by the copyright owner to German television to broadcast the film did not include authority to relay the film over cable diffusion networks outside Germany, or at least those existing in Belgium.

7 The Cour d'Appel then went on to examine in the light of Community law the argument of the Coditel companies that any prohibition on the transmission of films, the copyright in which has been assigned by the producer to a distribution company covering the whole Belgium, is contrary to the provisions of the EEC Treaty, in particular to Article 85 [81] and Articles 59 [49] and 60 [50]. After rejecting the argument based on Article 59 [49] 'in so far as it limits the possibility for a transmitting station established in a country which borders on Belgium, and which is the country of the persons for whom a service is intended, freely to provide that service'.

In the opinion of the appellant companies, Article 59 [49] must be understood to mean that it prohibits restrictions on freedom to provide services and not merely restrictions on the freedom of activity of those providing services, and that it covers all cases where the provision of a service involves or has involved at an earlier stage or will involve at a later state the crossing of intra-Community frontiers.

*    *    *

11 The second question [referred by the Cour d'Appel] raises the problem of whether Articles 59 [49] and 60 [50] of the Treaty prohibit an assignment, limited to the territory of a member-state, of the copyright in a film, in view of the fact that a series of such assignments might result in the partitioning of the Common Market as regards the undertaking of economic activity in the film industry.

12 A cinematographic film belongs to the category of literary and artistic works made available to the public by performances which may be infinitely repeated. In this respect the problems involved in the observance of copyright in relation to the requirements of the Treaty are not the same as those which arise in connection with literary and artistic works the placing of which at the disposal of the public is inseparable from the circulation of the material form of the works, as in the case of books or records.

13 In these circumstances the owner of the copyright in a film and his assigns have a legitimate interest in calculating the fees due in respect of the authorisation to exhibit the film on the basis of the actual or probable number of performances and in authorising a television broadcast of the film only after it has been exhibited in cinemas for a certain period of time. It appears from the file on the present case that the contract made between Les Films la Boétie and Ciné Vog stipulated that the exclusive right which was assigned included the right to exhibit the film *Le Boucher* publicly in Belgium by way of projection in cinemas and on television could not be exercised until 40 months after the first showing of the film in Belgium.

14 These facts are important in two regards. On the one hand, they highlight the

fact that the right of a copyright owner and his assigns to require fees for any showing of a film is part of the essential function of copyright in this type of literary and artistic work. On the other hand, they demonstrate that the exploitation of copyright in films and the fees attaching thereto cannot be regulated without regard being had to the possibility of television broadcasts of those films. The question whether an assignment of copyright limited to the territory of a member-State is capable of constituting a restriction on freedom to provide services must be examined in this context.

15 Whilst Article 59 [49] of the Treaty prohibits restrictions upon freedom to provide services, it does not thereby mean restrictions upon the exercise of certain economic activities which have their origin in the application of national legislation for the protection of intellectual property, save where such application constitutes a means of arbitrary discrimination or a disguised restriction on trade between member-states. Such would be the case if that application enable parties to an assignment of copyright to create artificial barriers to trade between member-States.

16 The effect of this is that, whilst copyright entails the right to demand fees for any showing or performance, the rules of the Treaty cannot in principle constitute an obstacle to the geographical limits which the parties to a contract of assignment have agreed upon in order to protect the author and his assigns in this regard. The mere fact that those geographical limits may coincide with national frontiers does not point to a different solution in a situation where television is organized in the member-states largely on the basis of statutory broadcasting monopolies, which indicates that a limitation other than the geographical field of application of an assignment is often impracticable.

17 The exclusive assignee of the performing right in a film for the whole of a member-State may therefore rely upon his right against cable television diffusion companies which have transmitted that film on their diffusion network having received it from a television broadcasting station established in another member-State without thereby infringing Community law.

18 Consequently the answer to the question referred to the Court by the Cour d'Appel, Brussels, should be that the provisions of the Treaty relating to the freedom to provide services do not preclude an assignee of the performing right in a cinematographic film in a member-State from relying upon his right to prohibit the exhibition of that film in that State, without his authority, by means of cable diffusion if the film so exhibited is picked up and transmitted after being broadcast in another member-State by a third party with the consent of the original owner of the right.

19 It is clear from the answer given to the second question that Community law, on the assumption that it applies to the activities of the cable diffusion companies which are the subject-matter of the dispute brought before the national court, has no effect upon the application by that court of the provisions of copyright legislation in a case such as this. Therefore there is no need to answer the first question.

# NOTES AND QUESTIONS

The *Coditel* case raised intellectual property issues (copyright) in the context of EC 49 and 50/TFEU 56 and 57. How were such articles relevant? How did the ECJ come to the conclusion that the copyright laws did not infringe EC 49/TFEU 56?

## § 14.05  INDIRECT RESTRICTIONS

### [A]  Police Powers

### MARC MICHEL JOSEMANS v. BURGEMEESTER VAN MAASTRICHT
Case C-137/09 NYR

[Mr. Josemans ran the 'Easy Going' coffee-shop in Maastricht, where cannabis could be sold and consumed without criminal prosecution. However, the city of Maastricht had restricted access to residents of the Netherlands to prevent narcotic "tourism"., The Mayor of Maastricht had declared the establishment in question temporarily closed following two reports attesting that persons who are not resident in the Netherlands had been admitted to it contrary to the provisions in force in that municipality (the "APV" law).]

51. As regards the applicability of Article 12 EC, [18] which lays down a general prohibition of all discrimination on grounds of nationality, it should be noted that that provision applies independently only to situations governed by European Union law for which the EC Treaty lays down no specific rules of non-discrimination . . .

52. As the principle of non-discrimination has been implemented, in the area of the freedom to provide services, by Article 49 EC [56], Article 12 EC [18] does not apply in circumstances such as those in the main proceedings.

53. As regards the applicability of Article 18 EC [21], that provision, which lays down generally the right for every citizen of the Union to move and reside freely within the territory of the Member States, finds specific expression in the provisions guaranteeing the freedom to provide services . . . As citizens of the European Union who do not reside in the Netherlands and wish to go into coffee-shops in the municipality of Maastricht to consume lawful goods there are to be regarded as 'persons for whom'services 'are intended' within the meaning of Article 49 EC [56] it is not necessary for the Court to rule on the interpretation of Article 18 EC [21].

54. Consequently, . . . , in the course of marketing narcotic drugs which are not distributed through channels strictly controlled by the competent authorities with a view to use for medical or scientific purposes, a coffee-shop proprietor may not rely on Articles 12 EC [18], 18 EC [21], 29 EC [35] or 49 EC [56] to object to municipal rules such as those at issue in the main proceedings, which prohibit the admission of persons who are non-resident in the Netherlands to such establishments. As regards the marketing of non-alcoholic beverages and food in those establishments, Article 49 EC [56] et seq. may be relied on by such a proprietor.

\*    \*    \*

57. It is common ground that, under the rules at issue in the main proceedings, only 'residents' are admitted to coffee-shops. That term covers, under Article 2.3.1.1(1)(d) of the APV, any person who has his actual place of residence in the Netherlands. Consequently, the proprietors of such establishments are not entitled to provide catering services to persons residing in other Member States and those persons are precluded from enjoying such services.

58. It is clear from the Court's case-law that the principle of equal treatment, of which Article 49 EC [56] embodies a specific instance, prohibits not only overt discrimination by reason of nationality but also all covert forms of discrimination which, by the application of other criteria of differentiation, lead in fact to the same result . . .

59. That is true, in particular, of a measure under which a distinction is drawn on the basis of residence, in that that requirement is liable to operate mainly to the detriment of nationals of other Member States, since non-residents are in the majority of cases foreigners . . .

60. It must, however, be examined whether such a restriction may be justified by legitimate interests which European Union law recognises.

\*    \*    \*

61. The German Government takes the view that the rules at issue in the main proceedings are justified by the derogating provisions set out in Article 46(1) EC in conjunction with Article 55 EC, namely grounds of public policy, public security or public health. The Burgemeester van Maastricht and the Belgian Government rely, in the alternative, on grounds of public policy and public security. According to the Netherlands Government, the need to combat drug tourism constitutes a public-interest objective for the purposes of the line of case-law initiated in 'Cassis de Dijon' (Case 120/78 Rewe-Zentral [1979] ECR 649).

62. While acknowledging the importance of the fight against drug tourism, the Commission submits that, as they are discriminatory, those rules can be compatible with European Union law only if they are covered by an express derogating provision, namely Article 46 EC [52] in conjunction with Article 55 EC [62]. The derogations provided for by those provisions should be interpreted restrictively. As regards more specifically grounds of public policy, they may be relied on only if there is a genuine and sufficiently serious threat to a fundamental interest of society . . .

63. In the present case, it is common ground that the rules at issue in the main proceedings are intended to put an end to the public nuisance caused by the large number of tourists wanting to purchase or consume cannabis in the coffee-shops in the municipality of Maastricht. According to the information provided by the Burgemeester van Maastricht at the hearing, the 14 coffee-shops in the municipality attract around 10 000 visitors per day and a little more than 3.9 million visitors per year, 70% of which are not resident in the Netherlands.

64. The Burgemeester van Maastricht and the Netherlands Government state that the problems associated with the sale of 'soft' drugs which arise in that commune,

such as the various forms of public nuisance and crime and the increasing number of illegal points of sale of drugs, including 'hard' drugs, have been exacerbated by drug tourism. The Belgian, German and French Governments refer to the public order problems to which that phenomenon, including the illegal export of cannabis, gives rise in Member States other than the Kingdom of the Netherlands, in particular in neighbouring States.

65. It must be pointed out that combating drug tourism and the accompanying public nuisance is part of combating drugs. It concerns both the maintenance of public order and the protection of the health of citizens, at the level of the Member States and also of the European Union.

66. Given the commitments entered into by the European Union and its Member States, there is no doubt that the abovementioned objectives constitute a legitimate interest which, in principle, justifies a restriction of the obligations imposed by European Union law, even under a fundamental freedom such as the freedom to provide services.

67. In that connection, it is important to bear in mind . . . that the need to combat drugs has been recognised by various international conventions which the Member States, and even the European Union, have cooperated on or acceded to. The preambles to those instruments mention the danger to the health and well-being of individuals constituted, in particular, by demand for and the illicit traffic in narcotic drugs and psychotropic substances, as well as their harmful effects on the economic, cultural and political bases of society.

68. Furthermore, the need to fight drugs, in particular by preventing drug addiction and punishing the illicit trafficking in such products or substances, has been set out in Article 152(1) EC and in Articles 29 EU and 31 EU. As regards provisions of secondary law, the first recital in the preamble to Framework Decision 2004/757 states that illicit drug trafficking poses a threat to health, safety and the quality of life of citizens of the European Union, and to the legal economy, stability and security of the Member States. Furthermore, as is apparent from paragraph 10 of this judgment, certain instruments of the European Union relate expressly to the prevention of drug tourism.

69. However, measures which restrict the freedom to provide services may be justified by the objective of combating drug tourism and the accompanying public nuisance only if they are suitable for securing the attainment of that objective and do not go beyond what is necessary in order to attain . . .

70. In that connection it is important to bear in mind that a restrictive measure can be considered to be suitable for securing the attainment of the objective pursued only if it genuinely reflects a concern to attain that objective in a consistent and systematic manner . . .

71. Mr Josemans calls into question the suitability and proportionality of the rules at issue in the main proceedings. They relate exclusively to coffee-shops. Under 'the AHOJG criteria', those establishments are required, unlike the illegal premises selling drugs in the municipality of Maastricht, to fight against the public nuisance caused by their customers. Furthermore, those rules are liable to drive drug tourists to use illegal channels.

72. The Commission expresses doubts as to the necessity of the rules at issue in the main proceedings and as to their consistency. It states that the national measures to combat the public nuisance caused by the consumption of drugs should be based on objective and non-discriminatory criteria. . . .

73. The Burgemeester van Maastricht and the Netherlands, Belgian and German Governments take the view, by contrast, that the rules at issue in the main proceedings constitute an appropriate and proportionate means of combating drug tourism and the accompanying public nuisance. The Burgemeester van Maastricht and the Netherlands Government state that the various measures adopted by municipalities applying a policy of tolerance with regard to coffee-shops in order to deal with that phenomenon have not achieved the objective pursued.

74. In the present case, it cannot be denied that the policy of tolerance applied by the Kingdom of the Netherlands with regard to the sale of cannabis encourages persons who are resident in other Member States to travel to that State, and more specifically to the municipalities in which coffee-shops are tolerated, in particular in border regions, in order to buy and consume that drug. Furthermore, according to the information in the case-file, some of those persons purchase cannabis in such establishments in order to export it illegally to other Member States.

75. It is indisputable that a prohibition on admitting non-residents to coffee-shops, such as that which is the subject-matter of the dispute in the main proceedings, constitutes a measure capable of substantially limiting drug tourism and, consequently, of reducing the problems it causes.

\*　　\*　　\*

78. It cannot be held to be inconsistent for a Member State to adopt appropriate measures to deal with a large influx of residents from other Member States who wish to benefit from the marketing — tolerated in that Member State — of products which are, by their very nature, prohibited in all Member States from being offered for sale.

79. As regards the scope of rules such as those at issue in the main proceedings, it is important to bear in mind that they apply only to establishments the main activity of which is the marketing of cannabis. They do not preclude a person who is not resident in the Netherlands from going, in the municipality of Maastricht, into other catering establishments in order to consume non-alcoholic beverages and food. According to the Netherlands Government, there are more than 500 such establishments.

80. As regards the possibility of adopting measures which are less restrictive of the freedom to provide services, according to the case-file, in the municipalities which apply a policy of tolerance with regard to coffee-shops, various measures relating to combating drug tourism and the accompanying public nuisance have been implemented, such as a restriction on the number of coffee-shops or their opening hours, the implementation of a card system which allows customers access to them or even a reduction in the amount of cannabis per person which may be bought. According to the information provided by the Burgemeester van Maastricht and the Netherlands Government, those measures have nevertheless proved to be insufficient and ineffective in the light of the objective pursued.

81. As regards more specifically the possibility of granting non-residents access to coffee-shops whilst refusing to sell cannabis to them, it must be pointed out that it is not easy to control and monitor with accuracy that that product is not served to or consumed by non-residents. Furthermore, there is a danger that such an approach would encourage the illegal trade in or the resale of cannabis by residents to non-residents inside coffee-shops.

82. Member States cannot be denied the possibility of pursuing the objective of combating drug tourism and the accompanying public nuisance by the introduction of general rules which are easily managed and supervised by the national . . . In the present case, nothing in the case-file gives grounds to assume that the objective pursued could be achieved to the extent envisaged by the rules at issue in the main proceedings by granting non-residents access to coffee-shops whilst refusing to sell them cannabis.

83. In such circumstances, it must be stated that rules such as those at issue in the main proceedings are suitable for attaining the objective of combating drug tourism and the accompanying public nuisance and do not go beyond what is necessary in order to attain it.

84. Having regard to all of the foregoing considerations, the answer to the second question is that Article 49 EC [56] must be interpreted as meaning that rules such as those at issue in the main proceedings constitute a restriction on the freedom to provide services laid down by the EC Treaty [TFEU]. That restriction is, however, justified by the objective of combating drug tourism and the accompanying public nuisance.

## NOTES AND QUESTIONS

1. This case dealt with a law that discriminated against nonresident *recipients* of services. Why could the Court not approach that discrimination in the same way that it had in *Van Binsbergen*?

2. The language above attempts to set out the logic with which the ECJ seeks to approach questions regarding the application of the TFEU provisions on citizenship rights and discrimination in general as opposed to specific economic rights. The logic is that the general prohibition in EC 12/TFEU 18 is effectively subsumed into the prohibition of restrictions on services that implements that principle in that context. Does this seem right to you? Could the same logic be applied to the provisions regarding workers or self-employed persons?

3. What do you think of the Court's reasoning regarding objective justification? Does it look like a step backward in terms of free movement? How might the question be answered in the U.S.?

## [B]    Taxation

### FKP SCORPIO KONZERTPRODUKTIONEN GMBH v. FINANZAMT HAMBURG-EIMSBUTTEL
Case C-290/04, 2006 ECJ CELEX LEXIS 547, [2006] ECR I-9461

[The German Tax law (EStG) provided that, in the case of persons with "partial liability to tax", (i.e. essentially non-residents) the tax on income of that kind was levied by means of retention at source. The retention amounted to 15% of the total receipts. Under Paragraph 50a(4), third, fifth and sixth sentences, of the EStG, business expenses were not deductible. The value added tax on the services provided in Germany by the person with partial tax liability also formed part of the income. The income tax was payable when the payment was made to the creditor. At that time the payment debtor had to make the retention of tax at source for the account of the payment creditor with partial liability to tax, the latter being the taxable person (tax debtor). The law however laid down certain special rules for the case in which a convention for the avoidance of double taxation applied.]

28. By its first question the national court asks essentially whether Articles 59 [56] and 60 [57] of the EEC Treaty must be interpreted as precluding national legislation under which a procedure of retention of tax at source is applied to payments made to providers of services not resident in the Member State in which the services are provided, while payments made to providers of services resident in that Member State are not subject to such a retention. The national court asks the Court to rule also on the corollary of such legislation, namely the liability incurred by a recipient of services who has failed to make the retention at source that he was required to make.

29. The legislation at issue in the main proceedings establishes a different tax system depending on whether the provider of services is established in Germany or in another Member State.

* * *

33. In the present case, as the referring court points out, the obligation on the recipient of services to make a retention at source of the tax on the payment made to a provider of services residing in another Member State and the fact that that recipient may in certain cases incur liability are liable to deter companies such as Scorpio from calling on providers of services residing in other Member States.

34. It follows that legislation such as that at issue in the main proceedings constitutes an obstacle to the freedom to provide services, prohibited in principle by Articles 59 [56] and 60 [57] of the EEC Treaty.

35. As the governments which have submitted observations and the Commission rightly submit, and as the Advocate General states in his Opinion, such legislation is nevertheless justified by the need to ensure the effective collection of income tax.

36. The procedure of retention at source and the liability rules supporting it constitute a legitimate and appropriate means of ensuring the tax treatment of the income of a person established outside the State of taxation and ensuring that the

income concerned does not escape taxation in the State of residence and the State where the services are provided. It should be recalled that at the material time, in 1993, no Community directive or any other instrument referred to in the case-file governed mutual administrative assistance concerning the recovery of tax debts between the Kingdom of the Netherlands and the Federal Republic of Germany.

37. Moreover, the use of retention at source represented a proportionate means of ensuring the recovery of the tax debts of the State of taxation.

38. The same is true of the potential liability of the recipient of services who is required to make such a retention, as that enables the absence of retention at source to be penalised if necessary. Since that liability constitutes the corollary of that method of collecting income tax, it too contributes in a proportionate manner to ensuring the effectiveness of collecting the tax.

39. It follows that Articles 59 [56] and 60 [57] of the EEC Treaty must be interpreted as not precluding:

- national legislation under which a procedure of retention of tax at source is applied to payments made to providers of services not resident in the Member State in which the services are provided, whereas payments made to providers of services resident in that Member State are not subject to such a retention;

- national legislation under which liability is incurred by a recipient of services who has failed to make the retention at source that he was required to make.

Question 2

40. Since this question is based on the same premiss as Question 3(d), namely that the payment creditor is a national of a non-member country, it will be examined together with that question.

Question 3(a)

41. The Bundesfinanzhof asks the Court whether Articles 59 [56] and 60 [57] of the EEC Treaty must be interpreted as precluding national legislation which does not allow a recipient of services who is the debtor of the payment made to a non-resident provider of services to deduct, when making the retention of tax at source, the business expenses of that service provider which are economically connected with his activities in the Member State in which the services are provided, whereas a provider of services residing in that State is taxable only on his net income, that is, the income received after deduction of business expenses.

\* \* \*

45. The Bundesfinanzhof . . . . wishes to know whether Articles 59 [56] and 60 [57] of the EEC Treaty . . . preclude national tax legislation which does not allow business expenses to be deducted from taxable income at the time when the payment debtor makes the retention at source of the tax, but gives a non-resident the possibility of being taxed on the basis of his net income in Germany in a procedure following, at his request, the procedure of retention at source, and of thus

obtaining a refund of any difference between that amount and that of the retention at source.

46. Starting from the Bundesfinanzhof's premiss, namely the existence at the material time of a refund procedure in which the business expenses of a non-resident provider of services could be taken into account subsequently, it should be recalled that, according to settled case-law of the Court, the application of the host Member State's national rules to providers of services is liable to prohibit, impede or render less attractive the provision of services to the extent that it involves expense and additional administrative and economic burdens . . .

47. In the case at issue in the main proceedings, the obligation, even where the non-resident provider of services has informed his payment debtor of the amount of his business expenses directly linked to his activity, to commence a procedure for the subsequent refund of those expenses is liable to impede the provision of services. In that commencing such a procedure involves additional administrative and economic burdens, and to the extent that the procedure is inevitably necessary for the provider of services, the tax legislation in question constitutes an obstacle to the freedom to provide services, prohibited in principle by Articles 59 [56] and 60 [57] of the EEC Treaty.

48. No argument has been advanced to justify the national legislation at issue in the main proceedings, in so far as it does not allow a recipient of services who is the debtor of the payment made to a non-resident provider of services to deduct, when making the retention of tax at source, the business expenses directly linked to the activity of the non-resident provider of services in the Member State in which the services are provided, if the provider of services has reported them to him.

49. The answer to Question 3(a) must therefore be that Articles 59 [56] and 60 [57] of the EEC Treaty must be interpreted as precluding national legislation which does not allow a recipient of services who is the debtor of the payment made to a non-resident provider of services to deduct, when making the retention of tax at source, the business expenses which that service provider has reported to him and which are directly linked to his activity in the Member State in which the services are provided, whereas a provider of services residing in that State is taxable only on his net income, that is, the income received after deduction of business expenses.

Question 3(b)

50. By this question, which is linked to the preceding one, the Bundesfinanzhof essentially asks whether Articles 59 [56] and 60 [57] of the EEC Treaty must be interpreted as not precluding national legislation under which only the business expenses directly linked to activities in the Member State in which the service is provided, which the service provider established in another Member State has reported to the payment debtor, are deducted in the procedure for retention at source, and any further business expenses can be taken into account in a subsequent refund procedure.

51. This question must be answered in the light of the considerations on the previous question and bearing in mind the fact that the Court does not have the material to make a comparison between the situations of resident and non-resident

providers of services. While the expenses which the provider of services has reported to his debtor must be deducted in the procedure for the retention of tax at source, Articles 59 [56] and 60 [57] of the EEC Treaty do not preclude the taking into account if appropriate of expenses that are not directly linked, within the meaning of the Gerritse line of case-law, to the economic activity that generated the taxable income, in a subsequent refund procedure.

52. The answer to Question 3(b) must therefore be that Articles 59 [56] and 60 [57] of the EEC Treaty must be interpreted as not precluding national legislation under which only the business expenses directly linked to the activity that generated the taxable income in the Member State in which the service is provided, which the service provider established in another Member State has reported to the payment debtor, are deducted in the procedure for retention at source, and expenses that are not directly linked to that economic activity can be taken into account if appropriate in a subsequent refund procedure.

Question 3(c)

53. By this question the Bundesfinanzhof asks the Court whether Articles 59 [56] and 60 [57] of the EEC Treaty must be interpreted as precluding a rule that the tax exemption granted under the Germany-Netherlands Convention to a non-resident provider of services who has carried on activity in Germany can be taken into account by the payment debtor in the procedure for retention of tax at source, or in a subsequent procedure for exemption or refund, or, in the circumstances referred to in paragraph 21 above, in proceedings for liability brought against him, only if a certificate of exemption stating that the conditions laid down to that end by that convention are satisfied is issued by the competent tax authority.

54. . . . [I]n the absence of unifying or harmonising measures adopted by the Community, the Member States remain competent to determine the criteria for taxation of income and wealth with a view to eliminating double taxation by means inter alia of international agreements . . .

55. However, as far as the exercise of the power of taxation so allocated is concerned, the Member States are obliged to comply with Community rules . . .

56. Although . . . the income derived from the artistic services at issue in the main proceedings was taxable not in Germany but only in the Netherlands under the Germany-Netherlands Convention, it must be stated, . . . that the obligation imposed on a provider of services residing in the Netherlands to request the competent German tax authority to issue a certificate of exemption in order to escape additional tax on his income in Germany constitutes, as pointed out in paragraph 49 above, a restriction on the freedom to provide services, because of the administrative steps that it requires the service provider to take.

57. Similarly, the obligation imposed on the recipient of services to produce that certificate of exemption in proceedings for liability brought against him is liable to deter him from calling on a provider of services established in another Member State. As Scorpio submits, the payment debtor has to make sure that his contracting partner has either personally initiated the procedure for exemption or refund (and, in the latter case, pays him the amount of the refund) or else given him

authorisation to start that procedure on his behalf. There is a risk that a provider of services established in another Member State will not be interested in taking those steps or will no longer be available once the contractual relationship has come to an end.

58. Consequently, the fact that the tax exemption in question can be taken into account, at the various stages of the taxation procedure mentioned by the Bundesfinanzhof, only on production of a certificate issued by the competent tax authority stating that the conditions laid down to that end by the Germany-Netherlands Convention are satisfied constitutes an obstacle to the freedom to provide services guaranteed by Articles 59 [56] and 60 [57] of the EEC Treaty.

59. That obstacle is, however, justified in order to ensure the proper functioning of the procedure for taxation at source.

60. As the Belgian Government inter alia argues and as the Advocate General states in point 90 of his Opinion, it appears to be important that the payment debtor can refrain from retaining tax at source only if he is certain that the provider of services satisfies the conditions for an exemption. The payment debtor cannot be required himself to clarify whether or not, in each individual case, the income in question is exempt under a convention for the avoidance of double taxation. Finally, authorising the payment debtor unilaterally to refrain from retaining the tax at source could, in the event of an error on his part, have the effect of compromising the collection of the tax from the payment creditor.

61. In the light of the above considerations, the answer to Question 3(c) must be that Articles 59 [56] and 60 of the EEC Treaty must be interpreted as not precluding a rule that the tax exemption granted under the Germany-Netherlands Convention to a non-resident provider of services who has carried on activity in Germany can be taken into account by the payment debtor in the procedure for retention of tax at source, or in a subsequent procedure for exemption or refund, or in proceedings for liability brought against him, only if a certificate of exemption stating that the conditions laid down to that end by that convention are satisfied is issued by the competent tax authority.

## NOTES AND QUESTIONS

Do you think that the Court in this case paid too much deference to national taxation prerogatives?

## FRANCOIS DE COSTER v. COLLEGE DES BOURGMESTRES ET ECHEVINS DE WATERMAEL-BOITSFORT

Case C-17/00, 2001 ECJ CELEX LEXIS 293, [2001] ECR I-9445.

[Articles 1 to 3 of the tax regulation on satellite dishes adopted by the municipal council of Watermael-Boitsfort (Belgium) on 24 June 1997 (the tax regulation) read as follows:

1. An annual municipal tax on satellite dishes is hereby introduced for the 1997 to 2001 financial years inclusive.

2. The rate of the tax is set at 5000 francs per satellite dish, whatever its size. The tax is due for the whole calendar year regardless of the date of installation of the dish during the tax year.

3. The tax is payable by the owner of the satellite dish on 1 January of the tax year . . . .

This tax regulation was repealed with effect from 1 January 1999 by a decision of the municipal Council of Watermael-Boitsfort meeting on 21 September 1999, prompted by the fact that in the course of infringement proceedings against Belgium, the Commission had sent the latter a reasoned opinion questioning the compliance of measures such as the tax regulation with EU law.]

5 Mr De Coster lodged at the College juridictionnel de la Region de Bruxelles-Capitale a complaint against the satellite dish tax charged him by the municipality of Watermael-Boitsfort for the 1998 financial year.

6 Mr De Coster considers that such a tax results in a restriction on the freedom to receive television programmes coming from other Member States which is contrary to Community law and especially to Article 59 [56] of the Treaty.

7 By letter of 27 April 1999 addressed to the College juridictionnel de la Region de Bruxelles-Capitale, the municipality of Watermael-Boitsfort stated that the tax on satellite dishes was introduced in an attempt to prevent their uncontrolled proliferation in the municipality and thereby preserve the quality of the environment.

\*      \*      \*

25 [I]t must be observed that although, as Community law stands at present, direct taxation does not as such fall within the purview of the Community, the powers retained by the Member States must nevertheless be exercised consistently with Community law (see, in particular, Case C-118/96 Safir 1998 ECR I-1897, paragraph 21).

26 In the context of freedom to provide services the Court has also recognised that a national tax measure restricting that freedom may constitute a prohibited measure . . .

27 Since the duty to abide by the rules relating to the freedom to provide services applies to the actions of public authorities . . . . it is, in that respect, irrelevant that the tax measure in question was adopted, as in the main proceedings, by a local authority and not by the State itself.

28 Furthermore, it is settled case-law that the transmission, and broadcasting, of television signals comes within the rules of the Treaty relating to the provision of services . . .

29 It must also be noted that, according to the case-law of the Court, Article 59 [56] of the Treaty requires not only the elimination of all discrimination on grounds of nationality against providers of services who are established in another Member State, but also the abolition of any restriction, even if it applies without distinction to national providers of services and to those of other Member States, which is liable to prohibit or further impede the activities of a provider of services established in

another Member State where he lawfully provides similar services . . .

30 Furthermore, the Court has already held that Article 59 [56] of the Treaty precludes the application of any national rules which have the effect of making the provision of services between Member States more difficult than the provision of services purely within one Member State . . .

31 In that regard it must be noted that the introduction of a tax on satellite dishes has the effect of a charge on the reception of television programmes transmitted by satellite which does not apply to the reception of programmes transmitted by cable, since the recipient does not have to pay a similar tax on that method of reception.

32 However, the Commission indicated in its written observations that whilst broadcasters established in Belgium enjoy unlimited access to cable distribution for their programmes in that Member State, broadcasters established in certain other Member States do not. The number of Danish, Greek, Italian, Finnish or Swedish channels which can be broadcast by cable in Belgium is thus particularly limited, the Commission noting in that regard a maximum of one channel per State, if any. It follows that most television broadcasting programmes transmitted from those Member States can only be received by satellite dishes.

33 In such circumstances, as the Commission correctly observes, a tax such as that introduced by the tax regulation is liable to dissuade the recipients of the television broadcasting services established in the municipality of Watermael-Boitsfort from seeking access to television programmes broadcast from other Member States, since the reception of such programmes is subject to a charge which does not apply to the reception of programmes coming from broadcasters established in Belgium.

34 Furthermore, as the Commission also observes, the introduction of such a tax is liable to hinder the activities of operators in the field of satellite transmission by imposing a charge on the reception of programmes transmitted by such operators which does not apply to the reception of programmes transmitted by the national cable distributors.

35 It follows from those considerations that the tax on satellite dishes introduced by the tax regulation is liable to impede more the activities of operators in the field of broadcasting or television transmission established in Member States other than the Kingdom of Belgium, while giving an advantage to the internal Belgian market and to radio and television distribution within that Member State.

36 . . . [T]he municipality of Watermael-Boitsfort nevertheless justifies the tax regulation by stating its concern to prevent the uncontrolled proliferation of satellite dishes in the municipality and thereby preserve the quality of the environment.

37 In that regard, it suffices to state that even if the need for protection relied on by the municipality of Watermael-Boitsfort is capable of justifying restriction of the freedom to provide services, and even if it is established that merely reducing the number of satellite dishes as anticipated by the introduction of a tax such as the one in question in the main proceedings is capable of meeting that need, the tax exceeds what is necessary to do so.

38 As the Commission observed, there are methods other than the tax in question

in the main proceedings, less restrictive of the freedom to provide services, which could achieve an objective such as the protection of the urban environment, for instance the adoption of requirements concerning the size of the dishes, their position and the way in which they are fixed to the building or its surroundings or the use of communal dishes. Moreover, such requirements have been adopted by the municipality of Watermael-Boitsfort, as is apparent from the planning rules on outdoor aerials adopted by that municipality and approved by regulation of 27 February 1997 of the government of the Brussels-Capital region . . .

39 In view of all of the above considerations the answer to the question submitted must be that Articles 59 [56], 60 [57] and 55 [62] of the Treaty must be interpreted as preventing the application of a tax on satellite dishes such as that introduced by Articles 1 to 3 of the tax regulation.

## NOTES AND QUESTIONS

Does the above decision suggest that a discriminatory element must be present to find that a local law in the host state constitutes a restriction on the provision of cross border services? Or is the discriminatory element what actually causes the restriction? Suppose that a charge had been placed on cable providers that equalized the impact of the charge on satellite dish owners?

## [C] Budgetary Matters

### V.G. MÜLLER-FAURÉ v. ONDERLINGE WAARBORGMAATSCHAPPIJ OZ ZORGVERZEKERINGEN UA AND E.E.M. VAN RIET v. ONDERLINGE WAARBORGMAATSCHAPPIJ ZAO ZORGVERZEKERINGEN
Case C-385/99, 2003 ECJ CELEX LEXIS 739, [2003] ECR I-4509

The Muller — Faure Case

20. While on holiday in Germany, Ms Müller-Fauré underwent dental treatment involving the fitting of six crowns and a fixed prosthesis on the upper jaw. The treatment was provided between 20 October and 18 November 1994 without recourse to any hospital facilities.

21. When she returned from her holiday, she applied to the Zwijndrecht Fund [one of the agencies that administered medical insurance for the Dutch state] for reimbursement of the costs of the treatment, which amounted to a total of DEM 7 444.59. By letter of 12 May 1995 the Fund refused reimbursement on the basis of the opinion of its advisory dental officer.

22. Ms Müller-Fauré sought the opinion of the Ziekenfonsraad, which is responsible for supervising the management and administration of sickness funds and which, on 16 February 1996, confirmed the Zwijndrecht Fund's decision on the ground that insured persons are entitled only to treatment itself and not to reimbursement of any related costs, except in exceptional circumstances which did not exist in this

case.

23. Ms Müller-Fauré then brought an action before the Arrondissementsrechtbank te Rotterdam (District Court, Rotterdam) (Netherlands). By judgment of 21 August 1997, that court upheld the Fund's decision, having also found that the case entailed no exceptional circumstances such as to justify reimbursement of the costs, given, in particular, the scale of the treatment and the fact that it extended over several weeks.

24. The Centrale Raad van Beroep points out that in any event only a limited part of the treatment received by Ms Müller-Fauré is covered by the Verstrekkingenbesluit and is therefore eligible for reimbursement. Furthermore, it finds that Ms Müller-Fauré voluntarily sought treatment from a dentist established in Germany while she was on holiday there because she lacked confidence in dental practitioners in the Netherlands. Such circumstances cannot, according to the case-law of the court concerned, provide grounds under the national legislation for reimbursement in respect of medical treatment undergone abroad without authorisation from the insured person's fund.


The Van Riet case

25. Ms Van Riet had been suffering from pain in her right wrist since 1985. On 5 April 1993, the doctor treating her requested that the Amsterdam Fund's medical adviser should grant authorisation for his patient to have an arthroscopy performed in Deurne hospital (Belgium) where that examination could be carried out much sooner than in the Netherlands. The Fund rejected that request by letters of 24 June and 5 July 1993 on the ground that the test could also be performed in the Netherlands.

26. In the meantime, Ms Van Riet had already had the arthroscopy carried out at Deurne hospital in May 1993 and, following that examination, the decision was taken to carry out an ulnar reduction to relieve the patient's pain. Care before and after the treatment, and the treatment itself, were provided in Belgium, partly in hospital and partly elsewhere. The Amsterdam Fund refused to reimburse the cost of the care, which amounted to a total of BEF 93 782. That decision was confirmed by the Ziekenfondsraad on the ground that there was no emergency nor any medical necessity such as to justify Ms Van Riet receiving treatment in Belgium, since appropriate treatment was available in the Netherlands within a reasonable period. The competent Arrondissementsrechtbank rejected as unfounded Ms Van Riet's action against the decision for the same reasons as the Amsterdam Fund.

27. The Centrale Raad van Beroep, before which the applicant in the main proceedings brought an appeal, states that, although it is not disputed that most of the treatment given to Ms Van Riet is indeed covered by the Verstrekkingenbesluit, the treatment was provided in Belgium without prior authorisation and without it being established that Ms Van Riet could not reasonably wait, for medical or other reasons, until the Amsterdam Fund had taken a decision on her application. Furthermore, in that court's view, the time which Ms Van Riet would have had to wait for the arthroscopy in the Netherlands was not unreasonable. The documents before the Court show that the waiting time was about six months.

\* \* \*

37. By its first question, the national court is essentially asking whether Articles 59 [56] and 60 [57] of the Treaty are to be interpreted as precluding legislation of a Member State, such as the legislation at issue in the main proceedings, which makes assumption of the costs of care provided in another Member State, by a person or an establishment with whom or which the insured person's sickness fund has not concluded an agreement, conditional upon prior authorisation by the fund.

38. It should be borne in mind, as a preliminary point, that it is settled case-law that medical activities fall within the scope of Article 60 [57] of the Treaty, there being no need to distinguish in that regard between care provided in a hospital environment and care provided outside such an environment (see, most recently, Smits and Peerbooms, paragraph 53).

39. The Court also found, in paragraphs 54 and 55 of Smits and Peerbooms, that the fact that the applicable rules are social security rules and, more specifically, provide, as regards sickness insurance, for benefits in kind rather than reimbursement does not mean that the medical treatment in question falls outside the scope of the freedom to provide services guaranteed by the EC Treaty. Indeed, in the disputes before the national court, the treatment provided in a Member State other than that in which the persons concerned were insured resulted in direct payment by the patient to the doctor providing the service or the establishment in which the care was provided.

40. Since medical services fall within the ambit of freedom to provide services for the purposes of Articles 59 [56] and 60 [57] of the Treaty, it is necessary to determine whether the legislation at issue in the main actions introduces restrictions on that freedom in making assumption of the costs of care provided in a Member State other than that in which the insured person's sickness fund is established, by a person or establishment which has not concluded an agreement with that fund, conditional upon prior authorisation by the fund.

41. In that regard the Court has already held, in paragraph 62 of the judgment in Smits and Peerbooms, that while the ZFW does not deprive insured persons of the possibility of using a service provider established in a Member State other than that in which the sickness fund covering the insured is situated, it does nevertheless make reimbursement of the costs thus incurred subject to prior authorisation, which may be given, as the referring court points out, only where provision of the care at issue, irrespective of whether it involves a hospital, is a medical necessity.

42. Since the requirement of medical necessity is in practice satisfied only where adequate treatment cannot be obtained without undue delay from a contracted doctor or hospital in the Member State in which the person is insured, this requirement by its very nature is liable severely to limit the circumstances in which such authorisation will be issued.

43. Admittedly, it is open to the Netherlands sickness insurance funds to enter into agreements with hospital establishments outside the Netherlands. In such a case no prior authorisation would be required in order for the cost of treatment provided by such establishments to be assumed under the ZFW. However, with the exception of hospitals situated in regions adjoining the Netherlands, it seems unlikely that a

significant number of hospitals in other Member States would ever enter into agreements with those sickness insurance funds, given that their prospects of admitting patients insured by those funds remain uncertain and limited.

44. The Court has therefore already held that rules such as those at issue in the main proceedings deter, or even prevent, insured persons from applying to providers of medical services established in Member States other than that of the insurance fund and constitute, both for insured persons and service providers, a barrier to freedom to provide services (Smits and Peerbooms, paragraph 69).

45. However, before coming to a decision on whether Articles 59 [56] and 60 [57] of the Treaty preclude rules such as those at issue in the main actions, it is appropriate to determine whether those rules can be objectively justified, which is the subject of the second question.

The second and third questions

46. By its second and third questions, which it is appropriate to examine together, the referring court is asking whether legislation such as that at issue in the main proceedings, which has restrictive effects on freedom to provide services, can be justified by the actual particular features of the national sickness insurance scheme, which provides not for reimbursement of costs incurred but essentially for benefits in kind and is based on a system of agreements intended both to ensure the quality of the care and to control the costs thereof. It also wishes to know whether the fact that the treatment at issue is provided in whole or in part in a hospital environment has any effect in that regard.

*     *     *

66. It is clear from the documents before the Court that the reasons put forward to justify the requirement for prior authorisation where sickness insurance is to cover benefits provided in a Member State other than that in which the person concerned is insured, whether within a hospital environment or not, are linked (i) to the protection of public health inasmuch as the system of agreements is intended to ensure that there is a high-quality, balanced medical and hospital service open to all, (ii) to the financial balance of the social security system in that a system of that kind also permits the managing authorities to control expenditure by adjusting it to projected requirements, according to preestablished priorities, and (iii) to the essential characteristics of the sickness insurance scheme in the Netherlands, which provides benefits in kind.

The risk that the protection of public health may be adversely affected

67. It is apparent from the Court's case-law that the objective of maintaining a high-quality, balanced medical and hospital service open to all, may fall within one of the derogations provided for in Article 56 [52] of the EC Treaty . . . . , in so far as it contributes to the attainment of a high level of health protection . . . In particular, that Treaty provision permits Member States to restrict the freedom to provide medical and hospital services in so far as the maintenance of treatment capacity or medical competence on national territory is essential for public health,

and even the survival of the population . . .

68. However, it is settled case-law that it is necessary, where justification is based on an exception laid down by the Treaty or indeed on an overriding general-interest reason, to ensure that the measures taken in that respect do not exceed what is objectively necessary for that purpose and that the same result cannot be achieved by less restrictive . . .

69. In this instance the arguments put forward to justify the requirement for prior authorisation seek to establish that, if it were open to patients to get treatment in a Member State other than that in which they are insured, without prior authorisation to that effect, the competent State could no longer guarantee that in its territory there would be a high-quality, balanced medical and hospital service open to all and hence a high level of public health protection.

70. As to the Danish Government's argument that the actual competence of practitioners, working in surgeries or in a hospital environment, would be undermined because of numerous journeys abroad for medical purposes, the Court finds that no specific evidence has been adduced in support of this argument.

71. The objective of maintaining a balanced medical and hospital service open to all is inextricably linked to the way in which the social security system is financed and to the control of expenditure, which are dealt with below.

The risk of seriously undermining the financial balance of the social security system

72. It must be recalled, at the outset, that, according to the Court's case-law, aims of a purely economic nature cannot justify a barrier to the fundamental principle of freedom to provide services . . .

73. However, in so far as, in particular, it could have consequences for the overall level of public-health protection, the risk of seriously undermining the financial balance of the social security system may also constitute per se an overriding general-interest reason capable of justifying a barrier of that kind . . .

74. It is self-evident that assuming the cost of one isolated case of treatment, carried out in a Member State other than that in which a particular person is insured with a sickness fund, can never make any significant impact on the financing of the social security system. Thus an overall approach must necessarily be adopted in relation to the consequences of freedom to provide health-related services.

75. In that regard, the distinction between hospital services and non-hospital services may sometimes prove difficult to draw. In particular, certain services provided in a hospital environment but also capable of being provided by a practitioner in his surgery or in a health centre could for that reason be placed on the same footing as non-hospital services. However, in the main actions, the fact that the care at issue is partly hospital treatment and partly non-hospital treatment has not given rise to disagreement between the parties to the main proceedings or on the part of the Member States which have submitted observations under Article 23 of the EC Statute of the Court of Justice or the Commission.

Hospital services

76. As regards hospital services, such as those provided to Ms Van Riet in Deurne hospital, the Court, in paragraphs 76 to 80 of the judgment in Smits and Peerbooms, made the following findings.

77. It is well known that the number of hospitals, their geographical distribution, the way in which they are organised and the facilities with which they are provided, and even the nature of the medical services which they are able to offer, are all matters for which planning must be possible.

78. As may be seen, in particular, from the system of agreements involved in the main actions, this kind of planning generally meets a variety of concerns.

79. For one thing, it seeks to achieve the aim of ensuring that there is sufficient and permanent accessibility to a balanced range of high-quality hospital treatment in the State concerned.

80. For another thing, it assists in meeting a desire to control costs and to prevent, as far as possible, any wastage of financial, technical and human resources. Such wastage would be all the more damaging because it is generally recognised that the hospital care sector generates considerable costs and must satisfy increasing needs, while the financial resources which may be made available for health care are not unlimited, whatever the mode of funding applied.

81. In those circumstances, a requirement that the assumption of costs, under a national social security system, of hospital treatment provided in a Member State other than that of affiliation must be subject to prior authorisation appears to be a measure which is both necessary and reasonable.

82. As regards specifically the system set up by the ZFW, the Court clearly acknowledged that, if insured persons were at liberty, regardless of the circumstances, to use the services of hospitals with which their sickness insurance fund had no agreement, whether those hospitals were situated in the Netherlands or in another Member State, all the planning which goes into the system of agreements in an effort to guarantee a rationalised, stable, balanced and accessible supply of hospital services would be jeopardised at a stroke . . .

83. Although Community law does not therefore in principle preclude a system of prior authorisation for this category of services, the conditions attached to the grant of such authorisation must none the less be justified in the light of the overriding considerations mentioned above and must satisfy the requirement of proportionality referred to in paragraph 68 above.

84. It likewise follows from settled case-law that a scheme of prior administrative authorisation cannot legitimise discretionary decisions taken by the national authorities, which are liable to negate the effectiveness of provisions of Community law, in particular those relating to a fundamental freedom such as that at issue in the main proceedings . . .

85. Thus, in order for a prior administrative authorisation scheme to be justified even though it derogates from a fundamental freedom of that kind, it must be based on objective, non-discriminatory criteria which are known in advance, in such a way

as to circumscribe the exercise of the national authorities' discretion, so that it is not used arbitrarily . . . Such a prior administrative authorisation scheme must likewise be based on a procedural system which is easily accessible and capable of ensuring that a request for authorisation will be dealt with objectively and impartially within a reasonable time and refusals to grant authorisation must also be capable of being challenged in judicial or quasi-judicial proceedings . . .

86. In the main actions, the disputes do not concern the actual cover provided by the Netherlands sickness insurance scheme for the medical and hospital treatment with which Ms Müller-Fauré and Ms Van Riet were provided. In those actions, what is disputed is whether it was a medical necessity for them to have the treatment at issue in Germany and Belgium respectively, rather than in the Netherlands. . . .

87. As the national court states, it follows from the wording of Article 9(4) of the ZFW and Article 1 of the Rhbz that in principle that condition applies irrespective of whether the request for authorisation relates to treatment in an establishment located in the Netherlands with which the insured person's sickness insurance fund has no agreement or in an establishment located in another Member State.

88. As regards hospital treatment carried out outside the Netherlands, the national court states that the condition concerning the necessity of the treatment is in practice interpreted as meaning that such treatment is not to be authorised unless it appears that appropriate treatment cannot be provided without undue delay in the Netherlands. The Netherlands Government explains that if Article 9(4) of the ZFW is read in conjunction with Article 1 of the Rhbz, authorisation must be refused solely where the care required by the insured person's state of health is available from contracted care providers.

89. The condition concerning the necessity of the treatment, laid down by the legislation at issue in the main proceedings, can be justified under Article 59 [56] of the Treaty, provided that the condition is construed to the effect that authorisation to receive treatment in another Member State may be refused on that ground only if treatment which is the same or equally effective for the patient can be obtained without undue delay from an establishment with which the insured person's sickness insurance fund has an agreement.

90. In order to determine whether treatment which is equally effective for the patient can be obtained without undue delay in an establishment having an agreement with the insured person's fund, the national authorities are required to have regard to all the circumstances of each specific case and to take due account not only of the patient's medical condition at the time when authorisation is sought and, where appropriate, of the degree of pain or the nature of the patient's disability which might, for example, make it impossible or extremely difficult for him to carry out a professional activity, but also of his medical history).

91. . . . [citing a previous case]

"thus construed, the condition concerning the necessity of treatment can allow an adequate, balanced and permanent supply of high-quality hospital treatment to be maintained on the national territory and the financial stability of the sickness insurance system to be assured;

were large numbers of insured persons to decide to be treated in other Member States even when the hospitals having agreements with their sickness insurance funds offer adequate identical or equivalent treatment, the consequent outflow of patients would be liable to put at risk the very principle of having agreements with hospitals and, consequently, undermine all the planning and rationalisation carried out in this vital sector in an effort to avoid the phenomena of hospital overcapacity, imbalance in the supply of hospital medical care and logistical and financial wastage."

92. However, a refusal to grant prior authorisation which is based not on fear of wastage resulting from hospital overcapacity but solely on the ground that there are waiting lists on national territory for the hospital treatment concerned, without account being taken of the specific circumstances attaching to the patient's medical condition, cannot amount to a properly justified restriction on freedom to provide services. It is not clear from the arguments submitted to the Court that such waiting times are necessary, apart from considerations of a purely economic nature which cannot as such justify a restriction on the fundamental principle of freedom to provide services, for the purpose of safeguarding the protection of public health. On the contrary, a waiting time which is too long or abnormal would be more likely to restrict access to balanced, high-quality hospital care.

Non-hospital services

93. As regards non-hospital medical services such as those supplied to Ms Müller-Fauré and, in part, to Ms Van Riet, no specific evidence has been produced to the Court, not even by the Zwijndrecht and Amsterdam Funds or the Netherlands Government, to support the assertion that, were insured persons at liberty to go without prior authorisation to Member States other than those in which their sickness funds are established in order to obtain those services from a non-contracted provider, that would be likely seriously to undermine the financial balance of the Netherlands social security system.

94. It is true that removal of the condition that there should be a system of agreements in respect of services supplied abroad adversely affects the ways in which health-care expenditure may be controlled in the Member State of affiliation.

95. However, the documents before the Court do not indicate that removal of the requirement for prior authorisation for that type of care would give rise to patients travelling to other countries in such large numbers, despite linguistic barriers, geographic distance, the cost of staying abroad and lack of information about the kind of care provided there, that the financial balance of the Netherlands social security system would be seriously upset and that, as a result, the overall level of public-health protection would be jeopardised which might constitute proper justification for a barrier to the fundamental principle of freedom to provide services.

96. Furthermore, care is generally provided near to the place where the patient resides, in a cultural environment which is familiar to him and which allows him to build up a relationship of trust with the doctor treating him. If emergencies are disregarded, the most obvious cases of patients travelling abroad are in border

areas or where specific conditions are to be treated. Furthermore, it is specifically in those areas or in respect of those conditions that the Netherlands sickness funds tend to set up a system of agreements with foreign doctors, as the observations submitted to the Court reveal.

97. Those various factors seem likely to limit any financial impact on the Netherlands social security system of removal of the requirement for prior authorisation in respect of care provided in foreign practitioners'surgeries.

98. In any event, it should be borne in mind that it is for the Member States alone to determine the extent of the sickness cover available to insured persons, so that, when the insured go without prior authorisation to a Member State other than that in which their sickness fund is established to receive treatment there, they can claim reimbursement of the cost of the treatment given to them only within the limits of the cover provided by the sickness insurance scheme in the Member State of affiliation.

The argument based on the essential characteristics of the Netherlands sickness insurance scheme

99. The Zwijndrecht Fund and the Netherlands, Spanish and Norwegian Governments have drawn attention to the fact that Member States are free to set up the social security system of their choice. In this instance, in the absence of prior authorisation, insured persons could apply freely to non-contracted care providers with the result that the existence of the Netherlands system of benefits in kind, the operation of which is in essence dependent upon the system of agreements, would be jeopardised. Furthermore, the Netherlands authorities would be obliged to introduce mechanisms for reimbursement into their method of organising access to health care since, instead of receiving free health services on national territory, the insured would have to advance the sums needed to pay for the services received and wait for some time before being reimbursed. Thus, Member States would be obliged to abandon the principles and underlying logic of their sickness insurance schemes.

100. In that regard it follows from settled case-law that Community law does not detract from the power of the Member States to organise their social security systems . . . Therefore, in the absence of harmonisation at Community level, it is for the legislation of each Member State to determine the conditions on which social security benefits are granted . . . However, it is nevertheless the case that the Member States must comply with Community law when exercising that power . . .

101. Two preliminary observations must be made on this point.

102. First, achievement of the fundamental freedoms guaranteed by the Treaty inevitably requires Member States to make some adjustments to their national systems of social security. It does not follow that this would undermine their sovereign powers in this field. It is sufficient in this regard to look to the adjustments which they have had to make to their social security legislation in order to comply with Regulation No 1408/71, in particular with the conditions laid down in Article 69 thereof regarding the payment of unemployment benefit to workers residing in the territory of other Member States when no national system provided for the grant of such benefits to unemployed persons registered with an employment agency in another Member State.

103. Second, as has already been made clear in paragraph 39 above, a medical service does not cease to be a provision of services because it is paid for by a national health service or by a system providing benefits in kind. The Court has, in particular, held that a medical service provided in one Member State and paid for by the patient cannot cease to fall within the scope of the freedom to provide services guaranteed by the Treaty merely because reimbursement of the costs of the treatment involved is applied for under another Member State's sickness insurance legislation which is essentially of the type which provides for benefits in kind . . . The requirement for prior authorisation where a person is subsequently to be reimbursed for the costs of that treatment is precisely what constitutes, as has already been stated in paragraph 44 above, the barrier to freedom to provide services, that is to say, to a patient's ability to go to the medical service provider of his choice in a Member State other than that of affiliation. There is thus no need, from the perspective of freedom to provide services, to draw a distinction by reference to whether the patient pays the costs incurred and subsequently applies for reimbursement thereof or whether the sickness fund or the national budget pays the provider directly.

104. It is in the light of those observations that it is appropriate to determine whether removal of the requirement for sickness insurance funds to grant prior authorisation for non-hospital health care provided in a Member State other than that of affiliation, is such as to call in question the essential characteristics of the system of access to health care in the Netherlands.

105. First, when applying Regulation No 1408/71, those Member States which have established a system providing benefits in kind, or even a national health service, must provide mechanisms for ex post facto reimbursement in respect of care provided in a Member State other than the competent State. That is the case, for example, where it has not been possible to complete the formalities during the relevant person's stay in that State (see Article 34 of Regulation (EEC) No 574/72 of the Council of 21 March 1972 fixing the procedure for implementing Regulation No 1408/71) or where the competent State has authorised access to treatment abroad in accordance with Article 22(1)(c) of Regulation No 1408/71.

106. Second . . ., insured persons who go without prior authorisation to a Member State other than the one in which their sickness fund is established to receive treatment there can claim reimbursement of the cost of the treatment received only within the limits of the cover provided by the sickness insurance scheme of the Member State of affiliation. Thus, in the present case, it is apparent from the documents before the Court that, in relation to the EUR 3 806.35 paid by Ms Müller-Fauré to a provider established in Germany, the Zwijndrecht Fund would in any event, given the extent of the insurance cover provided by the Fund, contribute only up to a maximum amount of EUR 221.03. Likewise, the conditions on which benefits are granted, in so far as they are neither discriminatory nor an obstacle to freedom of movement of persons, remain enforceable where treatment is provided in a Member State other than that of affiliation. That is particularly so in the case of the requirement that a general practitioner should be consulted prior to consulting a specialist.

107. Third, nothing precludes a competent Member State with a benefits in kind

system from fixing the amounts of reimbursement which patients who have received care in another Member State can claim, provided that those amounts are based on objective, non-discriminatory and transparent criteria.

108. Consequently, the evidence and arguments submitted to the Court do not show that removal of the requirement that sickness insurance funds grant prior authorisation to their insured to enable them to receive health care, in particular other than in a hospital, provided in a Member State other than that of affiliation would undermine the essential characteristics of the Netherlands sickness insurance scheme.

## NOTES AND QUESTIONS

1.  The Court here had to address the delicate and highly political balance between its extensive interpretation of EC 49/TFEU 56 and the demands of financial and policy constraints arising from the provision of comprehensive health care by national governments. How did the Court address these issues? Is the guidance clear?

2.  See also *The Queen, on the application of Yvonne Watts v. Bedford Primary Care Trust and Secretary of State for Health*, Case C-372/04, 2006 ECJ CELEX LEXIS 394, [2006] ECR I-4325, for a detailed discussion of the circumstances in which the existence of waiting lists under the UK National Health System may justify a patient's seeking medical care in another Member State. A patient may be entitled to reimbursement of the costs of such care if it could be shown that the patient's placing on the waiting list was not an exercise of reasonable judgment by the NHS. Additionally the court considered the requirement for pre-authorization of such treatment in another member-State, holding that such a system may be justified to the extent necessary for proper planning by the authority. In *Manuel Acereda Herrera v. Servicio Cantabro de Salud*, Case C-466/04, 2006 ECJ CELEX LEXIS 292, [2006] ECR 5341, the Court held that travel expenses incurred in seeking treatment in another Member State were not recoverable by the patient.

3.  For an explanation of this complex decision, see M. Flear, *Case C-385/99 V.G. Müller-Fauré v. Onderlinge Waarborgmaatschappij O.Z. Zorgverzekeringen U.A. and E.E.M. van Riet v. Onderlinge Waarborgmaatschappij Z.A.O. Zorgverzekeringen'* (2004) 41 CML REV. 209.

## § 14.06   THE SCOPE AND BOUNDARIES OF EC 49/TFEU 56

### [A]   Application to the Receipt of Services

### LUISI AND CARBONE v. MINISTERO DEL TESORO
Joined Cases 286/82 and 26/83, 1984 ECJ CELEX LEXIS 57, [1984] ECR 377

[Proceedings had been instituted by two Italian residents against decisions of the Ministro del Tesoro [Minister for the Treasury] imposing fines upon them for purchasing various foreign currencies for use abroad in an amount whose exchange value in Italian lire exceeded the maximum permitted by Italian law, which at that time was LIT 500 000 per annum for the export of foreign currency by residents for the purposes of tourism, business, education and medical treatment. Note that the provisions on the free movement of capital had not yet been adopted. Article 106 EEC [repealed} did however require the free movement of money for trade purposes, including tourism.

3 Before the national court the plaintiffs contested the validity of the provisions of Italian legislation on which the fines were based, on the ground that those provisions were incompatible with Community law. In Case 286/82 the plaintiff in the main proceedings, Mrs. Luisi, stated that she had exported the currency in question for the purpose of various visits to France and the Federal Republic of Germany as a tourist and in order to receive medical treatment in the latter country. In Case 26/83 the plaintiff in the main proceedings, Mr. Carbone, stated that the foreign currency purchased by him had been used for a stay of three months in the Federal Republic of Germany as a tourist. Both plaintiffs submitted that the restrictions on the export of means of payment in foreign currency for the purpose of tourism or medical treatment were contrary to the provisions of the EEC Treaty relating to current payments and the movement of capital.

\* \* \*

10 By virtue of Article 59 [56] of the Treaty, restrictions on freedom to provide such services are to be abolished in respect of nationals of Member States who are established in a Member State other than that of the person for whom the service is intended. In order to enable services to be provided, the person providing the service may go to the Member State where the person for whom it is provided is established or else the latter may go to the State in which the person providing the service is established. Whilst the former case is expressly mentioned in the third paragraph of Article 60 [57], which permits the person providing the service to pursue his activity temporarily in the Member State where the service is provided, the latter case is the necessary corollary thereof, which fulfils the objective of liberalizing all gainful activity not covered by the free movement of goods, persons and capital.

11 For the implementation of those provisions, Title II of the General Programme for the Abolition of Restrictions On Freedom to Provide Services . . . which was drawn up by the Council pursuant to Article 63 of the Treaty on 18 December 1961, envisages inter alia the repeal of provisions laid down by law, regulation or administrative action which in any Member State govern, for economic purposes, the entry, exit and residence of nationals of Member States, where such provisions are not justified on grounds of public policy, public security or public health and are liable to hinder the provision of services by such persons.

12 According to Article 1 thereof, Council Directive 64/221/EEC of 25 February 1964 on the coordination of special measures concerning the movement and residence of foreign nationals which are justified on grounds of public policy, public security or public health . . . applies inter alia to any national of a Member State who travels to another Member State "as a recipient of services". Council Directive 73/148/EEC of 21 May 1973 on the abolition of restrictions on movement and residence within the Community for nationals of Member States with regard to

establishment and the provision of services . . . grants both the provider and the recipient of a service a right of residence co-terminous with the period during which the service is provided.

13 By basing the General Programme for the Abolition of Restrictions on the Freedom to provide Services partly on Article 106 [deleted] of the Treaty, its authors showed that they were aware of the effect of the liberalization of services on the liberalization of payments. In fact, the first paragraph of that article provides that any payments connected with the movement of goods or services are to be liberalized to the extent to which the movement of goods and services has been liberalized between Member States.

14 Among the restrictions on the freedom to provide services which must be abolished, the General Programme mentions, in section C of Title III, impediments to payments for services, particularly where, according to section D of Title III and in conformity with Article 106 (2), the provision of such services is limited only by restrictions in respect of the payments therefor. By virtue of section B of Title V of the General Programme, those restrictions were to be abolished before the end of the first stage of the transitional period, subject to a proviso permitting limits on "foreign currency allowances for tourists" to be retained during that period. Those provisions were implemented by Council Directive 63/340/EEC of 31 May 1963 on the abolition of all prohibitions on or obstacles to payments for services where the only restrictions on exchange of services are those governing such payments . . . Article 3 of that directive also refers to foreign exchange allowances for tourists.

15 However, both the General Programme and the aforesaid directive reserve the right for Member States to verify the nature and genuineness of transfers of funds and of payments and to take all necessary measures in order to prevent contravention of their laws and regulations, "in particular as regards the issue of foreign currency to tourists".

16 It follows that the freedom to provide services includes the freedom, for the recipients of services, to go to another Member State in order to receive a service there, without being obstructed by restrictions, even in relation to payments and that tourists, persons receiving medical treatment and persons travelling for the purpose of education or business are to be regarded as recipients of services.

## NOTES AND QUESTIONS

1.   In introducing the concept that EC 49/TFEU 56 also applies to receipt of services, the Court has introduced an entirely new dimension to the article. What might be the implications of this judgment?

2.   According to the Court, recipients of services would include tourists, persons receiving medical treatment, and persons traveling for the purposes of education and business. This potentially opened up the services provisions to a very broad expansion. These restrictions were generally motivated by a need to control state expenditure.

## [B]   Remoteness

## THE SOCIETY FOR THE PROTECTION OF UNBORN CHILDREN IRELAND LTD v. STEPHEN GROGAN AND OTHERS
### Case C-159/90, 1991 ECJ CELEX LEXIS 409, [1991] ECR I-4865

[Proceedings were brought by the Society for the Protection of Unborn Children Ireland Ltd ("SPUC") against Stephen Grogan and fourteen other officers of students associations in connection with the distribution in Ireland of specific information relating to the identity and location of clinics in another Member State where medical termination of pregnancy is carried out.]

3 Abortion has always been prohibited in Ireland, first of all at common law, then by statute. The relevant provisions at present in force are Sections 58 and 59 of the Offences Against the Person Act 1861, as reaffirmed in the Health (Family Planning) Act 1979.

4 In 1983 a constitutional amendment approved by referendum inserted in Article 40, Section 3, of the Irish Constitution a third subsection worded as follows: "The State acknowledges the right to life of the unborn and, with due regard to the equal right to life of the mother, guarantees in its laws to respect, and, as far as practicable, by its laws to defend and vindicate that right."

5 According to the Irish courts . . . to assist pregnant women in Ireland to travel abroad to obtain abortions, inter alia by informing them of the identity and location of a specific clinic or clinics where abortions are performed and how to contact such clinics, is prohibited under Article 40.3.3 of the Irish Constitution.

6 SPUC, the plaintiff in the main proceedings, is a company incorporated under Irish law whose purpose is to prevent the decriminalization of abortion and to affirm, defend and promote human life from the moment of conception. In 1989/90 Stephen Grogan and the other defendants in the main proceedings were officers of students associations which issued certain publications for students. Those publications contained information about the availability of legal abortion in the United Kingdom, the identity and location of a number of abortion clinics in that country and how to contact them. It is undisputed that the students associations had no links with clinics in another Member State.

7 In September 1989 SPUC requested the defendants, in their capacity as officers of their respective associations, to undertake not to publish information of the kind described above during the academic year 1989/90. The defendants did not reply, and SPUC then brought proceedings in the High Court for a declaration that the distribution of such information was unlawful and for an injunction restraining its distribution.

* * *

16 In its first question, the national court essentially seeks to establish whether medical termination of pregnancy, performed in accordance with the law of the

State where it is carried out, constitutes a service within the meaning of Article 60 [57] of the EEC Treaty.

17 According to the first paragraph of that provision, services are to be considered to be "services" within the meaning of the Treaty where they are normally provided for remuneration, in so far as they are not governed by the provisions relating to freedom of movement for goods, capital or persons. Indent (d) of the second paragraph of Article 60 [57] expressly states that activities of the professions fall within the definition of services.

18 It must be held that termination of pregnancy, as lawfully practised in several Member States, is a medical activity which is normally provided for remuneration and may be carried out as part of a professional activity. . . .

19 SPUC, however, maintains that the provision of abortion cannot be regarded as being a service, on the grounds that it is grossly immoral and involves the destruction of the life of a human being, namely the unborn child.

20 Whatever the merits of those arguments on the moral plane, they cannot influence the answer to the national court's first question. It is not for the Court to substitute its assessment for that of the legislature in those Member States where the activities in question are practised legally.

21 Consequently, the answer to the national court's first question must be that medical termination of pregnancy, performed in accordance with the law of the State in which it is carried out, constitutes a service within the meaning of Article 60 [57] of the Treaty.

Second and third questions

22 Having regard to the facts of the case, it must be considered that, in its second and third questions, the national court seeks essentially to establish whether it is contrary to Community law for a Member State in which medical termination of pregnancy is forbidden to prohibit students associations from distributing information about the identity and location of clinics in another Member State where medical termination of pregnancy is lawfully carried out and the means of communicating with those clinics, where the clinics in question have no involvement in the distribution of the said information.

23 Although the national court's questions refer to Community law in general, the Court takes the view that its attention should be focused on the provisions of Article 59 [56] et seq. of the EEC Treaty, which deal with the freedom to provide services, and the argument concerning human rights, which has been treated extensively in the observations submitted to the Court.

24 As regards, first, the provisions of Article 59 [56] of the Treaty, which prohibit any restriction on the freedom to supply services, it is apparent from the facts of the case that the link between the activity of the students associations of which Mr Grogan and the other defendants are officers and medical terminations of pregnancies carried out in clinics in another Member State is too tenuous for the prohibition on the distribution of information to be capable of being regarded as a restriction within the meaning of Article 59 [56] of the Treaty.

25 The situation in which students associations distributing the information at issue in the main proceedings are not in cooperation with the clinics whose addresses they publish can be distinguished from the situation which gave rise to the judgment in GB-INNO-BM (Case C-362/88 GB-INNO-BM v. Confederation du Commerce Luxembourgeois 1990 I-667), in which the Court held that a prohibition on the distribution of advertising was capable of constituting a barrier to the free movement of goods and therefore had to be examined in the light of Articles 30 [34], 31 [deleted] and 36 [36] of the EEC Treaty.

26 The information to which the national court's questions refer is not distributed on behalf of an economic operator established in another Member State. On the contrary, the information constitutes a manifestation of freedom of expression and of the freedom to impart and receive information which is independent of the economic activity carried on by clinics established in another Member State.

27 It follows that, in any event, a prohibition on the distribution of information in circumstances such as those which are the subject of the main proceedings cannot be regarded as a restriction within the meaning of Article 59 [56] of the Treaty.

28 Secondly, it is necessary to consider the argument of the defendants in the main proceedings to the effect that the prohibition in question, inasmuch as it is based on a constitutional amendment approved in 1983, is contrary to Article 62 [deleted] the EEC Treaty, which provides that Member States are not to introduce any new restrictions on the freedom to provide services in fact attained at the date when the Treaty entered into force.

29 It is sufficient to observe, as far as that argument is concerned, that Article 62 [59], which is complementary to Article 59 [56], cannot prohibit restrictions which do not fall within the scope of Article 59 [56].

30 Thirdly and lastly, the defendants in the main proceedings maintain that a prohibition such as the one at issue is in breach of fundamental rights, especially of freedom of expression and the freedom to receive and impart information, enshrined in particular in Article 10(1) of the European Convention on Human Rights.

31 . . . [W]here national legislation falls within the field of application of Community law the Court, when requested to give a preliminary ruling, must provide the national court with all the elements of interpretation which are necessary in order to enable it to assess the compatibility of that legislation with the fundamental rights — as laid down in particular in the European Convention on Human Rights — the observance of which the Court ensures. However, the Court has no such jurisdiction with regard to national legislation lying outside the scope of Community law. In view of the facts of the case and of the conclusions which the Court has reached above with regard to the scope of Articles 59 [56] and 62 [deleted] of the Treaty, that would appear to be true of the prohibition at issue before the national court.

32 The reply to the national court's second and third questions must therefore be that it is not contrary to Community law for a Member State in which medical termination of pregnancy is forbidden to prohibit students associations from distributing information about the identity and location of clinics in another

Member State where voluntary termination of pregnancy is lawfully carried out and the means of communicating with those clinics, where the clinics in question have no involvement in the distribution of the said information.

## NOTES AND QUESTIONS

1.   Why did the Court consider that the activity of distributing information fell outside the scope of EU law here?

2.   Note the remark in paragraph 24 that the links between the information providers and the services in question (abortion operations) was too "tenuous". Do you agree?

## [C]   The Need for an Economic Activity

### CHRISTELLE DELIEGE v. LIGUE FRANCOPHONE DE JUDO ET DISCIPLINES ASSOCIEES ASBL, LIGUE BELGE DE JUDO ASBL, UNION EUROPEENNE DE JUDO AND FRANCOIS PACQUEE
Joined Cases C-51/96 and C-191/97, 2000 ECJ CELEX LEXIS 22, [2000] ECR I-2549

[Ms Deliège had practised judo since 1983 and had been declared Belgian champion on several occasions, European champion once and under-19 world champion once, as well as winning and being highly placed in international tournaments. The parties disagreed as to Ms Deliège's status: she claimed to practise judo professionally or semi-professionally whilst the responsible Sports bodies, the Belgian Judo Leagues contended that judo was a sport which, in Europe and in Belgium in particular, was practised by amateurs.

There had been a series of disagreements between Ms Deliège and the Belgian leagues over their failure to select her for international events including the Barcelona and Atlanta Olympics. In making their decisions, they applied a system of rules-based quotas as to how many players from a given category could be selected. Ms Deliège claimed that these rules interfered with her right to provide services in other Member States. In particular, the systematic requirement of a quota and selection at national level appeared to constitute a barrier to the freedom to pursue an activity of an economic nature.]

41 It is to be remembered at the outset that, having regard to the objectives of the Community, sport is subject to Community law only in so far as it constitutes an economic activity within the meaning of Article 2 of the Treaty . . . The Court has also recognised that sporting activities are of considerable social importance in the Community . . .

42 That case-law is also supported by the Declaration on Sport (Declaration 29) annexed to the final act of the Conference which adopted the text of the Amsterdam Treaty, which emphasises the social significance of sport and calls on the bodies of the European Union to give special consideration to the particular characteristics of

amateur sport. In particular, that declaration is consistent with the abovementioned case-law in so far as it relates to situations in which sport constitutes an economic activity.

43 It must be recalled that the Treaty provisions concerning freedom of movement for persons do not prevent the adoption of rules or practices excluding foreign players from certain matches for reasons which are not of an economic nature, which relate to the particular nature and context of such matches and are thus of sporting interest only, such as, for example, matches between national teams from different countries. The Court stressed, however, that that restriction on the scope of the provisions in question must remain limited to its proper objective and cannot be relied upon to exclude the whole of a sporting activity . . .

44 The selection rules at issue in the main proceedings do not relate to events between teams or selected competitors from different countries comprising only nationals of the State of which the Federation which selected them is a member, such as the Olympic Games or certain world or European championships, but reserve participation, by the national federation, in certain other international events of a high level to athletes who are affiliated to the federation in question, regardless of their nationality. The mere circumstance that the placings achieved by athletes in those competitions are taken into account in determining which countries may enter representatives for the Olympic Games cannot justify treating those competitions as events between national teams which might fall outside the scope of Community law.

45 The LFJ submits in particular that sports associations and federations are entitled freely to determine the conditions governing access to competitions which concern only amateur sportsmen.

46 In that regard, it is important to note that the mere fact that a sports association or federation unilaterally classifies its members as amateur athletes does not in itself mean that those members do not engage in economic activities within the meaning of Article 2 of the Treaty.

47 As regards the nature of the rules at issue, . . . the Community provisions on the free movement of persons and services not only apply to the action of public authorities but extend also to rules of any other nature aimed at regulating gainful employment and the provision of services in a collective manner. The abolition as between Member States of obstacles to freedom of movement for persons and to freedom to provide services would be compromised if the abolition of State barriers could be neutralised by obstacles resulting from the exercise, by associations or organisations not governed by public law, of their legal autonomy.

48 It follows that the Treaty, and in particular Articles 59 [56], 60 [57] and 66 [62] thereof, may apply to sporting activities and to the rules laid down by sports associations of the kind at issue in the main proceedings.

49 In view of the foregoing considerations and the conflicting views expressed before the Court, it is important to verify whether an activity of the kind engaged in by Ms Deliege is capable of constituting an economic activity within the meaning of Article 2 of the Treaty and more particularly, the provision of services within the meaning of Article 59 [56] of that Treaty.

50 In the context of judicial cooperation between national courts and the Court of Justice, it is for national courts to establish and to evaluate the facts of the case . . . and for the Court of Justice to provide the national court with such guidance on interpretation as may be necessary to enable it to decide the dispute . . .

51 In that connection, it is important to note first that the judgment making the reference in Case C-191/97 refers among other things to grants awarded on the basis of earlier sporting results and to sponsorship contracts directly linked to the results achieved by the athlete. Moreover, Ms Deliege stated to the Court — and produced supporting documents — that she had received, by reason of her sporting achievements, grants from the Belgian French-speaking Community and from the Belgian Inter-Federal and Olympic Committee and that she has been sponsored by a banking institution and a motor-car manufacturer.

52 As regards, next, the concepts of economic activities and the provision of services within the meaning of Articles 2 [repealed] and 59 [56] of the Treaty respectively, it must be pointed out that those concepts define the field of application of one of the fundamental freedoms guaranteed by the Treaty and, as such, may not be interpreted restrictively . . .

53 As regards more particularly the first of those concepts, . . . the pursuit of an activity as an employed person or the provision of services for remuneration must be regarded as an economic activity within the meaning of Article 2 of the Treaty.

54 However, . . . the work performed must be genuine and effective and not such as to be regarded as purely marginal and ancillary.

55 As regards the provision of services, under the first paragraph of Article 60 [57] services are considered to be services within the meaning of the Treaty where they are normally provided for remuneration, in so far as they are not governed by the provisions relating to freedom of movement for goods, capital and persons.

56 In that connection, it must be stated that sporting activities and, in particular, a high-ranking athlete's participation in an international competition are capable of involving the provision of a number of separate, but closely related, services which may fall within the scope of Article 59 [56] of the Treaty even if some of those services are not paid for by those for whom they are performed . . .

57 For example, an organiser of such a competition may offer athletes an opportunity of engaging in their sporting activity in competition with others and, at the same time, the athletes, by participating in the competition, enable the organiser to put on a sports event which the public may attend, which television broadcasters may retransmit and which may be of interest to advertisers and sponsors. Moreover, the athletes provide their sponsors with publicity the basis for which is the sporting activity itself.

58 Finally, as regards the objections expressed in the observations submitted to the Court according to which, first, the main proceedings concern a purely internal situation and, second, certain international events fall outside the territorial scope of the Treaty, it must be remembered that the Treaty provisions on the freedom to provide services are not applicable to activities which are confined in all respects within a single Member State . . . However, a degree of extraneity may derive in

particular from the fact that an athlete participates in a competition in a Member State other than that in which he is established.

59 It is for the national court to determine, on the basis of those criteria of interpretation, whether Ms Deliege's sporting activities, and in particular her participation in international tournaments, constitutes an economic activity within the meaning of Article 2 of the Treaty and, more particularly, the provision of services within the meaning of Article 59 [56] of the Treaty.

60 If it is assumed that Ms Deliège's activity can be classified as a provision of services, it is necessary to consider whether the selection rules at issue in the main proceedings constitute a restriction on the freedom to provide services within the meaning of Article 59 [56] of the Treaty.

\* \* \*

66 Although a selection system may prove more favourable to one category of athletes than another, it cannot be inferred from that fact alone that the adoption of that system constitutes a restriction on the freedom to provide services.

67 Accordingly, it naturally falls to the bodies concerned, such as organisers of tournaments, sports federations or professional athletes' associations, to lay down appropriate rules and to make their selections in accordance with them.

68 In that connection, it must be conceded that the delegation of such a task to the national federations, which normally have the necessary knowledge and experience, is the arrangement adopted in most sporting disciplines, which is based in principle on the existence of a federation in each country. Moreover, it must be pointed out that the selection rules at issue in the main proceedings apply both to competitions organised within the Community and to those taking place outside it and involve both nationals of Member States and those of non-member countries.

69 The answer to the questions submitted must therefore be that a rule requiring professional or semi-professional athletes or persons aspiring to take part in a professional or semi-professional activity to have been authorised or selected by their federation in order to be able to participate in a high-level international sports competition, which does not involve national teams competing against each other, does not in itself, as long as it derives from a need inherent in the organisation of such a competition, constitute a restriction on the freedom to provide services prohibited by Article 59 [56] of the Treaty.

## NOTES AND QUESTIONS

1.    Ms. Deliège was seeking to bring her position as an ostensible amateur judo practitioner within the scope of the Treaty provisions on services. Are the guidelines for determining the applicability of EC 49/TFEU 56 to such cases clear in the Court's judgment? What might be the impact of EC 18/TFEU 21 here?

2.    In what sense (if any) did the way the sport was governed fit with the notion that Treaty articles can only be invoked against Member States?

**3.** As regards the personal free movement rights of individuals, the EU has elaborated on the basic restrictions set out in EC 49/TFEU 56 through the adoption of legislation, in this case, initially Directive 64/221, OJ (SE) 1963-1964, 117, now replaced by Directive 2004/38/EC of the Parliament and Council of 29 April 2004, [2004] OJ L158/77 on the right of citizens of the Union and their family members to move and reside freely within the territory of the Member States, which applies to employees, the freedom of establishment and the provision or receipt of services. This directive is often invoked *in conjunction with* the Treaty articles on services.

**4.** In a previous case, *Bond van Adverteerders v. Netherlands*, the Court had ruled that the requirement for some form of remuneration did not imply that it should be paid by the service recipient. Here, Dutch law in general prohibited the relay of television broadcasts from other Member States that contained advertisements directed specifically to Dutch residents. The distribution of these broadcasts by cable was found to comprise a number of services within the meaning of EC 49 and 50/TFEU 56 and 57, even though the cable relay companies were not paid by the broadcasters (for whom the inter-State element of the services were provided) but through subscription fees from viewers.

## [D]    Relationship to Other Freedoms

### STATE v. SACCHI
Case 155/73, 1974 ECJ CELEX LEXIS 47, [1974] ECR 409

[Under Italian law television was at the time a monopoly granted by the State to Radio Audizione Italiana (hereinafter called RAI), which involved on the one hand a monopoly in televised commercial advertising and on the other hand the prohibition on any other person or undertaking from receiving, for the purpose of their retransmission, audiovisual signals transmitted either from the national territory or from foreign stations.

Mr. Sacchi, who operated an unauthorized television relay undertaking (Telebiella), alleged that this system did not conform with the EC Treaty insofar as cable television was concerned. After he refused to pay the license fee for receivers for television relay, a refusal which Italian law treats as an offense, he was charged with "being in possession, in premises open to the public outside of his place of residence, of several television sets used to receive transmissions by cable without having paid the prescribed license fee."]

4 The first two questions posed by the national court seek in essence to know whether the principle of the free movement of goods in the Common Market applies to television broadcasts, especially in their commercial aspects, and whether the exclusive right, granted to a limited company by a member-State, to carry out all kinds of television broadcasting including broadcasting for purposes of commercial publicity, constitutes a violation of that principle.

5 The answer is dictated by the prior solution to the question of whether television broadcasts must be assimilated to products or goods, within the meaning of Article 3 (a) [repealed] and 9 [28] and of the introductory rubric to Title 1 of the Second Part of the Treaty.

6 In the absence of express provisions to the contrary in the Treaty, a television broadcast must, because of its nature, be regarded as a supply of services. While it is not entirely excluded that services provided normally against remuneration may fall under the provisions relating to the free movement of goods, such, however, is only the case, as emerges from Article 60 [57], inasmuch as they are governed by such provisions. It follows that the transmission of television broadcasts, including those having a publicity character, belongs, as such, to the rules in the Treaty relating to supplies of services.

7 On the other hand, trade exchanges involving all materials, sound tapes, films and other products used for the broadcasting of television programmers, are subject to the rules relating to the free movement of goods. In consequence, even though the existence of an undertaking having a monopoly of commercial television broadcasts is not in itself contrary to the principle of the free movement of goods, such an undertaking would contravene this principle by discriminating in favor of national materials and products.

8 In the same way, the fact that an undertaking in a member-State enjoys the exclusive right in respect of commercial television broadcasts is not, as such, incompatible with the free movement of the products whose marketing these broadcasts seek to promote. It would be different if the exclusive right was used to give preference, within the Community, to certain types of trade or to certain economic operators in relation to others. As is emphasized by Article 3 of the Commission directive of 22 December 1969, dealing with the removal of measures similar in effect to quantitative import restrictions not covered by other provisions made under the EEC Treaty, measures governing the marketing of products, the restrictive effects of which would go beyond the proper effects of a simple commercial system, are capable of amounting to measures similar in effect to quantitative restrictions. This would in particular be the case when these restrictive effects are out of proportion to the aim pursued — in the present case, the organization, according to the law of a member-State, of television serving the public interest.

9 Because the sixth question concerns the interpretation of Article 37[37] of the Treaty, it must be examined in conjunction with the problems raised by the provisions relating to the free movement of goods, among which this Article is placed. This question asks whether Article 37 [37] (1) and (2) applies to a limited company to which a member-State has granted the exclusive right to carry out television broadcasts on its territory, including commercial broadcasts and transmission of films and documents produced in the other member-States.

10 Article 37 [37] deals with the organization of national monopolies which are commercial in character. It results, both from the position of this provision in the chapter on the elimination of quantitative restrictions and from the use of the words 'imports' and 'exports' in Article 37 [37](1)(ii) and of the word 'products' in Article 37 [37] (3) and (4), that it envisages exchanges of goods and cannot relate to a monopoly for supplies of services. Thus, by reason of its character as a supply of service, televised commercial publicity escapes the application of these provisions.

## NOTES AND QUESTIONS

**1.** EC 31/TFEU 37 is covered more fully in Chapter 16, *infra*. What was the significance of the reference to article 37 (EC 31/TFEU 37) in this case?

**2.** Does the *Sacchi* case provide guidance on whether the provisions relating to goods or services should take precedence in the event that both apply (per the examples given by the Court)? Does it matter, or would the answer be the same whichever set of rules applied? What is the effect of the wording of EC 50/TFEU 57?

**3.** In the *Josémans* case, *supra*, the Court considers that the provision of narcotics in cafés was a service, not a supply of goods:

> 48. In order to ascertain whether such an activity concerns free movement of goods or the freedom to provide services, it must be borne in mind that an establishment is defined in Article 2.3.1.1(1)(a)(3) of the APV as a space to which the public has access and where food and/or non-alcoholic beverages are provided commercially, whether or not by means of vending machines, for consumption on the premises.

> 49. In such circumstances, . . . marketing of non-alcoholic beverages and food in coffee-shops appears to constitute a catering activity characterised by an array of features and acts in which services predominate as opposed to the supply of the product itself . . .

> 50. Since the free movement of goods aspect is entirely secondary to that of the freedom to provide services and may be considered together with it, the Court will examine the rules at issue in the main proceedings only in the light of the latter fundamental freedom . . .

It seems clear this was a characterization that was necessary if the ECJ were to consider the case to be affected by EU rules. If it had considered that the provisions on free movement of goods were applicable, as there was no effect on free movement — the goods were all consumed on the premises in the Netherlands.

## [E]  Exercise of Official Authority

### JOSEP PEÑARROJA FA v. BUREAU OF THE COUR DE CASSATION
#### Joined Cases C-372/09 and C-373/09, 2011 [2011] ECR

[The facts of this case are set out in the earlier extract appearing in this Chapter]

41 By its second question in each of the two cases, the Cour de Cassation asks in essence whether, in cases where the legal position is as defined by the French Codes of Civil and Criminal Procedure, Law No 71-498 and Decree No 2004-1463, the duty which is entrusted to a professional who has been appointed as a court expert translator by a national court for the purposes of a dispute before it is covered by the term 'activities connected with the exercise of official authority' as used in the first paragraph of Article 45 EC [51]. If it was to be covered by such definition,

restrictions on freedom of movement of services would be justified under article 45 EC [51].

42 [T]he Court has consistently held that the first paragraph of Article 45 EC [51] applies only to activities which in themselves involve a direct and specific connection with the exercise of official authority.

43 [T]he duty of a court expert translator is to provide to a high standard an impartial translation from one language to another, not to give an opinion on the substance of the case.

44 The translations carried out by such an expert are therefore merely ancillary steps and leave the discretion of judicial authority and the free exercise of judicial power intact, so that such translation services cannot be regarded as activities connected with the exercise of official authority.

## NOTES AND QUESTIONS

The official authority exemption applies to both services and establishment and is thus also addressed in Chapter 15. What do you think of the Court's view as expressed in the above case? Could one make a case that the exception ought to have a different meaning or scope in the case of the cross border provision of services as opposed to services provided by a person established in the Member State where they are provided?

# Chapter 15

## MEASURES AFFECTING MOVEMENT OF BUSINESSES AND CAPITAL

### § 15.01  OVERVIEW

***Template*** Article 7, Sections 7.4 – 7.6

***Materials in this Chapter***: The right of establishment laid out in EC 43/TFEU 49 deals with the freedom for individuals and companies to establish their business or create a branch or subsidiary, in any other Member State. The basic prohibition set out in EC 43/TFEU 49 seems to mirror the prohibition in EC 49/TFEU 56 in that it appears again to be subject to harmonization of national regulation. In the case of establishment, however, the right to regulate at a national level is clearly a major obstacle to its widespread application, since it is absolutely clear that Member States retain the right to regulate businesses and companies desiring to establish a permanent presence within their territory. In the absence of harmonizing regulation at the Union level, it would seem that even though EC 43/TFEU 49 is directly applicable, it is likely to be of very limited effect. In fact, this situation ought not to be a surprise to U.S. readers because much professional and corporate regulation is also at a State level and many professional qualifications are not subject to mutual recognition or only as between certain states that operate on reciprocity. Yet we see that in the EU, the ECJ once again has extended the reach of these articles beyond the core prohibition against discrimination on grounds of nationality.

Establishment is closely linked to the movement of capital as a practical matter, in particular with regard to its relationship with the taxation competence of the Member States. Hence the inclusion of that subject in this chapter. Capital movements are covered by EC 56/TFEU 63 et seq. This freedom is by far the youngest, having really only been fully endorsed in the EC/TFEU as a result of the first TEU and the decision to move forward to a single currency. There is therefore relatively little case law. The biggest impact has been its encroachment into the taxation competences of the Member States. The cases in this chapter will illustrate how the ECJ has wrestled with the protections of those competences when addressing EC 56/TFEU 63 et seq.

***Harmonization action at the EU Level*** Perhaps in significant measure because of the perceived direct threat to people's livelihoods, the EU's attempts to harmonize rules relating to authorizations and qualifications to carry on a trade or profession were fraught with controversy and difficulty. Very little was achieved by the original deadline (the end of the transitional period), and the Court stepped in to assure at least some relaxation of rules that impeded cross-border provision of services and establishment. Thereafter, piecemeal legislation occurred over time, leading to an initial general directive on mutual recognition — Directive 89/48, [1989] OJ L19/16. This directive covered mutual recognition of higher education and professional qualifications for individuals who had completed all professional training in their home state. Where there were significant differences in education requirements, there was provision for additional testing. This directive was followed by Directive 92/51, which adopted the same mutual recognition approach for post-secondary educational requirements. These directives and subsequent ones covering various professions such as architects, doctors and nurses were eventually swept into a consolidating text in the form of Directive 2005/36, [2005] OJ L 255/22. The EU's website provides a helpful summary and is included in the materials below. It should be noted that Directive 2005/36 does not consolidate the two prior directives on legal practice, which dealt with authorization to practice, although it does embrace the recognition of qualifications.

***The relationship of establishment and the free movement of workers*** Although the "establishment" provisions of the Treaty address self-employed persons and companies, it is often the case that restrictions on movement relating to qualifications arise in relation to employed people, too. An airline pilot, a teacher or a plumber are just as likely to be availing themselves of the provisions relating to the free movement of workers. Yet the provisions relating to the latter, strictly speaking, only address the basic freedom of personal movement and not obstacles arising from disparities in professional or education qualifications required for a particular job. In practice, Union legislation has equated this situation to that of establishment, thus it might be more appropriate to describe the overall body of law that has developed in this area as designed to facilitate the pursuit of an occupation whether as a self-employed person or as an employed person. This should be kept in mind when considering the materials in this chapter as they relate to recognition of diplomas.

## § 15.02   THE RIGHT OF ESTABLISHMENT FOR INDIVIDUALS

### [A]   The Meaning of "Establishment"

### REINHARD GEBHARD v. CONSIGLIO DELL'ORDINE DEGLI AVVOCATI E PROCURATORI DI MILANO
Case C-55/94, 1995 ECJ CELEX LEXIS 443, [1995] ECR I-4165

[Mr Gebhard, a German national, had been authorized to practise as a Rechtsanwalt (lawyer) in Germany since 3 August 1977 and was a member of the Bar of Stuttgart, where he was an "independent collaborator" within a group of lawyers (Bürogemeinschaft) although he did not have an office of his own in Germany. He had resided since March 1978 in Italy, where he lived with his wife, an Italian national, and his three children. His income was taxed entirely in Italy, his country of residence. He had pursued professional activity there since taking up residence and used the term avvocato on his letterhead to describe his professional position. The Milan bar prohibited him from doing so and opened disciplinary proceedings. Mr Gebhard then applied to the Milan Bar Council to be entered on the roll of members of the Bar. His application was based on Council Directive 89/48/EEC of 21 December 1988 on a general system for the recognition of higher-education diplomas awarded on completion of professional education and training of at least three years' duration (OJ 1989 L 19, p. 16) (now superseded by Directive 2005/36) and on his having completed a ten-year training period in Italy. The disciplinary proceedings were completed by a decision of 30 December 1992 by which the Milan Bar Council imposed on Mr Gebhard the sanction of suspension from pursuing his professional activity for six months.]

22 The provisions of the chapter on services are subordinate to those of the chapter on the right of establishment in so far, first, as the wording of the first paragraph of Article 59 [56] assumes that the provider and the recipient of the service concerned are "established" in two different Member States and, second, as the first paragraph of Article 60 [57] specifies that the provisions relating to services apply only if those relating to the right of establishment do not apply. It is therefore necessary to consider the scope of the concept of "establishment".

23 The right of establishment, provided for in Articles 52 [49] to 58 [54] of the Treaty, is granted both to legal persons within the meaning of Article 58 [54] and to natural persons who are nationals of a Member State of the Community. Subject to the exceptions and conditions laid down, it allows all types of self-employed activity to be taken up and pursued on the territory of any other Member State, undertakings to be formed and operated, and agencies, branches or subsidiaries to be set up.

24 It follows that a person may be established, within the meaning of the Treaty, in more than one Member State in particular, in the case of companies, through the setting-up of agencies, branches or subsidiaries (Article 52 [49]) and, as the Court has held, in the case of members of the professions, by establishing a second professional base . . .

25 The concept of establishment within the meaning of the Treaty is therefore a very broad one, allowing a Community national to participate, on a stable and continuous basis, in the economic life of a Member State other than his State of origin and to profit therefrom, so contributing to economic and social interpenetration within the Community in the sphere of activities as self-employed persons . . .

26 In contrast, where the provider of services moves to another Member State, the provisions of the chapter on services, in particular the third paragraph of Article 60, envisage that he is to pursue his activity there on a temporary basis.

27 . . . [T]he temporary nature of the activities in question has to be determined in the light, not only of the duration of the provision of the service, but also of its regularity, periodicity or continuity. The fact that the provision of services is temporary does not mean that the provider of services within the meaning of the Treaty may not equip himself with some form of infrastructure in the host Member State (including an office, chambers or consulting rooms) in so far as such infrastructure is necessary for the purposes of performing the services in question.

28 However, that situation is to be distinguished from that of Mr Gebhard who, as a national of a Member State, pursues a professional activity on a stable and continuous basis in another Member State where he holds himself out from an

established professional base to, amongst others, nationals of that State. Such a national comes under the provisions of the chapter relating to the right of establishment and not those of the chapter relating to services.

## COMMISSION v. GERMANY
### (INSURANCE SERVICES)
### Case 205/84, 1986 ECJ CELEX LEXIS 100, [1986] ECR 3755

[The Commission brought proceedings against Germany regarding its regulation of the insurance industry. The first head of claim concerned all insurance business other than transport insurance, EU co-insurance and compulsory insurance. It addressed specifically the requirements of establishment and authorization imposed by the German legislation on EU insurers as providers of services within the meaning of the Treaty.]

18 According to the first paragraph of Article 59 [56] of the EEC Treaty, the abolition of restrictions on the freedom to provide services within the Community concerns all services provided by nationals of Member States who are established in a State of the Community other than that of the person for whom the services are intended. The first paragraph of Article 60 [57] provides that services are to be considered to be "services" within the meaning of the Treaty where they are normally provided for remuneration, insofar as they are not governed by the provisions relating to freedom of movement for goods, capital and persons. Those articles require the abolition of all restrictions on the free movement of the provision of services, as thus defined, subject nevertheless to the provisions of Article 61 [58] and those of Article 55 [52] and 56 [53] to which Article 66 [61] refers.

\*    \*    \*

21 [I]t must be acknowledged that an insurance undertaking of another Member State which maintains a permanent presence in the Member State in question comes within the scope of the provisions of the Treaty on the right of establishment, even if that presence does not take the form of a branch or agency, but consists merely of an office managed by the undertaking's own staff or by a person who is independent but authorized to act on a permanent basis for the undertaking, as would be the case with an agency. In light of the aforementioned definition contained in the first paragraph of Article 60 [57], such an insurance undertaking cannot therefore avail itself of Articles 59 [56] and 60 [57] with regard to its activities in the Member State in question.

\*    \*    \*

23 Finally, it should be mentioned that since the scope of Articles 59 [56] and 60 [57] is defined by reference to the places of establishment or of residence of the provider of the services and of the person for whom they are intended, special problems may arise where the risk covered by the insurance contract is situated on the territory of a Member State other than that of the policy holder, as the person for whom the services are intended. The Court of Justice does not propose in these proceedings to consider such problems, which were not the subject of argument before it. The following examination therefore concerns only insurance against risks situated in the Member State of the policy holder (hereinafter referred to as "the State in

which the service is provided"). It follows from the foregoing that in order to give judgment in these proceedings it is necessary to consider only the provision of services relating to contracts of insurance against risks situated in a Member State concluded by a policy holder established or residing in that State with an insurer who is established in another Member State and who does not maintain any permanent presence in the first State or direct his business activities entirely or principally toward the territory of that State.

\*     \*     \*

63 As regards the insurance sector in general, the Court has already held in this case that the requirement of establishment is incompatible with articles 59 [56] and 60 [57] of the Treaty. Consequently, such a requirement in relation to the leading insurer can find no basis in directive 78/473. It is therefore sufficient to consider whether the requirement that the leading insurer must be authorized in the country of the risk is in conformity with Community law.

64 In that respect consideration of the first head of claim has shown that the requirement that an insurance undertaking providing services must be authorized in the state in which the service is provided can be regarded as compatible with the Treaty only in so far as it is justified on grounds relating to the protection of the consumer both as a policy-holder and as an insured person. According to article 1 (2) thereof, Directive 78/473 concerns only insurance against risks which by reason of their nature or size call for the participation of several insurers for their coverage. Moreover, according to article 1 (1) the directive applies only to community co-insurance operations relating to certain of the risks listed in the annex to Directive 73/239. For example, it does not concern either life assurance or accident and sickness insurance or road traffic civil liability insurance. The Directive is concerned with insurance which is taken out only by large undertakings or groups of undertakings which are in a position to assess and negotiate insurance policies proposed to them. Consequently, the arguments based on consumer protection do not have the same force as in connection with other forms of insurance.

## NOTES AND QUESTIONS

1.   Do these two cases provide a clear determinant as to when a person is or is not established in another Member State?

2.   In *Insurance Services*, the Court ultimately held that a requirement of establishment for insurance companies based in other Member States was incompatible with EC 49 and 50/TFEU 56 and 57 as regards insured risks in the host state. Note, however, that while a requirement to have a presence in the host country seems clearly discriminatory, the lesser requirements mentioned by the court would not necessarily be considered to be so.

*Insurance Services* exemplified quite a widespread problem, namely the insistence of the Member States on control of out-of-state activities that have an effect within the state. Insurance is a particularly sensitive area because of the need to make sure that insurance companies engaged in direct insurance of risks within the state have the means to meet claims, failure of which might result in widespread economic dislocation. Other insurance cases decided by the European Court of Justice include *Commission v. Ireland*, Case 206/84, 1986 ECJ CELEX LEXIS 101, [1986] ECR 3817, *Commission v. France*, Case 220/83, 1986 ECJ CELEX LEXIS 19, [1986] ECR 3663, *Commission v. Denmark*, Case 252/83, 1986 ECJ CELEX LEXIS 23, [1986] ECR 3713.

3.   The requirement to have a physical presence in the host state has something of a parallel in the United States in the case of residence requirements regarding the practice of law. In *New Hampshire v. Piper*, 470 U.S. 274, 105 S. Ct. 1272, 84 L. Ed. 2d 205 (1985). Piper, a resident of Vermont, passed the New Hampshire bar exam but was refused admission because she lived out of state (actually only 400 yards from the state line). The majority held that the requirement violated the Privileges and Immunities Clause but Justice Rehnquist dissented in the following terms:

> The reason that the practice of law should be treated differently is that law is one occupation that does not readily translate across state lines. Certain aspects of legal practice are distinctly and intentionally nonnational; in this regard one might view this country's legal system as the antithesis of the norms embodied in the Art. IV Privileges and Immunities Clause. Put simply, the state has a substantial interest in creating its own set of laws responsive to its own local interests, and it is reasonable for a State to decide that those people who have been trained to analyze law and policy are better equipped to write those state laws and adjudicate cases arising under them.

## THE QUEEN v. SECRETARY OF STATE FOR TRANSPORT, EX PARTE FACTORTAME LTD AND OTHERS
### C-221/89, 1991 ECJ CELEX LEXIS 165, [1991] ECR I-3905

[For facts, see the summary in Chapter 3]

20 It must be observed . . . that the concept of establishment within the meaning of Article 52 [49] et seq. of the Treaty involves the actual pursuit of an economic activity through a fixed establishment in another Member State for an indefinite period.

21 Consequently, the registration of a vessel does not necessarily involve establishment within the meaning of the Treaty, in particular where the vessel is not used to pursue an economic activity or where the application for registration is made by or on behalf of a person who is not established, and has no intention of becoming established, in the State concerned.

22 However, where the vessel constitutes an instrument for pursuing an economic activity which involves a fixed establishment in the Member State concerned, the registration of that vessel cannot be dissociated from the exercise of the freedom of establishment.

23 It follows that the conditions laid down for the registration of vessels must not form an obstacle to freedom of establishment within the meaning of Article 52 [49]

et seq. of the Treaty.

24 The United Kingdom and Belgium argue, however, that the registration of a vessel in a Member State is not a conditio sine qua non of establishment in that State, since natural persons or companies are not precluded from operating vessels, even fishing vessels, for instance from the United Kingdom, in the context of operations linked to the territory of that State; establishment in the United Kingdom in that way would be possible in respect of any vessel registered in one of the other Member States.

25 That argument cannot be upheld. According to the second paragraph of Article 52 [49] of the Treaty, freedom of establishment includes, in the case of nationals of a Member State, "the right to take up and pursue activities as self-employed persons . . . under the conditions laid down for its own nationals by the law of the country where such establishment is effected . . .".

26 The United Kingdom, Belgium, Denmark and Greece consider that the Treaty does not preclude a nationality requirement of the type at issue in the main proceedings, because discrimination on grounds of nationality can arise only where, under the law of a Member State, persons are treated differently on account of their nationality. In contrast, in this case, what is involved is not discriminatory treatment on grounds of nationality but a condition for the grant of nationality, and the Member States are free to determine to whom they will grant or refuse their nationality, in the case of natural persons and ships alike.

27 In that connection, it must be observed that the concept of the "nationality" of ships, which are not persons, is different from that of the "nationality" of natural persons.

28 The prohibition of discrimination on grounds of nationality, which is set out in particular, as regards the right of establishment, in Article 52 of the Treaty, is concerned with differences of treatment as between natural persons who are nationals of Member States and as between companies who are treated in the same way as such persons by virtue of Article 58.

29 Consequently, in exercising its powers for the purposes of defining the conditions for the grant of its "nationality" to a ship, each Member State must comply with the prohibition of discrimination against nationals of Member States on grounds of their nationality.

30 It follows from the foregoing that a condition of the type at issue in the main proceedings which stipulates that where a vessel is owned or chartered by natural persons they must be of a particular nationality and where it is owned or chartered by a company the shareholders and directors must be of that nationality is contrary to Article 52 [49] of the Treaty.

31 Such a condition is also contrary to Article 221 [55] of the Treaty, under which Member States must accord nationals of the other Member States the same treatment as their own nationals as regards participation in the capital of companies or firms within the meaning of Article 58 [54].

32 As for the requirement for the owners, charterers, managers and operators of the vessel and, in the case of a company, the shareholders and directors to be

resident and domiciled in the Member State in which the vessel is to be registered, it must be held that such a requirement, which is not justified by the rights and obligations created by the grant of a national flag to a vessel, results in discrimination on grounds of nationality. The great majority of nationals of the Member State in question are resident and domiciled in that State and therefore meet that requirement automatically, whereas nationals of other Member States would, in most cases, have to move their residence and domicile to that State in order to comply with the requirements of its legislation. It follows that such a requirement is contrary to Article 52 [49].

33 It follows from the foregoing that it is contrary to the provisions of Community law and, in particular, to Article 52 [49] of the EEC Treaty for a Member State to stipulate as conditions for the registration of a fishing vessel in its national register: (a) that the legal owners and beneficial owners and the charterers, managers and operators of the vessel must be nationals of that Member State or companies incorporated in that Member State, and that, in the latter case, at least 75% of the shares in the company must be owned by nationals of that Member State or by companies fulfilling the same requirements and 75% of the directors of the company must be nationals of that Member State; and (b) that the said legal owners and beneficial owners, charterers, managers, operators, shareholders and directors, as the case may be, must be resident and domiciled in that Member State.

34 In this regard, it is sufficient to point out that a requirement for the registration of a vessel to the effect that it must be managed and its operations directed and controlled from within the Member State in which it is to be registered essentially coincides with the actual concept of establishment within the meaning of Article 52 [49] et seq. of the Treaty, which implies a fixed establishment. It follows that those articles, which enshrine the very concept of freedom of establishment, cannot be interpreted as precluding such a requirement.

35 Such a requirement, however, would not be compatible with those provisions if it had to be interpreted as precluding registration in the event that a secondary establishment or the centre for directing the operations of the vessel in the Member State in which the vessel was to be registered acted on instructions from a decision-taking centre located in the Member State of the principal establishment.

36 Consequently, the reply to the national court must be that it is not contrary to Community law for a Member State to stipulate as a condition for the registration of a fishing vessel in its national register that the vessel in question must be managed and its operations directed and controlled from within that Member State.

## NOTES AND QUESTIONS

1. This was the second of the three cases involving Factortame. An excerpt from the first case, including a description of the factual background, is set out in Chapter 3, *supra*; while the third case, involving damages for breach of EU law and which was joined with a case from Germany (*Brasserie du Pêcheur*), is set out in Chapter 9.

2. The Court here was dealing with a UK rule requiring that companies that owned vessels should be 75 percent owned by British nationals for that vessel to be

registered in the UK Shipping Register and thus treated as "British". The owning companies themselves were incorporated there. This rule was found to violate EC 43/TFEU 49, while the requirement that registration be conditional on the location of the vessel's management and direction of operations in the UK did not. This would mean then that using a company incorporated in the UK as a mere cipher through which instructions could be given from outside the UK would not be protected by EC 43/TFEU 49. Does this decision, then, stand for the proposition that a company's place of establishment is determined by where it has its central management and control? (Consider in this respect to paragraphs 35 and 36)

3.    For a comparison with United States law on this point, see, e.g., *Lewis v. BT Investment Managers*, 447 U.S. 27, 100 S. Ct. 2009, 64 L. Ed. 2d 702 (1980). Florida had enacted legislation prohibiting out-of-state banks from providing investment advisory services through a branch. This was held unanimously by the Supreme Court to be a violation of the dormant Commerce Clause.

## [B]    The Meaning of "Nationals of a Member State" in EC 43/TFEU 49

### J. KNOORS v. SECRETARY OF STATE FOR ECONOMIC AFFAIRS
Case 115/78, 1979 ECJ CELEX LEXIS 139, [1979] ECR 399

[The plaintiff, a Netherlands national residing in Belgium, was engaged, during lengthy residence in that Member State, as an employed person in a plumbing business and since 1970 had worked as a plumbing contractor as the head of an independent business. He had applied to the Netherland s for a license to carry on his trade there and was refused. He invoked Directive 64/427 claiming to be a "beneficiary" of its provisions relating to the right of establishment, and the Court concluded that he was, even though he was a national of the State against which he was invoking the directive.]

19 This interpretation [that he was a beneficiary of the directive] is justified by the requirements flowing from freedom of movement for persons, freedom of establishment and freedom to provide services, which are guaranteed by Articles 3(c), 48 [45], 52 [49] and 59 [56] of the Treaty.

20 In fact, these liberties, which are fundamental in the Community system, could not be fully realized if the Member States were in a position to refuse to grant the benefit of the provisions of Community law to those of their nationals who have taken advantage of the facilities existing in the matter of freedom of movement and establishment and who have acquired, by virtue of such facilities, the trade qualifications referred to by the directive in a Member State other than that whose nationality they possess.

21 In contesting this solution the Netherlands Government states, first, that the first paragraph of Article 52 [49] provides for the abolition of "restrictions on the freedom of establishment of nationals of a Member State in the territory of another Member State" and, secondly, that according to the second paragraph of the same article, freedom of establishment is to include the right to take up activities as

self-employed persons under the conditions laid down by the law of the country where such establishment is effected "for its own nationals".

22 t is claimed that those provisions of the Treaty show that the nationals of the host State are not regarded by the Treaty as being beneficiaries of the liberalization measures for which provision is made and that they therefore remain entirely subject to the provisions of their national legislation.

23 Moreover, the Netherlands Government draws attention to the risk that the nationals of a Member State might evade the application of their national provisions in the matter of training for a trade if they were authorized to avail themselves, as against their own national authorities, of the facilities created by the directive.

24 Although it is true that the provisions of the Treaty relating to establishment and the provision of services cannot be applied to situations which are purely internal to a Member State, the position nevertheless remains that the reference in Article 52 [49] to "nationals of a Member State" cannot be interpreted in such a way as to exclude from the benefit of Community law a given Member State's own nationals when the latter, owing to the fact that they have lawfully resided on the territory of another Member State and have there acquired a trade qualification which is recognized by the provisions of Community law, are, with regard to their State of origin, in a situation which may be assimilated to that of any other persons enjoying the rights and liberties guaranteed by the Treaty.

25 However, it is not possible to disregard the legitimate interest which a Member State may have in preventing certain of its nationals, by means of facilities created under the Treaty, from attempting wrongly to evade the application of their national legislation as regards training for a trade.

26 In this case, however, it should be borne in mind that, having regard to the nature of the trades in question, the precise conditions set out in Article 3 of Directive No 64/427, as regards the length of periods during which the activity in question must have been pursued, have the effects of excluding, in the fields in question, the risk of abuse referred to by the Netherlands Government.

27 Moreover, it should be emphasized that it is always possible for the Council, by virtue of the powers conferred upon it by Article 57 [53] of the Treaty, to remove the causes of any abuses of the law by arranging for the harmonization of the conditions of training for a trade in the various Member States.

## NOTES AND QUESTIONS

1.   What consequence did the ECJ's ruling have here for the meaning of the phrase "nationals of a Member State"?

2.   Why did the Dutch government object to Knoors' request?

## [C] Requirement for Compliance with Host State Regulation, and the Scope of Mutual Recognition

### REINHARD GEBHARD v. CONSIGLIO DELL'ORDINE DEGLI AVVOCATI E PROCURATORI DI MILANO
Case C-55/94, 1995 ECJ CELEX LEXIS 443, [1995] ECR I-4165

[The facts of this case are set out in the excerpt *supra.*]

31 The provisions relating to the right of establishment cover the taking-up and pursuit of activities (see, in particular, the judgment in Reyners, paragraphs 46 and 47). Membership of a professional body may be a condition of taking up and pursuit of particular activities. It cannot itself be constitutive of establishment.

32 It follows that the question whether it is possible for a national of a Member State to exercise his right of establishment and the conditions for exercise of that right must be determined in the light of the activities which he intends to pursue on the territory of the host Member State.

33 Under the terms of the second paragraph of Article 52 [49], freedom of establishment is to be exercised under the conditions laid down for its own nationals by the law of the country where establishment is effected.

34 In the event that the specific activities in question are not subject to any rules in the host State, so that a national of that Member State does not have to have any specific qualification in order to pursue them, a national of any other Member State is entitled to establish himself on the territory of the first State and pursue those activities there.

35 However, the taking-up and pursuit of certain self-employed activities may be conditional on complying with certain provisions laid down by law, regulation or administrative action justified by the general good, such as rules relating to organization, qualifications, professional ethics, supervision and liability . . . Such provisions may stipulate in particular that pursuit of a particular activity is restricted to holders of a diploma, certificate or other evidence of formal qualifications, to persons belonging to a professional body or to persons subject to particular rules or supervision, as the case may be. They may also lay down the conditions for the use of professional titles, such as avvocato.

36 Where the taking-up or pursuit of a specific activity is subject to such conditions in the host Member State, a national of another Member State intending to pursue that activity must in principle comply with them. It is for this reason that Article 57 [53] provides that the Council is to issue directives, such as Directive 89/48, for the mutual recognition of diplomas, certificates and other evidence of formal qualifications or, as the case may be, for the coordination of national provisions concerning the taking-up and pursuit of activities as self-employed persons.

37 It follows, however, from the Court's case-law that national measures liable to hinder or make less attractive the exercise of fundamental freedoms guaranteed by the Treaty must fulfil four conditions: they must be applied in a non-discriminatory manner; they must be justified by imperative requirements in the general interest;

they must be suitable for securing the attainment of the objective which they pursue; and they must not go beyond what is necessary in order to attain it . . .

## NOTES AND QUESTIONS

In an early decision, *Reyners* (appearing below in another context), the Court had seemed to hold that under EC 43/TFEU 49 in the context of the rules on establishment, only discrimination on grounds of nationality is prohibited. How has the Court's thinking evolved in *Gebhard*? Is the Court's reasoning in this case reconcilable with the wording of EC 43/TFEU 49?

## THIEFFRY v. CONSEIL DE L'ORDRE DES ADVOCATS DE PARIS
### Case 71/76, 1977 ECJ CELEX LEXIS 85, [1977] ECR, 765

[This case concerned the admission to the Ordre des Avocats auprès de la Cour de Paris (the Paris Bar) of a Belgian advocate, who is the holder of a Belgian diploma of Doctor of Laws which had been recognized by a French university as equivalent to the French licenciate's degree in law, and who subsequently obtained the "Certificat d'Aptitude à la Profession d'Avocat" (qualifying certificate for the profession of advocate), having sat and passed that examination, in accordance with French legislation.

Thieffry applied for admission to the Paris Bar, but by an order of 9 March 1976 the Conseil de l'Ordre (Bar Council) rejected his application on the ground he "offers no French diploma evidencing a licentiate's degree or a doctor's degree".]

4 It appears from the wording of [the Bar's] decision that the application for admission was refused solely by reason of the fact that, although the person concerned had obtained university recognition of the equivalence of his basic diploma and furthermore had acquired the Certificat d'Aptitude à la Profession d'Avocat, that was not enough for him to be treated in the same way as a holder of the diploma of the licentiate's degree or doctor's degree within the meaning of discrimination on grounds of nationality in this field, the equivalence of diplomas does not follow automatically from the application of its provisions, since such equivalence can result only from directives concerning recognition adopted pursuant to Article 57[53] of the Treaty, which do not yet exist for the profession of advocate.

\* \* \*

7 Under Article 3 [repealed] of the Treaty, the activities of the Community include, inter alia, the abolition of obstacles to freedom of movement for persons and services.

8 With a view to attaining this objective, the first paragraph of Article 52 [49] provides that restrictions on the freedom of establishment of nationals of a member-State in the territory of another member-State shall be abolished by progressive stages in the course of the transitional period.

9 Under the second paragraph of the same Article, freedom of establishment

includes the right to take up activities as self-employed persons, under the conditions laid down for its own nationals by the law of the country where such establishment is effected.

10 Article 53[deleted] emphasizes the irreversible nature of the liberalization achieved in this regard at any given time, by providing that member-States shall not introduce any new restrictions on the right of establishment in their territories of nationals of other member-States.

11 With a view to making it easier for persons to take up and pursue activities as self-employed persons, Article 57 [53] assigns to the Council the duty of issuing directives concerning, first, the mutual recognition of diplomas, and secondly, the coordination of the provisions laid down by law or administrative action in member-States concerning the taking up and pursuit of activities as self-employed persons.

12 That Article is therefore directed towards reconciling freedom of establishment with the application of national professional rules justified by the general good, in particular rules relating to organization, qualifications, professional ethics, supervision and liability, provided that such application is effected without discrimination.

13 In the General Programme for the abolition of restrictions on freedom of establishment, adopted in 18 December 1961 pursuant to Article 54 [deleted] of the Treaty, the Council proposed to eliminate not only overt discrimination, but also any form of disguised discrimination, by designating in Title III (b) as restrictions which are to be eliminated, 'Any requirements imposed, pursuant to any provision laid down by law, regulation or administrative action or in consequence of any administrative practice, in respect of the taking up or pursuit of an activity as a self-employed person where, although applicable irrespective of nationality, their effect is exclusively or principally to hinder the taking up or pursuit of such activity by foreign nationals.'

14 In the context of the abolition of restrictions on freedom of establishment, that programme provides useful guidance for the implementation of the relevant provisions of the Treaty.

15 It follows from the provisions cited taken as a whole that freedom of establishment, subject to observance of professional rules justified by the general good, is one of the objectives of the Treaty.

16 In so far as Community law makes no special provision, these objectives may be attained by measures enacted by the member-States, which under Article 5 [TEU 4] of the Treaty are bound to take 'all appropriate measures, whether general or particular, to ensure fulfillment of the obligations arising out of this Treaty or resulting from action taken by the institutions of the Community', and to abstain 'from any measure which could jeopardize the attainment of the objectives of this Treaty'.

17 Consequently, if the freedom of establishment provided for by Article 52 [49] can be ensured in a member-State either under the provisions of the laws and regulations in force, or by virtue of the practices of the public service or of professional bodies, a person subject to Community law cannot be denied the

practical benefit of that freedom solely by virtue of the fact that, for a particular profession, the directives provided for by Article 57 [53] of the Treaty have not yet been adopted.

18 Since the practical enjoyment of freedom of establishment can thus in certain circumstances depend upon national practice or legislation, it is incumbent upon the competent public authorities — including legally recognized professional bodies — to ensure that such practice or legislation is applied in accordance with the objective defined by the provisions of the Treaty relating to freedom of establishment.

19 In particular, there is an unjustified restriction of that freedom where, in a member-State, admission to a particular profession is refused to a person covered by the Treaty who holds a diploma which has been recognized as an equivalent qualification by the competent authority of the country of establishment and who furthermore has fulfilled the specific conditions regarding professional training in force in that country, solely by reason of the fact that the person concerned does not possess the national diploma corresponding to the diploma which he holds and which has been recognized as an equivalent qualification.

20 The national court specifically referred to the effect of a recognition of equivalence 'by the university authority of the country of establishment', and in the course of the proceedings the question has been raised whether a distinction should be drawn, as regards the equivalence of diplomas, between university recognition, granted with a view to permitting the pursuit of certain studies, and a recognition having 'civil effect', granted with a view to permitting the pursuit of a professional activity.

21 It emerges from the information supplied in this connection by the Commission and the governments which took part in the proceedings that the distinction between the academic effect and the civil effect of the recognition of foreign diplomas is acknowledged, in various forms, in the legislation and practice of several member-States.

22 Since this distinction falls within the ambit of the national law of the different States, it is for the national authorities to assess the consequences thereof, taking account, however, of the objectives of Community law.

23 In this connection it is important that, in each member-State, the recognition of evidence of a professional qualification for the purposes of establishment may be accepted to the full extent compatible with the observance of the professional requirements mentioned above.

24 Consequently, it is for the competent national authorities, taking account of the requirements of Community law set out above, to make such assessments of the facts as will enable them to judge whether a recognition granted by a university authority can, in addition to its academic effect, constitute valid evidence of a professional qualification.

25 The fact that national legislation provides for recognition of equivalence only for university purposes does not of itself justify the refusal to recognize such equivalence as evidence of a professional qualification.

26 This is particularly so when a diploma recognized for university purposes is

supplemented by a professional qualifying certificate obtained according to the legislation of the country of establishment.

27 In these circumstances, the answer to the question referred to the court should be that when a national of one member-State desirous of exercising a professional activity such as the profession of advocate in another member-State has obtained a diploma in his country of origin which has been recognized as an equivalent qualification by the competent authority under the legislation of the country of establishment and which has thus enabled him to sit and pass the special qualifying examination for the profession in question, the act of demanding the national diploma prescribed by the legislation of the country of establishment constitutes, even in the absence of the directives provided for in Article 57 [53], a restriction incompatible with the freedom of establishment guaranteed by Article 52 [49] of the Treaty.

## NOTES AND QUESTIONS

1.  In what way exactly had the French Bar apparently violated EC 43/TFEU 49 in *Thieffry?* How far could the court's rationale be extended? Note the Court's statement that "freedom of establishment, subject to observance of professional rules justified by the general good, is one of the objectives of the Treaty". What are the implications of this statement for the legal profession of any Member State?

2.  The court's opinion in *Thieffry* denied the Paris Bar Council any discretion to second-guess the determination by the University of Paris that a law degree from an institution in another EU state can be regarded as the equivalent of a French Law degree, even though the University of Paris has no customary role in the process of passing on qualifications for an advocate. Moreover, the substantial differences in legal education would appear to be a matter of legitimate concern for a host state in such a case. How, if at all, can the Court's opinion on this point be justified?

3.  Prior to the general directive described in note 4 *infra*, the EU had adopted a number of directives in the field of professions such as doctors and lawyers designed to establish the principle of mutual recognition and minimum standards of education that would facilitate such recognition. In the case of lawyers, Directive 98/5 [1998] OJ L 77/36 allows lawyers who meet the qualification and experience requirements to establish themselves in other Member States and provide advice on both home state and host state law, subject to certain exceptions regarding court appearances, real estate transactions and the like. After practice for three years in the host state, the lawyer may use the host state title. This does not mean, however, that cases do not continue to arise under the basic Treaty provisions. Thus, in *Irene Vlassopoulou v. Ministerium fur Justiz, Bundes- und Europaangelegenheiten Baden-Württemberg*, Case C-340/89, 1991 ECJ CELEX LEXIS 206 [1991] ECR I-2357, the Court dealt with the question of how a State or Bar organization should proceed where there was uncertainty as to the correspondence of foreign qualifications with the host state's requirements as regards a lawyer already in practice in the state of qualification. It held that EC 43/TFEU 49 requires the national authorities of the host state to examine in a fair way to what extent the knowledge and qualifications attested by the diploma obtained by the person concerned in his

country of origin correspond to those required by the rules of the host State, regardless of any formal recognition of equivalence.

In a somewhat disappointing display of apparent protectionist sentiment, the Lawyers directive was unsuccessfully challenged by Luxembourg: *Luxembourg v. Parliament and Council*, Case C-168/98, 2000 ECJ EUR-Lex LEXIS 921, [2000] ECR I-9131.

**4.** The following extract from the official EU website summarizes the provisions of the more general directive, 2005/36, on the recognition of professional qualifications:

### Allowing Member State nationals the freedom to provide services and the right of establishment

The recognition of professional qualifications enables beneficiaries to gain access in host Member States to the professions in which they are qualified, and to practice under the same conditions as nationals of that Member State in cases where these professions are regulated.

The Directive makes a distinction between "freedom to provide services" and "freedom of establishment" on the basis of criteria identified by the Court of Justice: duration, frequency, regularity and continuity of the provision of services.

### Facilitating temporary and occasional provision of cross-border services

Any nationals of a Community Member State legally established in a given Member State may provide services on a temporary and occasional basis in another Member State under their original professional title without having to apply for recognition of their qualifications. However, if service providers relocate outside of their Member State of establishment in order to provide services, they must also provide evidence of two years' professional experience if the profession in question is not regulated in that Member State.

The host Member State may require the service provider to make a declaration prior to providing any services on its territory and renew it annually including the details of any insurance cover or other means of personal or collective protection with regard to professional liability. The host Member State may also require that the first application be accompanied by certain documents listed in the Directive, such as proof of the nationality of the service provider, of their legal establishment, and of their professional qualifications.

If the host Member State requires *pro forma* registration with the competent professional association, this must occur automatically upon the competent authority which received the prior declaration forwarding the applicant's file to the professional organisation or body. For professions which have public health or safety implications and do not benefit from automatic recognition, the host Member State may carry out a prior check of the service provider's professional qualifications within the limits of the principle of proportionality.

In cases where the service is provided under the professional title of the Member State of establishment or under the formal qualification of the service provider, the competent authorities of the host Member State may require service providers to furnish the recipient of the service with certain information, particularly with regard to insurance coverage against the financial risks connected with any challenge to their professional liability.

The competent authorities shall ensure the exchange of all information necessary for complaints by a recipient of a service against a service provider to be correctly pursued. The host Member State may also ask the Member State of establishment for information regarding the service provider's legal establishment, good conduct, and the absence of any penalties for professional misconduct. With regard to both the temporary provision of services and permanent establishment in another Member State, the Directive provides for the proactive exchange of information relating to any serious circumstances which arose when the individual in question was established on their territory and which are liable to have consequences for the pursuit of the professional activities concerned. This exchange of information must, at any rate, be carried out in compliance with existing legislation on data protection.

**Improving the existing systems of recognition for the purpose of permanent establishment in another Member State**

On the other hand, "freedom of establishment" is the framework which applies when a professional enjoys the effective freedom to become established in another Member State in order to conduct a professional activity there on a stable basis. With respect to establishment, the Directive comprises the three existing systems of recognition:

- **General system for the recognition of professional qualifications (Chapter I of the Directive).** This system applies as a fallback to all the professions not covered by specific rules of recognition and to certain situations where the migrant professional does not meet the conditions set out in other recognition schemes. This general system is based on the principle of mutual recognition, without prejudice to the application of compensatory measures if there are substantial differences between the training acquired by the migrant and the training required in the host Member State. The compensatory measure may take the form of an adaptation period or an aptitude test. The choice between one or other of these tests is up to the migrant unless specific derogations exist;

- **System of automatic recognition of qualifications attested by professional experience (Chapter II of the Directive).** The industrial, craft and commercial activities listed in the Directive are subject, under the conditions stated, to the automatic recognition of qualifications attested by professional experience;

- **System of automatic recognition of qualifications for specific professions (Chapter III of the Directive).** The automatic recognition of training qualifications on the basis of coordination of the minimum training conditions covers the following professions: doctors, nurses responsible for general care, dental practitioners, specialised dental practitioners, veterinary surgeons, midwives, pharmacists and architects.

The three systems of recognition of qualifications, which are applicable in the context of establishment, are set out and examined in detail below.

**General system for the recognition of professional qualifications (Chapter I of the Directive).**

When, in a host Member State, access to or pursuit of a profession is regulated, i.e. subject to possession of specific professional qualifications, the competent authority in this Member State allows access to the profession in question and pursuit thereof under the same conditions as for nationals, provided that the applicant holds a training qualification obtained in another Member State which attests to a level of training at least equivalent to the level immediately below that required in the host Member State.

When, on the other hand, in the Member State of the applicant, access to a profession is not subject to possession of specific professional qualifications, the applicant should, in order to be able to gain access to the profession in a host Member State which does regulate that profession, provide proof of two years of full-time professional experience over the preceding ten years on top of the qualification.

The Directive distinguishes five levels of professional qualifications:

- **attestation of competence** which corresponds to general primary or secondary education, attesting that the holder has acquired general knowledge, or an attestation of competence issued by a competent authority in the home Member State on the basis of a training course not forming part of a certificate or diploma, or of three years professional experience;

- **certificate** which corresponds to training at secondary level, of a technical or professional nature or general in character, supplemented by a professional course;

- **diploma certifying successful completion of training at post-secondary level of a duration of at least one year,** or professional training which is comparable in terms of responsibilities and functions;

- **diploma certifying successful completion of training at higher or university level of a duration of at least three years** and less than four years;

- **diploma certifying successful completion of training at higher or university level of a duration of at least four years.**

On an exceptional basis, other types of training can be treated as one of the five levels.

The host Member State can make recognition of qualifications subject to the applicant's completing a compensation measure (aptitude test or adaptation period of a maximum of three years) if:

- the training is one year shorter than that required by the host Member State or

- the training received covers substantially different matters to those covered by the evidence of formal training required in the host Member State or

- the profession as defined in the host Member State comprises one or more regulated professional activities which do not exist in the corresponding profession in the applicant's home Member State, and that difference consists of specific training which covers substantially different matters from those covered by the completed by the migrant.

The host Member State must, in principle, offer the applicant the choice between an adaptation period and an aptitude test. The host Member State can only derogate from this requirement in the cases specifically provided for, or with the Commission's authorisation.

The Directive provides for representative professional associations at both national and European level to establish common platforms by determining measures to compensate for the substantial differences identified between the training requirements in at least two thirds of the Member States, and in all the Member States which regulate that profession. That is, the platform must make it possible to provide adequate guarantees as to the level of qualification. If such a platform is likely to make the recognition of professional qualifications easier, the Commission may submit it to the Member States and adopt an implementing measure under the comitology procedure (regulation). Once this implementing measure has been adopted, the Member States shall waive the imposition of compensatory measures on applicants who meet the platform's conditions.

By late 2010, three years after the Directive is transposed by the Member States, the Commission shall submit to the European Parliament and the Council a report on the provision of the Directive relating to common platforms and, if necessary, make appropriate proposals for amending it.

**System of automatic recognition of qualifications attested by professional experience in certain industrial, craft and commercial activities (Chapter II of the Directive)**

*     *     *

The elements taken into consideration for the recognition of professional experience are the duration and form of professional experience (in a self-employed or employed capacity) in the reference sector. Previous training is also taken into consideration and may reduce the amount of professional experience required. All previous training should, however, be proven by a certificate recognised by the Member State or judged by a competent professional body to be fully valid.

\*   \*   \*

Each Member State automatically recognises certificates of training giving access to professional activities as a doctor, nurse responsible for general care, dental practitioner, veterinary surgeon, midwife, pharmacist and architect, covered by Annex V to the Directive.

The Directive also adopts the principle of automatic recognition for medical and dental specialisations common to at least two Member States under existing law, but restricts futures additions to Directive 2005/36 of new medical specialisations — eligible for automatic recognition — to those that are common to at least two fifths of the Member States.

For the purposes of equivalence in qualifications, this Directive sets minimum training conditions for the following professions:

- **Doctor**: basic medical training precedes specialist medical training or the training of general practitioners.

**Basic medical training**: admission to basic medical training shall be contingent upon possession of a diploma or certificate providing access to universities or equivalent institutes which provide higher education and shall comprise a total of at least six years of study or 5 500 hours of theoretical and practical training provided by, or under the supervision of, a university.

**Specialist medical training**: admission to specialist medical training shall be contingent upon completion of six years of study in basic medical training and comprise full-time theoretical and practical training at a university or other recognised centre for a minimum duration which is not less than the duration referred to by the proposal in Annex V, point 5.1.4 (such as, for example, 5 years for the specialisation in general surgery).

**Training of general practitioners**: admission to general medical training shall be contingent upon completion of six years of study in basic medical training and comprise full-time practical training in an approved hospital, for a minimum duration of two years for any training of general practitioners leading to the award of evidence of formal qualifications issued before 1 January 2006, and of three years for certificates of training issued after that date.

[Others omitted]

\*   \*   \*

**Procedure for the mutual recognition of professional qualifications**

An individual application must be submitted to the competent authority in the host Member State, accompanied by certain documents and certificates as listed in the proposal (see Annex VII). According to the proposal, the competent authorities will in future have one month to acknowledge receipt of an application and to draw attention to any missing documents. A decision will have to be taken within three months of the date on which the application was received in full. Reasons will have to be given for any rejection and it will be possible for a rejection, or a failure to take a decision by the deadline, to be contested in the national courts.

Member State nationals shall be able to use the title conferred on them, and possibly an abbreviated form thereof, as well as the professional title of the corresponding host Member State. If a profession is regulated in the host Member State by an association or organisation (see Annex I), Member State nationals must be able to become members of that organisation or association in order to be able to use the title.

### Knowledge of languages

Member States may require migrants to have the knowledge of languages necessary for practising the profession. This provision must be applied proportionately, which rules out the systematic imposition of language tests before a professional activity can be practised. It should be noted that any evaluation of language skills is separate from the recognition of professional qualifications. It must take place after recognition, when actual access to the profession in question is sought.

### Administrative cooperation and other provisions

In order to facilitate the application of the above provisions, this proposal seeks close collaboration between the competent authorities in the host Member State and the home Member State, and the introduction of the following provisions:

- each Member State shall designate a coordinator to facilitate the uniform application of this directive;

- each Member State shall designate contact points by no later than 20 October 2007. These will have the task of providing citizens with such information as is necessary concerning the recognition of professional qualifications and to assist them in enforcing their rights, particularly through contact with the competent authorities to rule on requests for recognition;

- the nomination of Member States' representatives to the Committee on the recognition of professional qualifications. This comitology committee, which is chaired by the Commission representative, is to assist the Commission within the limits of the enforcement powers conferred on it by the Directive.

- The Commission shall consult with experts from the professional groups in an appropriate manner

Every two years, the Member States shall send a report to the Commission on the application of the system. If the application of one of the provisions of this Directive presents major difficulties in a particular area, the

Commission shall examine those difficulties in collaboration with the Member State concerned.

# ROBERT KOLLER v. OBERSTE BERUFUNGS- UND DISZIPLINARKOMMISSION (OBDK)
## Case 118/09, 2010 ECJ EUR-Lex LEXIS 1191 [2010] ECR NYR

[On 25 November 2002, Mr Koller, an Austrian national, obtained from the University of Graz (Austria) the degree of 'Magister der Rechtswissenschaften', namely a diploma awarded on completion of a cycle of university law studies lasting at least eight semesters. In November 2004, the Spanish Ministry of Education and Science recognised the degree of 'Magister der Rechtswissenschaften' as equivalent to that of 'Licenciado en Derecho', as the applicant had followed courses at the University of Madrid and passed additional examinations in accordance with the homologation procedure laid down by domestic Spanish law. On 14 March 2005, the Madrid Chamber of Lawyers, having established that Mr Koller held the degree of 'Licenciado en Derecho', authorised him to use the title 'abogado'. Mr Koller, then applied to take the aptitude test for the profession of lawyer in Austria.

At the time, the applicant was lawfully carrying on the profession of 'avocado' (lawyer) in Spain. His application was rejected and the applicant appealed to the Oberste Berufungs- und Disziplinarkommission (Appeals and Disciplinary Board; 'OBDK'). His appeal was rejected on the ground that in Spain, by contrast with the rules applicable in Austria, practical experience was not required in order to pursue the profession of a lawyer. The OBDK concluded that Mr Koller's application was designed to circumvent the requirement for five years' practical experience required by the Austrian rules.

Secondly, the OBDK took the view that the degree of 'Licenciado en Derecho' was not sufficient for admission to the aptitude test. In that respect, the second indent of Article 1(a) of Directive 89/48 of 21 December 1988 on a general system for the recognition of higher education diplomas awarded on completion of professional education and training of at least three years' duration, as amended by Directive 2001/19/EC of the European Parliament and of the Council of 14 May 2001 [now replaced by Directive 2005/06], differentiated between the successful completion of a cycle of post-secondary studies lasting at least three years and the professional training required in addition to that cycle of studies. In those circumstances, it was to be presumed that the aptitude test was a test limited to assessing the professional knowledge of the applicant. Since Mr Koller did not have any professional knowledge, he could not, in the view of the OBDK, be admitted to the aptitude test.]

37 By its second question, the referring court asks, in essence, whether Directive 89/48 as amended must be interpreted as precluding the competent authorities of the host Member State from refusing to authorise a person in a situation such as that of the applicant in the main proceedings to take the aptitude test for the profession of lawyer without proof of completion of the period of practical experience required by the legislation of that Member State.

38 As the holder of a 'diploma' within the meaning of Article 1(a) of Directive 89/48

as amended, a person such as Mr Koller enjoys, in accordance with Article 3, first paragraph, subparagraph (a), of that directive, access to the regulated profession of lawyer in the host Member State.

39 However, since the profession is one the exercise of which requires a precise knowledge of national law and an essential and constant element of which is the provision of advice and/or assistance concerning national law, Article 3 of Directive 89/48 as amended does not prevent the host Member State from requiring, pursuant to Article 4(1)(b) of the latter, that the applicant take an aptitude test, provided that State first verifies whether the knowledge acquired by the applicant in the course of his professional experience is capable of covering, in whole or in part, the substantial difference referred to in the first subparagraph of that latter provision.

40 Since the applicant is subject, in the host Member State, to an aptitude test whose very purpose is to ensure that he is capable of exercising the regulated profession in that Member State, the latter cannot, by virtue of Article 4 of Directive 89/48 as amended, deny to a person in a situation such as that of the applicant in the main proceedings authorisation to take such a test on the ground that he has not completed the period of practical experience required by the legislation of that Member State.

41 Therefore, the answer to the second question is that Directive 89/48 as amended must be interpreted as precluding the competent authorities of the host Member State from denying to a person in a situation such as that of the applicant in the main proceedings authorisation to take the aptitude test for the profession of lawyer without proof of completion of the period of practical experience required by the legislation of that Member State.

## NOTES AND QUESTIONS

1.   This case provides an insight into the EU legislation designed to require mutual recognition of diplomas and professional qualifications. It arose under the earlier directives on mutual recognition but the substance of the requirements is the same under Directive 2005/36.

2.   It appears that, as in *Knoors*, the regulatory authority here was concerned that Mr. Koller had used the mutual recognition procedure to circumvent the five years practical experience laid down by Austrian law. Perhaps there was a fear that allowing Mr. Koller to take the test (and assuming he passed), his admission would seriously undermine the Austrian practical experience requirement. Do you think this is a possible consequence of the ECJ's ruling? Is that an argument that the Austrian authorities can legitimately make?

3.   Would it have made a difference if the applicant was not carrying on the profession of lawyer in Spain? With respect to the practical experience, do you find the arguments of the Court convincing? What other grounds could have raised the Court to support its ruling?

## [D]   Justification of Restrictions Based on the General Interest

## ORDRE DES AVOCATS AU BARREAU DE PARIS v. KLOPP
### Case 107/83, 1984 ECJ CELEX LEXIS 264, [1984] ECR 2971

[Mr. Klopp, a German national and a member of the Düsseldorf Bar had applied to take the oath as an avocat and to be registered for the period of practical training at the Paris Bar while remaining a member of the Düsseldorf Bar and retaining his residence and chambers there. The Council of the Paris Bar Association rejected his application on the ground that although Mr. Klopp satisfied all the other requirements for admission as an advocate, especially as regards his personal and formal qualifications, he did not satisfy the provisions of Article 83 of Decree No. 72-468 and Article 1 of the Internal Rules of the Paris Bar, which provided that an advocate may establish chambers in one place only, which must be within the territorial jurisdiction of the tribunal de grande instance [regional court] with which he is registered.]

Article 83 of the decree also provided that "an advocate shall establish his chambers within the territorial jurisdiction of the tribunal de grande instance with which he is registered." Article 1 of the Internal Rules of the Paris Bar provided: that "in order to practice the profession, he must be a registered legal practitioner or trainee and must have his chambers in Paris or in the départements of Hauts de Seine, Seine-Saint-Denis or Val de Marne," and that "apart from his principal chambers he may establish a second set of chambers within the same geographical area."]

6 In substance, the question posed by the national Court is whether in the absence of a directive on the coordination of national provisions concerning access to and exercise of the legal profession Articles 52 [49] et seq. of the Treaty prevent the competent authorities of a Member State from denying pursuant to their national law and the rules of professional conduct in force there a national of another Member State the right to enter and to exercise the legal profession solely because he maintains at the same time professional chambers in another Member State.

7 The Paris Bar Council maintains first that Article 52 [49] of the Treaty has only partial direct effect inasmuch as it embodies the rule of equal treatment but does not necessarily apply to other cases. Accordingly, in the absence of directives the practical terms of free establishment depend on national law, unless the latter is discriminatory or constitutes a patently unreasonable obstacle or is objectively incompatible with the general interest.

8 The first paragraph of Article 52 [49] of the Treaty provides for the abolition of restrictions on the freedom of establishment of nationals of a Member State in the territory of another Member State.

\* \* \*

10 Nevertheless, . . . in laying down that freedom of establishment shall be attained at the end of the transitional period, Article 52[49] imposes an obligation to attain a precise result the fulfillment of which must be made easier by, but not made

dependent on, the implementation of a program of progressive measures. Consequently, the fact that the Council has failed to issue the directives provided for in Article 54 [50] and 57 [53] cannot serve to justify failure to meet the obligation.

11 It is therefore necessary to consider the scope of Article 52 [49] of the Treaty as a directly applicable rule of Community law with regard to the establishment in a Member State of a lawyer already established in another Member State and retaining his original establishment there.

12 The Paris Bar Council and the French Government maintain that Article 52 [49] of the Treaty makes access to and exercise of freedom of establishment depend on the conditions laid down by the Member State of establishment. Both Article 83 of Decree no. 72-468 and Article 1 of the Internal Rules of the Paris Bar (cited above) are applicable without distinction to French nationals and nationals of other Member States. Those provisions provide that an advocate may establish chambers in one place only.

13 In that respect the applicant objects in the first place that the national French legislation as applied is discriminatory and thus contrary to Article 52 [49] of the Treaty, for while the Paris Bar Association has allowed or tolerated the practice of certain of its members in having a second set of chambers in other countries it will not permit the applicant to establish himself in Paris while retaining his chambers in Düsseldorf.

14 However, according to the division of jurisdiction between the Court of Justice and the national court laid down in Article 177 [267] of the EEC Treaty it is for the national court to determine whether in practice the rules in question are discriminatory. The question put by the national court must therefore be answered without giving any opinion on the objection based on a discriminatory application of the national law in question.

15 In the second place, the applicant, the United Kingdom, the Danish Government and the Commission consider that the legislation of the Member State of establishment, although applicable to access to the profession and practice of law in that country, may not prohibit a lawyer who is a national of another Member State from retaining his chambers there.

16 The Paris Bar Council and the French Government object in that respect that Article 52 [49] of the Treaty requires the full application of the law of the Member State of establishment. The rule that an advocate may have his chambers in one place only is based on the need for advocates to genuinely practice before a court in order to ensure their availability to both the court and their clients. It should be respected as being a rule pertaining to the administration of justice and to professional ethics, objectively necessary and consistent with the public interest.

17 It should be emphasized that under the second paragraph of Article 52 [49] freedom of establishment includes access to and the pursuit of the activities of self-employed persons "under the conditions laid down for its own nationals by the law of the country where such establishment is effected." It follows from that provision and its context that in the absence of specific Community rules in the matter each Member State is free to regulate the exercise of the legal profession in its territory.

18 Nevertheless, that rule does not mean that the legislation of a Member State may require a lawyer to have only one establishment throughout the Community territory. Such a restrictive interpretation would mean that a lawyer once established in a particular Member State would be able to enjoy the freedom of the Treaty to establish himself in another Member State only at the price of abandoning the establishment he already had.

19 That freedom of establishment is not confined to the right to create a single establishment within the Community is confirmed by the very words of Article 52 [49] of the Treaty, according to which the progressive abolition of the restrictions on freedom of establishment applies to restrictions on the setting up of agencies, branches or subsidiaries by nationals of any Member State established in the territory of another Member State. That rule must be regarded as a specific statement of a general principle, applicable equally to the liberal professions, according to which the right of establishment includes freedom to set up and maintain, subject to observance of the professional rules of conduct, more than one place of work within the Community.

20 In view of the special nature of the legal profession, however, the second Member State must have the right, in the interests of the proper administration of justice, to require that lawyers enrolled at a Bar in its territory should practice in such a way as to maintain sufficient contact with their clients and the judicial authorities and abide by the rules of the profession. Nevertheless, such requirements must not prevent the nationals of other Member States from exercising properly the right of establishment guaranteed them by the Treaty.

21 In that respect it must be pointed out that modern methods of transport and telecommunications facilitate proper contact with clients and the judicial authorities. Similarly, the existence of a second set of chambers in another Member State does not prevent the application of the rules of ethics in the host Member State.

22 The question must therefore be answered to the effect that even in the absence of any directive coordinating national provisions governing access to and the exercise of the legal profession, Article 52 [49] et seq. of the EEC Treaty prevent the competent authorities of a Member State from denying, on the basis of the national legislation and the rules of professional conduct which are in force in that state, to a national of another Member State the right to enter and to exercise the legal profession solely on the ground that he maintains chambers simultaneously in another Member State.

## NOTES AND QUESTIONS

1. Why was the apparently justifiable internal French restriction in this case on establishing chambers outside the geographical scope of the courts where an individual was admitted to practice considered to be a violation of EC 43/TFEU 49? It was observed in the plaintiff's submission in *Klopp* that the French law prohibiting avocats from having chambers outside the region where he or she is registered did not prohibit in practice the establishment of chambers in other countries, so the French law was discriminatory. Was this relevant? What did the Court think of this argument?

**2.**  After the Court's decision, would Mr. Klopp be able to open a third office in France outside of the Paris region? This would amount to reverse discrimination, since French avocats at the time of the *Klopp* decision could not have offices outside the territorial jurisdiction of the court in which they were admitted.

**3.**  See also *Commission v. Belgium*, Case 221/85, 1987 ECJ CELEX LEXIS 169 [1987] ECR 719, and *Gullung v. Conseil de l'ordre des avocats*, Case 292/86, 1988 ECJ CELEX LEXIS 182 [1988] ECR 111, where the ECJ held that a requirement for lawyers to register themselves with the national bar (including national lawyers) might be discriminatory unless it was objectively justified.

**4.**  In his Paris practice would Klopp be required to follow the German rules of professional ethics, the French rules, or both? The Council of the Bars and Laws Societies of the European Community (CCBE) is an umbrella organization that includes all of the EU national bar associations that represent lawyers engaged in courtroom practice, as well as the law societies representing British and Irish solicitors. It does not include associations of notaries, legal advisors or house counsel. On October 28, 1988, the CCBE adopted the Code of Conduct for lawyers in the EU. Although the CCBE has no legislative authority, the Code of Conduct is not a purely advisory document. On the contrary, it is expected that it will be adopted as law in all Member States of the EU, and many Member States have already adopted it. The Code of Conduct constitutes a kind of minimum harmonization of professional conduct rules. For discussion, see Toulin, *A Worldwide Common Code of Professional Ethics?*15 FORDHAM INT'L LAW J. 673 (1991-92). A directive to facilitate establishment for lawyers was adopted in 1998: Directive 98/5, [1998] OJ L 77/36.

**5.**  Linguistic aptitude tests required for admission to practice of law in Luxembourg were questioned in *Grahame J. Wilson v. Ordre des avocats du Barreau de Luxembourg* Case C-506/04, 2006 ECJ CELEX LEXIS 501, [2006] ECR 8613. Here the Court considered the impact of Directive 98/5/EC in the following terms:

> 64 [T]he Community legislature sought to put an end to the differences in national rules on the conditions for registration with the competent authorities which gave rise to inequalities and obstacles to free movement
> . . .

> 65 In that context, Article 3 of Directive 98/5 provides that a lawyer who wishes to practise in a Member State other than that in which he obtained his professional qualification must register with the competent authority in that State, which must register him 'upon presentation of a certificate attesting to his registration with the competent authority in the home Member State'.

> 66 Given the objective of Directive 98/5, set out in paragraph 64 of this judgment, it must be held, as the United Kingdom Government and the Commission rightly submitted, that in Article 3 of that directive the Community legislature carried out a complete harmonisation of the prior conditions for the exercise of the right it confers.

67 It is thus apparent that presentation to the competent authority of the host Member State of a certificate attesting to registration with the competent authority of the home Member State is the only condition to which registration of the person concerned in the host Member State may be subject, enabling him to practise in the latter Member State under his home-country professional title.

68 That analysis is confirmed by the Explanatory Memorandum on the Proposal for a European Parliament and Council Directive to facilitate practice of the profession of lawyer on a permanent basis in a Member State other than that in which the qualification was obtained (COM (94) 572 final), in which, in the comments on Article 3, it is stated that '[r]egistration [with the competent authority of the host Member State] is an automatic entitlement where the applicant furnishes proof of his registration with the competent authority in his home Member State'.

69 As the Court has already noted, the Community legislature, with a view to making it easier for a particular class of migrant lawyers to exercise the fundamental freedom of establishment, did not opt for a system of prior testing of the knowledge of the persons concerned (see *Luxembourg* v. *Parliament and Council*, paragraph 43).

70 Thus Directive 98/5 does not allow the registration of a European lawyer with the competent authority of the host Member State to be conditional on a hearing designed to enable that authority to determine whether the person concerned is proficient in the languages of that Member State.

71 As Mr Wilson, the United Kingdom Government and the Commission submitted, the exclusion of a system of prior testing of the knowledge, particularly of languages, for European lawyers is, however, accompanied in Directive 98/5 by a set of rules intended to ensure, to a level acceptable in the Community, the protection of consumers and the proper administration of justice . . .

72 Thus, the purpose of the obligation imposed by Article 4 of Directive 98/5 on European lawyers to practise under their home-country professional title in the host Member State is, according to recital (9) in the preamble to that directive, to make clear the distinction between such lawyers and lawyers from the host Member State, so that clients are aware that the professional to whom they entrust the defence of their interests has not obtained his qualification in that Member State . . . and does not necessarily have the knowledge, in particular of languages, which is adequate to deal with the case.

73 As regards activities relating to representation and defence of a client in legal proceedings, Member States are permitted, in accordance with Article 5(3) of Directive 98/5, to require European lawyers practising under their home-country professional title to work in conjunction with a lawyer who practises before the judicial authority in question and who would, where necessary, be answerable to that authority or with an 'avoué' practising

before it. That option compensates for any lack of proficiency on the part of the European lawyer in the court languages of the host Member State.

74 Under Articles 6 and 7 of Directive 98/5, a European lawyer must comply not only with the rules of professional conduct applicable in his home Member State but also with those of the host Member State, failing which he will incur disciplinary sanctions and exposure to professional liability (see *Luxembourg* v. *Parliament and Council*, paragraphs 36 to 41). One of the rules of professional conduct applicable to lawyers is an obligation, like that provided for in the Code of Conduct adopted by the Council of the Bars and Law Societies of the European Union (CCBE), breach of which may lead to disciplinary sanctions, not to handle matters which the professionals concerned know or ought to know they are not competent to handle, for instance owing to lack of linguistic knowledge (see, to that effect, *Luxembourg* v. *Parliament and Council*, paragraph 42). Communication with clients, the administrative authorities and the professional bodies of the host Member State, like compliance with the rules of professional conduct laid down by the authorities of that Member State, requires a European lawyer to have sufficient linguistic knowledge or recourse to assistance where that knowledge is insufficient.

75 It is also important to point out, as did the Commission, that one of the objectives of Directive 98/5, according to recital (5) in the preamble, is, 'by enabling lawyers to practise under their home-country professional titles on a permanent basis in a host Member State, [to meet] the needs of consumers of legal services who, owing to the increasing trade flows resulting, in particular, from the internal market, seek advice when carrying out cross-border transactions in which international law, Community law and domestic laws often overlap'. Such international cases, like those to which the law of a Member State other than the host Member State is applicable, may not require a degree of knowledge of the languages of the latter Member State as high as that required to deal with matters in which the law of that Member State is applicable.

76 Finally, it must be observed that like treatment of European lawyers as lawyers of the host Member State, which Directive 98/5 is designed to facilitate, according to recital (14) in the preamble, requires, under Article 10, that the person concerned proves that he has effectively and regularly pursued for a period of at least three years an activity in the law of that State or, where the period is shorter, that he has other knowledge, training or professional experience relating to that law. Such a measure enables European lawyers wishing to integrate into the profession of the host Member State to become familiar with the language(s) of that Member State."

77 In light of the foregoing, the answer to Questions 3 and 4 must be that Article 3 of Directive 98/5 must be interpreted as meaning that the registration of a lawyer with the competent authority of a Member State other than the State where he obtained his qualification in order to practise

there under his home-country professional title cannot be made subject to a prior examination of his proficiency in the languages of the host Member State.

## [E]   The Public Service Exception

### JEAN REYNERS v. BELGIAN STATE
Case 2-74, [1974] ECR 631

[Reyners, a French national, had applied for admission to the Brussels (Belgium) Bar but was refused on the grounds that he was not a Belgian national.]

33 The Conseil d'Etat has also requested a definition of what is meant in the first paragraph of article 55 [51] by "activities which in that state are connected, even occasionally, with the exercise of official authority".

34 More precisely, the question is whether, within a profession such as that of avocat, only those activities inherent in this profession which are connected with the exercise of official authority are excepted from the application of the chapter on the right of establishment, or whether the whole of this profession is excepted by reason of the fact that it comprises activities connected with the exercise of this authority.

35 The Luxembourg government and the Ordre National des Avocats de Belgique consider that the whole profession of avocat is exonerated from the rules in the treaty on the right of establishment by the fact that it is connected organically with the functioning of the public service of the administration of justice.

36 This situation (it is argued) results both from the legal organization of the bar, involving a set of strict conditions for admission and discipline, and from the functions performed by the avocat in the context of judicial procedure where his participation is largely obligatory.

37 These activities, which make the advocate an indispensable auxiliary of the administration of justice, form a coherent whole, the parts of which cannot be separated.

38 The plaintiff in the main action, for his part, contends that at most only certain activities of the profession of avocat are connected with the exercise of official authority and that they alone therefore come within the exception created by article 55 [51] to the principle of free establishment.

39 The German, Belgian, British, Irish and Dutch governments, as well as the Commission, regard the exception contained in article 55 [51] as limited to those activities alone within the various professions concerned which are actually connected with the exercise of official authority, subject to their being separable from the normal practice of the profession.

40 Differences exist, however, between the Governments referred to as regards the nature of the activities which are thus excepted from the principle of the freedom of establishment, taking into account the different organization of the professions corresponding to that of avocat from one Member State to another.

41 The German government in particular considers that by reason of the compulsory connection of the Rechtsanwalt with certain judicial processes, especially as regards criminal or public law, there are such close connexions between the profession of Rechtsanwalt and the exercise of judicial authority that large sectors of this profession, at least, should be excepted from freedom of establishment.

42 Under the terms of the first paragraph of article 55 the provisions of the chapter on the right of establishment shall not apply 'so far as any given Member State is concerned, to activities which in that state are connected, even occasionally, with the exercise of official authority'.

43 Having regard to the fundamental character of freedom of establishment and the rule on equal treatment with nationals in the system of the treaty, the exceptions allowed by the first paragraph of article 55 [51] cannot be given a scope which would exceed the objective for which this exemption clause was inserted.

44 The first paragraph of article 55 [51] must enable Member States to exclude non-nationals from taking up functions involving the exercise of official authority which are connected with one of the activities of self-employed persons provided for in article 52 [49].

45 This need is fully satisfied when the exclusion of nationals is limited to those activities which, taken on their own, constitute a direct and specific connexion with the exercise of official authority.

46 An extension of the exception allowed by article 55 [51] to a whole profession would be possible only in cases where such activities were linked with that profession in such a way that freedom of establishment would result in imposing on the Member State concerned the obligation to allow the exercise, even occasionally, by non-nationals of functions appertaining to official authority.

47 This extension is on the other hand not possible when, within the framework of an independent profession, the activities connected with the exercise of official authority are separable from the professional activity in question taken as a whole.

48 In the absence of any directive issued under article 57 [53] for the purpose of harmonizing the national provisions relating, in particular, to professions such as that of avocat, the practice of such professions remains governed by the law of the various Member States.

49 The possible application of the restrictions on freedom of establishment provided for by the first paragraph of article 55 [51] must therefore be considered separately in connexion with each Member State having regard to the national provisions applicable to the organization and the practice of this profession.

50 This consideration must however take into account the Community character of the limits imposed by article 55 [51] on the exceptions permitted to the principle of freedom of establishment in order to avoid the effectiveness of the treaty being defeated by unilateral provisions of Member States.

51 Professional activities involving contacts, even regular and organic, with the courts, including even compulsory cooperation in their functioning, do not constitute, as such, connexion with the exercise of official authority.

52 The most typical activities of the profession of avocat, in particular, such as consultation and legal assistance and also representation and the defence of parties in court, even when the intervention or assistance of the avocat is compulsory or is a legal monopoly, cannot be considered as connected with the exercise of official authority.

53 The exercise of these activities leaves the discretion of judicial authority and the free exercise of judicial power intact.

54 It is therefore right to reply to the question raised that the exception to freedom of establishment provided for by the first paragraph of article 55 [51] must be restricted to those of the activities referred to in article 52 [49] which in themselves involve a direct and specific connexion with the exercise of official authority.

55 In any case it is not possible to give this description, in the context of a profession such as that of avocat, to activities such as consultation and legal assistance or the representation and defence of parties in court, even if the performance of these activities is compulsory or there is a legal monopoly in respect of it.

## NOTES AND QUESTIONS

**1.** What conclusions can be drawn from the Court's analysis in *Reyners* regarding the scope of the official authority exception in EC 45/TFEU 51? Note the difference in wording between this provision and EC 39/TFEU45 (and see the *Commission v. Belgium* case in Chapter 17 *infra*.)

**2.** The requirement by some States that only U.S. nationals could practice law was struck down by the U.S. Supreme Court in *Application of Griffiths*, 413 U.S. 717, 93 S. Ct. 2851, 37 L. Ed. 2d 910 (1973).

## COMMISSION v. BELGIUM
### Case C-47/08, 2011 2011 ECJ EUR-Lex LEXIS 832, [2011] ECR NYR

[The Commission brought seven actions for failure to fulfill obligations against six Member States (Belgium, Germany, Greece, France, Luxembourg, Portugal and Austria) because they reserve access to the profession of notary to their own nationals, which in the Commission's opinion is discrimination on grounds of nationality, prohibited by the EC Treaty and notably article EC 43/TFEU 49. The claim against Belgium serves as an example of the arguments in these cases.]

73 By its first head of claim, the Commission complains that the Kingdom of Belgium is blocking the establishment in its territory, for the purpose of practising as a notary, of nationals of other Member States by reserving access to that profession to its own nationals, in breach of Article 43 EC [49].

74 This head of claim thus concerns solely the nationality condition laid down by the Belgian legislation at issue for access to that profession, from the point of view of Article 43 EC [49].

— Substance

77 Article 43 EC [49] is one of the fundamental provisions of European Union law.

79 The freedom of establishment conferred on nationals of one Member State in the territory of another Member State includes in particular access to and exercise of activities of self-employed persons under the same conditions as are laid down by the law of the Member State of establishment for its own nationals. In other words, Article 43 EC [49] prohibits the Member States from laying down in their laws conditions for the pursuit of activities by persons exercising their right of establishment there which differ from those laid down for its own nationals.

80 Article 43 EC [49] is thus intended to ensure that all nationals of all Member States who establish themselves in another Member State for the purpose of pursuing activities there as self-employed persons receive the same treatment as nationals of that State, and it prohibits, as a restriction on freedom of establishment, any discrimination on grounds of nationality resulting from national legislation.

81 In the present case, the national legislation at issue reserves access to the profession of notary to Belgian nationals, thus enshrining a difference in treatment on the ground of nationality which is prohibited in principle by Article 43 EC [49].

82 The Kingdom of Belgium submits, however, that the activities of notaries are outside the scope of Article 43 EC [49] because they are connected with the exercise of official authority within the meaning of the first paragraph of Article 45 EC [51]. The Court must therefore begin by examining the concept of the exercise of official authority within the meaning of that provision, before going on to ascertain whether the activities of notaries in the Belgian legal system fall within that concept.

83 As regards the concept of the 'exercise of official authority' within the meaning of the first paragraph of Article 45 EC [51], the assessment of that concept must take account, in accordance with settled case-law, of the character as European Union law of the limits imposed by that provision on the permitted exceptions to the principle of freedom of establishment, so as to ensure that the effectiveness of the Treaty in the field of freedom of establishment is not frustrated by unilateral provisions of the Member States.

84 It is also settled case-law that the first paragraph of Article 45 EC [51] is an exception to the fundamental rule of freedom of establishment. As such, the exception must be interpreted in a manner which limits its scope to what is strictly necessary to safeguard the interests it allows the Member States to protect.

85 In addition, the Court has repeatedly held that the exception in the first paragraph of Article 45 EC [51] must be restricted to activities which in themselves are directly and specifically connected with the exercise of official authority.

87 It must be ascertained in the light of the above considerations whether the activities entrusted to notaries in the Belgian legal system involve a direct and specific connection with the exercise of official authority.

88 Account must be taken of the nature of the activities carried out by the members of the profession at issue.

89 The Kingdom of Belgium and the Commission agree that the principal activity of notaries in the Belgian legal system consists in the establishment of authentic instruments in due and proper form. In order to do this the notary must ascertain

that all the conditions required by law for drawing up the instrument are satisfied. Moreover, an authentic instrument has probative force and is enforceable.

90 It must be observed, in this respect, that the documents that may be authenticated under Belgian law are documents and agreements freely entered into by the parties. They decide themselves, within the limits laid down by law, the extent of their rights and obligations and choose freely the conditions which they wish to be subject to when they produce a document or agreement to the notary for authentication. The notary's intervention thus presupposes the prior existence of an agreement or consensus of the parties.

91 Furthermore, the notary cannot unilaterally alter the agreement he is called on to authenticate without first obtaining the consent of the parties.

92 The activity of authentication entrusted to notaries does not therefore, as such, involve a direct and specific connection with the exercise of official authority within the meaning of the first paragraph of Article 45 EC [51].

93 The fact that some documents and agreements are subject to mandatory authentication, in default of which they are void, cannot call that conclusion into question. It is normal for the validity of various documents to be subject, in national legal systems and in accordance with the rules laid down, to formal requirements or even compulsory validation procedures. That fact is not therefore enough to bear out the arguments of the Kingdom of Belgium.

94 The obligation of notaries to ascertain, before carrying out the authentication of a document or agreement, that all the conditions required by law for drawing up that document or agreement have been satisfied and, if that is not the case, to refuse to perform the authentication cannot call the above conclusion into question either.

95 It is true that, as the Kingdom of Belgium observes, the notary's verification of those facts pursues an objective in the public interest, namely to guarantee the lawfulness and legal certainty of documents entered into by individuals. However, the mere pursuit of that objective cannot justify the powers necessary for that purpose being reserved exclusively to notaries who are nationals of the Member State concerned.

96 Acting in pursuit of an objective in the public interest is not, in itself, sufficient for a particular activity to be regarded as directly and specifically connected with the exercise of official authority. It is not disputed that activities carried out in the context of various regulated professions frequently, in the national legal systems, involve an obligation for the persons concerned to pursue such an objective, without falling within the exercise of official authority.

97 However, the fact that notarial activities pursue objectives in the public interest, in particular to guarantee the lawfulness and legal certainty of documents entered into by individuals, constitutes an overriding reason in the public interest capable of justifying restrictions of Article 43 EC [49] deriving from the particular features of the activities of notaries, such as the restrictions which derive from the procedures by which they are appointed, the limitation of their numbers and their territorial jurisdiction, or the rules governing their remuneration, independence, disqualification from other offices and protection against removal, provided that those

restrictions enable those objectives to be attained and are necessary for that purpose.

98 It is also true that a notary must refuse to authenticate a document or agreement which does not satisfy the conditions laid down by law, regardless of the wishes of the parties. However, following such a refusal, the parties remain free to remedy the unlawfulness, amend the conditions in the document or agreement, or abandon the document or agreement.

99 As to the probative force and the enforceability of notarial acts, these indisputably endow those acts with significant legal effects. However, the fact that an activity includes the drawing up of acts with such effects does not suffice for that activity to be regarded as directly and specifically connected with the exercise of official authority within the meaning of the first paragraph of Article 45 EC [51].

102 As regards the enforceable nature of an authentic instrument, it must be observed, as the Kingdom of Belgium submits, that that enforceability enables the obligation embodied in the instrument to be enforced without the prior intervention of the court.

103 The enforceability of an authentic instrument does not, however, derive from powers possessed by the notary which are directly and specifically connected with the exercise of official authority. While the notary's endorsement of the authority to enforce on the authentic instrument does give it enforceable status, that status is based on the intention of the parties to enter into a document or agreement, after its conformity with the law has been checked by the notary, and to make it enforceable.

104 It must also be ascertained whether the other activities entrusted to notaries in the Belgian legal system, referred to by the Kingdom of Belgium, involve a direct and specific connection with the exercise of official authority.

105 As regards, first, the functions of notaries in connection with the attachment of immovable property, it must be recalled that the notary is principally responsible for implementing the sale by auction or by private treaty, if the latter has been authorised by the court, under the conditions determined by the court. The notary must also arrange the inspection of the premises and draw up the documentation, which indicates the date of the sale and contains a clause assigning the proceeds of the sale to the creditors.

106 It is thus clear that the notary does not have power to carry out the attachment himself. In addition, it is the court responsible for attachment proceedings which appoints the notary and entrusts him with carrying out the sale by auction or by private treaty and the determination of priorities. It is for the court to ensure that the provisions concerning means of enforcement are complied with. As follows from Article 1396 of the Judicial Code, the court may, even of its own motion, call for a report on the state of the procedure from the office-holders or officials authenticating the act or commissioned by the court. If disputes arise, the decision is for the court to take, the notary being obliged to draw up a statement of the objections, suspend all actions and refer the question to the court.

107 The functions of notaries in connection with the attachment of immovable

property can thus be seen to be exercised under the supervision of the court, to which the notary must refer any disputes, and which takes the final decision. Those functions cannot therefore be regarded as directly and specifically connected, as such, with the exercise of official authority.

108 The same conclusion follows, secondly, with respect to the functions entrusted to notaries under Articles 1186 to 1190 of the Judicial Code in connection with certain sales of immovable property. It is apparent from those provisions that the decision whether or not to authorise those sales is for the court.

109 As regards, thirdly, the activities of notaries in relation to inventories of deceased persons' estates and property in joint ownership or co-ownership, and to the affixing and removal of official seals, those activities are subject to authorisation by a magistrate. In the event of difficulties, the notary refers the question to the magistrate, pursuant to Article 1184 of the Judicial Code.

110 As regards, fourthly, the activities of notaries in relation to the judicial division of estates, it must be noted that it is for the court to order the division and refer the parties, if appropriate under conditions it determines, to a notary whose task it is, in particular, to prepare the inventory and establish the total estate and define the shares. It is also for the court to decide any dispute that may arise and to approve the liquidated account drawn up by the notary or to refer it to him for the purpose of drawing up a supplementary account or an account in accordance with the court's instructions. Consequently, those activities do not involve the notary in the exercise of official authority.

111 That is also the case, fifthly, with the procedure for ranking the creditors following a sale by auction. In that procedure the notary is responsible for drawing up the report of the distribution of the proceeds of sale or, if necessary, the priority of preferential rights and mortgages. Any disputes must be brought before the court.

113 Sixthly, as regards acts such as gifts inter vivos, wills, marriage contracts and statutory cohabitation agreements, which must be concluded by a notarial act if they are not to be void, reference is made to the considerations in paragraphs 90 to 103 above.

114 The same considerations apply, seventhly, in relation to acts constituting companies, associations and foundations, which must be done by authentic instrument if they are not to be void. It should be added, moreover, that those legal persons acquire legal personality only following the filing of the constituent act with the registry of the commercial court.

115 As regards, eighthly, the tax-collecting functions of notaries when they receive payment of registration fees or mortgage duties, these cannot be regarded in themselves as directly and specifically connected with the exercise of public authority. It should be pointed out in this respect that the collection is done by the notary on behalf of the person owing the tax, is followed by the remittal of the corresponding sums to the relevant State department, and is not therefore fundamentally different from the collection of value added tax.

123 In those circumstances, it must be concluded that the activities of notaries as

defined in the current state of the Belgian legal system are not connected with the exercise of official authority within the meaning of the first paragraph of Article 45 EC [51].

124 Consequently, the nationality condition required by Belgian legislation for access to the profession of notary constitutes discrimination on grounds of nationality prohibited by Article 43 EC [49].

125 In the light of all the above considerations, the first head of claim is well founded.

## NOTES AND QUESTIONS

1.  The profession of "notaire" does not have a real parallel in the Anglo-American legal system. The requirement that a notaire be involved in certain transactions is intended to assure a state interest in making sure documents are properly executed (so that, in particular, taxes can be properly assessed on the transaction).

2.  The ECJ does not consider that the acts to be perfomed by a notaire constitute an exercise of official authority. Why? Are the conclusions drawn by the Court convincing?

3.  The profession of notaire should not be equated with the office of notary public in the U.S. The latter office can and usually is performed by non-lawyers, but their duties are all associated with the exercise of official acts.

## § 15.03    ESTABLISHMENT AND THE REGULATION OF BUSINESS ENTITIES

### [A]    The Effect of EC 43/TFEU 49 on State Corporation Laws

## ÜBERSEERING BV v. NORDIC CONSTRUCTION COMPANY BAUMANAGEMENT GMBH (NCC)
### Case C-208/00, 2002 ECJ CELEX LEXIS 308, [2002] ECR I-9919

[Under Dutch law, where the plaintiff was incorporated, the legal status of companies is purely a matter of where it is incorporated and where it has its registered office. Überseering had however moved its central control and management to Germany and was entirely owned by German nationals. German law treats the latter as the basic test for legal capacity. The Plaintiff had sued the defendant in contract and the court refused to recognize it as having the capacity to bring an action because of the German rule.]

80 Überseering, which is validly incorporated in the Netherlands and has its registered office there, is entitled under Articles 43 EC [49] and 48 EC [54] to exercise its freedom of establishment in Germany as a company incorporated under Netherlands law. It is of little significance in that regard that, after the company

was formed, all its shares were acquired by German nationals residing in Germany, since that has not caused Überseering to cease to be a legal person under Netherlands law.

81 Indeed, its very existence is inseparable from its status as a company incorporated under Netherlands law since, as the Court has observed, a company exists only by virtue of the national legislation which determines its incorporation and functioning (see, to that effect, Daily Mail and General Trust, paragraph 19). The requirement of reincorporation of the same company in Germany is therefore tantamount to outright negation of freedom of establishment.

82 In those circumstances, the refusal by a host Member State (B') to recognise the legal capacity of a company formed in accordance with the law of another Member State (A') in which it has its registered office on the ground, in particular, that the company moved its actual centre of administration to Member State B following the acquisition of all its shares by nationals of that State residing there, with the result that the company cannot, in Member State B, bring legal proceedings to defend rights under a contract unless it is reincorporated under the law of Member State B, constitutes a restriction on freedom of establishment which is, in principle, incompatible with Articles 43 EC [49] and 48 EC [54].

As to whether the restriction on freedom of establishment is justified

83 Finally, it is appropriate to determine whether such a restriction on freedom of establishment can be justified on the grounds advanced by the national court and by the German Government.

84 The German Government has argued in the alternative, should the Court find that application of the company seat principle entails a restriction on freedom of establishment, that the restriction applies without discrimination, is justified by overriding requirements relating to the general interest and is proportionate to the objectives pursued.

85 In the German Government's submission, the lack of discrimination arises from the fact that the rules of law proceeding from the company seat principle apply not only to any foreign company which establishes itself in Germany by moving its actual centre of administration there but also to companies incorporated under German law which transfer their actual centre of administration out of Germany.

86 As regards the overriding requirements relating to the general interest put forward in order to justify the alleged restriction, the German Government maintains, first, that in other spheres, secondary Community law assumes that the administrative head office and the registered office are identical. Community law has thus recognised the merits, in principle, of a single registered and administrative office.

87 In the German Government's submission, the German rules of private international company law enhance legal certainty and creditor protection. There is no harmonisation at Community level of the rules for protecting the share capital of limited liability companies and such companies are subject in Member States other than the Federal Republic of Germany to requirements which are in some respects

much less strict. The company seat principle as applied by German law ensures that a company whose principal place of business is in Germany has a fixed minimum share capital, something which is instrumental in protecting parties with whom it enters into contracts and its creditors. That also prevents distortions of competition since all companies whose principal place of business is in Germany are subject to the same legal requirements.

88 The German Government submits that further justification is provided by the protection of minority shareholders. In the absence of a Community standard for the protection of minority-shareholders, a Member State must be able to apply to any company whose principal place of business is within its territory the same legal requirements for the protection of minority shareholders.

89 Application of the company seat principle is also justified by employee protection through the joint management of undertakings on conditions determined by law. The German Government argues that the transfer to Germany of the actual centre of administration of a company incorporated under the law of another Member State could, if the company continued to be a company incorporated under that law, involve a risk of circumvention of the German provisions on joint management, which allow the employees, in certain circumstances, to be represented on the company's supervisory board. Companies in other Member States do not always have such a body.

90 Finally, any restriction resulting from the application of the company seat principle can be justified on fiscal grounds. The incorporation principle, to a greater extent than the company seat principle, enables companies to be created which have two places of residence and which are, as a result, subject to taxation without limits in at least two Member States. There is a risk that such companies might claim and be granted tax advantages simultaneously in several Member States. By way of example, the German Government mentions the cross-border offsetting of losses against profits between undertakings within the same group.

91 The Netherlands and United Kingdom Governments, the Commission and the EFTA Surveillance Authority submit that the restriction in question is not justified. They point out in particular that the aim of protecting creditors was also invoked by the Danish authorities in Centros to justify the refusal to register in Denmark a branch of a company which had been validly incorporated in the United Kingdom and all of whose business was to be carried on in Denmark but which did not meet the requirements of Danish law regarding the provision and paying-up of a minimum amount of share capital. They add that it is not certain that requirements associated with a minimum amount of share capital are an effective way of protecting creditors.

92 It is not inconceivable that overriding requirements relating to the general interest, such as the protection of the interests of creditors, minority shareholders, employees and even the taxation authorities, may, in certain circumstances and subject to certain conditions, justify restrictions on freedom of establishment.

93 Such objectives cannot, however, justify denying the legal capacity and, consequently, the capacity to be a party to legal proceedings of a company properly incorporated in another Member State in which it has its registered office. Such a

measure is tantamount to an outright negation of the freedom of establishment conferred on companies by Articles 43 EC and 48 EC.

94 Accordingly, the answer to the first question must be that, where a company formed in accordance with the law of a Member State (A') in which it has its registered office is deemed, under the law of another Member State (B'), to have moved its actual centre of administration to Member State B, Articles 43 EC [49] and 48 EC [54] preclude Member State B from denying the company legal capacity and, consequently, the capacity to bring legal proceedings before its national courts for the purpose of enforcing rights under a contract with a company established in Member State B.

# NOTES AND QUESTIONS

1.  The *Überseering* case appears to provide a very clear ruling on the obligations of Member States to recognize the legal standing of companies incorporated in other Member States. What, however, would be the position if, under Dutch law, a company's legal capacity needed to be determined in the same way as in Germany? For a detailed analysis, see W.H. Roth, *From Centros to Überseering: Free Movement of Companies, Private International Law and Community Law* (2003) 52 ICLQ 177.

2.  In the United States, this issue has long been resolved under the Full Faith and Credit clause of the Constitution. For larger companies operating nationally, incorporated in Delaware, but with their seat of management in another state, this is indeed a long-established principle and it is somewhat perplexing that so long after the common market was created, the Member States should still seek to decline mutual recognition for legal entities. What might be behind such reluctance?

3.  After languishing for almost 30 years, a proposal to create a European Company status for companies wishing to operate across the Union with a uniform structure was finally enacted into law in 2001: Council Regulation 2157/2001 on the Statute for a European company (SE) [2001] OJ L 294/1. Because of its more relaxed provisions relating to worker participation versus the German Aktiengesell-schaft model, an increasing number of German AGs have been converting to this form. The principles of this new structure are described in the summary below, found on the EU official website:

## SUMMARY

### Regulation on the Statute for a European Company

The European Company (known by the Latin term "Societas Europaea" or SE) is now a reality some 30 years after the initial proposal. The new legislation should enter into force in 2004. Agreement on the SE is one of the priorities identified in the Financial Services Action Plan (FSAP).

### Formation

There is provision for four ways of forming a European Company: merger, formation of a holding company, formation of a joint subsidiary, or conversion of a public limited company previously formed under national law. Formation by merger is available only to public limited companies from different Member States. Formation of an SE holding company is available to public and private limited companies with their registered offices in different Member States or having subsidiaries or branches in Member States other than that of their registered office. Formation of a joint subsidiary is available under the same circumstances to any legal entities governed by public or private law.

### Minimum capital

The SE must have a minimum capital of EUR 120 000. Where a Member State requires a larger capital for companies exercising certain types of activity, the same requirement will also apply to an SE with its registered office in that Member State.

### Registered office

The registered office of the SE designated in the statutes must be the place where it has its central administration, that is to say its true centre of operations. The SE can easily transfer its registered office within the Community without — as is the case at present — dissolving the company in one Member State in order to form a new one in another Member State.

### Laws applicable

The order of precedence of the laws applicable to the SE is clarified.

### Registration and liquidation

The registration and completion of the liquidation of an SE must be disclosed for information purposes in the Official Journal of the European Communities. Every SE must be registered in the State where it has its registered office, in a register designated by the law of that State.

### Statutes [Charter and bylaws]

The Statutes of the SE must provide as governing bodies the general meeting of shareholders and either a management board and a supervisory board (two-tier system) or an administrative board (single-tier system).

Under the two-tier system the SE is managed by a management board. The member or members of the management board have the power to represent the company in dealings with third parties and in legal proceedings. They are appointed and removed by the supervisory board. No person may be a member of both the management board and the supervisory board of the same company at the same time.

However, the supervisory board may appoint one of its members to exercise the functions of a member of the management board if a vacancy arises. During such a period the function of the person concerned as a member of the supervisory board shall be suspended.

Under the single-tier system, the SE is managed by an administrative board. The member or members of the administrative board have the power to represent the company in dealings with third parties and in legal proceedings. The administrative board may delegate only the management to one or more of its members.

The following operations require the authorisation of the supervisory board or the deliberation of the administrative board:

- any investment project requiring an amount more than the percentage of subscribed capital;

- the setting-up, acquisition, disposal or closing down of undertakings, businesses or parts of businesses where the purchase price or disposal proceeds account for more than the percentage of subscribed capital;

- the raising or granting of loans, the issue of debt securities and the assumption of liabilities of a third party or suretyship for a third party where the total money value in each case is more than the percentage of subscribed capital;

- the conclusion of supply and performance contracts where the total turnover provided for therein is more than the percentage of turnover for the previous financial year;

- the percentage referred to above is to be determined by the Statutes of the SE. It may not be less than 5% nor more than 25%.

### Annual accounts

The SE must draw up annual accounts comprising the balance sheet, the profit and loss account and the notes to the accounts, and an annual report giving a fair view of the company's business and of its position; consolidated accounts may also be required.

### Taxation

In tax matters, the SE is treated the same as any other multinational, i.e. it is subject to the tax regime of the national legislation applicable to the company and its subsidiaries. SEs are subject to taxes and charges in all Member States where their administrative centres are situated. Thus their tax status is not totally satisfactory as there is still no adequate harmonisation at European level.

### Winding-up

Winding-up, liquidation, insolvency and suspension of payments are in large measure to be governed by national law. An SE which transfers its registered office outside the Community must be wound up on application by any person concerned or any competent authority.

### Council Directive supplementing the Statute for a European company with regard to the involvement of employees

### Definition

"Employee participation" does not mean participation in day-to-day decisions, which are a matter for the management, but participation in the supervision and strategic development of the company.

### Participation

- Several models of participation are possible: firstly, a model in which the employees form part of the supervisory board or of the administrative board, as the case may be; secondly, a model in which the employees are represented by a separate body; and finally, other models to be agreed between the management or administrative boards of the founder companies and the employees in those companies, the level of information and consultation being the same as in the case of the second model. The general meeting may not approve the formation of an SE unless one of the models of participation defined in the Directive has been chosen.

- The employees' representatives must be provided with such office space, financial and material resources, and other facilities as to enable them to perform their duties properly.

- If the two parties do not reach a satisfactory arrangement, a set of standard principles set out in the Annex to the Directive becomes applicable.

- With regard to a European company formed through a merger, the standard principles relating to worker participation will apply where at least 25% of the employees had the right to participate in decisions before the merger. Here a political agreement proved impossible until the Nice summit in December 2000. The compromise adopted by the Heads of State or Government allowed a Member State not to apply the Directive to SEs formed from a merger, in which case the SE could not be registered in the Member State in question unless an agreement had been concluded between the management and employees, or unless none of its employees had the right of participation before its formation.

### Employment contracts and pensions

Employment contracts and pensions are not covered by the Directive. With regard to occupational pension schemes, SEs are covered by the provisions laid down in the proposal for a directive on institutions for occupational schemes, presented by the Commission in October 2000, in particular in connection with the possibility of introducing a single pension scheme for all their employees in the European Union.

For the full text of the regulation see http://europa.eu/scadplus/leg/en/lvb/l26016.htm

## [B]   Abuse?

# CENTROS LTD AND ERHVERVS- OG SELSKABSSTYRELSEN
Case C-212/97, 1999 ECJ CELEX LEXIS 274, [1999] ECR I-1459

[The Danish Trade and Companies Board had refused to register a branch of Centros, a company incorporated in England but with no economic activity there.]

14 By its question, the national court is in substance asking whether it is contrary to Articles 52 [49] and 58 [54] of the Treaty for a Member State to refuse to register a branch of a company formed in accordance with the legislation of another Member State in which it has its registered office but where it does not carry on any business when the purpose of the branch is to enable the company concerned to carry on its entire business in the State in which that branch is to be set up, while avoiding the formation of a company in that State, thus evading application of the rules governing the formation of companies which are, in that State, more restrictive so far as minimum paid-up share capital is concerned.

15 As a preliminary point, it should be made clear that the Board does not in any way deny that a joint stock or private limited company with its registered office in another Member State may carry on business in Denmark through a branch. It therefore agrees, as a general rule, to register in Denmark a branch of a company formed in accordance with the law of another Member State. In particular, it has added that, if Centros had conducted any business in England and Wales, the Board would have agreed to register its branch in Denmark.

16 According to the Danish Government, Article 52 [49] of the Treaty is not applicable in the case in the main proceedings, since the situation is purely internal to Denmark. Mr and Mrs Bryde, Danish nationals, have formed a company in the United Kingdom which does not carry on any actual business there with the sole purpose of carrying on business in Denmark through a branch and thus of avoiding application of Danish legislation on the formation of private limited companies. It considers that in such circumstances the formation by nationals of one Member State of a company in another Member State does not amount to a relevant external element in the light of Community law and, in particular, freedom of establishment.

17 In this respect, it should be noted that a situation in which a company formed in accordance with the law of a Member State in which it has its registered office desires to set up a branch in another Member State falls within the scope of Community law. In that regard, it is immaterial that the company was formed in the first Member State only for the purpose of establishing itself in the second, where its main, or indeed entire, business is to be conducted (see, to this effect, Segers paragraph 16).

18 That Mr and Mrs Bryde formed the company Centros in the United Kingdom for the purpose of avoiding Danish legislation requiring that a minimum amount of share capital be paid up has not been denied either in the written observations or at the hearing. That does not, however, mean that the formation by that British company of a branch in Denmark is not covered by freedom of establishment for the purposes of Article 52 [49] and 58 [54] of the Treaty. The question of the application

of those articles of the Treaty is different from the question whether or not a Member State may adopt measures in order to prevent attempts by certain of its nationals to evade domestic legislation by having recourse to the possibilities offered by the Treaty.

19 As to the question whether, as Mr and Mrs Bryde claim, the refusal to register in Denmark a branch of their company formed in accordance with the law of another Member State in which its has its registered office constitutes an obstacle to freedom of establishment, it must be borne in mind that that freedom, conferred by Article 52 [49] of the Treaty on Community nationals, includes the right for them to take up and pursue activities as self-employed persons and to set up and manage undertakings under the same conditions as are laid down by the law of the Member State of establishment for its own nationals. Furthermore, under Article 58 [54] of the Treaty companies or firms formed in accordance with the law of a Member State and having their registered office, central administration or principal place of business within the Community are to be treated in the same way as natural persons who are nationals of Member States.

20 The immediate consequence of this is that those companies are entitled to carry on their business in another Member State through an agency, branch or subsidiary. The location of their registered office, central administration or principal place of business serves as the connecting factor with the legal system of a particular State in the same way as does nationality in the case of a natural person . . .

21 Where it is the practice of a Member State, in certain circumstances, to refuse to register a branch of a company having its registered office in another Member State, the result is that companies formed in accordance with the law of that other Member State are prevented from exercising the freedom of establishment conferred on them by Articles 52 [49] and 58 [54] of the Treaty.

22 Consequently, that practice constitutes an obstacle to the exercise of the freedoms guaranteed by those provisions.

23 According to the Danish authorities, however, Mr and Mrs Bryde cannot rely on those provisions, since the sole purpose of the company formation which they have in mind is to circumvent the application of the national law governing formation of private limited companies and therefore constitutes abuse of the freedom of establishment. In their submission, the Kingdom of Denmark is therefore entitled to take steps to prevent such abuse by refusing to register the branch.

24 It is true that according to the case-law of the Court a Member State is entitled to take measures designed to prevent certain of its nationals from attempting, under cover of the rights created by the Treaty, improperly to circumvent their national legislation or to prevent individuals from improperly or fraudulently taking advantage of provisions of Community law . . . .

25 However, although, in such circumstances, the national courts may, case by case, take account — on the basis of objective evidence — of abuse or fraudulent conduct on the part of the persons concerned in order, where appropriate, to deny them the benefit of the provisions of Community law on which they seek to rely, they must

nevertheless assess such conduct in the light of the objectives pursued by those provisions . . .

26 In the present case, the provisions of national law, application of which the parties concerned have sought to avoid, are rules governing the formation of companies and not rules concerning the carrying on of certain trades, professions or businesses. The provisions of the Treaty on freedom of establishment are intended specifically to enable companies formed in accordance with the law of a Member State and having their registered office, central administration or principal place of business within the Community to pursue activities in other Member States through an agency, branch or subsidiary.

27 That being so, the fact that a national of a Member State who wishes to set up a company chooses to form it in the Member State whose rules of company law seem to him the least restrictive and to set up branches in other Member States cannot, in itself, constitute an abuse of the right of establishment. The right to form a company in accordance with the law of a Member State and to set up branches in other Member States is inherent in the exercise, in a single market, of the freedom of establishment guaranteed by the Treaty.

28 In this connection, the fact that company law is not completely harmonised in the Community is of little consequence. Moreover, it is always open to the Council, on the basis of the powers conferred upon it by Article 54 [50] (3)(g) of the EC Treaty, to achieve complete harmonisation.

29 In addition, it is clear from paragraph 16 of Segers that the fact that a company does not conduct any business in the Member State in which it has its registered office and pursues its activities only in the Member State where its branch is established is not sufficient to prove the existence of abuse or fraudulent conduct which would entitle the latter Member State to deny that company the benefit of the provisions of Community law relating to the right of establishment.

30 Accordingly, the refusal of a Member State to register a branch of a company formed in accordance with the law of another Member State in which it has its registered office on the grounds that the branch is intended to enable the company to carry on all its economic activity in the host State, with the result that the secondary establishment escapes national rules on the provision for and the paying-up of a minimum capital, is incompatible with Articles 52 [49] and 58 [54] of the Treaty, in so far as it prevents any exercise of the right freely to set up a secondary establishment which Articles 52 [49] and 58 [54] are specifically intended to guarantee.

31 The final question to be considered is whether the national practice in question might not be justified for the reasons put forward by the Danish authorities.

32 Referring both to Article 56 [52] of the Treaty and to the case-law of the Court on imperative requirements in the general interest, the Board argues that the requirement that private limited companies provide for and pay up a minimum share capital pursues a dual objective: first, to reinforce the financial soundness of those companies in order to protect public creditors against the risk of seeing the public debts owing to them become irrecoverable since, unlike private creditors, they cannot secure those debts by means of guarantees and, second, and more

generally, to protect all creditors, whether public or private, by anticipating the risk of fraudulent bankruptcy due to the insolvency of companies whose initial capitalisation was inadequate.

33 The Board adds that there is no less restrictive means of attaining this dual objective. The other way of protecting creditors, namely by introducing rules making it possible for shareholders to incur personal liability, under certain conditions, would be more restrictive than the requirement to provide for and pay up a minimum share capital.

34 It should be observed, first, that the reasons put forward do not fall within the ambit of Article 56 [52] of the Treaty. Next, it should be borne in mind that, according to the Court's case-law, national measures liable to hinder or make less attractive the exercise of fundamental freedoms guaranteed by the Treaty must fulfil four conditions: they must be applied in a non-discriminatory manner; they must be justified by imperative requirements in the general interest; they must be suitable for securing the attainment of the objective which they pursue; and they must not go beyond what is necessary in order to attain it . . .

35 Those conditions are not fulfilled in the case in the main proceedings. First, the practice in question is not such as to attain the objective of protecting creditors which it purports to pursue since, if the company concerned had conducted business in the United Kingdom, its branch would have been registered in Denmark, even though Danish creditors might have been equally exposed to risk.

36 Since the company concerned in the main proceedings holds itself out as a company governed by the law of England and Wales and not as a company governed by Danish law, its creditors are on notice that it is covered by laws different from those which govern the formation of private limited companies in Denmark and they can refer to certain rules of Community law which protect them, such as the Fourth Council Directive 78/660/EEC of 25 July 1978 based on Article 54 [50](3)(g) of the Treaty on the annual accounts of certain types of companies (OJ 1978 L 222, p. 11), and the Eleventh Council Directive 89/666/EEC of 21 December 1989 concerning disclosure requirements in respect of branches opened in a Member State by certain types of company governed by the law of another State (OJ 1989 L 395, p. 36).

37 Second, contrary to the arguments of the Danish authorities, it is possible to adopt measures which are less restrictive, or which interfere less with fundamental freedoms, by, for example, making it possible in law for public creditors to obtain the necessary guarantees.

38 Lastly, the fact that a Member State may not refuse to register a branch of a company formed in accordance with the law of another Member State in which it has its registered office does not preclude that first State from adopting any appropriate measure for preventing or penalising fraud, either in relation to the company itself, if need be in cooperation with the Member State in which it was formed, or in relation to its members, where it has been established that they are in fact attempting, by means of the formation of the company, to evade their obligations towards private or public creditors established on the territory of a Member State concerned. In any event, combating fraud cannot justify a practice of

refusing to register a branch of a company which has its registered office in another Member State.

39 The answer to the question referred must therefore be that it is contrary to Articles 52 [49] and 58 [54] of the Treaty for a Member State to refuse to register a branch of a company formed in accordance with the law of another Member State in which it has its registered office but in which it conducts no business where the branch is intended to enable the company in question to carry on its entire business in the State in which that branch is to be created, while avoiding the need to form a company there, thus evading application of the rules governing the formation of companies which, in that State, are more restrictive as regards the paying up of a minimum share capital. That interpretation does not, however, prevent the authorities of the Member State concerned from adopting any appropriate measure for preventing or penalising fraud, either in relation to the company itself, if need be in cooperation with the Member State in which it was formed, or in relation to its members, where it has been established that they are in fact attempting, by means of the formation of a company, to evade their obligations towards private or public creditors established in the territory of the Member State concerned.

## NOTES AND QUESTIONS

1. The Danish Government had argued that the issue in this case was wholly internal to Denmark. Indeed, the only connection with another Member State for the individuals concerned was that they owned shares in the company for which they now wished to establish a branch in Denmark in order to trade solely in Denmark. How did the Court deal with this issue? Why was this situation not considered an abuse of the Treaty provisions? In that connection, see also *Kamer van Koophandel and Fabrieken voor Amsterdam v. Inspire Art Ltd*, Case C-167/01, 2003 ECJ CELEX LEXIS 380 [2003] ECR I-10155. In *Cadbury Schweppes plc and Cadbury Schweppes Overseas Ltd v. Commissioners of Inland Revenue*, Case C-196/04, 2006 ECJ CELEX LEXIS 445 [2006] ECR I-7995, the ECJ confirmed that it is not an abuse of the freedom of establishment for a company established in a Member State to set up and capitalize companies in another Member State solely to take advantage of a more favorable tax regime. The Court sought to explain the difference between justified exercise of EC 43/TFEU 49 rights and an abuse of those rights in the following terms:

> 50 It is also apparent from case-law that the mere fact that a resident company establishes a secondary establishment, such as a subsidiary, in another Member State cannot set up a general presumption of tax evasion and justify a measure which compromises the exercise of a fundamental freedom guaranteed by the Treaty . . .

> 51 On the other hand, a national measure restricting freedom of establishment may be justified where it specifically relates to wholly artificial arrangements aimed at circumventing the application of the legislation of the Member State concerned . . .

52 It is necessary, in assessing the conduct of the taxable person, to take particular account of the objective pursued by the freedom of establishment . . .

53 That objective is to allow a national of a Member State to set up a secondary establishment in another Member State to carry on his activities there and thus assist economic and social interpenetration within the Community in the sphere of activities as self-employed persons . . . To that end, freedom of establishment is intended to allow a Community national to participate, on a stable and continuing basis, in the economic life of a Member State other than his State of origin and to profit therefrom . . .

54 Having regard to that objective of integration in the host Member State, the concept of establishment within the meaning of the Treaty provisions on freedom of establishment involves the actual pursuit of an economic activity through a fixed establishment in that State for an indefinite period . . . Consequently, it presupposes actual establishment of the company concerned in the host Member State and the pursuit of genuine economic activity there.

55 It follows that, in order for a restriction on the freedom of establishment to be justified on the ground of prevention of abusive practices, the specific objective of such a restriction must be to prevent conduct involving the creation of wholly artificial arrangements which do not reflect economic reality, with a view to escaping the tax normally due on the profits generated by activities carried out on national territory.

2.    The practice of incorporating in England to avoid the capital contribution rules prevalent on the continent has become widespread and controversial. While one or two cases may not seem to cause particular concern when appraised against the rationale for such a requirement, a widespread practice could lead to a significant undermining of the host state's policy goal. Consider the practice of incorporating in Delaware where one reason for doing so is to take advantage of favorable governance rules and thus possibly subvert policy intentions of the state where business is actually to be conducted.

3.    The issues in the *Centros* case seem more closely analogous to the "full faith and credit" requirement of the U.S. Constitution than the Commerce Clause.

4.    For another case involving alleged abuse of the EU rules, see *Dionysios Diamantis v. Elliniko Dimosio (Greek State) and Organismos Ikonomikis Anasygkrotisis Epicheiriseon ae (OAE)*, Case C-373/97, 2000 ECJ CELEX LEXIS 97, [2000] ECR I-1705. Mr. Diamantis was a shareholder in the public limited liability company Plastika Kavalas AE (hereinafter Plastika Kavalas). At the beginning of the 1980s that company was facing serious financial difficulties, and the shareholders asked that it be placed under a scheme provided for in Greek law regarding special liquidation. The Minister for the National Economy decided however to place Plastika Kavalas under the scheme for provisional administration by a governmental agency — the OAE.

Under that provisional administration, the OAE decided to increase the capital of Plastika Kavalas and was issued with shares that gave it a 2/3 majority. Subsequently there were further changes and eventually the majority of shares were transferred to another company, Plastika Makedonias, which was then taken over by the Petzetakis Group.

Mr. Diamantis brought an action in the national court seeking a declaration that the alterations in the capital of the company were invalid, on the ground that they were contrary to Article 25 of the Second Council Directive 77/91/EEC on "coordination of safeguards which, for the protection of the interests of members and others, are required by Member States of companies within the meaning of the second paragraph of Article 58 [54] of the Treaty, in respect of the formation of public limited liability companies and the maintenance and alteration of their capital, with a view to making such safeguards equivalent" ([1977] OJ L 26, p. 1).

The Greek Government and the OAE pleaded abuse of rights by Mr. Diamantis due to the length of time that had elapsed and the shareholding changes that had not been objected to at the time, but the ECJ disagreed with that assertion, while suggesting another avenue to challenge Diamantis' action:

> 44 . . . Community law does not preclude national courts from applying a provision of national law which enables them to determine whether a right deriving from a Community law provision is being abused. However, in making that determination, it is not permissible to deem a shareholder relying on Article 25(1) of the Second Directive to be abusing his rights under that provision merely because he is a minority shareholder of a company subject to reorganisation measures, or has benefited from reorganisation of the company, or has not exercised his right of pre-emption, or was among the shareholders who asked for the company to be placed under the scheme applicable to companies in serious difficulties, or has allowed a certain period of time to elapse before bringing his action. In contrast, Community law does not preclude national courts from applying the provision of national law concerned if, of the remedies available for a situation that has arisen in breach of that provision, a shareholder has chosen a remedy that will cause such serious damage to the legitimate interests of others that it appears manifestly disproportionate.

## [C]   The Interplay of EC 43/TFEU 49 and States' Taxation Competences

### THE QUEEN v. H. M. TREASURY AND COMMISSIONERS OF INLAND REVENUE, EX PARTE DAILY MAIL AND GENERAL TRUST PLC
#### Case 81/87, 1988 ECJ CELEX LEXIS 371, [1988] ECR 5483

[The Daily Mail, a British newspaper, and General Trust PLC, a UK public corporation, sought a declaration that it was not required to obtain consent from the UK Treasury to move its central management and control out of the UK. The effect of such a move would be to remove it from the taxing jurisdiction.]

7 It is common ground that the principal reason for the proposed transfer of central management and control was to enable the applicant, after establishing its residence for tax purposes in the Netherlands, to sell a significant part of its non-permanent assets and to use the proceeds of that sale to buy its own shares, without having to pay the tax to which such transactions would make it liable under United Kingdom tax law, in regard in particular to the substantial capital gains on the assets which the applicant proposed to sell. After establishing its central management and control in the Netherlands the applicant would be subject to Netherlands corporation tax, but the transactions envisaged would be taxed only on the basis of any capital gains which accrued after the transfer of its residence for tax purposes.

*     *     *

11 The first question seeks in essence to determine whether Articles 52 [49] and 58 [54] of the Treaty give a company incorporated under the legislation of a Member State and having its registered office there the right to transfer its central management and control to another Member State. If that is so, the national court goes on to ask whether the Member State of origin can make that right subject to the consent of national authorities, the grant of which is linked to the company's tax position.

12 With regard to the first part of the question, the applicant claims essentially that Article 58 [54] of the Treaty expressly confers on the companies to which it applies the same right of primary establishment in another Member State as is conferred on natural persons by Article 52 [49]. The transfer of the central management and control of a company to another Member State amounts to the establishment of the company in that Member State because the company is locating its centre of decision-making there, which constitutes genuine and effective economic activity.

13 The United Kingdom argues essentially that the provisions of the Treaty do not give companies a general right to move their central management and control from one Member State to another. The fact that the central management and control of a company is located in a Member State does not itself necessarily imply any genuine and effective economic activity on the territory of that Member State and cannot therefore be regarded as establishment within the meaning of Article 52 [49] of the Treaty.

14 The Commission emphasizes first of all that in the present state of Community law, the conditions under which a company may transfer its central management and control from one Member State to another are still governed by the national law of the State in which it is incorporated and of the State to which it wishes to move. In that regard, the Commission refers to the differences between the national systems of company law. Some of them permit the transfer of the central management and control of a company and, among those, certain attach no legal consequences to such a transfer, even in regard to taxation. Under other systems, the transfer of the management or the centre of decision-making of a company out of the Member State in which it is incorporated results in the loss of legal personality. However, all the systems permit the winding-up of a company in one Member State and its reincorporation in another. The Commission considers that where the transfer of central management and control is possible under national

legislation, the right to transfer it to another Member State is a right protected by Article 52 [49] of the Treaty.

15 Faced with those diverging opinions, the Court must first point out, as it has done on numerous occasions, that freedom of establishment constitutes one of the fundamental principles of the Community and that the provisions of the Treaty guaranteeing that freedom have been directly applicable since the end of the transitional period. Those provisions secure the right of establishment in another Member State not merely for Community nationals but also for the companies referred to in Article 58 [54].

16 Even though those provisions are directed mainly to ensuring that foreign nationals and companies are treated in the host Member State in the same way as nationals of that State, they also prohibit the Member State of origin from hindering the establishment in another Member State of one of its nationals or of a company incorporated under its legislation which comes within the definition contained in Article 58 [54]. As the Commission rightly observed, the rights guaranteed by Articles 52 [49] et seq. would be rendered meaningless if the Member State of origin could prohibit undertakings from leaving in order to establish themselves in another Member State. In regard to natural persons, the right to leave their territory for that purpose is expressly provided for in Directive 73/148, which is the subject of the second question referred to the Court.

17 In the case of a company, the right of establishment is generally exercised by the setting-up of agencies, branches or subsidiaries, as is expressly provided for in the second sentence of the first paragraph of Article 52 [49]. Indeed, that is the form of establishment in which the applicant engaged in this case by opening an investment management office in the Netherlands. A company may also exercise its right of establishment by taking part in the incorporation of a company in another Member State, and in that regard Article 221 [344] of the Treaty ensures that it will receive the same treatment as nationals of that Member State as regards participation in the capital of the new company.

18 The provision of United Kingdom law at issue in the main proceedings imposes no restriction on transactions such as those described above. Nor does it stand in the way of a partial or total transfer of the activities of a company incorporated in the United Kingdom to a company newly incorporated in another Member State, if necessary after winding-up and, consequently, the settlement of the tax position of the United Kingdom company. It requires Treasury consent only where such a company seeks to transfer its central management and control out of the United Kingdom while maintaining its legal personality and its status as a United Kingdom company.

19 In that regard it should be borne in mind that, unlike natural persons, companies are creatures of the law and, in the present state of Community law, creatures of national law. They exist only by virtue of the varying national legislation which determines their incorporation and functioning.

20 As the Commission has emphasized, the legislation of the Member States varies widely in regard to both the factor providing a connection to the national territory required for the incorporation of a company and the question whether a company

incorporated under the legislation of a Member State may subsequently modify that connecting factor. Certain States require that not merely the registered office but also the real head office, that is to say the central administration of the company, should be situated on their territory, and the removal of the central administration from that territory thus presupposes the winding-up of the company with all the consequences that winding-up entails in company law and tax law. The legislation of other States permits companies to transfer their central administration to a foreign country but certain of them, such as the United Kingdom, make that right subject to certain restrictions, and the legal consequences of a transfer, particularly in regard to taxation, vary from one Member State to another.

21 The Treaty has taken account of that variety in national legislation. In defining, in Article 58 [54], the companies which enjoy the right of establishment, the Treaty places on the same footing, as connecting factors, the registered office, central administration and principal place of business of a company. Moreover, Article 220 [344] of the Treaty provides for the conclusion, so far as is necessary, of agreements between the Member States with a view to securing inter alia the retention of legal personality in the event of transfer of the registered office of companies from one country to another. No convention in this area has yet come into force.

22 It should be added that none of the directives on the coordination of company law adopted under Article 54 [51] (3) (g) of the Treaty deal with the differences at issue here.

23 It must therefore be held that the Treaty regards the differences in national legislation concerning the required connecting factor and the question whether — and if so how — the registered office or real head office of a company incorporated under national law may be transferred from one Member State to another as problems which are not resolved by the rules concerning the right of establishment but must be dealt with by future legislation or conventions.

24 Under those circumstances, Articles 52 [49] and 58 [54] of the Treaty cannot be interpreted as conferring on companies incorporated under the law of a Member State a right to transfer their central management and control and their central administration to another Member State while retaining their status as companies incorporated under the legislation of the first Member State.

25 The answer to the first part of the first question must therefore be that in the present state of Community law Articles 52 [49] and 58 [54] of the Treaty, properly construed, confer no right on a company incorporated under the legislation of a Member State and having its registered office there to transfer its central management and control to another Member State.

## NOTES AND QUESTIONS

1.   Why did the Court accept that EC 43/TFEU 49 did not guarantee a company the right to move its principal place of business to another Member State?

2.   There have been a number of other cases exploring the relationship between tax laws and the right of establishment.

For example, in *Futura Participations SA and Singer v. Administration des contributions*, Case C-250/95, 1997 ECJ CELEX LEXIS 267, [1997] ECR I-2471, Futura Participations S.A., based in Paris, had a branch named Singer in Luxembourg. A dispute arose with the Luxembourg authorities regarding the taxation of Singer. In principle, all income of a Luxembourg resident was taxable wherever arising. However, pursuant to Article 4(2) of the double taxation agreement between France and Luxembourg, where an undertaking had a permanent establishment in both contracting States (as in this case) each State may tax only the income arising from the activity of the permanent establishment located on its territory.

Under the Luxembourg tax law, resident taxpayers could deduct from the total amount of their net income losses carried forward from previous years, provided that they had kept proper accounts. Non-resident taxpayers were not obliged to keep separate accounts relating to their Luxembourg activities. If they did not keep such accounts, they were allowed to determine the amount of their taxable income in Luxembourg on the basis of an apportionment of their total income whereby a proportion of that income is treated as arising from the taxpayer's Luxembourg activities. Luxembourg law allowed non-resident taxpayers to deduct from the total of their net income previous losses carried forward from previous years, provided that they were "economically related to income received locally and that accounts are kept within the country".

Not having proper accounts for 1986, Singer determined its taxable income for that year on the basis of an apportionment of Futura's total income. In its tax declaration for that year, the branch also requested the tax authorities to set off against its 1986 income losses amounting to more than LFR 23 000 000 incurred between 1981 and 1986. Since Singer did not have proper accounts for that period either, the amount of the losses was also determined on the basis of an apportionment of all Futura's losses during that period. The Luxembourg tax authorities refused to allow a set-off on the ground that in Luxembourg law a non-resident taxpayer may carry forward a loss only if certain conditions laid down in Article 157(2) of the Luxembourg Law were respected and not on the basis of an apportionment.

The national court asked whether EC 52/TFEU 49 of the Treaty precluded a Member State from making the carrying forward of previous losses, requested by a taxpayer which had a branch in that State but was not resident there, subject to the condition that the losses must be economically related to the income earned by the taxpayer in that State and that, during the financial year in which the losses were incurred, the taxpayer must have kept and held in that State, in respect of activities he carried on there, accounts complying with the relevant national rules.

The Court held that:

> 43 . . . Article 52 [49] of the Treaty does not preclude a Member State from making the carrying forward of previous losses, requested by a taxpayer which has a branch in its territory but is not resident there, subject to the condition that the losses must be economically related to the income earned by the taxpayer in that State, provided that resident taxpayers do not receive more favourable treatment. On the other hand,

that article does preclude the carrying forward of losses from being made subject to the condition that, in the year in which the losses were incurred, the taxpayer must have kept and held in that State accounts relating to his activities carried on there which comply with the relevant national rules. The Member State concerned may, however, require the non-resident taxpayer to demonstrate clearly and precisely that the amount of the losses which he claims to have incurred corresponds, under its domestic rules governing the calculation of income and losses which were applicable in the financial year concerned, to the amount of the losses actually incurred in that State by the taxpayer.

In another case, *Marks & Spencer plc v. David Halsey (Her Majesty's Inspector of Taxes)*, Case C-446/03, 2005 ECJ CELEX LEXIS 734, [2005] ECR I-10837 the plaintiffs challenged the UK tax law that did not allow a parent company resident in the UK to deduct losses incurred by subsidiaries in other Member States. However, through the device of "group relief", such losses could be deducted from the parent company's taxable income in the case of its subsidiaries resident in the UK. The Court considered that the law did not infringe EC 43/TFEU 49 but with some caveats:

> 59. . . . [A]s Community law now stands, Articles 43 EC [49] and 48 EC [54] do not preclude provisions of a Member State which generally prevent a resident parent company from deducting from its taxable profits losses incurred in another Member State by a subsidiary established in that Member State although they allow it to deduct losses incurred by a resident subsidiary. However, it is contrary to Articles 43 EC [49] and 48 EC [54] to prevent the resident parent company from doing so where the non-resident subsidiary has exhausted the possibilities available in its State of residence of having the losses taken into account for the accounting period concerned by the claim for relief and also for previous accounting periods and where there are no possibilities for those losses to be taken into account in its State of residence for future periods either by the subsidiary itself or by a third party, in particular where the subsidiary has been sold to that third party.

Can you discern any common themes running through the Court's approach here?

## § 15.04   FREE MOVEMENT OF CAPITAL

### [A]   The Scope of EC 56/TFEU 63

## CRIMINAL PROCEEDINGS AGAINST LUCAS EMILIO SANZ DE LERA, RAIMUNDO DíAZ JIMÉNEZ AND FIGEN KAPANOGLU

Joined cases C-163/94, C-165/94 and C-250/94, 1995 ECJ EUR-Lex LEXIS 486,1995 ECR I-4821

[Each of the defendants had been apprehended at Madrid airport after security checks revealed that they were carrying large amounts of Spanish currency (pesetas at the time) that they were evidently intending to remove to non-Member States without having made a declaration of their intent as required by Spanish law. The Council had enacted a directive (the "directive") laying down rules within which the Member States could exercise their rights under EC 58/TFEU 65.]

19 Article 73b(1) [63] of the Treaty gave effect to the liberalization of capital movements between Member States and between Member States and non-member countries. To that end, it provides that . . . , all restrictions on the movement of capital between Member States and non-member countries are to be prohibited.

20 By virtue of Article 73d(1)(b) of the Treaty [65], Article 73b(1) [63] is to be without prejudice to the right of the Member States "to take all requisite measures to prevent infringement of national law and regulations, in particular in the field of taxation and the prudential supervision of financial institutions, or to lay down procedures for the declaration of capital movements for purposes of administrative or statistical information or to take measures which are justified on grounds of public policy or public security".

21 Pursuant to Article 73d(3) [65] of the Treaty, those measures and procedures "shall not constitute a means of arbitrary discrimination or a disguised restriction on the free movement of capital . . . as defined in Article 73b [63]".

22 It . . . [T]]he measures which are necessary to prevent the commission of certain infringements and are permitted by Article 4(1) of the directive, in particular those designed to ensure effective fiscal supervision and to prevent illegal activities such as tax evasion, money laundering, drug trafficking or terrorism, are also covered by Article 73d(1)(b).

23 It is therefore necessary to consider whether the requirement of an authorization or a prior declaration for the export of coins, banknotes or bearer cheques is necessary in order to uphold the objectives pursued and whether those objectives might be attained by measures less restrictive of the free movement of capital.

24 . . . [A]uthorization has the effect of suspending currency exports and makes them conditional in each case upon the consent of the administrative authorities, which must be sought by means of a special application.

25 The effect of such a requirement is to cause the exercise of the free movement of capital to be subject to the discretion of the administrative authorities and thus

be such as to render that freedom illusory . . .

26 However, the restriction on the free movement of capital resulting from that requirement could be eliminated without thereby detracting from the effective pursuit of the aims of those rules.

27 As the Commission has rightly pointed out, it would be sufficient to set up an adequate system of declarations indicating the nature of the planned operation and the identity of the declarant, which would require the competent authorities to proceed with a rapid examination of the declaration and enable them, if necessary, to carry out in due time the investigations found to be necessary to determine whether capital was being unlawfully transferred and to impose the requisite penalties if national legislation was being contravened.

28 Thus, unlike prior authorization, such a system of declarations would not suspend the operation concerned but would nevertheless enable the national authorities to carry out, in order to uphold public policy, effective supervision to prevent infringements of national law and regulations.

29 As regards the Spanish Government's argument that only a system of authorization makes it possible to establish that a criminal offence has been committed and impose penalties under criminal law, such considerations cannot justify the maintenance of measures which are incompatible with Community law.

30 It follows that Articles 73b(1) and 73d(1)(b) [63] of the Treaty preclude rules which make the export of coins, banknotes or bearer cheques conditional on prior authorization but do not by contrast preclude a transaction of that nature being made conditional on a prior declaration.

## NOTES AND QUESTIONS

It should be noted in the first instance that as this case illustrates EC 56/TFEU 63, which covers capital movements to third countries as well as within the Union. This contrasts with the other freedom of movement provisions, which all address intra-Union movements only. Why might capital be treated differently? Bearing in mind the facts of the above case, are there other aspects of this particular freedom that are noticeably different from the other freedoms?

## [B]　The Interrelation of EC 56/TFEU 63 and the Taxation Competences of the Member States

### PETRI MANNINEN
Case C-319/02, 2004 ECJ CELEX LEXIS 291, [2004] ECR I-7477

[Mr Manninen, a resident of Finland, questioned whether EC 56 and 58/TFEU 63 and 65 had the effect of precluding taxation in Finland on dividends received from a Swedish company. The profits distributed by that Swedish company in the form of dividends to Mr Manninen had already borne corporation tax in Sweden. The dividends also bore a tax in Sweden on revenue from capital by means of deduction at source. Since dividends distributed by foreign companies to Finnish taxpayers conferred no entitlement to a tax credit in Finland, they were subject in that Member State to income tax on revenue from capital at the rate of 29%. However, in accordance with Convention 26/1997 concluded between Member States of the Nordic Council for the avoidance of double taxation in the matter of income tax and wealth tax, the tax deducted at source in Sweden, the rate of which could not exceed 15% by virtue of Article 10 of that convention, was deductible from the tax due by way of income tax on revenue from capital from the fully taxable shareholder in Finland. Additionally Finnish law allowed a tax credit for corporation tax paid by Finnish companies but not foreign companies. Thus Mr Manninen was subject to Finnish tax on the dividend, while, had he received it from a Finnish company, he would have received a tax credit for the corporation tax paid by that company.]

18. In its questions, which may be examined together, the national court is asking in essence whether Articles 56 [63] EC and 58 [65] EC preclude legislation, such as that at issue in the main proceedings, whereby the right of a fully-taxable person in a Member State to the benefit of a tax credit on dividends paid to him by limited companies is excluded where those companies are not established in that State.

19. The first point to be made is that, although direct taxation falls within their competence, the Member States must none the less exercise that competence consistently with Community law . . .

20. As for whether tax legislation such as that at issue in the main proceedings involves a restriction on the free movement of capital within the meaning of Article 56 [63] EC, it should be noted that the tax credit under Finnish tax legislation is designed to prevent the double taxation of company profits distributed to shareholders by setting off the corporation tax due from the company distributing dividends against the tax due from the shareholder by way of income tax on revenue from capital. The end result of such a system is that dividends are no longer taxed in the hands of the shareholder. Since the tax credit applies solely in favour of dividends paid by companies established in Finland, that legislation disadvantages fully taxable persons in Finland who receive dividends from companies established in other Member States, who, for their part, are taxed at the rate of 29% by way of income tax on revenue from capital.

21. It is undisputed that the tax convention concluded between the States of the Nordic Council for the prevention of double taxation is not capable of eliminating that unfavourable treatment. That convention does not provide for any system for setting off corporation tax against income tax due on revenue from capital. It merely seeks to attenuate the effects of double taxation in the hands of the shareholder in relation to that latter tax.

22. It follows that the Finnish tax legislation has the effect of deterring fully taxable persons in Finland from investing their capital in companies established in another Member State.

23. Such a provision also has a restrictive effect as regards companies established in other Member States, in that it constitutes an obstacle to their raising capital in Finland. Since revenue from capital of non-Finnish origin receives less favourable tax treatment than dividends distributed by companies established in Finland, the

shares of companies established in other Member States are less attractive to investors residing in Finland than shares in companies which have their seat in that Member State . . .

24. It follows from the above that legislation such as that at issue in the main proceedings constitutes a restriction on the free movement of capital which is, in principle, prohibited by Article 56 [63] EC.

25. It must, however, be examined whether that restriction on the free movement of capital is capable of being justified having regard to the provisions of the EC Treaty.

26. It should be recalled in that respect that, in accordance with Article 58 [65](1)(a) EC, . . . Article 56 [63] shall be without prejudice to the right of Member States . . . to apply the relevant provisions of their tax law which distinguish between taxpayers who are not in the same situation with regard to . . . the place where their capital is invested'.

27. According to the Finnish, French and United Kingdom Governments, that provision clearly shows that Member States are entitled to reserve the benefit of the tax credit for dividends paid by companies established in their territory.

28. In that respect, it should be noted that Article 58 [65](1)(a) of the Treaty, which, as a derogation from the fundamental principle of the free movement of capital, must be interpreted strictly, cannot be interpreted as meaning that any tax legislation making a distinction between taxpayers by reference to the place where they invest their capital is automatically compatible with the Treaty. The derogation in Article 58 [65](1)(a) EC is itself limited by Article 58 [65](3) EC, which provides that the national provisions referred to in Article 58 [65](1) shall not constitute a means of arbitrary discrimination or a disguised restriction on the free movement of capital and payments as defined in Article 56 [63]'.

29. A distinction must therefore be made between unequal treatment which is permitted under Article 58 [65](1)(a) EC and arbitrary discrimination which is prohibited by Article 58 [65](3). In that respect, the case-law shows that, for national tax legislation like that at issue, which, in relation to a fully taxable person in the Member State concerned makes a distinction between revenue from national dividends and that from foreign dividends, to be capable of being regarded as compatible with the Treaty provisions on the free movement of capital, the difference in treatment must concern situations which are not objectively comparable or be justified by overriding reasons in the general interest, such as the need to safeguard the coherence of the tax system . . . In order to be justified, moreover, the difference in treatment between different categories of dividends must not go beyond what is necessary in order to attain the objective of the legislation.

30. The Finnish, French and United Kingdom Governments begin by arguing that the dividends paid are fundamentally different in character according to whether they come from Finnish or non-Finnish companies. Unlike profits distributed by non-Finnish companies, those paid in the form of dividends by companies established in Finland are subject to corporation tax in that Member State, conferring entitlement on the part of a shareholder who is fully taxable in Finland to the tax credit. The difference in treatment between dividends paid by companies established in that State and those paid by companies which do not satisfy that condition

is therefore justified, they argue, in the light of Article 58 [65](1)(a) EC.

31. The French Government further argues that the Finnish tax legislation conforms to the principle of territoriality and cannot therefore be regarded as contrary to the Treaty provisions on the free movement of capital . . .

32. In that regard, it needs to be examined whether, in accordance with Article 58 [65](1)(a) EC, the difference in treatment of a shareholder fully taxable in Finland according to whether he receives dividends from companies established in that Member State or from companies established in other Member States relates to situations which are not objectively comparable.

33. It should be noted that the Finnish tax legislation is designed to prevent double taxation of company profits by granting to a shareholder who receives dividends a tax advantage linked to the taking into account of the corporation tax due from the company distributing the dividends.

34. It is true that, in relation to such legislation, the situation of persons fully taxable in Finland might differ according to the place where they invested their capital. That would be the case in particular where the tax legislation of the Member State in which the investments were made already eliminated the risk of double taxation of company profits distributed in the form of dividends, by, for example, subjecting to corporation tax only such profits by the company concerned as were not distributed.

35. That is not the case here, however. As the order for reference shows, both dividends distributed by a company established in Finland and those paid by a company established in Sweden are, apart from the tax credit, capable of being subjected to double taxation. In both cases, the revenue is first subject to corporation tax and then — in so far as it is distributed in the form of dividends — to income tax in the hands of the beneficiaries.

36. Where a person fully taxable in Finland invests capital in a company established in Sweden, there is thus no way of escaping double taxation of the profits distributed by the company in which the investment is made. In the face of a tax rule which takes account of the corporation tax owed by a company in order to prevent double taxation of the profits distributed, shareholders who are fully taxable in Finland find themselves in a comparable situation, whether they receive dividends from a company established in that Member State or from a company established in Sweden.

37. It follows that the Finnish tax legislation makes the grant of the tax credit subject to the condition that the dividends be distributed by companies established in Finland, while shareholders fully taxable in Finland find themselves in a comparable situation, whether they receive dividends from companies established in that Member State or from companies established in other Member States.

38. Moreover, . . . the Finnish tax legislation cannot be regarded as an emanation of the principle of territoriality. . . . [T]hat principle does not preclude the granting of a tax credit to a person fully taxable in Finland in respect of dividends paid by companies established in other Member States . . .

39. In any event, having regard to Article 58 [65](1)(a) EC, the principle of

territoriality cannot justify different treatment of dividends distributed by companies established in Finland and those paid by companies established in another Member States, if the categories of dividends concerned by that difference in treatment share the same objective situation.

40. Secondly, the Finnish, French and United Kingdom Governments maintain that the Finnish tax legislation is objectively justified by the need to ensure the cohesion of the national tax system . . . In particular, they argue . . . . there is in this case a direct link between the taxation of the company's profits and the tax credit granted to the shareholder receiving the dividends. They point out that the tax credit is granted to the latter only on condition that that company has actually paid the tax on its profits. If that tax does not cover the minimum tax on the dividends to be distributed, that company is required to pay an additional tax.

41. The Finnish Government adds that, if a tax credit were to be granted to the recipients of dividends paid by a Swedish company to shareholders who were fully taxable in Finland, the authorities of that Member State would be obliged to grant a tax advantage in relation to corporation tax that was not levied by that State, thereby threatening the cohesion of the national tax system.

42. In that respect, it should be noted that, in paragraphs 28 and 21 respectively of the judgments in Bachmann and Commission v. Belgium, the Court of Justice acknowledged that the need to preserve the cohesion of a tax system might justify a restriction on the exercise of the fundamental freedoms guaranteed by the Treaty. However, for an argument based on such justification to succeed, a direct link had to be established between the tax advantage concerned and the offsetting of that advantage by a particular tax levy . . . As is shown [in two previous cases involving Belgian taxation], those judgments are based on the finding that, in Belgian law, there was a direct link, in relation to the same taxpayer liable to income tax, between the ability to deduct insurance contributions from taxable income and the subsequent taxation of sums paid by the insurers.

43. The case-law further shows that an argument based on the need to safeguard the cohesion of a tax system must be examined in the light of the objective pursued by the tax legislation in question . . .

44. As has already been noted in paragraph 33 of this judgment, the Finnish tax legislation is designed to prevent double taxation of company profits distributed to shareholders. The objective pursued is achieved by granting the taxpayer a tax credit calculated by reference to the rate of taxation of company profits by way of corporation tax (see paragraph 8 of this judgment). Having regard to the identical rate of tax on company profits and on revenue from capital, namely 29%, that tax system finally results in taxing, solely in the hands of companies established in Finland, the profits distributed by them to taxpayers who are fully taxable in Finland, the latter being simply exonerated from tax on the dividends received. Should the tax paid by a Finnish company which pays dividends turn out to be less than the amount of the tax credit, the difference is charged to that company by means of an additional tax.

45. Even if that tax legislation is thus based on a link between the tax advantage and the offsetting tax levy, in providing that the tax credit granted to the shareholder

fully taxable in Finland is to be calculated by reference to the corporation tax due from the company established in that Member State on the profits which it distributes, such legislation does not appear to be necessary in order to preserve the cohesion of the Finnish tax system.

46. Having regard to the objective pursued by the Finnish tax legislation, the cohesion of that tax system is assured as long as the correlation between the tax advantage granted in favour of the shareholder and the tax due by way of corporation tax is maintained. Therefore, in a case such as that at issue in the main proceedings, the granting to a shareholder who is fully taxable in Finland and who holds shares in a company established in Sweden of a tax credit calculated by reference to the corporation tax owed by that company in Sweden would not threaten the cohesion of the Finnish tax system and would constitute a measure less restrictive of the free movement of capital than that laid down by the Finnish tax legislation.

47. It should be noted furthermore that, in Bachmann and Commission v. Belgium, the purpose of the tax provisions in question was also to avoid double taxation. The possibility which Belgian legislation gave to physical persons to deduct payments made under life assurance contracts from their taxable income — with the end result of not taxing the income used to pay those contributions — was based on the justification that the capital constituted by means of those contributions would subsequently be taxed in the hands of its holders. In such a system, double taxation was avoided by postponing the sole taxation due until the time when the capital constituted by means of the exonerated contributions was paid. Coherence of the tax system necessarily required that, if the Belgian tax authorities were to allow the deductibility of life assurance contributions from taxable income, they had to be certain that the capital paid by the assurance company at the expiry of the contract would in fact subsequently be taxed. It is in that precise context that the Court of Justice then took the view that there were no less restrictive measures than those forming the subject-matter of Bachmann and Commission v. Belgium, which were capable of safeguarding the coherence of the tax system in question.

48. In the case at issue in the main proceedings here, however, the factual context is different. At the time when the shareholder fully taxable in Finland receives dividends, the profits thus distributed have already been subject to taxation by way of corporation tax, irrespective of whether those dividends come from Finnish or from Swedish companies. The objective pursued by the Finnish tax legislation, which is to eliminate the double taxation of profits distributed in the form of dividends, may be achieved by also granting the tax credit in favour of profits distributed in that way by Swedish companies to persons fully taxable in Finland.

49. Whilst, for the Republic of Finland, granting a tax credit in relation to corporation tax due in another Member State would entail a reduction in its tax receipts in relation to dividends paid by companies in other Member States, it has been consistently held in the case-law that reduction in tax revenue cannot be regarded as an overriding reason in the public interest which may be relied on to justify a measure which is in principle contrary to a fundamental freedom . . .

50. At the hearing, the Finnish and United Kingdom Governments referred to various practical obstacles which, in their submission, preclude a shareholder fully

taxable in Finland from being granted a tax credit corresponding to the corporation tax due from a company established in another Member State. They argued that the Treaty rules on the free movement of capital apply not only to movements of capital between Member States but also to movements of capital between Member States and non-member countries. According to those governments, bearing in mind the diversity of the tax systems in force, it is impossible in practice to determine exactly the amount of tax, by way of corporation tax, which has affected dividends paid by a company established in another Member State or in a non-member country. They argue that such impossibility is due in particular to the fact that the basis of assessment for corporation tax varies from one country to another and that rates of tax may vary from one year to the next. They further argue that dividends paid by a company do not necessarily arise from the profits of a given accounting year.

51. In that respect, it should first be noted that the case in the main proceedings does not in any way concern the free movement of capital between Member States and non-member countries. This case concerns the refusal by the tax authorities of a Member State to grant a tax advantage to a person fully taxable in that State where that person has received dividends from a company established in another Member State.

52. Moreover, the order for reference shows that, in Finland, the tax credit allowed to the shareholder is equal to 29/71ths of the dividends paid by the company established in that Member State. For the purposes of calculating the tax credit, the numerator of the fraction to be applied is thus equal to the rate of taxation of company profits by way of corporation tax, and the denominator is equal to the result obtained by deducting that same rate of taxation from the base of 100.

53. Finally, it should also be noted that in Finnish law the tax credit always corresponds to the amount of the tax actually paid by way of corporation tax by the company which distributes the dividends. Should the tax paid by way of corporation tax turn out to be less than the amount of the tax credit, the difference is charged to the company making the distribution by means of an additional tax.

54. In those circumstances, the calculation of a tax credit granted to a shareholder fully taxable in Finland, who has received dividends from a company established in Sweden, must take account of the tax actually paid by the company established in that other Member State, as such tax arises from the general rules on calculating the basis of assessment and from the rate of corporation tax in that latter Member State. Possible difficulties in determining the tax actually paid cannot, in any event, justify an obstacle to the free movement of capital such as that which arises from the legislation at issue in the main proceedings . . .

55. In the light of the above considerations, the answer to the questions referred must be that Articles 56 [63] EC and 58 [65] EC preclude legislation whereby the entitlement of a person fully taxable in one Member State to a tax credit in relation to dividends paid to him by limited companies is excluded where those companies are not established in that State.

## NOTES AND QUESTIONS

1.  This case marks something of a turning point in the ECJ's hitherto rather wary approach to direct taxation issues. It refers in the judgment to various prior cases and indicates why it had, in those particular cases, concluded that the national tax provision in question could be justified as a restriction on capital movement.

2.  Note that the *Futura* case mentioned earlier in this Chapter was based on EC 43/TFEU 49 (right of establishment), while *Manninen* was based on EC56/TFEU 63 (freedom of capital movement). What would explain the difference in EC Treaty/TFEU provisions chosen for the examination of the two cases?

3.  It is interesting to note the Court's comment that the Member States cannot assert a potential reduction in tax income as a ground for discriminatory treatment. This seems right, but what consequences could it have? Would the Finnish authorities in this case have had the option to remove the tax credit for Finnish taxpayers receiving dividends from Finnish companies?

4.  In another dividend double tax case, *Kerckhaert and Morres*, Case C-513/04, 2006 ECJ CELEX LEXIS 406, [2006] ECR I-10967, the Court stated:

> 16 In *Verkooijen*, *Lenz* and *Manninen*, the Court found that the laws of the Member States at issue did not treat in the same way dividend income from companies established in the Member State in which the taxpayer concerned was resident and dividend income from companies established in another Member State, thereby denying recipients of the latter dividends the tax benefits granted to the others. Having concluded that the situation of taxpayers receiving dividends from companies established in another Member State is not objectively different to that of taxpayers receiving dividends from companies established in the Member State in which they are resident, the Court held that the laws at issue amounted to restrictions of the fundamental freedoms guaranteed by the Treaty.

> 17 Contrary to the arguments submitted by Mr and Mrs Kerckhaert-Morres, the case in the main proceedings differs from those which gave rise to the judgments cited above inasmuch as the Belgian tax legislation does not make any distinction between dividends from companies established in Belgium and dividends from companies established in another Member State. Under Belgian law both are taxed at an identical rate of 25% by way of income tax.

> 18 In addition, the argument cannot be upheld that, in the present case, shareholders resident in Belgium are in a different situation depending on whether they receive dividends from a company established in Belgium or from a company established in another Member State, such that treating them in the same way, namely by applying a uniform rate of income tax, amounts to discrimination.

> 19 It is true that discrimination may consist not only in the application of different rules to comparable situations but also in the application of the same rule to different situations (see Case C-279/93 *Schumacker* [1995] ECR I-225, paragraph 30, and Case C-311/97 *Royal Bank of Scotland*

[1999] ECR I-2651, paragraph 26). However, in respect of the tax legislation of his State of residence, the position of a shareholder receiving dividends is not necessarily altered, in terms of that case-law, merely by the fact that he receives those dividends from a company established in another Member State, which, in exercising its fiscal sovereignty, makes those dividends subject to a deduction at source by way of income tax.

20 In circumstances such as those of the present case, the adverse consequences which might arise from the application of an income tax system such as the Belgian system at issue in the main proceedings result from the exercise in parallel by two Member States of their fiscal sovereignty.

What distinction was the Court making between this case and *Kerckhaert?*

**5.** For cases involving similar concerns around double taxation of corporate earnings, see, for example, *Test Claimants in Class IV of the ACT Group Litigation*, Case C-374/04, 2006 ECJ CELEX LEXIS 738 [2006] ECR I-11673. For differences in the tax treatment of charities, see *Centro di Musicologia Walter Stauffer*, Case C-386/04, 2006 ECJ CELEX LEXIS 929, [2006] ECR I-8203, where the ECJ held that charities recognized as such in their home Member State must be treated the same way in the host Member State, notwithstanding the provisions of EC 58/TFEU 63, if the difference is the result of arbitrary discrimination or a disguised restriction on the free movement of capital.

**6.** The free movement of capital provisions have also been asserted in relation to estate or death taxes. In *Heirs of M. E. A. van Hilten-van der Heijden v. Inspecteur van deBbelastingdienst/particulieren/ondernemingen buitenland te Heerlen*, Case C-513/03, 2006 ECJ CELEX LEXIS 84, [2006] ECR I-1957, Mrs. van Hilten-van der Heijden died on 22 November 1997. Of Netherlands nationality, she had been resident in the Netherlands until the start of 1988, then in Belgium and, since 1991, in Switzerland.

Her estate included immovable property situated in the Netherlands, Belgium and Switzerland and investments in quoted securities in the Netherlands, Germany, Switzerland and the United States of America, as well as bank accounts opened at Netherlands and Belgian branches of banking institutions established in the European Union and managed by them.

Her heirs were assessed inheritance tax calculated on the basis of Article 3(1) of the Dutch inheritance tax law of 1956. That law provided that the estate of a national of a Member State who dies within 10 years of ceasing to reside in that Member State is to be taxed as if that national had continued to reside in that Member State, while providing for relief in respect of the taxes levied in the State to which the deceased transferred his residence. The assessments were upheld by the Inspector after an appeal brought by four of the heirs who asserted that the rule in question here impeded the free movement of capital. The Court provided the following guidance:

> 44. In that regard, it follows from the caselaw that the measures prohibited by Article 73b [63](1) of the Treaty, as being restrictions on the movement of capital, include those which are likely to discourage non-residents from

making investments in a Member State or to discourage that Member State's residents to do so in other States or, in the case of inheritances, those whose effect is to reduce the value of the inheritance of a resident of a State other than the Member State in which the assets concerned are situated and which taxes the inheritance of those assets . . .

45. National legislation such as that in question in the main proceedings, which provides that the estate of a national of a Member State who dies within 10 years of ceasing to reside in that Member State is to be taxed as if that national had continued to reside in that Member State, while providing for relief in respect of the taxes levied in the State to which the deceased transferred his residence, does not constitute a restriction on the movement of capital.

46. By enacting identical taxation provisions for the estates of nationals who have transferred their residence abroad and of those who have remained in the Member State concerned, such legislation cannot discourage the former from making investments in that Member State from another State nor the latter from doing so in another Member State from the Member State concerned, and, regardless of the place where the assets in question are situated, nor can it diminish the value of the estate of a national who has transferred his residence abroad. The fact that such legislation covers neither nationals resident abroad for more than 10 years nor those who have never resided in the Member State concerned is irrelevant in that regard. Since it applies only to nationals of the Member State concerned, it cannot constitute a restriction on the movement of capital of nationals of the other Member States.

47. As regards the differences in treatment between residents who are nationals of the Member State concerned and those who are nationals of other Member States resulting from national legislation such as that in question in the main proceedings, it must be observed that such distinctions, for the purposes of allocating powers of taxation, cannot be regarded as constituting discrimination prohibited by Article 73b [63] of the Treaty. They flow, in the absence of any unifying or harmonising measures adopted in the Community context, from the Member States' power to define, by treaty or unilaterally, the criteria for allocating their powers of taxation (see to that effect, as regards Article 48 [45] of the EC Treaty . . .

48. Moreover, the Court has already had occasion to decide that, for the purposes of the allocation of powers of taxation, it is not unreasonable for the Member States to find inspiration in international practice and, particularly, the model conventions drawn up by the Organisation for Economic Cooperation and Development (OECD) . . . As the Netherlands Government observed, the legislation in question in the main proceedings complies with the commentaries in the Model Double Taxation Convention concerning Inheritances and Gifts (Report of the Fiscal Affairs Committee of the OECD, 1982). It is clear from the commentaries on Articles 4, 7, 9A and 9B of that model that that type of legislation is justified by the concern to prevent a form of tax evasion whereby a national of a State, in

contemplation of his death, transfers his residence to another State where the tax is lower. The commentaries state that double taxation is avoided by a system of tax credits and that, since prevention of tax evasion is justified only if the death occurs only a short time after the transfer of residence, the maximum permitted period is 10 years. The same commentaries state also that the scope can be extended to cover not only nationals of the State concerned but also residents who are not nationals of that State.

49. In that context, it must be observed that the mere transfer of residence from one State to another does not come within Article 73b [63] of the Treaty. As the Advocate General pointed out in point 58 of his Opinion, such a transfer of residence does not involve, in itself, financial transactions or transfers of property and does not partake of other characteristics of a capital movement as they appear from Annex I to Directive 88/361.

50. It follows that national legislation which would discourage a national who wishes to transfer his residence to another State, and thus hinder his freedom of movement, cannot for that reason alone constitute a restriction on the movement of capital within the meaning of Article 73b [63] of the Treaty.

51. The reply to the questions referred must therefore be that Article 73b [63] of the Treaty is to be interpreted as meaning that it does not preclude legislation of a Member State, such as that in question in the main proceedings, by which the estate of a national of that Member State who dies within 10 years of ceasing to reside in that Member State is to be taxed as if that national had continued to reside in that State, while enjoying relief in respect of inheritance taxes levied by other States.

## NOTES AND QUESTIONS

In paragraph 44, the ECJ notes that laws that are liable to discourage residents from making investments in other Member States are restrictions within the meaning of EC 56/TFEU 63. Restrictions on movements of capital to third countries are also within its scope. Yet the Court upheld the Dutch law. On what basis?

## [C]　Capital Movements and State Security

### ALFREDO ALBORE
Case C-423/98, 2000 ECJ CELEX LEXIS 383, [2000] ECR I-5965

[Mr Albore, a notary had brought suit to require the registration of ownership by German nationals of property situated in a territory designated by Italian law as being of military importance. The registration had been denied because the transactions required prefectural authorization which had not been obtained.]

18 Although no justification is mentioned in the order for reference and the Italian Government likewise has not mentioned any in its written observations, it is clear from the object of the legislation at issue that the contested measure may be

regarded as having been adopted in relation to public security, a concept which, within the meaning of the Treaty, includes the external security of a Member State . . .

19 However, the requirements of public security cannot justify derogations from the Treaty rules such as the freedom of capital movements unless the principle of proportionality is observed, which means that any derogation must remain within the limits of what is appropriate and necessary for achieving the aim in view . . .

20 Furthermore, under Article 73d (3) of the EC Treaty (now Article 58 [65] (3) EC), such requirements may not be relied on to justify measures constituting a means of arbitrary discrimination or a disguised restriction on the free movement of capital.

21 In that regard, a mere reference to the requirements of defence of the national territory, where the situation of the Member State concerned does not fall within the scope of Article 224 of the EC Treaty (now Article 297 EC [347], cannot suffice to justify discrimination on grounds of nationality against nationals of other Member States regarding access to immovable property on all or part of the national territory of the first State.

22 The position would be different only if it were demonstrated, for each area to which the restriction applies, that non-discriminatory treatment of the nationals of all the Member States would expose the military interests of the Member State concerned to real, specific and serious risks which could not be countered by less restrictive procedures.

23 In the absence of any evidence enabling the Court to examine whether the existence of such circumstances might be demonstrated in relation to the island of Ischia, it is for the national court to decide, in the case before it, whether or not there is sufficient justification within the meaning of the foregoing paragraph.

24 The answer to the question submitted must therefore be that Article 73b [63] of the Treaty precludes national legislation of a Member State which, on grounds relating to the requirements of defence of the national territory, exempts the nationals of that Member State, and only them, from the obligation to apply for an administrative authorisation for any purchase of real estate situated within an area of the national territory designated as being of military importance. The position would be different only if it could be demonstrated to the competent national court that, in a particular area, non-discriminatory treatment of the nationals of all the Member States would expose the military interests of the Member State concerned to real, specific and serious risks which could not be countered by less restrictive procedures.

## NOTES AND QUESTIONS

1.   This case concerned EC56/TFEU 63. The law in question here created a general requirement to obtain authorization for purchases of real estate in areas of military importance (close to frontiers) and then exempted Italian nationals from that obligation. Given the current state of integration in the EU, is it likely that any law discriminating against other Member States' nationals' ownership of real estate could be upheld?

**2.** State security is sometimes invoked as a ground for pre-approval of investments by non-nationals. See, for example, *Association Eglise de Scientologie de Paris and Scientology International Reserves Trust v. The Prime Minister*, Case C-54/99, 2000 ECJ CELEX LEXIS 471, [2000] ECR I-1355. The U.S. exercises similar controls to some extent, as was evident in the DP World (Dubai controlled) attempt to assume control of port assets in the U.S. owned by a British company that it was acquiring. Similarly, the attempted acquisition of Unocal by China National Offshore Oil Company was blocked. Such issues could assume a higher profile in the EU with its dependence on foreign energy, particularly Russian gas. However, it seems more likely that any moves to control investments will emanate from the EU level given their pan-European context.

**3.** In *Manfred Trummer and Peter Mayer*, Case C-222/97, 1999 ECJ CELEX LEXIS 278, [1999] ECR I-1661, an Austrian rule required that mortgages be denominated in the national currency, a rule that the ECJ considered contrary to EC 56/TFEU 63. The judgment is perhaps a little surprising since there could be some justifiable policy reasons for insisting that debts carrying a security interest should be in local currency. In fact, this might not be ruled out in other cases. However, in this particular instance, no justifications were put forward. It seems unlikely that the Court would take the position as far as the hypothetical question suggests since there are clearly good reasons for maintaining distinct currencies, indeed such a ruling would probably be entirely unacceptable from a political standpoint. Nonetheless, it is possible that this situation could evolve, particularly as the euro becomes more broadly used and understood outside the euro-zone.

### [D]  The Boundaries of Application of EC 56/TFEU 63

## COMMISSION v. GERMANY
(VOLKSWAGEN LAW),
Case C-112/05, 2007 ECJ EUR-Lex LEXIS 2392, [2007] ECR I-8995

[At issue was a law that had set up a special voting structure for shareholders in the Volkswagen company and which was designed to prevent a takeover and to give Germany and the Land of Lower Saxony greater protection and rights than the minority interest they held in the company could have justified under normal corporate ownership standards.]

18. In the absence of a Treaty definition of 'movement of capital' within the meaning of Article 56 [63](1) EC, the Court has previously recognised the nomenclature set out in Annex I to Council Directive 88/361/EEC of 24 June 1988 for the implementation of Article 67 [repealed] (OJ 1988 L 178, p. 5) as having indicative value. Movements of capital within the meaning of Article 56 [63](1) EC therefore include direct investments, that is to say, as that nomenclature and the related explanatory notes show, investments of any kind undertaken by natural or legal persons and which serve to establish or maintain lasting and direct links between the persons providing the capital and the undertakings to which that capital is made available in order to carry out an economic activity . . . As regards shareholdings in new or existing undertakings, as those explanatory notes confirm, the objective of establishing or maintaining lasting economic links presupposes that the shares held by

the shareholder enable him, either pursuant to the provisions of the national laws relating to companies limited by shares or in some other way, to participate effectively in the management of that company or in its control . . .

19. Concerning this form of investment, the Court has stated that national measures must be regarded as 'restrictions' within the meaning of Article 56 [63](1) EC if they are liable to prevent or limit the acquisition of shares in the undertakings concerned or to deter investors of other Member States from investing in their capital . . .

20. In the present case, the Federal Republic of Germany submits, in essence, that the VW Law is not a national measure within the meaning of the case-law referred to in the preceding three paragraphs. It also states that the disputed provisions of that Law, taken separately or as a whole, are not restrictions within the meaning of that case-law either.

\*　　\*　　\*

30. Having regard to the parties' arguments in relation to the first two complaints, and the cumulative effects of the two provisions of the VW Law which those complaints call in question, it is appropriate for the Court to examine the latter together.

The first and second complaints, based on the fact that the voting rights are capped at 20% and the blocking minority is fixed at 20%

\*　　\*　　\*

38. . . . . [T]he capping of voting rights is a recognised instrument of company law.

39. It is common ground, moreover, that, while the first sentence of Paragraph 134(1) of the Law on public limited companies lays down the principle that voting rights must be proportionate to the share of capital, the second sentence thereof allows a limitation on the voting rights in certain cases.

40. However . . . there is a difference between a power made available to shareholders, who are free to decide whether or not they wish to use it, and a specific obligation imposed on shareholders by way of legislation, without giving them the possibility to derogate from it.

41. In addition, the parties are in agreement that the first sentence of Paragraph 134(1) of the Law on public limited companies, as amended by the Law on the control and transparency of companies, removed the possibility of inserting a limitation on voting rights in the articles of association of listed companies. As the Commission has submitted, without being contradicted on this point by the German Government, since Volkswagen is a listed company, a ceiling on the voting rights cannot for that reason normally be inserted into its articles of association.

42. The Federal Republic of Germany submits that the limitation laid down in Paragraph 2(1) of the VW Law, since it applies without distinction to all shareholders, may be seen both as an advantage and as a disadvantage. While on the one hand there is the restriction on voting rights to which a shareholder holding more than 20% of the share capital is subject, on the other there is a corresponding protection against the influence of other possible shareholders having significant holdings, and

thus, the guarantee of effective participation in the company's management.

43. Prior to assessing this argument, it is appropriate to examine the effects of the cap on voting rights alongside the requirement contained in Paragraph 4(3) of the VW Law of a majority of over 80% of the share capital in order to pass certain resolutions of the general assembly of Volkswagen's shareholders.

44. . . . [S]uch resolutions include amendment of the company's articles of association, capital or financial structures, for which the Law on public limited companies fixes the required majority at a minimum of 75% of the share capital.

45. . . . [T]he percentage of 75% of the share capital provided for in the Law on public limited companies may be increased and fixed at a higher level by the particular company's articles of association. However, as the Commission has correctly noted, it is open to shareholders to decide whether or not to make use of that power. Conversely, the fact that the threshold of the required majority has been fixed by Paragraph 4(3) of the VW Law at more than 80% of the capital results, not from the will of the shareholders, but, as was held in Paragraph 29 of the present judgment, from a national measure.

46. This requirement, derogating from general law, and imposed by way of specific legislation, thus affords any shareholder holding 20% of the share capital a blocking minority.

47. Admittedly, . . . this power applies without distinction. In the same way as the cap on voting rights, it may operate both to the benefit and to the detriment of any shareholder in the company.

48. However, it is apparent from the file that, when the VW Law was adopted in 1960, the Federal State and the Land of Lower Saxony were the two main shareholders in Volkswagen, a recently privatised company, and each held 20% of its capital.

49. According to the information provided to the Court, while the Federal State has chosen to part with its interest in the capital of Volkswagen, the Land of Lower Saxony, for its part, still retains an interest in the region of 20%.

50. Paragraph 4(3) of the VW Law thus creates an instrument enabling the Federal and State authorities to procure for themselves a blocking minority allowing them to oppose important resolutions, on the basis of a lower level of investment than would be required under general company law.

51. By capping voting rights at the same level of 20%, Paragraph 2(1) of the VW Law supplements a legal framework which enables the Federal and State authorities to exercise considerable influence on the basis of such a reduced investment.

52. By limiting the possibility for other shareholders to participate in the company with a view to establishing or maintaining lasting and direct economic links with it which would make possible effective participation in the management of that company or in its control, this situation is liable to deter direct investors from other Member States.

53. This finding cannot be undermined by the argument advanced by the Federal Republic of Germany to the effect that Volkswagen's shares are among the most

highly-traded in Europe and that a large number of them are in the hands of investors from other Member States.

54. . . . [T]he restrictions on the free movement of capital which form the subject-matter of these proceedings relate to direct investments in the capital of Volkswagen, rather than portfolio investments made solely with the intention of making a financial investment . . .) and which are not relevant to the present action. As regards direct investors, it must be pointed out that, by creating an instrument liable to limit the ability of such investors to participate in a company with a view to establishing or maintaining lasting and direct economic links with it which would make possible effective participation in the management of that company or in its control, Paragraphs 2(1) and 4(3) of the VW Law diminish the interest in acquiring a stake in the capital of Volkswagen.

55. This finding is not affected by the presence, among Volkswagen's shareholders, of a number of direct investors, which, according to the Federal Republic of Germany, is similar to such a presence among the shareholders of other large undertakings. This circumstance is not such as to cast doubt on the fact that, because of the disputed provisions of the VW Law, direct investors from other Member States, whether actual or potential, may have been deterred from acquiring a stake in the capital of that company in order to participate in it with a view to establishing or maintaining lasting and direct economic links with it which would make possible effective participation in the management of that company or in its control, even though they were entitled to benefit from the principle of the free movement of capital and the protection which that principle affords them.

56. It must therefore be held that the combination of Paragraphs 2(1) and 4(3) of the VW Law constitutes a restriction on the movement of capital within the meaning of Article 56(1) EC [63].

The third complaint, based on the right to appoint two representatives to Volkswagen's supervisory board

*   *   *

59. Under Paragraph 4(1) of the VW Law, the Federal State and the Land of Lower Saxony are each entitled, on condition that they are shareholders in the company, to appoint two representatives as members of the supervisory board of Volkswagen, that is, a total of four persons.

60. Such an entitlement constitutes a derogation from general company law, which restricts the rights of representation conferred on certain shareholders to one third of the number of the shareholders' representatives on the supervisory board. As the Commission has argued without being contradicted on this point, in the case of Volkswagen, the supervisory board of which comprises 20 members, 10 of whom are appointed by the shareholders, the number of representatives who may be appointed by the Federal State and the Land of Lower Saxony may not exceed a maximum of three according to general company law.

61. This right of appointment is therefore a specific right, which derogates from general company law and is laid down by a national legislative measure for the sole benefit of the Federal and State authorities.

62. The right of appointment conferred on the Federal State and the Land of Lower Saxony thus enables them to participate in a more significant manner in the activity of the supervisory board than their status as shareholders would normally allow.

63. Even if, as the Federal Republic of Germany has observed, the right of representation of that Land is not disproportionate to the interest which it currently holds in the share capital of Volkswagen, the fact remains that both that Land and the Federal State have the right to appoint two representatives to the supervisory board of Volkswagen on condition that they hold shares in that company, irrespective of the extent of their holdings.

64. Paragraph 4(1) of the VW Law thus establishes an instrument which gives the Federal and State authorities the possibility of exercising influence which exceeds their levels of investment. As a corollary, the influence of the other shareholders may be reduced below a level commensurate with their own levels of investment.

65. The fact that the supervisory board, as the Federal Republic of Germany submits, is not a decision-making body, but a simple monitoring body, is not such as to undermine the position and influence of the Federal and State authorities concerned. While German company law assigns to the supervisory board the task of monitoring the company's management and of providing reports on that management to the shareholders, it confers significant powers on that body, such as the appointment and dismissal of the members of the executive board, for the purpose of performing that task. Furthermore, as the Commission has pointed out, approval by the supervisory board is necessary for a number of transactions, including, in addition to the setting-up and transfer of production facilities, the establishment of branches, the sale and purchase of land, investments and the acquisition of other undertakings.

66. By restricting the possibility for other shareholders to participate in the company with a view to establishing or maintaining lasting and direct economic links with it such as to enable them to participate effectively in the management of that company or in its control, Paragraph 4(1) of the VW Law is liable to deter direct investors from other Member States from investing in the company's capital.

67. For the same reasons as those set out in paragraphs 53 to 55 of this judgment, this finding cannot be undermined by the Federal Republic of Germany's argument that there is a keen investment interest in Volkswagen shares on the international financial markets.

68. In the light of the foregoing, it must be held that Paragraph 4(1) of the VW Law constitutes a restriction on the movement of capital within the meaning of Article 56 [63](1) EC.

69. The question of whether or not the Federal State and the Land of Lower Saxony make use of their right under Paragraph 4(1) is entirely irrelevant. It need merely be stated in this regard that the specific right, which derogates from the general law, conferred on those Federal and State authorities, to appoint representatives to the supervisory board of Volkswagen continues to exist in the German legal system.

Possible justification for the restrictions

\* \* \*

72. The free movement of capital may be restricted by national measures justified on the grounds set out in Article 58 EC [65] or by overriding reasons in the general interest to the extent that there are no Community harmonising measures providing for measures necessary to ensure the protection of those . . .

73. In the absence of such Community harmonisation, it is in principle for the Member States to decide on the degree of protection which they wish to afford to such legitimate interests and on the way in which that protection is to be achieved. They may do so, however, only within the limits set by the Treaty and must, in particular, observe the principle of proportionality, which requires that the measures adopted be appropriate to secure the attainment of the objective which they pursue and not go beyond what is necessary in order to attain it . . .

74. As regards the protection of workers' interests, invoked by the Federal Republic of Germany to justify the disputed provisions of the VW Law, it must be held that that Member State has been unable to explain, beyond setting out general considerations as to the need for protection against a large shareholder which might by itself dominate the company, why, in order to meet the objective of protecting Volkswagen's workers, it is appropriate and necessary for the Federal and State authorities to maintain a strengthened and irremovable position in the capital of that company.

75. In addition, as regards the right to appoint representatives to the supervisory board, it must be stated that, under German legislation, workers are themselves represented within that body.

76. Consequently, the Member State's justification based on the protection of workers cannot be upheld.

77. The same applies to the justification which the Federal Republic of Germany seeks to base on the protection of minority shareholders. While the desire to provide protection for such shareholders may also constitute a legitimate interest and justify legislative intervention, in accordance with the principles referred to in paragraphs 72 and 73 above, even if it were also liable to constitute a restriction on the free movement of capital, it must be held that, in the present case, such a desire cannot justify the disputed provisions of the VW Law.

78. It should be recalled, in this regard, that those provisions form part of a legal framework giving the Federal State and the Land of Lower Saxony the ability to exercise a greater level of influence than would normally be linked to their investment. However, the Federal Republic of Germany has not shown why, in order to protect the general interests of minority shareholders, it is appropriate or necessary to maintain such a position for the benefit of the Federal and State authorities.

79. It cannot be ruled out that, in certain special circumstances, the Federal and State authorities in question may use their position in order to defend general interests which might be contrary to the economic interests of the company

concerned, and therefore, contrary to the interests of its other shareholders.

80. Finally, to the extent to which the Federal Republic of Germany contends that the activity of an undertaking as large as Volkswagen may have such an impact on the general interest that it justifies the existence of statutory guarantees which go beyond the control measures provided for under general company law, it must be pointed out that, even if this argument were well founded, that Member State has failed to explain, beyond setting out general considerations as to the risk that shareholders may put their personal interests before those of the workers, why the provisions of the VW Law criticised by the Commission are appropriate and necessary to preserve the jobs generated by Volkswagen's activity.

# NOTES AND QUESTIONS

1.   What do you think of the Court's reasoning here in its dismissal of the arguments put forward by Germany? Is it possible to define with any precision what are the boundaries of the capital free movement provisions? Could they penetrate into essentially private arrangements (rather like EC 30/TFEU 36 impinged on the rights of individuals to assert intellectual property rights)?

2.   By contrast, in *Commission v. Belgium (Golden Share)*, Case C-503/99, 2002 ECJ CELEX LEXIS 793, [2002] ECR I-4809, the Court did uphold a measure by Belgium in which the Belgian government had privatized Distrigaz, the national gas distribution monopoly, but had retained a "golden share" enabling it to have the final say on certain matters regarded as of national importance. After first concluding that the practice of retaining golden shares fell within the provisions on the free movement of capital, the Court continued:

> 43 . . . [D]epending on the circumstances, certain concerns may justify the retention by Member States of a degree of influence within undertakings that were initially public and subsequently privatised, where those undertakings are active in fields involving the provision of services in the public interest or strategic . . .

> 44 However, those concerns cannot entitle Member States to plead their own systems of property ownership, referred to in Article 222 [345] of the Treaty, by way of justification for obstacles, resulting from privileges attaching to their position as shareholder in a privatised undertaking, to the exercise of the freedoms provided for by the Treaty. . . . [T]hat article does not have the effect of exempting the Member States'systems of property ownership from the fundamental rules of the Treaty.

> 45 The free movement of capital, as a fundamental principle of the Treaty, may be restricted only by national rules which are justified by reasons referred to in Article 73d [65](1) of the Treaty or by overriding requirements of the general interest and which are applicable to all persons and undertakings pursuing an activity in the territory of the host Member State. Furthermore, in order to be so justified, the national legislation must be suitable for securing the objective which it pursues and must not go beyond what is necessary in order to attain it, so as to accord with the principle of proportionality . . .

46 In the present case, the objective pursued by the legislation at issue, namely the safeguarding of energy supplies in the event of a crisis, falls undeniably within the ambit of a legitimate public interest. Indeed, the Court has previously recognised that the public-security considerations which may justify an obstacle to the free movement of goods include the objective of ensuring a minimum supply of petroleum products at all times . . . The same reasoning applies to obstacles to the free movement of capital, inasmuch as public security is also one of the grounds of justification referred to in Article 73d [65](1)(b) of the Treaty.

47 However, the Court has also held that the requirements of public security, as a derogation from the fundamental principle of free movement of capital, must be interpreted strictly, so that their scope cannot be determined unilaterally by each Member State without any control by the Community institutions. Thus, public security may be relied on only if there is a genuine and sufficiently serious threat to a fundamental interest of society . . .

48 It is necessary, therefore, to ascertain whether the legislation in issue enables the Member State concerned to ensure a minimum level of energy supplies in the event of a genuine and serious threat, and whether or not it goes beyond what is necessary for that purpose.

49 First of all, it should be noted that the regime in issue is one of opposition. It is predicated on the principle of respect for the decision-making autonomy of the undertaking concerned, inasmuch as, in each individual case, the exercise of control by the minister responsible requires an initiative on the part of the Government authorities. No prior approval is required. Moreover, in order for that power of opposition to be exercised, the public authorities are obliged to adhere to strict time-limits.

50 Next, the regime is limited to certain decisions concerning the strategic assets of the companies in question, including in particular the energy supply networks, and to such specific management decisions relating to those assets as may be called in question in any given case.

51 Lastly, the Minister may intervene pursuant to Articles 3 and 4 of the Royal Decrees of 10 and 16 June 1994 only where there is a threat that the objectives of the energy policy may be compromised. Furthermore, as the Belgian Government has expressly stated in its written pleadings and at the hearing, without being contradicted on the point by the Commission, any such intervention must be supported by a formal statement of reasons and may be the subject of an effective review by the courts.

52 The scheme therefore makes it possible to guarantee, on the basis of objective criteria which are subject to judicial review, the effective avail-ability of the lines and conduits providing the main infrastructures for the domestic conveyance of energy products, as well as other infrastructures for the domestic conveyance and storage of gas, including unloading and cross-border facilities. Thus, it enables the Member State concerned to intervene with a view to ensuring, in a given situation, compliance with the

public service obligations incumbent on SNTC and Distrigaz, whilst at the same time observing the requirements of legal certainty.

53 The Commission has not shown that less restrictive measures could have been taken to attain the objective pursued. There is no certainty that planning designed to encourage natural gas undertakings to conclude long-term supply contracts, to diversify their sources of supply or to operate a system of licences would be enough, on its own, to permit a rapid reaction in any particular situation. Moreover, the introduction of rules precisely defining the standards required of undertakings in the sector concerned, as proposed by the Commission, would appear to be even more restrictive than a right of opposition limited to specific situations.

54 As to the Commission's arguments concerning the gas directive, suffice it to note that the time-limit for transposition of that directive did not expire until 10 August 2000. Consequently, the Community framework which, according to the Commission, the directive is intended to establish as regards the exercise by Member States of powers in relation to the public service obligations imposed on undertakings in the sector concerned cannot in any event affect the present action, since the reasoned opinions were dated 18 December 1998 and the application was lodged on 22 December 1999.

55 The legislation in issue is therefore justified by the objective of guaranteeing energy supplies in the event of a crisis.

# Chapter 16

## STATE AIDS AND STATE ENTERPRISES

### § 16.01  OVERVIEW

*Template* Article 7, Sections 7.8 and 7.9

***Materials in this Chapter***: This chapter contains cases and materials relating to the restrictions imposed on Member States by the Treaty as regards both financial assistance to industry and the State's actual participation in the economy.

***Background*** Involvement of governments in economic activity remains widespread in Europe. Historically, and as a result of social-market policies, many basic industries were or are under state control or operated as a public service by companies holding exclusive concessions from the state: electricity, gas, telecommunications, postal services, railways, some forms of road transport, airlines, television and radio, coal, steel, even automobile manufacture, medical services and defense industries. The question of how far the EU should go in controlling or even breaking up such arrangements remains controversial, and indeed resulted in some changes to the draft Treaty of Lisbon language at the behest of France, which sees the encouragement of national "champions" as a key component of its domestic policy.

Government has also been heavily involved in attempting to direct investment and support employment by funding infrastructure projects, and by offering subsidies in various forms to private enterprise (e.g., cash payments, accelerated depreciation and tax holidays).

Such activities result in competition for jobs and investment. In recognition of this, the EC Treaty imposed various basic restrictions on the activities of the Member States and also created prescribed limits and express powers of enforcement at the EU level with regard to illegal subsidies. In addition, powers to grant aid from the EU budget have gradually evolved, to assist less advantaged regions and countries that needed support in order to maintain membership of the Exchange Rate Mechanism.

***State Aids*** Limitations on States' ability to provide financial aid to businesses are found in EC 87-89/TFEU 107-109. These provisions are designed to provide the assurance that Member State financial assistance does not distort competition, and that, where permissible, such assistance takes place within well-defined EU policy goals.

The state aid provisions in the TFEU are of broad application across all sectors, including the financial sector, and thus provided a legal basis for the Commission to assert at least some influence over the conduct of Member States during the financial crisis of late 2008 and early 2009. Although the Commission could have taken a much more central role in reviewing state actions, the political support would not have been there; and in any event its powers are largely of an "approve" or "disapprove" type rather than affirmative. The Commission did at least try to bring the various disparate Member State actions within a common framework under EC 87(3)(b)/TFEU 107 (3)(b) to the effect that, assuming certain principles were followed, the Commission would approve the actions as quickly as within 24 hours. The principles were:

- Non-discriminatory access to the aid;

- Aids should be limited in time;

- State support should be limited to what is necessary to deal with the specific liquidity problem;

- The private sector should be involved;

- Avoidance of market abuses by recipients of aid;

- Appropriate monitoring and follow-up.

The setting up of this simple common framework was due to the fact that, so far, neither the EU generally nor the Commission in particular have had the budgetary or fiscal powers that were needed to support banks in crisis. This may change in the aftermath of the Greek sovereign debt crisis. The EU developed an important funding policy (primarily financed by the Eurozone countries) initially based on EC 100/TFEU 122, in order to support Greece and the other eurozone countries in danger of defaulting on their loans. This provision allows for financial support to Member States in difficulties caused by "exceptional circumstances". As of the time of writing, the scheme is under revision with a view to creating a European Stability Mechanism for future destabilizing events (see Chapter 21, *infra*).

***State participation in the economy*** The EC Treaty/TFEU also contains provisions that place constraints on the Member States when they actually participate in economic activity directly.

EC 86/TFEU 106 has presented particular challenges. It is a specific recognition of the role played by the Member States and requires a balancing of such policies against the overriding free market principles of the rest of the EC Treaty. It does not in itself create any new obligations or rights. However, paragraph 1 essentially applies the competition provisions to the Member States when they are participating in the economy (directly, or through the grant of monopoly rights to private companies). Paragraph (2) then provides an exception to the application of the other provisions of the Treaty, and in particular the competition rules for companies that have a public service or revenue collection element, but such exemption only applies to the extent that without it, such companies would not be able to carry out their public duties.

Paragraph (3) of EC 86/TFEU 106 allows the Commission to issue "appropriate directives or decisions to Member States" in order to "ensure the application of the provisions of this Article." This provision has been invoked, for example, to enforce EC 87-89/TFEU 107-109 by ensuring that public undertakings'support by governments is "transparent" through disclosure in their accounts. See Commission Directive 80/723 O.J. 1980, L195/35. This Directive was the subject of a challenge by several Member States — see Chapter 6, *supra.*

Public procurement policy could also be included in this context, though action here has come through the harmonization powers granted in the context of the provisions on goods and services. The first directive on this subject was 71/305 (OJ 1971 L 185/5) on the coordination of procedures for the award of Public Works Contracts (building and civil engineering works). Directive 77/62 followed — on coordination of such procedures for the award of public supply contracts (supplemented by 80/767 implementing the GATT agreement of 1979). Directive 89/665 provided for remedies in the case of non-compliance and thus finally gave some teeth to the previous directives. In June 1993, new Directives, 93/36 on Public Supply contracts and 93/37 on Public works contracts replaced the original two. Directive 93/38 for the first time set up a regime also for utilities, whether public or privately owned. Directives 93/36 and 93/37 were replaced by Directive 2004/18, [2004] OJ L 134/114 and Directive 93/38 was replaced by Directive 2004/17 [2004] OJ L134/1. For an analysis of the new regime, see C.H. Bovis, *The new public procurement regime of the European Union: A critical analysis of policy, law and jurisprudence* (2005) 30 EL REV. 607.

The fundamental approach of these directives is to require state bodies to advertise their projected work and supply needs in the Official Journal and to ensure non-discrimination as between suppliers from different Member States in the selection process. In the latter case, the criteria relating to the tenderers themselves are (in the case of public bodies subject to 93/36 and 93/37) limited to probity, financial and economic standing and ability. As to the tender itself, selection must be based on either the lowest priced or the "economically most advantageous" bid.

***Comparison with the United States*** By contrast, in the United States there are no specific restrictions on the abilities of the states to offer incentives to industry to locate or continue operations within their territory. Moreover, although the court decisions indicate that a state's tax and regulatory policy may not, absent special justification, subject interstate business or nonresidents to worse treatment than intrastate business or residents are accorded, this prohibition appears inapplicable to state business subsidies limited to resident business. As suggested by Professor Jonathan Varat, in the United States, economic integration apparently "is being sacrificed for state autonomy in a way that political integration would not likely be." (J. Varat, *Economic Integration and Interregional Migration in the United States Federal System*, in M. TUSHNET (ED.), COMPARATIVE CONSTITUTIONAL FEDERALISM, EUROPE AND AMERICA, GREENWOOD, 1990, pp 36-37).

## § 16.02   FINANCIAL ASSISTANCE BY MEMBER STATES ("STATE AIDS")

### [A]   What Is an Aid?

**COMMISSION v. FRANCE**

(SOLIDARITY GRANT)

Case 290/83, [1985] ECR 439

[The Caisse Nationale de Crédit Agricole (National Agricultural Credit Fund), a private French organization, financed a large "solidarity grant" to poorer farmers that had been approved by the French government and agricultural trade organizations. The measures were notified to the Commission in compliance with EC 93/TFEU 108. The Commission originally initiated the procedure under that article. However, after the French government took the position that the grant was privately financed, the Commission broke off the procedure under EC 93/TFEU 108 and initiated an action against France under EC 226/TFEU 258.]

7 The Commission considers that there is no doubt that the State was the initiator of the decision taken by the Fund's governing board. In its view, the decision presents all the characteristics of a decision taken under pressure from the public authorities, and the fact that those authorities do not have a majority on the governing board is irrelevant in that respect.

8 The Commission refers in addition to the fact that the provisions of the French Code Rural concerning the Fund provide only for credit operations. Since under French law the Fund is a public body, it may not act ultra vires. That means, in particular, that it may not use its assets for purposes other than those provided for in its articles. If the Fund exceeds its powers, the Minister for Agriculture must intervene as the supervisory authority. The fact that he did not intervene proves, according to the Commission, that the State did not oppose the solidarity grant, despite its incompatibility with the powers conferred on the Fund.

9 In those circumstances, the Commission considers that the grant in question is a measure having an effect equivalent to State aid, which is incompatible with the Common Market and which comes within the scope of Article 5 [TEU 4] of the Treaty. By its action the French Government created a situation equivalent to that resulting from the grant of State aid and, in so doing, has not abstained from causing measures to be taken which are liable to jeopardize the attainment of the objectives of the Treaty. A Member State cannot avoid its obligations by entrusting to an economic agent the implementation of a measure which, if it were taken by the State directly, would be incompatible with the Treaty.

10 For its part, the French Government maintains that the notion of a measure having an effect equivalent to State aid is not one which is known to Community law. This construction, put forward by the Commission, cannot serve as a basis either for a procedure under Article 93 [108] or for an action under Article 169 [258] for a declaration that a State has failed to fulfill its obligations.

11 Nor, according to the French Government, does the measure in question

constitute State aid within the meaning of Article 92 [107] of the Treaty. There was no encouragement on the part of the authorities, in relation to which, moreover, the Fund enjoys complete autonomy. Neither the general rules governing public bodies in French administrative law nor the specific provisions governing the Fund give the Government the power to intervene as a supervisory authority in such circumstances.

12 It appears . . . that . . . decisions concerning, inter alia, the allocation of the Fund's profits do not become definitive until they have been approved by the public authorities.

13 According to Article 92 [107](1) of the Treaty, any aid granted by a Member State or through State resources in any form whatsoever which distorts or threatens to distort competition by favoring certain undertakings or the production of certain goods is, insofar as it affects trade between Member States, incompatible with the Common Market. By virtue of the generality of the terms employed in that provision any State measure, insofar as it has the effect of according aid in any form whatsoever, may be assessed on the basis of Article 92 [107] for its compatibility with the Common Market.

14 As is clear from the actual wording of Article 92 [107](1), aid need not necessarily be financed from State resources to be classified as State aid. In addition, as the Court of Justice ruled in its judgment of March 22, 1977 . . . the prohibition contained in Article 92 [107] covers all aid granted by a Member State or through State resources, and there is no necessity to draw any distinction according to whether the aid is granted directly by the State or by public or private bodies established or appointed by it to administer the aid.

15 It follows that Article 92 [107] of the Treaty covers aid which, like the solidarity grant in question, was decided and financed by a public body and the implementation of which is subject to the approval of the public authorities, the detailed rules for the grant of which correspond to those for ordinary State aid and which, moreover, was put forward by the Government as forming part of a body of measures in favor of farmers which were all notified to the Commission in pursuance of Article 98 [108](3).

16 For the purpose of assessing whether or not an aid coming within the scope of Article 92 [107] is compatible with the Common Market, Article 98 [108](2) of the Treaty set up a special procedure which lays down specific conditions and rules. Under that provision, the Commission may bring an action against the Member State concerned only if that State does not comply with a decision whereby the Commission requests it to abolish or alter the aid in question. Prior to that decision, the provision requires that the parties concerned be given notice to submit their observations, thereby guaranteeing the other Member States and the sectors concerned an opportunity to make their views known and allowing the Commission to be fully informed of all the facts of the case before taking its decision. Finally, Article 93 [108](2) provides that the Member States concerned may apply to the Council, which may, acting unanimously, decide that the aid in question is to be considered compatible with the Common Market.

17 It follows that the procedure laid down in Article 98 [108](2) provides all the

parties concerned with guarantees which are specifically adapted to the special problems created by State aid with regard to competition in the Common Market and which go much further than those provided in the preliminary procedure laid down in Article 169 of the Treaty in which only the Commission and the Member State concerned participate. Accordingly, although the existence of that specific procedure in no way prevents the compatibility of an aid scheme in relation to Community rules other than those contained in Article 92 [107] from being assessed under the procedure provided for in Article 169 [258], the Commission must, however, use the procedure laid down in Article 98 [108](2) if it wishes to establish that that scheme, as aid, is incompatible with the Common Market.

18 It follows from the foregoing that Articles 92 [107] and 98 [108] leave no scope for a parallel concept of "measures equivalent to aid" which are subject to different rules from those which apply to aid properly so-called.

19 In those circumstances, the application must be dismissed as inadmissible inasmuch as it is founded directly on Article 169 [258] of the Treaty and the Commission has failed to comply with the preliminary phase of the procedure laid down in Article 98 [108].

## NOTES AND QUESTIONS

1.    Why did the Court reject the concept of a measure equivalent to a state aid? Why did the Commission in fact need to make this argument?

2.    In *Kwekerij Gebroeders van der Kooy BV & Others v. Commission*, Joined Cases 67-68/85, 70/85, 1988 ECJ CELEX LEXIS 20, [1999] ECR 219, the Court held that a power company, created under private law but controlled by the state through 50 percent share ownership and subject to government control of its prices, was equivalent to the state for the purpose of establishing state aid under article 87(1). The aid at issue was the supply of natural gas at reduced prices to the horticultural industry. (This case also appears in Chapter 8, *supra*, in connection with actions under EC 230/TFEU 263.) See also *Amministrazione delle Finanze dello Stato v. Denkavit Italiana Srl*, Case 61/79, [1980] ECR 1205.

## ALTMARK TRANS GMBH AND ANOTHER v. NAHVERKEHRSGESELLSCHAFT ALTMARK GMBH
### Case C-280/00, 2003 ECJ CELEX LEXIS 98, [2003] ECR I-7747

[A German regional government in the state of Sachsen-Anhalt granted Altmark Trans GmbH licences to operate scheduled bus services (the decision). To operate those services Altmark Trans required additional financing from the public authorities. Nahverkehrsgesellschaft Altmark GmbH, an unsuccessful applicant for those licences alleged that Altmark Trans was not an economically viable undertaking, as it was unable to survive without public subsidies, and that therefore the licences granted to Altmark Trans were unlawful. The regional government rejected that complaint. On appeal, the Higher Administrative Court of Sachsen-Anhalt set aside the licences. It held that those subsidies were not compatible with EU law respecting state aid, in particular Council Regulation (EEC) 1191/69 (on action by Member States concerning the obligations inherent in the concept of a public service in transport by rail, road and inland waterway) (the regulation). A number of questions were subsequently referred to the ECJ on this point.]

84. Measures which, whatever their form, are likely directly or indirectly to favour certain undertakings . . . or are to be regarded as an economic advantage which the recipient undertaking would not have obtained under normal market conditions . . . are regarded as aid.

\*    \*    \*

87. . . .W]here a state measure must be regarded as compensation for the services provided by the recipient undertakings in order to discharge public service obligations, so that those undertakings do not enjoy a real financial advantage and the measure thus does not have the effect of putting them in a more favourable competitive position than the undertakings competing with them, such a measure is not caught by art 92 [107](1) of the Treaty.

88. However, for such compensation to escape classification as state aid in a particular case, a number of conditions must be satisfied.

89. First, the recipient undertaking must actually have public service obligations to discharge, and the obligations must be clearly defined. In the main proceedings, the national court will therefore have to examine whether the public service obligations which were imposed on Altmark Trans are clear from the national legislation and/or the licences at issue in the main proceedings.

90. Second, the parameters on the basis of which the compensation is calculated must be established in advance in an objective and transparent manner, to avoid it conferring an economic advantage which may favour the recipient undertaking over competing undertakings.

91. Payment by a Member State of compensation for the loss incurred by an undertaking without the parameters of such compensation having been established beforehand, where it turns out after the event that the operation of certain services in connection with the discharge of public service obligations was not economically viable, therefore constitutes a financial measure which falls within the concept of state aid within the meaning of art 92 [107](1) of the Treaty.

92. Third, the compensation cannot exceed what is necessary to cover all or part of the costs incurred in the discharge of public service obligations, taking into account the relevant receipts and a reasonable profit for discharging those obligations. Compliance with such a condition is essential to ensure that the recipient undertaking is not given any advantage which distorts or threatens to distort competition by strengthening that undertaking's competitive position.

93. Fourth, where the undertaking which is to discharge public service obligations, in a specific case, is not chosen pursuant to a public procurement procedure which would allow for the selection of the tenderer capable of providing those services at the least cost to the community, the level of compensation needed must be determined on the basis of an analysis of the costs which a typical undertaking, well run and adequately provided with means of transport so as to be able to meet the necessary public service requirements, would have incurred in discharging those

obligations, taking into account the relevant receipts and a reasonable profit for discharging the obligations.

94. It follows from the above considerations that, where public subsidies granted to undertakings expressly required to discharge public service obligations in order to compensate for the costs incurred in discharging those obligations comply with the conditions set out in paragraphs 89-93, above, such subsidies do not fall within art 92 [107](1) of the Treaty. Conversely, a state measure which does not comply with one or more of those conditions must be regarded as state aid within the meaning of that provision.

## NOTES AND QUESTIONS

1. How did the Court address the argument of the losing bidder that the winner needed the subsidy to survive?

2. There has been a stream of cases dealing with ever more subtle refinements of state assistance to industry. For example, in *Ferring SA v. Agence centrale des organismes de securite sociale (ACOSS)*, Case C-53/00, 2001 ECJ CELEX LEXIS 297, [2001] ECR I-9067, the Court held that an exemption from a tax on social security funding was only a state aid to the extent that the advantage in not being assessed the tax exceeds the additional costs that they bear in discharging the public service obligations imposed on them by national law.

One issue of particular complexity is whether investments in private enterprises by a State-owned enterprise can be considered an aid. In *France v. Commission (Aid to Stardust Marine)*, Case C-482/99, 2002 ECJ CELEX LEXIS 788, [2002] ECR I-4397 the ECJ, in considering the circumstances where a public undertaking might be acting for the State, the Court stated that:

51 . . . [F]or a measure to be capable of being classified as State aid within the meaning of Article 87 [107] (1) EC, it must be imputable to the State, which infers such imputability from the mere fact that that measure was taken by a public undertaking, cannot be accepted.

52 Even if the State is in a position to control a public undertaking and to exercise a dominant influence over its operations, actual exercise of that control in a particular case cannot be automatically presumed. A public undertaking may act with more or less independence, according to the degree of autonomy left to it by the State. That might be the situation in the case of public undertakings . . . Therefore, the mere fact that a public undertaking is under State control is not sufficient for measures taken by that undertaking, such as the financial support measures in question here, to be imputed to the State. It is also necessary to examine whether the public authorities must be regarded as having been involved, in one way or another, in the adoption of those measures.

53 On that point, it cannot be demanded that it be demonstrated, on the basis of a precise inquiry, that in the particular case the public authorities specifically incited the public undertaking to take the aid measures in question. In the first place, having regard to the fact that relations between

the State and public undertakings are close, there is a real risk that State aid may be granted through the intermediary of those undertakings in a non-transparent way and in breach of the rules on State aid laid down by the Treaty.

54 Moreover, it will, as a general rule, be very difficult for a third party, precisely because of the privileged relations existing between the State and a public undertaking, to demonstrate in a particular case that aid measures taken by such an undertaking were in fact adopted on the instructions of the public authorities.

55 For those reasons, it must be accepted that the imputability to the State of an aid measure taken by a public undertaking may be inferred from a set of indicators arising from the circumstances of the case and the context in which that measure was taken. In that respect, the Court has already taken into consideration the fact that the body in question could not take the contested decision without taking account of the requirements of the public authorities . . . or the fact that, apart from factors of an organic nature which linked the public undertakings to the State, those undertakings, through the intermediary of which aid had been granted, had to take account of directives issued by [a government committee].

56 Other indicators might, in certain circumstances, be relevant in concluding that an aid measure taken by a public undertaking is imputable to the State, such as, in particular, its integration into the structures of the public administration, the nature of its activities and the exercise of the latter on the market in normal conditions of competition with private operators, the legal status of the undertaking (in the sense of its being subject to public law or ordinary company law), the intensity of the supervision exercised by the public authorities over the management of the undertaking, or any other indicator showing, in the particular case, an involvement by the public authorities in the adoption of a measure or the unlikelihood of their not being involved, having regard also to the compass of the measure, its content or the conditions which it contains.

57 However, the mere fact that a public undertaking has been constituted in the form of a capital company under ordinary law cannot, having regard to the autonomy which that legal form is capable of conferring upon it, be regarded as sufficient to exclude the possibility of an aid measure taken by such a company being imputable to the State . . . The existence of a situation of control and the real possibilities of exercising a dominant influence which that situation involves in practice makes it impossible to exclude from the outset any imputability to the State of a measure taken by such a company, and hence the risk of an infringement of the Treaty rules on State aid, notwithstanding the relevance, as such, of the legal form of the public undertaking as one indicator, amongst others, enabling it to be determined in a given case whether or not the State is involved.

# PORTUGUESE REPUBLIC v. COMMISSION
## (AUTONOMOUS REGION OF THE AZORES)
## Case C-88/03, 2006 ECJ EUR-Lex LEXIS 1773, [2006] ECR I-7115

[The Commission brought proceedings against Portugal under EC 226/TFEU 258 regarding a system of taxation applicable in the Azores, Portuguese islands located in the middle of the Atlantic Ocean. The Azores have autonomous powers including taxation powers, and the central issue in the case was whether the lower tax rates applicable there were in fact state aids covered by EC 87/TFEU 107 or were, rather, simply a function of a general system of taxation of an autonomous region within a country where lower rates are applied by the authority for that region. Here, it was not a question of deciding which Treaty article applied, but whether the Member States' competence with regard to taxation could be overridden by the State aid provisions of the EC Treaty/TFEU.]

52. Article 87 [107] (1) EC prohibits State aid 'favouring certain undertakings or the production of certain goods', that is to say, selective aid . . . However, . . . the concept of State aid does not refer to State measures which differentiate between undertakings and which are, therefore, prima facie selective where that differentiation arises from the nature or the overall structure of the system of charges of which they are part . . .

53. Accordingly, it is appropriate to examine, first, whether the measures reducing the tax rates in question are selective in nature and, if necessary, to examine whether, as the Portuguese Government submits, those measures are justified by the nature and overall structure of the Portuguese tax system.

54. As regards the assessment of the condition of selectivity, which is a constituent factor in the concept of State aid, it is clear from settled case-law that Article 87 [107] (1) EC requires assessment of whether, under a particular statutory scheme, a State measure is such as to 'favour certain undertakings or the production of certain goods' in comparison with other undertakings which are in a legal and factual situation that is comparable in the light of the objective pursued by the measure in question . . .

55. Such an analysis is also required in respect of a measure adopted not by the national legislature but by an infra-State authority, since a measure adopted by a regional authority and not the central power is likely to constitute aid if the conditions laid down by Article 87 [107](1) EC are satisfied . . .

56. It is clear from the foregoing that in order to determine whether the measure at issue is selective it is appropriate to examine whether, within the context of a particular legal system, that measure constitutes an advantage for certain undertakings in comparison with others which are in a comparable legal and factual situation. The determination of the reference framework has a particular importance in the case of tax measures, since the very existence of an advantage may be established only when compared with 'normal' taxation. The 'normal' tax rate is the rate in force in the geographical area constituting the reference framework.

57. In that connection, the reference framework need not necessarily be defined within the limits of the Member State concerned, so that a measure conferring an

advantage in only one part of the national territory is not selective on that ground alone for the purposes of Article 87 [107](1) EC.

58. It is possible that an infra-State body enjoys a legal and factual status which makes it sufficiently autonomous in relation to the central government of a Member State, with the result that, by the measures it adopts, it is that body and not the central government which plays a fundamental role in the definition of the political and economic environment in which undertakings operate. In such a case it is the area in which the infra-State body responsible for the measure exercises its powers, and not the country as a whole, that constitutes the relevant context for the assessment of whether a measure adopted by such a body favours certain undertakings in comparison with others in a comparable legal and factual situation, having regard to the objective pursued by the measure or the legal system concerned.

59. The Commission's argument that such an analysis is rendered inadmissible by the wording of the Treaty and the well-established case-law in that field cannot be accepted.

60. It is true, as the Court has already ruled, that the fact that an aid programme has been adopted by a regional authority does not prevent the application of Article 87 [107](1) EC if the relevant conditions are satisfied . . . Furthermore, as the Commission stated, in paragraph 26 of the grounds of the contested decision, the text of the Treaty itself, which in Article 87 [107](3)(a) and (c) classifies measures intended to 'favour certain undertakings or the production of certain goods' as State aid which may be declared compatible, indicates that benefits whose scope is limited to part of the territory of the State subject to the rules on aid may constitute selective benefits. However, it cannot be inferred from that that a measure is selective, for the purposes of Article 87 [107](1) EC, on the sole ground that it is applicable only in a limited geographical area of a Member State.

61. Furthermore, it cannot be inferred from the judgment in Case C-156/98 Germany v. Commission [2000] ECR I-6857 that a measure the benefit of which is reserved for undertakings situated in certain regions is selective for that reason alone. In paragraph 23 of that judgment the Court held that the fact that a tax concession favoured certain undertakings situated in the new Länder or West Berlin prevented its being a general measure of tax or economic policy. However, the tax concession concerned had been adopted by the national legislature and was applicable to only some of the undertakings in a number of regions in Germany, namely those employing a maximum of 250 employees and whose head office and management were situated in the new Länder or West Berlin, by way of derogation from the national system which is otherwise homogeneous.

62. In order to determine the selectivity of a measure adopted by an infra-State body which, like the measure at issue, seeks to establish in one part of the territory of a Member State a tax rate which is lower than the rate in force in the rest of that State it is appropriate, as stated in paragraph 58 of this judgment, to examine whether that measure was adopted by that body in the exercise of powers sufficiently autonomous vis-à-vis the central power and, if appropriate, to examine whether that measure indeed applies to all the undertakings established in or all production of goods on the territory coming within the competence of that body.

63. . . . . [The] Advocate General specifically identified three situations in which the issue of the classification as State aid of a measure seeking to establish, in a limited geographical area, tax rates lower than the rates in force nationally may arise.

64. In the first situation, the central government unilaterally decides that the applicable national tax rate should be reduced within a defined geographic area. The second situation corresponds to a model for distribution of tax competences in which all the local authorities at the same level (regions, districts or others) have the autonomous power to decide, within the limit of the powers conferred on them, the tax rate applicable in the territory within their competence. The Commission has recognised, as have the Portuguese and United Kingdom Governments, that a measure taken by a local authority in the second situation is not selective because it is impossible to determine a normal tax rate capable of constituting the reference framework.

65. In the third situation described, a regional or local authority adopts, in the exercise of sufficiently autonomous powers in relation to the central power, a tax rate lower than the national rate and which is applicable only to undertakings present in the territory within its competence.

66. In the latter situation, the legal framework appropriate to determine the selectivity of a tax measure may be limited to the geographical area concerned where the infra-State body, in particular on account of its status and powers, occupies a fundamental role in the definition of the political and economic environment in which the undertakings present on the territory within its competence operate.

67. . . . . [I]n order that a decision taken in such circumstances can be regarded as having been adopted in the exercise of sufficiently autonomous powers, that decision must, first of all, have been taken by a regional or local authority which has, from a constitutional point of view, a political and administrative status separate from that of the central government. Next, it must have been adopted without the central government being able to directly intervene as regards its content. Finally, the financial consequences of a reduction of the national tax rate for undertakings in the region must not be offset by aid or subsidies from other regions or central government.

68. It follows that political and fiscal independence of central government which is sufficient as regards the application of Community rules on State aid presupposes, as the United Kingdom Government submitted, that the infra-State body not only has powers in the territory within its competence to adopt measures reducing the tax rate, regardless of any considerations related to the conduct of the central State, but that in addition it assumes the political and financial consequences of such a measure.

69. Since the Portuguese Government disputes the Commission's assessment of the selective nature of the tax reduction measures in question, it is necessary to examine whether those measures which favour undertakings liable for tax in the Azores Region fulfil the requirements set out in paragraphs 67 and 68 of this judgment.

70. In that connection, it must be observed that under the Constitution of the

Portuguese Republic the Azores form an autonomous region with its own political and administrative status and its own self-government institutions which have the power to exercise their own fiscal competence and adapt national fiscal provisions to regional specificities in accordance with Law No 13/98 and Decree No 2/99/A.

71. As far as concerns economic autonomy, the Portuguese Government, in answer to the Commission's arguments that the Autonomous Region of the Azores lacks autonomy on account of compensatory financial transfers from the central State, merely observed that the Commission had not submitted any evidence on the merits of those arguments, without itself demonstrating that the Autonomous Region of the Azores does not receive any State financing to make good the fall in tax revenue which may result from reductions in the tax rates.

72. In that regard, it must be observed that, under Article 5(1) of Law No 13/98 and in the context of the adaptation of the national tax system to regional specificities, the constitutional principle of national solidarity was stated to mean that the central State contributes, with the autonomous regional authorities, to the achievement of economic development and the correction of inequalities deriving from insularity and to economic and social convergence with the rest of the national territory.

73. According to Article 32 of that Law, the application of that principle gives rise to a duty incumbent on both the central and regional authorities to promote the correction of inequalities arising from insularity by reducing local tax burden and by an obligation to ensure an appropriate level of public services and private activities.

74. As the Portuguese Government recognises, it is as a corollary to that constitutional and legislative system that Decree No 2/99/A adapts the national tax system to regional specificities.

75. Although the reduction in tax revenue which may result, for the Azores region, from reductions in tax rates may affect the attainment of the objective, recognised by the Portuguese Government, of correcting inequalities in economic development, it is in any event offset by a financing mechanism which is centrally managed. In this case, that financing is expressly provided for in Article 5(2) of Law No 13/98 in the form of budgetary transfers.

76. It follows that the two aspects of the fiscal policy of the regional government, namely the decision to reduce the regional tax burden by exercising its power to reduce tax rates on revenue and the fulfilment of its task of correcting inequalities deriving from insularity, are inextricably linked and depend, from the financial point of view, on budgetary transfers managed by central government.

77. In that context, it must be held that the decision of the government of the Autonomous Region of the Azores to exercise its power to reduce the rates of national tax on revenue in order to allow economic operators in the region to overcome the structural disadvantages deriving from their insular situation on the periphery of the Community, was not adopted in accordance with all the requirements set out in paragraphs 67 and 68 of this judgment.

78. Accordingly, the relevant legal framework for determining the selectivity of the tax measures at issue cannot be defined exclusively within the geographical limits

of the Azores region. Those measures must be assessed in relation to the whole of Portuguese territory, in the context of which they appear to be selective.

79. It follows, as the Commission rightly held in the contested decision, that the reductions in the tax rates at issue are selective and not general measures.

## NOTES AND QUESTIONS

1. Does the above case suggest that political subdivisions of a Member State are not bound by the EC Treaty/TFEU provisions on State aids? Or is the Court making a different point?

2. The differentiation of aids from general systems of charges or taxation seems to involve some rather subtle distinctions. Are the ECJ's guidelines clear enough to give the requisite guidance? What should a Member State do if it is in doubt?

3. See also, *Union General de Trabajadores de la Rioja et al v. Comunidad Autonoma de la Rioja et al.* Joined Cases C-428/06 to C-434/06, 2008 ECJ EUR-Lex LEXIS 2235, [2008] ECR I-6747.

## [B]   Effect on Trade Between Member States

## PHILIP MORRIS HOLLAND BV v. COMMISSION
### Case 730/79, [1980] ECR 2671

[The Netherlands Government had informed the Commission of its intention to Philip Morris a sum]of more than 60 million guilders for an investment project providing a certain number of new jobs.]

3 The aim of the aid in question was to help the applicant to concentrate and develop its production of cigarettes by closing one of the two factories which it owns in the Netherlands and by raising the annual production capacity of the second located at Bergen-op-Zoom in the south of the country to 16 000 million cigarettes, thereby increasing the manufacturing capacity of the subsidiary by 40% and total production in the Netherlands by about 13%.

4 After the Commission had reviewed the proposed aid in accordance with the provisions of Article 98 [108] of the Treaty it adopted the disputed decision, which provides that the Kingdom of the Netherlands shall refrain from implementing its proposal, communicated to the Commission by letter dated 4 October 1978, to grant the "additional premium for major schemes" to investment made at Bergen-op-Zoom.

\*   \*   \*

9 The applicant maintains that, in order to decide to what extent specific aid is incompatible with the Common Market, it is appropriate to apply first of all the criteria for deciding whether there are any restrictions on competition under Articles 85 [101] and 86 [102] of the Treaty. The Commission must therefore first determine the "relevant market" and in order to do so must take account of the product, the territory and the period of time in question. It must then consider the

pattern of the market in question in order to be able to assess how far the aid in question in a given case affects relations between competitors. But these essential aspects of the matter are not found in the disputed decision. The decision does not define the relevant market either from the standpoint of the product or in point of time. The market pattern and moreover for that matter, the relations between competitors resulting therefrom which might in a given case be distorted by the disputed aid, have not been specified at all.

10 It is common ground that when the applicant has completed its planned investment it will account for nearly 50% of cigarette production in the Netherlands and that it expects to export over 80% of its production to other Member States. . .

.

11 When State financial aid strengthens the position of an undertaking compared with other undertakings competing in intra-Community trade the latter must be regarded as affected by that aid. In this case the aid which the Netherlands Government proposed to grant was for an undertaking organized for international trade and this is proved by the high percentage of its product which it intends to export to other Member States. The aid in question was to help to enlarge its production capacity and consequently to increase its capacity to maintain the flow of trade including that between Member States. On the other hand the aid is said to have reduced the cost of converting the production facilities and has thereby given the applicant a competitive advantage over manufacturers who have completed or intend to complete at their own expense a similar increase in the production capacity of their plant.

12 These circumstances, which have been mentioned in the recitals in the preamble to the disputed decision and which the applicant has not challenged, justify the Commission's deciding that the proposed aid would be likely to affect trade between Member States and would threaten to distort competition between undertakings established in different Member States.

13 It follows from the foregoing considerations that the first submission must be rejected in substance and also far as concerns the inadequacy of the statement of reasons on which the decision was based.

## NOTES AND QUESTIONS

1.    What criteria did the court use for assessing whether there was a distortion on competition and trade? Did it look at the two as separate criteria? Was there any merit in the plaintiff's argument that the same test in relation to the latter should be applied as applies to EC 81 and 82/TFEU 101 and 102 cases?

2.    The Court has also had occasion to consider the situation where the aid in question was actually designed to bolster exports. In *Belgium v. Commission (Aid to Tubemeuse)*, Case C-142/87, 1990 ECJ CELEX LEXIS 23, [1990] ECR I-959, Belgium had sought the annulment of a Commission Decision that had found that State financial assistance, amounting to some Bfr. 12 billion, granted to Tubemeuse by increasing its capital, taking out bonds and converting guaranteed loans into capital, constituted illegal aid. Belgium argued that even if the operations in question did constitute aid, that aid benefited exports to third countries, since

Tubemeuse exported 90 percent of its production to non-member countries (mostly the Soviet Union). Belgium argued first that the aid was thus governed by Article 132 of the EC Treaty, and not the State aid provisions. The Court considered that even if that were the case, the State aid provisions could apply. As to the volume of exports outside the EU, the Commission's decision indicated that, in the context of overall crisis affecting the seamless tube industry worldwide, Tubemeuse's stated intention was to withdraw from the Soviet market, which it considered to be insufficiently profitable, and to use the aid received to turn toward other markets.

**3.** Presumably if aid is mostly to benefit exports, it would be in the EU's interests to support it. How could this be achieved within the EU rules?

## ALTMARK TRANS GMBH AND ANOTHER v. NAHVERKEHRSGESELLSCHAFT ALTMARK GMBH
### Case C-280/00, 2003 ECJ CELEX LEXIS 98, [2003] ECR I-7747

[The facts are set out in the first excerpt from this case, *supra*]

77 . . . [I]t . . . is not impossible that a public subsidy granted to an undertaking which provides only local or regional transport services and does not provide any transport services outside its state of origin may none the less have an effect on trade between Member States.

78. Where a Member State grants a public subsidy to an undertaking, the supply of transport services by that undertaking may for that reason be maintained or increased with the result that undertakings established in other Member States have less chance of providing their transport services in the market in that Member State . . .

79. In the present case, that finding is not merely hypothetical, since, as appears in particular from the observations of the Commission, several Member States have since 1995 started to open certain transport markets to competition from undertakings established in other Member States, so that a number of undertakings are already offering their urban, suburban or regional transport services in Member States other than their state of origin.

\*   \*   \*

81. . . . [T]here is no threshold or percentage below which it may be considered that trade between Member States is not affected. The relatively small amount of aid or the relatively small size of the undertaking which receives it does not as such exclude the possibility that trade between Member States might be affected . . .

82. The second condition for the application of art 92 [107](1) of the Treaty, namely that the aid must be capable of affecting trade between Member States, does not therefore depend on the local or regional character of the transport services supplied or on the scale of the field of activity concerned.

## NOTES AND QUESTIONS

How did the Court approach the question of the effect on trade in this case? Would you consider the Court's approach expansive or literal? What was the relevance of the *de minimis* issue? Does this have similarities with the *Völk v. Verwaecke* approach *(supra*, Chapter 11) or are the issues really quite different here?

## [C]   Relationship with Other Treaty Provisions

## IANNELLI & VOLPI SPA v. DITTA PAOLO MERONI
### Case 74/76, [1977] ECR 557

[The defendant was an Italian purchaser of imported wallpaper. The plaintiff was an Italian vendor, which charged the purchaser a proportion of the levy which, on importing the goods into Italy, it had previously paid to the Ente Nazionale per la Cellulosa e per la Carta, (ENCC).]

2 ENCC is a body governed by Italian public law, whose object is to promote and regulate, in particular by means of subsidies, the production of cellulose and paper in this Member State. A large part of the aids administered by the ENCC consist of subsidies to newspaper publishers for the purpose of enabling them to obtain at a reduced price paper purchased from paper mills and used for publishing. The ENCC's operations are financed by levies charged on home-produced cellulose, paper and cardboard at various stages of their production or marketing and on similar imported products at the time of importation.

3 The above-mentioned Italian legal provisions allow the importer who has paid the levy to the ENCC to pass on a proportion thereof to the ultimate purchasers.

The defendant in the main action submits by way of justification for its refusal to pay this proportion, on the one hand, that the scheme for granting aid introduced by the legislative provisions in question is, considered as a whole, incompatible with the Treaty because it infringes Article 30 [34] of the Treaty, so that the scheme cannot legally justify the collection of the levies which the plaintiff was called upon to pay or consequently permit the plaintiff to pass on part of it to the purchaser and, on the other hand, that the levy itself constitutes discriminatory internal taxation in contravention of Article 95 [110] of the Treaty.

4 It is advisable to state that the alleged infringement of Article 30 [34] is due to the fact that the granting by the ENCC of subsidies to newspaper undertakings to enable them to obtain newsprint more cheaply was at the time subject to the condition that the newsprint in question was produced in Italy or imported by the ENCC, and not imported directly from another Member State. As far as concerns the levy charged by the ENCC, the infringement of Article 95 [90] arises because there was one basis of assessment for paper and cardboard and paper products (including wallpaper) if they were manufactured in Italy and another if they were imported.

5 The main point raised by the questions referred is whether a national court, when asked to rule on whether a system of State aids within the meaning of Article 92, [107] or some of its aspects, is compatible with the Treaty, may take account of a

possible infringement of Articles 30 [34] and 95 [110] and, if so, what are the criteria which make it possible to ascertain whether in circumstances such as those that arose in this case the said articles have in fact been infringed.

It should be pointed out that these questions refer to the situation that existed before the modification of the system of aids in question, which the Commission required to be carried out under the powers vested in it by Article 93 [108](2) of the Treaty and which the Italian State put into effect as from January 1, 1974 . . .

\*    \*    \*

8 The prohibition in Article 30 [34] of the Treaty of all quantitative restrictions in imports or measures having equivalent effect is aimed, on the one hand, at measures prohibiting imports in whole or in part and, on the other hand, as mentioned in Commission Directive No. 70/50/EEC of December 22, 1969 . . . , at "measures other than those applicable equally to domestic or imported products," which hinder imports that could otherwise take place, including measures that make the sale of imports "more difficult or costly than domestic production".

9 However wide the field of application of Article 30 [34] may be, it nevertheless does not include obstacles to trade covered by other provisions of the Treaty. In fact, since the legal consequences of the application or of a possible infringement of these various provisions must be determined having regard to their particular purpose in the context of all the objectives of the Treaty, they may be of a different kind, and this implies that their respective fields of application must be distinguished, except in those cases which may fall simultaneously within the field of application of two or more provisions of Community law. Thus obstacles which are of a fiscal nature or have equivalent effect and are covered by Articles 9 to 16 [28 to 32] and 95 [110] of the Treaty do not fall within the prohibition in Article 30 [34].

10 Similarly, the fact that a system of aids provided by the State or by means of State resources may, simply because it benefits certain national undertakings or products, hinder, at least indirectly, the importation of similar or competing products coming from other Member States is not in itself sufficient to put an aid as such on the same footing as a measure having an effect equivalent to a quantitative restriction within the meaning of Article 30 [34].

11 Moreover, it is apparent from both Article 92 [(1) and (3) [107] and the third subparagraph of Article 93(2) [108(3)] that the incompatibility of aids with the Common Market as provided for in Article 92(1) [107] is neither absolute nor unconditional. Article 92(2) [107] not only provides for exceptions but in addition both Article 92 [107] and Article 93 [108] give the Commission a wide discretion and the Council wide powers to permit State aid in derogation from the general prohibition in Article 92(1) [107].

12 The conclusion to be drawn from all these considerations is that the intention of the Treaty, in providing through Article 93 [108] for aid to be kept under constant review and supervised by the Commission, is that the finding that an aid may be incompatible with the Common Market is to be determined, subject to review by the Court of Justice, by means of an appropriate procedure which it is the Commission's responsibility to set in motion.

The parties concerned cannot therefore simply, on the basis of Article 92 [107] alone, challenge the compatibility of an aid with Community law before a national court or ask it to decide as to any incompatibility which may be the main issue in an action before it or may arise as a subsidiary issue. The effect of an interpretation of Article 30 [34] which is so wide as to treat an aid as such within the meaning of Article 92 [107] as being similar to a quantitative restriction referred to in Article 30 [34] would be to alter the scope of Articles 92 [107] and 93 [108] of the Treaty and to interfere with the system adopted in the Treaty for the division of powers by means of the procedure for keeping aids under constant review as described in Article 93 [108].

13 The prohibition of quantitative restrictions and measures having equivalent effect laid down in Article 30 [34] the Treaty is mandatory and explicit, and its application does not require any subsequent intervention by the Member States or the Community institutions. The prohibition therefore has direct effect and creates individual rights which the national courts must protect; this occurred at the end of the transitional period at the latest, that is to say on January 1, 1970, as the provisions of the second paragraph of Article 32 [deleted] of the Treaty indicate.

14 Those aspects of an aid which contravene specific provisions of the Treaty other than Articles 92 [107] and 93 [108] may be so indissolubly linked to the object of the aid that it is impossible to evaluate them separately, so that their effect on the compatibility or incompatibility of the aid viewed as a whole must of necessity be determined in the light of the procedure prescribed in Article 93 [108]. The situation, however, is otherwise if it is possible when a system of aid is being analyzed to separate those conditions or factors which, even though they form part of this system, may be regarded as not being necessary for the attainment of its object or for its proper functioning. In the latter case, there are no reasons based on the division of powers under Articles 92 [107] and 93 [108] which permit the conclusion to be drawn that, if other Treaty provisions, which have direct effect, are infringed, those provisions may not be invoked before a national court simply because the factor in question is an aspect of aid.

15 The fact that the inevitable consequence of the aid itself is often protection and therefore some partitioning of the market, as far as concerns the production of undertakings which do not derive any benefit from it, cannot imply that the aid produces restrictive effects which go beyond what is necessary to enable it to attain the objectives permitted by the Treaty. This is the position in the case of an arrangement whereby aid is granted to traders who obtain supplies of imported products through a State agency but is withheld when the products are imported direct, if this distinction is not clearly necessary for the attainment of the objective of the said aid or for its proper functioning.

16 Nevertheless, in answering the second question it must be stated that, if one of the constituent elements of a system of aids could be a measure having an effect equivalent to a quantitative restriction which is not necessary for the attainment of the object of the aid, the national courts are not entitled to make a declaration to the effect that the system of aids as a whole is incompatible with the Treaty or, consequently, to hold that for this reason alone that the levies which finance the aid are illegal, because they finance an aid incompatible with the Treaty.

17 Therefore the answer to the first three questions must be: (a) Article 30 [34] of the Treaty has direct effect and creates, at the end of the transitional period at the latest for all persons subject to Community law rights which the national courts must protect; (b) the aids referred to in Articles 92 [107] and 93 [108] of the Treaty do not as such fall within the field of application of the prohibition of quantitative restrictions on imports and measures having equivalent effect laid down in Article 30 [34] but those aspects of aid which are not necessary for the attainment of its object or for its proper functioning and which contravene this prohibition may for that reason be held to be incompatible with this provision; (c) the fact that an aspect of aid which is not necessary for the attainment of its object or for its proper functioning is incompatible with a provision of the Treaty other than Articles 92 [107] and 93 [108] does not in fact invalidate by reason of illegality the system of financing the said aid.

## DU PONT DE NEMOURS ITALIANA SPA v. UNITA SANITARIA LOCALE NO 2 DI CARRARA
### Case C-21/88, 1990 ECJ CELEX LEXIS 100, [1990] ECR I-889

[Italy imposed on all public bodies and authorities, as well as to bodies and companies in which the State has a shareholding, and including local health authorities situated throughout Italy, the obligation to obtain at least 30 per cent of their supplies from industrial and agricultural undertakings and small businesses established in Southern Italy in which the products concerned undergo processing.]

4 In accordance with the provisions of that national legislation, the local health authority laid down by decision of 3 June 1986 the conditions governing a restricted tendering procedure for the supply of radiological films and liquids. According to the special terms and conditions set out in the annex, it divided the contract into two lots, one, equal to 30 per cent of the total amount, being reserved to undertakings established in Southern Italy. Du Pont de Nemours Italiana challenged that decision before the Tribunale Amministrativo Regionale della Toscana, on the ground that it had been excluded from the tendering procedure for that lot because it did not have an establishment in Southern Italy. By decision of 15 July 1986 the local health authority proceeded to award the contract for the lot corresponding to 70 per cent of the total amount in question. Du Pont de Nemours Italiana also challenged that decision before the same court.

\* \* \*

19 In its second question, the national court seeks to establish whether in the event that the rules in question might be regarded as aid within the meaning of Article 92 that might exempt them from the prohibition set out in Article 30 [34].

20 In that regard, it is sufficient to recall that as the Court has consistently held (see, in particular, Case 103/84, EC COMMISSION v. ITALY) Article 92 [107] may in no case be used to frustrate the rules of the Treaty on the free movement of goods. It is clear from the relevant case law that those rules and the Treaty provisions relating to State aid have a common purpose, namely to ensure the free movement of goods between member-States under normal conditions of competition. As the Court made clear in the judgment cited above, the fact that a national

measure might be regarded as aid within the meaning of Article 92 [107] is therefore not a sufficient reason to exempt it from the prohibition contained in Article 30[28].

21 In the light of that case law — there being no need to consider whether the rules in question are in the nature of aid — it must be stated in answer to the national court's second question that the fact that national rules might be regarded as aid within the meaning of Article 92 [107] cannot exempt them from the prohibition set out in Article 30 [34].

## NOTES AND QUESTIONS

1.   Compare the Court's approach in *DuPont* and *Ianelli*. Is it possible to derive any general principles for deciding the apparent conflicts between the various articles?

2.   Other conflicts have arisen in the context of the relationship between EC 28/TFEU 34 and EC 90/TFEU 110, and EC 31/TFEU 37 and EC 86/TFEU 106. The Court's approach in the above two cases — very specific factual analysis — is repeated in these other areas. See, for example, *Compagnie Commerciale de l'Ouest and Others v. Receveur Principal des Douanes de la Pallice Port*, Joined Cases C-78/90 to C-83/90, 1992 ECJ CELEX LEXIS 156, [1992] ECR I-1847, where the ECJ stated:

> It must be observed that, in the circumstances referred to by the national court, the parafiscal charge at issue was introduced independently of the rules governing the import and marketing of oil in France and was unconnected with the exercise of the exclusive rights provided for by those rules.

> It must therefore be stated in reply to the national court that Article 37 [37] of the Treaty does not preclude the introduction of a parafiscal charge which is created independently of the rules governing the importation and marketing of petroleum in force in a Member State and is unconnected with the exercise of the exclusive rights provided for by those rules.

## § 16.03   PARTICIPATION BY THE STATE IN COMMERCIAL ACTIVITY

### [A]   State Monopolies

#### PUBBLICO MINISTERO v. MANGHERA
Case 59/75, [1976] ECR 91

[Manghera was accused of having violated the exclusive right of the Italian State monopoly in manufactured tobacco to import tobacco into Italy.]

3 The first question asks whether Article 37 [37] (1) of the Treaty is to be interpreted as meaning that, with effect from 31 December 1969 (the date when the transitional period expired), the trade monopoly should have been reorganized in

such a way as to eliminate even the possibility of any discrimination being practised against Community exporters, with the consequential extinction, with effect from 1 January 1970, of the exclusive right to import from other Member States.

4 Under Article 37 [37] (1) Member States must progressively adjust any State monopolies of a commercial character so as to ensure that when the transitional period has ended no discrimination regarding the conditions under which goods are procured and marketed exists between the nationals of Member States.

5 Without requiring the abolition of the said monopolies, this provision prescribes in mandatory terms that they must be adjusted in such a way as to ensure that when the transitional period has ended such discrimination shall cease to exist.

6 For the purposes of interpreting Article 37 [37] as regards the nature and scope of the adjustment prescribed it must be considered in its context in relation to the other paragraphs of the same article and in its place in the general scheme of the Treaty.

7 This article comes under the title on the free movement of goods and in particular under Chapter II on the abolition of quantitative restrictions between Member States. It applies to any body through which a Member State either directly or indirectly supervises, determines or appreciably influences imports or exports between Member States.

8 Furthermore, Article 37 [37] (2) refers to the obligation on all Member States to refrain as from the beginning of the transitional period from introducing any new measures likely to restrict the scope of the articles dealing with the abolition of customs duties and quantitative restrictions between Member States.

9 Article 37 [37] (3), moreover, provides that the time-table for adjustment provided for in paragraph (1) must be harmonized with the abolition of quantitative restrictions on the same products provided for in Articles 30 [34] to 34 [31]. It follows from these provisions and their structure that the obligation laid down in paragraph (1) aims at ensuring compliance with the fundamental rule of the free movement of goods throughout the common market, in particularly by the abolition of quantitative restrictions and measures having equivalent effect in trade between Member States.

10 This objective would not be attained if, in a Member State where a commercial monopoly exists, the free movement of goods from other Member States similar to those with which the national monopoly is concerned were not ensured.

11 The Council's Resolution of 21 April 1970 on national monopolies of a commercial character in manufactured tobacco itself refers to the obligation to abolish exclusive rights to import and market manufactured tobacco.

12 The exclusive right to import manufactured products of the monopoly in question thus constitutes, in respect of Community exporters, discrimination prohibited by Article 37 [37] (1).

13 The answer to the first question should therefore be that Article 37 [37] (1) of the EEC Treaty must be interpreted as meaning that as from 31 December 1969 every national monopoly of a commercial character must be adjusted so as to eliminate

the exclusive right to import from other Member States.

# NOTES AND QUESTIONS

**1.** Why did the Court conclude that all import monopolies are prohibited under EC 31/TFEU 37? Do you agree with this reasoning?

**2.** In *Criminal Proceedings against Harry Franzen*, Case C-189/95, 1997 ECJ CELEX LEXIS 254, [1997] ECR I-5909, the ECJ decided that a retail monopoly on the sale of alcoholic drinks in Sweden did not violate EC 31/TFEU 37. However, the law had also provided that importers and wholesalers must be licensed and meet certain conditions to receive such licenses. This requirement fell foul of EC 28 and 30/TFEU 34 and 36:

> 70 In a national system such as that in question in the main proceedings, only holders of production licences or wholesale licences are allowed to import alcoholic beverages, that is to say traders who fulfil the restrictive conditions to which issue of those licences is subject. According to the information provided to the Court during the proceedings, the traders in question must provide sufficient personal and financial guarantees to carry on the activities in question, concerning in particular their professional knowledge, their financial capacity and possession of storage capacity sufficient to meet the needs of their activities. Furthermore, the submission of an application is subject to payment of a high fixed charge . . . which is not reimbursed if the application is rejected. Finally, in order to keep his licence, a trader must pay an annual supervision fee, which is also high . . . for the basic amounts, depending on the kinds of beverage and the quantities produced or marketed).

> 71 The licensing system constitutes an obstacle to the importation of alcoholic beverages from other Member States in that it imposes additional costs on such beverages, such as intermediary costs, payment of charges and fees for the grant of a licence, and costs arising from the obligation to maintain storage capacity in Sweden.

> 72 According to the Swedish Government's own evidence, the number of licences issued is low (223 in October 1996) and almost all of these licences have been issued to traders established in Sweden.

> 73 Domestic legislation such as that in question in the main proceedings is therefore contrary to Article 30 [34] of the Treaty.

> 74 TheSwedish Government has, however, invoked Article 36 [36] of the EC Treaty. It maintains that its legislation was justified on grounds relating to the protection of human health.

> 75 It is indeed so that measures contrary to Article 30 [34] may be justified on the basis of Article 36 [36] of the Treaty. All the same . . . the domestic provisions in question must be proportionate to the aim pursued and not attainable by measures less restrictive of intra-Community trade.

76 Although the protection of human health against the harmful effects of alcohol, on which the Swedish Government relies, is indisputably one of the grounds which may justify derogation from Article 30 [34] of the Treaty . . . the Swedish Government has not established that the licensing system set up by the Law on Alcohol, in particular as regards the conditions relating to storage capacity and the high fees and charges which licence-holders are required to pay, was proportionate to the public health aim pursued or that this aim could not have been attained by measures less restrictive of intra-Community trade.

77 It must therefore be held that Articles 30 [34] and 36 [36] of the Treaty preclude domestic provisions allowing only traders holding a production licence or a wholesale licence to import alcoholic beverages on conditions such as those laid down by Swedish Legislation.

## HANSEN GMBH & CO. v. HAUPTZOLLAMT FLENSBURG
### Case 91/78, [1979] ECR 935

[The German Government had introduced a new law of May 2, 1976 relating to the marketing and sale of alcohol spirit beverages.

The plaintiff in this case was an undertaking which manufactured and distributed spirits and which marketed in the Federal Republic of Germany at the time in question imported spirits coming from various sources, of both EU and non-EU origin, either unprocessed or in the form of coupages. After the entry into force of the new law such spirits became liable to the tax on spirits of DM 1 650 per hectolitre of wine-spirit which is applicable uniformly, albeit under various designations, both to domestic spirits and to imported spirits.

The plaintiff, however, maintained that that equality of treatment was merely apparent, since it was clear from the preparatory stages of the new law that the increase in the rate of taxation from DM 1 500 to DM 1 650 per hectolitre had the sole objective of enabling the monopoly administration to make good its losses stemming from the marked difference which had arisen between, on the one hand, the purchase price which it is bound by law to pay to producers of spirits to which the monopoly applies and, on the other, the selling price of such spirits to consumers, as determined by market forces following prior judgements of the ECJ that held the prior monopoly on imports of such products infringed EC 37/TFEU 37. The plaintiff claimed that that practice was simply the continuation of the monopoly in spirits by other means and accordingly it is appropriate to apply EC 37/TFEU 37.

The question arose as to whether the new arrangement should be considered a state aid under EC 87 – 89/TFEU 107-109 the application of which would preempt the application of EC 31/TFEU 37.]

8 Article 37 [37] does not require the total abolition of State monopolies of a commercial character but only that they be so adjusted as to ensure that no discrimination regarding the conditions under which goods are procured and marketed exists between nationals of Member States.

It is further provided in Article 37 [37] (2) that the operations of a State monopoly shall not be employed to re-establish a customs barrier or quantitative restrictions in intra-Community trade.

Article 37 [37] remains applicable wherever, even after the adjustment prescribed in the Treaty, the exercise by a State monopoly of its exclusive rights entails a discrimination or restriction prohibited by that article.

In cases such as the present, which concerns an activity specifically connected with the exercise by a State monopoly of its exclusive right to purchase, process and sell spirits, the application of the provisions of Article 37 [37] cannot be excluded.

It thus appears that the national court was justified in requesting clarification of the relationship between Article 37 [37] and the provisions of the Treaty concerning official aids since the operations of the monopoly are closely linked with the support of certain categories of producer by means of purchase prices guaranteed by law.

9 A comparison between Article 37 [37] on the one hand and Articles 92 [107] and 98 [108] on the other shows that those provisions pursue the same objective, which is to ensure that the two categories of intervention on the part of a Member State, namely action by a State monopoly and the granting of aids, do not distort the conditions of competition within the common market or create discrimination against the products or trade of other Member States.

However, the application of those provisions presupposes distinct conditions peculiar to the two kinds of State measure which they are intended to govern and they differ furthermore as to their legal consequences, above all in that the intervention of the Commission plays a large part in the implementation of Articles 92 [107] and 98 [108] whilst Article 37 [37] is intended to be directly applicable.

A measure effected through the intermediary of a public monopoly which may also be considered as an aid within the meaning of Article 98 [108] is consequently governed both by the provisions of Article 37 [37] and by those applicable to State aids.

It follows that the operations of a State monopoly are not exempted from the application of Article 37 [37] by reason of the fact that they may at the same time be classified as an aid within the meaning of the Treaty.

It is therefore clear that in all cases where the arrangements for marketing a product such as spirits entail the intervention of a public monopoly acting pursuant to its exclusive right the specific provisions of Article 37 [37] are applicable, even if the relationship between the monopoly and producers may be in the nature of an aid.

10 The answer to the first question must therefore be that Article 37 [37] of the Treaty constitutes in relation to Articles 92 [107] and 98 [108] of that Treaty a lex specialis in the sense that State measures, inherent in the exercise by a State monopoly of a commercial character of its exclusive right must, even where they are linked to the grant of an aid to producers subject to the monopoly, be considered in the light of the requirements of Article 37 [37].

## NOTES AND QUESTIONS

1. How did the Court resolve the issue of the apparent overlap between the state aid provisions and EC 31/TFEU 37? What was the legal consequence of the Court's ruling? Which party would have been helped by a conclusion that EC 31/TFEU 37 was not applicable because of the alleged state aid preemption?

## [B]   Grants of Exclusive Rights to Public Undertakings or Concessionaires

### HÖFNER AND ELSER v. MACROTRON GMBH
### Case C-41/90, 1991 ECJ CELEX LEXIS 390, [1991] ECR I-1979

[Proceedings were brought by Messrs Höfner and Elser, recruitment consultants, against Macrotron GmbH, established in Munich. The dispute concerned fees claimed from that company by Messrs Höfner and Elser pursuant to a contract under which the latter were to assist in the recruitment of a sales director. Under a German law (the "AFG") only the Bundesanstalt für Arbeit (Federal Office for Employment] was permitted to act as recruitment agents but the Bundesanstalt had informally relaxed that monopoly with respect to executive recruitment. However, since the law had not changed, contracts made by private parties in violation of it were unenforceable.]

25 As regards the manner in which a public employment agency enjoying an exclusive right of employment procurement conducts itself in relation to executive recruitment undertaken by private recruitment consultancy companies, it must be stated that the application of Article 86 [102] of the Treaty cannot obstruct the performance of the particular task assigned to that agency in so far as the latter is manifestly not in a position to satisfy demand in that area of the market and in fact allows its exclusive rights to be encroached on by those companies.

26 Whilst it is true that Article 86 [102] concerns undertakings and may be applied within the limits laid down by Article 90 [106](2) to public undertakings or undertakings vested with exclusive rights or specific rights, the fact nevertheless remains that the Treaty requires the Member States not to take or maintain in force measures which could destroy the effectiveness of that provision . . . Article 90 [106](1) in fact provides that the Member States are not to enact or maintain in force, in the case of public undertakings and the undertakings to which they grant special or exclusive rights, any measure contrary to the rules contained in the Treaty, in particular those provided for in Articles 85 [101] to 94 [109].

27 Consequently, any measure adopted by a Member State which maintains in force a statutory provision that creates a situation in which a public employment agency cannot avoid infringing Article 86 [102] is incompatible with the rules of the Treaty.

28 It must be remembered, first, that an undertaking vested with a legal monopoly may be regarded as occupying a dominant position within the meaning of Article 86 [102] of the Treaty . . . and that the territory of a Member State, to which that monopoly extends, may constitute a substantial part of the common market . . .

29 Secondly, the simple fact of creating a dominant position of that kind by granting

an exclusive right within the meaning of Article 90 [106](1) is not as such incompatible with Article 86 [102] of the Treaty . . . A Member State is in breach of the prohibition contained in those two provisions only if the undertaking in question, merely by exercising the exclusive right granted to it, cannot avoid abusing its dominant position.

30 Pursuant to Article 86 [102](b), such an abuse may in particular consist in limiting the provision of a service, to the prejudice of those seeking to avail themselves of it.

31 A Member State creates a situation in which the provision of a service is limited when the undertaking to which it grants an exclusive right extending to executive recruitment activities is manifestly not in a position to satisfy the demand prevailing on the market for activities of that kind and when the effective pursuit of such activities by private companies is rendered impossible by the maintenance in force of a statutory provision under which such activities are prohibited and non-observance of that prohibition renders the contracts concerned void.

*   *   *

34 . . . [A] public employment agency engaged in employment procurement activities is subject to the prohibition contained in Article 86 [102] of the Treaty, so long as the application of that provision does not obstruct the performance of the particular task assigned to it. A Member State which has conferred an exclusive right to carry on that activity upon the public employment agency is in breach of Article 90 [106](1) of the Treaty where it creates a situation in which that agency cannot avoid infringing Article 86 [102] of the Treaty. That is the case, in particular, where the following conditions are satisfied:

- the exclusive right extends to executive recruitment activities;

- the public employment agency is manifestly incapable of satisfying demand prevailing on the market for such activities;

- the actual pursuit of those activities by private recruitment consultants is rendered impossible by the maintenance in force of a statutory provision under which such activities are prohibited and non-observance of that prohibition renders the contracts concerned void;

- the activities in question may extend to the nationals or to the territory of other Member States.

## NOTES AND QUESTIONS

1.   How does one make sense of the test regarding breach of EC 86/TFEU 106 (1) where one is confronted with an undertaking that falls within article 86(2)? Put another way, since paragraph (2) allows the disapplication of EC 81 or 82/TFEU101 or 102 to the extent that the undertaking would otherwise be obstructed in its task, does the Court's approach nonetheless operate to render the State liable where it can be concluded that the undertaking will necessarily violate the competition law? Does the *Höfner* case offer a clear analytical path for reaching a conclusion?

**2.** How good, in your view, were the chances that the plaintiffs in the above case would be able to prevail before the German court?

**3.** See also *Société Civile Agricole du Centre d'Insemination de la Crespelle v. Cooperative d'Elevage et d'Insemination Artificielle du Département de la Mayenne*, Case C-323/93, 1994 ECJ CELEX LEXIS 401, [1994] ECR I-5077, where the Court considered a French law, pursuant to which artificial insemination of animals was to be carried out by approved insemination centers. In the Mayenne department, the Mayenne cooperative had the exclusive rights to carry out insemination and brought proceedings against La Crespelle, which carried out such activities in breach of the exclusive concession granted to the cooperative. Questions arose as to the compatibility of the exclusive right with EC 82/TFEU 102, read in conjunction with EC 86/TFEU 106(1). The ECJ sustained its approach that the grant was acceptable.

## CRIMINAL PROCEEDINGS AGAINST SILVANO RASO AND OTHERS
Case C-163/96, 1998 ECJ CELEX LEXIS 281, [1998] ECR I-533

[Mr Raso and 10 other persons, the legal representatives of La Spezia Container Terminal SRL (hereinafter LSCT'), the concessionaire for a terminal within the port of La Spezia, and four other undertakings authorised to carry out dock work there were accused of having unlawfully used and supplied labor in breach of an Italian law of 1994, which granted the exclusive right to supply temporary labor to certain companies that had been reconstituted after the prior law was found to be in breach of the EC Treaty. These companies in their reconstituted form were also in competition with other dock companies that were required to obtain any temporary labor from them.]

27 [I]t should be recalled that although merely creating a dominant position by granting exclusive rights within the meaning of Article 90 [106](1) of the Treaty is not in itself incompatible with Article 86 [102], a Member State is in breach of the prohibitions contained in those two provisions if the undertaking in question, merely by exercising the exclusive rights granted to it, is led to abuse its dominant position or when such rights are liable to create a situation in which that undertaking is led to commit such abuses . . .

28 In view of that it is clear that in so far as the scheme laid down by the 1994 Law does not merely grant the former dock-work company now reconstituted the exclusive right to supply temporary labour to terminal concessionaires and to other undertakings authorised to operate in the port but also enables it, as stated in paragraph 17 of this judgment, to compete with them on the market in dock services, such former dock-work company now reconstituted will have a conflict of interest.

29 That is because merely exercising its monopoly will enable it to distort in its favour the equal conditions of competition between the various operators on the market in dock-work services . . .

30 The result is that the company in question is led to abuse its monopoly by imposing on its competitors in the dock-work market unduly high costs for the

supply of labour or by supplying them with labour less suited to the work to be done.

31 In those circumstances a legal framework such as that which results from the 1994 Law must be regarded as being in itself contrary to Article 90 [106](1) in conjunction with Article 86 [102] of the Treaty. In that regard, it is therefore immaterial that the national court did not identify any particular case of abuse by the reconstituted former dock-work company . . .

32 In the light of those considerations the reply to the third question must be that Articles 86 [102] and 90 [106] of the Treaty must be interpreted as precluding a national provision which reserves to a dock-work company the right to supply temporary labour to other undertakings operating in the port in which it is established, when that company is itself authorised to carry out dock work.

## NOTES AND QUESTIONS

1.   As regards the circumstances that would lead to liability of the Member State under EC 86/TFEU 106(1), does the Court change course here compared with the *Höfner* case? Compare *Elliniki Radiophonia Tileorassi Anonimi v. Dimotiki Etairia Pliroforissis (DEP) and Sotinos Kouvelas*, Case C-260/89, [1991] ECR 2925, where the Court considered that EC 82/TFEu 102 should apply where state measures "are liable to create a situation in which [the monopoly] is led to infringe article 86 [102]". Is the test in *Höfner* more or less restrictive?

## [C]   Services of General Economic Interest

### CRIMINAL PROCEEDINGS AGAINST PAUL CORBEAU
Case C-320/91, 1993 ECJ CELEX LEXIS 195, [1993] ECR I-2533

[Under Belgian law the Regie des Postes . . . . (Post Office) had an exclusive right to collect, carry and distribute throughout Belgium all correspondence of whatever nature, and to lay down penalties for any infringement of that exclusive right. Mr Corbeau provided, within the City of Liège and the surrounding areas, a service consisting in collecting mail from the address of the sender and distributing it by noon on the following day, provided that the addressee is located within the district concerned. As regards correspondence destined for addressees outside that district, Mr Corbeau collected it from the sender's address and sent it by post.]

8 . . . [A] body such as the Regie des Postes, which has been granted exclusive rights as regards the collection, carriage and distribution of mail, must be regarded as an undertaking to which the Member State concerned has granted exclusive rights within the meaning of Article 90 [106](1) of the Treaty.

9 Next it should be recalled that the Court has consistently held that an undertaking having a statutory monopoly over a substantial part of the common market may be regarded as having a dominant position within the meaning of Article 86 [102] of the Treaty. . . .

10 However, Article 86 [102] applies only to anti-competitive conduct engaged in by undertakings on their own initiative, not to measures adopted by States. . . .

11 . . . [A]lthough the mere fact that a Member State has created a dominant position by the grant of exclusive rights is not as such incompatible with Article 86 [102], the Treaty none the less requires the Member States not to adopt or maintain in force any measure which might deprive those provisions of their effectiveness. . . .

12 Thus Article 90 [106](1) provides that in the case of public undertakings to which Member States grant special or exclusive rights, they are neither to enact nor to maintain in force any measure contrary to the rules contained in the Treaty with regard to competition.

13 That provision must be read in conjunction with Article 90 [106](2) which provides that undertakings entrusted with the operation of services of general economic interest are to be subject to the rules on competition in so far as the application of such rules does not obstruct the performance, in law or in fact, of the particular tasks assigned to them.

14 That latter provision thus permits the Member States to confer on undertakings to which they entrust the operation of services of general economic interest, exclusive rights which may hinder the application of the rules of the Treaty on competition in so far as restrictions on competition, or even the exclusion of all competition, by other economic operators are necessary to ensure the performance of the particular tasks assigned to the undertakings possessed of the exclusive rights.

15 As regards the services at issue in the main proceedings, it cannot be disputed that the Regie des Postes is entrusted with a service of general economic interest consisting in the obligation to collect, carry and distribute mail on behalf of all users throughout the territory of the Member State concerned, at uniform tariffs and on similar quality conditions, irrespective of the specific situations or the degree of economic profitability of each individual operation.

16 The question which falls to be considered is therefore the extent to which a restriction on competition or even the exclusion of all competition from other economic operators is necessary in order to allow the holder of the exclusive right to perform its task of general interest and in particular to have the benefit of economically acceptable conditions.

17 The starting point of such an examination must be the premise that the obligation on the part of the undertaking entrusted with that task to perform its services in conditions of economic equilibrium presupposes that it will be possible to offset less profitable sectors against the profitable sectors and hence justifies a restriction of competition from individual undertakings where the economically profitable sectors are concerned.

18 Indeed, to authorize individual undertakings to compete with the holder of the exclusive rights in the sectors of their choice corresponding to those rights would make it possible for them to concentrate on the economically profitable operations and to offer more advantageous tariffs than those adopted by the holders of the exclusive rights since, unlike the latter, they are not bound for economic reasons to offset losses in the unprofitable sectors against profits in the more profitable sectors.

19 However, the exclusion of competition is not justified as regards specific services dissociable from the service of general interest which meet special needs of economic operators and which call for certain additional services not offered by the traditional postal service, such as collection from the senders' address, greater speed or reliability of distribution or the possibility of changing the destination in the course of transit, in so far as such specific services, by their nature and the conditions in which they are offered, such as the geographical area in which they are provided, do not compromise the economic equilibrium of the service of general economic interest performed by the holder of the exclusive right.

20 It is for the national court to consider whether the services at issue in the dispute before it meet those criteria.

21 The answer to the questions referred to the Court by the Tribunal Correctionnel de Liège should therefore be that it is contrary to Article 90 [106] of the EEC Treaty for legislation of a Member State which confers on a body such as the Regie des Postes the exclusive right to collect, carry and distribute mail, to prohibit, under threat of criminal penalties, an economic operator established in that State from offering certain specific services dissociable from the service of general interest which meet the special needs of economic operators and call for certain additional services not offered by the traditional postal service, in so far as those services do not compromise the economic equilibrium of the service of general economic interest performed by the holder of the exclusive right. It is for the national court to consider whether the services in question in the main proceedings meet those criteria.

## NOTES AND QUESTIONS

**1.** Does the Court in some way contradict itself in holding that the grant of exclusive rights here has to be limited to those necessary for the performance of the concessionnaire's task? What has happened to the basic principle that EC 86 (1)/TFEU 106 does not prohibit the grant of exclusive rights per se? Or is the point here that the concessionaire had the right to prevent others from performing services that it was not itself performing? What are the implications of such a conclusion? Could the Member State in that case rectify the situation by broadening the scope of the concessionnaire's activities?

**2.** In a later case, *Commune Almelo v. NV Energiebedrijf Ijsselmij*, Case 393/92, 1994 ECJ CELEX LEXIS 154, [1994] ECR I-1477, at issue were various arrangements to supply and purchase electricity concluded between the Dutch electricity producers (who operate under a non-exclusive government concession) and distributors. Under Article 2 of the standard terms embodying these arrangements, the purchaser had to undertake to buy electricity from the local producer, to use it for its own purposes or for distribution and not to supply it outside its own territory. The Court held that the producers' obligation — to ensure the supply of electricity in their part of Dutch territory — was a service of general economic interest and that the importation prohibition might well be legitimate if it was necessary to ensure that the producers' obligation to supply on non-discriminatory terms to all customers was to be fulfilled (in other words "importation" from another producer into the assigned territory could mean that the most profitable areas were "cherry picked", leaving the local companies only with the uneconomic activities).

*Almelo* concerned an examination of contractual provisions in private law contracts and the producers had *not* been granted exclusive rights, so any breach of EC 82/TFEU 102 could have arisen only from the de facto existence of a "collective dominant position" of the producers resulting from the web of restrictive agreements, not from any action by the Dutch government. However, perhaps the agreements themselves could be attacked under EC 81/TFEU 102. In sum, the Court explicitly accepted that private companies with special rights of general economic interest may maintain anticompetitive arrangements and that these are indeed necessary for the performance of their task. *Almelo* does not, then, undermine the basic premise apparent in *Corbeau* that the *grant of exclusivity* by a Member State is *per se* illegal under article 86(2) if not necessary for the performance of the specific service entrusted.

3.    If a key economic activity, such as the operation of a port or pipeline, is in the hands of a single operator, the question arises whether it must be made available for third parties to use on reasonable terms. Usually such "monopolies" are, in one sense or another, operated as a result of a state concession — or at least could not be operated without special rights such as the ability to compulsorily purchase land. Even if such facilities are considered to fall under EC 86/TFEU 106(2), the grant to its owner or operator of the exclusive right to use it could be considered outside the exception of that paragraph, while if there were no such explicit grant, then the owner might itself be liable for breach of EC 82/TFEU 102 (since it could no longer rely on state action as a defense). This then opens the way for third parties to demand access on reasonable terms, since denial would be a violation of the Treaty by the Member State or the owner as the case may be.

This approach is exemplified in the following Commission decision, which addressed the refusal by the Danish government to permit the construction by the Swedish group Stena Rederi AB of a private commercial port in the immediate vicinity of the port of Roedby. The Commission's legal assessment in its decision read as follows:

>    The refusal to allow 'Euro-Port A/S', a subsidiary of the Swedish group 'Stena Rederi AB' (Stena) to operate from Roedby has the effect of eliminating a potential competitor on the Roedby-Puttgarden route and hence of strengthening the joint dominant position of DSB and DB on that route.

>    According to the case law of the Court, an abuse within the meaning of Article 86 [102] is committed in cases where, without any objective necessity, an undertaking holding a dominant position on a particular market reserves to itself an ancillary activity which might be carried out by another undertaking as part of its activities on a neighbouring but separate market, with the possibility of eliminating all competition from such undertaking. . . .

>    Thus an undertaking that owns or manages and uses itself an essential facility, i.e. a facility or infrastructure without which its competitors are

unable to offer their services to customers, and refuses to grant them access to such facility is abusing its dominant position.

Consequently, an undertaking that owns or manages an essential port facility from which it provides a maritime transport service may not, without objective justification, refuse to grant a shipowner wishing to operate on the same maritime route access to that facility without infringing Article 86 [102].

According to the case-law of the Court . . . . Article 90 [106] (1) prohibits Member States from placing, by law, regulation or administrative provision, public undertakings and undertakings to which they grant exclusive rights in a position in which those undertakings could not place themselves by their own conduct without infringing Article 86 [102]. The Court added that, where the extension of the dominant position of a public undertaking or an undertaking to which the State has granted exclusive rights resulted from a State measure, such a measure constituted an infringement of Article 90 [106], read in conjunction with Article 86 [102] of the Treaty. This principle was confirmed in the judgment of 17 November 1992 in Cases C-271, 281 and 289/90 (paragraph 36).

Thus, for the reasons given above, any firm in the same position as DSB which refused to grant another shipping operator access to the port it controlled would be abusing a dominant position. Where, as in the present case, a Member State has refused such access and has strengthened the effects of the refusal by also refusing to authorize the construction of a new port, it constitutes a State measure in breach of Article 90 [106], read in conjunction with Article 86 [102].

Article 90 [106]

The Commission considers that the application of the competition rules in the present case does not impede the particular task entrusted to the public undertaking DSB namely to organize rail services and manage the port facilities at Roedby. Therefore the exception provided for in Article 90 [106] (2) does not apply.

The Commission is not aware that DSB has been entrusted with particular tasks other than that referred to above. If (as the letter of 22 February 1993 from the Danish authorities appears to indicate) DSB is indeed subject to a 'transport obligation' the Commission points out that neither their nature nor scope has been specified by the Danish authorities. Consequently, the exception provided for in Article 90 [106] (2) does not justify maintaining the monopoly held by DB and DSB on the Roedby-Puttgarden route.

Since this decision there has been a flow of directives issued either under EC 86/TFEU 106 (3) or by the Council and Parliament under the harmonization provisions, intended to introduce competition in the infrastructure industries, including gas, telecommunications and electricity. Progress in implementation has been slow due to resistance from many vested interests. However, this is now considered a cornerstone of policy for the EU. See P. D. Cameron, *The internal market in energy: Harnessing the new regulatory regime*, (2005) 30 E.L REV. 631.

In a number of cases the Court has upheld activities that would otherwise fall under EC 82/TFEU 102.

For example, in *Albany International BV v. Stichting Bedrijfspensioenfonds Textielindustrie*, Case C-67/96, 1999 ECJ CELEX LEXIS 83, [1999] ECR I-5751, the Court held that EC 82 and 86/TFEU 102 and 106 do not preclude the public authorities from conferring on a pension fund the exclusive right to manage a supplementary pension scheme in a given sector. Furthermore the exclusive right of a sectoral pension fund to manage supplementary pensions in a given sector and the resultant restriction of competition may be justified under EC 86/TFEU106(2) of the Treaty as a measure necessary for the performance of a particular social task of general interest with which that fund has been entrusted.

In *Deutsche Post v. GZS Deutsche Post v. Citicorp*, Case C-147/97, 2000 ECJ CELEX LEXIS 73, [2000] ECR I-825, the ECJ upheld legislation that permitted the application of internal rate charges to bulk mail posted in the Netherlands in order to take advantage of lower postal rates in that country. The mailings had originated in Germany, were mailed in the Netherlands, but were intended for German recipients. The ECJ considered that since under normal procedures ("Terminal Dues") Deutsche Post, which had a monopoly on the delivery of mail in Germany, would be unable to recover the full cost from the Netherlands post office for delivering such mail (under agreements relating to international mail delivery) a law that entitled it to add a border crossing surcharge was not a violation of EC 82/TFEU 102, notwithstanding that the senders had no choice but to pay the charge as long as the charge allowed for any payment received from the Netherlands postal service.

## [D]   Use of the Private Sector to Carry Out a State Policy

### PASCAL VAN EYCKE v. ASPA NV
#### Case 267/86, 1988 ECJ CELEX LEXIS 174, [1988] ECR 4769

[A dispute had arisen between Mr van Eycke, the plaintiff, and ASPA NV, a Belgian financial institution, concerning the rate of interest payable on a savings deposit which the plaintiff intended to make with ASPA. It is apparent from the documents before the Court that, after learning of the interest rates on savings deposits advertised by ASPA, the plaintiff went there in order to make a deposit on the terms advertised. When ASPA subsequently informed him that it was required, by virtue of a Royal Decree of 13 March 1986, to apply terms that were less favourable than those offered in its advertisement, the plaintiff brought an action before the national court for a declaration that ASPA could not rely on that royal decree in order to justify a change in its terms regarding savings deposits, on the ground that the decree was contrary to EC 81/TFEU 101 et seq.]

3 In order better to understand that Royal Decree, it should be viewed in its legal and economic context. In Belgium there has for many years been a tax exemption in respect of part of the income from savings deposits; that exemption was introduced for social reasons and in order to encourage saving, and is governed by

the basic rules set out in section 19(7) of the Income Tax Code.

4 When, at the beginning of the 1980s, a growing number of savings establishments introduced a policy of high interest rates, the Belgian Government sought to limit the scope of the tax exemption and, by the Act of 28 December 1983, made it subject to a number of conditions to be laid down by Royal Decree.

5 The Royal Decree of 29 December 1983, adopted in implementation of that Act, in substance made the grant of tax exemption subject to two conditions: the yield on savings accounts was to comprise, first, interest at a basic rate not exceeding the lowest average rate applicable on the market in question and, secondly, a fidelity or growth premium which could be fixed freely by each financial institution.

6 The Belgian monetary authorities subsequently came to the view that competition on fidelity or growth premiums was too vigorous and ran counter the general trend towards lower interest rates which characterised other forms of saving. Since the maintenance of a high level of interest on savings deposits led, according to the authorities, to the maintenance of an equally high level of interest on lending, which adversely affected the country's economic performance and the public debt, the Belgian Banking committee issued a recommendation in September 1985 to financial institutions designed to limit the yield on savings deposits. That led to the conclusion of 30 December 1985 of a self-regulatory agreement between the banks, private savings banks and public credit institutions setting the rate of interest and premiums at a maximum of 7 per cent.

7 Since not all the financial institutions adhered to that agreement, the Minister of Finance decided to introduce a system in which the public authorities would themselves determine the conditions for the tax exemption.

8 That system was established by the above-mentioned Royal Decree of 13 March 1986, which fixed the maximum level of both the basic rate of interest and the rate of the fidelity or growth premium.

\*    \*    \*

16 . . . Articles 85 [101] and 86 [102] of the Treaty per se are concerned only with the conduct of undertakings and not with national legislation. The Court has consistently held, however, that Articles 85 [101] and 86 [102] of the Treaty, in conjunction with Article 5 [TEU 4], require the member-States not to introduce or maintain in force measures, even of a legislative nature, which may render ineffective the competition rules applicable to undertakings. Such would be the case, the Court has held, if a member-State were to require or favour the adoption of agreements, decisions or concerted practices contrary to Article 85 [101] or to reinforce their effects, or to deprive its own legislation of its official character by delegating to private traders responsibility for taking decisions affecting the economic sphere.

17 . . . [B]efore the adoption of the legislation in question there were agreements between banks or concerted practices designed to restrict the yield on savings deposits. However, it is not apparent either from those findings or from the observations submitted to the Court that the legislation in question was intended to require or favour the adoption of new restrictive agreements or the implementation

of new practices. In order to assess the true scope of that legislation in the light of the criteria laid down by the Court in its case-law it is therefore necessary merely to ascertain, first, whether it may be regarded as intended to reinforce the effects of pre-existing agreements and, secondly, whether there are circumstances capable of depriving the legislation of its official character.

18 With regard to the first point it is sufficient to note that, as the Court has consistently held, legislation may be regarded as intended to reinforce the effects of pre-existing agreements, decisions or concerted practices only if it incorporates either wholly or in part the terms of agreements concluded between undertakings and requires or encourages compliance on the part of those undertakings. Although the prospect of losing the entire benefit of the preferential tax treatment for savings deposits constitutes a significant inducement to comply with the legislation in question, it is not apparent from any of the findings made by the national court in its judgment that such legislation merely confirmed both the method of restricting the yield on deposits and the level of maximum rates adopted under pre-existing agreements, decisions or practices. However, it is for the national court to enquire further into that point if it considers that there may be doubts in that regard.

19 With regard to the second point, it is apparent from the legislation in question that the authorities reserved to themselves the power to fix the maximum rates of interest on savings deposits and did not delegate that responsibility to any private trader. That legislation thus has an official character which cannot be called in question by the mere fact, emphasised by the plaintiff in the main proceedings, that according to the preamble to the Royal Decree of 13 March 1986 the Decree was adopted following consultations with the representatives of associations of credit establishments.

20 The answers to the first and second questions must therefore be that national legislation which restricts the benefit of an exemption from income tax in respect of interest on a certain category of savings deposits solely to deposits on which the interest rates and premiums paid do not exceed the maximum levels fixed by legislation is not incompatible with the obligations imposed on the member-States by Article 5 [TEU 4] of the EEC Treaty in conjunction with Articles 3(f) [repealed] and 85 [101], subject to review by the national court in order to ascertain whether the legislation in question did not merely confirm both the method of restricting the yield on deposits and the level of maximum interest rates adopted under pre-existing agreements, decisions or concerted practices.

## NOTES AND QUESTIONS

1.   Could paragraph 3 of article 3 of Regulation 1/2003 be read to address the sort of issue that arose in *Van Eycke*?

2.   Did the Court in *Van Eycke* in any way suggest that EC 81/TFEU 101 could apply to Member States? How would you define the duty of the Member States in relation to EU Competition policy based on the ECJ's judgment here? Is it possible that EC 81 and 82/TFEU 101 and 102 might also act to prevent national governments from enacting or enforcing legislation in areas other than competition law? (Another case on this subject is *Verband der Sachversicherer v. Commission*,

Case 45/85, 1987 ECJ CELEX LEXIS 140, [1987] ECR 405.)

**3.** In the *Sun/Bulk Oil* case, set out in Chapter 12, *supra*, the argument was made that the UK policy prohibiting oil exports to Israel might be unlawful as a contravention of EC 81/TFEU 101:

> 43 Bulk further argues that the destination clause included in the British contracts, which incorporates by reference the United Kingdom Government's policy, is contrary to Article 85 [101] of the Treaty. That is to say, the agreements and concerted practices which resulted from the United Kingdom policy, in particular the insertion of a destination clause in all contracts, were agreements between undertakings which were intended to restrict or distort competition within the Common Market and which affected trade between member-States. The United Kingdom policy thus authorises and even requires oil companies to infringe Article 85 [101] of the Treaty, contrary to Article 3(f), 5 [TEU 4] and 85 [101] of the Treaty.

> 44 As has just been stated, a measure such as that in question which is specifically directed at exports of oil to a non-member country is not in itself likely to restrict or distort competition within the Common Market. It cannot therefore affect trade within the Community and infringe Articles 3(f), 5 [TEU 4] and 85 [101] of the Treaty.

> 45 The answer to the first part of the question must therefore be that Articles 34 [35] and 85 [101] of the Treaty, upon their proper construction, do not prevent a member-State from adopting a policy restricting or prohibiting exports of oil to a non-member country on the basis of Article 10 of Regulation 2603/69.

Did the Court appear to accept that such an argument had any merit, although clearly unsuccessful in this case?

**4.** In *In re Vitamin C Antitrust Litigation*, 06-mdl-1738, a U.S. court had to deal with somewhat the same issues with respect to Chinese manufacturers of vitamins who concerted pricing behavior within a committee of a Chamber of Commerce that was still essentially an arm of the Government. The Chinese Government argued that the actions of the manufacturers were effectively coerced and therefore they could not be considered to have voluntarily conspired to violate U.S. antitrust laws. The subcommittee in question was apparently authorized by an official document but the court noted that it was "difficult to differentiate between a cartel that was voluntarily formed by its members, who then had to seek governmental approval, and a cartel that was mandated by governmental fiat." (See Opinion at 19.)

## CONSORZIO INDUSTRIE FIAMMIFERI (CIF) v. AUTORITÀ GARANTE DELLA CONCORRENZA E DEL MERCATO
### Case C-198/01, 2003 ECJ CELEX LEXIS 390, [2003] ECR I-8055

[Italian national legislation in 1923 had introduced a regime for the manufacture and sale of matches by establishing a consortium of domestic match manufacturers, the CIF. The decree conferred on the consortium a commercial monopoly consisting of the exclusive right to manufacture and sell matches for consumption on the Italian domestic market. In addition, the CIF was authorised to use the special government seals necessary for the application of manufacturing duty on matches (introduced by Royal Decree No 560/1923). Those seals were to be allocated between the member undertakings so that they could affix them to the boxes of matches produced.

Thus the CIF came into being as a consortium, membership of which was compulsory and restricted and which was established by Italian law for the production and sale of the matches necessary to satisfy national demand. The arrangement in its original form was struck down as unconstitutional by the Italian Constitutional court in 1983 and a new agreement was entered into between CIF and the Italian state in 1992 after the fiscal monopoly was abolished. The price of matches was to be set by the government minister while the CIF quota-allocation committee was authorized to set sales quotas among the members.

The Italian Competition Authority opened a proceeding following a complaint from a German match manufacturer who was alleging that it was experiencing difficulties in distributing its products on the Italian market. It was empowered to investigate both under Italian competition law and EC law. In its final decision in 2000, the Authority found that the conduct adopted by the operators on the Italian market for matches, although being a more or less direct consequence of the legislation was none the less partly attributable to autonomous economic decisions. The CIF challenged the Authority's decision in the Italian courts.]

63 The CIF submits that, by requiring it to allocate quotas between the member undertakings? regardless of the rules and criteria by reference to which the quotas are set? the Italian legislature eliminated *ab initio* any opportunity which those undertakings might have had to engage in competition in order to win larger market shares.

64 It explains that Article 4 of the 1992 agreement requires match production to be allocated between member undertakings by a committee, the quota allocation committee, composed of representatives from the industry and presided over by an official from the State Monopolies Board, appointed by the Finance Minister.

65 Therefore, quite apart from the quota actually awarded to each undertaking, the quota-allocation system imposed by the legislature eliminates in principle competition between the member undertakings, which must in any event comply with the production quota allocated. Consequently, any competitive effort intended to increase production is futile.

66 . . . [I]t is appropriate to consider first whether national legislation of the kind at issue in the main proceedings precludes undertakings from engaging in autonomous conduct which remains capable of preventing, restricting or distorting competition and, if it does, to go on to ascertain whether any additional restrictions for which the undertakings are blamed are actually attributable to the Member State concerned.

67 . . . [T]he possibility of excluding particular anti-competitive conduct from the scope of Article 81 [101] (1) EC on the ground that it has been required of the undertakings in question by existing national legislation or that the legislation has

precluded all scope for any competitive conduct on their part has been only partially accepted by the Court of Justice . . .

68 . . . [P]rice competition does not constitute the only effective form of competition or that to which absolute priority must in all circumstances be given . . .

69 Consequently, pre-determination of the sales price of matches by the Italian State does not, on its own, rule out all scope for competitive conduct. Even if limited, competition may operate through other factors.

70 Third, although the Italian legislation at issue in the main proceedings confers on the CIF, a consortium membership of which is compulsory for manufacturers, power to allocate production between the member undertakings, it does not set out either the rules or the criteria by reference to which allocation is to be carried out. In addition . . . it seems that the CIF's commercial monopoly was abolished as early as 1983 when the prohibition on non-members of the consortium manufacturing and selling matches was lifted.

71 In those circumstances, the remaining competition between the member undertakings is liable to distortion going beyond that already brought about by the legal obligation itself.

72 In that regard, the investigation carried out by the Authority revealed a system of ongoing and *ad hoc* transfers of production quotas and agreements on exchanges of quotas between the undertakings, that is to say agreements which were not provided for by the law.

73 In addition, the Commission referred to a fixed quota of about 15% set aside for imports. In its submission, that quota was not set by national law and thus the CIF enjoyed autonomous decision-making power in that regard.

74 The Commission also submits that the agreement concluded between the CIF and Swedish Match, which, as early as 1994, enabled Swedish Match to supply significant quantities of matches for the CIF to sell in Italy in return for Swedish Match's undertaking not to enter the Italian market directly, bears witness to the CIF's freedom of action as regards business decisions.

75 It is for the referring court to assess whether there are any grounds for such assertions.

## NOTES AND QUESTIONS

1.  How did the Court view the quota allocation process — did it excuse the companies from all competition?

2.  Conflicts between antitrust law and state law occur in the U.S. also. The issue may arise as to the legal position where a state actively *condones* a practice otherwise potentially *violative* of federal anti-trust law. It seems that a two-pronged test is applied: First, is the activity being carried on in compliance with the "clearly articulated and affirmatively expressed" policy of the state? Second, is the state engaging in active supervision? See *Southern Motor Carriers Rate Conference Inc. v. United States*, 471 U.S. 48 (1985), and *Town of Hallie v. City of Eau Claire*, 471 U.S. 34 (1985).

3. As the *Fiammiferi* case suggests, in the EU context, state-mandated action will generally cause an agreement to fall outside the scope of EC 81/TFEU 101 on the grounds that the parties had no free will in the matter. However, clearly it was difficult to establish that this was so in that case. See also *BNIC v. Clair*, Case 123/83, [1985] ECR 391. Here, the Bureau National Interprofessional du Cognac encompassed members of a wine growers' group and a dealers' group. The Court stated:

> 16 The Board maintains that the agreement between the two groups was not made on the initiative of undertakings but under the aegis, and according to the procedure laid down in the internal rules, of the Board, which, according to French administrative case law, constitutes an institution of public law in view of the manner in which it was created, the rules concerning its financing, organization, functioning and the appointment of its members and the public service mission entrusted to it. Consequently, its activity is not covered by Article 85 [101] of the Treaty.

> 17 That argument cannot be accepted. Article 85 [101] states that it applies to agreements between undertakings and decisions by associations of undertakings. As the defendant in the main proceedings and the Commission have rightly observed, the legal framework within which such agreements are made and such decisions are taken and the classification given to that framework under the various national legal systems are irrelevant as far as the applicability of the Community rules on competition and in particular Article 85 [101] of the Treaty are concerned.

> 18 The Board observes that the members who attended its general meeting and who negotiated and concluded the agreement in question were all appointed by the Minister for Agriculture. Thus, they do not represent the various trade organizations from which they come, and the agreement made between them cannot be regarded as an agreement between associations of undertakings.

> 19 That argument cannot be accepted. Article 85 [101] must be interpreted as covering such an agreement, since it was negotiated and concluded by persons who, although appointed by the public authorities, were, apart from the two appointed directly by the minister, proposed for appointment by the trade organizations directly concerned and who consequently must be regarded as in fact representing those organizations in the negotiation and conclusion of the agreement.

4. State liability for causing private parties to breach EC 81 or 82/TFEU 101 and 102 was originally established in *INNO v. ATAB*, 13/77, [1977] ECR 2115.

5. For a commentary on this complex case, see P. Nebbia, *Case C-198/01, Consorzio Industrie Fiammiferi (CIF) v. Autorità Garante della Concorrenza e del Mercato'* (2004) 41 CML REV. 839.

# Part VI

# CITIZENSHIP AND FUNDAMENTAL RIGHTS

# Chapter 17

# FREE MOVEMENT AND NON-DISCRIMINATION

## § 17.01  OVERVIEW

**Template** Article 8, Sections 8.1 and 8.2; Charter of Fundamental Rights, Article 45

***Materials in this chapter*** This chapter concentrates on the two fundamental rights that comprise the core elements of EU citizenship: free movement for all Union citizens and non-discrimination on grounds of nationality. These rights cover all nationals of the Member States, but free movement rights are more developed and extensive for those who engage in economic activity. In this chapter, while free movement rights include those for anyone engaged in an economic activity, those more extensive rights are addressed in the context of free movement for "workers", which may seem a somewhat anachronistic term but one now imbued with precise meaning in EU law.

The difference between the rights for citizens in general compared with workers (as well as others exercising economic freedoms) comes down to their respective entitlement to state benefits such as unemployment pay, health insurance, education and other social support. Workers who have exercised free movement rights are to be treated on an equal basis with nationals of the host state in this regard. It is quite evident of course that without equal treatment in this area (including for family members), workers would be prevented or at least heavily dissuaded from taking work in another Member State. By contrast, the right of citizens in general to exercise free movement and residence in another Member State is conditioned on their not becoming a charge on public finances at least for an initial five-year period after they have taken up residence.

There is now a highly developed body of law (both as regards EU legislation and extensive judicial interpretation) relating to state benefits for EU workers. This chapter alludes to this topic but does not address it in any detail. Rather, the materials have been chosen to illustrate the extent of the free movement right as it may be affected by measures that create restrictions on either inbound or outbound movement. Such measures range from direct immigration rules through to laws that on their face have nothing to do with immigration or emigration controls. Parallels with the development of the law relating to the other freedoms will be evident.

The chapter then addresses *citizenship* rights of free movement, focusing on the scope of application (i.e., that there must be an EU context in which rights are asserted) and the condition regarding there being no charge on public finances.

The last section contains materials dealing with non-discrimination on grounds of nationality where the materials provide examples of direct and indirect discrimination and also address what is meant by the reference to the "scope of application of the Treaties" in EC 12/TFEU 18.

***Legitimate restrictions on free movement*** The abolition of immigration and residence restrictions has always been subject to exceptions based on public policy, public security or public health. The EU has legislated extensively on how these exceptions are to be applied by the Member States. This legislation has gradually rendered it less necessary for individuals to invoke the fundamental rights of the Treaty when they are denied entry or faced with expulsion. It is more likely today that an individual will be invoking a directive, national implementing legislation or Union regulations.

***Comparison with U.S.*** In the EU, nationality was and remains a status conferred by each Member State and thus movement between Member States was and is treated as an immigration matter, which clearly distinguishes the EU from the U.S. or any other conventional federation. As noted above, historically in the EU, the relaxation of immigration between Member States was based entirely on economic factors. In this connection although there is a considerable degree of overlapping protection, U.S. enforcement of political unification and free interstate migration and the constitutional limitations on state barriers to interstate movements of goods and services are less stringent than those restricting state interference with interstate movement of people. This suggests that in the United States, personal movement interstate is a more fundamental freedom than interstate commercial activity.

In the same vein, Professor Lawrence Tribe has noted that "the negative implications of the U.S. commerce clause derive principally from a political theory of union, not from an economic theory of free trade. The function of the clause is to ensure national solidarity, not economic efficiency."

For a parallel in the U.S. to the kinds of issues that arise in the cases in this chapter, one might look to requirements for residence, or a minimum residence period, in a state, to receive benefits, exercise a profession or run for public office. Such rules would not violate the privileges and immunities clause or the Fourteenth Amendment to the U.S. Constitution when applied in a balanced and proportionate manner.

***An historical perspective on immigration restrictions*** Paradoxically, the need to legislate rights of free movement and residence seems to be a fairly recent development. At the time the U.S. Constitution was adopted, there were virtually no generalized constraints on movement of people and this was generally true also in Europe, i.e., passport and immigration controls were largely unknown. Only quite recently (the early part of the twentieth century) were such controls introduced in Europe. See, in this regard, K. Lewin, *The Free Movement of Workers*, 2 CML REV. 300 (1964).

If restrictions on movement between sovereign nations are a relatively recent phenomenon requiring treaties between nations to remove them, then it is a further paradox that restrictions on movement of nationals *within* sovereign states also became a reality in some countries during the twentieth century, even in peacetime. This was the case within the former Soviet Union and the Communist countries of Eastern and Central Europe, where citizens were often restricted from moving freely within the territory, at least for the purposes of taking up residence, without obtaining official approval.

***Evolution of EU Citizenship*** Over the nearly 50 years of existence of the European Communities and now the European Union, there has been a gradual shift toward integration going beyond the purely economic realm. As already observed, this shift picked up momentum with the TEU, which created the status of EU citizenship.

EU citizenship is not the same as EU nationality — there is no such thing. Nationality is still a matter for each Member State. Hence unlike the United States, freedom of movement and residence does not flow from a unified federal base. Instead, the key premise of EU citizenship is that any EU Member State national should, by virtue of that nationality, have the right to reside in any other Member State. As TFEU 20 states, EU citizenship is additional to nationality.

Although one might conclude that EU citizenship today grants a right for any national of any Member State to reside anywhere in the EU and enjoy the rights and privileges accorded to nationals of the host state, the wording of TFEU 21 indicates that they do not actually go this far. The right of residence is "subject to the limitations and conditions laid down in this Treaty." So an important question is whether or to what degree the rights of individuals are extended beyond the exercise of economic activity.

In this regard, the ECJ case law has been of crucial importance in developing the matter. Indeed, in the past few years, the ECJ case law has been developing at a steady rate in the field of EU citizenship and on the free movement of persons, including on the free movement of persons from third countries. Several important cases have recently been decided: (*Metock*, Case C-127/08, 2008 ECJ EUR-Lex LEXIS 1951, [2008] ECR I-6241; *Grunkin and Paul*, Case C-353/06, 2008 ECJ EUR-Lex LEXIS 2141, [2008] ECR I-7639; *Vatsouras* Case C-22/08, 2009 ECJ EUR-Lex LEXIS 455, [2009] ECJ I-4585; and *Foerster* Case C-158/07, 2008 ECJ EUR-Lex 2144, [2008], ECR I-8507.). This area is now one of the legal areas in which judgments are very much awaited, since the ECJ is, with regard to the free movement of persons, once again almost truly playing the role of a legislator.

***The political implications of free movement*** EU law on free movement has become a lightning rod for those opposed to further development of the EU. The opportunity for people looking for work to move from the new central European Member States to the prosperous western Member States has aroused many concerns about threats to jobs and wage levels (this notwithstanding the transitional arrangements that permit them to derogate from the free movement provisions of the Treaties). Immigration from both within and outside the EU, and the threat of immigration from Turkey if it becomes a member, are just as contentious. From a legal/constitutional perspective, the issues are exacerbated by the introduction of the provisions on citizenship in the TEU. Altogether, this has become the area of EU law that today most closely touches the general population and is capable of generating extremely strong political shockwaves. The "Turkish question" also played a significant part in the rejection of the Constitution Treaty.

Immigration, at least illegal immigration, is of course an issue of current significance in the United States as well, but without the added dimension of internal movement, since freedom of movement and the right to reside anywhere within the United States have always been basic principles of the federal structure. Citizenship and nationality are conferred at the federal level. States therefore cannot invoke prohibitions on movement based on nationality, while the federal government has responsibility for immigration control for nationals of other countries.

For a more detailed account of this subject see for example E. GUILD, THE LEGAL ELEMENTS OF EUROPEAN IDENTITY (Kluwer, 2004). See also M. Dougan, *The constitutional dimension to the case law on Union citizenship* (2007) 1 EL REV. 613.

In a recent report by the Commission on "Citizenship of the Union", COM (2008) 85 Final, can be found a great many interesting statistics including the percentages of the populations of each Member State now comprised of nationals of other Member States. (In the UK, this figure is 2.1%)

***Abolition of internal border controls and treatment of third country nationals***
The Schengen Conventions (more generally described in Chapter 2) were designed to establish a system of controls at the EU's external borders so that, once an individual has cleared immigration at that checkpoint, he or she should be able to move around freely within the Union space. This arrangement was rendered into Union law by Regulation 562/2006 [2006] OJ L105/1 establishing a Union borders code. The code does not entirely eliminate internal border checks. Thus, article 21 provides that police checks at borders may be permissible as long as they do not amount to systematic border control and are based on specific information resulting in spot checks. For this internal space to be effective, the Union also has adopted a uniform visa application system: Regulation 810/2009, [2009] OJ L 243/1. Since the UK and Ireland do not operate within the Schengen system, however, the uniform system does apply to visas for those countries, a matter that has caused some consternation within the tourist trade, in that third country nationals requiring visas (such as nationals of China) may decide not to visit the UK because an extra layer of bureaucracy has to be dealt with. Applications for asylum within the EU are addressed by Regulation 343/2003, [2003] OJ L. 50/1, while Directive 2005/85 [2005] OJ L 326/13 addresses the right to remain in the EU pending consideration of the application and Directive 2003/9 [2003] OJ L31/18 deals with their treatment during this period. Directive 2004/83 [2004] OJ L 304/12 lays down minimum standards for granting asylum.

The right of non-EU nationals to reside permanently within the EU is governed by Directive 2003/109, [2003] OJ L 16/44.

***Discrimination on grounds of nationality*** In a system of nation states each conferring its own nationality, the different treatment of nationals versus foreigners is a permitted and necessary consequence of the status of nationality. Nationals and non-nationals are not in the same situation and thus restrictions on entry and residence do not constitute discrimination. This was exemplified in the *Van Duyn* case in this chapter. For this reason, while the TFEU prohibits discrimination on grounds of nationality, this cannot be regarded as a "fundamental right" in the same way that the rights described in the following chapters are. One may think of it logically as being the necessary corollary to free movement, in that it applies once that right has been exercised or in conjunction with that right. It is thus in a different category from the rights listed in article 21 (1) of the Charter of Fundamental Rights. While the Charter specifically mentions it as a fundamental right (article 21(2), it simply repeats the formula in the TFEU, which limits the prohibition to circumstances within the scope of application of that Treaty. The materials will illustrate, however, that as a result of the developing implications of citizenship, this form of discrimination can arise in cases quite independent of the exercise of free movement rights.

***Discrimination or free movement rights?*** The nature of some types of restrictions arising out of Member State measures can result in both the provisions on free movement and the rule against discrimination being applicable. As noted already, the right of states to exclude non-nationals is by its very nature discriminatory. The TFEU restricts this right through its statement that restrictions on free movement are to be eliminated, but does not eliminate it altogether given the exceptions built into EC 39/TFEU 45. By contrast, the prohibition on discrimination conceptually relates to the situation where foreigners have exercised free movement rights and seek to take up, or have taken up, employment. This prohibition is not subject to the exceptions that apply to the free movement provisions.

In practice this distinction has become confused in cases where a Member State measure has an indirect discriminatory effect that makes the exercise of free movement rights more difficult for non-nationals. Does this then mean that the measure should be considered as restricting free movement and thus potentially justified under one of the exceptions? Or is the indirect discriminatory effect to be considered as simply triggering the prohibition on discrimination, in which case no exceptions are permitted? The Court has taken both approaches, as will be seen from the *Clean Car* and *Angonese* cases in this chapter, and it is not easy to distinguish the approaches from a logical standpoint.

## § 17.02   RIGHT OF FREE MOVEMENT FOR WORKERS

### [A]   Who is a "Worker"?

#### LEVIN v. STAATSSECRETARIS VAN JUSTITIE
Case 53/81, 1982 ECJ EUR-LEXIS 184; [982] ECR 35

[Mrs Levin, a British national and the wife of a national of a non-member country had applied for a permit to reside in the Netherlands. This was refused because at the time she was considered by the Dutch authorities not to be a "worker" Subsequently she found a low-paying part-time job but the permit was again denied in the first place because she did not earn enough to support her household. She argued that in any event, she and her husband had property and income more than sufficient to support themselves, even without pursuing such employment activity, but this seems only to have reinforced the authorities' second reason for denial, namely that her employment was merely being used as a means to enable her husband to reside in the Netherlands.]

14 In conformity with this view the recitals in the preamble to Regulation (EEC) No 1612/68 contain a general affirmation of the right of all workers in the Member States to pursue the activity of their choice within the Community, irrespective of whether they are permanent, seasonal or frontier workers or workers who pursue their activities for the purpose of providing services. Furthermore, although article 4 of directive 68/36/EEC grants the right of residence to workers upon the mere production of the document on the basis of which they entered the territory and of a confirmation of engagement from the employer or a certificate of employment, it does not subject this right to any condition relating to the kind of employment or to the amount of income derived from it.

15 An interpretation which reflects the full scope of these concepts is also in conformity with the objectives of the Treaty which include, according to articles 2 and 3, the abolition, as between member states, of obstacles to freedom of movement for persons, with the purpose inter alia of promoting throughout the Community a harmonious development of economic activities and a raising of the standard of living. Since part-time employment, although it may provide an income lower than what is considered to be the minimum required for subsistence, constitutes for a large number of persons an effective means of improving their living conditions, the effectiveness of Community law would be impaired and the achievement of the objectives of the Treaty would be jeopardized if the enjoyment of rights conferred by the principle of freedom of movement for workers were reserved solely to persons engaged in full-time employment and earning, as a result, a wage at least equivalent to the guaranteed minimum wage in the sector under consideration.

16 It follows that the concepts of "worker" and "activity as an employed person" must be interpreted as meaning that the rules relating to freedom of movement for workers also concern persons who pursue or wish to pursue an activity as an employed person on a part-time basis only and who, by virtue of that fact obtain or would obtain only remuneration lower than the minimum guaranteed remuneration in the sector under consideration. In this regard no distinction may be made between those who wish to make do with their income from such an activity and those who supplement that income with other income, whether the latter is derived from property or from the employment of a member of their family who accompanies them.

17 It should however be stated that whilst part-time employment is not excluded from the field of application of the rules on freedom of movement for workers, those rules cover only the pursuit of effective and genuine activities, to the exclusion of activities on such a small scale as to be regarded as purely marginal and ancillary. It follows both from the statement of the principle of freedom of movement for workers and from the place occupied by the rules relating to that principle in the system of the Treaty as a whole that those rules guarantee only the free movement of persons who pursue or are desirous of pursuing an economic activity.

* * *

21 . . . [T]he advantages which Community law confers in the name of [free movement for workers] may be relied upon only by persons who actually pursue or seriously wish to pursue activities as employed persons. They do not, however mean that the enjoyment of this freedom may be made to depend upon the aims pursued by a national of a Member State in applying for entry upon and residence in the territory of another Member State, provided that he there pursues or wishes to pursue an activity which meets the criteria specified above, that is to say, an effective and genuine activity as an employed person.

22 Once this condition is satisfied, the motives which may have prompted the worker to seek employment in the member state concerned are of no account and must not be taken into consideration.

## NOTES AND QUESTIONS

1.  Given the Court's reasoning here, was Mrs. Levin to be considered a worker or not? Was there not a strong hint here that EU rights were being abused? Referring to the *Leclerc* case (Chapter 13), does not the Court take a dim view of such "abuse"?

2.  Other cases have addressed a variety of situations where a person might well be on the margin of what is meant by the EU term "worker" See, for example, *Lair v. Universtät Hanover*, Case 39-86 1988 ECJ EUR-Lex LEXIS 116 [1988] ECR 3161, where a French national residing in Germany had become a student at the Hanover University after having been employed for two years some time previously, and with sporadic employment thereafter, she was considered by the ECJ to be a worker.

3.  Given the supervening development of European citizenship, would persons like Mrs. Levin need today to take employment to gain residence rights?

## [B]  Direct Restrictions on Free Movement of Workers

### LYNNE WATSON AND ALLESSANDRO BELMANN
#### Case 118/75, [1976] ECR 1185

[Criminal proceedings had been brought against a British national who spent several months in Italy and an Italian national who gave her accommodation. Ms Watson had failed to register with the police in violation of Italian law. The Court was not provided with information as to the basis of Ms Watson's residence but gave an interpretation based on assumption that she had status as a person exercising the economic right of free movement.]

16 By creating the principle of freedom of movement for persons and by conferring on any person falling within its ambit the right of access to the territory of the Member States, for the purposes intended by the Treaty, Community law has not excluded the power of Member States to adopt measures enabling the national authorities to have an exact knowledge of population movements affecting their territory.

17 Under the terms of Article 8 (2) of Directive No 68/360 and Article 4 (2) of

Directive 73/148, the competent authorities in the Member States may require nationals of the other Member States to report their presence to the authorities of the State concerned.

18 Such an obligation could not in itself be regarded as an infringement of the rules concerning freedom of movement for persons.

However, such an infringement might result from the legal formalities in question if the control procedures to which they refer were such as to restrict the freedom of movement required by the Treaty or to limit the right conferred by the Treaty on nationals of the Member States to enter and reside in the territory of any other Member State for the purposes intended by Community law.

19 In particular as regards the period within which the arrival of foreign nationals must be reported, the provisions of the Treaty are only infringed if the period fixed is unreasonable.

20 Among the penalties attaching to failure to comply with the prescribed declaration and registration formalities, deportation, in relation to persons protected by Community law, is certainly incompatible with the provisions of the Treaty since, as the Court has already confirmed in other cases, such a measure negates the very right conferred and guaranteed by the Treaty.

21 As regards other penalties, such as fines and detention, whilst the national authorities are entitled to impose penalties in respect of a failure to comply with the terms of provisions requiring foreign nationals to notify their presence which are comparable to those attaching to infringements of provisions of equal importance by nationals, they are not justified in imposing a penalty so disproportionate to the gravity of the infringement that it becomes an obstacle to the free movement of persons.

22 In so far as national rules concerning the control of foreign nationals do not involve restrictions on freedom of movement for persons and on the right conferred by the Treaty on persons protected by Community law, to enter and reside in the territory of the Member States, the application of such legislation, where it is based upon objective factors, cannot constitute 'discrimination on grounds of nationality', prohibited under Article 7[18] of the Treaty.

23 Provisions which require residents of the host State to inform the public authorities of the identity of foreign nationals for whom they provide accommodation, and which are for the most part connected with the internal order of the State, can only be called into question from the point of view of Community law if they place an indirect restriction on freedom of movement for persons.

The foregoing observations concerning the obligations imposed on nationals of other Member States are therefore equally valid as regards to the above mentioned requirement.

## NOTES AND QUESTIONS

**1.** In light of the subsequent development of Union citizenship, is it appropriate that Member States should be able to maintain laws requiring registration of non-nationals?

**2.** The principles in *Watson* also apply generally to spouses of EU citizens. See *Commission v. Belgium*, Case 321/87, 1989 ECJ CELEX LEXIS 159, [1989] ECR 997, although this was not the case where the non-citizen has entered the State unlawfully. In *Secretary of State for the Home Department v. Akrich*, Case C-109/01, 2003 ECJ CELEX LEXIS 358, [2003] ECR I-9607, the Court also held that, in order to benefit from the rights of entry into and residence in a Member State, the non-Union spouse of a Union citizen must be lawfully resident in a Member State when he moves to another Member State. As noted in Chapter 5, in *Metock e.a. v. Minister for Justice, Equality and Law Reform* Case C-127/08, 2008 ECJ EUR-Lex LEXIS 1951, [2008] ECR I-6241, the Court reconsidered its judgment in *Akrich* and stated that such rights could not be placed under the condition of prior lawful residence even for a spouse who would have entered the territory of that Member State unlawfully.

## VAN DUYN v. HOME OFFICE
### Case 41/74 [1974] ECR 1337

[See the excerpt from this case in Chapter 5 for the factual background. For current directive provisions see Directive 2004/38 [2004] OJ L 158/77, articles 28-33, appearing in the Documentary Supplement]

16 [T]he Court is asked to rule whether Article 48[45] of the Treaty and Article 3 of Directive 64/221 must be interpreted as meaning that a Member State, in the performance of its duty to base a measure taken on grounds of public policy exclusively on the personal conduct of the individual concerned is entitled to take into account as matters of personal conduct:

(a) the fact that the individual is or has been associated with some body or organization the activities of which the member-State considers contrary to the public good but which are not unlawful in that State;

(b) the fact that the individual intends to take employment in the member-State with such a body or organization it being the case that no restrictions are placed upon nationals of the member-State who wish to take similar employment with such a body or organization.

17 It is necessary, first, to consider whether association with a body or an organization can in itself constitute personal conduct within the meaning of Article 3 of Directive 64/221. Although a person's past association cannot, in general, justify a decision refusing him the right to move freely within the Community, it is nevertheless the case that present association, which reflects participation in the activities of the body or of the organization as well as identification with its aims and its designs, may be considered a voluntary act of the person concerned and, consequently, as part of his personal conduct within the meaning of the provision cited.

18 This third question further raises the problem of what importance must be attributed to the fact that the activities of the organization in question, which are considered by the member-State as contrary to the public good, are not however prohibited by national law. It should be emphasized that the concept of public policy in the context of the Community and where, in particular, it is used as a justification for derogating from the fundamental principle of freedom of movement for workers, must be interpreted strictly, so that its scope cannot be determined unilaterally by each member-State without being subject to control by the institutions of the Community. Nevertheless, the particular circumstances justifying recourse to the concept of public policy may vary from one country to another and from one period to another, and it is therefore necessary in this matter to allow the competent national authorities an area of discretion within the limits imposed by the Treaty.

19 It follows from the above that where the competent authorities of a member-State have clearly defined their standpoint as regards the activities of a particular organization and where, considering it to be socially harmful, they have taken administrative measures to counteract these activities, the member-State cannot be required, before it can rely on the concept of public policy, to make such activities unlawful, if recourse to such a measure is not thought appropriate in the circumstances.

20 The question raises finally the problem of whether a member-State is entitled, on grounds of public policy, to prevent a national of another member-State from taking gainful employment within its territory with a body or organization, it being the case that no similar restriction is placed upon its own nationals.

21 In this connection, the Treaty, while enshrining the principle of freedom of movement for workers without any discrimination on grounds of nationality, admits, in Article 48 [45] (3), limitations justified on grounds of public policy, public security or public health to the rights deriving from this principle. Under the terms of the provision cited above, the right to accept offers of employment actually made, the right to move freely within the territory of member-State for this purpose, and the right to stay in a member-State for the purpose of employment are, among others, all subject to such limitations. Consequently, the effect of such limitations, when they apply, is that leave to enter the territory of a member-State and the right to reside there may be refused to a national of another member-State.

22 Furthermore, it is a principle of international law, which the EEC Treaty cannot be assumed to disregard in the relations between Member States, that a State is precluded from refusing its own nationals the right of entry or residence.

23 It follows that a member-State, for reasons of public policy, can, where it deems necessary, refuse a national of another member-State the benefit of the principle of freedom of movement for workers in a case where such a national proposes to take up a particular offer of employment even though the member-State does not place a similar restriction upon its own nationals . . .

24 Accordingly, the reply to the third question must be that Article 48[45] of the EEC Treaty and Article 3 (1) of Directive 64/221 are to be interpreted as meaning that a member-State, in imposing restrictions justified on grounds of public policy, is entitled to take into account, as a matter of personal conduct of the individual

concerned, the fact that the individual is associated with some body or organization the activities of which the member-State considers socially harmful but which are not unlawful in that State, despite the fact that no restriction is placed upon nationals of the said member-State who wish to take similar employment with these same bodies or organizations.

## NOTES AND QUESTIONS

**1.** In *Van Duyn* the Court found that the British Government had not violated article 48 (EC39/TFEU 45) of the Treaty in excluding Ms. Van Duyn. Why wasn't this exclusion a violation of EC 12/TFEU18? How, precisely, did the ECJ justify its position regarding non-nationals?

**2.** In *Adoui v. Belgium*, Joined Cases 115 & 116/81 [1982] ECR 1665, two prostitutes appealed against the Belgian authorities' refusal to grant them a residence permit in Belgium, where they were seeking to practice their trade. The ECJ held that Member States could not deny residence to non-nationals for conduct which, if practiced by a state's nationals, was not subject to repressive measures or other steps to combat it.

Are *Van Duyn* and *Adoui* consistent in their approach to the scope for applying restrictions on entry (and consequent residence) to non-nationals that could not be applied to nationals?

**3.** On the formalities linked to the entry to another country, see also *Wijsenbeek* Case C-378/97, which recognized the obligation to produce an ID card to prove that the individual is indeed a national of one of the Member States, and *Salah Oulane* Case C-215/03, 2005 ECJ EUR-Lex LEXIS 330, [2005] ECR I-1215, in which the Court watered down its previous *Wijsenbeek* ruling. The *Salah Oulane* judgment's operative part states:

> . . . [T]he recognition by a Member State of the right of residence of a recipient of services who is a national of another Member State may not be made subject to his production of a valid identity card or passport, where his identity and nationality can be proven unequivocally by other means.

> 2. It is contrary to Article 49 EC [56] for nationals of a Member State to be required in another Member State to present a valid identity card or passport in order to prove their nationality, when the latter State does not impose a general obligation on its own nationals to provide evidence of identity, and permits them to prove their identity by any means allowed by national law.

> 3. A detention order with a view to deportation in respect of a national of another Member State, imposed on the basis of failure to present a valid identity card or passport even when there is no threat to public policy, constitutes an unjustified restriction on the freedom to provide services and is therefore contrary to Article 49 EC [56].

> 4. It is for nationals of a Member State residing in another Member State in their capacity as recipients of services to provide evidence establishing

that their residence is lawful. If no such evidence is provided, the host Member State may undertake deportation, subject to the limits imposed by EU law.

4. Regulation 1612/68 was adopted to ensure that the laws of the Member States were modified as necessary to ensure free movement for workers (e.g., regarding the grant of work and entry permits etc.) Regulation 1408/71 covers social security matters. Social security rights are based on where the claimant resides, with qualifying periods, where required, being taken into account wherever they occurred within the EU. Obviously the ability of workers to move from state to state is limited to the extent that they could not ensure that their families also could move and enjoy the same rights as nationals. There are many decided cases in this area of derivative rights.

## THE QUEEN v. IMMIGRATION APPEAL TRIBUNAL, EX PARTE GUSTAFF DESIDERIUS ANTONISSEN
### Case C-292/89, 1991 ECJ EUR-Lex LEXIS 189, [1991] ECR I-745.

[Mr Antonissen, a Belgian national, arrived in the United Kingdom in October 1984. He had not yet found work there when, on 30 March 1987, he was sentenced to two terms of imprisonment for unlawful possession of cocaine and possession of that drug with intent to supply. He was released on parole on 21 December 1987. The Secretary of State decided to deport him considering that this would be "conducive to the public good". Mr Antonissen appealed to the relevant Tribunal which however took the view that, since he had been seeking employment in the United Kingdom for more than six months, he could no longer be treated as a worker under EU rules. Mr Antonissen sought judicial review in the High Court, which then referred questions to the ECJ regarding the right of the UK to execute the deportation.

9 . . . [I]t has been argued that, according to the strict wording of Article 48 [45] of the Treaty, Community nationals are given the right of move freely within the territory of the Member States for the purpose only of accepting offers of employment actually made (Article 48 [45] (3)(a) and (b)) whilst the right to stay in the territory of a Member State is stated to be for the purpose of employment (Article 48 [45] (3)(c)).

10 Such an interpretation would exclude the right of a national of a Member State to move freely and to stay in the territory of the other Member States in order to seek employment there, and cannot be upheld.

11 Indeed . . . freedom of movement for workers forms one of the foundations of the Community and, consequently, the provisions laying down that freedom must be given a broad interpretation . . .

12 Moreover, a strict interpretation of Article 48 [45](3) would jeopardize the actual chances that a national of a Member State who is seeking employment will find it in another Member State, and would, as a result, make that provision ineffective.

13 It follows that Article 48 [45] (3) must be interpreted as enumerating, in a non-exhaustive way, certain rights benefiting nationals of Member States in the

context of the free movement of workers and that that freedom also entails the right for nationals of Member States to move freely within the territory of the other Member States and to stay there for the purposes of seeking employment.

14 Moreover, that interpretation of the Treaty corresponds to that of the Community legislature, as appears from the provisions adopted in order to implement the principle of free movement, in particular Articles 1 and 5 of Regulation (EEC) No 1612/68 . . . which presuppose that Community nationals are entitled to move in order to look for employment, and hence to stay, in another Member State.

15 It must therefore be ascertained whether the right, under Article 48 [45] and the provisions of Regulation No 1612/68. . . . to stay in a Member State for the purposes of seeking employment can be subjected to a temporal limitation.

16 In that regard, it must be pointed out in the first place that the effectiveness of Article 48 [45] is secured in so far as Community legislation or, in its absence, the legislation of a Member State gives persons concerned a reasonable time in which to apprise themselves, in the territory of the Member State concerned, of offers of employment corresponding to their occupational qualifications and to take, where appropriate, the necessary steps in order to be engaged.

17 The national court referred to the declaration recorded in the Council minutes at the time of the adoption of the aforesaid Regulation No 1612/68 and of Council Directive 68/360/EEC (of the same date) on the abolition of restrictions on movement and residence within the Community for workers of Member States and their families . . . That declaration reads as follows:

"Nationals of a Member State as referred to in Article 1 [of the directive] who move to another Member State in order to seek work there shall be allowed a minimum period of three months for the purpose; in the event of their not having found employment by the end of that period, their residence on the territory of this second State may be brought to an end.

However, if the above-mentioned persons should be taken charge of by national assistance (social welfare) in the second State during the aforesaid period they may be invited to leave the territory of this second State."

18 However, such a declaration cannot be used for the purpose of interpreting a provision of secondary legislation where, as in this case, no reference is made to the content of the declaration in the wording of the provision in question. The declaration therefore has no legal significance.

19 For their part, the United Kingdom and the Commission argue that, under Article 69(1) of Council Regulation (EEC) No 1408/71 on the application of social security schemes to employed persons, to self-employed persons and to members of their families moving within the Community . . . the Member States may limit to three months the period during which nationals from other Member States may stay in their territory in order to seek employment. According to the provision in question, an unemployed person who has acquired entitlement to benefits in a Member State and goes to another Member State to seek employment there retains entitlement to those benefits for a maximum period of three months.

20 That argument cannot be upheld. As the Advocate General has rightly observed,

there is no necessary link between the right to employment benefit in the Member State of origin and the right to stay in the host State.

21 In the absence of a Community provision prescribing the period during which Community nationals seeking employment in a Member State may stay there, a period of six months, such as that as laid down in the national legislation at issue in the main proceedings, does not appear in principle to be insufficient to enable the persons concerned to apprise themselves, in the host Member State, of offers of employment corresponding to their occupational qualifications and to take, where appropriate, the necessary steps in order to be engaged and, therefore, does not jeopardize the effectiveness of the principle of free movement. However, if after the expiry of that period the person concerned provides evidence that he is continuing to seek employment and that he has genuine chances of being engaged, he cannot be required to leave the territory of the host Member State.

## NOTES AND QUESTIONS

1. The Treaty does not describe any right to move to another Member State to seek work, yet the Court here upheld that right. What was the Court's rationale? What might it take for a person to satisfy the authorities that he or she meets the requirements laid out in paragraph 21?

2. In the United States, a leading case is *Edwards v. California*, 314 U.S. 160 (1941), where California had made it a crime to bring indigents into the State. Such restrictions were held to violate the dormant Commerce Clause principle. However, Justice Douglas took the view that the right of free movement is more fundamental, being derived from the Privileges and Immunities clause of the Constitution:

> . . . I am of the opinion that the right of persons to move freely from State to State occupies a more protected position in our constitutional system than does the movement of cattle, fruit, steel and coal across state lines. While the opinion of the Court expresses no view on that issue, the right involved is so fundamental that I deem it appropriate to indicate the reach of the constitutional question which is present. The right to move freely from State to State is an incident of *national* citizenship protected by the privileges and immunities clause of the Fourteenth Amendment against state interference. Mr. Justice Moody, in *Twining v. New Jersey*, 211 U.S. 78, 211 U.S. 97, stated,

> "Privileges and immunities of citizens of the United States . . . are only such as arise out of the nature and essential character of the National Government, or are specifically granted or secured to all citizens or persons by the Constitution of the United States."

> And he went on to state that one of those rights of *national* citizenship was "the right to pass freely from State to State." . . . Now it is apparent that this right is not specifically granted by the Constitution. Yet, before the Fourteenth Amendment, it was recognized as a right fundamental to the national character of our Federal government. It was so decided in 1867 by *Crandall v. Nevada*, 6 Wall. 35. In that case, this Court struck down a Nevada tax "upon every person leaving the State" by common carrier. Mr.

Justice Miller, writing for the Court, held that the right to move freely throughout the nation was a right of national citizenship. That the right was implied did not make it any the less "guaranteed" by the Constitution. *Id.*, p. 73 U. S. 47. To be sure, he emphasized that the Nevada statute would obstruct the right of a citizen to travel to the seat of his national government or its offices throughout the country. *And see United States v. Wheeler*, 254 U. S. 281, 254 U. S. 299. But there is not a shred of evidence in the record of the *Crandall* case that the persons there involved were en route on any such mission any more than it appears in this case that Duncan entered California to interview some federal agency. The point which Mr. Justice Miller made was merely in illustration of the damage and havoc which would ensue if the States had the power to prevent the free movement of citizens from one State to another. This is emphasized by his quotation from Chief Justice Taney's dissenting opinion in the *Passenger Cases*, 7 How. 283, 48 U.S. 283:

"We are all citizens of the United States, and, as members of the same community, must have the right to pass and repass through every part of it without interruption, as freely as in our own States."

The conclusion that the right of free movement is a right of *national* citizenship stands on firm historical ground. If a state tax on that movement, as in the *Crandall* case, is invalid, *a fortiori* a state statute which obstructs or in substance prevents that movement must fall. That result necessarily follows unless perchance a State can curtail the right of free movement of those who are poor or destitute. But to allow such an exception to be engrafted on the rights of *national* citizenship would be to contravene every conception of national unity. It would also introduce a caste system utterly incompatible with the spirit of our system of government. It would permit those who were stigmatized by a State as indigents, paupers, or vagabonds to be relegated to an inferior class of citizenship. It would prevent a citizen because he was poor from seeking new horizons in other States. It might thus withhold from large segments of our people that mobility which is basic to any guarantee of freedom of opportunity. The result would be a substantial dilution of the rights of *national* citizenship, a serious impairment of the principles of equality. Since the state statute here challenged involves such consequences, it runs afoul of the privileges and immunities clause of the Fourteenth Amendment.

## [C]  Indirect Restrictions on Free Movement of Workers

### CRIMINAL PROCEEDINGS v. CHOQUET
### Case 16/78, [1978] ECR 2293

[Mr Choquet was a French national living in Germany, where he was employed as an electrician. He was being prosecuted for driving a motor vehicle without a driving license valid under German law. In its reference, the national court asked questions relating to the apparent discrimination against non-nationals arising from the requirement to take a local driving test.]

4. The Court file shows that when the police carried out a check on the occasion of a road traffic accident in which the accused was involved he produced a driving license issued by the French authorities.

The German administration does not regard that driving license as being valid, whereas according to the provisions of the national road traffic rules a holder of a foreign driving license who has been established for more than one year in the territory of the Federal Republic of Germany is obliged to obtain a German driving license.

However, according to the information supplied during these proceedings, in that case the conditions to which the issue of the driving license are subject are simplified as compared with the procedure for the issue of the domestic driving license and do not as a general rule lead to a fresh driving test.

. . . [I]t should be pointed out, in the first place, that the Commission in a proposal for a directive on the harmonization of the laws relating to motor vehicle driving licenses, which it submitted to the Council on 5 December 1975 . . . indicated that Article 75 [71] (1) I of the Treaty relating to the implementation of a common transport policy was the legal basis of the measures proposed.

That article, which authorizes the Council to lay down "any . . . appropriate provisions" in transport matters, could indicate a solution to the dispute only by way of implementing measures adopted by the Council, and at the present stage there are none.

It must nevertheless be appreciated that national rules relating to the issue and mutual recognition of driving licences by the Member States exert an influence, both direct and indirect, on the exercise of the rights guaranteed by the provisions of the Treaty relating to freedom of movement for workers, to establishment and, subject to the reference contained in Article 61 [51](1) of the Treaty, to the provision of services in general.

In fact, taking into account the importance of individual means of transport, the possession of a driving licence duly recognized by the host State may affect the actual pursuit by persons subject to Community law of a large number of occupations for employed or self-employed persons.

5 It is apparent therefore that, even in the absence of any specific Community law provisions in this field, the Amtsgericht was right to refer its question asking the Court to rule on the possible effect of the requirements for the issue or recognition of driving licences on freedom of movement for workers, to which must be added the freedom of establishment and the freedom to provide services, which are all guaranteed by the Treaty.

6 The rules regarding the issue of driving licences, including the determination of the conditions under which a foreign driving licence may be recognized or exchanged for a domestic driving licence, fall primarily within the scope of the responsibilities devolving upon the Member States, within their national territory, concerning the safety of highway traffic.

7 A comparative study of the present position in this field in the Member States makes it clear that their laws on the issue of driving licences — especially as far as

concerns the rules for driving tests, the frequency of medical examinations, the term of validity of driving licences and the definition of the different classes of motor vehicles — differ to such an extent that the mere recognition of driving licenses for the benefit of persons who elect to reside permanently within the territory of a Member State other than the State which issued them with a driving licence cannot be contemplated unless the requirements for the issue of those driving licences are harmonized to a sufficient extent.

In these circumstances the requirements imposed by a Member State on persons established within its territory, in so far as the recognition of driving licences issued by other Member States is concerned, cannot be regarded as amounting in themselves to an obstacle to freedom of movement for workers, to freedom of establishment or to the liberalization of the provision of services.

Consequently, controls designed to guarantee to Member States that the holder of a driving license issued by another Member State who is established within their territory satisfies the requirements laid down for their own nationals by the legislation applicable in that field cannot in principle be regarded as a requirement which is incompatible with the rules of the Treaty.

8 Legislative provisions of this kind could be considered to contravene Community law only if their application were to cause persons in one Member State who had obtained a driving licence in another Member State such difficulties that those persons would in fact be hindered in the free exercise of the rights which Articles 48[45], 52[49] and 59[56] of the Treaty guarantee them in connexion with the free movement of persons, freedom of establishment and freedom to provide services.

Insistence on a driving test which clearly duplicates a test taken in another Member State for the classes of vehicle which the person concerned wishes to drive, or linguistic difficulties arising out of the procedure laid down for the conduct of any checks, or the imposition of exorbitant charges for completing the requisite formalities could all be examples of this. Such obstacles to the recognition of a driving licence issued by another Member State are not in fact in due proportion to the requirements for the safety of highway traffic.

9 The answer to the question referred must therefore be that it is not in principle incompatible with Community law for one Member State to require a national of another Member State, who is permanently established in its territory, to obtain a domestic driving licence for the purpose of driving motor vehicles, even if he is in possession of a driving licence issued by the authorities in his State of origin.

However, such a requirement may be regarded as indirectly prejudicing the exercise of the right of freedom of movement, the right of freedom of establishment or the freedom to provide services guaranteed by Articles 48[45], 52[49] and 59[56] of the Treaty respectively, and consequently as being incompatible with the Treaty, if it appears that the conditions imposed by national rules on the holder of a driving licence issued by another Member State are not in due proportion to the requirements of road safety.

## NOTES AND QUESTIONS

**1.** It is interesting to note that linguistic difficulties could be one reason why a driving test might be considered to impose an unreasonable burden. How would a Member State be required to deal with that?

**2.** Suppose the *Choquet* case had come before the courts in a State of the United States. How do you think the courts would analyze the issue and with what results?

## UNION ROYALE BELGE DES SOCIETES DE FOOTBALL ASSOCIATION ASBL AND OTHERS v. JEAN-MARC BOSMAN
### Case C-415/93, 1995 ECJ CELEX LEXIS 220, [1995] ECR I-4921

[The Belgian Football Association (URBSFA), in line with international practices and requirements laid down by UEFA and FIFA (European and international football federations), required a (professional) football club to make a payment to another club if the former wished to hire a player whose contract with the latter had come to an end. This arrangement required the issuance of a transfer certificate by URBSFA to the new club. Bosman's contract with a Belgian club had ended and he sought employment with a club in France. URBSFA refused to certify the transfer ostensibly on concerns about the financial standing of the French club. Bosman sued URBSFA and others for damages and claimed (among other things) that the transfer rules infringed his EU right to free movement. The Court addressed several important questions, the first being whether national football associations, being private, fall within the requirements of EC 39/TFEU 45]

88 UEFA considers that the disputes pending before the national court concern a purely internal Belgian situation which falls outside the ambit of Article 48 [45] of the Treaty. They concern a Belgian player whose transfer fell through because of the conduct of a Belgian club and a Belgian association.

89 . . . [T]he provisions of the Treaty concerning the free movement of workers, and particularly Article 48 [45], cannot be applied to situations which are wholly internal to a Member State, in other words where there is no factor connecting them to any of the situations envisaged by Community law.

90 However, it is clear from the findings of fact made by the national court that Mr Bosman had entered into a contract of employment with a club in another Member State with a view to exercising gainful employment in that State. By so doing, as he has rightly pointed out, he accepted an offer of employment actually made, within the meaning of Article 48 [45](3)(a).

91 Since the situation in issue in the main proceedings cannot be classified as purely internal, the argument put forward by UEFA must be dismissed.

Existence of an obstacle to freedom of movement for workers

92 It is thus necessary to consider whether the transfer rules form an obstacle to freedom of movement for workers prohibited by Article 48 [45] of the Treaty.

93 As the Court has repeatedly held, freedom of movement for workers is one of the fundamental principles of the Community and the Treaty provisions guaranteeing

that freedom have had direct effect since the end of the transitional period.

94 The Court has also held that the provisions of the Treaty relating to freedom of movement for persons are intended to facilitate the pursuit by Community citizens of occupational activities of all kinds throughout the Community, and preclude measures which might place Community citizens at a disadvantage when they wish to pursue an economic activity in the territory of another Member State . . .

95 In that context, nationals of Member States have in particular the right, which they derive directly from the Treaty, to leave their country of origin to enter the territory of another Member State and reside there in order there to pursue an economic activity . . .

96 Provisions which preclude or deter a national of a Member State from leaving his country of origin in order to exercise his right to freedom of movement therefore constitute an obstacle to that freedom even if they apply without regard to the nationality of the workers concerned . . .

97 The Court has also stated . . . that even though the Treaty provisions relating to freedom of establishment are directed mainly to ensuring that foreign nationals and companies are treated in the host Member State in the same way as nationals of that State, they also prohibit the Member State of origin from hindering the establishment in another Member State of one of its nationals or of a company incorporated under its legislation which comes within the definition contained in Article 58 [55]. The rights guaranteed by Article 52 [49] et seq. of the Treaty would be rendered meaningless if the Member State of origin could prohibit undertakings from leaving in order to establish themselves in another Member State. The same considerations apply, in relation to Article 48 [45] of the Treaty, with regard to rules which impede the freedom of movement of nationals of one Member State wishing to engage in gainful employment in another Member State.

98 It is true that the transfer rules in issue in the main proceedings apply also to transfers of players between clubs belonging to different national associations within the same Member State and that similar rules govern transfers between clubs belonging to the same national association.

99 . . . . [T]hose rules are likely to restrict the freedom of movement of players who wish to pursue their activity in another Member State by preventing or deterring them from leaving the clubs to which they belong even after the expiry of their contracts of employment with those clubs.

100 Since they provide that a professional footballer may not pursue his activity with a new club established in another Member State unless it has paid his former club a transfer fee agreed upon between the two clubs or determined in accordance with the regulations of the sporting associations, the said rules constitute an obstacle to freedom of movement for workers.

101 As the national court has rightly pointed out, that finding is not affected by the fact that the transfer rules adopted by UEFA in 1990 stipulate that the business relationship between the two clubs is to exert no influence on the activity of the player, who is to be free to play for his new club. The new club must still pay the fee in issue, under pain of penalties which may include its being struck off for debt,

which prevents it just as effectively from signing up a player from a club in another Member State without paying that fee.

102 Nor is that conclusion negated by the case-law of the Court cited by URBSFA and UEFA, to the effect that Article 30 [34] of the Treaty does not apply to measures which restrict or prohibit certain selling arrangements so long as they apply to all relevant traders operating within the national territory and so long as they affect in the same manner, in law and in fact, the marketing of domestic products and of those from other Member States . . .

103 It is sufficient to note that, although the rules in issue in the main proceedings apply also to transfers between clubs belonging to different national associations within the same Member State and are similar to those governing transfers between clubs belonging to the same national association, they still directly affect players' access to the employment market in other Member States and are thus capable of impeding freedom of movement for workers. They cannot, thus, be deemed comparable to the rules on selling arrangements for goods which in Keck and Mithouard were held to fall outside the ambit of Article 30 [34] of the Treaty . . .

104 . . . [T]he transfer rules constitute an obstacle to freedom of movement for workers prohibited in principle by Article 48 [45] of the Treaty. It could only be otherwise if those rules pursued a legitimate aim compatible with the Treaty and were justified by pressing reasons of public interest. But even if that were so, application of those rules would still have to be such as to ensure achievement of the aim in question and not go beyond what is necessary for that purpose . . .

Existence of justifications

105 First, URBSFA, UEFA and the French and Italian Governments have submitted that the transfer rules are justified by the need to maintain a financial and competitive balance between clubs and to support the search for talent and the training of young players.

106 In view of the considerable social importance of sporting activities and in particular football in the Community, the aims of maintaining a balance between clubs by preserving a certain degree of equality and uncertainty as to results and of encouraging the recruitment and training of young players must be accepted as legitimate.

107 As regards the first of those aims, Mr Bosman has rightly pointed out that the application of the transfer rules is not an adequate means of maintaining financial and competitive balance in the world of football. Those rules neither preclude the richest clubs from securing the services of the best players nor prevent the availability of financial resources from being a decisive factor in competitive sport, thus considerably altering the balance between clubs.

108 As regards the second aim, it must be accepted that the prospect of receiving transfer, development or training fees is indeed likely to encourage football clubs to seek new talent and train young players.

109 However, because it is impossible to predict the sporting future of young

players with any certainty and because only a limited number of such players go on to play professionally, those fees are by nature contingent and uncertain and are in any event unrelated to the actual cost borne by clubs of training both future professional players and those who will never play professionally. The prospect of receiving such fees cannot, therefore, be either a decisive factor in encouraging recruitment and training of young players or an adequate means of financing such activities, particularly in the case of smaller clubs.

110 Furthermore . . . the same aims can be achieved at least as efficiently by other means which do not impede freedom of movement for workers.

111 It has also been argued that the transfer rules are necessary to safeguard the worldwide organization of football.

112 However, the present proceedings concern application of those rules within the Community and not the relations between the national associations of the Member States and those of non-member countries. In any event, application of different rules to transfers between clubs belonging to national associations within the Community and to transfers between such clubs and those affiliated to the national associations of non-member countries is unlikely to pose any particular difficulties . . . [T]he rules which have so far governed transfers within the national associations of certain Member States are different from those which apply at the international level.

113 Finally, the argument that the rules in question are necessary to compensate clubs for the expenses which they have had to incur in paying fees on recruiting their players cannot be accepted, since it seeks to justify the maintenance of obstacles to freedom of movement for workers simply on the ground that such obstacles were able to exist in the past.

114 The answer to the first question must therefore be that Article 48 [45] of the Treaty precludes the application of rules laid down by sporting associations, under which a professional footballer who is a national of one Member State may not, on the expiry of his contract with a club, be employed by a club of another Member State unless the latter club has paid to the former club a transfer, training or development fee.

## NOTES AND QUESTIONS

1.    The clubs sought to argue that the EC Treaty/TFEU requirements relating to free movement should not apply to internal transfers within a Member State — citing the *Keck & Mithouard* analogy from the context of the free movement of goods. How was *Keck* allegedly relevant? How did the Court deal with this argument? Given that the rules in question were actually directed at the movement of players from one club to another, in what way could they still be considered "indirect" restrictions?

2.    The indirect nature of restriction on free movement enables the court to engage in an examination of objective justification, just as it does in the case of indirect restrictions on the other freedoms. Do you think the ECJ was right in rejecting the arguments for justification of the transfer restrictions or should it

have referred this factual question back to the national court?

3. For the practical consequences of this judgment, see STEFAAN VAN DEN BOGAERT, PRACTICAL REGULATION OF THE MOBILITY OF SPORTSMEN IN THE EU POST BOSMAN (Kluwer 2005).

## CLEAN CAR AUTOSERVICE GESMBH v. LANDESHAUPTMANN VON WIEN
### Case C-350/96, 1998 ECJ CELEX LEXIS 339, 1998 ECR I-2521

[The facts of this case are summarized in Chapter 4 but are summarized again here for convenience. Under Austrian law, the non-resident owner of a company doing business in Austria was required to appoint a manager who was resident in Austria. Clean Car had applied to the Magistrat der Stadt Wien (Vienna City Council) to register for the trade of maintenance and care of motor vehicles (service station). When making that application, it stated that it had appointed Mr Rudolf Henssen, a German national residing in Berlin, as general manager; it further indicated that Mr Henssen was actively seeking to rent accommodation in Austria and that the declaration relating to his residence there would be forwarded in due course. The Vienna City Council denied Clean Car a business permit because the person appointed as manager did not yet have a residence in Austria.]

18 Next, it must be noted that Article 48(1) states, in general terms, that freedom of movement for workers is to be secured within the Community. Under Article 48(2) and (3), such freedom of movement is to entail the abolition of any discrimination based on nationality between workers of the Member States as regards employment, remuneration and other conditions of work and employment, and to entail the right, subject to limitations justified on grounds of public policy, public security or public health, to accept offers of employment actually made, to move freely within the territory of Member States for that purpose, to stay in a Member State in order to be employed there under the same conditions as nationals of that State and to remain there after such employment.

19 Whilst those rights are undoubtedly enjoyed by those directly referred to — namely, workers — there is nothing in the wording of Article 48 to indicate that they may not be relied upon by others, in particular employers.

20 It must further be noted that, in order to be truly effective, the right of workers to be engaged and employed without discrimination necessarily entails as a corollary the employer's entitlement to engage them in accordance with the rules governing freedom of movement for workers.

21 Those rules could easily be rendered nugatory if Member States could circumvent the prohibitions which they contain merely by imposing on employers requirements to be met by any worker whom they wish to employ which, if imposed directly on the worker, would constitute restrictions on the exercise of the right to freedom of movement to which that worker is entitled under Article 48 [45] of the Treaty.

\* \* \*

27 The Court has consistently held that the rules of equal treatment prohibit not

only overt discrimination based on nationality but also all covert forms of discrimination which, by applying other distinguishing criteria, achieve in practice the same result . . .

28 It is true that [the Austrian law] applies without regard to the nationality of the person to be appointed as manager.

29 However . . . national rules under which a distinction is drawn on the basis of residence are liable to operate mainly to the detriment of nationals of other Member States, as non-residents are in the majority of cases foreigners.

30 A requirement that nationals of the other Member States must reside in the State concerned in order to be appointed managers of undertakings exercising a trade is therefore such as to constitute indirect discrimination based on nationality, contrary to Article 48 [45](2) of the Treaty.

31 It would be otherwise only if the imposition of such a residence requirement were based on objective considerations independent of the nationality of the employees concerned and proportionate to a legitimate aim pursued by the national law . . .

*     *     *

33 In their written observations, the Landeshauptmann von Wien and the Austrian Government have explained that the residence requirement is intended to ensure that the manager can be served with notice of the fines which may be imposed upon him and that they can be enforced against him. The intention is also to ensure that the manager satisfies the other requirement imposed on him by [the Austrian law], namely that he must be in a position to act effectively as such in the business.

34 In that regard, the residence requirement must be held either to be inappropriate for ensuring that the aim pursued is achieved or to go beyond what is necessary for that purpose.

35 In the first place, the fact that the manager resides in the Member State in which the undertaking is established and exercises its trade does not itself necessarily ensure that he will be in a position to act effectively as manager in the business. A manager residing in the State but at a considerable distance from the place at which the undertaking exercises its trade should normally find it more difficult to act effectively in the business than a person whose place of residence, even if in another Member State, is at no great distance from that at which the undertaking exercises its trade.

36 Secondly, other less restrictive measures, such as serving notice of fines at the registered office of the undertaking employing the manager and ensuring that they will be paid by requiring a guarantee to be provided beforehand, would make it possible to ensure that the manager can be served with notice of any such fines imposed upon him and that they can be enforced against him.

37 Finally, it must be added, even such measures as those just indicated are not justified by the aims in question if the service of notice of fines imposed on a manager resident in another Member State and their enforcement against him are guaranteed by an international convention concluded between the Member State in which the undertaking exercises its trade and that in which the manager resides.

38 It must be concluded, therefore, that the residence requirement in question constitutes indirect discrimination.

39 As regards the justifications based on Article 48 [45](3) of the Treaty, to which the national court has also referred, it must be observed that a general rule of the kind in issue in the main proceedings cannot be justified on any grounds of public security or public health.

40 As regards the justification on grounds of public policy, also envisaged in Article 48 [45](3) of the Treaty, . . . . In so far as it may justify certain restrictions on the free movement of persons subject to Community law, recourse to the concept of public policy as used in that provision presupposes, in any event, the existence, in addition to the perturbation of the social order which any infringement of the law involves, of a genuine and sufficiently serious threat affecting one of the fundamental interests of society.

41 Here, however, it does not appear from the documents in the case that any such interest is liable to be affected if the owner of an undertaking is free to appoint, for the purpose of exercising that undertaking's trade, a manager who does not reside in the Member State concerned.

42 It is thus also impossible for a national provision such as that in issue in the main proceedings, which requires any worker appointed as manager for the exercise of a trade to reside in the State concerned, to be justified on grounds of public policy within the meaning of Article 48 [45](3) of the Treaty.

43 In view of the foregoing considerations, the answer to the second question must be that Article 48 [45] of the Treaty precludes a Member State from providing that the owner of an undertaking exercising a trade on the territory of that State may not appoint as manager a person not resident there.

## NOTES AND QUESTIONS

1.    The Court makes the point that employers may also invoke EC 39/TFEU 45 if the State measure has the effect of preventing workers from exercising their free movement rights. In this connection the Court references its observations in the *Bosman* case that organizations operating rules that impede free movement for workers may invoke the exceptions listed in EC 39/TFEU 45. What is the logic that the Court is following here?

2.    As indicated in the Overview, the unstated question before the Court was whether a State measure requiring residence within the State acted like a barrier to entry for foreigners, which then would be justified if one of the exceptions mentioned above applied, or whether the finding that there was indirect discrimination here simply violated the prohibition on discrimination. The Court explicitly referenced the exceptions to free movement rights so obviously thought that the State measure here fell into the first category. Does that conclusion make sense to you?

3.    The United States is not immune from attempts by the states to restrict benefits to residents who have lived for a qualifying period in the state. Attempts by the states to restrict benefits to residents who have lived for a qualifying period in

the state have generally been struck down as infringing the constitutional right to travel. The landmark decision is *Shapiro v. Thompson*, 394 U.S. 618 (1969), where the Supreme Court reviewed the constitutionality of two state statutes and a District of Columbia statute that denied welfare benefits to persons who had not resided within the jurisdiction for at least one year. The Court struck down these statutes on the ground that they infringed a constitutional right to travel. Although stating that it had "no occasion to ascribe the source of this right to travel interstate to a particular constitutional provision" the Court noted that past decisions had grounded it on the commerce clause; the privileges and immunities clause of Article IV, section 2, clause 1; the privileges or immunities clause of the Fourteenth Amendment; and the due process clause of the Fifth Amendment. In later cases the Supreme Court has indicated that a state may require persons to be residents of the state to receive benefits, but it has consistently applied close judicial scrutiny to durational residency requirements. See, e.g., *Zobel v. Williams*, 457 U.S. 55 (1982) (invalidating state distribution of state money to citizens in varying amounts based upon the length of each citizen's residence). For discussion, see JOHN E. NOWAK AND RONALD D. ROTUNDA, CONSTITUTIONAL LAW 929-33 (5th ed. West Pub. Co. 1995).

## [D]  The Boundaries of the Prohibition on Free Movement Restrictions

### MOSER v. LAND BADEN WÜRTTEMBERG
#### Case 180/83 [1984] ECR 3723

[The Land (state) of Baden-Württemberg had refused to allow Mr. Moser to undertake the postgraduate training necessary to secure entry, after passing the second state examination, to the post of teacher at primary-and secondary-school level because, contrary to the requirements of the Land's legislation regarding access to employment in the public service, there was insufficient certainty as regards Mr. Moser's loyalty to the Basic Law of the Federal Republic of Germany, by reason of his membership of the German Communist Party.]

12 In the three questions submitted to the Court of Justice, the Arbeitsgericht asks essentially whether Article 48 [45] of the Treaty covers a situation such as that in which Mr. Moser finds himself and, more particularly, whether a person in such a situation may rely on Article 48[45] to prevent the application to him of legislation, such as that in force in the Land, by virtue of which persons as regards whose loyalty to the Basic Law there is insufficient certainty are denied access to the vocational training necessary to enable them to become teachers in primary and secondary education.

13 The reply to those questions depends, in the first place, on the determination of the scope of Article 48[45] of the Treaty.

14 . . . [T]hat provision aims, in implementation of the general principle laid down in Article 7, to abolish in the legislation of the Member State provisions regarding employment, remuneration and other conditions of work and employment by virtue of which a worker who is a national of another Member State is subject to more severe treatment or is placed in an unfavorable situation in law or in fact as compared with the situation of a national in the same circumstances.

15 It follows that the provisions of the Treaty concerning the free movement of workers and particularly Article 48 [45] cannot be applied to situations which are wholly internal to a Member State, in other words, where there is no factor connecting them to any of the situations envisaged by Community law.

16 The case described by the national court concerns, as the German Government has correctly pointed out, a German national who has always lived and maintained his residence in the Federal Republic of Germany and who contests the refusal by the German authorities to allow him access, under the legislation of that State, to a particular kind of vocational training.

17 In order to establish a connection with the Community provisions, Mr. Moser claimed in the observations which he submitted to the Court of Justice that the application to him of the German legislation in question, by making it impossible for him to complete his training as a teacher, entails the result that he is precluded from applying for teaching posts in schools in the other Member States.

18 That argument cannot be upheld. A purely hypothetical prospect of employment in another Member State does not establish a sufficient connection with Community law to justify the application of Article 48[45] of the Treaty.

19 It follows that there is no factor connecting a personal situation of the kind referred to by the national court with the provisions of Community law on the free movement of workers.

20 It must therefore be held in reply to the questions submitted by the national court that Article 48 [45] of the EEC Treaty does not apply to situations which are wholly internal to a Member State, such as that of a national of a Member State who has never resided or worked in another Member State, and that such a person cannot rely on Article 48 [45] to prevent the application to him of the legislation of his own country.

## VOLKER GRAF v. FILZMOSER MASCHINENBAU GMBH
### Case C-190/98, 2000 ECJ CELEX LEXIS 286, [2000] ECR I-493

[Mr Graf, a German national, sued to obtain compensation from Filzmoser on termination of his employment. Pursuant to Austrian law the payment was denied because he had voluntarily resigned. In fact he had resigned to take up employment in Germany and the entitlement to such payments only applied in the case of termination by the employer.]

13 By its question, the national court essentially asks whether Article 48 [45] of the Treaty precludes national provisions which deny a worker entitlement to compensation on termination of employment if he terminates his contract of employment himself in order to take up employment in another Member State, when those provisions grant him entitlement to such compensation if the contract ends without the termination being at his own initiative or attributable to him.

\* \* \*

18 [I]t is clear from the Court's case-law, in particular from the judgment in Bosman, . . . that Article 48 [45] of the Treaty prohibits not only all discrimination,

direct or indirect, based on nationality but also national rules which are applicable irrespective of the nationality of the workers concerned but impede their freedom of movement.

19 According to Mr Graf, the loss of compensation on termination of employment where the worker himself terminates the contract constitutes such an obstacle to freedom of movement for workers, comparable to the obstacle which was at issue in Bosman. In his submission, it is largely immaterial in this connection whether the worker suffers a financial loss because he changes employer or the new employer is required to make a payment in order to take him on.

20 By contrast, the other parties who have submitted observations to the Court maintain that national legislation applicable irrespective of the nationality of the workers concerned which is liable to dissuade the latter from deciding to exercise their right to freedom of movement does not necessarily constitute an obstacle to freedom of movement for workers.

21 In that regard, the Court has held on numerous occasions that the Treaty provisions relating to freedom of movement for persons are intended to facilitate the pursuit by Community nationals of occupational activities of all kinds through-out the Community, and preclude measures which might place Community nation-als at a disadvantage when they wish to pursue an economic activity in the territory of another Member State . . .

22 Nationals of Member States have in particular the right, which they derive directly from the Treaty, to leave their country of origin to enter the territory of another Member State and reside there in order to pursue an economic activity . . .

23 Provisions which, even if they are applicable without distinction, preclude or deter a national of a Member State from leaving his country of origin in order to exercise his right to freedom of movement therefore constitute an obstacle to that freedom. However, in order to be capable of constituting such an obstacle, they must affect access of workers to the labour market.

24 Legislation of the kind at issue in the main proceedings is not such as to preclude or deter a worker from ending his contract of employment in order to take a job with another employer, because the entitlement to compensation on termination of employment is not dependent on the worker's choosing whether or not to stay with his current employer but on a future and hypothetical event, namely the subsequent termination of his contract without such termination being at his own initiative or attributable to him.

25 Such an event is too uncertain and indirect a possibility for legislation to be capable of being regarded as liable to hinder freedom of movement for workers where it does not attach to termination of a contract of employment by the worker himself the same consequence as it attaches to termination which was not at his initiative or is not attributable to him . . .

26 In view of all the foregoing considerations, the answer to the question submitted must be that Article 48 [45] of the Treaty does not preclude national provisions which deny a worker entitlement to compensation on termination of employment if he terminates his contract of employment himself in order to take up employment

in another Member State, when those provisions grant him entitlement to such compensation if the contract ends without the termination being at his own initiative or attributable to him.

## NOTES AND QUESTIONS

1. Compare *Moser* and *Graf*. Do you think there has been a shift in the Court's approach to rules that appear to be outside the boundaries of the TFEU prohibition? What did the ECJ mean by rules that affect "access of workers to the labour market"? Is this in effect the test for determining whether a rule falls within the TFEU 45 prohibition?

2. There have been quite a number of other cases, where sometimes the ECJ has found a restriction on free movement by a State on its own nationals and sometimes not: see, for example, *F.C. Terhoeve v. Inspecteur van de Belastingdienst Particulieren/Ondernemingen buitenland* Case C-18/95, 1999 ECJ CELEX LEXIS 40, [1999] ECR I-345; *Commission v. Denmark*, Case C-464/02, 2005 ECJ CELEX LEXIS 390, [2005] ECR I-7929. See also *De Cuyper* case, which implicated also EC 18 EC/TFEU 21; *Ministère Public v. André Gauchard*, Case 20/87, 1987 ECJ CELEX LEXIS 445, [1987] ECR 48 and *Friedrich Kremzow v. Austria*, Case C-299/95, 1997 ECJ CELEX LEXIS 286,[1997] ECR I-2629 (discussed in Chapter 4).

## [E]  The Public Service Exemption

### COMMISSION v. BELGIUM
(PUBLIC SERVICE EMPLOYMENT)
Case 149/79, [1980] ECR 3881

[The Commission had found Belgium to be in breach of EEC Article 48 (EC 39/TFEU 45 by denying non-nationals employment in alleged public service positions.]

2 In its reasoned opinion and application to the Court the Commission referred generally to "various vacancies" advertised by the Société Nationale des Chemins de Fer Belges [Belgian National Railway Company] and the Société Nationale des Chemins de Fer Vicinaux [National Local Railway Company] concerning posts for unskilled workers, and to vacancies advertised "during recent years" by the City of Brussels and the Commune of Auderghem and the Commission gave only a brief indication of the posts involved. Through information requested by the Court during the written and oral procedures and produced by the Government of the Kingdom of Belgium and after the Commission had specified the posts during the oral procedure without challenge from the Belgian government, it became possible to establish an exact list of the posts in issue.

3 From that information and that list it emerges that the vacancies referred to concern posts for trainee locomotive drivers, loaders, platelayers, shunters and traveled with the national railways and unskilled workers with the local railways as well as posts for hospital nurses, children's nurses, night-watchmen, plumbers,

carpenters, electricians, garden hands, architects, and supervisors with the City of Brussels and the Commune of Auderghem. Nevertheless the information obtained during the inquiry has not enabled the Court to gain a precise idea of the nature of the duties involved in the posts for which it has been possible to draw up a precise list.

4 Those posts were in actual fact offered between 1973 and 1977 through public notices or newspaper advertisements by the public undertakings and local authorities referred to above, and among the conditions required for recruitment the advertisements stipulated the possession of Belgian nationality.

9 Article 48 [45] (4) of the Treaty provides that "the provisions of this article shall not apply to employment in the public service".

10 That provision removes from the ambit of Article 48 [45] (1) to (3) a series of posts which involve direct or indirect participation in the exercise of powers conferred by public law and duties designed to safeguard the general interests of the State or of other public authorities. Such posts in fact presume on the part of those occupying them the existence of a special relationship of allegiance to the State and reciprocity of rights and duties which form the foundation of the bond of nationality.

11 The scope of the derogation made by Article 48 [45] (4) to the principles of freedom of movement and equality of treatment laid down in the first three paragraphs of the article should therefore be determined on the basis of the aim pursued by that article. However, determining the sphere of application of Article 48 [45] (4) raises special difficulties since in the various Member States authorities acting under powers conferred by public law have assumed responsibilities of an economic and social nature or are involved in activities which are not identifiable with the functions which are typical of the public service yet which by their nature still come under the sphere of application of the Treaty. In these circumstances the effect of extending the exception contained in Article 48 [45] (4) to posts which, whilst coming under the State or other organizations governed by public law, still do not involve any association with tasks belonging to the public service properly so called, would be to remove a considerable number of posts from the ambit of the principles set out in the Treaty and to create inequalities between Member States according to the different ways in which the State and certain sectors of economic life are organized.

12 Consequently it is appropriate to examine whether the posts covered by the action may be associated with the concept of public service within the meaning of Article 48 [45] (4), which requires uniform interpretation and application throughout the Community. It must be acknowledged that the application of the distinguishing criteria indicated above gives rise to problems of appraisal and demarcation in specific cases. It follows from the foregoing that such a classification depends on whether or not the posts in question are typical of the specific activities of the public service in so far as the exercise of powers conferred by public law and responsibility for safeguarding the general interests of the State are vested in it.

13 Where, in the case of posts which, although offered by public authorities, are not within the sphere to which Article 48 [45] (4) applies, a worker from another Member State is, like a national worker, required to satisfy all other conditions of

recruitment, in particular concerning the competence and vocational training required, the provisions of the first three paragraphs of Article 48 [45] and Regulation No. 1612/68 do not allow him to be debarred from those posts simply on the grounds of his nationality.

14 In support of the argument put forward by the Belgian Government and supported by the interveners to the effect that the exception clause in Article 48 [45] (4) of the Treaty has general scope covering all the posts in the administration of a Member State, that government has invoked the special provisions of Article 8 of Regulation No. 1612/68 by which a worker from another Member State "may be excluded from taking part in the management of bodies governed by public law and from holding an office governed by public law".

15 Far from supporting the case of the Belgian Government that provision confirms on the contrary the interpretation of Article 48 [45](4) given above. Indeed, as the Belgian Government itself admits, Article 8 of Regulation No. 1612/68 is not intended to debar workers from other Member States from certain posts, but simply permits them to be debarred in some circumstances from certain activities which involve their participation in the exercise of powers conferred by public law, such as — to use the examples given by the Belgian Government itself — those involving "the presence of trade-union representatives on the boards of administration of many bodies governed by public law with powers in the economic sphere".

16 The Belgian Government further mentions that the constitutional laws of certain Member States refer expressly to the problem of employment in the public service, the principle being the exclusion of non-nationals, save for any possible derogations. Such is also, it claims, the effect of Article 6 of the Belgian Constitution by which "Belgians . . . only shall be admitted to civil and military posts save in special cases for which exception may be made." The Belgian Government has itself stated that it does not deny that "Community rules override national rules" but it believes that the similarity between the constitutional laws of those Member States should be used as an aid to interpretation to cast light on the meaning of Article 48 [45] (4) and to reject the interpretation given to that provision by the Commission, which would have the effect of creating conflict with the constitutional provisions referred to.

17 The French Government has propounded an argument of similar tenor, drawing attention to the principles applied in French law on the public service, which is founded on a comprehensive idea based on the requirement of French nationality as a condition of entry to any post in the public service appertaining to the State, municipalities or other public establishments, without any possibility of making a distinction on the basis of the nature and the characteristics of the post in question.

18 It is correct that Article 48 [45] (4) is indeed intended to operate, in the scheme of the provisions on freedom of movement for workers, to take account of the existence of provisions of the kind mentioned. But at the same time, as is admitted in the observations of the French Government, the demarcation of the concept of "public service" within the meaning of Article 48 [45] (4) cannot be left to the total discretion of the Member States.

19 Irrespective of the fact that the wording of the Belgian Constitution does not rule out the possibility of exceptions being made to the general requirement of the

possession of Belgian nationality, it should be recalled, as the Court has constantly emphasized in its case-law, that recourse to provisions of the domestic legal systems to restrict the scope of the provisions of Community law would have the effect of impairing the unity and efficacy of that law and consequently cannot be accepted. That rule, which is fundamental to the existence of the Community, must also apply in determining the scope and bounds of Article 48 [45] (4) of the Treaty. Whilst it is true that that provision takes account of the legitimate interest which the Member States have in reserving to their own nationals a range of posts connected with the exercise of powers conferred by public law and with the protection of general interests, at the same time it is necessary to ensure that the effectiveness and scope of the provisions of the Treaty on freedom of movement of workers and equality of treatment of nationals of all Member States shall not be restricted by interpretations of the concept of public service which are based on domestic law alone and which would obstruct the application of Community rules.

20 Finally, the Belgian and French Governments argue that the exclusion of foreign workers from posts which do not at the outset involve any participation in the exercise of powers conferred by public law becomes necessary, for instance, if recruitment takes place on the basis of service regulations and the holders of the posts are eligible for a career which in the higher grades involves duties and responsibilities involving the exercise of powers conferred by public law. The German and British Governments add that such an exclusion is also necessitated by the fact that flexibility in assignment to posts is a characteristic of the public service and the duties and responsibilities of an employee may consequently change, not only on promotion, but also after a transfer within the same branch, or to a different branch at the same level.

21 Those objections do not however take account of the fact that, in referring to posts involving the exercise of powers conferred by public law and the conferment of responsibilities for the safeguarding of the general interests of the State, Article 48 [45] (4) allows Member States to reserve to their nationals by appropriate rules entry to posts involving the exercise of such powers and such responsibilities within the same grade, the same branch or the same class.

22 The argument of the German Government on that last point, to the effect that any exclusion of nationals of other Member States from promotion or transfer to certain posts in the public service would have the effect of creating discrimination within such service, does not take into consideration the fact that the interpretation which that government puts on Article 48 [45] (4), and which has the effect of debarring those nationals from the totality of posts in the public service, involves a restriction on the rights of such nationals which goes further than is necessary to ensure observance of the objectives of the provision as construed in the light of the foregoing considerations.

23 The Court takes the view that, in general, so far as the posts in dispute are concerned, information available in this case, which has been provided by the parties during the written and oral procedures, does not enable a sufficiently accurate appraisal to be made of the actual nature of the duties involved so as to make it possible to identify, in the light of the foregoing considerations, those of the

posts which do not come within the concept of public service within the meaning of Article 48 [45] (4) of the Treaty.

24 In these circumstances the Court does not consider itself to be in a position at this stage to give a decision on the allegation that the Belgian Government has failed to fulfil its obligations. Consequently it invites the Commission and the Kingdom of Belgium to re-examine the issue between them in the light of the foregoing considerations and to report to the Court, either jointly or separately, within a specified period, either any solution to the dispute which they succeed in reaching together or their respective viewpoints, having regard to the matters of law arising from this judgment. An opportunity will be provided for the interveners to submit their observations to the Court on any such report or reports at the appropriate time.

## NOTES AND QUESTIONS

1. Under Belgian law, posts in the "public service" could be limited to Belgian nationals. The law was applied to all sorts of posts: unskilled workers, railwaymen, nurses, plumbers, electricians and architects, whether they were employed by the central or local government. The Court ruled that the concept of public service applied only to the exercise of official authority by employees safeguarding the general interest of the state. Only higher levels and not lower levels of a post could be regarded as exercising official authority. In the above case, the Court took a very narrow view of the public service exception. How did the Court justify this interpretation?

2. To the same effect, see *Commission v. France*, Case 307/84, 1986 ECJ CELEX LEXIS 132, [1986] ECR 1725 (nurses in public hospitals not within scope of EC 39/TFEU 45(4)); *Allué & Coonan v. Università degli studi di Venezia*, Case 33/88, 1989 ECJ CELEX LEXIS 323, [1989] ECR 159, (teachers in state university not "employees in the public service" within EC 39/TFEU 45(4)). In *Sotgiu v. Deutsche Bundespost*, Case 152/73, [1974] ECR 153, rules of the German post office granted extra allowances to workers living apart from their families in Germany, and the German Government relied on EC 39 [45](4) in response to a charge that the rules violated the Treaty because of their discriminatory nature. The Court held that the exception provided by EC 39/TFEU 45(4) did not apply to all employment in the public service, but only to those activities that involved the exercise of official authority. Further, it applied only to conditions of access; once access was granted, no discriminatory conditions of employment are permitted. How does this fit with the argument that certain parts could be reserved for nationals?

3. In the U.S., nationality requirements of course become relevant only with respect to non-U.S. nationals. In *Bernal v. Fainter*, 467 U.S. 216 (1984), the U.S. Supreme Court struck down a Texas statute that required notaries public to be U.S. citizens on the ground that it violated the Equal Protection Clause of the Fourteenth Amendment of the U.S. Constitution. In doing so the Court applied a "strict scrutiny" test and held that notaries public do not perform functions that "go to the heart of representative government." In contrast, the U.S. Supreme Court has consistently applied a "rational basis" test to federal legislative distinctions between citizens and aliens and between different kinds of aliens, with the result

that such distinctions have been upheld. See, e.g., *Mathews v. Diaz*, 426 U.S. 67 (1976).

At the same time, residency requirements can have the same consequence as nationality as between the various states. In *McCarthy v. Philadelphia Civil Service Commission*, 424 U.S. 645 (1976), the Supreme Court upheld the constitutionality of a regulation of the City of Philadelphia that required that city employees be residents of the city. McCarthy's employment with the Philadelphia Fire Department had been terminated after he moved his permanent residence from Philadelphia to New Jersey. In response to his argument that the city's regulation violated his right to travel interstate, the Court distinguished cases like *Shapiro* on the ground that these cases involved a statutory requirement of residency in the state of at least one year *before* becoming eligible to receive benefits or to vote. Here, by contrast, there was a bona fide requirement of *continuing* residence in the state in order to remain in *public* employment.

# § 17.03   FREE MOVEMENT AND RESIDENCE AS A CITIZENSHIP RIGHT

## [A]   Need for a Connection with Union Law

### KUNQIAN CATHERINE ZHU AND MAN LAVETTE CHEN v. SECRETARY OF STATE FOR THE HOME DEPARTMENT
#### Case C-200/02, 2004 ECJ CELEX LEXIS 493, [2004] ECR I-9925

7 [M]rs Chen and her husband, both of Chinese nationality, work for a Chinese undertaking established in China. Mrs Chen's husband is a director and the majority shareholder of that company. For the purposes of his work, he travels frequently to various Member States, in particular the United Kingdom.

8 The couple's first child was born in the People's Republic of China in 1998. Mrs Chen, who wished to give birth to a second child, entered the United Kingdom in May 2000 when she was about six months pregnant. She went to Belfast in July of the same year and Catherine was born there on 16 September 2000. The mother and her child live at present in Cardiff, Wales (United Kingdom).

9 Under section 6(1) of the Irish Nationality and Citizenship Act of 1956, which was amended in 2001 and applies retroactively as from 2 December 1999, Ireland allows any person born on the island of Ireland [including Northern Ireland, part of the United Kingdom] to acquire Irish nationality. Under section 6(3), a person born in the island of Ireland is an Irish citizen from birth if he or she is not entitled to citizenship of any other country.

10 Under those rules, Catherine was issued with an Irish passport in September 2000. According to the order for reference, Catherine is not entitled, on the other hand, to acquire United Kingdom nationality since, in enacting the British Nationality Act 1981, the United Kingdom departed from the jus soli, so that birth in the territory of that Member State no longer automatically confers United Kingdom nationality.

11 It is common ground that Mrs Chen took up residence in the island of Ireland in order to enable the child she was expecting to acquire Irish nationality and, consequently, to enable her to acquire the right to reside, should the occasion arise, with her child in the United Kingdom.

12 The referring court also observes that Ireland forms part of the Common Travel Area within the meaning of the Immigration Acts, so that, because Irish nationals do not as a general rule have to obtain a permit to enter and reside in the United Kingdom, Catherine, in contrast to Mrs Chen, may move freely within the United Kingdom and within Ireland. Aside from Catherine's right of free movement limited to those two Member States, neither of the appellants in the main proceedings is entitled to reside in the United Kingdom under its domestic legislation.

13 The order for reference also makes it clear that Catherine is dependent both emotionally and financially on her mother, that her mother is her primary carer, that Catherine receives private medical services and child-care services in return for payment in the United Kingdom, that she lost the right to acquire Chinese nationality by virtue of having been born in Northern Ireland and her subsequent acquisition of Irish nationality and, as a result, that she only has the right to enter Chinese territory under a visa allowing residence for a maximum of 30 days per visit; that the two appellants in the main proceedings provide for their needs by reason of Mrs Chen's employment, that the appellants do not rely upon public funds in the United Kingdom and there is no realistic possibility of their becoming so reliant, and, finally, that the appellants are insured against ill health.

14 The Secretary of State for the Home Department's refusal to grant a long-term residence permit to the two appellants in the main proceedings was based on the fact that Catherine, a child of eight months of age, was not exercising any rights arising from the EC Treaty such as those laid down by Regulation 5(1) of the EEA Regulations and the fact that Mrs Chen was not entitled to reside in the United Kingdom under those regulations.

\*     \*     \*

24 . . . [T]he national court would like to know whether Catherine might have a right to long-term residence under Article 18 EC [21] and under Directive 90/364, which, subject to certain conditions, guarantees such a right for nationals of Member States to whom it is not available under other provisions of Community law, and for members of their families.

25 By virtue of Article 17(1) EC [20], every person holding the nationality of a Member State is a citizen of the Union. Union citizenship is destined to be the fundamental status of nationals of the Member States . . .

26 As regards the right to reside in the territory of the Member States provided for in Article 18(1) EC [21], it must be observed that that right is granted directly to every citizen of the Union by a clear and precise provision of the Treaty. Purely as a national of a Member State, and therefore as a citizen of the Union, Catherine is entitled to rely on Article 18(1) EC [21]. That right of citizens of the Union to reside in another Member State is subject to the limitations and conditions imposed by the Treaty and by the measures adopted to give it effect . . .

\*   \*   \*

34 The United Kingdom Government contends, finally, that the appellants in the main proceedings are not entitled to rely on the Community provisions in question because Mrs Chen's move to Northern Ireland with the aim of having her child acquire the nationality of another Member State constitutes an attempt improperly to exploit the provisions of Community law. The aims pursued by those Community provisions are not, in its view, served where a national of a non-member country wishing to reside in a Member State, without however moving or wishing to move from one Member State to another, arranges matters in such a way as to give birth to a child in a part of the host Member State to which another Member State applies its rules governing acquisition of nationality jure soli. It is, in their view, settled case-law that Member States are entitled to take measures to prevent individuals from improperly taking advantage of provisions of Community law or from attempting, under cover of the rights created by the Treaty, illegally to circumvent national legislation. That rule, which is in conformity with the principle that rights must not be abused, was in their view reaffirmed by the Court in its judgment in Case C-212/97 Centros 1999 ECR I1459.

35 That argument must also be rejected.

36 It is true that Mrs Chen admits that the purpose of her stay in the United Kingdom was to create a situation in which the child she was expecting would be able to acquire the nationality of another Member State in order thereafter to secure for her child and for herself a long-term right to reside in the United Kingdom.

37 Nevertheless, under international law, it is for each Member State, having due regard to Community law, to lay down the conditions for the acquisition and loss of nationality . . .

38 None of the parties that submitted observations to the Court has questioned either the legality, or the fact, of Catherine's acquisition of Irish nationality.

39 Moreover, it is not permissible for a Member State to restrict the effects of the grant of the nationality of another Member State by imposing an additional condition for recognition of that nationality with a view to the exercise of the fundamental freedoms provided for in the Treaty . . .

40 However, that would be precisely what would happen if the United Kingdom were entitled to refuse nationals of other Member States, such as Catherine, the benefit of a fundamental freedom upheld by Community law merely because their nationality of a Member State was in fact acquired solely in order to secure a right of residence under Community law for a national of a non-member country.

41 Accordingly, in circumstances like those of the main proceedings, Article 18 EC [21] and Directive 90/364 confer on a young minor who is a national of a Member State, is covered by appropriate sickness insurance and is in the care of a parent who is a third-country national having sufficient resources for that minor not to become a burden on the public finances of the host Member State, a right to reside for an indefinite period in that State.

The right of residence of a person in Mrs Chen's situation

42 Article 1(2)(b) of Directive 90/364, which guarantees dependent' relatives in the ascending line of the holder of the right of residence the right to install themselves with the holder of the right of residence, regardless of their nationality, cannot confer a right of residence on a national of a non-member country in Mrs Chen's situation either by reason of the emotional bonds between mother and child or on the ground that the mother's right to enter and reside in the United Kingdom is dependent on her child's right of residence.

43 According to the case-law of the Court, the status of dependent' member of the family of a holder of a right of residence is the result of a factual situation characterised by the fact that material support for the family member is provided by the holder of the right of residence . . .

44 In circumstances such as those of the main proceedings, the position is exactly the opposite in that the holder of the right of residence is dependent on the national of a non-member country who is her carer and wishes to accompany her. In those circumstances, Mrs Chen cannot claim to be a dependent' relative of Catherine in the ascending line within the meaning of Directive 90/364 with a view to having the benefit of a right of residence in the United Kingdom.

45 On the other hand, a refusal to allow the parent, whether a national of a Member State or a national of a non-member country, who is the carer of a child to whom Article 18 EC [21] and Directive 90/364 grant a right of residence, to reside with that child in the host Member State would deprive the child's right of residence of any useful effect. It is clear that enjoyment by a young child of a right of residence necessarily implies that the child is entitled to be accompanied by the person who is his or her primary carer and accordingly that the carer must be in a position to reside with the child in the host Member State for the duration of such residence . . .

46 For that reason alone, where, as in the main proceedings, Article 18 EC [21] and Directive 90/364 grant a right to reside for an indefinite period in the host Member State to a young minor who is a national of another Member State, those same provisions allow a parent who is that minor's primary carer to reside with the child in the host Member State.

47 The answer to be given to the national court must therefore be that, in circumstances like those of the main proceedings, Article 18 EC [21] and Directive 90/364 confer on a young minor who is a national of a Member State, is covered by appropriate sickness insurance and is in the care of a parent who is a third-country national having sufficient resources for that minor not to become a burden on the public finances of the host Member State, a right to reside for an indefinite period in that State. In such circumstances, those same provisions allow a parent who is that minor's primary carer to reside with the child in the host Member State.

## NOTES AND QUESTIONS

**1.** This is a most peculiar case. Does the decision make sense? Did Catherine Chen actually exercise a free movement right by moving from Northern Ireland to Wales (both being parts of one Member State, the UK)?

**2.** Would the Court have ruled differently if Catherine Chen had been born in England as opposed to Northern Ireland? If the answer is yes, would that give rise to injustice in your opinion? And does the court's ruling create an anomaly in that residents of the host state have fewer rights than nationals who move their residence to the host state?

**3.** On what legal basis does the decision that Mrs. Chen should be allowed to reside in the UK rely?

**4.** Note that Directive 90/364 has been repealed and replaced by Directive 2004/38/EC (described *infra*). For a useful commentary, see Bjørn Kunoy, '*A union of national citizens: The origins of the Court's lack of avant-gardisme in the Chen case*' (2006) 43 CML REV. 179.

## [B]   Effect on State Competences in Other Areas — Legitimate Purpose and Proportionality

## K. TAS-HAGEN AND R. A. TAS v. RAADSKAMER WUBO VAN DE PENSIOEN- EN UITKERINGSRAAD
Case C-192/05, 2006 ECJ EUR-Lex LEXIS 2496, 2006 ECR I-10451.

[Mrs Tas-Hagen was born in 1943 in what was at the time the Dutch East Indies and went to the Netherlands in 1954. In 1961 she acquired Netherlands nationality. In 1987, after having become incapable of working and thereby forced to terminate her professional career, she took up residence in Spain. While still resident in the Netherlands, Mrs Tas-Hagen applied, for the grant of a periodic civilian war injury benefit and an allowance to cover various expenses. This application was based on health problems resulting from the events that she had experienced in the Dutch East Indies during the Japanese occupation and during the Bersiap period following that occupation. Her application was denied since she was not resident in the Netherlands. Mr Tas was born in the Dutch East Indies in 1931. In 1947 he took up residence in the Netherlands. From 1951 to 1971 he held Indonesian nationality. He regained Netherlands nationality in 1971. In 1983 Mr Tas was declared wholly incapable of work on grounds of mental health. In 1987 Mr Tas took up residence in Spain. He also submitted an application for civilian war injury benefits.]

The ECJ began by establishing that EC 18/TFEU 21 was applicable because the benefits were denied specifically on the grounds that the applicants were not resident, having exercised their citizenship right to take up residence in Spain.]

32. . . . In making payment of the benefit to civilian war victims conditional on the fact that applicants are resident in the territory of the Netherlands at the time when their application is submitted, [the Dutch law] is liable to dissuade Netherlands nationals in a situation such as that of the applicants in the main proceedings from exercising their freedom to move and to reside outside the Netherlands.

33. Such a restriction can be justified, with regard to Community law, only if it is based on objective considerations of public interest independent of the nationality of the persons concerned and is proportionate to the legitimate objective of the national provisions . . .

34. As to the first condition, which concerns the existence of objective considerations of public interest, it is apparent from the order for reference that the limitation by the [Dutch law], by means of the condition of residence, of the number of persons likely to be eligible for the benefits introduced by that Law results from the Netherlands legislature's wish to limit the obligation of solidarity with civilian war victims to those who had links with the population of the Netherlands during and after the war. The condition of residence is therefore an expression of the extent to which such victims are connected to Netherlands society.

35. Admittedly, this aim of solidarity may constitute an objective consideration of public interest. It is still necessary for the condition of proportionality outlined in paragraph 33 above to be met. It follows from the case-law that a measure is proportionate when, while appropriate for securing the attainment of the objective pursued, it does not go beyond what is necessary in order to attain it . . .

36. With regard to benefits that are not covered by Community law, Member States enjoy a wide margin of appreciation in deciding which criteria are to be used when assessing the degree of connection to society, while at the same time complying with the limits imposed by Community law.

37. However, a condition of residence such as that in issue in the main proceedings cannot be characterized as an appropriate means by which to attain the objective sought.

38. . . . [A] criterion requiring residence cannot be considered a satisfactory indicator of the degree of connection of applicants to the Member State granting the benefit when it is liable, as is the case with the criterion in issue in the main proceedings, to lead to different results for persons resident abroad whose degree of integration into the society of the Member State granting the benefit is in all respects comparable.

39. Consequently, the setting of a residence criterion such as that used in the main proceedings, based solely on the date on which the application for the benefit is submitted, is not a satisfactory indicator of the degree of attachment of the applicant to the society which is thereby demonstrating its solidarity with him. It follows that this condition of residence fails to comply with the principle of proportionality referred to in paragraphs 33 and 35 above.

40. In the light of the foregoing considerations, the answer to the question must be that Article 18 [21] (1) EC is to be interpreted as precluding legislation of a Member State under which it refuses to grant to one of its nationals a benefit for civilian war victims solely on the ground that, at the time at which the application was submitted, the person concerned was resident, not in the territory of that Member State, but in the territory of another Member State.

# NOTES AND QUESTIONS

**1.**   Was it not reasonable for the Dutch authorities to insist on residence in the Netherlands when all of the circumstances giving rise to the benefit scheme were occasioned by reason of residence in a Dutch colony covered by it?

**2.**   In the United States, the Supreme Court has frequently struck down laws laying down residence requirements as a condition of eligibility for benefits. See, for example, *Shapiro v. Thompson*, 394 U.S. 618, 89 S. Ct. 1322, 22 L. Ed.2d 600 (1969). It was not clear whether the Court's objections were based on the privileges and immunities clause or the commerce clause; however, in the later case of *Saenz v. Roe*, 526 U.S. 489, 119 S. Ct. 1518, 143 L. Ed. 2d 689 (1999), the Court made clear that equal treatment of new residents versus established residents was required by the privileges and immunities language of Amendment XIV.

**3.**   With *K. Tas-Hagen and R. A. Tas v. Raadskamer WUBO van de Pensioen-en Uitkeringsraad*, compare *De Cupyer*, Case C-406/04, 2006 ECJ CELEX LEXIS 372, [2006] ECR I-6947, concerning legislation on the award of unemployment benefits that required the person concerned to be resident on national territory. In that case, the payments were subject to Regulation 1408/71, which restricted the right of the paying Member State to deny benefits to persons who move to other Member States to seek work (and cease to maintain a residence in the home state). However, there was a public interest exception that the Belgian authorities were able to invoke, based on the need to monitor ongoing eligibility — that would be difficult when the applicant is no longer within the jurisdiction.

**4.**   Denial of educational grants to study in another Member State based on a requirement that the study should be a continuation of a course already taken for at least one year in the student's home state has also been found incompatible with EC 18/TFEU 21 on the grounds of disproportionality to the objectives of such a rule: *Rhiannon Morgan v. Bezirksregierung Köln*, Case C-11/06, 2007 ECJ EUR-Lex LEXIS 2646, [2007] ECR I-9161, and *Iris Bucher v. Landrat des Kreises Düren*, Case C-12/06, 2007 ECJ EUR-Lex LEXIS 2646, [2007] ECR 9161.

**5.**   Not all citizenship cases regarding free movement involve some form of denial of State benefits. In *Grunkin and Paul*, Case C-353/06, 2008 ECJ EUR-Lex LEXIS 2141 [2008] ECR I-7639, the ECJ accepted the reference regarding the use of double-barreled surnames in Germany that it had previously rejected in the *Niebühl* case (described in Chapter 9 *supra.)* The referring Court asked whether the refusal of the Registrar in Germany to accept the child's name, given and registered in Denmark, violated EU law. The consequence of the refusal was that the child would have different names in Denmark and Germany. This the ECJ considered to be a significant burden on the right of free movement accorded by EC 18/TFEU 21 and held the German requirement to be incompatible with that article.

## [C]  Conditions and Limitations in the Treaties and Union Legislation — the "Public Burden" Condition

### BAUMBAST v. SECRETARY OF STATE FOR THE HOME DEPARTMENT
Case C-413/99, 2002 ECJ CELEX LEXIS 3461, [2002] ECR I-7091

16 Mrs Baumbast, a Colombian national, married Mr Baumbast, a German national, in the United Kingdom in May 1990. Their family consists of two daughters, the elder, Maria Fernanda Sarmiento, Mrs Baumbast's natural daughter, who is a Colombian national and the younger, Idanella Baumbast, who has dual German and Colombian nationality.

*    *    *

18 In June 1990, the members of the Baumbast family were granted residence permits/documents valid for five years. Between 1990 and 1993, Mr Baumbast pursued an economic activity in the United Kingdom, initially as an employed person and then as head of his own company. However, since that company failed and he was unable to obtain a sufficiently well-paid job in the United Kingdom, he has been employed since 1993 by German companies in China and Lesotho. Although Mr Baumbast has from time to time sought work in the United Kingdom since that date, his employment situation had not changed at the time of the order for reference.

19 During the material period, Mr and Mrs Baumbast owned a house in the United Kingdom and their daughters went to school there. They did not receive any social benefits and, having comprehensive medical insurance in Germany, they traveled there, when necessary, for medical treatment.

20 In May 1995, Mrs Baumbast applied for indefinite leave to remain in the United Kingdom for herself and for the other members of her family. In January 1996, the Secretary of State refused to renew Mr Baumbast's residence permit and the residence documents of Mrs Baumbast and her children.

21 On 12 January 1998, that refusal was brought before the Immigration Adjudicator (United Kingdom). He found that Mr Baumbast was neither a worker nor a person having a general right of residence under Directive 90/364. As regards the children, the Adjudicator decided that they enjoyed an independent right of residence under Article 12 of Regulation No 1612/68. Moreover, he held that Mrs Baumbast enjoyed a right of residence for a period co-terminous with that during which her children exercised rights under Article 12 of that regulation. According to the Adjudicator, Mrs Baumbast's rights flowed from the obligation on Member States under that provision to encourage all efforts to enable children to attend courses in the host Member State under the best possible conditions.

*    *    *

86 . . . [t]he application of the limitations and conditions acknowledged in Article 18(1) EC [21] in respect of the exercise of that right of residence is subject to judicial review. Consequently, any limitations and conditions imposed on that right

do not prevent the provisions of Article 18(1) EC [21] from conferring on individuals rights which are enforceable by them and which the national courts must protect . . .

87 As regards the limitations and conditions resulting from the provisions of secondary legislation, Article 1(1) of Directive 90/364 provides that Member States can require of the nationals of a Member State who wish to enjoy the right to reside within their territory that they themselves and the members of their families be covered by sickness insurance in respect of all risks in the host Member State and have sufficient resources to avoid becoming a burden on the social assistance system of the host Member State during their period of residence.

88 As to the application of those conditions for the purposes of the Baumbast case, it is clear from the file that Mr Baumbast pursues an activity as an employed person in non-member countries for German companies and that neither he nor his family has used the social assistance system in the host Member State. In those circumstances, it has not been denied that Mr Baumbast satisfies the condition relating to sufficient resources imposed by Directive 90/364.

89 As to the condition relating to sickness insurance, the file shows that both Mr Baumbast and the members of his family are covered by comprehensive sickness insurance in Germany. The Adjudicator seems to have found that that sickness insurance could not cover emergency treatment given in the United Kingdom. It is for the national tribunal to determine whether that finding is correct in the light of Regulation (EEC) No 1408/71 of the Council of 14 June 1971 on the application of social security schemes to employed persons and their families moving within the Community (OJ, English Special Edition 1971 (II), p. 416). Particular reference should be made to Article 19(1)(a) of that regulation which ensures, at the expense of the competent Member State, the right for an employed or self-employed person residing in the territory of another Member State other than the competent State whose condition requires treatment in the territory of the Member State of residence to receive sickness benefits in kind provided by the institution of the latter State.

90 In any event, the limitations and conditions which are referred to in Article 18 EC [21] and laid down by Directive 90/364 are based on the idea that the exercise of the right of residence of citizens of the Union can be subordinated to the legitimate interests of the Member States. In that regard, according to the fourth recital in the preamble to Directive 90/364 beneficiaries of the right of residence must not become an unreasonable' burden on the public finances of the host Member State.

91 However, those limitations and conditions must be applied in compliance with the limits imposed by Community law and in accordance with the general principles of that law, in particular the principle of proportionality. That means that national measures adopted on that subject must be necessary and appropriate to attain the objective pursued . . .

92 In respect of the application of the principle of proportionality to the facts of the Baumbast case, it must be recalled, first, that it has not been denied that Mr Baumbast has sufficient resources within the meaning of Directive 90/364; second,

that he worked and therefore lawfully resided in the host Member State for several years, initially as an employed person and subsequently as a self-employed person; third, that during that period his family also resided in the host Member State and remained there even after his activities as an employed and self-employed person in that State came to an end; fourth, that neither Mr Baumbast nor the members of his family have become burdens on the public finances of the host Member State and, fifth, that both Mr Baumbast and his family have comprehensive sickness insurance in another Member State of the Union.

93 Under those circumstances, to refuse to allow Mr Baumbast to exercise the right of residence which is conferred on him by Article 18(1) EC [21] by virtue of the application of the provisions of Directive 90/364 on the ground that his sickness insurance does not cover the emergency treatment given in the host Member State would amount to a disproportionate interference with the exercise of that right.

94 The answer to the first part of the third question must therefore be that a citizen of the European Union who no longer enjoys a right of residence as a migrant worker in the host Member State can, as a citizen of the Union, enjoy there a right of residence by direct application of Article 18(1) EC [21]. The exercise of that right is subject to the limitations and conditions referred to in that provision, but the competent authorities and, where necessary, the national courts must ensure that those limitations and conditions are applied in compliance with the general principles of Community law and, in particular, the principle of proportionality.

## NOTES AND QUESTIONS

1.    The Court bases its assessment of the UK procedure in issue here on the need to apply the public burden exception in accordance with the principle of proportionality. How did that principle come into play in the particular circumstances of this case?

2.    For an analysis of this and related cases, see D. Martin, *Comments on D'Hoop, Gräbner and Baumbast* (2003), 5 EUROPEAN JOURNAL OF MIGRATION AND LAW 143.

3.    In a later case, *Vatsouras*, Cases C-22/08 and C-23/08, 2009 ECJ EUR-Lex LEXIS 455, [2009] ECR I-NYR, the Court held that a job seeker (who does not enjoy the protection of TFEU 45 and its legislative progeny as regards entitlement to benefits) who has established genuine links with the labor market of a Member State can receive a benefit of a financial nature intended to facilitate access to employment. Indeed, independently of its status under national law, such a benefit is not "social assurance" which Member States may continue to refuse to job-seekers under the public burden exception to citizenship rights.

## § 17.04   EU LEGISLATION ON FREE MOVEMENT

### DIRECTIVE 2004/38
[2004] OJ 158/77

[The principal EU legislation dealing with non discrimination for those who exercise the right of free movement to take up work or self employment is now contained in the directive referenced above, known as the "Citizenship directive", which covers both economic and citizenship free movement rights. The following summary appears on the EU's website.]

The Directive merges into a single instrument all the legislation on the right of entry and residence for Union citizens. . . . This simplification will make it easier not only for the general public but also for public authorities to exercise their rights. The Directive also sets out to reduce to the bare minimum the formalities which Union citizens and their families must complete in order to exercise their right of residence.

### General provisions

This proposal is designed to regulate:

- the conditions in which Union citizens and their families exercise their right to move and reside freely within the Member States;

- the right of permanent residence;

- restrictions on the aforementioned rights on grounds of public policy, public security or public health.

### Right to move and right of residence for up to three months

All Union citizens have the right to enter another Member State by virtue of having an identity card or valid passport. Under no circumstances can an entry or exit visa be required. Where the citizens concerned do not have travel documents, the host Member State must afford them every facility in obtaining the requisite documents or having them sent.

Family members who do not have the nationality of a Member State enjoy the same rights as the citizen who they have accompanied. They may be subject to a short stay visa requirement under Regulation (EC) No 539/2001. Residence permits will be deemed equivalent to short-stay visas.

For stays of less than three months, the only requirement on Union citizens is that they possess a valid identity document or passport. The host Member State may require the persons concerned to register their presence in the country within a reasonable and non-discriminatory period of time.

**Right of residence for more than six months**

The right of residence for more than six months remains subject to certain conditions. Applicants must:

- either be engaged in economic activity (on an employed or self-employed basis);

- or have sufficient resources and sickness insurance to ensure that they do not become a burden on the social services of the host Member State during their stay. The Member States may not specify a minimum amount which they deem sufficient, but they must take account of personal circumstances;

- or be following vocational training as a student and have sufficient resources and sickness insurance to ensure that they do not become a burden on the social services of the host Member State during their stay;

- or be a family member of a Union citizen who falls into one of the above categories.

Residence permits are abolished for Union citizens. However, Member States may require them to register with the competent authorities within a period of not less than three months as from the date of arrival. Proof of registration will be issued immediately on presentation of:

- an identity card or valid passport;

- proof that the above conditions are complied with (see Article 9 of the Directive on the proof required for each category of citizen).

Union citizens engaged in training must show, by means of a statement or any other means, that they have sufficient resources for themselves and for the members of their families to ensure that they do not become a burden on the social services of the host Member State. This will be sufficient to prove that they comply with the resources condition.

Family members of Union citizens who are not nationals of a Member State must apply for a residence permit for family members of Union citizens. These permits are valid for at least five years from their date of issue.

The death of the Union citizen, his or her departure from the host Member State, divorce, annulment of marriage or termination of partnership does not affect the right of family members who are not nationals of a Member State to continue residing in the Member State in question, subject to certain conditions.

**Right of permanent residence**

Union citizens acquire the right of permanent residence in the host Member State after a five-year period of uninterrupted legal residence, provided that an expulsion decision has not been enforced against them. This right of permanent residence is no longer subject to any conditions. The same rule applies to family members who are not nationals of a Member State and who have lived with a Union citizen for five years. The right of permanent residence is lost only in the event of more than two successive years' absence from the host Member State.

Union citizens who so request receive a document certifying their right to permanent residence. The Member States issue to third country family members permanent residence permits which are valid indefinitely and renewable automatically every ten years no later than six months after the application is made. Citizens can use any form of evidence generally accepted in the host Member State to prove that they have been continuously resident.

## Common provisions on the right of residence and right of permanent residence

Union citizens qualifying for the right of residence or the right of permanent residence and the members of their family also benefit from equal treatment with host-country nationals in the areas covered by the Treaty. However, the host Member State is not obliged to grant entitlement to social security during the first three months of residence to persons other than employed or self-employed workers and the members of their family. Equally, host Member States are not required, prior to the acquisition of the permanent right of residence, to grant maintenance aid for studies, including for vocational training, in the form of grants or loans to these same persons. Family members, irrespective of their nationality, will be entitled to engage in economic activity on an employed or self-employed basis.

## Restrictions on the right of entry and the right of residence on grounds of public policy, public security or public health

Union citizens or members of their family may be expelled from the host Member State on grounds of public policy, public security or public health. Under no circumstances may an expulsion decision be taken on economic grounds. Measures affecting freedom of movement and residence must comply with the proportionality principle and be based exclusively on the personal conduct of the individual concerned; previous criminal convictions do not automatically justify such measures.

Such conduct must represent a sufficiently serious and present threat which affects the fundamental interests of the state. The mere fact that the entry documents used by the individual concerned have expired does not constitute grounds for expulsion.

In any event, before taking an expulsion decision, the Member State must assess a number of factors such as the period for which the individual concerned has been resident, his or her age, degree of integration and family situation in the host Member State and links with the country of origin. Only in exceptional circumstances, for overriding considerations of public security, can expulsion orders be served on a Union citizen if he has resided in the host country for ten years or if he is a minor.

The person concerned by a decision refusing leave to enter or reside in a Member State must be notified of that decision. The grounds for the decision must be given and the person concerned must be informed of the appeal procedures available to them. Except in emergencies, the subject of such decisions must be allowed at least one month in which to leave the Member State.

Lifelong exclusion orders cannot be issued under any circumstances. Persons concerned by exclusion orders can apply for the situation to be reviewed after a maximum of three years. The Directive also makes provision for a series of procedural guarantees. In particular the individuals concerned have access to judicial review and, where appropriate, to administrative review in the host Member State."

# NOTES AND QUESTIONS

At the end of 2008, the Commission published a report that indicated a significant failure on the part of Member States to implement the directive, as summarized in the following press release:

> Vice-president Jacques Barrot, Commissioner in charge for Justice, Freedom and Security, stated "Free movement of persons constitutes one of the fundamental freedoms of the internal market, to the benefit of EU citizens, of the Member States and of the competitiveness of European economy. Flaws in the implementation of EU law in this field might result in a breach of the principles laying at the very core basis of the European construction. This is why the Commission will step up its efforts to ensure that EU citizens and their families effectively and fully enjoy their rights under the Directive. The Commission will use fully its powers under the Treaty to achieve this result, launching infringement proceedings when necessary, providing guidance to the Member States and ensuring that EU citizens are informed of their rights."

> Directive 2004/38 provides a single legal instrument on free movement of EU citizens and their family members. The Directive lays down simple administrative formalities and gives to EU citizens and their families a right of permanent residence after five years of residence in the host Member State. The Directive extends family reunification rights to registered partners under certain conditions.

> Member States had to bring into force the laws and administrative provisions necessary to comply with the Directive by 30 April 2006. One of the roles of the Commission is to make sure that EU laws are effectively implemented at national or local level for the benefits of EU citizens. Now, after two and a half years, it is time to take stock of how Member States fulfilled this obligation.

> All Member States have adopted national laws to protect the right of EU citizens and their families to move and reside freely within the EU.

> Although national laws in some areas treat EU citizens and their families better than EU law requires, not one single Member State has transposed the Directive effectively and correctly in its entirety. Not one Article of the Directive has been transposed effectively and correctly by all Member States.

> The overall transposition of the Directive is rather disappointing.

Only Cyprus, Greece, Finland, Portugal, Malta, Luxembourg and Spain have correctly adopted more than 85% of provisions of the Directive.

Austria, Denmark, Estonia, Slovenia and Slovakia, on the other hand, have correctly adopted less than 60% of provisions of the Directive.

This is mitigated by the fact that incorrectly transposed provisions of the Directive seem to be, at least in a number of cases, correctly applied by the national courts and authorities, despite the absence of written and clear guidelines for the exercise of judicial and administrative discretion in this area.

The problems revealing persistent violation of the core rights of EU citizens exercising their right to free movement within the EU are mostly related to:

• the right of entry and residence of third country family members *(problems with entry visas or when crossing the border, conditions attached to the right of residence not foreseen in the Directive and delayed issue of residence cards)*,

• the requirement for EU citizens to submit with the applications for residence additional documents not foreseen in the Directive.

The responsibility for ensuring that the rights of EU citizens are guaranteed and that EU citizens are informed of their rights lies with the Member States.

The Commission will continue working at technical level with the Member States. This work has already identified a number of issues that require further discussion and clarification, especially as regards the issues of criminality and abuse.

The Commission intends to offer information and assistance by issuing guidelines in the first half of 2009 on a number of issues identified as problematic in transposition or application.

The Commission will also encourage and support Member States to launch awareness-raising campaigns to inform EU citizens of their rights under the Directive.

## § 17.05    FREE MOVEMENT WITHIN A MEMBER STATE

### ROLAND RUTILI v. MINISTRE DE L'INTERIEUR
Case 36-75, 1975 ECJ EUR-Lex LEXIS 152, [1975] ECR 1219

[Rutili, an Italian national, who had exercised his free movement rights as a worker to reside in France, was a known trade union agitator. The French government sought to imposed restrictions on his movement with French territory justified on grounds of public policy.]

47 The reservation contained in article 48 [45](3) concerning the protection of public

policy has the same scope as the rights the exercise of which may, under that paragraph, be subject to limitations.

48 It follows that prohibitions on residence under the reservation inserted to this effect in article 48 [45] (3) may be imposed only in respect of the whole of the national territory.

49 On the other hand, in the case of partial prohibitions on residence, limited to certain areas of the territory, persons covered by Community law must, under article 7 [18] of the Treaty and within the field of application of that provision, be treated on a footing of equality with the nationals of the Member State concerned.

50 It follows that a Member State cannot, in the case of a national of another Member State covered by the provisions of the Treaty, impose prohibitions on residence which are territorially limited except in circumstances where such prohibitions may be imposed on its own nationals.

51 The answer to the second question must, therefore, be that an appraisal as to whether measures designed to safeguard public policy are justified must have regard to all rules of Community law the object of which is, on the one hand, to limit the discretionary power of member states in this respect and, on the other, to ensure that the rights of persons subject thereunder to restrictive measures are protected.

52 These limitations and safeguards arise, in particular, from the duty imposed on member states to base the measures adopted exclusively on the personal conduct of the individuals concerned, to refrain from adopting any measures in this respect which service ends unrelated to the requirements of public policy or which adversely affect the exercise of trade union rights and, finally, unless this is contrary to the interests of the security of the State involved, immediately to inform any person against whom a restrictive measure has been adopted of the grounds on which the decision taken is based to enable him to make effective use of legal remedies.

53 In particular, measures restricting the right of residence which are limited to part only of the national territory may not be imposed by a member state on nationals of other member states who are subject to the provisions of the treaty except in the cases and circumstances in which such measures may be applied to nationals of the state concerned.

## NOTES AND QUESTIONS

1. The Charter of Fundamental Rights, article 45 specifically, declares that citizens of the Union have the right to move freely within the territory of the Member States. The *Rutili* case above arose, of course, under the provisions of the EC Treaty as an issue relating to the scope of Member State rights, on grounds of public policy, to impose conditions on persons who had exercised the free movement right *between* Member States. Compare in this regard, *Ministre de L'Interieur v. Olazabal*, Case C-100/01, 2002 ECJ CELEX LEXIS 591, [2002] ECR I-10981, where the ECJ stated:

35 The defendant in the main proceedings . . . has been sentenced in France to 18 months' imprisonment and a four-year ban on residence for conspiracy to disturb public order by intimidation or terror. The documents before the Court show that the administrative police measures taken against him, the legality of which forms the subject-matter of the main proceedings, were motivated by the fact that he formed part of an armed and organised group whose activity constitutes a threat to public order in French territory. Prevention of such activity may, moreover, be regarded as falling within the maintenance of public security.

36 Furthermore, it should be noted that, in Rutili, the national court had doubts as to whether a particular situation such as that of Mr Rutili, who had exercised trade union rights, allowed the adoption of a measure designed to preserve public order. In this case, by contrast, the referring court starts from the premiss that reasons of public order preclude the residence of the migrant worker in question on part of the territory, and that, without the possibility of imposing a measure prohibiting residence in that part of the territory, they could justify a measure prohibiting residence in the whole of the territory.

37 In those circumstances, it is necessary to examine whether Article 48 [45] of the Treaty precludes a Member State from imposing on a migrant worker who is a national of another Member State administrative police measures limiting his right of residence to part of the national territory.

38 . . . [I]t does not follow from the wording of Article 48 [45](3) of the Treaty that limitations on the free movement of workers justified on grounds of public policy (ordre public) must always have the same territorial scope as rights conferred by that provision. Nor does secondary legislation preclude that interpretation. Even if Article 6(1)(a) of Directive 68/360 requires the residence card to be valid for the whole of the territory of the Member State which issues it, Article 10 of the same directive allows derogations to be made from that provision, particularly on grounds of public policy.

39 It should be remembered that the reservation provided for in Article 48 [45](3) of the Treaty opens the possibility to Member States, faced with a genuine and sufficiently serious threat affecting a fundamental interest of society, to place restrictions on the free movement of workers . . .

40 The Court has held many times that the reservations contained in Article 48 [45] of the Treaty and Article 56 of the EC Treaty [52] . . . permit Member States to adopt, with respect to nationals of other Member States, and in particular on the grounds of public policy, measures which they cannot apply to their own nationals, inasmuch as they have no authority to expel the latter from the territory or to deny them access thereto . . .

41 In situations where nationals of other Member States are liable to banishment or prohibition of residence, they are also capable of being subject to less severe measures consisting of partial restrictions on their right of residence, justified on grounds of public policy, without it being

necessary that identical measures be capable of being applied by the Member State in question to its own nationals.

42 It should, however, be remembered that a Member State cannot, by virtue of the public policy reservation contained in Articles 48 [45] and 56 [52] of the Treaty, adopt measures against a national of another Member State by reason of conduct which, when engaged in by nationals of the first Member State, does not give rise to punitive measures or other genuine and effective measures intended to combat that conduct.

43 It must also be remembered that a measure restricting one of the fundamental freedoms guaranteed by the Treaty may be justified only if it complies with the principle of proportionality. In that respect, such a measure must be appropriate for securing the attainment of the objective which it pursues and must not go beyond what is necessary in order to attain it . . .

44 It is for the national courts to determine whether the measures taken in this case do in fact relate to individual conduct which constitutes a genuine and sufficiently serious threat to public order or public security, and whether they comply with the principle of proportionality.

45 The answer to the question referred must therefore be that neither Article 48 [45] of the Treaty nor the provisions of secondary legislation which implement the freedom of movement for workers preclude a Member State from imposing, in relation to a migrant worker who is a national of another Member State, administrative police measures limiting that worker's right of residence to a part of the national territory, provided

- that such action is justified by reasons of public order or public security based on his individual conduct;

- that, by reason of their seriousness, those reasons could otherwise give rise only to a measure prohibiting him from residing in, or banishing him from, the whole of the national territory; and

- that the conduct which the Member State concerned wishes to prevent gives rise, in the case of its own nationals, to punitive measures or other genuine and effective measures designed to combat it.

How might one distinguish *Rutili* and *Olazebal?* The Court noted that at least the State should be able to impose restrictions on its own nationals for the same reasons if it is to do so for non-nationals. Does this seem to conflict with Article 45 of the Charter?

## § 17.06   DISCRIMINATION ON GROUNDS OF NATIONALITY

### [A]   Direct Discrimination

## MARIA MARTINEZ SALA v. FREISTAAT BAYERN
### Case C-85/96, 1998 ECJ CELEX LEXIS 13186, [1998] ECR I-2691

[Questions were raised in proceedings between Mrs Martinez Sala and Freistaat Bayern (State of Bavaria) concerning the latter's refusal to grant her a child allowance.]

13 Mrs Martinez Sala, born on 8 February 1956, is a Spanish national who has lived in Germany since May 1968. She had various jobs there at intervals between 1976 and 1986 and was in employment again from 12 September 1989 to 24 October 1989. Since then she has received social assistance from the City of Nuremberg and the Landratsamt Nurnberger Land (Nuremberg Rural District Authority) under the Bundessozialhilfegesetz (Federal Social Welfare Law).

14 Until 19 May 1984, Mrs Martinez Sala obtained from the various competent authorities residence permits which ran more or less without interruption. There-after, she obtained only documents certifying that the extension of her residence permit had been applied for. In its order for reference, the Bayerisches Landessozialgericht points out that the European Convention on Social and Medical Assistance of 11 December 1953 did not, however, allow her to be deported. A residence permit expiring on 18 April 1995 was issued to Mrs Martinez Sala on 19 April 1994, and this permit was extended for a further year on 20 April 1995.

15 In January 1993, that is to say during the period in which she did not have a residence permit, Mrs Martinez Sala applied to Freistaat Bayern for child-raising allowance for her child born during that month.

16 Freistaat Bayern, by decision of 21 January 1993, rejected her application on the ground that she did not have German nationality, a residence entitlement or a residence permit.

\*    \*    \*

[The Court first considered whether Mrs Sala was a "worker" under the relevant EC legislation and determined that this question would need to be remanded for further consideration by the national court].

46 By its fourth question the referring court seeks to ascertain whether Community law precludes a Member State from requiring nationals of other Member States to produce a formal residence permit in order to receive a child-raising allowance.

47 This question is based on the assumption that the appellant in the main proceedings has been authorised to reside in the Member State concerned.

48 Under the BErzGG, in order to be entitled to German child-raising allowance, the claimant, besides meeting the other material conditions for its grant, must be permanently or ordinarily resident in German territory.

49 A national of another Member State who is authorised to reside in German

territory and who does reside there meets this condition. In that regard, such a person is in the same position as a German national residing in German territory.

50 However, the BErzGG provides that, unlike German nationals, a non-national, including a national of another Member State, must be in possession of a certain type of residence permit in order to receive the benefit in question. It is common ground that a document merely certifying that an application for a residence permit has been made is not sufficient, even though such a certificate warrants that the person concerned is entitled to stay.

51 The referring court points out, moreover, that delays in granting residence permits for purely technical administrative reasons can materially affect the substance of the rights enjoyed by citizens of the European Union'.

52 Whilst Community law does not prevent a Member State from requiring nationals of other Member States lawfully resident in its territory to carry at all times a document certifying their right of residence, if an identical obligation is imposed upon its own nationals as regards their identity cards . . . the same is not necessarily the case where a Member State requires nationals of other Member States, in order to receive a child-raising allowance, to be in possession of a residence permit for the issue of which the administration is responsible.

53 For the purposes of recognition of the right of residence, a residence permit can only have declaratory and probative force . . . However, the case-file shows that, for the purposes of the grant of the benefit in question, possession of a residence permit is constitutive of the right to the benefit.

54 Consequently, for a Member State to require a national of another Member State who wishes to receive a benefit such as the allowance in question to produce a document which is constitutive of the right to the benefit and which is issued by its own authorities, when its own nationals are not required to produce any document of that kind, amounts to unequal treatment.

55 In the sphere of application of the Treaty and in the absence of any justification, such unequal treatment constitutes discrimination prohibited by Article 6 [18] of the EC Treaty.

*    *    *

62 Article 8 [17] (2) of the Treaty attaches to the status of citizen of the Union the rights and duties laid down by the Treaty, including the right, laid down in Article 6 [18] of the Treaty, not to suffer discrimination on grounds of nationality within the scope of application ratione materiae of the Treaty.

63 It follows that a citizen of the European Union, such as the appellant in the main proceedings, lawfully resident in the territory of the host Member State, can rely on Article 6 of the Treaty in all situations which fall within the scope ratione materiae of Community law, including the situation where that Member State delays or refuses to grant to that claimant a benefit that is provided to all persons lawfully resident in the territory of that State on the ground that the claimant is not in possession of a document which nationals of that same State are not required to have and the issue of which may be delayed or refused by the authorities of that State.

64 Since the unequal treatment in question thus comes within the scope of the Treaty, it cannot be considered to be justified: it is discrimination directly based on the appellant's nationality and, in any event, nothing to justify such unequal treatment has been put before the Court.

65 The answer to the fourth question must therefore be that Community law precludes a Member State from requiring nationals of other Member States authorised to reside in its territory to produce a formal residence permit issued by the national authorities in order to receive a child-raising allowance, whereas that Member State's own nationals are only required to be permanently or ordinarily resident in that Member State.

## NOTES AND QUESTIONS

In *Sala* the Court did not rule on the question whether Mrs. Sala enjoyed rights as a worker. It did, however, determine that she was protected from discrimination on grounds of nationality because the German government had granted her residence rights. In what way was the German requirement to produce evidence of status discriminatory?

## [B]   Indirect Discrimination

### FINANZAMT KÖLN — ALTSTADT v. ROLAND SCHUMACKER
Case C-279/93, 1995 ECJ CELEX LEXIS 186, [1995] ECR I-225

[In Germany, the Einkommensteuergesetz (Law on income tax, hereinafter 'the EStG') applied different tax regimes to employed persons according to their residence. Residents were permitted certain allowances and benefits that reduced their taxes. Under Paragraph 1(1) of the EStG, natural persons who had their permanent residence or usual abode in Germany were subject there to tax on all their income ('unlimited taxation'). However, under Paragraph 1(4) natural persons with no permanent residence or usual abode in Germany were subject to tax only on the part of their income arising in Germany ('limited taxation'). Under Paragraph 49 (1) (4), such income of German origin included in particular income from employment in Germany. Some of the above benefits were withheld from those employed persons who were subject only to limited taxation.]

28 . . . National rules . . . under which a distinction is drawn on the basis of residence in that non-residents are denied certain benefits which are, conversely, granted to persons residing within national territory, are liable to operate mainly to the detriment of nationals of other Member States. Non-residents are in the majority of cases foreigners.

29 In those circumstances, tax benefits granted only to residents of a Member State may constitute indirect discrimination by reason of nationality.

30 It is also settled law that discrimination can arise only through the application of different rules to comparable situations or the application of the same rule to different situations.

31 In relation to direct taxes, the situations of residents and of non-residents are not, as a rule, comparable.

32 Income received in the territory of a Member State by a non-resident is in most cases only a part of his total income, which is concentrated at his place of residence. Moreover, a non-resident's personal ability to pay tax, determined by reference to his aggregate income and his personal and family circumstances, is more easy to assess at the place where his personal and financial interests are centred. In general, that is the place where he has his usual abode. Accordingly, international tax law, and in particular the Model Double Taxation Treaty of the Organization for Economic Cooperation and Development (OECD), recognizes that in principle the overall taxation of taxpayers, taking account of their personal and family circumstances, is a matter for the State of residence.

33 The situation of a resident is different in so far as the major part of his income is normally concentrated in the State of residence. Moreover, that State generally has available all the information needed to assess the taxpayer's overall ability to pay, taking account of his personal and family circumstances.

34 Consequently, the fact that a Member State does not grant to a non-resident certain tax benefits which it grants to a resident is not, as a rule, discriminatory since those two categories of taxpayer are not in a comparable situation.

35 Accordingly, Article 48 [45] of the Treaty does not in principle preclude the application of rules of a Member State under which a non-resident working as an employed person in that Member State is taxed more heavily on his income than a resident in the same employment.

36 The position is different, however, in a case such as this one where the non-resident receives no significant income in the State of his residence and obtains the major part of his taxable income from an activity performed in the State of employment, with the result that the State of his residence is not in a position to grant him the benefits resulting from the taking into account of his personal and family circumstances.

37 There is no objective difference between the situations of such a non-resident and a resident engaged in comparable employment, such as to justify different treatment as regards the taking into account for taxation purposes of the taxpayer's personal and family circumstances.

38 In the case of a non-resident who receives the major part of his income and almost all his family income in a Member State other than that of his residence, discrimination arises from the fact that his personal and family circumstances are taken into account neither in the State of residence nor in the State of employment.

39 The further question arises whether there is any justification for such discrimination.

40 The view has been advanced, by those Member States which have submitted observations, that discriminatory treatment regarding the taking into account of personal and family circumstances and the availability of "splitting" was justified by the need for consistent application of tax regimes to non-residents. That justification, based on the need for cohesion of the tax system, was upheld by the Court in

Case C-204/90 Bachmann v. Belgium 1992 ECR I-249, paragraph 28). According to those Member States, there is a link between the taking into account of personal and family circumstances and the right to tax worldwide income. Since the taking into account of those circumstances is a matter for the Member State of residence, which is alone entitled to tax worldwide income, they contend that the State on whose territory the non-resident works does not have to take account of his personal and family circumstances since otherwise the personal and family circumstances of the non-resident would be taken into account twice and he would enjoy the corresponding tax benefits in both States.

41 That argument cannot be upheld. In a situation such as that in the main proceedings, the State of residence cannot take account of the taxpayer's personal and family circumstances because the tax payable there is insufficient to enable it to do so. Where that is the case, the Community principle of equal treatment requires that, in the State of employment, the personal and family circumstances of a foreign non-resident be taken into account in the same way as those of resident nationals and that the same tax benefits should be granted to him.

42 The distinction at issue in the main proceedings is thus in no way justified by the need to ensure the cohesion of the applicable tax system.

43 At the hearing, the Finanzamt argued that administrative difficulties prevent the State of employment from ascertaining the income which non-residents working in its territory receive in their State of residence.

44 That argument likewise cannot be upheld.

45 Council Directive 77/799/EEC of 19 December 1977 concerning mutual assistance by the competent authorities of the Member States in the field of direct taxation (OJ 1977 L 336, p. 15) provides for ways of obtaining information comparable to those existing between tax authorities at national level. There is thus no administrative obstacle to account being taken in the State of employment of a non-resident's personal and family circumstances.

46 More particularly, it must be pointed out that the Federal Republic of Germany grants frontier workers resident in the Netherlands and working in Germany the tax benefits resulting from the taking into account of their personal and family circumstances, including the "splitting tariff". Provided that they receive at least 90% of their income in Germany, those Community nationals are treated in the same way as German nationals under the German Law of 21 October 1980 implementing the additional protocol of 13 March 1980 to the Double Taxation Treaty between the Federal Republic of Germany and the Kingdom of the Netherlands of 16 June 1959.

47 The answer to be given to the second and third questions is therefore that Article 48 [45] of the Treaty must be interpreted as precluding the application of rules of a Member State under which a worker who is a national of, and resides in, another Member State and is employed in the first State is taxed more heavily than a worker who resides in the first State and performs the same work there when, as in the main action, the national of the second State obtains his income entirely or almost exclusively from the work performed in the first State and does not receive in the second State sufficient income to be subject to taxation there in a manner enabling

his personal and family circumstances to be taken into account.

## NOTES AND QUESTIONS

1.  The prohibition on discrimination enters the Court's analysis at two different levels here. First, it is necessary to ascertain whether the national rule predominantly affects non-nationals. Having determined that it does, the Court then goes on to ascertain whether the national measure is in fact discriminatory, i.e., whether in all the circumstances the rule treats different situations alike or the same situations differently. As suggested in the Overview, it is possible to regard such cases as falling under the prohibition on restrictions of free movement or as violating the non-discrimination rule. Which approach did the Court follow, and why?

2.  In *Ritter-Coulais v. FA Germersheim*, Case C-152/03, 2006 ECJ CELEX LEXIS 73, [2006] ECR 1711, the Court concluded that EC 39/TFEU 45 could apply to discriminatory tax treatment of German nationals by the German government when they worked in Germany but lived in France. See also *Turpeinen*, Case C-520/04, 2006 ECJ CELEX LEXIS 989, [2006] ECR I-10685. How might such treatment be regarded in the U.S.?

## ROMAN ANGONESE v. CASSA DI RISPARMIO DI BOLZANO SPA
### Case C-281/98, 2000 ECJ CELEX LEXIS 321, [2000] ECR I-4139

[As noted in the excerpt from the case in Chapter 4, Mr Angonese, an Italian national whose mother tongue was German applied to take part in a competition for a post with a private banking undertaking in Bolzano, the Cassa di Risparmio.]

38 According to the order for reference, the Cassa di Risparmio accepts only the Certificate as evidence of the requisite linguistic knowledge and the Certificate can be obtained only in one province of the Member State concerned.

39 Persons not resident in that province therefore have little chance of acquiring the Certificate and it will be difficult, or even impossible, for them to gain access to the employment in question.

40 Since the majority of residents of the province of Bolzano are Italian nationals, the obligation to obtain the requisite Certificate puts nationals of other Member States at a disadvantage by comparison with residents of the province.

41 That is so notwithstanding that the requirement in question affects Italian nationals resident in other parts of Italy as well as nationals of other Member States. In order for a measure to be treated as being discriminatory on grounds of nationality under the rules relating to the free movement of workers, it is not necessary for the measure to have the effect of putting at an advantage all the workers of one nationality or of putting at a disadvantage only workers who are nationals of other Member States, but not workers of the nationality in question.

42 A requirement, such as the one at issue in the main proceedings, making the right to take part in a recruitment competition conditional upon possession of a language diploma that may be obtained in only one province of a Member State and

not allowing any other equivalent evidence could be justified only if it were based on objective factors unrelated to the nationality of the persons concerned and if it were in proportion to the aim legitimately pursued.

43 The Court has ruled that the principle of non-discrimination precludes any requirement that the linguistic knowledge in question must have been acquired within the national territory. . . .

44 So, even though requiring an applicant for a post to have a certain level of linguistic knowledge may be legitimate and possession of a diploma such as the Certificate may constitute a criterion for assessing that knowledge, the fact that it is impossible to submit proof of the required linguistic knowledge by any other means, in particular by equivalent qualifications obtained in other Member States, must be considered disproportionate in relation to the aim in view.

## NOTES AND QUESTIONS

1. Mr. Angonese was an Italian national, and yet he was able to invoke EC 39/TFEU 45 in respect of a situation that appeared wholly internal to the Italian province of Bolzano. Why then did the Court rule that the Bank's requirement was discriminatory on grounds of nationality?

2. In contrast to the *Clean Car* case earlier in this Chapter, the Court, having found the Bank's requirement to be indirectly discriminatory, simply followed that conclusion by declaring it an infringement of the prohibition on discrimination rather than a restriction on free movement rights. How might one rationalize this conclusion compared with *Clean Car*?

## CRIMINAL PROCEEDINGS AGAINST HORST OTTO BICKEL AND ULRICH FRANZ
### Case C-274/96, 1998 ECJ CELEX LEXIS 316, [1998] ECR I-7637

[Mr Bickel was a truck driver of Austrian nationality, resident at Nuziders in Austria. On 15 February 1994, while driving his lorry at Castelbello in the Trentino-Alto Adige Region of Italy, he was stopped by a carabinieri patrol and charged with driving while under the influence of alcohol. Mr Franz, a German national resident at Peissenberg in Germany, visited the Trentino-Alto Adige as a tourist. On 5 May 1995, in the course of a customs inspection, he was found to be in possession of a type of knife that was prohibited. There is a large German-speaking population in this area (as already noted in the *Angonese* case) and therefore the residents are entitled to have judicial proceedings conducted in German. This facility however was not available to non-residents of the province.]

21 The Italian Government contends that the only nationals upon whom the right in question is conferred are those who are both residents of the Province of Bolzano and members of its German-speaking community, the aim of the rules in issue being to recognise the ethnic and cultural identity of persons belonging to the protected minority. Accordingly, the right of that protected minority to the use of its own language need not be extended to nationals of other Member States who are present, occasionally and temporarily, in that region, since provision has been made

to enable such persons to exercise the rights of the defence adequately, even where they have no knowledge of the official language of the host State.

22 The Commission points out that the right to have proceedings conducted in German is not accorded to all Italian nationals, but only to those who are resident in the Province of Bolzano and who belong to its German-speaking community. Accordingly, it is for the national court to determine whether the rules in issue genuinely give rise to discrimination on grounds of nationality, to identify the group of persons discriminated against and then to determine whether such discrimination is justifiable by reference to objective circumstances.

23 The documents before the Court show that the Italian rules restrict the right to have proceedings conducted in German to German-speaking citizens of the Province of Bolzano. It follows that German-speaking nationals of other Member States, particularly Germany and Austria — such as Mr Bickel and Mr Franz — who travel or stay in that province cannot require criminal proceedings to be conducted in German despite the fact that the national rules provide that the German language is to have the same status as Italian.

24 In those circumstances, it appears that German-speaking nationals of other Member States travelling or staying in the Province of Bolzano are at a disadvantage by comparison with Italian nationals resident there whose language is German. Whereas a member of the latter group may, if charged with an offence in the Province of Bolzano, have the proceedings conducted in German, a German-speaking national from another Member State, travelling in that province, is denied that right.

25 Even on the assumption that, as the Italian Government maintains, German-speaking nationals of other Member States who are resident in the Province of Bolzano may rely on the rules in issue and submit their pleadings in German — so that there is no discrimination on grounds of nationality as between residents of the region — Italian nationals are at an advantage by comparison with nationals of other Member States. The majority of Italian nationals whose language is German are in a position to demand that German be used throughout the proceedings in the Province of Bolzano, because they meet the residence requirement laid down by the rules in issue; the majority of German-speaking nationals of other Member States, on the other hand, cannot avail themselves of that right because they do not satisfy that requirement.

26 Consequently, rules such as those in issue in the main proceedings, which make the right, in a defined area, to have criminal proceedings conducted in the language of the person concerned conditional on that person being resident in that area, favour nationals of the host State by comparison with nationals of other Member States exercising their right to freedom of movement and therefore run counter to the principle of non-discrimination laid down in Article 6 [18] of the Treaty.

27 A residence requirement of that kind can be justified only if it is based on objective considerations independent of the nationality of the persons concerned and is proportionate to the legitimate aim of the national provisions . . .

28 However, it is clear from the order for reference that this is not the position in the case of the rules in issue.

29 The Italian Government's contention that the aim of those rules is to protect the ethno-cultural minority residing in the province in question does not constitute a valid justification in this context. Of course, the protection of such a minority may constitute a legitimate aim. It does not appear, however, from the documents before the Court that that aim would be undermined if the rules in issue were extended to cover German-speaking nationals of other Member States exercising their right to freedom of movement.

30 Furthermore, it should be recalled that Mr Bickel and Mr Franz pointed out at the hearing, without being contradicted, that the courts concerned are in a position to conduct proceedings in German without additional complications or costs.

31 Consequently, the answer to the second part of the question referred for a preliminary ruling must be that Article 6 [18] of the Treaty precludes national rules which, in respect of a particular language other than the principal language of the Member State concerned, confer on citizens whose language is that particular language and who are resident in a defined area the right to require that criminal proceedings be conducted in that language, without conferring the same right on nationals of other Member States travelling or staying in that area, whose language is the same.

## NOTES AND QUESTIONS

1.    If the individuals in this case had been French, for example, but came from Alsace Lorraine and spoke a dialect of German as well as French, could they have insisted on proceedings being conducted in German?

2.    In *Ministère Public v. Mutsch*, Case 137/84, [1985] ECR 2682, the Court held that:

> The principle of the free movement of workers . . . requires that a worker who is a national of one Member State and habitually resides in another Member State have a right to demand that criminal proceedings against him be conducted in a language other than the language normally used in proceedings before the court that tries him, if workers who are nationals of the host Member State have the right in the same circumstances. Such a right is based on the notion of social advantage within the meaning of article 7(2) of Regulation 1612/68.

3.    In *Groener v. Minister for Education*, Case C-379/87, 1989 ECJ EUR-Lex LEXIS 202, [1989] ECR 3967, Ms. Groener, a German national, had been employed part-time as an art teacher in the Dublin College of Marketing and Design. She applied for a full-time position but failed a proficiency test in the Irish language. Irish is not spoken by the entire population but the Government promotes a policy of teaching it in schools as a means of expressing national identity and culture. Full-time educators at a college level were required to pass the Irish proficiency exam. Ms. Groener of course had not been educated at a grade/High School level in Ireland and thus was at a considerable disadvantage. The Court struggled to reconcile the Irish law with the EU prohibition on non-discrimination in the following terms:

19 The EEC Treaty does not prohibit the adoption of a policy for the protection and promotion of a language of a Member State which is both the national language and the first official language. However, the implementation of such a policy must not encroach upon a fundamental freedom such as that of the free movement of workers. Therefore, the requirements deriving from measures intended to implement such a policy must not in any circumstances be disproportionate in relation to the aim pursued and the manner in which they are applied must not bring about discrimination against nationals of other Member States.

20 The importance of education for the implementation of such a policy must be recognized. Teachers have an essential role to play, not only through the teaching which they provide but also by their participation in the daily life of the school and the privileged relationship which they have with their pupils. In those circumstances, it is not unreasonable to require them to have some knowledge of the first national language.

21 It follows that the requirement imposed on teachers to have an adequate knowledge of such a language must, provided that the level of knowledge required is not disproportionate in relation to the objective pursued, be regarded as a condition corresponding to the knowledge required by reason of the nature of the post to be filled within the meaning of the last subparagraph of Article 3(1) of Regulation No 1612/68.

22 It must also be pointed out that where the national provisions provide for the possibility of exemption from that linguistic requirement where no other fully qualified candidate has applied for the post to be filled, Community law requires that power to grant exemptions to be exercised by the Minister in a non-discriminatory manner.

23 Moreover, the principle of non-discrimination precludes the imposition of any requirement that the linguistic knowledge in question must have been acquired within the national territory. It also implies that the nationals of other Member States should have an opportunity to retake the oral examination, in the event of their having previously failed it, when they again apply for a post of assistant lecturer or lecturer.

## [C]   "Within the Scope of Application of the Treaties"

### IAN WILLIAM COWAN v. TRESOR PUBLIC
Case 186/871989, ECJ EUR-Lex LEXIS 144, [1989] ECR 195

[Mr Cowan, a British citizen claimed compensation from the French state for injury resulting from a violent assault suffered by him at the exit of a metro station during a brief stay in Paris. The French law that provided for compensation to victims of crimes required that the claimant be of French nationality or resident in France.]

5 Mr Cowan . . . relied on the prohibition of discrimination laid down, in particular, in Article 7 [18] of the EEC Treaty. He argued that the conditions set out above were discriminatory and that such conditions prevented tourists from going freely to another Member State to receive services there. The representative of the

Treasury and the Ministère Public replied that the rules in question treated resident foreigners in the same way as French nationals and that to distinguish their situation from that of tourists was compatible with Community law, which itself makes periods spent by nationals of one Member State in another Member State subject to different conditions according to the length of the stay.

\*    \*    \*

10 By prohibiting "any discrimination on grounds of nationality" Article 7 [18] of the Treaty requires that persons in a situation governed by Community law be placed on a completely equal footing with nationals of the Member State. In so far as this principle is applicable it therefore precludes a Member State from making the grant of a right to such a person subject to the condition that he reside on the territory of that State — that condition is not imposed on the State's own nationals.

11 It should also be emphasized that the right to equal treatment is conferred directly by Community law and may not therefore be made subject to the issue of a certificate to that effect by the authorities of the relevant Member State. . . .

\*    \*    \*

13 It follows that in so far as the prohibition of discrimination is applicable it precludes a Member State from making the award of a right to a person in a situation governed by Community law subject to the condition that he hold a residence permit or be a national of a country which has entered into a reciprocal agreement with that Member State.

The scope of the prohibition of discrimination

14 Under Article 7[18] of the Treaty the prohibition of discrimination applies "within the scope of application of this Treaty" and "without prejudice to any special provisions contained therein". This latter expression refers particularly to other provisions of the Treaty in which the application of the general principle set out in that article is given concrete form in respect of specific situations. Examples of that are the provisions concerning free movement of workers, the right of establishment and the freedom to provide services.

15 On that last point, in its judgment of 31 January 1984 in Joined Cases 286/82 and 26/83 Luisi and Carbone v. Ministero del Tesoro ((1984)) ECR 377, the Court held that the freedom to provide services includes the freedom for the recipients of services to go to another Member State in order to receive a service there, without being obstructed by restrictions, and that tourists, among others, must be regarded as recipients of services.

16 At the hearing the French Government submitted that as Community law now stands a recipient of services may not rely on the prohibition of discrimination to the extent that the national law at issue does not create any barrier to freedom of movement. A provision such as that at issue in the main proceedings, it says, imposes no restrictions in that respect. Furthermore, it concerns a right which is a manifestation of the principle of national solidarity. Such a right presupposes a closer bond with the State than that of a recipient of services, and for that reason

it may be restricted to persons who are either nationals of that State or foreign nationals resident on the territory of that State.

17 That reasoning cannot be accepted. When Community law guarantees a natural person the freedom to go to another Member State the protection of that person from harm in the Member State in question, on the same basis as that of nationals and persons residing there, is a corollary of that freedom of movement. It follows that the prohibition of discrimination is applicable to recipients of services within the meaning of the Treaty as regards protection against the risk of assault and the right to obtain financial compensation provided for by national law when that risk materializes. The fact that the compensation at issue is financed by the Public Treasury cannot alter the rules regarding the protection of the rights guaranteed by the Treaty.

18 The French Government also submitted that compensation such as that at issue in the main proceedings is not subject to the prohibition of discrimination because it falls within the law of criminal procedure, which is not included within the scope of the Treaty.

19 Although in principle criminal legislation and the rules of criminal procedure, among which the national provision in issue is to be found, are matters for which the Member States are responsible, . . . Community law sets certain limits to their power. Such legislative provisions may not discriminate against persons to whom Community law gives the right to equal treatment or restrict the fundamental freedoms guaranteed by Community law.

20 In the light of all the foregoing the answer to the question submitted must be that the prohibition of discrimination laid down in particular in Article 7 [18] of the EEC Treaty must be interpreted as meaning that in respect of persons whose freedom to travel to a Member State, in particular as recipients of services, is guaranteed by Community law that State may not make the award of State compensation for harm caused in that State to the victim of an assault resulting in physical injury subject to the condition that he hold a residence permit or be a national of a country which has entered into a reciprocal agreement with that Member State.

## NOTES AND QUESTIONS

1. In *Cowan*, the Court stated that the rights of a person exercising an economic freedom — here a British tourist, as a recipient of services in France, could not be subject to the condition that such person must hold a French residence permit, while French nationals were automatically entitled to compensation whether resident in France or not. How would the Court have viewed the situation if the law had in fact prescribed residence as the criterion?

2.

Note also the remarks of the Court in *Brian Francis Collins v. Secretary of State for Work and Pensions*, Case C-138/02, 2004 ECJ CELEX LEXIS 135, [2004] ECR I-2703, cited in the above case:

[W]hen Community law guarantees a natural person the freedom to go to another Member State the protection of that person from harm in the Member State in question, on the same basis as that of nationals and persons residing there, is a corollary of that freedom of movement. It follows that the prohibition of discrimination is applicable to recipients of services within the meaning of the Treaty as regards protection against the risk of assault and the right to obtain financial compensation provided for by national law when that risk materialises.

# FRANCOISE GRAVIER v. CITY OF LIEGE
## Case 293/83, [1985] ECR 593

[Francoise Gravier, a student at the Academie Royale des Beaux Arts, Liège, claimed that the City of Liège should be prohibited from requiring her to pay a fee called the "minerval" (enrolment fee) which students of Belgian nationality were not required to pay. The City of Liège joined as third parties the Belgian State, which issued the circulars requiring that the fee be charged, and the Communauté Française, the regional institution responsible for art education.]

19 The first remark which must be made in that regard is that although educational organization and policy are not as such included in the spheres which the Treaty has entrusted to the Community institutions, access to and participation in courses of instruction and apprenticeship, in particular vocational training, are not unconnected with Community law.

20 Article 7 of Regulation No 1612/68 of the Council of 15 October 1968 on freedom of movement for workers within the Community . . . provides that a worker who is a national of a Member State and who is employed in another Member State is to have access to training in vocational schools and retraining centres in that country by virtue of the same right and under the same conditions as national workers. Article 12 of the regulation provides that the children of such workers are to be admitted to that State's general educational apprenticeship and vocational training courses under the same conditions as the nationals of that State.

21 With regard more particularly to vocational training, Article 128 [148] of the Treaty provides that the Council is to lay down general principles for implementing a common vocational training policy capable of contributing to the harmonious development both of the national economies and of the Common Market. The first principle established in Council Decision No 63/266/EEC of 2 April 1963 laying down those general principles . . . states that "the general principles must enable every person to receive adequate training, with due regard for freedom of choice of occupation, place of training and place of work".

22 The particular attention which the Community institutions have given to problems of access to vocational training and its improvement throughout the Community may be seen, moreover, in the "general guidelines" which the Council laid down in 1971 for drawing up a Community programme on vocational training (Official Journal, English Special Edition, Second Series IX, p 50), in the resolution of the Council and of the Ministers of Education meeting within the Council of 13 December 1976 concerning measures to be taken to improve the preparation of young people for work and to facilitate their transition from education to working

life (Official Journal No C 308, p 1) and the Council resolution of 11 July 1983 concerning vocational training policies in the European Community in the 1980s (Official Journal No C 193, p 2).

23 The common vocational training policy referred to in Article 128 [148] of the Treaty is thus gradually being established. It constitutes, moreover, an indispensible element of the activities of the Community, whose objectives include inter alia the free movement of persons, the mobility of labour and the improvement of the living standards of workers.

24 Access to vocational training is in particular likely to promote free movement of persons throughout the Community, by enabling them to obtain a qualification in the Member State where they intend to work and by enabling them to complete their training and develop their particular talents in the Member State whose vocational training programmes include the special subject desired.

25 It follows from all the foregoing that the conditions of access to vocational training fall within the scope of the Treaty.

26 The answer to the first question must therefore be that the imposition on students who are nationals of other Member States, of a charge, a registration fee or the so-called "minerval" as a condition of access to vocational training, where the same fee is not imposed on students who are nationals of the host Member State, constitutes discrimination on grounds of nationality contrary to Article 7 [18] of the Treaty.

## NOTES AND QUESTIONS

1.   Given the introductory phrase of EC 12/TFEU 18, how did the Court bring Ms. Gravier within the ambit of invocable EC Treaty provisions? Does this interpretation seem expansive?

2.   When moving away from the "free movement of workers" toward the "free movement of citizens" the ECJ broadened its case law to job seekers and students. In order to do so it combined the provisions on citizenship and on non-discrimination (see following section) that entitled it to state that student grants or unemployment allowances should be non-discriminatory between EU citizens, also arguing that these were potential workers. See *Grzelczyk* Case C-184/99, 2001 ECJ EUR-Lex LEXIS 956 [2001] ECR I-6193; *Vatsouras* Cases C-22/08 and C-23/08, 2009 ECJ EUR-Lex LEXIS 455 [2009] ECR I-NYR; *Foerster* Case C-158/07, 2008 ECJ EUR-Lex LEXIS 2144 [2008] ECR I-NYR; and *Bidar*, Case C-209/03, 2005 ECJ EUR-Lex LEXIS 62 [2005] ECR I-2119.

## THE QUEEN (ON THE APPLICATION OF DANY BIDAR) v. LONDON BOROUGH OF EALING AND SECRETARY OF STATE FOR EDUCATION AND SKILLS
### Case C-209/03, 2005 ECJ CELEX LEXIS 98, [2005] ECR I-2119

[Mr Bidar was a student at the London School of Economics. He was denied a government sponsored student loan since he was a French national. He had been living in the UK for more than three years with his grandmother. Under the UK

Education support regulations, entitlement to a loan is dependent on at least three years residence in the UK. Additionally, the applicant must be treated under the regulations as "settled" in the UK. While persons exercising the economic rights of free movement were so treated, the Mr Bidar had neither exercised such rights himself nor was he a family member of a person who had.]

30. . . . [T]he national court wishes to know whether assistance granted to students to cover their maintenance costs is within the scope of application of the Treaty within the meaning of the first paragraph of Article 12 EC [18], which states that, without prejudice to any special provisions contained in the Treaty, any discrimination on grounds of nationality is prohibited within that scope of application.

31. In that context, the national court wishes to know whether assistance granted to students to cover their maintenance costs is within the scope of application of the Treaty within the meaning of the first paragraph of Article 12 EC [18], which states that, without prejudice to any special provisions contained in the Treaty, any discrimination on grounds of nationality is prohibited within that scope of application.

32. To assess the scope of application of the Treaty within the meaning of Article 12 EC [18], that article must be read in conjunction with the provisions of the Treaty on citizenship of the Union. Citizenship of the Union is destined to be the fundamental status of nationals of the Member States, enabling those who find themselves in the same situation to receive the same treatment in law irrespective of their nationality, subject to such exceptions as are expressly provided for . . .

33. According to settled case-law, a citizen of the European Union lawfully resident in the territory of the host Member State can rely on Article 12 EC [18] in all situations which fall within the scope ratione materiae of Community law . . .

34. Those situations include those involving the exercise of the fundamental freedoms guaranteed by the Treaty and those involving the exercise of the right to move and reside within the territory of the Member States, as conferred by Article 18 EC [21] . . .

35. Moreover, there is nothing in the text of the Treaty to suggest that students who are citizens of the Union, when they move to another Member State to study there, lose the rights which the Treaty confers on citizens of the Union . . .

36. . . . [A] national of a Member State who goes to another Member State and pursues secondary education there exercises the freedom to move guaranteed by Article 18 EC [21].

37. Furthermore, a national of a Member State who, like the claimant in the main proceedings, lives in another Member State where he pursues and completes his secondary education, without it being objected that he does not have sufficient resources or sickness insurance, enjoys a right of residence on the basis of Article 18 EC [21] and Directive 90/364.

38. With regard to social assistance benefits . . . a citizen of the Union who is not economically active may rely on the first paragraph of Article 12 EC [18] where he has been lawfully resident in the host Member State for a certain time or possesses a residence permit.

39. It is true that the Court held in Lair and Brown (paragraphs 15 and 18 respectively) that at the present stage of development of Community law assistance given to students for maintenance and for training falls in principle outside the scope of the EEC Treaty for the purposes of Article 7 thereof later Article 6 of the EC Treaty, now, after amendment, Article 12 EC [18] '. In those judgments the Court considered that such assistance was, on the one hand, a matter of education policy, which was not as such included in the spheres entrusted to the Community institutions, and, on the other, a matter of social policy, which fell within the competence of the Member States in so far as it was not covered by specific provisions of the EEC Treaty.

40. However, since judgment was given in Lair and Brown, the Treaty on European Union has introduced citizenship of the Union into the EC Treaty and added to Title VIII (now Title XI) of Part Three a Chapter 3 devoted inter alia to education and vocational training . . .

41. Thus Article 149(1) EC [165] gives the Community the task of contributing to the development of quality education by encouraging cooperation between Member States and, if necessary, by supporting and supplementing their action, while fully respecting the responsibility of those States for the content of teaching and the organisation of education systems and their cultural and linguistic diversity.

42. Under paragraphs 2 and 4 of that article, the Council may adopt incentive measures, excluding any harmonisation of the laws and regulations of the Member States, and recommendations aimed in particular at encouraging the mobility of students and teachers . . .).

43. In view of those developments since the judgments in Lair and Brown, it must be considered that the situation of a citizen of the Union who is lawfully resident in another Member State falls within the scope of application of the Treaty within the meaning of the first paragraph of Article 12 EC [18] for the purposes of obtaining assistance for students, whether in the form of a subsidised loan or a grant, intended to cover his maintenance costs.

44. That development of Community law is confirmed by Article 24 of Directive 2004/38, which states in paragraph 1 that all Union citizens residing in the territory of another Member State on the basis of that directive are to enjoy equal treatment within the scope of the Treaty'. In that the Community legislature, in paragraph 2 of that article, defined the content of paragraph 1 in more detail, by providing that a Member State may in the case of persons other than workers, self-employed persons, persons who retain such status and members of their families restrict the grant of maintenance aid in the form of grants or loans in respect of students who have not acquired a right of permanent residence, it took the view that the grant of such aid is a matter which, in accordance with Article 24(1), now falls within the scope of the Treaty.

45. That interpretation is not invalidated by the argument put forward by the governments which have submitted observations and by the Commission concerning the limitations and conditions referred to in Article 18 EC [21]. Those governments and the Commission observe that, while citizenship of the Union enables nationals of the Member States to rely on the first paragraph of Article 12

EC [18] when they exercise the right to move and reside within the territory of those States, their situation falls within the scope of application of the Treaty within the meaning of Article 12 EC [18] only, in accordance with Article 18(1) EC [21], subject to the limitations and conditions laid down in the Treaty and by the measures adopted to give it effect, which include those laid down by Directive 93/96. Since Article 3 of that directive excludes the right to payment of maintenance grants on the part of students benefiting from the right of residence, those grants are still outside the scope of the Treaty.

46. In this respect, it is indeed the case that students who go to another Member State to start or pursue higher education there and enjoy a right of residence there for that purpose under Directive 93/96 cannot base any right to payment of maintenance assistance on that directive.

47. However, Article 3 of Directive 93/96 does not preclude a national of a Member State who, by virtue of Article 18 EC [21] and Directive 90/364, is lawfully resident in the territory of another Member State where he intends to start or pursue higher education from relying during that residence on the fundamental principle of equal treatment enshrined in the first paragraph of Article 12 EC [18].

48. In a context such as that of the main proceedings where the right of residence of the applicant for assistance is not contested, the assertion, made by some of the governments which have submitted observations, that Community law allows a Member State to take the view that a national of another Member State who has recourse to social assistance no longer fulfils the conditions of his right of residence and if appropriate to take measures, within the limits imposed by Community law, for the removal of that national . . . is moreover immaterial.

49. In the light of all the foregoing, the answer to Question 1 must be that assistance, whether in the form of subsidised loans or of grants, provided to students lawfully resident in the host Member State to cover their maintenance costs falls within the scope of application of the Treaty for the purposes of the prohibition of discrimination laid down in the first paragraph of Article 12 EC [18].

## NOTES AND QUESTIONS

1.   Consider the Court's rationale for determining that the circumstances of this case fell within the scope of the application of the Treaties. What might this mean for future cases that on their face do not involve any exercise of economic activity? Does it "open the floodgates"?

2.   For analysis of this decision, see O. Golynker, *Analysis and Reflections — Student loans: The European concept of social justice according to Bidar*, (2006) 31 EL REV. 390.

3.   In *Foerster*, C-158/07, 2008 ECJ EUR-Lex LEXIS 2144 [2008] ECR I-8507, the Court followed up on its judgment in *Bidar* by stating the conditions under which students are entitled to a maintenance grant. The Court considered that the application to students of a requirement of five years' prior residence was an appropriate condition to deliver a maintenance grant to a non-national.

## DAVID CHARLES HAYES AND JEANNETTE KAREN HAYES
## v. KRONENBERGER GMBH

Case C-323/95, 1997 ECJ CELEX LEXIS 292, [1997] ECR I-1711

[Mr and Mrs Hayes, a partnership under English civil law, sued Kronenberger GmbH, a German company in liquidation, for sums owed. Kronenberger asked Mr. and Mrs. Hayes to furnish security for costs under Paragraph 101(1) of the Zivilprozessordnung (German Code of Civil Procedure, or "ZPO"). According to that provision, foreign nationals who act as plaintiffs in proceedings brought before German courts must, upon application by the defendant, give security for costs and lawyers' fees. Paragraph 110(2)(1) of the ZPO provides, however, that this obligation does not apply where the plaintiff is a national of a State which does not require such security to be given by German nationals. The Saarlandisches Oberlandesgericht observed that whilst courts in the United Kingdom tended no longer to require nationals of Member States of the European Union to furnish security for costs, this did not amount to a consistent practice guaranteeing the reciprocity required by Paragraph 110(2)(1) of the ZPO.]

12 It must . . . first be considered whether a provision of a Member State requiring nationals of another Member State to furnish security for costs when intending to bring judicial proceedings against one of its nationals or a company established in that country, where its own nationals are not subject to that requirement, falls within the scope of application of the Treaty.

13 It has been consistently held that, whilst, in the absence of Community legislation, it is for the internal legal order of each Member State to lay down the detailed procedural rules for legal proceedings intended fully to safeguard the rights which individuals derive from Community law, Community law nevertheless imposes limits on that competence . . . Such legislative provisions may not discriminate against persons to whom Community law gives the right to equal treatment or restrict the fundamental freedoms guaranteed by Community law . . .

14 It must be held that a national procedural rule, such as the one described above, is liable to affect the economic activity of traders from other Member States on the market of the State in question. Although it is, as such, not intended to regulate an activity of a commercial nature, it has the effect of placing such traders in a less advantageous position than nationals of that State as regards access to its courts. Since Community law guarantees such traders free movement of goods and services in the common market, it is a corollary of those freedoms that they must be able, in order to resolve any disputes arising from their economic activities, to bring actions in the courts of a Member State in the same way as nationals of that State . . .

15 . . . Articles 59 [56] and 60 [50] of the EC Treaty preclude a Member State from requiring security for costs to be given under a provision such as Paragraph 110 of the ZPO by a member of a profession established in another Member State who brings an action before one of its courts, on the sole ground that he is a national of another Member State.

16 It is important to note however that . . . national legislative provisions which fall within the scope of application of the Treaty are, by reason of their effects on

intra-Community trade in goods and services, necessarily subject to the general principle of non-discrimination laid down by the first paragraph of Article 6 of the Treaty [18], without there being any need to connect them with the specific provisions of Articles 30 [34], 36 [36], 59 [66] and 66 [74] of the Treaty.

17 It must therefore be held that a rule of domestic civil procedure, such as the one at issue in the main proceedings, falls within the scope of the Treaty within the meaning of the first paragraph of Article 6 [18] and is subject to the general principle of non-discrimination laid down by that article in so far as it has an effect, even though indirect, on trade in goods and services between Member States. Such an effect is liable to arise in particular where security for costs is required where proceedings are brought to recover payment for the supply of goods . . .

18 In so far as it prohibits any discrimination on grounds of nationality', Article 6 [18] of the Treaty requires persons in a situation governed by Community law and nationals of the Member State concerned to be treated absolutely equally.

19 A provision such as the one at issue in the main proceedings obviously entails direct discrimination on the basis of nationality. Under that provision, a Member State does not require its own nationals to furnish security even if they have no assets or residence in that State.

20 Kronenberger and the Swedish Government consider, however, that the principle of non-discrimination does not preclude a requirement for foreign plaintiffs to furnish security where any order for judicial costs cannot be enforced in the country of the plaintiff's domicile. In that event, it is argued, the security is designed to avoid a foreign plaintiff being able to bring judicial proceedings without running any financial risk should he lose his case.

\*   \*   \*

24 . . . [W]ithout its being necessary to consider whether that situation might warrant the imposition of security for costs on non-residents where such a risk exists, suffice it to say that, in so far as the provision at issue imposes different treatment depending on the plaintiff's nationality, it does not comply with the principle of proportionality. On the one hand, it cannot secure repayment of judicial costs in every trans-frontier case, since security cannot be imposed on a German plaintiff not residing in Germany and having no assets there. On the other, it is disproportionate to the objective pursued in that a non-German plaintiff who resides and has assets in Germany could also be required to furnish security.

25 The answer to the national court's question must therefore be that Article 6 [18] of the Treaty must be interpreted as precluding a Member State from requiring security for costs to be furnished by a national of another Member State who has brought an action in one of its civil courts against one of its nationals where that requirement may not be imposed on its own nationals who have neither assets nor a residence in that country, in a situation where the action is connected with the exercise of fundamental freedoms guaranteed by Community law.

## NOTES AND QUESTIONS

**1.** The Court considered only EC 12/TFEU 18 in answering the questions posed and noted that the article applied in the context of the exercise of the free movement of goods and services provisions of the EC Treaty/TFEU. Could or should it have considered other provisions as well, specifically those relating to EU Citizenship, and might this have made any difference? Suppose the English plaintiffs here had sued a German company in relation to a contractual relationship existing only in Germany, as for example the refund of a deposit they paid on a lease to enable their child to obtain accommodation while doing a study semester in Germany. Would this then be outside the scope of EC 12/TFEU 18 since no inter-state transaction within the scope of the EC Treaty/TFEU was involved? Or do you think the Court would inevitably find such a connection?

**2.** See also *Commission v. Italy*, Case C-224/00, 2002 ECJ CELEX LEXIS 313, [2002] ECR I-2965, where a national rule requiring security to be provided by non-residents for payment of fines was upheld due to the absence of any international arrangements to require enforcement in another Member State; and *Johannes v. Johannes*, Case C-430/97, 1999 ECJ CELEX LEXIS 348, [199] ECR I-3475, where, under principles of private international law, the use of nationality as a connecting factor for choice of law was considered acceptable (apportionment of pension rights in divorce proceedings).

## EGON SCHEMPP v. FINANZAMT MÜNCHEN
### Case C-403/03, 2005 ECJ CELEX LEXIS 325, [2005] ECR I-6421

[Under divorce arrangements, Mr. Schempp, a German national and resident, paid maintenance to his ex-wife, who had taken up residence in Austria. In general, German Tax Law allowed deduction of maintenance payments by the payor since under German law the recipient was liable to tax (whether tax is actually paid or not). However, under Austrian law the recipient is not taxed, and therefore the German authorities denied Mr. Schempp's deduction.]

13. The first point to examine is whether the situation at issue in the main proceedings falls within the scope of Community law.

14. It should be recalled that the first paragraph of Article 12 EC [18] prohibits, within the scope of application of the Treaty, and without prejudice to any special provisions contained therein, any discrimination on grounds of nationality.

15. To assess the scope of application of the Treaty within the meaning of Article 12 EC [18], that article must be read in conjunction with the provisions of the Treaty on citizenship of the Union. Citizenship of the Union is destined to be the fundamental status of nationals of the Member States, enabling those who find themselves in the same situation to receive the same treatment in law irrespective of their nationality, subject to such exceptions as are expressly provided for . . .

16. Under Article 17(1) EC [20], every person holding the nationality of a Member State is a citizen of the Union. Mr Schempp, as a German national, thus has such citizenship.

17. As the Court has already held, Article 17(2) EC [20] attaches to the status of

citizen of the Union the rights and duties laid down by the Treaty, including the right to rely on Article 12 EC [18] in all situations falling within the material scope of Community law. . . .

18. Those situations include those involving the exercise of the fundamental freedoms guaranteed by the Treaty and those involving the exercise of the right to move and reside within the territory of the Member States, as conferred by Article 18 EC [21] . . .

19. While in the present state of Community law direct taxation falls within the competence of the Member States, the latter must none the less exercise that competence in accordance with Community law, in particular the provisions of the Treaty concerning the right of every citizen of the Union to move and reside freely within the territory of the Member States, and therefore avoid any overt or covert discrimination on the basis of nationality . . .

20. However, it also follows from the case-law that citizenship of the Union, established by Article 17 EC [20], is not intended to extend the material scope of the Treaty to internal situations which have no link with Community law . . .

21. According to the German and Netherlands Governments, the main proceedings relate to such a situation. The person relying on Article 12 EC [18], in the present case Mr Schempp, did not make use of his right of free movement laid down by Article 18 EC [21]. His former spouse did indeed exercise such a right. The present case, however, does not concern her taxation but that of Mr Schempp. The German Government therefore observes that in the present case the only factor external to the Federal Republic of Germany is the fact that Mr Schempp is paying maintenance to a person resident in another Member State. Since maintenance payments have no effect on intra-Community trade in goods and services, however, the situation does not fall within Article 12 EC [18].

22. On this point, it must be observed that, contrary to the submissions of the German and Netherlands Governments, the situation of a national of a Member State who, like Mr Schempp, has not made use of the right to freedom of movement cannot, for that reason alone, be assimilated to a purely internal situation . . .

23. While it is correct that Mr. Schempp has not exercised such a right, it is nevertheless common ground that his former spouse, by establishing her residence in Austria, exercised the right granted by Article 18 EC [21] to every citizen of the Union to move and reside freely in the territory of another Member State.

24 . . . [S]ince, for the purposes of determining the deductibility of maintenance paid by a taxpayer resident in Germany to a recipient resident in another Member State, the national legislation at issue in the main proceedings takes account of the fiscal treatment of those payments in the State of residence of the recipient, it necessarily follows that the exercise in the present case by Mr. Schempp's former spouse of her right to move and reside freely in another Member State under Article 18 EC [21] was such as to influence her former husband's capacity to deduct the maintenance payments made to her from his taxable income in Germany.

25. It follows from all the foregoing that, since the exercise by Mr. Schempp's former spouse of a right conferred by the Community legal order had an effect on

his right to deduct in his Member State of residence, such a situation cannot be regarded as an internal situation with no connection with Community law.

27. It is common ground that if Mr. Schempp's former spouse had been resident in Germany he would have been entitled to deduct the maintenance payments made to her. Since, however, she was resident in Austria, the German tax authorities refused him that deduction.

28. It is settled case-law that the principle of non-discrimination requires that comparable situations must not be treated differently unless such treatment is objectively justified . . .

29. It must therefore be examined whether the situation of Mr. Schempp, who pays maintenance to his former spouse resident in Austria without being able to deduct those payments in his income tax declaration, can be compared to that of a person who makes such payments to a former spouse resident in Germany and enjoys that tax advantage.

30. Under the third sentence of Paragraph 1a(1)(1) of the EStG, the deductibility in Germany of maintenance payments by a taxpayer resident in that Member State to a recipient resident in another Member State is conditional on their being taxed in that other Member State.

31. It follows that since, in the main proceedings, the maintenance payments were not taxed in the Member State of residence of Mr. Schempp's former spouse, he was not allowed to deduct those payments from his income in Germany.

32. In those circumstances, it is apparent that the unfavourable treatment of which Mr. Schempp complains in fact derives from the circumstance that the tax system applicable to maintenance payments in his former spouse's Member State of residence differs from that applied in his own Member State of residence.

33. As the Netherlands Government points out, if his former spouse had chosen to reside in a Member State, such as the Netherlands, in which — contrary to the situation in Austria — maintenance payments are taxed, Mr. Schempp would have been entitled under the national legislation at issue in the present case to deduct the maintenance payments made to her.

34. It is settled case-law that Article 12 EC [18] is not concerned with any disparities in treatment, for persons and undertakings subject to the jurisdiction of the Community, which may result from divergences existing between the various Member States, so long as they affect all persons subject to them in accordance with objective criteria and without regard to their nationality . . .

35. It follows that, contrary to Mr. Schempp's claims, the payment of maintenance to a recipient resident in Germany cannot be compared to the payment of maintenance to a recipient resident in Austria. The recipient is subject in each of those two cases, as regards taxation of the maintenance payments, to a different tax system.

36. Consequently, the fact that a taxpayer resident in Germany is not able, under Paragraph 1a(1)(1) of the EStG, to deduct maintenance paid to his former spouse resident in Austria does not constitute discrimination within the meaning of Article

12 EC [18].

37. According to Mr. Schempp, the unequal treatment of which he is the subject in the present case derives, however, from the fact that, while deductibility of maintenance paid to a person resident in Germany is not conditional on that person actually paying tax, actual payment of tax is required for deductibility of maintenance paid to a person resident in the territory of another Member State.

38. However, it must be recalled that in the present proceedings the national court solely asks the Court whether Community law precludes a taxpayer resident in Germany from being unable to deduct the maintenance paid to his former spouse resident in Austria. Consequently, for the purpose of providing the national court with an interpretation which will be of use to it in giving its decision in the main proceedings, it must be concluded that the point raised by Mr. Schempp, in that it concerns the payment of maintenance to a recipient resident in another Member State in which maintenance payments are taxable, does not arise in the present case, as it is common ground that maintenance payments are not taxable in Austria.

39. As to the undisputed fact that, if Mr. Schempp's former spouse had resided in Germany, he would have been entitled to deduct the maintenance paid to her, even though in such a case the maintenance would not have been taxed because his former spouse's income in Germany during the period in question was below the tax thresholds applied by German tax legislation, that cannot call into question the conclusion in paragraph 36 above. As the Commission of the European Communities rightly observes, the non-taxation of maintenance payments on those grounds in Germany cannot be equated to the non-taxation of the maintenance in Austria on the ground of its non-taxable character in that Member State, since the fiscal consequences which attach to each of those situations as regards the taxation of income are different for the taxpayers concerned.

Application of Article 18 EC [21]

40. Under Article 18(1) EC, [21] every citizen of the Union shall have the right to move and reside freely within the territory of the Member States, subject to the limitations and conditions laid down in the Treaty and by the measures adopted to give it effect'.

41. As a national of a Member State and hence a citizen of the Union, Mr. Schempp is entitled to rely on that provision.

42. In his observations, Mr. Schempp submits that Article 18(1) EC protects not only the right to move and settle in other Member States but also the right to choose one's residence. He submits that, since the maintenance payments are not deductible from taxable income where the recipient resides in another Member State, the recipient could be subject to a certain pressure not to leave Germany, thus constituting a restriction on the exercise of the rights guaranteed by Article 18(1) EC. That pressure could materialise specifically at the time when the amount of the maintenance is determined, since that determination takes the tax implications into account.

43. On this point, it is clear that, as the German and Netherlands Governments and

the Commission submit, the national legislation in question does not in any way obstruct Mr Schempp's right, as a citizen of the Union, to move and reside in other Member States under Article 18(1) EC [21].

44. As has been observed, it is true that the transfer of his former spouse's residence to Austria entailed unfavourable tax consequences for Mr. Schempp in his Member State of residence.

45. However, the Court has already held that the Treaty offers no guarantee to a citizen of the Union that transferring his activities to a Member State other than that in which he previously resided will be neutral as regards taxation. Given the disparities in the tax legislation of the Member States, such a transfer may be to the citizen's advantage in terms of indirect taxation or not, according to circumstances

. . .

46. The same principle applies a fortiori to a situation such as that at issue in the main proceedings where the person concerned has not himself made use of his right of movement, but claims to be the victim of a difference in treatment following the transfer of his former spouse's residence to another Member State.

47. In those circumstances, the answer to the questions referred must be that the first paragraph of Article 12 EC [18] and Article 18(1) EC [21] must be interpreted as not precluding a taxpayer resident in Germany from being unable, under national legislation such as that at issue in the main proceedings, to deduct from his taxable income in that Member State the maintenance paid to his former spouse resident in another Member State in which the maintenance is not taxable, where he would be entitled to do so if his former spouse were resident in Germany.

## NOTES AND QUESTIONS

1. How did the Court arrive at the decision that the circumstances here were within the scope of EU law? Given the reasoning, how might one now define what that requirement really means? Does it actually have any substance anymore? Could a person make the case that her taxes are so high that they reduce her financial ability to exercise her free movement rights, thus bringing such a situation within the scope of the Treaty? (Consider in this connection the *Kremzow* case in Chapter 4)

2. What was the Court's reasoning as to why under EU law it was acceptable that the German Tax Law required that Mr. Schempp's maintenance payments be taxed? As Mr. Schempp pointed out, since income taxation occurs only at the state level, the impact of differences in taxes and tax rules from one Member State to another could have a significant influence on a person's willingness to relocate. How did the court react to that argument?

3. For a commentary on the above case law, see S. Kingston, A *light in the darkness: Recent developments in the ECJ's direct tax jurisprudence*, (2007) 44 CML REV. 1321. As to current and future developments, see I. Begg, *Future fiscal arrangements of the European Union* (2004) 41 CML REV. 775.

# Chapter 18

# EQUALITY
_____

## § 18.01  OVERVIEW

***Template*** Article 8, Section 8.2 and Charter Article 21

***Materials in this Chapter*** Chapter III of the Charter is titled "Equality" and its first provision, article 21(1), contains a seemingly sweeping prohibition of discrimination. This is rather deceptive. It is necessary to recall once again that, by virtue of TEU 6, which renders the Charter of equal legal value as the Treaties, it "shall apply [only] to the institutions of the Union, Union acts and any situation involving the implementation of Union law." Moreover, it may not be interpreted as extending the competences of the Union. Thus, while the Charter is a useful reference for identifying rights, it is more descriptive of existing EU principles than prescriptive. The materials here describe principles that are already embedded in EU law and in specific legislation that extends them to the Member States.

***EU law on equality*** As already noted, the EEC Treaty had contained from the beginning one fundamental prohibition reflecting the notion of equality: the original EEC 119 (EC 141/TFEU 157) provision prohibiting discrimination in pay based on gender. The ECJ's finding in *Defrenne* that this provision is directly applicable was controversial at the time (as discussed in Chapter 4) and at odds with the Commission's historical guidance. The Treaty of Amsterdam introduced two new paragraphs to the article. Paragraph 3 gave the Council and Parliament legislative power to extend sex equality requirements beyond pay (i.e., equal opportunity and equal treatment generally for men and women in employment). Paragraph 4 allowed Member States to provide for specific advantages for the underrepresented sex.

Amsterdam also introduced a provision (EC 13/TFEU 19) granting the Council power (with the consent of the Parliament) to adopt legislation to combat discrimination as described in article 21 of the Charter. However, once again this power was limited to the powers conferred by the Treaties on the Union. This, so far, has meant that implementing legislation has focused on discrimination in employment and related areas.

Article 21(2) of the Charter addresses discrimination on grounds of nationality but essentially defers to the similar prohibition in the TFEU. As noted in Chapter 17, the prohibition of discrimination on grounds of nationality is necessary because such discrimination gets in the way of the internal market and arises from the artificial status of nationality created by the international system of nation states. It is not prohibited, therefore, because it is perceived as an affront to human freedom and dignity. On the contrary, it is a closely guarded right of each nation state. It is thus of a different character altogether from the types of discrimination addressed in Article 21(1).

***Legislation relating to gender discrimination in employment*** It is worth re-emphasizing that EC 141/TFEU 157 does not depend on any inter-state jurisdictional requirement. It reaches directly into the national legal systems to prohibit gender discrimination in pay even by private employers, whether or not there is any impairment of the free movement of workers.

Long before the extensions of Union legislative authority in the Amsterdam Treaty to other forms of discrimination, the (then) EEC had adopted a series of directives relating to *gender discrimination.*

The first was a directive on equal pay (Directive 75/117. That Directive arguably extended EC 141/TFEU 157 to cover work to which equal value is attributed (thus moving beyond the very limited prohibition recognized by the Court in the *Defrenne* case (Chapter 4) on discrimination in pay for the same work).

This was followed by Directive 76/207, which extended the prohibition to other forms of discrimination in employment. It was amended in 1986 by Directive 86/613 [1986] OJ L 359/56 to also cover self-employed individuals and in 2002 by Directive 2002/73 1 to also include a prohibition on sexual harassment.

Directive 97/80 [1997] OJ L 14/6 (the so-called "burden of proof directive) incorporated an ECJ judgment — *Union of Commercial and Clerical Employees v. Danish Employers' Association ex parte Danfoss*, Case 109/88 [1989] ECR 3199 — in which the Court held that where a pay system indirectly results in a pay difference between men and women and cannot be readily explained by some objective factor, it is for the employer to prove that the system is not in fact discriminatory.

Outside the specific scope of EC 141/TFEU 157, measures were also adopted under EC 235/TFEU 268 Directive 79/7 addressing gender discrimination in the context of State Social Security schemes (which in Europe extend to unemployment benefits, heath insurance, retirement and work-related injury). The purpose here was to require Member States over time to adjust their state systems to eliminate discrimination with respect to qualifying periods, contributions and calculation of benefits. However, the directive stopped short of requiring Member States to align the age for men and women for state pensions, a highly sensitive political issue. Directive 86/378 applied the same concepts to private employer benefit schemes, including the exception for old age pensions.

With the exception of the State Social Security directive, all of the above have now been consolidated in Directive 2006/54 (reproduced in the documentary supplement).

***Legislation on other forms of discrimination*** Action on the *other forms of discrimination* described in Article 21(1) of the Charter came in 2000 with Directive 2000/43 on racial and ethnic origin discrimination (which includes discrimination in education, benefits and public housing), followed quickly by the Framework Employment Directive, Directive 2000/78 addressing the remaining types of discrimination.

***Comparison with the U.S.*** The equal protection provisions of the U.S. Constitution and the U.S. Civil Rights Act are probably together the body of fundamental law in the U.S. comparable to the EU principles of equality. In fact, the Civil Rights Act analogy is particularly apposite since it was enacted under the Commerce Clause, just as the EU rules apply, at least today, to the economic agenda embodied in the EU Treaties.

## § 18.02  GENDER DISCRIMINATION — EQUAL PAY FOR EQUAL WORK

### [A]  Indirect Discrimination

### J. P. JENKINS v. KINGSGATE (CLOTHING PRODUCTIONS) LTD
Case 96/80, [1981] ECR 911

[A dispute had arisen between a female employee working part-time and her employer, a manufacturer of women's clothing, against whom she claimed that she was receiving an hourly rate of pay lower than that paid to one of her male colleagues employed full-time on the same work. For current relevant directive provisions see Directive 2006/54, [2006] OJ L204, articles 2 and 4, reproduced in the Documentary Supplement.]

3 Mrs. Jenkins took the view that such a difference in pay contravened the equality clause incorporated into her contract of employment by virtue of the [U.K.] Equal Pay Act 1970, section 1 (2) (a) of which provides for equal pay for men and women in every case where "a woman is employed on like work with a man in the same employment".

4 The Industrial Tribunal, hearing the case at first instance, held in its decision of 5 February 1979 that in the case of part-time work the fact that the weekly working hours amounted, as in that case, to 75% of the full working hours was sufficient to constitute a "material difference" between part-time work and full-time work within the meaning of section 1 (3) of the above-mentioned Act, according to which:

"An equality clause shall not operate in relation to a variation between the woman's contract and the man's contract if the employer proves that the variation is genuinely due to a material difference (other than the difference of sex) between her case and his".

5 Mrs. Jenkins appealed against that decision to the Employment Appeal Tribunal, which decided that the dispute raised problems concerning the interpretation of Community law and referred a number of questions to the Court for a preliminary ruling.

6 According to the information in the order making the reference, prior to 1975 the employer did not pay the same wages to male and female employees but the hourly rates of pay were the same whether the work was part-time or full-time. From November 1975 the pay for full-time work (that is to say, the pay for those working 40 hours per week) became the same for male and female employees but the hourly

rate for part-time work was fixed at a rate which was 10% lower than the hourly rate of pay for full-time work.

7 The part-time workers employed by the employer in question were apparently all female with the exception of a sole male part-time worker who had just retired and who at the time had been authorized to continue working, exceptionally and for short periods, after the normal age of retirement.

*    *    *

9 It appears from the first three questions and the reasons stated in the order making the reference that the national court is principally concerned to know whether a difference in the level of pay for work carried out part-time and the same work carried out full-time may amount to discrimination of a kind prohibited by Article 119 [157] of the Treaty when the category of part-time workers is exclusively or predominantly comprised of women.

10 The answer to the questions thus understood is that the purpose of Article 119 [157] is to ensure the application of the principle of equal pay for men and women for the same work. The differences in pay prohibited by that provision are therefore exclusively those based on the difference of the sex of the workers. Consequently the fact that part-time work is paid at an hourly rate lower than pay for full-time work does not amount per se to discrimination prohibited by Article 119 [157] provided that the hourly rates are applied to workers belonging to either category without distinction based on sex.

11 If there is no such distinction, therefore, the fact that work paid at time rates is remunerated at an hourly rate which varies according to the number of hours worked per week does not offend against the principle of equal pay laid down in Article 119 [157] of the Treaty in so far as the difference in pay between part-time work and full-time work is attributable to factors which are objectively justified and are in no way related to any discrimination based on sex.

12 Such may be the case, in particular, when by giving hourly rates of pay which are lower for part-time work than those for full-time work the employer is endeavoring, on economic grounds which may be objectively justified, to encourage full-time work irrespective of the sex of the worker.

13 By contrast, if it is established that a considerably smaller percentage of women than of men perform the minimum number of weekly working hours required in order to be able to claim the full-time hourly rate of pay, the inequality in pay will be contrary to Article 119 [157] of the Treaty where, regard being had to the difficulties encountered by women in arranging to work that minimum number of hours per week, the pay policy of the undertaking in question cannot be explained by factors other than discrimination based on sex.

14 Where the hourly rate of pay differs according to whether the work is part-time or full-time it is for the national courts to decide in each individual case whether, regard being had to the facts of the case, its history and the employer's intention, a pay policy such as that which is at issue in the main proceedings although represented as a difference based on weekly working hours is or is not in reality discrimination based on the sex of the worker.

15 The reply to the first three questions must therefore be that a difference in pay between full-time workers and part-time workers does not amount to discrimination prohibited by Article 119 [157] of the Treaty unless it is in reality merely an indirect way of reducing the level of pay of part-time workers on the ground that that group of workers is composed exclusively or predominantly of women.

# NOTES AND QUESTIONS

**1.** *Jenkins* illustrates some of the complexities that have arisen under EC141/ TFEU 157. When, according to the Court, would discrimination between full-time and part-time employees violate EC 141/TFEU 157?

**2.** *Jenkins* left the question of "objective justification" of differences between full and part-time workers for resolution by the national courts. In *Bilka-Kaufhaus GmbH v. Karin Weber von Hartz*, Case 170/84, 1986 ECJ CELEX LEXIS 92, [1986] ECR 1607, an occupational pension scheme stipulated that employees could only receive a pension if they had worked full-time for 15 years. The Court here seemed to impose a greater burden on the employee to show discrimination:

> If the national court finds that the measures chosen by [the employer] correspond to a real need on the part of the undertaking, are appropriate with a view to achieving the objectives pursued and are necessary to that end, the fact that the measures affect a far greater number of women than men is not sufficient to show that they constitute an infringement of article 119 [157].

Then, in the later *Danfoss* case and as now captured by Directive 97/80, the Court effectively shifted the burden of proof where the reasons for differences in pay were not obvious:

> . . . [T]he Equal Pay Directive must be interpreted as meaning that where an undertaking applies a system of pay which is totally lacking in transparency, it is for the employer to prove that his practice in the matter of wages is not discriminatory, if a female worker establishes, in relation to a relatively large number of employees, that the average pay for women is less than that for men" Does this principle raise other Fundamental Rights issues? (See also *B.F. Cadman v. Health & Safety Executive*, Case C-17/05, 2006 ECJ CELEX LEXIS 549, [2006] ECR I-9583.)

**3.** Compare *Corning Glass Works v. Brennan*, 417 U.S. 188, 94 S. Ct. 2223, 41 L. Ed. 2d 1 (1974), where the U.S. Supreme Court also put the burden of proof on the employer to show objective factors that would justify a pay differential in a case where the Department of Labor sued Corning because it paid night shift production inspectors more than day shift production inspectors, and all the day shift inspectors were women, while most night shift inspectors were men.

## [B]   The Meaning of "Pay"

# BARBER v. GUARDIAN ROYAL EXCHANGE ASSURANCE GROUP
## Case 262/88, 1990 ECJ CELEX LEXIS 147, [1990] ECR I-1889

[Mr Barber was a member of the pension fund established by the Guardian which applied a non-contributory scheme, that is to say a scheme wholly financed by the employer. That scheme, which was a 'contracted-out' scheme, that is to say it was approved under the UK Social Security Pensions Act 1975, involved the contractual waiver by members of the earnings-related part of the State pension scheme, for which the scheme in question was a substitute. Members of a scheme of that kind paid to the State scheme only reduced contributions corresponding to the basic flat-rate pension payable under the latter scheme to all workers regardless of their earnings.

Under the Guardian's pension scheme, the normal pensionable age was fixed for the category of employees to which Mr Barber belonged at 62 for men and at 57 for women. That difference was equivalent to that which exists under the State social security scheme, where the normal pensionable age is 65 for men and 60 for women. Members of the Guardian's pension fund were entitled to an immediate pension on attaining the normal pensionable age provided for by that scheme.

If an individual was terminated for lack of work ("redundancy" in the British terminology) the full pensionable age was reduced to 55 for men and 50 for women.

Mr Barber was made redundant when he was age 52. The Guardian paid him the statutory redundancy payment and an ex gratia payment. He would have been entitled to a retirement pension as from the date of his 62nd birthday. A woman in the same position as Mr Barber would have received an immediate retirement pension as well as the statutory redundancy payment and that the total value of those benefits would have been greater than the amount paid to Mr Barber. Mr Barber claimed discrimination under EEC 119 (EC 141/TFEU 157).

For current legislation on this matter see Directive 2006/54, [2006] OJ L 204, Articles 2 and 5-9.

12 As the Court has held, the concept of pay, within the meaning of the second paragraph of Article 119 [157], comprises any other consideration, whether in cash or in kind, whether immediate or future, provided that the worker receives it, albeit indirectly, in respect of his employment from his employer. . . . Accordingly, the fact that certain benefits are paid after the termination of the employment relationship does not prevent them from being in the nature of pay, within the meaning of Article 119 [157] of the Treaty.

13 As regards, in particular, the compensation granted to a worker in connection with his redundancy, it must be stated that such compensation constitutes a form of pay to which the worker is entitled in respect of his employment, which is paid to him upon termination of the employment relationship, which makes it possible to facilitate his adjustment to the new circumstances resulting from the loss of his

employment and which provides him with a source of income during the period in which he is seeking new employment.

14 It follows that compensation granted to a worker in connection with his redundancy falls in principle within the concept of pay for the purposes of Article 119 [157] of the Treaty.

15 At the hearing, the United Kingdom argued that the statutory redundancy payment fell outside the scope of Article 119 [157] of the Treaty because it constituted a social security benefit and not a form of pay.

16 In that regard it must be pointed out that a redundancy payment made by the employer, such as that which is at issue, cannot cease to constitute a form of pay on the sole ground that, rather than deriving from the contract of employment, it is a statutory or ex gratia payment.

17 In the case of statutory redundancy payments it must be borne in mind that. . . . Article 119 [157] of the Treaty also applies to discrimination arising directly from legislative provisions. This means that benefits provided for by law may come within the concept of pay for the purposes of that provision.

18 Although it is true that many advantages granted by an employer also reflect considerations of social policy, the fact that a benefit is in the nature of pay cannot be called in question where the worker is entitled to receive the benefit in question from his employer by reason of the existence of the employment relationship.

19 In the case of ex gratia payments by the employer, it is clear . . . that Article 119 [157] also applies to advantages which an employer grants to workers although he is not required to do so by contract.

20 Accordingly, without there being any need to discuss whether or not the directive on equal treatment is applicable, the answer to the first question must be that the benefits paid by an employer to a worker in connection with the latter's compulsory redundancy fall within the scope of the second paragraph of Article 119 [157], whether they are paid under a contract of employment, by virtue of legislative provisions or on a voluntary basis.

The second question

21 In view of the answer given to the first question, the second question must be understood as seeking in substance to ascertain whether a retirement pension paid under a contracted-out private occupational scheme falls within the scope of Article 119 [157] of the Treaty, in particular where that pension is awarded in connection with compulsory redundancy.

22 . . . [C]onsideration in the nature of social security benefits is not in principle alien to the concept of pay. However, the Court pointed out that this concept, as defined in Article 119 [157], cannot encompass social security schemes or benefits, in particular retirement pensions, directly governed by legislation without any element of agreement within the undertaking or the occupational branch concerned, which are compulsorily applicable to general categories of workers.

23 The Court noted that those schemes afford the workers the benefit of a statutory

scheme, to the financing of which workers, employers and possibly the public authorities contribute in a measure determined less by the employment relationship than by considerations of social policy.

24 In order to answer the second question, therefore, it is necessary to ascertain whether those considerations also apply to contracted-out private occupational schemes such as that referred to in this case.

25 In that regard it must be pointed out first of all that the schemes in question are the result either of an agreement between workers and employers or of a unilateral decision taken by the employer. They are wholly financed by the employer or by both the employer and the workers without any contribution being made by the public authorities in any circumstances. Accordingly, such schemes form part of the consideration offered to workers by the employer.

26 Secondly, such schemes are not compulsorily applicable to general categories of workers. On the contrary, they apply only to workers employed by certain undertakings, with the result that affiliation to those schemes derives of necessity from the employment relationship with a given employer. Furthermore, even if the schemes in question are established in conformity with national legislation and consequently satisfy the conditions laid down by it for recognition as contracted-out schemes, they are governed by their own rules.

27 Thirdly, it must be pointed out that, even if the contributions paid to those schemes and the benefits which they provide are in part a substitute for those of the general statutory scheme, that fact cannot preclude the application of Article 119 [157]. It is apparent from the documents before the Court that occupational schemes such as that referred to in this case may grant to their members benefits greater than those which would be paid by the statutory scheme, with the result that their economic function is similar to that of the supplementary schemes which exist in certain Member States, where affiliation and contribution to the statutory scheme is compulsory and no derogation is allowed. In its judgment of 13 May 1986 in Case 170/84 Bilka-Kaufhaus v. Weber von Hartz ((1986)) ECR 1607, the Court held that the benefits awarded under a supplementary pension scheme fell within the concept of pay, within the meaning of Article 119 [157].

28 It must therefore be concluded that, unlike the benefits awarded by national statutory social security schemes, a pension paid under a contracted-out scheme constitutes consideration paid by the employer to the worker in respect of his employment and consequently falls within the scope of Article 119 [157] of the Treaty.

29 That interpretation of Article 119 [157] is not affected by the fact that the private occupational scheme in question has been set up in the form of a trust and is administered by trustees who are technically independent of the employer, since Article 119 [157] also applies to consideration received indirectly from the employer.

30 The answer to the second question submitted by the Court of Appeal must therefore be that a pension paid under a contracted-out private occupational scheme falls within the scope of Article 119 [157] of the Treaty.

The third and fifth questions

31 In these questions the Court of Appeal seeks in substance to ascertain, in the first place, whether it is contrary to Article 119 [157] of the Treaty for a man made compulsorily redundant to be entitled only to a deferred pension payable at the normal pensionable age when a woman in the same position receives an immediate retirement pension as a result of the application of an age condition that varies according to sex in the same way as is provided for by the national statutory pension scheme. Secondly, the Court of Appeal wishes to ascertain, in substance, whether equal pay must be ensured at the level of each element of remuneration or only on the basis of a comprehensive assessment of the consideration paid to workers.

32 In the case of the first of those two questions thus formulated, it is sufficient to point out that Article 119 [157] prohibits any discrimination with regard to pay as between men and women, whatever the system which gives rise to such inequality. Accordingly, it is contrary to Article 119 [157] to impose an age condition which differs according to sex in respect of pensions paid under a contracted-out scheme, even if the difference between the pensionable age for men and that for women is based on the one provided for by the national statutory scheme.

33 As regards the second of those questions, it is appropriate to refer to [prior judgments], in which the Court emphasized the fundamental importance of transparency and, in particular, of the possibility of a review by the national courts, in order to prevent and, if necessary, eliminate any discrimination based on sex.

34 With regard to the means of verifying compliance with the principle of equal pay, it must be stated that if the national courts were under an obligation to make an assessment and a comparison of all the various types of consideration granted, according to the circumstances, to men and women, judicial review would be difficult and the effectiveness of Article 119 [157] would be diminished as a result. It follows that genuine transparency, permitting an effective review, is assured only if the principle of equal pay applies to each of the elements of remuneration granted to men or women.

35 The answer to the third and fifth questions submitted by the Court of Appeal must therefore be that it is contrary to Article 119 [157] of the Treaty for a man made compulsorily redundant to be entitled to claim only a deferred pension payable at the normal pensionable age when a woman in the same position is entitled to an immediate retirement pension as a result of the application of an age condition that varies according to sex in the same way as is provided for by the national statutory pension scheme. The application of the principle of equal pay must be ensured in respect of each element of remuneration and not only on the basis of a comprehensive assessment of the consideration paid to workers.

## NOTES AND QUESTIONS

1.   The "contracted out" pension plan referred to was a form of substitution of the state pension scheme by a private scheme operated by an employer. As such, it was argued by the employer and the UK government that it was not "pay" as contemplated by article 119 (EC 141/TFEU 157). Does that not seem reasonable?

What was the Court's response?

**2.** See also *G.C. Ten Oever v. Stichting Bedrijfspensioenfonds voor het Glazen-wassers — en Schoonmaakbedrijf*, Case C-109/91, 1993 ECJ CELEX LEXIS 120, [1993] ECR I-4879, where the ECJ applied the temporal limitation of *Barber* so as to apply only to benefits payable in respect of periods of employment subsequent to May 17, 1990. It confirmed further that a survivor's pension provided for by an occupational pension scheme funded by employers and employees was covered by EC 141/TFEU 157. (In this case, the scheme only allowed a survivor's benefit to be payable to a widow.)

**3.** See also *Sarah Margaret Richards v. Secretary of State for Work and Pensions*, Case C-423/04, 2006 ECJ CELEX LEXIS 190, [2006] ECR I-3585, where the Court, while acknowledging the permissible discrimination in retirement age for statutory pensions, rejected an argument that the UK could treat a person who had become a woman after a sex change operation as a man for the purposes of such legislation, when in fact it had issued a formal certificate confirming the change.

## § 18.03   EQUAL TREATMENT FOR MEN AND WOMEN IN EMPLOYMENT

### [A]   Affirmative Action

## KATARINA ABRAHAMSSON AND LEIF ANDERSON v. ELISABET FOGELQVIST
### Case C-407/98, 2000 ECJ CELEX LEXIS 377, [2000] ECR I-5539

[At issue in this case was a provision of Swedish law, Regulation 1995: 936 article 3 of which stated:

> When appointments are made, the provisions of Article 15a of Chapter 4 of Regulation 1993:100 shall be replaced by the following provisions.

> A candidate belonging to an under-represented sex who possesses sufficient qualifications in accordance with the first paragraph of Article 15 of Chapter 4 of Regulation 1993:100 must be granted preference over a candidate of the opposite sex who would otherwise have been chosen ("positive discrimination") where it proves necessary to do so in order for a candidate of the under-represented sex to be appointed.

> Positive discrimination must, however, not be applied where the difference between the candidates' qualifications is so great that such application would give rise to a breach of the requirement of objectivity in the making of appointments.

This law was part of an effort to boost the number of female professors in state universities.

Also in issue was EU Directive 76/207 (now replaced by Directive 2006/54). Article 2(1) and (4) of that directive had provided:

1. For the purposes of the following provisions, the principle of equal treatment shall mean that there shall be no discrimination whatsoever on grounds of sex either directly or indirectly by reference in particular to marital or family status. . . .

4. This Directive shall be without prejudice to measures to promote equal opportunity for men and women, in particular by removing existing inequalities which affect women's opportunities in the areas referred to in Article 1(1).

Mr Anderson had been passed over for a vacancy for the chair of Professor of Hydrospheric Sciences in the University of Goteborg in favor of a Ms Fogelqvist.

*[The current legislation on this subject can be found in Directive 2006/54, [2006] OJ L 204, Article 3]*

44 The issue raised by the first question is whether Article 2(1) and (4) precludes national legislation, such as the Swedish legislation at issue in the main proceedings, under which a candidate for a public post who belongs to the under-represented sex and possesses sufficient qualifications for that post must be chosen in preference to a candidate of the opposite sex who would otherwise have been appointed, where this is necessary to secure the appointment of a candidate of the under-represented sex and the difference between the respective merits of the candidates is not so great as to give rise to a breach of the requirement of objectivity in making appointments.

45 . . . [T]he national legislation at issue in the main proceedings enables preference to be given to a candidate of the under-represented sex who, although sufficiently qualified, does not possess qualifications equal to those of other candidates of the opposite sex.

46 As a rule, a procedure for the selection of candidates for a post involves assessment of their qualifications by reference to the requirements of the vacant post or of the duties to be performed.

47 . . . [I]t is legitimate for the purposes of that assessment for certain positive and negative criteria to be taken into account which, although formulated in terms which are neutral as regards sex and thus capable of benefiting men too, in general favour women. Thus, it may be decided that seniority, age and the date of last promotion are to be taken into account only in so far as they are of importance for the suitability, qualifications and professional capability of candidates. Similarly, it may be prescribed that the family status or income of the partner is immaterial and that part-time work, leave and delays in completing training as a result of looking after children or dependants in need of care must not have a negative effect.

48 The clear aim of such criteria is to achieve substantive, rather than formal, equality by reducing de facto inequalities which may arise in society and, thus, in accordance with Article 141(4) EC [157] to prevent or compensate for disadvantages in the professional career of persons belonging to the under-represented sex.

49 It is important to emphasise in that connection that the application of criteria such as those mentioned in paragraph 47 above must be transparent and amenable

to review in order to obviate any arbitrary assessment of the qualifications of candidates.

50 As regards the selection procedure at issue in the main proceedings, it does not appear from the relevant Swedish legislation that assessment of the qualifications of candidates by reference to the requirements of the vacant post is based on clear and unambiguous criteria such as to prevent or compensate for disadvantages in the professional career of members of the under-represented sex.

51 On the contrary, under that legislation, a candidate for a public post belonging to the under-represented sex and possessing sufficient qualifications for that post must be chosen in preference to a candidate of the opposite sex who would otherwise have been appointed, where that measure is necessary for a candidate belonging to the under-represented sex to be appointed.

52 It follows that the legislation at issue in the main proceedings automatically grants preference to candidates belonging to the under-represented sex, provided that they are sufficiently qualified, subject only to the proviso that the difference between the merits of the candidates of each sex is not so great as to result in a breach of the requirement of objectivity in making appointments.

53 The scope and effect of that condition cannot be precisely determined, with the result that the selection of a candidate from among those who are sufficiently qualified is ultimately based on the mere fact of belonging to the under-represented sex, and that this is so even if the merits of the candidate so selected are inferior to those of a candidate of the opposite sex. Moreover, candidatures are not subjected to an objective assessment taking account of the specific personal situations of all the candidates. It follows that such a method of selection is not such as to be permitted by Article 2(4) of the Directive.

54 In those circumstances, it is necessary to determine whether legislation such as that at issue in the main proceedings is justified by Article 141(4) EC [157].

55 In that connection, it is enough to point out that, even though Article 141(4) EC [157] allows the Member States to maintain or adopt measures providing for special advantages intended to prevent or compensate for disadvantages in professional careers in order to ensure full equality between men and women in professional life, it cannot be inferred from this that it allows a selection method of the kind at issue in the main proceedings which appears, on any view, to be disproportionate to the aim pursued.

56 The answer to the first question must therefore be that Article 2(1) and (4) of the Directive and Article 141(4) EC [157] preclude national legislation under which a candidate for a public post who belongs to the under-represented sex and possesses sufficient qualifications for that post must be chosen in preference to a candidate of the opposite sex who would otherwise have been appointed, where this is necessary to secure the appointment of a candidate of the under-represented sex and the difference between the respective merits of the candidates is not so great as to give rise to a breach of the requirement of objectivity in making appointments.

## NOTES AND QUESTIONS

**1.** In *Kalanke v. Freie Hansestadt Bremen*, Case C-450/93, [1995] ECR I-3051, the Court had indicated that article 2(4) of the earlier directive needed to be interpreted narrowly as an exception to the general principle of non-discrimination. It determined that "national rules which guarantee women absolute and unconditional priority for appointment or promotion go beyond promoting equal opportunities and overstep the limits of the exception . . ." In that case the rules automatically gave priority to women in sectors where they were underrepresented, assuming they were, however, as equally qualified as male candidates. How does this case compare with *Foglqvist*? Is affirmative action favoring the appointment of women in practical terms prohibited?

**2.** In *Joseph Griesmar v. Ministre de l'Economie, des Finances et de l'Industrie et Ministre de la Fonction publique, de la Réforme de l'Etat et de la Décentralisation*, Case C-366/99, 2001 ECJ CELEX LEXIS 710, [2001] ECR I-9383, the Court held that in matters of equal pay, factors designed to favor women with children were contrary to the principle of equal pay. In this case, it considered a service credit related to the period during which a woman was bringing up children. It amounted to one year for each legitimate child, each natural child of recognized paternity, and every other child who, at the date of retirement from the service, had been brought up under the conditions and for the period specified in the law. Given the now-binding legal force of Article 21 of the Charter, will Member States be permanently barred from affirmative action of this kind?

## [B]  Occupational Requirements

## JOHNSTON v. CHIEF CONSTABLE, ROYAL ULSTER CONSTABULARY
Case 222//84, 1986 ECJ EUR-Lex LEXIS 105, [1986] ECR 1651

[The Plaintiff, a policewoman in Northern Ireland, was not offered a renewal of her contract of employment as a result of a policy adopted by the Chief Constable to exclude females from regular police work due to the requirement that police officers in the province were required to be armed. This, of course, was a response to the sectarian violence that had claimed the lives of many police officers. For reasons described in the judgment, including a general ground of public safety, he was opposed to arming female officers. Johnston sought redress in an Industrial Tribunal for unfair dismissal, invoking article 2(2) of Directive 76/207 which stated that discrimination was permissible for "occupational activities . . . for which, by reason of their nature or the context in which they are carried out, the sex of the worker constitutes a determining factor."

For the current law see Directive 2006/54, [2006] OJ L 204, Article 14, found in the Documentary Supplement.]

26 . . . [T]he only articles in which the Treaty provides for derogations applicable in situations which may involve public safety are articles 36 [36], 48 [45], 56 [52], 223 [346] and 224 [347] which deal with exceptional and clearly defined cases. Because of their limited character those articles do not lend themselves to a wide

interpretation and it is not possible to infer from them that there is inherent in the Treaty a general proviso covering all measures taken for reasons of public safety. If every provision of Community law were held to be subject to a general proviso, regardless of the specific requirements laid down by the provisions of the Treaty, this might impair the binding nature of Community law and its uniform application.

                                    *    *    *

34 Since . . . it is expressly provided that the sex discrimination order is to apply to employment in the police and since in this regard no distinction is made between men and women in the specific provisions that are applicable, the nature of the occupational activity in the police force is not a relevant ground of justification for the discrimination in question. What must be examined, however, is the question whether, owing to the specific context in which the activity described in the industrial tribunal's decision is carried out, the sex of the person carrying out that activity constitutes a determining factor.

35 . . . [T]he policy towards women in the RUC full-time reserve was adopted by the Chief Constable because he considered that if women were armed they might become a more frequent target for assassination and their fire-arms could fall into the hands of their assailants, that the public would not welcome the carrying of fire-arms by women, which would conflict too much with the ideal of an unarmed police force, and that armed policewomen would be less effective in police work in the social field with families and children in which the services of policewomen are particularly appreciated. The reasons which the Chief Constable thus gave for his policy were related to the special conditions in which the police must work in the situation existing in Northern Ireland, having regard to the requirements of the protection of public safety in a context of serious internal disturbances.

36 As regards the question whether such reasons may be covered by article 2 (2) of the Directive, it should first be observed that that provision, being a derogation from an individual right laid down in the Directive, must be interpreted strictly. However, it must be recognized that the context in which the occupational activity of members of an armed police force are carried out is determined by the environment in which that activity is carried out. In this regard, the possibility cannot be excluded that in a situation characterized by serious internal disturbances the carrying of fire-arms by policewomen might create additional risks of their being assassinated and might therefore be contrary to the requirements of public safety.

37 In such circumstances, the context of certain policing activities may be such that the sex of police officers constitutes a determining factor for carrying them out. If that is so, a Member State may therefore restrict such tasks, and the training leading thereto, to men. In such a case, as is clear from article 9 (2) of the Directive, the Member States have a duty to assess periodically the activities concerned in order to decide whether, in the light of social developments, the derogation from the general scheme of the Directive may still be maintained.

38 [I]n determining the scope of any derogation from an individual right such as the equal treatment of men and women provided for by the Directive, the principle of proportionality, one of the general principles of law underlying the Community legal

order, must be observed. That principle requires that derogations remain within the limits of what is appropriate and necessary for achieving the aim in view and requires the principle of equal treatment to be reconciled as far as possible with the requirements of public safety which constitute the decisive factor as regards the context of the activity in question.

39 [I]t is for the national court to say whether the reasons on which the Chief Constable based his decision are in fact well founded and justify the specific measure taken in Mrs. Johnston's case. it is also for the national court to ensure that the principle of proportionality is observed and to determine whether the refusal to renew Mrs Johnston's contract could not be avoided by allocating to women duties which, without jeopardizing the aims pursued, can be performed without fire-arms.

40 . . . Article 2 (2) of Directive No. 76/207 must be interpreted as meaning that in deciding whether, by reason of the context in which the activities of a police officer are carried out, the sex of the officer constitutes a determining factor for that occupational activity, a Member State may take into consideration requirements of public safety in order to restrict general policing duties, in an internal situation characterized by frequent assassinations, to men equipped with fire-arms.

## NOTES AND QUESTIONS

1. What is your reaction to the court's guidance here? Were the Chief Constable's concerns just a smokescreen?

2. What was the purpose of the Court's remarks in paragraph 26?

3. Keep in mind that Directive 2006/54, as the successor to 76/207, is not directly effective (per the Court's decision in *Marshall*, Chapter 5). Thus, cases such as *Johnston* would not as such arise in a private employment context. However, per the *Von Colson* doctrine (Chapter 9) there may still be scope for individuals to invoke it in that context, and of course there is also the possibility of damages against a Member State that has failed properly to implement it.

## GABRIELE HABERMANN-BELTERMANN v. ARBEITERWOHLFAHRT, BEZIRKSVERBAND NDB./OPF. E.V.
### Case C-421/92, 1994 ECJ CELEX LEXIS 173, [1994] ECR I-1657

[Mrs. Habermann-Beltermann, a nurse qualified in the care of the elderly, applied for a post as a night attendant in a home for the aged. For family reasons, she was able to work at night only. An employment contract between Mrs. Habermann-Beltermann and the Arbeiterwohlfahrt was signed on 23 March 1992, with effect from 1 April 1992. The contract stipulated that Mrs. Habermann-Beltermann was to be assigned night-time work only. She was absent from work because of illness from 29 April to 12 June 1992. A medical certificate dated 29 May 1992 stated that she was pregnant. It was alleged that the pregnancy began on 11 March 1992. Under the law for the protection of mothers, pregnant women were not to be assigned nighttime work. Article 2(3) of Directive 76/207 (now article 28 of Directive 2006/54) reserved to Member States the right to retain or introduce provisions intended to protect women in connection with "pregnancy and maternity", that article recognizes the legitimacy, in terms of the principle of equal treatment, first, of protecting a woman's biological condition during and after pregnancy and, second, of protecting the special relationship between a woman and her child over the period which follows pregnancy and childbirth.

For the current legislation on this subject see Directive 2006/54, [2006] OJ L 204, Article 28, found in the Documentary Supplement.]

11 The questions submitted relate to an employment contract for an indefinite period for the performance of night-time work, concluded between an employer and a pregnant employee, both of whom were unaware of the pregnancy. In its questions, the national court seeks essentially to ascertain whether Article 2(1), read in conjunction with Articles 3(1) and 5(1) of the directive, are to be interpreted as precluding such a contract, first, from being held to be void on account of the prohibition on night-time work which applies, by virtue of national law, during pregnancy and breastfeeding and, secondly, from being avoided by the employer on account of a mistake on his part as to the essential personal characteristics of the other party at the time when the contract was concluded.

*    *    *

21 In the first place, so far as concerns the purpose of Article 2(3) of the directive, by reserving to Member States the right to retain or introduce provisions which are intended to protect women in connection with "pregnancy and maternity", that article recognizes the legitimacy, in terms of the principle of equal treatment, first, of protecting a woman's biological condition during and after pregnancy and, second, of protecting the special relationship between a woman and her child over the period which follows pregnancy and childbirth . . .

22 . . . [T]he directive leaves Member States with a discretion as to the social measures which must be adopted in order to guarantee, within the framework laid down by the directive, the protection of women in connection with pregnancy and maternity and to offset the disadvantages which women, by comparison with men, suffer with regard to the retention of employment.

23 In this case, the questions submitted for a ruling relate to a contract for an indefinite period and the prohibition on night-time work by pregnant women therefore takes effect only for a limited period in relation to the total length of the contract.

24 In the circumstances, to acknowledge that the contract may be held to be invalid or may be avoided because of the temporary inability of the pregnant employee to perform the night-time work for which she has been engaged would be contrary to the objective of protecting such persons pursued by Article 2(3) of the directive, and would deprive that provision of its effectiveness.

25 Accordingly, termination of a contract for an indefinite period on grounds of the woman's pregnancy, whether by annulment or avoidance, cannot be justified by the fact that she is temporarily prevented, by a statutory prohibition imposed because of pregnancy, from performing night-time work.

26 . . . Directive 76/207/EEC precludes an employment contract for an indefinite

period for the performance of night-time work concluded between an employer and a pregnant employee, both of whom were unaware of the pregnancy, from being held to be void on account of the statutory prohibition on night-time work which applies, by virtue of national law, during pregnancy and breastfeeding, or from being avoided by the employer on account of a mistake on his part as to the essential personal characteristics of the woman at the time when the contract was concluded.

## NOTES AND QUESTIONS

**1.**  What was the precise issue here? Was the ECJ calling into question the validity of the German law? Would Mrs. Belterman have had a claim for discrimination if the employer had known about her pregnancy and declined on that ground to employ her initially?

**2.**  For a review of case law relating to gender equality through 2006, see C. Costello, G. Davies, *The case law of the Court of Justice in the field of sex equality since 2000* (2006) 43 CML REV. 1567.

## [C]  Remedies

## M. HELEN MARSHALL v. SOUTHAMPTON AND SOUTH-WEST HAMPSHIRE AREA HEALTH AUTHORITY
### Case C-271/91, 1993 ECJ CELEX LEXIS 174, [1993] ECR I-4367

[This second case brought by Helen Marshall regarding her wrongful dismissal arose because the Industrial Tribunal, to which the Court of Appeal remitted the case to consider the question of compensation, assessed Miss Marshall's financial loss at £18, 405, including £7 710 by way of interest, and awarded her compensation of £19, 405, including a sum of £1,000 compensation for injury to feelings. It applied caps on compensation as required by the applicable UK law. This case also involved Directive 76/207 [1976] OJ L 39/40 which was an earlier and less comprehensive version of Directive 2006/54. It will be recalled from Chapter 3 that the provisions of a directive cannot create obligations for individuals, thus for private employers, but that Marshall was employed by a government run entity and was thus able to invoke article 6 of the directive against it.

For the current legislation in this area see Directive 2006/54 [2006] OJ L 204, Articles 17, 18 and 25]

22 Article 6 of the Directive puts Member States under a duty to take the necessary measures to enable all persons who consider themselves wronged by discrimination to pursue their claims by judicial process. Such obligation implies that the measures in question should be sufficiently effective to achieve the objective of the Directive and should be capable of being effectively relied upon by the persons concerned before national courts.

23 As the Court held in the judgment in Case 14/83 Von Colson and Kamann v. Land Nordrhein-Westfalen 1984 ECR 1891, at paragraph 18, Article 6 does not prescribe a specific measure to be taken in the event of a breach of the prohibition of discrimination, but leaves Member States free to choose between the different

solutions suitable for achieving the objective of the Directive, depending on the different situations which may arise.

24 However, the objective is to arrive at real equality of opportunity and cannot therefore be attained in the absence of measures appropriate to restore such equality when it has not been observed. As the Court stated in paragraph 23 of the judgment in Von Colson and Kamann, cited above, those measures must be such as to guarantee real and effective judicial protection and have a real deterrent effect on the employer.

25 Such requirements necessarily entail that the particular circumstances of each breach of the principle of equal treatment should be taken into account. In the event of discriminatory dismissal contrary to Article 5(1) of the Directive, a situation of equality could not be restored without either reinstating the victim of discrimination or, in the alternative, granting financial compensation for the loss and damage sustained.

26 Where financial compensation is the measure adopted in order to achieve the objective indicated above, it must be adequate, in that it must enable the loss and damage actually sustained as a result of the discriminatory dismissal to be made good in full in accordance with the applicable national rules.

*        *        *

30 [T]he fixing of an upper limit of the kind at issue in the main proceedings cannot, by definition, constitute proper implementation of Article 6 of the Directive, since it limits the amount of compensation a priori to a level which is not necessarily consistent with the requirement of ensuring real equality of opportunity through adequate reparation for the loss and damage sustained as a result of discriminatory dismissal.

31 With regard to the . . . question relating to the award of interest, suffice it to say that full compensation for the loss and damage sustained as a result of discriminatory dismissal cannot leave out of account factors, such as the effluxion of time, which may in fact reduce its value. The award of interest, in accordance with the applicable national rules, must therefore be regarded as an essential component of compensation for the purposes of restoring real equality of treatment.

32 Accordingly, the reply to be given to the first and second questions is that the interpretation of Article 6 of the Directive must be that reparation of the loss and damage sustained by a person injured as a result of discriminatory dismissal may not be limited to an upper limit fixed a priori or by excluding an award of interest to compensate for the loss sustained by the recipient of the compensation as a result of the effluxion of time until the capital sum awarded is actually paid.

## NOTES AND QUESTIONS

1.   Was the claim here essentially one for failure to implement the directive or for the underlying gender discrimination, or are they one and the same thing?

2.   For what reasons was the cap on damages considered contrary to article 6? Presumably the cap had been introduced by UK law for valid policy reasons, so why

shouldn't these be taken into account?

**3.**   What consequences might ensue from this ruling as regards claims against private employers? Would it be incumbent on the State at this point to remove all statutory limitations on damages for dismissal based on gender grounds?

**4.**   See Chapter 9 *supra* regarding the question of whether or when national courts might have to create or supplement national procedures or remedies when dealing with EU law in connection with specific individual rights granted by EU legislation.

## § 18.04   SUPPLY OF AND ACCESS TO GOODS AND SERVICES

### DIRECTIVE 2004/113
[2004] OJ L 373/37

**implementing the principle of equal treatment between men and women in the access to and supply of goods and services**

### Article 1

#### Purpose

The purpose of this Directive is to lay down a framework for combating discrimination based on sex in access to and supply of goods and services, with a view to putting into effect in the Member States the principle of equal treatment between men and women.

### Article 2

#### Definitions

For the purposes of this Directive, the following definitions shall apply:

(a) direct discrimination: where one person is treated less favourably, on grounds of sex, than another is, has been or would be treated in a comparable situation;

(b) indirect discrimination: where an apparently neutral provision, criterion or practice would put persons of one sex at a particular disadvantage compared with persons of the other sex, unless that provision, criterion or practice is objectively justified by a legitimate aim and the means of achieving that aim are appropriate and necessary;

(c) harassment: where an unwanted conduct related to the sex of a person occurs with the purpose or effect of violating the dignity of a person and of creating an intimidating, hostile, degrading, humiliating or offensive environment;

(d) sexual harassment: where any form of unwanted physical, verbal, non-verbal or physical conduct of a sexual nature occurs, with the purpose or effect of violating the dignity of a person, in particular when creating an intimidating, hostile, degrading, humiliating or offensive environment.

## Article 3

### Scope

1. Within the limits of the powers conferred upon the Community, this Directive shall apply to all persons who provide goods and services, which are available to the public irrespective of the person concerned as regards both the public and private sectors, including public bodies, and which are offered outside the area of private and family life and the transactions carried out in this context.

2. This Directive does not prejudice the individual's freedom to choose a contractual partner as long as an individual's choice of contractual partner is not based on that person's sex.

3. This Directive shall not apply to the content of media and advertising nor to education.

4. This Directive shall not apply to matters of employment and occupation. This Directive shall not apply to matters of self-employment, insofar as these matters are covered by other Community legislative acts.

## Article 4

### Principle of equal treatment

1. For the purposes of this Directive, the principle of equal treatment between men and women shall mean that

(a) there shall be no direct discrimination based on sex, including less favourable treatment of women for reasons of pregnancy and maternity;

(b) there shall be no indirect discrimination based on sex.

2. This Directive shall be without prejudice to more favourable provisions concerning the protection of women as regards pregnancy and maternity.

3. Harassment and sexual harassment within the meaning of this Directive shall be deemed to be discrimination on the grounds of sex and therefore prohibited. A person's rejection of, or submission to, such conduct may not be used as a basis for a decision affecting that person.

4. Instruction to direct or indirect discrimination on the grounds of sex shall be deemed to be discrimination within the meaning of this Directive.

5. This Directive shall not preclude differences in treatment, if the provision of the goods and services exclusively or primarily to members of one sex is justified by a legitimate aim and the means of achieving that aim are appropriate and necessary.

## Article 5

### Actuarial factors

1. Member States shall ensure that in all new contracts concluded after 21 December 2007 at the latest, the use of sex as a factor in the calculation of premiums and benefits for the purposes of insurance and related financial services shall not result in differences in individuals' premiums and benefits.

2. Notwithstanding paragraph 1, Member States may decide before 21 December 2007 to permit proportionate differences in individuals' premiums and benefits where the use of sex is a determining factor in the assessment of risk based on relevant and accurate actuarial and statistical data. The Member States concerned shall inform the Commission and ensure that accurate data relevant to the use of sex as a determining actuarial factor are compiled, published and regularly updated. These Member States shall review their decision five years after 21 December 2007, taking into account the Commission report referred to in Article 16, and shall forward the results of this review to the Commission.

3. In any event, costs related to pregnancy and maternity shall not result in differences in individuals' premiums and benefits.

Member States may defer implementation of the measures necessary to comply with this paragraph until two years after 21 December 2007 at the latest. In that case the Member States concerned shall immediately inform the Commission.

## Article 6

### Positive action

With a view to ensuring full equality in practice between men and women, the principle of equal treatment shall not prevent any Member State from maintaining or adopting specific measures to prevent or compensate for disadvantages linked to sex.

## Article 7

### Minimum requirements

1. Member States may introduce or maintain provisions which are more favourable to the protection of the principle of equal treatment between men and women than those laid down in this Directive.

2. The implementation of this Directive shall in no circumstances constitute grounds for a reduction in the level of protection against discrimination already afforded by Member States in the fields covered by this Directive.

## CHAPTER II

## REMEDIES AND ENFORCEMENT

### Article 8

### Defence of rights

1. Member States shall ensure that judicial and/or administrative procedures, including where they deem it appropriate conciliation procedures, for the enforcement of the obligations under this Directive are available to all persons who consider themselves wronged by failure to apply the principle of equal treatment to them, even after the relationship in which the discrimination is alleged to have occurred has ended.

2. Member States shall introduce into their national legal systems such measures as are necessary to ensure real and effective compensation or reparation, as the Member States so determine, for the loss and damage sustained by a person injured as a result of discrimination within the meaning of this Directive, in a way which is dissuasive and proportionate to the damage suffered. The fixing of a prior upper limit shall not restrict such compensation or reparation.

3. Member States shall ensure that associations, organisations or other legal entities, which have, in accordance with the criteria laid down by their national law, a legitimate interest in ensuring that the provisions of this Directive are complied with, may engage, on behalf or in support of the complainant, with his or her approval, in any judicial and/or administrative procedure provided for the enforcement of obligations under this Directive.

4. Paragraphs 1 and 3 shall be without prejudice to national rules on time limits for bringing actions relating to the principle of equal treatment.

### Article 9

### Burden of proof

1. Member States shall take such measures as are necessary, in accordance with their national judicial systems, to ensure that, when persons who consider themselves wronged because the principle of equal treatment has not been applied to them establish, before a court or other competent authority, facts from which it may be presumed that there has been direct or indirect discrimination, it shall be for the respondent to prove that there has been no breach of the principle of equal treatment.

2. Paragraph 1 shall not prevent Member States from introducing rules of evidence, which are more favourable to plaintiffs.

3. Paragraph 1 shall not apply to criminal procedures.

4. Paragraphs 1, 2 and 3 shall also apply to any proceedings brought in accordance with Article 8(3).

5. Member States need not apply paragraph 1 to proceedings in which it is for the court or other competent authority to investigate the facts of the case.

Article 10

Victimisation

Member States shall introduce into their national legal systems such measures as are necessary to protect persons from any adverse treatment or adverse consequence as a reaction to a complaint or to legal proceedings aimed at enforcing compliance with the principle of equal treatment.

Article 11

Dialogue with relevant stakeholders

With a view to promoting the principle of equal treatment, Member States shall encourage dialogue with relevant stakeholders which have, in accordance with national law and practice, a legitimate interest in contributing to the fight against discrimination on grounds of sex in the area of access to and supply of goods and services.

*    *    *

Article 14

Penalties

Member States shall lay down the rules on penalties applicable to infringements of the national provisions adopted pursuant to this Directive and shall take all measures necessary to ensure that they are applied. The penalties, which may comprise the payment of compensation to the victim, shall be effective, proportionate and dissuasive. Member States shall notify those provisions to the Commission by 21 December 2007 at the latest and shall notify it without delay of any subsequent amendment affecting them.

# NOTES AND QUESTIONS

1. This directive explicitly prohibits discrimination based on gender with respect to actuarial calculations. In *Association Belge des Consommateurs Test-Achats ASBL et al v. Conseil des Ministres*, Case C-236/09 2011 ECJ EUR-Lex LEXIS 66, [2011] ECR I-NYR the Court concluded that the directive prohibited discrimination in insurance premiums in life insurance after 2012, the end of the transitional period mentioned in the directive. It would have been contrary to

articles 21 and 23 of the Charter of Fundamental Rights to allow such discrimination to persist indefinitely as could be implied from the language of Article 5(2). This case caused a furore in the insurance industry. Does the decision actually make sense? Could one have found any way to a different conclusion? Note that the Charter has modified application in the United Kingdom and Poland. Does that mean that such discrimination could continue in that Member State?

2. How far does this directive reach? Does it apply to every single act of discrimination, including any that does not have any connection with the Treaties?

## § 18.05  OTHER FORMS OF DISCRIMINATION

### [A]  The Effect of Directive 2000/78 on the Scope of Application of EU Fundamental Rights

### DIRECTIVE 2000/78
establishing a general framework for equal treatment in employment and occupation
[2000] OJ L 303

Article 1

Purpose

The purpose of this Directive is to lay down a general framework for combating discrimination on the grounds of religion or belief, disability, age or sexual orientation as regards employment and occupation, with a view to putting into effect in the Member States the principle of equal treatment.

Article 2

Concept of discrimination

1. For the purposes of this Directive, the "principle of equal treatment" shall mean that there shall be no direct or indirect discrimination whatsoever on any of the grounds referred to in Article 1.

2. For the purposes of paragraph 1:

(a) direct discrimination shall be taken to occur where one person is treated less favourably than another is, has been or would be treated in a comparable situation, on any of the grounds referred to in Article 1;

(b) indirect discrimination shall be taken to occur where an apparently neutral provision, criterion or practice would put persons having a particular religion or belief, a particular disability, a particular age, or a particular sexual orientation at a particular disadvantage compared with other persons unless:

(i) that provision, criterion or practice is objectively justified by a legitimate aim and the means of achieving that aim are appropriate and necessary, or

(ii) as regards persons with a particular disability, the employer or any person or organisation to whom this Directive applies, is obliged, under national legislation, to take appropriate measures in line with the principles contained in Article 5 in order to eliminate disadvantages entailed by such provision, criterion or practice.

3. Harassment shall be deemed to be a form of discrimination within the meaning of paragraph 1, when unwanted conduct related to any of the grounds referred to in Article 1 takes place with the purpose or effect of violating the dignity of a person and of creating an intimidating, hostile, degrading, humiliating or offensive environment. In this context, the concept of harassment may be defined in accordance with the national laws and practice of the Member States.

4. An instruction to discriminate against persons on any of the grounds referred to in Article 1 shall be deemed to be discrimination within the meaning of paragraph 1.

5. This Directive shall be without prejudice to measures laid down by national law which, in a democratic society, are necessary for public security, for the maintenance of public order and the prevention of criminal offences, for the protection of health and for the protection of the rights and freedoms of others.

## Article 3

### Scope

1. Within the limits of the areas of competence conferred on the Community, this Directive shall apply to all persons, as regards both the public and private sectors, including public bodies, in relation to:

(a) conditions for access to employment, to self-employment or to occupation, including selection criteria and recruitment conditions, whatever the branch of activity and at all levels of the professional hierarchy, including promotion;

(b) access to all types and to all levels of vocational guidance, vocational training, advanced vocational training and retraining, including practical work experience;

(c) employment and working conditions, including dismissals and pay;

(d) membership of, and involvement in, an organisation of workers or employers, or any organisation whose members carry on a particular profession, including the benefits provided for by such organisations.

2. This Directive does not cover differences of treatment based on nationality and is without prejudice to provisions and conditions relating to the entry into and residence of third-country nationals and stateless persons in the territory of Member States, and to any treatment which arises from the legal status of the third-country nationals and stateless persons concerned.

3. This Directive does not apply to payments of any kind made by state schemes or similar, including state social security or social protection schemes.

4. Member States may provide that this Directive, in so far as it relates to discrimination on the grounds of disability and age, shall not apply to the armed forces.

## WERNER MANGOLD v. RUDIGER HELM
### Case C-144/04, 2005 ECJ CELEX LEXIS 607, [2005] ECR I-9981

[Mr Mangold, who was 56, was employed by Mr Helm, a German lawyer, for a fixed term running from the following July until early 2004. The employment contract stated that its term was fixed solely because of Mr Mangold's age. German legislation introduced in 2002 (the so-called Hartz law) required the use of fixed term employment contracts to be objectively justified except in the case of workers who had reached the age of 52. This legislation allegedly was adopted under Directive 1999/70 concerning a framework agreement concluded by the EU Employers and Unions Federations as to the use of fixed term contracts. The intent of the German legislation was to provide workers over that age an opportunity to find employment where, if employers had to employ them on a permanent basis, their chances of obtaining employment were significantly less due to the social burdens imposed on employers with respect to regular employees. Germany took advantage of the three years extension provided in article 18 of Directive 2000/78 to maintain the Hartz law in place until 2006.]

74 . . . Directive 2000/78 does not itself lay down the principle of equal treatment in the field of employment and occupation. Indeed, in accordance with Article 1 thereof, the sole purpose of the directive is to lay down a general framework for combating discrimination on the grounds of religion or belief, disability, age or sexual orientation', the source of the actual principle underlying the prohibition of those forms of discrimination being found, as is clear from the third and fourth recitals in the preamble to the directive, in various international instruments and in the constitutional traditions common to the Member States.

75. The principle of non-discrimination on grounds of age must thus be regarded as a general principle of Community law. Where national rules fall within the scope of Community law, which is the case with Paragraph 14(3) of the TzBfG, as amended by the Law of 2002, as being a measure implementing Directive 1999/70 (see also, in this respect, paragraphs 51 and 64 above), and reference is made to the Court for a preliminary ruling, the Court must provide all the criteria of interpretation needed by the national court to determine whether those rules are compatible with such a principle . . .

76. Consequently, observance of the general principle of equal treatment, in particular in respect of age, cannot as such be conditional upon the expiry of the period allowed the Member States for the transposition of a directive intended to lay down a general framework for combating discrimination on the grounds of age, in particular so far as the organisation of appropriate legal remedies, the burden of proof, protection against victimisation, social dialogue, affirmative action and other specific measures to implement such a directive are concerned.

77. In those circumstances it is the responsibility of the national court, hearing a dispute involving the principle of non-discrimination in respect of age, to provide, in a case within its jurisdiction, the legal protection which individuals derive from the

rules of Community law and to ensure that those rules are fully effective, setting aside any provision of national law which may conflict with that law . . .

78. Having regard to all the foregoing, the reply to be given to the second and third questions must be that Community law and, more particularly, Article 6(1) of Directive 2000/78, must be interpreted as precluding a provision of domestic law such as that at issue in the main proceedings which authorises, without restriction, unless there is a close connection with an earlier contract of employment of indefinite duration concluded with the same employer, the conclusion of fixed-term contracts of employment once the worker has reached the age of 52.

It is the responsibility of the national court to guarantee the full effectiveness of the general principle of non-discrimination in respect of age, setting aside any provision of national law which may conflict with Community law, even where the period prescribed for transposition of that directive has not yet expired.

## NOTES AND QUESTIONS

1.     The German law was intended to make it more attractive for employers to hire older individuals by expressly permitting fixed term employment contracts. Yet in this case the law was alleged to discriminate *against* older workers by reason of this very fact. (It may be recalled from Chapter 9 that there was a strong suspicion that the whole case had been contrived to enable this challenge to occur — Mr. Mangold only worked a couple of hours a week and he and Mr. Helm shared the same views regarding the German law.) The Court did not question the validity of the social objective but nonetheless concluded the German law was contrary to EU law. What caused it to reach this conclusion?

2.     Since Directive 2000/78 could not have horizontal direct effect, the Court was obliged to look to other principles in determining whether the rights asserted here were part of EU law. Thus, the Court said that the principle underlying the prohibition it laid down derived from "various international instruments" and "the constitutional traditions common to the Member States." And that "[t]he principle of non-discrimination on grounds of age must thus be regarded as a general principle of Community law." It was thus "the responsibility of the national court to guarantee the full effectiveness of the general principle of non-discrimination in respect of age, setting aside any provision of national law which may conflict with Community law, even where the period prescribed for transposition of [Directive 2000/78] has not yet expired." How is this to be reconciled with the underlying principle that EU rights only apply in the application of EU law? Recall for example that in *Faccini Dori v. Recreb*, Case C-91/92, 1994 ECJ CELEX LEXIS 102, [1994] ECR I-3325 the Court observed that the EU was competent "to enact obligations for individuals with immediate effect . . . only where it is empowered to adopt regulations."

3.     Contrast *Mangold* with the case of *Birgit Bartsch v. Bosch und Siemens Hausgeräte (BSH) Altersfürsorge GmbH*. Case C-427/06, 2008 ECJ EUR-Lex LEXIS 2169, [2008] ECR I-7245, the plaintiff had complained that a private employer's pension plan discriminated on the basis of age because it did not allow payment of a survivor's benefit to a spouse of a deceased employee/retiree who was

more than 15 years younger than the employee. This rule was expressly endorsed by German government guidelines dating back to 1984. The Court held that there was no connection with EU law as matters stood at the time and therefore the situation was outside the scope of EU law. While a framework for implementing EC 13/TFEU [19] is contained in Directive 2000/78, that was not sufficient to bring age discrimination within the scope of EU law because at the time, the directive's deadline for transposition had not yet passed. The German Guidelines were clearly not a measure implementing that directive since they had been adopted many years earlier. The ECJ distinguished the case from *Mangold* in the following terms:

> In that case [*Mangold*], the national rules in question were a measure implementing a Community directive, namely, Council Directive 1999/ 70/EC of 28 June 1999 concerning the framework agreement on fixed-term work concluded by ETUC, UNICE and CEEP (OJ 1999 L 175, p. 43), by means of which those rules were thus brought within the scope of Community law (see *Mangold*, paragraph 75). By contrast, the guidelines at issue in the main proceedings do not correspond to measures transposing Community provisions.

4.    The *Mangold* case caused an uproar in legal and political circles in Germany, prompting a strong written protest by the ex-President of the German Supreme Court claiming that the ECJ had seriously overstepped its jurisdiction.

## LISA JACQUELINE GRANT v. SOUTH-WEST TRAINS LTD
### Case C-249/96, 1998 ECJ CELEX LEXIS 308, [1998] ECR I-621

[Ms Grant sued her employer South-West Trains Ltd (hereinafter SWT') concerning the refusal by SWT of travel concessions for Ms Grant's female partner. Ms Grant was employed by SWT, a company which operated railways in the Southampton region. Clause 18 of her contract of employment, entitled Travel facilities', stated:

> You will be granted such free and reduced rate travel concessions as are applicable to a member of your grade. Your spouse and dependants will also be granted travel concessions. Travel concessions are granted at the discretion of the employer and will be withdrawn in the event of their misuse.

The Staff Travel Facilities Privilege Ticket Regulations, provided in Clause 8 ("Spouses") that:

> Privilege tickets are granted to a married member of staff. . . for one legal spouse but not for a spouse legally separated from the employee . . .

> Privilege tickets are granted for one common law opposite sex spouse of staff . . . subject to a statutory declaration being made that a meaningful relationship has existed for a period of two years or more . . .

Ms Grant applied for travel concessions for her female partner, with whom she declared she had had a meaningful relationship' for over two years. SWT refused to allow the benefit sought, on the ground that for unmarried persons travel concessions could be granted only for a partner of the opposite sex.]

24 In the light of all the material in the case, the first question to answer is whether a condition in the regulations of an undertaking such as that in issue in the main proceedings constitutes discrimination based directly on the sex of the worker. If it does not, the next point to examine will be whether Community law requires that stable relationships between two persons of the same sex should be regarded by all employers as equivalent to marriages or stable relationships outside marriage between two persons of opposite sex. Finally, it will have to be considered whether discrimination based on sexual orientation constitutes discrimination based on the sex of the worker.

25 First, it should be observed that the regulations of the undertaking in which Ms Grant works provide for travel concessions for the worker, for the worker's spouse', that is, the person to whom he or she is married and from whom he or she is not legally separated, or the person of the opposite sex with whom he or she has had a "meaningful" relationship for at least two years, and for the children, dependent members of the family, and surviving spouse of the worker.

26 The refusal to allow Ms Grant the concessions is based on the fact that she does not satisfy the conditions prescribed in those regulations, more particularly on the fact that she does not live with a spouse' or a person of the opposite sex with whom she has had a meaningful' relationship for at least two years.

27 That condition, the effect of which is that the worker must live in a stable relationship with a person of the opposite sex in order to benefit from the travel concessions, is, like the other alternative conditions prescribed in the undertaking's regulations, applied regardless of the sex of the worker concerned. Thus travel concessions are refused to a male worker if he is living with a person of the same sex, just as they are to a female worker if she is living with a person of the same sex.

28 Since the condition imposed by the undertaking's regulations applies in the same way to female and male workers, it cannot be regarded as constituting discrimination directly based on sex.

29 Second, the Court must consider whether, with respect to the application of a condition such as that in issue in the main proceedings, persons who have a stable relationship with a partner of the same sex are in the same situation as those who are married or have a stable relationship outside marriage with a partner of the opposite sex.

30 Ms Grant submits in particular that the laws of the Member States, as well as those of the Community and other international organisations, increasingly treat the two situations as equivalent.

31 While the European Parliament, as Ms Grant observes, has indeed declared that it deplores all forms of discrimination based on an individual's sexual orientation, it is nevertheless the case that the Community has not as yet adopted rules providing for such equivalence.

32 As for the laws of the Member States, while in some of them cohabitation by two persons of the same sex is treated as equivalent to marriage, although not completely, in most of them it is treated as equivalent to a stable heterosexual relationship outside marriage only with respect to a limited number of rights, or

else is not recognised in any particular way.

33 The European Commission of Human Rights for its part considers that despite the modern evolution of attitudes towards homosexuality, stable homosexual relationships do not fall within the scope of the right to respect for family life under Article 8 of the Convention . . . and that national provisions which, for the purpose of protecting the family, accord more favourable treatment to married persons and persons of opposite sex living together as man and wife than to persons of the same sex in a stable relationship are not contrary to Article 14 of the Convention, which prohibits inter alia discrimination on the ground of sex . . .

34 In another context, the European Court of Human Rights has interpreted Article 12 of the Convention as applying only to the traditional marriage between two persons of opposite biological sex. . . .

35 It follows that, in the present state of the law within the Community, stable relationships between two persons of the same sex are not regarded as equivalent to marriages or stable relationships outside marriage between persons of opposite sex. Consequently, an employer is not required by Community law to treat the situation of a person who has a stable relationship with a partner of the same sex as equivalent to that of a person who is married to or has a stable relationship outside marriage with a partner of the opposite sex.

## TADAO MARUKO v. VERSORGUNGSANSTALT DER DEUTSCHEN BÜHNEN
### Case C-267/06, 2008 ECJ EUR-Lex LEXIS 2148, [2008] ECR I-1757

[Recently enacted German law had established the status of a registered life partnership for same sex couples. One legal consequence of this new status was that the survivor of such a partnership was entitled to a state widow or widower's pension. In this case Mr Maruko's partner had died and he claimed an occupational private pension entitlement under the private pension scheme operated by the defendant, the "VddB" or German Theatre Pension Institution. The Court found that this was not a state scheme but was "pay" thus, a rationale similar to the occupational pension scheme in *Barber*. Mr Maruko was denied the pension by the Institution on the grounds that he was not a surviving spouse.]

63. Mr Maruko and the Commission maintain that refusal to grant the survivor's benefit at issue in the main proceedings to surviving life partners constitutes indirect discrimination within the meaning of Directive 2000/78, since two persons of the same sex cannot marry in Germany and, consequently, cannot qualify for that benefit, entitlement to which is reserved to surviving spouses. In their opinion, spouses and life partners are in a comparable legal situation which justifies the granting of that benefit to surviving life partners.

64. According to the VddB, there is no constitutional obligation to treat marriage and life partnership identically, so far as concerns the law of social security or pensions. Life partnership is an institution sui generis and represents a new form of civil status. It cannot be inferred from the German legislation that there is any obligation to grant equal treatment to life partners, on the one hand, and spouses, on the other.

The Court's reply

65. In accordance with Article 1 thereof, the purpose of Directive 2000/78 is to combat, as regards employment and occupation, certain forms of discrimination including that on grounds of sexual orientation, with a view to putting into effect in the Member States the principle of equal treatment.

66. Under Article 2 of Directive 2000/78, the 'principle of equal treatment' means that there is to be no direct or indirect discrimination whatsoever on any of the grounds referred to in Article 1 of the Directive. According to Article 2(2)(a) of Directive 2000/78, direct discrimination occurs where one person is treated less favourably than another person who is in a comparable situation, on any of the grounds referred to in Article 1 of the Directive. Article 2(2)(b)(i) states that indirect discrimination occurs where an apparently neutral provision, criterion or practice would put persons having a particular religion or belief, a particular disability, a particular age, or a particular sexual orientation at a particular disadvantage compared with other persons unless that provision, criterion or practice is objectively justified by a legitimate aim and the means of achieving that aim are appropriate and necessary.

67. It is clear from the information provided in the order of reference that, from 2001 — the year when the LPartG, in its initial version, entered into force — the Federal Republic of Germany altered its legal system to allow persons of the same sex to live in a union of mutual support and assistance which is formally constituted for life. Having chosen not to permit those persons to enter into marriage, which remains reserved solely to persons of different sex, that Member State created for persons of the same sex a separate regime, the life partnership, the conditions of which have been gradually made equivalent to those applicable to marriage.

68. The referring court observes that the Law of 15 December 2004 contributed to the gradual harmonisation of the regime put in place for the life partnership with that applicable to marriage. By that law, the German legislature introduced amendments to Book VI of the Social Security Code — statutory old age pension scheme, by adding inter alia a fourth paragraph to Paragraph 46 of that Book, from which it is clear that life partnership is to be treated as equivalent to marriage as regards the widow's or widower's pension referred to in that provision. Analogous amendments were made to other provisions of Book VI.

69. The referring court considers that, in view of the harmonisation between marriage and life partnership, which it regards as a gradual movement towards recognising equivalence, as a consequence of the rules introduced by the LPartG and, in particular, of the amendments made by the Law of 15 December 2004, a life partnership, while not identical to marriage, places persons of the same sex in a situation comparable to that of spouses so far as concerns the survivor's benefit at issue in the main proceedings.

70. However, the referring court finds that entitlement to that survivor's benefit is restricted, under the provisions of the VddB Regulations, to surviving spouses and is denied to surviving life partners.

71. That being the case, those life partners are treated less favourably than surviving spouses as regards entitlement to that survivor's benefit.

72. If the referring court decides that surviving spouses and surviving life partners are in a comparable situation so far as concerns that survivor's benefit, legislation such as that at issue in the main proceedings must, as a consequence, be considered to constitute direct discrimination on grounds of sexual orientation, within the meaning of Articles 1 and 2(2)(a) of Directive 2000/78.

73. It follows from the foregoing that the answer to the third question must be that the combined provisions of Articles 1 and 2 of Directive 2000/78 preclude legislation such as that at issue in the main proceedings under which, after the death of his life partner, the surviving partner does not receive a survivor's benefit equivalent to that granted to a surviving spouse, even though, under national law, life partnership places persons of the same sex in a situation comparable to that of spouses so far as concerns that survivor's benefit. It is for the referring court to determine whether a surviving life partner is in a situation comparable to that of a spouse who is entitled to the survivor's benefit provided for under the occupational pension scheme managed by the VddB.

## NOTES AND QUESTIONS

Why did Ms. Grant's claim fail under EU law while Mr. Maruko's succeeded? How did the Directive affect the situation? Did this mean that the directive itself created obligations for private parties?

## [B] The Justifications Under Article 6 of Directive 2000/78

### DIRECTIVE 2000/78
establishing a general framework for equal treatment in employment and occupation
[2000] OJ L 303

#### Article 6

Justification of differences of treatment on grounds of age

1. Notwithstanding Article 2(2), Member States may provide that differences of treatment on grounds of age shall not constitute discrimination, if, within the context of national law, they are objectively and reasonably justified by a legitimate aim, including legitimate employment policy, labour market and vocational training objectives, and if the means of achieving that aim are appropriate and necessary.

Such differences of treatment may include, among others:

(a) the setting of special conditions on access to employment and vocational training, employment and occupation, including dismissal and remuneration conditions, for young people, older workers and persons with caring responsibilities in order to promote their vocational integration or ensure their protection;

(b) the fixing of minimum conditions of age, professional experience or seniority in service for access to employment or to certain advantages linked to employment;

(c) the fixing of a maximum age for recruitment which is based on the training requirements of the post in question or the need for a reasonable period of employment before retirement.

2. Notwithstanding Article 2(2), Member States may provide that the fixing for occupational social security schemes of ages for admission or entitlement to retirement or invalidity benefits, including the fixing under those schemes of different ages for employees or groups or categories of employees, and the use, in the context of such schemes, of age criteria in actuarial calculations, does not constitute discrimination on the grounds of age, provided this does not result in discrimination on the grounds of sex.

# FÉLIX PALACIOS DE LA VILLA v. CORTEFIEL SERVICIOS SA

## Case C-411/05, 2007 ECJ EUR-Lex LEXIS 3333, [2007] ECR I-08531

[From 1980 until 2001 compulsory retirement of workers who had reached a certain age was used by the Spanish legislature as a mechanism to absorb unemployment. Due to an improving labor market (unfortunately now reversed due to the financial crisis of 2009/10) the Spanish legislature went from regarding compulsory retirement as an instrument favoring employment policy to viewing it as a burden on the social security system, so that it decided to replace the policy of encouraging compulsory retirement with measures intended to promote the implementation of a system of flexible retirement.

Consequently, and also in the context of implementing Directive 2000/78, Spain enacted a new Workers'statute that provided that workers could not to be discriminated against directly or indirectly, when seeking employment or once in employment, on the basis of sex, marital status, age within the limits laid down by this Law, racial or ethnic origin, social status, religion or beliefs, political ideas, sexual orientation, membership or lack of membership of a trade union or on the basis of their language on Spanish territory.

As a result of many disputes about the legality of clauses in existing collective agreements authorising the compulsory retirement of workers, Spain subsequently enacted a further law (Law 14/2005) that reintroduced the mechanism for compulsory retirement, but laid down in that respect different conditions depending on whether the definitive or transitional rules of that law were applicable. For the future, it provided that collective agreements could contain clauses providing for the termination of a contract of employment on the grounds that a worker has reached the normal retirement age stipulated in social security legislation, provided that the following requirements were satisfied:

"(a) such a measure must be linked to objectives which are consistent with employment policy and are set out in the collective agreement, such as increased stability in employment, the conversion of temporary contracts into permanent contracts, sustaining employment, the recruitment of new workers, or any other objectives aimed at promoting the quality of employment.

(b) a worker whose contract of employment is terminated must have completed the minimum contribution period, or a longer period if a clause to that effect is contained in the collective agreement, and he must have satisfied the conditions laid down in social security legislation for entitlement to a retirement pension under his contribution regime."

As concerned collective agreements concluded before its entry into force, the single transitional provision of Law 14/2001 ('the single transitional provision'), imposed only the second of the conditions, excluding any reference to the pursuit of an aim relating to employment policy.

Mr Palacios de la Villa brought proceedings against his employer, Cortefiel Servicios SA ('Cortefiel'), concerning the automatic termination of his contract of employment by reason of the fact that he had reached the age-limit for compulsory retirement, set at 65 years of age by national law. The Court first determined that in principle the mandatory retirement age fell within the notion of age discrimination under the Directive.]

53. In this case, . . . [the Court found that] the single transitional provision, which allows the inclusion of compulsory retirement clauses in collective agreements, was adopted, at the instigation of the social partners, as part of a national policy seeking to promote better access to employment, by means of better distribution of work between the generations.

54. It is true, as the national court has pointed out, that [Article 6] does not expressly refer to an objective of that kind.

55. However, that fact alone is not decisive.

56. It cannot be inferred from Article 6(1) of Directive 2000/78 that the lack of precision in the national legislation at issue as regards the aim pursued automatically excludes the possibility that it may be justified under that provision.

57. In the absence of such precision, it is important, however, that other elements, taken from the general context of the measure concerned, enable the underlying aim of that law to be identified for the purposes of judicial review of its legitimacy and whether the means put in place to achieve that aim are appropriate and necessary.

58. In this case, it is clear from the referring court's explanations that, first, the compulsory retirement of workers who have reached a certain age was introduced into Spanish legislation in the course of 1980, against an economic background characterised by high unemployment, in order to create, in the context of national employment policy, opportunities on the labour market for persons seeking employment.

59. Secondly, such an objective was expressly set out in the Tenth Additional Provision.

60. Thirdly, after the repeal, in the course of 2001, of the Tenth Additional Provision, and following signature by the Spanish Government and employers' and trade union organisations of the Declaration for Social Dialogue 2004 relating to competitiveness, stable employment and social cohesion, the Spanish legislature reintroduced the compulsory retirement mechanism by Law 14/2005. The aim of Law 14/2005 itself is to create opportunities in the labour market for persons seeking employ-

ment. Its single article thus makes it possible, in collective agreements, to include clauses authorising the termination of an employment contract on the ground that the worker has reached retirement age, provided that that measure is 'linked to objectives which are consistent with employment policy and are set out in the collective agreement', such as 'the conversion of temporary contracts into permanent contracts [or] the recruitment of new workers'.

61. In that context, and given the numerous disputes concerning the repercussions of repeal of the Tenth Additional Provision on compulsory retirement clauses contained in collective agreements concluded under Law 8/1980, both in its original version and that approved by Royal Legislative Decree 1/1995, together with the ensuing legal uncertainty for the social partners, the single transitional provision of Law 14/2005 confirmed that it was possible to set an age-limit for compulsory retirement in accordance with those collective agreements.

62. Thus, placed in its context, the single transitional provision was aimed at regulating the national labour market, in particular, for the purposes of checking unemployment.

63. That assessment is further reinforced by the fact that, in this case, the third paragraph of Article 19 of the collective agreement expressly mentions the 'interests of promoting employment' as an objective of the measure established by that provision.

64. The legitimacy of such an aim of public interest cannot reasonably be called into question, since employment policy and labour market trends are among the objectives expressly laid down in the first subparagraph of Article 6(1) of Directive 2000/78 and, in accordance with the first indent of the first paragraph of Article 2 EU and Article 2 EC, the promotion of a high level of employment is one of the ends pursued both by the European Union and the European Community.

65. Furthermore, the Court has already held that encouragement of recruitment undoubtedly constitutes a legitimate aim of social policy . . . and that assessment must evidently apply to instruments of national employment policy designed to improve opportunities for entering the labour market for certain categories of workers.

66. Therefore, an objective such as that referred to by the legislation at issue must, in principle, be regarded as 'objectively and reasonably' justifying 'within the context of national law', as provided for by the first subparagraph of Article 6(1) of Directive 2000/78, a difference in treatment on grounds of age laid down by the Member States.

67. It remains to be determined whether, in accordance with the terms of that provision, the means employed to achieve such a legitimate aim are 'appropriate and necessary'.

68. It should be recalled in this context that, as Community law stands at present, the Member States and, where appropriate, the social partners at national level enjoy broad discretion in their choice, not only to pursue a particular aim in the field of social and employment policy, but also in the definition of measures capable of achieving it . . .

69. As is already clear from the wording, 'specific provisions which may vary in accordance with the situation in Member States', in recital 25 in the preamble to Directive 2000/78, such is the case as regards the choice which the national authorities concerned may be led to make on the basis of political, economic, social, demographic and/or budgetary considerations and having regard to the actual situation in the labour market in a particular Member State, to prolong people's working life or, conversely, to provide for early retirement.

70. Furthermore, the competent authorities at national, regional or sectoral level must have the possibility available of altering the means used to attain a legitimate aim of public interest, for example by adapting them to changing circumstances in the employment situation in the Member State concerned. The fact that the compulsory retirement procedure was reintroduced in Spain after being repealed for several years is accordingly of no relevance.

71. It is, therefore, for the competent authorities of the Member States to find the right balance between the different interests involved. However, it is important to ensure that the national measures laid down in that context do not go beyond what is appropriate and necessary to achieve the aim pursued by the Member State concerned.

72. It does not appear unreasonable for the authorities of a Member State to take the view that a measure such as that at issue in the main proceedings may be appropriate and necessary in order to achieve a legitimate aim in the context of national employment policy, consisting in the promotion of full employment by facilitating access to the labour market.

73. Furthermore, the measure cannot be regarded as unduly prejudicing the legitimate claims of workers subject to compulsory retirement because they have reached the age-limit provided for; the relevant legislation is not based only on a specific age, but also takes account of the fact that the persons concerned are entitled to financial compensation by way of a retirement pension at the end of their working life, such as that provided for by the national legislation at issue in the main proceedings, the level of which cannot be regarded as unreasonable.

74. Moreover, the relevant national legislation allows the social partners to opt, by way of collective agreements — and therefore with considerable flexibility — for application of the compulsory retirement mechanism so that due account may be taken not only of the overall situation in the labour market concerned, but also of the specific features of the jobs in question.

75. In the light of those factors, it cannot reasonably be maintained that national legislation such as that at issue in the main proceedings is incompatible with the requirements of Directive 2000/78.

76. Given the foregoing interpretation of Directive 2000/78, there is no need for the Court to give a ruling in relation to Article 13 EC — also referred to in the first question — on the basis of which that directive was adopted.

77. In the light of all the foregoing considerations, the answer to the first question must be that the prohibition on any discrimination on grounds of age, as implemented by Directive 2000/78, must be interpreted as not precluding national

legislation, such as that at issue in the main proceedings, pursuant to which compulsory retirement clauses contained in collective agreements are lawful where such clauses provide as sole requirements that workers must have reached retirement age, set at 65 by national law, and must have fulfilled the conditions set out in the social security legislation for entitlement to a retirement pension under their contribution regime, where

- the measure, although based on age, is objectively and reasonably justified in the context of national law by a legitimate aim relating to employment policy and the labour market, and

- it is not apparent that the means put in place to achieve that aim of public interest are inappropriate and unnecessary for the purpose.

## NOTES AND QUESTIONS

1.    The introduction of Social Security government retirement benefits in the United States in the 1930s was justified under the Commerce Clause on the grounds that it would encourage older workers to retire and thus open up jobs for younger people. This was the same objective pursued by the original Spanish law. The Directive was found to provide the latitude necessary to allow the collective agreement based on that law to benefit from the exceptions listed in article 6 of the Directive. Do you think the enactment of the Charter might have an impact on that conclusion in future cases? How about the European Convention? Is it surprising that the Court was willing to accept the "lack of precision" regarding the justification for the collective agreement rule?

2.    Note once again that the protection against age discrimination was asserted against a private employer, thus reinforcing the position suggested in *Mangold* and *Maruko*, above.

## [C]   Racial and Ethnic Discrimination

### COUNCIL DIRECTIVE 2000/43/EC
implementing the principle of equal treatment between persons irrespective of racial or ethnic origin

Article 1

Purpose

The purpose of this Directive is to lay down a framework for combating discrimination on the grounds of racial or ethnic origin, with a view to putting into effect in the Member States the principle of equal treatment.

Article 2

Concept of discrimination

1. For the purposes of this Directive, the principle of equal treatment shall mean that there shall be no direct or indirect discrimination based on racial or ethnic origin.

2. For the purposes of paragraph 1:

(a) direct discrimination shall be taken to occur where one person is treated less favourably than another is, has been or would be treated in a comparable situation on grounds of racial or ethnic origin;

(b) indirect discrimination shall be taken to occur where an apparently neutral provision, criterion or practice would put persons of a racial or ethnic origin at a particular disadvantage compared with other persons, unless that provision, criterion or practice is objectively justified by a legitimate aim and the means of achieving that aim are appropriate and necessary.

3. Harassment shall be deemed to be discrimination within the meaning of paragraph 1, when an unwanted conduct related to racial or ethnic origin takes place with the purpose or effect of violating the dignity of a person and of creating an intimidating, hostile, degrading, humiliating or offensive environment.

In this context, the concept of harassment may be defined in accordance with the national laws and practice of the Member States.

4. An instruction to discriminate against persons on grounds of racial or ethnic origin shall be deemed to be discrimination within the meaning of paragraph 1.

Article 3

Scope

1. Within the limits of the powers conferred upon the Community, this Directive shall apply to all persons, as regards both the public and private sectors, including public bodies, in relation to:

(a) conditions for access to employment, to self-employment and to occupation, including selection criteria and recruitment conditions, whatever the branch of activity and at all levels of the professional hierarchy, including promotion;

(b) access to all types and to all levels of vocational guidance, vocational training, advanced vocational training and retraining, including practical work experience;

(c) employment and working conditions, including dismissals and pay;

(d) membership of and involvement in an organisation of workers or employers, or any organisation whose members carry on a particular profession, including the benefits provided for by such organisations;

(e) social protection, including social security and healthcare;

(f) social advantages;

(g) education;

(h) access to and supply of goods and services which are available to the public, including housing.

## Article 4

### Genuine and determining occupational requirements

Notwithstanding Article 2(1) and (2), Member States may provide that a difference of treatment which is based on a characteristic related to racial or ethnic origin shall not constitute discrimination where, by reason of the nature of the particular occupational activities concerned or of the context in which they are carried out, such a characteristic constitutes a genuine and determining occupational requirement, provided that the objective is legitimate and the requirement is proportionate.

## NOTES AND QUESTIONS

1.   It will be noted that this directive extends beyond discrimination in employment. Could it be invoked against the 2011 French law that prohibits the wearing of the burqa, the Muslim garb that covers a woman's entire body (including her face), or is that more likely to be considered religious discrimination? Is it discrimination at all in the context of societal norms that expect people to be open with each other?

2.   Could the justifications provided for in article 4 allow the situation where an employer refuses to employ persons of a particular race or ethnic background because his customers would object? In *Centrum for Gelijkheid van Kansen v. Firma Feryn*, Case 54/07, 2008 ECJ EUR-Lex LEXIS 1947, [2008] ECR I-5187, the ECJ suggested not. But suppose this were connected to, say, an ability to communicate with customers?

## § 18.06   ECONOMIC EQUALITY

### ROYAL SCHOLTEN-HONIG (HOLDINGS) LTD v. INTERVENTION BOARD FOR AGRICULTURAL PRODUCE; TUNNEL REFINERIES LTD v. INTERVENTION BOARD FOR AGRICULTURAL PRODUCE
#### Joined Cases 103 and 145/77, [1978] ECR 2037

[At issue was the validity inter alia of Council Regulations (EEC) Nos 1111/77 of 17 May 1977 laying down common provisions for isoglucose and 1110/77 of the same date amending Regulation (EEC) No 3330/74 on the common organization of the market in sugar. There was a serious sugar surplus of production in the EC and the common organization therefore sought to constrain production and reduce intervention costs by allocating quotas, designated as A, B and C, which represented gradations of support for sugar sales. Thus, quantities sold under Quota A enjoyed intervention price protection; quota B quantities were subject to a production levy which at the relevant time meant that about 26% of total A and B production was subject to the levy; quota C production could be sold only outside the EC at world prices. Isoglucose produced chemically from cereal starches, was in some areas a competitor for sugar made from cane and beets and had originally been part of the sugar organization but was separated out by the regulations in issue.]

26 The prohibition of discrimination laid down in [EC34(2)/TFEU 40(2)] is merely a specific enunciation of the general principle of equality which is one of the fundamental principles of community law.

27 That principle requires that similar situations shall not be treated differently unless the differentiation is objectively justified.

28 It must therefore be ascertained whether isoglucose is in a situation comparable to that of other products of the starch industry, in particular in the sense that they can be substituted for isoglucose in the specific use to which the latter product is normally put.

[The Court analyzed the effects of the regulation and charges on isoglucose vs. sugar and found that isoglucose had been discriminated against.]

83 Accordingly the provisions of Regulation No 1111/77 establishing the production levy system for isoglucose offend against the general principle of equality of which the prohibition on discrimination set out in Article 40 (3) of the Treaty is a specific expression.

## NOTES AND QUESTIONS

1.   The court says the sort of economic discrimination at issue in this case is an example of the principle of equality, but the case is specific to the prohibition on discrimination in the context of the common agricultural policy. Is the Court suggesting that it would apply this principle to any EU act potentially? In the above case, the action sought annulment of the regulation. The Court did so, thus confirming that legislation that discriminates in violation of a specific article in the Treaty by imposing an unfair burden on one group of economic operators versus another is indeed unlawful. Contrast this with the cases in Chapter 8 dealing with the notion that a lawful act might give rise to an EU-based action for damages where a party had suffered unusual and specific damage (*Dorsch*). Is this another expression of a general concept of a prohibition on economic discrimination or are these different issues altogether?

2.   This case was one of many that were spawned by the disastrous attempt by the EU to regulate the isoglucose market, but other market regulation has also been overturned by the court on discrimination grounds: See, e.g., *Bela-Mühle Josef Bergmann KG v. Grows-Farm GmbH*, Case 114/76, [1977] ECR 1211.

## § 18.07  EQUALITY AND DEMOCRATIC RIGHTS

### MATTHEWS v. UNITED KINGDOM
(App. no. 24833/94) EUROPEAN COURT OF HUMAN RIGHTS (1998) 28
EHRR 361, [1999] ECHR 24833/94

[The facts underlying this judgment, and the special status of Gibraltar are set out in chapter 6, *supra*. The judgment refers to the prior decision of the "Commission" This was the European Commission on Human Rights which acted as a first reviewer of an application. It has since been abolished.]

The [UK] Government submitted that, even if Article 3 of Protocol No. 1 could be said to apply to the European Parliament, the absence of elections in Gibraltar in 1994 did not give rise to a violation of that provision but instead fell within the State's margin of appreciation. They pointed out that in the 1994 elections the United Kingdom had used a single-member constituency, "first-past-the-post" system. It would have distorted the electoral process to constitute Gibraltar as a separate constituency, since its population of approximately 30,000 was less than 5% of the average population per European Parliament seat in the United Kingdom. The alternative of redrawing constituency boundaries so as to include Gibraltar within a new or existing constituency was no more feasible, as Gibraltar did not form part of the United Kingdom and had no strong historical or other link with any particular United Kingdom constituency.

The applicant submitted that she had been completely deprived of the right to vote in the 1994 elections. She stated that the protection of fundamental rights could not depend on whether or not there were attractive alternatives to the current system.

\* \* \*

The Court recalls that the rights set out in Article 3 of Protocol No. 1 are not absolute, but may be subject to limitations. The Contracting States enjoy a wide margin of appreciation in imposing conditions on the right to vote, but it is for the Court to determine in the last resort whether the requirements of Protocol No. 1 have been complied with. It has to satisfy itself that the conditions do not curtail the right to vote to such an extent as to impair its very essence and deprive it of effectiveness; that they are imposed in pursuit of a legitimate aim; and that the means employed are not disproportionate. In particular, such conditions must not thwart "the free expression of the people in the choice of the legislature" . . .

The Court makes it clear at the outset that the choice of electoral system by which the free expression of the opinion of the people in the choice of the legislature is ensured — whether it be based on proportional representation, the "first-past-the-post" system or some other arrangement — is a matter in which the State enjoys a wide margin of appreciation. However, in the present case the applicant, as a resident of Gibraltar, was completely denied any opportunity to express her opinion in the choice of the members of the European Parliament. The position is not analogous to that of persons who are unable to take part in elections because they live outside the jurisdiction, as such individuals have weakened the link between themselves and the jurisdiction. In the present case, as the Court has found . . . the legislation which emanates from the European Community forms part of the legislation in Gibraltar, and the applicant is directly affected by it.

In the circumstances of the present case, the very essence of the applicant's right to vote, as guaranteed by Article 3 of Protocol No. 1, was denied.

It follows that there has been a violation of that provision.

## NOTES AND QUESTIONS

1. What might be the implications of the ECHR court's involving itself in a question relating to EU rights? Does this look like a very narrow issue or the beginning of a significant new development? Consider in this regard how the ECHR might come into play once the EU has acceded to it.

2. The UK, to comply with the ECHR judgment, enacted legislation that combined Gibraltar with one of the constituencies within mainland Britain, thus enabling those who were entitled to vote in European elections per the *Matthews* judgment to do so. Given the special status of Gibraltar, Spain subsequently challenged this action on the grounds that the vote had been extended to persons who were not citizens of the EU, but this claim was unsuccessful. See *Spain v. United Kingdom* Case C-145/04, 2006 ECJ CELEX LEXIS 444, [2006] ECR I-7917.

## M. G. EMAN AND O. B. SEVINGER V COLLEGE VAN BURGEMEESTER EN WETHOUDERS VAN DEN HAAG
### Case C-300/04, 2006 ECJ CELEX LEXIS 446, [2006] ECR I-8055

[Mr Eman and Mr Sevinger, both of Netherlands nationality and resident in Oranjestad (Aruba), brought suit against the defendants concerning the latter's rejection of their application for registration on the register of electors for the election of members of the European Parliament on 10 June 2004. Aside from the Treaty provisions the applicants also relied on Article 5 of Directive 93/109 which provides:

If, in order to vote or to stand as candidates, nationals of the Member State of residence must have spent a certain minimum period as a resident in the electoral territory of that State, Community voters and Community nationals entitled to stand as candidates shall be deemed to have fulfilled that condition where they have resided for an equivalent period in other Member States. This provision shall apply without prejudice to any specific conditions as to length of residence in a given constituency or locality.'

Dutch law required residence in the Netherlands, but Aruba was not considered to be part of the Netherlands for this purpose. Thus the applicants were denied the right to register to vote.

56. The appellants in the main proceedings and the Commission claim, however, that the Netherlands Electoral Law infringed the principle of equal treatment in that it confers the right to vote and to stand as a candidate in elections to the European Parliament on all Netherlands nationals resident in a non-member country, whereas such a right is not conferred on Netherlands nationals resident in the

Netherlands Antilles or Aruba.]

57. In that regard, it must be observed that the principle of equal treatment or nondiscrimination, which is one of the general principles of Community law, requires that comparable situations must not be treated differently and that different situations must not be treated in the same way unless such treatment is objectively justified (Joined Cases C453/03, C11/04, C12/04 and C194/04 ABNA and Others 2005 ECR I10423, paragraph 63, and Case C344/04 IATA and ELFAA 2006 ECR 1403, paragraph 95).

58. Here, the relevant comparison is between a Netherlands national resident in the Netherlands Antilles or Aruba and one residing in a non-member country. They have in common that they are Netherlands nationals who do not reside in the Netherlands. Yet there is a difference in treatment between the two, the latter having the right to vote and to stand as a candidate in elections to the European Parliament held in the Netherlands whereas the former has no such right. Such a difference in treatment must be objectively justified.

59. At the hearing, the Netherlands Government stated that the Netherlands Electoral Law's objective was to enable Netherlands nationals from the Netherlands residing abroad to vote, since those nationals are assumed still to have links with Netherlands society. However, it is also apparent from that Government's explanations at the hearing that a Netherlands national who transfers his residence from Aruba to a non-member country has the right to vote in the same way as a Netherlands national transferring his residence from the Netherlands to a non-member country, while a Netherlands national resident in Aruba does not have that right.

60. In that regard, the objective pursued by the Netherlands legislature consisting in the conferment of the right to vote and stand for election on Netherlands nationals who have or have had links with the Netherlands falls within that legislature's discretion as regards the holding of the elections. However, the Netherlands Government has not sufficiently demonstrated that the difference in treatment observed between Netherlands nationals resident in a non-member country and those resident in the Netherlands Antilles or Aruba is objectively justified and does not therefore constitute an infringement of the principle of equal treatment.

61. Having regard to those matters, the answer to the third question must be that while, in the current state of Community law, there is nothing which precludes the Member States from defining, in compliance with Community law, the conditions of the right to vote and to stand as a candidate in elections to the European Parliament by reference to the criterion of residence in the territory in which the elections are held, the principle of equal treatment prevents, however, the criteria chosen from resulting in different treatment of nationals who are in comparable situations, unless that difference in treatment is objectively justified.

\*     \*     \*

65. By its fifth question, the Raad van State asks whether Community law imposes requirements as to the nature of the legal redress (rechtsherstel) to be provided if the national court — on the basis of, inter alia, the answers given by the Court to

the above questions — were to conclude that persons resident or living in the Netherlands Antilles and Aruba and having Netherlands nationality were wrongly refused registration for the election of the members of the European Parliament of 10 June 2004.

66. In that regard, it is clear from Article 12 of the 1976 Act that the European Parliament rules only on disputes relating to elections which may arise out of the provisions of the 1976 Act other than those arising out of the national provisions to which it refers. Since the determination of who are entitled to the right to vote and to stand as a candidate in elections to the European Parliament comes within the powers of each Member State, it follows that disputes relating to the national provisions defining those entitled to that right are also a matter of national law.

67. Thus, in the absence of Community legislation in respect of disputes relating to the right to vote and stand for election to the European Parliament, it is for the domestic legal system of each Member State to designate the courts having jurisdiction and to determine the detailed procedural rules governing actions at law intended to safeguard the rights which individuals derive from Community law, provided, first, that those rules are not less favourable than those governing rights which originate in domestic law (principle of equivalence) and, second, that they do not render impossible or excessively difficult in practice the exercise of rights conferred by the Community legal order (principle of effectiveness) . . .

68. As regards possible legal redress (rechtsherstel) for a person who, because of a national provision which is contrary to Community law, is refused registration on the register of electors for the election of Members of the European Parliament, it is likewise in accordance with the requirements and detailed rules of national law that such redress can take place, it being understood that those conditions and rules must comply with the principles of equivalence and effectiveness . . . In order to determine the appropriate redress, the national court may usefully refer to the detailed rules for legal redress laid down in cases of infringement of the national rules in the context of elections to the institutions of the Member State.

69. In that context, it must also be recalled that the principle of liability on the part of a Member State for damage caused to individuals as a result of breaches of Community law for which it can be held responsible is inherent in the system of the Treaty, and that a Member State is thus required to make reparation for the damage caused where the rule of law infringed is intended to confer rights on individuals, the breach is sufficiently serious and there is a direct causal link between the breach of the obligation resting on the State and the damage sustained by the injured parties . . . although this does not mean that the State cannot incur liability under less strict conditions on the basis of national law . . .

70. Subject to the right of reparation which flows directly from Community law where the conditions referred to in the previous paragraph are satisfied, it is on the basis of rules of national law on liability that the State must make reparation for the consequences of the loss and damage caused, provided that the conditions for reparation of loss and damage laid down by national law are not less favourable than those relating to similar domestic claims and are not so framed as to make it, in practice, impossible or excessively difficult to obtain reparation . . .

71. The reply to the fifth question must therefore be that it is for the national law of each Member State to determine the rules allowing legal redress for a person who, because of a national provision that is contrary to Community law, has not been entered on the electoral register for the election of the members of the European Parliament of 10 June 2004 and has therefore been excluded from participation in those elections. Those remedies, which may include compensation for the loss caused by the infringement of Community law for which the State may be held responsible, must comply with the principles of equivalence and effectiveness.

## NOTES AND QUESTIONS

1.  The Dutch nationals in this case relied on the principle of equal treatment to justify their right to vote under European law principles. Given cases such as *Moser*, (Chapter 17 *supra*) does the Court's ruling here represent a clear manifestation of supplemental rights conferred on EU citizens by the status of EU citizenship over and above the rights deriving from the EC Treaty/TFEU?

2.  What do you think of the Court's response to the question of legal redress? Is it surprising, perhaps, that the right of compensation seems to be a matter of national law?

# Chapter 19

# CITIZENS' RIGHTS

## § 19.01   OVERVIEW

***Template*** Article 8 Section 9.2 and Charter Articles 39-44

***The term "Citizens' Rights"*** The Charter brings together a number of rights under the heading of "Citizens' Rights". This is rather confusing if read as referring to the rights of EU citizens deriving specifically from that status. In fact, the term "Citizens' " is being used in the Charter only generically to describe what might more accurately be called rights pertaining to the individual's interaction with or participation in EU institutions. They are not necessarily dependent on EU citizenship. Thus, the right to good administration is a general right available to nationals and non-nationals alike; while voting rights are obviously linked to citizenship. The rights derived from EU citizenship — in particular the rights of free movement and residence (Chapter 17) might, since they are additional to the status of nationality, more appropriately be regarded as descriptive of the individual's interaction, under EU law, with the *Member States*.

***Materials in this Chapter***: This chapter contains materials addressing two of the enumerated "citizens' rights" in the Charter: the "right to good administration" and the right of access to EU documents. The former term was introduced by the Charter and does not occur anywhere in the Treaties. However, the elements of it are well developed in EU law, having largely taken shape through the individual's interaction with the EU under the competition provisions, which, as noted already in Chapter 7, have historically been the area where the EU has exercised the most notable degree of executive authority. This will gradually change over time as the EU sets up more and more specialized agencies. (These are mentioned in Chapter 2). One may note as well that the expansion of EU competence has also brought the EU into play in areas of national security and criminal law (see the *Modjahedines* case in this Chapter, for example).

The right of access to documents has been a more recent development, having first surfaced in the 1990s and now captured in EU legislation. This is an area of particular interest for the Member States that themselves already have a highly developed system of open government. Two of the leading cases on the current legislation were taken up by Sweden on behalf of individual litigants and prompted rather dramatic reversals by the ECJ of General Court decisions that had come down against the individuals.

***Relationship with the "Justice" provisions of the Charter*** The Charter rightly references "justice" in the context of criminal law. However, many of the principles that form the basis of a just criminal system can be "translated" into the administrative context as, for example, the right to a fair hearing and the presumption of innocence. At the same time, the nature of the administrative task imposed on an EU institution cannot be viewed as based on principles of justice as such. An institution may be called on to act as both investigator and decisionmaker — the competition rules are the clearest example. The parallels need to be tempered by the nature of the administrative task. Indeed, the EU Courts have approached the subject not from the desire to see justice done, but rather from the need to ensure that the institution properly carries out its task to the highest possible standard. The "right to good administration" is therefore a very apt description for the law in this area.

***Relationship with the criteria in EC 230/TFEU 263*** As noted already in various places in this book, the European Court has the power to review EU acts based on the criteria laid down in EC 230/TFEU 263. These criteria are reflective of their origins in the French administrative law system. The EU Courts seem not to pay much attention to which of these categories they are relying on and they have therefore been largely overtaken by the more extensive development of fundamental rights as a principle of EU law based on the duty of the Court to see that the law is observed, now enshrined in TEU 19.

***U.S. Comparison*** Much of what appears under the "right of good administration" finds its parallel in U.S. administrative law, and in particular the Administrative Procedure Act (APA). This in turn may be regarded as a particular manifestation of the constitutional requirements for "due process" as developed in the administrative law context.

***Other enumerated Citizens' rights*** Citizens' rights include the right to compensation. Given the separate provisions in the TFEU itself relating to the action for damages, this topic is addressed in Chapter 8 on Judicial Protection.

As explained on the EU Website:

> The position of European Ombudsman was created by the original TEU. The Ombudsman "acts as an intermediary between the citizen and the EU authorities. He is entitled to receive and investigate complaints from EU citizens, businesses and organisations, and from anyone residing or having their registered office in an EU country. He helps to uncover 'maladministration' in the European Union institutions and bodies. 'Maladministration' means poor or failed administration — in other words, when an institution fails to act in accordance with the law, or fails to respect the principles of good administration, or violates human rights. Some examples are:
>
> - unfairness,
> - discrimination,
> - abuse of power,
> - lack or refusal of information,
> - unnecessary delay,
> - incorrect procedures.

The Ombudsman carries out investigations following a complaint or on his own initiative. He operates completely independently and impartially. He does not request or accept instructions from any government or organisation.

## § 19.02  THE RIGHT TO GOOD ADMINISTRATION

### [A]  Timely Action

**JCB SERVICE v. COMMISSION**

Case T-67/01, 2004 ECJ CELEX LEXIS 20, [2004] ECR II-49

[JCB Service manufactured among other things, backhoe loaders and held substantial market shares globally including a 60% share of the UK market. It had originally notified its distribution agreements to the Commission for clearance or exemption under Regulation 17/62 (now repealed and replaced by Regulation 1/2003 — see Chapter 6). However, while there was some back and forth between JCB and the Commission over an extended time period, the Commission did not formally act on the request for an exemption. Then, prompted by a complaint from a French distributor of JCB parts that had been sued by JCB under French unfair competition law, the Commission began proceedings against JCB in 1996. It issued a statement of objections but overlooked completely the original 1973 notification which had the effect under regulation 17 of rendering JCB immune from fines. This then prompted a second statement of objections and eventually a decision adverse to JCB in 2000, finally rejecting the request of exemption. JCB sought annulment of the decision based *inter alia* on the Commission's delay of 27 years. The CFI/General Court decision was upheld on appeal:

Case C-167/04 P, 2006 ECJ EUR-Lex LEXIS 2176, [2006] ECR I-08935.]

36. The need to act within a reasonable time in conducting administrative proceedings relating to competition policy is a general principle of Community law whose observance is ensured by the Community judicature . . . and which is incorporated, as an element of the right to good administration, in Article 41(1) of the Charter of fundamental rights of the European Union proclaimed in Nice on 7 December 2000 (OJ 2000 C 364, p. 1). Accordingly, while it is not necessary to rule on the applicability as such of Article 6(1) of the ECHR to administrative proceedings before the Commission relating to competition policy, it must be considered whether, in the present case, the Commission has breached the general principle of Community law that decisions must be adopted within a reasonable time in the procedure leading to the adoption of the contested decision.

37. In considering this plea, a distinction must be made between the two sets of administrative proceedings at issue, namely, first, consideration of the agreements notified in 1973, which was concluded by the rejection, in Article 2 of the contested decision, of the application for exemption, and, second, investigation of the complaint made in 1996, the conclusions of which are set out in the other articles of the operative part of the contested decision relating to the infringement.

38. As regards the proceedings which followed notification in 1973, according to the

documents on the file, the Commission filed the notified agreements in 1992 without taking a decision and it was only JCB's reply to the first statement of objections which led the defendant to reconsider those agreements in the course of the investigation of the complaint. It is abundantly clear that the fact that those proceedings lasted 27 years breaches the obligation of the administration to adopt a position and close proceedings, once opened, within a reasonable time. However, regrettable as such a breach is, it cannot have affected either the lawfulness of the rejection of the application for exemption or the proper conduct of the proceedings to establish that there was an infringement.

39. As regards the rejection of an application for exemption, which is a separate decision from that finding that there was an infringement, it is settled case-law that the mere fact of not having been adopted within a reasonable time cannot render unlawful a decision taken by the Commission following notification of an agreement . . .

40. Infringement of the principle that the Commission must act within a reasonable time, if established, would justify the annulment of a decision taken following administrative proceedings in competition matters only in so far as it also constituted an infringement of the rights of defence of the undertakings concerned. Where it has not been established that the undue delay has adversely affected the ability of the undertakings concerned to defend themselves effectively, failure to comply with the principle that the Commission must act within a reasonable time cannot affect the validity of the administrative procedure . . .

41. As regards the decision finding an infringement, suffice it to note that care is taken in that decision not to base findings on matters which were notified and to establish that the practices of which JCB is accused are different from those stipulated by the notified agreements. Consequently, the fact that the agreements were notified long ago cannot affect the lawfulness of the infringement proceedings relating to matters other than those notified.

42. Moreover, JCB Service does not argue that the length of time which elapsed resulted in any particular procedural irregularity and confines itself to submitting that the Commission's conduct reveals poor management of the file. No inference of relevance to the consideration of the claims for annulment can therefore be drawn from the length of time which has elapsed since the notifications made in 1973.

43. As regards the investigation of the complaint referred to the Commission on 15 February 1996, the total duration of the procedure, 4 years, 10 months and 6 days, does not appear excessive given the complexity of the case, which involves several Member States and covers 5 heads of infringement, and the need to draw up a second statement of objections . . .

44. Even if that length of time were held excessive, that finding would be such as to entail the annulment of the relevant articles of the contested decision only if it were established that it gave rise to an infringement of the rights of defence . . .

45. However, it must be noted that the applicant does not argue that the Commission's alleged failure to act within a reasonable time in investigating the complaint gave rise, in the present case, to an infringement of the rights of defence. As was confirmed at the hearing, JCB Service confines itself to arguing that the

length of the procedure reveals the Commission's partiality and mismanagement of the file and thereby demonstrates the unlawfulness of the contested decision. Against that background, and without it being necessary to rule on the alleged excessive length of the investigation of the complaint, it must be held that the plea as it is argued cannot entail the total or partial annulment of the operative part of the contested decision.

46. It follows from the foregoing observations that the plea, which is not such as to affect the lawfulness of the contested decision, either with regard to the application for exemption or with regard to the infringement, must be rejected as inoperative.

## NOTES AND QUESTIONS

1. In light of the CFI's/General Court's reasoning, delay in adopting a decision or a failure to take a decision might lead to the annulment of an eventual action if the rights of the defense were infringed. What do you think the Court meant by this? Can you think of some examples? Is this a sound approach in terms of ensuring proper conduct by the Commission?

2. Could JCB have invoked EC 232/TFEU 265?

3. For another case involving timely action, see *SCK and FNK v. Commission* Case T-213/95 and T-18/96, 1997 ECJ CELEX LEXIS 90, [1997] ECR II-1739.

## [B]  Presumption of Innocence?

### JCB SERVICE v. COMMISSION
Case T-67/01 2004 ECJ CELEX LEXIS 20, [2004] ECR II-49

[The facts are set out in the extract above. JCB claimed a breach of the right to be heard, which was governed, as regards the application of EC 81/TFEU 101 EC and EC 82/TFEU 102, by the provisions of Article 19(1) of former Regulation No 17 and by those of former Regulation No 99/63 on the hearings provided for in Article 19(1) and (2) of Regulation No 17 (OJ, English Special Edition, 1963-1964 p. 47). Those provisions required that undertakings concerned by a proceeding for the establishment of infringements are afforded the opportunity, in the course of the administrative procedure, of effectively making known their views on all the objections dealt with in the decision . . . JCB also relied on the principle of the presumption of innocence which is part of the EU legal order and applies to the procedures relating to infringements of the competition rules applicable to undertakings that may result in the imposition of fines or periodic penalty payments. Under Article 15(5) of Regulation 17, the operation of notified agreements could not incur fines with respect to the period starting with the date of notification until the Commission determined otherwise. JCB argued that because the Commission had made two attempts at a statement of objections, and for other reasons, it was biased against JCB.]

53. As regards the principle of the presumption of innocence, the mere fact that the Commission adopted two successive statements of objections cannot suffice to establish that that principle was breached. Moreover, a general presumption of the

guilt of the undertaking concerned can be attributed to the Commission only if the findings of fact it made in the decision were not supported by the evidence it furnished.

54. As an example of the Commission's alleged partiality, JCB Service mentions, first, a memorandum of 16 May 1995 from the Sales Development Director, sent to the managers of the companies in the group, which states that the prohibition of parallel imports is contrary to the decisions of the Commission and the case-law of the Court of Justice. It alleges that the Commission used that document as evidence that JCB was aware of Community law, which constitutes an aggravating factor. However JCB cannot claim that it was unaware of the requirements of Community competition law, as, moreover, attested by its notification of its agreements as soon as the United Kingdom of Great Britain and Northern Ireland joined the European Community. JCB's concern over the compatibility of its agreements and practices with Community law, which emerges from the memorandum mentioned above, is an objective finding of fact, which is, moreover, not disputed by the applicant. The fact that the Commission has taken account of the document in question and the conduct which it records does not therefore reveal partiality on its part.

55. JCB submits, second, that the Commission misinterpreted the letter of 13 April 1995 from Berkeley JCB [a distributor] to JCB Sales mentioned in recital 89 of the contested decision. That correspondence records the fact that that distributor might be approached "by both end users and agents". Even if the Commission had misinterpreted that part of the sentence in stating in recital 143 of the contested decision that "overseas end-users and their duly appointed agents" were referred to, that possible inaccuracy did not in itself demonstrate partiality but, at worst, betrayed a poor understanding of the document.

56. Third, JCB takes the view that, in any event, the Commission assumed its guilt. It complains, for instance, that it did not take account of the judgment of the Cour d'appel de Paris of 8 April 1998, which was in its favour. That judgment, which held that Central Parts used the JCB sign without authorisation and deleted the serial numbers from JCB machines, concluded that Central Parts had engaged in acts of unfair competition against JCB. The Commission also misinterpreted the "Rouviere dispute", named after a customer of Central Parts, an unauthorised dealer who bought a JCB machine from Central Parts and subsequently repaired it badly. The fact that the author of a complaint in a procedure applying Regulation No 17 might have engaged in misconduct for which it was sentenced by a court is irrelevant to the infringements actually alleged against JCB which are, moreover, separate.

57. JCB Service submits, fourth, that the transcript of the interview held on 6 November 1996 on the premises of the unauthorised distributor, Watling JCB, between officials of the Competition DG and the distributor's representatives made by staff of that directorate constituted exculpatory evidence which the Commission was wrong not to take into account.

58. According to the transcript of that interview, which was placed on the court file during these proceedings, as indicated in paragraphs 27, 28 and 30 above, the information given to the Commission by Watling JCB during that interview concerns, inter alia, the way in which restrictions imposed on out-of territory sales were implemented, relations between the applicant and the JCB Dealer Associa-

tion, service support fees and the drawing up of retail price lists. In the picture of relations between the JCB group and one of its distributors which emerges from that interview, no element can be clearly pinpointed as evidence as to whether or not the practices of the distribution network constitute infringements. It seems, therefore, that it cannot be argued that the Commission excluded the document from its examination of the elements of the infringement in order to suppress exculpatory evidence. Moreover, the Commission states that it excluded that document because it had doubts about the lawfulness of the circumstances in which it was obtained, which seems a plausible explanation here.

59. Accordingly, in the light of the circumstances described above and the content of the transcript in question, the Commission's decision to exclude that document from the file is not sufficient to prove the allegation of partiality made against the Commission in dealing with the case.

60. In conclusion, there is nothing in the conduct of the administrative procedure to indicate that the Commission interpreted the documents and the facts in a tendentious or biased manner or exhibited partiality in its conduct towards JCB. The plea of breach of the principle of the presumption of innocence in consideration of the evidence must therefore be rejected.

## NOTES AND QUESTIONS

**1.** The CFI/General Court seems to have accepted here without question that a presumption of innocence applies in administrative proceedings. Does the Charter support such a view? What other provisions of the Charter might be applicable here?

**2.** Consider the arguments made by JCB to support its position that the Commission was biased. Given the nature of competition proceedings (see, in this regard, Chapter 7) did they perhaps have more merit than the Court was prepared to accept?

### [C]   Right to a Fair Hearing and the Right to Effective Judicial Protection

### ORGANISATION DES MODJAHEDINES DU PEUPLE D'IRAN v. COUNCIL
#### Case T-228/02, [2006] ECR II-4665

[This is another case dealing with the measures taken by the Union to freeze assets of suspected terrorist groups following the 9/11 attacks in the U.S. The Council had adopted a regulation (2580/2001) under which it had then adopted a decision to freeze the funds of the plaintiff organization. The applicants complained that they had not been given a chance to make their case within the procedure followed for adopting decisions as to who should be included in the list. See also the *Kadi* case in Chapter 3. Case T-228/02 was not appealed.]

114 It is appropriate first, to define the purpose of the safeguard of the right to a fair hearing in the context of the adoption of a decision to freeze funds under Article

2(3) of Regulation No 2580/2001, distinguishing between an initial decision to freeze funds referred to in Article 1(4) of Common Position 2001/931 ('the initial decision to freeze funds') and any subsequent decision to maintain a freeze of funds, following a periodic review, as referred to in Article 1(6) of that common position ('subsequent decisions to freeze funds').

115 In that context, it should be noted, first, that the right to a fair hearing only falls to be exercised with regard to the elements of fact and law which are liable to determine the application of the measure in question to the person concerned, in accordance with the relevant rules.

116 In the circumstances of the present case, the relevant rules are laid down in Article 2(3) of Regulation No 2580/2001, according to which the Council, acting by unanimity, is to establish, review and amend the list of persons, groups and entities to which that regulation applies, in accordance with the provisions laid down in Article 1(4) to (6) of Common Position 2001/931. Thus, in accordance with Article 1(4) of Common Position 2001/931, the list is to be drawn up on the basis of precise information or material in the relevant file which indicates that a decision has been taken by a competent authority in respect of the persons, groups and entities concerned, irrespective of whether it concerns the instigation of investigations or prosecution for a terrorist act, an attempt to perpetrate, participate in or facilitate such an act based on serious and credible evidence or clues, or condemnation for such deeds. 'Competent authority' is understood to mean a judicial authority, or, where judicial authorities have no jurisdiction in the relevant area, an equivalent competent authority in that area. Moreover, the names of persons and entities in the list are to be reviewed at regular intervals and at least once every six months to ensure that there are grounds for keeping them in the list, as provided for by Article 1(6) of Common Position 2001/931.

117 As rightly pointed out by the Council and the United Kingdom, the procedure which may culminate in a measure to freeze funds under the relevant rules therefore takes place at two levels, one national, the other Community. In the first phase, a competent national authority, in principle judicial, must take in respect of the party concerned a decision complying with the definition in Article 1(4) of Common Position 2001/931. If it is a decision to instigate investigations or to prosecute, it must be based on serious and credible evidence or clues. In the second phase, the Council, acting by unanimity, must decide to include the party concerned in the disputed list, on the basis of precise information or material in the relevant file which indicates that such a decision has been taken. Next, the Council must, at regular intervals, and at least once every six months, ensure that there are grounds for keeping the party concerned in the list. Verification that there is a decision of a national authority meeting that definition is an essential precondition for the adoption, by the Council, of an initial decision to freeze funds, whereas verification of the consequences of that decision at the national level is imperative in the context of the adoption of a subsequent decision to freeze funds.

118 Accordingly, the observance of the right to a fair hearing in the context of the adoption of a decision to freeze funds is also liable to arise at those two levels . . .

119 The right of the party concerned to a fair hearing must be effectively safeguarded in the first place as part of the national procedure which led to the

adoption, by the competent national authority, of the decision referred to in Article 1(4) of Common Position 2001/931. It is essentially in that national context that the party concerned must be placed in a position in which he can effectively make known his view of the matters on which the decision is based, subject to possible restrictions on the right to a fair hearing which are legally justified in national law, particularly on grounds of public policy, public security or the maintenance of international relations . . .

120 Next, the right of the party concerned to a fair hearing must be effectively safeguarded in the Community procedure culminating in the adoption, by the Council, of the decision to include or maintain it on the disputed list, in accordance with Article 2(3) of Regulation No 2580/2001. As a rule, in that area, the party concerned need only be afforded the opportunity effectively to make known his views on the legal conditions of application of the Community measure in question, namely, where it is an initial decision to freeze funds, whether there is specific information or material in the file which shows that a decision meeting the definition laid down in Article 1(4) of Common Position 2001/931 was taken in respect of him by a competent national authority and, where it is a subsequent decision to freeze funds, the justification for maintaining the party concerned in the disputed list.

121 However, provided that the decision in question was adopted by a competent national authority of a Member State, the observance of the right to a fair hearing at Community level does not usually require, at that stage, that the party concerned again be afforded the opportunity to express his views on the appropriateness and well-foundedness of that decision, as those questions may only be raised at national level, before the authority in question or, if the party concerned brings an action, before the competent national court. Likewise, in principle, it is not for the Council to decide whether the proceedings opened against the party concerned and resulting in that decision, as provided for by the national law of the relevant Member State, was conducted correctly, or whether the fundamental rights of the party concerned were respected by the national authorities. That power belongs exclusively to the competent national courts or, as the case may be, to the European Court of Human Rights . . .

122 Nor, if the Community measure to freeze funds is adopted on the basis of a decision by a national authority of a Member State concerning investigations or prosecutions (rather than on the basis of a decision of condemnation), does the observance of the right to a fair hearing require, as a rule, that the party concerned be afforded the opportunity effectively to make known his views on whether that decision is 'based on serious and credible evidence or clues', as required by Article 1(4) of Common Position 2001/931. Although that element is one of the legal conditions of application of the measure in question, the Court finds that it would be inappropriate, in the light of the principle of sincere cooperation referred to in Article 10 EC [TEU 4], to make it subject to the exercise of the right to a fair hearing at Community level.

123 The Court notes that, under Article 10 EC [TEU 4], relations between the Member States and the Community institutions are governed by reciprocal duties to cooperate in good faith . . .

124 In a case of application of Article 1(4) of Common Position 2001/931 and Article

2(3) of Regulation No 2580/2001, provisions which introduce a specific form of cooperation between the Council and the Member States in the context of combating terrorism, the Court finds that that principle entails, for the Council, the obligation to defer as far as possible to the assessment conducted by the competent national authority, at least where it is a judicial authority, both in respect of the issue of whether there are 'serious and credible evidence or clues' on which its decision is based and in respect of recognition of potential restrictions on access to that evidence or those clues, legally justified under national law on grounds of overriding public policy, public security or the maintenance of international relations. . . .

125 However, these considerations are valid only in so far as the evidence or clues in question were in fact assessed by the competent national authority referred to in the preceding paragraph. If, on the other hand, in the course of the procedure before it, the Council bases its initial decision or a subsequent decision to freeze funds on information or evidence communicated to it by representatives of the Member States without it having been assessed by the competent national authority, that information must be considered as newly-adduced evidence which must, in principle, be the subject of notification and a hearing at Community level, not having already been so at national level.

126 It follows from the foregoing that, in the context of relations between the Community and its Member States, observance of the right to a fair hearing has a relatively limited purpose in respect of the Community procedure for freezing funds. In the case of an initial decision to freeze funds, it requires, in principle, first, that the party concerned be informed by the Council of the specific information or material in the file which indicates that a decision meeting the definition given in Article 1(4) of Common Position 2001/931 has been taken in respect of it by a competent authority of a Member State, and also, where applicable, any new material referred to in paragraph 125 above and, second, that it must be placed in a position in which it can effectively make known its view on the information or material in the file. In the case of a subsequent decision to freeze funds, observance of the right to a fair hearing similarly requires, first, that the party concerned be informed of the information or material in the file which, in the view of the Council, justifies maintaining it in the disputed lists, and also, where applicable, of any new material referred to in paragraph 125 above and, second, that it must be afforded the opportunity effectively to make known its view on the matter.

127 At the same time, however, certain restrictions on the right to a fair hearing, so defined in terms of its purpose, may legitimately be envisaged and imposed on the parties concerned, in circumstances such as those of the present case, where what are in issue are specific restrictive measures, consisting of a freeze of the financial funds and assets of the persons, groups and entities identified by the Council as being involved in terrorist acts.

128 The Court therefore finds . . . that notification of the evidence adduced and a hearing of the parties concerned, before the adoption of the initial decision to freeze funds, would be liable to jeopardise the effectiveness of the sanctions and would thus be incompatible with the public interest objective pursued by the Community pursuant to Security Council Resolution 1373 (2001). An initial measure freezing

funds must, by its very nature, be able to benefit from a surprise effect and to be applied with immediate effect. Such a measure cannot, therefore, be the subject-matter of notification before it is implemented . . .

129 However, in order for the parties concerned to be able to defend their rights effectively, particularly in legal proceedings which might be brought before the Court of First Instance, it is also necessary that the evidence adduced against them be notified to them, in so far as reasonably possible, either concomitantly with or as soon as possible after the adoption of the initial decision to freeze funds (see also paragraph 139 below).

130 In that context, the parties concerned must also have the opportunity to request an immediate re-examination of the initial measure freezing their funds . . . The Court recognises, however, that such a hearing after the event is not automatically required in the context of an initial decision to freeze funds, in the light of the possibility that the parties concerned also have immediately to bring an action before the Court of First Instance, which also ensures that a balance is struck between observance of the fundamental rights of the persons included in the disputed list and the need to take preventive measures in combating international terrorism . . .

131 It must be emphasised, however, that the considerations just mentioned are not relevant to subsequent decisions to freeze funds adopted by the Council in connection with the re-examination, at regular intervals, at least every six months, of the justification for maintaining the parties concerned in the disputed list, provided for by Article 1(6) of Common Position 2001/931. At that stage, the funds are already frozen and it is accordingly no longer necessary to ensure a surprise effect in order to guarantee the effectiveness of the sanctions. Any subsequent decision to freeze funds must accordingly be preceded by the possibility of a further hearing and, where appropriate, notification of any new evidence.

132 The Court cannot accept the viewpoint put forward by the Council and the United Kingdom on this point at the oral hearing, to the effect that the Council need only hear the parties concerned, in the context of the adoption of a subsequent decision to freeze funds, if they have previously made an express request to that effect. Under Article 1(6) of Common Position 2001/931, the Council may only adopt such a decision after having ensured that maintaining the parties concerned in the disputed list remains justified, which implies that it must afford them the opportunity effectively to make known their views on the matter.

133 Next, the Court recognises that, in circumstances such as those of this case, where what is at issue is a temporary protective measure restricting the availability of the property of certain persons, groups and entities in connection with combating terrorism, overriding considerations concerning the security of the Community and its Member States, or the conduct of their international relations, may preclude the communication to the parties concerned of certain evidence adduced against them and, in consequence, the hearing of those parties with regard to such evidence, during the administrative procedure . . .

134 Such restrictions are consistent with the constitutional traditions common to the Member States, as submitted by the Council and the United Kingdom, who have

pointed out that exceptions to the general right to be heard in the course of an administrative procedure are permitted in many Member States on grounds of public interest, public policy or the maintenance of international relations, or when the purpose of the decision to be taken is or could be jeopardised if the right is observed . . .

135 They are, moreover, consistent with the case-law of the European Court of Human Rights which, even in the more stringent context of adversarial criminal proceedings subject to the requirements of Article 6 of the ECHR, acknowledges that, in cases concerning national security and, more specifically, terrorism, certain restrictions on the right to a fair hearing may be envisaged, especially concerning disclosure of evidence adduced or terms of access to the file . . .

136 In the present circumstances, those considerations apply above all to the 'serious and credible evidence or clues' on which the national decision to instigate an investigation or prosecution is based, in so far as they may have been brought to the attention of the Council, but it is also conceivable that the restrictions on access may concern the specific content or the particular grounds for that decision, or even the identity of the authority that took it. It is even possible that, in certain, very specific circumstances, the identification of the Member State or third country in which a competent authority has taken a decision in respect of a person may be liable to jeopardise public security, by providing the party concerned with sensitive information which it could misuse.

137 It follows from all of the foregoing that the general principle of observance of the right to a fair hearing requires, unless precluded by overriding considerations concerning the security of the Community or its Member States, or the conduct of their international relations, that the evidence adduced against the party concerned, as identified in paragraph 126 above, should be notified to it, in so far as possible, either concomitantly with or as soon as possible after the adoption of an initial decision to freeze funds. Subject to the same reservations, any subsequent decision to freeze funds must, in principle, be preceded by notification of any new evidence adduced and a hearing. However, observance of the right to a fair hearing does not require either that the evidence adduced against the party concerned be notified to it before the adoption of an initial measure to freeze funds, or that that party automatically be heard after the event in such a context.

*   *   *

— The right to effective judicial protection

152 Lastly, with respect to the safeguard relating to the right to effective judicial protection, this is effectively ensured by the right the parties concerned have to bring an action before the Court against a decision to freeze their funds, pursuant to the fourth paragraph of Article 230 EC [263] . . .

153 Thus the judicial review of the lawfulness of a decision to freeze funds taken pursuant to Article 2(3) of Regulation No 2580/2001 is that provided for in the second paragraph of Article 230 EC [263], under which the Community Courts have jurisdiction in actions for annulment brought on grounds of lack of competence, infringement of an essential procedural requirement, infringement of the EC Treaty or of any rule of law relating to its application or misuse of powers.

154 As part of that review, and having regard to the grounds for annulment put forward by the party concerned or raised by the Court of its own motion, it is for the Court to ensure, inter alia, that the legal conditions for applying Regulation No 2580/2001 to a particular scenario, as laid down in Article 2(3) of that regulation and, by reference, either Article 1(4) or Article 1(6) of Common Position 2001/931, depending on whether it is an initial decision or a subsequent decision to freeze funds, are fulfilled. That implies that the judicial review of the lawfulness of the decision in question extends to the assessment of the facts and circumstances relied on as justifying it, and to the evidence and information on which that assessment is based . . . The Court must also ensure that the right to a fair hearing is observed and that the requirement of a statement of reasons is satisfied and also, where applicable, that the overriding considerations relied on exceptionally by the Council in order to not to respect those rights are well founded.

155 In the present case, that review is all the more imperative because it constitutes the only procedural safeguard ensuring that a fair balance is struck between the need to combat international terrorism and the protection of fundamental rights. Since the restrictions imposed by the Council on the right of the parties concerned to a fair hearing must be offset by a strict judicial review which is independent and impartial. . . . the Community Courts must be able to review the lawfulness and merits of the measures to freeze funds without it being possible to raise objections that the evidence and information used by the Council is secret or confidential.

156 Although the European Court of Human Rights recognises that the use of confidential information may be necessary when national security is at stake, that does not mean, in its view, that national authorities are free from any review by the national courts simply because they state that the case concerns national security and terrorism . . .

157 The Court finds that, here also, inspiration may be drawn from the provisions of Directive 2004/38. . . . Article 31(1) of that directive provides that the persons concerned are to have access to judicial and, where appropriate, administrative means of redress in the host Member State to appeal against or seek review of any decision taken against them on the grounds of public policy, public security or public health. Moreover, Article 31(3) of that directive provides that the means of redress are to allow for an examination of the lawfulness of the decision, as well as of the facts and circumstances on which the proposed measure is based.

158 The question whether the applicant and/or its lawyers may be provided with the evidence and information alleged to be confidential, or whether they may be provided only to the Court, in accordance with a procedure which remains to be defined so as to safeguard the public interests at issue whilst affording the party concerned a sufficient degree of judicial protection, is a separate issue on which it is not necessary for the Court to rule in the present action . . .

159 Lastly, it is true that the Council enjoys broad discretion in its assessment of the matters to be taken into consideration for the purpose of adopting economic and financial sanctions on the basis of Articles 60 EC [75], 301 EC [215] and 308 EC [352], consistent with a common position adopted on the basis of the CFSP. Because the Community Courts may not, in particular, substitute their assessment of the evidence, facts and circumstances justifying the adoption of such measures for that

of the Council, the review carried out by the Court of the lawfulness of decisions to freeze funds must be restricted to checking that the rules governing procedure and the statement of reasons have been complied with, that the facts are materially accurate, and that there has been no manifest error of assessment of the facts or misuse of power. That limited review applies, especially, to the Council's assessment of the factors as to appropriateness on which such decisions are based . . .

## NOTES AND QUESTIONS

1.   To what extent did the CFI/General Court suggest that the courts or authorities of the Member States were bound to follow EU principles here when hearing any claims at the State level? Why did the Court reject the proposition that the hearing at EU level should require investigation of the evidence adduced at the state level?

2.   Why did the Court draw a distinction between an initial decision to freeze funds and a subsequent decision to maintain the freeze?

3.   What conditions did the Court consider essential to satisfy the right to effective judicial protection? In this regard, did the Court pay enough respect to the principle that national security is a matter solely for the Member States as stated in TEU 4?

4.   In Case T-256/07, *People's Mojahedin Organization of Iran, v. Council*, 2008 ECJ EUR-Lex LEXIS 1959, [2008] ECR II-1951, the plaintiffs again prevailed in challenging the Council decision that had been adopted notwithstanding a ruling by the British Proscribed Organisations Appeal Commission overturning a decision by the British Home Secretary to so designate them, ruling that it was unreasonable and perverse. The Council then adopted a third decision based on "new information concerning the group" that apparently had come to light after the Home Secretary's action had been annulled in the UK. In *People's Mojahedin Organization of Iran v. Council*, Case T-284/08, 2009 ECJ EUR-Lex LEXIS 841, [2008] ECR 334 this Council decision was annulled for failing to give the group a fair hearing. At that point the Council gave up, much to the annoyance of the Iranian Government, which had considered the organization to be terrorist in character. See also *Yassin Abdullah Kadi and Al Barakaat International Foundation v. Council*, Joined Cases C-402/05 P and C-415/05 P, 2008 ECJ EUR-Lex LEXIS 1954, [2008] ECR 6351, discussed in Chapter 3.

## [D]   Access to Files

## BPB INDUSTRIES PLC AND BRITISH GYPSUM LTD v. COMMISSION
### Case C-310/93 P, 1995 ECJ CELEX LEXIS 189, [1995] ECR I-865

[This case concerned an appeal from a Commission decision in proceedings under EC 82/TFEU 102. As in *JCB*, the applicable regulation at the time was Regulation 17/62, now repealed and replaced by Regulation 1/2003. The principles described in this case are now embodied in Article 27 of Regulation 1/2003 and Articles 15 and

16 of Regulation 773/2004.]

13 The appellants maintained before the Court of First Instance . . . that the Decision should be annulled since the Commission had failed to disclose to them all the relevant documents which were in its possession, to their considerable detriment.

14 In reaching its conclusion that the rights of the defence were observed during the course of the administrative procedure, the Court of First Instance noted that the Commission had, in its Twelfth Report on Competition Policy (pp. 40 and 41), imposed on itself a number of rules concerning access to the file in competition cases and that it had therefore been held, in Case T-7/89 Hercules Chemicals v. Commission 1991 ECR II-1711, paragraphs 53 and 54, that the Commission "has an obligation to make available to the undertakings involved in Article 85(1) [101] proceedings all documents, whether in their favour or otherwise, which it has obtained during the course of the investigation, save where the business secrets of other undertakings, the internal documents of the Commission or other confidential information are involved" (paragraph 29 of the judgment under appeal).

15 The Court of First Instance further pointed out that . . . it had held that "the procedure for access to the file in competition cases is intended to enable the addressees of a statement of objections to examine evidence in the Commission's file so that they are in a position effectively to express their views on the conclusions reached by the Commission in its statement of objections on the basis of that evidence" (paragraph 30 of the judgment under appeal).

16 The Court of First Instance went on to note that, in pursuance of the abovementioned commitments which the Commission had imposed upon itself, the statement of objections sent to the appellants was accompanied by an annex containing a list summarizing all the 2, 095 documents which made up the Commission's file, specifying, for each document or group of documents, whether it was accessible to the appellants or not and identifying six categories of documents which were not made accessible to them: first, documents for purely internal Commission purposes; secondly, certain correspondence with third-party undertakings; thirdly, certain correspondence with the Member States; fourthly, certain published information and studies; fifthly, certain reports of verifications; and, sixthly, a reply to a request for information made under Article 11 of Regulation No 17 . . .

17 In paragraph 33, the Court of First Instance held:

"It is thus apparent that the applicants have no real grounds for complaining that the Commission did not make accessible to them certain purely internal documents, which the Court of First Instance has already decided did not have to be disclosed. The same applies necessarily to certain correspondence with the Member States and published documents and studies. The same applies again to the reports of verifications, the answer to a request for information made by the Commission and certain correspondence with third-party undertakings, to which the Commission was entitled to refuse access by reason of their confidential nature. An undertaking to which a statement of objections has been addressed, and which occupies a dominant position in the market, may, for that very reason, adopt retaliatory measures against a competing undertaking, a supplier or a customer, who has collaborated in the investigation carried out by the Commission. Finally, for the same reason, the applicants cannot maintain that the complaint submitted to the Commission under Article 3 of Regulation No 17 was wrongly made only partially available to them (documents 1 to 233). Accordingly, the Commission's refusal to disclose those documents to the applicants cannot, in this case, affect the legality of the Decision."

18 In support of their plea the appellants state, first, that the Court of First Instance wrongly held that the Commission complied with its obligation to make available all documents, whether in their favour or otherwise, in its files which were not of a confidential nature.

19 Secondly, the appellants argue that the Court of First Instance should itself have examined the documents in the file.

20 Thirdly, the appellants criticize the Court of First Instance for having upheld the Commission's non-disclosure of certain documents on the sole and inadequate ground that if they had been disclosed, retaliatory measures might have been taken against the supplier of the information. In their view, to deny flatly to the undertakings concerned any access to any of the information contained in a document which is not strictly confidential violates the principle of proportionality.

21 When considering whether this plea is well-founded, it must first be borne in mind that observance of the rights of the defence requires, inter alia, that the undertaking concerned must have been enabled to express its views effectively on the documents used by the Commission to support its allegation of an infringement . . .

22 The appellants do not deny that the Court of First Instance could, without infringing the principle of observance of the rights of the defence, hold that the Commission is not obliged to disclose internal documents and other confidential information. They merely allege that the Court of First Instance misapplied that principle when it considered that the documents referred to in paragraph 33 of the judgment under appeal fell within the specified categories of documents not to be disclosed or, at the very least, failed to give sufficient reasons for that finding.

23 Finally . . . the appellants did not complain before the Court of First Instance that an incriminating document was not disclosed but rather that the documents which were not disclosed might have been helpful to their case. The criterion for non-disclosure, they claimed, should not be whether the Commission relies on a document but whether the document is truly confidential . . .

24 It must therefore be determined whether the Court of First Instance was entitled to find that the documents not disclosed fell within the categories of documents which the Commission may legitimately refuse to disclose by reason of their confidential nature.

25 As regards the refusal to disclose to the appellants the purely internal Commission documents, the correspondence with the Member States and the published documents and studies, it is enough to point out that the Court of First Instance was entitled to hold both that the first two categories of documents were

of a confidential nature and that the third category concerned documents which were, by definition, accessible to the appellants.

26 With regard to the correspondence with third-party undertakings and the answer to a request for information, it must be recognized that an undertaking holding a dominant position on the market might adopt retaliatory measures against competitors, suppliers or customers who have collaborated in the investigation carried out by the Commission. That being so, it is clear that third-party undertakings which submit documents to the Commission in the course of its investigations and consider that reprisals might be taken against them as a result can do so only if they know that account will be taken of their request for confidentiality.

27 The Court of First Instance was therefore right to consider that the Commission was entitled to refuse access to such documents on the ground that they were confidential.

28 Finally, the appellants have acknowledged in their appeal that the reports of verifications relate to inspections carried out in third-party undertakings. In that regard, suffice it to observe that documents capable of providing evidence of infringements by third parties, unrelated, moreover, to the present case, are obviously not to be disclosed to the appellants.

29 As regards the appellants' complaint that the Court of First Instance did not give sufficient reasons for its decision concerning the Commission's refusal to make the abovementioned documents available to them, it is to be noted that their allegations concerning a supposed infringement of the rights of the defence were merely "uncertain and hypothetical", as the Court of First Instance found in paragraph 35 of the judgment under appeal.

30 In view of that finding, the reasoning of the judgment under appeal, as summarized in paragraphs 14 to 17 above, clearly shows the grounds on which the Court of First Instance based its rejection of those allegations. Nor, in those circumstances, can the Court of First Instance be criticized, as it is by the appellants, for having looked in a general way at the type of documents in issue without of its own accord looking at each document not disclosed in order to verify the arguments relied on by the Commission for not having made them available.

31 Finally, the appellants complain that the Court of First Instance did not hold that the Commission should at the very least have made non-confidential summaries of certain documents available to them.

32 That complaint, too, must be dismissed, since it has not been established either that such summaries were requested by the appellants or that such a request would have been justified.

33 It follows from all the foregoing that the appellants cannot justifiably claim that the Court of First Instance infringed the principle of the observance of the rights of the defence and that their fourth plea in law must be dismissed as unfounded.

The alternative plea in law

34 With regard to the alternative plea, suffice it to point out that it is not for this Court, when ruling on questions of law in the context of an appeal, to substitute, on grounds of fairness, its own assessment for that of the Court of First Instance exercising its unlimited jurisdiction to rule on the amount of fines imposed on undertakings for infringements of Community law.

35 Since none of the appellants' pleas in law can be upheld, the appeal must be dismissed in its entirety.

# NOTES AND QUESTIONS

1.   From this case, and keeping in mind Regulation 773/2004 (discussed in part in Chapter 7 and appearing in the Documentary Supplement) to what extent does a defendant in a EC 81 and 82/TFEU 101 or 102 proceeding have rights regarding the access to files?

2.   Julian Joshua, in a 1995 paper titled "Attitudes to Anti-Trust Enforcement in the EU and U.S.: Dodging the Traffic Warden, or Respecting the Law?" *ec.europa.eu/?/eali./competition/speeches/text/sp1995_044_en.html* makes some observations on U.S. criminal practice with regard to file access:

> The U.S. adjudicatory model gives no support to the notion of general access. Most agency proceedings have no procedure for discovery at all. Contrary to assertions made by British lawyers to the House of Lords Select Committee, the Federal Trade Commission does *not* make its full file available to all parties. The FTC does permit parties to obtain discovery under the supervision of the Administrative Law Judge but 'fishing expeditions' are out. A few head notes from FTC dockets convey the general flavour:
>
> *"General Access to FTC Records. Good cause, that is, real or actual need was not shown for the production of confidential information in the Commission's files, since the respondent, in effect, was asking for general access to confidential investigational files merely to see whether something useful to its defence may turn up. The respondent did not show in any specific way that the material was necessary to its defense, and it did not seek any specific material relating to any specific defense.*
>
> Relying on the traditional confidentiality of the FTC's investigational files, the informer's privilege and the attorney's work product rule, and FTC hearing examiner denied production of documents contained in FTC files. Even assuming relevance of the documents sought, the examiner said, the fact that material sought by the company is not being offered in evidence by the government, doubt as to its necessity in establishing a defense was shown. The motions could therefore be denied as premature."

In *Brady v. Maryland* the Supreme Court had held that:

*"the suppression by the prosecution of evidence favourable to an accused on request violates due process when the evidence is material either to guilt or punishment."*

Disclosure is however required only if the unused evidence is both favourable to the accused and material to guilt or punishment.

In *U.S. v. Agurs* the Supreme Court explained that:

*"[a] fair analysis of the holding in BRADY indicates that implicit in the requirement of materiality is a concern that the suppressed evidence might have affected the outcome of the trial."*

The Supreme Court has also made it clear on several occasions that

*"the prosecutor is not required to deliver his entire file to defense counsel, but only to disclose evidence favourable to the accused that, if suppressed, would deprive the defendant of a fair trial."*

Attempts to obtain blanket disclosure on grounds of general prosecution 'bias' have therefore invariably failed.

The Supreme Court has also rejected as imposing an impossible burden on the government any rule that the prosecution commits reversible error by any failure to disclose evidence favourable to the accused no matter how insignificant. Even if it transpires that relevant material has not been disclosed, such failure does not call for automatic reversal. The *Brady* requirement is aimed at ensuring that a real miscarriage of justice does not occur:

*"[a] constitutional error occurs, and the conviction must be reversed, only if the evidence is material in the sense that its suppression undermines confidence in the outcome of the trial."*

Evidence is not to be considered 'material' unless there is a reasonable probability that had the evidence been disclosed to the defence, the result of the proceeding would have been different. In the American trial context this means that it would have to be so convincing that it might well have caused the jury to reach a different verdict. The test laid down by the Supreme Court in *Bagley* for Brady material is thus very similar to that of the ECJ (*mutatis mutandis*) in cases like *Telefunken* and *Pioneer* to non-disclosure of documents relied on in the decision. A decision will not be annulled for non-disclosure of documents *"of secondary importance to the infringement found"*.

If non-disclosure of evidence actually relied on by the Commission does necessarily lead to automatic annulment, how can this extreme sanction be the logical result for allegedly "exculpatory" material, particularly where it has not even been shown to exist?

Courts in the United States have been equally insistent that due process does not require the creation of and adherence to complicated sets of rules and procedures:

"Once it is determined that due process applies the question remains what process is due. We turn that question, fully realizing as our cases regularly do that the interpretation and application of the Due Process Clause are intensely practical matters and that "[t]he very nature of due process negates any concept of inflexible procedures universally applicable to every imaginable situation".

The U.S. Supreme Court has identified three distinct factors which have to be considered in determining the procedural incidents required by due process in any given case. It is particularly useful when it is agreed that due process requires some additional procedural safeguards over and above those provided for in the legislation. The Court will consider and weigh: (1) the private interest that will be affected by the official action; (2) the fairness and reliability of the existing procedures and the probable value, if any, of additional or substitute procedural safeguards; and (3) the public interests including the function involved and the fiscal or administrative burdens that the additional or substitute procedural requirements would entail. The determination of the appropriate measure of due process in a particular case is thus to be seen as a complex balancing operation. The benefit of the incremental procedural safeguard proposed has to be compared with the additional cost it will entail, not only in financial, but also in practical terms.

See also B. Doherty, *Playing Poker with the Commission: Right of access to the Commission's File in Competition Cases* [1994], 1 ECLR 8.

## [E]   The Right Against Self Incrimination/Right to Silence

## ORKEM SA (CDF CHIMIE SA) v. COMMISSION, SOLVAY & CIE v. COMMISSION
Joined Cases 374/87 and 27/88, 1989 ECJ CELEX LEXIS 319, [1989] ECR 3283

[Orkem was the addressee of a decision under former Regulation 17/62 by the Commission requiring it to answer certain questions in connection with an investigation under EC 81/TFEU 101 (formerly article 85 of the EC Treaty). It objected that the questions would require it to "incriminate itself". The Regulation 17 article references are substantially reproduced in Regulation 1/2003. Requests for information are now made under Article 18 of that Regulation.]

18 The applicant claims, essentially, that the Commission used the contested decision to compel it to incriminate itself by confessing to an infringement of the competition rules and to inform against other undertakings. By doing so, the Commission has, in its view, infringed the general principle that no one may be compelled to give evidence against himself, which forms part of Community law in so far as it is a principle upheld by the laws of the Member States, by the European Convention for the Protection of Human Rights and Fundamental Freedoms of 4 November 1950 (hereinafter referred to as "the European Convention") and by the International Covenant on Civil and Political Rights of 19 December 1966 (United

Nations Treaty Series, Vol. 999, p. 71), hereinafter referred to as "the International Covenant). It has thus, in the applicant's view, infringed the rights of the defence.

19 In considering whether that submission is well founded, it should be recalled that . . . , the aim of the powers given to the Commission by Regulation No 17 is to enable it to carry out its duty under the EEC Treaty of ensuring that the rules on competition are applied in the common market. The function of those rules, as is apparent from the fourth recital in the preamble to the Treaty, Article 3(f) [repealed] and Articles 85 and 86 [101 and 102], is to prevent competition from being distorted to the detriment of the public interest, individual undertakings and consumers. The exercise of the powers given to the Commission by Regulation No 17 contributes to the maintenance of the system of competition intended by the Treaty which undertakings have an absolute duty to comply with.

20 The rules necessary for the application of Articles 85 [101] and 86 [102], introduced by the Council, prescribe two successive but clearly separate procedures: first, a preparatory investigation procedure, and secondly, a procedure involving submissions by both parties initiated by the statement of objections.

21 The sole purpose of the preliminary investigation procedure is to enable the Commission to obtain the information and documentation necessary to check the actual existence and scope of a specific factual and legal situation . . .

22 For that purpose, Regulation No 17 conferred on the Commission wide powers of investigation and imposed on undertakings the obligation to cooperate in the investigative measures.

23 Thus, Article 11(1) of Regulation No 17 empowers the Commission to obtain all necessary information from undertakings and Article 11(5) authorizes it to require, by decision, that information be supplied to it where an undertaking does not supply the information requested or supplies incomplete information.

24 If the Commission considers that the information thus obtained justifies such a course of action, it sends a statement of objections to the undertaking concerned, thus initiating the inter partes procedure governed by Regulation No 99/63 of the Commission of 25 July 1963 on the hearings provided for in Article 19(1) and (2) of Council Regulation No 17 . . .

25 For the purposes of that inter partes procedure, Article 19 of Regulation No 17 and Regulation No 99/63 provide in particular that the undertaking concerned is entitled to make known in writing and, if appropriate, orally its views on the objections raised against them . . . In any decision which the Commission might be prompted to adopt on conclusion of the procedure, it will be entitled to set out only those objections on which the undertaking concerned has had an opportunity of making known its views.

26 In the course of the preliminary investigation procedure, Regulation No 17 expressly accords only certain guarantees to the undertaking under investigation. Thus, a decision requiring information to be supplied may be taken only after a prior request has proved unsuccessful. Similarly, a decision fixing the definitive amount of a fine or penalty payment, in a case where the undertaking concerned fails to supply the information required by the decision, may be adopted only after

the undertaking in question has been given an opportunity to make its views known.

27 On the other hand, Regulation No 17 does not give an undertaking under investigation any right to evade the investigation on the ground that the results thereof might provide evidence of an infringement by it of the competition rules. On the contrary, it imposes on the undertaking an obligation to cooperate actively, which implies that it must make available to the Commission all information relating to the subject-matter of the investigation.

28 In the absence of any right to remain silent expressly embodied in Regulation No 17, it is appropriate to consider whether and to what extent the general principles of Community law, of which fundamental rights form an integral part and in the light of which all Community legislation must be interpreted, require, as the applicant claims, recognition of the right not to supply information capable of being used in order to establish, against the person supplying it, the existence of an infringement of the competition rules.

29 In general, the laws of the Member States grant the right not to give evidence against oneself only to a natural person charged with an offence in criminal proceedings. A comparative analysis of national law does not therefore indicate the existence of such a principle, common to the laws of the Member States, which may be relied upon by legal persons in relation to infringements in the economic sphere, in particular infringements of competition law.

30 As far as Article 6 of the European Convention is concerned, although it may be relied upon by an undertaking subject to an investigation relating to competition law, it must be observed that neither the wording of that article nor the decisions of the European Court of Human Rights indicate that it upholds the right not to give evidence against oneself.

31 Article 14 of the International Covenant, which upholds, in addition to the presumption of innocence, the right (in paragraph 3(g)) not to give evidence against oneself or to confess guilt, relates only to persons accused of a criminal offence in court proceedings and thus has no bearing on investigations in the field of competition law.

32 It is necessary, however, to consider whether certain limitations on the Commission's powers of investigation are implied by the need to safeguard the rights of the defence which the Court has held to be a fundamental principle of the Community legal order . . .

33 . . . [W]hilst it is true that the rights of the defence must be observed in administrative procedures which may lead to the imposition of penalties, it is necessary to prevent those rights from being irremediably impaired during preliminary inquiry procedures which may be decisive in providing evidence of the unlawful nature of conduct engaged in by undertakings and for which they may be liable. Consequently, although certain rights of the defence relate only to contentious proceedings which follow the delivery of the statement of objections, other rights must be respected even during the preliminary inquiry.

34 Accordingly, whilst the Commission is entitled, in order to preserve the useful effect of Article 11(2) and (5) of Regulation No 17, to compel an undertaking to

provide all necessary information concerning such facts as may be known to it and to disclose to it, if necessary, such documents relating thereto as are in its possession, even if the latter may be used to establish, against it or another undertaking, the existence of anti-competitive conduct, it may not, by means of a decision calling for information, undermine the rights of defence of the undertaking concerned.

35 Thus, the Commission may not compel an undertaking to provide it with answers which might involve an admission on its part of the existence of an infringement which it is incumbent upon the Commission to prove.

36 The foregoing criteria must be observed in considering the questions to which the Commission, by means of the contested decision, required the applicant to give an answer.

37 The questions in Section I [of the Commission's decision] relating to meetings of producers, which are intended only to secure factual information on the circum-stances in which such meetings were held and the capacity in which the participants attended them, and also the requirement of disclosure of documents in the applicant's possession relating thereto, are not open to criticism.

38 The questions on prices in Section II [of the Commission's decision] relate essentially to the measures taken in order to determine and maintain price levels satisfactory to all the participants at the meetings. Whilst those questions are not open to criticism in so far as the Commission seeks factual clarification as to the subject-matter and implementation of those measures, the position is different as regards those which relate to the purpose of the action taken and the objective pursued by those measures. In that respect, sub-question 1I, which seeks clarifi-cation on "every step or concerted measure which may have been envisaged or adopted to support such price initiatives", is such as to compel the applicant to acknowledge its participation in an agreement whose object was to fix selling prices and which was capable of preventing or restricting competition, or to state that it intended to achieve that objective.

39 The same finding applies to Questions 1 and 2 of Section III concerning the quotas, targets or shares allocated to the producers. By requiring disclosure of the "details of any system or method which made it possible to attribute sales targets or quotas to the participants" and details of "any method facilitating annual monitoring of compliance with any system of targets in terms of volume or quotas", the Commission endeavoured to obtain from the applicant an acknowledgment of its participation in an agreement intended to limit or control production or outlets or to share markets.

40 No such criticism may be made against Question 3 in Section III, which deals with the information disclosed by the undertaking to the other producers regarding the production and sale of the product in question or against the questions in Section IV on the statements forwarded to, and statistics provided by, Fides, since those questions were intended only to elicit factual information on the functioning of the system for the exchange of statistical and other information.

41 It must be concluded that, by requiring the undertaking to which the decision was addressed to acknowledge, in response to Questions II(1)I and III(1) and (2) of

the request for information, that it had infringed Article 85 of the EEC Treaty [101], the Commission undermined the applicant's rights of defence.

42 The contested decision must therefore be annulled as regards Questions II(1)(c) and III(1) and (2); the remainder of the application must be dismissed

## NOTES AND QUESTIONS

1. Given the administrative nature of the proceeding here, are you surprised by the Court's views in this case on the right not to have to give evidence against oneself? What was the basis of the Court's conclusion that such a right constituted part of the "rights of defence" available to the applicant? Did the Court accept that Orkem had the right not to be forced to incriminate itself? From what source or sources did the Court draw? Are these the same sources the Court has drawn on in past decisions in finding that a particular fundamental right is part of EU Law? In the United States, the courts have recognized that the act of producing documents in response to a subpoena may be considered to be within the privilege against self-incrimination. See *United States v. Hubbell* 530 U.S. 27 (2000). Would that carry any weight in proceedings such as those in *Orkem*?

2. What problems can arise if the parties choose to take advantage of the leniency program relating to EC 81 and 82/TFEU 101 and 102 (see Chapter 7)?

3. In the United States, the right against self-incrimination may be invoked only by individuals. See *United States v. White*, 322 U.S. 694 (1944) and *Bellis v. United States* 417 U.S. 85 (1974), where the Court stated that the privilege is "limited to its historic function of protecting only the natural individual from compulsory incrimination through his own testimony or personal records."

The right may be asserted in a civil proceeding if the individual has a reasonable belief that the incriminating information might lead to a criminal prosecution or a criminal-type penalty. Whether the penalty is criminal or not requires an assessment of its purpose or effect: *Flemming v. Nestor*, 363 U.S. 603 (1960). Since in Europe the EU has no criminal powers, there could be no such exposure at the EU level, but this could arise if the acts in question were capable of prosecution as criminal offenses in any Member State. See also *United States v. Ward*, 448 U.S. 242 (1980) and *Kennedy v. Mendoza-Martinez*, 372 U.S. 144 (1963).

4. For an analysis of the impact of current Regulation 1/2003 on due process in competition proceedings, see A. Andreangeli, *The impact of the Modernisation Regulation on the guarantees of due process in competition proceedings*. (2006) 31 EL REV. 342.

## § 19.03　RIGHT OF ACCESS TO DOCUMENTS

## [A]　EU Legislation

## REGULATION (EC) NO 1049/2001 REGARDING PUBLIC ACCESS TO EUROPEAN PARLIAMENT, COUNCIL AND COMMISSION DOCUMENTS [2001] OJ L 145

Article 1

Purpose

The purpose of this Regulation is:

(a) to define the principles, conditions and limits on grounds of public or private interest governing the right of access to European Parliament, Council and Commission (hereinafter referred to as "the institutions") documents provided for in Article 255 of the EC Treaty in such a way as to ensure the widest possible access to documents,

(b) to establish rules ensuring the easiest possible exercise of this right, and

(c) to promote good administrative practice on access to documents.

Article 2

Beneficiaries and scope

1. Any citizen of the Union, and any natural or legal person residing or having its registered office in a Member State, has a right of access to documents of the institutions, subject to the principles, conditions and limits defined in this Regulation.

2. The institutions may, subject to the same principles, conditions and limits, grant access to documents to any natural or legal person not residing or not having its registered office in a Member State.

3. This Regulation shall apply to all documents held by an institution, that is to say, documents drawn up or received by it and in its possession, in all areas of activity of the European Union.

4. Without prejudice to Articles 4 and 9, documents shall be made accessible to the public either following a written application or directly in electronic form or through a register. In particular, documents drawn up or received in the course of a legislative procedure shall be made directly accessible in accordance with Article 12.

5. Sensitive documents as defined in Article 9(1) shall be subject to special treatment in accordance with that Article.

6. This Regulation shall be without prejudice to rights of public access to documents

held by the institutions which might follow from instruments of international law or acts of the institutions implementing them.

## Article 3

### Definitions

For the purpose of this Regulation:

(a) "document" shall mean any content whatever its medium (written on paper or stored in electronic form or as a sound, visual or audiovisual recording) concerning a matter relating to the policies, activities and decisions falling within the institution's sphere of responsibility;

(b) "third party" shall mean any natural or legal person, or any entity outside the institution concerned, including the Member States, other Community or non-Community institutions and bodies and third countries.

## Article 4

### Exceptions

1. The institutions shall refuse access to a document where disclosure would undermine the protection of:

(a) the public interest as regards:

- public security,

- defence and military matters,

- international relations,

- the financial, monetary or economic policy of the Community or a Member State;

(b) privacy and the integrity of the individual, in particular in accordance with Community legislation regarding the protection of personal data.

2. The institutions shall refuse access to a document where disclosure would undermine the protection of:

- commercial interests of a natural or legal person, including intellectual property,

- court proceedings and legal advice,

- the purpose of inspections, investigations and audits,

unless there is an overriding public interest in disclosure.

3. Access to a document, drawn up by an institution for internal use or received by an institution, which relates to a matter where the decision has not been taken by the institution, shall be refused if disclosure of the document would seriously undermine the institution's decision-making process, unless there is an overriding public interest in disclosure.

Access to a document containing opinions for internal use as part of deliberations and preliminary consultations within the institution concerned shall be refused even after the decision has been taken if disclosure of the document would seriously undermine the institution's decision-making process, unless there is an overriding public interest in disclosure.

4. As regards third-party documents, the institution shall consult the third party with a view to assessing whether an exception in paragraph 1 or 2 is applicable, unless it is clear that the document shall or shall not be disclosed.

5. A Member State may request the institution not to disclose a document originating from that Member State without its prior agreement.

6. If only parts of the requested document are covered by any of the exceptions, the remaining parts of the document shall be released.

7. The exceptions as laid down in paragraphs 1 to 3 shall only apply for the period during which protection is justified on the basis of the content of the document. The exceptions may apply for a maximum period of 30 years. In the case of documents covered by the exceptions relating to privacy or commercial interests and in the case of sensitive documents, the exceptions may, if necessary, continue to apply after this period.

## Article 5

### Documents in the Member States

Where a Member State receives a request for a document in its possession, originating from an institution, unless it is clear that the document shall or shall not be disclosed, the Member State shall consult with the institution concerned in order to take a decision that does not jeopardise the attainment of the objectives of this Regulation.

The Member State may instead refer the request to the institution.

## Article 6

### Applications

1. Applications for access to a document shall be made in any written form, including electronic form, in one of the languages referred to in Article 314 of the EC Treaty and in a sufficiently precise manner to enable the institution to identify the document. The applicant is not obliged to state reasons for the application.

2. If an application is not sufficiently precise, the institution shall ask the applicant to clarify the application and shall assist the applicant in doing so, for example, by providing information on the use of the public registers of documents.

3. In the event of an application relating to a very long document or to a very large number of documents, the institution concerned may confer with the applicant informally, with a view to finding a fair solution.

4. The institutions shall provide information and assistance to citizens on how and where applications for access to documents can be made.

## Article 7

### Processing of initial applications

1. An application for access to a document shall be handled promptly. An acknowledgement of receipt shall be sent to the applicant. Within 15 working days from registration of the application, the institution shall either grant access to the document requested and provide access in accordance with Article 10 within that period or, in a written reply, state the reasons for the total or partial refusal and inform the applicant of his or her right to make a confirmatory application in accordance with paragraph 2 of this Article.

2. In the event of a total or partial refusal, the applicant may, within 15 working days of receiving the institution's reply, make a confirmatory application asking the institution to reconsider its position.

3. In exceptional cases, for example in the event of an application relating to a very long document or to a very large number of documents, the time-limit provided for in paragraph 1 may be extended by 15 working days, provided that the applicant is notified in advance and that detailed reasons are given.

4. Failure by the institution to reply within the prescribed time-limit shall entitle the applicant to make a confirmatory application.

## Article 8

### Processing of confirmatory applications

1. A confirmatory application shall be handled promptly. Within 15 working days from registration of such an application, the institution shall either grant access to the document requested and provide access in accordance with Article 10 within that period or, in a written reply, state the reasons for the total or partial refusal. In the event of a total or partial refusal, the institution shall inform the applicant of the remedies open to him or her, namely instituting court proceedings against the institution and/or making a complaint to the Ombudsman, under the conditions laid down in Articles 230 and 195 of the EC Treaty, respectively.

2. In exceptional cases, for example in the event of an application relating to a very long document or to a very large number of documents, the time limit provided for in paragraph 1 may be extended by 15 working days, provided that the applicant is notified in advance and that detailed reasons are given.

3. Failure by the institution to reply within the prescribed time limit shall be considered as a negative reply and entitle the applicant to institute court proceedings against the institution and/or make a complaint to the Ombudsman, under the relevant provisions of the EC Treaty.

## Article 9

### Treatment of sensitive documents

1. Sensitive documents are documents originating from the institutions or the agencies established by them, from Member States, third countries or International Organisations, classified as "TRES SECRET/TOP SECRET", "SECRET" or "CONFIDENTIEL" in accordance with the rules of the institution concerned, which protect essential interests of the European Union or of one or more of its Member States in the areas covered by Article 4(1)(a), notably public security, defence and military matters.

2. Applications for access to sensitive documents under the procedures laid down in Articles 7 and 8 shall be handled only by those persons who have a right to acquaint themselves with those documents. These persons shall also, without prejudice to Article 11(2), assess which references to sensitive documents could be made in the public register.

3. Sensitive documents shall be recorded in the register or released only with the consent of the originator.

4. An institution which decides to refuse access to a sensitive document shall give the reasons for its decision in a manner which does not harm the interests protected in Article 4.

5. Member States shall take appropriate measures to ensure that when handling applications for sensitive documents the principles in this Article and Article 4 are respected.

6. The rules of the institutions concerning sensitive documents shall be made public.

7. The Commission and the Council shall inform the European Parliament regarding sensitive documents in accordance with arrangements agreed between the institutions.

## Article 10

### Access following an application

1. The applicant shall have access to documents either by consulting them on the spot or by receiving a copy, including, where available, an electronic copy, according to the applicant's preference. The cost of producing and sending copies may be charged to the applicant. This charge shall not exceed the real cost of producing and sending the copies. Consultation on the spot, copies of less than 20 A4 pages and direct access in electronic form or through the register shall be free of charge.

2. If a document has already been released by the institution concerned and is easily accessible to the applicant, the institution may fulfil its obligation of granting access to documents by informing the applicant how to obtain the requested document.

3. Documents shall be supplied in an existing version and format (including

electronically or in an alternative format such as Braille, large print or tape) with full regard to the applicant's preference.

## Article 11

### Registers

1. To make citizens' rights under this Regulation effective, each institution shall provide public access to a register of documents. Access to the register should be provided in electronic form. References to documents shall be recorded in the register without delay.

2. For each document the register shall contain a reference number (including, where applicable, the interinstitutional reference), the subject matter and/or a short description of the content of the document and the date on which it was received or drawn up and recorded in the register. References shall be made in a manner which does not undermine protection of the interests in Article 4.

3. The institutions shall immediately take the measures necessary to establish a register which shall be operational by 3 June 2002.

## Article 12

### Direct access in electronic form or through a register

1. The institutions shall as far as possible make documents directly accessible to the public in electronic form or through a register in accordance with the rules of the institution concerned.

2. In particular, legislative documents, that is to say, documents drawn up or received in the course of procedures for the adoption of acts which are legally binding in or for the Member States, should, subject to Articles 4 and 9, be made directly accessible.

3. Where possible, other documents, notably documents relating to the development of policy or strategy, should be made directly accessible.

4. Where direct access is not given through the register, the register shall as far as possible indicate where the document is located.

## Article 13

### Publication in the Official Journal

1. In addition to the acts referred to in Article 254(1) and (2) of the EC Treaty [297] and the first paragraph of Article 163 of the Euratom Treaty, the following documents shall, subject to Articles 4 and 9 of this Regulation, be published in the Official Journal:

(a) Commission proposals;

(b) common positions adopted by the Council in accordance with the procedures referred to in Articles 251 [294] and 252 [repealed] of the EC Treaty [TFEU] and the reasons underlying those common positions, as well as the European Parliament's positions in these procedures;

(c) framework decisions and decisions referred to in Article 34(2) of the EU Treaty [repealed];

(d) conventions established by the Council in accordance with Article 34(2) of the EU Treaty [repealed];

(e) conventions signed between Member States on the basis of Article 293 of the EC Treaty [293];

(f) international agreements concluded by the Community or in accordance with Article 24 of the EU Treaty [TEU 37].

2. As far as possible, the following documents shall be published in the Official Journal:

(a) initiatives presented to the Council by a Member State pursuant to Article 67(1) of the EC Treaty [repealed] or pursuant to Article 34(2) of the EU Treaty [repealed];

(b) common positions referred to in Article 34(2) of the EU Treaty [repealed];

(c) directives other than those referred to in Article 254(1) and (2) of the EC Treaty [297], decisions other than those referred to in Article 254(1) of the EC Treaty [297], recommendations and opinions.

3. Each institution may in its rules of procedure establish which further documents shall be published in the Official Journal.

## Article 14

### Information

1. Each institution shall take the requisite measures to inform the public of the rights they enjoy under this Regulation.

2. The Member States shall cooperate with the institutions in providing information to the citizens.

## Article 15

### Administrative practice in the institutions

1. The institutions shall develop good administrative practices in order to facilitate the exercise of the right of access guaranteed by this Regulation.

2. The institutions shall establish an interinstitutional committee to examine best

practice, address possible conflicts and discuss future developments on public access to documents.

## Article 16

### Reproduction of documents

This Regulation shall be without prejudice to any existing rules on copyright which may limit a third party's right to reproduce or exploit released documents.

## Article 17

### Reports

Each institution shall publish annually a report for the preceding year including the number of cases in which the institution refused to grant access to documents, the reasons for such refusals and the number of sensitive documents not recorded in the register.

2. At the latest by 31 January 2004, the Commission shall publish a report on the implementation of the principles of this Regulation and shall make recommendations, including, if appropriate, proposals for the revision of this Regulation and an action programme of measures to be taken by the institutions.

## NOTES AND QUESTIONS

1.  Since the Council is a legislative organ of the EU, one might start from the premise that all its deliberations ought to be public, as are those of the Parliament or any democratically elected body. Yet until Lisbon, the precise opposite was true. Now, the Council's legislative deliberations are supposed to be open to the public. However, executive sessions are still closed. Mirroring this reluctance to open up the Council to the public gaze, until 1994 there was no right of access to documents. The gradual opening up of access has now produced some significant changes as evidenced by the ECJ's decisions below.

2.  The current legislation relating to access is based on language in the EC Treaty introduced by the Treaty of Amsterdam. Prior to this, access had been governed by a Decision of the council adopted on 20 December 1993 — Decision 93/731 on public access to Council documents ([1993] OJ L 340, p. 43), the aim of which was to implement the principles established by a Code of Conduct that had itself been introduced as a result of changes introduced by the TEU. A number of cases were decided under the prior legislation and these established the principle that the Council must give reasons for denying access that the Court can review.

## [B]   Disclosure of Legal Advice

## SWEDEN AND MAURIZIO TURCO v. COUNCIL

Joined cases C-39/05 P and C-52/05 P, 2008 ECJ EUR-Lex LEXIS 2927;2008 ECR I-4723

[The applicant had requested *inter alia* a copy of a legal opinion given by the Council's legal service in connection with a proposal for a Council directive laying down minimum standards for the reception of applicants for asylum in Member States. The CFI/General Court had ruled against him and Sweden, as an advocate of transparency appealed to the ECJ, which overturned the lower court.]

37. As regards the exception relating to legal advice laid down in the second indent of Article 4(2) of Regulation No 1049/2001, the examination to be undertaken by the Council when it is asked to disclose a document must necessarily be carried out in three stages, corresponding to the three criteria in that provision.

38. First, the Council must satisfy itself that the document which it is asked to disclose does indeed relate to legal advice and, if so, it must decide which parts of it are actually concerned and may, therefore, be covered by that exception.

39. The fact that a document is headed 'legal advice/opinion' does not mean that it is automatically entitled to the protection of legal advice ensured by the second indent of Article 4(2) of Regulation No 1049/2001. Over and above the way a document is described, it is for the institution to satisfy itself that that document does indeed concern such advice.

40. Second, the Council must examine whether disclosure of the parts of the document in question which have been identified as relating to legal advice 'would undermine the protection' of that advice.

41. In that regard, it must be pointed out that neither Regulation No 1049/2001 nor its travaux préparatoires throw any light on the meaning of 'protection' of legal advice. Therefore, that term must be interpreted by reference to the purpose and general scheme of the rules of which it forms part.

42. Consequently, the exception relating to legal advice laid down in the second indent of Article 4(2) of Regulation No 1049/2001 must be construed as aiming to protect an institution's interest in seeking legal advice and receiving frank, objective and comprehensive advice.

43. The risk of that interest being undermined must, in order to be capable of being relied on, be reasonably foreseeable and not purely hypothetical.

44. Third and last, if the Council takes the view that disclosure of a document would undermine the protection of legal advice as defined above, it is incumbent on the Council to ascertain whether there is any overriding public interest justifying disclosure despite the fact that its ability to seek legal advice and receive frank, objective and comprehensive advice would thereby be undermined.

45. In that respect, it is for the Council to balance the particular interest to be protected by non-disclosure of the document concerned against, inter alia, the public interest in the document being made accessible in the light of the advantages

stemming, as noted in recital 2 of the preamble to Regulation No 1049/2001, from increased openness, in that this enables citizens to participate more closely in the decision-making process and guarantees that the administration enjoys greater legitimacy and is more effective and more accountable to the citizen in a democratic system.

46. Those considerations are clearly of particular relevance where the Council is acting in its legislative capacity, as is apparent from recital 6 of the preamble to Regulation No 1049/2001, according to which wider access must be granted to documents in precisely such cases. Openness in that respect contributes to strengthening democracy by allowing citizens to scrutinize all the information which has formed the basis of a legislative act. The possibility for citizens to find out the considerations underpinning legislative action is a precondition for the effective exercise of their democratic rights.

47. It is also worth noting that, under the second subparagraph of Article 207(3) EC [240], the Council is required to define the cases in which it is to be regarded as acting in its legislative capacity, with a view to allowing greater access to documents in such cases. Similarly, Article 12(2) of Regulation No 1049/2001 acknowledges the specific nature of the legislative process by providing that documents drawn up or received in the course of procedures for the adoption of acts which are legally binding in or for the Member States should be made directly accessible.

The requirements to be satisfied by the statement of reasons

48. The reasons for any decision of the Council in respect of the exceptions set out in Article 4 of Regulation No 1049/2001 must be stated.

49. If the Council decides to refuse access to a document which it has been asked to disclose, it must explain, first, how access to that document could specifically and effectively undermine the interest protected by an exception laid down in Article 4 of Regulation No 1049/2001 relied on by that institution and, secondly, in the situations referred to in Article 4(2) and (3) of that regulation, whether or not there is an overriding public interest that might nevertheless justify disclosure of the document concerned.

50. It is, in principle, open to the Council to base its decisions in that regard on general presumptions which apply to certain categories of documents, as considerations of a generally similar kind are likely to apply to requests for disclosure relating to documents of the same nature. However, it is incumbent on the Council to establish in each case whether the general considerations normally applicable to a particular type of document are in fact applicable to a specific document which it has been asked to disclose.

57. . . . . [T]he Court of First Instance did not require the Council to have checked whether the reasons of a general nature on which it relied were in fact applicable to the legal opinion whose disclosure was requested. Secondly, as will be apparent from the considerations concerning the third part of this plea which follow, the Court of First Instance erred in holding that there was a general need for confidentiality in respect of advice from the Council's legal service relating to legislative matters.

*   *   *

59. As regards, first, the fear expressed by the Council that disclosure of an opinion of its legal service relating to a legislative proposal could lead to doubts as to the lawfulness of the legislative act concerned, it is precisely openness in this regard that contributes to conferring greater legitimacy on the institutions in the eyes of European citizens and increasing their confidence in them by allowing divergences between various points of view to be openly debated. It is in fact rather a lack of information and debate which is capable of giving rise to doubts in the minds of citizens, not only as regards the lawfulness of an isolated act, but also as regards the legitimacy of the decision-making process as a whole.

60. Furthermore, the risk that doubts might be engendered in the minds of European citizens as regards the lawfulness of an act adopted by the Community legislature because the Council's legal service had given an unfavourable opinion would more often than not fail to arise if the statement of reasons for that act was reinforced, so as to make it apparent why that unfavourable opinion was not followed.

61. Consequently, to submit, in a general and abstract way, that there is a risk that disclosure of legal advice relating to legislative processes may give rise to doubts regarding the lawfulness of legislative acts does not suffice to establish that the protection of legal advice will be undermined for the purposes of the second indent of Article 4(2) of Regulation No 1049/2001 and cannot, accordingly, provide a basis for a refusal to disclose such advice.

62. As regards, secondly, the Council's argument that the independence of its legal service would be compromised by possible disclosure of legal opinions issued in the course of legislative procedures, it must be pointed out that that fear lies at the very heart of the interests protected by the exception provided for in the second indent of Article 4(2) of Regulation No 1049/2001. As is apparent from paragraph 42 of this judgment, that exception seeks specifically to protect an institution's interest in seeking legal advice and receiving frank, objective and comprehensive advice.

63. However, in that regard, the Council relied before both the Court of First Instance and the Court on mere assertions, which were in no way substantiated by detailed arguments. In view of the considerations which follow, there would appear to be no real risk that is reasonably foreseeable and not purely hypothetical of that interest being undermined.

64. As regards the possibility of pressure being applied for the purpose of influencing the content of opinions issued by the Council's legal service, it need merely be pointed out that even if the members of that legal service were subjected to improper pressure to that end, it would be that pressure, and not the possibility of the disclosure of legal opinions, which would compromise that institution's interest in receiving frank, objective and comprehensive advice and it would clearly be incumbent on the Council to take the necessary measures to put a stop to it.

65. As regards the Commission's argument that it could be difficult for an institution's legal service which had initially expressed a negative opinion regarding a legislative act in the process of being adopted subsequently to defend the lawfulness of that act if its opinion had been published, it must be stated that such

a general argument cannot justify an exception to the openness provided for by Regulation No 1049/2001.

66. In view of those considerations, there appears to be no real risk that is reasonably foreseeable and not purely hypothetical that disclosure of opinions of the Council's legal service issued in the course of legislative procedures might undermine the protection of legal advice within the meaning of the second indent of Article 4(2) of Regulation No 1049/2001.

67. In any event, in so far as the interest in protecting the independence of the Council's legal service could be undermined by that disclosure, that risk would have to be weighed up against the overriding public interests which underlie Regulation No 1049/2001. . . . [S]uch an overriding public interest is constituted by the fact that disclosure of documents containing the advice of an institution's legal service on legal questions arising when legislative initiatives are being debated increases the transparency and openness of the legislative process and strengthens the democratic right of European citizens to scrutinize the information which has formed the basis of a legislative act, as referred to, in particular, in recitals 2 and 6 of the preamble to Regulation No 1049/2001.

68. It follows from the above considerations that Regulation No 1049/2001 imposes, in principle, an obligation to disclose the opinions of the Council's legal service relating to a legislative process.

69. That finding does not preclude a refusal, on account of the protection of legal advice, to disclose a specific legal opinion, given in the context of a legislative process, but being of a particularly sensitive nature or having a particularly wide scope that goes beyond the context of the legislative process in question. In such a case, it is incumbent on the institution concerned to give a detailed statement of reasons for such a refusal.

70. In that context, it must also be borne in mind that, under Article 4(7) of Regulation No 1049/2001, an exception can only apply for the period during which protection is justified on the basis of the content of the document.

71. Having regard to all those considerations, it is apparent that the Court of First Instance erred in holding, in paragraphs 77 to 80 of the judgment under appeal, that the contested decision could comply with the obligation to give reasons and be justified by reference to a general need for confidentiality which applies to legal advice relating to legislative questions.

## NOTES AND QUESTIONS

1. The CFI/General Court had said that it did not consider that the nature of the document sought, i.e., a legal opinion, in and of itself meant that it did not need to be provided to the applicant. Did the ECJ find any fault with that conclusion? Note that although the opinion had been provided in connection with a potential legislative act, the decision to deny access was executive in nature. Does that have something to do with the ECJ's conclusions (compare the cases concerning review of legislation versus executive acts in Chapter 8)?

2. The CFI/General Court has itself had experiences with unwanted consequences of access to documents: in *Svenska Journalistforbundet v. Council*, Case T-174/95, 1998 ECJ CELEX LEXIS 59, [1998] ECR II-2289, the applicant applied for access to 20 documents in relation to the establishment of the European Police Office ("Europol"). The Council adopted a decision denying access to most of the documents requested and the applicant then sought annulment of that decision. The documents provided by the Council in its defense of the action for annulment of its decision were subsequently published on the internet. The Court took a dim view of this action:

> 130 [T]he Council drew the attention of the Court to the fact that certain pertinent documents, including the Council's defence, had been published on the Internet. It considers that the applicant's conduct was prejudicial to the proper course of the procedure. The Council laid particular stress on the fact that the text of the defence had been edited by the applicant before it was placed on the Internet. Furthermore, the names and contact details of the Council's Agents in the case were given and the public encouraged to send their comments on the case to those Agents. The Council requested the Court to take any measures which might be appropriate in order to avoid further such action on the part of the applicant.

> 131 . . . [T]he applicant's lawyers explained that they had played no role in the placing of the defence and other documents concerning the case on the Internet. They had no knowledge of those facts before receiving the letter from the Registry of the Court of First Instance. They had immediately asked the applicant to remove all the documents from the Internet, and informed it that they would no longer be able to represent it if that was not done.

> 132 . . . [T]he applicant confirmed that it had placed the documents on the Internet without informing its lawyers. It explained that the editing of the defence had been carried out for purely practical reasons and that its intention was not to alter its contents or weaken the Council's case. It simply wanted to shorten the defence by not reproducing certain passages in view of the time required to put the defence on the Internet. It had no intention of putting pressure on the Council and added that the names and contact details of the Council's Agents were included simply because they knew about the case, not to encourage the public to contact them directly as individuals.

> 133 The applicant undertook to refrain from placing on the Internet or in any other way making available to the public any further documents exchanged between the parties in the case. It would thenceforth restrict itself to normal media reports on the case. The applicant further indicated that it had taken the decision to have the defence withdrawn from the Internet. However, the document had been placed on the Internet by an independent organisation, Gravande Journalister (an association of Swedish investigative reporters and editors), which refused to withdraw it. Under Swedish law the applicant had no legal means of forcing that

association to withdraw the document and the latter was therefore responsible for keeping the defence on the Internet.

134 . . . [T]he Swedish Government explained that the Legal Director at the Ministry of Justice had received a copy of the defence from the applicant and the Legal Director had subsequently released a copy to a journalist without any objection on the applicant's part. In doing so, the Legal Director had taken into account the fact that the applicant had already published a detailed report on the main elements of the defence and had given the names of the representatives of the Council concerned. Another factor in that decision was that the document had not been transmitted to the Swedish Government by a Community institution, but by a private individual who had the right to dispose of the document and had already demonstrated his willingness to disseminate it. The Ministry was in no way involved in the publication of the defence on the Internet and the newspaper's action in that respect was regarded as a provocation.

Findings of the Court

135 Under the rules which govern procedure in cases before the Court of First Instance, parties are entitled to protection against the misuse of pleadings and evidence. Thus . . . no third party, private or public, may have access to the case-file or to the procedural documents without the express authorisation of the President, after the parties have been heard. Moreover . . . the President may exclude secret or confidential documents from those furnished to an intervener in a case.

136 These provisions reflect a general principle in the due administration of justice according to which parties have the right to defend their interests free from all external influences and particularly from influences on the part of members of the public.

137 It follows that a party who is granted access to the procedural documents of other parties is entitled to use those documents only for the purpose of pursuing his own case and for no other purpose, including that of inciting criticism on the part of the public in relation to arguments raised by other parties in the case.

138 In the present case, it is clear that the actions of the applicant in publishing an edited version of the defence on the Internet in conjunction with an invitation to the public to send their comments to the Agents of the Council and in providing the telephone and telefax numbers of those Agents, had as their purpose to bring pressure to bear upon the Council and to provoke public criticism of the Agents of the institution in the performance of their duties.

139 These actions on the part of the applicant involved an abuse of procedure which will be taken into account in awarding costs (see below, paragraph 140), having regard, in particular, to the fact that this incident led to a suspension of the proceedings and made it necessary for the parties in the case to lodge additional submissions in this respect.

## [C]  Documents of the Member States

## SWEDEN v. COMMISSION AND OTHERS
Case C-64/05 P.2007 ECJ EUR-Lex LEXIS 1898. [2007] ECR I-11389

[This was another appeal by Sweden on behalf of private applicants that had lost an application to the CFI/General Court for disclosure of documents. The applicant in the original CFI/General Court proceeding, IFAW, a non-governmental organisation active in the field of the protection of animal welfare and nature conservation, requested access to various documents the Commission had received in connection with the examination a project concerning the Muhlenberger Loch site which consisted of the enlargement of the Daimler Chrysler Aerospace Airbus GmbH factory and the reclamation of part of the estuary for a runway extension. Its earlier requests had been made under Commission Decision 94/90 but after the entry into force of Regulation 1049/2001. Once again, the ECJ overturned the decision of the CFI/General Court's decision.]

47. . . . In contrast to Article 9(3), Article 4(5) does not make the prior agreement of the Member State an absolute condition of the disclosure of a document, but makes the possible need for such agreement subject to a prior expression of will by the Member State concerned. In those circumstances the use of the expression 'may request' simply emphasises that that provision gives the Member State an option, and only the actual exercise of that option in a particular case has the consequence of making the prior agreement of the Member State a necessary condition of the future disclosure of the document in question.

*　　*　　*

54. Moreover, recitals 2 and 3 in the preamble to that regulation show that its aim is to improve the transparency of the Community decision-making process, since such openness inter alia guarantees that the administration enjoys greater legitimacy and is more effective and more accountable to the citizen in a democratic system.

55. . . . [I]t is precisely the concern to improve the transparency of the Community decision-making process that explains that, as provided by Article 2(3) of the regulation, the right of access to documents held by the Parliament, the Council and the Commission extends not only to documents drawn up by those institutions but also to documents received from third parties, including the Member States, as expressly stated by Article 3(b) of the regulation.

56. By so providing, the Community legislature . . . abolished the authorship rule that had applied previously. As may be seen from [prior rules] on public access to European Parliament documents (OJ 1997 L 263, p. 27), such a rule meant that, where the author of a document held by an institution was a natural or legal person, a Member State, another Community institution or body, or any other national or international organisation, the request for access to the document had to be made directly to the author of the document.

*　　*　　*

58. . . . [T]o interpret Article 4(5) of Regulation No 1049/2001 as conferring on the Member State a general and unconditional right of veto, so that it can oppose, in an entirely discretionary manner and without having to give reasons for its decision, the disclosure of any document held by a Community institution simply because it originates from that Member State, is not compatible with the objectives mentioned in paragraphs 53 to 56 above.

\* \* \*

62. It must be stressed in this respect that, as the Kingdom of Sweden submitted at the hearing and the Advocate General observed in point 42 of his Opinion, the creation of a discretionary right of veto for the Member States would in those circumstances have the potential effect of excluding from the provisions of Regulation No 1049/2001 an especially important class of documents that could form the basis of the Community decision-making process and cast light on it.

63. . . . [B]oth in their capacity as members of the Council and as participants in many committees set up by the Council or the Commission, the Member States constitute an important source of information and documentation intended to contribute to the Community decision-making process.

64. It follows that the right of public access would potentially be frustrated, to that extent, without any objective reason. The effectiveness of that right would thereby be substantially reduced . . .

65. . . . [T]here is nothing in Regulation No 1049/2001 to support the Court of First Instance's conclusion that the Community legislature intended by Article 4(5) of that regulation to enact a sort of conflict-of-laws rule for the purpose of preserving the application of national rules, or even, as suggested by the Commission, the policies of the Member States, concerning access to documents originating from the Member States, at the expense of the specific rules laid down in that field by the regulation.

\* \* \*

70. . . . [A]s regards the fact that recital 15 in the preamble to Regulation No 1049/2001 states that it is not the object or the effect of the regulation to amend national legislation on access to documents, that — contrary to the view taken by the Court of First Instance in paragraph 57 of the judgment under appeal — is not capable of affecting the scope to be given to Article 4(5) of the regulation. Read as a whole and in conjunction with Article 5 of the regulation, to which it relates, that recital is intended solely to recall that requests for access to documents held by the national authorities, including documents that originate from Community institutions, remain governed by the national rules applicable to those authorities, without the provisions of Regulation No 1049/2001 taking the place of those rules, subject to the requirements laid down by Article 5 imposed by the obligation of loyal cooperation under Article 10 EC [TEU 4].

71. Moreover, documents which a Member State transmits to a third party do not remain subject exclusively to the legal order of that State. As the Kingdom of Sweden rightly submits, a Community institution, as an external authority distinct from the Member States, is part of a legal order with rules of its own as regards

access to the documents in its possession. It follows in particular that the rules governing such access cannot have the effect of amending national law, which . . . governs the conditions of access to a document held by a national authority.

*     *     *

75. . . . Article 4(5) of Regulation No 1049/2001 cannot be interpreted as conferring on the Member State a general and unconditional right of veto, so that it could in a discretionary manner oppose the disclosure of documents originating from it and held by an institution, with the effect that access to such documents would cease to be governed by the provisions of that regulation and would depend only on the provisions of national law.

76. On the contrary, several factors militate in favour of an interpretation of Article 4(5) to the effect that the exercise of the power conferred by that provision on the Member State concerned is delimited by the substantive exceptions set out in Article 4(1) to (3), with the Member State merely being given in this respect a power to take part in the Community decision. Seen in that way, the prior agreement of the Member State referred to in Article 4(5) resembles not a discretionary right of veto but a form of assent confirming that none of the grounds of exception under Article 4(1) to (3) is present.

77. Beside the fact that such an interpretation is compatible both with the objectives pursued by Regulation No 1049/2001, as set out in paragraphs 53 to 56 above, and with the need, noted in paragraph 66 above, to interpret Article 4 of the regulation strictly, it can also be justified by the more immediate legislative context of Article 4(5) of the regulation.

78. It should be observed that, while Article 4(1) to (3) of Regulation No 1049/2001 clearly lists substantive exceptions that may justify, or as the case may be require, a refusal to communicate the document that has been asked for, Article 4(5) confines itself to requiring the prior agreement of the Member State concerned where that State has made a specific request to that effect.

*     *     *

83. . . . [W]hile the decision-making process thus established by Article 4(5) of Regulation No 1049/2001 requires the institution and the Member State involved to confine themselves to the substantive exceptions laid down in Article 4(1) to (3) of the regulation, it is none the less possible for the legitimate interests of the Member States to be protected on the basis of those exceptions and by virtue of the special rules for sensitive documents laid down in Article 9 of the regulation.

84. In particular, there is nothing to exclude the possibility that compliance with certain rules of national law protecting a public or private interest, opposing disclosure of a document and relied on by the Member State for that purpose, could be regarded as an interest deserving of protection on the basis of the exceptions laid down by that regulation . . .

*     *     *

88. The institution cannot accept a Member State's objection to disclosure of a document originating from that State if the objection gives no reasons at all or if the

reasons are not put forward in terms of the exceptions listed in Article 4(1) to (3) of Regulation No 1049/2001. Where, despite an express request by the institution to the Member State to that effect, the State still fails to provide the institution with such reasons, the institution must, if for its part it considers that none of those exceptions applies, give access to the document that has been asked for.

89. Finally, as is apparent in particular from Articles 7 and 8 of the regulation, the institution is itself obliged to give reasons for a decision to refuse a request for access to a document. Such an obligation means that the institution must, in its decision, not merely record the fact that the Member State concerned has objected to disclosure of the document asked for, but also set out the reasons relied on by that Member State to show that one of the exceptions to the right of access in Article 4(1) to (3) of the regulation applies. That information will allow the person who has asked for the document to understand the origin and grounds of the refusal of his request and the competent court to exercise, if need be, its power of review.

\* \* \*

93. . . . Article 4(5) of Regulation No 1049/2001 . . . did not aim to establish a division between two powers, one national and the other of the Community, with different purposes. As pointed out in paragraph 76 above, that provision creates a decision-making procedure the sole object of which is to determine whether access to a document should be refused under one of the substantive exceptions listed in Article 4(1) to (3) of the regulation, a decision-making procedure in which both the Community institution and the Member State concerned play a part, in the terms stated in paragraph 76.

94. In such a case it is within the jurisdiction of the Community judicature to review, on application by a person to whom the institution has refused to grant access, whether that refusal was validly based on those exceptions, regardless of whether the refusal results from an assessment of those exceptions by the institution itself or by the relevant Member State. From the point of view of the person concerned, the Member State's intervention does not affect the Community nature of the decision that is subsequently addressed to him by the institution in reply to the request he has made for access to a document in its possession.

## NOTES AND QUESTIONS

1. The above case raises the complex issue of how the EU regime on access to documents interacts with Member State laws and requirements regarding their documents. The regulation was held by the CFI/General Court to allow the Commission to deny access to a German government document. The ECJ firmly rejected the apparent deference given to the Member States by the lower court. In doing so it pointed out that the Regulation substantially increased the right of access by abolishing the "authorship" rule (i.e., that the author's consent had to be obtained if the document had not originated with an EU institution). What was the significance of this change? For a commentary, see B. Driessen: *Analysis and Reflections — Access to Member State documents in EC law: A comment* (2007) 31 EL REV. 906.

**2.**   See also *Association de la presse internationale a.s.b.l. v. Commission of the European Communities*, Case T-36/04, 2007 ECJ CELEX LEXIS 532, [2007] ECR II NYR.

**3.**   For more general commentary, see J. Heliskoski, P. Leino, *Darkness at the break of noon: The case law on Regulation No. 1049/2001 on access to documents* (2006) 43 CML REV. 735; M.E. de Leeuw: *Openness in the legislative process in the European Union* (2007) 32 EL REV. 295; and P. Cabral, *Analysis and Reflections — Access to Member State documents in EC law*, (2006) 31 EL REV. 378; B. Driessen, *The Council of the European Union and access to documents*, (2005)30 EL REV. 675. See also the *Bavarian Lager* case described in Chapter 19 regarding the interaction of the public access rules with privacy legislation.

# Chapter 20

# HUMAN RIGHTS

## § 20.01  OVERVIEW

***Template*** Article 8 Section 8.2 and Charter, Articles 1-19, 27-38 and 47-50

***Materials in this Chapter***: The Charter catalogues what we might loosely term Human Rights into "Freedoms", "Dignity", "Solidarity" and "Justice." The cases and materials illustrate how these rights interact with Union law and also with the law of the Member States when the latter implement Union law or seek to take advantage of exceptions permitted by the Treaties. Interaction with Union law to date has often taken the form of an apparent collision between human rights and the economic free movement rights. The cases and materials also illustrate how some human rights may collide with others: the example so far evident in Union law can be found in the tension between the right to privacy and the right to free expression.

***Relevance in Union law*** It is clear that the rights described in this chapter vary considerably in their history, relevance and application in the EU system. Rights such as the freedom of expression have so far been of very limited impact, since the TEU and the TFEU do not amount to a constitution of general application, and the EU does not have any legislative powers (yet) that extend into or significantly impinge on such areas. Thus, such rights are of somewhat peripheral importance still today, though increasingly used to evaluate Member State actions taken in implementation of EU law. As a result of the transfer of the PJCC provisions to the TFEU, one can imagine that matters will look very different in the future. Other rights are extremely well developed, particularly the right to respect for private life and in particular the protection of personal data, where comprehensive EU legislation exists today.

***Comparison with the United States*** As a general matter, these rights, as articulated in the Charter, may look somewhat odd to the U.S. reader. Many seem to be more like aspirational principles than the simple statements found in the Bill of Rights. In practice, however, the difference may be less pronounced. The Charter spells out limitations and overriding public interests. In the U.S., by contrast, the Bill of Rights leaves such an exercise to the courts, which have developed extensive case law to accommodate situations where, for various reasons, the rights must arrive at certain boundaries.

Another contrast of course is the explicit endorsement of social democracy, particularly with regard to union rights and social security. One may object that such rights ought not to be classified as "fundamental" since they are not necessarily endorsed as constitutional rights by states that otherwise espouse freedom and justice — the United States of course being the obvious candidate.

## § 20.02   FREEDOMS

### [A]   Expression

## LASERDISKEN APS v. KULTURMINISTERIET
### Case C-479/04, 2006 ECJ CELEX LEXIS 447, [2006] ECR I-8089

[Laserdisken was a commercial company selling inter alia copies of cinemato-graphic works to individual purchasers through its sales outlets in Denmark. Until the end of 2002, those copies were mostly imported by the company from other Member States but also from non-member countries. The products included special editions, such as original American editions, or editions filmed using special techniques. Another major part of the product range consisted of cinematographic works which were not or would not be available in Europe. These works had historically not been protected by Danish copyright law because Denmark treated the copyright as "exhausted" when the work was placed on the market in any country. (The doctrine of exhaustion as it has developed in EU law is addressed in Chapter 13.) However, Danish law was changed to implement Directive 2001/29 which required Member States to limit the principle of exhaustion to works first placed on the market by the rights holder within the EU only.

Article 4 of the Directive read as follows:

> 1. Member States shall provide for authors, in respect of the original of their works or of copies thereof, the exclusive right to authorise or prohibit any form of distribution to the public by sale or otherwise.

> 2. The distribution right shall not be exhausted within the Community in respect of the original or copies of the work, except where the first sale or other transfer of ownership in the Community of that object is made by the rightholder or with his consent.

Prior to transposition of Directive 2001/29, section 19 of the Danish Law on copyright provided that '[w]hen a copy of a work is, with the copyright holder's consent, sold or in some other manner transferred to another party, the copy may be distributed further'. To implement the directive, Denmark amended section 19 to read as follows:

> 'When a copy of a work is, with the copyright holder's consent, sold or in some other manner transferred to another party within the European Economic Area, the copy may be distributed further. As regards further distribution in the form of lending or rentals, the provision in the first sentence shall also apply to sales or other forms of transfer to other parties outside the European Economic Area."

Having lost significant revenue following the above amendment to Danish copyright law, Laserdisken brought legal proceedings against the Danish Govern-ment claiming that section 19 of the Danish law, as amended in the context of the transposition of Article 4(2) of Directive 2001/29, did not apply. According to

Laserdisken, the new provisions of section 19 had a significant effect on its imports and sales of DVDs lawfully marketed outside the EEA.

The ECJ first confirmed that the Directive restricted the principle of exhaustion to works first placed on the market in the EU. Laserdisken maintained that this limitation infringed article 10 of the ECHR by restricting the right of individuals to receive information.]

60 According to Laserdisken, Article 4(2) of Directive 2001/29 has the effect of depriving citizens of the Union of their right to receive information, in breach of Article 10 of the European Convention for the Protection of Human Rights and Fundamental Freedoms, signed in Rome on 4 November 1950 ('the ECHR'). Laserdisken also pleads disregard of the freedom of copyright holders to communicate their ideas.

\* \* \*

63 First, the argument that there has been a breach of the freedom of expression guaranteed by Article 10 of the ECHR because copyright holders are prevented from communicating their ideas must be rejected. According to Article 4(2) of Directive 2001/29, the right of distribution is exhausted provided that the copyright holder has given his consent to the first sale or other transfer of ownership. That holder is, therefore, in a position to exercise his control over the first placing on the market of the object covered by that right. In that context, freedom of expression clearly cannot be relied upon to have the rule of exhaustion invalidated.

64 Secondly, regarding the freedom to receive information, even if the exhaustion rule laid down in Article 4(2) of Directive 2001/29 may be capable of restricting that freedom, it nevertheless follows from Article 10(2) of the ECHR that the freedoms guaranteed by Article 10(1) may be subject to certain limitations justified by objectives in the public interest, in so far as those derogations are in accordance with the law, motivated by one or more of the legitimate aims under that provision and necessary in a democratic society, that is to say justified by a pressing social need and, in particular, proportionate to the legitimate aim pursued . . .

65 In the present case, the alleged restriction on the freedom to receive information is justified in the light of the need to protect intellectual property rights, including copyright, which form part of the right to property.

66 It follows that the argument that there has been a breach of freedom of expression must be rejected.

## NOTES AND QUESTIONS

1. What was the essence of Laserdisken's argument here with respect to freedom of expression? Did the Court offer any rationale for why intellectual property rights should trump this fundamental right? Or was the plaintiff's argument itself so devoid of merit as not to warrant such an exercise?

2. In *Bernard Connolly v. Commission*, Case C-274/99 P, 2001 ECJ CELEX LEXIS 687, [2001] ECR I-1611, Mr. Connolly, an official of the Commission was Head of Unit 3, "EMS: National and Community Monetary Policies", in Directorate

D, "Monetary Affairs" in the Directorate-General for Economic and Financial Affairs (DG II). While on leave on personal grounds in the summer of 1985, Mr. Connolly published a book titled *The Rotten Heart of Europe — The Dirty War for Europe's Money* without requesting prior permission from the Commission. Early in September of that year, a series of articles concerning the book was published in the European and, in particular, the British press. This led to disciplinary proceedings.

Mr. Connolly invoked the right of free expression in the proceedings and subsequent appeal to the CFI/General Court and then the ECJ. The Court found that he could not have failed to be aware that he would be refused permission on the same grounds as those on which permission had previously been refused in respect of articles of similar content, and his conduct had seriously prejudiced the Communities' interests and damaged the institution's image and reputation. The CFI/General Court observed that the book at issue contained numerous aggressive, derogatory and frequently insulting statements, which were detrimental to the honor of the persons and institutions to which they referred and which had been extremely well publicized, particularly in the press. The Court also noted Mr. Connolly's high-ranking grade and that the book at issue publicly expressed the applicant's fundamental opposition to the Commission's policy, which it was his responsibility to implement, namely bringing about economic and monetary union, an objective that was laid down in the EC Treaty/TFEU.

The Advocate General describes essentially a four-step process of analysis for examining a law or rule that may restrict the freedom of expression:

1. Does it actually interfere with the freedom of expression?

2. Does it serve one of the enumerated legitimate purposes?

3. Is it sufficiently precise that individuals can know whether they are obeying the law or not?

4. Even if all of the above are satisfied, is the restriction necessary in a democratic society?

Connolly was ultimately unsuccessful on all grounds of appeal. An interesting parallel in the U.S. is *McAuliffe v. City of New Bedford*, 155 Mass. 216, 29 N.E. 517 (1892), in which Justice Holmes famously remarked that "[t]he petitioner may have a constitutional right to talk politics, but he has no constitutional right to be a policeman."

## VEREINIGTE FAMILIAPRESS ZEITUNGSVERLAGS- UND VERTRIEBS GMBH v. HEINRICH BAUER VERLAG
### Case C-368/95, 1997 ECJ CELEX LEXIS 316, [1997] ECR I-3689

*[For the facts of this case, see the note to the* Keck *case in Chapter 13,* supra.]

13 The Austrian Government and the Commission argue, however, that the aim of the national legislation in question is to maintain press diversity, which is capable of constituting an overriding requirement for the purposes of Article 30 [34].

14 They point out that shortly after the Gesetz über die Deregulierung des Wettbewerbs (Law on the Deregulation of Competition) entered into force in Austria in 1992 and liberalized inter alia the organization of prize competitions, fierce competition set in between periodicals publishers, as a result of their offering larger and larger gifts, in particular the chance to take part in prize competitions.

15 Fearing that small publishers might not be able to resist that cut-throat competition in the long term, in 1993 the Austrian legislature excluded the press from [the new law] which . . . authorizes to a certain extent the organization of prize competitions and draws linked to the sale of products or the supply of services.

16 . . . [T]he Austrian Government pointed out in particular that, given the relatively low selling price of periodicals, especially of daily newspapers, there was a risk, in spite of the limits to prizes set by [the new law], that consumers would attach more importance to the chance of winning than to the quality of the publication . . .

17 The Austrian Government and the Commission also point to the very high degree of concentration of the press in Austria. The Austrian Government states that in the early 1990s the market share of the largest press group was 54.5% in Austria, as compared with only 34.7% in the United Kingdom and 23.9% in Germany.

18 Maintenance of press diversity may constitute an overriding requirement justifying a restriction on free movement of goods. Such diversity helps to safeguard freedom of expression, as protected by Article 10 of the European Convention on Human Rights and Fundamental Freedoms, which is one of the fundamental rights guaranteed by the Community legal order . . .

19 However, . . . the provisions of national law in question must be proportionate to the objective pursued and that objective must not be capable of being achieved by measures which are less restrictive of intra-Community trade.

\* \* \*

24 [I]t is to be noted that where a Member State relies on overriding requirements to justify rules which are likely to obstruct the exercise of free movement of goods, such justification must also be interpreted in the light of the general principles of law and in particular of fundamental rights . . .

25 Those fundamental rights include freedom of expression, as enshrined in Article 10 of the European Convention for the Protection of Human Rights and Fundamental Freedoms . . .

26 A prohibition on selling publications which offer the chance to take part in prize games competitions may detract from freedom of expression. Article 10 of the European Convention for the Protection of Human Rights and Fundamental Freedoms does, however, permit derogations from that freedom for the purposes of maintaining press diversity, in so far as they are prescribed by law and are necessary in a democratic society . . .

27 . . . [I]t must therefore be determined whether a national prohibition such as that in issue in the main proceedings is proportionate to the aim of maintaining press diversity and whether that objective might not be attained by measures less

restrictive of both intra-Community trade and freedom of expression.

28 To that end, it should be determined, first, whether newspapers which offer the chance of winning a prize in games, puzzles or competitions are in competition with those small press publishers who are deemed to be unable to offer comparable prizes and whom the contested legislation is intended to protect and, second, whether such a prospect of winning constitutes an incentive to purchase capable of bringing about a shift in demand.

29 It is for the national court to determine whether those conditions are satisfied on the basis of a study of the Austrian press market.

30 In carrying out that study, it will have to define the market for the product in question and to have regard to the market shares of individual publishers or press groups and the trend thereof.

31 Moreover, the national court will also have to assess the extent to which, from the consumer's standpoint, the product concerned can be replaced by papers which do not offer prizes, taking into account all the circumstances which may influence the decision to purchase, such as the presence of advertising on the title page referring to the chance of winning a prize, the likelihood of winning, the value of the prize or the extent to which winning depends on a test calling for a measure of ingenuity, skill or knowledge.

32 The Belgian and Netherlands Governments consider that the Austrian legislature could have adopted measures less restrictive of free movement of goods than an outright prohibition on the distribution of newspapers which afford the chance of winning a prize, such as blacking out or removing the page on which the prize competition appears in copies intended for Austria or a statement that readers in Austria do not qualify for the chance to win a prize.

33 The documents before the Court suggest that the prohibition in question would not constitute a barrier to the marketing of newspapers where one of the above measures had been taken. If the national court were nevertheless to find that this was the case, the prohibition would be disproportionate.

34 In the light of the foregoing considerations, the answer to be given to the national court's question must be that Article 30 [34] of the EC Treaty is to be interpreted as not precluding application of legislation of a Member State the effect of which is to prohibit the distribution on its territory by an undertaking established in another Member State of a periodical produced in that latter State containing prize puzzles or competitions which are lawfully organized in that State, provided that that prohibition is proportionate to maintenance of press diversity and that that objective cannot be achieved by less restrictive means. This assumes, inter alia, that the newspapers offering the chance of winning a prize in games, puzzles or competitions are in competition with small newspaper publishers who are deemed to be unable to offer comparable prizes and the prospect of winning is liable to bring about a shift in demand. Furthermore, the national prohibition must not constitute an obstacle to the marketing of newspapers which, albeit containing prize games, puzzles or competitions, do not give readers residing in the Member State concerned the opportunity to win a prize. It is for the national court to determine

whether those conditions are satisfied on the basis of a study of the national press market concerned.

## NOTES AND QUESTIONS

This case exemplifies the sort of conflict that may in future become more common, between the economic freedoms in the TFEU, the equal weight of the Charter, and public interest considerations built into the freedoms themselves. Unlike the other cases in this section, it was here that authorities asserted a *restriction* on the press based on freedom of speech as a justification. How did the ECJ work through these various considerations?

## [B]　The Right to Property

## R. v. MINISTRY OF AGRICULTURE, FISHERIES AND FOOD EX PARTE BOSTOCK
### Case 2/92, 1994 ECJ CELEX LEXIS 95, [1994] ECR I-955

[A dispute had arisen between Mr. Bostock, a former tenant farmer, and the Ministry of Agriculture, Fisheries and Food concerning an application for compensation for the loss incurred by reason of the transfer to the landlord of the farm, on expiry of the tenancy, of a reference quantity originally allocated to the tenant under the system of additional levies on milk. Reference quantities were to set quotas for milk production on individual land holdings under the Common organization of the market for dairy products. The quotas were fixed on the basis of actual production in a reference year. As a general principle, since the reference quantity related to a specific farm, it was not transferable if the tenant surrendered the lease (i.e. the tenant could not take it with him to another property.]

3 Mr. Bostock had been the tenant on the farm since 1962. At that time, the farm had 40 cows and corresponding facilities. Over the years Mr. Bostock made substantial improvements to the farm. In particular, he increased the milk production capacity in 1967.

4 Following introduction of the system of additional milk levies by Regulation 856/84 and the implementing provisions, Mr. Bostock received a reference quantity under the new arrangements. On 25 March 1985 he surrendered his tenancy. The reference quantity was accordingly transferred to the landlord of the farm pursuant to Article 5(3) of Regulation 1371/84.

5 No compensation was paid to Mr. Bostock in respect of that transfer. At the time when the tenancy was surrendered, the "outgoers' scheme" of the [EU's] milk quota system . . . did not provide for any such compensation. However, . . . the Agriculture Act 1986, which came into force on 25 September 1986, provides from that date for payment of compensation by a landlord to a tenant.

6 In May 1990 Mr. Bostock brought proceedings against the Ministry of Agriculture, Fisheries and Food in which, in essence, he sought a declaration that the United Kingdom was under an obligation to provide for payment of compensation to tenants whose leases had expired between April 1984 and September 1986. He

submits that in failing to implement a compensation scheme for outgoing tenants during the period from April 1984 to September 1986 the United Kingdom was in breach of the above Community regulations and/or the fundamental principles of respect for property, unjust enrichment and non-discrimination. He goes on to argue that, in the absence of such a scheme, an outgoing tenant may rely directly on the provisions of Community law in support of a claim for compensation from his landlord.

*    *    *

10 Nothing in the regulations referred to by the national court requires Member States to introduce a scheme for the payment by a landlord of compensation to an outgoing tenant, or directly confers on a tenant a right to such compensation, in respect of the reference quantity transferred to the landlord on the expiry of a lease.

The general principles of law

11 The general principles of Community law relied on by Mr. Bostock include in particular the right to property and the principle of non-discrimination. He contends that those principles are breached where, in a position such as that in the main proceedings, a tenant is unable to obtain any compensation for the loss flowing from the transfer of the reference quantity. Mr. Bostock adds that the relationship between private parties constitutes, in relation to milk quotas, a 'natural context' for application of the principle of respect for property and avoidance of unjust enrichment.

*    *    *

18 Mr Bostock argues that the right to property is a fundamental right which requires a Member State to introduce a scheme for payment by a landlord of compensation to an outgoing tenant, or indeed confers directly on the tenant a right to compensation from the landlord.

19 That argument cannot be accepted. The right to property safeguarded by the Community legal order does not include the right to dispose, for profit, of an advantage, such as the reference quantities allocated in the context of the common organization of a market, which does not derive from the assets or occupational activity of the person concerned . . .

20 It follows that the protection of the right to property guaranteed by the Community legal order does not require a Member State to introduce a scheme for payment of compensation by a landlord to an outgoing tenant and does not confer a right to such compensation directly on the tenant.

## NOTES AND QUESTIONS

1.   How would you define the right to property invoked in *Bostock*? What might the case tell us about the Court's view on the definition of "property"? Since compensation rules were subsequently introduced, does that not suggest that Bostock's argument had more merit than the Court was prepared to concede?

**2.** In an earlier case, *Wachauf*, the Court dealt with a situation where a dairy farmer's lease had expired (rather than surrendered). Under the EU common organization for dairy products at the time, a farmer who ceased to carry on dairy farming and gave an undertaking never to resume it would have created the right to a compensation payment — rather like the U.S. legislation that pays farmers to leave land fallow. In the case of a tenancy, however, the rules required that the lessor consent to the cessation. Wachauf's landlord had originally granted consent but then realized that it would eliminate the reference quantity that would have transferred to him and therefore withdrew it. Wachauf had built up the farm by his own labours and the ECJ was clear that for him to lose the right to compensation because of the landlord consent rule relating to leased property would have violated fundamental rights, but it is not clear which ones. No reference to property rights as such is found in the judgment. In any event, the Court found that the EU regulations did not preclude compensation in such cases.

**3.** The Court has continued to uphold EU legislation in the agricultural and fisheries sectors involving alleged deprivation of property rights: see, for example, *Booker Aquacultur Ltd and Hydro Seafood GSP Ltd. V. The Scottish Ministers*, Joined Cases C-20 & 64/00 [2003] ECR I-913.

## THE QUEEN AND SECRETARY OF STATE FOR HEALTH v. BRITISH AMERICAN TOBACCO (INVESTMENTS) LTD AND IMPERIAL TOBACCO LTD, SUPPORTED BY JAPAN TOBACCO INC. AND JT INTERNATIONAL SA
### Case C-491/01, 2002 ECJ EUR-Lex LEXIS 1961, [2002] ECR I-11453

[This case concerned a preliminary ruling over Directive 2001/37/EC regarding the manufacture, presentation and sale of tobacco products (OJ 2001 L 194, p. 26). Japan Tobacco Inc was the holder of a trademark for cigarettes named 'Mild Seven". The European Court of Justice was asked to state whether Article 7 of the directive — read in conjunction with the 27th recital in the preamble — was invalid due to its contravening the right of property.

Recital 27 provided that

> The use on tobacco product packaging of certain texts, such as "low-tar", "light", "ultra-light", "mild", names, pictures and figurative or other signs, may mislead the consumer into the belief that such products are less harmful and give rise to changes in consumption. Smoking behavior and addiction, and not only the content of certain substances contained in the product before consumption, also determine the level of inhaled substances. In order to ensure the proper functioning of the internal market, and given the development of proposed international rules, the prohibition of such use should be provided for at Community level, giving sufficient time for introduction of this rule.

Article 5 of the Directive laid down labelling requirements, including in particular the requirement that the product packaging must show the tar, nicotine and carbon monoxide yields in such a way as to cover certain percentages of its surface, and that the packaging must carry warnings concerning the risks to health posed by tobacco products, except tobacco for oral use and other smokeless tobacco products. In particular, Article 5(6)(e) of the Directive provides that the text of the warnings and indications of yields must be printed in the official language or languages of the Member State where the product is placed on the market.

Article 7 of the Directive, entitled 'Product descriptions', was worded as follows:

'With effect from 30 September 2003, and without prejudice to Article 5(1), texts, names, trade marks and figurative or other signs suggesting that a particular tobacco product is less harmful than others shall not be used on the packaging of tobacco products.]

27. Japan Tobacco Inc. is the trade mark owner and JT International SA is the exclusive licensee of the 'Mild Seven' trade mark for cigarettes. Japan Tobacco submits that Article 7 of the Directive, in so far as it is to be interpreted as applying to established trade marks, will preclude Japan Tobacco from having the benefit of or using, within the Community, the intellectual property in the 'Mild Seven' trade mark, which, when that provision enters into force, will cause severe damage to the value of the brand worldwide.

*     *     *

143. The claimants in the main proceedings maintain that Articles 5 and 7 of the Directive infringe Article 295 EC [345], the fundamental right to property and/or Article 20 of the TRIPs Agreement, which provides that use of a trade mark in the course of trade is not to be unjustifiably encumbered by special requirements such as its use in a manner detrimental to its capability to distinguish the goods or services of one undertaking from those of other undertakings. They claim that the very large size of the new health warnings required by Article 5 of the Directive constitutes a serious infringement of their intellectual property rights. Those warnings will dominate the overall appearance of tobacco product packaging and so curtail or even prevent the use of their trade marks by the manufacturers of those products. Likewise, they claim that the absolute prohibition on using the descriptive terms referred to in Article 7 of the Directive will deprive them of a number of their trade marks because they will no longer be permitted to use them.

144. According to Japan Tobacco, Article 7 of the Directive prohibits it from exercising its intellectual property rights by preventing it from using its trade mark Mild Seven in the Community and by depriving it of the economic benefit of its exclusive licences for that trade mark. Such a result entails infringement of the right to property, which is recognised to be a fundamental human right in the Community legal order, protected by the first subparagraph of Article 1 of the First Protocol to the European Convention on Human Rights ("ECHR") and enshrined in Article 17 of the Charter of Fundamental Rights of the European Union.

147. With regard, first of all, to Article 295 EC [345], it must be borne in mind that according to that provision the Treaty 'shall in no way prejudice the rules in Member States governing the system of property ownership'. That provision merely recognises the power of Member States to define the rules governing the system of property ownership and does not exclude any influence whatever of Community law on the exercise of national property rights . . .

148. It must be stated that in the circumstances of the present case the Directive does not impinge in any way on the rules governing the system of property ownership in the Member States within the meaning of Article 295 EC [345] which is irrelevant in relation to any effect produced by the Directive on the exercise by the manufacturers of tobacco products of their trademark rights over those products.

149. As regards the validity of the Directive in respect of the right to property, the Court has consistently held that, while that right forms part of the general principles of Community law, it is not an absolute right and must be viewed in relation to its social function. Consequently, its exercise may be restricted, provided that those restrictions in fact correspond to objectives of general interest pursued by the Community and do not constitute a disproportionate and intolerable interference, impairing the very substance of the rights guaranteed . . .

150. . . . . [T]he only effect produced by Article 5 of the Directive is to restrict the right of manufacturers of tobacco products to use the space on some sides of cigarette packets or unit packets of tobacco products to show their trade marks, without prejudicing the substance of their trade mark rights, the purpose being to ensure a high level of health protection when the obstacles created by national laws on labelling are eliminated. In the light of this analysis, Article 5 constitutes a proportionate restriction on the use of the right to property compatible with the protection afforded that right by Community law.

151. . . . . Article 7 of the Directive is intended to ensure, in a manner in keeping with the principle of proportionality, a high level of health protection on the harmonisation of the provisions applicable to the description of tobacco products.

152. While that article entails prohibition, in relation only to the packaging of tobacco products, on using a trade mark incorporating one of the descriptors referred to in that provision, the fact remains that a manufacturer of tobacco products may continue, notwithstanding the removal of that description from the packaging, to distinguish its product by using other distinctive signs. In addition, the Directive provides for a sufficient period of time between its adoption and the entry into force of the prohibition under Article 7.

153. In light of the foregoing, it must be held that the restrictions on the trade mark right which may be caused by Article 7 of the Directive do in fact correspond to objectives of general interest pursued by the Community and do not constitute a disproportionate and intolerable interference, impairing the very substance of that right.

\*   \*   \*

157. It follows from the foregoing considerations concerning Question 1(d) that the Directive is not invalid by reason of infringement of Article 295 EC [345] or the fundamental right to property.

## NOTES AND QUESTIONS

**1.** The court refers to a standard for balancing public policy that permits restrictions as long as they "do not constitute a disproportionate and intolerable interference, impairing the very substance of that [property] right." Is that not precisely what happened here? Under article 7 the plaintiffs would in future be prohibited from using their trademark on the packaging of their goods.

**2.** In *Yassin Abdullah Kadi and Al barakaat International Foundation v. Council*, Joined Cases C-402/05 P and C-415/05 P, 2008 ECJ EUR-Lex LEXIS 1954, [2008] ECR I-6351 (for which the factual background is set out in the extract in Chapter 4) the ECJ gave the notion of "disproportionate and intolerable interference" a different connotation. Where the Plaintiff's property was interfered with (as here by the freezing of assets) the imposition of the restrictive measures was found to constitute "an unjustified restriction of his right to property" because there had been a failure to accord the plaintiff any guarantee enabling him to put his case to the competent authorities. This is a quite different angle compared with the *Tobacco* case, which focused on a balancing of competing policy objectives (intellectual property protection versus the right to property). In *Kadi*, the ECJ did not question that the policy objective (anti-terrorism) would have trumped the right to property. Despite the discussion of the right to property, therefore, this aspect of *Kadi* was really about due process.

## BOSPHORUS HAVA YOLLARI TURIZM VE TICARET AS v. MINISTER FOR TRANSPORT, ENERGY AND COMMUNICATIONS AND OTHERS
### Case C-84/95, 1996 ECJ CELEX LEXIS 489, [1996] ECR I-3953

[Bosphorus Airways was a Turkish company which operated principally as an air charterer and travel organizer. It leased for a period of four years two aircraft owned by the Yugoslav national airline JAT. The agreement, known as a "dry lease", provided for the leasing of the aircraft only and excluded cabin and flight crew, who were provided by Bosphorus Airways. That company thus had complete control of the day-to-day management of the aircraft for that period. However, JAT remained the owner of the aircraft.

The transaction between Bosphorus Airways and JAT had been entered into in complete good faith and was not intended to circumvent the sanctions against the Federal Republic of Yugoslavia which had been decided by United Nations resolutions and implemented in the Community by Regulation No 990/93. Furthermore, in application of those sanctions, the rent due under the lease was paid into blocked accounts, and was thus not paid to JAT. Finally, the aircraft were used exclusively by Bosphorus Airways for flights between Turkey on the one hand and several Member States and Switzerland on the other.

When one of the aircraft was preparing to take off following maintenance operations at Dublin Airport, the Irish Government directed it to be impounded under Article 8 of Regulation No 990/93 on the ground that it was an aircraft in which a majority or controlling interest was held by a person or undertaking in or operating from the Federal Republic of Yugoslavia.

The first paragraph of Article 8 of Regulation No 990/93 provides:

All vessels, freight vehicles, rolling stock and aircraft in which a majority or controlling interest is held by a person or undertaking in or operating from the Federal Republic of Yugoslavia (Serbia and Montenegro) shall be impounded by the competent authorities of the Member States.]

19 Bosphorus Airways submits, in the second place, that to interpret the first paragraph of Article 8 of Regulation No 990/93 as meaning that an aircraft whose day-to-day operation and control are carried out under a lease by a person or undertaking not based in or operating from the Federal Republic of Yugoslavia must nevertheless be impounded because it belongs to an undertaking based in that republic, would infringe Bosphorus's fundamental rights, in particular its right to peaceful enjoyment of its property and its freedom to pursue a commercial activity, in that it would have the effect of destroying and obliterating its air charter and travel organization business.

20 That interpretation, according to Bosphorus Airways, would also infringe the principle of proportionality, since the owner of the aircraft in question has already been penalized by the rent being held in blocked accounts and the impounding of the aircraft was therefore a manifestly unnecessary penalty, disproportionate with respect to a wholly innocent party.

21 It is settled case-law that the fundamental rights invoked by Bosphorus Airways are not absolute and their exercise may be subject to restrictions justified by objectives of general interest pursued by the Community. . . .

22 Any measure imposing sanctions has, by definition, consequences which affect the right to property and the freedom to pursue a trade or business, thereby causing harm to persons who are in no way responsible for the situation which led to the adoption of the sanctions.

23 Moreover, the importance of the aims pursued by the regulation at issue is such as to justify negative consequences, even of a substantial nature, for some operators.

24 The provisions of Regulation No 990/93 contribute in particular to the implementation at Community level of the sanctions against the Federal Republic of Yugoslavia adopted, and later strengthened, by several resolutions of the Security Council of the United Nations. The third recital in the preamble to Regulation No 990/93 states that "the prolonged direct and indirect activities of the Federal Republic of Yugoslavia (Serbia and Montenegro) in, and with regard to, the Republic of Bosnia-Herzegovina are the main cause for the dramatic developments in the Republic of Bosnia-Herzegovina"; the fourth recital states that "a continuation of these activities will lead to further unacceptable loss of human life and material damage and to a further breach of international peace and security in the region"; and the seventh recital states that "the Bosnian Serb party has hitherto not accepted, in full, the peace plan of the International Conference on the Former Yugoslavia in spite of appeals thereto by the Security Council".

25 It is in the light of those circumstances that the aim pursued by the sanctions assumes especial importance, which is, in particular, in terms of Regulation No

990/93 and more especially the eighth recital in the preamble thereto, to dissuade the Federal Republic of Yugoslavia from "further violating the integrity and security of the Republic of Bosnia-Herzegovina and to induce the Bosnian Serb party to cooperate in the restoration of peace in this Republic".

26 As compared with an objective of general interest so fundamental for the international community, which consists in putting an end to the state of war in the region and to the massive violations of human rights and humanitarian international law in the Republic of Bosnia-Herzegovina, the impounding of the aircraft in question, which is owned by an undertaking based in or operating from the Federal Republic of Yugoslavia, cannot be regarded as inappropriate or disproportionate.

## NOTES AND QUESTIONS

1. Do you think the standard adopted for proportionality here created an unfair result for Bosphorus?

2. Bosphorus challenged the Irish action in the European Court of Human Rights, which (as indicated in the *Modjahedines* case above) issued its decision on June 30 2005. The Court's summary of its decision reads as follows:

The European Court of Human Rights has today delivered at a public hearing a judgment in the case of *"Bosphorus Airways" v. Ireland* (application no. 45036/98). The Court held unanimously that there had been **no violation of Article 1 of Protocol No. 1** (protection of property) to the European Convention on Human Rights. (The judgment is available in English and French.)

### 3. Summary of the judgment

### Complaint

Bosphorus Airways complained that the manner in which Ireland implemented the sanctions regime to impound its aircraft was a reviewable exercise of discretion within the meaning of Article 1 of the Convention and a violation of Article 1 of Protocol No. 1.

\* \* \*

### Decision of the Court

Article 1

It was not disputed that the impoundment of the aircraft leased by Bosphorus Airways was implemented by the Irish authorities on its territory following a decision by the Irish Minister for Transport. In such circumstances Bosphorus Airways fell within the "jurisdiction" of the Irish State.

Article 1 of Protocol No. 1

Legal basis for the impoundment of the aircraft

The Court observed that, once adopted, EC Regulation 990/93 was "generally applicable" and "binding in its entirety" (under Article 189, now Article 249, of the EC Treaty), so that it applied to all Member States, none of whom could lawfully depart from any of its provisions. In addition, its "direct applicability" was not, and in the Court's view could not be, disputed. The Regulation became part of Irish domestic law with effect from 28 April 1993, when it was published in the Official Journal, prior to the date of the impoundment and without the need for implementing legislation.

The Court considered it entirely foreseeable that a Minister for Transport would implement the impoundment powers contained in Article 8 of EC Regulation 990/93. The Irish authorities rightly considered themselves obliged to impound any departing aircraft to which they considered Article 8 of EC Regulation 990/93 applied. Their decision that it did so apply was later confirmed, among other things, by the ECJ

The Court also agreed with the Irish Government and the European Commission that the Supreme Court had no real discretion to exercise, either before or after its preliminary reference to the ECJ.

The Court concluded that the impugned interference was not the result of an exercise of discretion by the Irish authorities, either under EC or Irish law, but rather amounted to compliance by the Irish State with its legal obligations flowing from EC law and, in particular, Article 8 of EC Regulation 990/93.

Was the impoundment justified?

The Court found that the protection of fundamental rights by EC law could have been considered to be, and to have been at the relevant time, "equivalent" to that of the Convention system. Consequently, a presumption arose that Ireland did not depart from the requirements of the Convention when it implemented legal obligations flowing from its membership of the EC. Such a presumption could be rebutted if, in a particular case, it was considered that the protection of Convention rights was manifestly deficient. In such cases, the interest of international cooperation would be outweighed by the Convention's role as a "constitutional instrument of European public order" in the field of human rights.

The Court took note of the nature of the interference, of the general interest pursued by the impoundment and by the sanctions regime and of the ruling of the ECJ, a ruling with which the Supreme Court was obliged to and did comply. It considered it clear that there was no dysfunction of the mechanisms of control of the observance of Convention rights.

In the Court's view, therefore, it could not be said that the protection of Bosphorus Airways' Convention rights was manifestly deficient. It followed that the presumption of Convention compliance had not been rebutted and that the impoundment of the aircraft did not give rise to a violation of Article 1 of Protocol No. 1.

## [C]   Respect for Family Life

## MARY CARPENTER v. SECRETARY OF STATE FOR THE HOME DEPARTMENT
### Case C-60/00, 2002 ECJ CELEX LEXIS 261, [2002] ECR I-6279

[Mrs. Carpenter, a national of the Philippines, was given leave to enter the United Kingdom as a visitor on 18 September 1994 for six months. She overstayed that leave and failed to apply for any extension of her stay. On 22 May 1996 she married Peter Carpenter, a United Kingdom national. Mr. Carpenter ran a business selling advertising space in medical and scientific journals and offering various administrative and publishing services to the editors of those journals. The business was established in the UK, where the publishers of the journals for which he sells advertising space were based. A significant proportion of the business was conducted with advertisers established in other Member States of the European Community. Mr. Carpenter traveled to other Member States for the purpose of his business.

On 15 July 1996 Mrs. Carpenter applied to the Secretary of State for leave to remain in the UK as the spouse of a national of that Member State. Her application was refused by a decision of the Secretary of State of 21 July 1997.

The Secretary of State also decided to make a deportation order against Mrs. Carpenter removing her to the Philippines. Under that decision it was open to Mrs. Carpenter to leave the United Kingdom voluntarily. If she did not do so, the Secretary of State would sign the deportation order and Mrs. Carpenter would have to obtain its revocation before she could seek leave to enter the United Kingdom as the spouse of a UK citizen.

Mrs. Carpenter appealed against the decision to make a deportation order to an Immigration Adjudicator (United Kingdom), arguing that the Secretary of State was not entitled to deport her because she was entitled to a right to remain in the United Kingdom under EU law. She maintained that since her husband's business required him to travel around in other Member States, providing and receiving services, he could do so more easily as she was looking after his children from his first marriage, so that her deportation would restrict her husband's right to provide and receive services.

The Immigration Adjudicator was satisfied that Mrs. Carpenter's marriage was genuine and that she played an important part in the upbringing of her stepchildren. He also accepted that she could be indirectly responsible for the increased success of her husband's business and that her husband was a provider of services for the purposes of Community law. According to the Immigration Adjudicator, Mr. Carpenter had the right to travel to other Member States to provide services and to be accompanied for that purpose by his spouse. However, while he was resident in the United Kingdom, he could not be considered to be exercising any freedom of movement within the meaning of EU law. The Immigration Adjudicator therefore dismissed Mrs. Carpenter's appeal by decision of 10 June 1998.

On Mrs. Carpenter's appeal to the Immigration Appeal Tribunal, that Tribunal considered that the issue of EU law raised by the proceedings before it was whether it was contrary to EU law and, in particular, EC 49/TFEU 56, for the Secretary of State to refuse to grant a right of residence to, and to decide to deport Mrs. Carpenter where, first, Mr. Carpenter was exercising his freedom to provide services in other Member States, and second, the childcare and homemaking performed by Mrs. Carpenter might indirectly assist and facilitate Mr. Carpenter's exercise of his rights under EC 49/TFEU 56, by providing him with economic assistance which permitted him to spend greater time on his business.]

28 It is to be noted, at the outset, that the provisions of the Treaty relating to the freedom to provide services, and the rules adopted for their implementation, are not applicable to situations which do not present any link to any of the situations envisaged by Community law . . .

29 As is apparent from paragraph 14 of this judgment, a significant proportion of Mr Carpenter's business consists of providing services, for remuneration, to advertisers established in other Member States. Such services come within the meaning of services' in Article 49 EC [56] both in so far as the provider travels for that purpose to the Member State of the recipient and in so far as he provides cross-border services without leaving the Member State in which he is established . . .

\* \* \*

37 . . . Mr. Carpenter is exercising the right freely to provide services guaranteed by Article 49 EC [56]. The services provided by Mr. Carpenter make up a significant proportion of his business, which is carried on both within his Member State of origin for the benefit of persons established in other Member States, and within those States.

38 In that context it should be remembered that the Community legislature has recognised the importance of ensuring the protection of the family life of nationals of the Member States in order to eliminate obstacles to the exercise of the fundamental freedoms guaranteed by the Treaty, as is particularly apparent from the provisions of the Council regulations and directives on the freedom of movement of employed and self-employed workers within the Community . . .

39 It is clear that the separation of Mr. and Mrs. Carpenter would be detrimental to their family life and, therefore, to the conditions under which Mr. Carpenter exercises a fundamental freedom. That freedom could not be fully effective if Mr. Carpenter were to be deterred from exercising it by obstacles raised in his country of origin to the entry and residence of his spouse . . .

40 A Member State may invoke reasons of public interest to justify a national measure which is likely to obstruct the exercise of the freedom to provide services only if that measure is compatible with the fundamental rights whose observance the Court ensures . . .

41 The decision to deport Mrs. Carpenter constitutes an interference with the exercise by Mr. Carpenter of his right to respect for his family life within the

meaning of Article 8 of the Convention for the Protection of Human Rights and Fundamental Freedoms, signed at Rome on 4 November 1950 (hereinafter the Convention'), which is among the fundamental rights which, according to the Court's settled case-law, restated by the Preamble to the Single European Act and by Article 6(2) EU, are protected in Community law.

42 Even though no right of an alien to enter or to reside in a particular country is as such guaranteed by the Convention, the removal of a person from a country where close members of his family are living may amount to an infringement of the right to respect for family life as guaranteed by Article 8(1) of the Convention. Such an interference will infringe the Convention if it does not meet the requirements of paragraph 2 of that article, that is unless it is in accordance with the law', motivated by one or more of the legitimate aims under that paragraph and necessary in a democratic society', that is to say justified by a pressing social need and, in particular, proportionate to the legitimate aim pursued . . .

43 A decision to deport Mrs. Carpenter, taken in circumstances such as those in the main proceedings, does not strike a fair balance between the competing interests, that is, on the one hand, the right of Mr. Carpenter to respect for his family life, and, on the other hand, the maintenance of public order and public safety.

44 Although, in the main proceedings, Mr. Carpenter's spouse has infringed the immigration laws of the United Kingdom by not leaving the country prior to the expiry of her leave to remain as a visitor, her conduct, since her arrival in the United Kingdom in September 1994, has not been the subject of any other complaint that could give cause to fear that she might in the future constitute a danger to public order or public safety. Moreover, it is clear that Mr. and Mrs. Carpenter' s marriage, which was celebrated in the United Kingdom in 1996, is genuine and that Mrs. Carpenter continues to lead a true family life there, in particular by looking after her husband's children from a previous marriage.

45 In those circumstances, the decision to deport Mrs. Carpenter constitutes an infringement which is not proportionate to the objective pursued.

46 In view of all the foregoing, the answer to the question referred to the Court is that Article 49 EC [56], read in the light of the fundamental right to respect for family life, is to be interpreted as precluding, in circumstances such as those in the main proceedings, a refusal, by the Member State of origin of a provider of services established in that Member State who provides services to recipients established in other Member States, of the right to reside in its territory to that provider's spouse, who is a national of a third country.

## NOTES AND QUESTIONS

1. Describe how the EU right to respect for family life was relevant to the Carpenters' situation.

2. Is this judgment stretching the notion of freedom to provide services as a basis for residence entitlements beyond reasonable limits? What implications might this have for the internal laws of the Member States more generally? Does it make sense to tie the rights to the supply of services at all?

**3.** In *Parliament v. Council* Case C-540/03, 2006 ECJ CELEX LEXIS 529, [2006] ECR I-5769, the Parliament challenged the final subparagraph of article 4(1), article 4(6) and article 8 of directive 2003/86 on family reunification (within the context of personal free movement), as regards inter alia the provisions allowing Member States to insist on a residence requirement for the sponsor not exceeding two years. The court considered the effect of article 8 ECHR in the following terms:

102. The coexistence of different situations, according to whether or not Member States choose to make use of the possibility of imposing a waiting period of two years, or of three years where their legislation in force on the date of adoption of the Directive takes their reception capacity into account, merely reflects the difficulty of harmonising laws in a field which hitherto fell within the competence of the Member States alone. As the Parliament itself acknowledges, the Directive is important for applying the right to family reunification in a harmonised fashion. In the present instance, it does not appear that the Community legislature exceeded the limits imposed by fundamental rights in permitting Member States which had, or wished to adopt, specific legislation to adjust certain aspects of the right to reunification.

103. Consequently, Article 8 of the Directive cannot be regarded as running counter to the fundamental right to respect for family life or to the obligation to have regard to the best interests of children, either in itself or in that it expressly or impliedly authorises the Member States to act in such a way.

104. In the final analysis, while the Directive leaves the Member States a margin of appreciation, it is sufficiently wide to enable them to apply the Directive's rules in a manner consistent with the requirements flowing from the protection of fundamental rights . . .

105. It should be remembered that, in accordance with settled case-law, the requirements flowing from the protection of general principles recognised in the Community legal order, which include fundamental rights, are also binding on Member States when they implement Community rules, and that consequently they are bound, as far as possible, to apply the rules in accordance with those requirements . . .

106. Implementation of the Directive is subject to review by the national courts since, as provided in Article 18 thereof, the Member States shall ensure that the sponsor and/or the members of his/her family have the right to mount a legal challenge where an application for family reunification is rejected or a residence permit is either not renewed or is withdrawn or removal is ordered'. If those courts encounter difficulties relating to the interpretation or validity of the Directive, it is incumbent upon them to refer a question to the Court for a preliminary ruling in the circumstances set out in Articles 68 EC [repealed] and 234 EC [267].

Is the Court suggesting perhaps that the circumstances in which the Member States could actually exercise in full the derogation in the directive might be very limited?

**4.** See also *Commission v. Spain (Third Country Nationals)* Case C-503/03, 2006 ECJ CELEX LEXIS 171, [2006] ECR I-1097.

## [D] Privacy and Protection of Personal Data

## DIRECTIVE 95/46

of the European Parliament and of the Council of 24 October 1995 on the protection of individuals with regard to the processing of personal data and on the free movement of such data.

[1995] OJ L 281

### SUMMARY

**(European Union website: Summaries of European Union legislation)**

This Directive applies to data processed by automated means (e.g. a computer database of customers) and data contained in or intended to be part of non automated filing systems (traditional paper files).

It does not apply to the processing of data:

- by a natural person in the course of purely personal or household activities;

- in the course of an activity which falls outside the scope of Community law, such as operations concerning public security, defence or State security.

The Directive aims to protect the rights and freedoms of persons with respect to the processing of personal data by laying down guidelines determining when this processing is lawful.

The guidelines relate to:

- the **quality** of the data: personal data must be processed fairly and lawfully, and collected for specified, explicit and legitimate purposes. They must also be accurate and, where necessary, kept up to date;

- the **legitimacy** of data processing: personal data may be processed only if the data subject has unambiguously given his/her consent or processing is necessary:

  - for the performance of a contract to which the data subject is party or;

  - for compliance with a legal obligation to which the controller is subject or;

  - in order to protect the vital interests of the data subject or;

  - for the performance of a task carried out in the public interest or;

  - for the purposes of the legitimate interests pursued by the controller;

special **categories** of processing: it is forbidden to process personal data revealing racial or ethnic origin, political opinions, religious or philosophical beliefs, trade-union membership, and the processing of data concerning health or sex life. This provision comes with certain qualifications concerning, for example, cases where processing is necessary to protect the vital interests of the data subject or for the purposes of preventive medicine and medical diagnosis;

**information** to be given to the data subject: the controller must provide the data subject from whom data are collected with certain information relating to himself/herself (the identity of the controller, the purposes of the processing, recipients of the data etc.);

the data subject's **right of access** to data: every data subject should have the right to obtain from the controller:

- confirmation as to whether or not data relating to him/her are being processed and communication of the data undergoing processing;

- the rectification, erasure or blocking of data the processing of which does not comply with the provisions of this Directive in particular, either because of the incomplete or inaccurate nature of the data, and the notification of these changes to third parties to whom the data have been disclosed.

**exemptions and restrictions**: the scope of the principles relating to the quality of the data, information to be given to the data subject, right of access and the publicising of processing may be restricted in order to safeguard aspects such as national security, defence, public security, the prosecution of criminal offences, an important economic or financial interest of a Member State or of the European Union or the protection of the data subject;

the **right to object** to the processing of data: the data subject should have the right to object, on legitimate grounds, to the processing of data relating to him/her. He/she should also have the right to object, on request and free of charge, to the processing of personal data that the controller anticipates being processed for the purposes of direct marketing. He/she should finally be informed before personal data are disclosed to third parties for the purposes of direct marketing, and be expressly offered the right to object to such disclosures;

the **confidentiality and security of processing**: any person acting under the authority of the controller or of the processor, including the processor himself, who has access to personal data must not process them except on instructions from the controller. In addition, the controller must implement appropriate measures to protect personal data against accidental or unlawful destruction or accidental loss, alteration, unauthorised disclosure or access;

the **notification** of processing to a supervisory authority: the controller must notify the national supervisory authority before carrying out any processing operation. Prior checks to determine specific risks to the rights and freedoms of data subjects are to be carried out by the supervisory authority following receipt of the notification. Measures are to be taken to ensure that processing operations are publicised and the supervisory authorities must keep a register of the processing operations notified.

Every person shall have the right to a **judicial remedy** for any breach of the rights guaranteed him by the national law applicable to the processing in question. In addition, any person who has suffered damage as a result of the unlawful processing of their personal data is entitled to receive compensation for the damage suffered.

Transfers of personal data from a Member State to a third country with an adequate level of protection are authorised. However, they may not be made to a third country which does not ensure this level of protection, except in the cases of the derogations listed.

The Directive aims to encourage the drawing up of national and Community codes of conduct intended to contribute to the proper implementation of the national and Community provisions.

Each Member State is to provide one or more independent public authorities responsible for monitoring the application within its territory of the provisions adopted by the Member States pursuant to the Directive.

A Working Party on the Protection of Individuals with regard to the Processing of Personal Data is set up, composed of representatives of the national supervisory authorities, representatives of the supervisory authorities of the Community institutions and bodies, and a representative of the Commission.

## TIETOSUOJAVALTUUTETTU v. SATAKUNNAN MARKKINAPÖRSSI OY, SATAMEDIA OY
### Case C-73/07, 2008 ECJ EUR-Lex LEXIS 1980, [2008] ECR I-9831

[The facts underlying this reference are set out below. The basic question considered by the ECJ touched on the interplay between the Data Protection Directive and the fundamental right to freedom of expression, which is handled in the directive by Article 9, which reads as follows:

Article 9

Processing of personal data and freedom of expression

Member States shall provide for exemptions or derogations from the provisions of this Chapter, Chapter IV and Chapter VI for the processing of personal data carried out solely for journalistic purposes or the purpose of artistic or literary expression only if they are necessary to reconcile the right to privacy with the rules governing freedom of expression.]

25 For several years, Markkinapörssi has collected public data from the Finnish tax authorities for the purposes of publishing extracts from those data in the regional editions of the *Veropörssi* newspaper each year.

26 The information contained in those publications comprises the surname and given name of approximately 1.2 million natural persons whose income exceeds certain thresholds as well as the amount, to the nearest EUR 100, of their earned and unearned income and details relating to wealth tax levied on them. That

information is set out in the form of an alphabetical list and organised according to municipality and income bracket.

27 According to the order for reference, the *Veropörssi* newspaper carries a statement that the personal data disclosed may be removed on request and without charge.

28 While that newspaper also contains articles, summaries and advertisements, its main purpose is to publish personal tax information.

29 Markkinapörssi transferred personal data published in the *Veropörssi* newspaper, in the form of CD-ROM discs, to Satamedia, which is owned by the same shareholders, with a view to those data being disseminated by a text-messaging system. In that connection, those companies signed an agreement with a mobile telephony company which put in place, on Satamedia's behalf, a text-messaging service allowing mobile telephone users to receive information published in the *Veropörssi* newspaper on their telephone, for a charge of approximately EUR 2. Personal data are removed from that service on request.

30 The Tietosuojavaltuutettu and the Tietosuojalautakunta, who are the Finnish authorities responsible for data protection, supervise the processing of personal data and have the regulatory powers laid down in the Law on personal data.

31 Following complaints from individuals alleging infringement of their right to privacy, on 10 March 2004, the Tietosuojavaltuutettu responsible for investigating the activities of Markkinapörssi and Satamedia requested the Tietosuojalautakunta to prohibit the latter from carrying on the personal data processing activities at issue.

32 That request having been rejected by the Tietosuojalautakunta, the Tietosuojavaltuutettu brought proceedings before the Helsingin hallinto-oikeus (Administrative Court, Helsinki), which also rejected his application. The Tietosuojavaltuutettu then brought an appeal before the Korkein hallinto-oikeus (Supreme Administrative Court).

*     *     *

50 By its second question, the national court asks, in essence, whether Article 9 of the directive should be interpreted as meaning that the activities referred to at points (a) to (d) of the first question, relating to data from documents which are in the public domain under national legislation, must be considered as activities involving the processing of personal data carried out solely for journalistic purposes. The national court states that it seeks clarification as to whether the fact that the principal aim of those activities is the publication of the data in question is relevant to the determination of that issue.

51 . . . [T]he provisions of a directive must be interpreted in the light of the aims pursued by the directive and the system it establishes . . .

52 In that regard, it is not in dispute that, as is apparent from Article 1 of the directive, its objective is that the Member States should, while permitting the free flow of personal data, protect the fundamental rights and freedoms of natural

persons and, in particular, their right to privacy, with respect to the processing of personal data.

53 That objective cannot, however, be pursued without having regard to the fact that those fundamental rights must, to some degree, be reconciled with the fundamental right to freedom of expression.

54 Article 9 of the directive refers to such a reconciliation. As is apparent, in particular, from recital 37 in the preamble to the directive, the object of Article 9 is to reconcile two fundamental rights: the protection of privacy and freedom of expression. The obligation to do so lies on the Member States.

55 In order to reconcile those two 'fundamental rights' for the purposes of the directive, the Member States are required to provide for a number of derogations or limitations in relation to the protection of data and, therefore, in relation to the fundamental right to privacy, specified in Chapters II, IV and VI of the directive. Those derogations must be made solely for journalistic purposes or the purpose of artistic or literary expression, which fall within the scope of the fundamental right to freedom of expression, in so far as it is apparent that they are necessary in order to reconcile the right to privacy with the rules governing freedom of expression.

56 In order to take account of the importance of the right to freedom of expression in every democratic society, it is necessary, first, to interpret notions relating to that freedom, such as journalism, broadly. Secondly, and in order to achieve a balance between the two fundamental rights, the protection of the fundamental right to privacy requires that the derogations and limitations in relation to the protection of data provided for in the chapters of the directive referred to above must apply only in so far as is strictly necessary.

57 In that context, the following points are relevant.

58 First, as the Advocate General pointed out at point 65 of her Opinion and as is apparent from the legislative history of the directive, the exemptions and derogations provided for in Article 9 of the directive apply not only to media undertakings but also to every person engaged in journalism.

59 Secondly, the fact that the publication of data within the public domain is done for profit-making purposes does not, prima facie, preclude such publication being considered as an activity undertaken 'solely for journalistic purposes'. As Markkinapörssi and Satamedia state in their observations and as the Advocate General noted at point 82 of her Opinion, every undertaking will seek to generate a profit from its activities. A degree of commercial success may even be essential to professional journalistic activity.

60 Thirdly, account must be taken of the evolution and proliferation of methods of communication and the dissemination of information. As was mentioned by the Swedish Government in particular, the medium which is used to transmit the processed data, whether it be classic in nature, such as paper or radio waves, or electronic, such as the internet, is not determinative as to whether an activity is undertaken 'solely for journalistic purposes'.

61 It follows from all of the above that activities such as those involved in the main proceedings, relating to data from documents which are in the public domain under

national legislation, may be classified as 'journalistic activities' if their object is the disclosure to the public of information, opinions or ideas, irrespective of the medium which is used to transmit them. They are not limited to media undertakings and may be undertaken for profit-making purposes.

62 The answer to the second question should therefore be that Article 9 of the directive is to be interpreted as meaning that the activities referred to at points (a) to (d) of the first question, relating to data from documents which are in the public domain under national legislation, must be considered as activities involving the processing of personal data carried out 'solely for journalistic purposes', within the meaning of that provision, if the sole object of those activities is the disclosure to the public of information, opinions or ideas. Whether that is the case is a matter for the national court to determine.

## NOTES AND QUESTIONS

**1.** Consider the Court's analysis of what constitutes a "journalistic purpose." Does the party seeking to release the data have to be a journalist? (The question has also arisen in the context of the First Amendment in the U.S. and is at the heart of the Wikileaks controversy.)

**2.** The Privacy Directive was adopted on the basis of the harmonization provisions relative to the preservation of the internal market. As such, it applies to the Member States. How would you connect it to the Charter, if at all?

**3.** The directive applies only to situations covered by EU law (Article 3) and gives certain examples where it would not apply, including criminal law. In light of the movement of "PJCC" matters into the TFEU, is this still accurate?

## PRODUCTORES DE MÚSICA DE ESPAÑA (PROMUSICAE) v. TELEFÓNICA DE ESPAÑA SAU
### Case C-275/06, 2008 ECJ EUR-Lex LEXIS 2035, [2008] ECR I-271

[Promusicae had sought to obtain information from the Spanish Telephone company about individuals suspected of violating copyright through filesharing of copyrighted materials. Restrictions on the disclosure of personal information were imposed by Spanish law that implemented Directive 2000/31/EC on certain legal aspects of information society services, in particular electronic commerce, in the Internal Market ("Directive on electronic commerce"), and Directive 2002/58/EC concerning the processing of personal data and the protection of privacy in the electronic communications sector ("Directive on privacy and electronic communications"). However, Spain had also implemented Directive 2001/29/EC on the harmonisation of certain aspects of copyright and related rights in the information society, and Directive 2004/48/EC on the enforcement of intellectual property rights.

The national court asked the ECJ whether these various directives required the Member States to lay down, in a situation such as that in the main proceedings, an obligation to communicate personal data in order to ensure effective protection of copyright in the context of civil proceedings. The ECJ held that they did not, but then went on to consider the interplay of EU fundamental rights, and in particular the right to property and the right to an effective remedy and the privacy rights of the individual.]

61 The national court refers in its order for reference to Articles 17 and 47 of the Charter, the first of which concerns the protection of the right to property, including intellectual property, and the second of which concerns the right to an effective remedy. By so doing, that court must be regarded as seeking to know whether an interpretation of those directives to the effect that the Member States are not obliged to lay down, in order to ensure the effective protection of copyright, an obligation to communicate personal data in the context of civil proceedings leads to an infringement of the fundamental right to property and the fundamental right to effective judicial protection.

62 It should be recalled that the fundamental right to property, which includes intellectual property rights such as copyright . . . and the fundamental right to effective judicial protection constitute general principles of Community law . . .

63 However, the situation in respect of which the national court puts that question involves, in addition to those two rights, a further fundamental right, namely the right that guarantees protection of personal data and hence of private life.

64 According to recital 2 in the preamble to Directive 2002/58, the directive seeks to respect the fundamental rights and observes the principles recognised in particular by the Charter. In particular, the directive seeks to ensure full respect for the rights set out in Articles 7 and 8 of that Charter. Article 7 substantially reproduces Article 8 of the European Convention for the Protection of Human Rights and Fundamental Freedoms signed at Rome on 4 November 1950, which guarantees the right to respect for private life, and Article 8 of the Charter expressly proclaims the right to protection of personal data.

65 The present reference for a preliminary ruling thus raises the question of the need to reconcile the requirements of the protection of different fundamental rights, namely the right to respect for private life on the one hand and the rights to protection of property and to an effective remedy on the other.

66 The mechanisms allowing those different rights and interests to be balanced are contained, first, in Directive 2002/58 itself, in that it provides for rules which determine in what circumstances and to what extent the processing of personal data is lawful and what safeguards must be provided for, and in the three directives mentioned by the national court, which reserve the cases in which the measures adopted to protect the rights they regulate affect the protection of personal data. Second, they result from the adoption by the Member States of national provisions transposing those directives and their application by the national authorities . . . .

67 As to those directives, their provisions are relatively general, since they have to be applied to a large number of different situations which may arise in any of the Member States. They therefore logically include rules which leave the Member States with the necessary discretion to define transposition measures which may be adapted to the various situations possible . . .

68 That being so, the Member States must, when transposing the directives

mentioned above, take care to rely on an interpretation of the directives which allows a fair balance to be struck between the various fundamental rights protected by the Community legal order. Further, when implementing the measures transposing those directives, the authorities and courts of the Member States must not only interpret their national law in a manner consistent with those directives but also make sure that they do not rely on an interpretation of them which would be in conflict with those fundamental rights or with the other general principles of Community law, such as the principle of proportionality . . .

69 Moreover, it should be recalled here that the Community legislature expressly required, in accordance with Article 15(1) of Directive 2002/58, that the measures referred to in that paragraph be adopted by the Member States in compliance with the general principles of Community law, including those mentioned in Article 6(1) and (2) EU.

70 In the light of all the foregoing, the answer to the national court's question must be that Directives 2000/31, 2001/29, 2004/48 and 2002/58 do not require the Member States to lay down, in a situation such as that in the main proceedings, an obligation to communicate personal data in order to ensure effective protection of copyright in the context of civil proceedings. However, Community law requires that, when transposing those directives, the Member States take care to rely on an interpretation of them which allows a fair balance to be struck between the various fundamental rights protected by the Community legal order. Further, when implementing the measures transposing those directives, the authorities and courts of the Member States must not only interpret their national law in a manner consistent with those directives but also make sure that they do not rely on an interpretation of them which would be in conflict with those fundamental rights or with the other general principles of Community law, such as the principle of proportionality.

## NOTES AND QUESTIONS

1.   What does this case tell us about the nature of EU fundamental rights given that these are indeed supposed to be applicable within an autonomous body of law (Chapter 3)? Does it imply that national variations have an important part to play here? Or is this a complete abdication by the ECJ of its responsibilities?

2.   At the EU level, legislation on protection of personal data in the form of Regulation 45/2001, [2001] OJ L8/1 was put to the test in *The Bavarian Lager Co. Ltd. v. Commission*, Case T194/04, 2007 ECJ EUR-Lex LEXIS 1873, [2007] ECR II-4523. The Commission had started an EC 226/TFEU 258 proceeding against the UK regarding concerns about UK rules relating to the importation of foreign beers (these were rules purporting to regulate "tied houses arrangements" of the type in issue in the *Delimitis* case (*supra* Chapter 11.) In the course of this proceeding a meeting was arranged with UK officials and the matter was subsequently closed. The applicant in this case sought to find out who from the European Confederation of Brewers had attended the meeting, asserting article EC 255/TFEU 15 and Regulation 1045/2001 (reproduced in the Documentary Supplement). The conflict that arose here was thus potentially between the basic principles of Privacy enshrined in Directive 95/46 and the right of access to documents (see chapter 12).

Here though, it was not the individuals who sought protection under the privacy rules, but the Commission itself, based on Regulation 45/2001 EC and Article 8 of the ECHR. The CFI/General Court rejected that position on the principle that the disclosure in question did not undermine the private life of the individuals in question:

> 114 It should also be noted that, in accordance with the case-law of the European Court of Human Rights, 'private life' is a broad concept that does not lend itself to an exhaustive definition. Article 8 of the ECHR also protects the right to identity and personal development and also the right of any individual to establish and develop relationships with other human beings and with the outside world. There is no reason in principle to exclude professional or business activities from the concept of 'private life' . . . There is thus an area of interaction between the individual and others which, even in a public context, may fall within the concept of 'private life' . . .

> 115 In order to determine whether there has been a breach of Article 8 of the ECHR, it needs to be determined, first, whether there has been an interference in the private life of the person concerned and, secondly, if so, whether that interference is justified. In order to be justified, it must be in accordance with the law, pursue a legitimate aim and be necessary in a democratic society. Concerning that latter condition, in order to determine whether a disclosure is 'necessary in a democratic society', it needs to be examined whether the grounds relied on in justification are 'relevant and sufficient', and whether the measures adopted are proportionate to the legitimate aims pursued. In cases concerning the disclosure of personal data, the European Court of Human Rights has recognised that the competent authorities have to be granted a certain discretion in order to establish a fair balance between competing public and private interests. That margin of discretion is, however, accompanied by judicial review, and its breadth is to be determined by reference to factors such as the nature and importance of the interests at stake and the seriousness of the interference . . .

> 116 Any decision taken pursuant to Regulation No 1049/2001 must comply with Article 8 of the ECHR, in accordance with Article 6(2) EU. In that regard it should be noted that Regulation No 1049/2001 determines the general principles and the limits which, for reasons of public or private interest, govern the exercise of the right of access to documents, in accordance with Article 255(2) EC. Therefore, Article 4(1)(b) of that regulation provides an exception designed to ensure protection of the privacy and integrity of the individual.

> 117 Moreover, exceptions to the principle of access to documents must be interpreted restrictively. The exception under Article 4(1)(b) of Regulation No 1049/2001 concerns only personal data that are capable of actually and specifically undermining the protection of privacy and the integrity of the individual.

118 It should also be emphasised that the fact that the concept of 'private life' is a broad one, in accordance with the case-law of the European Court of Human Rights, and that the right to the protection of personal data may constitute one of the aspects of the right to respect for private life . . . does not mean that all personal data necessarily fall within the concept of 'private life'.

119 A fortiori, not all personal data are by their nature capable of undermining the private life of the person concerned. In recital 33 of Directive 95/46, reference is made to data which are capable by their nature of infringing fundamental freedoms or privacy and which should not be processed unless the data subject gives his explicit consent, which implies that not all data are of that nature. Such sensitive data may be included in those referred to by Article 10 of Regulation No 45/2001, concerning processing relating to particular categories of data, such as those revealing racial or ethnic origin, religious or philosophical beliefs, or data concerning health or sex life.

120 It follows from the whole of the above that, in order to be able to determine whether the exception under Article 4(1)(b) of Regulation No 1049/2001 applies, it is necessary to examine whether public access to the names of the participants at the meeting of 11 October 1996 is capable of actually and specifically undermining the protection of the privacy and the integrity of the persons concerned.

## § 20.03  DIGNITY

### OMEGA SPIELHALLEN- UND AUTOMATENAUFSTELLUNGS-GMBH v. OBERBÜRGERMEISTERIN DER BUNDESSTADT BONN
Case C-36/02, 2004 ECJ CELEX LEXIS 458, [2004] ECR I-9609

[Omega, a German company, had, since 1 August 1994, been operating an installation known as a "laserdrome", normally used for the practice of "laser sport" in Bonn (Germany). Omega having obtained Court authorisation to use it on a provisional basis. The equipment used by Omega in its establishment, which included sub-machine-gun-type laser targeting devices and sensory tags fixed either in the firing corridors or to jackets worn by players, was initially developed from a children's toy freely available on the market. That equipment having proved technically inadequate, Omega turned to equipment supplied by the British company Pulsar International Ltd. Even before the public opening of the "laserdrome", a part of the population had manifested its opposition to the project. It was subsequently banned by the Bonn Police.]

28. . . . In this case, the documents before the Court show that the grounds relied on by the Bonn police authority in adopting the prohibition order expressly mention the fact that the activity concerned constitutes a danger to public policy. Moreover, reference to a danger to public policy also appears in [the relevant German law] empowering police authorities to take necessary measures to avert that danger.

29. In these proceedings, it is undisputed that the contested order was adopted independently of any consideration linked to the nationality of the providers or recipients of the services placed under a restriction. In any event, since measures for safeguarding public policy fall within a derogation from the freedom to provide services set out in Article 46 EC [52], it is not necessary to verify whether those measures are applied without distinction both to national providers of services and those established in other Member States.

30. However, the possibility of a Member State relying on a derogation laid down by the Treaty does not prevent judicial review of measures applying that derogation . . . In addition, the concept of public policy' in the Community context, particularly as justification for a derogation from the fundamental principle of the freedom to provide services, must be interpreted strictly, so that its scope cannot be determined unilaterally by each Member State without any control by the Community institutions . . .

31. The fact remains, however, that the specific circumstances which may justify recourse to the concept of public policy may vary from one country to another and from one era to another. The competent national authorities must therefore be allowed a margin of discretion within the limits imposed by the Treaty . . .

32. In this case, the competent authorities took the view that the activity concerned by the prohibition order was a threat to public policy by reason of the fact that, in accordance with the conception prevailing in public opinion, the commercial exploitation of games involving the simulated killing of human beings infringed a fundamental value enshrined in the national constitution, namely human dignity. According to the Bundesverwaltungsgericht, the national courts which heard the case shared and confirmed the conception of the requirements for protecting human dignity on which the contested order is based, that conception therefore having to be regarded as in accordance with the stipulations of the German Basic Law.

33. It should be recalled in that context that, according to settled case-law, fundamental rights form an integral part of the general principles of law the observance of which the Court ensures, and that, for that purpose, the Court draws inspiration from the constitutional traditions common to the Member States and from the guidelines supplied by international treaties for the protection of human rights on which the Member States have collaborated or to which they are signatories. The European Convention on Human Rights and Fundamental Freedoms has special significance in that respect . . .

34. As the Advocate General argues in paragraphs 82 to 91 of her Opinion, the Community legal order undeniably strives to ensure respect for human dignity as a general principle of law. There can therefore be no doubt that the objective of protecting human dignity is compatible with Community law, it being immaterial in that respect that, in Germany, the principle of respect for human dignity has a particular status as an independent fundamental right.

35. Since both the Community and its Member States are required to respect fundamental rights, the protection of those rights is a legitimate interest which, in principle, justifies a restriction of the obligations imposed by Community law, even

under a fundamental freedom guaranteed by the Treaty such as the freedom to provide services . . .

36. However, measures which restrict the freedom to provide services may be justified on public policy grounds only if they are necessary for the protection of the interests which they are intended to guarantee and only in so far as those objectives cannot be attained by less restrictive measures . . .

37. It is not indispensable in that respect for the restrictive measure issued by the authorities of a Member State to correspond to a conception shared by all Member States as regards the precise way in which the fundamental right or legitimate interest in question is to be protected. Although, in paragraph 60 of Schindler, the Court referred to moral, religious or cultural considerations which lead all Member States to make the organisation of lotteries and other games with money subject to restrictions, it was not its intention, by mentioning that common conception, to formulate a general criterion for assessing the proportionality of any national measure which restricts the exercise of an economic activity.

38. On the contrary, as is apparent from well-established case-law subsequent to Schindler, the need for, and proportionality of, the provisions adopted are not excluded merely because one Member State has chosen a system of protection different from that adopted by another State . . .

39. In this case, it should be noted, first, that, according to the referring court, the prohibition on the commercial exploitation of games involving the simulation of acts of violence against persons, in particular the representation of acts of homicide, corresponds to the level of protection of human dignity which the national constitution seeks to guarantee in the territory of the Federal Republic of Germany. It should also be noted that, by prohibiting only the variant of the laser game the object of which is to fire on human targets and thus play at killing' people, the contested order did not go beyond what is necessary in order to attain the objective pursued by the competent national authorities.

40. In those circumstances, the order of 14 September 1994 cannot be regarded as a measure unjustifiably undermining the freedom to provide services.

41. In the light of the above considerations, the answer to the question must be that Community law does not preclude an economic activity consisting of the commercial exploitation of games simulating acts of homicide from being made subject to a national prohibition measure adopted on grounds of protecting public policy by reason of the fact that that activity is an affront to human dignity.

## NOTES AND QUESTIONS

1.   Describe how the principle of Human Dignity came into play here as a matter of EU law.

2.   What does the Court say about the implications of possible variations among the laws of the Member States in applying the principle of Human Dignity? Since these are EU principles applied in connection with the implementation of EU law, should there not be uniformity?

3. For an analysis, see M. Bulterman and H.R. Kranenborg, *Analysis and Reflections — What if rules on free movement and human rights collide? About laser games and human dignity: The Omega case*, (2006) 31 EL REV. 93.

## § 20.04 SOLIDARITY

### LAVAL UN PARTNERI LTD v. SVENSKA BYGGNADSARBETAREFÖRBUNDET, SVENSKA BYGGNADSARBETAREFÖRBUNDETS AVD. 1, BYGGETTAN, SVENSKA ELEKTRIKERFÖRBUNDET
Case 341/05, 2007 ECJ EUR-Lex LEXIS 2399, [2007] ECR I-11767

[Laval was a Latvian company that provided workers at sites in Sweden where its former subsidiary, Baltic, had construction contracts. At Vaxholm, Baltic was engaged in the building of a school for the municipality.

In Sweden, collective agreements for recognition of bargaining rights between unions and employers and for terms and conditions (other than wages) are negotiated but are not mandatory, nor is it mandatory that a collective agreement cover all employers in the sector. However, once a collective agreement is in place, wage negotiations occur within the context of such agreement and the law (here referred to by its abbreviation MBL) provides for a fall-back mechanism to determine wages for the workers covered by the agreement, if agreement cannot be reached through negotiation or mediation. Swedish law prohibits strikes, lockouts or other actions by either side to amend a collective agreement. It also prohibits industrial action by employers or workers covered by a collective agreement intended to force *other* parties to enter into collective agreements. As a result of a case decided by the Swedish labor tribunal (known as the *Britannia* case), this prohibition was held to extend to industrial action intended to force non-Swedish parties to amend foreign collective agreements insofar they would cover work performed in Sweden, provided that a similar prohibition existed in the foreign country in question. However, the effects of the *Britannia* decision were modified by an amendment to the MBL that removed the prohibition with respect to action where the "link with [Sweden] is too tenuous for the MBL to be deemed to apply directly to the terms and conditions of employment in question." This had the result of causing collective action that would have been illegal in the case of Swedish companies not to be illegal in the case of action against foreign companies.

Directive 96/71 (the directive n issue in the *Wolff* case in Chapter 14) laid down certain minimum levels of protection for EU workers who are seconded to work in another Member State (the "host state"). In essence, the directive required that the seconded workers should be entitled to the same level of protection as existed for workers in the host state. In the present case, since collective agreements were not mandatory in Sweden, Latvian workers were not entitled to the same terms and conditions as Swedish workers covered by collective agreements with Swedish employers, though the Latvian employer and the Swedish union were under an obligation to negotiate in good faith in order to try and reach such agreement.

Laval started the negotiation process but wanted to include wage negotiations in it rather than sign up to a collective agreement first and then be faced with the possibility of having an unacceptable level of wage costs imposed on it potentially via the default procedure. These negotiations eventually broke down and the Swedish Union, Byggnads and its affiliates, Byggettan and Elektrikerna started industrial action against Laval by blockading the Vexholm site. This was then extended to cover other sites where Baltic had contracts. Eventually the Vexholm contract was terminated and Baltic was declared bankrupt. Laval then sued the unions for damages. It questioned whether the MBL violated the directive or EC 49/TFEU 56. The ECJ first considered the effect of the directive and concluded that because it required only laws or collective agreements of general application to be applied to foreign seconded workers, it could not be held to apply to a situation where the rights and duties of employers and workers were governed by a collective agreement of the kind in issue here. Moreover, Swedish law did not lay down any minimum wage, so the directive's provisions on that issue were not applicable. It then went on to consider the impact of EC 49/TFEU 56 on two questions posed by the Swedish court.]

89. According to the observations of the Danish and Swedish Governments, the right to take collective action constitutes a fundamental right which, as such, falls outside the scope of Article 49 EC [56] and Directive 96/71.

90. In that regard, it must be recalled that the right to take collective action is recognised both by various international instruments which the Member States have signed or cooperated in. . . .

91. Although the right to take collective action must therefore be recognised as a fundamental right which forms an integral part of the general principles of Community law the observance of which the Court ensures, the exercise of that right may none the less be subject to certain restrictions. As is reaffirmed by Article 28 of the Charter of Fundamental Rights of the European Union, it is to be protected in accordance with Community law and national law and practices.

92. Although it is true, as the Swedish Government points out, that the right to take collective action enjoys constitutional protection in Sweden, as in other Member States, nevertheless . . . under the Swedish constitution, that right — which, in that Member State, covers the blockading of worksites — may be exercised unless otherwise provided by law or agreement.

93. In that regard, the Court has already held that the protection of fundamental rights is a legitimate interest which, in principle, justifies a restriction of the obligations imposed by Community law, even under a fundamental freedom guaranteed by the Treaty, such as the free movement of goods . . .

94. As the Court held, in Schmidberger and Omega, the exercise of the fundamental rights at issue, that is, freedom of expression and freedom of assembly and respect for human dignity, respectively, does not fall outside the scope of the provisions of the Treaty. Such exercise must be reconciled with the requirements relating to rights protected under the Treaty and in accordance with the principle of proportionality . . .

95. It follows from the foregoing that the fundamental nature of the right to take collective action is not such as to render Community law inapplicable to such action,

taken against an undertaking established in another Member State which posts workers in the framework of the transnational provision of services.

96. It must therefore be examined whether the fact that a Member State's trade unions may take collective action in the circumstances described above constitutes a restriction on the freedom to provide services, and, if so, whether it can be justified.

97. It should be noted that, in so far as it seeks to abolish restrictions on the freedom to provide services stemming from the fact that the service provider is established in a Member State other than that in which the service is to be provided, Article 49 EC [56] became directly applicable in the legal orders of the Member States on expiry of the transitional period and confers on individuals rights which are enforceable by them and which the national courts must protect . . .

98. Furthermore, compliance with Article 49 EC [56] is also required in the case of rules which are not public in nature but which are designed to regulate, collectively, the provision of services. The abolition, as between Member States, of obstacles to the freedom to provide services would be compromised if the abolition of State barriers could be neutralised by obstacles resulting from the exercise of their legal autonomy by associations or organisations not governed by public law . . .

99. In the case in the main proceedings, it must be pointed out that the right of trade unions of a Member State to take collective action by which undertakings established in other Member States may be forced to sign the collective agreement for the building sector — certain terms of which depart from the legislative provisions and establish more favourable terms and conditions of employment as regards the matters referred to in Article 3(1), first subparagraph, (a) to (g) of Directive 96/71 and others relate to matters not referred to in that provision — is liable to make it less attractive, or more difficult, for such undertakings to carry out construction work in Sweden, and therefore constitutes a restriction on the freedom to provide services within the meaning of Article 49 EC [56].

100. The same is all the more true of the fact that, in order to ascertain the minimum wage rates to be paid to their posted workers, those undertakings may be forced, by way of collective action, into negotiations with the trade unions of unspecified duration at the place at which the services in question are to be provided.

101. It is clear from the case-law of the Court that, since the freedom to provide services is one of the fundamental principles of the Community . . . a restriction on that freedom is warranted only if it pursues a legitimate objective compatible with the Treaty and is justified by overriding reasons of public interest; if that is the case, it must be suitable for securing the attainment of the objective which it pursues and not go beyond what is necessary in order to attain it . . .

102. The Swedish Government and the defendant trade unions in the main proceedings submit that the restrictions in question are justified, since they are necessary to ensure the protection of a fundamental right recognised by Community law and have as their objective the protection of workers, which constitutes an overriding reason of public interest.

103. In that regard, it must be pointed out that the right to take collective action for

the protection of the workers of the host State against possible social dumping may constitute an overriding reason of public interest within the meaning of the case-law of the Court which, in principle, justifies a restriction of one of the fundamental freedoms guaranteed by the Treaty . . .

104. It should be added that, according to Article 3(1)(c) and (j) EC [repealed], the activities of the Community are to include not only an 'internal market character-ised by the abolition, as between Member States, of obstacles to the free movement of goods, persons, services and capital', but also 'a policy in the social sphere'. Article 2 EC [3] states that the Community is to have as its task, inter alia, the promotion of 'a harmonious, balanced and sustainable development of economic activities' and 'a high level of employment and of social protection'.

105. Since the Community has thus not only an economic but also a social purpose, the rights under the provisions of the EC Treaty on the free movement of goods, persons, services and capital must be balanced against the objectives pursued by social policy, which include, as is clear from the first paragraph of Article 136 EC [151], inter alia, improved living and working conditions, so as to make possible their harmonisation while improvement is being maintained, proper social protection and dialogue between management and labour.

106. In the case in the main proceedings, Byggnads and Byggettan contend that the objective of the blockade carried out against Laval was the protection of workers.

107. In that regard, it must be observed that, in principle, blockading action by a trade union of the host Member State which is aimed at ensuring that workers posted in the framework of a transnational provision of services have their terms and conditions of employment fixed at a certain level, falls within the objective of protecting workers.

108. However, as regards the specific obligations, linked to signature of the collective agreement for the building sector, which the trade unions seek to impose on undertakings established in other Member States by way of collective action such as that at issue in the case in the main proceedings, the obstacle which that collective action forms cannot be justified with regard to such an objective. In addition to what is set out in paragraphs 81 and 83 of the present judgment, with regard to workers posted in the framework of a transnational provision of services, their employer is required, as a result of the coordination achieved by Directive 96/71, to observe a nucleus of mandatory rules for minimum protection in the host Member State.

109. Finally, as regards the negotiations on pay which the trade unions seek to impose, by way of collective action such as that at issue in the main proceedings, on undertakings, established in another Member State which post workers temporar-ily to their territory, it must be emphasised that Community law certainly does not prohibit Member States from requiring such undertakings to comply with their rules on minimum pay by appropriate means . . .

110. However, collective action such as that at issue in the main proceedings cannot be justified in the light of the public interest objective . . . . where the negotiations on pay, which that action seeks to require an undertaking established in another Member State to enter into, form part of a national context characterised by a lack

of provisions, of any kind, which are sufficiently precise and accessible that they do not render it impossible or excessively difficult in practice for such an undertaking to determine the obligations with which it is required to comply as regards minimum pay . . .

111. In the light of the foregoing, the answer to the first question must be that Article 49 EC [56] and Directive 96/71 are to be interpreted as precluding a trade union, in a Member State in which the terms and conditions of employment covering the matters referred to in Article 3(1), first subparagraph, (a) to (g) of that directive are contained in legislative provisions, save for minimum rates of pay, from attempting, by means of collective action in the form of a blockade ('blockad') of sites such as that at issue in the main proceedings, to force a provider of services established in another Member State to enter into negotiations with it on the rates of pay for posted workers and to sign a collective agreement the terms of which lay down, as regards some of those matters, more favourable conditions than those resulting from the relevant legislative provisions, while other terms relate to matters not referred to in Article 3 of the directive.

*   *   *

112. . . . . [T]he national court is [also] asking, in essence, whether, where there is a prohibition in a Member State against trade unions undertaking collective action with the aim of having a collective agreement between other parties set aside or amended, Articles 49 EC [56] and 50 EC [57] preclude that prohibition from being subject to the condition that such action must relate to terms and conditions of employment to which the national law applies directly, thereby making it impossible for an undertaking which posts workers to that Member State in the framework of the provision of services and which is bound by a collective agreement subject to the law of another Member State to enforce such a prohibition vis-à-vis those trade unions.

113. That question concerns the application of the provisions of the MBL which introduced a system to combat social dumping, pursuant to which a service provider is not entitled, in the Member State in which it provides its services, to expect any account to be taken of the obligations under collective agreements to which it is already subject in the Member State in which it is established. It follows from such a system that collective action is authorised against undertakings bound by a collective agreement subject to the law of another Member State in the same way as such action is authorised against undertakings which are not bound by any collective agreement.

114. It is clear from settled case-law that the freedom to provide services implies, in particular, the abolition of any discrimination against a service provider on account of its nationality or the fact that it is established in a Member State other than the one in which the service is provided . . .

115. It is also settled case-law that discrimination can arise only through the application of different rules to comparable situations or the application of the same rule to different situations . . .

116. In that regard, it must be pointed out that national rules, such as those at issue in the case in the main proceedings, which fail to take into account, irrespective of

their content, collective agreements to which undertakings that post workers to Sweden are already bound in the Member State in which they are established, give rise to discrimination against such undertakings, in so far as under those national rules they are treated in the same way as national undertakings which have not concluded a collective agreement.

117. It follows from Article 46 EC [52], which must be interpreted strictly, that discriminatory rules may be justified only on grounds of public policy, public security or public health . . .

118. It is clear from the order for reference that the application of those rules to foreign undertakings which are bound by collective agreements to which Swedish law does not directly apply is intended, first, to allow trade unions to take action to ensure that all employers active on the Swedish labour market pay wages and apply other terms and conditions of employment in line with those usual in Sweden, and secondly, to create a climate of fair competition, on an equal basis, between Swedish employers and entrepreneurs from other Member States.

119. Since none of the considerations referred to in the previous paragraph constitute grounds of public policy, public security or public health within the meaning of Article 46 EC [52], applied in conjunction with Article 55 EC [62], it must be held that discrimination such as that in the case in the main proceedings cannot be justified.

## NOTES AND QUESTIONS

1. The Court refers to "social dumping", a shorthand way of describing the practice by which a business in one Member State might import cheaper labor from another Member State to circumvent collective agreements and other labor arrangements. To what extent does the Court accept that national legislation to combat this practice is valid under EU law? Does the Court's view suggest a bias against Unions and workers' rights?

2. Consider the Court's response to the arguments made by the intervenors that the defendants were exercising fundamental rights that could not be overridden by the EC Treaty/TFEU? Does that response seem compatible with the earlier cases such as *Internationale Handelsgesellschaft* (Chapter 3), where the basic issue of the relationship of EU law with fundamental rights was first considered?

3. In *International Transport Workers' Federation, Finnish Seamen's Union, v. Viking Line ABP, OÜ Viking Line Eesti*, Case C–438/05, 2007 ECJ EUR-Lex LEXIS 2396, [2007] ECR I-10779, the Court held that the right to strike embedded in article 28 of the Charter did not prevail over the right of an employer to avail itself of EC 43/TFEU 49 (freedom of establishment). Here, a union representing seamen had sought to prevent the employer from transferring the registration of its vessels to another Member State. The Court stated:

> 44 Although the right to take collective action, including the right to strike, must therefore be recognised as a fundamental right which forms an integral part of the general principles of Community law the observance of which the Court ensures, the exercise of that right may none the less be

subject to certain restrictions. As is reaffirmed by Article 28 of the Charter of Fundamental Rights of the European Union, those rights are to be protected in accordance with Community law and national law and practices. In addition, as is apparent from paragraph 5 of this judgment, under Finnish law the right to strike may not be relied on, in particular, where the strike is *contra bonos mores* or is prohibited under national law or Community law.

45 In that regard, the Court has already held that the protection of fundamental rights is a legitimate interest which, in principle, justifies a restriction of the obligations imposed by Community law, even under a fundamental freedom guaranteed by the Treaty, such as the free movement of goods . . .

46 However, in *Schmidberger* and *Omega*, the Court held that the exercise of the fundamental rights at issue, that is, freedom of expression and freedom of assembly and respect for human dignity, respectively, does not fall outside the scope of the provisions of the Treaty and considered that such exercise must be reconciled with the requirements relating to rights protected under the Treaty and in accordance with the principle of proportionality (see, to that effect, *Schmidberger*, paragraph 77, and *Omega*, paragraph 36).

47 It follows from the foregoing that the fundamental nature of the right to take collective action is not such as to render Article 43 EC [49] inapplicable to the collective action at issue in the main proceedings.

See also *Finalarte Sociedade de Construção Civil Ld^a, Portugaia Construções Ld^a, and Engil Sociedade de Construção Civil SA v. Urlaubs- und Lohnausgleichskasse der Bauwirtschaft and Urlaubs- und Lohnausgleichskasse der Bauwirtschaft v. Amilcar Oliveira Rocha, Tudor Stone Ltd, Tecnamb-Tecnologia do Ambiante Ld^a, Turiprata Construções Civil Ld^a, Duarte dos Santos Sousa and Santos & Kewitz Construções Ld^a* Joined cases C-49/98, C-50/98, C-52/98 to C-54/98 and C-68/98 to C-71/98, 2001 ECJ EUR-Lex LEXIS 1016, [2001] ECR I-7831, where the Court again referenced the principle of proportionality as the guiding principle in balancing fundamental rights against EU free movement rights.

4.   The Charter provisions on solidarity were part of the reason why the UK obtained a sort of derogation in Protocol No. UK. UK law protecting collective action is quite weak compared with the laws of other Member States. The protocol provides (also in relation to Poland) that:

*Article 1*

1. The Charter does not extend the ability of the Court of Justice of the European Union, or any court or tribunal of Poland or of the United Kingdom, to find that the laws, regulations or administrative provisions, practices or action of Poland or of the United Kingdom are inconsistent with the fundamental rights, freedoms and principles that it reaffirms.

2. In particular, and for the avoidance of doubt, nothing in Title IV of the Charter creates justiciable rights applicable to Poland or the United

Kingdom except in so far as Poland or the United Kingdom has provided for such rights in its national law.

*Article 2*

To the extent that a provision of the Charter refers to national laws and practices, it shall only apply to Poland or the United Kingdom to the extent that the rights or principles that it contains are recognised in the law or practices of Poland or of the United Kingdom.

Given the Court's rulings on the application of general principles of law protecting fundamental rights (*Internationale Handelsgesellschaft*, Chapter 3, and *Hauer*, Chapter 4) does the exclusion actually have any significance? Does the first article mean that the Court would have to provide one interpretation for these two Member States and a different one for everyone else?

## § 20.05  JUSTICE

### [A]  Right to a Fair Trial and Effective Remedy

#### CRIMINAL PROCEEDINGS AGAINST MARIA PUPINO
Case C-105/03, 2005 ECJ CELEX LEXIS 774, [2005] ECR I-5285

[The reference in this case was made in the context of criminal proceedings against Mrs Pupino, a nursery school teacher charged with inflicting injuries on pupils aged less than five years at the time of the facts. At issue was the compatibility of Italian criminal procedure with a Framework Decision of the European Union. (Recall from Chapter 5 that Framework Decisions were adopted under the PJCC when it was still part of the TEU. They resembled directives but were not subject to ECJ interpretation except where the Member State had accepted such jurisdiction, and were not capable of having any direct effect. As a result of the removal of PJCC to the TFEU, EU action will in future proceed via directives.) The Public Prosecutor had asked the Court to take the evidence of eight victims under a special procedure available at the preliminary stage of a two part process whereby they could be questioned in special surroundings appropriate to their age. However, Mrs Pupino objected to this and the Court rejected the prosecutor's request because the special procedure only applied:

a) where there are reasonable grounds for believing that the witness cannot be heard in open court by reason of illness or serious impediment;

b) where, on the basis of specific facts, there are reasonable grounds for believing that the witness is vulnerable to violence, threats, offers or promises of money or other benefits, to induce him or her not to testify or to give false testimony.

The national court examined the Framework Decision and decided that it needed an interpretation from the ECJ on the possible impact of this act on the Italian law. It referenced the following provisions:

2. Each Member State shall ensure that victims who are particularly vulnerable can benefit from specific treatment best suited to their circumstances.'

3. Each Member State shall safeguard the possibility for victims to be heard during proceedings and to supply evidence. Each Member State shall take appropriate measures to ensure that its authorities question victims only insofar as necessary for the purpose of criminal proceedings.

\* \* \*

8. (4) Each Member State shall ensure that, where there is a need to protect victims — particularly those most vulnerable — from the effects of giving evidence in open court, victims may, by decision taken by the court, be entitled to testify in a manner which will enable this objective to be achieved, by any appropriate means compatible with its basic legal principles.]

The Framework Decision

6. Under Article 2 of the Framework Decision, headed Respect and recognition':

1. Each Member State shall ensure that victims have a real and appropriate role in its criminal legal system. It shall continue to make every effort to ensure that victims are treated with due respect for the dignity of the individual during proceedings and shall recognise the rights and legitimate interests of victims with particular reference to criminal proceedings.

2. Each Member State shall ensure that victims who are particularly vulnerable can benefit from specific treatment best suited to their circumstances.'

7. Article 3 of the Framework Decision, headed Hearings and provision of evidence' provides:

Each Member State shall safeguard the possibility for victims to be heard during proceedings and to supply evidence.

Each Member State shall take appropriate measures to ensure that its authorities question victims only insofar as necessary for the purpose of criminal proceedings.'

8. Article 8 of the Framework Decision, headed Right to protection', provides in paragraph 4:

Each Member State shall ensure that, where there is a need to protect victims — particularly those most vulnerable — from the effects of giving evidence in open court, victims may, by decision taken by the court, be entitled to testify in a manner which will enable this objective to be achieved, by any appropriate means compatible with its basic legal principles.'

9. Under Article 17 of the Framework Decision, each Member State is required to bring into force the laws, regulations and administrative provisions necessary to comply with the Framework Decision not later than 22 March 2002'.

National legislation

10. [The Italian Code of Criminal Procedure; the CPP'] . . . provides:

1. During the preliminary enquiry, the Public Prosecutor's Office and the person being examined may ask the judge to take evidence under special arrangements:

a) where there are reasonable grounds for believing that the witness cannot be heard in open court by reason of illness or serious impediment;

b) where, on the basis of specific facts, there are reasonable grounds for believing that the witness is vulnerable to violence, threats, offers or promises of money or other benefits, to induce him or her not to testify or to give false testimony.

*    *    *

11. Under Article 398(5a) of the CPP:

. . . [W]here the evidence involves minors under 16, the judge shall determine by order the place, time and particular circumstances for hearing evidence where a minor's situation makes it appropriate and necessary. In such cases, the hearing can be held in a place other than the court, in special facilities or, failing that, at the minor's home. The witness statements must be fully documented by the use of sound and audiovisual recording equipment. Where recording equipment or technical personnel are not available, the judge shall use the expert report or technical advice procedures. The interview shall also be minuted. The recordings shall be transcribed only at the request of the parties.'

Factual background and the question referred

12. The order for reference shows that, in the criminal proceedings against Mrs Pupino, it is alleged that, in January and February 2001, she committed several offences of misuse of disciplinary measures' within the meaning of Article 571 of the Italian Criminal Code (the CP') against a number of her pupils aged less than five years at the time, by such acts as regularly striking them, threatening to give them tranquillisers and to put sticking plasters over their mouths, and forbidding them from going to the toilet. She is further charged that, in February 2001, she inflicted serious injuries', as referred to in Articles 582, 585 and 576 of the CP, in conjunction with Article 61(2) and (11) thereof, by hitting a pupil in such a way as to cause a slight swelling of the forehead. The proceedings before the Tribunale di Firenze are at the preliminary enquiry stage.

*    *    *

50. By its question, the national court essentially asks whether, on a proper interpretation of Articles 2, 3 and 8(4) of the Framework Decision, a national court must be able to authorise young children, who, as in this case, claim to have been victims of maltreatment, to give their testimony in accordance with arrangements ensuring them an appropriate level of protection, outside the public trial and before it is held.

51. Article 3 of the Framework Decision requires each Member State to safeguard the possibility for victims to be heard during proceedings and to supply evidence,

and to take appropriate measures to ensure that its authorities question victims only insofar as necessary for the purpose of criminal proceedings.

52. Articles 2 and 8(4) of the Framework Decision require each Member State to make every effort to ensure that victims are treated with due respect for their personal dignity during proceedings, to ensure that particularly vulnerable victims benefit from specific treatment best suited to their circumstances, and to ensure that where there is a need to protect victims, particularly those most vulnerable, from the effects of giving evidence in open court, victims may, by decision taken by the court, be entitled to testify in a manner enabling that objective to be achieved, by any appropriate means compatible with its basic legal principles.

53. The Framework Decision does not define the concept of a victim's vulnerability for the purposes of Articles 2(2) and 8(4). However, independently of whether a victim's minority is as a general rule sufficient to classify such a victim as particularly vulnerable within the meaning of the Framework Decision, it cannot be denied that where, as in this case, young children claim to have been maltreated, and maltreated, moreover, by a teacher, those children are suitable for such classification having regard in particular to their age and to the nature and consequences of the offences of which they consider themselves to have been victims, with a view to benefiting from the specific protection required by the provisions of the Framework Decision referred to above.

54. None of the three provisions of the Framework Decision referred to by the national court lays down detailed rules for implementing the objectives which they state, and which consist, in particular, in ensuring that particularly vulnerable victims receive specific treatment best suited to their circumstances', and the benefit of special hearing arrangements that are capable of guaranteeing to all victims treatment which pays due respect to their individual dignity and gives them the opportunity to be heard and to supply evidence, and in ensuring that those victims are questioned only insofar as necessary for the purpose of criminal proceedings'.

55. Under the legislation at issue in the main proceedings, testimony given during the preliminary enquiries must generally be repeated at the trial in order to acquire full evidential value. It is, however, permissible in certain cases to give that testimony only once, during the preliminary enquiries, with the same probative value, but under different arrangements from those which apply at the trial.

56. In those circumstances, achievement of the aims pursued by the abovementioned provisions of the framework decision require that a national court should be able, in respect of particularly vulnerable victims, to use a special procedure, such as the Special Inquiry for early gathering of evidence provided for in the law of a Member State, and the special arrangements for hearing testimony for which provision is also made, if that procedure best corresponds to the situation of those victims and is necessary in order to prevent the loss of evidence, to reduce the repetition of questioning to a minimum, and to prevent the damaging consequences, for those victims, of their giving testimony at the trial.

57. It should be noted in that respect that, according to Article 8(4) of the Framework Decision, the conditions for giving testimony that are adopted must in

any event be compatible with the basic legal principles of the Member State concerned.

58. Moreover, in accordance with Article 6(2) EU, the Union must respect fundamental rights, as guaranteed by the European Convention for the Protection of Human Rights and Fundamental Freedoms signed in Rome on 4 November 1950 (the Convention'), and as they result from the constitutional traditions common to the Member States, as general principles of law.

59. The Framework Decision must thus be interpreted in such a way that fundamental rights, including in particular the right to a fair trial as set out in Article 6 of the Convention and interpreted by the European Court of Human Rights, are respected.

60. It is for the national court to ensure that — assuming use of the Special Inquiry and of the special arrangements for the hearing of testimony under Italian law is possible in this case, bearing in mind the obligation to give national law a conforming interpretation — the application of those measures is not likely to make the criminal proceedings against Mrs Pupino, considered as a whole, unfair within the meaning of Article 6 of the Convention, as interpreted by the European Court of Human Rights . . .

61. In the light of all the above considerations, the answer to the question must be that Articles 2, 3 and 8(4) of the Framework Decision must be interpreted as meaning that the national court must be able to authorise young children, who, as in this case, claim to have been victims of maltreatment, to give their testimony in accordance with arrangements allowing those children to be guaranteed an appropriate level of protection, for example outside the trial and before it takes place. The national court is required to take into consideration all the rules of national law and to interpret them, so far as possible, in the light of the wording and purpose of the Framework Decision.

## NOTES AND QUESTIONS

1.   Does the Court provide any useful guidance to the national court here regarding the application of fundamental rights?

2.   What consequences might have ensued if the Court had found the Framework Decision to be incompatible with the principles set out in the European Convention?

## [B]   Double Jeopardy

### CRIMINAL PROCEEDINGS AGAINST LEOPOLD HENRI VAN ESBROECK.
Case C-436/04, 2006 ECJ CELEX LEXIS 576, [2006] ECR I-2333

[Mr Van Esbroeck, a Belgian national, was sentenced by a court in Bergen, Norway to five years' imprisonment for illegally importing, on 1 June 1999, narcotic drugs (amphetamines, cannabis, MDMA and diazepam) into Norway. After having served part of his sentence, Mr Van Esbroeck was released conditionally on 8 February 2002 and escorted back to Belgium. On 27 November 2002, a prosecution was brought against Mr Van Esbroeck in Belgium, as a result of which he was sentenced to one year's imprisonment, in particular for illegally exporting the above listed products from Belgium on 31 May 1999. That judgment was upheld on appeal. The courts applied Article 36(2)(a) of the Convention implementing the Schengen Agreement, according to which each of the offences enumerated in that article, which include the import and export of narcotic drugs, are to be regarded as a distinct offence if committed in different countries. The defendant lodged an appeal on a point of law against that judgment and pleaded infringement of the ne bis in idem principle, enshrined in Article 54 of the Convention implementing the Schengen Agreement (OJ 2000 L 239) ("CISA"). The CISA became part of EU Law for the then 13 fully participating states pursuant to Protocol No 1 of the Amsterdam Treaty, while articles 54 and 71 were enacted on the basis of articles 31, 32 and 34 TEU. Other states including Norway subsequently acceded to the CISA.]

25. By the second question the national court is effectively asking what the relevant criterion is for the purposes of the application of the concept of the same acts' within the meaning of Article 54 of the CISA and, more precisely, whether the unlawful acts of exporting from one Contracting State and importing into another the same narcotic drugs as those which gave rise to the criminal proceedings in the two States concerned are covered by that concept.

26. In that regard, the Czech Government submitted that identity of the acts means identity of their legal classification and of the protected legal interests.

27. In the first place, however, the wording of Article 54 of the CISA, "the same acts", shows that that provision refers only to the nature of the acts in dispute and not to their legal classification.

28. It must also be noted that the terms used in that article differ from those used in other international treaties which enshrine the ne bis in idem principle. Unlike Article 54 of the CISA, Article 14(7) of the International Covenant on Civil and Political Rights and Article 4 of Protocol No 7 to the European Convention for the Protection of Human Rights and Fundamental Freedoms use the term offence', which implies that the criterion of the legal classification of the acts is relevant as a prerequisite for the applicability of the ne bis in idem principle which is enshrined in those treaties.

29. . . . . . [N]owhere in Title VI of the Treaty on European Union relating to police and judicial cooperation in criminal matters (Articles 34 and 31 of which were stated to be the legal basis for Articles 54 to 58 of the CISA), or in the Schengen Agreement or the CISA itself, is the application of Article 54 of the CISA made conditional upon characterization, or at the least approximation, of the criminal laws of the Member States.

30. There is a necessary implication in the ne bis in idem principle, enshrined in that article, that the Contracting States have mutual trust in their criminal justice systems and that each of them characterises the criminal law in force in the other Contracting States even when the outcome would be different if its own national law were applied . . .

31. It follows that the possibility of divergent legal classifications of the same acts in two different Contracting States is no obstacle to the application of Article 54 of the CISA.

32. For the same reasons, the criterion of the identity of the protected legal interest cannot be applicable since that criterion is likely to vary from one Contracting State to another.

33. The above findings are further reinforced by the objective of Article 54 of the CISA, which is to ensure that no one is prosecuted for the same acts in several Contracting States on account of his having exercised his right to freedom of movement . . .

34. As pointed out by the Advocate General in point 45 of his Opinion, that right to freedom of movement is effectively guaranteed only if the perpetrator of an act knows that, once he has been found guilty and served his sentence, or, where applicable, been acquitted by a final judgment in a Member State, he may travel within the Schengen territory without fear of prosecution in another Member State on the basis that the legal system of that Member State treats the act concerned as a separate offence.

35. Because there is no characterization of national criminal laws, a criterion based on the legal classification of the acts or on the protected legal interest might create as many barriers to freedom of movement within the Schengen territory as there are penal systems in the Contracting States.

36. In those circumstances, the only relevant criterion for the application of Article 54 of the CISA is identity of the material acts, understood in the sense of the existence of a set of concrete circumstances which are inextricably linked together.

37. As regards, more particularly, a situation such as that at issue in the main proceedings, it must be observed that such a situation may, in principle, constitute a set of facts which, by their very nature, are inextricably linked.

38. However, the definitive assessment in that regard belongs, as rightly pointed out by the Netherlands Government, to the competent national courts which are charged with the task of determining whether the material acts at issue constitute a set of facts which are inextricably linked together in time, in space and by their subject-matter.

39. Contrary to the submissions made by the Slovak Government, that interpretation can be reconciled with Article 71 of the CISA which provides for the adoption, by the Contracting States, of all the measures necessary to combat illegal trafficking of narcotic drugs.

40. As rightly submitted by the Netherlands Government, the CISA does not lay down an order of priority amongst the different provisions, and, in addition, Article 71 of the Convention does not contain any element which might restrict the scope of Article 54, which enshrines, within the Schengen territory, the ne bis in idem principle, which is characterized in the case-law as a fundamental principle of Community law . . .

41. It follows that the reference made in Article 71 of the CISA to existing United

Nations Conventions cannot be understood as hindering the application of the ne bis in idem principle laid down in Article 54 of the CISA, which prevents only the plurality of proceedings against a person for the same acts and does not lead to characterization within the Schengen territory.

42. In the light of the above, the answer to the second question must be that Article 54 of the CISA must be interpreted as meaning that:

- the relevant criterion for the purposes of the application of that article of the CISA is identity of the material acts, understood as the existence of a set of facts which are inextricably linked together, irrespective of the legal classification given to them or the legal interest protected;

- punishable acts consisting of exporting and importing the same narcotic drugs and which are prosecuted in different Contracting States to the CISA are, in principle, to be regarded as the same acts' for the purposes of Article 54 of the Convention, the definitive assessment in that respect being the task of the competent national courts.

## NOTES AND QUESTIONS

1.   The Court refers to the concern that, if the same act could give rise to different criminal characterizations in different Member States, this would impair free movement of persons. This seems to make sense for the purpose of the Schengen arrangements, but does it pose a threat to the cultural diversity of the Member States? There might be quite different perceptions of the seriousness of a crime and how it should be punished.

2.   Prior to Lisbon, the Council had been adopting Framework Decisions relating to criminal matters at a rapid rate. In 2008, seven were adopted in November/December covering the definition of organized crime, standards for criminalization of expressions of racism and xenophobia, terrorism, protection of personal data in the context of police and judicial cooperation, evidence warrants, and mutual recognition of judgments imposing custodial sentences, as well as probation measures and alternative sanctions. Future measures, of course, will be in the form of directives.

# RELATIONS BETWEEN THE MEMBER STATES

# Chapter 21

# DUTIES OF COOPERATION AMONG THE MEMBER STATES

## § 21.01  OVERVIEW

*Template*: Article 9

***Some general comments on Part VII and Template Article 9*** In the United States Constitution, there is very little that addresses the relationships between States. The most notable example is Article IV, Sections 1 and 2, addressing respectively requiring that full faith and credit be accorded to official and judicial proceedings of other states and the obligation of extradition between states. In other respects the Constitution is focused on establishing the federal government.

In the European Union, by contrast, and as already noted in Chapter 2 *supra*, the Treaties recognize the continued existence of the Member States as sovereign states under international law where the principal areas of sovereign power — taxation, public order, justice and defense — remain predominantly matters for the Member States. Yet, as these areas interact in increasingly fundamental ways with the scope of Union powers, it is not surprising that the Treaties have begun to address them and even to open up the possibilities of greater Union involvement or substitution.

***Cooperation in economic relations*** There is probably no greater topical illustration of continuing Member State powers than in the area of economic policy. As indicated in Section 9.3 of the Template, economic policy remains a Member State competence, with only a weak obligation of coordination. As indicated in Chapter 7, this is mirrored by a Union competence to facilitate such coordination. Admittedly, the eurozone members were obliged to observe the Stability and Growth Pact (EC 104/TFEU 126 adopted to form the basis of economic cohesion, but when both France and Germany themselves violated it in 2003, it became evident that neither was prepared to endorse legal proceedings against the other in the Council. The Commission sued the Council to try to enforce the Pact (*Commission v. Council*, Case 27/04, [2004] ECR I-6649), but the Court sidestepped the issue by holding that the Council had discretion whether to act or not, at least in the short term. The upshot was an amendment to the Pact confirming it was essentially unenforceable and thereby reemphasizing the sovereignty of the Member States over economic policy.

What of the effect of TEU 4 in this area? This states the basic requirement that, in accordance with the principle of sincere cooperation, the Member States will assist each other in carrying out "tasks arising under the Treaties". (This is a separate obligation from the sincere cooperation owed to *the Union* itself, which was used so effectively by the ECJ in developing the system of remedies in state courts for breaches of EU law — *Von Colson* — addressed in Chapter 9.) The duty of the Member States to each other seems too vague a provision to have any independent force on its own, but at the same time it does underpin the concept that the Member States are required to support each other in a general sense in all matters, including economic policy. One may therefore wonder whether it might be of some influence in dealing with the prolonged crisis affecting the eurozone, which (as of the time of writing) is suffering from the absence of fiscal cohesion. In that regard, there is arguably some doubt as to the legality of positions taken by Member States such as the UK that have been unwilling to provide financial support for measures taken by eurozone states. This is admittedly a political issue that is not capable of solution through any legal process, however much the legal arguments might look appealing. At the same time, it seems likely that the powers of the Member States using the euro will need to be progressively subordinated to Union action if the eurozone is to be preserved.

The EU sovereign debt crisis of 2008/9 forced action by the Member States in the field of economic policy, demonstrating dramatically the linkage between fiscal and monetary affairs. In response to that crisis, the Member States decided to create a "bailout facility", in its permanent form to be called the European Stability Mechanism (ESM). Given the prohibition of such action under EC 105/TFEU 125, the ESM proposal (intended to be operational by July 2013) required an amendment to the TFEU under the procedure laid down in TEU 48(6) and required ratification by all Member States:

DECISION 2011/199/EU OF THE EUROPEAN COUNCIL,

. . .

Whereas:

(1) Article 48(6) of the Treaty on European Union (TEU) allows the European Council, acting by unanimity after consulting the European Parliament, the Commission and, in certain cases, the European Central Bank, to adopt a decision amending all or part of the provisions of Part Three of the Treaty on the Functioning of the European Union (TFEU). Such a decision may not increase the competences conferred on the Union in the Treaties and its entry into force is conditional upon its subsequent approval by the Member States in accordance with their respective constitutional requirements.

(2) At the meeting of the European Council of 28 and 29 October 2010, the Heads of State or Government agreed on the need for Member States to establish a permanent crisis mechanism to safeguard the financial stability of the euro area as a whole and invited the President of the European Council to undertake consultations with the members of the European Council on a limited treaty change required to that effect.

(3) On 16 December 2010, the Belgian Government submitted, in accordance with Article 48(6), first subparagraph, of the TEU, a proposal for revising Article 136 of the TFEU by adding a paragraph under which the

Member States whose currency is the euro may establish a stability mechanism to be activated if indispensable to safeguard the stability of the euro area as a whole and stating that the granting of any required financial assistance under the mechanism will be made subject to strict conditionality. At the same time, the European Council adopted conclusions about the future stability mechanism (paragraphs 1 to 4).

(4) The stability mechanism will provide the necessary tool for dealing with such cases of risk to the financial stability of the euro area as a whole as have been experienced in 2010, and hence help preserve the economic and financial stability of the Union itself. At its meeting of 16 and 17 December 2010, the European Council agreed that, as this mechanism is designed to safeguard the financial stability of the euro area as whole, Article 122(2) of the TFEU will no longer be needed for such purposes. The Heads of State or Government therefore agreed that it should not be used for such purposes.

(5) On 16 December 2010, the European Council decided to consult, in accordance with Article 48(6), second subparagraph, of the TEU, the European Parliament and the Commission, on the proposal. It also decided to consult the European Central Bank. The European Parliament, the Commission and the European Central Bank, respectively, adopted opinions on the proposal.

(6) The amendment concerns a provision contained in Part Three of the TFEU and it does not increase the competences conferred on the Union in the Treaties,

HAS ADOPTED THIS DECISION:

## Article 1

The following paragraph shall be added to Article 136 of the Treaty on the Functioning of the European Union:

"3. The Member States whose currency is the euro may establish a stability mechanism to be activated if indispensable to safeguard the stability of the euro area as a whole. The granting of any required financial assistance under the mechanism will be made subject to strict conditionality.". . . .

This measure once again emphasizes that in the field of economic policy, it is the Member States who have the competence. Yet, given the ability to impose strict conditions, its use is likely to put the budgetary and financial policy of the Member States who participate in the euro under intense scrutiny, thus in a practical sense seriously undermining their economic sovereignty and independence. It is unclear, at this stage, whether the intense focus on government borrowing and spending will fade away once the EU sovereign debt crisis ends — or, as some experts believe, once the euro collapses — or whether the EU sovereign debt crisis sets the stage for a new area of EU construction in which the Member States will eventually have to transfer their economic and financial competences to the EU. This could, for example, involve a Union tax on financial transactions and harmonization of corporation tax.

***Cooperation in Justice and public order*** In Chapter 2 it was noted that one of the significant areas of responsibility transferred from the TEU to the TFEU by the Lisbon Treaty was Union action to support justice and police cooperation. This suggests a dramatic shift in the scope of Union activity from a largely economic focus to internal affairs in general — the area of freedom, security and justice (AFSJ). However, while the Union is given real powers in this area, TFEU 81-89 are all based on promoting *cooperation among the Member States*. These provisions therefore might be seen as a concrete example of the general obligation of sincere cooperation mentioned above. They could result in or necessitate harmonization of laws, but such efforts are designed to support continued *national* administration by ensuring that national law enforcement is not subverted by the loss of ability of national authorities to control the movement of people, goods and capital within the territory covered by the Union. Mutual recognition of criminal procedures and enforcement is a key element.

Similarly, in the area of civil law, the TFEU provisions are designed primarily to give the Union power to promote the national administration of justice through the recognition and enforcement of judgments. The Treaties themselves have never contained anything equivalent as such to the "full faith and credit" clause of Article IV, Section 1 of the United States Constitution, although TEU 4 has sometimes been argued to have a role here. However, as noted above, the second sentence of the U.S. Full Faith and Credit clause — granting powers to the Congress to make laws — is somewhat reflected in what is now TFEU 81.

EU action in this area began with the so-called Brussels Convention of 1968 and has now been supplanted by EU regulations, notably Regulation 44/2000 on the Recognition and Enforcement of Judgments in Civil and Commercial Matters. There is a significant body of case law under these measures now, which deserves separate treatment outside the scope of this work. The casebook by Bermann, Goebel, Davey and Fox mentioned in the reading materials in Chapter 2 is recommended on this subject. Some aspects of this legislation will likely have effects on matters arising under Union law, including the developing area of civil damages actions for breach of the competition rules, quite likely involving choices of venue and applicable law. This subject thus connects back to questions in this regard raised in Chapter 9 and is not dealt with separately here.

***Materials in this Chapter*** As noted above, Member States continue to have full sovereign state status, act in international organizations, enter into treaties and the like, even among themselves. This of course looks a very strange situation for those familiar with conventional federal structures and does create some quite unique legal issues.

This chapter explores various aspects of the public international law consequences of this situation. This phenomenon triggers a number of interactions with the Union and Treaty obligations in the context of public international law:

- In what ways do the obligations under the Treaties change the way in which international law governs relations between the States?

- Do pre-existing international treaty obligations undertaken by the Member States continue to apply in their relations with third countries? What happens if they conflict with EU law?

- Disputes between Member States

The Chapter also provides an illustration of the duties of cooperation under the AFSJ.

## § 21.02   APPLICATION OF INTERNATIONAL LAW TO INTER-STATE RELATIONS

### COMMISSION v. LUXEMBOURG AND BELGIUM
#### (MILK PRODUCTS)
Joined Cases 90, 91/63, [1964] ECR 625
[No paragraph numbering appears in the original]

[After complaining for several years to no avail, the Commission brought an article 226 action claiming that a new tax on the import of certain milk products, levied by Belgium and Luxembourg in 1958, constituted an infringement of article 12 [25], the so-called "standstill" provision barring the introduction of new customs duties on intra-EU trade. Belgium and Luxembourg admitted they had violated article 12[25] but attempted to justify the tax on the ground it was necessary to protect their markets. They pointed out that the EU had failed to create in due time a market organization under the Common Agricultural Policy for the milk products at issue.]

The defendants, arguing that the application is inadmissible, complain that the Community failed to comply with the obligations falling on it by reason of the Resolution of the Council of 4 April 1962, and was thus responsible for the continuance of the alleged infringement of the Treaty, which should have ceased before the issue of the reasoned opinion under Article 169 [226]. In their view, since international law allows a party, injured by the failure of another party to perform its obligations, to withhold performance of its own, the Commission has lost the right to plead infringement of the Treaty. However this relationship between the obligations of parties cannot be recognized under Community law.

In fact the Treaty is not limited to creating reciprocal obligations between the different natural and legal persons to whom it is applicable, but establishes a new legal order which governs the powers, rights and obligations of the said persons, as well as the necessary procedures for taking cognizance of and penalizing any breach of it. Therefore, except where otherwise expressly provided, the basic concept of the Treaty requires that the Member States shall not take the law into their own hands. Therefore the fact that the Council failed to carry out its obligations cannot relieve the defendants from carrying out theirs.

The application is therefore admissible.

[The Court ruled for the Commission on the merits of the case]

# COMMISSION v. FRANCE
## (MUTTON AND LAMB)
### Case 232/78, [1979] ECR 2729

[The Commission sought a declaration that the French Republic, by continuing . . . to apply its restrictive national system to the importation of mutton and lamb from the United Kingdom, has failed to fulfil its obligations under EC 25/TFEU 30 and under EC 28/TFEU 34.]

6 The French Government does not dispute the fact that this system is incompatible with the Treaty provisions relating to the elimination of obstacles to the free movement of goods within the Community. However, with a view to justifying the maintenance of this system and its application to imports of mutton and lamb from the United Kingdom it puts forward in substance three arguments. First it emphasizes the serious social and economic effects on the economy of certain economically less-favoured areas for which sheep-rearing is an important source of wealth, of discontinuing the national organization of the market. Secondly, it draws attention to the progress made in the work being carried out with a view to setting up a common organization of the market in mutton and lamb and stresses the harmful effects of interposing a phase of free trade between the discontinuance of the national organization and replacing it by a common organization. Finally it points to the inequality in the field of competition deriving from the fact that it would have to abolish its own organization of the market even though in the United Kingdom a national organization of the market based on the system of "deficiency payments", which results in subsidizing exports of mutton and lamb to France, would remain intact in the sector under consideration.

7 Although the Court is aware of the genuine problems which the French authorities have to solve in the sector under consideration and of the desirability of achieving the establishment, in the shortest possible time, of a common organization of the market in mutton and lamb, it must again draw attention to the fact that, . . . after the expiration of the transitional period of the EEC Treaty, and, as far as the new Member States are concerned, after the expiration of the time-limits for the transition specifically provided for in the Act of Accession, a national organization of the market must no longer operate in such a way as to prevent the Treaty provisions relating to the elimination of restrictions on intra-Community trade from having full force and effect, since the Community institutions are henceforth responsible for the requirements of the markets concerned. The expiration of the time-limits for the transition implies therefore that those matters and sectors specifically assigned to the Community are the responsibility of the Community so that, although it is still necessary to take special measures, a decision to adopt them can no longer be made unilaterally by the Member States concerned; they must be adopted within the Community system which is designed to guarantee that the general public interest of the Community is protected.

8 Consequently it is for the competent institutions and for them alone to adopt within the appropriate periods the requisite measures with a view to finding, in a Community context, a comprehensive solution of the problem of the market in mutton and lamb and of the special difficulties which arise in this connection in certain areas. Nevertheless, the fact that this work has not yet been successful is

not a sufficient justification for the maintenance by a Member State of a national organization of the market which includes features which are incompatible with the requirements of the Treaty relating to the free movement of goods, such as bans on imports and levying dues on imported products, under any designation whatsoever.

9 The French Republic cannot justify the existence of such a system with the argument that the United Kingdom, for its part, has maintained a national organization of the market in the same sector. If the French Republic is of the opinion that that system contains features which are incompatible with Community law it has the opportunity to take action, either within the Council, or through the Commission, or finally by recourse to judicial remedies with a view to achieving the elimination of such incompatible features. A Member State cannot under any circumstances unilaterally adopt, on its own authority, corrective measures or measures to protect trade designed to prevent any failure on the part of another Member State to comply with the rules laid down by the Treaty.

10 The Court must therefore conclude that the national organization of the market in mutton and lamb maintained by the French authorities is incompatible with the Treaty.

## NOTES AND QUESTIONS

**1.** In the above two cases, did the ECJ in any sense consider general international law principles to be part of EU Law?

**2.** In the early case of *Fédération Charbonnière de Belgique v. High Authority*, 8/55 [1954-56] ECR 245, the ECJ had resort to "a rule of interpretation generally accepted in both international and national law". It might be argued that cases arising under the ECSC Treaty may be relevant today, given the similarities in a narrower field with the EC Treaty. However, its narrow scope would have likely caused the ECJ to look for principles of interpretation wherever they may exist whilst in the EU the autonomy of the system can cause such interpretative techniques to be redundant. Do you agree?

**3.** In its approach to interpretation, the European Court of Justice has tended to develop its own methodology. This would have been inevitable even if there had been a common law influence from the outset because the Treaties were, after all, creative of public international law. Common lawyers, therefore, would probably have favored the use of traditional public international law interpretative technique. The Court of Justice, however, while starting from that point, rapidly moved in new directions, drawing heavily on the various techniques used in domestic civil law systems to fill out apparent gaps in the civil codes. The Court has used a variety of interpretative techniques.

Note that in *Fédération Charbonnière*, the Court of Justice was asked whether the High Authority had price fixing powers beyond those specifically set out in the Treaty. The Advocate General argued that "although the Treaty . . . was concluded in the form of an international treaty and although it unquestionably is one, it is nevertheless, from a material point of view, the charter of the Community, since the rules of law which derive from it constitute the internal law of that Community." [1954-1956] ECR at 277. Thus he concluded that it was the responsibility of the

High Authority to "ensure that the objectives set out in this Treaty are attained" and that consequently article 8 ECSC permitted it to set prices, a result that the Court confirmed.

## § 21.03 DUTY OF COOPERATION IN ADJUSTING EXISTING TREATY RELATIONS WITH THIRD COUNTRIES

### BUDEJOVICKY BUDVAR, NARODN I PODNIK v. RUDOLF AMMERSIN GMBH
Case C-216/01, 2003 ECJ CELEX LEXIS 399, [2003] ECR I-13617

[Budjovicky Budvar, narodn i podnik ("Budvar"), a brewery established in the town of eske Budjovice (Czech Republic), sought an injunction against Rudolf Ammersin GmbH ("Ammersin"), a company established in Vienna (Austria) which ran a drink distribution business, prohibiting Ammersin from marketing beer produced by the brewery Anheuser-Busch Inc. ("Anheuser-Busch"), established in Saint Louis (United States), under the name American Bud on the ground that, pursuant to various bilateral agreements between the Czech Republic and the Republic of Austria, in that Member State the name "Bud" is reserved for beer produced in the Czech Republic. A bilateral convention between the former Czechoslovakia and Austria had been entered into before Austria acceded to the EC Treaty. The Convention required Parties to assure exclusive use for designations of origin. One question that had to be answered was whether or to what extent Austria, having become in the meantime a Member State, could apply the Convention requirement notwithstanding that it would otherwise be in breach of TFEU 34.]

144. It follows from the first paragraph of Article 307 EC [351] that rights and obligations under an agreement concluded between a Member State and a non-member country before the date of accession of that Member State are not affected by the Treaty provisions.

145. The purpose of that provision is to make clear, in accordance with the principles of international law, that application of the EC Treaty does not affect the duty of the Member State concerned to respect the rights of non-member countries under an earlier agreement and to perform its obligations thereunder . . .

146. Consequently, in order to determine whether a Community rule may be deprived of effect by an earlier international agreement, it is necessary to examine whether that agreement imposes on the Member State concerned obligations whose performance may still be required by the non-member country which is party to it . . .

147. In the present case, it is common ground that protection of the name Bud is provided for by the bilateral instruments at issue, which were concluded between the Czechoslovak Socialist Republic and the Republic of Austria well before the latter's accession to the European Union.

148. It also appears from the bilateral instruments at issue, in particular Article 7(1) of the bilateral convention, that they impose on the Republic of Austria obligations

whose performance could have been required by the Czechoslovak Socialist Republic.

149. However, the question arises whether under those instruments the Czech Republic has acquired rights which it can still require the Republic of Austria to respect.

150. It should be recalled that following its break-up on 1 January 1993, the Czech and Slovak Federative Republic, which had itself replaced the Czechoslovak Socialist Republic, ceased to exist and that two new independent States, namely the Czech Republic and the Slovak Republic, succeeded it on the respective parts of its territory.

151. The question therefore arises whether, in the context of such a succession of States, the bilateral instruments at issue concluded by the Czechoslovak Socialist Republic remained in force following the break-up of the Czech and Slovak Federative Republic, in particular with respect to rights inuring to the benefit of the Czech Republic, such as the ones at issue in the main proceedings, with the effect that those rights and the corresponding obligations on the Republic of Austria remained in force after that break-up and were consequently still in force at the date of the Republic of Austria's accession to the European Union.

152. It is common ground that at the date of the break-up, there was a widely accepted international practice based on the principle of the continuity of treaties. According to that practice, unless one of the State parties to a bilateral agreement indicates its intention to renegotiate or denounce the agreement, the agreement is considered in principle to remain in force in relation to the States succeeding the State which has broken up.

153. At least as far as concerns the specific case of the complete break-up of States, and notwithstanding the possibility of denouncing or renegotiating agreements, it is apparent that the principle of the continuity of treaties, thus understood, constitutes a reference principle which was widely accepted at the time of the break-up in question.

154. In any event, and without there being any need for the Court to decide the question whether at the time of the break-up of the Czech and Slovak Federative Republic that principle of the continuity of treaties was a customary rule of international law, it cannot be denied that application of that principle in the international practice of the law of treaties was, at that time, fully consistent with international law.

155. In those circumstances, it must be ascertained whether both the Republic of Austria and the Czech Republic actually intended to apply the principle of the continuity of treaties to the bilateral instruments at issue and whether there is any evidence of their intentions in that regard during the period between the date of the break-up and that of the Republic of Austria's accession to the European Union.

156. As is clear from, in particular, the resolution of the Czech National Council of 17 December 1992 and from Article 5 of Constitutional Law No 4/1993 . . . the Czech Republic expressly accepted the principle of the automatic continuity of treaties.

157. As to the Republic of Austria's position, it appears traditionally to have advocated what is known as the "tabula rasa "principle, whereby, with the exception of treaties relating to territory or cases where there is an express agreement to the contrary, the succession of a new State to a contracting State automatically results in the expiry of the treaties concluded by the latter.

158. However, the question arises whether in a situation of succession of States such as that resulting from the complete break-up of the former State and, in particular, in relation to the bilateral instruments at issue, the Republic of Austria intended to apply the principle referred to in the preceding paragraph of this judgment.

159. . . . [I]t seems clear from both the case-law of the Austrian courts and the fact that, in particular in relation to the Czech Republic, the Republic of Austria denounced certain agreements concluded with the Czechoslovak Socialist Republic, but solely with regard to the future, that there are indications in the approach of that Member State, also during the period between the break-up of the Czech and Slovak Federative Republic and the Republic of Austria's accession to the European Union, to show that it had moved away from applying the "tabula rasa" principle.

160. The Austrian practice as regards the States succeeding the Czech and Slovak Federative Republic seems to be based on a pragmatic approach, according to which bilateral agreements remain in force unless they have been denounced by one or other of the parties. Such an approach leads to results which are very similar to those resulting from application of the principle of the continuity of treaties.

161. In that regard, it is for the national court to ascertain whether, at any time between the break-up of the Czech and Slovak Federative Republic, which took place on 1 January 1993, and the Federal Chancellor's communication in 1997, the Republic of Austria indicated its intention to renegotiate or denounce the bilateral instruments at issue.

162. If confirmed by the national court, that would be particularly significant because, as has been pointed out in paragraph 156 above, at the time of the break-up of its predecessor State, the Czech Republic clearly expressed the point of view that agreements concluded with that predecessor State remained in force. The Czech Republic thus expressly reserved the right to enforce against the Republic of Austria the rights accorded to it under the bilateral instruments at issue in its capacity as the successor State.

163. The importance of such a circumstance is, moreover, corroborated by the purpose of the first paragraph of Article 307 EC [351], the aim of which is to allow a Member State to respect the rights which can be asserted against it by non-member countries on the basis of an agreement which predates that State's accession to the European Union in cases such as the one at issue in the main proceedings (see paragraph 145 above).

164. It is for the national court to ascertain whether, in the case at issue in the main proceedings, both the Republic of Austria and the Czech Republic actually intended to apply the principle of the continuity of treaties to the bilateral instruments at issue.

165. As regards the Republic of Austria, it should again be made clear that it cannot

be ruled out a priori that a declaration of intention in that regard, even where made after a certain delay (that is, not until 1997), can nevertheless be taken into account for the purpose of definitively establishing the intention of that Member State to accept the Czech Republic as contracting party to the bilateral instruments at issue and to find that, in the present case, application of those instruments comes within the scope of the first paragraph of Article 307 EC [351].

166. It would be otherwise if, at any time prior to the Federal Chancellor's communication, the Republic of Austria had already clearly expressed the contrary intention.

167. If, having carried out the checks that are necessary having regard, in particular, to the criteria set out in this judgment, the national court were to reach the conclusion that at the date of the Republic of Austria's accession to the European Union that Member State was bound to the Czech Republic by the bilateral instruments at issue, it would follow that those instruments can be regarded as acts concluded before the date of the Republic of Austria's accession to the European Union for the purposes of the first paragraph of Article 307 EC [351].

168. It should be added that, in accordance with the second paragraph of that provision, the Member States are required to take all appropriate steps to eliminate the incompatibilities between an agreement concluded before a Member State's accession and the Treaty.

169. It follows that the national court must ascertain whether a possible incompatibility between the Treaty and the bilateral convention can be avoided by interpreting that convention, to the extent possible and in compliance with international law, in such a way that it is consistent with Community law.

170. If it proves impracticable to interpret an agreement concluded prior to a Member State's accession to the European Union in such a way that it is consistent with Community law then, within the framework of Article 307 EC [351], it is open to that State to take the appropriate steps, while, however, remaining obliged to eliminate any incompatibilities existing between the earlier agreement and the Treaty. If that Member State encounters difficulties which make adjustment of an agreement impossible, an obligation to denounce that agreement cannot therefore be excluded (see Commission v. Portugal, paragraph 58).

171. In that regard, it should be noted that Article 16(3) of the bilateral convention provides that the two contracting parties may denounce the convention by giving notice of at least one year, issued in writing and through diplomatic channels.

172. Pending the success of one of the methods referred to in the second paragraph of Article 307 EC [351] in eliminating any incompatibilities between an agreement predating the accession of the Member State concerned to the European Union and the Treaty, the first paragraph of that article permits that State to continue to apply such an agreement in so far as it contains obligations which remain binding on that State under international law.

173. In the light of the foregoing, the answer to the third and fourth questions must be that the first paragraph of Article 307 EC [351] is to be interpreted as permitting a court of a Member State, subject to the findings to be made by that court having

regard inter alia to the criteria set out in this judgment, to apply the provisions of bilateral agreements such as those at issue in the main proceedings, concluded between that State and a non-member country and according protection to a name from the non-member country, even where those provisions prove to be contrary to the Treaty rules, on the ground that they concern an obligation resulting from agreements concluded before the date of the accession of the Member State concerned to the European Union. Pending the success of one of the methods referred to in the second paragraph of Article 307 EC [351] in eliminating any incompatibilities between an agreement predating that accession and the Treaty, the first paragraph of that article permits that State to continue to apply such an agreement in so far as it contains obligations which remain binding on that State under international law.

## NOTES AND QUESTIONS

1.   Article 34(1) of the Vienna Convention on Succession of States in respect of Treaties of 23 August 1978 provides:

When a part or parts of the territory of a State separate to form one or more States, whether or not the predecessor State continues to exist:

(a) any treaty in force at the date of the succession of States in respect of the entire territory of the predecessor State continues in force in respect of each successor State so formed;

(b) any treaty in force at the date of the succession of States in respect only of that part of the territory of the predecessor State which has become a successor State continues in force in respect of that successor State alone.

In the *Budvar* case, what was Austria's obligation in terms of its compliance with EU law here? Was this an issue of EU law, international law or Austrian law?

2.   In *Commission v. Finland (Bilateral Investment Treaties)*, Case C-118/07, 2009 ECJ EUR-Lex LEXIS 1052, 2009 ECR I-10889, the Commission successfully argued that Finland had breached its treaty obligations, notwithstanding the text of EC 307/TFEU 351, by not taking action to amend bilateral investment treaties with various countries so as to enable the immediate effect of any actions taken by the Council under EC 57, 59 and 60/TFEU 64,66 and 75. A primary objective of such treaties is to remove restrictions on capital movements between the parties to them and Finland, when bound by these liberalizing measures, might have been prevented from assuring the implementation of restrictive measures authorized by the Council. (This has particular significance with respect to Council actions regarding the freezing of bank accounts of alleged terrorist organizations, such as those at issue in the *Al Barakaat* case below.) The Court stated:

27 Under the first paragraph of Article 307 EC, the rights and obligations arising from an agreement concluded before the date of accession of a Member State between it and a third country are not affected by the provisions of the Treaty. The purpose of that provision is to make it clear, in accordance with the principles of international law, that application of the

Treaty is not to affect the duty of the Member State concerned to respect the rights of third countries under a prior agreement and to perform its obligations . . .

28 However, the second paragraph of Article 307 EC obliges the Member States to take all appropriate steps to eliminate incompatibilities with Community law which have been established in agreements concluded prior to their accession. Under that provision, the Member States are required, where appropriate, to assist each other to that end and, where appropriate, to adopt a common attitude.

29 The provisions of Articles 57(2) EC, 59 EC and 60(1) EC confer on the Council the power to restrict, in certain specific circumstances, movements of capital and payments between the Member States and third countries.

30 In order to ensure the effectiveness of those provisions, measures restricting the free movement of capital must be capable, where adopted by the Council, of being applied immediately with regard to the States to which they relate.

31 Accordingly, . . . those powers of the Council, which consist in the unilateral adoption of restrictive measures with regard to third countries on a matter which is identical to or connected with that covered by an earlier agreement concluded between a Member State and a third country, reveal an incompatibility with that agreement where, first, the agreement does not contain a provision allowing the Member State concerned to exercise its rights and to fulfil its obligations as a member of the Community and, second, there is also no international-law mechanism which makes that possible.

32 As regards the abovementioned agreement, the Republic of Finland, does not put forward any mechanism which would enable it to fulfil its Community obligations. Furthermore, in any event, the possibility, relied on by the States intervening, of taking other steps made available under international law such as the suspension or the denunciation of the agreement at issue or of certain provisions of that agreement is too uncertain in its effects to guarantee that the measures adopted by the Council could be effectively applied within the prescribed period.

33 It is common ground that, in the case referred to, the Republic of Finland has not taken any steps, within the period prescribed by that institution in its reasoned opinion, with respect to the third country concerned to eliminate the risk of conflict to which the application of the agreement concerned may give rise with measures liable to be adopted by the Council pursuant to Articles 57(2) EC [64], 59 EC [66] and 60(1) EC [67].

34 It should be added that . . . the incompatibilities with the Treaty which the investment agreements with the third countries give rise to and which preclude the application of restrictions to the movement of capital and to payments which the Council may adopt pursuant to Articles 57(2) EC [64],

59 EC [66] and 60(1) EC [67] are not limited to the defendant Member State in this case.

35 It should therefore be stated that, in accordance with the second paragraph of Article 307 EC [351], the Member States are required, where necessary, to assist each other to eliminate the incompatibilities established between the agreements concluded by the Member States prior to their accession and Community law and, where appropriate, to adopt a common attitude. In the context of its duty under Article 211 EC [TEU 17] to ensure that the provisions of the Treaty are applied, it is for the Commission to take any steps which might facilitate mutual assistance between the Member States concerned and their adoption of a common attitude.

Since it requires the agreement of both parties to a treaty to amend it, what was the scope of Finland's duty here, particularly if the other country refused to accept an amendment? If there were termination provisions in such agreements, was it up to Finland to terminate, even if that meant its own nationals might then have to deal with restrictions imposed by the other country?

## § 21.04    RESOLUTION OF DISPUTES BETWEEN MEMBER STATES

### COMMISSION v. IRELAND
(NUCLEAR REPROCESSING)
Case C-459/03, 2006 ECJ CELEX LEXIS 238, [2006] ECR I-4635

[For background see the extract of this case in Chapter 12]

59. The Commission raises three heads of complaint in its action. First, it claims that, by bringing proceedings against the United Kingdom under the Convention, Ireland has failed to respect the exclusive jurisdiction vested in the Court by Article 292 EC [344] [344] to rule on any dispute concerning the interpretation and application of Community law. Second, the Commission argues that Ireland has breached Articles 292 EC [344] and 193 EA by referring to the Arbitral Tribunal a dispute which requires for its resolution the interpretation and application of measures of Community law. Third, the Commission alleges that Ireland has failed to comply with its duty of cooperation under Article 10 EC [TEU 4] by exercising a competence which belongs to the Community and that it has failed in that duty under Articles 10 EC [TEU 4] and 192 EA by failing first to inform or consult with the competent Community institutions.

\*    \*    \*

80. It is necessary to specify at the outset that, by its first head of complaint, the Commission is criticising Ireland for failing to respect the exclusive jurisdiction of the Court by bringing before the Arbitral Tribunal a dispute between it and another Member State concerning the interpretation and application of provisions of the Convention involving obligations assumed by the Community in the exercise of its external competence in regard to protection of the environment, and for thereby breaching Article 292 EC [344]. The articles of the EAEC Treaty to which the

Commission refers in its submissions relate to the second and third heads of complaint.

81. Under Article 300(7) EC [218], agreements concluded under the conditions set out in that Article shall be binding on the institutions of the Community and on Member States'.

82. The Convention was signed by the Community and subsequently approved by Decision 98/392. It follows that, according to settled case-law, the provisions of that convention now form an integral part of the Community legal order . . .

83. The Convention was concluded by the Community and all of its Member States on the basis of shared competence.

84. The Court has already ruled that mixed agreements have the same status in the Community legal order as purely Community agreements, as these are provisions coming within the scope of Community competence . . .

85. From this the Court has concluded that, in ensuring respect for commitments arising from an agreement concluded by the Community institutions, the Member States fulfil, within the Community system, an obligation in relation to the Community, which has assumed responsibility for the due performance of that agreement (Case C-13/00 Commission v. Ireland, paragraph 15).

\*    \*    \*

121. It follows that the provisions of the Convention relied on by Ireland in the dispute relating to the MOX plant and submitted to the Arbitral Tribunal are rules which form part of the Community legal order. The Court therefore has jurisdiction to deal with disputes relating to the interpretation and application of those provisions and to assess a Member State's compliance with them . . .

122. It is, however, necessary to determine whether this jurisdiction of the Court is exclusive, such as to preclude a dispute like that relating to the MOX plant being brought by a Member State before an arbitral tribunal established pursuant to Annex VII to the Convention.

123. The Court has already pointed out that an international agreement cannot affect the allocation of responsibilities defined in the Treaties and, consequently, the autonomy of the Community legal system, compliance with which the Court ensures under Article 220 EC. That exclusive jurisdiction of the Court is confirmed by Article 292 EC [344] [344], by which Member States undertake not to submit a dispute concerning the interpretation or application of the EC Treaty to any method of settlement other than those provided for therein . . .

124. It should be stated at the outset that the Convention precisely makes it possible to avoid such a breach of the Court's exclusive jurisdiction in such a way as to preserve the autonomy of the Community legal system.

125. It follows from Article 282 of the Convention that, as it provides for procedures resulting in binding decisions in respect of the resolution of disputes between Member States, the system for the resolution of disputes set out in the EC Treaty must in principle take precedence over that contained in Part XV of the Convention.

126. It has been established that the provisions of the Convention in issue in the dispute concerning the MOX plant come within the scope of Community competence which the Community exercised by acceding to the Convention, with the result that those provisions form an integral part of the Community legal order.

127. Consequently, the dispute in this case is indeed a dispute concerning the interpretation or application of the EC Treaty, within the terms of Article 292 EC [344] [344].

128. Furthermore, as it is between two Member States in regard to an alleged failure to comply with Community-law obligations resulting from those provisions of the Convention, this dispute is clearly covered by one of the methods of dispute settlement established by the EC Treaty within the terms of Article 292 EC [344], namely the procedure set out in Article 227 EC [259].

129. In addition, it is not open to dispute that proceedings such as those brought by Ireland before the Arbitral Tribunal fall to be described as a method of settlement of a dispute within the terms of Article 292 EC [344] inasmuch as, under Article 296 of the Convention, the decisions delivered by such a tribunal are final and binding on the parties to the dispute.

130. Ireland contends, however, by way of alternative submission, that, if the Court were to conclude that the provisions of the Convention invoked before the Arbitral Tribunal form an integral part of Community law, that conclusion would also be unavoidable with regard to the provisions of the Convention dealing with dispute settlement. Consequently, it submits, the initiation of proceedings before an arbitral tribunal referred to in Article 287(1)(c) of the Convention constitutes a method of dispute settlement provided for in the EC Treaty, within the terms of Article 292 EC [344].

131. That argument must be rejected.

132. As has been pointed out in paragraph 123 of the present judgment, an international agreement such as the Convention cannot affect the exclusive jurisdiction of the Court in regard to the resolution of disputes between Member States concerning the interpretation and application of Community law. Furthermore, as indicated in paragraphs 124 and 125 of the present judgment, Article 282 of the Convention precisely makes it possible to avoid such a breach occurring, in such a way as to preserve the autonomy of the Community legal system.

133. It follows from all of the foregoing that Articles 220 EC [259] and 292 EC [344] precluded Ireland from initiating proceedings before the Arbitral Tribunal with a view to resolving the dispute concerning the MOX plant.

134. This finding cannot be brought into question by the fact that the application by Ireland instituting proceedings before the Arbitral Tribunal also relates to certain obligations of the United Kingdom concerning the risks connected with terrorism.

135. Without it being necessary to rule on the question as to whether that part of the dispute comes within the scope of Community law, suffice it to hold that, as follows from paragraph 120 of the present judgment, a significant part of the dispute in this case between Ireland and the United Kingdom relates to the interpretation or application of Community law. It is for the Court, should the need

arise, to identify the elements of the dispute which relate to provisions of the international agreement in question which fall outside its jurisdiction.

136. As the jurisdiction of the Court is exclusive and binding on the Member States, the arguments put forward by Ireland concerning the advantages which arbitration proceedings under Annex VII to the Convention would present in comparison with an action brought before the Court under Article 227 EC [259] cannot be accepted.

137. Even if they were assumed to have been demonstrated, such advantages could not in any event justify a Member State in avoiding its Treaty obligations with regard to judicial proceedings intended to rectify an alleged breach of Community law by another Member State . . .

138. Finally, with regard to the arguments put forward by Ireland concerning urgency and the possibility of obtaining interim measures under Article 290 of the Convention, suffice it to point out that, under Article 243 EC, the Court may prescribe any necessary interim measures in cases before it. It is evident that such measures may therefore be ordered in the context of proceedings brought under Article 227 EC [259].

139. In the light of all of the foregoing, the first head of complaint must be upheld.

The second head of complaint

140. By its second head of complaint, the Commission contends that the submission by Ireland of instruments of Community law for interpretation and application by the Arbitral Tribunal amounts to a breach of Article 292 EC [344] and, in regard to the measures relied on which come within the ambit of the EAEC Treaty, a breach of Article 193 EA.

\*    \*    \*

146. It is common ground that, in its statement of claim and in its written submissions to the Arbitral Tribunal, Ireland invoked a number of Community measures.

147. In addition to the Convention for the Protection of the Marine Environment of the North-East Atlantic, the measures in question are essentially, in regard to the EC Treaty, Directives 85/337 and 90/313 and, in regard to the EAEC Treaty, Directives 80/836, 92/3 and 96/29.

148. It is also common ground that those Community measures were invoked by Ireland pursuant to Article 293(1) of the Convention, which provides that a tribunal such as the Arbitral Tribunal is to apply this Convention and other rules of international law not incompatible with this Convention'.

149. As the Advocate General has noted in points 49 and 50 of his Opinion, it follows from the different passages in the pleadings lodged by Ireland before the Arbitral Tribunal that that Member State presented those Community measures not only as relevant for the purpose of clarifying the meaning of the general provisions of the Convention in issue in the dispute but also as rules of international law to be applied by the Arbitral Tribunal pursuant to Article 293 of the Convention.

150. Thus, as the United Kingdom Government has submitted without being challenged on this point, Ireland argued inter alia before the Arbitral Tribunal that the 1993 environmental statement did not meet the requirements of Directive 85/337 and that the United Kingdom's refusal to disclose the operating plan for the MOX plant meant that it was not possible to evaluate the justification for that plant, as required under Directive 96/29, in addition to the contention that this refusal amounted to a breach of Article 6 of Directive 80/836 and of Article 6 of Directive 96/29.

151. It thus appears that Ireland submitted instruments of Community law to the Arbitral Tribunal for purposes of their interpretation and application in the context of proceedings seeking a declaration that the United Kingdom had breached the provisions of those instruments.

152. That is at variance with the obligation imposed on Member States by Articles 292 EC [344] and 193 EA to respect the exclusive nature of the Court's jurisdiction to resolve disputes concerning the interpretation and application of provisions of Community law, in particular by having recourse to the procedures set out in Articles 227 EC [TEU 19] and 142 EA for the purpose of obtaining a declaration that another Member State has breached those provisions.

153. Therefore, as some of the measures in question come within the scope of the EC Treaty and others within the scope of the EAEC Treaty, it must be held that there has been a breach of Articles 292 EC [344] and 193 EA.

154. It must also be pointed out that the institution and pursuit of proceedings before the Arbitral Tribunal, in the circumstances indicated in paragraphs 146 to 150 of the present judgment, involve a manifest risk that the jurisdictional order laid down in the Treaties and, consequently, the autonomy of the Community legal system may be adversely affected.

155. That risk exists even though, as Ireland avers, it has given a formal assurance that it has not called on, and will not call on, the Arbitral Tribunal to examine or appraise, pursuant to Article 293 of the Convention or any other provision, whether the United Kingdom has breached any rule of Community law.

156. Furthermore, the existence of that risk renders entirely irrelevant the fact that Ireland may have called on the Arbitral Tribunal to apply Community law by way of renvoi or by recourse to any other technique.

157. The second head of complaint must accordingly be regarded as being well founded.

The third head of complaint

158. By its third head of complaint, the Commission submits, first, that Ireland has failed to comply with the duty of cooperation under Article 10 EC [TEU 4] inasmuch as, by instituting proceedings under the Convention on the basis of provisions falling within the competence of the Community, Ireland exercised a competence which belongs to the Community. Second, the Commission contends that Ireland also failed in its duty of cooperation under both Article 10 EC [TEU 4] and Article 192 EA by bringing those proceedings unilaterally without having first informed

and consulted the competent Community institutions.

* * *

168. The Commission first of all criticises Ireland for having failed in its duty of cooperation under Article 10 EC [TEU 4] inasmuch as, by bringing arbitral proceedings under the Convention, Ireland exercised a competence which belongs to the Community.

169. The obligation devolving on Member States, set out in Article 292 EC [344], to have recourse to the Community judicial system and to respect the Court's exclusive jurisdiction, which is a fundamental feature of that system, must be understood as a specific expression of Member States' more general duty of loyalty resulting from Article 10 EC [TEU 4].

170. The unavoidable conclusion must also be drawn that this first part of the third head of complaint has the same subject-matter as the first head of complaint since it focuses on the same conduct on the part of Ireland, that is to say, the bringing by that Member State of the proceedings before the Arbitral Tribunal in contravention of Article 292 EC [344].

171. It is for that reason unnecessary to find that there has been a failure to comply with the general obligations contained in Article 10 EC [TEU 4] that is distinct from the failure, already established, to comply with the more specific Community obligations devolving on Ireland pursuant to Article 292 EC [344].

# NOTES AND QUESTIONS

1.   Article 282 of the Convention reads:

*Obligations under general, regional or bilateral agreements*

If the States Parties which are parties to a dispute concerning the interpretation or application of this Convention have agreed, through a general, regional or bilateral agreement or otherwise, that such dispute shall, at the request of any party to the dispute, be submitted to a procedure that entails a binding decision, that procedure shall apply in lieu of the procedures provided for in this Part, unless the parties to the dispute otherwise agree.

2.   *Commission v. Ireland* indicates a number of principles that must be used in determining whether a Member State must now treat a matter as one of internal EU law within the exclusive purview of EU procedures and institutions or whether, on the contrary the Member State could still regard the matter as falling within international law. What are these principles?

For discussion of the role of EC 10/TEU 4 and its impact on mixed agreements and the EU duties of the Member States in relation to their own competences in mixed agreements, see the further excerpt from this case in Chapter 12. Does this case suggest that Member States are now restricted in their freedom to take *any* action *vis-à-vis* other Member States whether or not any competence has been transferred to the EU? For example, does a border dispute between two Member

States, even if not entailing any EU legal issues, now require settlement within an EU framework? (Consider, for example, the long-running dispute between Spain and the UK over Gibraltar; or between the Member States bordering the North Sea regarding exploitation of hydrocarbons). Is not the whole purpose of the Union to "internalize" international disputes?

## § 21.05    EXTRADITION AND FULL FAITH AND CREDIT

### ADVOCATEN VOOR DE WERELD VZW V LEDEN VAN DE MINISTERRAAD
2007 ECJ EUR-Lex LEXIS 2352;2007 ECR I-3633

[The Advocaten voor de Wereld VZW ('Advocaten voor de Wereld') brought an action before the Belgian Arbitragehof (Court of Arbitration) seeking the annulment of the Belgian Law implementing the Framework Directive on the European arrest warrant in particular Articles 3, 5(1) and (2) and 7. Recital (5) in the preamble to the Framework Decision provided:

> The objective set for the Union to become an area of freedom, security and justice leads to abolishing extradition between Member States and replacing it by a system of surrender between judicial authorities. Further, the introduction [*4] of a new simplified system of surrender of sentenced or suspected persons for the purposes of execution or prosecution of criminal sentences makes it possible to remove the complexity and potential for delay inherent in the present extradition procedures. Traditional cooperation relations which have prevailed up till now between Member States should be replaced by a system of free movement of judicial decisions in criminal matters, covering both pre-sentence and final decisions, within an area of freedom, security and justice.

Recital (6) in the preamble to the Framework Decision was worded as follows:

> The European arrest warrant provided for in this Framework Decision is the first concrete measure in the field of criminal law implementing the principle of mutual recognition which the European Council referred to as the "cornerstone" of judicial cooperation.

Article 1 of the Framework Decision, which was adopted on the basis of Article 31(1)(a) and (b) TEU and Article 34(2)(b) TEU [now both repealed], provided:

> 1. The European arrest warrant is a judicial decision issued by a Member State with a view to the arrest and surrender by another Member State of a requested person, for the purposes of conducting a criminal prosecution or executing [*6] a custodial sentence or detention order.

> 2. Member States shall execute any European arrest warrant on the basis of the principle of mutual recognition and in accordance with the provisions of this Framework Decision.

3. This Framework Decision shall not have the effect of modifying the obligation to respect fundamental rights and fundamental legal principles as enshrined in Article 6 of the Treaty on European Union.

Article 2 of the Framework Decision provided:

1. A European arrest warrant may be issued for acts punishable by the law of the issuing Member State by a custodial sentence or a detention order for a maximum period of at least 12 months or, where a sentence has been passed or a detention order has been made, for sentences of at least four months.

2. The following offences, if they are punishable in the issuing Member State by a custodial sentence or a detention order for a maximum period of at least three years and as they are defined by the law of the issuing Member State, shall, under the terms of this Framework Decision and without verification of the double criminality of the act, give rise to surrender pursuant to a European arrest warrant:

- participation in a criminal organisation,

- terrorism,

- trafficking in human beings,

- sexual exploitation of children and child pornography,

- illicit trafficking in narcotic drugs and psychotropic substances,

- illicit trafficking in weapons, munitions and explosives,

- corruption,

- fraud, including that affecting the financial interests of the European Communities within the meaning of the Convention of 26 July 1995 on the protection of the European Communities' financial interests,

- laundering of the proceeds of crime,

- counterfeiting currency, including of the euro,

- computer-related crime,

- environmental crime, including illicit trafficking in endangered animal species and in endangered plant species and varieties,

- facilitation of unauthorised entry and residence,

- murder, grievous bodily injury,

- illicit trade in human organs and tissue,

- kidnapping, illegal restraint and hostage-taking,

- racism and xenophobia,

- organised or armed robbery,

- illicit trafficking in cultural goods, including antiques and works of art,

- swindling,

- racketeering [*8] and extortion,

- counterfeiting and piracy of products,

- forgery of administrative documents and trafficking therein,

- forgery of means of payment,

- illicit trafficking in hormonal substances and other growth promoters,

- illicit trafficking in nuclear or radioactive materials,

- trafficking in stolen vehicles,

- rape,

- arson,

- crimes within the jurisdiction of the International Criminal Court,

- unlawful seizure of aircraft/ships,

- sabotage.

44. Advocaten voor de Wereld contends, in contrast to all of the other parties which have submitted observations in these proceedings, that, to the extent to which it dispenses with verification of the requirement of the double criminality of the offences mentioned in it, Article 2(2) of the Framework Decision is contrary to the principle of equality and non-discrimination and to the principle of legality in criminal matters.

45. It must be noted at the outset that, by virtue of Article 6 EU, the Union is founded on the principle of the rule of law and it respects fundamental rights, as guaranteed by the European Convention for the Protection of Human Rights and Fundamental Freedoms, signed in Rome on 4 November 1950, and as they result from the constitutional provisions common to the Member States, as general principles of Community law. It follows that the institutions are subject to review of the conformity of their acts with the Treaties and the general principles of law, just like the Member States when they implement the law of the Union . . .

46. It is common ground that those principles include the principle of the legality of criminal offences and penalties and the principle of equality and non-discrimination, which are also reaffirmed respectively in Articles 49, 20 and 21 of the Charter of Fundamental Rights of the European Union, proclaimed in Nice on 7 December 2000 (OJ 2000 C 364, p. 1).

47. It is accordingly a matter for the Court to examine the validity of the Framework Decision in the light of those principles.

The principle of the legality of criminal offences and penalties

48. According to Advocaten voor de Wereld, the list of more than 30 offences in respect of which the traditional condition of double criminality is henceforth abandoned if those offences are punishable in the issuing Member State by a

custodial sentence or detention order for a maximum period of at last three years is so vague and imprecise that it breaches, or at the very least is capable of breaching, the principle of legality in criminal matters. The offences set out in that list are not accompanied by their legal definition but constitute very vaguely defined categories of undesirable conduct. A person deprived of his liberty on foot of a European arrest warrant without verification of double criminality does not benefit from the guarantee that criminal legislation must satisfy conditions as to precision, clarity and predictability allowing each person to know, at the time when an act is committed, whether that act does or does not constitute an offence, by contrast to those who are deprived of their liberty otherwise than pursuant to a European arrest warrant.

49. The principle of the legality of criminal offences and penalties (nullum crimen, nulla poena sine lege), which is one of the general legal principles underlying the constitutional traditions common to the Member States, has also been enshrined in various international treaties, in particular in Article 7(1) of the European Convention for the Protection of Human Rights and Fundamental Freedoms . . .

50. This principle implies that legislation must define clearly offences and the penalties which they attract. That condition is met in the case where the individual concerned is in a position, on the basis of the wording of the relevant provision and with the help of the interpretative assistance given by the courts, to know which acts or omissions will make him criminally liable . . .

51. In accordance with Article 2(2) of the Framework Decision, the offences listed in that provision give rise to surrender pursuant to a European arrest warrant, without verification of the double criminality of the act, 'if they are punishable in the issuing Member State by a custodial sentence or a detention order for a maximum period of at least three years and as they are defined by the law of the issuing Member State'.

52. Consequently, even if the Member States reproduce word-for-word the list of the categories of offences set out in Article 2(2) of the Framework Decision for the purposes of its implementation, the actual definition of those offences and the penalties applicable are those which follow from the law of 'the issuing Member State'. The Framework Decision does not seek to harmonise the criminal offences in question in respect of their constituent elements or of the penalties which they attract.

53. Accordingly, while Article 2(2) of the Framework Decision dispenses with verification of double criminality for the categories of offences mentioned therein, the definition of those offences and of the penalties applicable continue to be matters determined by the law of the issuing Member State, which, as is, moreover, stated in Article 1(3) of the Framework Decision, must respect fundamental rights and fundamental legal principles as enshrined in Article 6 EU, and, consequently, the principle of the legality of criminal offences and penalties.

54. It follows that, in so far as it dispenses with verification of the requirement of double criminality in respect of the offences listed in that provision, Article 2(2) of the Framework Decision is not invalid on the ground that it infringes the principle of the legality of criminal offences and penalties.

## NOTES AND QUESTIONS

1. As between sovereign states, the concept of double criminality (that an act for which extradition is sought must be a crime in both the state of refuge and the requesting state) is almost universal. Thus, for example, suppose the United States sought to extradite an individual from the UK for violations of the U.S. antitrust laws that are criminal offences. The UK, however, did not at the time penalize such actions with criminal sanctions. Within the United States, the Article IV Section 2 requires that a state hosting a fugitive from justice in another state where treason, a felony, or "other Crime" is alleged is required to surrender the fugitive at the request of the state having jurisdiction.

2. Under the umbrella, now, of the AFSJ provisions in the TFEU, the equivalent of the recognition clause in the U.S. Constitution regarding civil judgments is found in Regulation 44/2001, [2001] OJ L 12/1. This regulation lays down the jurisdictional bases upon which national courts may assert jurisdiction.

3. In *Sfakianakis AEVE v. Elliniko Dimosio*, Joined Cases C-23/04 to C-25/04, 2006 ECJ CELEX LEXIS 56, [2006] ECR I-1265, the Court was asked to rule in the following circumstances: During the period before Hungary became a Member State, an Association Agreement was in place between it and the EU. This agreement was treated as part of the EU legal order for the matters within its scope.

A question had arisen as to the validity of certain certificates of origin confirming that vehicles had been manufactured in Hungary and therefore would benefit from the favorable customs tariff treatment under the agreement. Under well-established procedures, the Greek authorities would have had to accept certificates of origin that came from the Hungarian customs authorities. However, in this case, the authenticity of the documents having been questioned, the matter was referred to the Hungarian courts who confirmed some of the certificates. The Greek authorities declined to accept these rulings and imposed duties, which the importer, Sfakianakis, then challenged in the Greek Courts. The referring court asked whether the Greek Customs Authorities were bound to recognize the decision of the Hungarian court. By implication, since the Greek court was asked to rule on the Customs action, it needed to know whether it was itself bound to recognize the Hungarian ruling, which effectively held that Hungarian law complied with the Association Agreement. The ECJ ruled that the Greek authorities should recognize the Hungarian decision:

> 28 As the Court has held on several occasions, the right to an effective judicial remedy is a general principle of Community law which underlies the constitutional traditions common to the Member States . . . Since the Association Agreement is an integral part of the Community legal order, it is therefore for the competent authorities of the Member States to uphold the right to an effective legal remedy in respect of the application of the customs scheme provided for by that agreement (see, to that effect, Case 12/86 *Demirel* [1987] ECR 3719, . . .)

\* \* \*

32 In the light of the foregoing, . . . the customs authorities of the State of import are bound to take account of judicial decisions delivered in the State of export on actions brought against the results of verifications of the validity of goods movement certificates conducted by the customs authorities of the State of export, once they have been informed of the existence of those actions and the content of those decisions, regardless of whether the verification of the validity of the movement certificates was carried out at the request of the customs authorities of the State of import.

Note that situations like this are not covered by Regulation 44/2001 [2001] OJ L 12 (which replaced for most purposes the Convention of 27 September 1968 on Jurisdiction and the Enforcement of Judgments in Civil and Commercial Matters), because they do not concern enforcement or other effects of a judgment in the other state but only the binding effect of the first state's judgment on the second state. One could imagine that in most cases it is unlikely that a court would want to question the determination of another Member State's court with respect to the compatibility of the latter's law with EU law, but it might if it believed there had been a fundamental mistake or miscarriage of justice. The likelihood would be much stronger if the first court had ruled on the compatibility of its own state's law.

This case suggests that a "full faith and credit" obligation exists under Union law between the courts of the Member States as regards recognition of official acts by other Member States. See also TFEU 61(3) and (4).

# TABLE OF CASES

[References are to pages]

[References are to pages]

[References are to pages]

[References are to pages]

# INDEX

[References are to sections.]

## A

**AGRICULTURE** (See INTERNAL COMPE-
TENCES, subhead: Agriculture and fisheries)

**ARTICLE 6**
Justifications under Article 6 of directive 2000/78
. . . 18.05[B]

**AUTONOMY OF UNION LAW**
Generally . . . 3.01
Doctrine of supremacy in national courts
    Acceptance of ECJ's view of supremacy
      . . . 3.03[A]
    Constitutional obstacle, other . . . 3.03[E]
    ECJ's view of supremacy, acceptance of
      . . . 3.03[A]
    EU law, unilateral determinations on scope and
      meaning of . . . 3.03[F]
    Fundamental rights, conflict with . . . 3.03[B]
    Procedural obstacle, other . . . 3.03[E]
    Restrictions on transfer of sovereignty
      . . . 3.03[C]
    Sovereignty, restrictions on transfer of
      . . . 3.03[C]
    Time rule, last in . . . 3.03[D]
ECJ, as developed by
    Constitutional principles, effect on
      . . . 3.02[C]
    Effect on
      Constitutional principles . . . 3.02[C]
      National constitutions . . . 3.02[C]
    National constitutions, effect on . . . 3.02[C]
    National law, consequences of applying su-
      premacy doctrine in . . . 3.02[D]
    Primacy doctrine position of Member States in
      international law, effects of . . . 3.02[E]
    Primacy of Union law . . . 3.02[B]
    Sovereign rights to union, transfer of
      . . . 3.02[A]
    Supremacy doctrine in national law, conse-
      quences of application . . . 3.02[D]
    Supremacy of Union law . . . 3.02[B]
National courts, Union's institutions in . . . 3.04
Union's institutions in national courts . . . 3.04

## B

**BUDGETARY MATTERS**
Free movement of services . . . 14.05[C]

**BUSINESSES AND CAPITAL, MEASURES AF-
FECTING MOVEMENT OF**
Generally . . . 15.01
Capital, free movement of (See subhead: Free move-
ment of capital)
EC 56/TFEU 63
    Boundaries of application of . . . 15.04[D]

**BUSINESSES AND CAPITAL, MEASURES AF-
FECTING MOVEMENT OF**—Cont.
EC 56/TFEU 63—Cont.
    Member States taxation competences and, in-
      terrelation of . . . 15.04[B]
    Scope of . . . 15.04[A]
    Taxation competences of Member States and,
      interrelation of . . . 15.04[B]
Establishment and regulation of business entities
    Abuse . . . 15.03[B]
    EC 43/TFEU 49
      State corporation laws, EC 43/TFEU 49
        effect on . . . 15.03[A]
      States' taxation competences and, inter-
        play of . . . 15.03[C]
    State corporation laws, effect of EC 43/TFEU
      49 on . . . 15.03[A]
    States' taxation competences, interplay of EC
      43/TFEU 49 and . . . 15.03[C]
Free movement of capital
    Capital movements and state security
      . . . 15.04[C]
    EC 56/TFEU 63 (See subhead: EC 56/TFEU
      63)
      Taxation competences of Member States
        and, interrelation of . . . 15.04[B]
    Member States taxation competences and EC
      56/TFEU 63, interrelation of . . . 15.04[B]
    Scope of EC 56/TFEU 63 . . . 15.04[A]
    State security, capital movements and
      . . . 15.04[C]
    Taxation competences of Member States and
      EC 56/TFEU 63, interrelation of
      . . . 15.04[B]
Individuals, right of establishment for (See subhead:
  Right of establishment for individuals)
Right of establishment for individuals
    EC 43/TFEU 49, "Nationals of a Member
      State" in . . . 15.02[B]
    Establishment . . . 15.02[A]
    General interest, justification of restrictions
      based on . . . 15.02[D]
    Host state regulation, requirement for compli-
      ance with . . . 15.02[C]
    Mutual recognition, scope of . . . 15.02[C]
    "Nationals of a Member State" in EC
      43/TFEU 49 . . . 15.02[B]
    Public service exception . . . 15.02[E]

**BUSINESS LICENSES**
Free movement of services . . . 14.03

[References are to sections.]

# C

**CAPITAL, MEASURES AFFECTING MOVE-MENT OF** (See BUSINESSES AND CAPITAL, MEASURES AFFECTING MOVEMENT OF)

**CITIZENSHIP RIGHTS** (See FREE MOVEMENT AND NON-DISCRIMINATION, subhead: Residence as citizenship right and free movement)

**CITIZENS' RIGHTS**
Generally . . . 19.01
Documents, right of access to
Disclosure of legal advice . . . 19.03[B]
EU Legislation . . . 19.03[A]
Legal advice, disclosure of . . . 19.03[B]
Member States, documents of . . . 19.03[C]
Good administration, right to
Effective judicial protection, right to
. . . 19.02[C]
Fair hearing, right to . . . 19.02[C]
Files, access to . . . 19.02[D]
Innocence, presumption of . . . 19.02[B]
Presumption of innocence . . . 19.02[B]
Self incrimination, right against . . . 19.02[E]
Silence, right to . . . 19.02[E]
Timely action . . . 19.02[A]

**CIVIL LAW**
Shared powers . . . 11.06

**COMPETITION LAW** (See EXECUTIVE POWERS, subhead: Competition law, enforcement of)

**CONSTITUTIONAL DOCUMENTS AND PRINCIPLES**
Generally . . . 4.01
Fundamental rights
Charter, impact of . . . 4.03[B]
European convention
Fundamental freedoms, protection of
. . . 4.03[C]
Human rights, protection of . . . 4.03[C]
General principles of law common to Member
States . . . 4.03[A]
Impact of charter . . . 4.03[B]
Law common to Member States, general principles of . . . 4.03[A]
Limits of EU fundamental rights . . . 4.03[D]
Member States, general principles of law common to . . . 4.03[A]
Reach of EU fundamental rights . . . 4.03[D]
International law role in EU legal system, Interaction of international law with EU laws
National level, at . . . 4.04[A]
Union level, at . . . 4.04[B]
Treaties
Concept of direct effect . . . 4.02[A]
Direct applicability . . . 4.02[C]
Direct effect, concept of . . . 4.02[A]
Directly effective provisions create obligations
for individuals . . . 4.02[B]

**CRIMINAL LAW**
Shared powers . . . 11.06

**CURRENCY**
Generally . . . 2.06[E]

**CUSTOMS DUTIES**
Generally . . . 13.02

# D

**DAMAGES**
Actions for, EU law in national court (See NATIONAL COURTS, EU LAW IN, subhead: Damages, actions for)
Claims for damages against EU institutions (See JUDICIAL PROTECTION, subhead: Claims for damages against EU institutions)

**DEMOCRATIC RIGHTS**
Generally . . . 18.07

**DIGNITY**
Generally . . . 20.03

**DIRECTIVE 2000/78**
EU fundamental rights, effect on scope of application of . . . 18.05[A]
Justifications under Article 6 of directive 2000/78
. . . 18.05[B]

**DISCRIMINATION**
Equality, other forms of discrimination in (See EQUALITY, subhead: Discrimination, other forms of)
Free movement (See FREE MOVEMENT AND NON-DISCRIMINATION, subhead: Discrimination on grounds of nationality)
Gender discrimination
Indirect discrimination . . . 18.02[A]
"Pay," meaning of . . . 18.02[B]
Imports, discrimination against (See GOODS, MEASURES AFFECTING FREE MOVEMENT OF, subhead: Discrimination against imports)
Nationality, discrimination on grounds of (See FREE MOVEMENT AND NON-DISCRIMINATION, subhead: Discrimination on grounds of nationality)

**DOMESTIC PRODUCTS**
Intent to protect . . . 13.05[B]

**DUTIES OF COOPERATION AMONG MEMBER STATES**
Generally . . . 21.01
Existing treaty relations with third countries, adjusting . . . 21.03
Extradition . . . 21.05
Full faith . . . 21.05
International law to inter-state relations, application
of . . . 21.02
Inter-state relations, application of International law
to . . . 21.02
Resolution of disputes between Member States
. . . 21.04
Third countries, adjusting existing treaty relations
with . . . 21.03

[References are to sections.]

# E

[References are to sections.]

[References are to sections.]

[References are to sections.]

[References are to sections.]

[References are to sections.]